EXODUS
1–18

VOLUME 2

THE ANCHOR BIBLE is a fresh approach to the world's greatest classic. Its object is to make the Bible accessible to the modern reader; its method is to arrive at the meaning of biblical literature through exact translation and extended exposition, and to reconstruct the ancient setting of the biblical story, as well as the circumstances of its transcription and the characteristics of its transcribers.

THE ANCHOR BIBLE is a project of international and interfaith scope: Protestant, Catholic, and Jewish scholars from many countries contribute individual volumes. The project is not sponsored by any ecclesiastical organization and is not intended to reflect any particular theological doctrine. Prepared under our joint supervision, THE ANCHOR BIBLE is an effort to make available all the significant historical and linguistic knowledge which bears on the interpretation of the biblical record.

THE ANCHOR BIBLE is aimed at the general reader with no special formal training in biblical studies; yet it is written with the most exacting standards of scholarship, reflecting the highest technical accomplishment.

This project marks the beginning of a new era of cooperation among scholars in biblical research, thus forming a common body of knowledge to be shared by all.

William Foxwell Albright
David Noel Freedman
GENERAL EDITORS

THE ANCHOR BIBLE

EXODUS
1–18

◆

A New Translation
with Introduction and Commentary

WILLIAM H. C. PROPP

THE ANCHOR BIBLE
Doubleday
New York   London   Toronto   Sydney   Auckland

THE ANCHOR BIBLE
PUBLISHED BY DOUBLEDAY
a division of Random House, Inc.

THE ANCHOR BIBLE, DOUBLEDAY, and the portrayal of an anchor
with a dolphin are registered trademarks of Doubleday, a division of
Random House, Inc.

A hardcover edition of this book was published
in 1999 by Doubleday

Original Jacket Illustration by Margaret Chodos-Irvine

The Library of Congress has catalogued the hardcover edition as follows:

Library of Congress Cataloging-in-Publication Data
Bible. O.T. Exodus I–XVIII. English. Propp. 1998.
    Exodus 1–18: a new translation with introduction and commentary /
by William H. C. Propp.
    p. cm. — (The Anchor Bible; v. 2)
Includes bibliographical references and index.
1. Bible. O.T. Exodus I–XVIII—Commentaries. I. Propp, William
Henry Covici. II. Title. III. Series: Bible. English. Anchor Bible.
1964; v. 2.
BS192.2.A1   1964 .G3 vol. 2
[BS1243 1998]
220.7'7 s—dc21
[222'.12077]   97-37301
                                           CIP

ISBN-13: 978-0-385-51975-5
ISBN-10: 0-385-51975-3

PRINTED IN THE UNITED STATES OF AMERICA

BVG 01

For Lovers of the Bible

ACKNOWLEDGMENTS

◆

I am deeply grateful to the friends who undertook to read some or all of this work in manuscript, and favored me with helpful criticism: Francis I. Andersen, Louis Bookheim, Anna Propp Covici, the late Pascal Covici, Jr., Richard Elliot Friedman, David M. Goodblatt, Ronald S. Hendel, James G. Propp, Theodore Propp, Miriam Sherman, Donald F. Tuzin and John W. Wright. Kevin G. O'Connell made me the princely gift of his unpublished notes on Exodus 1–5, from which I learned much. I must acknowledge the contributions of students over many years in my Exodus Seminar at the University of California, San Diego: Mari Chernow, Augusto C. Feliú, the late Lois Garber, Jeffrey C. Geoghegan, Michael M. Homan, Daniel Kirsch, Risa Levitt Kohn, Raquel Tashman, Andrew Welch and Chien-pei Mark Yu. It is chiefly for them and their successors that I have written this book. My most heartfelt thanks go to my editor and colleague David Noel Freedman, whose incisive commentary on this commentary has spared those to whom it is dedicated much foolishness.

W. H. C. P.

CONTENTS

◆

LIST OF ABBREVIATIONS AND TERMS

◆

I. SYMBOLS, ABBREVIATIONS AND TERMS

. . .	omitted or unreadable words
[ ]	reconstructed or restored text
*	reconstructed, unattested or erroneous form
<	develops out of
>	develops into
†	original reading in doubt; translation follows *BHS*
††	translation does not follow *BHS*

I	first dictionary definition
I-	first radical (pe' of tri-literal root)
1	first person
1 Chr	1 Chronicles
1 Cor	1 Corinthians
1 Enoch	Ethiopic Apocalypse of Enoch, c. 100 B.C.E. (*OTP* 1.13–89)
1 Esdr	1 Esdras
1 Kgs	1 Kings
1 Pet	1 Peter
1QExod	DSS Exodus (DJD 1.50–51)
1QIsa^a	DSS Isaiah (Burrows 1950–51)
1QM	DSS *Milḥāmâ (War Scroll)* (Sukenik 1955: pll. 16–34)
1QpHab	DSS *Pesher on Habbakuk* (Cross et al. 1972: 149–63)
1QS	DSS *1QSerek* (Burrows 1950–51)
1 Sam	1 Samuel
1 Thess	1 Thessalonians

1 Tim	1 Timothy
II	second dictionary definition
II-	second radical ('ayin of tri-literal root)
2	second person
2 Bar	2 Baruch
2 Chr	2 Chronicles
2 Cor	2 Corinthians
2 Esdr	2 Esdras
2 Kgs	2 Kings
2 Pet	2 Peter
2QExod^{a-b}	DSS Exodus (DJD 3.49–56)
2 Sam	2 Samuel
2 Thess	2 Thessalonians
2 Tim	2 Timothy
III-	third radical (lamedh of tri-literal root)
3	third person
3 Enoch	Hebrew Apocalypse of Enoch, c. 500 C.E. (*OTP* 1.255–315)
4 Bar	4 Baruch
4QBibPar	DSS biblical paraphrase (DJD 5.1–6)
4QDt^{j}	DSS Deuteronomy (Duncan 1992; DJD 14.75–91)
4QDt^{q}	DSS Deuteronomy (Skehan 1954; DJD 14.137–42)
4QExod^{b-g}	DSS Exodus (DJD 12.79–146)
4QGen-Exod^{a}	DSS Genesis-Exodus (DJD 12.1–30)
4QMezG–Q	DSS Mezuzah (DJD 6.31–91)
4QMišmārôt	DSS calendrical text (Talmon and Knohl 1995)
4QpaleoExod^{m}	DSS Exodus (DJD 9.53–130)
4QpaleoGen-Exod^{l}	DSS Genesis-Exodus (DJD 9.17–50)
4QPhylA–R	DSS phylacteries (DJD 6.48–77)
4QPs^{b}	DSS Psalms (Skehan 1964)
4QReworked Pentateuch^{c}	DSS periphrastic Torah (DJD 13.255–318)
4QSam^{a}	DSS Samuel (unpublished; for readings, see provisionally McCarter 1980, 1984)
8QPhyl	DSS phylactery (DJD 3.149–56)
11QTemple	DSS *Temple Scroll* (Yadin 1983)

a   first half of a verse

Abarbanel   Isaac ben Judah Abarbanel, Iberian Jewish philosopher, commentator, 1437–1508 C.E.

ad sensum   a commonsense reading or correction

Adv. haeres.   Epiphanius, *Adversus haereses*

a fortiori   how much more so

AHI   G. I. Davies, *Ancient Hebrew Inscriptions* (Cambridge: Cambridge University, 1991)

Akedah   Binding of Isaac (Genesis 22)

Akkadian   Mesopotamian Semitic language; main dialects Assyrian (north) and Babylonian (south)

ʾaleph   first letter of the Hebrew alphabet

Aleppo Codex   important biblical MS written c. 925 C.E.; not extant for Exodus

alloform   alternate form

Amarna   Egyptian site yielding tablets containing Egyptian diplomatic correspondence (fourteenth century B.C.E.)

Amon   Chief god of New Kingdom Egypt

ʿAnatu   Ugaritic goddess of passion

ANEP   J. B. Pritchard, ed. *The Ancient Near East in Pictures Relating to the Old Testament* (Princeton, N.J.: Princeton University, 1969)

ANET   J. B. Pritchard, ed. *Ancient Near Eastern Texts Relating to the Old Testament* (Princeton, N.J.: Princeton University, 1950)

ANET[3]   *ANET*, third edition with Supplement (1969)

Ant.   Josephus, *Jewish Antiquities*

anthropocentrism   focus on humanity

anthropomorphism   imputing human traits to nonhuman beings

Ap.   Josephus, *Against Apion*

apodictic   law phrased as direct command

apotropaic   repelling evil forces

apud   cited at second hand from

Aquila   Jewish translator of Bible into Greek, c. 125 C.E.

Arabic   Semitic language; also, daughter translation of LXX

Aramaic   Semitic language of Syria, closely akin to Hebrew

archaic   old-fashioned

archaistic	artificially made to look old-fashioned
Aristobulus	lost historical work on Judaism, c. 150 B.C.E. (*OTP* 2.837–42)
ARM	Archives royales de Mari (Mari tablets)
ʿārōb	swarming insects
Artapanus	Jewish historian, c. 200 B.C.E. (*OTP* 2.897–903)
Ashkenazic	pertaining to Central and East European Jewry
assimilation	becoming similar or identical
asyndeton	underuse of conjunctions
ʾAṯiratu	Ugaritic chief goddess
ʿAṯtaru	Ugaritic god of the morning star
Augustine	Bishop of Hippo, Christian theologian, 354–430 C.E.
autograph	original MS
ʿayin	sixteenth letter of the Hebrew alphabet
b	second half of a verse
b.	Babylonian Talmud
B. Bat.	tractate *Baba Batra*
B. Qam.	tractate *Baba Qamma*
Baʿlu	"Lord," Ugaritic storm god; also called Haddu
Bar	Baruch (Apocrypha)
B.C.E.	Before the Common Era (= B.C.)
BDB	F. Brown, S. R. Driver, C. A. Briggs, *A Hebrew and English Lexicon of the Old Testament* (Boston/New York: Houghton, Mifflin, 1907)
Bek.	tractate *Bekorot*
Bekhor Shor	Joseph ben Isaac Bekhor Shor, French Jewish exegete, twelfth century C.E.
ben Naphthali	scantily attested school of Massoretes
Ber.	tractate *Berakot*
beth	second letter of the Hebrew alphabet
BHS	*Biblia Hebraica Stuttgartensia* (Stuttgart: Deutsche Bibelgesellschaft, 1983)
Bib. Ant.	Pseudo-Philo, *Biblical Antiquities*, c. 50 C.E. (*OTP* 2.304–77)
byform	alternate form
c.	approximately (*circa*)

CAD	*The Assyrian Dictionary of the Oriental Institute of the University of Chicago (Chicago Assyrian Dictionary)* (Chicago: Oriental Institute, 1956–)
Cairo Genizah	repository for discarded scrolls in Ezra Synagogue of Cairo (since eighth century C.E.)
Calvin	John Calvin, Protestant reformer and Bible commentator, 1509–64 C.E.
Cant	Canticles, Song of Songs
cantillation	Massoretic musical/accentual/syntactic notation (trope)
case ending	final vowel in some Semitic languages indicating grammatical function for nouns and adjectives
casuistic	law phrased as a condition ("if . . . then")
CD	Damascus Covenant (Rabin 1958)
C.E.	Common Era (= A.D.)
cf.	compare (*confer*)
chiasm	symmetrical ABB′A′ structure
chthonian	pertaining to the underworld
Clementine edition	1502 edition of Vg
Clement of Alexandria	Titus Flavius Clemens, Christian theologian, third century C.E.
clipping	misdivision of morphemes
cognate	etymologically related
cognate accusative	direct object sharing root of verb
cohortative	first-person command/exhortation
Col	Colossians
composite text	Torah composed of JEDP sources
conflation	combination
conjectural emendation	emendation without textual basis
construct	bound form of noun or adjective (*səmîkût*)
continuous writing	omitting spaces between words
corvée	mass forced labor
cosmogony	cosmic creation
D	source of Deuteronomy
daghesh	point placed in letter to indicate doubling or, in *bgdkpt*, plosive pronunciation

daleth   fourth letter of the Hebrew alphabet

Dan   Daniel

Day of Expiation   Yom Kippur (tenth day of seventh month)

defective   written without *matres lectionis*

Deity   translation for *'ĕlōhîm* 'God' (NOTE to 1:17)

Demetrius   Demetrius the Chronographer, biblical commentator, c. 200
                  B.C.E. (*OTP* 2.848–54)

desacralization   making sacred goods available for human use

De spec. leg.   Philo, *De specialibus legibus*

Deut   Deuteronomy

Deuteronomistic   pertaining to the editorial stratum of the Deuteronomistic
                  History

Deuteronom(ist)ic   pertaining to either D or Dtr

Deuteronomistic History   Deuteronomy through 2 Kings

Deut. Rab.   *Deuteronomy Rabba*, midrashic compendium

direct object marker   preposition *'ēt*

dittography   accidental double writing

DJD   Discoveries in the Judaean Desert (Oxford: Clarendon Press)

Documentary Hypothesis   theory that Torah is composed of several sources

doublet   second version of an account

DSS   Dead Sea Scroll(s)

Dtr   Deuteronomistic History

dual   noun form indicating a pair (e.g., *yādayim* 'two hands')

durative   describing ongoing action

E   Elohistic source

EA   El Amarna (Egypt)

Eccl   Ecclesiastes, Qohelet

eisegesis   reading into a text

ellipsis   omission of a word or words that are nevertheless to be
                  understood

Elohist   author of E

enclitic (mem)   final *m* attached to words in Hebrew and Ugaritic, signifi-
                  cance uncertain

enjambment   discrepancy between versification and syntax

Enūma eliš   Babylonian creation myth

epanalepsis	resumptive repetition (*Wiederaufnahme*)
Eph	Ephesians
Epiphanius	Epiphanius of Constantia, Palestinian Church Father, fourth century C.E.
Epist. ad Fabiolem	Jerome, *Epistola ad Fabiolem*
eponymous	that for which something or someone is named
ʿErub.	tractate *ʿErubin*
Eschaton	the end of time
Esth	Esther
Ethiopic	Geʿez, classical Semitic language of Ethiopia
etiology	explanation of origins
Eupolemus	Jewish historian, c. 150 B.C.E. (*OTP* 2.865–72)
Eusebius	Eusebius of Caesarea, Christian theologian and historian, c. 260–339 C.E.
exegesis	interpretation
exilic	pertaining to the Jews' Babylonian exile, 587–539 B.C.E.
Exod	Exodus
Exod. Rab.	*Exodus Rabba*, midrashic compendium
expansion	scribal addition
Ezek	Ezekiel
Ezekiel the Tragedian	author of *Exagōgē*, Greek play based on Exodus, c. 200 B.C.E. (*OTP* 2.808–19)
f.	feminine
fem.	(the same)
fig.	figure
first hand	the original text of a MS, later altered
Fragmentary Targum	imperfectly preserved Palestinian Targum(s) (Klein 1980)
Gal	Galatians
Gaonic	describing the early post-Talmudic period, c. 600–1100 C.E.
Gen	Genesis
gentilic	suffixed -*î* indicating national origin (e.g., *miṣrî* 'Egyptian'); also called *niṣbe*
gimel	third letter of the Hebrew alphabet
Giṭ.	tractate *Giṭṭin*

GKC	*Gesenius' Hebräische Grammatik*, 28th ed., ed. E. Kautzsch, trans. A. E. Cowley (Oxford: Clarendon, 1910)
gloss	explanatory textual insertion
Greater J	supposed Yahwistic document present in Genesis through 2 Samuel (Friedman 1998)
Gt	Semitic verbal conjugation, often passive
guttural	fricative consonant pronounced in back of throat; in Hebrew, 'aleph, he', ḥeth, 'ayin
Hab	Habakkuk
habitual	describing repeated action
Haddu	Ugaritic storm god; also called Baʕlu
Haggadah	Jewish Passover liturgy
Hammurapi Code	Babylonian law code, c. 1800 B.C.E.
haplography	accidental omission due to sequence of similar letters or words
harmonization	resolution of contradiction
ḥarṭummîm	term for Egyptian magicians
he'	fifth letter of the Hebrew alphabet
he' syncope	loss of *h* between vowels
Heb	Hebrews
Hecataeus	Hecataeus of Abdera, Hellenistic historian, c. 300 B.C.E.
hendiadys	two coordinated words conveying a single concept
ḥeth	eighth letter of the Hebrew alphabet
Hexapla	Origen's compilation of Hebrew and Greek versions of the Bible
high place	Israelite local temple
Hiph'il	causative conjugation of the Hebrew verb
Hithpa'el	reflexive conjugation of the Hebrew verb
Hittite(s)	dominant civilization in Anatolia c. 1600–1200 B.C.E.
Ḥizquni	Hezekiah ben Manoah, French Jewish commentator, mid-thirteenth century C.E.
hollow root	verbal root with middle waw or yodh
homeograph	identically spelled
homoioarkton	consecutive words or phrases with same initial letter(s)
homoioteleuton	consecutive words or phrases with same final letter(s)

Hoph'al	passive-causative conjugation of the Hebrew verb
Horus	Egyptian falcon god, symbol of royalty
Hos	Hosea
Ḥul.	tractate Ḥullin
Hurrian	obscure but populous people attested from late third millennium to late second millennium throughout the Near East
hysteron proteron	narrating events in reverse order
ibn Ezra	Abraham ibn Ezra, itinerant Jewish commentator and poet, 1089–1164 C.E.
ibn Janaḥ	Jonah ibn Janaḥ, Spanish Jewish grammarian and lexicographer, eleventh century C.E.
ʾIlu	"God," Ugaritic high deity
imitatio dei	imitation of God
imperative	command
imperfect	Hebrew prefix conjugation of verb (yiktōb)
Inanna	Sumerian goddess of passion
inclusio	framing through repetition of words or phrases
incongruence	grammatical nonagreement
ingressive	action beginning to take place
inner-Greek	within the transmission of LXX
inverted syntax	in Hebrew, subject before verb
Irenaeus	early Church Father, c. 140–202 C.E.
Isa	Isaiah
Isis	Egyptian goddess, mother of Horus
Israel's Sons	the nation of Israel (bənê yiśrāʾēl)
J	Yahwistic source
Jas	James
Jdt	Judith
JE	combination of J and E
Jer	Jeremiah
Jerome	Christian theologian, translator of Vg, c. 347–419 C.E.
Josephus	Flavius Josephus, Jewish soldier and historian, c. 37–95 C.E.
Josh	Joshua
Jub	Jubilees, c. 150 B.C.E. (OTP 2.52–142)

Judg	Judges
jussive	third-person command
KAI	H. Donner and W. Röllig, *Kanaanäische und aramäische Inschriften* (Wiesbaden: Harrassowitz, 1962)
kaph	eleventh letter of the Hebrew alphabet
Kassite	formerly nomadic people dominating Babylonia c. 1600–1200 B.C.E.
KB	L. Köhler and W. Baumgartner, *Lexikon in Veteris Testamenti libros* (Leiden: Brill, 1958)
Kenn	MS collated by Kennicott (1776–80)
Kethibh	written (but not pronounced) (scribal annotation)
Ketub.	tractate *Ketubot*
KJV	King James Version
KTU	M. Dietrich, O. Loretz, J. Sanmartín, *Die keilalphabetischen Texte aus Ugarit* (AOAT 24. Kevelaer: Butzon & Bercker; Neukirchen-Vluyn: Neukirchener Verlag, 1976)
L	Leningrad Codex
l.	line
Lam	Lamentations
lamedh	twelfth letter of the Hebrew alphabet
Late Antiquity	c. 300–750 C.E.
Late Bronze Age	c. 1550–1200 B.C.E.
LCL	Loeb Classical Library
lectio brevior	shorter reading
lectio difficilior	more difficult reading
lectio facilior	easier reading
Leitwort	theme word
Leningrad Codex	St. Petersburg Museum biblical MS B 19a, written 1009 C.E.
Lev	Leviticus
Lev. Rab.	*Leviticus Rabba*, midrashic compendium
lexeme	word
locative/directive	suffixed -*â* indicating goal of motion (e.g., '*arṣâ* 'groundward')
Lucianic	family of LXX MSS evincing correction toward proto-MT

Luzzatto	Samuel David Luzzatto, Italian Jewish philosopher, commentator, 1800–65 C.E.
LXX	Septuagint, Greek Pentateuch
LXX^A	codex Alexandrinus
LXX^B	codex Vaticanus
LXX^F	codex Ambrosianus
LXX^M	codex Coislinianus
m.	masculine
m.	Mishnah
Maimonides	R. Moses Maimonides (Rambam), Spanish-Egyptian Jewish theologian, 1135–1204 C.E.
Mak.	tractate *Makkot*
Makš.	tractate *Makširin* (= *Mašqin*)
Mal	Malachi
mappiq	point indicating consonantal he' (as in *lāh* 'to her')
masc.	masculine
Massoretes	scribes who established MT, c. 700–900 C.E.
Massoretic Text	canonical Jewish Hebrew Bible
maṣṣôt	unleavened bread
Maṣṣôt	Festival of Unleavened Bread, antecedent to Jewish Passover
mater (pl. *matres*) *lectionis*	nonpronounced he', waw and yodh (*'ēm qərî'â*)
Matt	Matthew
medial he'	root with he' in middle ('ayin-he')
Meg.	tractate *Megilla*
Mek.	*Mekilta*, midrashic compendium on Exodus
Melito	Melito of Sardis, Christian theologian, second century C.E.
mem	thirteenth letter of the Hebrew alphabet
Memar Marqah	early Samaritan midrash (MacDonald 1963)
Men.	tractate *Menaḥot*
Menaḥem ben Saruq	Spanish Jewish lexicographer, tenth century C.E.
menorah	Tabernacle candelabrum
Merneptah	Egyptian ruler in late thirteenth century B.C.E., son of Ramesses II
məṣōrā'	afflicted by skin disease; "leper"

metathesis   reversal

metri causa   for the meter's sake

mezuzah, mezuzoth   box containing scriptural verses affixed to Jews'
                     doorposts

Mic   Micah

Middle Bronze Age   c. 2100–1550 B.C.E.

Middle Kingdom   Egypt c. 2000–1650 B.C.E.

Midianite Hypothesis   theory that Yahwism originated among the Midianites

midrash   para-biblical Jewish legend

Moses   Philo, *Life of Moses*

MS(S)   manuscript(s)

MT   Massoretic Text

n.   note

Nah   Nahum

nasal   consonants *m* and *n*

n.d.   no date; indicates unpublished MS

NEB   *New English Bible*

Ned.   tractate *Nedarim*

Neh   Nehemiah

New Kingdom   Egypt c. 1570–1070 B.C.E.

Niphꜥal   passive-reflexive conjugation of Hebrew verb

Nisan   first month (March-April) in Jewish-Babylonian calendar

nişbe   Arabic/Semitic gentilic suffix

NJV   New Jewish Version (*Tanakh* [Philadelphia: Jewish Publica-
                    tion Society, 1985])

Northwest Semitic   Amorite, Ugaritic, Aramaic, Phoenician, Canaanite,
                     Moabite, Ammonite, Edomite, Hebrew

nota accusativi   direct object marker (*'ēt*)

Num   Numbers

nun   fourteenth letter of the Hebrew alphabet

nun assimilation   tendency of *n* to become identical to following consonant

Nuphꜥal   internal passive conjugation of Niphꜥal

OB   Old Babylonian period, c. 2000–1600 B.C.E.

Obad   Obadiah

OED	Oxford English Dictionary (Oxford: Oxford University, 1971)
OG	Old Greek; the Greek Old Testament
Old Latin	Vetus Latina, early Latin translation of LXX
Oral Torah	Jewish laws not in Torah but traditionally believed to be of Mosaic origin
Origen	Christian theologian, biblical scholar, c. 185–253 C.E.
Osiris	Egyptian god of dead, father of Horus, brother-husband of Isis
OTP	J. H. Charlesworth, ed. *The Old Testament Pseudepigrapha* (2 vols.; Garden City, N.Y.: Doubleday, 1985)
P	the Priestly source
p.	page/plural
pace	in respectful dissent with
paleo-Hebrew script	the original, preexilic form of the Hebrew alphabet
parablepsis	skip of the eye
paragogic nun	archaic suffix attached to 2 m.p. and 3 m.p. imperfect verbs (*yiktōbûn*)
paronomasia	wordplay
pars pro toto	part for the whole
passim	here and there
Passover	Jewish festival on Nisan 15–21
pausal	special form of word used at major syntactic breaks
pe'	seventeenth letter of the Hebrew alphabet
Pentateuch	Torah
perfect	the suffix conjugation of the Hebrew verb (*kātab*)
pericope	section of text
peripheral Akkadian	Akkadian written outside of Mesopotamia proper
Pesaḥ	Israelite festival antecedent to Jewish Passover
Pesaḥ.	tractate *Pesaḥim*
pətûḥâ	paragraph break in MT
PG	Patrologia graeca
Phil	Philippians
Philo	Philo of Alexandria, Hellenistic Jewish writer and philosopher, c. 20 B.C.E.–50 C.E.
Philo of Byblos	author of *Phoenician History*, c. 70–160 C.E.
Phlm	Philemon

phylacteries	capsules containing scriptural verses worn by Jews in prayer and study (*təpillîn*)
Pi'el	Hebrew verbal conjugation with doubled middle radical
PL	Patrologia latina
pl.	plural; plate
plene	full use of *matres lectionis*
plus	a longer text
pointing	the Hebrew vocalization, *niqqûd*
polysyndeton	overuse of conjunctions
postexilic	after 539 B.C.E.
Praep. evangelica	Eusebius, *Praeparatio evangelica*
preexilic	before 587 B.C.E.
preterite	past tense, punctual/completed action
Priestly Writer	author of P
privately	personal communication
Proppian	conforming to the schema of V. I. Propp (1968)
proto-MT	standard Jewish Bible prior to c. 700 C.E.
Proto-Semitic	ancestor of Semitic languages
Prov	Proverbs
Ps	Psalms
Pu'al	passive of Pi'el conjugation
punctator	scribe who inserted vocalization
Qal	base form of Hebrew verb (Pa'al)
Qal Passive	internal passive of the Qal
Qara'ites	literalistic Jewish sect, c. 765 C.E. to present
Qere	pronounced (though not written) (scribal annotation)
Qidd.	tractate *Qiddušin*
Qimḥi	David Qimḥi, Provençal Jewish commentator and grammarian, c. 1160–1235 C.E.
qoph	nineteenth letter of the Hebrew alphabet
Quaest. in Exod.	Philo, *Quaestiones et solutiones in Exodum*
R	Redactorial stratum of Torah
R.	Rabbi
radical	root letter/consonant

Ramban	R. Moses ben Nachman (Nachmanides), Spanish Jewish commentator, 1194–1270 C.E.
Ramesses II	Egyptian ruler in mid-thirteenth century B.C.E.
Rashbam	R. Samuel ben Meir, French Jewish commentator on Bible and Talmud, c. 1080–1174 C.E.
Rashi	R. Solomon ben Isaac, French Jewish commentator on Bible and Talmud, 1040–1105 C.E.
Reᶜ	Egyptian sun god
received text	MT
Redactor	final editor of Torah
Redactor^{JE}	editor who produced JE
resh	twentieth letter of the Hebrew alphabet
resumptive repetition	repetition framing a digression (epanalepsis, *Wiederaufnahme*)
Rev	Revelation
Rom	Romans
Roš Haš.	tractate *Roš Haššana*
Rosh Hashanah	Jewish New Year (first day of seventh month)
Rō(’)š haššānâ	(the same)
Rossi	MS collated by de Rossi (1784–85)
RSP	*Ras Shamra Parallels I, II, III* (AnOr 49, 50, 51; Rome: Pontifical Biblical Institute, 1972, 1975, 1981)
RSV	Revised Standard Version
s.	singular
Saadiah	Saadiah ben Joseph Gaon, Babylonian Jewish scholar, 882–942 C.E.
Šabb.	tractate *Šabbat*
Sadducee	late Hellenistic and early Roman era Jewish sect
ṣadhe	eighteenth letter of the Hebrew alphabet
Sahidic Coptic	daughter translation of LXX
Sam	Samaritan Torah
Samaritans	sect/community of Jews from middle first millennium B.C.E. until present
Samaritan Tg.	translation of Torah into Samaritan Aramaic
Samariticon	translation of Sam into Greek

samekh   fifteenth letter of the Hebrew alphabet

Sammael   malefic angel

Sanh.   tractate *Sanhedrin*

ṣāraʿat   skin disease; "leprosy"

Sargon   Sargon of Akkad, Mesopotamian ruler c. 2300 B.C.E.

Sebhirin   tentative marginal correction or scruple, "one might think" (scribal annotation)

secondary   added later

Second Isaiah   Isaiah 34–35, 40–66

Second Rabbinic Bible   Venice edition, ed. Jacob ben Ḥayyim (1524 C.E.)

Septuagint   Greek Torah (third century B.C.E.)

Seti I   Egyptian ruler c. 1291–1279 B.C.E.

sətûmâ   space to separate textual units

Sforno   Obadiah ben Jacob Sforno, Italian Jewish commentator, c. 1470–1550 C.E.

Shelters   Israelite-Jewish festival of Sukkot

shin   twenty-first letter of the Hebrew alphabet

sin   alternative pronunciation of twenty-first letter of the Hebrew alphabet

Sir   Wisdom of Jesus ben Sira

Soncino Bible (1488)   first printed Hebrew Bible

Sop.   tractate *Soperim*

South Semitic   Arabic and Ethiopic

Spinoza   Baruch (Benedict) Spinoza, Dutch Jewish philosopher, 1632–77 C.E.

spirantization fricative pronunciation of intervocalic plosive (e.g., veth vs. beth, khaph vs. kaph, etc.)

square script   Aramaic alphabet used for writing Hebrew since c. 400 B.C.E.

stichometry   division of poetry into lines

Strom.   Clement of Alexandria, *Stromata*

sublinear correction   scribal correction beneath the line

Suk.   tractate *Sukka*

Sumerian   dominant civilization of Mesopotamia c. 3000–2000 B.C.E.

Sybilline Oracles 5   Egyptian Jewish work c. 100 C.E. (*OTP* 1.393–405)

Symmachus   Jewish reviser of LXX to proto-MT (c. 200 C.E.)

synecdoche	part for the whole
Synoptic(s)	Gospels of Matthew, Mark and Luke
Syr	Syriac Bible
SyrHex	Syro-Hexapla
Syriac	Christian Aramaic dialect
Syro-Hexapla	translation of Hexapla into Syriac
t.	Tosephta
Taʿan.	tractate *Taʿanit*
Tannaʾim	Rabbis cited in Mishnah
Targum	Jewish Aramaic Bible translation
Targumic Tosephta	collection of marginal variants in Targumic MSS
taw	twenty-second letter of the Hebrew alphabet
Tendenz	bias
Tertullian	early Christian writer, c. 155–220 C.E.
Test. Dan	*Testament of Dan* (OTP 1.808–10)
ṭeth	ninth letter of the Hebrew alphabet
Tetragrammaton	divine name *yhwh*
t-form	Semitic verbal conjugation with prefixed or internal *t*, generally passive
Tg.	Targum
Tg. Neb.	Targum Jonathan to the Prophets
Tg. Neofiti I	Palestinian Targum to the Torah
Tg. Onqelos	literalistic Targum to the Torah
Tg. Ps.-Jonathan	midrashic Palestinian Targum to the Torah
theodicy	theological speculation about divine justice
Theodotion	Jewish revision of LXX to proto-MT (c. 50 B.C.E.)
theomachy	battle between gods
third	obscure term for a soldier (*šālîš*)
Three, the	Symmachus, Aquila, Theodotion
Tiglath Pileser III	Assyrian ruler 744–727 B.C.E.
T. Levi	Testament of Levi, c. 150 B.C.E. (*OTP* 1.788–95)
Tob	Tobit
Torah	first five books of Bible
tractate	division of the Talmud

Tract. theolog.-pol.   Spinoza, *Tractatus theologico-politicus*

transhumance   seasonal migration between lowlands and highlands

trope   cantillation

Tudḫaliyas IV   Hittite ruler c. 1250 B.C.E.

type   model; prefiguration

Ugarit   city in N. Syria, flourished c. 1400–1200 B.C.E.

ultima   final syllable

Unleavened Bread   festival in the first month, days 15–21 (*Maṣṣôt*)

Ur-text   original text

v   verse

Versions   surviving witnesses to biblical text

Vetus Latina   early Latin translation of LXX

Vg   Vulgate

vocalization   Hebrew vowel points (*niqqûd*)

vocative lamedh lamedh prefix in Hebrew and Ugaritic indicating direct address

Vorlage   Hebrew text underlying translation

vs.   versus

Vulgate   translation of Bible into Latin by Jerome

War   Josephus, *Jewish War*

waw   sixth letter of the Hebrew alphabet, often a conjunction

waw consecutive   conjunction before verb to indicate sequence of events (*wāw hahippûk*)

Weeks   Israelite-Jewish festival of Shavuot

Wiederaufnahme   resumptive repetition (= epanalepsis)

Wis   Wisdom of Solomon

witness   any biblical MS or translation

XQPhyl1   phylactery from Qumran, exact provenience unknown (Yadin 1969: 36)

y.   Palestinian/Jerusalem Talmud

Yahweh   God's name

Yahwism   Israelite religion

Yahwist   author of J

Yebam.   tractate *Yebamot*

yodh — tenth letter of the Hebrew alphabet

Yôm hakkippūrîm — Yom Kippur, Day of Expiation (tenth of seventh month)

Yom Kippur — (same)

Zadokite — descendant of Zadok, high priest under King Solomon

zayin — seventh letter of the Hebrew alphabet

Zebaḥ. — tractate *Zebaḥim*

Zech — Zechariah

Zeph — Zephaniah

zeugma — incongruous attachment of a single modifier to two incompatible antecedents

Zimri-Lim — King of Mari c. 1775–1760 B.C.E.

II. BIBLIOGRAPHICAL ABBREVIATIONS

AB — Anchor Bible

ABD — *Anchor Bible Dictionary*

ABRL — Anchor Bible Reference Library

AfO — *Archiv für Orientforschung*

AGJU — Arbeiten zur Geschichte des antiken Judentums und des Urchristentums

AJBI — *Annual of the Japanese Biblical Institute*

AJSL — *American Journal of Semitic Languages and Literature*

AJT — *American Journal of Theology*

AnBib — Analecta biblica

AnOr — Analecta orientalia

AnSt — *Anatolian Studies*

AOAT — Alter Orient und Altes Testament

AOS — American Oriental Series

ARW — *Archiv für Religionswissenschaft*

ASAE — *Annales du Service des Antiquités de l'Égypt*

ASAESup — *ASAE*, Supplements

ASOR — American Schools of Oriental Research

ASORDS — ASOR Dissertation Series

ATANT — Abhandlungen zur Theologie des Alten Testaments

BA	*Biblical Archaeologist*
BARev	*Biblical Archaeology Review*
BASOR	*Bulletin of the American Schools of Oriental Research*
BBB	Bonner biblische Beiträge
Bib	*Biblica*
BibOr	Biblica et orientalia
BKAT	Biblischer Kommentar: Altes Testament
BN	*Biblische Notizen*
BRev	*Bible Review*
BWANT	Beiträge zur Wissenschaft vom Neuen und Alten Testament
BZ	*Biblische Zeitschrift*
BZAW	Beihefte zur ZAW
CahRB	Cahiers de la *Revue biblique*
CBQ	*Catholic Biblical Quarterly*
CBQMS	CBQ Monograph Series
ConBOT	Coniectanea biblica, Old Testament
CRAIBL	*Comptes rendus de l'Académie des inscriptions et belles-lettres*
DBSup	*Dictionnaire de la Bible, Supplément*
diss.	dissertation
DJD	Discoveries in the Judaean Desert
Ebib	Études bibliques
ed.	edited by
EM	*'Enṣiqlôpedyâ miqrā'ît*
EncJud	*Encyclopaedia judaica*
ErFor	Erträge der Forschung
ErIsr	Eretz Israel
EstBib	*Estudios bíblicos*
et al.	and others (*et alii*)
ETL	*Ephemerides theologicae lovanienses*
ExpTim	*Expository Times*
FRLANT	Forschungen zur Religion und Literatur des Alten und Neuen Testaments
Fs.	Festschrift
HAR	*Hebrew Annual Review*

HAT	Handbuch zum Alten Testament
HKAT	Handkommentar zum Alten Testament
HR	*History of Religions*
HSM	Harvard Semitic Monographs
HSS	Harvard Semitic Studies
HTR	*Harvard Theological Review*
HUCA	*Hebrew Union College Annual*
IB	*Interpreter's Bible*
ICC	International Critical Commentary
IDB	*Interpreter's Dictionary of the Bible*
IEJ	*Israel Exploration Journal*
Int	*Interpretation*
IOS	*Israel Oriental Studies*
JA	*Journal asiatique*
JANES(CU)	*Journal of the Ancient Near Eastern Society (of Columbia University)*
JAOS	*Journal of the American Oriental Society*
JBL	*Journal of Biblical Literature*
JCS	*Journal of Cuneiform Studies*
JEA	*Journal of Egyptian Archaeology*
JJS	*Journal of Jewish Studies*
JNES	*Journal of Near Eastern Studies*
JNSL	*Journal of Northwest Semitic Languages*
JPOS	*Journal of the Palestine Oriental Society*
JQR	*Jewish Quarterly Review*
JSem	*Journal for Semitics*
JSOT	*Journal for the Study of the Old Testament*
JSOT/ASORMS	JSOT/ASOR Monograph Series
JSOTSup	JSOT, Supplements
JSS	*Journal of Semitic Studies*
JTS	*Journal of Theological Studies*
Leš	*Lešonénu*
M.A.R.I.	*MARI, Annales de Recherches Interdisciplinaires*
NedTT	*Nederlands theologisch tijdschrift*

n.f.	*neue Folge* (new series)
NJBC	*The New Jerome Bible Commentary*
NRT	*La nouvelle revue théologique*
NTS	*New Testament Studies*
OBO	Orbis biblicus et orientalis
OIP	Oriental Institute Publications
OLZ	*Orientalische Literaturzeitung*
Or	*Orientalia*
orig.	original edition
OTL	Old Testament Library
OTS	*Oudtestamentische Studiën*
PEQ	*Palestine Exploration Quarterly*
PJ	*Palästina-Jahrbuch*
pub.	published
RA	*Revue d'assyriologie et d'archéologie orientale*
RB	*Revue biblique*
RHR	*Revue de l'histoire des religions*
RivB	*Rivista biblica*
RSP	*Ras Shamra Parallels*
SANT	Studien zum Alten und Neuen Testament
SBL	Society of Biblical Literature
SBLDS	SBL Dissertation Series
SBLMS	SBL Monograph Series
SBLMasS	SBL Massoretic Studies
SBLSCS	SBL Septuagint and Cognate Studies
SBLTT	SBL Texts and Translations
SBLWAW	SBL Writings from the Ancient World
SBS	Stuttgarter Bibelstudien
SBT	Studies in Biblical Theology
ScrHier	Scripta hierosolymitana
SJOT	*Scandinavian Journal of the Old Testament*
SNTSMS	Society for New Testament Studies Monograph Series
ST	*Studia theologica*
STDJ	Studies on the Texts of the Desert of Judah

StudBib	Studia Biblica
TA	*Tel Aviv*
TDOT	*Theological Dictionary of the Old Testament*
TLZ	*Theologische Literaturzeitung*
UF	*Ugarit-Forschungen*
Ug	*Ugaritica*
VT	*Vetus Testamentum*
VTSup	VT, Supplements
WBC	Word Biblical Commentary
WMANT	Wissenschaftliche Monographien zum Alten und Neuen Testament
WO	*Die Welt des Orients*
ZA	*Zeitschrift für Assyriologie*
ZAH	*Zeitschrift für althebräistik*
ZAW	*Zeitschrift für die alttestamentliche Wissenschaft*
ZDMG	*Zeitschrift der deutschen morgenländischen Gesellschaft*
ZDMGSup	ZDMG, Supplements
ZDPV	Zeitschrift des deutschen Palästina-Vereins
ZTK	*Zeitschrift für Theologie und Kirche*

TRANSLITERATION SYSTEM

◆

My Hebrew transliteration slightly modifies a system familiar to scholars, though fairly inscrutable to the uninitiated. Its advantage is a near one-to-one correspondence to Massoretic symbols. It probably does not, however, reflect the Massoretes' actual pronunciation, still less the ancient Israelites'.

I do not generally indicate "weak" daghesh in *bgdkpt*; when necessary, however, I show spirantization by over- or underlining. *Matres lectionis* are indicated either by circumflex (*â, î, ê, ô, û*) or by a letter in parentheses (*h* or *y*). Quiescent 'aleph retained by historical spelling is often put within parentheses, e.g., *rō(')š* 'head.' Parenthetical shewa—(*ə*)—indicates a shewa that might or might not have been vocalic in Massoretic Hebrew. Like other grammarians, I consider so-called lamedh-he' roots to be lamedh-yodh (e.g., the root "to build" is *bny*, not *bnh*). Here are the alphabetic consonants and vowel points:

HEBREW TRANSLITERATION

	Consonants				Vowel Points		
Letter	Medial Position	Final Position	Transliteration		Vowel	Pointing	Transliteration
'aleph	א		'		vocal šəwā'	אְ	ə
beth	בּ		b		qāmeṣ	אָ	ā
gimel	ג		g		pataḥ	אַ	a
daleth	ד		d		ḥātēp pataḥ	אֲ	ă
he	ה		h		ḥîreq	אִ	i*
waw	ו		w		ḥîreq yôd	אִי	î
zayin	ז		z		ṣērê	אֵ	ē
ḥeth	ח		ḥ		ṣērê yôd	אֵי	ê
teth	ט		ṭ		səgōl	אֶ	e
yodh	י		y		ḥātēp səgōl	אֱ	ĕ
kaph	כ	ך	k		ḥōlem	אֹ	ō
lamedh	ל		l		ḥōlem wāw	וֹ	ô

*ḥîreq—rarely i long ḥireq

mem	מ	ם	m	qāmeṣ qāṭôn	אָ	o
nun	נ	ן	n	ḥātēp qāmeṣ	אֳ	ŏ
samekh	ס		s	qibbûṣ	אֻ	u**
ʿayin	ע		ʿ	šûreq	ו	û
pe	פ	ף	p			
ṣadhe	צ	ץ	ṣ			
qoph	ק		q			
resh	ר		r			
shin	שׁ		š			
sin	שׂ		ś			
taw	ת		t			

**qibbûs—rarely û long qibbûṣ

And here is the first verse of MT Exodus in transliteration: *wəʾēlle(h) šəmôt bənê yiśrāʾēl habbāʾîm miṣrāymâ ʾēt yaʿăqōb ʾîš ûbêtô bāʾû.*

EXODUS 1–18
A TRANSLATION

◆

PART I. ISRAEL IN EGYPT (EXODUS 1:1–11:10)

I. *As ever they oppressed him, so he multiplied* (1:1–14)

1 ¹And these are the names of Israel's sons coming to Egypt with Jacob; man and his *house* they came; ²Reuben, Simeon, Levi and Judah, ³Issachar, Zebulon and Benjamin, ⁴Dan and Naphtali, Gad and Asher. ⁵Now, all of the *soul* coming from Jacob's *thigh* was seventy *souls*. But Joseph was in Egypt. ⁶And Joseph died, and all his brothers, and all that generation. ⁷But Israel's sons bore fruit and swarmed and multiplied and proliferated greatly, greatly, so the land was filled with them.

⁸Then arose a new king over Egypt who did not know Joseph. ⁹And he said to his people: "See: the people of Israel's Sons is greater and mightier than we. ¹⁰Let us be wise concerning him, lest he multiply and, it may happen, should war come, he too be added to our enemies and fight against us and go up from the land." ¹¹So they set over him corvée masters in order to oppress him with their tasks, and he built storage cities for Pharaoh: Pithom and Raamses. ¹²But as ever they oppressed him, so he multiplied and so he burst out, and they dreaded from before Israel's Sons. ¹³And Egypt made Israel's Sons work through duress, ¹⁴for they embittered their lives through hard work in mortar and in bricks, and with all work in the field—in short, all their work with which they worked them through duress.

II. *If he is a son, kill him* (1:15–21)

1 ¹⁵And Egypt's king said to the Hebrew midwives—of whom the name of the one was Shiphrah and the name of the second Puah—¹⁶and he said, "In your helping the Hebrew women give birth, then look upon the *two stones*. If he is a son, kill him, but if she is a daughter, she may live." ¹⁷But the midwives feared the Deity and did not do as what Egypt's king spoke to them; and they let the boys live.

¹⁸Then Egypt's king called to the midwives and said to them, "Why did you do this thing and allow the boys to live?"

¹⁹And the midwives said to Pharaoh, "The Hebrew women are not at all like the Egyptian women, but they are lively. Before the midwife comes to them they bear."

N.B.: The following translation of Exodus 1–18 is based upon a reconstructed Hebrew text diverging from that found in printed Bibles. All differences are explained under TEXTUAL NOTES. On the hyperliteral style, see INTRODUCTION, pp. 40–41.

20And Deity graced the midwives, and the people multiplied and proliferated greatly. 21And it happened, because the midwives feared the Deity, that he made *houses* for them.

III. *For I drew him from the waters* (1:22–2:10)

1   22Now, Pharaoh commanded all his people, saying, "All the son born, throw him into the Nile, but all the daughter let live."

2   1Then a man from Levi's *house* went and *took* Levi's daughter. 2And the woman conceived and bore a son and saw him, how he was good, and she hid him three *moons*. 3But she could conceal him no longer, so she took for him a vessel of papyrus and tarred it with tar and with pitch, and put the boy in it and set in the rushes on the Nile's *lip*. 4And his sister stationed herself from a distance to know what would be done to him.

5Now, Pharaoh's daughter went down to wash by the Nile, and her maids were going on the Nile's *arm*. And she saw the vessel among the rushes and sent her maidservant, and she took it. 6And she opened and saw him—the boy—and, see: a child crying! And she pitied him and said, "This is from the Hebrews' boys."

7And his sister said to Pharaoh's daughter, "Shall I go and call for you a nursing woman from the Hebrews, so that she may suckle the boy for you?"

8And Pharaoh's daughter said to her, "Go." And the lass went and called the boy's mother.

9And Pharaoh's daughter said to her, "Cause this boy to go and suckle him for me, and I, I will pay your wage." So the woman took the boy and suckled him.

10And the boy grew, and she brought him to Pharaoh's daughter, and he was to her as a son. And she called his name "Moses" and said, "For I drew him from the waters."

IV. *Who set you as a man, ruler and judge?* (2:11–15a)

2   11And it happened in those days, and Moses grew. And he went out to his brothers and looked upon their tasks and saw an Egyptian man striking a Hebrew man from his brothers. 12And he turned like this and like this, and he saw that there was no man. Then he struck the Egyptian and hid him in the sand.

13And he went out on the second day, and, see: two Hebrew men fighting. And he said to the evil one, "Why do you strike your fellow?"

14But he said, "Who set you as a man, ruler and judge over us? To kill me, do you *say*, as you killed the Egyptian?"

And Moses feared and *said*, "The affair has become known after all."

15aAnd Pharaoh heard this affair and sought to kill Moses. So Moses fled from Pharaoh's *face* and settled in the land of Midian.

V. *A sojourner in a foreign land* (2:15b–23a)

2 ¹⁵ᵇAnd he settled beside the well.

¹⁶Now, Midian's priest had seven daughters; and they came and drew and filled the troughs to water their father's flock. ¹⁷But the shepherds came and expelled them. Then Moses arose and saved them and watered their flock.

¹⁸And they returned to Reuel their father, and he said, "Why have you hastened to come today?"

¹⁹And they said, "An Egyptian man rescued us from the shepherds' *arm*, and he also drew, drew for us and watered the flock."

²⁰And he said to his daughters, "So where is he? Why is it you left the man? Call to him, that he may eat food."

²¹So Moses agreed to settle with the man. And he gave his daughter Zipporah to Moses. ²²And she bore a son, and he called his name Gershom, for he said, "A sojourner was I in a foreign land."

²³ᵃAnd it happened in those many days, and Egypt's king died.

VI. *And Deity remembered his covenant* (2:23b–25)

2 ²³ᵇAnd Israel's Sons moaned from the work and screamed, and their plea ascended to the Deity from the work. ²⁴And Deity heard their groan, and Deity remembered his covenant with Abraham, with Isaac and with Jacob. ²⁵And Deity saw Israel's Sons, and he made himself known to them.

VII. *Yahweh the Hebrews' deity happened upon us* (3–4)

3 ¹Moses, meanwhile, was herding the flock of Jethro, his father-in-law, Midian's priest, and he drove the flock behind the wilderness, and he came to the Deity's mountain, to Horeb. ²And Yahweh's Messenger appeared to him as a fire flame from within the bush. And he saw, and, see: the bush burning with fire, but the bush not consumed. ³So Moses said, "I would turn and see this great vision. Why does not the bush burn?"

⁴And Yahweh saw that he turned to see, and Deity called to him from within the bush and said, "Moses, Moses."

And he said, "See me."

⁵And he said, "Do not approach hither. Pull your sandals from upon your feet, for the place on which you are standing, it is holiness ground." ⁶And he said, "I am your father's deity, Abraham's deity, Isaac's deity and Jacob's deity."

Then Moses hid his face, for he was afraid to gaze at the Deity. ⁷And Yahweh said, "I have seen, seen the humiliation of my people who are in Egypt, and their scream have I heard from *the face of* his overseers; I indeed know his pains. ⁸So I will descend/have descended to rescue him from Egypt's *arm* and to bring him up from that land to a land good and broad, to a land flowing of milk and honey, to the place of the Canaanite and the Hittite and the Amorite and the Perizzite and the Hivvite and the Jebusite. ⁹And now, see: the scream of Israel's Sons has come to me, and I have also seen the oppression with which Egypt are oppressing them. ¹⁰And now, go, for I send you to Pharaoh, and take my people, Israel's Sons, out from Egypt."

¹¹But Moses said to the Deity, "Who am I that I should go to Pharaoh, or that I should take Israel's Sons out from Egypt?"

¹²And he said, "Because I will be with you. And this is the sign for you that I, I sent you. When you take the people out from Egypt, you will serve the Deity at this mountain."

¹³But Moses said to the Deity, "Suppose I come to Israel's Sons and say to them, 'Your fathers' deity has sent me to you,' and they say to me, 'What is his name?'—what should I say to them?"

¹⁴Then Deity said to Moses, "I will be who I will be." And he said, "Thus you will say to Israel's Sons: '"I-will-be" has sent me to you.'"

¹⁵And Deity further said to Moses, "Thus you will say to Israel's Sons: 'Yahweh your fathers' deity, Abraham's deity, Isaac's deity and Jacob's deity—he has sent me to you'; this is my name to eternity, and this is my designation age (by) age. ¹⁶Go, and you will gather Israel's elders and say to them, 'Yahweh your fathers' deity appeared to me, the deity of Abraham, Isaac and Jacob, saying: "I acknowledge, acknowledge you and what is done to you in Egypt. ¹⁷And I have said, 'I will take you up from Egypt's oppression to the land of the Canaanite and the Hittite and the Amorite and the Perizzite and the Hivvite and the Jebusite, to a land flowing of milk and honey.'"' ¹⁸And they will heed your voice, and you will come, you and Israel's elders, to Egypt's king and say to him, 'Yahweh the Hebrews' deity happened upon us. And now, we would go a three days' way into the wilderness and sacrifice to Yahweh our deity.' ¹⁹But I, I know that Egypt's king will not allow you to go, unless by a strong arm. ²⁰So I will send my arm and strike Egypt with all my wonders which I will work in his midst, and afterward he will release you. ²¹And I will set this people's favor in Egypt's eyes, and it will happen, when you go, you will not go emptily. ²²But a woman will ask of her neighbor woman and of the woman sojourner of her house silver objects and gold objects and robes. And you will place on your sons and on your daughters, and you will despoil Egypt."

4 ¹But Moses answered and said, "And suppose they do not believe me and do not heed my voice, but say, 'Yahweh did not appear to you'?"

²Then Yahweh said to him, "What's this in your hand?"

And he said, "A rod."

³And he said, "Throw it groundward."

So he threw it groundward, and it became a snake, and Moses fled from its *face*.

⁴Then Yahweh said to Moses, "Send out your hand and grasp its tail."

So he sent out his hand and seized it, and it became a rod in his hand. ⁵"So that they will believe that Yahweh their fathers' deity, Abraham's deity, Isaac's deity and Jacob's deity appeared to you."

⁶And Yahweh further said to him, "Bring your arm into your bosom."

So he put his arm into his bosom. Then he removed it, and, see: his arm was *maṣōrā‛* like snow. [7]Then he said, "Return your arm to your bosom."

So he returned his arm to his bosom. Then he removed it from his bosom, and, see: it returned like his flesh. [8]"And it will happen, if they do not believe you and do not heed the first sign's voice, then they will believe the latter sign's voice. [9]But it will happen, if they do not believe even these two signs nor heed your voice, then you will take from the Nile's waters and pour on the dry land. And they will become, the waters you take from the Nile, they will become blood on the dry land."

[10]But Moses said to Yahweh, "Please, my Lordship, I am not a words man, not yesterday nor the day before nor since your speaking to your slave, but I am heavy of mouth and heavy of tongue."

[11]But Yahweh said to him, "Who made/makes for Man a mouth or who makes dumb or deaf or percipient or blind? Is it not I, Yahweh? [12]And now, go, for I, I will be with your mouth and will guide you in what you will speak."

[13]Then he said, "Please, my Lordship, send through the hand you would send."

[14]Then Yahweh's *nose* grew angry at Moses. And he said, "Is there not Aaron, your brother Levite? I know that he will speak, speak, and, moreover, see: him coming out to meet you, and he will see you and rejoice in his heart. [15]And you will speak to him and put the words in his mouth. And I, I will be with your mouth and with his mouth, and I will teach you what you will do. [16]And he, he will speak for you to the people; and it will happen, he, he will be for you as a mouth, and you, you will be for him as Deity. [17]And this rod you will take in your hand, with which you may work the signs."

[18]So Moses went and returned to Jether his father-in-law and said to him, "I would go and return to my brothers who are in Egypt and see if they still live."

And Jethro said to Moses, "Go in peace."

[19]And Yahweh said to Moses in Midian, "Go, return to Egypt, for all the men seeking your *soul* have died."

[20]So Moses took his *woman* and his sons and mounted them on the ass, and he returned to the land of Egypt. And Moses took the Deity's rod in his hand.

[21]And Yahweh said to Moses, "In your going to return to Egypt, *see* all the wonders which I have put into your hand, and work them to Pharaoh's *face*. But I, I will strengthen his heart, and he will not release the people. [22]And you will say to Pharaoh, 'Thus has Yahweh said: "My son, my firstborn, is Israel. [23]And I have said to you, 'Release my son that he may serve me.' And if you refuse to release him, see: I am going to kill your son, your firstborn."'"

[24]And it happened on the way, at the night-stop, and Yahweh met him and sought to put him to death. [25]But Zipporah took a flint and severed her son's foreskin and applied to his *legs* and said, "For you are a bridegroom/son-in-law of bloodiness to me."

[26]And he slackened from him. Then she said, "A bridegroom/son-in-law of bloodiness by circumcision."

[27]And Yahweh said to Aaron, "Go to meet Moses to the wilderness."

So he went and met him at the Deity's mountain and kissed him. [28]And Moses told to Aaron all Yahweh's words with which he sent him, and all the signs which he commanded him.

[29]And Moses and Aaron went and assembled all the elders of Israel's Sons. [30]And Aaron spoke all the words that Yahweh had spoken to Moses, and he did the signs before the people's eyes. [31]And the people trusted, and they heard that Yahweh acknowledged Israel's Sons and that he beheld their oppression. And they knelt and bowed down.

VIII. *A sword in their hand to kill us* (5:1–6:1)

5 [1]And afterwards Moses and Aaron came and said to Pharaoh, "Thus has Yahweh Israel's deity said: 'Release my people, that they may celebrate to me in the wilderness.'"

[2]But Pharaoh said, "Who is Yahweh, that I should heed his voice by releasing Israel? I have not known Yahweh; moreover, Israel I will not release."

[3]Then they said, "The Hebrews' deity happened upon us. We would go a three days' way into the wilderness and sacrifice to Yahweh our deity, lest he strike us with the plague or with the sword."

[4]But Egypt's king said to them, "Why, Moses and Aaron, should you distract the people from his work? Go to your tasks." [5]And Pharaoh said, "See: the land's people are now many, and you will interrupt them from their tasks."

[6]So on that day Pharaoh commanded those overseeing the people and his officers, saying, [7]"Do not continue to give the people straw to brickmake the bricks as yesterday and the day before. They, they shall go and scrabble straw for themselves. [8]But the volume of the bricks they were producing yesterday and the day before you shall lay upon them; do not deduct from it. For they are lax; therefore they cry, saying, 'We would go sacrifice to our deity.' [9]Let the work be hard upon the men; so let them do it, and not look to words of deceit."

[10]Then the people's overseers and his officers went out and said to the people, saying, "Thus has Pharaoh said: 'I am not going to give you straw. [11]You, you go get for yourselves straw from wherever you can find, for not a whit is deducted from your work.'"

[12]So the people scattered in all the land of Egypt to scrabble stubble for the straw, [13]and the overseers were urging, saying, "Finish your tasks, a day's matter in its day, just as when the straw was being given to you." [14]And the officers of Israel's Sons, whom Pharaoh's overseers had placed over them, were beaten, saying, "Why have you not completed your quota of brickmaking as yesterday and the day before, both yesterday and today?"

[15]And the officers of Israel's Sons came and cried to Pharaoh, saying, "Why do you do so to your slaves? [16]Straw is not being given to your slaves, yet 'Bricks,' they say to us, 'make!' Now, see: your slaves are being beaten, and your people is the fault."

¹⁷But he said, "Lax are you, lax; therefore you are saying, 'We would go sacrifice to Yahweh.' ¹⁸And now, go work; and straw will not be given to you, but the full volume of bricks you must give."

¹⁹And the officers of Israel's Sons saw them in trouble, saying, "Do not deduct from your bricks, a day's matter in its day." ²⁰And they encountered Moses and Aaron stationed to meet them in their going out from with Pharaoh. ²¹And they said to them, "May Yahweh look on you and judge, who have fouled our odor in Pharaoh's eyes and in his slaves' eyes, placing a sword in their hand to kill us."

²²So Moses returned to Yahweh and said, "My Lordship, for what have you done badly to this people? For what is it you sent me? ²³For ever since I came to Pharaoh to speak in your name, it has gone badly for this people, and rescued, you have not rescued your people."

6 ¹And Yahweh said to Moses, "Now you will see what I will do to Pharaoh. For by a strong arm he will release them, and by a strong arm he will expel them from his land."

IX. *I am Yahweh* (6:2–7:7)

6 ²And Deity spoke to Moses and said to him, "I am Yahweh. ³Now, I appeared to Abraham, to Isaac and to Jacob in God Shadday, but I, my name Yahweh, was not known to them. ⁴And I both made stand my covenant with them to give them the land of Canaan, the land of their sojournings in which they sojourned; ⁵and I also have heard the groan of Israel's Sons, because the Egyptians are making them work, and I have remembered my covenant. ⁶Therefore, say to Israel's Sons: 'I am Yahweh. And I will take you out from under Egypt's burdens. And I will rescue you from their work. And I will redeem you with an extended limb and with great judgments. ⁷And I will take you to me as a people, and I will become to you as a deity. And you will know that I am Yahweh your deity, who takes you out from under Egypt's burdens. ⁸And I will bring you to the land that I raised my arm to give it to Abraham, to Isaac and to Jacob, and I will give it to you as an inheritance. I am Yahweh.'" ⁹And Moses spoke so to Israel's Sons. But they did not heed Moses, from shortness of spirit and from hard work.

¹⁰Then Yahweh spoke to Moses, saying, ¹¹"Come, speak to Pharaoh Egypt's king, so that he will release Israel's Sons from his land."

¹²But Moses spoke before Yahweh, saying, "If Israel's Sons have not heeded me, then how will Pharaoh heed me, as I am uncircumcised of lips?"

¹³And Yahweh spoke to Moses and to Aaron and commanded them to Israel's Sons and to Pharaoh Egypt's king, to take Israel's Sons from the land of Egypt.

¹⁴These are the heads of their fathers' house. The sons of Reuben Israel's firstborn: Hanoch and Pallu, Hezron and Carmi; these are Reuben's families.

[15]And Simeon's sons: Jemuel and Jamin and Ohad and Jachin and Zohar and Shaul the Canaanitess's son; these are Simeon's families. [16]And these are the names of Levi's sons in their generations: Gershon and Kohath and Merari; and the years of Levi's life: seven and thirty and one hundred year. [17]Gershon's sons: Libni and Shimei in their families. [18]And Kohath's sons: Amram and Yizhar and Hebron and Uzziel; and the years of Kohath's life: three and thirty and one hundred year. [19]And Merari's sons: Mahli and Mushi. These are the Levite's families in their generations. [20]And Amram took Jochebed his aunt as a *woman* for him, and she bore him Aaron and Moses; and the years of Amram's life: six and thirty and one hundred year. [21]And Yizhar's sons: Korah and Nepheg and Zichri. [22]And Uzziel's sons: Mishael and Elizaphan and Sithri. [23]And Aaron took Elisheba Amminadab's daughter, Nahshon's sister, as a *woman* for him, and she bore him Nadab and Abihu, Eleazar and Ithamar. [24]And Korah's sons: Assir and Elkanah and Abiasaph. These are the Korahite's families. [25]And Eleazar Aaron's son took for himself (one) of Putiel's daughters as a *woman* for him, and she bore him Phinehas. These are the heads of the Levites' fathers in their families. [26]That is Aaron and Moses to whom Yahweh said, "Take Israel's Sons out from the land of Egypt by their brigades." [27]They are the speakers to Pharaoh Egypt's king to take Israel's Sons out from Egypt; that is Moses and Aaron.

[28]And it happened, on the day Yahweh spoke to Moses in the land of Egypt, [29]and Yahweh spoke to Moses, saying, "I am Yahweh. Speak to Pharaoh Egypt's king all that I speak to you."

[30]But Moses said before Yahweh, "As I am uncircumcised of lips, then how will Pharaoh heed me?"

7 [1]And Yahweh said to Moses, "See: I have made you a deity to Pharaoh, and Aaron your brother will be your prophet. [2]You, you will speak all that I command you, and Aaron your brother will speak to Pharaoh, that he should release Israel's Sons from his land. [3]But I, I will harden Pharaoh's heart and multiply my signs and my wonders in the land of Egypt. [4]And Pharaoh will not listen to you, and I will lay my arm upon Egypt and take out my brigades, my people, Israel's Sons, from the land of Egypt with great judgments. [5]And Egypt will know that I am Yahweh, in my extending my arm over Egypt. And I will take out Israel's Sons from their midst."

[6]And Moses and Aaron did, as Yahweh commanded them, so they did. [7]And Moses was a *son of* eighty years, and Aaron was a *son of* three and eighty years, in their speaking to Pharaoh.

X. But Pharaoh's heart was strong; he did not release Israel's Sons (7:8–11:10)

7 [8]And Yahweh said to Moses and to Aaron, saying, [9]"When Pharaoh speaks to you, saying, 'Give yourselves a wonder,' then say to Aaron, 'Take your rod and cast before Pharaoh. Let it become a serpent.'"

¹⁰And Moses and Aaron came to Pharaoh and did so, as Yahweh commanded. And Aaron cast his rod before Pharaoh and before his slaves, and it became a serpent. ¹¹But Pharaoh, too, called to the sages and to the wizards, and they, too, Egypt's ḥarṭummîm, did with their mysteries likewise. ¹²And each threw down his rod and they became serpents. And Aaron's rod swallowed their rods. ¹³But Pharaoh's heart was strong, and he did not heed them, as Yahweh had spoken.

¹⁴And Yahweh said to Moses, "Pharaoh's heart is firm; he has refused to release the people. ¹⁵Go to Pharaoh in the morning; see: (him) going out to the waters. And you will station yourself to meet him on the Nile's *lip*, and the rod that turned into a snake you will take in your hand. ¹⁶And you will say to him, 'Yahweh the Hebrews' deity sent me to you, saying, "Release my people, that they may serve me in the wilderness"—but, see: you have not hearkened till now. ¹⁷Thus has Yahweh said: "By this you may know that I am Yahweh. See: I am going to strike with the rod that is in my hand upon the waters that are in the Nile, and they will turn to blood. ¹⁸And the fish that is in the Nile will die, and the Nile will reek, and Egypt will be unable to drink waters from the Nile."'"

¹⁹And Yahweh said to Moses, "Say to Aaron, 'Take your rod and extend your arm over Egypt's waters—over their rivers, over their "niles" and over their marshes and over every reservoir of their waters, that they become blood.' And blood will be in all the land of Egypt, in the stocks and in the stones."

²⁰And Moses and Aaron did so, as Yahweh commanded. And he raised with the rod and struck the waters that were in the Nile to Pharaoh's eyes and to his slaves' eyes, and all the waters that were in the Nile were turned to blood. ²¹And the fish that was in the Nile died, and the Nile reeked, and Egypt were not able to drink waters from the Nile, and the blood was in all the land of Egypt. ²²But Egypt's ḥarṭummîm did likewise with their mysteries, and Pharaoh's heart was strong, and he did not heed them, as Yahweh had spoken. ²³And Pharaoh turned and came into his house and did not set his heart to this either. ²⁴And all Egypt dug waters to drink from the Nile's surroundings, for they could not drink from the Nile's waters.

²⁵And seven days were filled after Yahweh's smiting the Nile. ²⁶And Yahweh said to Moses, "Come to Pharaoh, and you will say to him, 'Thus has Yahweh said: "Release my people, that they may serve me. ²⁷For if you refuse to release, see: I am going to strike all your territory with the frogs. ²⁸And the Nile will breed frogs, and they will ascend and come into your house and into your bed room and onto your bed and into your slaves' house and among your people and into your ovens and into your dough pans. ²⁹And upon you and upon your slaves and upon your people the frogs will ascend."'"

8 ¹And Yahweh said to Moses, "Say to Aaron, 'Extend your arm with your rod over the rivers, over the "niles" and over the marshes, and raise the frogs upon the land of Egypt.'"

²And Aaron extended his arm over Egypt's waters, and the frog ascended and covered the land of Egypt. ³But the ḥarṭummîm did likewise with their mysteries,

and they raised up the frogs upon the land of Egypt. ⁴And Pharaoh called to Moses and to Aaron and said, "Pray to Yahweh, that he remove the frogs from me and from my people, and I will release the people, that they may sacrifice to Yahweh."

⁵And Moses said, "Assume honor over me as to for when I should pray for you and for your slaves and for your people, to cut off the frogs from you and from your houses; only in the Nile they will remain."

⁶And he said, "For tomorrow."

And he said, "According to your word, that you may know that none is like Yahweh our deity. ⁷And the frogs will depart from you and from your houses and from your slaves and from your people; only in the Nile they will remain."

⁸And Moses and Aaron went out from with Pharaoh, and Moses cried to Yahweh on the matter of the frogs that he put upon Pharaoh. ⁹And Yahweh did according to Moses' word, and the frogs died from the houses, from the yards and from the fields. ¹⁰And they piled them as heaps, heaps, and the land reeked. ¹¹But Pharaoh saw that there was respite, and he made firm his heart, and he did not heed them, as Yahweh had spoken.

¹²And Yahweh said to Moses, "Say to Aaron, 'Extend your rod and strike the dirt of the land, that it become lice in all the land of Egypt.'"

¹³And they did so. And Aaron extended his arm with his rod and struck the dirt of the land, and the louse became on man and on animal; all the dirt of the land became lice in all the land of Egypt. ¹⁴And the ḥarṭummîm did likewise with their mysteries, to bring forth the lice, but they were not able. And the louse became on man and on animal. ¹⁵And the ḥarṭummîm said to Pharaoh, "It is a divine finger." But Pharaoh's heart was strong, and he did not heed them, as Yahweh had spoken.

¹⁶And Yahweh said to Moses, "Rise early in the morning and station yourself before Pharaoh; see: (him) going out to the waters. And you will say to him, 'Thus has Yahweh said: "Release my people, that they may serve me. ¹⁷For if you do not release my people, see: I am going to send against you and against your slaves and against your people and into your houses the ʿārōb; and Egypt's houses will be full of the ʿārōb, as well as the land on which they are. ¹⁸But I will separate on that day the land of Goshen, on which my people stands, and there will be no ʿārōb there, that you may know that I am Yahweh in the land's midst. ¹⁹For I will put a redemption between my people and between your people; tomorrow this sign will occur."'"

²⁰And Yahweh did so, and heavy ʿārōb came to Pharaoh's house and his slaves' house. And in all the land of Egypt the land was being devastated from before the ʿārōb.

²¹And Pharaoh called to Moses and to Aaron and said, "Go, sacrifice to your deity in the land."

²²But Moses said, "It is not possible to do so, for Egypt's abomination we would sacrifice to Yahweh our deity. If we sacrifice Egypt's abomination to their eyes, will they not stone us? ²³A three days' way we would go into the wilderness and sacrifice to Yahweh our deity as he may say to us."

²⁴But Pharaoh said, "I, I will release you, that you may sacrifice to Yahweh your deity in the wilderness. Only far, do not go far. Pray for me."

²⁵And Moses said, "See: I am going out from with you, and I will pray to Yahweh, and the ʿārōb will leave from Pharaoh, from his slaves and from his people tomorrow. Only let not Pharaoh continue to toy by not releasing the people to sacrifice to Yahweh."

²⁶And Moses went out from with Pharaoh and prayed to Yahweh. ²⁷And Yahweh did according to Moses' word and removed the ʿārōb from Pharaoh, from his slaves and from his people; not one remained. ²⁸But Pharaoh made firm his heart this time, too, and did not release the people.

9 ¹And Yahweh said to Moses, "Come to Pharaoh, and you will speak to him: 'Thus has Yahweh the Hebrews' deity said: "Release my people, that they may serve me. ²For if you refuse to release, and you still hold them, ³see: Yahweh's arm is about to be upon your cattle that are in the field, upon the horses, upon the asses, upon the camels, upon the herd and upon the flock— a very heavy plague. ⁴But Yahweh will separate between Israel's cattle and between Egypt's cattle, and of all belonging to Israel's Sons no thing will die."'" ⁵And Yahweh set a time, saying, "Tomorrow Yahweh will do this thing in the land."

⁶And Yahweh did this thing on the next day. And all Egypt's cattle died, and of Israel's Sons' cattle not one died. ⁷And Pharaoh sent, and, see: so much as one of Israel's cattle had not died. But Pharaoh's heart was firm, and he did not release the people.

⁸And Yahweh said to Moses and to Aaron, "Take for yourselves oven ash, the fullness of your fists, and let Moses cast it heavenward to Pharaoh's eyes. ⁹And it will become dust over all the land of Egypt, and it will become upon man and upon animal a šəḥîn blossoming with boils in all the land of Egypt."

¹⁰So they took the oven ash and stood before Pharaoh, and Moses threw it heavenward, and there was a šəḥîn of boils blossoming upon man and upon animal. ¹¹And the ḥarṭummîm could not stand before Moses because of the šəḥîn, for the šəḥîn was upon the ḥarṭummîm and upon all Egypt. ¹²But Yahweh strengthened Pharaoh's heart, and he did not heed them, as Yahweh had spoken to Moses.

¹³And Yahweh said to Moses, "Rise early in the morning and station yourself before Pharaoh. And you will say to him, 'Thus has Yahweh the Hebrews' deity said: "Release my people, that they may serve me. ¹⁴For this time I am going to send all these my afflictions against you and against your slaves and against your people, in order that you may know that none is like me in all the world. ¹⁵For now, I could have sent forth my arm and smitten you and your people with the plague, so that you would have vanished from the land. ¹⁶However, for this I have let you stand: in order to show you my strength, and to tell my *name* in all the world. ¹⁷You still exalt yourself over my people without releasing them. ¹⁸See: I am going to rain at this time tomorrow very heavy hail, whose like never was in Egypt from the day, her founding, and until now. ¹⁹And now send, shelter your cattle and all in the field that is yours. Every man or animal

that will be found in the field and will not have been gathered into the house—
then the hail will descend upon them and they will die.'"
²⁰He who feared Yahweh's word from Pharaoh's slaves, he sheltered his slaves
and his cattle in the houses. ²¹But he who did not put his heart to Yahweh's
word, then he left his slaves and his cattle in the field.
²²And Yahweh said to Moses, "Extend your arm toward the heavens, and let
there be hail in all the land of Egypt, upon man and upon animal and upon
all the field's herbage in the land of Egypt."
²³So Moses extended his rod toward the heavens, and Yahweh, he gave *voices*
and hail, and fire went groundward, and Yahweh rained hail on the land of
Egypt. ²⁴And there was hail, and fire caught up within the hail, very heavy,
whose like was not in Egypt since she became a nation. ²⁵And the hail struck
in the land of Egypt everything that was in the field, from man and to animal,
and all the field's herbage the hail struck, and every tree of the field it smashed.
²⁶Only in the land of Goshen, where Israel's Sons were, there was no hail.
²⁷And Pharaoh sent and called to Moses and to Aaron and said to them, "I
have been wrong this time. The justified one is Yahweh, and the guilty are I
and my people. ²⁸Pray to Yahweh, that it will be enough of being divine *voices*
and hail, and I will release you, and you will not continue to stand still."
²⁹And Moses said to him, "As my leaving the city, I will spread my hands to
Yahweh. The *voices* will cease, and the hail will be no more, that you may
know that the earth is Yahweh's. ³⁰But you and your slaves, I know that you do
not yet fear before Yahweh Deity."
³¹Now, the flax and the barley were smitten, for the barley was young ears
and the flax was buds. ³²But the wheat and the emmer were not smitten, for
they were *dark*.
³³And Moses left the city from with Pharaoh and spread his hands to Yahweh, and the *voices* and the hail ceased, and rain was not shed groundward.
³⁴And Pharaoh saw that the rain and the hail and the *voices* had ceased, and he
continued to do wrong, and he made firm his heart, he and his slaves. ³⁵And
Pharaoh's heart was strong, and he did not release Israel's Sons, as Yahweh had
spoken through Moses' hand.
10   ¹And Yahweh said to Moses, "Come to Pharaoh, for I, I have made
firm his heart and his slaves' heart, so that I might set these my signs in his
core, ²and so that you may tell into your son's ears and your son's son's how I
lorded it in Egypt, and my signs that I set among them, that you may know
that I am Yahweh."
³And Moses and Aaron came to Pharaoh and said to him, "Thus has Yahweh
the Hebrews' deity said: 'Until when do you refuse to humble yourself before
me? Release my people, that they may serve me. ⁴For if you refuse to release
my people, see: I am going to bring tomorrow locust in your territory. ⁵And it
will cover the land's *eye*, and one will not be able to see the earth, and it will
eat the excess of the remnant remaining to you from the hail, and it will eat
every tree that sprouts for you from the field. ⁶And they will fill your houses
and your slaves' houses and all Egypt's houses—that which your fathers and

your fathers' fathers never saw, from the day of their being upon the ground until this day.'" And he turned and went from with Pharaoh.

⁷And Pharaoh's slaves said to him, "Until when will this be a snare to us? Release the men, that they may serve Yahweh their deity. Don't you yet know that Egypt is dying?"

⁸So Moses and Aaron were brought back to Pharaoh, and he said to them, "Go, serve Yahweh your deity. *Who and who* are going?"

⁹And Moses said, "With our youths and with our elders we would go, with our sons and with our daughters, with our flocks and with our herds we would go, for it is Yahweh's festival for us."

¹⁰But he said to them, "May Yahweh be so with you, as I would release you and your dependents. See, for evil is before your face. ¹¹Not so. Go, you males, and serve Yahweh, for that is what you are seeking," and he expelled them from before Pharaoh.

¹²And Yahweh said to Moses, "Extend your arm over the land of Egypt with the locust, and let it ascend upon the land of Egypt and eat all the land's herbage, all that the hail left behind."

¹³So Moses extended his rod over the land of Egypt, and Yahweh, he drove a *forward* wind into the land, all that day and all the night. The morning happened, and the *forward* wind bore the locust, ¹⁴and the locust ascended over all the land of Egypt and alit in all the territory of Egypt, very heavy. Before it there was never such locust as it, and after it never will be such. ¹⁵And it covered all the land's *eye*, so that the land was dark, and it ate all the land's herbage and all the tree's fruit that the hail had left; not any greenery was left on the tree or on the field's herbage in all the land of Egypt.

¹⁶And Pharaoh hurried to call to Moses and to Aaron and said, "I have wronged Yahweh your deity and you. ¹⁷And now, *lift* my fault only this time, and pray to Yahweh your deity that he remove from upon me just this death."

¹⁸So he went out from with Pharaoh and prayed to Yahweh. ¹⁹And Yahweh turned back a very strong sea wind, and it bore the locust and blew it into the Suph Sea. Not one locust was left in all Egypt's territory. ²⁰But Yahweh strengthened Pharaoh's heart, and he did not release Israel's Sons.

²¹And Yahweh said to Moses, "Extend your arm into the heavens, and let there be darkness over the land of Egypt." ²²And Moses extended his arm into the heavens, and there was a darkness of gloom in all the land of Egypt three days. ²³Man could not see his *brother*, and no man stood up *from under himself* three days. But for all Israel's Sons there was light in their dwellings.

²⁴And Pharaoh called to Moses and said, "Go serve Yahweh. Only your flock and your herd will be detained. Your dependents, too, may go with you."

²⁵But Moses said, "Both will you, you put into our hand *slaughter sacrifices* and *ascending sacrifices* that we may make to Yahweh our deity, ²⁶and also our own cattle will go with us; not a hoof will remain. For from them we will take to serve Yahweh our deity, since we, we do not know with what we will serve Yahweh until our arrival there."

²⁷But Yahweh strengthened Pharaoh's heart, and he did not release them.

²⁸Then Pharaoh said to him, "Go from before me. Watch yourself, see my face no more. For on the day of your seeing my face you will die."

²⁹And Moses said, "You spoke right. I will see your face no more."

11   ¹And Yahweh said to Moses, "Yet one more plague I will bring upon Pharaoh and upon Egypt. After this, he will release you from here; when he releases completely, he will expel, expel you. ²Speak in the people's ears, that they should ask, man of his friend and woman of her friend, silver objects and gold objects. ³And Yahweh will put the people's favor in Egypt's eyes. Also, the man Moses will be very great in the land of Egypt, in Pharaoh's slaves' eyes and in the people's eyes."

⁴And Moses said, "Thus has Yahweh said: 'At midnight I am going to set forth in Egypt's midst. ⁵And every firstborn in the land of Egypt will die, from the firstborn of Pharaoh sitting on his throne to the firstborn of the maidservant that is behind the two millstones, and every animal firstborn. ⁶And a great cry will be in Egypt, whose like never happened nor whose like will ever recur. ⁷But for all Israel's Sons not a dog will *sharpen his tongue,* from man to animal, that you may know that Yahweh will separate between Egypt and between Israel.' ⁸And all these your slaves will go down to me and bow to me, saying, 'Go out, you and all the people that are at your *feet,*' and then I will go out," and he went out from with Pharaoh with anger of *nose.*

⁹And Yahweh said to Moses, "Pharaoh will not heed you, that my wonders may be multiplied in the land of Egypt."

¹⁰And Moses and Aaron, they did all these wonders before Pharaoh. But Yahweh strengthened Pharaoh's heart, and he did not release Israel's Sons from his land.

PART II. LIBERATION FROM EGYPT
(EXODUS 12:1–15:21)

XI. *And you will observe this day as an eternal rule* (12:1–13:16)

12   ¹And Yahweh said to Moses and to Aaron in the land of Egypt, saying, ²"This month is for you a *head* of months; it is the first for you of the year's months. ³Speak to all Israel's congregation, saying, 'On the tenth of this month, and they will take for themselves, (each) man a sheep/goat for a fathers'-house, a sheep/goat for the house. ⁴But if the house is insufficient for being for a sheep/goat, then he and his neighbor, the one nearest his house, will take; in proportion to the *souls,* (each) man according to what he eats, you will apportion the sheep/goat. ⁵A perfect male sheep/goat, *son of* a year, shall be for you; from the sheep or from the goats you will take. ⁶And it will be for you as a kept thing until the fourteenth day of this month. Then all the community of Israel's congregation will slaughter it *between the two evenings.* ⁷And they will take from the blood and put onto the two doorposts and onto the lintel, onto

the houses in which they will eat it. ⁸And they will eat the meat in this night, fire-roasted; with unleavened bread and bitter lettuce they will eat it. ⁹Do not eat from it raw or cooked, boiled in water; but rather fire-roasted, its head with its shanks and with its innards. ¹⁰And leave none of it over until morning, but what remains of it until morning in fire you must burn. ¹¹And thus you will eat it: your loins girt, your sandals on your feet and your staff in your hand, and you will eat it frantically. It is *Pesaḥ* for Yahweh.

¹²'And I will pass through the land of Egypt in this night and strike every firstborn in the land of Egypt, from man and to animal, and upon all Egypt's gods I will execute judgments; I am Yahweh. ¹³And the blood will be for you as a sign on the houses where you are. And I will see the blood and protect over you, and harm from destruction will not be upon you in my striking the land of Egypt.

¹⁴'And this day will be for you as a memorial, and you will celebrate it as a festival for Yahweh *to your ages*; as an eternal rule you will celebrate it. ¹⁵Seven days you will eat unleavened bread. Even on the first day you will eliminate leaven from your houses, for anyone eating what is leavened, then that *soul* will be cut off from Israel, from the first day until the seventh day. ¹⁶And on the first day a calling of holiness, and on the seventh day a calling of holiness will be for you. Any work may not be done on them; only what is eaten by any *soul*, it alone may be done for you. ¹⁷And you will observe the Unleavened Bread, for on the *bone* of this day I took your brigades out from the land of Egypt. And you will observe this day *to your ages* as an eternal rule. ¹⁸In the first (month), on the fourteenth day of the month in the evening, you will eat unleavened bread, until the twenty-first day of the month in the evening. ¹⁹Seven days leaven will not be found in your houses. For anyone eating what is leavened, then that *soul* will be cut off from Israel's community, among the sojourner and among the land's native. ²⁰Anything leavened you will not eat. In all your dwellings, eat unleavened bread.'"

²¹Then Moses called to all Israel's elders and said to them, "Draw out, take for yourselves small cattle for your families and slaughter the *Pesaḥ*. ²²And you will take a marjoram bunch and dip in the sheep's/goat's blood and apply to the lintel and to the two doorposts from the blood that is in the bowl/threshold. But you, do not go out, (any) man from his house's doorway, until morning. ²³And Yahweh will pass to harm Egypt and will see the blood on the lintel and on the two doorposts, and Yahweh will protect over the doorway and will not allow the Destroyer to come into your houses for harm. ²⁴And you will observe this matter as a rule for you and for your sons to eternity. ²⁵And it will happen, when you come to the land that Yahweh will give to you as he has spoken, then you will observe this service. ²⁶And it will happen, when your sons say to you, 'What is this service to you?' ²⁷then you will say, 'It is the *Pesaḥ slaughter sacrifice* for Yahweh, who protected over Israel's Sons' houses in Egypt in his harming Egypt, but our houses he rescued.'"

And the people knelt and bowed. ²⁸And Israel's Sons went and did; as Yahweh commanded Moses and Aaron, so they did.

²⁹And it happened at half the night, and Yahweh, he struck every firstborn in the land of Egypt, from the firstborn of Pharaoh sitting on his throne to the firstborn of the captive that was in the *pit house*, and every animal firstborn. ³⁰And Pharaoh arose by night, he and his slaves and all Egypt, and there was a great cry in Egypt, for there was no house that there was not a dead one there. ³¹And he called to Moses and to Aaron by night and said, "Rise, go out from my people's midst, both you and Israel's Sons, and go serve Yahweh according to your speaking. ³²Both your flocks and your herds take, as you have spoken, and go. And bless me, too."

³³So Egypt *grew strong* concerning the people, hastening to release them from the land, for they said, "We all are dead." ³⁴And the people picked up its dough before it could rise, their dough pans wrapped in their robes upon their shoulder.

³⁵And Israel's Sons had done according to Moses' word and asked silver objects and gold objects and robes. ³⁶And Yahweh had put the people's favor in Egypt's eyes, and they lent to them, and they despoiled Egypt.

³⁷And Israel's Sons set forth from Raamses to Succoth, about six hundred thousand *foot-men*—the males, besides the dependents. ³⁸And also many foreigners went up with them, and flock and herd—very *heavy* cattle. ³⁹And they baked the dough which they took out from Egypt as cakes of unleavened bread, because it had not risen, because they had been expelled from Egypt and could not tarry, and also they had made no provisioning for themselves.

⁴⁰And the dwelling of Israel's Sons that they dwelt in Egypt: thirty year and four hundred year. ⁴¹And it happened at the end of thirty year and four hundred year, and it happened on the *bone* of this day, all Yahweh's brigades went out from the land of Egypt. ⁴²It is a night of observance for Yahweh, as he takes them out from the land of Egypt; it, this night, is for Yahweh an observance for all Israel's Sons *to their ages.*

⁴³And Yahweh said to Moses and Aaron, "This is the *Pesaḥ* Rule: any foreigner's son may not eat of it. ⁴⁴And any man's slave, a purchase by silver, and you will circumcise him; then he may eat of it. ⁴⁵A resident or a hireling may not eat of it. ⁴⁶In one house it must be eaten; do not take from the house from the meat to the outside, and a bone of it you must not break. ⁴⁷All Israel's congregation must do it. ⁴⁸And when a sojourner sojourns with you and would do a *Pesaḥ* for Yahweh, every male of him must be circumcised, and then he may approach to do it and be like the land's native. But any uncircumcised may not eat of it. ⁴⁹One Direction will be for the native and for the sojourner residing in your midst."

⁵⁰And all Israel's sons did; as Yahweh commanded Moses and Aaron, so they did. ⁵¹And it happened on the *bone* of this day, Yahweh took Israel's Sons out from the land of Egypt in their brigades.

13 ¹And Yahweh spoke to Moses, saying; ²"Sanctify to me every firstborn, *loosening* of every womb among Israel's Sons, among man and among animal—he is for me."

³And Moses said to the people, "Remember this day, when you went out from Egypt, from a slaves' house, for with arm strength Yahweh took you out from this; and anything leavened may not be eaten.

⁴"Today you are going out in the month of the New Grain. ⁵And it will happen, when Yahweh brings you to the land of the Canaanite and the Hittite and the Amorite and the Hivvite and the Jebusite, which he swore to your fathers to give to you, a land flowing of milk and honey, then you will serve this service in this month. ⁶Six days you will eat unleavened bread, and on the seventh day will be a festival for Yahweh. ⁷Unleavened bread you will eat for the seven days, and anything leavened may not be seen for you, and leaven may not be seen for you in all your territory. ⁸And you will tell to your son on that day, saying, 'For the sake of what Yahweh did for me in my going out from Egypt.' ⁹And it will be for you as a sign on your arm and as a memorial *between your eyes*, so that Yahweh's Direction will be in your mouth, for with a strong arm Yahweh took you out from Egypt.

¹⁰"And you will observe this rule at its occasion, *from days to days*. ¹¹And it will happen, when Yahweh brings you to the Canaanite's land, as he swore to your fathers, and gives it to you, ¹²then you will make each *loosening* of the womb pass over to Yahweh, and each *loosening*, animal spawn, that may be for you, the males, to Yahweh. ¹³But each *loosening* of an ass you will redeem with a sheep/goat, or, if you do not redeem, then *neck* it; and each human firstborn among your sons you will redeem. ¹⁴And it will happen, when your son asks you tomorrow, saying, 'What is this?' then you will say to him, 'With arm strength Yahweh took us out from Egypt, from a slaves' house. ¹⁵And it happened, when Pharaoh was too hard to release us, then Yahweh killed each firstborn in the land of Egypt, from the human firstborn and to the animal firstborn. Therefore I sacrifice to Yahweh each *loosening* of the womb, the males, and each firstborn of my sons I redeem.' ¹⁶And it will be as a sign on your arm and as a circlet *between your eyes*, for with arm strength Yahweh took us out from Egypt."

XII. *But Israel's sons walked on the dry land in the Sea's midst* (13:17–15:21)

13 ¹⁷And it happened, in Pharaoh's releasing the people, and Deity did not lead them the way of the land of Philistines, although it was near, but Deity said, "Lest the people repent in their seeing war and return to Egypt." ¹⁸And Deity sent the people around the way of the wilderness of/toward the Suph Sea; and resolute went up Israel's Sons from Egypt. ¹⁹And Moses took Joseph's bones with him, for he had adjured, adjured Israel's Sons, saying, "Deity will acknowledge, acknowledge you, and you will take up my bones from here with you."

²⁰And they set forth from Succoth and camped at Etham, on the wilderness's edge. ²¹And Yahweh was going before them by day in a cloud pillar to lead them the way, and by night in a fire pillar to illuminate for them, going by

day and by night. ²²The cloud pillar would not depart by day, nor the fire pillar by night, before the people.

14   ¹And Yahweh spoke to Moses, saying, ²"Speak to Israel's Sons, that they should turn back and camp before Pi-hahiroth between Migdol and between the Sea before Baal-zephon; opposite it you will camp by the Sea. ³And Pharaoh will say of Israel's Sons, 'They are confused in the land; the wilderness has closed against them.' ⁴And I will strengthen Pharaoh's heart, and he will pursue after them. And I will glorify myself over Pharaoh and over all his force, and Egypt will know that I am Yahweh." And they did so.

⁵And it was told to Egypt's king that the people had fled. And Pharaoh's and his slaves' heart was reversed concerning the people, and they said, "What is this we did, that we released Israel from our service?"

⁶And he harnessed his chariotry and his people he took with him, ⁷and he took six hundred choice chariotry and all Egypt's chariotry, and *thirds* over all of it. ⁸And Yahweh strengthened the heart of Pharaoh, Egypt's king, and he pursued after Israel's Sons, and Israel's Sons were going out with raised arm. ⁹And Egypt pursued after them and overtook them encamped by the Sea, all the horse of Pharaoh's chariotry and his horsemen and his force, at Pi-hahiroth before Baal-zephon.

¹⁰And Pharaoh, he led near. And Israel's Sons raised their eyes and they saw, and, see: Egypt setting forth after them. And they feared greatly. And Israel's Sons cried to Yahweh. ¹¹And they said to Moses, "Is it from a lack of no graves in Egypt that you took us to die in the wilderness? What is this you did to us, by taking us out from Egypt? ¹²Is not this the word that we spoke to you in Egypt, saying, 'Let us alone that we may serve Egypt'? For serving Egypt is better for us than our dying in the wilderness."

¹³And Moses said to the people, "Do not fear. Station yourselves and see Yahweh's salvation that he will make for you today. For, as you have seen Egypt today, you will see them no more to eternity. ¹⁴Yahweh, he will fight for you; and you, you will be still."

¹⁵And Yahweh said to Moses, "(For) what do you cry to me? Speak to Israel's Sons, that they should set forth. ¹⁶And you, raise your rod and extend your arm over the Sea and split it, and Israel's Sons will go in the Sea's midst on the dry land. ¹⁷And I, see, I am going to strengthen Egypt's heart, and they will come after them. And I will glorify myself over Pharaoh and over all his force, over his chariotry and over his horsemen, ¹⁸and Egypt will know that I am Yahweh, through my glorification over Pharaoh, over his chariotry and over his horsemen."

¹⁹And the Deity's Messenger going before Israel's camp set forth and went behind them, and the cloud pillar set forth from before them and stood behind them. ²⁰And it came between Egypt's camp and between Israel's camp. And there was the cloud and the dark, and it illumined the night. And *this one* did not approach *this one* all the night.

²¹And Moses extended his arm over the Sea, and Yahweh conducted the Sea with a mighty *forward* wind all the night, and he made the Sea into the dry

ground, and the waters were split. ²²And Israel's Sons entered in the Sea's midst on the dry land, and the waters for them a wall from their right and from their left. ²³And Egypt pursued and came after them, all Pharaoh's horse, his chariotry and his horsemen, into the Sea's midst.

²⁴And it happened during the morning watch, and Yahweh looked down toward Egypt's camp from inside a pillar of fire and cloud. And he panicked Egypt's camp, ²⁵and he diverted/bound/removed his chariot wheel and made him drive with heaviness. And Egypt said, "I must flee from Israel's *face*, for Yahweh is the fighter for them against Egypt."

²⁶And Yahweh said to Moses, "Extend your arm over the Sea, and its waters will return upon Egypt, upon his chariotry and upon his horsemen."

²⁷And Moses extended his arm over the Sea, and the Sea returned *at morning's turning* to its original course, and Egypt setting forth to meet it. And Yahweh tumbled Egypt in the Sea's midst. ²⁸And the waters returned and covered the chariotry and the horsemen of all Pharaoh's force coming after them into the Sea; so much as one of them did not remain. ²⁹But Israel's Sons had walked on the dry land in the Sea's midst, and the waters for them a wall from their right and from their left.

³⁰So Yahweh saved on that day Israel from Egypt's *arm*, and Israel saw Egypt dead at the Sea's *lip*. ³¹And Israel saw the great *arm* that Yahweh made in Egypt, and the people feared Yahweh and trusted in Yahweh and in Moses his slave.

15   ¹Then sang Moses and Israel's Sons this song of Yahweh, and they said, saying:

I would sing of Yahweh, for he acted exaltedly, exaltedly!
Horse and his driver he hurled into the Sea.

²My strength and my power/music is Yah;
And he was for me as salvation.

This is my god, and I exalt him,
My father's deity, and I elevate him:
³Yahweh Man of War, Yahweh is his name.

⁴Pharaoh's chariots and his force he cast into the Sea.
And the choice of his *thirds* were sunk in the Suph Sea.

⁵Deeps, they cover them;
They went down in the depths like stone.

⁶Your right hand, Yahweh, strong in might,
Your right hand, Yahweh, you shatter enemy.

⁷And in your pride's greatness you break down your *uprisers*.
You release your anger; it consumes them as straw.

⁸And with your nostrils' breath waters were piled;
Streams stood like a heap.
Deeps congealed in Sea's heart.

⁹Enemy said,
"I'll pursue, overtake,
Apportion spoil.

My gullet will be full of them.
I'll *empty* my sword.
My hand will dispossess them."

¹⁰You blew with your breath; Sea covered them.
They sank like lead in strong waters.

¹¹Who as you among gods, Yahweh,
Who as you is strong in holiness,
Dreadful of glory, worker of wonder?

¹²You extended your right arm;
Earth swallows them.

¹³You led by your grace the people which you redeemed;
You guided by your might to your holiness's pasture/camp/tent.

¹⁴Peoples heard. They shudder.
Convulsion seized Philistia's inhabitants.

¹⁵Then perturbed were Edom's princes.
Moab's *rams*, quaking seizes them.
Liquefied were all Canaan's inhabitants.

¹⁶Upon them fall fear and terror.
At your limb's greatness they are still as stone,

Till crosses your people, Yahweh,
Till crosses the people which you have gotten.

¹⁷May you bring them and plant them in your property mountain,
The firm seat for your sitting/throne/dwelling you devised, Yahweh,
The sanctum, my Lordship, your hands founded.

¹⁸Yahweh, he will reign, ever and eternity.

¹⁹For Pharaoh's horse, with his chariotry and his horsemen, entered the Sea, and Yahweh brought back upon them the Sea's waters. But Israel's Sons walked on the dry land in the Sea's midst.
²⁰And Miriam the prophetess, Aaron's sister, took the drum in her hand, and all the women went forth behind her with drums and with dances. ²¹And Miriam sang back to them:

"Sing of Yahweh, for he acted exaltedly, exaltedly!
Horse and his driver he hurled into the Sea."

PART III. SOJOURN IN THE WILDERNESS
(EXODUS 15:22–18:27)

XIII. *I, Yahweh, am your healer* (15:22–26)

15   ²²And Moses made Israel set forth from the Suph Sea, and they went out
into the Shur Wilderness and went three days into the wilderness, but did not
find waters. ²³And they arrived at Marah (Bitter), but could not drink waters
from Marah because they were bitter; therefore one called its name Marah.
²⁴And the people complained against Moses, saying, "What will we drink?"

²⁵So he cried to Yahweh, and Yahweh taught him a tree, and he threw into
the waters, and the waters were sweetened.

There he set for him rule and law, and there he tested him. ²⁶And he said,
"If you listen, listen to Yahweh your deity's voice, and what is straight in his
eyes you do, and give ear to his commands and observe all his rules, all the
disease that I set in Egypt I will not set upon you. Rather, I, Yahweh, am your
healer."

XIV. *Bread from the heavens* (15:27–16:36)

15   ²⁷And they came to Elim, and there were twelve *eye-springs* of water there
and seventy date palms. And they camped there by the water.

16   ¹And they set forth from Elim, and all the congregation of Israel's Sons
came to the Sin Wilderness that is between Elim and between Sinai on the
fifteenth day of the second month of their going out from the land of Egypt.

²Then all the congregation of Israel's Sons complained against Moses and
against Aaron in the wilderness, ³and Israel's Sons said to them, "Who would
give our dying by Yahweh's hand in the land of Egypt, in our sitting by the
meat pot, in our eating bread to satiety! Instead, you have taken us out into
this wilderness to let all this community die of hunger."

⁴Then Yahweh said to Moses, "See: I am going to rain down for you bread
from the heavens; and the people may go out and collect a day's matter in its
day, so that I may test him: will he walk by my Direction or not? ⁵And it will
happen on the sixth day, and they will prepare what they take in, and there
will be a second amount, in addition to what they collect day (by) day."

⁶Then Moses and Aaron said to all of Israel's Sons, "Evening: and you will
know that Yahweh, he has taken you out from the land of Egypt; ⁷and morning: and you will see Yahweh's Glory, in his hearing your complaints against
Yahweh—for what are we, that you complain against us?" ⁸And Moses said,

"In Yahweh's giving you in the evening meat to eat, and bread in the morning to satiety, in Yahweh's hearing your complaints that you complain against him — and what are we? Not against us are your complaints, but against Yahweh."

[9]Then Moses said to Aaron, "Say to all the congregation of Israel's Sons, 'Approach before Yahweh, for he has heard your complaints.'"

[10]And it happened, with Aaron's speaking to all the congregation of Israel's Sons, and they faced toward the wilderness, and, see: Yahweh's Glory appeared in the cloud. [11]And Yahweh spoke to Moses, saying, [12]"I have heard the complaints of Israel's Sons. Speak to them, saying, 'Between the two evenings you will eat meat, and in the morning you will be sated with bread, that you may know that I am Yahweh your deity.'"

[13]And it happened in the evening, and the quail ascended and covered the camp, and in the morning the dew layer was about the camp. [14]And the dew layer ascended, and, see: on the wilderness's surface, fine as rime, fine as frost on the earth. [15]And Israel's Sons saw and said, (each) man to his *brother*, "That is What (*mān*)?" for they did not know what that was.

And Moses said to them, "That is the bread that Yahweh has given you for food. [16]This is the word that Yahweh commanded: 'Gather of it (each) man according to his consumption, an *'ōmer* per *skull*; the number of your *souls*, (each) man for those in his tent, you may take.'"

[17]And Israel's Sons did so. And they gathered, he who did much and he who did little. [18]And they measured it in the *'ōmer*, and he who did much had no surplus, and he who did little had no deficit. (Each) man according to his consumption they gathered.

[19]And Moses said to them, "Let (each) man not leave any of it until morning." [20]But they did not heed Moses, and men left (some) of it until morning, and it bred worms and stank. And Moses was furious at them.

[21]And they collected it by morning by morning, (each) man according to his consumption, but the sun grew hot, and it melted. [22]And it happened on the sixth day, they collected a second amount of bread, the two *'ōmer* for the one, and all the congregation's leaders came and told to Moses. [23]And he said to them, "That is what Yahweh spoke. Tomorrow is a Sabbatical, a Sabbath of holiness for Yahweh. Whatever you would bake, bake; and whatever you would cook, cook; and all the remainder set by you as a kept thing until the morning."

[24]So they set it by until the morning, as Moses commanded, and it did not stink, and a worm was not in it. [25]And Moses said, "Eat it today, for today is a Sabbath for Yahweh. Today you will not find it in the field. [26]Six days you may collect it; but on the seventh day, Sabbath, it will not be in it."

[27]And it happened on the seventh day, (some) of the people went out to collect but did not find. [28]And Yahweh said to Moses, "Until when do you refuse to observe my commandments and my directions? [29]See that Yahweh, he has given you the Sabbath; therefore he gives you on the sixth day two days' bread. Sit, (each) man *under himself*; let (each) man not go out from his place on the seventh day." [30]So the people stopped on the seventh day.

³¹And Israel's House called its name *mān* ("What?"). And it was like white coriander seed, and its taste like a wafer in honey. ³²And Moses said, "This is the word that Yahweh commanded: 'An ʿ*ōmer*-ful of it as a kept thing for your ages, so that they may see the bread that I fed you in the wilderness in my taking you out from the land of Egypt.'"

³³And Moses said to Aaron, "Take one container and put there the ʿ*ōmer*-ful of *mān* and set it before Yahweh as a kept thing for your ages," ³⁴as Yahweh commanded to Moses. And Aaron set it before the Covenant as a kept thing.

³⁵So Israel's Sons ate the *mān* forty years, until their coming to a habitable land; the *mān* they ate, until their coming to the land of Canaan's edge.

³⁶And the ʿ*ōmer*: it is the tenth of the *'ēpâ*.

XV. *Is there Yahweh in our midst or not?* (17:1–7)

17   ¹And all the congregation of Israel's Sons set forth from the Sin Wilderness on their settings forth at Yahweh's *mouth*, and they camped in Rephidim. And there was no water for the people's drinking, ²so the people quarreled with Moses and they said, "Give us water that we may drink."

But Moses said to them, "(For) what would you quarrel with me? (For) what would you test Yahweh?"

³But the people thirsted there for water, and the people complained against Moses and said, "For what is it you brought us up from Egypt, to let me and my children and my cattle die of thirst?"

⁴So Moses cried to Yahweh, saying, "What can I do for this people? Yet a little more and they will stone me!"

⁵And Yahweh said to Moses, "Cross before the people and take with you (some) of Israel's elders; and your rod, with which you struck the Nile, you shall take in your hand and go. ⁶See: I will be standing before you there, upon the mountain, in Horeb. And you will strike the mountain, and waters will go out from it, and the people will drink."

And Moses did so, to the eyes of Israel's Sons' elders. ⁷And he called the place-name Massah (Testing) and Meribah (Quarrel), on account of Israel's Sons' quarrel and on account of their testing Yahweh, saying, "Is there Yahweh in our midst or not?"

XVI. *I will eradicate, eradicate the name Amalek from under the heavens* (17:8–16)

17   ⁸And Amalek came and fought with Israel at Rephidim. ⁹And Moses said to Joshua, "Choose for us men, and go forth, fight against Amalek tomorrow. I will be standing on the mountain's *head*, and the Deity's rod in my hand."

¹⁰So Joshua did as Moses said to him, to fight against Amalek. And Moses, Aaron and Hur, they ascended the mountain's *head*. ¹¹And it would happen,

whenever Moses lifted his arms, then Israel would prevail. But whenever he rested his arms, then Amalek would prevail. ¹²And Moses' arms grew heavy, so they took a stone and put under him, and he sat on it. And Aaron and Hur supported his arms, on this side one and on this side one, and his arms were steadiness until the sun's *entry*. ¹³And Joshua cut down Amalek and his people by the sword's *mouth*.

¹⁴And Yahweh said to Moses, "Write this (as) a memorandum in the document and put into Joshua's ears, that I will eradicate, eradicate the name Amalek from under the heavens."

¹⁵And Moses built an altar and called its name, "Yahweh Is My Flag(pole)," ¹⁶and he said, "For an arm (is?) on Yah's *kēs*." Yahweh has had a war with Amalek *since age (by) age*.

XVII. *Men of competence, fearing Deity, men of reliability, hating gain* (18)

18 ¹And Jethro, Midian's priest, Moses' father-in-law, heard all that Deity did for Moses and for Israel his people, that Yahweh had taken Israel out from Egypt. ²And Jethro, Moses' father-in-law, took Zipporah, Moses' *woman* since her marriage-gift, ³and her two sons, of whom the name of the one was Gershom—for he said, "A sojourner was I in a foreign land"—⁴and the name of the one was Eliezer—for, "My father's deity was as my help and rescued me from Pharaoh's sword." ⁵And Jethro, Moses' father-in-law, and his sons and his *woman* came to Moses, to the wilderness where he was camping, to the Deity's mountain. ⁶And he said to Moses, "I, your father-in-law Jethro, am coming to you, and your *woman* and her two sons with her."

⁷And Moses went out to meet his father-in-law, and he bowed and kissed him. And they inquired, (each) man of his fellow, about well-being, and they entered into the tent. ⁸And Moses told his father-in-law all that Yahweh did to Pharaoh and to Egypt on Israel's behalf: all the hardship that befell them on the way, and Yahweh rescued them. ⁹And Jethro rejoiced over all the good that Yahweh did for Israel, that he rescued him from Egypt's hand. ¹⁰And Jethro said, "Blessed is Yahweh who rescued his people from Egypt's hand and from Pharaoh's hand. ¹¹Now I know that Yahweh is greater than all the gods, for in the affair when they dealt wickedly with them—"

¹²And Jethro, Moses' father-in-law, took *ascending offering* and *slaughter sacrifices* for Deity, and Aaron and (some) of Israel's elders came to eat food with Moses' father-in-law before the Deity.

¹³And it happened on the next day, and Moses sat to judge the people, and the people stood about Moses from the morning till the evening. ¹⁴And Jethro, Moses' father-in-law, saw all that he was doing for the people, and he said, "What is this thing that you are doing for the people? Why are you sitting by yourself, and all the people standing about you, from morning till evening?"

¹⁵And Moses said to his father-in-law, "Because the people come to me to consult Deity. ¹⁶Whenever they have a matter coming to me, then I judge between a man and between his fellow, and I make known the Deity's rules and his directions."

¹⁷But Moses' father-in-law said to him, "The thing that you are doing is not good. ¹⁸You will wither, wither, both you and this people that is with you, for the thing is too heavy for you; you cannot do it by yourself. ¹⁹Now, listen to my voice—I will advise you—and may Deity be with you. You, be for the people *opposite* the Deity, and you, you will bring the matters to the Deity, ²⁰and you will clarify for them the rules and the directions, and make known to them the way they must walk in, and the deed that they must do. ²¹And you, you must see from all the people men of competence, fearing Deity, men of reliability, hating gain, and you will place over them rulers of thousands, rulers of hundreds, rulers of fifties and rulers of tens, ²²and they may judge the people at any time. And it will happen, all the big matters they will bring to you, and all the small matters they will judge themselves. And it will lighten from upon you, and they will bear with you. ²³If this thing you do, and Deity commands you, then you will be able to stand, and also all this people upon its place will come in well-being."

²⁴And Moses listened to his father-in-law's voice and did all that he said. ²⁵And Moses selected men of competence from all Israel and set them heads over the people—rulers of thousands, rulers of hundreds, rulers of fifties and rulers of tens. ²⁶And they would judge the people at any time; the difficult matters they would bring to Moses, and all the small matters they would judge themselves.

²⁷Then Moses released his father-in-law, and he went him away to his land.

INTRODUCTION

◆

I. ABOUT EXODUS

◆

SYNOPSIS

The second book of the Torah[1] is called in Hebrew (*'ēlle[h]*) *šəmôt* '(these are the) names of' and in Greek *Exodos* 'road out, exit' (Latinized as *Exodus*). Exodus recounts the further fortunes of Jacob's sons and daughters, settled in Egypt as Pharaoh's honored guests (Genesis 45–50). After an unspecified time, perhaps some three centuries, the Egyptians grow alarmed at the Hebrews' proliferation. A new Pharaoh first enslaves them and then plots to kill all male newborns. Through an unusual sequence of events, one child is spared and raised in Pharaoh's own palace. This is Moses.

Venturing outside, Moses kills an Egyptian taskmaster. He flees into the desert, weds a Midianite and becomes a father. At Mount Horeb (also later called "Sinai"), Moses encounters God in a talking, burning bush. God reveals his true name, Yahweh, and grants Moses the power to work miracles with his rod. God sends Moses back to liberate the Israelites and to bring them through the desert to the land long promised to their ancestors: Canaan. On the road to Egypt, however, Yahweh attacks Moses, who is saved by a rite of circumcision performed by his wife upon their son.

Once in Egypt, Moses confronts yet another Pharaoh, who only mocks and increases Israel's suffering. But Moses works signs and wonders against Egypt, the Ten Plagues, and the king's resistance gradually erodes. The last straw is the death of the firstborn, from which Israel is spared when they anoint their door frames with lambs' blood.

Pharaoh finally releases Israel, but almost immediately repents his leniency. Moses leads the people to the Sea, with the Egyptian cavalry close behind. Yahweh parts the waters for Israel, and drowns the Egyptians when they in turn attempt the passage. Led by Moses and his sister, Miriam, the people break into song.

The Israelites then trek through the wilderness to God's mountain. On the way, their trust in Moses and Yahweh is repeatedly tested. God sends Manna and quails to feed the people, and at Horeb he creates a spring to slake their

---

[1] "Torah" refers to the first five books of the Bible. They are also called the "Five Books of Moses" and the "Pentateuch" (Greek for "five-part work").

thirst. With divine help, Israel beats back the Amalekites' attack. Moses and his father-in-law, Jethro, establish the Israelite judiciary at the mountain, and Yahweh begins to reveal the terms of a Covenant between himself and Israel, which the people ratify by acclamation. The tribal leaders dine before God. Moses receives the Covenant Tablets and instructions for building God's earthly habitation, the Tabernacle.

In Moses' absence, however, the people backslide, making and worshiping the Golden Calf. Moses assuages God's wrath but smashes the Tablets. The Covenant is renewed, and more laws follow. The Meeting Tent is built under the inspired direction of the craftsman Bezalel; it is consecrated two weeks before the anniversary of the departure from Egypt. Exodus concludes with the settling of Yahweh's Glory upon the Tabernacle.

EXODUS AS NARRATIVE

Why is Exodus so satisfying a story? Students of folklore and literature have isolated a relatively small number of narrative templates underlying most traditional tales. Taken as a whole, Exodus hews to a well-known plot type: the heroic adventure story or fairy tale, classically analyzed by V. I. Propp (1968).[2] Admittedly, Exodus is far too complex to be laid neatly onto Propp's grid of thirty-one "functions," each occurring in proper order and distributed among seven character types.[3] For one thing, there is not one Hero, but three: Moses, Israel and Yahweh.[4] Moreover, other independent tale types obtrude into the narrative. Nevertheless, the overall sequence of events follows Propp closely:

1. *The initial situation* (Propp function α). This slot is filled by the genealogy in 1:1–5 (one of Propp's own examples is the enumeration of family members).
2. *A family member is absent;* e.g., there is a change of generations (function β²).[5] This slot is filled by 1:6, the passing of Joseph's generation.

---

[2] Propp recognized, and subsequent research has confirmed, the broad applicability of his model. On Propp and the Bible, see Milne (1988). He is no relation of the present author.

[3] These are the Villain, the Hero, the Donor, the Helper, the Sought-for Person, the Dispatcher and the False Hero. In Propp's analysis, a role may be played by more than one character; i.e., there might be several Villains or Helpers. Conversely, one character may play more than one role; e.g., the Donor and Helper might be the same person. Propp also allows for the combination of several stories into a single complex tale. It is important to remember that not all functions or character types must be present in a Proppian tale. It is the sequence of the functions that is (relatively) fixed.

[4] In much of Exodus, Israel is a Hero in its own right. But vis-à-vis Moses, Israel is the Sought-for Person requiring rescue, comparable to a captive princess in a fairy tale. On Yahweh as Hero of the story, see below.

[5] Raised numerals after functions refer to subtypes. For example, function A is any act of villainy; function A¹ is abduction, function A² is theft, etc.

3. *The Villain harms a family member,* e.g., by depriving him of liberty (function A^{15}). Israel is enslaved (1:11–14).

At this point, several extraneous tales interrupt the Proppian flow: the mid-wives story (1:15–21), Moses' birth (1:22–2:10), his excursion outside the palace (2:11–15a) and his Midianite sojourn (2:15b–22). These are independent tale types: the Hoodwinked Villain, the Floating Foundling, the Disillusioned Prince and the Sojourner's Tale.[6] The last three take Moses into the desert, where we rejoin the Proppian sequence.[7]

4. *The misfortune is made known* and responded to (function B). Yahweh takes note of Israel's oppression and resolves to act (2:23b–25).
5. *The Hero is tested or interrogated* and given a task by the Donor-Helper, whom he encounters accidentally (function D^{1-2}). The Burning Bush (chaps. 3–4) fills this slot.
6. *The Hero is granted a magic agent* (function F). Moses receives the divine rod and various miracles (4:17).
7. *The Hero is relocated to the vicinity of the Sought-for Person* (function G). Moses heads back to Egypt at God's command to rescue Israel (4:18–23).
8. *The Hero is branded,* e.g., given a protective mark by a princess (function J^1).[8] For Hero Moses, this slot is filled by the Bloody Bridegroom episode (4:24–26).
9. *The Hero and Villain fight,* sometimes repeatedly (function H). This slot is filled by the contest of wills between Moses and Pharaoh, and in particular by the Plagues (5:1–12:42).
10. *The Hero is branded* (function J). Near the battle's end, the Israelites' homes receive the protecting paschal blood, another symbolic wound (12:1–28).
11. *The Villain is defeated* (function I). Pharaoh is defeated with the death of the firstborn (12:29–30).
12. *The initial misfortune/lack is removed;* e.g., the captive is freed (function K^{10}). Israel is liberated (12:31–42).
13. *The Hero returns/flees homeward* (function ↓). Moses and Israel leave Egypt (12:30–42; 13:17–22).
14. *The Hero is pursued* (function Pr^1). Pharaoh musters his army to recapture Israel (14:2–10).
15. *The Hero is rescued* (function Rs). This slot is filled by the Sea event (14:15–15:21).

---

[6] See COMMENTS to 1:15–21; 1:22–2:10; 2:11–15a; 3–4.

[7] The transference of Moses into the wilderness in effect serves as Propp function ↑, whereby the Hero leaves home.

[8] Despite Propp's insistence on sequence, close examination of his examples proves that the order of functions H, I and J is somewhat fluid (cf. Milne 1988: 282 n. 19). In Exodus, the sequence is JHJI, with J repeated because both Moses and Israel are Heroes.

At this point, Exodus again deviates from Propp's schema. But the similarities are nonetheless enlightening. In some fairy tales, when the Hero returns home, he is assigned a difficult task (function M). After passing an ordeal (function N) and vanquishing all rivals (function Ex), he undergoes a change of status (function T), marries a princess and ascends the throne (function W). It seems to me that these, too, are present in Exodus, albeit slightly disguised. The theme of Yahweh testing Israel dominates 15:23–17:16. The nations of Amalek and Midian (i.e., Jethro) show up near God's mountain, but are not the Chosen (17:8–18:27).[9] Israel alone is transfigured into a "priestly kingdom" (19:6) and joined in a permanent union with God by the Covenant. In a sense, Yahweh and Israel get married.[10] They do not, however, live happily ever after.

EXODUS AND CANAANITE MYTH

In the foregoing analysis, the Hero of Exodus was defined as Moses/Israel, with Yahweh the Donor-Helper. What if we consider Yahweh the Hero? Later biblical references to the Liberation generally emphasize God's role, barely mentioning Moses at all. In fact, the Exodus story is often described as a battle between Yahweh and Pharaoh over who shall possess Israel.

In this aspect, the tradition has quite a specific prototype: the Canaanite myth of the storm god Baʿlu, biblical Baal, which itself has been compared to a Proppian fairy tale (Sasson 1981: 84; Forsyth 1987). In the beginning of the story, Baʿlu lacks a permanent abode. A rival deity, Prince Sea, dispatches two envoys demanding the gods' submission and the delivery of Baʿlu as hostage. With two magic clubs provided by the divine craftsman Koṯaru, Baʿlu defeats and probably dries up Sea, whereupon he is acclaimed king. Having amassed riches, Koṯaru builds a mountaintop palace where Baʿlu hosts a banquet and thunders to rout his enemies (KTU 1.1–4; ANET 129–35).

The resemblance to Exodus is unmistakable. Yahweh and Israel lack a permanent abode. Yahweh sends two messengers to demand that Pharaoh hand over Israel.[11] God vanquishes his adversary through two magic rods, drying the Sea. He then leads Israel to his mountain abode, where the elders dine before him, where his eternal kingship is proclaimed and where he reveals himself in thunder. The craftsman Bezalel builds Yahweh's dwelling out of the people's amassed treasures.[12]

---

[9] The Midrash even imagines God offering the Torah to various nations, i.e., Proppian False Heroes. Of these, only Israel, the True Hero, is willing to accept the Law (Ginzberg 1928: 3.80–82).

[10] The Bible frequently compares the Covenant to a marriage, both implicitly (e.g., Exod 34:14–15; Num 15:39; Deut 31:16) and explicitly (Isa 57:8; Jer 2:2, 20–25; Ezekiel 16; Hosea 1–3) (Adler 1989).

[11] Here, briefly, Yahweh plays the role of Sea, rather than of Baʿlu.

[12] For further discussion of the Exodus and Canaanite myth, see COMMENTS to 13:17–15:21; 17:1–7; 35–40.

EXODUS AND INITIATION

Propp (1984: 116–23) observes that the heroic fairy tale in many ways resembles a rite of passage. In the archetypical (male) initiation, the candidate withdraws from society to undergo a harrowing, transforming experience. His near-death and quasi-rebirth bind him to the gods, on the one hand, and to society, on the other, both vertically (to the ancestors) and horizontally (to adult contemporaries) (van Gennep 1960; Turner 1967: 93–111).

Israel's migration from Egypt to Canaan has also been compared to a rite of passage (Haldar 1950: 5; Talmon 1966: 50, 54; Cohn 1981: 7–23; Hendel 1989: 375). Israel performs a special blood ritual, the *Pesaḥ*, and leaves Egypt. This night marks the Hebrews' change of social status—from slavery to freedom—and change of location—from Egypt to the desert. Soon afterward they cross the Sea, representing the bounds of the known, to enter the wilderness proper (cf. Liverani 1990b: 52–55). In Turner's evocative terminology, the desert is "liminal," the threshold between one space/time/state and another. In one sense, it is huge—one can wander there for forty years. In another sense, its breadth is infinitesimal; it is No-place.[13] During their liminal period, the Israelites enter into a Covenant binding the tribes one to another and all to their common ancestral deity. During the next forty years, Israel will be repeatedly tried and many will be killed. The people metaphorically and literally mature, as a new generation replaces the old. At the other end of their journey, Israel experiences symbolic rebirth in another water-crossing, now of the Jordan, followed by another paschal rite (Josh 5:10–12). This *Pesaḥ* is preceded by circumcision, a typical initiatory mutilation (see Propp 1987b, 1993). Finally, Israel conquers the land to take its place among nations.

The Exodus tradition differs from the rite of passage in one crucial respect, however. In the typical initiation, the candidate returns to his starting point. He, not his home, has changed. But in Exodus–Deuteronomy, the people move from Egypt to Canaan. To fit the initiation pattern as defined by van Gennep and Turner, we should consider Israel's entire absence from Canaan, from Joseph to Joshua, as their liminal period. No less than the wilderness, Egypt is the crucible in which Israel is refined (Deut 4:20; 1 Kgs 8:51; Jer 11:4), from which it emerges a great people (Exod 1:7, 8, 12).[14]

Given the analogies, one might suspect that the Exodus-Wandering-Conquest tradition somehow grew out of actual rites of passage.[15] To be sure,

---

[13] Both the Suph Sea and the Jordan River are parted/dried by God and crossed by Israel (Exodus 14–15; Joshua 3–4). By making Sea and river poetically parallel, Ps 66:6 and 114:3, 6 imply their quasi-identity. Thereby, the intervening desert collapses into nonexistence.

[14] This qualification also affects my comparison of Exodus to a Proppian tale, in which the Hero infallibly returns to his home. In fact, Israel's full Proppian tale is the journey from Canaan to Egypt and back again narrated in Genesis–Joshua. The trek to Sinai recounted in Exodus is a return to Canaan in miniature, foreshadowing the actual resettlement (cf. Smith 1997 *passim*).

[15] Cf. Propp's (1984: 116–23) opinion that fairy tales originate in rites of initiation.

the once-popular doctrine that myths are the ghosts of dead rituals has been repeatedly called into question (e.g., by Fontenrose 1966). In fact, rituals generate myths, myths generate rituals, and both in any case spring from common fonts in the human soul. We must judge each case separately.

Although the Bible mentions no rites of male adolescent initiation explicitly, circumcision and/or *Pesaḥ* may once have served this function (Propp 1987b, 1993; COMMENT to chaps. 3–4). If so, the Exodus story may indeed have evolved out of (or alongside) a ritual. But it is best to keep an open mind, as initiation can be an independent literary theme. And we must also reckon with the historical kernel of the Exodus tradition (see APPENDIX B, vol. II).

THEMES IN EXODUS

Several themes and words recur to unify the Book of Exodus. Fire (*'ēš*) is the medium in which Yahweh appears on the terrestrial plane: in the Burning Bush (3:2), in the cloud pillar (13:21–22; 14:24), atop Mount Sinai (19:18; 24:17) and upon the Tabernacle (40:38). "It is possible to epitomize the entire story of Exodus as the movement of the fiery manifestation of the divine presence" (Greenberg 1969: 16–17).

Prominent, too, is the root *kbd*, connoting heaviness, glory, wealth and firmness (cf. Fox 1986: 77). Moses suffers from *heavy* mouth (4:10) and arms (17:12); Pharaoh's *firmness* of heart (7:14; 8:11, 28; 9:7, 34; 10:1) makes Israel's labor *heavy* (5:9). Yahweh in response sends *heavy* plagues (8:20; 9:3, 18, 24; 10:14), so that he may be *glorified* over Pharaoh (14:4, 17, 18). The culmination is the descent of Yahweh's fiery *kābôd* 'Glory,' described as a *"heavy* cloud," first upon Sinai and later upon the Tabernacle (19:16; 24:16–17; 29:43; 33:18, 22; 40:34–38; cf. 16:7, 10).

Also important in chaps. 3–15, particularly in the Song of the Sea (15:1–18), are the nouns *yād* 'hand/arm,' *zərôaʿ* 'arm' and *yāmîn* 'right hand/arm,' describing the limbs of Pharaoh, Egypt, Moses, Aaron and especially God. "Arm" in Hebrew connotes power, mighty act and visible memorial (NOTES to 14:30, 31 and 15:12). Moses' rod in particular symbolizes the divine arm (COMMENT to chaps. 3–4, pp. 227–29). The culmination of this theme is 14:31, "And Israel saw the great *arm* that Yahweh made in Egypt, and the people feared Yahweh and trusted in Yahweh and in Moses his slave."

Even more significant is the theme of Yahweh's *šēm* 'name,' connoting his fame, posterity, memorial, concept and essence (3:13, 15; 5:23; 6:3; 9:16; 15:3; 20:7, 24; 33:12, 17, 19; 34:5, 14). The Burning Bush, the Plagues, the drowning of Pharaoh's host—all teach Yahweh's "name," which he reveals explicitly in 6:2: "I am Yahweh." At the Sea, Moses and Israel exult, "Yahweh Man of War . . . is his name." The climax of this theme is 33:12, 17, 19; 34:5–7, where Moses receives the fullest revelation of God's name and qualities that man may bear. Never again will the foreigner scoff, "Who is Yahweh? . . . I have not known Yahweh" (5:2).

Yahweh's *fire*, his *Glory*, his *arm* and his *name*—all are the means whereby he is *known* in the world. The most prominent theme word in Exodus is *yāda'*, a verb connoting knowledge, experience, duty and love (Fretheim 1991a: 14–15). The kings of Egypt "know" neither Joseph (1:8) nor God (5:2). Yahweh "knows" Israel and their suffering (3:7; 32:22). Egypt, Jethro and all Israel learn to "know" Yahweh and his name (2:25; 6:3, 7; 7:5, 17; 8:6, 18; 9:14, 29; 10:2; 11:7; 14:4, 18; 16:6, 12; 18:11; 29:46; 31:13; 33:12, 13, 16, 17). The theme may even take us back to Genesis 2–3, where humanity attains the capacity to "know" at the cost of eternal life.

Finally, we have the verb *'ābad* 'work, make, serve, worship' and its derived nouns *'ebed* 'slave' and *'ăbōdâ* 'labor, worship.' Pharaoh forces Israel to *work* as *slaves* (1:13, 14; 2:23; 5:9, 11; 6:5, 6, 9; 14:5, 12); the people beg leave to *worship* Yahweh (3:12; 4:23; 7:16, 26; 8:15, 16; 9:1, 13; 10:3, 7, 8, 11, 24, 26; 12:31; 13:3, 14; 20:2). Eventually, they build the Tabernacle, site of Yahweh's *worship* (27:19; 30:16; 35:21, 24; 36:1, 3, 5; 38:21; 39:32, 40, 42). Israel, Moses and Aaron are Yahweh's *slaves* (4:10; 14:31; 32:13), contrasted with Pharaoh's *slaves*, i.e., the Egyptian court (5:15, 16; 7:28, 29; 8:5, 7, 17, etc.). "The book of Exodus moves from slavery to worship . . . from the enforced construction of buildings for Pharaoh to the glad and obedient offering . . . for a building for the worship of God" (Fretheim 1991a: 1). The root *'bd*, too, takes us back to Eden, where humanity was created for light work (Gen 2:15) and whence it was expelled for hard labor (Gen 3:17–19, 23).

EXODUS AS DIPTYCH

Exodus is a bipartite work whose center is somewhat difficult to determine[16]. One could find the hinge in 13:16, where, on the fifteenth day of the first month, the Hebrews leave Egypt proper. The Book of Exodus ends almost exactly a year later, when the Tabernacle is consecrated on the first day of the first month (40:2, 17). Or one could regard as pivotal the arrival at Mount Sinai, which inaugurates a new epoch in Israel's history (19:1–2). Greenberg (1969: 3) defines the halves as chaps. 1–19, the historical background to the Covenant, and chaps. 20–40, the establishment of the Covenant itself.

For many, however, the natural turning point falls after 15:21 (cf. Pedersen 1940: 728–31; Fohrer 1964). Israel has crossed the Sea, Egypt has drowned and Moses and Miriam have sung their Song. Exod 1:1–15:21 tells the story of

---

[16]Not all would recognize a simple two-panel structure. Clifford (1990: 44) finds two *interlocking* halves: 1:1–15:21 and 12:37–40:38. (One could alternatively define the interlocking units as 1:1–18:27 and 15:22–40:38.) Others might regard Exodus as a triptych (1:1–15:21; 15:22–18:27; 19:1–40:38), a tetraptych (1:1–15:21; 15:22–18:27; 19:1–24:18; 25:1–40:38) (Sarna 1986: 6–7) or even a pentaptych (1:1–6:27; 6:28–15:21; 15:22–18:27; chaps. 19–31; 32–40 (Fokkelman 1987: 57–58).

Israel under Pharaoh's dominion; 15:22–40:37 tells of Israel under Yahweh's dominion (cf. Watts 1992: 48–49). More or less framing the first panel are female characters (1:15–2:10; 15:20–21), the theme of drowning (1:22–2:10; 14–15) and Egypt's fear of Israel (1:10; 14:25) (Watts p. 49; Blum 1990: 9, 17 n. 35). Watts (pp. 56, 206–20) observes, moreover, that hymns such as 15:1b–18, 21 often conclude narrative units in ancient Near Eastern literature, including the Bible (cf. Genesis 49; Deuteronomy 32–33; Judges 5; 2 Samuel 22–23; 1 Chronicles 16; Judith 16; Tobit 13; Luke 1–2). He compares these to the "show-stopper" numbers of musical theater (pp. 187–89).

I think this is almost but not quite right. M. S. Smith (1996: 30, 39) has shown that the center of Exodus is not really the empty space between 15:21 and 22. The "midpoint" is no point at all, but rather all of 15:1–21. The Song of the Sea begins with Egypt in the Sea, essentially summarizing Exodus 1–14; it concludes with Israel camped about King Yahweh's mountain sanctum, anticipating the Covenant (chaps. 19–24, 33–34) and the Tabernacle building (chaps. 25–31, 35–40).[17] Watts himself shows that Exod 15:1–21 and other "inset psalms" not merely are retrospective but also point forward to the fulfillment of hope (e.g., 1 Sam 2:1–10; Isaiah 38; Jonah 2; Daniel 2). In short, the Song of the Sea both concludes the first half of Exodus and opens the second half.[18]

---

[17] The two halves of Exodus are to a degree structurally symmetrical. The first panel features double revelations to Moses and Israel, the second revelation (chaps. 6–7) more efficacious than the first (chaps. 3–4). The second panel features two Covenants, the first abortive (chaps. 19–24, 32) and the second permanent (chaps. 33–34) (cf. Smith 1996, 1997: 144–261).

[18] The breaking of this two-volume commentary between Exodus 18 and 19 does not, therefore, reflect my understanding of the structure of Exodus. It rather arises from the anticipated length of each volume.

II. ABOUT THIS COMMENTARY

◆

AIMS

My basic approach to the Bible is anthropological. My goal is to understand, as best we can, Israelite social institutions and perceptions of reality. This orientation will be most apparent in my use of the methods of folktale analysis and in my interpretation of *Pesaḥ-Maṣṣôt* as a rite of purification and riddance (COMMENT to 12:1–13:16). I am also interested in how aspects of the Bible and Israelite culture relate to the ancient Near Eastern milieu(s) from and against which they arose. And I am very interested in words: their contextual meanings, their semiconscious resonances and their ultimate etymologies. Lastly, I am interested in history. What reality underlies the accounts? How, when, where and why did Israel emerge as a nation?

PARTITION

For convenient discussion, I have divided Exodus into units of varying length. Our oldest Hebrew manuscripts already break up the text with blank spaces (on *pətûḥâ* 'open' and *sətûmâ* 'closed' sections, see Tov 1992: 50–51). The familiar division, first into chapters and later into numbered verses, was imposed by Christians upon the *Latin* Bible beginning about 1200 C.E. (Loewe 1969: 147–48). Appreciating the convenience, Jews later adopted slightly variant versions of the system for their own Hebrew Bibles.[19] Given its recent origin, I have felt free to ignore the chapter-and-verse structure in my partition. Instead, I insert breaks at major changes of scene, time or subject.

After partition, the next step is to translate.

---

[19]This is why chapter and verse in Hebrew Bibles, and in works based upon Hebrew Bibles, do not always conform to Christian translations. This commentary cites chapter and verse according to the Hebrew edition of *BHS*, which in Exodus diverges from Christian Bibles only in chaps. 8 and 22 (English 8:1; 22:1 = Hebrew 7:26; 21:37).

TRANSLATION

My English version of Exodus is for private study, not community reading. When torn between fidelity and felicity, I have leaned heavily toward the former, even at the frequent expense of English grammar and usage. The legitimate justification for the fluid translation is that, assuming the exemplar was elegant by ancient Israelite canons, we render it best through elegant, or at least idiomatic, English. This principle underlies the translations of NJV and Durham (1987). In contrast, the literalistic approach, exemplified in Greek by Aquila (c. 125 C.E.), in German by Buber and Rosenzweig (1934), in French by Chouraqui (1975) and in English by Fox (1986, 1995) and Korsak (1992), to an extent conveys the experience of reading the original. And it preserves ambiguities without imposing solutions—a major advantage for a scholarly edition. Lastly, hyperliteral rendering maintains a necessary sense of temporal and cultural distance between reader and text.[20]

An innovation of this edition is the literal rendering of such idioms as "the Sea's *lip*" or "the *bone* of this day," in order to exhume the dead metaphors buried in paraphrases like "the seashore" or "this very day."[21] To assist the reader, these oddities will be italicized and accompanied by a NOTE. My fidelity is not slavish, however, when the result would be unintelligible—unless the original is unintelligible. I am especially free with the Hebrew conjunction *wa-/û-*, employing "and," "or," "but," "so," "now," "when," "then," "if," "for" or nothing at all, as the context may warrant.[22] I have also waged a private war against "of," the bane of English Bible translation. For Hebrew *banê yiśrā'ēl* and *'ōhel mô'ēd*, why say "the Sons of Israel" or "the Tent of Meeting" and not "Israel's Sons" or "Meeting Tent"? Another innovation is the use of repetition to reflect the infinitive absolute or an emphatic pronoun in the original: e.g., "I will eradicate, eradicate" (*māḥō[h] 'emḥe[h]*) or "and you, you will be silent" (*wa'attem taḥărîšûn*).

The Massoretic Hebrew Bible (MT) contains a complex system of punctuation, the trope or cantillation, often helpful in interpreting syntax. But these

---

[20] For further elaboration of my theories of translation, see Propp (1996).

[21] Most of these in fact involve body parts. To be sure, some may question to what extent Israelites were aware of the literal meaning. I assume that, as long as expressions were etymologically transparent, speakers were at least semiconscious. When I speak of my "body" of work, I have a specific image in mind; when I refer to my "corpus," I do not.

[22] While the King James Version and its imitators begin almost every sentence with "and," Fox and Chouraqui generally do not translate waw before a verb (waw consecutive) at all. Here is my position: both approaches successfully capture the effect of the Hebrew, forcing readers to decide the relation of successive clauses in time or logic (parataxis). Since the Hebrew conjunction conveys both more and less information than English "and," I would prefer not to translate it; a comma would suffice. The resulting staccato style would recapture some of the original's pace. But because my text-critical discussion often deals precisely with the presence or absence of a conjunction, I have taken pains to render *wa-/û* in some fashion, lest readers following the English become confused.

symbols differ in function from modern punctuation signs—e.g., there is no question mark or quotation mark—and they were not present in the autograph. For the sake of readability, I have punctuated and paragraphed my translation by the conventions for modern English.

The transcription of proper nouns is a problem for all biblical translators, burdened by such traditional spellings as "Isaac" and "Jerusalem" for *yiṣḥāq* and *yərûšāla(y)im*. I have resisted the temptation to transliterate Hebrew names à la Fox (1986, 1995), since many would become unrecognizable to most readers, and since MT enshrines medieval, not ancient, Hebrew pronunciation. Rendering literally all etymologically transparent names (e.g., *yiṣḥāq* = "He laughs") would have comported with my overall approach but would have imposed too many inconveniences upon the reader. Instead, I preserve the traditional "Moses," "Aaron," etc.

After the translation of each portion comes the discussion entitled "Analysis," divided into three sub-sections: TEXTUAL NOTES, SOURCE ANALYSIS and REDACTION ANALYSIS. These I implore the general reader to skip, as they are both technical and dull.

TEXTUAL NOTES

Readers too rarely ask how ancient (or modern) works have reached their hands, and whether they have arrived intact. For the Bible, we do not possess the original manuscript of a single book. Rather, we have copies of copies of copies, to the nth degree. Some may have been dictated orally to facilitate mass production; some may have been written from memory; most were probably reproduced by visual inspection, as required by Jewish law (*b. Meg.* 18b; *y. Meg.* 4:1, 74d). Despite the safeguards of professional scribedom, the transmission process was fraught with peril at every step. We cannot simply flourish a Hebrew Bible and call it "*the* text." In fact, even printed editions differ in trivial ways (Tov 1992: 6–8).

The aim of textual criticism is to restore, insofar as is possible, the original words of the first edition, the lost "parent" of all extant textual witnesses. Or so we pretend. In fact, even for modern works, defining "original" can be difficult. Do we give priority to the author's manuscript, the author's corrected proofs, the first printed edition or a later version revised by the author's own hand (see Parker 1984)? Comparable complications probably apply to ancient works.[23]

Skipping over numerous problems, I will now summarize the evolution of the pentateuchal text. Sometime after the Jews' return from the Babylonian Exile

---

[23] E.g., what if the editor of the Torah produced several copies, each differing slightly from the others and from his source documents? What if, soon after redaction, a second scribe consulted those still-extant sources and corrected the Torah accordingly?

in 539,[24] the first Torah was assembled by a scribe whom we call the Redactor. Like a modern synagogue scroll, it contained no vowels or cantillation, only consonants and probably blank spaces to separate words and major sections.[25] The letters were in the paleo-Hebrew alphabet, not the "square" Aramaic script used today. Unlike a modern Torah, the original was probably written on five separate rolls. Ever after, the text was considered sacrosanct; it has undergone minimal development. The era of composition was over.[26]

The Torah became the constitution of the nation of Judah, and ultimately of world Jewry. It was transcribed into contemporary Aramaic letters c. 300 (see Tov 1992: 218–20) and copied and recopied by hundreds of scribes of varying competence, who introduced countless changes into the text, mostly minor and inadvertent. These were in turn perpetuated in "daughter" MSS—although meticulous proofreading was later mandated to control the spread of error. Whether some copyists were known to be more careful than others, so that their work possessed greater authority, we do not know. It is a reasonable assumption that prior to 70 C.E., master copies were kept in the Jerusalem Temple (cf. Deut 17:18; y. Taʿan. 4:68a; b. Pesaḥ. 112a; b. Ketub. 19b, 106a).

Meanwhile, in Alexandria, Egypt, Hellenized Jews had translated the Torah into Greek, producing the Septuagint (LXX) in the third century B.C.E.[27] Again, we do not possess the original LXX, but copies of copies[28] handed down in the Christian churches. Our oldest complete biblical MSS are Greek translations from the fourth century C.E., although LXX fragments from the second and first centuries B.C.E. have been recovered (Tov 1992: 136). The various witnesses to LXX may be compared to reconstruct, more or less, the original Greek.[29] If we then *retranslate this work into Hebrew*, we obtain a text often different from that preserved among the Jews. Some differences are the result of translators' license, others of translators' error, but many are faithful renditions of a lost Hebrew text, the LXX *Vorlage* (German: "what lay before").

Though their numbers have considerably dwindled, in Roman days, the Samaritans were an important and populous subgroup of Jews. The Samaritan

---

[24]Unless otherwise indicated, dates throughout this commentary are B.C.E.

[25]On the question of whether the autograph contained word divisions or instead employed "continuous writing," see Tov (1992: 108–9). My text-critical discussion often entertains the possibility of continuous writing, as when I posit the migration of letters between words, but the matter is truly vexed.

[26]This last statement requires qualification. Here and there, wide divergence among the Versions shows that the biblical text underwent true literary development even after the first editing (Tov 1992: 313–49). We will encounter this problem in Exodus 35–40, the building of the Tabernacle, where the Greek and the Hebrew accounts differ considerably.

[27]Over the next few centuries, the rest of the Hebrew Bible and Apocrypha were put into Greek as well. Often the entire Greek Old Testament is loosely called the "Septuagint." Outside the Torah, however, I shall use the term "Old Greek" (OG).

[28]And copies of translations of copies—in Latin, Ethiopic, Coptic, Arabic and other languages.

[29]A complicating factor is that some LXX MSS were revised in Late Antiquity to the Jews' Hebrew Bible. These "corrections" must be undone in order to recover the original LXX. They shed light, however, on the pre-medieval Hebrew text.

Pentateuch (Sam) differs from LXX and the standard Jewish Torah (MT), frequently agreeing with one against the other—unless the question is one of specifically Samaritan doctrine. Scholars date the prototype of Sam to c. 100 B.C.E., based primarily on its paleo-Hebrew script and affinities with some Dead Sea Scrolls (Sanderson 1986: 28–35). Like LXX, Sam is not one MS, but a family of closely affiliated MSS.

During the past fifty years, the Qumran caves near the Dead Sea have yielded hundreds of scrolls and scroll fragments dating from the mid-third century B.C.E. to 68 C.E. Among these are over a dozen MSS of Exodus, all fragmentary, all different from one another and all in partial agreement and disagreement with LXX, Sam and MT. Phylacteries and mezuzoth from Qumran and Masada also contain portions of Exodus 12–13 and 20.[30]

LXX, the Dead Sea Scrolls, Sam and MT jointly attest to a spectrum of readings in Greco-Roman times. These textual witnesses cannot be derived one from another. They rather share a common source, the object of our text-critical quest. It may not be the pentateuchal autograph, only an intermediate exemplar, but textual criticism can take us no further.

To this point, the picture is much as we would expect: MSS increasingly diverge the more they are removed from their ancient prototype. But the picture appears to change abruptly in the early second century C.E. Scrolls from Wadi Murabba'at and Naḥal Ḥever are almost identical to the later MT, and all subsequent evidence attests to the relative homogeneity of the biblical text throughout the (non-Samaritan) Jewish world (Cross 1964). Can it be that all variant MSS were suppressed in a *coup*, from one end of the Diaspora to the other? If not, what really happened?

Rabbinic Judaism arose after the Second Temple was destroyed by the Romans in 70 C.E. This crisis unleashed certain tendencies, stifling others. A group of sages known to posterity as the Tanna'im became, in the late first and early second Christian centuries, *the* arbiters for succeeding generations of what was Jewish and what was not (Cohen 1987: 214–31). Dissident groups such as the Samaritans and later the Qara'ites were excluded from the fold. I suggest, then, that we imagine a wave phenomenon, coincident with the rise of Tanna'itic hegemony, resulting in the near-total standardization of all Hebrew MSS.[31] This version naturally required a few centuries to expel its rivals from the far-flung reaches of the Diaspora. But it so far outstripped its competitors in prestige, the Tanna'itic Bible became the natural basis for all scholarly

---

[30]These amulets are valuable textual witnesses, subject to one caution: by Jewish law, they may be written from memory. A degree of variation is therefore expected.

[31]In fact, the proto-Tanna'itic Bible had apparently attained considerable authority *before* the destruction of the Second Temple (Tov 1992: 187–97). Some 60 percent of the Qumran scrolls are of this type, as are all the texts from Masada (destroyed 73 C.E.). Moreover, as we have noted, Rabbinic tradition records that Temple scribes were entrusted with correcting biblical MSS (*b. Pesaḥ.* 112a; *b. Ketub.* 19b, 106a), presumably in conformity to the three scrolls of the Temple courtyard, which themselves differed trivially (see Tov pp. 32–33). Thus the Tanna'im accelerated and consummated a process already under way.

work on the Hebrew text, whether by the Rabbis, the Qara'ites or the Church Fathers. Deviant MSS were no doubt preserved by some communities until they wore out. But they were not copied or cited by the experts of the day; hence, their readings have not been passed down. The *appearance*, from our perspective, of the Jews instantaneously adopting a uniform biblical text is probably the combined result of natural selection and the incompleteness of the record.[32]

After the Dead Sea Scrolls, we possess no Hebrew biblical MSS until the early Middle Ages. For the interim, we have only the indirect testimony of ancient translations and citations. A Targum (*Tg.*) is a Jewish translation of the Bible into Aramaic, the vernacular of the pre-Islamic Near East. Dating Targumic literature is extremely difficult (Alexander 1992). Our three complete Targumim of the Torah are the fairly literal *Tg. Onqelos* (c. 100 C.E.?), the far freer *Tg. Neofiti I* (c. 300 C.E.?) and the much-embellished *Tg. Pseudo-Jonathan* (completed c. 700 C.E. but with older antecedents). There are also Targumic fragments from the Cairo Genizah (Klein 1986) and the so-called *Fragmentary Targum* (Klein 1980), akin to *Neofiti I* and *Pseudo-Jonathan*.[33] These translations vary from MT in minor but interesting ways, confirming that the standardization of the Bible was an uneven process, and less thorough than surviving Hebrew MSS might suggest. The same is evident from deviant scriptural citations in the Talmuds (see Aptowitzer 1970).

Other translations roughly contemporary with the *Tgs.* and of comparable utility are the Vulgate (Vg) of St. Jerome, the Peshiṭta or Syriac Version (Syr) and "the Three." Vg was produced c. 400 C.E. and generally supports either MT or LXX; hence, it is of little independent value for the textual critic. Syr (c. 200 C.E.) often differs from both MT and LXX, but it is also less literal, especially in younger MSS. Closest of all to MT, and therefore of least value for us, are "the Three": Jewish revisions of LXX ascribed to "Theodotion" (c. 50 B.C.E.),[34] Aquila (c. 125 C.E.) and Symmachus (c. 200 C.E.), fragmentarily preserved in the original Greek and in Syriac translation.

Throughout Late Antiquity and the early Middle Ages, the Hebrew biblical text was undergoing near-total standardization, down to the merest details. Perhaps as early as c. 700 C.E., groups of Rabbinic and Qara'ite Jews confirmed the basic consonantal text, refined safeguards for accurate copying and developed symbols enshrining received pronunciation,[35] cantillation, syntactical

---

[32]And there is another factor. By law, not only must biblical MSS be copied from older texts, they must also be corrected to existing texts (*haggāhâ*). Over time, this would inevitably create uniformity, irrespective of the antiquity of particular readings, just as interbreeding produces genetic homogeneity in laboratory animals.

[33]The Samaritans have their own Targumic tradition, often helpful in elucidating the Samaritan Torah. Targumic literature exists at Qumran, too, but not for Exodus.

[34]The attribution is spurious, for the historical Theodotion lived in the late second century C.E.

[35]The familiar Hebrew vowel pointing, the "Tiberian" vocalization, is only one of three basic Massoretic systems. The other two, the "Palestinian" and "Babylonian," are less well attested (see Tov 1992: 39–49).

analysis,[36] even scribal quirks.[37] The era of the Massoretes (< *ba'ălê hammassôrâ* 'tradition experts') reached its peak c. 900 C.E. Massoretic texts became standard for all Jewish communities retaining knowledge of Hebrew, except for the Samaritans. One should remember, however, that, despite its standardization, MT is an abstraction, a type of text attested in about six thousand medieval exemplars that disagree in numerous but relatively minor ways (Tov 1992: 23). Properly speaking, *a* Massoretic text is any biblical text accompanied by vocalization, trope and marginal annotation in the style of the Massoretes.

Few ancient variant readings survive in the MT tradition; most differences among MSS are new mistakes or developments, and in any case are rarely more serious than "Egypt" vs. "land of Egypt" (Goshen-Gottstein 1967: 280 n. 4, 285, 287). But we should remain open-minded and alert. Individual readings, though generally transmitted "genetically" from parent to daughter MS, may also leap "infectiously" from MS to MS, as when a scribe compares existing texts or consults his memory. Thus, even if Rabbinic authority prevented deviant MSS from being reproduced *in toto*, individual variants apparently found shelter here and there in otherwise Massoretic texts. We in fact find sporadic agreement between MT MSS and LXX, Sam, the Dead Sea Scrolls, etc.[38] In any case, since there is no such thing as *the* MT, it is arbitrary to select one prestigious text—the Aleppo Codex, the Leningrad Codex, the Second Rabbinic Bible, etc.—as sole witness.

By and large, the invention of printing halted the evolution of the Hebrew biblical text. Since the Second Rabbinic Bible (Venice, 1524), all published editions have differed in only the most minor of details, such as optional spellings.[39]

How, then, do we reconstruct the elusive autograph, some 2,500 years old? It is plain that disagreement among biblical MSS, though a perennial theological embarrassment, is our most precious resource. We begin by culling variants, first from the families of Hebrew MSS—MT,[40] Sam[41] and the Dead Sea

---

[36]On the "trope," see Tov (1992: 67–71). As with the vocalization, several systems competed in the Middle Ages.

[37]Large, small, suspended, broken or dotted letters, final letters in midword, etc. (Tov 1992: 54–58). Even before 700 C.E., the Talmuds attest to the Jews' concern with exact spelling and letter form.

[38]Because virtually all involve synonymous readings—"Pharaoh" vs. "Egypt's king," etc.— Goshen-Gottstein (1967) is doubtless right to see the hand of coincidence; i.e., the same variant has arisen twice spontaneously. But we must consider each case on its own merits.

[39]For a selection of variants from earlier printed editions, see Ginsburg (1994).

[40]The Hebrew edition used by me and most scholars, *Biblia Hebraica Stuttgartensia* (BHS), is based on the "Leningrad Codex" (B 19a). This MS has no unique claim to authority, but is our oldest dated and complete exemplar of MT (1009 C.E.). Readings from other MSS are cited from Kennicott (1776–80), de Rossi (1784–85) and the BHS apparatus—but only selectively, as when they appear to support another ancient witness. A better procedure would have been to compare all MT MSS among themselves prior to bringing other traditions to bear—the approach of the Hebrew University Bible Project—but this would have been prohibitively laborious.

[41]Sam is cited from the edition of von Gall (1918), the Samaritan Targum from Tal (1981). For corrections to von Gall, see Baillet (1982).

Scrolls.[42] We then turn to the ancient translations—witnesses to LXX,[43] "the Three,"[44] Vg,[45] Syr[46] and *Tgs.*[47]—which must be translated back into Hebrew to be made useful.

And there is one more step. While we lack pre-Roman-era biblical MSS, Hebrew inscriptions going back to the tenth century B.C.E. prove that Israelite spelling conventions and letter shapes changed considerably over time. Some problems of interpretation arise, and others resolve themselves, once we readjust the orthography to ancient norms.

Having assembled a gamut of variant readings, we must judge among them. Here it is helpful to know the observed foibles of scribes (see Tov 1992: 233–91):

1. A scribe may inadvertently transpose letters or words (metathesis).
2. A scribe may inadvertently drop material between similar sequences of letters (haplography).
3. A scribe may inadvertently duplicate sequences of letters (dittography).
4. A scribe may confuse similar-*looking* letters or words. Far less often, he may confuse similar-*sounding* letters or words, giving rise to the suspicion that, Jewish law notwithstanding, texts were occasionally dictated or written from memory (cf. *b. Meg.* 18b; *y. Meg.* 4:1, 74d).
5. A scribe may misdivide words. This phenomenon suggests that the autograph lacked word divisions, like phylacteries and mezuzoth. But, since no surviving MS or Israelite inscription employs "continuous writing," we might also attribute misdivision to the occasional crowding of words.
6. A scribe may deliberately shorten a text to eliminate a perceived redundancy. This is far more common in translation than in Hebrew transmission.
7. A scribe may expand a text for various reasons: to supply information (e.g., identify speakers), update language or spelling or replace a rare word with one more familiar. Sometimes, he may incorporate a variant from another MS, or make an interlinear or marginal remark that a later copyist will naively insert into the body of the text.

In the absence of obvious mechanical error (types 1–5), critics generally favor the shorter reading (*lectio brevior*) over the longer, and the more difficult reading (*lectio difficilior*) over the expected—provided that the short or difficult reading also makes sense, and taking into account the peculiarities of each

---

[42]Most of these are published in the series "Discoveries in the Judaean Desert" (DJD).

[43]I have consulted both the Cambridge (Brooke and McLean 1909) and Göttingen (Wevers 1991) editions of LXX. In addition, Wevers's commentaries on LXX Exodus (1990, 1992) are invaluable.

[44]Cited from Field (1875), which requires some updating. On Theodotionic Exodus, see O'Connell (1972).

[45]R. Weber, *Biblia Sacra* (Stuttgart: Deutsche Bibelgesellschaft, 1983).

[46]*The Old Testament in Syriac I, 1* (Leiden: Brill, 1977).

[47]I have used the editions of Sperber (1959), Rieder (1974), Diez-Macho (1970) and Klein (1980) for *Tgs. Onqelos, Ps.-Jonathan, Neofiti I* and the *Fragmentary Targum*, respectively.

manuscript tradition.[48] The "rules" cannot be and never are applied mechanically, however. In the final analysis, textual criticism is neither science nor art, but a form of divination, i.e., a pseudo-science in which the honest practitioner does not fully believe.

Accordingly, although we proceed *as if* attempting to reconstruct the original, our aspirations must be considerably humbler. More often than not, the result of our labors is a spectrum of possible readings, some not even attested but rather invented by the critic to solve a problem (conjectural emendation). The mark † before a TEXTUAL NOTE indicates that, although my translation follows standard MT (i.e., *BHS*), there is room for doubt. Where the translation diverges from *BHS*, the TEXTUAL NOTE is preceded by ††.

However copious, my TEXTUAL NOTES do not contain *all* variants. I have been selective, focusing on those affecting translation and interpretation. But I have taken pains to incorporate most of the evidence from the newly published Dead Sea Scrolls, since it is not available in previous commentaries. I generally do not treat matters of optional spelling (e.g., *šmwt* vs. *šmt*) or of minor, synonymous readings (*'el* vs. *lə-*, omission or addition of *'ēt*, etc.).

After TEXTUAL NOTES comes SOURCE ANALYSIS, wherein we delve beneath the surface of the (supposed) pristine text.

SOURCE ANALYSIS

My earlier reference to the editing of the Torah after the Babylonian Exile probably surprised some readers. Judeo-Christian tradition records that Moses penned the Torah at God's dictation in the fifteenth century B.C.E. The critical enterprise called SOURCE ANALYSIS has impugned the credibility of this belief, however.

Many cultures tell of a founder-hero wielding unusual powers and authority who established mores for future generations. The motif's universality obliges the historian to regard such stories skeptically. For the Torah, there is ample evidence that Moses did not write Genesis, Exodus, Leviticus, Numbers and Deuteronomy, at least not in the form we have them. First, the Torah's spelling conforms, on the whole, to norms of the fifth to third centuries B.C.E., a millennium after Moses supposedly lived (Andersen and Forbes 1986; Tov 1992: 224). Thus, even if Moses was the author, later scribes must have updated the spelling, like modern editors of Shakespeare.

This fact alone would not trouble some traditionalists, although the Torah's letter-for-letter accuracy is an article of faith for many Orthodox Jews. A greater

---

[48] For example, Syr is more given to both accidental haplography and deliberate expansion than the other Versions. Sam expands primarily for two purposes: to harmonize divergent or incomplete accounts of the same event, and to reinforce matters of Samaritan doctrine. LXX, though fairly literal, occasionally compresses in the interests of economy or expands in the interests of clarity. And most variation in the MT family involves either optional spellings or nonsensical miswritings; deliberate changes are rare.

difficulty is the presence of ostensible reflections upon the Mosaic era from the perspective of a later age. For example, Gen 12:6; 13:7 recall of the Patriarchal period, "the Canaanite was *then* in the land"—whereas, from Moses' viewpoint, the Canaanites should be *still* in the land. Similarly, Gen 36:31 tells of "kings who reigned in the land of Edom before a king ruled for Israel's Sons," even though Moses supposedly lived centuries before the Israelite monarchy. Deuteronomy repeatedly calls Transjordan "the Jordan's *other* side," although Moses is standing *in Transjordan* (Deut 1:1, 5; 3:8, 20, 25; 4:41, 46, 47, 49; 11:30). And the Torah narrates Moses' death and claims that none like him ever arose again, once more betraying the perspective of a later time (Deut 34:5–12).

Tradition lightly dispels these difficulties, invoking Moses' prophetic powers. The logic is unassailable, if only we allow for the supernatural. In theory, a true prophet could have predicted the Canaanites' demise, the coronation of Saul, his own death and Persian-period spelling. But the critical historian is rather drawn to conclude that the Mosaic authorship of the Torah is just another legend, or at best an exaggeration. In fact, the Pentateuch never explains how it came to be written.[49] The earliest allusions to a Mosaic Pentateuch come from the postexilic period, when most scholars date the Torah's editing and promulgation (Ezra 3:2; 6:18; 7:6; Neh 1:7, 8; 8:1, 14; 9:14; 10:30; 13:1, etc.).

If Moses did not write the Torah, who did? Most likely several people, for, as is well known, the Pentateuch is rife with internal contradictions and duplications (doublets). Each, taken alone, proves nothing; traditional Jewish and Christian scholars have effectively dealt with most of them piecemeal. Cumulatively, they constitute a major challenge to the tradition of a single Author. It rather appears that an editor (or multiple editors) produced the Torah by combining several written sources of diverse origin, relatively unretouched, into a composite whole. This is the Documentary Hypothesis.[50]

The number of sources appears to have been small. First, no story is told more than three times. Second, it is hard to imagine an editor countenancing so many duplications and inconsistencies were he at liberty to weave together isolated fragments from dozens of documents. Third and most important, if we arrange the doublets in four columns and then read across, continuity and consistency replace contradiction and redundancy. These columns approximate the original sources.[51]

---

[49] Moses is said to have inscribed or commanded a "Direction" (*tôrâ*) in Deut 1:5; 4:8, 44; 27:3, 8, 26; 28:58, 61; 29:20, 28; 30:10; 31:9, 11, 12, 24, 26; 32:46; 33:4. But there is no reason, apart from the claim of tradition, to find here an allusion to the whole Pentateuch. Deuteronomy itself is the more likely referent.

[50] For a pellucid exposition of the evidence, see Friedman (1987, 1992).

[51] This is an oversanguine picture of source analysis. While it is true that we can eliminate almost all blatant contradictions, to demonstrate continuity within each reconstructed document is more difficult. Moreover, different readers have different senses of what constitutes unacceptable contradiction or duplication. I, personally, am untroubled by small inconsistencies, while German scholars as a class demand maximal efficiency and consistency from the pristine documents.

While the exact process by which the Torah coalesced is impossible to reconstruct, here is a commonly accepted model which I think pretty close to the truth. After the demise of the Northern Kingdom of Israel (721 B.C.E. [2 Kings 17]), refugees brought south to Judah a document telling the national history from a Northern perspective (Procksch 1906; Friedman 1987, 1992). We call this text "E" and its author the "Elohist," because God is called (hā)'ĕlōhîm '(the) Deity'[52] prior to Moses' day and sporadically thereafter. In Judah, a scribe we call "Redactor^JE" combined E with a parallel, southern version, "J," which calls God "Yahweh"[53] throughout (except in some dialogue). We call J's author the "Yahwist." The composite of J and E is known as "JE."

Precisely a century later (621 B.C.E.), a work called "D," essentially the Book of Deuteronomy, was promulgated to supplement JE. It purports to be Moses' final testament deposited in the Tabernacle (Deut 31:24–26) and rediscovered after centuries of neglect (2 Kings 22). In fact, D appears to be a rewritten law code of Northern origin, with stylistic and ideological affinities to E. The author/editor of D, the Deuteronomistic Historian, also continued Israel's history down to his own era, producing the first edition of Deuteronomy through 2 Kings (a second edition was made in the Exile [Cross 1973: 275–89]). Some think JE was also reworked, so that the Deuteronomistic work properly began with Creation (e.g., Fuss 1972; Rendtorff 1990; Blum 1990; Johnstone 1990, 1992). If so, however, the editor added relatively little in Genesis–Numbers.

If D was intended to complement and complete JE, another work, the Priestly source (P), attempted to supplant JE with its own partisan account of cosmic and national origins (Friedman 1981). The date of P is disputed, with most scholars favoring a late preexilic, exilic or early postexilic date (i.e., c. 700–400). Subsequently, a second priestly writer, the final Redactor (R), thwarted P's purpose by combining it with JE, inserting additional genealogical and geographical material (Friedman 1981, 1987). The Redactor also detached D from Joshua–2 Kings, producing the Pentateuch.[54]

For Exodus, our main concern is with P, E and J, although there is some D-like language, too (see SOURCE ANALYSES to 12:1–13:16, 15:22–26; and chaps. 19–24, 32, 33–34 and APPENDIX A). It is likely, moreover, that the Song of the Sea (15:1b–18) originally circulated independently and should thus be considered another source. P is the document most easily recognized, thanks to its characteristic vocabulary, style and agenda (McEvenue 1971; Paran 1989; Levitt Kohn 1997). P's main concern is mediating the gulf between God's

---

[52] On this translation, rather than "God," see NOTE to 1:17.

[53] In German *Jahweh* — hence "J."

[54] Many scholars detect the Priestly hand in Joshua (e.g., Blenkinsopp 1976; Lohfink 1978), while Friedman (1998) argues that the Yahwistic source continues through Joshua, Judges and Samuel. If so, we may require more complex scenarios: e.g., Redactor^JE used only half of J, leaving the second part for the Deuteronomistic Historian; or the priestly Redactor edited Genesis–2 Kings, but inserted very little into Samuel–Kings, just as the Deuteronomistic Historian may have incorporated JE virtually unretouched into his longer work (Freedman 1962: 717).

holiness and the profane world through priestly sacrifice. P stresses distinctions of clean and unclean, the centrality of Tabernacle service and the exclusive right of the house of Aaron to officiate. Its rather austere Deity sends no angelic messengers. P also evinces a scholarly interest in chronology and genealogy. Since P's "voice" seems somehow louder than JE's, in my translation it appears in **boldface**.[55] In JE, in contrast, sacrifice is offered by a variety of men in a variety of places. There is more interest in narrative and character portrayal, less in ritual, chronology and genealogy. God communicates through angels, dreams or direct revelation. JE is set in regular typeface.[56]

The most striking difference among J, E and P involves the divine name. E and P hold that the name "Yahweh" was first revealed to Moses (3:14–15 [E]; 6:2–3 [P]). Previously, God was called "God (*'ēl*)," "God Shadday (*'ēl šadday*)" or "(the) Deity (*[hā]'ĕlōhîm*)." In J, however, the earliest generations of humanity already use the name "Yahweh" (Gen 4:26, etc.); Moses is merely granted a more detailed revelation of God's attributes (Exod 34:6–7). Consequently, virtually any text prior to the Burning Bush containing the name "Yahweh" is from J. When it comes to the Mountain of Lawgiving, however, J and P line up against E and D: J and P call it "Sinai," while in E and D it is "Horeb." A final difference between J and E is that the former calls Moses' father-in-law "Reuel," while the latter uses "Jethro" (Jethro/Reuel does not appear in P or D).

Because separating J from E is difficult outside of Genesis,[57] prudence would dictate partitioning Exodus simply between P and JE. I have nevertheless undertaken the dubious task of disentangling J from E, because the results are surprising. If J is the dominant voice in Genesis, in Exodus we probably have more E than J. This flies in the face of all previous scholarship, which unanimously ascribes the bulk of non-Priestly Exodus to J (but now see R. Friedman 1998: 314). This is simply an unexamined dogma, however, put baldly in Noth's (1948: 28) methodological postulate: "In *Zweifelsfalle eher für J als für E zu entscheiden ist*" (emphasis in original).[58] Why? Jettisoning the axiom, we find far more E than J in Exodus. Recurring idioms, characters and themes all point to the Elohist.[59]

---

[55] I also put in boldface the contribution of R, whose style is so similar to P's that some scholars do not distinguish between them (for a critique, see Propp 1997). On Knohl's (1987, 1995) partition of P into two strata, see APPENDIX A, vol. II.

[56] Because neither J nor E is fully preserved, because their styles are very similar and because it is particularly hard to separate them in Exodus (see below), I do not distinguish J from E by typeface.

[57] Even in Genesis, some deny the existence of an Elohistic source (e.g., Rudolph 1938; Carr 1996; cf. Van Seters 1992). But I find E necessary to explain the complementary distribution of divine names and doublets (see, e.g., Speiser 1964: xx–xxxvii).

[58] In dubious cases, one must opt for J rather than for E.

[59] D. N. Freedman (privately) observes that, unlike J, the Elohistic and Priestly sources regard the revelation to Moses as epoch-making. We might therefore expect E and P to provide more detail about Moses and the Exodus, and consequently to be better represented in Exodus than in Genesis.

The chain of evidence begins with 3:15–17, the classic Elohistic text in which God first reveals his name to Moses at "the Deity's mountain . . . Horeb" (3:1): "And Deity further said to Moses, 'Thus you will say to Israel's Sons: "Yahweh your fathers' deity . . . has sent me to you"; this is my name to eternity, and this is my designation age (by) age. Go, and you will gather Israel's elders and say to them, "Yahweh your fathers' deity appeared to me . . . saying: '. . . I acknowledge, acknowledge you (*pāqōd pāqadtî 'etkem*) and what is done to you in Egypt . . . I will take you up (*'aʿăle[h] 'etkem*) [from Egypt].'"'" The reference to *'ĕlōhîm* (v 15) creates a presumption of Elohistic authorship, confirmed by the explicit allusion to Gen 50:24–25 (E): "And Joseph said to his brothers, 'I am dying, but Deity will acknowledge, acknowledge you (*pāqōd yipqōd 'etkem*) and take you up (*wahe'ĕlâ 'etkem*) from this land to the land which he swore to Abraham, to Isaac and to Jacob.' So Joseph adjured Israel's sons, saying, 'Deity (*'ĕlōhîm*) will acknowledge, acknowledge you (*pāqōd yipqōd . . . 'etkem*); and you will take up my bones from here.'"

From 3:15–16, we also learn that the elders are Moses' assistants in E. In 3:18, Moses is told to take them before Pharaoh, to announce that "Yahweh the Hebrews' deity happened upon us." He delivers this message in chap. 5, which must also be E, even though the elders are unaccountably absent.

We will skip, for the moment, the rest of the Burning Bush scene and the Ten Plagues. Exod 13:17–19 recounts Israel's departure from Egypt, again invoking Gen 50:25 by the key terms *pāqōd yipqōd 'etkem* and *'ĕlōhîm:* "And it happened, in Pharaoh's releasing the people, and Deity did not lead them the way of the land of Philistines. . . . And Moses took Joseph's bones with him, for he had adjured, adjured Israel's sons, saying, 'Deity (*'ĕlōhîm*) will acknowledge, acknowledge you (*pāqōd yipqōd 'etkem*).'" E is also present in the following account of the Sea event, where the non-Priestly material seems composed of two strands. One is presumably E and the other J (see SOURCE ANALYSIS to 13:17–15:22).

After the Sea, the Massah-Meribah episode (17:2–7) mentions Horeb and the elders, both signs of E. And we meet a valuable cross-reference in 17:5: Moses is to strike the rock with "your rod, with which you struck the Nile," i.e., turned it to blood. I would infer that the non-Priestly plague of blood (7:14–18, 20b–21a, 23–24) is Elohistic, along with the rest of the JE Plagues cycle (on the unity of the non-P plagues, see SOURCE ANALYSIS to 7:8–11:10). This includes the non-Priestly paschal legislation associated with the tenth plague, which features the elders (12:21–23, 25–27).

The plague of blood contains yet another cross-reference: Moses is to use "the rod that turned into a snake" (7:15). This takes us back to the Burning Bush, where Moses' rod, also called "the Deity's rod" (4:20), underwent such a transformation (4:2–5). This wonder is part of a continuous account of how Aaron came to be Moses' spokesman (4:2–16), and, confirming our thesis, Aaron plays a minor role in Exodus 5 and the Elohistic portions of chaps. 7–12. The references to the divine rod and Jethro (not Reuel) in 4:17–18 are further signs of E.

Returning to Exodus 17, we note that the Amalek incident (vv 8–16) refers to *maṭṭē(h) hā'ĕlōhîm* 'the Deity's rod' an expression paralleled in 4:20. Present are not only Moses and Aaron but also Hur and Joshua, whom we may add to our Elohistic *dramatis personae*. Exodus 18 mentions "the Deity's mountain" and Jethro, both signs of E. And chaps. 19–20, the theophany at Sinai/Horeb, is composed of several strands, one of which includes *'ĕlōhîm* (19:3, 17, 19; 20:1, 19–21) and the elders (19:7) and should be E. Exod 24:13–14 and chap. 32 also display the earmarks of E: Aaron, Hur, Joshua, the elders and "the Deity's mountain." Exod 33:6 names "Horeb," while 33:7–11 tells of Joshua assisting Moses in the Meeting Tent (cf. 24:13).

This does not exhaust the Elohistic matter in Exodus. Most commentators ascribe to E the midwives story (1:15–21), which mentions *'ĕlōhîm* and the fear of God (cf. Wolff 1975). Other episodes (Marah, Manna) may also be Elohistic, but the evidence is less clear (see SOURCE ANALYSES to 15:22–26 and 15:27–16:36).

Admittedly, my thesis is neither proven nor provable. Quite possibly, both J and E told of Aaron, Joshua, the elders and/or the divine rod, in which case partition becomes impossible. But I would point to the attractive simplicity of my analysis, and would in any case submit that Noth's axiom needs reconsideration. Simplicity is crucial—for I do not insist that the classical JEPD hypothesis is correct. It is merely the *simplest* model that accounts for most of the evidence. Under SOURCE ANALYSIS, while I justify source assignments in detail, I also air many doubts. My intention is to expose the Documentary Hypothesis in both strength and weakness. Having undertaken source criticism in a fairly traditional mode in the body of the commentary, I shall assess its success or failure in APPENDIX A (vol. II). There I will consider challenges to the standard model[60] and also the vexed matter of the sources' dates.

After taking the Torah apart, our next task is to reassemble it under REDACTION ANALYSIS.

REDACTION ANALYSIS

Exodus is really five different works: the entire Book of Exodus, P, JE, J and E.[61] REDACTION ANALYSIS traces the evolution of Exodus from its original, hypothetical components into the book as we have it. Attempting to make sense of the whole, we will discover nuances of which the editors themselves may have been unaware, but which were often remarked upon by traditional Christian and Jewish interpreters.

---

[60] I will especially weigh the possibility that some of my "Elohistic" stratum is rather connected with the "Proto-Genesis" redactional layer detected in Genesis by Carr (1996).

[61] Strictly speaking, the portions of Exodus ascribed to J, E, P and probably JE are not true "books," i.e., independent scrolls, but segments of longer works.

How were the editors able, psychologically, to incorporate contradictory accounts and laws? Perhaps they felt that, in recording dimly remembered events of antiquity, it was safest to preserve multiple versions. And if, as many think, the Torah's compilation was concurrent with the coalescence of Israelite and Judean society (e.g., Friedman 1987), reliance upon multiple sources might have enhanced its authority. At any rate, at the expense of coherence and consistency, the Torah has achieved richness, mystery and an appeal to multiple sensibilities.

Some regard the final Redactor as an artist, even a genius. I do not. He was a writer, i.e., a scribe, but not an author. His raw materials were already highly polished works of art, which he had but to transcribe. As for the arrangement of the text, most of his decisions were dictated by his sources.[62] Nevertheless, the end product is art of the highest caliber—or so our Judeo-Christian conditioning obliges us to feel.

NOTES AND COMMENTS

The bulk of the commentary is taken up by NOTES and COMMENTS, whose scope is less restricted than TEXTUAL CRITICISM, SOURCE ANALYSIS and REDACTION ANALYSIS. Under NOTES, I explore various technical matters of interpretation: the meanings and etymologies of words, syntactic analysis, wordplay, resonances with other passages—in fact, any issue that can be dealt with briefly. I reserve COMMENTS for more general or extended discussions. NOTES and COMMENTS will be the sections of greatest interest for most readers.

APPENDICES

There are five appendices which will appear in volume II, each devoted to a meta-issue raised by Exodus.

APPENDIX A questions the validity of the Documentary Hypothesis and the source-critical enterprise. We will ask how many strata the Torah contains, when and where they were written and whether they are better conceived as independent documents or as editorial layers. We will also see how the hypothesis has weathered recent challenges and try to establish limits for what source critics may reasonably claim as the fruit of their labors.

APPENDIX B addresses the date and historicity of Israel's departure from Egypt. We will consider matters of chronology and geography, and how the

---

[62]Here the Redactor differs from the collage artist, whose achievement is the use of found materials, not necessarily *objets d'art*, in surprising and affecting ways.

Exodus tradition squares with contemporary archaeology's picture of emergent Israel.

APPENDIX C characterizes Israelite monotheism and attempts to discover its historical origins. Connections with the ancient Egyptian and Semitic cultural milieus will be explored, along with the emergence of Covenant theology. God's names will also be discussed.

APPENDIX D provides an overview of the Exodus theme in the Bible, particularly in the Prophets.

APPENDIX E contains additions, corrections and afterthoughts to volume I.

CONCLUSION

My main intent has been to write a useful work. I have fancied myself the moderator of a vast, millennial colloquium. Josephus, Aqiba, Origen, Rashi, Calvin, Wellhausen and Albright are here, alongside some outsiders too prominent not to be invited: Baruch Spinoza, Sigmund Freud, Cecil B. De Mille, etc. Each injects a word, but I control the discussion and have written up the proceedings.

The result, like Exodus itself, is a pastiche. Rather than summarize and evaluate my predecessors' works, I have often cannibalized (or, if you prefer, recycled), lifting insights from original contexts and putting them to uses of which their authors would surely disapprove.[63] So I hereby apologize to the living and the dead. Sometimes I merely cite an important treatment without responding, so that students may know where to find further discussion.[64] Consequently, these volumes should be regarded, not as the last, but as the first word on Exodus.

Finally: an innovation of which I am quite proud is labeling extreme lines of conjecture SPECULATION. Controlled fantasy is relatively benign, and indeed it prepares us for future discoveries. Speculation is harmful only when it parades as certainty.

---

[63]To illustrate: when I say "cf. Jones," I am not necessarily quoting or even agreeing with Jones. Rather, I am indicating that Jones has said something similar or relevant to my own point. In contrast, "see Jones" or simply "Jones" conveys my endorsement.

[64]In these respects, my work differs from Greenberg (1969) and Childs (1974), who are more interested in the history of interpretation for its own sake. In particular, my commentary gives a misleading impression of medieval Jewish exegesis, from which I have culled only insights relevant for the modern critic.

BIBLIOGRAPHY

◆

BIBLIOGRAPHY

◆

Whenever possible, I cite English editions of foreign-language works, even if they appeared decades after the original writing: e.g., Loewenstamm 1992a was first published in 1965 (Hebrew), while Jacob 1992 was completed, but never published, in 1945 (German). The inconvenience this method imposes upon the specialist is, I think, outweighed by its convenience for the non-scholarly English reader, for whom this work is also intended. This bibliography gives all original publication dates, providing a clearer sense of the history of scholarship. Modern Hebrew titles will be transliterated according to my method for Biblical Hebrew; see pp. xxxix–xl above.

Abba, R.
   1961   The Divine Name Yahweh. *JBL* 80: 320–28.
Abou-Assaf, A., P. Bordreuil, and A. R. Millard
   1982   *La statue de Tell Fekheryeh*. Études Assyriologiques 7. Paris: Recherche sur les civilisations.
Ackerman, J. S.
   1974   The Literary Context of the Moses Birth Story (Exodus 1–2). Pp. 74–119 in *Literary Interpretations of Biblical Narratives*, ed. K. R. R. Gros Louis et al. Nashville: Abingdon.
Ackerman, S.
   1992   *Under Every Green Tree: Popular Religion in Sixth-Century Judah*. HSM 46. Atlanta: Scholars Press.
   1993   Child Sacrifice: Returning God's Gift. *BRev* 9.3: 20–28, 56.
Ackroyd, P. R.
   1986   *Yāḏ*. TDOT 5.397–426. Grand Rapids, Mich.: Eerdmans.
Adamson, P. B.
   1988   Some Infective and Allergic Conditions in Ancient Mesopotamia. *RA* 82: 163–77.
Adler, E. J.
   1989   The Background for the Metaphor of Covenant as Marriage in the Hebrew Bible. Ph.D. diss., University of California, Berkeley.
Aejmelaeus, A.
   1986   Function and Interpretation of *ky* in Biblical Hebrew. *JBL* 105: 193–229.

Aharoni, Y.
1979   The Land of the Bible. 2d ed. Philadelphia: Westminster.
1981   Arad Inscriptions. Jerusalem: Israel Exploration Society.
Ahitub, S.
1968   Mōše(h). Haššēm. EM 5.495–96. Jerusalem: Bialik Institute.
1971   Pāsēaḥ. EM 6.514. Jerusalem: Bialik Institute.
1982   Tôšāb. EM 8.507–8. Jerusalem: Bialik Institute.
Ahuviah, A.
1991   Šēšet yāmîm tilqəṭūhû. Beit Mikra 36: 226–29.
Aimé-Giron, N.
1941   Baʿal Ṣapon et les dieux Taḫpanḫès dans un nouveau papyrus
        Phénicien. ASAE 40: 433–60.
Albrektson, B.
1968   On the Syntax of ʾhyh ʾšr ʾhyh in Exodus 3:14. Pp. 15–28 in Words
        and Meanings, ed. P. R. Ackroyd and B. Lindars. Cambridge:
        Cambridge University.
Albright, W. F.
1920   A Revision of Early Hebrew Chronology. JPOS 1: 49–79.
1924   Contributions to Biblical Archaeology and Philology. JBL 43:
        363–93.
1927   The Names "Israel" and "Judah," with an Excursus on the Etymol-
        ogy of Tôdâh and Tôrâh. JBL 46: 151–85.
1944   The Oracles of Balaam. JBL 63: 207–33.
1950a   A Catalogue of Early Hebrew Lyric Poems (Psalm LXVIII). HUCA
        23.1: 1–39.
1950b   Baal-Zephon. Pp. 1–14 in Festschrift Alfred Bertholet, ed. W. Baum-
        gartner et al. Tübingen: Mohr (Siebeck).
1954   Northwest Semitic Names in a List of Egyptian Slaves from the
        Eighteenth Century B.C. JAOS 74: 222–33.
1956   The Refrain "And God Saw ki tob" in Genesis. Pp. 22–26 in Mé-
        langes bibliques rédigés en l'honneur de André Robert. Travaux de
        l'Institut Catholique de Paris 4. Paris: Bloud & Gay.
1962   Kənaʿan, kənaʿānî. EM 4.196–202. Jerusalem: Bialik Institute.
1963   Jethro, Hobab and Reuel in Early Hebrew Tradition. CBQ 25:
        1–11.
1968   Yahweh and the Gods of Canaan. Jordan Lectures on Comparative
        Religion 7. Garden City, N.Y.: Doubleday.
Alexander, P. S.
1992   Targum, Targumim. ABD 6.320–31. New York: Doubleday.
Alonso-Schökel, L.
1988   A Manual of Hebrew Poetics. Subsidia Biblica 11. Rome: Pontifical
        Biblical Institute.
Alquier, J., and P. Alquier
1931   Stèles votives à Saturne découvertes près de N'gaous (Algérie).
        CRAIBL 1931: 21–26.

Alt, A.
1968   *Essays on Old Testament History and Religion.* Garden City, N.Y.: Doubleday.
Alter, R. B.
1981   *The Art of Biblical Narrative.* New York: Basic Books.
1985   *The Art of Biblical Poetry.* New York: Basic Books.
Andersen, F. I., and A. D. Forbes
1983   "Prose Particle" Counts of the Hebrew Bible. Pp. 165–83 in *The Word of the Lord Shall Go Forth,* ed. C. L. Meyers and M. O'Connor. Fs. D. N. Freedman. Winona Lake, Ind.: Eisenbrauns.
1986   *Spelling in the Hebrew Bible.* BibOr 41. Rome: Pontifical Biblical Institute.
Andersen, F. I., and D. N. Freedman
1980   *Hosea.* AB 24. Garden City, N.Y.: Doubleday.
Andrae, W.
1947/52   Der kultische Garten. WO 1: 485–94.
Andreasen, N-E. A.
1972   *The Old Testament Sabbath. A Tradition-Historical Investigation.* SBLDS 7. Missoula, Mont.: Printing Department, University of Montana.
Ap-Thomas, D. R.
1983   All the King's Horses? Pp. 135–51 in *Proclamation and Presence²,* ed. J. I. Durham and J. R. Porter. Macon, Ga.: Mercer University.
Aptowitzer, V.
1930–31   Bêt hammiqdāš šel maʿălâ ʿal pî hāʾaggādâ. *Tarbiz* 2: 137–53.
1970   *Das Schriftwort in der rabbinischen Literatur.* Orig. pub. 1906–15. New York: KTAV.
Armayor, O. K.
1978   Did Herodotus Ever Go to Egypt? *Journal of the American Research Center in Egypt* 15: 59–73.
Assmann, J.
1995   *Egyptian Solar Religion in the New Kingdom.* London/New York: Kegan Paul International.
Astour, M. C.
1966   Some New Divine Names from Ugarit. *JAOS* 86: 277–84.
1967   *Hellenosemitica.* 2d ed. Leiden: Brill.
Attridge, H. W., and R. A. Oden, Jr.
1976   *The Syrian Goddess.* SBLTT 9. Missoula, Mont.: Scholars Press.
1981   *Philo of Byblos: The Phoenician History.* CBQMS 9. Washington, D.C.: Catholic Biblical Association of America.
Auerbach, E.
1958   Die Feste im alte Israel. *VT* 8: 1–18.
1959   Der Wechsel des Jahres-Anfangs in Juda. *VT* 9: 113–21.
1960   Die Umschaltung vom judäischen auf dem babylonischen Kalendar. *VT* 10: 69–70.

1975 *Moses.* German orig. 1953. Detroit: Wayne State University.
Auffret, P.
1983 Essai sur la structure littéraire d'Ex 14. *EstBib* 41: 53–82.
Avalos, H.
1990 Exodus 22:9 and Akkadian Legal Formulae. *JBL* 109: 116–17.
1995 *Illness and Health Care in the Ancient Near East.* HSM 54. Atlanta: Scholars Press.
Avigad, N.
1969 Qəbûṣat ḥôtāmôt ʿibriyyîm. Pp. 1–9 in W. F. *Albright Volume.* ErIsr 9. Jerusalem: Israel Exploration Society.
1972 Excavations in the Jewish Quarter of the Old City of Jerusalem, 1971. *IEJ* 22: 193–200.
1983 *Discovering Jerusalem.* Hebrew orig. 1980. Nashville: Thomas Nelson.
Avishur, Y.
1981 *RWM (RMM)-BNH* bəʾûgārîtît ûb(ə)miqrāʾ. *Leš* 45: 270–79.
Axelsson, L. E.
1987 *The Lord Rose up from Seir.* ConBOT 25. Lund: Almqvist & Wiksell.
Baentsch, B.
1903 *Exodus-Leviticus-Numeri.* HKAT. Göttingen: Vandenhoeck & Ruprecht.
Baillet, M.
1982 Corrections à l'édition de von Gall du Pentateuch samaritain. Pp. 23–35 in *Von Kanaan bis Kerala,* ed. W. C. Delsman et al. Fs. J. P. M. van der Ploeg. AOAT 211. Kevelaer: Butzon & Bercker; Neukirchen-Vluyn: Neukirchener Verlag.
Bakir, A.
1952 *Slavery in Pharaonic Egypt.* ASAESup 18. Cairo: Institut Français d'Archéologie.
Ball, C. J.
1899 *Light from the East.* London: Eyre & Spottiswoode.
Baltzer, K.
1971 *The Covenant Formulary.* German orig. 1960. Oxford: Blackwell.
1987 Liberation from Debt Slavery After the Exile in Second Isaiah and Nehemiah. Pp. 477–84 in *Ancient Israelite Religion,* ed. P. D. Miller, Jr., P. D. Hanson, and S. D. McBride. Fs. F. M. Cross. Philadelphia: Fortress.
Barkay, G.
1992 The Priestly Benediction on Silver Plaques from Ketef Hinnom in Jerusalem. *TA* 9: 139–92.
Barker, M.
1991 *The Gate of Heaven.* London: SPCK.
Barré, M. L.
1992 "My Strength and My Song" in Exodus 15:2. *CBQ* 54: 623–37.

Barth, J.
1894   Die Nominalbildung in den semitischen Sprachen. Leipzig: Hinrichs.
Batto, B. F.
1983   The Reed Sea: Requiescat in Pace. JBL 10: 27–35.
1992   Slaying the Dragon. Louisville: Westminster/John Knox.
Baumgarten, J. M.
1989   4Q500 and the Ancient Conception of the Lord's Vineyard. JJS 40:
        1–6.
Beale, G. K.
1984   An Exegetical and Theological Consideration of the Hardening of
        Pharaoh's Heart in Exodus 4–14 and Romans 9. Trinity Journal 5:
        129–54.
Beck, P.
1990   ʿal ṣalmît mittēl dān. Pp. 87–93 in Ruth Amiran Volume. ErIsr 21.
        Jerusalem: Israel Exploration Society.
Becking, B.
1994   Elisha: "Shaʿ is my God?" ZAW 106: 113–16.
Beegle, D. M.
1972   Moses, the Servant of Yahweh. Grand Rapids, Mich.: Eerdmans.
Beer, G.
1911   Die Bitterkräuter beim Paschafest. ZAW 31: 152–53.
1939   Exodus. HAT 3. Tübingen: Mohr (Siebeck).
Bender, A.
1903   Das Lied Exodus 15. ZAW 23: 1–48.
Ben-Ḥayyim, Z.
1961   ʿIbrît waʾărāmît nôsaḥ šômərôn III.1. Jerusalem: Academy of the
        Hebrew Language.
1967   ʿIbrît waʾărāmît nôsaḥ šômərôn III.2. Jerusalem: Academy of the
        Hebrew Language.
Ben-Reuben, S.
1984   "Wayyikbad lēb parʿō(h)." Beit Mikra 97: 112–13.
Ben-Shabbat, S.
1956–57 Heʿārôt lammaʾămār "ḥătan dāmîm" mēʾēt Dr. J. Blau. Tarbiz
        26: 213.
Benz, F. C.
1972   Personal Names in the Phoenician and Punic Inscriptions. Studia
        Pohl 8. Rome: Pontifical Biblical Institute.
Berlin, A.
1985   The Dynamics of Biblical Parallelism. Bloomington: University of
        Indiana.
Bertman, S.
1964   A Note on the Reversible Miracle. HR 3: 323–27.
Beyerlin, W.
1965   Origins and History of the Oldest Sinaitic Traditions. German orig.
        1961. Oxford: Blackwell.

Bickermann, E.
    1968   *Chronology of the Ancient World*. London: Thames & Hudson.
    1976   *Studies in Jewish and Christian History*. AGJU 9. Leiden: Brill.
Biella, J. C.
    1982   *Dictionary of Old South Arabic*. HSS 25. Chico, Calif.: Scholars
            Press.
Bienamé, G.
    1984   *Moïse et le don de l'eau dans la tradition juive ancienne*. AnBib 98.
            Rome: Pontifical Biblical Institute.
Bird, P.
    1987   The Place of Women in the Israelite Cultus. Pp. 397–419 in *Ancient Israelite Religion*, ed. P. D. Miller, Jr., P. D. Hanson, and S. D.
            McBride. Fs. F. M. Cross. Philadelphia: Fortress.
Blau, J.
    1956–57 Ḥătan dāmîm. *Tarbiz* 26: 1–3.
    1957   Über die t-Form des Hifʿil im Bibelhebräisch. *VT* 7: 385–88.
    1977   "Weak" Phonetic Change and the Hebrew *ŚÎN*. *HAR* 1: 67–119.
    1987–88 Kǝlûm ništammǝrû ʿiqbôtā(y)w šel hazzûgî bitḥûm hakkin-
            nûyîm wǝhappōʿal bǝʾibrît hammiqrāʾ. *Leš* 52: 165–68.
Blenkinsopp, J.
    1976   The Structure of P. *CBQ* 38: 275–92.
    1992   *The Pentateuch*. ABRL. New York/London/Toronto/Sydney/Auck-
            land: Doubleday.
Blum, E.
    1990   *Studien zur Komposition des Pentateuch*. BZAW 189. Berlin/New
            York: de Gruyter.
Blum, R., and E. Blum
    1990   Zipporah und ihr *ḥtn dmym*. Pp. 41–54 in *Die Hebräische Bibel
            und ihre zweifache Nachgeschichte*, ed. E. Blum, C. Macholz, and
            E. W. Stegemann. Fs. R. Rendtorff. Neukirchen-Vluyn: Neukirche-
            ner Verlag.
Bodenheimer, F. S.
    1947   The Manna of Sinai. *BA* 10: 2–6.
Bodenheimer, F. S., and E. Swirski
    1957   *The Aphidoidea of the Middle East*. Jerusalem: Weizmann Science
            Press.
Borowski, O.
    1987   *Agriculture in Iron Age Israel*. Winona Lake, Ind.: Eisenbrauns.
Bottéro, J.
    1981   L'ordalie en Mésopotamie ancienne. *Annali della Scuola Normale
            Superiore di Pisa*. Classe di lettere e filosofia, serie III,3. 11: 1005–67.
Brekelmans, C.
    1954   Exodus XVIII and the Origins of Yahwism in Israel. *OTS* 10:
            215–24.

1966   Die sogenannten deuteronomischen Elemente in Genesis bis Numeri. Pp. 90–96 in *Volume du congrès, Geneve, 1965*. VTSup 15. Leiden: Brill.
Brenner, A.
1994   Who's Afraid of Feminist Criticism? Who's Afraid of Biblical Humor? The Case of the Obtuse Foreign Ruler in the Hebrew Bible. *JSOT* 63: 38–55.
Brenner, M. L.
1991   *The Song of the Sea: Ex 15:1–21*. BZAW 195. Berlin/New York: de Gruyter.
Brettler, M. Z.
1989   *God Is King: Understanding an Israelite Metaphor*. JSOTSup 76. Sheffield: JSOT.
Brichto, H. C.
1974   Kin, Cult, Land and Afterlife—a Biblical Complex. *HUCA* 44: 1–54.
1976   On Slaughter and Sacrifice, Blood and Atonement. *HUCA* 47: 19–55.
Bright, J.
1951   The Date of the Prose Sermons of Jeremiah. *JBL* 70: 15–35.
1983   *A History of Israel*. 3d ed. Philadelphia: Fortress.
Brin, G.
1977   The Firstling of Unclean Animals. *JQR* 68: 1–15.
Brock, S. P.
1973   An Unrecognised Occurrence of the Month Name Ziw (2 Sam. xxi 9). *VT* 12: 100–3.
1982   An Early Interpretation of *pāsaḥ*: *'aggēn* in the Palestinian Targum. Pp. 27–34 in *Interpreting the Hebrew Bible*, ed. J. A. Emerton and S. C. Reif. Fs. E. I. J. Rosenthal. Cambridge: Cambridge University.
Brock-Utne, A.
1934   Eine religionsgeschichtliche Studie zu dem ursprünglichen Passahopfer. *ARW* 31: 272–78.
Brodsky, H.
1990   Locusts in the Book of Joel. *BRev* 6.4: 33–39.
Bron, F.
1979   *Recherches sur les inscriptions phéniciennes de Karatepe*. Hautes Études Orientales 11. Geneva: Droz.
Brongers, H. A., and A. S. van der Woude
1965–66   Wat is de Betekenis van 'Ābnāyim in Exodus 1:16? *NedTT* 20: 241–54.
Bronznick, N. M.
1977   Hassēmanṭîqâ šel haššôreš *ḥlš* ləhistaʿăpûyyôtā(y)w. *Leš* 41: 163–75.
1991–92   Milləšôn ḥăkāmîm lilšôn miqrāʾ. *Beit Mikra* 37: 202–13.

Brooke, A. E., and N. McLean
1909   *The Old Testament in Greek. I,2.* Cambridge Septuagint. Cambridge: Cambridge University.
Brown, R. E.
1994   *The Death of the Messiah.* ABRL. New York: Doubleday.
Brownlee, W. H.
1977   The Ineffable Name of God. *BASOR* 226: 39–46.
Buber, M.
1946   *Moses.* Oxford/London: East & West Library.
Buber, M., and F. Rosenzweig
1934   *Die Schrift.* Berlin: Schocken.
Buccellati, G.
1966   *The Amorites of the Ur III Period.* Naples: Instituto Orientale di Napoli.
Buis, P.
1978   Les conflits entre Moïse et Israël dans Exode et Nombres. *VT* 28: 257–70.
Burns, R. J.
1983   *Exodus Leviticus Numbers.* Old Testament Message 3. Wilmington: Glazier.
1987   *Has the Lord Indeed Spoken Only Through Moses?* SBLDS 84. Atlanta: Scholars Press.
Burrows, M.
1950–51   *The Dead Sea Scrolls of St. Mark's Monastery.* New Haven, Conn.: American Schools of Oriental Research.
Burton, R. F.
1856   *Personal Narrative of a Pilgrimage to El-Medinah and Meccah.* New York: Putnam.
Caloz, M.
1968   Exode XIII,3–16 et son rapport au Deutéronome. *RB* 75: 5–62.
Campbell, A. F.
1975   *Ruth.* AB 7. Garden City, N.Y.: Doubleday.
1979   Psalm 78: A Contribution to the Theology of Tenth Century Israel. *CBQ* 41: 51–79.
Canaan, T.
1926   Mohammedan Saints and Sanctuaries in Palestine. *JPOS* 6: 117–58.
1963   Das Blut in den Sitten und im Aberglauben des palästinischen Arabers. *ZDPV* 79: 8–23.
Caquot, A.
1978   D^{c}bash. *TDOT* 3.128–31. Grand Rapids, Mich.: Eerdmans.
Carlson, R. A.
1969   Élie à l'Horeb. *VT* 19: 416–39.
Carmichael, C.
1974   *The Laws of Deuteronomy.* Ithaca, N.Y.: Cornell University.

Carr, D. M.
 1996   *Reading the Fractures of Genesis.* Louisville: Westminster/John Knox.
Carroll, R. P.
 1969   The Elijah-Elisha Sagas: Some Remarks on Prophetic Succession in Ancient Israel. *VT* 19: 400–15.
Casalis, M.
 1976   The Dry and the Wet: A Semiological Analysis of Creation and Flood Myths. *Semiotica* 17: 35–67.
Cassin, E.
 1968   *La splendeur divine.* École practique des hautes études, Sorbonne. Civilisations et sociétés 8. Paris; Mouton.
Cassuto, U.
 1961   *A Commentary on the Book of Genesis 1.* Hebrew orig. 1944. Jerusalem: Magnes.
 1967   *A Commentary on the Book of Exodus.* Hebrew orig. 1951. Jerusalem: Magnes.
 1975   *Biblical and Oriental Studies.* Jerusalem: Magnes.
Charlesworth, J. H.
 1983   *The Old Testament Pseudepigrapha 1.* Garden City, N.Y.: Doubleday.
 1985   *The Old Testament Pseudepigrapha 2.* Garden City, N.Y.: Doubleday.
Charpin, D., and J.-M. Durand
 1986   Fils de Sim'al. Les origines tribales des rois de Mari. *RA* 80: 141–83.
Chiera, E.
 1934   *Sumerian Epics and Myths.* OIP 15. Chicago: University of Chicago.
Childs, B. S.
 1962   *Myth and Reality in the Old Testament.* London: SCM.
 1965   The Birth of Moses. *JBL* 84: 109–22.
 1970   A Traditio-Historical Study of the Reed Sea Tradition. *VT* 20: 406–18.
 1974   *The Book of Exodus.* OTL. Philadelphia: Westminster.
Chouraqui, A.
 1975   *Noms.* Paris: Desclée de Brouwer.
Chwolson, D.
 1965   *Die Ssabier und der Ssabismus.* Orig. pub. 1856. Amsterdam: Oriental Press.
Clark, G. R.
 1993   *The Word Ḥesed in the Hebrew Bible.* JSOTSup 157. Sheffield: JSOT.
Clements, R. E.
 1965   *God and Temple.* Philadelphia: Fortress.

Clifford, R. J.
  1972   *The Cosmic Mountain in Canaan and the Old Testament.* HSM 4.
          Cambridge, Mass.: Harvard University.
  1981   In Zion and David a New Beginning: An Interpretation of Psalm
          78. Pp. 121–41 in *Traditions in Transformation,* ed. B. Halpern and
          J. D. Levenson. Winona Lake, Ind.: Eisenbrauns.
  1990   Exodus. Pp. 44–60 in *NJBC,* ed. R. E. Brown, J. A. Fitzmyer, and
          R. E. Murphy. Englewood Cliffs, N.J.: Prentice-Hall.
Cloete, W. T. W.
  1989   The Concept of Metre in Old Testament Studies. *JSem* 1: 39–53.
Coats, G. W.
  1967   The Traditio-Historical Character of the Reed Sea Motif. *VT* 17:
          253–65.
  1968   *Rebellion in the Wilderness.* Nashville: Abingdon.
  1969   The Song of the Sea. *CBQ* 31: 1–17.
  1970   Self-Abasement and Insult Formulas. *JBL* 89: 14–26.
  1988   *Moses. Heroic Man, Man of God.* JSOTSup 57. Sheffield: JSOT.
Cody, A.
  1968   Exodus 18,12: Jethro Accepts a Covenant with the Israelites. *Bib*
          49: 153–66.
  1969   *A History of Old Testament Priesthood.* Rome: Pontifical Biblical
          Institute.
Cogan, M.
  1968   A Technical Term for the Exposure of Infants. *JNES* 27: 133–35.
Cogan, M., and H. Tadmor
  1988   *II Kings.* AB 11. Garden City, N.Y.: Doubleday.
Cohen, C.
  1972   Hebrew *tbh:* Proposed Etymologies. *JANESCU* 4: 37–51.
Cohen, M. E.
  1993   *The Cultic Calendars of the Ancient Near East.* Bethesda, Md.:
          CDL.
Cohen, S. J. D.
  1987   *From the Maccabees to the Mishnah.* Library of Early Christianity.
          Philadelphia: Westminster.
Cohn, R. L.
  1981   *The Shape of Sacred Space.* AAR Studies in Religion 23. Chico,
          Calif.: Scholars Press.
Cole, R. A.
  1973   *Exodus.* Downers Grove, Ill.: InterVarsity.
Collins, T.
  1978   *Line-Forms in Hebrew Poetry.* Studia Pohl Series Major 7. Rome:
          Pontifical Biblical Institute.
Coogan, M. D.
  1978   *Stories from Ancient Canaan.* Philadelphia: Westminster.

Coote, R. B.
1991   *In Defense of Revolution: The Elohist History.* Minneapolis: Fortress.
Coote, R. B., and D. R. Ord
1989   *The Bible's First History.* Philadelphia: Fortress.
Copisarow, M.
1962   The Ancient Egyptian, Greek and Hebrew Concept of the Red Sea. *VT* 12: 1–13.
Coppens, J.
1947   Miscellanées bibliques. *ETL* 23: 173–90.
Couroyer, B.
1955   L'origine égyptienne du mot "Pâque." *RB* 62: 481–96.
1960   Un égyptianisme biblique: "Depuis la fondation de l'Égypte." *RB* 67: 42–48.
Cowley, A. E.
1920   A Hittite Word in Hebrew. *JTS* 21: 326–27.
1923   *Aramaic Papyri of the Fifth Century B.C.* Oxford: Clarendon.
Craigie, P. C.
1972   Psalm XXIX in the Hebrew Poetic Tradition. *VT* 22: 143–51.
Cross, F. M.
1958   *The Ancient Library of Qumran.* Garden City, N.Y.: Doubleday.
1961a   The Development of the Jewish Scripts. Pp. 133–202 in *The Bible and the Ancient Near East,* ed. G. E. Wright. Fs. W. F. Albright. Garden City, N.Y.: Doubleday.
1961b   The Priestly Tabernacle. Pp. 201–21 in *The Biblical Archaeologist Reader I,* ed. D. N. Freedman and G. E. Wright. Garden City, N.Y.: Doubleday.
1964   The History of the Biblical Text in the Light of Discoveries in the Judaean Desert. *HTR* 57: 281–99.
1973   *Canaanite Myth and Hebrew Epic.* Cambridge, Mass.: Harvard University.
1974   Leaves from an Epigraphist's Notebook. *CBQ* 36: 486–94.
1981   The Priestly Tabernacle in the Light of Recent Research. Pp. 169–80 in *Temples and High Places in Biblical Times,* ed. A. Biran. Jerusalem: Hebrew Union College–Jewish Institute of Religion.
1983   The Epic Traditions of Early Israel: Epic Narrative and the Reconstruction of Early Israelite Institutions. Pp. 13–39 in *The Poet and the Historian,* ed. R. E. Friedman. HSS 26. Chico, Calif.: Scholars Press.
1985   A Literate Soldier: Lachish Letter III. Pp. 41–47 in *Biblical and Related Studies Presented to Samuel Iwry,* ed. A. Kort and S. Morschauser. Winona Lake, Ind.: Eisenbrauns.
1988   Reuben, First-Born of Jacob. *ZAW* 100 (Supplement): 46–64.
1994   4QExod^b. Pp. 79–95 in *Qumran Cave 4.VII,* ed. E. Ulrich et al. DJD 12. Oxford: Clarendon.

Cross, F. M., et al.
1972   Scrolls from Qumrân Cave I. Jerusalem: Albright Institute of Archaeological Research and the Shrine of the Book.
Cross, F. M., and D. N. Freedman
1952   Early Hebrew Orthography. New Haven, Conn.: American Oriental Society. Originally Ph.D. diss., Johns Hopkins University, 1948.
1955   The Song of Miriam. JNES 14: 237–50.
1975   Studies in Ancient Yahwistic Poetry. SBLDS 21. Missoula, Mont.: Scholars Press. Originally Ph.D. diss., Johns Hopkins University, 1950.
Cross, F. M., and R. J. Saley
1970   Phoenician Incantations on a Plaque of the Seventh Century B.C. from Arslan Tash in Upper Syria. BASOR 197: 42–49.
Crowfoot, G. M., and L. Baldensperger
1931   Hyssop. PEQ 63: 89–98.
Crüsemann, F.
1978   Der Widerstand gegen das Königtum. WMANT 49. Neukirchen-Vluyn: Neukirchener Verlag.
Curtiss, S. I.
1903   Ursemitische Religion im Volksleben des heutigen Orients. Leipzig: Hinrichs.
Dahood, M.
1962   Nādâ "to Hurl" in Ex 15,16. Bib 43: 248–49.
1966   Psalms I. AB 16. Garden City, N.Y.: Doubleday.
1969   Psalms II. AB 17. Garden City, N.Y.: Doubleday.
1970   Psalms III. AB 17A. Garden City, N.Y.: Doubleday.
1971   Hebrew-Ugaritic Lexicography IX. Bib 52: 337–56.
1972   Hebrew-Ugaritic Lexicography X. Bib 52: 386–403.
1978   Exodus 15,2 ʾanwēhû and Ugaritic šnwt. Bib 59: 260–61.
1981   Vocative lamedh in Exodus 2,14 und [sic] Merismus in 34,21. Bib 62: 413–15.
Daiches, S.
1921   The meaning of ʿm hʾrṣ. JQR 12: 33–34.
1929   The Meaning of ʿm hʾrṣ in the Old Testament. JTS 30: 245–49.
Dalley, S.
1989   Myths from Mesopotamia. Oxford/New York: Oxford University.
Dalman, G.
1928   Arbeit und Sitte in Palästina I. Gütersloh: Bertelsmann.
Damrosch, D.
1987   The Narrative Covenant. San Francisco: Harper & Row.
Daniélou, J.
1960   From Shadows to Reality: Studies in the Biblical Typology of the Fathers. French orig. 1950. Westminster, Md.: Newman.
Daube, D.
1963   The Exodus Pattern in the Bible. London: Faber & Faber.

Davies, G. F.
1992   *Israel in Egypt*. JSOTSup 135. Sheffield: JSOT.
Davies, G. H.
1967   *Exodus*. Torch Bible Commentaries. London: SCM.
Davies, G. I.
1974   The Hebrew Text of Exodus VIII 19 (EVV. 23): An Emendation. *VT* 24: 489–92.
1983   The Wilderness Itineraries and the Composition of the Pentateuch. *VT* 33: 1–13.
Davila, J.
1991   The Name of God at Moriah: An Unpublished Fragment from 4QGenExod[a]. *JBL* 110: 577–82.
1994   4QGen-Exod[a]. Pp. 7–30 in *Qumran Cave 4.VII*, ed. E. Ulrich et al. DJD 12. Oxford: Clarendon.
Day, J.
1985   *God's Conflict with the Sea*. Cambridge: Cambridge University.
1992   Asherah. *ABD* 1.483–87. New York: Doubleday.
Day, P. L.
1988   *An Adversary in Heaven*. HSM 43. Atlanta: Scholars Press.
Dayan, M.
1977   Qərîʿat yam sûp ləʾôr maddəʿê haṭṭebaʿ. *Beit Mikra* 23: 162–76.
Decker, W.
1975   Bad. *Lexicon der Ägyptologie* 1.598–99. Wiesbaden: Harrassowitz.
Delcor, M.
1990   *Environnement et Tradition de l'Ancien Testament*. AOAT 228. Kevelaer: Butzon & Bercker; Neukirchen-Vluyn: Neukirchener Verlag.
Della Vida, L.
1944   El ʿElyon in Genesis 14 18–20. *JBL* 63: 1–9.
De Mille, C. B.
1956   *The Ten Commandments*. Paramount Pictures.
Dhorme, E. P.
1920–23 L'emploi métaphorique des noms de parties du corps en hébreu et en akkadien. *RB* 29: 465–506; 30: 374–99; 517–40; 31: 215–33, 489–517; 32: 185–212.
Dietrich, M., O. Loretz, and J. Sanmartín
1973   Die ugaritischen Verben *MRR* I, *MRR* II und *MRR* III. *UF* 5: 119–22.
Diez-Macho, A.
1970   *Neophyti 1.II*. Madrid/Barcelona: Consejo Superior de Investigaciones Científicas.
Dillmann, A.
1880   *Exodus und Leviticus*. Kurzgefasstes exegetisches Handbuch. Leipzig: Hirzel.
Dossin, G.
1938   Les archives épistolaires du palais de Mari. *Syria* 19: 105–26.

Doughty, C. M.
1936   *Travels in Arabia Deserta.* New York: Random House.
Dozy, R. P. A.
1881   *Supplément aux dictionnaires arabes.* Leiden: Brill.
Driver, S. R.
1891   *An Introduction to the Literature of the Old Testament.* New York: Scribner.
1895   *A Critical and Exegetical Commentary on Deuteronomy.* 3d ed. ICC. Edinburgh: Clark.
1904   *The Book of Genesis.* New York: Gorham.
1911   *The Book of Exodus.* Cambridge Bible for Schools and Colleges. Cambridge: Cambridge University.
Dumbrell, W.
1972   Exodus 4:24–26: A Textual Re-examination. *HTR* 65: 285–90.
Dumermuth, F.
1964   Folkloristisches in der Erzählung von den ägyptischen Plagen. *ZAW* 76: 323–24.
Dumoulin, P.
1994   *Entre la Manne et l'Eucharistie: Étude de Sg 16,15–17,1a.* AnBib 132. Rome: Pontifical Biblical Institute.
Duncan, J. A.
1989   A Critical Edition of Manuscripts from Qumran Cave IV. Ph.D. diss., Harvard University.
1992   Considerations of 4QDt^j in Light of the "All Souls Deuteronomy" and Cave 4 Phylactery Texts. Pp. 199–215 in *The Madrid Qumran Congress: Proceedings of the International Congress on the Dead Sea Scrolls, Madrid 18–21 March, 1991.* STDJ. Leiden/New York/ Cologne: Brill; Madrid: Editorial Complutense.
Dupont-Sommer, A.
1948   Ostraca araméens d'Éléphantine. *ASAE* 48: 109–30.
Durand, J.-M.
1993   Le mythologème du combat entre le dieu de l'orage et la mer en Mésopotamie. *M.A.R.I.* 7: 41–61.
Durham, J. I.
1987   *Exodus.* WBC 3. Waco, Tex.: Word Books.
Eakin, F. E., Jr.
1967   The Reed Sea and Baalism. *JBL* 86: 378–84.
Ebeling, E.
1931   *Tod und Leben.* Berlin/Leipzig: de Gruyter.
1932   Aussetzung. *Reallexikon der Assyriologie* 1.322. Berlin/Leipzig: de Gruyter.
Edwards, D. R.
1992   Dress and Ornamentation. *ABD* 2.232–38. New York: Doubleday.
Edzard, E. O.
1959   Altbabylonische *nawûm.* *ZA* 19: 168–73.

1965   Sebettu. Pp. 124–25 in *Wörterbuch der Mythologie I. Götter und Mythen im Vorderen Orient*, ed. W. Häussig. Stuttgart: Klett.

Eerdmans, B. D.
1910   *Das Buch Exodus.* Giessen: Töpelmann.

Ehrlich, A. B.
1908   *Randglossen zur hebräischen Bibel 1.* Leipzig: Hinrichs.
1969   *Mikrâ ki-Pheschutô 1.* Orig. pub. 1899. New York: KTAV.

Eichrodt, W.
1970   *Ezekiel.* OTL. German orig. 1965–66. Philadelphia: Westminster.

Eilberg-Schwartz, H.
1990   *The Savage in Judaism.* Bloomington/Indianapolis: University of Indiana.
1994   *God's Phallus.* Boston: Beacon Press.

Eising, H.
1986   Y^eōr. *TDOT* 5.359. Grand Rapids, Mich.: Eerdmans.

Eissfeldt, O.
1932   *Baal Zaphon, Zeus Kasios und der Durchzug der Israeliten durchs Meer.* Halle: Niemeyer.
1945–48   Mein Gott. *ZAW* 61: 3–16.
1955   Zwei verkannte militär-technische Termini. *VT* 5: 235–38.
1961   Die älteste Erzählung vom Sinaibund. *ZAW* 73: 137–46.
1965   *The Old Testament.* 3d ed. German orig. 1964. Oxford: Blackwell.

Eliade, M.
1954   *The Myth of the Eternal Return.* Bollingen Series 46. New York: Bollingen Foundation.

Ellenbogen, M.
1977   Linguistic Archaeology, Semantic Integration, and the Recovery of Lost Meanings. Pp. 93–95 (English) in *Proceedings of the Sixth World Congress of Jewish Studies Vol. I*, ed. A. Shinan. Jerusalem: Jerusalem Academic Press.

Elliger, K.
1966   *Kleine Schriften zum Alten Testament.* Theologische Bücherei 32. Munich: Chr. Kaiser.

Elman, Y.
1976   The Akkadian Cognate of Hebrew *šǝḥîn. JANESCU* 8: 33–36.

Elwoude, J.
1994   The Use of *'ēt* in Non-Biblical Hebrew Texts. *VT* 44: 170–82.

Emerton, J. A.
1966   "Spring and Torrent" in Ps LXXIV 15. Pp. 122–33 in *Volume du congrés, Genève, 1965.* VTSup 15. Leiden: Brill.
1982   Leviathan and *ltn:* The Vocalization of the Ugaritic Word for the Dragon. *VT* 32: 327–31.

Engnell, I.
1969   *A Rigid Scrutiny.* Nashville: Vanderbilt University.

Erman, A.
   1927   *The Literature of the Ancient Egyptians.* German orig. 1923. London: Methuen & Co.
   1969   *Life in Ancient Egypt.* Orig. pub. 1894. Bronx, N.Y.: Blom.
Euting, J.
   1896   *Tagbuch einer Reise in Inner-Arabien.* Leiden: Brill.
Ewald, H.
   1876   *The Antiquities of Israel.* German orig. 1866. London: Longmans, Green.
Eyre, C. J.
   1992   Yet Again the Wax Crocodile: P. Westcar 3,12ff. *JEA* 78: 280–81.
Falkenstein, A., and W. von Soden
   1953   *Sumerische und akkadische Hymnen und Gebete.* Zurich/Stuttgart: Artemis.
Fensham, F. C.
   1964   Did a Treaty Between the Israelites and the Kenites Exist? *BASOR* 175: 51–54.
   1971   Father and Son as Terminology for Treaty and Covenant. Pp. 121–35 in *Near Eastern Studies in Honor of William Foxwell Albright,* ed. H. Goedicke. Baltimore/London: Johns Hopkins University.
Field, F.
   1875   *Origenis Hexaplorum quae supersunt.* Oxford: Clarendon.
Fields, W. W.
   1992   The Motif "Night as Danger" Associated with Three Biblical Destruction Narratives. Pp. 17–32 in *"Sha'arei Talmon,"* ed. M. Fishbane and E. Tov. Fs. S. Talmon. Winona Lake, Ind.: Eisenbrauns.
Finkelstein, I.
   1988   *The Archaeology of the Israelite Settlement.* Jerusalem: Israel Exploration Society.
Firmage, E.
   1992   Zoology. *ABD* 6.1109–67. New York: Doubleday.
Fishbane, M.
   1979   *Text and Texture.* New York: Schocken.
   1985   *Biblical Interpretation in Ancient Israel.* Oxford: Clarendon.
   1992   The Well of Living Water: A Biblical Motif and Its Ancient Transformations. Pp. 3–16 in *"Sha'arei Talmon,"* ed. M. Fishbane and E. Tov. Fs. S. Talmon. Winona Lake, Ind.: Eisenbrauns.
   1994   Arm of the Lord: Biblical Myth, Rabbinic Midrash, and the Mystery of History. Pp. 271–92 in *Language, Theology, and the Bible,* ed. S. E. Ballentine and J. Barton. Fs. J. Barr. Oxford: Clarendon.
Fisher, L. R.
   1965   Creation at Ugarit and in the Old Testament. *VT* 15: 313–24.
Fitzmyer, J. A.
   1979   *A Wandering Aramean.* SBLMS 25. Chico, Calif.: Scholars Press.

Flusser, D., and S. Safrai
1980 Who Sanctified the Beloved in the Womb. *Immanuel* 11: 46–55.
Fohrer, G.
1957 *Elia.* ATANT. Zurich: Zwingli.
1964 *Überlieferung und Geschichte des Exodus.* BZAW 91. Berlin: Töpelmann.
Fokkelman, J. P.
1987 Exodus. Pp. 56–65 in *The Literary Guide to the Bible,* ed. R. Alter and F. Kermode. Cambridge, Mass.: Belknap.
Fontenrose, J.
1959 *Python.* Berkeley: University of California.
1966 *The Ritual Theory of Myth.* Berkeley: University of California.
Foresti, F.
1982 Composizione e Redazione Deuteronomistica in Ex 15,1–18. *Lateranum* 48: 41–69.
Forsyth, N.
1987 *The Old Enemy: Satan and the Combat Myth.* Princeton, N.J.: Princeton University.
Fox, E.
1986 *Now These Are the Names.* New York: Schocken.
1995 *The Five Books of Moses.* New York: Schocken.
Frankfort, H.
1978 *Kingship and the Gods.* Chicago: University of Chicago.
Frazer, J. G.
1911 *The Golden Bough IV. The Dying God.* London: Macmillan.
Fredriksson, H.
1945 *Jahwe als Krieger.* Lund: Ohlsson.
Freedman, D. N.
1960 The Name of the God of Moses. *JBL* 79: 151–56.
1962 Pentateuch. *IDB* 3.711–27. Nashville/New York: Abingdon.
1969 The Burning Bush. *Bib* 50: 245–46.
1980 *Pottery, Poetry, and Prophecy.* Winona Lake, Ind.: Eisenbrauns.
1981 Temple Without Hands. Pp. 21–30 in *Temples and High Places in Biblical Times,* ed. A. Biran. Jerusalem: Hebrew Union College–Jewish Institute of Religion.
Fretheim, T. E.
1991a *Exodus.* Interpretation. Louisville: John Knox.
1991b The Plagues as Ecological Signs of Historical Disaster. *JBL* 110: 385–96.
Freund, J.
1989 Zikkārôn ûṣ(ə)dāqâ. *Beit Mikra* 118: 202–6.
Friedman, R. E.
1977 The Biblical Expression *Mastîr Pānîm. HAR* 1: 139–47.
1981 *The Exile and Biblical Narrative.* Chico, Calif.: Scholars Press.
1986 Deception for Deception. *BRev* 2.1: 22–31, 68.

1987   *Who Wrote the Bible?* New York: Summit.
1992   Torah. *ABD* 6.605–22. New York: Doubleday.
1995   *The Disappearance of God.* Boston/New York/Toronto/London: Little, Brown.
1998   *The Hidden Book in the Bible.* San Francisco: HarperCollins.
Fritz, V.
1970   *Israel in der Wüste.* Marburger Theologische Studien 7. Marburg: Elwert.
1990   Weltalter und Lebenszeit: Mythische Elemente in der Geschichts- schreibung Israels und bei Hesiod. *ZTK* 87: 145–62.
Frymer-Kensky, T.
1977a   The Judicial Ordeal in the Ancient Near East. Ph.D. diss., Yale University.
1977b   The Atrahasis Epic and Its Significance for Our Understanding of Genesis 1–9. *BA* 40: 147–55.
1992   *In the Wake of the Goddesses.* New York: Free Press.
Füglister, N.
1963   *Die Heilsbedeutung des Pascha.* SANT. Munich: Kösel.
1977   Sühne durch Blut—Zur Bedeutung von Leviticus 17,11. Pp. 143–64 in *Studien zum Pentateuch,* ed. G. Braulik. Fs. W. Korn- feld. Vienna/Freiburg/Basel: Herder.
Fuss, W.
1972   *Die deuteronomistische Pentateuchsredaktion in Exodus 3–17.* BZAW 126. Berlin: de Gruyter.
Gall, A. von
1918   *Der Hebräische Pentateuch der Samaritaner.* Giessen: Töpelmann.
Gallery, L. M.
1978   The Garden of Ancient Egypt. Pp. 43–49 in *Immortal Egypt,* ed. D. Schmandt-Besserat. Malibu: Undena.
Gandz, S.
1970   *Studies in Hebrew Astronomy and Mathematics.* New York: KTAV.
Gardiner, A.
1957   *Egyptian Grammar.* 3d ed. Oxford: Griffith Institute, Ashmolean Museum.
Garofalo, S.
1937   L'epinicio di Mosè (Esodo 15). *Bib* 18: 1–22.
Garr, W. R.
1992   The Grammar and Interpretation of Exodus 6:3. *JBL* 111: 385– 408.
Garsiel, M.
1992   *Biblical Names: A Literary Study of Midrashic Derivations and Puns.* Hebrew orig. 1987. Ramat-Gan: Bar-Ilan University.
Gaster, T. H.
1936–37 Notes on 'The Song of the Sea (Exodus XV.).' *ExpTm* 48: 45.
1949   *Passover. Its History and Traditions.* New York: Schuman.

1962a   Angel. *IDB* 1.128–34. Nashville: Abingdon.
1962b   Demon. *IDB* 1.817–24. Nashville: Abingdon.
1962c   Sacrifices and Offerings, OT. *IDB* 4.147–59. Nashville: Abingdon.
1969   *Myth, Legend, and Custom in the Old Testament.* New York: Harper & Row.
Gevirtz, S.
1961   West Semitic Curses and the Problem of the Origins of Hebrew Law. *VT* 11: 137–58.
Ghillany, F. W.
1842   *Die Menschenopfer der alten Hebräer.* Nuremberg: Schrag.
Gibson, J. C. L.
1978   *Canaanite Myths and Legends.* 2d ed. Edinburgh: Clark.
Ginsberg, H. L.
1982   *The Israelian Heritage of Judaism.* New York: Jewish Theological Seminary of America.
Ginsburg, C. D.
1894   *ʿEśrîm wəʾarbāʿâ siprê haqqōdeš.* London: Hebrat môṣîʾê ləʾôr tôrat yhwh hattəmîmâ.
Ginzberg, L.
1928   *The Legends of the Jews.* Philadelphia: Jewish Publication Society.
Glatt, D. A.
1993   *Chronological Displacement in Biblical and Related Literatures.* SBLDS 139. Atlanta: Scholars Press.
Glueck, N.
1967   *Ḥesed in the Bible.* German orig. 1927. Cincinnati: Hebrew Union College.
Goldin, J.
1971   *The Song at the Sea.* New Haven, Conn./London: Yale University.
Goldstein, B. R., and A. Cooper
1990   The Festivals of Israel and Judah and the Literary History of the Pentateuch. *JAOS* 110: 19–31.
Goldstein, J. A.
1976   *I Maccabees.* AB 41. Garden City, N.Y.: Doubleday.
Gomes, E. H.
1911   *Seventeen Years Among the Sea Dyaks of Borneo.* London: Seeley.
Good, E. M.
1970   Exodus XV 2. *VT* 20: 358–59.
Good, R. M.
1983   *The Sheep of His Pasture.* HSM 29. Chico, Calif.: Scholars Press.
Goodenough, E. R.
1964   *Jewish Symbols in the Greco-Roman Period. Volume Eleven. Symbolism in the Dura Synagogue.* Bollingen Series 37. New York: Bollingen Foundation.
Gordon, C. H.
1965   *Ugaritic Textbook.* AnOr 38. Rome: Pontifical Biblical Institute.

Gordon, C. H., and N. H. Tur-Sinai
1965   Ḥōdeš. *EM* 3.35–40. Jerusalem: Bialik Institute.
Görg, M.
1986   "Der starke Arm Pharaos"—Beobachtungen zum Belegspektrum einer Metapher in Palästina und Ägypten. Pp. 323–30 in *Hommages à François Daumas*. Montpellier: Université de Montpellier.
1988   *Paesaḥ* (Pascha): Fest des "schlagenden" Gottes? *BN* 43: 7–11.
Gorman, F. H.
1990   *The Ideology of Ritual*. JSOTSup 91. Sheffield: JSOT.
Goshen-Gottstein, M. H.
1967   Hebrew Biblical Manuscripts: Their History and Place in the HUBP Edition. *Bib* 48: 243–90.
Gottwald, N. K.
1979   *The Tribes of Yahweh*. Maryknoll, N.Y.: Orbis.
Gray, G. B.
1936   Passover and Unleavened Bread: The Laws of J, E, and D. *JTS* 37: 241–53.
1971   *Sacrifice in the Old Testament*. Orig. pub. 1925. New York: KTAV.
Gray, J.
1950–52 Canaanite Mythology and Hebrew Tradition. *Transactions of the Glasgow University Oriental Society* 14: 47–57.
1965   *The Legacy of Canaan*. VTSup 5. Leiden: Brill.
Greenberg, M.
1955   *The Ḥab/piru*. AOS 39. New Haven, Conn.: American Oriental Society.
1959   The Biblical Concept of Asylum. *JBL* 78: 125–32.
1969   *Understanding Exodus*. New York: Behrman House.
1971   The Redaction of the Plague Narrative in Exodus. Pp. 243–52 in *Near Eastern Studies in Honor of William Foxwell Albright*, ed. H. Goedicke. Baltimore: Johns Hopkins University.
1983a *Ezekiel*. AB 22. Garden City, N.Y.: Doubleday.
1983b Ezekiel's Vision: Literary and Iconographic Aspects. Pp. 159–68 in *History, Historiography and Interpretation*, ed. H. Tadmor and M. Weinfeld. Jerusalem: Magnes; Leiden: Brill.
Greenfield, J. C.
1959   Lexicographical Notes II. *HUCA* 30: 141–51.
1969   Some Glosses on the Keret Epic. Pp. 60–65 (English section) in *W. F. Albright Volume*. ErIsr 9. Jerusalem: Israel Exploration Society.
Greenstein, E. L.
1974   Two Variations of Grammatical Parallelism in Canaanite Poetry and their Psycholinguistic Background. *JANES* 6: 87–105.
1989   The Syntax of Saying "Yes" in Biblical Hebrew. *JANES* 19: 51–59.
Grelot, P.
1975   Quatre cents trente ans (Ex 12,40). Note sur les Testaments de Lévi et de ʿAmram. Pp. 559–70 in *Homenaje a Juan Prado*, ed. L. Alvarez

Verdes and E. J. Alonso Hernández. Madrid: Consejo Superior de Investigaciones Científicas.

Gressmann, H.
1913   *Mose und seine Zeit.* Göttingen: Vandenhoeck & Ruprecht.

Griffiths, J. G.
1953   The Egyptian Derivation of the Name Moses. *JNES* 12: 225–31.

Grønbaek, J. H.
1964   Juda und Amalek: Überlieferungsgeschichtliche Erwägungen zu Exodus 17, 8–16. *ST* 18: 26–45.

Groot, J. de
1943   The Story of the Bloody Husband (Exodus IV 24–26). *OTS* 2: 10–17.

Gruber, M. I.
1986   Hebrew *Qědēšāh* and Her Canaanite Cognates. *UF* 18: 133–48.
1989   Breast-Feeding Practices in Biblical Israel and in Old Babylonian Mesopotamia. *JANES* 19: 61–83.

Grünwaldt, K.
1992   *Exil und Identität. Beschneidung, Passa und Sabbat in der Priesterschrift.* Athenäums Monografien: Theologie. BBB 85. Frankfurt am Main: Hain.

Gunkel, H.
1895   *Schöpfung und Chaos in Urzeit und Endzeit.* Göttingen: Vandenhoeck & Ruprecht.
1910   *Genesis.* 3d ed. Göttinger Handkommentar zum Alten Testament 1.1. Göttingen: Vandenhoeck & Ruprecht.

Gunn, D. M.
1982   The "Hardening of Pharaoh's Heart": Plot, Character and Theology in Exodus 1–14. Pp. 72–96 in *Art and Meaning: Rhetoric in Biblical Literature,* ed. D. J. A. Clines et al. JSOTSup 19. Sheffield: JSOT.

Gunneweg, A. H. J.
1965   *Leviten und Priester.* FRLANT 89. Göttingen: Vandenhoeck & Ruprecht.

Guthe, H.
1918   Passahfest nach Dtn 16. Pp. 217–32 in *Abhandlungen zur semitischen Religionskunde und Sprachwissenschaft,* ed. W. Frankenberg and F. Küchler. BZAW 33. Giessen: Töpelmann.

Haag, H.
1971   *Vom alten zum neuen Pascha.* SBS 49. Stuttgart: KBW.

Haak, R. D.
1982   A Study and New Interpretation of QṢR NPŠ. *JBL* 101: 161–67.

Habel, N. C.
1965   Form and Significance of the Call Narratives. *ZAW* 77: 297–323.

Hackett, J. A.
1980   *The Balaam Text from Deir 'Alla.* HSM 31. Chico, Calif.: Scholars Press.

Halbe, J.
1975   Erwägungen zu Ursprung und Wesen des Massotfestes. ZAW 87: 324–46.
Haldar, A.
1950   The Notion of the Desert in Sumero-Accadian and West-Semitic Religions. Uppsala Universitets Årsskrift 3. Uppsala: Almqvist & Wiksell.
Hall, R. G.
1992   Circumcision. ABD 1.1025–31. New York: Doubleday.
Hallo, W. W.
1991   The Book of the People. Brown Judaic Studies 225. Atlanta: Scholars Press.
Hallo, W. W., and J. J. A. van Dijk
1968   The Exaltation of Inanna. Yale Near Eastern Researches 3. New Haven, Conn.: Yale University.
Halpern, B.
1983   The Emergence of Israel in Canaan. SBLMS 29. Chico, Calif.: Scholars Press.
1988   The First Historians. San Francisco: Harper & Row.
1991   Jerusalem and the Lineages in the Seventh Century BCE: Kinship and the Rise of Individual Moral Liability. Pp. 11–107 in Law and Ideology in Monarchic Israel, ed. B. Halpern and D. W. Hobson. JSOTSup 124. Sheffield: JSOT.
1992a   Settlement of Canaan. ABD 5.1120–43. New York: Doubleday.
1992b   The Baal (and the Asherah) in Seventh-Century Judah: Yhwh's Retainers Retired. Pp. 115–54 in Konsequente Traditionsgeschichte, ed. R. Bartelmus et al. Fs. K. Baltzer. OBO 126. Fribourg: Editions universitaires; Göttingen: Vandenhoeck & Ruprecht.
1993   The Exodus and the Israelite Historian. Pp. 89*–96* in Avraham Malamat Volume. ErIsr 24. Jerusalem: Israel Exploration Society.
Hamlin, E. J.
1974   The Liberator's Ordeal. A Study of Exodus 4:1–9. Pp. 33–42 in Rhetorical Criticism: Essays in Honor of James Muilenburg, ed. J. J. Jackson and M. Kessler. Pittsburgh: Pickwick.
Handy, L. K.
1992   Lilith. ABD 4.324–25. New York: Doubleday.
Haneman, G.
1980   ʿAl mašmǝʿût habbiṭṭûy "ben kāk wǝkāk šānîm" wǝhaddômîm lô. Pp. 103–9 in Studies in Hebrew and Semitic Languages Dedicated to the Memory of Prof. Eduard Yechezkel Kutscher, ed. G. B. Sarfatti et al. Ramat-Gan: Bar-Ilan University.
Haran, M.
1962   Shiloh and Jerusalem: The Origin of the Priestly Tradition in the Pentateuch. JBL 81: 14–24.
1976   Šbt, mimmoḥǝrat haššabbāt. EM 7.517–21. Jerusalem: Bialik Institute.

1978   *Temples and Temple Service in Ancient Israel.* Oxford: Clarendon.
1981   Behind the Scenes of History: Determining the Date of the Priestly Source. *JBL* 100: 321–33.
Harris, R.
1965   The Journey of the Divine Weapon. Pp. 217–24 in *Studies in Honor of Benno Landsberger on his Seventy-fifth Birthday,* ed. H. G. Güterbock and T. Jacobsen. Assyriological Studies 16. Chicago: University of Chicago.
Hartom, E. S.
1954   Bəkôr, bəkôrâ. *EM* 2.123–26. Jerusalem: Bialik Institute.
Haupt, P.
1904   Moses' Song of Triumph. *AJSL* 20: 149–72.
1909   Der Name Jahwe. *OLZ* 12: 211–14.
Hauser, A. J.
1987   Two Songs of Victory: A Comparison of Exodus 15 and Judges 5. Pp. 265–84 in *Directions in Biblical Hebrew Poetry,* ed. E. R. Follis. JSOTSup 40. Sheffield: JSOT.
Hay, L. S.
1964   What Really Happened at the Sea of Reeds? *JBL* 83: 397–403.
Hayes, J. H., and J. M. Miller
1977   *Israelite and Judaean History.* London: SCM.
Heidel, A.
1951   *The Babylonian Genesis.* 2d ed. Chicago/London: University of Chicago.
Helck, W.
1971   *Die Beziehungen Ägyptens zu Vorderasien im 3. und 2. Jahrtausend v. Chr.* 2d ed. Ägyptologische Abhandlungen 5. Wiesbaden: Harrassowitz.
Heltzer, M.
1978   *Goods, Prices and the Organization of Trade in Ugarit.* Wiesbaden: Reichert.
Hempel, J.
1957   "Ich bin der Herr, dein Arzt" (Ex. 15,26). *TLZ* 82: 809–26.
Hendel, R. S.
1985   "The Flame of the Whirling Sword": A Note on Genesis 3:24. *JBL* 104: 671–74.
1987a *The Epic of the Patriarch.* HSM 42. Atlanta: Scholars Press.
1987b Of Demigods and the Deluge: Toward an Interpretation of Genesis 6:1–4. *JBL* 106: 13–26.
1989   Sacrifice as a Cultural System: The Ritual Symbolism of Exodus 24,3–8. *ZAW* 101: 366–90.
1995a 4Q252 and the Flood Chronology of Genesis 7–8: A Text-Critical Solution. *Dead Sea Discoveries* 2: 72–79.
1995b Tangled Plots in Genesis. Pp. 35–51 in *Fortunate the Eyes That See.* Fs. D. N. Freedman. Grand Rapids, Mich.: Eerdmans.

Henninger, J.
1955   Ist der sogenannte Nilus-Bericht eine brauchbare religionsge-
       schichtliche Quelle? *Anthropos* 50: 81–148.
1956   Zum Verbot des Knochenzerbrechens bei den Semiten. Pp. 448–
       59 in *Studi orientalistici in onore di Giorgio Levi della Vida*.
       Pubblicazioni dell'Instituto per l'Oriente 52. Rome: Instituto per
       l'Oriente.
1968   Primitialopfer und Neujahrsfest. Pp. 147–89 in *Anthropica*. Fs. P. W.
       Schmidt. Studia Instituti Anthropos 21. St. Augustin bei Bonn:
       Anthropos-Institut.
1972   Premiers-nés. *DBSup* 8.461–82. Paris: Letouzey & Ané.
1975   *Les fêtes de printemps chez les Sémites et la Pâque israélite*. Ebib.
       Paris: LeCoffre.
Herrmann, S.
1973   *Israel in Egypt*. German orig. 1970. SBT 2.27. Naperville, Ill.:
       Allenson.
Herrmann, W.
1992   Ex 17.7bβ und die Frage nach der Gegenwart Jahwes in Israel.
       Pp. 46–55 in *Alttestamentliche Glaube und biblische Theologie*, ed.
       J. Hausmann and H.-J. Zobel. Fs. H. D. Preuss. Stuttgart/Berlin/
       Köln: Kohlhammer.
Herzberg, W.
1979   Polysemy in the Hebrew Bible. Ph.D. diss., New York University.
Hestrin, R., and M. Dayagi-Mendels
1979   *Inscribed Seals: First Temple Period*. Jerusalem: Israel Museum.
Hillers, D. R.
1967   Delocutive Verbs in Biblical Hebrew. *JBL* 86: 320–24.
Hirsch, S.
1933   *Sheep and Goats in Palestine*. Tel Aviv: Palestine Economic Society.
Hoffner, H. A., Jr.
1990   *Hittite Myths*. SBLWAW 2. Atlanta: Scholars Press.
1995   Oil in Hittite Texts. *BA* 58: 108–14.
Höfner, M.
1970   Die vorislamischen Religionen Arabiens. Pp. 233–402 in *Die
       Religionen Altsyriens, Altarabiens und der Mandäer*, ed. H. Gese,
       M. Höfner, K. Rudolph. Die Religionen der Menschheit 10,2.
       Stuttgart: Kohlhammer.
Hoftijzer, J., and G. van der Kooij
1976   *Aramaic Texts from Deir ʿAlla*. Documenta et Monumenta Orien-
       tis Antiqui 19. Leiden: Brill.
Holl, A. F. C., and T. E. Levy
1993   From the Nile Valley to the Chad Basin: Ethnoarchaeology of
       Shuwa Arab Settlements. *BA* 56: 166–79.
Holzinger, H.
1900   *Exodus*. Kurzer Hand-commentar zum Alten Testament 2. Tübin-
       gen: Mohr (Siebeck).

Hooke, S. H.
1938   *The Origins of Early Semitic Ritual.* Schweich Lectures 1935. London: Oxford University.
Hornung, E.
1982   *Conceptions of God in Ancient Egypt: The One and the Many.* Ithaca, N.Y.: Cornell University.
Hort, G.
1957–58 The Plagues of Egypt. *VT* 69: 84–103; 70: 48–59.
Houtman, C.
1983   Exodus 4:24–26 and Its Interpretation. *JNSL* 11: 81–103.
1986   On the Meaning of *ûbāʿeṣîm ûbāʾăbānîm* in Exodus VII 19. *VT* 36: 347–52.
1989   "YHWH Is My Banner"—"A 'Hand' on the 'Throne' of YH." *OTS* 25: 110–20.
Huddlestun, J. R.
1992   Red Sea. *ABD* 5.633–42. New York: Doubleday.
Huffmon, H. B.
1966   The Treaty Background of Hebrew *yādaʿ*. *BASOR* 181: 31–37.
Huffmon, H. B., and S. B. Parker
1966   A Further Note on the Treaty Background of Hebrew *yādaʿ*. *BASOR* 184: 36–38.
Hulse, E. V.
1975   The Nature of Biblical "Leprosy" and the Use of Alternate Medical Terms in Modern Translations of the Bible. *PEQ* 107: 87–105.
Humbert, P.
1958   *Opuscules d'un hébraïsant.* Mémoires de l'Université de Neuchâtel 26. Neuchâtel: Université de Neuchâtel.
Hummel, H. D.
1957   Enclitic *Mem* in Early Northwest Semitic, Especially Hebrew. *JBL* 76: 85–107.
Hurowitz, V.
1989   Isaiah's Impure Lips and Their Purification in Light of Mouth Purification and Mouth Purity in Akkadian Sources. *HUCA* 60: 39–89.
1990   The Etymology of Biblical Hebrew *ʿayin* "appearance" in Light of Akkadian *šiknu*. *ZAH* 3: 90–94.
1992   *I Have Built You an Exalted House.* JSOTSup 115. JSOT/ASORMS 5. Sheffield: JSOT.
Hyatt, J. P.
1971   *Commentary on Exodus.* New Century Bible. London: Marshall, Morgan & Scott.
Irwin, W. A.
1961   Where Shall Wisdom Be Found? *JBL* 80: 131–42.
Israel, F.
1979   Miscellanea Idumea. *RivB* 27: 171–203.

Jacob, B.
   1992   *The Second Book of the Bible: Exodus.* Trans. W. Jacob. German orig. (unpublished) 1945. Hoboken, N.J.: KTAV.
Jacob, I., and W. Jacob
   1992   Flora. *ABD* 2.803–17. New York: Doubleday.
Jacobsen, T.
   1968   The Battle Between Marduk and Tiamat. *JAOS* 88: 104–8.
   1987a The Graven Image. Pp. 15–32 in *Ancient Israelite Religion*, ed. P. D. Miller, Jr., P. D. Hanson, and S. D. McBride. Fs. F. M. Cross. Philadelphia: Fortress.
   1987b *The Harps That Once....* New Haven, Conn./London: Yale University.
Janzen, J. G.
   1983   Kugel's Adverbial *kî ṭôb*: An Assessment. *JBL* 102: 99–106.
   1989   The Root *prꜥ* in Judges v 2 and Deuteromony xxxii 42. *VT* 39: 393–406.
   1992   Song of Moses, Song of Miriam: Who Is Seconding Whom? *CBQ* 54: 211–20.
Jaubert, A.
   1953   Le calendrier des Jubilés et de la secte de Qumrân. Ses origines bibliques. *VT* 3: 250–64.
   1957   *La date de la Cène.* Ebib: Paris: Lecoffre.
Jaussen, A.
   1948   *Coutumes des Arabes au pays de Moab.* Paris: Librarie d'Amérique et d'Orient.
Jenks, A. W.
   1977   *The Elohist and North Israelite Traditions.* SBLMS 22. Missoula, Mont.: Scholars Press.
Jeremias, Joachim
   1932   *Die Passahfeier der Samaritaner.* BZAW 59. Giessen: Töpelmann.
Jeremias, Jorg
   1965   *Theophanie: Die Geschichte einer alttestamentlichen Gattung.* WMANT. Neukirchen-Vluyn: Neukirchener Verlag.
Johnson, A. R.
   1953   The Primary Meaning of $\sqrt{g^{\jmath}l}$. Pp. 67–77 in *Congress Volume, Copenhagen 1953.* VTSup 1. Leiden: Brill.
Johnson, L. T.
   1992   Tongues, Gift of. *ABD* 6.596–600. New York: Doubleday.
Johnson, M. D.
   1969   *The Purpose of the Biblical Genealogies.* SNTSMS 8. Cambridge: Cambridge University.
Johnstone, W.
   1990   *Exodus.* Old Testament Guides. Sheffield: JSOT.
   1992   The Two Theological Versions of the Passover Pericope in Exodus. Pp. 160–78 in *Text as Pretext*, ed. R. P. Carroll. Fs. R. Davidson. JSOTSup 138. Sheffield: JSOT.

Joüon, P.
1965   *Grammaire de l'hébreu biblique.* Rome: Pontifical Biblical Institute.
Junker, H.
1950   Der Blutbräutigam. Pp. 120–28 in *Alttestamentliche Studien*, ed. H. Junker and H. Botterweck. Fs. F. Nötscher. BBB 1. Bonn: Hanstein.
Kang, S.-M.
1989   *Divine War in the Old Testament and the Ancient Near East.* BZAW 177. Berlin: de Gruyter.
Kaplan, L.
1981   "And the Lord Sought to Kill Him" (Exod 4:24) Yet Once Again. *HAR* 5: 65–74.
Katzenstein, H. J.
1982   Gaza in the Egyptian Texts of the New Period. *JAOS* 102: 111–13.
Kaufmann, Y.
1942–56 *Tôlǝdôt hā'ĕmûnâ hayyiśrǝ'ēlît.* Jerusalem: Bialik Institute.
1960   *The Religion of Israel.* Chicago: University of Chicago.
Kedar-Kopfstein, B.
1978   *Dām. TDOT* 3.234–50. Grand Rapids, Mich.: Eerdmans.
Keel, O.
1972   Erwägungen zum Sitz im Leben des vormosaischen Pascha und zur Etymologie von *pesaḥ. ZAW* 84: 414–34.
1974   *Wirkmachtige Siegeszeichen im Alten Testament.* OBO 5. Freiburg/Göttingen: Vandenhoeck & Ruprecht.
1978   *The Symbolism of the Biblical World.* German orig. 1972. New York: Seabury.
Kennicott, B.
1776–80 *Vetus Testamentum Hebraicum.* Oxford: Clarendon.
Kikawada, I. M.
1975   Literary Convention of the Primaeval History. *AJBI* 1: 3–21.
Kilmer, A. D.
1972   The Mesopotamian Concept of Overpopulation and Its Solution as Reflected in the Mythology. *Or* 41: 160–77.
King, J. R.
1987   The Joseph Story and Divine Politics: A Comparative Study of a Biographic Formula from the Ancient Near East. *JBL* 106: 577–94.
Kitchen, K.
1966   *Ancient Orient and Old Testament.* Downers Grove, Ill.: InterVarsity.
1982   *Pharaoh Triumphant.* Monumenta Hannah Sheen Dedicata II. Warminster: Aris & Phillips.
Klein, J.
1992   Akitu. *ABD* 1.138–40. New York: Doubleday.
Klein, M. L.
1980   *The Fragment-Targums of the Pentateuch.* AnBib 76. Rome: Pontifical Biblical Institute.

1986   *Genizah Manuscripts of Palestinian Targum to the Pentateuch I.* Cincinnati: Hebrew Union College.

Kloos, C.
1986   *Yhwh's Combat with the Sea: A Canaanite Tradition in the Religion of Ancient Israel.* Amsterdam: van Oorschot; Leiden: Brill.

Knight, G. A. F.
1976   *Theology as Narrative. A Commentary on the Book of Exodus.* Edinburgh: Handsel.

Knobloch, F. W.
1992   Adoption. *ABD* 1.76–79. New York: Doubleday.

Knohl, I.
1987   The Priestly Torah Versus the Holiness School: Sabbath and the Festivals. *HUCA* 58: 65–117.
1995   *The Sanctuary of Silence: The Priestly Torah and the Holiness School.* Minneapolis: Fortress.

Koenig, J.
1963   Sourciers, thaumaturges et scribes. *RHR* 164: 17–38, 165–80.

Koenig, Y.
1985   Égypt et Israël: quelques points de contact. *JA* 273: 1–10.

Kohata, F.
1986   *Jahwist und Priesterschrift in Exodus 3–14.* BZAW 166. Berlin: de Gruyter.

Kohler, K.
1910   Verbot des Knochenzerbrechens. *ARW* 13: 153–54.

Köhler, L.
1934   Kleinigkeiten. *ZAW* 52: 160.
1957   *Old Testament Theology.* German orig. 1953. Philadelphia: Westminster.

Kopf, L.
1976   *Studies in Arabic and Hebrew Lexicography.* Jerusalem: Magnes.

Korsak, M. P.
1992   *At the Start . . . Genesis Made New.* European Series, Louvain Cahiers 124. Louvain: Leuvense Schrijfversaktie.

Kosmala, H.
1962   The "Bloody Husband." *VT* 12: 14–28.

Krahmalkov, C. R.
1981   A Critique of Professor Goedicke's Exodus Theories. *BARev* 7.5: 51–54.

Kramer, S. N.
1981   *History Begins at Sumer.* 3d ed. Philadelphia: University of Pennsylvania.
1986   *In the World of Sumer.* Detroit: Wayne State University.

Kraus, H.-J.
1951   Gilgal. Ein Beitrag zur Kulturgeschichte Israels. *VT* 1: 181–99.
1966   *Worship in Israel.* German orig. 1962. Richmond: John Knox.

Kreuzer, S.
1991   Zur Priorität und Auslegungsgeschichte von Exodus 12,40 MT. ZAW 103: 252–58.

Kselman, J. S.
1978   The Recovery of Poetic Fragments from the Pentateuchal Priestly Source. *JBL* 97: 161–73.

Kugel, J. L.
1980   The Adverbial Use of *kî ṭôb*. *JBL* 99: 433–35.
1981   *The Idea of Biblical Poetry.* New Haven, Conn.: Yale University.

Kuhl, C.
1952   Die "Wiederaufnahme"—ein literarkritisches Prinzip? ZAW 64: 1–11.

Kutler, L.
1984   A "Strong" Case for Hebrew Mar. *UF* 16: 111–18.

Kutsch, E.
1958   Erwägungen zur Geschichte der Passafeier und des Massotfestes. ZTK 55: 1–35.
1977   Der sogenannte "Blutbräutigam." Erwägungen zu Ex 4,24–26. ZDMGSup 4: 122–23.

Laaf, P.
1970   *Die Pascha-Feier Israels.* BBB 36. Bonn: Hanstein.

Labuschagne, C. J.
1966   *The Incomparability of Yahweh in the Old Testament.* Pretoria Oriental Series 5. Leiden: Brill.
1982   The Meaning of *bᵉyād rāmā* in the Old Testament. Pp. 143–48 in *Von Kanaan bis Kerala,* ed. W. C. Delsman et al. Fs. J. P. M. van der Ploeg. AOAT 211. Kevelaer: Butzon & Bercker; Neukirchen-Vluyn: Neukirchener Verlag.

Lachs, S. T.
1976   Exodus IV 11: Evidence for an Emendation. *VT* 26: 249–50.

Lagrange, M. J.
1899   Deux chants de guerre. *RB* 8: 532–52.

Lalouette, C.
1986   *Thèbes ou la naissance d'un empire.* Paris: Fayard.

Lambdin, T. O.
1953   Egyptian Loan Words in the Old Testament. *JAOS* 73: 145–55.

Lambert, W. G.
1992   Enuma Elish. *ABD* 2.526–28. New York: Doubleday.

Lambert, W. G., and A. R. Millard
1969   *Atra-ḫasis. The Babylonian Story of the Flood.* Oxford: Clarendon.

Landström, B.
1970   *Ships of the Pharaohs.* Garden City, N.Y.: Doubleday.

Lane, E. W.
1863–93   *Arabic-English Lexicon.* London: Williams & Norgate.

1978   *An Account of the Manners and Customs of the Modern Egyptians.*
        Orig. pub. 1836. The Hague/London: East-West.
Langdon, S.
1935   *Babylonian Menologies and the Semitic Calendars.* London: Oxford
        University.
Lauha, A.
1945   *Die Geschichtsmotive in den alttestamentlichen Psalmen.* Annales
        Academiae Scientiarum Fennicae B 56. Helsinki: Finnische Liter-
        aturgesellschaft.
1963   Das Schilfmeermotif im Alten Testament. Pp. 32–46 in *Congress
        Volume, Bonn 1962,* ed. G. W. Anderson et al. VTSup 9. Leiden:
        Brill.
Lauth, F. J.
1871   Moses-Osarsyph. ZDMG 25: 139–48.
Lawton, P.
1985   Irony in Early Exodus. ZAW 97: 414.
Layard, A. H.
1849   *Nineveh and Its Remains.* 3d ed. London: Murray.
Layton, S.C.
1990   *Archaic Features of Canaanite Personal Names in the Hebrew
        Bible.* HSM 47. Atlanta: Scholars Press.
Le Déaut, R.
1963   *La nuit pascale.* AnBib 22. Rome: Pontifical Biblical Institute.
Lehmann, M. R.
1969   Biblical Oaths. ZAW 81: 74–92.
Leibowitz, N.
1976   *Studies in Shemot I.* Jerusalem: World Zionist Organization.
Leslau, W.
1958   *Ethiopic and South Arabic Contributions to the Hebrew Lexicon.*
        Berkeley/Los Angeles: University of California.
Levenson, J. D.
1985   *Sinai and Zion.* Minneapolis/Chicago/New York: Winston.
1988   *Creation and the Persistence of Evil.* San Francisco: Harper &
        Row.
1993a   *The Hebrew Bible, the Old Testament, and Historical Criticism.*
        Louisville: Westminster/John Knox.
1993b   *The Death and Resurrection of the Beloved Son.* New Haven,
        Conn./London: Yale University.
Levi, J.
1987   *Die Inkongruenz im Hebräisch.* Wiesbaden: Harrassowitz.
Levi-Strauss, C.
1978   *The Origin of Table Manners.* French orig. 1968. New York: Harper
        & Row.
Levine, B. A.
1974   *In the Presence of the Lord.* Studies in Judaism and Late Antiquity 5.
        Leiden: Brill.

1981a Review of J.-M. de Tarragon, Le culte à Ugarit. RB 88: 245–50.
1981b The Deir ʿAlla Plaster Inscriptions. JAOS 101: 195–205.
1989   Leviticus. JPS Torah Commentary. Philadelphia: Jewish Publica-
       tion Society.
1993   Numbers 1–20. AB 4. New York: Doubleday.
Levitt Kohn, R.
1997   A New Heart and a New Soul: Ezekiel, the Exile and the Torah.
       Ph.D. diss., University of California, San Diego.
Lewis, B.
1980   The Sargon Legend. ASORDS 4. Cambridge, Mass.: American
       Schools of Oriental Research.
Lewy, J.
1944   The Old West Semitic Sun-god Ḥammu. HUCA 18: 429–88.
Licht, J. S.
1962   Malʾak-h(aśśēm), malʾākîm. EM 4.975–90. Jerusalem: Bialik Insti-
       tute.
1968a Maṣṣâ. EM 5.225–28. Jerusalem: Bialik Institute.
1968b Mārôr. EM 5.454–55. Jerusalem: Bialik Institute.
1971a ʿŌmer. EM 6.299–302. Jerusalem: Bialik Institute.
1971b Pesaḥ. EM 6.514–26. Jerusalem: Bialik Institute.
1973   Hannissāyôn bəmiqrāʾ ûb(ə)yahădût šel təqûpat habbayit haśśēnî.
       Jerusalem: Magnes.
Lichtenstein, M. H.
1984   Biblical Poetry. Pp. 105–27 in Back to the Sources, ed. B. W. Holtz.
       New York: Summit.
Lichtheim, M.
1973   Ancient Egyptian Literature—Volume I: The Old and Middle
       Kingdoms. Berkeley: University of California.
1976   Ancient Egyptian Literature—Volume II: The New Kingdom. Berke-
       ley: University of California.
1980   Ancient Egyptian Literature—Volume III: The Late Period. Berke-
       ley: University of California.
Lipiński, E.
1963   Yāhweh mâlāk. Bib 44: 405–60.
1965   La royauté de Yahwé dans la poésie et le culte de l'ancien Israel. 2d
       ed. Brussels: Paleis der Academiën.
1969   La fête de l'ensevelissement et de la résurrection de Melqart.
       Pp. 30–58 in Actes de la XVIIe Rencontre Assyriologique Internatio-
       nale, ed. A. Finet. Ham-sur-Heure: Comité belge de recherches
       en Mésopotamie.
1973   L'étymologie de "Juda." VT 23: 380–81.
Liverani, M.
1979   Un' ipotesi sul nome di Abramo. Henoch 1: 9–17.
1990a A Seasonal Pattern for the Amarna Letters. Pp. 337–48 in Linger-
       ing over Words, ed. T. Abusch, J. Huehnergard, and P. Steinkeller.
       Fs. W. L. Moran. Atlanta: Scholars Press.

1990b *Prestige and Interest* History of the Ancient Near East/Studies 1. Padua: Sargon.

Loewe, R.
1969   The Medieval History of the Latin Vulgate. Pp. 102–54 in *The Cambridge History of the Bible Volume 2*, ed. G. W. H. Lampe. Cambridge: Cambridge University.

Loewenstamm, S. A.
1950   ʾĔlîšebaʿ. *EM* 1 3ː1–52. Jerusalem: Bialik Institute.
1958   Review of C. F. A. Schaeffer, *Ugaritica* III. *IEJ* 8: 138–40.
1962a Kārēt, hikkārēt. *EM* 4.330–32. Jerusalem: Bialik Institute.
1962b Maṭṭe(h). *EM* 4.825–32. Jerusalem: Bialik Institute.
1965   Yitrô. *EM* 3.954–57. Jerusalem: Bialik Institute.
1969a "The Lord Is My Strength and My Glory." *VT* 19: 464–70.
1969b The Expanded Colon in Ugaritic and Biblical Verse. *JSS* 14: 176–96.
1975   The Making and Destruction of the Golden Calf—a Rejoinder. *Bib* 56: 330–43.
1992a *The Evolution of the Exodus Tradition.* Hebrew orig. 1965. Jerusalem: Magnes.
1992b The Story of Moses' Birth. Pp. 201–21 in *From Babylon to Canaan*, ed. Y. Avishur and J. Blau. Jerusalem: Magnes.

Lohfink, N.
1963   *Das Hauptgebot.* AnBib 20. Rome: Pontifical Biblical Institute.
1968   *The Christian Meaning of the Old Testament.* German orig. 1965. Milwaukee: Bruce.
1978   Die Priesterschrift und die Geschichte. Pp. 189–225 in *Congress Volume, Göttingen 1977.* VTSup 29. Leiden: Brill.
1994   *Theology of the Pentateuch.* Fortress: Minneapolis.

Long, B. O.
1968   *The Problem of Etiological Narrative in the Old Testament.* BZAW 108. Berlin: Töpelmann.
1987   Framing Repetitions in Biblical Historiography. *JBL* 106: 385–99.

Löw, I.
1967   *Die Flora der Juden.* Orig. pub. 1924–34. Hildesheim: Olms.

Lübbe, J. C.
1990   Hebrew Lexicography: A New Approach. *JSem* 2: 1–15.

Lucas, A., and J. R. Harris
1962   *Ancient Egyptian Materials and Industries.* 4th ed. London: Arnold.

Luckenbill, D. D.
1926–27 *Ancient Records of Assyria and Babylonia* II. New York: Greenwood.

Lundbom, J. R.
1978   God's Use of the *Idem per Idem* to Terminate Debate. *HTR* 71: 193–201.

MacDonald, J.
1963   *Memar Marqah.* BZAW 84. Berlin: Töpelmann.

Macintosh, A. A.
1971   Exodus VIII 19, Distinct Redemption and the Hebrew Roots *pdh* and *pdd*. *VT* 21: 548–55.
Macuch, R.
1969   *Grammatik des samaritanischen Hebräisch.* Studia Samaritana 1. Berlin: de Gruyter.
Mahler, E.
1947   *Études sur le calendrier égyptien.* Annales du Musée Guimet 24. Paris: Leroux.
Maiberger, P.
1983   *Das Manna.* Ägypten und Altes Testament 6. Wiesbaden: Harrassowitz.
Maier, W. A., III
1986   *ʾAšerah: Extrabiblical Evidence.* HSM 37. Atlanta: Scholars Press.
Malamat, A.
1954   Gədûd. *EM* 2.432–34. Jerusalem: Bialik Institute.
1956   Nîṣənê nəbûʾâ bitʿûdôt mārî. Pp. 74–84 in *Yitzhak Ben-Zvi Volume.* ErIsr 4. Jerusalem: Israel Exploration Society.
1988   Pre-monarchical Social Institutions in Israel in the Light of Mari. Pp. 165–76 in *Congress Volume, Jerusalem 1986,* ed. J. A. Emerton. VTSup 40. Leiden: Brill.
1989   *Mari and the Early Israelite Experience.* Schweich Lectures 1984. Oxford: Oxford University.
Malul, M.
1990   Adoption of Foundlings in the Bible and Mesopotamian Documents: A Study of Some Legal Metaphors in Ezekiel 16:1–7. *JSOT* 46: 97–126.
Mandelkern, S.
1937   *Veteris Testamenti Concordantiae.* Leipzig: Schocken.
Mann, T. W.
1971   The Pillar of Cloud in the Reed Sea Narrative. *JBL* 90: 15–30.
1977   *Divine Presence and Guidance in Israelite Traditions: The Typology of Exaltation.* Johns Hopkins Near Eastern Studies. Baltimore: Johns Hopkins University.
1988   *The Book of the Torah.* Atlanta: John Knox.
1996   Passover: The Time of Our Lives. *Int* 50: 240–50.
Margalit, B.
1982   Ugaritic Lexicography I. *RB* 89: 418–26.
Margalith, O.
1977–78   Wəkōl rekeb miṣrayim wəšālišīm ʿal kullô (šəmôt yʺd, z). *Beit Mikra* 23: 68–72.
Martin-Achard, R.
1992   Isaac. *ABD* 3.462–70. New York: Doubleday.
Marzal, A.
1963   Consideraciones sobre la raíz ugarítica "*ṭlṭ.*" *Bib* 44: 343–51.

Masetti-Rouault, M. G.
    n.d.   The King, Death and the Enemy in Assyrian Royal Inscriptions. Forthcoming in *JAOS*.
Mastin, B. A.
    1979   Was the *Šāliš* the Third Man in the Chariot? Pp. 125–54 in *Studies in the Historical Books of the Old Testament*. VTSup 30. Leiden: Brill.
May, H. G.
    1936   The Relation of the Passover to the Festival of Unleavened Cakes. *JBL* 55: 65–82.
Mazar, B.
    1965   The Sanctuary of Arad and the Family of Hobab the Kenite. *JNES* 24: 297–303.
    1968   Miskənôt, ʿārê miskənôt. *EM* 5.165–67. Jerusalem: Bialik Institute.
McBride, S. D.
    1969   The Deuteronomic Name Theology. Ph.D. diss., Harvard University.
    1990   Transcendent Authority: The Role of Moses in Old Testament Traditions. *Int* 44: 229–39.
McCarter, P. K., Jr.
    1973   The River Ordeal in Israelite Literature. *HTR* 66: 403–12.
    1980   *I Samuel*. AB 8. Garden City, N.Y.: Doubleday.
    1984   *II Samuel*. AB 9. Garden City, N.Y.: Doubleday.
McCarthy, C.
    1981   *The Tiqqune Sopherim*. OBO 36. Freiburg: Universitäts Verlag; Göttingen: Vandenhoeck & Ruprecht.
McCarthy, D. J.
    1966   Plagues and the Sea of Reeds: Exodus 5–14. *JBL* 85: 137–58.
    1969   The Symbolism of Blood and Sacrifice. *JBL* 88: 166–76.
    1978   Exod 3:14: History, Philology and Theology. *CBQ* 40: 311–22.
McCoy, F. W., and G. Heiken
    1990   Thera. *Archaeology* 43.3: 42–49.
McEvenue, S. E.
    1971   *The Narrative Style of the Priestly Writer*. AnBib 50. Rome: Pontifical Biblical Institute.
McKay, J. W.
    1972   The Date of Passover and Its Significance. *ZAW* 84: 435–47.
McKenzie, J. L.
    1959   The Elders in the Old Testament. *Bib* 40: 522–40.
McNeile, A. H.
    1908   *The Book of Exodus*. Westminster Commentaries. London: Methuen.
Meier, S. A.
    1988   *The Messenger in the Ancient Semitic World*. HSM 45. Atlanta: Scholars Press.

Melamed, E. Z.
1961   "Break-up" of Stereotype Phrases as an Artistic Device in Biblical
        Poetry. Pp. 115–53 in *Studies in the Bible*, ed. C. Rabin. ScrHier 8.
        Jerusalem: Magnes.
Melnyk, J. L. R.
1993   When Israel Was a Child: Ancient Near Eastern Adoption Formu-
        las and the Relationship Between God and Israel. Pp. 245–59 in
        History and Interpretation, ed. M. P. Graham, W. P. Brown, and
        J. K. Kuan. Fs. J. H. Hayes. JSOTSup 173. Sheffield: JSOT.
Mendelsohn, I.
1962   On Corvée Labor in Ancient Canaan and Israel. *BASOR* 167: 31–
        35.
Mendenhall, G. E.
1954a   Law and Covenant in Israel and in the Ancient Near East. *BA* 17:
        26–46, 49–76.
1954b   Puppy and Lettuce in Northwest-Semitic Covenant Making.
        BASOR 133: 26–30.
1958   The Census Lists of Numbers 1 and 26. *JBL* 77: 52–66.
1973   *The Tenth Generation.* Baltimore/London: Johns Hopkins Univer-
        sity.
Meshel, Z.
1971   *Dərôm Sînay.* Jerusalem: Šêrûtê hôṣā'â lə'ôr yiśrə'ēliyyîm.
1981   A Religious Center at Kuntillet-Ajrud, Sinai. P. 161 in *Temples and
        High Places in Biblical Times*, ed. A. Biran. Jerusalem: Hebrew
        Union College–Jewish Institute of Religion.
Mesnil du Buisson, R. du
1939   Une tablette magique de la région du moyen Euphrate. Pp. 421–
        34 in *Mélanges syriens offerts à M. René Dussaud I.* Bibliothèque
        archéologique et historique 30. Paris: Geuthner.
Mettinger, T. N. D.
1982   *The Dethronement of Sabaoth.* ConBOT 18. Lund: Gleerup.
1984   YHWH SABAOTH—the Heavenly King on the Cherubim
        Throne. Pp. 109–38 in *Studies in the Period of David and Solomon
        and Other Essays*, ed. T. Ishida. Winona Lake, Ind.: Eisenbrauns.
1988   *In Search of God.* Swedish orig. 1987. Philadelphia: Fortress.
Metzger, M.
1970   Himmlische und irdische Wohnstatt Jahwes. *UF* 2: 139–58.
1983   Gottheit, Berg und Vegetation in vorderorientalischer Bildtradi-
        tion. *ZDPV* 99: 54–94.
1992   Der Weltenbaum in vorderorientalischer Bildtradition. Pp. 1–34 in
        Unsere Welt—Gottes Schöpfung, ed. W. Härle, M. Marquardt, and
        W. Nethöfel. Fs. E. Wölfel. Marburger Theologische Studien 32.
        Marburg: Elwert.
Meyer, E.
1906   *Die Israeliten und ihre Nachbarstämme.* Halle: Niemeyer.

Meyer, L.
    1983   *The Message of Exodus*. Minneapolis: Augsburg.
Meyers, C. L.
    1976   *The Tabernacle Menorah*. ASORDS 2. Missoula, Mont.: Scholars Press.
    1987   A Terracotta at the Harvard Semitic Museum and Disc-Holding Female Figures Reconsidered. *IEJ* 37: 116–22.
    1991   Of Drums and Damsels: Women's Performance in Ancient Israel. *BA* 54: 16–27.
    1994   Miriam the Musician. Pp. 207–30 in *A Feminist Companion to Exodus to Deuteronomy*, ed. A. Brenner. The Feminist Companion to the Bible 6. Sheffield: Sheffield Academic Press.
Midant-Reynes, B., and F. Braunstein-Silvestre
    1977   Le chameau en Égypte. *Or* 46: 337–62.
Middlekoop, P.
    1967   The Significance of the Story of the "Bloody Husband" (Ex. 4:24–26). *The South East Asia Journal of Theology* 8: 34–38.
Milgrom, J.
    1976   Israel's Sanctuary: The Priestly Picture of Dorian Gray. *RB* 83: 390–99.
    1990   *Numbers*. JPS Torah Commentary. Philadelphia: Jewish Publication Society.
    1991   *Leviticus 1–16*. AB 3. Garden City, N.Y.: Doubleday.
Milik, J. T.
    1977   Tefillin, Mezuzot, Targums. DJD 6: 31–91. Oxford: Clarendon.
Miller, P. D., Jr.
    1965   Fire in the Mythology of Canaan and Israel. *CBQ* 27: 256–61.
    1970a   Ugaritic *ġzr* and Hebrew ʿ*zr* II. *UF* 2: 159–75.
    1970b   Animal Names as Designations in Ugaritic and Hebrew. *UF* 2: 177–86.
    1970c   Apotropaic Imagery in Proverbs 6:20–22. *JNES* 29: 129–30.
    1973   *The Divine Warrior in Early Israel*. HSM 5. Cambridge, Mass.: Harvard University.
Milne, P. J.
    1988   *Vladimir Propp and the Study of Structure in Hebrew Biblical Narrative*. Sheffield: Sheffield Academic Press.
Mitchell, T. C.
    1969   The Meaning of the Noun Ḥtn in the Old Testament. *VT* 19: 93–112.
Moberly, R. W. L.
    1992   *The Old Testament of the Old Testament*. Overtures to Biblical Theology. Minneapolis: Fortress.
Montgomery, J. A.
    1935   Ras Shamra Notes IV: The Conflict of Baal and the Waters. *JAOS* 55: 268–77.

Moor, J. C. de
1971 *The Seasonal Pattern in the Ugaritic Myth of Baʿlu.* AOAT 16. Kevelaer: Butzon & Bercker; Neukirchen-Vluyn: Neukirchener Verlag.
1972 *New Year with Canaanites and Israelites.* Kampen: Kok.
Moore, G. F.
1901 *Judges.* ICC. New York: Scribner.
Morag, S.
1972 Pronunciation of Hebrew. *EncJud* 13.1120–45. Jerusalem: Keter.
Moran, W. L.
1961 The Hebrew Language in Its Northwest Semitic Background. Pp. 54–72 in *The Bible and the Ancient Near East*, ed. G. E. Wright. Garden City, N.Y.: Doubleday.
1962 Some Remarks on the Song of Moses. *Bib* 43: 317–27.
1963 The End of the Unholy War and the Anti-Exodus. *Bib* 44: 333–42.
1971 Atrahasis: The Babylonian Story of the Flood. *Bib* 52: 51–61.
1987 Some Considerations of Form and Interpretation in *Atra-Ḫasis*. Pp. 245–55 in *Language, Literature and History*, ed. R. Rochberg-Halton. Fs. E. Reiner. AOS 67. New Haven, Conn.: American Oriental Society.
1992 *The Amarna Letters.* French orig. 1987. Baltimore/London: Johns Hopkins University.
Morenz, S.
1973 *Egyptian Religion.* German orig. 1960. Ithaca, N.Y.: Cornell University.
Moreshet, M.
1980 ʿAl binyan nûpʿal bəʿibrît habbātar-miqrāʾît. Pp. 126–39 in *Studies in Hebrew and Semitic Languages Dedicated to the Memory of Professor Eduard Yechezkel Kutscher*, ed. G. B. Sarfatti et al. Ramat-Gan: Bar-Ilan University.
Morgenstern, J.
1916 The Bones of the Paschal Lamb. *JAOS* 36: 146–53.
1917 The Origin of Maṣṣoth and the Maṣṣoth Festival. *AJT* 21: 275–93.
1924 The Three Calendars of Ancient Israel. *HUCA* 1: 13–78.
1927 The Oldest Document of the Hexateuch. *HUCA* 4: 1–138.
1931–32 The Book of the Covenant, III. *HUCA* 8–9: 47–48.
1935 Supplementary Studies in the Calendars of Ancient Israel. *HUCA* 10: 1–148.
1949 The Despoiling of the Egyptians. *JBL* 68: 2–3.
1963 The "Bloody Husband" (?) (Exod. 4:24–26) Once Again. *HUCA* 34: 35–70.
1966 *The Rites of Birth, Marriage, Death and Kindred Occasions Among the Semites.* Cincinnati: Hebrew Union College Press.
Mowinckel, S.
1952 Die vermeintliche "Passahlegende" Ex. 1–15. *ST* 5: 66–88.
1953 *Religion und Kultus.* Göttingen: Vandenhoeck & Ruprecht.

1961   The Name of the God of Moses. *HUCA* 32: 121–33.

Muilenburg, J.
1961   The Linguistic and Rhetorical Usages of the Particle *ky* in the Old Testament. *HUCA* 32: 135–60.
1966   A Liturgy on the Triumphs of Yahweh. Pp. 233–51 in *Studia Biblica et Semitica*. Fs. T. C. Vriezen. Wageningen: Veenman.

Mull, K. V., and C. S. Mull
1992   Biblical Leprosy—Is It Really? *BRev* 8.2: 33–39, 62.

Murray, G. W.
1935   *Sons of Ishmael*. London: Routledge.

Musil, A.
1928   *The Manners and Customs of the Rwala Bedouins*. American Geographical Society Oriental Explorations and Studies 6. New York: American Geographical Society.

Na'aman, N.
1988   The List of David's Officers (*šālîšîm*). *VT* 38: 71–79.

Newby, P. H.
1980   *Warrior Pharaohs*. London/Boston: Faber & Faber.

Niccacci, A.
1990   *The Syntax of the Verb in Classical Hebrew Prose*. JSOTSup 86. Sheffield: JSOT.

Nicolsky, N. M.
1927   Pascha im Kulte des jerusalemischen Tempels. *ZAW* 45: 171–90, 241–53.

Niditch, S.
1987   *Underdogs and Tricksters: A Prelude to Biblical Folklore*. San Francisco: Harper & Row.
1993   *Folklore and the Hebrew Bible*. Guides to Biblical Scholarship. Minneapolis: Fortress.

Niehoff, M.
1992   Do Biblical Characters Talk to Themselves? Narrative Modes of Representing Inner Speech in Early Biblical Fiction. *JBL* 111: 577–95.

Niehr, H.
1986   *Herrschen und Richten: Die Wurzel špṭ im alten Orient und im Alten Testament*. Forschung zur Bibel 54. Würzburg: Echter.

Nilsson, M. P.
1920   *Primitive Time-Reckoning*. Lund: Gleerup.

Nims, C. F.
1950   Bricks Without Straw. *BA* 13: 22–28.

Norin, S. I. L.
1977   *Er spaltete das Meer*. ConBOT 9. Lund: Gleerup.

Noth, M.
1928   *Die israelitischen Personennamen*. Stuttgart: Kohlhammer.
1940   Der Wallfahrtsweg zum Sinai. *PJ* 36: 5–28.

1948   *Überlieferungsgeschichte des Pentateuch.* 2d ed. Stuttgart: Kohlhammer.
1960   *The History of Israel.* 2d ed. German orig. 1958. New York: Harper & Row.
1962   *Exodus.* German orig. 1959. OTL. Philadelphia: Westminster.
1972   *A History of Pentateuchal Traditions.* German orig. 1948. Englewood Cliffs, N.J.: Prentice-Hall.
1981   *The Deuteronomistic History.* German orig. 1943. JSOTSup 15. Sheffield: JSOT.
Nötscher F.
1953   Zum emphatischen Lamed. *VT* 3: 372–80.
O'Connell, K. G.
1972   *The Theodotionic Revision of the Book of Exodus.* HSM 3. Cambridge, Mass.: Harvard University.
1984   The List of Seven Peoples in Canaan: A Fresh Analysis. Pp. 221–42 in *The Answers Lie Below: Essays in Honor of Lawrence Edmond Toombs,* ed. H. O. Thompson. Lanham, Md.: University Press of America.
n.d.   Unpublished commentary on Exodus 1–5.
O'Connor, M.
1980   *Hebrew Verse Structure.* Winona Lake, Ind.: Eisenbrauns.
Oden, R. A., Jr.
1977   *Studies in Lucian's De Syria Dea.* HSM 15. Missoula, Mont.: Scholars Press.
1992   Cosmogony, Cosmology. *ABD* 1.1162–71. New York: Doubleday.
Oertel, F.
1970   *Herodots Ägyptischer Logos und die Glaubwürdigkeit Herodots.* Antiquitas Reihe 1: Abhandlugen zur alten Geschichte 18. Bonn: Habelt.
Oesch, J. M.
1979   *Petucha und Setuma.* OBO 27. Göttingen: Vandenhoeck & Ruprecht.
Oesterley, W. O. E.
1933   Early Hebrew Festival Rituals. Pp. 111–46 in *Myth and Ritual,* ed. S .H. Hooke. London: Oxford University.
Ogden, G. S.
1967   Notes on the Use of *hwyh* in Exodus IX 3. *VT* 17: 483–84.
1992   Idem per Idem: Its Use and Meaning. *JSOT* 53: 107–20.
Olivarri, E.
1971–72   La celebración de la Pascua y Acimos en la legislación del Antiguo Testamento. *EstBib* 30: 231–68; 31: 17–41, 293–320.
Olyan, S.
1982   Zadok's Origins and the Tribal Politics of David. *JBL* 101: 177–93.
1989   *Asherah and the Cult of Yahweh in Israel.* SBLMS 34. Atlanta: Scholars Press.

1991   The Israelites Debate Their Options at the Sea of Reeds: *LAB* 10:3, Its Parallels, and Pseudo-Philo's Ideology and Background. *JBL* 110: 75–91.

O'Neil, W. M.
1975   *Time and the Calendars*. Sydney: Sydney University.

Oppenheim, A. L.
1943   Akkadian *pul(u)ḫ(t)u* and *melammu*. *JAOS* 63: 31–34.
1965   On Royal Gardens in Mesopotamia. *JNES* 24: 328–33.

Oren, E. D.
1987   The "Ways of Horus" in North Sinai. Pp. 69–119 in *Egypt, Israel, Sinai: Archaeological and Historical Relationships in the Biblical Period*, ed. A. F. Rainey. Tel Aviv: Tel Aviv University.

O'Toole, R. F.
1992   Last Supper. *ABD* 4.234–41. New York: Doubleday.

Otten, H.
1973   *Eine althethitische Erzählung um die Stadt Zalpa*. Studien zu den Boğazköy-Texten 17. Wiesbaden: Harrassowitz.

Otto, E.
1975   *Das Mazzotfest in Gilgal*. BWANT 107. Stuttgart: Kohlhammer.
1976   Erwägungen zum überlieferungsgeschichtlichen Ursprung und "Sitz im Leben" des jahwistischen Plagenzyklus. *VT* 26: 3–27.

Paran, M.
1989   *Forms of the Priestly Style in the Pentateuch* (Hebrew). Jerusalem: Magnes.

Pardee, D.
1978   The Semitic Root *mrr* and the Etymology of Ugaritic *mr(r)* ‖ *brk*. *UF* 10: 249–88.

Parker, H.
1984   *Flawed Texts and Verbal Icons*. Evanston, Ill.: Northwestern University.

Parker, R. A.
1950   *The Calendars of Ancient Egypt*. Studies in Oriental Civilization 26. Chicago: University of Chicago.

Parker, S. B.
1971   Exodus XV 2 Again. *VT* 21: 373–79.
1972   The Ugaritic Deity Rāpiʾu. *UF* 4: 97–104.

Parpola, S.
1987   Neo-Assyrian Treaties from the Royal Archives of Nineveh. *JCS* 39: 161–89.

Parpola, S., and K. Watanabe
1988   *Neo-Assyrian Treaties and Loyalty Oaths*. State Archives of Assyria 2. Helsinki: Helsinki University.

Parron, T.
1937   *Shadow on the Land*. New York: Reynal & Hitchcock.

Patrick, D.
1976   Traditio-History of the Reed Sea Account. *VT* 26: 248–49.
Patterson, O.
1982   *Slavery and Social Death.* Cambridge, Mass.: Harvard University.
Paul, S. M.
1992a   Polysensuous Polyvalency in Poetic Parallelism. Pp. 147–63 in "*Sha'arei Talmon*," ed. M. Fishbane and E. Tov. Fs. S. Talmon. Winona Lake, Ind.: Eisenbrauns.
1992b   Exodus 1:21: "To Found a Family." A Biblical and Akkadian Idiom. *MAARAV* 8: 139–42.
1995   The "Plural of Ecstasy" in Mesopotamian and Biblical Love Poetry. Pp. 585–97 in *Solving Riddles and Untying Knots,* ed. Z. Zevit, S. Gitin, and M. Sokoloff. Fs. J. C. Greenfield. Winona Lake, Ind.: Eisenbrauns.
Peckham, B.
1987   Phoenicia and the Religion of Israel: The Epigraphic Evidence. Pp. 79–99 in *Ancient Israelite Religion,* ed. P. D. Miller, Jr., P. D. Hanson, and S. D. McBride. Fs. F. M. Cross. Philadelphia: Fortress.
1993   *History and Prophecy.* New York: Doubleday.
Pedersen, J.
1934   Passahfest und Passahlegende. *ZAW* 52: 161–75.
1940   *Israel. Its Life and Culture III–IV.* Danish orig. 1934. London: Oxford University.
Perlitt, L.
1969   *Bundestheologie im Alten Testament.* WMANT 36. Neukirchen-Vluyn. Neukirchener Verlag.
Perrot, C.
1969   *Petuḥot et Setumot,* Étude sur les alinéas du Pentateuque. *RB* 76: 50–91.
Pfeiffer, R. H.
1941   *Introduction to the Old Testament.* 3d ed. New York: Harper.
Piganiol, A.
1963   Le rôti et le bouilli. Pp. 369–71 in *A Pedro Bosch-Gimpera,* ed. S. Genovés. Mexico: Instituto Nacional de Antropología e Historia, Universidad Nacional Autónoma de México.
Pixley, G. V.
1987   *On Exodus. A Liberation Perspective.* Spanish orig. 1983. Maryknoll: Orbis.
Plastaras, J.
1966   *The God of Exodus.* Milwaukee: Bruce.
Poethig, E. B.
1985   The Victory Song Tradition of the Women of Israel. Ph.D. diss., Union Theological Seminary.

Pomeroy, S. B.
    1975   *Goddesses, Whores, Wives, and Slaves.* New York: Schocken.
Pope, M. H.
    1955   *El in the Ugaritic Texts.* VTSup 2. Leiden: Brill.
    1962a Number, Numbering, Numbers. *IDB* 3.561–67. Nashville: Abingdon.
    1962b Seven, Seventh, Seventy. *IDB* 4.294–95. Nashville: Abingdon.
    1966   Marginalia to M. Dahood's *Ugaritic-Hebrew Philology. JBL* 85: 455–66.
    1973   *Job.* 3d ed. AB 15. Garden City, N.Y.: Doubleday.
Porten, B.
    1968   *Archives from Elephantine.* Berkeley: University of California.
    1990   The Calendar of Aramaic Texts from Achaemenid and Ptolemaic Egypt. Pp. 13–32 in *Irano-Judaica II,* ed. A. Netzer and S. Shaked. Jerusalem: Məkôn Ben-Ṣəbî.
Porten, B., and A. Yardeni
    1986   *Textbook of Aramaic Documents from Ancient Egypt.* Winona Lake, Ind.: Eisenbrauns.
Porter, B. H., and S. D. Ricks
    1990   Names in Antiquity: Old, New, and Hidden. Vol. 1, pp. 501–22 in *By Study and Also by Faith,* ed. J. M. Lundquist and S. D. Ricks. Fs. H. W. Nibley. Salt Lake City: Deseret.
Powell, M. A.
    1992   Weights and Measures. *ABD* 6.897–908. New York: Doubleday.
Preuss, H. D.
    1968   "Ich will mit dir sein." *ZAW* 80: 139–73.
Procksch, O.
    1906   *Das nordhebräische Sagenbuch: Die Elohimquelle.* Leipzig: Hinrichs.
Propp, V. I.
    1968   *The Morphology of the Folktale.* 2d ed. Russian orig. 1928. Austin/London: University of Texas.
    1984   *Theory and History of Folklore.* Theory and History of Literature 5. Minneapolis: University of Minnesota.
Propp, W. H. C.
    1987a *Water in the Wilderness.* HSM 40. Atlanta: Scholars Press.
    1987b The Origins of Infant Circumcision in Israel. *HAR* 11: 355–70.
    1987c On Hebrew *Śāde(h),* "Highland." *VT* 37: 230–36.
    1987d The Skin of Moses' Face—Transfigured or Disfigured? *CBQ* 49: 375–86.
    1988   The Rod of Aaron and the Sin of Moses. *JBL* 107: 19–26.
    1990   Eden Sketches. Pp. 189–203 in *The Hebrew Bible and Its Interpreters,* ed. W. H. Propp, B. Halpern and D. N. Freedman. Biblical and Judaic Studies from the University of California, San Diego 1. Winona Lake, Ind.: Eisenbrauns.

1992a Gershon. *ABD* 2.994–95. New York: Doubleday.
1992b Ithamar. *ABD* 3.579–81. New York: Doubleday.
1993 That Bloody Bridegroom. *VT* 43: 495–518.
1996 Review of *The Five Books of Moses* (E. Fox) and *Genesis* (R. Alter). *BRev* 12.5: 10, 14–15.
1997 The Priestly Source Recovered Intact? *VT* 46: 458–78.

Qimron, E.
1972 Hahabḥānâ bên wāw ləyôd bitʿûdôt midbar yəhûdâ. *Beit Mikra* 18: 102–12.
1986 *The Hebrew of the Dead Sea Scrolls.* HSS 29. Atlanta: Scholars Press.
1988 Məqôrô šel binyān nûpʿal. *Leš* 52: 178–79.

Quaegebeur, J.
1985 On the Egyptian Equivalent of Biblical *Ḥarṭummîm.* Pp. 162–72 in *Pharaonic Egypt*, ed. S. Israelit-Groll. Jerusalem: Magnes.

Rabenau, K. von
1966 Die beiden Erzählungen vom Schilfmeerwunder in Exod. 13,17–14,31. Pp. 7–29 in *Theologische Versuche*, ed. P. Wätzel and G. Schille. Berlin: Evangelische Verlagsanstalt.

Rabin, C.
1958 *The Zadokite Documents.* 2d ed. Oxford: Clarendon.
1961 Etymological Miscellanea. Pp. 384–400 in *Studies in the Bible*, ed. C. Rabin. ScrHier 8. Jerusalem: Magnes.
1963 Hittite Words in Hebrew. *Or* 32: 113–39.
1977 Hamitic Languages as a Source of Semitic Etymologies. Pp. 329–40 (English section) in *Proceedings of the Sixth World Congress of Jewish Studies Vol. I*, ed. A. Shinan. Jerusalem: Jerusalem Academic Press.

Rad, G. von
1951 *Der Heilige Krieg im alten Israel.* ATANT 20. Zurich: Zwingli.
1962 *Old Testament Theology.* German orig. 1957. New York: Harper & Row.
1965 *The Problem of the Hexateuch and Other Essays.* Edinburgh: Oliver & Boyd.

Rainey, A. F.
1970 Compulsory Labour Gangs in Ancient Israel. *IEJ* 20: 191–202.
1978 *El Amarna Tablets 359–379.* 2d ed. AOAT 8. Levelaer: Butzon & Bercker; Neukirchen-Vluyn: Neukirchener Verlag.

Rank, O.
1952 *The Myth of the Birth of the Hero.* German orig. 1909. New York: Brunner.

Redford, D. B.
1967 The Literary Motif of the Exposed Child. *Numen* 14: 209–28.
1970 *A Study of the Biblical Story of Joseph.* VTSup 20. Leiden: Brill.
1987 An Egyptological Perspective on the Exodus Narrative. Pp. 137–61 in *Egypt, Israel, Sinai: Archaeological and Historical Relationships in the Biblical Period*, ed. A. F. Rainey. Tel Aviv: Tel Aviv University.

1992   *Egypt, Canaan, and Israel in Ancient Times.* Princeton, N.J.:
        Princeton University.
Reichert, A.
1977   Israel, the Firstborn of God: A Topic of Early Deuteronomic The-
        ology. Pp. 341–49 in *Proceedings of the Sixth World Congress of
        Jewish Studies Vol. I,* ed. A. Shinan. Jerusalem: Jerusalem Aca-
        demic Press.
Rendsburg, G.
1982   Dual Personal Pronouns and Dual Verbs in Hebrew. *JQR* 73: 38–61.
Rendtorff, R.
1990   *The Problem of the Process of Transmission in the Pentateuch.* Ger-
        man orig. 1977. JSOTSup 89. Sheffield: JSOT.
Reviv, H.
1982   Śākîr. *EM* 8.285–87. Jerusalem: Bialik Institute.
1989   *The Elders in Ancient Israel.* Hebrew orig. 1983. Jerusalem:
        Magnes.
Reymond, P.
1958   *L'eau, sa vie, et sa signification dans l'Ancien Testament.* VTSup 6.
        Leiden: Brill.
Richardson, M. E. J.
1978   Ugaritic Place Names with Final -y. *JSS* 23: 298–315.
Richter, W.
1970   *Die sogennanten vorprophetischen Berufungsberichte.* FRLANT
        101. Göttingen: Vandenhoeck & Ruprecht.
Rieder, D.
1974   *Targûm yônātān ben ʿuzzîʾēl.* Jerusalem: American Academy for
        Jewish Studies.
Rihbany, A. M.
1927   *Morgenländische Sitten im Leben Jesu.* Basel: Reinhardt.
Ringgren, H.
1977   Gāʾal. *TDOT* 2.350–55. Grand Rapids, Mich.: Eerdmans.
1978   Hûʾ. *TDOT* 3.341–44, 346–52. Grand Rapids, Mich.: Eerdmans.
Ripinsky, M. P.
1983   Camel Ancestry and Domestication in Egypt and the Sahara.
        Archaeology 36.3: 21–27.
Roberts, J. J. M.
1971   The Hand of Yahweh. *VT* 21: 244–51.
Robertson, D. A.
1969   The Morphemes -y (i) and -w (ō) in Biblical Hebrew. *VT* 19: 211–23.
1972   *Linguistic Evidence in Dating Early Hebrew Poetry.* SBLDS 3.
        Missoula, Mont.: Society of Biblical Literature.
1977   *The Old Testament and the Literary Critic.* Philadelphia: Fortress.
Robinson, B. P.
1986   Zipporah to the Rescue: A Contextual Study of Exodus IV 24–26.
        VT 36: 447–61.

Robinson, H. W.
1967 *Corporate Personality in Ancient Israel.* Philadelphia: Fortress.
Rochberg-Halton, F.
1992 Calendars. Ancient Near East. *ABD* 1.810–14. New York: Doubleday.
Romerowski, S.
1990 Que signifie le mot *ḥesed? VT* 60: 89–103.
Rosen, S. A.
1996 *Lithics After the Stone Age.* Walnut Creek, Calif.: Altamira.
Rosenberg, R.
1980 The Concept of Biblical Sheol Within the Context of Ancient Near Eastern Beliefs. Ph.D. diss., Harvard University.
Rossi, J. B. de
1784–85 *Variae Lectiones Veteris Testamenti Librorum.* Parma: ex Regio Typographeo.
Rost, L.
1943 Weidewechsel und altisraelitischer Festkalendar. *ZDPV* 66: 205–16.
Rozelaar, M.
1952 The Song of the Sea. *VT* 2: 221–28.
Rudolph, W.
1938 *Der "Elohist" von Exodus bis Josua.* BZAW 68. Berlin: Töpelmann.
Rüger, H. P.
1970 Zum Text von Sir 40 10 und Ex 10 21. *ZAW* 82: 103–9.
Rummel, S.
1981 Narrative Structures in the Ugaritic Texts. Pp. 223–332 in *RSP* III, ed. S. Rummel. AnOr 51. Rome: Pontifical Biblical Institute.
Rustum-Shehadeh, L. A.
1969 The Sibilants in the West Semitic Languages of the Second Millennium B.C. Ph.D. diss., Harvard University.
Rylaarsdam, J. C.
1962 Booths, Feast of. *IDB* 1.455–58. Nashville: Abingdon.
Safrai, S.
1965 *Hāʿălîyâ ləregel bîmê bayit šēnî.* Tel Aviv: Am Hassefer.
Sakenfeld, K. D.
1978 *The Meaning of Hesed in the Hebrew Bible.* HSM 17. Missoula, Mont.: Scholars Press.
Sanderson, J. E.
1986 *An Exodus Scroll from Qumran: 4QpaleoExod^m and the Samaritan Tradition.* HSS 30. Atlanta: Scholars Press.
1994 4QExod^c. Pp. 97–125 in *Qumran Cave 4.VII,* ed. E. Ulrich et al. DJD 12. Oxford: Clarendon.
Särko, P.
1993 "The Third Man"—David's Heroes in 2 Sam 23,8–39. *SJOT* 7: 108–24.

Sarna, N. M.
    1986   *Exploring Exodus.* New York: Schocken.
Sasson, J.
    1966   Circumcision in the Ancient Near East. *JBL* 85: 473–76.
    1968   Bovine Symbolism and the Exodus Narrative. *VT* 18: 380–87.
    1981   Literary Criticism, Folklore Scholarship, and Ugaritic Literature.
            Pp. 81–98 in *Ugarit in Retrospect,* ed. G. D. Young. Winona Lake,
            Ind.: Eisenbrauns.
Sasson, V.
    1983   An Unrecognized "Smoke Signal" in Isaiah XXX 27. *VT* 33:
            90–95.
Sauneron, S.
    1962   *Les fêtes religieuses d'Esna.* Esna 5. Cairo: Institut Français
            d'Archéologie Orientale.
Savran, G. W.
    1988   *Telling and Retelling: Quotation in Biblical Narrative.* Blooming-
            ton: Indiana University.
Saydon, P. P.
    1964   Meanings and Uses of the Particle *'t. VT* 14: 192–210.
Schaeffer, C. F.-A.
    1938   Les fouilles de Ras Shamra—Ugarit. Neuvième campagne (prin-
            temps 1937). Rapport sommaire. XIII. Fouilles sur le sommet du
            Djebel Akra et aux ruines du couvent de Saint-Barnabé. *Syria* 19:
            323–27.
Schäfer, H.
    1957   Das Niederschlagen der Feinde. *Wiener Zeitschrift für die Kunde
            des Morgenlandes* 54: 168–76.
Scharbert, J.
    1981   Das "Schilfmeerwunder" in den Texten des Alten Testaments.
            Pp. 395–417 in *Mélanges bibliques et orientaux en l'honneur de
            M. Henri Cazelles,* ed. A. Caquot and M. Delcor. AOAT 212. Keve-
            laer: Butzon & Bercker; Neukirchen-Vluyn: Neukirchener Verlag.
    1989   *Exodus.* Die Neue Echter Bibel. Würzburg: Echter.
Schart, A.
    1990   *Mose und Israel im Konflikt.* OBO 98. Freiburg; Universitäts Ver-
            lag; Göttingen: Vandenhoeck & Ruprecht.
Schild, E.
    1954   On Exodus iii 14—"I Am That I Am." *VT* 4: 296–302.
Schildenberger, J.
    1961   Psalm 78 (77) und die Pentateuchquellen. Pp. 231–56 in *Lex
            Tua Veritas,* ed. H. Gross and F. Mussner. Fs. H. Junker. Trier:
            Paulinus.
Schley, D. G.
    1990   The *šālišîm:* Officers or Special Three-Man Squads? *VT* 40: 321–26.
    1992   David's Champions. *ABD* 2.49–52. New York: Doubleday.

Schmid, H. H.
1976   *Der sogenannte Jahwist.* Zurich: Theologischer Verlag Zürich.
Schmid, Herbert
1965   Mose, Der Blutbräutigam. *Judaica* 21: 113–18.
Schmidt, Hans
1931   Das Meerlied. Ex 15 2–19. ZAW 49: 59–66.
Schmidt, L.
1990   *Beobachtungen zu der Plagenerzählung in Exodus VII 14–XI 10.*
        StudBib 4. Leiden: Brill.
Schmidt, W. H.
1983   *Exodus, Sinai und Mose.* ErFor 191. Darmstadt: Wissenschaft-
        liche Buchgesellschaft.
1988   *Exodus 1.* BKAT 2.1. Neukirchen-Vluyn: Neukirchener Verlag.
Schmitt, H.-C.
1989   Tradition der Prophetenbücher in den Schichten der Plagen-
        erzählung Ex 7,1–11,10. Pp. 196–216 in *Prophet und Propheten-
        buch*, ed. V. Fritz, K.-F. Pohlmann, and H.-C. Schmitt. Fs. O. Kaiser.
        BZAW 185. Berlin: de Gruyter.
1990   Die Geschichte vom Sieg über die Amalekiter Ex 17,8–16 als theo-
        logische Lehrerzählung. ZAW 102: 335–44.
Schneemann, G.
1980   Deutung und Bedeutung der Beschneidung nach Ex. 4,24–26.
        TLZ 105: 794.
Schott, S.
1950   *Altägyptische Liebeslieder.* Die Bibliothek der alten Welt. Zurich:
        Artemis.
Schulman, A. R.
1957   Egyptian Representations of Horsemen and Raiding in the New
        Kingdom. *JNES* 16: 263–71.
Seale, M.
1974   *The Desert Bible.* London: Weidenfeld & Nicolson.
Segal, J. B.
1957   Intercalations and the Hebrew Calendar. *VT* 7: 250–307.
1963   *The Hebrew Passover.* London: Oxford University.
1982   Šānâ. *EM* 8.197–209. Jerusalem: Bialik Institute.
Seger, J. D.
1992   Limping About the Altar. Pp. 120*–27* in *A. Biran Volume.* ErIsr
        23. Jerusalem: Israel Exploration Society.
Seidl, T.
1991   *ʾăšr* als Konjunktion. Pp. 445–69 in *Text, Methode und Grammatik*,
        ed. W. Gross et al. Fs. W. Richter. St. Ottilien: EOS.
Seow, C. L.
1989   *Myth, Drama, and the Politics of David's Dance.* HSM 44. Atlanta:
        Scholars Press.
1992   Hosts, Lord of. *ABD* 3.304–7. New York: Doubleday.

Shanks, H.
1981   The Exodus and the Crossing of the Red Sea, According to Hans
        Goedicke. *BARev* 7.5: 42–50.
Shinan, A.
1992   *Targûm wə'aggādâ bô.* Jerusalem: Magnes.
Siebert-Hommes, J.
1992   Die Geburtsgeschichte des Mose innerhalb des Erzählzusammen-
        hangs von Exodus i und ii. *VT* 42: 398–404.
Siegfried, C.
1884   Die Aussprache des Hebräischen bei Hieronymus. *ZAW* 4: 34–83.
Sierksma, F.
1951   Quelques remarques sur la circoncision en Israel. *OTS* 9: 136–69.
Silbermann, A. M., and M. Rosenbaum
1934   *Chumash with Targum Onkelos, Haphtaroth and Rashi's Commen-
        tary.* Jerusalem: Silbermann Family.
Ska, J.-L.
1979   La sortie d'Égypt (Ex 7–14) dans le récit sacerdotal (P^g) et la tradi-
        tion prophétique. *Bib* 60: 191–215.
1981   Séparation des eaux et de la terre ferme dans le récit sacerdotal.
        NRT 113: 512–32.
1994   Note sur la traduction de *wᵉlō'* en Exode iii 19b. *VT* 44: 60–65.
Skehan, P. W.
1954   A Fragment of the "Song of Moses" (Deut 32) from Qumran.
        BASOR 136: 12–15.
1959   Qumran and the Present State of Old Testament Studies: The
        Masoretic Text. *JBL* 78: 21–33.
1964   A Psalm Manuscript from Qumran (4QPs^b). *CBQ* 26: 313–22.
Skinner, J.
1910   *A Critical and Exegetical Commentary on Genesis.* ICC. New
        York: Scribner.
Smend, R.
1912   *Die Erzählung des Hexateuch auf ihre Quellen untersucht.* Berlin:
        Reimer.
Smend, R.
1978   *Die Entstehung des Alten Testaments.* Theologische Wissenschaft 1.
        Stuttgart/Berlin/Köln/Mainz: Kohlhammer.
Smith, G. H.
1912   *The Early Poetry of Israel in Its Physical and Social Origins.* Lon-
        don: Oxford University.
Smith, H. P.
1906   Some Ethnological Parallels to Exodus iv. 24–25. *JBL* 25: 14–24.
Smith, M. S.
1990   *The Early History of God.* San Francisco: Harper & Row.
1996   The Literary Arrangement of the Priestly Redaction of Exodus: A
        Preliminary Investigation. *CBQ* 58: 25–50.

1997   The Pilgrimage Pattern in Exodus. JSOTSup 239. Sheffield: Shef-
        field Academic Press.
Smith, W. R.
1881   The Old Testament in the Jewish Church. Edinburgh: Black.
1927   Lectures on the Religion of the Semites. 3d ed. New York:
        Macmillan.
Snaith, N. H.
1947   The Jewish New Year Festival: Its Origins and Development. Lon-
        don: Society for Promoting Christian Knowledge.
1965   Yam-Sôp: The Sea of Reeds: The Red Sea. VT 15: 395–98.
Snell, B.
1971   Tragicorum Graecorum Fragmenta I. Göttingen: Vandenhoeck &
        Ruprecht.
Soden, W. von
1964   Jahwe "Er ist, Er erweist sich." WO 3: 177–87.
1967   Kleine Beiträge zum Ugaritischen und Hebräischen. Pp. 291–300
        in Hebräische Wortforschung. Fs. W. Baumgartner. VTSup 16.
        Leiden: Brill.
1970   Mirjām-Maria "Gottesgeschenk." UF 2: 269–72.
Soggin, J. A.
1960   Kultätiologische Sagen und Katechese im Hexateuch. VT 10:
        341–47.
1966   Gilgal, Passah und Landnahme. VTSup 15: 263–77.
1985   Das Wunder am Meer und in der Wüste (Exodus, cc. 14–15).
        Pp. 379–85 in Mélanges bibliques et orientaux en l'honneur de
        M. Mathias Delcor, ed. A. Caquot et al. AOAT 215. Kevelaer:
        Butzon & Bercker; Neukirchen-Vluyn: Neukirchener Verlag.
Sourdel, D.
1952   Les cultes du Hauran à l'époque romaine. Institut Français
        d'Archéologie de Beyrouth, Bibliothèque archéologique et his-
        torique 53. Paris: Imprimerie Nationale/Geuthner.
Speir, S.
1960   PQH Ex. IV 11. VT 10: 347.
Speiser, E. A.
1941   Introduction to Hurrian. New Haven, Conn.: American Schools of
        Oriental Research.
1964   Genesis. AB 1. Garden City, N.Y.: Doubleday.
1965   Pālil and Congeners: A Sampling of Apotropaic Symbols. Pp. 389–
        93 in Studies in Honor of Benno Landsberger on his Seventy-fifth
        Birthday, ed. H. G. Güterbock and T. Jacobsen. Assyriological
        Studies 16. Chicago: University of Chicago.
Spencer, A. J.
1979   Brick Architecture in Ancient Egypt. Warminster: Aris & Phillips.
Sperber, A.
1959   The Bible in Aramaic I. Leiden: Brill.

Sperling, S. D.
1992 Blood. *ABD* 1.761–63. New York: Doubleday.
Stager, L. E.
1980 The Rite of Child Sacrifice at Carthage. Pp. 1–11 in *New Light on Ancient Carthage*, ed. J. G. Pedley. Ann Arbor: University of Michigan.
1985 The Archaeology of the Family in Ancient Israel. *BASOR* 260: 1–35.
n.d. Jerusalem and the Garden of Eden. Forthcoming in L. E. Stager, *A Heap of Broken Images*. Louisville: Westminster/John Knox.
Stamm, J. J.
1939 *Die akkadische Namengebung.* Mitteilungen der vorderasiatisch-aegyptischen Gesellschaft 44. Leipzig: Hinrichs.
Steingrimsson, S. Ö.
1979 *Vom Zeichen zur Geschichte. Eine literar- und formkritische Untersuchung von Ex 6,28–11,10.* ConBOT 14. Lund: Gleerup.
Stek, J. H.
1986 What Happened to the Chariot Wheels of Exod 14:25? *JBL* 105: 293–94.
Stendebach, F. J.
1973 Das Verbot des Knochenzerbrechens bei den Semiten. *BZ* n.f. 17: 29–38.
Stern, P. D.
1989 1 Samuel 15: Towards an Ancient View of the War-Ḥerem. *UF* 21: 413–20.
Sternberg, M.
1985 *The Poetics of Biblical Narrative.* Bloomington: Indiana University.
Stiebing, W. H., Jr.
1987 The Israelite Exodus and the Volcanic Eruption of Thera. *Catastrophism and Ancient History* 9: 69–79.
Stolz, F.
1970 *Strukturen und Figuren im Kult von Jerusalem.* BZAW 118. Berlin: de Gruyter.
1972 Die Bäume des Gottesgartens auf dem Libanon. *ZAW* 84: 141–56.
Stuart, D. K.
1976 *Studies in Early Hebrew Meter.* HSM 13. Missoula, Mont.: Scholars Press.
Sukenik, E. L.
1955 *The Dead Sea Scrolls of the Hebrew University.* Jerusalem: Hebrew University and Magnes.
Tadmor, H.
1958 Historical Implications of the Correct Rendering of Akkadian *dâku. JNES* 17: 129–41.
1962 Krônôlôgyâ. *EM* 4.247–310. Jerusalem: Bialik Institute.

1980 Treaty and Oath in the Ancient Near East: A Historian's Approach. Pp. 127–52 in *Humanizing America's Iconic Book: Society of Biblical Literature Centennial Addresses,* ed. G. M. Tucker and D. A. Knight. Chico, Calif.: Scholars Press.

Tal, A.
1981 *Targûm haššômərônî lattôrâ.* Tel Aviv: Tel Aviv University.

Tallqvist, K. L.
1966 *Assyrian Personal Names.* Orig. pub. 1914. Acta Societatis Scientarum Fennicae 48.1. Hildesheim: Olms.

Talmon, S.
1954a Hătan dāmîm. Pp. 93–96 in *U. Cassuto Volume.* ErIsr 3. Jerusalem: Israel Exploration Society.
1954b A Case of Abbreviation Resulting in Double Readings. *VT* 4: 206–8.
1958a Divergences in Calendar-Reckoning in Ephraim and Judah. *VT* 8: 48–74.
1958b The Calendar Reckoning of the Sect from the Judaean Desert. Pp. 162–99 in *Aspects of the Dead Sea Scrolls,* ed. C. Rabin and Y. Yadin. ScrHier 4. Jerusalem: Magnes.
1964 Aspects of the Textual Transmission of the Bible in the Light of Qumran Manuscripts. *Textus* 4: 95–132.
1966 The "Desert Motif" in the Bible and in Qumran Literature. Pp. 31–63 in *Biblical Motifs,* ed. A. Altmann. Cambridge, Mass.: Harvard University.
1978a har; gibhʿāh. *TDOT* 3.427–47. Grand Rapids, Mich.: Eerdmans.
1978b The Presentation of Synchroneity and Simultaneity in Biblical Narratives. Pp. 9–26 in *Studies in Hebrew Narrative Art,* ed. J. Heinemann, S. Werses. ScrHier 27. Jerusalem: Magnes.
1978c The "Comparative Method" in Biblical Interpretation—Principles and Problems. Pp. 320–56 in *Congress Volume, Göttingen 1977.* VTSup 29. Leiden: Brill.
1984 Yad wašem: An Idiomatic Phrase in Biblical Literature and Its Variations. *Hebrew Studies* 25: 8–17.
1986 *King, Cult and Calendar in Ancient Israel.* Jerusalem: Magnes.
1990 "400 Jahre" oder "vier Generationen" (Gen 15,13–15): Geschichtliche Zeitangaben oder literarische Motive? Pp. 13–25 in *Die Hebräische Bibel und ihre zweifache Nachgeschichte,* ed. E. Blum, C. Macholz, and E. W. Stegemann. Fs. R. Rendtorff. Neukirchen-Vluyn: Neukirchener Verlag.
1994 The Reckoning of the Day in the Biblical and Early Post-Biblical Periods; From Morning or from Evening? Pp. 109–20 in *The Bible in the Light of Its Interpreters,* ed. S. Japhet. Jerusalem: Magnes.

Talmon, S., and I. Knohl
1995 A Calendrical Scroll from a Qumran Cave: Mišmarot Bᵃ, 4Q321. Pp. 267–301 in *Pomegranates and Golden Bells,* ed. D. P. Wright,

D. N. Freedman, and A. Hurvitz. Fs. J. Milgrom. Winona Lake, Ind.: Eisenbrauns.

Talmon, S., and W. W. Fields
1989   The Collocation *mštyn bqyr ʿšwr wʿzwb* and Its Meaning. *ZAW* 101: 85–112.

Tarragon, J.-M. de
1980   *Le culte à Ugarit.* CahRB 19. Paris: Gabalda.
1991   La pointe de flèche inscrite des Pères Blancs de Jérusalem. *RB* 98: 244–51.

Tawil, H.
1980   Azazel the Prince of the Steppe: A Comparative Study. *ZAW* 92: 43–59.

Thiele, E. R.
1951   *The Mysterious Numbers of the Hebrew Kings.* Chicago: University of Chicago.

Thierry, G. J.
1948   The Pronunciation of the Tetragrammaton. *OTS* 5: 30–42.

Thomas, D. W.
1941   A Note on *Lîqqăhat* in Proverbs xxx. 17. *JTS* 42: 154–55.
1948   A Note on *wayyēdaʿ ʾĕlōhîm* in Exod. II. 25. *JTS* 49: 143–44.

Thompson, R. J.
1970   *Moses and the Law in a Century of Criticism Since Wellhausen.* VTSup 19. Leiden: Brill.

Thompson, S.
1955   *Motif-Index of Folk-Literature.* Bloomington: Indiana University.

Thompson, T. L.
1974   *The Historicity of the Patriarchal Narratives.* BZAW 133. Berlin: de Gruyter.
1978   The Background of the Patriarchs. *JSOT* 9: 2–43.
1987   *The Origin Tradition of Ancient Israel.* JSOTSup 55. Sheffield: JSOT.

Thompson, T. L., and D. Irvin
1977   The Joseph and Moses Narratives. Pp. 149–212 in *Israelite and Judaean History,* ed. J. H. Hayes and J. M. Miller. London: SCM.

Tigay, J. H.
1978   "Heavy of Mouth" and "Heavy of Tongue": On Moses' Speech Difficulty. *BASOR* 231: 57–67.
1979   On the Term Phylacteries (Matt 23:5). *HTR* 72: 45–53.
1982a *Təpillîn. EM* 8.883–95. Jerusalem: Bialik Institute.
1982b On the Meaning of *ṭ(w)ṭpt. JBL* 101: 321–31.

Tournay, R.
1949   Les psaumes complexes (suite). *RB* 56: 37–60.
1957   Le nom du "Buisson ardent." *VT* 7: 410–13.
1958   Recherches sur la chronologie des Psaumes. *RB* 65: 321–57.

Tov, E.
  1979   Loan Words, Homophony and Transliterations in the Septuagint. *Bib* 60: 216–36.
  1981   *The Text-Critical Use of the Septuagint in Biblical Research.* Jerusalem: Simor.
  1992   *Textual Criticism of the Hebrew Bible.* Minneapolis: Fortress; Aasen-Maastricht: Van Gorcum.
Towers, J. R.
  1959   The Red Sea. *JNES* 18: 150–53.
Trible, P.
  1984   *Texts of Terror.* Overtures to Biblical Theology 13. Philadelphia: Fortress.
Tromp, N.
  1969   *Primitive Conceptions of Death and the Nether World in the Old Testament.* BibOr 21. Rome: Pontifical Biblical Institute.
Trumbull, H. C.
  1885   *The Blood Covenant.* New York: Scribner.
  1906   *The Threshold Covenant.* 2d ed. New York: Scribner.
Turner, V.
  1967   *The Forest of Symbols.* Ithaca, N.Y.: Cornell University.
Valentin, H.
  1978   *Aaron.* OBO 18. Göttingen: Vandenhoeck & Ruprecht.
VanderKam, J. C.
  1992   Calendars. *ABD* 1.814–20. New York: Doubleday.
Van der Ploeg, J.
  1954   Les šōṭᵉrîm d'Israël. *OTS* 10: 185–96.
  1961   Les anciens dans l'ancien Testament. Pp. 175–91 in *Lex Tua Veritas,* ed. H. Gross and F. Mussner. Fs. H. Junker. Trier: Paulinus.
Van der Toorn, K.
  1988   Ordeal Procedures in the Psalms and the Passover Meal. *VT* 38: 427–45.
Van Dijk, J.
  1983   *LUGAL UD ME-LÁM-bi NIR-ĞÁL.* Leiden: Brill.
Van-Dijk-Hemmes, F.
  1994   Some Recent Views on the Presentation of the Song of Miriam. Pp. 200–6 in *A Feminist Companion to Exodus to Deuteronomy,* ed. A. Brenner. The Feminist Companion to the Bible 6. Sheffield: Sheffield Academic Press.
Vanel, A.
  1965   *L'Iconographie du dieu de l'orage.* CahRB 7. Paris: Gabalda.
Van Gennep, A.
  1960   *The Rites of Passage.* French orig. 1909. Chicago: University of Chicago.

Van Houten, C.
  1991   *The Alien in Israelite Law*. JSOTSup 107. Sheffield: JSOT.
Van Seters, J.
  1972   Confessional Reformulation in the Exilic Period. *VT* 22: 448–59.
  1983   The Place of the Yahwist in the History of Passover and Massot. *ZAW* 95: 167–82.
  1986   The Plagues of Egypt. *ZAW* 98: 31–39.
  1992   *Prologue to History*. Louisville: Westminster/John Knox.
  1994   *The Life of Moses. The Yahwist as Historian in Exodus-Numbers*. Louisville: Westminster/John Knox.
Van Zijl, P. J.
  1972   *Baal*. AOAT 10. Neukirchen-Vluyn: Neukirchener Verlag.
Vater, A. M.
  1980   Narrative Patterns for the Story of Commissioned Communication in the Old Testament. *JBL* 99: 365–82.
Vaux, R. de
  1937   Les textes de Ras Shamra et l'Ancien Testament. *RB* 46: 526–55.
  1961   *Ancient Israel*. New York: McGraw Hill.
  1964   *Les sacrifices de l'Ancien Testament*. CahRB 1. Paris: Gabalda.
  1970   The Revelation of the Divine Name YHWH. Pp. 48–75 in *Proclamation and Presence*, ed. J. I. Durham and J. R. Porter. Richmond, Va.: John Knox.
  1978   *The Early History of Israel*. French orig. 1973. Philadelphia: Westminster.
Vawter, B.
  1977   *Genesis: A New Reading*. Garden City, N.Y.: Doubleday.
Velde, H. te
  1967   *Seth, God of Confusion*. Probleme der Ägyptologie 6. Leiden: Brill.
Vermes, G.
  1956   *Discovery in the Judean Desert*. New York: Desclee.
  1957–58 Baptism and Jewish Exegesis: New Light from Ancient Sources. *NTS* 4: 308–19.
  1961   *Scripture and Tradition in Judaism*. Studia Post-Biblica 4. Leiden: Brill.
Vervenne, M.
  1987   The Protest Motif in the Sea Narrative (Ex 14,11–12). Form and Structure of a Pentateuchal Pattern. *ETL* 63: 257–71.
  1993   "The Blood Is the Life and the Life Is the Blood": Blood as Symbol of Life and Death in Biblical Tradition (Gen 9,4). Pp. 451–70 in *Ritual and Sacrifice in the Ancient Near East*, ed. J. Quaegebeur. Orientalia Lovaniensia Analecta 55. Leuven: Peeters.
  1994   The Question of "Deuteronomic" Elements in Genesis to Numbers. Pp. 243–68 in *Studies in Deuteronomy*, ed. F. G. Martínez

et al. Fs. C. J. Labuschagne. VTSup 53. Leiden/New York/Köln: Brill.

Vorländer, H.
1975 *Mein Gott.* AOAT 23. Kevelaer: Butzon & Bercker; Neukirchen-Vluyn: Neukirchener Verlag.

Vries, S. J. de
1968 The Origin of the Murmuring Tradition. *JBL* 87: 51–58.

Vriezen, T. C.
1950 'Ehje 'ašer 'ehje. Pp. 498–512 in *Festschrift Alfred Bertholet*, ed. W. Baumgartner et al. Tübingen: Mohr.
1967 Exodusstudien. Exodus I. *VT* 17: 334–53.

Wakeman, M. K.
1973 *God's Battle with the Monster.* Leiden: Brill.

Waldman, N. M.
1974 Words for "Heat" and Their Extended Meanings. *Gratz College Annual of Jewish Studies* 3: 43–48.
1976 A Comparative Note on Exodus 15:14–16. *JQR* 66: 189–92.
1989 *The Recent Study of Hebrew.* Cincinnati: Hebrew Union College; Winona Lake, Ind.: Eisenbrauns.

Waltke, B. K., and M. O'Connor
1990 *An Introduction to Biblical Hebrew Syntax.* Winona Lake, Ind.: Eisenbrauns.

Wambacq, B. N.
1976 Les origines de la *Pesah* israélite. *Bib* 57: 206–24, 301–26.
1980 Les Maṣṣôt. *Bib* 61: 31–54.
1981 Pesaḥ—Maṣṣôt. *Bib* 62: 499–518.

Ward, W. A.
1974 The Semitic Biconsonantal Root *SP* and the Common Origin of Egyptian *ČWF* and Hebrew *SÛP*: "Marsh(-Plant)." *VT* 24: 339–49.
1980 Egypto-Semitic MR, "Be Bitter, Strong." *UF* 12: 357–60.

Watson, W. G. E.
1977 Ugaritic and Mesopotamian Literary Texts. *UF* 9: 273–84.
1984 *Classical Hebrew Poetry.* JSOTSup 26. Sheffield: JSOT.
1985 Internal Parallelism in Classical Hebrew Verse. *Bib* 66: 365–83.
1989 Internal or Half-Line Parallelism in Classical Hebrew Again. *VT* 39: 44–66.

Watts, J. D. W.
1957 The Song of the Sea—Exod XV. *VT* 7: 371–80.

Watts, J. W.
1992 *Psalm and Story.* JSOTSup 139. Sheffield: JSOT.
1993 "This Song." Conspicuous Poetry in Hebrew Prose. Pp. 345–58 in *Verse in Ancient Near Eastern Prose*, ed. J. C. de Moor and W. G. E. Watson. AOAT 42. Kevelaer: Butzon & Bercker; Neukirchen-Vluyn: Neukirchener Verlag.

Weems, R. J.
1992   The Hebrew Women Are Not Like the Egyptian Women: The Ideology of Race, Gender and Sexual Reproduction in Exodus 1. *Semeia* 59: 25–33.

Weidner, E. F.
1941–44   Šilkan(ḫe)ni, König von Muṣri, ein Zeitgenosse Sargons II. *AfO* 14: 40–53.

Weimar, P.
1980   *Die Berufung des Mose.* OBO 32. Göttingen: Vandenhoeck & Ruprecht.
1985   *Die Meerwundererzählung.* Ägypten und Altes Testament 9. Wiesbaden: Harrassowitz.

Weinfeld, M.
1968   Nēkār, nokrî, nokriyyâ. *EM* 5.866–67. Jerusalem: Bialik Institute.
1972   *Deuteronomy and the Deuteronomic School.* Oxford: Clarendon.
1973   "Rider of the Clouds" and "Gatherer of the Clouds." *JANESCU* 5: 421–26.
1977a   bᶜrîth. *TDOT* 2.253–79. Grand Rapids, Mich.: Eerdmans.
1977b   Judge and Officer in Ancient Israel and in the Ancient Near East. *IOS* 7: 65–88.
1978–79   Nôsāpôt liktôbôt ʿAǧrûd. *Shnaton* 5–6: 237–39.
1983   Divine Intervention in War in Ancient Israel and in the Ancient Near East. Pp. 121–47 in *History, Historiography and Interpretation,* ed. H. Tadmor and M. Weinfeld. Jerusalem: Magnes; Leiden: Brill.

Welch, A. C.
1927   On the Method of Celebrating Passover. *ZAW* 45: 24–29.

Wellhausen, J.
1885   *Prolegomena to the History of Ancient Israel.* German orig. 1883. Edinburgh: Black.
1897   *Reste arabischen Heidentums.* 2d ed. Berlin: Reimer.
1899   *Die Composition des Hexateuchs und der historischen Bücher des Alten Testaments.* 3d ed. Berlin: Reimer.

Wensinck, A.
1925   *Arabic New-Year and the Feast of Tabernacles.* Amsterdam: Koninklijke Akademie van Wetenschappen.

West, M. L.
1971   *Early Greek Philosophy and the Orient.* London: Oxford University Press.

Wevers, J. W.
1990   *Notes on the Greek Text of Exodus.* SBLSCS 30. Atlanta: Scholars Press.
1991   *Exodus.* Göttingen Septuagint II,1. Göttingen: Vandenhoeck & Ruprecht.

1992   *Text History of the Greek Exodus*. Abhandlungen der Akademie der Wissenschaften in Göttingen, Philologisch-historische Klasse, 3rd series, 192; MSU XXI. Göttingen: Vandenhoeck & Ruprecht.
White, S. A.
1992   4Q364 & 365: A Preliminary Report. Pp. 217–28 in *The Madrid Qumran Congress: Proceedings of the International Congress on the Dead Sea Scrolls, Madrid 18–21 March, 1991*. STDJ 11. Leiden/ New York/Köln: Brill; Madrid: Editorial Complutense.
Wifall, W.
1980   The Sea of Reeds as Sheol. *ZAW* 92: 325–32.
Wijngards, J.
1965   HWŞYʾ and HʿLH: A Twofold Approach to the Exodus. *VT* 15: 91–102.
Wilcke, C.
1977   Die Anfänge der akkadischen Epen. *ZA* 67: 153–216.
Willis, T. M.
1990   Elders in Pre-exilic Israelite Society. Ph.D. diss., Harvard University.
Wilson, I.
1985   *Exodus the True Story*. San Francisco: Harper & Row.
Wilson, J. A.
1948   The Oath in Ancient Egypt. *JNES* 7: 129–56.
Wilson, R. R.
1977   *Genealogy and History in the Biblical World*. Yale Near Eastern Researches 7. New Haven, Conn.: Yale University.
1979   The Hardening of Pharaoh's Heart. *CBQ* 41: 18–36.
1980   *Prophecy and Society in Ancient Israel*. Philadelphia: Fortress.
Wimmer, J. F.
1967   Tradition Reinterpreted in Ex 6,2–7,7. *Augustinianum* 7: 407–18.
Wiseman, D. J.
1983   Mesopotamian Gardens. *AnSt* 33: 137–44.
Wit, C. de
1973   La circoncision chez les anciens Egyptiens. *Zeitschrift für Ägyptische Sprache und Altertumskunde* 99: 41–48.
Wold, D. J.
1978   The Meaning of the Biblical Penalty *Kareth*. Ph.D. diss., University of California, Berkeley.
Wolf, C. U.
1947   Traces of Primitive Democracy in Ancient Israel. *JANES* 6: 98–108.
Wolff, H. W.
1975   The Elohistic Fragments in the Pentateuch. Pp. 67–82 in *The Vitality of the Old Testament*, ed. W. Brueggemann and H. W. Wolff. Atlanta: John Knox.
Wolters, A.
1990   Not Rescue but Destruction: Rereading Exodus 15:8. *CBQ* 52: 223–40.

Worden, T.
1953   The Literary Influence of the Ugaritic Fertility Myth on the Old Testament. VT 3: 273–97.

Wright, D. P.
1987   The Disposal of Impurity. SBLDS 101. Atlanta: Scholars Press.

Wright, G. E.
1953   Deuteronomy. IB 2.311–537. New York/Nashville: Abingdon.

Yadin, Y.
1969   Tefillin from Qumran. Jerusalem: Israel Exploration Society and the Shrine of the Book.
1983   The Temple Scroll. Hebrew orig. 1977. Jerusalem: Israel Exploration Society.

Yalon, H.
1968   Mābô' ləniqqûd hammišnâ. Jerusalem: Bialik Institute.

Yardeni, A.
1991   Remarks on the Priestly Blessing on Two Ancient Amulets from Jerusalem. VT 41: 176–85.

Yaron, R.
1959   Redemption of Persons in the Ancient Near East. Revue internationale des droits de l'Antiquité 3è Série 6: 155–76.

Yeivin, I.
1980   Introduction to the Tiberian Massorah. SBLMasS 5. Chico, Calif.: Scholars Press.

Yellin, D.
1926   A Hitherto Unnoticed Meaning of NPL. JPOS 6: 164–66.

Zadok, R.
1986   Die nichthebräischen Namen der Israeliten vor dem hellenistischen Zeitalter. UF 17: 387–98.

Zakovitch, Y.
1980   A Study of Precise and Partial Derivations in Biblical Etymology. JSOT 15: 31–50.

Zenger, E.
1981   Tradition und Interpretation in Exodus XV 1–21. Pp. 452–83 in Congress Volume, Vienna 1980. VTSup 32. Leiden: Brill.
1982   Israel am Sinai. Alterberge: CIS.

Zevit, Z.
1975–76   The Priestly Redaction and Interpretation of the Plague Narrative in Exodus. JQR 66: 193–211.
1990   Three Ways to Look at the Ten Plagues. BRev 6.3: 16–23, 42–44.

Ziegler, J.
1950   Die Hilfe Gottes "am Morgen." Pp. 281–88 in Alttestamentliche Studien, ed. H. Junker and J. Botterweck. Fs. F. Nötscher. Bonn: Hanstein.

Zimmerli, W.
1977   Der "Prophet" im Pentateuch. Pp. 197–211 in *Studien zum Pentateuch*, ed. G. Braulik. Fs. W. Kornfeld. Vienna/Freiburg/Basel: Herder.
1979   *Ezekiel 1*. German orig. 1969. Hermeneia. Philadelphia: Fortress.
1982   *I Am Yahweh*. Atlanta: John Knox.
1983   *Ezekiel 2*. German orig. 1969. Hermeneia. Philadelphia: Fortress.
Zohary, M.
1982   *Plants of the Bible*. Cambridge: Cambridge University.

ANALYSIS, NOTES AND COMMENTS

◆

PART I. ISRAEL IN EGYPT
(EXODUS 1:1–11:10)

I. *As ever they oppressed him, so he multiplied* (1:1–14)

◆

1 [1(R)]And these are the names of Israel's sons coming to Egypt with Jacob; man and his *house* they came: [2]Reuben, Simeon, Levi and Judah, [3]Issachar, Zebulon and Benjamin, [4]Dan and Naphtali, Gad and Asher. [5]Now, all of the *soul* coming from Jacob's *thigh* was seventy *souls*. But Joseph was in Egypt. [6(J?)]And Joseph died, and all his brothers, and all that generation. [7(R/P)]But Israel's sons bore fruit and swarmed and multiplied and proliferated greatly, greatly, so the land was filled with them.

[8(J)]Then arose a new king over Egypt who did not know Joseph. [9]And he said to his people: "See: the people of Israel's Sons is greater and mightier than we. [10]Let us be wise concerning him, lest he multiply and, it may happen, should war come, he too be added to our enemies and fight against us and go up from the land." [11]So they set over him corvée masters in order to oppress him with their tasks, and he built storage cities for Pharaoh: Pithom and Raamses. [12]But as ever they oppressed him, so he multiplied and so he burst out, and they dreaded from before Israel's Sons. [13(P)]And Egypt made Israel's Sons work through duress, [14]for they embittered their lives through hard work in mortar and in bricks, and with all work in the field—in short, all their work with which they worked them through duress.

ANALYSIS

TEXTUAL NOTES

†1:1. *And.* We do not know if *wə-* 'and' is original. MT and Sam have the conjunction; LXX and Kenn 108, 264 do not (probably also 4QpaleoGen-Exod[l]). It seems that originally Vg, too, lacked the conjunction, since early

MSS transliterate the Hebrew name of the book as *(h)e(l)lesmoth* = *'ēlle[h]*
šəmôt 'these are the names'); only sixteenth-century editions, reflecting rena-
scent Christian Hebraism, read *ueelle* = *wə'ēlle[h]* 'and these'). Gen 46:8 similarly begins "And these are the names of Israel's sons coming to Egypt" in all
traditions; Lev 1:1 and Num 1:1 also begin with "and" in all the Versions. Most
witnesses, however, including MT, lack "and" in Deut 1:1.

There are two possibilities for Exod 1:1 — either (a) "and" has been inserted
into the MT-Sam tradition but was originally lacking, or (b) "and" is original
but has fallen out of the Greek tradition, either because of its absence in
the Hebrew *Vorlage* of LXX or by choice of the translator. If scenario (a) is
correct, the conjunction might have been inserted in imitation of Gen 46:8
and in the interests of emphasizing the continuity between Genesis and Exodus (Jacob 1992: 3). If, on the other hand, scenario (b) is correct, "and" might
have been dropped to stress the independence of Exodus, or because it does
not determine the tense of a verb as in Leviticus (*wayyiqrā['*]) and Numbers
(*waydabbēr*).

†*with Jacob.* In MT, this phrase is joined to the following, thus: "With Jacob
came man and his *house.*" This is possible, but feels unidiomatic. I rather connect "man and his *house*" to "coming to Egypt."

LXX and 4QExod[b] read "with Jacob *their father,*" presumably adding *'byhm*
as an explanatory gloss. But conceivably *'byhm* fell out of the MT tradition
through homoioarkton with the following *'yš*.

1:2. *Simeon.* Sam has "*and* Simeon."

†*and Judah.* LXX lacks the conjunction and thus divides Jacob's sons into
three groups (assuming the absence of Joseph; see below) — sons of wives, sons
of first concubine, sons of second concubine — with the last name in each set
preceded by "and." In contrast, MT highlights *yəhûdâ*, the eponymous ancestor of the *yəhûdîm* 'Judeans, Jews' (A. Welch, privately). Jacob (1992: 4)
suggests that the pause at Judah also reflects Leah's pause from childbirth after
bearing Judah (Gen 29:35).

It is difficult to decide which version is original. Note that: (a) the name
"Levi" ends with the letters *wy*; (b) "and Judah" begins *wy*, and (c) *w* and *y* were
often indistinguishable in Roman-period Hebrew script (Cross 1961a; Qimron
1972). This environment could have induced either the omission or the addition of the conjunction *w-*. But Qumran, Sam and Syr supply still more conjunctions in 1:2–4, even in the absence of letters resembling *w/y*. In light of
the general tendency to fill out the text, we might opt for the LXX *lectio brevior*
as slightly more likely to be authentic. But my translation follows MT.

†1:3. *Issachar, Zebulon.* Sam, Syr and perhaps 4QGen-Exod[a] precede both
names with *w-* 'and.'

and Benjamin. 4QExod[b] has "*Joseph* and Benjamin," while omitting "but
Joseph was in Egypt" in v 5. Thus vv 2–4 become a complete catalog of Jacob's
sons; Joseph's prior descent into Egypt is ignored. If this variant is authentic,
then Joseph surely was dropped from the MT-LXX tradition by design, not accident. The ultimate judgment depends on our assessment of v 5b (see below).

1:4. *and Naphtali.* "And" is missing in Kenn 129.

†1:5. *coming from Jacob's thigh.* LXX simply reads **ləyaʿăqōb* 'from Jacob' (cf. Gen 46:26, 27), as perhaps did 4QExod[b] (Cross 1994: 84, 85). We cannot decide whether Exod 1:5 (MT) has been influenced by Gen 46:26, or Exod 1:5 (LXX) by Gen 46:26, 27 (Cross 1958: 137–38 n. 31). The difference is not trivial, however. Gen 46:26–27 properly distinguishes the *descendants* of Jacob, which exclude the patriarch, from the *house* of Jacob, which includes him. It is the latter that numbers seventy. In contrast, the MT of 1:5 is paradoxical: Jacob implicitly comes from his own *"thigh."* But I have, with reservations, translated following MT.

†*was.* Sam has *wyhyw* 'were.'

†*seventy.* Three times the Torah gives the total of Israelites who migrated to Egypt (Gen 46:27; Exod 1:5; Deut 10:22), but the textual witnesses disagree:

(a) MT Gen 46:27; Exod 1:5; Deut 10:22 have "seventy." Gen 46:1–24 lists seventy-one male descendants of Jacob; from these must be subtracted Er and Onan, who died young (v 12), and Joseph and his two sons, already in Egypt (v 20). Thus, sixty-six "sons" of Jacob accompany him to Egypt. Adding Jacob, Joseph and his two sons makes seventy male members of the "house of Jacob" (v 27).

(b) 4QExod[b] has *ḥmš wšbʿym* 'five-and-seventy' for Exod 1:5.

(c) 4QGen-Exod[a] reads *[šbʿym] wḥmš* '[seventy]-and-five' for Exod 1:5.

(d) LXX Gen 46:27 reads "seventy-five," featuring five additional names in the lineages of Manasseh and Ephraim (Gen 46:20). The subtotals, however, are incorrect. LXX Gen 46:22 gives the total of Rachel's descendants as eighteen, while in fact there are nineteen names; and in LXX Gen 46:27, the descendants of Joseph are nine, though only eight are named. LXX Exod 1:5, too, reads "seventy-five," and MSS vary between "seventy" and "seventy-five" for Deut 10:22.

(e) Jub 44:33 has "seventy."

(f) Ezekiel the Tragedian l. 2 has "seventy."

(g) Josephus (*Ant.* 2.214) has "seventy."

(h) Acts 7:14 has "seventy-five."

Seventy is a common number in biblical and cognate literatures (Pope 1962b). Cassuto (1967: 8) compares in particular the seventy sons of the Ugaritic goddess ʾАṯiratu (cf., too, the 77/88 children of Ashertu in the Canaanite-Hittite myth of Elkunirša [Hoffner 1990: 69]) and the seventy sons of Gideon (Judg 8:30) and Ahab (2 Kgs 10:1). If the tally of Hebrew immigrants to Egypt is based in legend rather than fact, we should expect such a round number, with a later pedant listing persons by name and calculating subtotals by tribe. At a still later stage, a scribe in the early LXX-Qumran tradition would have filled out Gen 46:20 from another genealogy (e.g., Numbers 26) and adjusted Gen 46:22, 27; Exod 1:5 accordingly. He may have been motivated by the consideration that, since Ephraim and Manasseh are Jacob's adopted sons (Gen 48:5–6), their descendants, too, should be included in Genesis 46, even down to Ephraim's grandchild (this raises a chronological problem, however: did Jacob already have great-great-grandchildren [O'Connell n.d.]?).

Another factor in the change of an even seventy to seventy-five might have been enhanced verisimilitude. We may compare the "about 600,000" Israelites of 12:37 (E) becoming 625,550 in P (38:26). Similarly, 400 years in Egypt (Gen 15:13 [J]) become 430 in P (Exod 12:40–41).

Still, the very oddity of the figure seventy-five could betoken its authenticity. If so, a proto-MT scribe deleted the sons of Manasseh and Ephraim in Gen 46:20, and a later copyist, finding only seventy names in Genesis 46, emended Gen 46:27; Exod 1:15; Deut 10:22 to "seventy." But it is more characteristic of scribes, when making conscious alterations, to add than to subtract. On the whole, "seventy" is the more probable reading.

For the inconsistency of LXX MSS in Deut 10:22, there are two possible explanations. Either the original LXX had "seventy," and later scribes removed the contradiction with LXX Genesis 46; Exod 1:5 in some MSS; alternatively, the original LXX had "seventy-five" in all three passages, but only Deut 10:22 was corrected to MT in certain traditions.

SPECULATION: The inconsistency of Deut 10:22 in the Greek MSS raises the possibility that the confusion between "seventy" and "seventy-five" in the Versions reflects an inconsistent Ur-text. That is, the original MS of the Torah may have contained both figures, which all traditions have harmonized in various directions.

A final piece of evidence indirectly proves that the reading "seventy" existed in the Roman period, corroborating Jubilees and Ezekiel the Tragedian. We know that Deut 32:8 originally read, "In the Highest One's distributing land to nations, in his dividing Man's sons, he set peoples' boundaries according to the number of bənê 'ĕlōhîm" (LXX; 4QDt[j] [cf. 4QDt[q]]; Old Latin; a Syro-Hexaplaric MS [Cambridge University Oriental MS 929]; see Skehan 1959; Day 1985: 175; Duncan 1989: 110; Tov 1992: 269). Bənê 'ĕlōhîm may be rendered "the sons of Deity," "the sons of gods" or, simply, "the gods." Today we call such beings "angels." There was a widespread Jewish belief that each nation had its own god or guardian angel (Deut 4:19; Judg 11:24; Mic 4:5; Psalm 82 [Loewenstamm 1992a: 115–16 n. 68]; Dan 10:13, 20; Ben Sira 17:17; Jub 15:31–32; 3 Enoch 17:8; cf. 1 Sam 26:19).

MT, however, refers not to "sons of Deity," but to "sons of Israel." Evidently, a scandalized scribe censored the potentially polytheistic verse. Loewenstamm compares the bowdlerization of "sons of god(s)" (bənê 'ēlîm) of Ps 29:1 into "families of nations" in Ps 96:7 = 1 Chr 16:28.

Where did a copyist find the gall to censor Scripture? Presumably in the consideration that, after all, he was not really changing anything. There were seventy nations (e.g., 1 Enoch 89:59; m. Soṭa 7:5; contrast 3 Enoch 17:8), therefore seventy tutelary deities (cf. the seventy sons of Ugaritic 'Aṭiratu). And there were *seventy* sons of Jacob (Tournay 1949: 53; Knight 1976: 3; Day 1985: 146–49, 174–75; Blenkinsopp 1992: 144). In fact, Israel's population is often compared to the number of stars, sometimes associated with the angels, though the figure in mind is not seventy but either 600,000 or infinity (Gen 15:5; 22:17; etc.) (cf. Halpern 1992b: 145, 147 n. 7). For further consideration of Yahweh's celestial retinue, see NOTE to 15:11 and APPENDIX C (vol. II).

†*souls*. Missing in LXX, which thus exhibits greater similarity to Gen 46:27. Either reading could be original (but see the following).

†*But Joseph was in Egypt*. So MT, Sam, 4QGen-Exod[a] and 4QpaleoGen-Exod[l]. The phrase was evidently missing, however, from 4QExod[b]. Hence, as it includes Joseph in v 2, 4QExod[b] gives the (false) impression that Joseph entered Egypt with Jacob. This is so unexpected, it could be original. In that case, one or possibly two later hands emended the text in consideration of Joseph's prior descent into Egypt, adding "but Joseph was in Egypt" and simultaneously or subsequently excising Joseph from v 3 (Cross 1994: 85).

To complicate matters further, LXX places "but Joseph was in Egypt" at the end of v 4. The presence of the phrase in two different places in two different traditions can only have come about if, behind either MT or LXX, lay a MS that, like 4QExod[b], omitted these words. Later, in one tradition or the other, a corrector reinserted the words — in the wrong place. Indeed, the phrase *wywsp hyh bmṣrym* could easily have fallen out, either from v 4b (LXX) by homoioarkton with *wyhy* or from v 5b by homoioteleuton with *šb'ym*. The latter process would also account for the loss of *npš* 'soul' in the LXX *Vorlage* (see previous TEXTUAL NOTE). Since the arrangement in LXX is slightly more natural (*lectio facilior*), MT may be superior (O'Connell n.d.). But we really cannot decide. Indeed, it is possible that the phrase was not in the original text at all, as in 4QExod[b] (cf. Cross 1958: 137 n. 31).

1:7. *bore fruit and swarmed and multiplied*. LXX "increased and became many and became common" may reflect a *Vorlage* inverting *wyšrṣw* 'and swarmed' and *wyrbw* 'and multiplied' (cf. Wevers 1990: 3). We cannot be sure, however, since Greek *ginesthai chydaios* 'become common' is never otherwise equivalent to Hebrew *šāraṣ*.

1:8. *new king*. Sam, *Tgs.*, Symmachus, Aquila and Theodotion agree with MT, but LXX and *Bib. Ant.* 9:1 have "*another* king," presumably a paraphrase and possibly derived from Judg 2:10: "*another* generation arose." Davila (1994: 19), however, proposes an inner-Greek corruption: *neōteros* 'younger' > *heterōs* 'another.'

1:10. *him*. In vv 10–12, MT and 4QGen-Exod[a] speak of Israel in the collective singular, while LXX, Syr, *Fragmentary Targum* and *Tgs. Onqelos* and *Ps.-Jonathan* use the plural. Sam, although it begins with the singular (*'lyw*), soon switches to the plural (*'nwtm*); 2QExod[a] uses plural verbs in v 12 (see below). MT, containing the least expected reading, is likely correct. The ambivalence may be attributable to the double subject of v 9: *'am* 'people' and *bənê* 'Sons' (R. Levitt Kohn, privately). Indeed, *'am* itself is inherently ambiguous, being both singular and plural.

come. Citing incongruence in grammatical number, many emend MT *tiqre(ʾ)nâ* to *tiqrāʾēnnû* 'befall *us*,' following LXX, Sam, Syr and *Tg. Onqelos.* But interchange of *w* and *h* would be anomalous. More likely, these Versions are misinterpreting *-nâ* as the Aramaic suffix *-nāʾ* 'us.' See further NOTE.

†1:11. *they set.* LXX has *"he* [Pharaoh] set." If LXX is correct, then the plural of MT and Sam reflects harmonization with the plural *yəʿannû* 'they oppressed' (v 12).

†*Pithom and Raamses.* Ancient witnesses show great variety in their treatment of these names. *Tgs. Ps.-Jonathan* and *Neofiti I* identify the cities as Tanis and Pelusium. LXX transliterates the names, adding "and On, that is, Heliopolis," probably a gloss by an Alexandrian scribe desirous of magnifying his ancestors' achievements; Josephus (*Ant.* 2.203), in the same spirit, even throws in the Pyramids! The third/second-century B.C.E. historian Artapanus refers to the building of Heliopolis and Tessan, the latter probably an error for either Saïs (= Tanis) or Goshen. Sam and Sibylline Oracle 5:182 call Pithom "Python"; *Sam. Tg.* reads *pywm.* MT's "Pithom and Raamses" is the best reading, as these are the names of actual Egyptian cities (see APPENDIX B, vol. II).

1:12. *oppressed him.* 2QExod[a] reads "oppressed *them*" (*ʾwtm* [*sic*]), supporting LXX and the Targumim. I follow MT, however; see TEXTUAL NOTE to v 10.

†*he multiplied.* Sam has *yprh* 'he was fruitful,' vs. MT *yrbh* 'he multiplied.' Sam has been influenced by *pārû* 'bore fruit' (v 7), by the visual and aural similarity of *yprh* and *yrbh* and perhaps by the following *yprṣ.* 2QExod[a], along with LXX and the Targumim, support MT "multiplied," but have the verb in the plural, as throughout vv 10–12. But the reading of MT and 4QGen-Exod[a], *kēn yirbe(h),* creates a fine play with v 10: "lest he multiply . . . so he multiplied" (Cassuto 1967: 11; Greenberg 1969: 33).

so he burst out. LXX paraphrases (?): "so they became very, very mighty" (*wyʿmṣw bmʾd mʾd*), and 2QExod[a] has a variant *wkn yšrṣw* 'and so they teemed.' Both readings are secondary, influenced by v 7. 4QGen-Exod[a] also has a plus, no longer legible.

they dreaded. LXX, the Targumim and most likely 2QExod[a] (Tov 1992: 131–32) have "the *Egyptians* dreaded." This is evidently a secondary insertion to signal a change of subject, the more necessary as these Versions put all the verbs in the plural.

1:13. *Egypt.* All the ancient translations paraphrase: "the Egyptians," not only here but wherever *miṣrayim* connotes persons, rather than a land (future instances will not be noted). In general, the Hebrew original is prone to collective language, which the Versions explicitly pluralize; many examples will appear under TEXTUAL NOTES below.

†*made . . . work.* Though vocalized as a Hiphʿil in standard MT (*wayyaʿăbidû*), the verb could also be read as a Qal *wayyaʿabdû,* with no difference in meaning (cf. Kenn 185 [first hand]).

†1:14. *they embittered.* 4QGen-Exod[a] uniquely reads *wymrr* 'and he (Egypt) embittered.' This *lectio difficilior* could be correct.

SOURCE ANALYSIS

Exod 1:1–5a might be Priestly, but more likely comes from the Redactor (Fohrer 1964: 9; Friedman 1987: 250). The case for P is as follows: "These are the names" is otherwise a Priestly cliché (Gen 25:13; 36:10; 46:8, etc.; also Gen 36:40 [J]). R's signature is "these are the *generations*" (Gen 2:4; 5:1; 6:9; etc.) (Friedman 1981: 44–132; 1987: 227). Furthermore, Exod 1:5 closely resembles Gen 46:26–27 (P), "All of the *soul* coming of Jacob to Egypt, coming out from his *thigh*, besides the *women* [wives] of Jacob's sons, all of the *soul* was sixty-six. And Joseph's sons that were born to him in Egypt were two; all of the *soul* of Jacob's house coming to Egypt was seventy." Arguably, then, Exod 1:1–5a is from P, 1:1a being identical to Gen 46:8a (P).

But these arguments are not quite compelling. Since 1:2–3 is not a genealogy, but a list, "names" would be more appropriate than "generations" for R as well as P. As for the similarity to Genesis 46, it is as easy to imagine the Redactor quoting P as to picture P repeating itself. Moreover, without the intervening JE matter, Exod 1:1 follows too closely upon Gen 46:27 (P) to belong to the same document. On the contrary, Exod 1:1–5a seems composed for exactly the purpose it now serves: to introduce the second book of the Torah and summarize the essentials for readers unfamiliar with Genesis. This would have to be the work of the Redactor, the creator of the five-scroll Torah (see INTRODUCTION). Thus, while formally distinct from the *tôlədôt* 'generations' passages, 1:1–5a continues the Redactor's pattern of using name lists to mark generational transitions (Davies 1992: 24).

In fact, the author of 1:1–5a appears to have misconstrued Gen 46:26–27 (A. Welch, privately). According to Gen 46:26, the number of persons "coming from Jacob's *thigh*" is sixty-six; seventy is the sum of his *household*, including himself (Gen 46:27). By collapsing Gen 46:26 and 27 (P), Exod 1:1–5a shows that its author missed this distinction, i.e., was not the Priestly Writer. But MT may be incorrect in 1:5a (see TEXTUAL NOTE).

Exod 1:5b, too, is Redactorial. Were the half-verse Priestly, it would originally have flowed out of Gen 50:13 as follows: "His [Jacob's] sons carried him to the land of Canaan and buried him in the cave of the field of Machpelah, which field Abraham had bought as a burial-property from Ephron the Hittite in Mamre's presence, *but Joseph was in Egypt*"—i.e., Joseph did not attend his father's burial. This seems forced, however; certainly Joseph goes back to Canaan in J (Gen 50:4–11, 14). And if the phrase "Joseph was in Egypt" originally stood at the end of v 4 (LXX), it is all the more clearly from R, being embedded in Redactorial matter (see TEXTUAL NOTES).

Skipping v 6 for the moment, I would assign 1:7 to either P or R. Typically Priestly idioms are *pārû* 'bore fruit,' *(way)yišrəṣû* 'swarmed,' *(way)yirbû* 'multiplied,' *(wat)timmālē'* 'was filled' and *bim'ōd mə'ōd* 'very, very' (see McNeile 1908: xii–xiii). On the other hand, the verb *(way)yaʿaṣmû* 'proliferated' is not typical of P, but rather appears in JE (vv 9, 20), again paired with *rbb/rby* 'to be great, many.' Such a mixing of Priestly and JE language could be indicative of R (cf. Van Seters 1994: 19). That 1:7 follows v 6 (J) so well also suggests it is from the editorial R stratum.

Exod 1:6 is non-Priestly and originally flowed directly into 1:8, skipping v 7. The resulting sentence—"And Joseph died, and all his brothers, and all that generation, and there arose a new king over Egypt, who did not know Joseph"—strikingly resembles Judg 2:8a–10: "And Joshua died . . . and also all that generation were gathered to their fathers, and another generation arose after them, who did not know Yahweh . . ." (Vriezen 1967). Whatever the explanation for this phenomenon (common authorship, common source, common idiom, common Deuteronomistic editing [see Blum 1990: 102–3; APPENDIX A, vol. II]), it decisively links 1:6 to v 8, without v 7.

Exod 1:6, 8–12 comes from a single source. One sign of unity, at least between vv 10 and 12, is the parallelism "lest it multiply . . . so it multiplied (Cassuto 1967: 11; Greenberg 1969: 33). And the repeated verb ʿny 'oppress' connects 1:12 with v 11. Considerable evidence links the passage to the Yahwist. First, E already described Joseph's death in Gen 50:26 (Schmidt 1988: 21). Moreover, the root ʿny seems to connect vv 11–12 with Gen 15:13 (J) (cf. Fishbane 1979: 64). Ackerman (1974: 81) compares the sequence hinnē(h) . . . hābâ 'see . . . let us' (vv 9–10) to Gen 11:6–7 (J): hēn . . . hābâ (see also Davies 1992: 56). And the Egyptians' self-fulfilling fear, that Israel might multiply and leave Egypt (v 8), recalls Genesis 11 (J): humans bring about their dispersion by taking steps to prevent it, building the Tower of Babel. Furthermore, 1:10 contains the root śnʾ 'hate,' shown by Friedman (1998) to be characteristic of the Greater J corpus, though it appears elsewhere, especially in legal materials. And Ackerman (1974: 80) finds punning between vv 8 and 10—yôsēp, nôsap—and wordplay is characteristic of J (cf. especially Gen 30:24 [J]). Finally, since Exod 1:15–21 (E) envisions two Hebrew midwives serving a presumably small Hebrew population, the non-Priestly description of Israel's proliferation in 1:6, 8–12 should be Yahwistic.

Still, one could muster arguments for assigning 1:6, 8–12 to E. Friedman (1987: 66), for example, finds in the "corvée masters" (v 11) an Elohistic polemic against Solomon's conscription. One might also invoke the similarity of vv 9, 11 (hinnē[h] . . . ʿam . . . rab . . . bəsiblōtām) to 5:5 (hēn rabbîm . . . ʿam . . . missiblōtām) (E). Schmidt (1988: 21), moreover, compares v 12 to Num 22:3, "And Moab feared the people greatly, for it was great (rbb), and Moab dreaded (qwṣ) Israel's sons," which may be Elohistic (Friedman 1987: 253). And 1:9 (ʿam . . . rab wəʿāṣûm) is echoed in 1:20b (wayyireb hāʿām wayyaʿaṣmû), probably Elohistic (see SOURCE ANALYSIS to 1:15–21, however)—but rbb and ʿṣm are often parallel in biblical and Ugaritic literature (RSP 1.516). Lastly, 1:8–12 flows easily into the Elohistic midwife story (1:15–21).

Exod 1:13–14 is clearly Priestly. The redundant style of v 14 is characteristic of P. And the word perek 'duress' is restricted to P (Lev 25:43, 46, 53) and Ezekiel (34:4).

We may now compare and contrast the Priestly and Yahwistic accounts of Israel's enslavement. P merely reports that the Egyptians impressed Israel into servitude (1:13–14). According to J, however, the Egyptians, forgetting all they owed the Hebrews and fearing the fertility of a free Israel, attempted simultaneously to exploit and oppress them. But their fear of Israel grew greater, not less, as the slaves continued to multiply. The sources differ in one detail: while J describes the Hebrews as having *built* the *city* of Raamses (1:11), P says they *inhabited* the *"land* of Raamses" (Gen 47:11; Exod 12:37; cf. Num 33:5 [R]).

REDACTION ANALYSIS

With the combination of JE and P, the break between the patriarchal and Mosaic ages became sharper, if only because Genesis and Exodus were now written on separate scrolls. Only later, we assume, did Jews set down the entire Pentateuch on one huge roll. Since Exodus 1 now opened a new volume, it became desirable to provide a partial summary of Genesis. Thus in 1:1–5, the Redactor tells of eleven Hebrew families descending into Egypt to join a twelfth, led by their common ancestor Jacob-Israel. The initial "and," if original, signals to readers that Exodus is a sequel (see TEXTUAL NOTE).

Rather than make up his own words, the Redactor adapted older Priestly material—specifically, Gen 46:8–27. First, in Exod 1:1a, he reproduced Gen 46:8a *verbatim* ("and these are the names of Israel's sons coming to Egypt"). Then, as we have seen, Gen 46:26–27 was compacted somewhat carelessly in Exod 1:5 (SOURCE ANALYSIS). From the negative statement "besides [i.e., not counting] the *women* of Jacob's sons" (Gen 46:26), an explanation of the total seventy, the Redactor inferred that "man and his *house* they came." He then listed the sons, albeit not in the order of Genesis 46 (see NOTE to 1:2). The parenthetical, almost defensive "but Joseph was in Egypt," if original, assures us that nobody has been forgotten; in fact, the tally of Gen 46:27 includes Joseph's Egyptian-born sons. In this manner, the editor, exercising great restraint, manufactured a prologue to his new book without presuming to work from whole cloth.

One inevitable and striking effect of the combination of parallel sources: the aggregation of verbs connoting fertility (vv 7 [R/P], 9, 12 [J], 20 [E]). These signal the fulfillment of God's promise to the Patriarchs (Gen 15:5; 17:2, 4–6; 22:17; 32:13).

Lastly, in the composite text, "Egypt made [them] work (*wayyaʿăbidû*)" (1:13 [P]) echoes the prediction that Israel would work for a foreign nation (*waʿăbādûm, yaʿăbōdû*) (Gen 15:13–14 [J]; cf. Fishbane 1979: 64). Redaction thus reinforces the evocation of God's covenant with Abraham, raising expectations of redemption.

NOTES

1:1. *these are the names.* The Bible enumerates Jacob's sons in various orders. Exod 1:1–5 most closely resembles Gen 35:23–26, which groups the sons roughly by their mothers' rank: chief wife Leah, second wife Rachel, Rachel's maid Bilhah, Leah's maid Zilpah (Bilhah precedes Zilpah either because she bore first [Gen 30:4–13] or else to create an implicit chiasm: sons of Leah, Rachel, Rachel's maidservant, Leah's maidservant [D. N. Freedman, privately]). The major difference from Gen 35:23–26 is that Joseph receives special treatment in Exod 1:5 (but see TEXTUAL NOTE).

Egypt. Hebrew *miṣrayim* corresponds to Akkadian-Arabic *miṣr(u)*. Like many place-names (*'eprayim, maḥănayim, qarnayim, qiryātayim,* etc.), *miṣrayim* appears dual. Does it refer to Upper and Lower Egypt? Or is *-ayim* rather some sort of locative suffix (cf. GKC §88c)? Although the true etymology of *miṣr* is unknown, the Israelites probably associated it with the roots *ṣwr* and *ṣrr,* connoting distress and hostility (Ezek 30:16; Ps 78:42; 106:11). Sometimes Egypt is called *māṣôr,* homophonous with terms for "distress," "fortress" and "siege."

house. Bayit connotes "household, family."

1:2. *Reuben.* The name appears to mean "Look, a son!"

Simeon. "Obedient," describing either the bearer of the name or the god attentive to his worshiper's prayer (Freedman, privately).

Levi. There is a large literature on the etymology of *lēwî,* most finding a connection with the Levites' sacred office (see Cody 1969: 29–33). Among the proposals are "Attached one," i.e., to God (cf. Gen 29:34; Num 18:2, 4; Zech 2:15); "Whirling dancer" (< *lwy* 'twist') and "the One of serpents" (Luther *apud* Meyer 1906: 426). Others see a borrowing from South Arabian *lw'* 'consecrated person' (see discussion of de Vaux 1961: 369–70). Levin (*apud* Waldman 1989: 10) even makes a connection with Greek *laos* 'people.' To my knowledge, no one has suggested that *lēwî* indeed means "attached person" in the sense of "sojourner, resident alien." Thus *lēwî* would be quasi-synonymous with *gēr;* cf. Isa 14:1: *wənilwâ haggēr 'ălêhem wənispəḥû 'al-bêt ya'ăqōb* 'the sojourner will be joined (*lwy*) to them and they will be attached to Jacob's House.' Owning no tribal territory, all Levites were in effect sojourners. We read of Levite *gērîm* in Judges 17, 19; and Deuteronomy often conjoins "the Levite and the sojourner" (14:29; 16:11, 14; 26:11, 12, 13). Cody (1969: 55) describes the early Levites as "*gērîm* with priestly specialization" (so also Gunneweg 1965 *passim*). This interpretation, though unprovable, fits the evidence and does not require that the Levites originated as a sacred tribe.

Judah. The etymology of *yəhûdâ* remains uncertain. The name exists in the variants *yəhûdî* (Jer 36:14, 21–23), *yəhûdît* (Gen 26:34), *yohdāy/yahdî* (1 Chr 2:47) and *yəhûd* (Josh 19:45). The last is also the Aramaic name of the nation of Judah (Dan 2:25; 5:13; 6:14; Ezra 5:1, 8; 7:14). Assyrian sources call Judah *ya-ú-di, ya-a-ḫu-du* or *ya-ku-du.*

Albright (1920: 68 n. 1) derives *yəhûdâ* from an Arabic root referring to religious guidance or consecration, while Lipiński (1973) invokes an Arabic root denoting ravines. Lewy (1944: 479) parses *yəhûdâ* as Hurrian, "Pertaining to Yahweh," in which case we would have to posit an original **yahuz(z)i* (cf. Speiser 1941: 116). The simplest explanation, though not without difficulties, remains Albright's (1927: 168–78) later opinion: *yəhûdâ* is short for **yəhûdə'ēl* 'May God be praised.'

1:3. *Issachar.* *Yiśśākār* seems to consist of the elements *yiš* 'there is' and *śākār* 'wage, reward' (note the ben Naphthali vocalization *yiśśākār* [Tov 1992: 46]).

Zebulon. *Zəbûlūn* means "Elevated, lordly." As a divine epithet, it is associated particularly with Canaanite Baal.

Benjamin. *Binyāmîn* means "Son of the *right hand* (i.e., the south)," presumably because Benjamin was the southernmost tribe of Israel before the incorporation of Judah (Halpern 1983: 9–12, 118–20, 146–59, 173–77). The same personal name appears at Mari as *bi-ni-ya-mi-na* (ARM XXII.328.16). The Mari texts also frequently mention an ethnic group "Sons of the South" (*DUMU*^mcš *ya-mi-na*), of disputed pronunciation and relation to biblical Benjamin (see Tadmor 1958: 130 n. 12; Malamat 1989: 31, 35 n. 29).

1:4. *Dan.* "He judged, vindicated" or perhaps simply "Judge" (cf. *dānî'ēl* 'God is my Judge' [?]). The name *'ăbîdān* (Num 1:12) means either "My father has judged" or "My father is Dan," in which case Dan is really a divine name.

Naphtali. "Wrestler" or "Twisted."

Gad and Asher. The names *gād* and *'āšēr* may both refer to fortune. *Gad* (*sic*) is also a Phoenician-Aramean deity memorialized in the place-names Baal Gad (Josh 11:17) and Gaddah (Josh 15:27). The feminine of Asher, *'ăšērâ*, is a goddess worshiped throughout the Near East (see Maier 1986).

1:5. *soul.* Like English "soul," Hebrew *nepeš* means "spirit," "person," "life" and "living being." A less literalistic rendering of v 5a might be "all the life coming from Jacob's *thigh* was seventy persons." But more likely, *nepeš* is used collectively, as if a plural: "all the *persons.*"

thigh. As in Gen 24:2, 9 (J); 46:26 (P); 47:29 (J); Judg 8:30, *yārēk* is a euphemism for the genitals; cf. Hebrew *raglayim* 'legs, feet, pudenda' and Akkadian *birkān* 'knees, testicles.' But *yārēk* may also denote the loin (the lower back), perhaps considered, as in English, the engine of virility.

seventy. On the divergent traditions about the number of Jacob's descendants, see TEXTUAL NOTE. Later we will read of seventy elders, corresponding to the seventy Israelite clans (24:1, 9; Num 11:24–25). See also NOTE to 15:27.

1:6. *Joseph died.* Joseph did not necessarily die first, but his death was more noteworthy than his brothers' (Calvin).

and all that generation. This seems redundant. The sense might be "*that is,* all that generation." Or the intent may be to include Joseph's *Egyptian* contemporaries, most notably his royal patron.

1:7. *sons.* Since Hebrew uses *bānîm* 'sons' to include daughters, "Israel's sons" are the whole family, male and female. There is nevertheless good reason to stress the masculine terminology: Israelite identity descended through the male line, in contrast to later Jewish practice.

swarmed. *Šāraṣ*, ordinarily said of animals, is used of humans only here and in Gen 9:7 (P); cf. the comparison of humanity to fish and reptiles/insects (*remeś*) in Hab 1:14. The diction of 1:7 may suggest that the Egyptians view the Israelites as vermin (Knight 1976: 4); compare their loathing in 1:12. The animal metaphor implicit in "swarmed" complements the vegetable image "bore fruit."

proliferated. The root ʿṣm can also mean "be mighty," but numbers, not strength, are at issue here (cf. Jer 15:8; Ps 105:24). In Exod 1:9, on the other hand, ʿāṣûm is better rendered "mighty," since it parallels "great," and the subject is potential war. Liverani (1990b: 222 n. 26) observes that, in general, pastoral tribalists idealize intensive reproduction, while urban agriculturalists tend to define blessing as the accumulation of goods.

the land. Hāʾāreṣ must be Egypt. Some argue for the Land of Raamses, where, according to P (Gen 47:11), the Israelites had been settled by Joseph's Pharaoh (Hyatt 1971: 57). But that was *before* the population explosion. After such an accumulation of verbs denoting increase, a statement that the Israelites filled the region of Egypt they had previously inhabited would be anticlimactic. Rather, the echo of Gen 1:28; 9:1, "bear fruit and multiply and fill the land [i.e., the world]," implies that here, too, "the land" is a broad region (Jacob 1992: 9); see also COMMENT.

1:8. *new king.* "There arose a king that did not know Joseph" would have sufficed. Why a "*new* king"? Many speculate that the "new king" has founded a new dynasty (e.g., Josephus *Ant.* 2.202; Durham 1987: 7). A more conservative interpretation would be that the "new king," like the "new wife" of Deut 24:5, has not been king for very long. His headstrong action would exemplify the folly of youth upon attaining power (cf. 1 Kgs 12:1-19). The simplest explanation, however, is that this "new king" contrasts with the old king, Joseph's Pharaoh; accordingly, LXX and *Bib. Ant.* 9:1 paraphrase: "another king."

did not know Joseph. In other words, the new king ignored Joseph's former salvation of Egypt and did not acknowledge the benefits conferred upon the Hebrew vizier and his kin (Bekhor Shor). On the theory that 1:8 reflects the historical reversion from Hyksos (i.e., Semitic) to native Egyptian rule, see APPENDIX B (vol. II).

1:9. *his people.* This might refer to the king's advisers, or perhaps the entire people. In any case, Pharaoh is not the only culprit. All Egypt is implicated in the oppression of Israel, as is clear from the plurals in 1:11-14 (Jacob 1992: 10).

people of Israel's Sons. The text adds the seemingly unnecessary ʿam 'people' to signal that, henceforth, bənê yiśrāʾēl are no longer Jacob's twelve sons, but a great people (among others, Greenberg 1969: 20)—hence my capitalization. There may be, moreover, an effort to balance the "people" of Israel against ʿammô 'his [Pharaoh's] people,' to emphasize that the conflict is between two sovereign nations (Fox 1986: 11). ʿAm bənê yiśrāʾēl is grammatically ambiguous; it could also be interpreted "Israel's Sons *have become* a people."

greater and mightier than we. In the immediate context, one is tempted to render, "*too* great and mighty for us," a less extravagant claim (Holzinger 1900: 2; McNeile 1908: 3). Parallel passages, however, support our translation (Num 14:12; Deut 9:14; Ps 105:24; cf. Deut 7:1; 9:1; 11:23; *KTU* 1.3.i.12)

(Greenberg 1969: 20). Thus 1:9 makes the historically preposterous claim that the Israelites became more powerful than the Egyptians (but see APPENDIX B [vol. II] on the Hyksos dominion over Egypt).

Pharaoh's paranoia is ludicrous, yet sinister. Demagogues often credit weak minorities with vast powers. Elsewhere, the Bible depicts the Egyptian ruling class as obsessively xenophobic (Gen 42:9, 12; 43:32; 46:34). Egyptian sources attest to their tight control on immigration and emigration (Greenberg 1969: 21–22).

1:10. *be wise.* Most render *niṯḥakkəmâ* as "let us deal shrewdly" (RSV) or the like, without conveying the reflexivity of the Hithpaʿel conjugation. In Eccl 7:16, at least, *hiṯḥakkēm* means "be wise," not "act wisely." Perhaps the verb in Exod 1:10 means "take counsel together," again stressing the complicity of all Egypt (cf. NOTES to vv 9, 11). Ackerman (1974: 80) even finds an ironical reference to the legendary wisdom of Egypt (cf. Isa 19:11–12; Acts 7:22): Pharaoh's "wisdom" leads to his people's decimation.

But it is indeed initially shrewd of the Egyptians to convert their problem— Israel's fertility—into an asset—slavery. Were the Hebrews assaulted outright, they might launch the very attack the Egyptians fear (Ramban). Moreover, in the early years of his reign, an unscrupulous ruler might be wise to foment xenophobia in order to unite his people; Childs (1974: 15) calls attention to the telltale "us . . . them" language.

him. Hebrew employs collective language far more often than does English. There is no neuter gender; all nouns are either masculine or feminine.

lest he multiply. Cassuto (1967: 11) and Greenberg (1969: 33) catch the assonance between *pen-yirbe(h)* 'lest he multiply' (v 10) and *kēn yirbe(h)* 'so he multiplied' (v 12).

come. Most puzzling is the form *tiqre(ʾ)nâ* (Kenn 181, 277 *tqrʾn*) (< *qrʾ* II = *qry* 'befall'; compare Gen 42:4 and Arad Ostracon 24:16 [*AHI* 2.024]). The verb is ostensibly plural, though its antecedent *milḥāmâ* 'war' is singular. Sforno infers that the language is elliptical: "war" implies the "evils and troubles of any war." Cassuto (1967: 10), taking up a suggestion as old as Gesenius and Ewald (*apud* Dillmann 1880: 6), more plausibly invokes the energic suffix *-na* of Arabic and Ugaritic. (Here the energic may be dependent on the preceding *pen* 'lest, suppose,' just as jussive clauses often feature *nāʾ*, probably another energic vestige [Gordon 1965: 72].) Other traces of the energic, all in biblical poetry, are briefly treated by Cross and Freedman (1975: 19, 112); the most pertinent, cited already by Rashbam, is *tišlaḥnâ* 'she [sic] sent' (Judg 5:26). (Dahood [1971: 348], too, recognizes the energic in Exod 1:10, but derives the verb from *qrʾ* I 'call' in the Qal Passive, rendering, "when war is declared.")

If *tiqre(ʾ)nâ* is in fact an archaism, its presence in prose is surprising. Does the author convey Pharaoh's hauteur by making him speak a highfalutin dialect of Hebrew (cf. Jacob 1992: 12; NOTE to 5:2)?

fight against us. Here Pharaoh betrays his ignorance, not only of Joseph but of Joseph's god (cf. 5:2, etc.), who is responsible for all of Israel's successes

(Gen 41:16). It is Yahweh who will fight against Egypt. Israel will be completely passive (14:14, 25; 15:1–18), not to say cowardly (14:10–12).

go up from the land. We might expect the Egyptians to fear that Israel would conquer the land. Some even attempt to read *ʿālâ min-hāʾāreṣ* in this way (see Schmidt 1988: 3–4). The best effort is Bekhor Shor's, taking *min* 'from' as comparative: "he will become more exalted *than* the land" (cf. Deut 28:43). But Bekhor Shor himself finds this forced and prefers the plain sense: the Israelites might function as a fifth column and help an enemy to overthrow their oppressors, then take advantage of the chaos and leave. (We might alternatively consider the final two clauses of v 10 as chronologically reversed [hysteron proteron]: Israel might leave the land, join Egypt's enemies and then march back in triumph.)

But I am not sure we can or should rationalize Pharaoh's concerns. The Yahwist is clearly foreshadowing future events. By making an exodus the king's worst fear, the author ensures that Pharaoh's worst fear will be realized (cf. Childs 1974: 15; Davies 1992: 41). For the irony, compare Gen 11:4, 8 (J): the people build a tower to prevent their dispersion, thereby bringing about their dispersion. Indeed, it probably never occurred to the Yahwist or his sources that the Hebrews might have wished to remain in Egypt as rulers, since that is not what happened in fact and tradition.

SPECULATION: Those who favor interpreting "the land" (v 7) as the "Land of Raamses," which I reject (see NOTE), might read similarly in v 10: Pharaoh simply fears that Israel might leave its ghetto.

1:11. they set. The Egyptian people as a whole is explicitly implicated in the oppression, at least in MT (see TEXTUAL NOTE) (Maimonides *apud* Jacob 1992: 16); cf. Deut 26:6, "the Egyptians mistreated us."

corvée. I.e., conscription of men for massive labor projects. Schmidt (1988: 34) suggests that *mas* refers collectively to the workers, rather than to the institution itself, like peripheral Akkadian *massu*. In ancient Egypt, Canaan and monarchic Israel, commoners were periodically impressed for the execution of massive public and royal works (Bakir 1952; Mendelsohn 1962; Rainey 1970; for Israelite epigraphic evidence, see *AHI* 100.782). If the author (or his source) was aware that native Egyptians, too, were subject to the corvée, perhaps he regarded its imposition on Israel, not as a special act of hostility, but as the removal of an exemption (cf. Gen 47:21 [LXX; Sam]).

to oppress. The verb *ʿinnâ* can also mean "humiliate." Possibly, the point is that Israel is degraded socially through conscription. But more likely, the reference is to physical coercion.

Pharaoh's measure seems something of a *non sequitur*: how would oppression reduce the population? One first thinks of ill health and workplace accidents, but Bekhor Shor suggests that the people would simply be too fatigued to copulate.

their tasks. Who is "their"? LXX avoids the question by ignoring the pronominal suffix on *siblōtām*. Holzinger (1900: 2) observes that "their" should refer to the Egyptians, since Israel is grammatically singular in the sentence; cf., too, *siblōt miṣrayim* 'Egypt's burdens' (6:6, 7 [P]). On the other hand, elsewhere in JE, the suffix on "tasks" refers to the Israelites (2:11 [J]; 5:5 [E]).

The exact nuance of *səbālōt* is uncertain. Its singular, *sēbel*, is cognate to Mari Akkadian *sablum* 'labor gang,' and so perhaps *bəsiblotām* means "in their labor gangs" (cf. our discussion of *mas* 'corvée/conscripts' above).

storage cities. The ancient translations are divided in their understanding of *miskənôt*. The Targumim have *'ôṣārā'* 'storehouse,' while LXX renders *ochyrai* 'fortified' (also Calvin; Mazar 1968). Probably we would do best to combine the two approaches and take *miskənôt* as fortified storage cities (see 2 Chr 32:27–28, "Hezekiah . . . made for himself treasuries for silver and for gold . . . and *miskənôt* for the harvest of grain and wine and oil").

Pharaoh. The royal epithet underwent considerable semantic evolution within Egyptian before Hebrew borrowed it. In the third millennium, *pr-ʿ3* 'big house' described the royal palace proper. By 1500, however, it denoted the reigning king of Egypt, and by the ninth century, it was prefixed directly to the monarch's name. In the eighth century, *pr-ʿ3* was treated as if it were one of the ruler's names. Thereafter, *pr-ʿ3* became a functional equivalent of "king."

Although the Bible names later rulers of Egypt—e.g., Shishak, Hophra, Necho—the Egyptian monarchs of Genesis and Exodus are anonymous; or, rather, "Pharaoh" is treated as the name borne by each. Thus we do not find "*the* Pharaoh" (**happarʿō[h]*) or "*Egypt's* Pharaoh" (**parʿō[h] miṣrayim*), but "Pharaoh, king of Egypt." The Aramaic "Adon Letter" (*KAI* 266; sixth century) may similarly use "Pharaoh, the lord of kings" as a name, but this is not quite clear. The Assyrian annals of Sargon II (eighth century) mention "Pir'u, king of Muṣri," which ought to mean "Pharaoh, king of Egypt," an exact parallel to Hebrew *parʿō(h) melek miṣrayim* (Luckenbill 1926–27: 2.7, 26–27, 105). Strangely, however, this appears not to be an Egyptian Pharaoh, but rather a Sinaitic prince whose name or epithet, coincidentally or purposely, resembles a native Egyptian title (Weidner 1941–44: 45–46). The King Pheros mentioned in Herodotus *Histories* 2.111 may be yet another survival.

Pithom and Raamses. On these cities, see APPENDIX B, vol. II.

1:12. *so he multiplied.* Jacob (1992: 15) observes that fecundity is a characteristic survival strategy of oppressed classes. On the echo of v 9, see NOTE.

they dreaded. The Egyptians' attempt to alleviate their fear of Israel through persecution has the opposite effect, magnifying the Hebrews' population and Egypt's corresponding dread (Bekhor Shor). *Qwṣ* also describes the Moabites' reaction to Israel's great population (Num 22:3). The root, which also exists in a dialectal variant, *qwṭ*, conveys both fear and loathing.

1:13. *Egypt.* Biblical Hebrew often uses *miṣrayim* 'Egypt' collectively to denote the citizens thereof.

made . . . work. Or "enslaved" (*wayya'ăbidû*).

duress. Perek appears only in P (Exod 1:13, 14; Lev 25:43, 46, 53) and Ezek 34:4. The root *prk* means "rub, crumble" and here connotes the abuse of slaves.

1:14. *Hard work in mortar and in bricks.* Cassuto (1967: 12) shows that this, rather than the usual "with labor, mortar and bricks," is the correct and logical translation.

all work in the field. Deut 11:10 also recalls that the Israelites farmed in Egypt, but evidently not under duress as here. The labor required to irrigate, plow, sow, tend and reap the Nile delta is, of course, immense.

in short. This is one of several possible renderings of emphatic *'et-* (see Saydon 1964: 201, but also Davies 1992: 41–42). Alternatively, we might see *'et-* as signaling apposition and leave it untranslated.

their work. The pronominal suffix ("their") might refer either to the Hebrews or to the Egyptians (cf. NOTE to 1:11 "their tasks").

worked. I.e., "made them work."

COMMENT

REPRODUCTION AND MENACE

The language describing Israel's proliferation has resonances harking back to Genesis, especially within P (Ackerman 1974: 76–78). "Israel's sons bore fruit and swarmed and multiplied and proliferated greatly, greatly, so the land was filled with them" (1:7 [P]) echoes God's command to the first humans: "Bear fruit and multiply and fill the land" (Gen 1:28 [P]). And again, after the Flood subsides, God commands Noah and his family, "Bear fruit and multiply and fill the land . . . swarm in the land" (Gen 9:1, 7 [P]). The Priestly Writer's choice of language hints that the events of Exodus represent a new beginning for Yahweh and humanity, as momentous as the Flood or Creation itself. Conversely, one may regard the Flood and Creation as foreshadowing Israel's birth (cf. Fox 1986: 12; Schmidt 1988: 29–30; Fretheim 1991a: 25).

Why the emphasis on Israel's prodigious fertility? At the most simplistic level, if 70 male ancestors entered Egypt and 600,000 left, Israelite historians would naturally have inferred a high reproductive rate (cf. Tanhuma *Šəmôt* 5).

Second: both J and P record God's promises of numerous descendants to the Patriarchs (Gen 15:5 [J]; 17:2, 6 [P]; 22:17 [E?]; 26:4, 24 [J]; 32:13 [J/E]; 48:4 [P]). Now Yahweh, presumably at work behind the scenes, redeems these promises (Fretheim 1991a: 25).

Third: Egypt was anciently renowned for its agricultural fertility (Gen 13:10 [J]; Diodorus Siculus *Bibliotheca Historica* 1.10; for further references, see Luzzatto [on 12:37], Dillmann 1880: 3 and Jacob 1992: 9). In the Land of the Nile, Israel finally overcomes the sterility that had blighted the Matriarchs and

Patriarchs. Moses will be the first biblical hero since Abraham conceived without difficulty.

Fourth: Israel's fertility constitutes a threat for Egypt. In Gen 1:28, humanity is commanded, "Bear fruit and multiply and fill the land *and subdue it*." After the Flood, the mandate is repeated, "Bear fruit and multiply and fill the land; *the fear and dread of you* will be upon every creature of the land" (Gen 9:1–2). When the Hebrews bear fruit, multiply and fill the land (of Egypt), it is as if Pharaoh recalls Genesis; he knows what comes next. But Israel is destined to subdue, not Egypt, but the land of Canaan (Josh 18:1).

Fifth: fertility bears a threat for Israel. In stories in which a barren woman finally bears, temporary danger to the child often ensues (e.g., Isaac, Jacob, Joseph, the Shunammite's son [2 Kgs 4:8–37]) (Ackerman 1993). The corporate "person" Israel also belongs to this group. After the lifting of matriarchal sterility, danger (and salvation) should follow.

Moreover, studies of the overpopulation motif in ancient literature show how human reproduction threatens the established order. It must be suppressed by the gods (Moran 1971, 1987; Kilmer 1972; Frymer-Kensky 1977b; Hendel 1987b). Exodus 1, too, follows the mythic pattern, with Pharaoh, Egypt and Israel, respectively, paralleling the gods, the world and humanity (see further under COMMENT to 2:1–10).

S P E C U L A T I O N: Archaeology informs us that early Israel experienced explosive population growth in the Canaanite highlands during the twelfth and eleventh centuries (Finkelstein 1988: 193–94; APPENDIX B, vol. II). The causes are still unclear, but the tradition of Israel's proliferation in Egypt may dimly reflect this historical process.

DARK CENTURIES

Unremarked, centuries pass in 1:7. According to Gen 15:13 (J), Israel would be "slaves in a land not theirs and will serve them, and they will oppress them four hundred year." Later events prove four centuries to be the duration, not of the oppression, but of the entire Egyptian sojourn (cf. 12:40–41). Israel's enslavement falls fairly late in this period, only after they grow numerous.

Gen 15:16 (J) also predicts that a "fourth generation" would return to Canaan. Some scholars, halfway embracing the Bible's historicity, conclude that the real duration of the Egyptian residence was about a century, i.e., four twenty-five-year generations (e.g., Sarna 1986: 8). It is arbitrary, however, to accept biblical genealogies and yet balk at their Methuselan life spans. In fact, we should mistrust both the family trees and the chronologies, the former on comparative-anthropological grounds (Wilson 1977) and the latter on medical-archaeological grounds: humans have never lived that long. Since the Israelites attributed extended life spans to their most prominent forebears, the tradition of four generations lasting four hundred years is at least internally consistent, if unhistorical (see also NOTE to 12:40). (The notion of long-lived ancestors is not carried through rigorously, however; the death of an entire generation during the forty years' wandering presupposes a longevity briefer than ours, as was doubtless the case.)

The four centuries in Egypt pass without a tale worth telling. As with much of Israel's desert period and the later Babylonian captivity, the Bible appears to consider this sojourn devoid of noteworthy events. Its sole importance is as a time of incubation for Israel. In contrast, the momentous events demarcating the beginning and end of the four hundred years—Jacob's descent and the Exodus—are fully described.

THE SHAME OF SERVITUDE?

Exod 1:8–12 explains how Israel came to be a slave people, how free shepherds were impressed as manual laborers (Loewenstamm 1992a: 23). The tradition mitigates the potential shame in several ways. The Hebrew slaves were descended from royal clients, voluntary and esteemed immigrants to Egypt. They were enslaved not because of crime, debt or capture, nor were they sold. Rather, they were illegitimately conscripted, out of fear. The theme of Egypt's dread would have gratified Israelite readers in whose day Egypt hardly felt threatened by its puny neighbor.

We must not, however, exaggerate the disgrace of servile origins. The Egyptian captivity is the necessary background to Yahweh's mighty salvation, and it sets in relief Israel's later glory under David and Solomon. In the Bible, Israel's mean origins are more a source of pride than of embarrassment.

II. *If he is a son, kill him* (1:15–21)

1   [15(E)]And Egypt's king said to the Hebrew midwives—of whom the name of the one was Shiphrah and the name of the second Puah—[16]and he said, "In your helping the Hebrew women give birth, then look upon the *two stones*. If he is a son, kill him, but if she is a daughter, she may live." [17]But the midwives feared the Deity and did not do as what Egypt's king spoke to them; and they let the boys live.

[18]Then Egypt's king called to the midwives and said to them, "Why did you do this thing and allow the boys to live?"

[19]And the midwives said to Pharaoh, "The Hebrew women are not at all like the Egyptian women, but they are lively. Before the midwife comes to them they bear."

[20]And Deity graced the midwives, and the people multiplied and proliferated greatly. [21]And it happened, because the midwives feared the Deity, that he made *houses* for them.

ANALYSIS

TEXTUAL NOTES

†1:15. *Hebrew midwives.* I.e., midwives of Hebrew extraction. Many commentators, following LXX and Josephus (*Ant.* 2.206), read **limyallədōt hāʿibriyyōt* 'to the Hebrews' midwives,' potentially describing non-Israelites employed by the Hebrews (Holzinger 1900: 3; McNeile 1908: 5; Greenberg 1969: 26–27). I prefer MT *lamyallədōt hāʿibriyyōt* for two reasons: (a) the women's names are not Egyptian, but Hebrew or a related dialect (Luzzatto; see NOTE to 1:15); (b) their brave defiance of Pharaoh implies they are Hebrews themselves, not "righteous gentiles."

Shiphrah . . . Puah. Syr reverses the names.

1:16. *he said.* Syr and some LXX MSS add "to them."

†*she.* L and many other MT MSS read *hyʾ* (Kennicott 1776–80: 107), while the printed MT has *hwʾ*. In the Massoretic Torah, both *hîʾ* 'she' and *hûʾ* 'he' are usually spelled *hwʾ*, differing only in pointing. Because Roman-period Hebrew script often did not distinguish *w* from *y* (Cross 1961a; Qimron 1972), later scribes apparently feared to sort out the waws and yodhs in the Torah's sacrosanct consonantal text—but only for these pronouns. Because *hûʾ* is more common than *hîʾ*, copyists almost always wrote *hwʾ*. Later, the Massoretic punctators added vowels to restore the distinction, simply superimposing the vowels of *hîʾ* (Qere) on the consonants of *hûʾ* (Kethibh). The result is the hybrid *hi(w)ʾ*, which is to be read *hîʾ*.

†*she may live.* While MT has the unusual form *wḥyh* (see NOTE), Sam has the expected and synonymous *wḥyth*. LXX, however, has "save her," while Syr reads "let her live." Ordinarily, we would dismiss this as paraphrase, perhaps inspired by 1:22. But we might also reconstruct **[wḥyy]tnh* 'then you (f. pl.) may let live' (Piʿel) in 4QExod[b], thus recovering a potential *Vorlage* for both LXX and Syr (cf. Cross 1994: 86). While the verses are probably by different authors, the parallel in 1:22 (J) would also lead us to expect a Piʿel verb, not a Qal, in 1:16 (E).

†1:18. *Egypt's king.* Sam substitutes "Pharaoh."

midwives. Presumably independently, the Sahidic Coptic version of LXX and 4QExod[b] expand: "the *Hebrew* midwives."

1:19. *the midwife.* Some Sam MSS and Kenn 69 (first hand) read *hmyldwt* 'the midwives,' an assimilation to the plural elsewhere in the passage.

1:20. *the midwives.* Syr adds "because they did this thing."

multiplied . . . proliferated. In MT, the first verb is singular (*wayyireb*), the second plural (*wayyaʿaṣmû*). As "people" (*ʿam*) can be construed as singular or plural, and as verbs preceding plural subjects are often singular, there is no need to follow Sam, Tg. Ps.-Jonathan and some Syr MSS, which make "multiplied" plural (as if **wayyirbû*).

†1:21. *he made.* The subject of MT *wayya'aś* is God, but LXX reads "*they made houses* for themselves (*heautais*)" (cf. *Tg. Ps.-Jonathan; Fragmentary Targum*). If LXX is not just translating freely, its *Vorlage* probably had the ostensibly masculine plural **wy'św*, rather than the proper feminine plural **wt'śynh*, to resemble MT *wy'ś* (on gender incongruence, see following).

†*for them.* Since we would expect **lāhen* (f.) for MT *lāhem* (m.), perhaps the similar-looking mem and nun were confused in paleo-Hebrew script (the nasals *m* and *n* are also liable to be aurally confused in any period). Some have seen in *lāhem* a survival of the hypothetical dual **lahimā* (Rendsburg 1982: 43). But why only on this word in an entire story about two women? The most likely explanation is that Biblical Hebrew is simply inconsistent and tends to substitute the masculine for the feminine plural, as becomes the rule in Rabbinic Hebrew (see GKC §135o; Levi 1987; Blau 1987–88). Alternatively, one could take *Israel* as the antecedent in the original text, prior to redaction (see SOURCE ANALYSIS).

SOURCE ANALYSIS

The divine name *'ĕlōhîm* 'Deity' (vv 17, 20) indicates we are in either E or P (see INTRODUCTION, p. 50). Lacking any other diagnostic features of P, the narrative is most likely Elohistic. In particular, the theme of God-fearing (vv 17, 21) is typical of E (cf. Gen 20:8, 11; 22:12; Exod 3:6; 18:21; 20:18, 20; Wolff 1975).

There may also be a second source in 1:15–21, presumably J. Exod 1:20–21 is slightly strange in both content and grammar (see NOTES). Moreover, v 20b ("the people multiplied and proliferated greatly") resembles vv 9, 12 (J) (also v 7 [P]). One might hypothesize that vv 20–21 conflate two older texts, respectively from E and J: "and it happened, because the midwives feared the Deity, that Deity graced the midwives" (reversing vv 20 and 21); and "the people multiplied and proliferated greatly, and he/they (see TEXTUAL NOTE) made *houses* for them." If so, then the reference to "Levi's house" in 2:1 (J) picks up "houses" in 1:21b.

E, unlike J and P, provides no motive for Pharaoh's malice. Either it is gratuitous, or more likely the background has been omitted by Redactor^JE. In E, Israel presumably has not burgeoned to the extent envisioned by the Yahwist and Priestly Writer. Only two midwives serve the whole nation.

REDACTION ANALYSIS

Unless I have erred in assigning 1:8–12 entirely to J, there is a gap in E between Gen 50:26 and Exod 1:15. In this interval, the rise of a wicked king must have been narrated, an account dropped by Redactor^JE in favor of J.

By adding 1:15–21 to the J account, Redactor^JE improved the story considerably. Pharaoh now adopts successive stratagems to kill the Hebrews' infants. First, he privately instructs the midwives in detail (E). Then, thwarted, he publicly and curtly commands his own folk to expose the babies (J).

Redaction also created a problem, however. How can only two women service the mighty nation envisioned by J? Ibn Ezra concludes that Shiphrah and Puah are actually heads of guilds, supervising a mighty staff.

In the composite text, E's midwives episode concretely illustrates the paradox of 1:12 (J): "As they oppressed him, so he multiplied." And the roots *rbb*, *ʿṣm* 'to be numerous' (v 20b) refer back to Pharaoh's fears in v 9 (J).

NOTES

1:15. *Hebrew.* The Bible calls Israelites "Hebrews" (*ʿibrîm*) primarily in two contexts: (a) when they are interacting with non-Israelites and (b) when an individual Israelite is a slave. To explain this pattern, we might suppose that *ʿibrî* once bore mildly derogatory connotations of servitude and that Israelites used the term before foreigners in self-deprecation. Only later did they adopt *ʿibrî* as an all-purpose ethnic designation (compare the etymology of "Slav," originally meaning "slave"). It is also possible, however, that the texts referring to the "Hebrew slave" (Gen 39:17; Exod 21:2; cf. Deut 15:12; Jer 34:9, 14) implicitly contrast him with the foreign slave and that the term has no inherent connotation of servitude. (On the hypothesized connection between the *ʿibrîm* and the *ʿab/pirū(ma)* of the ancient Near East, see APPENDIX B, vol. II.)

Shiphrah. The same name appears in a Thirteenth Dynasty (eighteenth-century) list of Egyptian slaves (Albright 1954: 229). It would mean "Beauty" in Hebrew or a related Canaanite dialect.

Puah. Pûʿâ may be the same name as *pġt*, the heroine of the Ugaritic Legend of Aqhat (*ANET* 149-55). It probably means "Lass."

1:16. *two stones.* 'Obnayim is of uncertain meaning. It looks to be the dual of *'eben* 'stone,' although we would expect **'abnayim* (Jacob 1992: 19). In Jer 18:3, *'obnayim* denotes a potter's wheel, but that cannot work here (*pace* Cassuto 1967: 14). There are, however, at least three plausible interpretations of "two stones": (a) the *testicles* proving the child's gender (so, among others, Durham 1987: 12; cf. archaic-English "stones"); (b) *pedestals* upon which women rested their legs during birth (Saadiah; Hyatt 1971: 61); (c) the *bricks* on which Egyptian midwives may have deposited newborns (Ofele *apud* Holzinger 1900: 3; Brongers and van der Woude 1965-66: 247-49). For further literature on these and other proposals, see Schmidt (1988: 5-6).

I incline toward theory (a), since the evidence for (c) is scant and, were (b) correct, we would expect "*between* the two stones." But approach (a) also has difficulties. Nowhere else does Hebrew literature call testicles "stones." More important, the context suggests that both boys and girls possess or are associated with *'obnayim.* Note that, to determine sex, the midwives "look upon, inspect" (*rā'â ʿal*), rather than simply see (*rā'â 'et*) the *'obnayim.* This suggests a fourth explanation: "two stones" are pudenda in general.

she may live. The seemingly masculine (*wā)ḥāyâ* has provoked comment since the Middle Ages. The expected feminine *ḥāyɔtâ in fact appears in

Sam, but is suspect as *lectio facilior*. There are at least five ways to interpret the consonants *ḥyh*: (a) as a pausal form of **ḥayyâ*, an alternate feminine perfect of the root *ḥyy* (GKC §76*i*); (b) as a Qal infinitive absolute **ḥāyō(h)* (cf. Saadiah); (c) as a Piʿel infinitive absolute **ḥayyē(h)/ḥayyō(h)*; (d) as a Piʿel imperative **ḥayyūḥā* (cf. LXX; Syr). The wisest course, however, is (e) to accept gender incongruence as common in Hebrew (Levi 1987). It is curious, and probably not a coincidence, that v 19 features another anomalous derivative of this root: *ḥāyôt* 'lively' (see NOTE).

1:17. *feared*. Biblical writers often exploit the similarity of the roots *yrʾ* 'fear' and *rʾy* 'see, look upon' (e.g., 14:13, 30–31; 1 Sam 12:16–18; 1 Kgs 3:28). Here Pharaoh's command is "look upon" (*wrʾytn*), but the women instead "feared" (*wtyrʾn*), an anagram (Cassuto 1967: 14). Ackerman (1974: 87) detects the element of surprise in 1:17. In the context, we might expect the object of "fear" to be Pharaoh, not God.

the Deity. *ʾĔlōhîm* is a plural common noun literally meaning "gods." How could zealous monotheists have denoted their sole divinity with a plural? The most convincing explanation is that *ʾĕlōhîm* exemplifies the plural of abstraction (GKC §124*g*), hence my rendering "Deity" (< Late Latin *deitas* 'godhood'). Such plurals, including *ʾĕlōhîm*, often take singular modifiers (GKC §145*h*). For further discussion of *ʾĕlōhîm* and its Near Eastern parallels, see APPENDIX C, vol. II.

God is called "*the* Deity" (*hāʾĕlōhîm*) in vv 17, 21, but simply "Deity" (*ʾĕlōhîm*) in vv 20, 21. What is the difference? D. N. Freedman (privately) notes that the definite article tends to appear where "Deity" is grammatically oblique, and is omitted where "Deity" is nominative. There are exceptions, and probably other conditioning factors such as word order; nevertheless, the observation seems to be basically valid.

1:19. *at all*. I have taken *kî* as asseverative. It might also be regarded as a particle introducing direct quotation, or as the start of the midwives' self-exculpation: "because. . . . "

lively. If the MT vocalization is accurate, *ḥāyôt* is a feminine plural of an unattested **ḥāye(h)* 'lively' (Luzzatto). The idea may be that the women are so vital that their labor is fast and easy (note that *ḥyy* often connotes recovery from illness). Many, however, emend to **ḥayyôt* 'animals' (e.g., *b. Soṭa* 11b; Gressmann 1913: 7; Ehrlich 1908: 261; Scharbert 1989: 15). If this is correct, the text implicitly contrasts *ʿibriyyōt . . . *ḥayyôt* 'Hebrew . . . animals' and *nāšîm miṣriyyōt* 'Egyptian women.' We have already seen the Israelites compared to vermin in vv 7, 12. Oppressors typically justify their own inhumanity by explicitly or implicitly impugning their victims' humanity. A physical asset such as ease of childbirth, seen through the lens of prejudice, appears bestial.

Still other explanations of *ḥywt* have been proffered, but none convinces. Rabbinic Hebrew *ḥayyâ* (Aramaic *ḥayyǝtāʾ*) means both "midwife" and "woman in labor," but it is hard to accept the interpretation of Symmachus, Jerome and Rashi—"they themselves are midwives/know midwifery"—or that of LXX,

Theodotion and Aquila—"they give birth." Neither does the paraphrase (?) of
Tg. Onqelos, "they are wise," recommend itself.

1:20. *graced*. Or "was beneficent toward" (*wayyêṭeb*).

1:21. *houses*. *Bāttîm* does not refer to domiciles, for which the verb should
be "built" (*bny*), not "made" (*ʿśy*). Rather, "houses" are probably families. The
idiom "make a house" refers to founding a lineage in Akkadian (Paul 1992b)
and Hebrew (1 Sam 25:28; 2 Sam 7:11; 1 Kgs 2:24; cf. Gen 16:2; 30:3; Jer 12:16
[Luzzatto]). Luzzatto and Hyatt (1971: 61) also speculate that midwives were
typically barren women. If so, the reward of Shiphrah and Puah is both miraculous and appropriate. Having risked their lives to save children, they earn the
privilege of motherhood.

The theory that Shiphrah and Puah founded clans explains their memori-
alization in Exodus (Ehrlich 1969: 135). But why do we never read of their
descendants? Perhaps, rather, they simply attained the legal status of males, owning property independently (cf. Num 27:1–11; 36; Job 42:15). Their "houses"
are households.

Another possibility, following ibn Ezra's lead, is that "houses" are staff (see
REDACTION ANALYSIS). Since in E, Israel's population burgeons *after*
Shiphrah and Puah thwart Pharaoh, the overburdened midwives would soon
have required assistants. But this reads far too much into a basically straight-
forward text.

A final possibility, under the assumption that vv 20–21 are composite, is
that the "houses" are really the tribes of Israel, at least in J (see SOURCE
ANALYSIS). This interpretation is unlikely, however, for the composite text
(*pace* Calvin).

COMMENT

PHARAOH'S SINISTER LOGIC

To eradicate Israel, the king of Egypt adopts a curious but sensible plan: male
infanticide. Were genocide Pharaoh's sole aim, he could order all Hebrews slain
on the spot. But he would thereby lose thousands of slaves. The logical expedient is the one Pharaoh employs in both E (1:15–21) and J (1:22). *Bib. Ant.* 9:1
reconstructs the king's reasoning as follows: "Let us kill their males, and we will
keep their females so that we may give them to our slaves as wives. And whoever
is born from them will be a slave and will serve us" (also Calvin on 2:10). At
times, the Israelites themselves treated prisoners of war comparably, killing all
the men and confiscating the women (Num 31:1–18; Deut 20:14; 21:10–14;
Judg 21:11–14; 1 Kgs 11:15; cf. Judg 5:30). This has remained a common practice worldwide (Patterson 1982: 120–22).

The theme of 1:15–21, endangerment of Israelite lineage by death and assimilation, flows directly from Genesis. Note the barrenness of Sarah (Gen 11:30),

Rebekah (Gen 25:21) and Rachel (Gen 29:31); the near-deaths of Abraham (Gen 12:12), Isaac (Genesis 22; 26:7) and Jacob (Gen 27:41), and the recurring fear of miscegenation (Gen 12:10–20; 20; 24:3–8; 26:1–11, 34; 27:46–28:9; 34). The suspense over Israel's survival continues through Exodus, growing ever keener until the final rescue in chaps. 14–15. (The theme returns in 32:10, when God himself proposes to eradicate Israel.)

In addition, the particular threat to the Hebrew males foreshadows the events of the paschal night, when all the male firstborn of Egypt are slain in retaliation. (See p. 439 for the suggestion that Pharaoh reenacts the role of an ancient demon threatening newborns.) And, in the context of the Christian Bible, the endangerment of the Hebrew boys also anticipates the Slaughter of the Innocents prior to Jesus' birth (Matthew 2). The rescued infant savior Moses is a "type" of Jesus himself.

DECEPTION AND DELIVERANCE; FEMALE SAVIORS

Like other biblical acts of defiance, the midwives' heroism involves an element of the sneaky. Ostensibly powerless, they do not openly flout Pharaoh, but deceive him instead. Israelite writers were not puritanical about prevarication in a good cause; the Bible tells many stories in which a weak party tricks a stronger, or in which characters engage in reciprocal, even competitive, trickery (Friedman 1986; Niditch 1987; Frymer-Kensky 1992: 136–39). For 1:15–21, some suggest that Pharaoh, fearing a rebellion, attempts to dupe the Hebrew mothers into believing their offspring are stillborn (Calvin). If so, Shiphrah and Puah are merely repaying the monarch in his own false coin. For Meyer (1983: 33), on the other hand, Pharaoh is intentionally depicted as moronic and ignorant of childbirth. He easily falls victim to his own prejudice (cf. Jacob 1992: 21).

Exodus 1 opens with the fertility of Israel's "sons." But it concludes with mothers and midwives. For Burns (1983: 25–31), these symbolize the life principle (note *ḥyy* 'live' in 1:16, 17, 19, 22; on women and life, cf. Gen 3:20). The prominence of women will continue through Exodus 2 (Moses' birth, infancy and adolescence) and Exodus 4 (Zipporah rescues Moses). Giving life to the nascent nation, Shiphrah and Puah, Moses' mother and sister—even Pharaoh's daughter, her servant and Zipporah—are all midwives and "mothers in Israel" (cf. Judg 5:7).

III. *For I drew him from the waters* (1:22–2:10)

1   [22(J)]Now, Pharaoh commanded all his people, saying, "All the son born, throw him into the Nile, but all the daughter let live."

2 ¹Then a man from Levi's *house* went and *took* Levi's daughter. ²And the woman conceived and bore a son and saw him, how he was good, and she hid him three *moons*. ³But she could conceal him no longer, so she took for him a vessel of papyrus and tarred it with tar and with pitch, and put the boy in it and set in the rushes on the Nile's *lip*. ⁴And his sister stationed herself from a distance to know what would be done to him.

⁵Now, Pharaoh's daughter went down to wash by the Nile, and her maids were going on the Nile's *arm*. And she saw the vessel among the rushes and sent her maidservant, and she took it. ⁶And she opened and saw him — the boy — and, see: a child crying! And she pitied him and said, "This is from the Hebrews' boys."

⁷And his sister said to Pharaoh's daughter, "Shall I go and call for you a nursing woman from the Hebrews, so that she may suckle the boy for you?"

⁸And Pharaoh's daughter said to her, "Go." And the lass went and called the boy's mother.

⁹And Pharaoh's daughter said to her, "Cause this boy to go and suckle him for me, and I, I will pay your wage." So the woman took the boy and suckled him.

¹⁰And the boy grew, and she brought him to Pharaoh's daughter, and he was to her as a son. And she called his name "Moses" and said, "For I drew him from the waters."

ANALYSIS

TEXTUAL NOTES

1:22. *his people*. Acts 7:19; Jub 47:2 and possibly Ezekiel the Tragedian 12–13 report that the Israelites were commanded to immerse their children themselves, as Moses' mother in fact does (see COMMENT). This is probably midrash, rather than reflective of a variant "*the* people" (**hā'ām*), referring to the Hebrews.

†*son . . . daughter*. LXX, Sam, Tgs. Onqelos and Ps.-Jonathan and *Bib. Ant.* 9:1 add "of the Hebrews." Dillmann (1880: 12) thinks this the original reading, but there is no evident reason why a copyist should have omitted *l'brym*. It is easier to imagine a hypercritical scribe inserting it to answer the frivolous question "Did Pharaoh's command apply to *Egyptian* children as well?" (cf. *Exod. Rab.* 1:18; NOTES to 1:22 and 2:6).

2:1. *Levi's daughter*. At the end of v 1, LXX adds "and he had her," with some MSS further expanding: "as a wife" (cf. *Tg. Ps.-Jonathan; Fragmentary Targum*). There is no reason to consider either plus original.

2:2. *the woman*. LXX has simply "she."

three. For MT-Sam *šlšh*, 4QGen-Exodᵃ has the more common *šlšt*.

2:3. *she could*. LXX "*they* could no longer conceal him" sounds like a scribe's answer to the question "What about the father?" (cf. Loewenstamm 1992b: 202).

††*conceal him*. The Massoretic vocalization *haṣṣapînô*, with daghesh in the ṣadhe, is anomalous (see also NOTE to 15:17). Presumably, the intended form is *haṣpînô, with daghesh in the pe'. The dot's migration may have been caused

by momentarily confusing the Hiph'il prefix *ha-* with the definite article *ha-*; only the latter doubles the following consonant.

she took. LXX and Sam specify *"his mother* took." In LXX, at least, this is necessary, since the preceding verb is plural (see above).

tarred it. We would expect a mappiq in the suffix of *wattaḥmərâ*; for parallels, see GKC §91e.

put the boy in it. 4QExod^b continues: "and she said to her maidservant (*šphth*), 'Go.'" The verse then concludes as in MT. Cross (1994: 89) conjectures that a variant of v 5 somehow migrated within the text. But v 5 calls the servant *'āmâ*, not *šiphâ*. I would rather see midrash at work: the interpolator could not imagine a mother with the fortitude to abandon her child herself. He intentionally enhanced the parallelism between Moses' mother and Pharaoh's daughter by giving the mother her own servant. But it is remotely possible that 4QExod^b is in fact original, all other witnesses having suffered corruption by homoioarkton (*wt['mr] . . . wt[śm]*).

2:4. stationed herself. The anomalous *wattētaṣṣab* is generally emended to **wattityaṣṣēb,* but see NOTE.

to know. For MT *lədē'â,* 4QGen-Exod^a, 4QExod^b and Sam (Baillet 1982: 28) have the more common infinitive *ld't.*

2:5. sent her maidservant. Syr has "her maidservants." This is unlikely to reflect a variant *Vorlage,* but is rather a confusion with *'amhātāh,* used earlier in the verse to render *na'ărōte(y)hā* 'her maids.'

†*2:6. opened and saw him.* This is the reading of MT and Syr. Sam, however, reads "opened it and saw" (*wtptḥh wtr'*), placing the objectival suffix on the first verb rather than the second. While this could be correct, it is more likely an alteration due to (a) the presence of a suffix at the end of v 5 and (b) a desire to avoid redundancy with "the boy." LXX and *Tgs. Onqelos* and *Ps.-Jonathan* appear to have the shortest reading, with no suffix on either verb, but these Versions do not always follow the Hebrew rigidly in this respect. In 4QExod^b, the first verb is not legible, while the second is *wtr'h* 'and saw,' without an objectival suffix (also Kenn 600) (cf. Qimron 1986: 45).

†*the boy.* LXX does not reflect *'et-hayyeled.* Either it is an addition in MT, or, more likely, "she saw the boy, and, see: a child crying" seemed redundant to the original translator, who abbreviated (Wevers 1990: 14). The presence or absence of an objectival suffix on *wtr'(hw)* 'and saw (him)' (previous TEXTUAL NOTE) is probably related to the presence or absence of "the boy." That is, in some MSS, *wtr'/wtr'h/wtr'hw* was followed by *whnh* 'and, see:,' without an intervening *'t hyld* 'the boy.' Corruption occurred amid the clustering of the Hebrew letters he and waw.

†*and, see: a child crying.* D. N. Freedman (privately) conjectures that the original was not *whnh n'r bkh* (MT), but *whnh hn'r bkh* 'and, see: the child crying' (= Kenn 111); i.e., a he' was lost through haplography. LXX expands: "in the vessel."

she pitied him. 4QExod^b, Sam and LXX expand, *"Pharaoh's daughter* pitied him," resolving an ambiguity (see NOTE).

†2:7. *suckle*. For the MT-Sam jussive *wətêniq*, 4QExod^b uses the converted perfect *whynqh* (Cross 1994: 89). If 4QExod^b is correct, then MT and Sam have anticipated *wt(y)nqhw* (v 9). But, conversely, the scribe of 4QExod^b may have adapted a slightly unusual reading to the norm.

†2:9. *Cause . . . to go*. Standard MT has *hêlîkî*, rather than the expected **hôlîkî*. Several MT MSS (Kennicott 1776–80: 108) and a Cairo Genizah MS (BHS) read *hlyky*, while Sam has an ultra-defective *hlky*. We find a similar ambiguity in Gen 8:17, where the Kethibh is *hwṣ'* and the Qere *hyṣ'* (**hêṣê'*). 4QExod^b is unclear, with either *hwlky* or *hylky*. What is the correct reading? On the one hand, MT *hêlîkî* might be an error induced by the following *hêniqihû* and the similarity of Roman-period waw and yodh (GKC §69x; O'Connell n.d.). On the other hand, the root **ylk* might be an authentic byform of *hlk* 'go, walk' (KB).

†*suckle*. Standard MT *wattənîqēhû* is ostensibly the Hiph'il of a hollow root **nwq/nyq* (ibn Ezra), where we would rather have expected **wattēnîqēhû* (< *ynq*). In fact, MSS of both Sam and MT read *wtynqhw* (Kennicott 1776–80: 109). Conversely, in v 7, where standard MT has the expected *wtynq* 'so that she may suckle,' many MT MSS read *wtnyq* (< **nwq/nyq*) (Kennicott p. 108).

†2:10. *the boy*. For MT *hayyeled*, Sam has the synonymous *hn'r*. Moses is indeed called *na'ar* in 2:6, but elsewhere the story calls him *yeled*. On the one hand, as the more difficult reading, Sam might be correct. On the other hand, the sevenfold repetition of *yeled*, if meaningful, requires MT (see SOURCE ANALYSIS).

†*grew*. Given the context, I would consider a conjectural emendation **wayyiggāmēl* 'and (he) was weaned,' vs. *wayyigdal* 'and (he) grew.' The text could have been corrupted by anticipation of *wayyigdal* in v 11. See also NOTE.

SOURCE ANALYSIS

While there is no trace of P, it is somewhat difficult to decide between J and E for 1:22–2:10. But I do not find more than one hand (for discussion of the two-source analysis, see Fohrer 1964: 18–19; Schmidt 1988: 51–53). Although Coote (1991: 39–40) ascribes the passage to E, most opt for J, discerning a Yahwistic version of the threat to the infant males (cf. 1:15–21 [E]) (Holzinger 1900: 5; McNeile 1908: 5–6). Each story has a happy ending, but in E, all the Israelite babies are rescued, while J saves Moses alone and forgets the others. (Later tradition remedies this oversight: Pharaoh's decree expires after Moses' birth [e.g., Jub 47:3].) Other scholars, however, regard 1:22–2:10 as originally a sequel to 1:15–21, not a doublet: Pharaoh first tries to kill the babies through the midwives, then through his own henchmen (e.g., Childs 1974: 7). This, at any rate, is the import in the received text.

There is a simple reason for our difficulty in identifying the source of 1:22–2:10. Both J and E probably told of Moses' birth. But Redactor^JE suppressed one account in favor of the other—whether because the stories were so similar as to be redundant or so different as to be irreconcilable or not of equal interest. It is not easy to tell which version is preserved.

The lexical evidence is ambivalent. In support of J, some note that *tēbâ* 'vessel' otherwise appears only in the J-P Flood story, denoting Noah's ark (Genesis 6–9). And the substance with which Moses' basket is smeared, *ḥēmār*, is referred to only in Exod 2:3, Gen 11:3 (J) and Gen 14:10 (source unknown). But these arguments are not very strong.

And one can frame a lexical counterargument for E. In 2:5, the princess's maidservant is called *'āmâ*, rather than *šipḥâ*. At least in Genesis, only E uses *'āmâ* (Gen 20:17; 21:10, 12, 13; 30:3; 31:33). However, *'āmâ*, used metaphorically, is common in parts of Joshua–1 Kings that Friedman (1998) attributes to the Yahwist (Judg 9:18; 19:19; 1 Sam 1:11, 16; 25:24, 25, 28, 31, 41; 2 Sam 6:20, 22; 14:15, 16; 20:17; 1 Kgs 1:13, 17). The lexical argument is again inconclusive.

We could look instead to characteristic narrative motifs. The princess's trip to the Nile, where she meets Moses' sister "standing" (*tēttaṣṣab*), recalls Pharaoh's excursions to the Nile (7:14; 8:16 [E]), where he meets the "standing" Moses (*niṣṣabtā, hityaṣṣēb*). But this evidence, too, is weak.

Other arguments are equally unconvincing. Friedman (1987: 71–74, 79–80) ascribes to E a special reverence for Moses and a loyalty to the Levites (pp. 71–74). Thus the story of Moses' birth to a Levite couple should be Elohistic. On the other hand, Friedman (p. 86) also observes the Yahwist's sympathy for women. Is 1:22–2:10 therefore Yahwistic?

A better way to determine the vignette's authorship may be to link it with contiguous passages of known provenance. The reference to Reuel (as opposed to Jethro) in 2:18 is a likely indicator of J (see below). This implies that 2:15b–22 is entirely Yahwistic, since it brings Moses to the well where he meets Reuel's daughters (notice the sequence "he sat . . . he arose," binding vv 15 and 17). Exod 2:15b–22, in turn, is of a piece with vv 11–15a (see SOURCE ANALYSES of these passages). If we can prove that vv 1–10 flow directly into vv 11–22, we can assign the former to J.

One theme in particular connects all of 1:22–2:22, suggesting the hand of a single writer. The confusion over Moses' ethnic affiliation in 2:11–22 (J)—is he Egyptian, Midianite or Hebrew?—is explained by the story of his adoption in 1:22–2:10 (see COMMENT). Yet even this could be the product of editing, assuming both J and E told of Moses' rearing in the Egyptian court.

A curious device, however, strengthens the case for the original unity of 1:22–2:22. In 1:22–2:10, *yeled* 'child' occurs seven times (vv 4, 6, 7, 8, 9 [2x], 10 [but not in Sam]), plus the plural *yaldê* (v 6) (I am not counting *yillôd* in 1:22). In 2:11–22, on the other hand, *'îš* 'man' is repeated seven times (vv 11 [2x], 12, 14, 19, 20, 21), plus the plural *'ănāšîm* (v 13) (cf. Greenberg 1969: 55). (On the ambiguity of 7/8, compare the parallelism of seven and eight in biblical and Ugaritic poetry.) That the author is thinking in sevens is evident also in the number of Reuel's daughters (Siebert-Hommes 1992: 402). If not coincidental, the pattern signifies that, whereas 1:22–2:10 treats Moses' *childhood*, 2:11–22 tells of his *manhood*. And if the Reuel vignette is Yahwistic, so, too, must be Moses' exposure and adoption.

REDACTION ANALYSIS

For 1:22–2:10, the combination of sources adds meaning, without introducing blatant contradiction. Moses' father, mother and sister, anonymous in J, acquire names from P and R: Amram, Jochebed and Miriam (6:18–20; Num 26:59). By deferring Moses' genealogy to Exodus 6, however, the Redactor preserves the suspense of the original J (see COMMENT).

The change in Miriam's status is particularly complex. In J, Moses is protected by an anonymous sister. In E, Moses has a kinswoman Miriam, who supports him in song (15:20–21) but also quarrels with him (Numbers 12). In JE, there is no reason to equate these women. When P is added, however, they merge, lending poignancy to the eventual alienation of brother and sister.

The combination of J and P also enhances the sense that Moses' birth is a world-transforming event. According to 2:2, Moses' mother "saw him, how he was good." With redaction, these words echo the refrain of Genesis 1 (P), "and Deity saw how good" (in fact, Kenn 69, 89, 109 heighten the similarity by omitting *hû'* in Exodus). And, like God's first Creation, Moses is soon threatened by water but preserved in a *tēbâ* 'ark, container.' Thus 1:22–2:10 recapitulates the Flood as well as Creation (see COMMENT).

NOTES

1:22. *the son . . . the daughter.* Habbēn and habbat are collective, equivalent to the plural (Holzinger 1900: 4). That the command is not explicitly limited to *Hebrew* boys is presumably an authorial oversight (see TEXTUAL NOTES to 1:22 and 2:6). Jacob (1992: 22) implausibly imagines Pharaoh dementedly commanding the murder of his own people (so also *b. Soṭa* 12a; Rashi)!

throw. Cogan (1968) correctly observes that *hišlîk* can be a technical term for abandoning a child without implication of violent, malicious hurling (cf. Gen 21:15; Ezek 16:5). But he errs in seeing that as Pharaoh's intent here. The contrasting treatment of the daughters (*təḥayyûn*) shows that the king is indeed bent upon murder. But, whereas Pharaoh speaks of literal casting into the water in order to drown the sons, Moses' mother reinterprets his command à la Cogan, to connote exposure with the possibility of adoption. She does not *throw* her son in the Nile—but *sets* him in a basket among the rushes (Jacob 1992: 22–23, 28; Loewenstamm 1992b: 205–7), perhaps hoping that he would be adopted (Sforno).

Nile. Yə'ōr is a borrowing of Egyptian *itrw* 'river' (on the quiescence of the *t*, see Lambdin 1953: 151). Yə'ōr possesses extended meanings of "river," "channel" and even "tunnel" (Job 28:10; compare *minhārâ* 'tunnel' < *nāhār* 'river').

live. After v 22, Hebrew MSS insert a space (*sətûmâ*). Thus, when the chapters were numbered by medieval Christian scribes, our verse was judged more closely connected to the midwives story than to Moses' exposure. This is contrary to common sense. The break after 1:22 serves two positive functions, however: (a) it creates suspense across the chapter break; (b) it binds together two stories of originally independent authorship. The spacing system, employed already at Qumran, is of high antiquity (Perrot 1969). For all we know, the division of Exodus 1 from 2 goes back to Redactor[JE] himself.

2:1. *a man*. The anonymity of all the characters in 1:22–2:10, except for Moses at the very end, is frequently noted. The text tantalizes by concealing the child's identity—but who else could it be?—until he is safe.

On the other hand, the parents' tribal affiliation is made explicit. Moses is of known extraction, not a bastard foundling (Loewenstamm 1992b: 204). That the parents are Levites is particularly important, for that tribe would become ancient Israel's priestly caste (32:29; Deut 18:1–8; Judg 17:7–13; see COMMENTS to 6:2–7:7 and 32). From the Israelite reader's perspective, Moses' pure-Levite pedigree qualifies him for religious leadership (Durham 1987: 16).

took. I.e., married.

Levi's daughter. There are two possible translations of *bat-lēwî*. At issue is whether *bat* is definite or indefinite. Despite occasional exceptions, a noun in construct to a definite noun is itself definite, witness the preposition *'et* in 2:1. Hence, *bat-lēwî* should mean "Levi's daughter." In P, at least, Moses' mother, Jochebed, is literally "Levi's daughter" and her husband's aunt (6:20; Num 26:59; see NOTE to 6:20). Nevertheless, LXX renders *bat-lēwî* as "one of Levi's daughters," and Vg follows loosely in this vein: "a wife of his extraction." These Versions apparently take *bat-lēwî* as indefinite, either "a daughter of Levi" (see Joüon [1965: 431 §139b–c] for parallels) or possibly "a certain daughter of Levi" (see NOTE to 2:15). "A daughter of Levi" need not be biological, any more than "Israel's sons" are Jacob's immediate offspring. Thus, according to the LXX of 2:1, Moses' mother is merely her Levite husband's kinswoman. But this interpretation seems forced, probably motivated by concern over consanguinity (an aunt-nephew union is incestuous by Priestly canons [Lev 18:12; 20:19]); cf. NOTE to 6:20. If 2:1 referred merely to a female Levite, we would have expected **mibbənōt lēwî* 'from Levi's daughters.'

There is notable wordplay in 2:1 between *bêt* 'house' and *bat* 'daughter.' *Wayyēlek 'îš mibbêt lēwî* can be interpreted both as "a man from Levi's house went" and "a man went from Levi's house" (cf. Jacob 1992: 24). The former is the primary sense, but, by the secondary interpretation, the man leaves Levi's *b(y)t* 'house' to join Levi's *bt* 'daughter,' returning, as it were, to his starting point.

2:2. *conceived and bore a son*. Many commentators note that Moses' conception seems to be his mother's first, yet he has an older sister (v 4) (e.g., Knobel *apud* Dillmann 1880: 13). Is Moses merely the first *male* conception (the fraternity of Moses and Aaron comes from P [6:20], not J), or has Moses' father taken more than one wife (Dillmann 1880: 13; Jacob 1992: 24)? Calvin unconvincingly solves the problem by translating *wayyēlek . . . wayyiqqaḥ* (v 1) as "had gone . . . had taken," despite the use of waw consecutive.

All these speculations are overly rationalistic (Loewenstamm 1992b: 219–21). "Conceived and bore (a son)" is a cliché, exampled twenty-six times in the Bible (Gen 4:1, 17; 21:2, etc.) and twice in Ugaritic (*KTU* [1.5.v.22]; 11.5). When speaking of birth, a biblical author might reflexively refer to conception, creating for modern readers the misimpression that Moses is a firstborn. Rather, as it were, years pass between vv 1 and 2.

Saw him, how he was good. For this interpretation of *kî ṭôb,* see Albright (1956); Kugel (1980), but also Janzen (1983); Davies (1992: 88). Although Luzzatto supposes that Moses is a placid child and hence easily hidden, more likely *ṭôb* means "viable, healthy." Alternatively, *ṭôb* might connote beauty, as perhaps in 1 Kgs 20:3, "your good(ly) sons."

Why are we told that Moses is "good"? Would his mother have discarded him had he not been "good"? Presumably not. But in an age of high infant mortality, abandoning a healthy child would have been all the more bitter. We have mentioned under REDACTION ANALYSIS the echo of Genesis 1: like God, Moses' mother inspects her creation for signs of imperfection and finds none (Rashbam). Making the same connection more imaginatively, *b. Soṭa* 12a claims that the entire house was filled with light upon Moses' birth (cf. Gen 1:4).

three moons. "Moons" are months. The number three is probably used stereotypically to express the passage of a few months; compare Gen 38:24; 2 Sam 6:11; 24:13 and the ubiquitous formulae "three days" (e.g., 3:18; 15:22) and "on the third day" (19:11, 16, etc.). At any rate, with the lapse of time, the family's secret grows more difficult to keep (Jub 47:3; Philo *Moses* 1.10; Josephus *Ant.* 2.9.219).

2:3. vessel. *Tēbâ* has only two uses in the Bible: to denote Noah's ark (Genesis 6–8) and Moses' basket. It may be a loanword from Egyptian *tbt* 'container,' which also found its way into Greek as *thibis* 'basket.' In Rabbinic Hebrew, *tēbâ* refers to any chest, including the synagogue ark housing the Torah scrolls.

papyrus. Like *tēbâ, gōme*ʾ is a loanword (< Egyptian *qmꜣ* [Lambdin 1953: 149]). It appears only here and in Isa 18:2; 35:7; Job 8:11. On the use of papyrus in boat-making, see Isa 18:2; Job 9:26. And on Egyptian techniques for making papyrus boxes (not baskets!), see Lucas and Harris (1962: 130).

tar. This need not be true bitumen, mostly imported from the Dead Sea area, but any sort of resin or pitch. Since the Egyptians seem not to have used such caulking on their vessels (Herodotus *Histories* 2.96; Landström 1970: 19), this feature of the story may derive from Mesopotamian tradition (see COMMENT).

put. Moses' mother obeys Pharaoh's decree in her own way. She "puts" (*śām*) rather than "throws" (*hišlîk*) the boy—and not into the middle of the Nile, but among the rushes near the shore (see NOTE to 1:22 and COMMENT).

the rushes on the Nile's lip. "Lip" (*śāpâ*) here means "shore." Since, however, v 10 implies that the container is in the water, "on the *lip*" does not mean "on the riverbank" (*pace* LXX). More likely, the reference is to the offshore shallows (Ezekiel the Tragedian 17; Redford 1967: 218). Indeed, why seal the vessel at all, unless it is meant for immersion? Moreover, the stereotypical Floating Foundling Tale requires that the baby be deposited in water (Loewenstamm 1992b: 205–7)—although the Moses story deviates significantly from the type (see COMMENT).

Sûp 'rushes' is either cognate to or derived from New Kingdom Egyptian *ṯwf(y)* (Lambdin 1953: 153), possibly via Phoenician (Ward 1974). Bekhor Shor observes that a container made from rushes would be well camouflaged by the shore. Copisarow (1962: 7) and Ward (p. 343) argue that here *sûp* should be rendered "marsh," the former citing LXX *helos* 'swamp' and the latter invoking a similar usage of Egyptian *ṯwf(y)* and Arabic *sawfa*. However that may be, the use of *sûp* to describe where Moses is deposited foreshadows Israel's salvation at the Suph Sea (see COMMENT).

2:4. *his sister.* Who is she? Moses has a sibling Miriam in P and a kinswoman Miriam in E (see NOTE to 4:14). But since the Yahwist never again refers to this sister, it is futile to inquire after her name in J or JE. For the redacted Torah, one naturally identifies her as Miriam (see REDACTION ANALYSIS above).

stationed herself. Ibn Ezra calls *wattētaṣṣab* a "strange word." Critical commentators are virtually unanimous in restoring, after Sam, **wattityaṣṣēb* (e.g., GKC §71). Blau (1957) persuasively argues, however, that MT features the rare *t*-form of the Hiph'il (cf. 2 Sam 22:27; Jer 12:5; 22:15)—although we might rather have expected **wattētāṣab*. LXX translates/paraphrases, "kept watch," a common nuance of the root *yṣb/nṣb* (cf., e.g., *maṣṣāb* 'garrison'). There is great pathos in the image of the sister standing sentry, perhaps only to watch her infant brother perish (cf. Calvin).

2:5. *Pharaoh's daughter.* Perhaps, if the Yahwist is to be situated in preexilic Jerusalem, his sympathetic portrayal of Pharaoh's daughter is a nod to another Egyptian princess, Solomon's wife (1 Kgs 3:1–2; 11:1) (see APPENDIX A, vol. II).

went down. From the dry land to the water (ibn Ezra).

to wash by the Nile. Hay'ōr might denote a minor branch of the Nile, or even a man-made channel (O'Connell n.d.). Pharaoh's daughter does not fully immerse herself "in the Nile" (that would be **bay'ōr* [cf. Jacob 1992: 27]). She is rather on the bank, perhaps being doused by her maids (cf. Josephus *Ant.* 2.224; Luzzatto); Decker (1975) refers to Egyptian bathing jugs and sieves. Alternatively, she could be standing in the shallows or on stairs (Ramban). At any rate, she sends a servant into the deeper waters to fetch the basket.

Why is Pharaoh's daughter bathing at all, and why in the Nile? Herodotus (*Histories* 2.37) considered the Egyptians fanatical bathers. But, with occasional exceptions, they dipped themselves in pools rather than the river (Greenberg 1969: 200; Decker 1975). This discrepancy should not trouble us, however; Pharaonic hygiene was likely beyond the Yahwist's expertise (see also NOTE to 7:15). Since he needed to get Moses from the Nile to the palace, why not via a bathing princess? (Was there also an intent to titillate [cf. 2 Sam 11:2]?)

arm. Hebrew *yād* 'arm, hand' (see NOTE to 2:15) frequently bears the nuance "side."

she took it. Here and in v 6, it is unclear whether "she" is Pharaoh's daughter or her servant.

2:6. *child*. *Naʿar*, which usually denotes an older boy but sometimes an infant (Judg 13:8; 2 Sam 12:16), is perhaps used to limit the quasi-synonymous *yeled* to seven occurrences (see SOURCE ANALYSIS). Rashbam further suggests that *naʿar* is more gender-specific than *yeled*, although both are grammatically masculine. Thus the princess first perceives a "child" (*yeled*), then discovers it to be a "boy" (*naʿar*).

crying. Thereby evoking the princess's compassion (Bekhor Shor).

she pitied him. The subject might be either the maid or the princess. But Sam and LXX specify "Pharaoh's daughter," probably correctly. Arguably, the sister's impetuosity (v 7) implies that she has already seen signs of sympathy in the princess (O'Connell n.d.), and, in any case, the servant's feelings are irrelevant to the narrative (D. N. Freedman, privately). Coats (1988: 44) catches the *double entente* in *wattaḥmōl*, which can mean both "pitied" and "spared."

said. Classical Hebrew has no special verb for "think," using instead *ʾmr* 'say' (Niehoff 1992). Here one assumes the princess is silently speculating.

the Hebrews' boys. The princess infers Moses' ethnicity either from his garb (F. I. Andersen, privately) or more likely from his presence in the Nile (Holzinger 1900: 6; Ehrlich 1969: 136). Some Jewish exegetes suppose, however, that the princess perceives Moses' *circumcision* (e.g., *Exod. Rab.* 1:24; Rashbam). Admittedly, circumcision was not performed upon Egyptian infants, but rather upon boys (Wit 1973; Schmidt 1988: 70). But the biblical mandate for infant circumcision (Genesis 17) comes from P, not J. I find the plain sense preferable: any abandoned child must be Hebrew. This resolves the ambiguity we noted in TEXTUAL NOTE and NOTE to 1:22: Hebrew babies alone are subject to the Pharaonic decree (L. Bookheim, privately).

2:8. *Go*. Ackerman (1974: 93) sees this response as reflecting "a feeling of supreme authority, a brusque manner in dealing with underlings." But in Biblical Hebrew, one usually answers in the affirmative by repeating the question's initial verb (Greenstein 1989). The princess is essentially saying, "Yes."

2:9. *Cause . . . to go*. *Hêlîkî/*hôlîkî* (see TEXTUAL NOTE) is the causative of the root *hlk* 'go, walk.' There are at least three possible renderings: (a) "take him away" (Targumim); (b) "guide him"; (c) "teach him to walk." The first is the most likely. LXX, however, translates the verb as "guard," presumably in the sense of "take away and keep." A fanciful but interesting reading parses the consonants *hylyky* as *hēʾ lêkî* 'this is yours' (*Exod. Rab.* 1:25; *b. Soṭa* 12b; also Syr *hʾ lky*) (cf. *hēʾ lākem*, Gen 47:23). By this theory, the erudite princess speaks not only Hebrew (v 10) but also Aramaic!

suckle. In Near Eastern antiquity as in Tudor England (*Romeo and Juliet* I.iii.22–36), children were weaned at about three years of age (Childs 1965: 111–12; Gruber 1989); cf. "Instruction of Any" (Lichtheim 1976: 141; *ANET* 420); 2 Macc 7:27. Interestingly, when Hannah takes the newly weaned Samuel to Shiloh, she brings a three-year-old bull to sacrifice (1 Sam 1:24, with LXX, Syr, and 4QSam^a [McCarter 1980: 57]). Was the beast of the same age as Samuel, perhaps even a vicarious offering? However that may be, Exod 2:9 implies that Moses' personality has a chance to develop under his Hebrew mother's tutelage.

2:10. *grew*. Even if MT is correct (see TEXTUAL NOTE), the context makes it clear that "grew" connotes weaning. Compare Gen 21:8, *wayyigdal hayyeled wayyiggāmal* 'the boy grew and was weaned.'

was . . . as a son. *Wayhî-lāh ləbēn* probably refers to adoption, whether *de facto* or *de jure* (on language of adoption, cf. 2 Sam 7:14 and parallels; Ruth 4:16–17; Esth 2:7, 15); see further under COMMENT. Jacob (1992: 30–32), however, argues that the princess merely becomes Moses' protector and sponsor; and, admittedly, we might have expected less ambiguous language, e.g., "she took him for herself as a son" (cf. Esth 2:7). Jacob also observes that, tradition notwithstanding (Acts 7:22, etc.), there is no explicit evidence Moses was raised as an Egyptian prince.

Jacob's reading is not convincing, however. Why must Moses' mother masquerade as a wet nurse, unless another is filling the maternal role? Why does Moses "go out to his brothers" (2:11), unless he has been raised apart from them (Luzzatto)? And why do the Midianites mistake Moses for an Egyptian (2:19)? Lastly, in the archetypical foundling tale, there is always an adoptive parent (see COMMENT). The conventional interpretation remains the most likely.

she called. A child is ordinarily named by either its mother (Gen 29:32–30:24; 35:18; 1 Sam 1:20) or its father (Gen 16:15; 17:19; Exod 2:22; 18:3–4). There might even be disagreement between the parents (Gen 35:18). Accordingly, we might have expected to learn the boy's name in 2:2. But the author tightens the suspense, keeping the endangered child as anonymous as the supporting cast until the happy end. Then, by naming Moses, the princess acts as *de facto* mother.

Moses. *Mōše(h)* derives from Egyptian *mose* '(is) born'; the root is familiar from such names as Thutmosis, Ramesses, etc. (Griffiths 1953). Usually, there is a god before the elements *mś*, but *mś* can stand alone as a personal name. Some voice reservations—we might admittedly have expected **mōse(h)*, not *mōše(h)*—but they present no credible alternative. The likelihood of Hurrian, Kassite (Zadok 1986: 393) or Sumerian (Astour 1967: 229–33; Sasson 1968) derivation is surely low. If Moses' name is not Hebrew, what could it be but Egyptian? For a summary of the difficulties, see Ahitub (1968), who ultimately and sensibly embraces the Egyptian etymology.

Although our author ascribes Moses' name to an *Egyptian* princess (reflecting dim awareness of the true derivation?), he makes it a *Hebrew* pun (cf. the *Greek* wordplay in Susannah 54–55, set in *Babylonia*). The Israelites delighted in inventing imaginatively spurious etymologies (Zakovitch 1980; Garsiel 1992). In 2:10, as if often noted, the pun is suitably remote. Hebrew "drawn" should be *māšûy*, not *mōše(h)* (e.g., ibn Ezra)—unless *mōše(h)* is a rare Qal passive participle (cf. *'uk[k]al* in 3:2 [D. N. Freedman, privately]). *Mōše(h)* should rather mean "drawer (from water)."

Isa 63:11 in fact seems to interpret Moses' name in just this way (Greenberg 1969: 43; Jacob 1992: 35): "Then he remembered ancient days, the drawer (*mōše[h]*) of his people, the shepherd of his flock; where is he that raised them from the Sea?" (clauses transposed for clarity). The crucial phrase *mōše(h)* *'ammô* is absent from the Greek, but, at least in MT, the prophet regards Moses' name as foreshadowing his vocation. Moreover, Luzzatto and Fohrer (1964: 22) observe that 2 Sam = Ps 18:17 also uses *mšy* (Hiph'il) to connote rescue from water. *Mōše(h)* may thus have been tantamount to "Savior" (Sforno). If so, it is ironic yet fitting that Moses receives his name from his own Egyptian savior.

I drew. To solve the "problem" of the princess's Hebrew expertise, some Jewish commentators make the mother the subject of "(she) said," rendering *məšîtihû* as "you drew" (Ḥizquni; Abarbanel; see Jacob 1992: 32). This is grammatically possible, but far-fetched.

COMMENT

FEMALE SAVIORS

Pharaoh's efforts to crush the Hebrews are continually frustrated. The greater the oppression, the more they thrive. After Pharaoh reiterates his command that all infant boys be slain, Israel's savior is finally born. But his own survival is in immediate jeopardy.

Given the focus on procreation in 1:1–2:10, it is not surprising that females shine. Like the preceding midwives narrative, 1:22–2:10 features the saving actions of women—Levi's daughter, Pharaoh's daughter, Moses' sister and the princess's maidservant. (In 4:24–26, we will meet another protectress: Zipporah.) True, two males, the fathers of the princess and of Moses, set events into motion by respectively making a decree and taking a wife. But they play no further part. Rather, although Pharaoh would kill the Hebrews' sons and spare their daughters, it is daughters—Levi's daughter, her own daughter and even Pharaoh's daughter—who thwart his plans (Fretheim 1991a: 36–37; Weems 1992: 30; Brenner 1994: 43).

There is a nice symmetry among the female characters. Moses' sister, presumably deputized by the mother to guard the basket in the reeds, parallels the princess's servant, dispatched by the princess to fetch the basket from the reeds. And Levi's daughter, Moses' biological mother, parallels Pharaoh's daughter, his adoptive mother (cf. Siebert-Hommes 1992: 402).

IRONIES

Our story is laced with ironies, both comic and tragic (Childs 1974: 115; Lawton 1985; Sarna 1986: 28–29). Moses' mother complies with the decree of drowning—in a fashion. Reinterpreting the verb *hišlîk* 'throw,' she gently places Moses in a vessel and sets him among the rushes (Sforno; see NOTE to 1:22). Pharaoh's law, moreover, failed to say that a baby, once deposited in the Nile, might not be extracted by another party (Jacob 1992: 22–23). Herodotus (*Histories* 4.154) tells a comparable tale of one Themison: commanded to throw a princess into the sea, she merely immerses her briefly and thereby saves her life.

A further, oft-noted irony is that Moses' mother and sister trick Pharaoh's daughter into hiring the mother to nurse her own child—for pay! As a bonus, the princess even adopts the boy into the royal family (on the theme of the hoodwinked foreigner, see COMMENT to 1:15–21).

There are also grimmer ironies, and significant connections with the Exodus tradition. The encounter between Moses' sister and Pharaoh's daughter at the Nile foreshadows, at least in the composite text, the riverside meetings of Pharaoh and Moses (7:14; 8:16 [E]; cf. Fuss 1972: 134; Fretheim 1991a: 114). And Origen considers the plague of the bloody Nile (7:14–24) recompense for Pharaoh's decree in 1:22 to fill the river with infant corpses (*Homiliae in Exodum* 4.6). O'Connell (n.d.) feels an additional resonance between Pharaoh's measures against the Israelite males and the later death of the Egyptian firstborn. Finally, Sarna (1986: 28–29) observes that the Egyptians will be drowned in the Suph Sea, as they had conspired to drown Israel in the Nile River (cf. Wis 18:5; *Mek. Šîrātā'* 4). To make the analogy blatant, Moses' basket rests among the *sûp* 'reeds' (cf. Jub 48:14; *Bib. Ant.* 9:10). (The comeuppance is all the more apt, because Hebrew *yām* and *nāhār* are not mutually exclusive, unlike English "sea" and "river" [Keel 1978: 21].) Moses' rescue from the water can thus be interpreted as foreshadowing chaps. 14–15, where Moses leads Israel up from the Sea (Fretheim 1991a: 37, 40). The Midrash implicitly makes the connection by setting both events on the same date (e.g., *b. Soṭa* 12b; *Exod. Rab.* 1:24). Indeed, one might regard Pharaoh's daughter as symbolizing God himself, who rescues Israel from the waters and claims him as a son (see NOTE to 4:22); her servant, then, represents Moses.

THEMATIC STRUCTURE

Our passage is unified by the repetition of two roots: *lqḥ* 'take' and *yld* 'bear.' The man of Levi *takes* a wife (2:1), the woman *takes* a vessel (2:3), the maidservant *takes* the vessel (2:5) and the mother *takes* the boy back (2:9). Pharaoh condemns every son *born* to death (1:22); the woman *bears* a son (2:2), and *yeled* 'child' occurs eight times (vv 4, 6 [2x], 7, 8, 9 [2x], 10; see SOURCE ANALYSIS).

The section is also enclosed by a subtle device. After the formulaic "conceived and bore a son" (2:2), we automatically expect "and called his name" (cf. Gen 21:2–3; 29:32, 33, 34, 35, etc.). The displacement of the cliché to v 10 injects both suspense (who is this child?) and surprise (the name is given by an Egyptian!). And it also creates a frame around the intervening narrative and a sense of closure at the end.

THE FLOATING FOUNDLING

The historical Moses is most unlikely to have endured so traumatic an infancy. Any folklorist recognizes the tale of an imperiled child of illustrious lineage, abandoned by its natural parents and raised in obscurity by foster parents, only at length to come into its own. This is, more or less, the biography of Oedipus, Romulus, King Arthur, Snow White, Tarzan, Superman and innumerable less familiar heroes (Rank 1952; Redford 1967; Lewis 1980: 149–276). Three parallels deserve particular attention, since they come from the ancient Near East and feature babies set adrift. The most famous is a mid-seventh-century Assyrian pseudo-autobiography of Sargon of Akkad (c. 2300):

Sargon, mighty king, king of Agade, I—
My mother is an *ēnetu* (a priestess prohibited from reproducing),
My father I do not know . . .
The *ēnetu*, a mother, conceived me,
In secret she bore me.
She put me in a vessel of reeds,
She caulked my opening(s?) with bitumen.
She cast me into the [ri]ver
From which I could not rise [see Lewis 1980: 25, 46–47, 80 n. 114].
The river bore me be[fore] Aqqi,
It carried [me] to the water drawer.
Aqqi the water drawer (*dālû*), in dip[ping his] b[ucke]t,
Lo, he raised [me] up.
Aqqi the water drawer, to [his] (adopted) sonship
[L]o, he raised [me].
Aqqi the water drawer, to his gardening
[L]o, [he] set [me].
[During] my gardening
Lo, Ishtar fell in love with [me]—
For [fifty]-five years
Lo, I wield[ed] the kingship. (ll. 1–13)
(For original text and restorations, see Lewis 1980: 24–25.)

The analogies to the Moses story are clear. Moses' anonymous parents are identified only by tribal affiliation; Sargon's anonymous parents are identified only by occupation and region. Moses' mother is a Levite, later the priestly caste of Israel; Sargon's mother is a priestess. Moses' mother may not keep her child; Sargon's mother may not bear a child at all. Moses' father is inactive; Sargon's father is absent and unknown. Moses and Sargon are each set in or by a periodically inundating river in a reed vessel coated with bitumen. Both accounts resonate with the Flood traditions of their respective civilizations (Cohen 1972; Lewis 1980: 46; see below). Moses and Sargon are each rescued and adopted by strangers, and come under female protection. Both men are divinely elected to lead their peoples. Each story has a character whose name or title associates him with drawing from water: *mōše(h)* (Moses) and *dālû* 'water-drawer' (his name Aqqi 'I poured' [?] may also be relevant [cf. Lewis 1980: 48]). Finally, as Sargon becomes an apprentice gardener until his election by Ishtar, so Moses becomes an indentured shepherd until called by Yahweh (Exodus 3–4).

Another oft-cited parallel to 1:22–2:10 comes from Ptolemaic Egypt. Here all the characters are divine:

> Seth was ranging about looking for Horus when he was a child in his nest at Khemmis. His mother hid him in a papyrus-(thicket), and Nephthys' mat (?) was over him. She hid (him) as 'Child-who-is-in-the-papyrus-(thicket). . . . Another version: he was sailing about in a boat of papyrus, and Isis said to Thoth, "Let me see my son who is hidden in the marshes."
> (Translation from Redford 1967: 222.)

Though much is unclear, we recognize a threatened child secreted by his mother in the rushes of the Nile delta or sailing in a papyrus vessel. But the resemblance to the Moses story is less impressive than in the case of Sargon.

The oldest known example of the Floating Foundling motif comes from sixteenth-century Anatolia (Otten 1973; Lewis 1980: 156; Hoffner 1990: 62–63). The Hittite story begins with a queen who, ashamed at birthing thirty sons within a single year, deposits them in a vessel coated with oil (Hoffner 1995: 112). She then abandons them to the river. Later the children are rescued from the sea and raised by gods. They eventually discover their true identity and return home.

To go on endlessly with parallels from ancient Greece, India and Rome, not to mention later literature, would be pointless; Lewis (1980: 149–209) summarizes sixty-four tales, and even he is selective. Though there is dependence between some of the examples, others come from regions or times so remote that we must regard them as spontaneous creations. Even where direct influence is demonstrable, we must still ask what motivated the borrowing. What is the power of this archetypical tale?

The abandonment of children is probably universal, as are mechanisms for adoption. Mesopotamian texts, our oldest sources, refer to real or symbolic abandonment (Ebeling 1932; Childs 1965: 111; Cohen 1972; Lewis 1980: 54–55; Malul 1990; for further bibliography, see Knobloch 1992). Somewhat surprisingly, however, the Torah contains no legislation concerning adoption.

The practice surely existed in ancient Israel (*pace* Jacob 1992: 30). We read several times of elevating a *relative* to sonship, no doubt the preferred course in a tribal society (e.g., Gen 48:5–20; Esth 2:7; see de Vaux 1961: 51–52). There is also ample if indirect evidence for the adoption of strangers. On the mundane level, the best-known example is Abram's provisional adoption of a servant as his heir (Gen 15:2–3). There is also the story of Solomon's judgment: a childless woman attempts to fraudulently acquire another's son (1 Kgs 3:16–28). Judg 17:11 may describe a *de facto* adoption—"the Levite agreed to live with the man, and the lad was to him like one of his sons"—although we might have expected *libnô 'as his son' (cf. 2 Sam 9:11, where Mephibosheth clearly is *not* adopted). At the cosmic level, Ps 2:6–8 describes Yahweh's adoption of the Davidic king: "I have anointed my king on Zion, my holy mountain. . . . He [Yahweh] has said to me [the king]], 'You are my son; I have begotten you today. Ask of me, and I will make the nations your inheritance, your possession the ends of the earth'" (cf. 2 Sam 7:14 and parallels; Ps 89:27–28). In this coronation liturgy, we find reflected a ritual for human adoption, complete with a detailing of inheritance rights.

Like the king, all Israel is sometimes regarded as Yahweh's foster child: e.g., Deut 14:1; Jer 31:9, 20; Hos 11:1 (Melnyk 1993). According to Deut 32:10–20, Yahweh found Israel in the desert, embraced him, taught and loved him, treated him as a bird treats its young, led him and suckled him, and considered the people his own children. Ezek 16:4–14 similarly describes Israel as an abandoned baby girl, taken in, washed and cherished by Yahweh. Both texts, like Exod 1:22–2:10, presuppose the adoption of exposed infants. And Jer 3:19 envisions Yahweh's future adoption of Israel, including specification of the inheritance: "How would I set you among (my) sons and give you a pleasant land. . . . You would call me 'my Father.'" Lastly, the frequent claim that Israel is "called by Yahweh's name" (e.g., Deut 28:10; Jer 14:9, etc.) may betoken their adoption (cf. Gen 48:16).

In societies practicing exposure and adoption, childhood fears of abandonment, and suspicions (or hopes) of being a foundling, would be widespread. Tales of adoption would be particularly fascinating. Listeners would identify with the endangered infant, who embodies their primal fears and fantasies (cf. Rank 1952: 64–69). And parents would also empathize with the infant's terrified mother and father.

That so many protagonists of myth and legend should be raised by foster parents makes sense. Heroes often transgress normally uncrossable boundaries in nature or society. For example, when Mowgli and Tarzan are adopted by beasts, they acquire animal as well as human virtues. Similarly, the prince reared by poor folk (or vice versa as in Exodus) is able to combine a natural mastery with the common touch. Buber (1946: 35) writes apropos of Moses (and doubtless of himself): "The liberator . . . has to be introduced into the stronghold of the aliens, into that royal court by which Israel has been enslaved; and he must grow up there. This is a kind of liberation which cannot be brought about by anyone who grew up as a slave, nor yet by anyone who is not connected with the slaves, but only by one of the latter who has been brought up in the midst of the aliens and has received an education equipping him with all their wisdoms and powers, and thereafter 'goes forth to his brethren and observes their burdens.'"

A common but not universal feature of the abandoned-hero tale is the exposure in a vessel on a river. This, too, has deep psychological resonance. Rank (1952: 69–70) interprets Moses' coated, floating container as a sort of inside-out womb, from which he is reborn to his foster mother. Rank's intuition that the river represents amniotic fluid can be supported, to an extent, by parallels from Near Eastern literature. Hammurapi Code §185 speaks of adopting a son *ina mêšu* 'from his water,' i.e., from birth (for other texts, see *CAD* M II, 2.b'). This idiom probably underlies the Sargon tradition. Moreover, as Hos 12:4–5 makes clear, Jacob's wrestling with an angel in a river (Gen 32:25–32) parallels his wrestling with his brother *in utero* (Gen 25:22). The very nation of Israel is, in a sense, born in the Sea (Exodus 14–15), whose waters Job 38:8–9 likens to amniotic fluid. We may also compare the symbolic rebirth by baptism in the conversion rites of Judaism and Christianity (cf. Origen *Homiliae in Exodum* 2.4). Matt 3:13–17; Mark 1:9–11; Luke 3:21–22; John 1:33–34; 3:5 explicitly associate immersion and sonship.

We must leave open the question of whether the Moses story depends directly upon an Assyrian, Egyptian or Hittite prototype. Only the last clearly antedates the Bible. But the Sargon story, which may be older than the tablets on which it survives, is the closest to Exodus, and direct influence is not impossible. We know that Sargon's fame had spread eastward to Elam, westward to Egypt and northward to Anatolia, so why not to Canaan (see Lewis 1980: 109–47)? But whether Israel inherited the Floating Foundling Tale or created it anew, its truth must be sought within the human psyche, not in historical fact.

A DIFFERENT HERO

As Loewenstamm (1992b), Sarna (1986: 30–31) and others emphasize, Moses' exposure and adoption in fact deviate significantly from the heroic pattern. This is not surprising. Few specimens of any folktale will be "ideal," possessing all the features cataloged by folklorists. Each will be unique, reflecting its societal and narrational contexts. Exodus 2 follows the type in many particulars, but is highly original in other respects. Moses is not really separated from his family, at least initially, and Pharaoh's daughter knows he is a Hebrew, although whether she and he hide his identity is unclear (see COMMENT to 2:11–15a). The pathos of abandonment is minimal: the child is not set adrift in the Nile, to be menaced by crocodiles or to float out to sea. Rather, he rests securely in the shallows, his sister standing sentry. He is not raised in obscurity, safe from his foes, but as a prince in the court of his would-be murderer. Whereas the typical hero eventually leaves his lowly environment to assume his rightful glory, Moses flees the Pharaonic court to discover his path first among desert nomads and later among slaves.

SPECULATION: Despite my overall skepticism, it is barely possible that the unusual motif of adoption by a princess dimly reflects actual events. Not all Asiatics in New Kingdom Egypt were enslaved. Since at least the reign of Thutmosis III, foreign princesses were married to Egyptian nobles, and Canaanite princelings were raised as pampered hostages at the royal court, *the better to ensure their fathers' loyalty, and to cultivate the princes' future*

sympathies (see Helck 1971: 350–52; Redford 1992: 198, 224; on commoners raised at court in earlier times, see Erman 1969: 77–78). Such foreign
guests could also prove useful for meddling in local politics, as the stories
of Hadad of Edom (1 Kgs 11:14–22) and Jeroboam of Israel (1 Kgs 11:40)
illustrate. The case of the former is particularly striking for its parallels to
the Joseph and Moses stories (cf. Van Seters 1994: 32):

> And he [Pharaoh] gave him [Hadad] a house and food . . . and land. And
> Hadad found much favor in Pharaoh's eyes, and he gave him a wife, the
> sister of his own wife Tahpenes the queen. And Tahpenes' sister bore
> Genubath his son, and Tahpenes weaned him in Pharaoh's house. And
> Genubath was in Pharaoh's house among Pharaoh's sons. (1 Kgs 11:18–20)

If the historical Moses was the scion of a leading Hebrew family reared in
the Egyptian court, we could easily explain his Egyptian name as well as his
influence among Hebrews and (if Exodus may be believed) Egyptians. We
would also understand why his fictional biography deviates from the norm.
For more facts and speculations about the historical Exodus and Moses, see
APPENDIX B, vol. II.

MOSES' ARK

The Sargon tradition is not the only Mesopotamian text resembling the early
chapters of Exodus. There is also a marked similarity to the legend of the
Flood survivor Atra-ḫasīs (Lambert and Millard 1969; on the relation with
Exodus, see Kikawada 1975 and Batto 1992: esp. 30–31). The plot is as follows:
The minor gods, weary of digging ditches, go on strike and waken their master
Enlil. Humanity is created as a substitute labor force, and Enlil returns to his
sleep. But the humans prove so fecund and active that Enlil is recurrently
disturbed—somewhat like a new parent. He tries various methods to curb the
infestation of these formerly useful beings: first plague, then drought. Each
time, the friendly god Ea helps Atra-ḫasīs save himself and humanity. Enlil finally sends the Deluge. But Ea secretly advises Atra-ḫasīs to build a boat of
reed and pitch and to board his family and various animals. When the waters
subside, Atra-ḫasīs debarks under the protection of the goddess Ishtar, despite
Enlil's continued hostility. To limit subsequent human proliferation, the gods
create sterility, celibate orders of priestesses and a baby-killing she-demon. We
do not possess the end of the Old Babylonian *Epic of Atra-ḫasīs*, but, in a later
version, the survivor and his wife are accepted into the company of the gods
and granted immortality (*Gilgamesh* tablet XI [*ANET* 93–95]).

In turn, Exod 1:1–2:10 could be epitomized as follows: The Israelites are
fruitful and overpopulate the land, irritating the king. He adopts successive
measures to suppress them: first servitude, then killing babies at birth. But the
plan is foiled. A savior is set adrift in an "ark" (*tēbâ*) of reed and pitch, from

which he will safely emerge, protected by a princess from the king's wrath and even elevated to quasi-royal status.

What do we make of the similarities? Do they simply reflect shared story-telling conventions? Or is Exodus based upon *Atra-ḫasis?* The last possibility cannot be ruled out *a priori.* The great popularity of the Mesopotamian Flood tradition is witnessed by the numerous versions found throughout the ancient Near East, including the two intermingled accounts of Noah's ark in Genesis 6–9 (J and P; for documentary analysis, see any critical commentary). More-over, as we have just seen, Exod 1:22–2:10 may depend upon another Meso-potamian tradition, the Birth of Sargon.

But I must register a caveat. Exod 1:1–2:10 stems from, not one writer, but three. Most of the similarities to *Atra-ḫasis* come from J, yet it is the compos-ite JE that is closest to the Babylonian epic. It is difficult to imagine Redac-tor^JE consciously mimicking a foreign Flood story. (Conceivably, there was an Israelite Flood account even closer to *Atra-ḫasis* than Genesis 6–9, but this is sheerest speculation.)

The real explanation for the similarity of the Mesopotamian and biblical tra-ditions is probably more complicated. On the one hand, given that *Atra-ḫasis* and Exod 1:1–2:10 are both about population control, narrative necessity creates certain similarities. We should expect a futile attempt or attempts to eradicate the offensive humans, each followed by a salvation. The combination of J and E would entail an accumulation of dangers and escapes reminiscent of *Atra-ḫasis,* even in the absence of direct influence. (On the overpopulation motif, see also COMMENT to 1:1–14.)

On the other hand, the resemblances between Atra-ḫasis' ark and Moses' basket have a different origin. Exod 1:22–2:10 alludes to an Israelite Flood tradition—witness the term *tēbâ* 'vessel' (see NOTE to 2:3)—ultimately based upon a Mesopotamian prototype. The Sargon legend, too, refers to the origi-nal Babylonian Flood tradition, featuring a saving, pitch-besmeared reed ves-sel with a *bābu* 'opening' (Cohen 1972: 43–44; Lewis 1980: 46). Moreover, that Sargon's mother must surrender her child to the waters is an appropriate punishment for a lapsed *ēn(e)tu;* for that office, according to *Atra-ḫasis,* was instituted after the Flood precisely to limit reproduction.

In short, Exod 1:1–2:10 is related to, but not directly dependent upon, the Babylonian *Epic of Atra-ḫasis.*

WHERE IS GOD?

The Deity makes no appearance in the first two chapters of Exodus. In fact, he is barely mentioned. As in the stories of Joseph, David and Esther, the pivotal role of coincidence may suggest that God is invisibly at work, turning seeming setbacks into triumphs (Philo *Moses* 1.12; cf. Gen 45:5–9; 50:20). But the text reserves Yahweh's grand entrance for his revelation to Moses (Exodus 3–4 [JE]; 2:23b–25 and 6:2–8 [P]).

IV. Who set you as a man, ruler and judge? (2:11–15a)

2   [11(J)]And it happened in those days, and Moses grew. And he went out to his brothers and looked upon their tasks and saw an Egyptian man striking a Hebrew man from his brothers. [12]And he turned like this and like this, and he saw that there was no man. Then he struck the Egyptian and hid him in the sand. [13]And he went out on the second day, and, see: two Hebrew men fighting. And he said to the evil one, "Why do you strike your fellow?" [14]But he said, "Who set you as a man, ruler and judge over us? To kill me, do you *say*, as you killed the Egyptian?"

And Moses feared and *said*, "The affair has become known after all." [15a]And Pharaoh heard this affair and sought to kill Moses. So Moses fled from Pharaoh's *face* and settled in the land of Midian.

ANALYSIS

TEXTUAL NOTES

†2:11. *those days.* 4QExod[b] and LXX have "those *many* days"; i.e., they add *hrbym* after *hymym*. The word is presumably borrowed from 2:23, although haplography by homoioteleuton (*-ym . . . -ym*) cannot be excluded (Cross 1994: 89).

to his brothers. LXX adds "Israel's Sons."

from his brothers. LXX again adds "Israel's Sons," and this time so does Syr.

2:13 *he went out.* 4QExod[b] and some Syr MSS add "and he saw" (*wyr'*). O'Connell (n.d.) observes the similar sequence "went out . . . and saw" in v 11, which could have motivated an expansion in v 13. Moreover, *wayyar(')* *wəhinnē(h)* 'and he saw and, see' is a ubiquitous formula and thus *lectio facilior* (Gen 8:13; 15:17; 19:28; 22:13, etc.). MT is preferable.

2:14. *said.* 4QExod[b], Syr and a few witnesses to LXX add "to him."

and judge. 4QExod[b] and Sam read *wlš(w)pṭ* 'and *as* a judge.'

†*as you killed the Egyptian.* LXX and Syr insert, in a variety of places, "yesterday" (cf. Acts 7:28; Jub 47:12). This variant, absent in MT, Sam and 4QExod[b], might be secondary. If original, however, *'tm(w)l* 'yesterday' fell out by homoioarkton before *'t-hmṣry* 'the Egyptian' (D. N. Freedman, privately).

feared. 4QExod[b] and Kenn 95 add *m'(w)d(h)* 'very.'

The affair. LXX and possibly 4QExod[b] read *hdbr hzh* 'this affair' (Cross 1994: 90).

†*Has become known.* Perhaps the MT perfect *nôdaʿ* should be revocalized as a participle **nôdāʿ* 'is known.'

after all. On LXX, see NOTE.

†2:15. *settled in the land of Midian.* So MT; LXX and Syr have different readings. Syr has "he *went* to the land of Midian," while LXX reads "he settled in the land of Midian; *going into the land of Midian.* . . ." The simplest explanation is that there existed two Hebrew variants: *wayyēšeb bə'ereṣ midyān* (MT) and **wayyēlek 'el-'ereṣ midyān* (Syr *Vorlage*). LXX has combined the two, albeit with reversed temporal order (hysteron proteron; i.e., Moses should first *go* to Midian and then *settle* there). If the Syr *Vorlage* is original, MT has brought *wayyēšeb* forward from later in the verse. But MT *yšb* 'settle, sit' links consecutive episodes in 2:15a, 15b, just as *gdl* 'grow, grow up' connects vv 10, 11. My translation follows MT, since Syr is unsupported by Hebrew evidence. (Finally: it is not impossible that the original was an unattested **wayyēlek 'el-'ereṣ midyān wayyēšeb bə'ereṣ midyān* 'and he went to the land of Midian and settled in the land of Midian,' which suffered metathesis in LXX and haplography in MT and Syr.)

SOURCE ANALYSIS

Source attribution for Exodus 2, as we have already seen, is inherently difficult. There is only one account of Moses' arrival in Midian, where both J and E locate his first encounter with God (chaps. 3–4). But there is strong evidence for the Yahwistic authorship of vv 11–15a: namely, its continuity with 2:15b–22 (J; see below).

One sign of unitary authorship in 2:11–22 as a whole is the striking repetition of *'îš* 'man': 2:11 (2x), 12, 13 (plural *'ănāšîm*), 14, 19, 20, 21. In all, the singular occurs seven times plus one plural. As we have observed, this mechanical method of unifying two episodes may symbolize Moses' maturation and socialization, in contrast to the repeated *yeled* 'child' of the preceding unit (see SOURCE ANALYSIS to 1:22–2:10).

Moreover, pervading chap. 2 is the theme of Moses' ambiguous nationality (see COMMENT). While this could be the happy by-product of redaction, design by a single author seems more likely.

Furthermore, 4:19 (J) refers explicitly to the events of 2:11–15a: "All the men seeking your *soul* have died." Some find here a contradiction, since in 2:15a only Pharaoh seeks Moses' life (NOTE to 4:19). But more likely, 2:15a implies that Pharaoh gives orders to have Moses killed. It is these henchmen, along with their boss, whose obituary we read in 4:19. Still, we must be cautious. Assuming that 18:4 "my father's deity . . . rescued me from Pharaoh's sword," is Elohistic, E, too, must have told of hostility between Moses and the king.

REDACTION ANALYSIS

Redactor^JE eliminated E's version of Moses' arrival in Midian. J and E must have been either so different as to be irreconcilable or so similar as to be redundant. At any rate, the combination of J and E allows Moses to undergo maturation. The impetuous youth of J grows into a man "very humble, more than all humanity that is on the earth's *face*" (Num 12:3 [E]). The man with no right to serve as "ruler and judge" (2:14 [J]) himself appoints "rulers" and "judges" (18:21–26 [E]).

NOTES

2:11. *grew*. I.e., "grew up" (cf. Gen 21:20; 1 Sam 3:19), or, in our context, "continued to grow." To the double *wayyigdal* 'grew,' Jacob (1992: 141) compares 1 Sam 2:21; 3:19; see also Gen 21:8, 20. By later tradition, Moses was forty (Acts 7:23) or forty-two years old (Jub 47:1; 48:1) when he fled Egypt. Here, however, one gets the impression of an impetuous, aggressive youth.

their tasks. Alternatively, "their labor gangs"; see NOTE to 1:11.

an Egyptian man striking. This is a stereotypical scene in Egyptian art as far back as c. 3000 B.C.E.: Pharaoh wields the mace against hapless outlanders (e.g., ANEP 91–92; see Schäfer 1957). One imagines that, for the Israelite reader, the verbal icon of an Egyptian beating an Asiatic resonated as strongly as the visual image.

2:12. *like this and like this*. We would say "here and there" or "this way and that."

there was no man. There are two ways to take this (*Exod. Rab.* 1:29; *Lev. Rab.* 32:4; Cassuto 1967: 22; Jacob 1992: 37–38). Either Moses is skulking, making sure there are no witnesses—the usual interpretation—or he is looking for someone else to save the Hebrew.

In support of the latter reading, we can cite several parallels from Second Isaiah: "And I saw, and there was no man" (Isa 41:28); "Why have I come, and there is no man? . . . Is my own arm too short to redeem?" (Isa 50:2); "And Yahweh saw, and it was bad in his eyes, that there was no justice. And he saw that there was no man, and he was horrified, that there was none to interfere. So his arm gave him victory, and his righteousness supported him" (Isa 59:15b–16); "And I gazed, and there was no helper; and I was desolate, with no supporter. So my arm saved me, and my wrath, it supported me" (Isa 63:5). Compare also Judg 12:3, "I saw that you were not saving, so I put my *soul* in my [own] hands"; 2 Sam 22:42, "They gaze, but there is no savior; to Yahweh, but he did not answer them." So, too, Moses may be seeking someone else to intervene.

Still, Moses' hiding the body and perturbed aside, "the affair has become known after all," imply intentional stealth. In v 12, then, it seems he is indeed peering about for possible witnesses, not helpers. Or we might synthesize the two interpretations: the absence of bystanders both forces Moses to act and gives him hope of impunity. But, whatever the reason for Moses' circumspection, it is the reaction of an ordinary human, far from stereotypical heroic impetuosity (see COMMENT).

struck. Hebrew *hikkâ* may imply lethal force, but often does not (e.g., vv 11, 13). Later the Hebrew combatant truly names Moses' deed: *hāragtā* 'you killed' (v 14).

2:13. *the second day.* Either the next day, or the second day with which the narrative is concerned. (The variant "yesterday" [2:14] does not help, since *'etmôl* can also mean "in the past" [see TEXTUAL NOTE].)

fighting. Though the language is unspecific, the context shows that this is the same situation Moses encountered the first day: not an equal fight, but one man beating another.

evil one. I.e., the one Moses presumes is in the wrong, the aggressor (Bekhor Shor; Jacob 1992: 38; cf. Deut 25:1; 1 Kgs 8:32; Prov 24:24). The term *rāšāʿ* has judicial connotations (e.g., Isa 5:23), and Moses' question is an implicit condemnation, hence the indignant "Who appointed you as . . . judge?" (v 14).

fellow. Here *rēaʿ* connotes "fellow Hebrew."

2:14. *as a man.* Feeling this to be an awkward locution (LXX simply omits "man"), Dahood (1981: 413–14) interprets "O man," with rare vocative lamedh. This is possible for MT but is excluded for Sam's *l'yš śr wlšpṭ*. In any event, Dahood's reading is unnecessarily exotic. There are many parallels to *'îš śar wəšōpēṭ*: *'ănāšîm 'aḥîm* 'men, brothers' (Gen 13:8); *'îš kōhēn* 'a man, a priest' (Lev 21:9); *'îš nābî'* 'a man, a prophet' (Judg 6:8); *'îš sārîs* 'a man, a eunuch' (Jer 38:7); *'îš gēr ʿămālēqî* 'a man, an Amalekite sojourner' (2 Sam 1:13), and *'îš ṣar wə'ôyēb* 'a man, an adversary and enemy' (Esth 7:6) (Dillmann 1880: 17; Childs 1974: 28).

ruler and judge. Both *śar* and *šōpēṭ* bear many nuances. The former can designate a member of the nobility or a royal official, while the latter refers to a judge or war leader, like the protagonists in the Book of Judges or the Punic rulers known in Latin transcription as *suf(f)etes*. "Ruler and judge" is a prosaic example of the redundancy beloved of biblical poets; the analogous word pair from Ugaritic verse is *zbl-ṭpt* 'ruler-judge' (Cassuto 1967: 23). *Śar* and *šōpēṭ* are not quite synonyms, however. Moses acts as "judge" when he decides who is in the wrong and as "ruler" when he executes justice.

Who do the Hebrews think Moses is? If the slave regards him as an Egyptian, his question is tantamount to "What right have you Egyptians to enslave us?" Assuming, however, he recognizes Moses as a fellow Hebrew (see COMMENT), he is asking, "Who appointed you as tribal elder to judge and intervene in an internal quarrel?" *Śārîm* 'rulers' are connected with *zəqēnîm* 'elders' (Num 22:7, 14; Judg 8:6, 14, 16; Isa 3:14), while *šōpəṭîm* 'judges' are elsewhere mentioned with *šōṭərîm* 'officers' (Deut 16:18), in turn associated with *zəqēnîm* (Num 11:16; Deut 29:9; 31:28). Josh 8:33; 23:2; 24:1 list elders, officers, clan heads and judges together. These men are the standing authority in Israel before Yahweh commissions Moses (see COMMENT to Exodus 3–4, pp. 232–33). The Hebrews' words recall the Sodomites' question apropos of Lot: "Should one come to sojourn and pass judgment?" (Gen 19:9 [J]).

say. I.e., propose, intend. The verb *'āmar* often connotes mental action; see NOTE to *"said"* below.

feared. Previously, Moses "saw" (*wyr'*) (vv 11, 12); now he "feared" (*wyyr'*).

said. I.e., thought. Biblical Hebrew lacks a verb meaning "to think" prefacing indirect speech. Instead, one "says" one's thoughts, if only in one's heart (Niehoff 1992).

affair. Literally "word." *Dābār* sometimes bears judicial overtones (e.g., 18:16, 19, 22, 26).

after all. This is a rough interpretation of emphatic *'ākēn*, expressing surprise. LXX, which treats the sentence as a question, perhaps reads **hăkēn*.

2:15. *face.* Hebrew routinely uses *pānîm* in the sense of "presence" or "proximity."

Midian. The land of Midian is off the eastern coast of the Gulf of Aqaba. For more information on Midian and the Midianites, see APPENDIX B, vol. II.

COMMENT

THE DISILLUSIONED PRINCE

Surprisingly, the Bible tells us nothing about Moses' childhood (Jacob 1992: 43). Later legend inevitably remedies this reticence with tales of supernatural precocity (Driver 1911: 11–12; Ginzberg 1928: 2.269–89; Philo *Moses* 1.18–31). Still, despite sporadic idealization, Moses remains human throughout the Torah. From the story of his unlikely adoption, the plot skips directly to his young adulthood. We assume that, in the interim, Moses was raised as an Egyptian prince (see NOTE to 2:10). But our text shows little interest in his life before he meets Yahweh, just as Israel's experience in Egypt is of no concern until after Yahweh's first contact through Moses.

Like the tale of Moses' exposure, 2:11–15a seems to adapt a common folkloric pattern: a naive prince ventures outside the palace to witness the common life and is permanently transformed. One thinks of various monarchs who, in fact or legend, traverse their realms incognito (Thompson 1955: motif P14.19)—though Moses is not a prince masquerading as a commoner, but a slave masquerading as a prince. We especially recall Siddhartha, who like Moses leaves his royal estate to view human misery and subsequently undergoes a spiritual transformation.

The differences between the two stories are telling. Siddhartha's tale is always recounted dramatically, with emphasis on his soft life prior to enlightenment. The Yahwist, however, scarcely hints at this, and spares barely a dozen sentences for the entire incident. Unlike Siddhartha, Moses does not meet misery by accident but seeks it from the start. Moreover, the suffering that moves him is not the unfairness and pain of the entire human condition, but a specific situation of social injustice. He is therefore initially drawn to violence, not escape, as a remedy. Like Siddhartha, Moses forsakes luxury and attains illumination (at a sacred shrub, no less!). But the source of his wisdom is revelation, not introspection. Both men return to their societies to share their experiences. Yet the Israelite solution — Law — differs radically from the Buddha's.

There are also fundamental differences between the functions of these stories within Yahwism and Buddhism. The Buddha's enlightenment is a model for the adept. Nowhere, however, does the Torah enjoin imitation of Moses as a religious exercise.

While the best-known parallels are postbiblical, we can cite at least one ancient Near Eastern example of the tale of the Disillusioned Prince. In the Sumerian poem "Gilgamesh and the Land of the Living," the king tells his god, "In my city man dies, oppressed is the heart, / Man perishes, heavy is the heart, / I peered over the wall, / Saw dead bodies floating in the river's waters, / As for me, I too will be served thus" (Kramer 1986: 191). The hero then goes on a quest to attain eternal fame, a theme developed further by the Akkadian *Epic of Gilgamesh* (ANET³ 72–99, 503–7; Dalley 1989: 39–153). *Gilgamesh*, too, describes a self-indulgent monarch who discovers his fear of death and goes on several journeys. But, unlike Moses and the Buddha, Gilgamesh's compassion is primarily for himself. The Sumerian despot is no religious innovator, sharing his enlightenment with humanity. He is rather humanity itself, with all its potential and limitation. The message of Mesopotamian religion is resignation, whereas Buddhism and Yahwism offer positive solutions to ennui and despair.

CRIME AND PUNISHMENT

In 2:11–15, Moses intervenes in parallel incidents, narrated with typical biblical concision that says little and implies much. We are told, not what Moses feels, but what he does. If one day he precipitously goes to see his brothers' labors, we know his disquiet and commiseration have been growing. If he strikes an Egyptian, we know he is outraged. If he hides the body, we know he is afraid. The style of narration invites the reader into characters' minds, precisely by *not* divulging their thoughts.

In the first episode, Moses sees an Egyptian striking a Hebrew. The severity of the beating is uncertain, as *hikkâ* 'hit' can also mean "kill." But the intent and effect are probably not lethal (see NOTE to 2:12). Since Moses has gone out to behold Israel's tasks, Rashi infers that the culprit is one of the corvée masters (1:11). This may be so, but the aggressor is called simply "an Egyptian man." The author is not primarily depicting the relationship between slaves and their bosses, but between Israel and Egypt.

Moses gazes around, either in hopes of finding someone else to save the Hebrew or, failing that, to ascertain the absence of witnesses (NOTE to 2:12). Then he kills (*hikkâ*) the Egyptian. Lexically, we might say, the Egyptian gets his just deserts, blow for blow (Cassuto 1967: 22). But the beating he receives differs from the beating he was dispensing, and Moses' act is morally wrong.

Lamech once boasted he would "kill a man for wounding me, and a child for hitting me" (Gen 4:23 [J]). If this is unacceptable, how much less entitled is Moses to kill for the wounding of a stranger! By biblical law, moderately drubbing a slave is permissible (21:20–21). Thus, for all Moses or we know, the Hebrew deserves his punishment.

It is not killing per se that disturbs the author; the Torah is no pacifist tract. There are military victories and bloody executions; the Levites (32:26–29) and Phinehas (Numbers 25) are even rewarded for (justifiable) homicide with sacred offices. There is, however, a world of difference between killing in obedience to Yahweh and killing to avenge a beating. And Moses does not even sin boldly. The Levites and Phinehas do not peer this way and that before striking.

Thus, Moses' violence is not that of the macho soldier. Were he the typical hero, his youthful deed would start him on a life of conquests (for midrashim on Moses' military prowess, see Ginzberg 1928: 2.283–89). He would eventually challenge the armies of Egypt and personally defeat Pharaoh. Then he would lead his people in triumph to the promised land, which he would conquer and rule in splendor. Instead, the hero who accomplishes all this is "Yahweh Man of War" (15:3).

At any rate, despite the lack of witnesses, the news gets around, presumably spread by the rescued Hebrew (O'Connell n.d.). When Moses subsequently sees two Hebrews fighting, he can no more forbear from this conflict than from the first. By styling one of the adversaries "the evil one," the author emphasizes the parallel with the first incident. Here is another act of oppression, the more heinous because victim and aggressor are compatriots.

Whether he has learned a lesson about rashness, or whether he is more patient with Hebrews than with Egyptians, this time Moses does not shoot first and ask questions later. He makes the inquiry he should have made the first time: has the apparent aggressor good cause? But Moses is rebuffed with rude words that implicitly admit guilt. The malfeasant saves himself from a beating or worse by shocking Moses with the revelation that his own crime is known. Instantly, he ceases to worry about the beaten slave and begins to think of his own safety. By breaking off, the text implies that Moses quits the scene at once, leaving matters unresolved.

An interesting question is whether the fighting Hebrews recognize Moses as a compatriot. Moses asks the aggressor in 2:13, "Why do you strike your fellow (Hebrew)?" as if feigning not to be an Israelite. Moreover, he is said to resemble an Egyptian, at least to Midianites (2:19 [J]). But nomad shepherdesses might not be experts on Egyptian fashion, and "Why do you strike your fellow?" could also be said by an Israelite. Indeed, from the wicked Hebrew's question, "Do you *say* to kill me as you killed the Egyptian?" (v 14), some infer that he knows Moses is an Israelite (e.g., Greenberg 1969: 45). But how else would a Hebrew ask this question? Might he not so describe any Egyptian, irrespective of his interlocutor? The best evidence that the wicked Hebrew recognizes Moses is his question "Who set you as a man, ruler and judge over us?" These words would be presumptuous addressed to an Egyptian lordling. But they would make sense directed to a pretentious Hebrew usurping the tribal elders' authority. Thus, when Moses fears that "the affair has become known," he may be speaking, not just of his homicide, but also of his slave birth (Auerbach 1975: 18).

The guilty Hebrew's question is well taken, even if the source is personally objectionable (cf. Hendel 1987a: 147). In fact, no one has made Moses the judge and ruler of Israel; he is a vigilante. Plastaras (1966: 45) contrasts the biblical judges, moved to violence by Yahweh's spirit (Judg 6:34; 11:29; 14:19; 15:14-17; 1 Sam 11:6-7). Besides Moses, another self-appointed judge is Absalom, attempting to usurp the authority of his father, David (2 Sam 15:2-6) (cf. Niehr 1986: 135).

Our story sets up Moses' appointment in the next chapter. It shows the futility of attempting to rescue Israel without divine aid. Moses cannot kill each taskmaster individually; his initial intervention only alienates both the Egyptians and his own people. At the Burning Bush, Yahweh will give Moses an answer for the wicked Hebrew—"Yahweh, your fathers' deity . . . has sent me" (3:15)—but even during his commissioning, Moses will still doubt his legitimacy in the eyes of Israel (3:11-4:10 [mostly E]; 6:12 [P], 30 [R]). He continues to rely on the elders to confirm his authority (see COMMENT to Exodus 3-4, pp. 232-33).

Viewed from this perspective, the seemingly minor altercations in Exodus 2 set up the remainder of the Pentateuch. They show the necessity for a society governed by divinely inspired law (tôrâ), not rough justice. Moses the vigilante, with his instinct for equity, must become Moses the prophetic Lawgiver. The impetuous youth will mature into the archetype of humility (Numbers 11-12), so popular an arbiter that he must delegate his judicial authority to other "rulers" and "judges" (Exod 18:13-26). Conversely, Israelite hostility toward Moses, first articulated by the wicked Hebrew, becomes a Leitmotiv for the rest of the Torah. As one Israelite malfeasant questions the authority of the man who rescued one Israelite from one Egyptian, so the Israelite people will continually question the authority of him who saved all Israel from Egypt (cf. Acts 7:35-53; on the "murmuring tradition," see Coats 1968).

We are used to finding escapist entertainment in the lone hero, above any law, single-handedly righting society's wrongs. In five verses, the Yahwist presents a more realistic analysis of crime and punishment. He characteristically does justice to all sides of a moral dilemma. The author must sympathize with Moses' act (cf. Acts 7:25). Yet he acknowledges that homicide is sordid, difficult to conceal and liable to bring ill upon the perpetrator. I shall argue below that Yahweh in fact nearly executes Moses for this very crime (4:24-26); see COMMENT to Exodus 3-4, pp. 233-38; Propp (1993).

WHO'S IN CONTROL?

Yahweh does not summon Moses to Midian. Rather, like all events so far in Exodus, Moses' flight is "providential." What if he had not killed the Egyptian?

Suppose his crime had gone undetected? It is up to us to infer, or not to infer, that the hidden Deity is guiding events, drawing Moses toward the rendezvous in the wilderness. And, unbeknownst to Moses, his flight from Egypt to meet Jethro and Yahweh at Mount Horeb foreshadows the emigration of the entire Hebrew nation (Schmidt 1988: 82).

V. A sojourner was I in a foreign land (2:15b–23a)

2   [15b(J)]And he settled beside the well.
[16]Now, Midian's priest had seven daughters; and they came and drew and filled the troughs to water their father's flock. [17]But the shepherds came and expelled them. Then Moses arose and saved them and watered their flock.
[18]And they returned to Reuel their father, and he said, "Why have you hastened to come today?"
[19]And they said, "An Egyptian man rescued us from the shepherds' *arm*, and he also drew, drew for us and watered the flock."
[20]And he said to his daughters, "So where is he? Why is it you left the man? Call to him, that he may eat food."
[21]So Moses agreed to settle with the man. And he gave his daughter Zipporah to Moses. [22]And she bore a son, and he called his name Gershom, for he said, "A sojourner was I in a foreign land."
[23a(?)]And it happened in those many days, and Egypt's king died.

ANALYSIS

TEXTUAL NOTES

2:16. *seven daughters.* LXX adds "tending the flock of their father Jothor," i.e., Jethro (some MSS read Ragouēl = Reuel). Since Jethro is not properly introduced until 3:1 (E), his mention here in LXX is probably secondary. 4QExod[b] adds that the girls were tending sheep (rw'[w]t), but then the fragment breaks off.

†*their father's flock.* 4QExod[b], Sam and Kenn 69, 80, 109 prefix the optional direct object marker *'ēt*. This could be an expansion, but *'t* may alternatively have dropped by homoioteleuton with *lhšqwt* 'to water.'

†2:17. *expelled them.* The final letter of *waygārəšûm* should theoretically be nun (feminine plural), not mem (masculine plural). This may merely be a "mistake" (a better word might be "choice") on the part of the original author, or an error committed by a later scribe (*m* and *n* sound similar and, in the old Hebrew script, look similar). Another source of confusion may have been the

mention of Gershom in v 22. On the phenomenon of gender incongruence in biblical Hebrew, see Levi (1987); compare NOTE to 2:17 "their flock."

and watered. LXX "*he drew for them* and watered" is probably an expansion based upon v 19.

2:18. *Reuel.* Some LXX MSS read "Jothor" = Jethro, presumably a harmonization with chap. 3; cf. v 16.

said. LXX and Syr add "to them."

to come. Syr instead has "to water," presumably an interpretive alteration.

2:19. *they said.* Syr adds "to him."

2:20. *So.* Syr does not reflect the conjunction *wə-*.

Call to. LXX and Rossi 554 begin with the conjunction *wə-*, while Syr prefixes "Go!"

†2:21. *Zipporah.* At the end of the verse, LXX, Sam, Kenn 603 and Syr add "for a wife." While this would be a natural expansion (cf. NOTE to 2:1), in this instance, *l'šh* 'for a wife' might be original, assuming it dropped because of visual similarity to *lmšh* 'to Moses.'

†2:22. *she bore.* LXX has "*conceiving in the womb, the woman* bore," as if loosely translating *wattahar hā'iššâ wattēled,* as in 2:2 (MT). This could be correct, assuming haplography by homoioarkton (*wt . . . wt*).

he called. Some MSS of MT and Tg. Onqelos (de Rossi 1784–85: 48) read *wtqr'* 'and *she* called.' On which parent names a child, see NOTE to 2:10.

Gershom. Syr "Gershon" is a confusion with Levi's son (6:16). On the relationship between Gershom and Gershon, see COMMENT to 6:2–7:7.

†*foreign land.* At the end of v 22, LXX MSS and Syr append, in various ways, Moses' other son, Eliezer, who first appears in 18:4. This is probably an addition to explain "sons" in 4:20 (O'Connell n.d.), itself likely an old corruption (see NOTE).

SOURCE ANALYSIS

This vignette seems to be from one hand, except perhaps the last half-verse. There is no trace of Priestly style. Since v 22, the naming of Gershom, is a doublet of 18:3 (E), and since Moses' father-in-law is Reuel, not Jethro, we are probably in J (see INTRODUCTION, pp. 50–51). Our episode parallels J's other well-side courtship scenes: Genesis 24 (Abraham's servant and Rebekah) and 29 (Jacob and Rachel). It also resembles Genesis 18–20 (J) in its idealized depiction of nomadic hospitality. Moreover, the term *rahat* 'trough' appears only in Exod 2:16 and Gen 30:38, 41 (J).

We cannot, however, assign v 23a to a source. It might be J's echo of v 15 and prelude to 4:19, E's introduction to 3:1, P's introduction to vv 23b–25 or R's link between J and P. If v 23a comes from J, Pharaoh's death means that it is safe for Moses to return. If it is Elohistic or Priestly, the implication is that, despite the tyrant's death, the Hebrews have no respite, for Egypt's wickedness is not limited to a single ruler (Bekhor Shor; Calvin). And if v 23a is editorial, both meanings operate simultaneously.

REDACTION ANALYSIS

If the Elohist's Moses was born in Egypt, we must assume that Redactor[JE] discarded E's account of the journey to Midian. This editorial procedure contrasts with that of the final Redactor, who was willing, for example, to preserve two versions of Jacob's journey to Aram (Gen 27:41–45 [J]; 28:1–7 [P]).

Exod 2:15b–23a once again shows Moses willing to intercede violently on behalf of the wronged. In the redacted text, his zeal for justice anticipates his two great achievements: liberating Israel and handing down a law code (*tôrâ*). The early chapters of Exodus prove that Moses, his frailties notwithstanding, was a fit vessel for Yahweh's spirit.

NOTES

2:15. *settled.* As *yšb* can mean both "sit" and "dwell" (v 21), it is slightly unclear whether Moses becomes a literal or a figurative "squatter" by the well. Most likely, he simply sits down, waiting for an invitation home (Calvin). If so, the two halves of v 15 use *yšb* in distinct ways: "reside" and "sit down." For the stylistic device, Jacob (1992: 40) compares *gdl* 'grow, grow up' in 2:10–11 and *śym* 'cause to be, set' in Gen 48:20.

the well. I.e., "a certain well" (Sforno). Hebrew often uses the definite article when an object is definite for the speaker but indefinite for the audience (cf. Joüon 1965: 425–26 §137m–o).

2:16. *Midian's priest.* The verse could have begun, "The seven daughters of Midian's priest came. . . ." By opening with a parenthesis, the writer signals that it is the priest who is of most interest, not his daughters. And by keeping him temporarily nameless, the author makes Reuel's identity a subject of mild suspense, like that of the foundling in 1:22–2:10.

If Reuel/Jethro is a priest, what god does he serve? Since he resides near Mount Horeb (3:1; 18), confesses Yahweh's greatness (18:10–11) and leads Israel in sacrifice (18:12), the biblical authors probably considered him a Yahweh-worshiper (cf. NOTE to 18:11). On the implications for the history of Israelite religion, see APPENDIX C, vol. II.

seven daughters. On this stereotypical number, see Pope (1962b) and Jacob (1992: 40); for seven children, compare 1 Sam 2:5; Jer 15:9; Job 1:2; 42:13; Ruth 4:15; 2 Maccabees 7; Matt 22:23. Groups of seven females are characteristic of Canaanite literature; cf. Ḥawrān's seven wives (Arslan Tash amulet [Cross and Saley 1970: 45]) and the seven Kôṭarātu of Ugarit, divine patronesses of marriage and childbirth. In Exodus, too, seven young women may symbolize matrimony and procreation.

came and drew and filled. The rapid-fire verbs *wattābō(')nâ wattidlenâ wattəmalle(')nâ* may suggest efficiency (cf. Ackerman 1974: 103). Two other examples of this staccato style, both from J, are Gen 25:34 and 27:14 (see also NOTE to Exod 15:9).

Many cultures consign water-drawing, a menial but essential task, either to servants (Deut 29:10; Josh 9:21, 27; Ruth 2:9) or to women: for Israel, see Gen 24:11, 13, 43–46; 1 Sam 9:11; Nah 3:14; cf. John 4:6–30; for Ugarit, see *KTU* 1.12.ii.60; 1.14.iii.9, v.1; for Greece, see *Iliad* 6:457; *Odyssey* 10:105–8; Herodotus *Histories* 3.14, 5.12, 6.137; Pomeroy (1975: 30, 43, 72, 80); for the Bedouin, see Doughty (1936: 1.498, 636); Holl and Levy (1993: 176). The spring was, logically enough, a popular singles' spot (Genesis 24, 29; Exodus 2; cf. John 4; Alter 1981: 51–58; Davies 1992: 146–48; COMMENT below).

2:17. *the shepherds.* I.e., certain shepherds, those of whom we shall speak.

expelled them. Waygārašûm chimes with Gershom in v 22 (on the grammatical difficulty, see TEXTUAL NOTE).

arose. Although the verb qām here as elsewhere connotes the inception of an action (cf. English "went and"), in v 17, the literal meaning "stood up" is equally in effect, assuming Moses was previously seated (v 15b).

their flock. Ṣō(')n denotes a group of sheep, goats or both. The pronominal suffix on ṣō(')nām 'their flock' is ostensibly masculine, even though the suffix on "saved them" (wayyôšî'ān) is feminine. Since it is unlikely that Moses also waters the repulsed shepherds' flocks, we have yet another case of random incongruence (see Levi 1987) or, less likely, scribal error (cf. TEXTUAL NOTE to 2:17 "expelled them").

2:18. *Reuel.* The meaning of the name rə'û'ēl is not quite certain. 'Ēl clearly means "god." Rə'û, which also stands alone as an ethnic/geographical name (Gen 11:18–21), probably means "kinsman" (cf. rēa' 'kinsman' and the name rē'î 'My kinsman'). As a whole, rə'û'ēl resembles the name "Samuel," also of contested significance. If š(ə)mû'ēl means "Name (i.e., offspring, reminder?) of God" (< *šmu-'ili), then Reuel should mean "Kinsman of God" (< *ri'u-'ili). If, however, Samuel signifies "God is his *name* (i.e., personal deity)" (< *šmuhu 'ilu; cf. Cross 1973: 11), then Reuel probably means "God is his kinsman" (< *ri'uhu 'ilu). For a general treatment of biblical names of this shape, see Layton (1990: 49–105).

Whatever its etymology, the name "Reuel" appears in several contexts. Besides the priest of Midian, we find a Benjaminite (1 Chr 9:8), a Gadite (Num 2:14, etc.) (also called də'û'ēl), an Arab tribe related to Midian (Gen 25:3 [LXX]) and an Edomite clan (Gen 36:4, 10, 13, 17; also epigraphic r'l [Israel 1979: 174]). The first two are not directly relevant here, but the Arab-Edomite tribe could indeed be reflected and personified in Moses' father-in-law, presumably their ancestor (on tribal names common to Arabs, Edomites and Hebrews, see APPENDIX B, vol. II).

In E, Moses' father-in-law is called "Jethro" (3:1, etc.). In J, he is "Reuel." To complicate matters, Num 10:29 (J) mentions "Hobab, Reuel's son, Moses' father-in-law." One might assume that here Reuel is the father-in-law, but Judg 4:11 calls *Hobab* Moses' father-in-law (see further below). In fact, there may be a fourth name, Qeni (Judg 1:16; cf. *Mek. Yitrô* 1), although this is better emended to *ḥaqqênî* 'the Kenite' (cf. 1 Sam 5:6) or to "Hobab the Kenite" (OG).

As for the two names in J, Reuel and Hobab, at least seven different explanations have been proffered: (a) Reuel's presence in 2:18 is a scribal insertion (Holzinger 1900: 6–7; Meyer 1906: 45); (b) Reuel is really the girls' *grand*father or ancestor (*Tg. Ps.-Jonathan*; Ramban; Luzzatto; Sarna 1986: 36); (c) Hobab is actually Moses' brother-in-law (*ḥātān*), not father-in-law (*ḥōtēn*) (ibn Ezra; for further literature, see Moore 1901: 33); (d) Hobab is Moses' son-in-law (also *ḥātān*), married to an otherwise unknown daughter of Moses (Albright 1963: 7 n. 22); (e) the Yahwist was confused; (f) the Yahwist incorporated contradictory traditions; (g) either the Reuel or the Hobab allusion comes from a source neither Yahwistic nor Elohistic (cf. Morgenstern 1927: 47 n. 58).

To further confuse us, while the Torah calls Reuel, Hobab and Jethro *Midianites*, Judg 4:11 calls the sons of Hobab *Kenites*. Are Kenites and Midianites the same (the usual view), is one a subgroup of the other or is the tradition simply muddled? Schmidt (1988: 87) observes that one Hanoch is the son of Cain, the presumed ancestor of the Kenites (Gen 4:17 [J]), while another is Midian's offspring (Gen 25:4 [E]).

hastened . . . today. Ackerman (1974: 104) infers from "today" that the conflict with the shepherds is recurrent. The girls return early because, for once, they have not had to wait. A woman running home from a well to prepare for a stranger's visit is a narrative cliché (cf. Gen 24:28; 29:12; Judg 13:10) (Scharbert 1989: 19).

2:19. *arm.* Or "hand"; on *yād*, see NOTE to 3:19.

drew, drew for us. In vv 16–17, we are told that the *women* drew. Aside from authorial blunder, there are two possible explanations for the contradiction (Ackerman 1974: 104). Often biblical authors tell a story partly in the narrator's voice and partly in a character's (see Savran 1988). Probably, then, we are to infer that, after the aggressive shepherds had consumed all the girls' water, Moses drew more (cf. Bekhor Shor). But it is also possible that the Yahwist is portraying the excited shepherdesses as exaggerating the stranger's virtues (Ehrlich 1908: 266). Since drawing water was a task for women or slaves (NOTE to 2:16), Moses' reported behavior is an act of implicit self-deprecation, a condescension evocative of medieval chivalry.

2:20. *where is he?* There may be mild humor in Reuel chiding his daughters for not taking the stranger in. Picture the astonished Moses, as the reward for his gallantry, stranded by the spring! But it may well have been unmaidenly to offer hospitality (Calvin).

food. Leḥem can also mean "bread." The Midianite priest will again serve (sacrificial) *leḥem* to Moses, along with the leaders of Israel, in 18:12 (E).

2:21. *Moses agreed.* It is characteristic of Hebrew narrative to abridge. Thus we are not told explicitly that the women obeyed their father, or that Reuel invited Moses to stay. Yet these facts are nonetheless clear (Cassuto 1967: 25–26).

to settle. As in Gen 29:19, to "settle with" (*yāšab 'et/ʿim*) may imply residence as a working family member, not as a guest (Sforno).

Zipporah. The name means "Bird." The marriage of Zipporah and Moses reunites two sundered branches of the house of Abraham: Midian is descended from Keturah (Gen 25:1–4) and Israel from Sarah (Durham 1987: 240).

2:22. *called his name.* Like the previous episode (1:22–2:10), 2:11–22 closes with a naming (Blenkinsopp 1992: 146).

Gershom. The etymology of *gēršōm* is uncertain. Exod 2:22 (J) and 18:3 (E) derive the first syllable from *gēr* 'sojourner' (hence the Massoretic vocalization *gēr-* rather than the expected *ger-*). But what is *šōm?* Scharbert (1989: 19) posits a hypothetical *šōm 'wilderness,' hence, "Sojourner of the wilderness." Judg 17:7 suggests a different approach, however. We read there that the itinerant Levite Jonathan son of Gershom (cf. Judg 18:30) "sojourned there" (*gār-šām* or perhaps *gēr-šām*). So, too, in Exod 2:22, Gershom is probably meant to sound like "Sojourner there," i.e., *gēr-šām* (Rashbam; cf. *Gērsam* in LXX). And there is further wordplay. Given Moses' fugitive status, it is difficult not to think of *grš* 'expel' (Dillmann 1880: 21; Sarna 1986: 37). In fact, the verb *waygārəšûm* 'and expelled them' (v 17) may pun with Gershom (see TEXTUAL NOTE). Joseph, too, gives his sons Ephraim and Manasseh names evocative of exile (Gen 41:51–52).

Still, all the above is mere etymological midrash; the true derivation of *gēršōm* remains unknown. Consult Propp (1992a) for various possibilities, and add another: "Client of the (divine) Name," assuming *šōm* = *šēm* (cf. Aramaic *šum*) (on *gēr* in names, cf. Smith 1927: 79, 531 [note by S. A. Cook]). Gershom appears to be a variant of *gēršôn* son of Levi (6:16; see COMMENT to 6:2–7:7).

sojourner . . . in a foreign land. Which land: Egypt (Durham 1987: 24; Jacob 1992: 42) or Midian (Greenberg 1969: 49)? Or is the text deliberately ambiguous (Fretheim 1991a: 42)? By translating Moses' words in the present tense, LXX makes the "foreign land" Midian. But the perfect *hāyîtî* shows that, whether Moses is thinking of his recent sojourn in Midian or of his youth in Egypt, he considers himself home at last, in Reuel's tent. He is no longer a *gēr*, or at least less of one.

2:23. *those many days.* The diction may imply that Moses' years spent in Midian outnumber those of his childhood and adolescence, called merely "those days" (v 11).

Egypt's king died. It is a narrational cliché, no doubt born of political reality, for an exile to return home after the death of a hostile king; cf. the Egyptian "Tale of Sinuhe" (*ANET* 18–22) (Scharbert 1989: 19).

COMMENT

THE LOCAL WATERING HOLE

Moses flees eastward to one of the sparsely populated deserts of Asia, beyond Egypt's jurisdiction. He camps at an oasis. A lone refugee, he needs both water and allies.

When the locals arrive, Moses encounters opposed parties of unequal strength. In the ancient and modern Middle East, water rights are often bitterly contested. Several biblical wells bear names associated with enmity: Ein Mishpat 'Well of Judgment' (Gen 14:7); Beersheba 'Well of Oath' (Gen 21:25–31; 26:25–33); Esek 'Enmity' and Sitnah 'Hostility' (Gen 26:20–21); Massah 'Testing' and Meribah 'Strife' (Exod 17:1–7; Num 20:2–13). As he had previously intervened in paradigmatic situations of foreign oppression (2:11–12) and civil strife (2:13–14), now Moses attempts partially to redress female subjugation (Fretheim 1991a: 45), in a sense returning the protection he received from women in 1:22–2:10 (see COMMENT). This time, however, Moses exercises restrained violence in a good cause, and the outcome is positive. No one is killed (so far as we are told), and Moses wins a wife and the protection of a prestigious leader. His calm demeanor after the incident stands in marked contrast to his furtive behavior after the earlier conflicts. The text stresses, instead of Moses' martial prowess, his compassion and quasi-medieval courtesy.

The location of the altercation is significant. The spring is a popular female symbol in the Bible, representing a wife (Prov 1:15–16), a prostitute (Prov 23:27) or, if sealed, a virgin (Gen 29:2–10; Cant 4:12). (Cant 1:2 even develops a good pun between šqy 'drink,' nšq 'kiss' and šwq/šqq 'lust.') In Exodus, the well arguably represents Zipporah, from whom Moses drives off other men and for whom he performs an act of kindness (cf. Alter 1981: 52). The watering of the flock may also foreshadow Moses' miraculous production of water for Israel (15:22–26; 17:1–7; Num 20:2–13) (Fretheim 1991a: 43).

We may wonder why Reuel is so quick to bestow his daughter on a violent if well-intentioned stranger. Is he motivated by anything more than gratitude? Moses' Egyptian garb may create an initial impression of wealth and power, but his very presence in Midian would belie such an inference. More likely, if we may impute to Reuel an ulterior motive, he lacks enough sons to protect his flocks and daughters (Reuel does have a son in Num 10:29, however; see Noth 1962: 36). Thus, by acquiring a doughty son-in-law, Reuel acts both graciously and prudently. According to E (3:1) and presumably J, too, Moses enters his father-in-law's service as a shepherd, perhaps, like Jacob, to provide labor in lieu of a bride-price (for Mesopotamian and Hittite parallels, see ANET 162 §25, 190 §36). Moses might even expect to inherit his father-in-law's sacred office—which in a way he does (cf. Gressmann 1913: 19).

Ehrlich (1908: 265–66) and Coats (1988: 51) observe the lack of a love story in 2:15b–22. Despite the promising derring-do at the beginning of their relationship, Moses' marriage to Zipporah seems rather perfunctory. Moses' strongest ties are not with his wife, but with his father-in-law (see COMMENT to chap. 18, p. 635). It is not entirely surprising that Mek. ʿămālēq 3 (on Exod 18:2) registers Moses' early divorce from Zipporah. However that may be, the Moses-Zipporah story contrasts with the sensitively depicted romances of Jacob and Rachel (Gen 29:1–30 [J]) and Isaac and Rebekah (Gen 24:67 [J]).

Why the difference? The Patriarchs' and Matriarchs' greatest accomplishments are procreative. Moses' achievements are political and religious; in fact, he twice declines to father a new nation (32:10; Num 14:12) and receives no postmortem ancestral worship (Deut 34:6). His private life is of little concern to biblical tradition.

MOSES AND MIDIAN

One of the strangest and most significant of Israel's early traditions is the alliance between Moses and the Midianites/Kenites. This tribe plainly provoked strong feelings, both positive and negative. Genesis paints a nasty picture: Cain (*qayin*), from whose name *qênî* 'Kenite' seems derived, is the first murderer and fratricide (Gen 4:1–16 [J]). The Kenites are among the nations whom Israel is to dispossess (Gen 15:19 [J]). Midianite traders kidnap Joseph (Gen 37:28a [E]). Later in JE, however, there seem to be no hard feelings. Moses is related by marriage to the priest of Midian (Exodus 2–4; 18), himself a Yahweh-worshiper (18:9–12), the inventor of the Israelite judiciary (18:13–26) and their guide in the desert (Num 10:29; cf. 1 Sam 15:6). In a similar vein, Judg 4:17–21 and 5:24–27 commemorate the heroism of Jael, a Kenite by marriage (Judg 4:11). Again on the negative side, however, are the recurrent skirmishes between Israel and Midian in the premonarchic period (Josh 13:21; Judg 6:1–8:12).

P's treatment of Midian is particularly harsh. Although there is no evidence that Midianites still interacted with Israel in his time (see APPENDIX A, vol. II), the Priestly Writer was sufficiently outraged by their role in JE to: (a) omit Moses' Midianite sojourn, (b) ignore the tradition that Moses' wife was Midianite, (c) convert the seductresses of Baal Peor from Moabites into Midianites (Num 25:3–15) and (d) make the benevolent Balaam of JE (Numbers 22–24) an archfiend (Num 31:16). P in fact mandates the wholesale slaughter of Midian (Num 25:16–18; 31). Why should the Priestly Writer have cared?

Perhaps he simply was outraged by Jethro's sacred office in JE—in 18:12 (E), Jethro takes precedence over Aaron himself! Perhaps, too, he intended his aspersions of Midian to besmirch Moses, who is married to a Midianite in JE (but not in P!) (on P's complex attitude toward Moses, see COMMENT to 6:2–7:7). Finally, the Kenites were associated with Arad, where a temple stood in the late preexilic period (Mazar 1965). We may *a priori* assume this structure offended the Priestly Writer, an advocate of centralized worship. By denigrating the Midianites, P may be obliquely impugning the Arad cult (compare P's critique of the Korahites [Numbers 16–17], also active at Arad [Aharoni 1981: 180–82; *AHI* 2.049.1]).

STRANGER IN A STRANGE LAND

Exod 2:15b–23a tells the familiar story of a young man growing up. Moses has been undergoing a sort of identity crisis throughout Exodus 2. The son of Hebrew refugees from Canaan, nursed by a Hebrew mother, raised as an Egyptian princeling, speaking to Hebrews as an Egyptian but addressed by them as an Israelite, exiled from Egypt but mistaken for an Egyptian, now a Midianite by marriage—who is he? The author does not sow these doubts so much in his protagonist's mind as in ours. But Moses' aside, "A sojourner was I in a foreign land," betrays consciousness of his ambiguous status.

Exod 2:22 sounds like the happy ending of a folktale. Moses has won a wife, fathered a child and found a home. Surely his travails and wanderings are over. Events, however, expose the irony in his words. Moses is about to discover that he is *still* a "sojourner in a foreign land."

Moses' statement also proves to be prophetic. "Sojourner in a foreign land" would be an eloquent epitaph for one who was a stranger in Egypt, in Midian and in the wilderness, who was never fully accepted by his own people, who died before reaching Canaan and who was buried, not in ancestral soil, but in an unknown grave.

VI. *And Deity remembered his covenant* (2:23b–25)

2 [23b(P)]And Israel's Sons moaned from the work and screamed, and their plea ascended to the Deity from the work. [24]And Deity heard their groan, and Deity remembered his covenant with Abraham, with Isaac and with Jacob. [25]And Deity saw Israel's Sons, and he made himself known to them.

ANALYSIS

TEXTUAL NOTES

2:23. *from the work.* The Versions expand upon this in various ways, all utilizing material from 1:13–14. Syr adds "heavy"; *Tgs. Onqelos* and *Ps.-Jonathan* have "that was heavy upon them," and some LXX MSS add "hard."

†*screamed.* Where MT has *wyzʿqw*, Sam, Kenn 110, 600 (marg.) and 4QpaleoGen-Exod[l] have the synonymous *wyṣʿqw*.

2:24. *their groan.* For MT *nʾqtm*, Sam has *nqʾtm*—a simple misspelling of a rare word.

Isaac. Some MT MSS (Kenn 69, 150; Rossi 265, 419, 592), Sam, LXX, *Tg. Ps.-Jonathan*, Syr and some MSS of *Tg. Onqelos* read "*and* with Isaac" (de Rossi 1784–85: 48).

†2:25. *Deity saw Israel's Sons.* While MT *wyrʾ (wayyar[ʾ]) ʾlhym ʾt (ʾet) bny yśrʾl* is probably correct, it is worth considering a conjectural emendation **wyrʾ*

(wayyērāʾ) ʾlhym ʾl (ʾel) bny yśrʾl 'and Deity appeared to Israel's Sons.' The emended text makes slightly better sense, matches the following Niphʿal (see below) and exhibits stricter parallelism with 6:2–3 (P), into which 2:25 originally flowed. Compare, too, 1 Sam 2:27: "I revealed, revealed myself (niglêtî) to your father's house when they were in Egypt, slaves to Pharaoh" (see OG).

†the made himself known to them. So LXX and Kenn 391, reading wywdʿ ʾlyhm (wayyiwwādāʿ ʾălêhem) for MT wydʿ ʾlhym (wayyēdaʿ ʾĕlōhîm) 'and Deity knew.' Schmidt (1988: 79) combines LXX and MT: *wywdʿ ʾlhym 'and Deity made himself known.' The Greek is probably wholly correct, however (Scharbert 1989: 20; Blenkinsopp 1992: 150); cf. Ezek 20:5, "and I . . . made myself known to them (wāʾiwwādāʿ lāhem) in the land of Egypt" (Propp 1997). Still, there is room for doubt; in defense of MT, see Thomas (1948); Greenberg (1969: 54); Blum (1990: 240 n. 43).

SOURCE ANALYSIS

Since Yahweh is called "(the) Deity," we are in either E or P. God also "remembers" covenants in Gen 9:15–16; Exod 6:5; Lev 26:42, 45 (all P), while he "hears" Israel's cry in Exod 6:5 (P). Hence, our passage is Priestly, the original sequel to 1:14 (the oppression of the Hebrews) and introduction to 6:2 (Yahweh's revelation to Moses).

REDACTION ANALYSIS

Exod 2:23b–25 separates the charming tale of Moses and Reuel from the epoch-making encounter in chaps. 3–4. It momentarily lifts us to Heaven for a glimpse into the divine mind, before returning to earth with Moses in Midian (Cassuto 1967: 30). What has happened, literary-historically, is that the Redactor detached vv 23b–25 from 6:2 (P), into which they originally flowed, in order to introduce the JE bush revelation. In its present location, 2:23b–25 demonstrates Yahweh's universal scope: he attends to Egypt and forthwith appears in Midian. It also reminds the reader, in the midst of a pastoral interlude, that Israel's suffering continues unalleviated. Even Pharaoh's death (v 23a) has brought no relief (Bekhor Shor). The reader is also reassured that, even if Moses' career appears to have fizzled, God's plan will continue to unfold (cf. Mann 1988: 81).

To my taste, this look behind the scenes impairs the effectiveness of what follows. In JE, the encounter at the bush must have possessed a surreal suddenness absent in the redacted text. But a sort of suspense has been building throughout chaps. 1–2: where is God? Exod 2:23b–25 assures us that Israel is not forsaken.

NOTES

2:23. *from the work.* There is probable *double entente. Min* 'from' can mean either "out of" or "because of."

screamed. Z*ʿq/ṣʿq* sometimes has a connotation of legal accusation (Daube 1963: 27). But here the reference is more to cries of pain—*ʾnḥ, zʿq, nʾq*—and less to haling Egypt into the divine court. It is unclear whether the Hebrews in fact cry out to God or just cry out (cf. Plastaras 1966: 27). The diction may indicate that their scream rises on its own to Yahweh and is accepted as petition (cf. 3:7, 9). Plasataras (pp. 49–59) draws interesting comparisons between this passage and ritual lamentation, discerning in 2:23–15:21 as a whole a traditional sequence of lament, salvation oracle and thanksgiving.

2:24. *remembered.* God's remembering (*zkr*) his covenant is a typical Priestly concept (see SOURCE ANALYSIS), found sporadically elsewhere (e.g., Jer 14:21; Ezek 16:60). P will later mandate periodic trumpeting to provoke Yahweh's memory (Num 10:1–10).

Whether said of God or a man, "remembered" does not necessarily imply forgetfulness (e.g., Num 15:39; Lachish Ostracon 2:4 [*AHI* 1.002.4]). Rather, it connotes devoting one's full attention to a thing already known, often after receiving aural or visual stimulation. Still, from the Hebrews' perspective, Yahweh's long silence does suggest an unconscionable absence of mind.

2:25. *Deity saw Israel's Sons.* This statement follows awkwardly upon v 24, in which Yahweh hears and remembers. We would rather expect God's hearing and sight to *precede* memory; cf. 3:7: "I have *seen, seen* the humiliation of my people . . . their scream have I *heard* . . . I indeed *know* his pains." Apparently, we have hysteron proteron.

Moreover, we might expect God to see Israel's *suffering* or the like (cf. 3:7, 9), not to see Israel itself. In fact, the Targumim supply "oppression" in 2:25. But Schmidt (1988: 98) proffers as a parallel 1 Sam 9:16, "For I have seen my people, for its cry has come before me."

COMMENT

INTRODUCING: GOD

Formally, the most striking feature of this passage is its fourfold (fivefold in MT) repetition of *ʾĕlōhîm* 'Deity.' Leibowitz (1976: 19) writes, "It represents a foregrounding of the progressive re-appearance of God as a factor in the life of Israel, the progressive breaking down of barriers and resumption of the link between the upper and lower worlds. . . . The . . . re-appearance of the Divine name in the text signalled the end of the period of His estrangement from the world. No longer would He work from behind the scenes but would act openly in full public view bursting forth into the arena of history. . . ."

In fact, it is not quite clear that Yahweh is behind the events of chaps. 1–2. The author(s) may have cultivated theories of the interplay of chance, fate, prescience and divine causation that were more nuanced, on the one hand, or totally undeveloped, on the other. Suffice it to say that so far, God's interference has been at most indirect.

P's conception of God is often described as less anthropomorphic than J's. This is a distortion. J's Deity may be more intimate with humans than P's. But in J, Yahweh appears to Abram as a fire (Gen 15:17), while P's God creates humanity in his physical likeness (Gen 1:26, 27; cf. Ezek 1:26). In all sources, God possesses quasi-human faculties and limitations.

The Israelites, like other ancient Near Easterners, were not given to self-conscious theologizing. They never formulated explicit doctrines of divine omniscience and omnipotence (Levenson 1988). In 2:23b–25, God perceives Israel's plight with his senses, which in turn prompt his memory. We are tempted to ask the blasphemous question "Has God forgotten?"

Our passage is the first indication in the Book of Exodus that Israel's suffering will be neither meaningless nor interminable. A supernatural consciousness is about to resume control of events, if it has not been behind them all along. The reader who has not read Genesis is apprised of what is going on. And even those who know the Patriarchal saga are reassured that Yahweh will honor his oath to the Fathers. The days of Egypt's dominion are numbered, even if the biblical characters do not yet know it. The only uncertainties pertain to when Pharaoh will release Israel and whether the slaves will depart gladly or regretfully.

Although they may be the product of scribal error (see TEXTUAL NOTE), the final words of chapter 2 in MT, "and Deity knew," strike an eerie and ominous note. What did Deity know? Presumably, his ancient obligation to Israel, the full extent of Egypt's misdeeds, and that the time of recompense had come.

VII. Yahweh the Hebrews' deity happened upon us (3–4)

3 [1(E)]Moses, meanwhile, was herding the flock of Jethro, his father-in-law, Midian's priest, and he drove the flock behind the wilderness, and he came to the Deity's mountain, to Horeb. [2(J?)]And Yahweh's Messenger appeared to him as a fire flame from within the bush. And he saw, and, see: the bush burning with fire, but the bush not consumed. [3]So Moses said, "I would turn and see this great vision. Why does not the bush burn?"

[4]And Yahweh saw that he turned to see, [(E)]and Deity called to him [(E/RJE)]from within the bush [(E)]and said, "Moses, Moses."

And he said, "See me."

[5(J)]And he said, "Do not approach hither. Pull your sandals from upon your feet, for the place on which you are standing, it is holiness ground." [6(E?)]And he said, "I am your father's deity, Abraham's deity, Isaac's deity and Jacob's deity." [(E/J)]Then Moses hid his face, for he was afraid to gaze at the Deity. [7(J/RJE)]And Yahweh said, [(E?)]"I have seen, seen the humiliation of my people who are in Egypt, and their scream have I heard from *the face of* his overseers; I indeed know his pains. [8(E?)]So I will descend/have descended to rescue him from Egypt's *arm* and to bring him up from that land to a land good and broad, to a land flowing of milk and honey, to the place of the Canaanite and the Hittite and the Amorite and the Perizzite and the Hivvite and the Jebusite. [9(J?)]And now, see: the scream of Israel's Sons has come to me, and I have also seen the oppression with which Egypt are oppressing them. [10(E)]And now, go, for I send you to Pharaoh, and take my people, Israel's Sons, out from Egypt."

[11]But Moses said to the Deity, "Who am I that I should go to Pharaoh, or that I should take Israel's Sons out from Egypt?"

[12]And he said, "Because I will be with you. And this is the sign for you that I, I sent you. When you take the people out from Egypt, you will serve the Deity at this mountain."

[13]But Moses said to the Deity, "Suppose I come to Israel's Sons and say to them, 'Your fathers' deity has sent me to you,' and they say to me, 'What is his name?'—what should I say to them?"

[14]Then Deity said to Moses, "I will be who I will be." And he said, "Thus you will say to Israel's Sons: '"I-will-be" has sent me to you.'"

[15]And Deity further said to Moses, "Thus you will say to Israel's Sons: 'Yahweh your fathers' deity, Abraham's deity, Isaac's deity and Jacob's deity—he has sent me to you'; this is my name to eternity, and this is my designation age (by) age. [16]Go, and you will gather Israel's elders and say to them, 'Yahweh your fathers' deity appeared to me, the deity of Abraham, Isaac and Jacob, saying: "I acknowledge, acknowledge you and what is done to you in Egypt. [17]And I have said, 'I will take you up from Egypt's oppression to the land of the Canaanite and the Hittite and the Amorite and the Perizzite and the Hivvite and the Jebusite, to a land flowing of milk and honey.'"' [18]And they will heed your voice, and you will come, you and Israel's elders, to Egypt's king and say to him, 'Yahweh the Hebrews' deity happened upon us. And now, we would go a three days' way into the wilderness and sacrifice to Yahweh our deity.' [19]But I, I know that Egypt's king will not allow you to go, unless by a strong arm. [20]So I will send my arm and strike Egypt with all my wonders which I will work in his midst, and afterward he will release you. [21(J?)]And I will set this people's favor in Egypt's eyes, and it will happen, when you go, you will not go emptily. [22]But a woman will ask of her neighbor woman and of the woman sojourner of her house silver objects and gold objects and robes. And you will place on your sons and on your daughters, and you will despoil Egypt."

4 [1(E)]But Moses answered and said, "And suppose they do not believe me and do not heed my voice, but say, 'Yahweh did not appear to you'?"

²Then Yahweh said to him, "What's this in your hand?"
And he said, "A rod."
³And he said, "Throw it groundward."
So he threw it groundward, and it became a snake, and Moses fled from its *face*.
⁴Then Yahweh said to Moses, "Send out your hand and grasp its tail."
So he sent out his hand and seized it, and it became a rod in his hand. ⁵"So that they will believe that Yahweh their fathers' deity, Abraham's deity, Isaac's deity and Jacob's deity appeared to you."
⁶And Yahweh further said to him, "Bring your arm into your bosom."
So he put his arm into his bosom. Then he removed it, and, see: his arm was *maṣōrāʿ* like snow. ⁷Then he said, "Return your arm to your bosom."
So he returned his arm to his bosom. Then he removed it from his bosom, and, see: it returned like his flesh. ⁸"And it will happen, if they do not believe you and do not heed the first sign's voice, then they will believe the latter sign's voice. ⁹But it will happen, if they do not believe even these two signs nor heed your voice, then you will take from the Nile's waters and pour on the dry land. And they will become, the waters you take from the Nile, they will become blood on the dry land."
¹⁰But Moses said to Yahweh, "Please, my Lordship, I am not a words man, not yesterday nor the day before nor since your speaking to your slave, but I am heavy of mouth and heavy of tongue."
¹¹But Yahweh said to him, "Who made/makes for Man a mouth or who makes dumb or deaf or percipient or blind? Is it not I, Yahweh? ¹²And now, go, for I, I will be with your mouth and will guide you in what you will speak."
¹³Then he said, "Please, my Lordship, send through the hand you would send."
¹⁴Then Yahweh's *nose* grew angry at Moses. And he said, "Is there not Aaron, your brother Levite? I know that he will speak, speak, and, moreover, see: him coming out to meet you, and he will see you and rejoice in his heart. ¹⁵And you will speak to him and put the words in his mouth. And I, I will be with your mouth and with his mouth, and I will teach you what you will do. ¹⁶And he, he will speak for you to the people; and it will happen, he, he will be for you as a mouth, and you, you will be for him as Deity. ¹⁷And this rod you will take in your hand, with which you may work the signs."
¹⁸So Moses went and returned to Jether his father-in-law and said to him, "I would go and return to my brothers who are in Egypt and see if they still live."
And Jethro said to Moses, "Go in peace."
¹⁹⁽ᴶ⁾And Yahweh said to Moses in Midian, "Go, return to Egypt, for all the men seeking your *soul* have died."
²⁰So Moses took his *woman* and his sons and mounted them on the ass, ⁽ᴶ/ᴱ⁾and he returned to the land of Egypt. ⁽ᴱ⁾And Moses took the Deity's rod in his hand.
²¹And Yahweh said to Moses, "In your going to return to Egypt, *see* all the wonders which I have put into your hand, and work them to Pharaoh's *face*.

(R/E)But I, I will strengthen his heart, and he will not release the people. ²²(E)And you will say to Pharaoh, 'Thus has Yahweh said: "My son, my firstborn, is Israel. ²³And I have said to you, 'Release my son that he may serve me.' And if you refuse to release him, see: I am going to kill your son, your firstborn."'"

²⁴(J)And it happened on the way, at the night-stop, and Yahweh met him and sought to put him to death. ²⁵But Zipporah took a flint and severed her son's foreskin and applied to his *legs* and said, "For you are a bridegroom/son-in-law of bloodiness to me."

²⁶And he slackened from him. Then she said, "A bridegroom/son-in-law of bloodiness by circumcision."

²⁷(E)And Yahweh said to Aaron, "Go to meet Moses to the wilderness."

So he went and met him at the Deity's mountain and kissed him. ²⁸And Moses told to Aaron all Yahweh's words with which he sent him, and all the signs which he commanded him.

²⁹And Moses and Aaron went and assembled all the elders of Israel's Sons. ³⁰And Aaron spoke all the words that Yahweh had spoken to Moses, and he did the signs before the people's eyes. ³¹And the people trusted, and they heard that Yahweh acknowledged Israel's Sons and that he beheld their oppression. And they knelt and bowed down.

ANALYSIS

TEXTUAL NOTES

†3:1. *behind the wilderness*. Because this is so awkward (see NOTE), we might consider a conjectural emendation **wayyinhag 'aḥar ḥaṣṣō(')n hammidbār* 'and he drove behind the flock into the wilderness,' from which MT *wayyinhag 'et-ḥaṣṣō(')n 'aḥar hammidbār* 'and he drove the flock behind the wilderness' developed by metathesis. For the phrase "behind the flock," cf. 2 Sam 7:8; Amos 7:15; Cant 1:8; for *hammidbār* 'into the wilderness,' cf. Num 14:25; Josh 8:20. Admittedly, *nāhag 'aḥar* 'drove behind' is unparalleled.

†*to the Deity's mountain*. Both here and in the parallel 1 Kgs 19:8, most major LXX MSS read simply "to Mount Horeb," i.e., **'l hr ḥrb*, vs. MT-Sam *'l hr h'lhym ḥ(w)rbh*. If MT-Sam is original, perhaps the Greek translators felt theological discomfort with the concept of "the Deity's mountain." Or, given the similarity of he' and ḥeth, perhaps parablepsis occurred between *hr* and *ḥrbh* (although the result, theoretically, should have been an impossible **'l ḥrbh*). Lastly, it is possible that LXX is original and that MT-Sam contains a secondary gloss. Until **'l hr ḥrb* turns up in a Hebrew MS, however, the safer course is to follow MT-Sam.

3:2. *flame*. MT *labbat* (< *lbb*) occurs only here, while Sam has the expected *lhbt* (< *lhb*). Ehrlich (1908: 267) suggests that *blbt 'š* is a miswriting of **blb h'š* 'in the fire's heart,' but there are ways to explain MT without positing corruption (see NOTE).

3:4. *Yahweh.* Sam has "Deity," but other Versions support MT.

Deity. Here LXX and *Tg. Onqelos* reflect "Yahweh," while Sam supports MT. Thus Sam has "Deity" twice, while LXX and *Tg. Onqelos* have "Yahweh" twice. The mixed reading of MT is the most likely (Beegle 1972: 65).

3:5. *Pull your sandals from upon your feet.* Some MSS of MT and of Sam, LXX, *Fragmentary Targum* and *Tgs. Onqelos* and *Ps.-Jonathan* read the singular *na'alkā* 'your sandal,' instead of standard MT *nə'āle(y)kā* 'your sandals' (de Rossi 1784–85: 48). The use of the singular must be distributive: "each sandal." See also TEXTUAL NOTE.

your feet. Most Sam MSS reading "sandal" in the singular (previous TEXTUAL NOTE) here have "foot," i.e., *rglk* (vs. *rglyk*), as do *Tgs. Onqelos* and *Ps.-Jonathan* and many exemplars of MT (de Rossi 1784–85: 48). LXX is surprising: although most MSS read "sandal," they nevertheless have "feet" (cf. 1 Kgs 2:5 [MT]).

3:6. *he said.* Most LXX MSS add "to him."

your father's. Sam "your fathers'" (*'btyk*) (also Acts 7:32) is probably influenced by Deut 1:21; 6:3; 12:1; 27:3 (O'Connell n.d.).

†*Isaac's deity.* Here and in 3:15; 4:5, Sam, LXX, Kenn 1, 69, 253, Rossi 262 and 606 insert "and."

and Jacob's deity. Syr omits "and" here and in 3:15; 4:5.

hid his face. As usually with this idiom, LXX renders, "*turned aside* his face" (see Friedman 1977).

3:7. *said.* LXX adds "to Moses" as an explanatory plus.

their . . . his. *'Am* 'people' can be treated as both singular and plural, even within the same clause. LXX levels plurals throughout (omitting the pronominal suffix on "overseers"), while *Tg. Onqelos* has the plural suffix on all the nouns. The mixed reading of MT and Sam is presumably original (see also next TEXTUAL NOTE).

this pains. Sam and Vg read "his pain," i.e., *mk'bw* for MT *mk'byw* (on LXX-Syr "their pain," see previous TEXTUAL NOTE). There was a transitional stage of Hebrew orthography when it was possible to interpret *mk'bw* as either singular or plural (Andersen and Forbes 1986: 62). Since, moreover, the next word begins with *w* (identical to *y* in Herodian script), haplography to create Sam and dittography to create MT are equally possible.

†3:8. *I will descend/have descended.* It is difficult to choose between Sam **w'rdh* (future) (cf. *Samaritan Tg.*) and MT *wā'ērēd* (past). One could also emend MT to **wə'ērēd* (future). See NOTE.

to a land. Some LXX MSS insert "and lead them in."

Canaanite . . . Jebusite. After "the Perizzite," Sam and LXX add "and the Girgashite" (cf. 3:17). For a text-critical overview of this polymorphous list, see (provisionally) O'Connell (1984), adding the scrolls published since in DJD (see also Kennicott 1776–80: 110 *et passim*).

3:10. *Pharaoh.* LXX adds "Egypt's king."

†*take . . . out.* For the imperative *whwṣ'* of MT and 4QGen-Exod[a], Sam reads the converted perfect *whwṣ't* 'and *you will* take out.' Whichever is the

original, the following *'et* was surely involved in the corruption. Either *whwṣ'* *'t* became *whwṣ't 't* or vice versa.

Egypt. LXX expands, "*the land of* Egypt," as do a few witnesses to MT and to the Targumim (de Rossi 1784–85: 49).

3:11. *Deity.* Vetus Latina and *Tg. Onqelos* appear to reflect "Yahweh" (similarly in 3:13, 14, 15).

Pharaoh. LXX adds "Egypt's king."

Israel's Sons. Syr often paraphrases, "those of Israel's House" (also 9:4, 6; 11:7; 14:10; 15:22). Contrast 16:31.

Egypt. LXX reads "*the land of* Egypt."

3:12. *he said.* Some LXX witnesses specify the subject as "Deity" or "Yahweh," and the addressee as "Moses" or "him." Syr likewise has "*the Deity* said to him."

for you. Not reflected in Syr.

the people. LXX and Rossi 264 read "*my* people," as in v 10.

3:13. *to the Deity. Tg. Onqelos* and Vetus Latina ostensibly reflect "before Yahweh."

to them. 4QExod^b and Kenn 248 have *'lyhm*, vs. MT *lhm*. The meaning is unaffected, but our preference for variety favors MT, since we find both *'ălêkem* and *'ălēhem* later in the verse.

Your fathers'. Syr and some LXX witnesses prefix "the Lord." LXX "*our* fathers'" reflects an inner-Greek corruption *hymōn > hēmōn*. This has the effect of making Moses identify himself with the Hebrews, whereas in MT he stands aloof (Wevers 1990: 33).

3:14. *to Israel's Sons.* For MT and 4QGen-Exod^a *lbny*, Sam, 4QExod^b, many MT MSS (Kennicott 1776–80: 111; de Rossi 1784–85: 40) and the Soncino Bible (1488) read *'l bny*, with no difference in meaning. This latter reading anticipates v 15 *'el-bǝnê yiśrā'ēl*.

3:15. *further said.* 4QExod^b, Kenn 69, 111 and perhaps some witnesses to LXX and *Tg. Onqelos* put *'ôd* after *'ĕlōhîm*, not, as in MT, before. The variation is probably random, although mechanical error is conceivable, assuming *'wd* dropped after *wy'mr* by daleth-resh confusion (homoioteleuton) and was reinserted in the wrong place.

Thus. 4QExod^a reads *ky* 'indeed, when,' vs. *kh* 'thus' in all other witnesses. In v 14, where 4QExod^a supports MT, some Sam MSS likewise have *ky* for *kh*.

Isaac's deity. So standard MT and 4QExod^b. 4QGen-Exod^a, some MT MSS (de Rossi 1784–85: 49), Sam and LXX insert "and." For MT-Sam *yṣḥq*, 4QExod^b has *yṣhq* (cf. MT Jer 33:26; Amos 7:9, 16; Ps 105:9).

and Jacob's deity. Syr omits "and."

age (by) age. For MT *lǝdōr dōr*, Sam and Kenn 84, 89, 277, 293 (first hand) read the more common *ld(w)r wd(w)r*, with the conjunction. The original, succinct form of the idiom is preserved in Ugaritic: *dr.dr*.

†3:16. *Israel's elders.* 4QExod^b, Sam, LXX and Syr read "the elders of Israel's Sons," as in MT Exod 4:29. This is possibly correct, assuming *bny* 'sons of' fell

out after *zqny* 'elders of' through homoioteleuton (Cross 1994: 92). On the other hand, a shorter reading is generally preferable, and there seems to be a tendency to expand this phrase in the Versions (cf. TEXTUAL NOTES to 3:18, 4:29, 12:21 and 17:6).

the deity of Abraham, Isaac and Jacob. 4QExod^b and LXX conform to other lists of the Patriarchs, reading "Abraham's deity and Isaac's deity and Jacob's deity" (cf. Kenn 3, 150, 199). Sam and Syr resemble MT, but insert "and" before "Isaac."

3:17. *said.* 4QExod^b and Sam append an otiose cohortative suffix to the verb: *w'(w)mrh.*

†*and the Perizzite.* 4QExod^b lacks the conjunction, perhaps rightly. 4QExod^b (see Cross 1994: 93), Sam and LXX add "and the Girgashite" (cf. 3:8); for further discussion, see O'Connell (1984). Many MSS of MT lack the conjunction before "the Hittite" (Kennicott 1776–80: 111).

†*and the Hivvite.* Again, 4QExod^b may correctly omit the conjunction.

3:18. *Israel's elders.* Syr and a few LXX MSS read "elders of Israel's *Sons*," while *bny* 'Sons' is added above the line in 4QExod^b in the first scribe's hand (cf. TEXTUAL NOTE to 3:16).

Egypt's king. LXX inserts "Pharaoh."

say. The verb is plural in 4QExod^b, MT, Sam, Syr and *Tg. Onqelos* but singular in LXX, Kenn 189 and Rossi 419, presumably because "and you will come" (*ûbā[']tā*) is singular.

†*Yahweh.* The divine name is omitted both times by some LXX MSS. This might reflect either an originally shorter text or contamination from 5:3.

††*Hebrews'.* Sam and many MT MSS (Kennicott 1776–80: 111) preserve the original reading *h'brym.* Standard MT *h'bryym* is later form better attested at Qumran (see Qimron 1986: 31–32).

happened upon. While standard MT reads *niqrâ,* Sam and many MT MSS (Kennicott 1776–80: 111) have *nqr'* (cf. MT 5:3). The meaning is the same, as III-'aleph and III-yodh roots are often confused. Note, for example, that MT *lqr't* 'toward' (< *qry*) is more correctly spelled *lqrt* in the Siloam inscription (AHI 4.116.4) (for other examples, see BDB pp. 896–97). The LXX *Vorlage* also apparently read *nqr'* in 3:18, hence LXX's improbable translation "called" (< *qr'*).

And now. Missing in Kenn 189, Sam and LXX.

3:19. *Egypt's king.* LXX inserts "Pharaoh."

to go. For the rare infinitive *lhlk,* 4QExod^b reads ordinary *[l]lkt.* The more difficult MT is preferable.

unless. For the slightly unusual MT *wəlō'* 'unless,' Sam has the nonsensical *hlw'* 'is it not?' 4QExod^b and perhaps the LXX *Vorlage* read *ky 'm,* the more common way to say "unless." MT is preferable, but 4QExod^b is nonetheless helpful in determining the meaning (see NOTE).

3:20. *in his midst.* LXX, *Tg. Onqelos* and Syr, which routinely render "Egypt" as "the Egyptians," have "in *their* midst."

3:21. *you will . . . go.* Sam uses the paragogic nun (*tlkwn*) to match the first verb.

emptily. For the MT adverb *ryqm*, some Sam MSS invert yodh and resh, reading the adjective *rqym* 'empty.'

3:22. *a woman.* I.e., each woman. Sam reads "he will ask, a man from his friend and a woman from her friend, her neighbor," adapted from 11:2.

and gold objects. LXX reads simply "and gold," probably for a smoother rendering (cf. 11:2; 12:35).

†4:1. *my voice.* For MT *bəqôlî*, Sam and Kenn 1, 99 (first hand), 136, 155, 225 have *lq(w)ly* (cf. v 8). The meaning is unaffected.

†*Yahweh.* The dominant LXX tradition reads "the God," probably reflecting **'ĕlōhîm*; other witnesses (e.g., MT) have "Yahweh," and LXX^A combines both. It is difficult to decide whether "Yahweh" or "Deity" is original. At issue is the relationship among 3:16, 4:1 and 4:5. In MT, all three verses speak of *Yahweh* appearing to Moses; LXX, however, features more variety, calling God "Yahweh" in 3:16, "God" in 4:1 and neither in 4:5 (see also TEXTUAL NOTES to 4:30, 31). On the one hand, this diversity could be a sign of originality. On the other hand, perhaps the LXX *Vorlage* changed *yhwh* to **'lhym* 'Deity' in 4:1 because of confusion with the following **'l(y)hm* 'to them' (see next TEXTUAL NOTE). Note that, in chap. 19, where the two divine names also cluster thickly, LXX seems to prefer "Deity." In light of the uncertainties involved in reconstructing the LXX *Vorlage*, my translation here follows MT. (On the consequences of this indeterminacy for the cogency of the Documentary Hypothesis, see APPENDIX A, vol. II).

†*to you.* LXX adds the question "What should I say to them?" This could have existed in the *Vorlage* as **mh 'mr 'l(y)hm*, lost in proto-MT by homoioteleuton with the preceding **l' nr'h 'lyk 'lhym* (MT *yhwh*; see above) 'Deity did not appear to you.' But I incline toward the shorter reading of MT, taking LXX as a borrowing from 3:13, whether before or after translation into Greek.

4:2. *What's this.* Sam and many MT MSS (Kennicott 1776–80: 112) have the expected *mh zh*, for standard MT *mzh* (*mazze[h]*). The prefixal form of the interrogative pronoun also appears in Isa 3:15; Ezek 8:6; Mal 1:13; 1 Chr 15:13. On the possibility that MT contains a graphic pun, see NOTE.

4:3. *Throw it.* 4QExod^b expands by adding the particle *n'*.

4:4. *grasp.* For MT and Sam *'ḥz*, 4QExod^b has the synonymous *hḥzq*. Doubtless *'ḥz* is original, *hḥzq* having been brought forward from later in the verse (*wayyaḥăzeq*).

†4:5. *Yahweh.* The divine name is missing in LXX^B, perhaps correctly (see TEXTUAL NOTES to 4:1, 30, 31).

†*Isaac's deity.* LXX, Sam and Rossi 592 insert "and."

and Jacob's deity. Syr lacks "and."

4:6. *to him.* For MT-Sam *lw*, 4QExod^b has the synonymous *'lyw*. Some Syr MSS specify "to Moses."

Then he removed it. Some LXX MSS insert a command to remove the hand.
Sam, 4QGen-Exod[a] and LXX also add "from his bosom" (*mḥyqw*), as do some
MT MSS (Kenn 75, 109; Rossi 26, 262, 296, 419) and, most likely, 4QExod[b]
(Cross 1994: 93). While this is probably an expansion based upon the following verse, it is possible that "from his bosom," positing an original spelling
*mḥyqh, fell out by homoioteleuton with *wywṣ'h* 'then he removed it.'
4:7. *he said.* Syr expands: *"the Lord* said."
4:8. *if they do not believe you.* Although the fragment is incomplete, 4QExod[b]
apparently begins 4:8 with *lm'n* 'so that,' as in v 5.
4:9. *even.* Instead of "even," LXX has "you," borrowed from v 8.
will become . . . will become. Sam and perhaps Syr read *yhyw* for the second
whyw, with no difference in meaning; LXX simplifies by omitting altogether
one "will become."
4:11. *him.* LXX specifies "Moses."
makes. For the rare *yāśûm* (MT), Sam has the more common *yśym* (on waw-
yodh confusion, see Cross 1961a; Qimron 1972).
Yahweh. Some LXX witnesses read "the Deity."
4:12. *I will be with.* Here and in v 15, LXX "I will open" seems to be a paraphrase but conceivably reflects a variant *Vorlage *'eptaḥ/'eptəḥâ 'et* (vs. MT
'ehye[h] 'im), possibly derived from Ezek 3:27.
4:13. *he said.* Some LXX MSS and Syr specify "Moses said."
4:14. *said.* Some Syr MSS add "to him."
speak. LXX adds "for you" (cf. v 16).
4:15. *I will be with.* As in v 12, LXX reads "I will *open*."
†4:16. *and it will happen, he, he will be.* Though not impossible, the phrase
whyh hw' yhyh is sufficiently awkward that one suspects an ancient corruption
of **whw'/whw'h yhyh* 'and he, he will be.'
4:18. *Jether.* For standard MT *yeter*, Kenn 150, Rossi 16, Sam, Vg and Tg.
Ps.-Jonathan have *yitrô*, i.e., "Jethro." See NOTE to 3:1.
4:19. *Yahweh said to Moses.* LXX expands at the beginning of v 19, "after
those many days Egypt's king died," repeating 2:23.
†*to Egypt.* "To" is only implied in standard MT but is explicit in Sam *mṣrymh*
(also Kenn 69, 132, 150, 158 [first hand], 184, 650 B, 683; Rossi 262, 592). Other
MT MSS (Kenn 5, 109 [first hand]; Rossi 3, 264) read *bmṣrym* 'into Egypt.'
†4:20. *his sons.* On the possibility that the original read "his son," see NOTE.
ass. LXX takes *haḥămôr* as a collective, rendering "asses" (Wevers 1990: 51).
See NOTE.
he returned. Syr has *"went and* returned"; cf. vv 18, 19, 21.
†*the land of Egypt.* LXX and Syr omit "the land of." This shorter reading
could be original but is more likely a harmonization with v 19. Sam, in contrast to MT *'arṣâ*, reads simply *'rṣ* without the locative suffix (cf. GKC §118d–g;
Joüon 1965: 372 [§125n]).
†4:21. *In your going to return.* *Bəlektəkā lāšûb* is somewhat odd, implying
that Moses is to "see" the wonders while on his way. We might have expected

simply *bəšûbəkā 'upon your return,' or the like. Conceivably, we should read *bəlektô lāšûb 'in *his* going to return to Egypt, Yahweh said. . . .' See also NOTE.

hand. LXX and Syr read "hands," i.e., *yāde(y)kā, for MT yādəkā.

4:23. *my son.* LXX and Kenn 248, perhaps independently, read "my people," assimilating to the refrain of the following chapters: "release my people" (5:1; 7:16, 26; 8:16; 9:1, 13; 10:3).

him. Syr specifies "my son." LXX has "release *them*"; see previous TEXTUAL NOTE.

4:24. *on the way.* Syr has "*Moses was* on the way."

Yahweh. Aquila has "the Deity." The paraphrase "the Lord's angel" (LXX; *Tg. Onqelos*) attempts to mitigate the shock of the episode (Wevers 1990: 54; Tov 1992: 127–28). *Tg. Ps.-Jonathan* and a Targumic Tosephta call him a "destroying angel" in v 25 (Klein 1986: 1.173), while Jub 48:2 ventures to replace the Deity with the archfiend Mastemah.

met him. Syr has "met *Moses*."

4:25. *applied to his legs.* On the Versions, see NOTES.

bridegroom/son-in-law . . . to me. Samaritan *Tg.* has *ḥm* 'father-in-law,' as if reading *ḥtn* as *ḥōtēn* (MT *ḥătan*). Uncertainty as to the vocalization may also underlie the double rendering of *Fragmentary Targum* and *Tg. Ps.-Jonathan*: "The son-in-law (Hebrew *ḥātān*) sought to circumcise, but the father-in-law (*ḥōtēn*) restrained him." And even the more literalistic translations resort to paraphrase. *Tg. Onqelos* reads "by the blood of this circumcision a bridegroom has been given to us," while LXX has "may the blood of my son's circumcision stand."

The basis for this last rendering is uncertain. Dumbrell (1972: 288–89) supposes that the translator, reading *h* for *ḥ*, understood *ḥuttan 'was put.' (This would also account for *Tg. Onqelos.*) Alternatively, if Greek *histēmi 'stand' here connotes clotting (Wevers 1990: 55; cf. English "sta[u]nch"), it is remotely possible that the translator read a passive participle of *ḥtm 'seal,' which in Syriac and Arabic can describe the healing of wounds (cf. Lev 15:3), and which for later Judaism connotes circumcision (e.g., Rom 4:11; Bar 4:6; *Tg. Cant* 3:8).

††4:26. *he slackened.* I would revocalize *wyrp* as *wayyerep (Hiphʿil; cf. Deut 9:14; Judg 11:37; 1 Sam 11:3; 2 Kgs 4:27; Ps 37:8; Job 7:19). The implied object of "slacken" is "anger" or the like (cf. Judg 8:3 "their spirit became slack").

from him. Sam reads "from *her*" (*mmnh*); i.e., Zipporah, too, was attacked.

A bridegroom/son-in-law of bloodiness by circumcision. Here *Tg. Onqelos* provides an interpretive paraphrase: "but for the blood of this circumcision, the bridegroom would deserve killing." LXX, as in the previous verse, reads "may the blood of my son's circumcision stand."

4:27. *Aaron.* 4QBibPar adds "saying" (*l'mr*).

Moses. Some Syr MSS specify "your brother."

at the Deity's mountain. Some Syr MSS add "in Horeb," as in 3:1.

kissed him. LXX "kissed *each other*" is interpretive.

4:28. *commanded him.* Syr and *Tg. Ps.-Jonathan* add "to do."

4:29. *went.* While MT puts the verb in the singular, Sam and Syr have the plural, like the following *wayya'aspû* 'and (they) assembled.' Either way, the sense is plural (GKC §146f-h). Featuring the more varied phraseology, MT is preferable (cf. TEXTUAL NOTE to v 31).

†*all the elders.* Some witnesses to LXX omit "all," as does Rossi 18. This shorter reading could be original, since *kol* appears in the next verse.

Sons. Bny is absent in Kenn 69, 95, 101, 168 and Rossi 10, 274, 408, 611, 766. Ordinarily, we would prefer this shorter reading, but the lack of parallels in other traditions suggests rather than *bny* fell out by homoioteleuton after *zqny* 'elders'; contrast TEXTUAL NOTES to 3:16, 18.

4:30. *spoke.* Some Syr MSS expand: "to them."

the words. LXX, Kenn 155, 248 and Rossi 265, 554 read "*these* words," a ubiquitous phrase in the Torah (Gen 15:1; 20:8; 22:1, etc.). The shorter, more unusual reading of standard MT is preferable.

Yahweh. Most LXX MSS read "the Deity"; see TEXTUAL NOTE to 4:31.

4:31. *trusted.* The verb is singular in MT, LXX and Tg. Onqelos but plural in Sam and Syr. Since the next verb is plural (in MT, not in LXX), MT contains the most varied and preferable reading (*'am* 'people' can be singular or plural). In both vv 29 and 31, a plural subject is preceded by a singular and followed by a plural verb (GKC §145).

†*heard.* For MT *wyšm'w* 'heard,' LXX has "rejoiced," i.e., **wyśmḥw*—perhaps rightly. Either way, the discrepancy implies that at some point the text was memorized or dictated, rather than visually copied, since *ḥ* and *'* are similar in sound, not shape (cf. Ps 97:11, where *zārūa'* 'planted' might be an error for *zōrēaḥ/zāraḥ* 'shines'). *Š* and *ś* are indistinguishable in unpointed script and are pronounced identically by some Jewish communities (e.g., the Samaritans [Macuch 1969: 1.84–85, 128–30], Jerome's informants [Siegfried 1884: 66] and others [Morag 1972: 1133–34]). If LXX is secondary, perhaps the translators were troubled by an exegetical problem; see NOTE.

†*Yahweh.* Again, most LXX witnesses have "the Deity." We have found this phenomenon throughout chap. 4 (vv 1, 5, 30, 31), and argued that at least in vv 1 and 5, LXX may be superior to MT.

they. LXX specifies "the people," presumably an explanatory plus.

knelt and bowed down. Syr and some LXX witnesses add "before the Lord."

SOURCE ANALYSIS

Exodus 3–4 is a key passage for the documentary analysis of the Torah, affording crucial evidence for the existence of the J and E sources (see INTRODUCTION, pp. 47–52, and APPENDIX A, vol. II). But precisely at this point we part with our faithful mentor, the divine name, and rely on less trustworthy guides to source assignment. We are not altogether without resources—distinguishing P from JE remains easy and a subject of near-consensus—but separating J from E will henceforth always be difficult, sometimes impossible. (For an overdetailed treatment of Exodus 3–4 and the history of its source analysis, see Weimar 1980; for arguments against partitioning the passage at all, see Blum 1990: 22–28.)

Let us start with the (relatively) known and proceed to the unknown. I give the opening and closing sections of Exodus 3–4 to the Elohist. Exod 3:1 calls Moses' father-in-law Jethro, rather than Hobab or Reuel, and refers to "the Deity's mountain, Horeb," rather than "Mount Sinai" (see INTRODUCTION, pp. 50–52). Exod 4:27–31 is also Elohistic, mentioning "the Deity's mountain" (v 27) and continuing the *pqd* 'acknowledge' (v 31) theme from Gen 50:24–25; Exod 3:16. (Blum [1990: 32–35], however, attributes the motif to a Deuteronomistic editor; see APPENDIX A, vol. II). We should also note the possible appearance of *hā'ĕlōhîm* 'the Deity' in the original text of 4:30, 31 (see TEXTUAL NOTES).

That Aaron is Moses' interpreter in E helps us to assign 4:1–17, which explains how Aaron comes to be summoned into the wilderness. Note, again, that the original text may have called God "Deity" in 4:1 (TEXTUAL NOTE). Exod 4:1–17, moreover, displays several links with Numbers 12 (E): the phrase "*maṣōrāʿ* like snow" (4:6; Num 12:10), the theme of seeing God (4:1, 5; Num 12:6, 8 [also Exod 3:6, 16]) and the overall question of Moses' legitimacy as prophet. Lastly, 4:14, "moreover, see: him coming out to meet you" is reminiscent of Gen 32:7, "moreover, he is going to meet you" (E?).

As for 4:18–26, we may assign to E both v 18 (Moses' father-in-law is *Jether* [= Jethro]) and the end of v 20 ("the Deity's rod" is evidently the implement of 4:2–4, 17 [E]; see NOTE). Moses' (feigned?) desire to see his "brothers" (4:18) is thus fulfilled when he meets Aaron his "brother" Levite (4:27 [E]). Note, too, that in 17:5–6 Moses uses his rod at *Horeb*, a sign of E.

Exod 4:19 and the first part of v 20, on the other hand, should be Yahwistic. V 19 presumes none of the preceding transactions of Moses and Yahweh, but refers back to the events of 2:11–15 (J), in particular echoing 2:15a 'sought to kill.' Exod 4:20a, 24–26, Moses' departure from Midian with his family, is also Yahwistic; it contradicts 18:1–5 (E), according to which Jethro has kept his daughter and grandchildren with him. Although many consider 4:24–26 an excerpt from another, unknown source (Smith 1906; Gressmann 1913: 57; Sierksma 1951: 144; Talmon 1954a; Kosmala 1962; Morgenstern 1963: 66–70; Eissfeldt 1965: 192–93; Robinson 1986), I give it, too, to J (with Kutsch 1977). (Note, however, the similar use of *higgîaʿ* 'apply to' in 4:25 and 12:22 [E].) The words "and he returned to the land of Egypt" (middle of v 20) fit either J or E and perhaps stood originally in both.

We have accounted for all of chap. 4 except vv 21–23. I assign 4:21a to E, assuming the "wonders . . . in your hand" are the miracles of 4:1–9, all performed by or upon Moses' hand. One may object that in v 21 the wonders are for Pharaoh, whereas in vv 1–9 they are for the people (cf. v 30). I think, however, that 4:21a refers not only to the tricks of 4:1–9 but also to the Plagues of Exodus 7–11 (NOTE to 4:21). Certainly, the threat to Pharaoh's firstborn (4:22–23) features phrases that will resound throughout the Elohistic Plagues cycle ("release . . . if you refuse to release"). Exod 4:21b, which foretells the "strengthening" (*ḥzq*) of Pharaoh's heart, also foreshadows the Plagues, but is probably Redactorial (see REDACTION ANALYSIS below; also SOURCE ANALYSIS to Exodus 7:8–11:10).

A last wrinkle in chap. 4: Redactor[JE] may have reversed the Elohistic matter in vv 21 and 20. If so, E originally read, "And Yahweh said to Moses, 'In your going to return to Egypt, *see* all the wonders which I have put into your hand, and work them to Pharaoh's *face*,' and Moses took the Deity's rod in his hand." This yields a more coherent text but is obviously speculative.

Chap. 3 is harder to analyze than chap. 4; Redactor[JE] apparently manipulated his sources with great freedom. An additional complication is that the Versions often disagree in reading "Yahweh" or "(the) Deity," heretofore our basic criterion for distinguishing E from J. I provisionally assume that, since MT displays in this respect more variety than the other Versions, the latter have harmonized, while the received Hebrew text is more accurate. Also: it is easier for a translator to interchange divine appellations than for a copyist. Nonetheless, this phenomenon must remain an obstacle to any definitive source analysis (see APPENDIX A, vol. II).

We have already assigned 3:1 to E. Most give vv 2–4a to J, since the divine name "Yahweh" appears in vv 2, 4a (MT) (e.g., McNeile 1908: xv; Friedman 1987: 250). Conversely, the latter part of v 4 is considered Elohistic, since it calls the deity *ʾĕlōhîm*. Many, however, would attribute "from within the bush" to R[JE], under the assumption that the Burning Bush is proper to J (e.g., Noth 1962: 38 n.; Fuss 1972: 28; Richter 1970: 66). This is not the only analysis possible. One could assign 2–4a entirely to E, citing, on the one hand, E's previous mention of *malʾak yahwe(h)* 'Yahweh's Messenger' (Gen 22:11 [but see Davila 1991]), and, on the other hand, Sam "and *Deity* saw" (3:4a). Since, however, 3:7–10 seems composite (see below), 3:1–4 probably likewise combines Yahwistic and Elohistic descriptions of Moses' encounter with God.

Exod 3:5–6a is equally difficult. V 6b is probably Elohistic, since it refers to "the Deity" and the fear of God (Fuss 1972: 33). V 5, however, is Yahwistic by Friedman's (1998) theory of the Greater J, since it is repeated almost *verbatim* in Josh 5:15. Fuss (1972: 38) and Weimar (1980: 30), feeling a contradiction between the two commands in v 5, hypercritically divide the verse between authors; but surely the sense is "Do not approach hither *until* you have pulled your sandals. . . ."

It is hard to assign v 6a; it is as natural a continuation of v 5 (J) as an introduction to 6b (E). McNeile (1908: xiii) argues that the repeated "and he said" in vv 5–6 betokens a source change. But there are many parallels where multiple authorship is unlikely (Thierry 1948: 38; see below). A better argument for the Elohistic authorship of v 6a is that Moses' words in v 13 (E) presuppose awareness that he is addressing the Patriarchal god.

Exod 3:7–10 is also extremely difficult. At least 3:10 may with high probability be assigned to E, since it flows into v 11 (E; see below). Moreover, the phrase *ləkâ waʾešlāḥăkā* 'go, for I send you' (v 10) also appears in Gen 37:13 (E). As for 3:7–9, only one thing is certain: vv 7 and 9 are doublets. But which belongs to which source, and to which is v 8 connected? We might argue that the repeated "and now" (3:9, 10) points to a change in source and hence that v 9 is Yahwistic. But Greenberg (1969: 73–74) finds a parallel in 2 Sam 7:28–29, where the first "and now" has the sense of "whereas" (in fact, the sequence begins in 2 Sam 7:25; cf., too, Gen 45:5, 8; Josh 14:10–12; 1 Sam 24:21–22 [Jacob 1992: 59; Blum 1990: 23]). So we need not discern a documentary seam between vv 9 and 10. Exod 3:7 resembles 4:31 (E), speaking of Yahweh beholding (*rā'â*) Israel's oppression (*'ŏnî*); moreover, the reference to *nōgəśîm* 'overseers' anticipates chap. 5 (E). Yet the verse begins with a reference to Yahweh, ordinarily a sign of J. Thus, if v 7 is Elohistic, perhaps "Yahweh said" was added by Redactor[JE].

By elimination, v 9 should be J. As for v 8, the list of nations might be assigned to E on the basis of the similarity to 3:17 (E). But J cites the same list in 34:11; and, one might object, why should the Elohist repeat himself after so short an interval in 3:8, 17? In contrast, a positive argument for Yahwistic authorship of v 8 is that Gen 11:5, 7 and 18:21 (J) also speak of Yahweh's descent (*yrd*) to correct human behavior; the Deity similarly descends upon Sinai in Exod 19:11, 18, 20 (J). But this is most pertinent if "to descend" in 3:8 means to move from heaven to earth, whereas it may mean "go down (to Egypt)" (see NOTE). Overall, I find the evidence associating v 8 with E slightly stronger; note the recurrence of *hiṣṣîl* 'rescue' in 5:23 (E). If v 8 is Yahwistic, however, we must suppose it originally *followed* v 9: "And now, see: the scream of Israel's Sons has come to me, and I have also seen the oppression with which Egypt are oppressing them. So I will descend/have descended to rescue him from Egypt's *arm* and to bring him up from that land. . . ."

Given the repetition of *'ĕlōhîm* (but see TEXTUAL NOTES), 3:11–15 seems to be entirely Elohistic (Friedman 1987: 250). Note, too, that "this mountain" (v 12) refers back to "the Deity's mountain" in v 1 (E). The redundancy of vv 14–15 "Deity said. . . . And he said. . . . Deity further said" suggests editorial interference to most (e.g., Fohrer 1964: 40; Weimar 1980: 47; Schmidt 1988: 131–34). Thierry (1948: 38), however, cites numerous parallels (Gen 1:29; 9:8, 12, 17; 15:3, etc.). Still, it is possible that vv 14–15 have been expanded secondarily to exploit the assonance between the divine name "Yahweh" and *hāyâ* 'to be' (see NOTES and COMMENT).

In 3:16–20, we are still on *terra firma*. V 16 directly quotes Gen 50:24–25 (E), emphasizing the root *pqd* 'acknowledge' (cf. also Exod 4:31; 13:19). Moreover, 3:16 goes with 4:1 (E): "Yahweh . . . appeared to me. . . . Yahweh did not appear to you." I also give 3:18 to E, since God's instructions seem to be executed in 5:1–3 (E), although the elders are forgotten (COMMENT to chap. 5). In corroboration, note that "the Hebrews' deity" is also mentioned in 5:3; 7:16; 9:1, 13; 10:3 (E). And 3:17 is likewise Elohistic, since it connects vv 16 and 18. Exod 3:19–20, however, could conceivably be Yahwistic, the continuation of vv 9, 8 (in that order; see above). But 3:19–20 follows quite well upon v 18 (E) and, more important, refers to the Plagues narrative, which I will apportion between P and E. Hence, vv 19–20, too, are probably Elohistic (against Fuss [1972: 51–52], who considers "strong arm" and "midst" Deuteronomistic expressions). The fulfillment of 3:20 comes in 13:17 (E).

We encounter problems again in 3:21–22 and the associated 11:2–3; 12:35–36. These three passages respectively predict, mandate and report the despoiling of the Egyptians. While 3:12–22 fits its context well enough, the other two passages seem more like insertions into Elohistic material. I tentatively assign all three texts to J, noting the explicit prediction of Israel's departure with "much property" in Gen 15:14 (J?). But this is not much to go on; perhaps 3:21–22; 11:2–3; 12:35–36 are E after all, or an editor's insertion. (Blum [1990: 33] again invokes a Deuteronomistic editor, comparing the laws of manumission in Deut 15:13.)

It is hazardous to characterize J and E in chaps. 3–4, given the uncertainties of source assignment. By my analysis, both J and E describe Moses conversing with Yahweh in Midian. In each source, Moses performs a special act—removing his sandals (J) or hiding his face (E)—because of the site's sanctity. In both J and E, Yahweh announces that he has perceived Israel's suffering and is going to save them from Egypt. But here there is a telling difference: in E, God first sees, then hears (3:7); in J, he first hears, then sees (3:9). In other words, for E, Yahweh is the initiator; in J, he reacts to Israel's plaint. In J, because the Deity is the actual savior, Moses needs no assistance. E, on the other hand, stresses Moses' responsibility and his proportionally greater self-doubt. He must rely upon Aaron's eloquence and the elders' authority to persuade his own people and Pharaoh (see COMMENT). A final, formal difference between the sources is that in E Yahweh commands Moses to return to Egypt during their first conversation. In J, however, God sends him back in a subsequent communication, once the coast is clear (4:19).

REDACTION ANALYSIS

If my source analysis is correct, the Elohist is well represented in the early chapters of Exodus. As Redactor[JE] used J as his basic source for the Patriarchal epoch, so he preferred E's account of the Exodus. But much crucial information is preserved only from J: who Moses is, why he is in Midian and how he becomes son-in-law to the local priest.

The transition point from a J-based narrative to an E-based narrative is Exodus 3–4, where both documents are mixed together almost beyond recovery, and neither is complete. For example, we do not know where J's Bush theophany occurs, except that it is in or near Midian (4:19) upon "holiness ground" (3:5). In E, the meeting takes place on Mount Horeb itself, where the Covenant between Yahweh and his people will be reaffirmed and expanded. Thus in the combined JE, the Burning Bush is transplanted onto God's own mountain (this may already have been the case for E, assuming it, too, mentioned the Bush; see SOURCE ANALYSIS). Exodus 3–4 becomes a foreshadowing of the fiery theophany at Sinai/Horeb (see COMMENT).

We may perhaps reconstruct Redactor[JE]'s logic in his disposition of J and E in 3:7–10. Because of their redundancy, he separated v 7 (E?) from 9 (J?) by v 8 (E?). This created an ABA'B' structure (divine perception/response//divine perception/response) in vv 7–10, with an implicit parallelism between Yahweh's efforts (v 8) and Moses' (v 10). Moreover, he produced a symmetry of content between vv 7 and 9: Yahweh sees suffering/hears a cry//hears a cry/ sees suffering (Greenberg 1969: 99). For 3:7–18 as a whole, Blum (1990: 12 n. 11) observes the editor's use of sources to frame the revelation of the divine name in vv 11–15. Notable is the symmetry of vv 7–10 and 16–18 in both content and form: milk and honey/nations//nations/milk and honey. (Many, but not I, believe that only Deuteronom[ist]ic writers use the expression "land flowing of milk and honey" [e.g., Schmidt 1988: 137–39; Blum 1990: 32]; see APPENDIX A, vol. II.)

We again find composite JE in 4:18–31. Here Redactor^{JE} has been very active, making at least one surprising choice: placing v 19 after v 18. The reverse would have made more sense; indeed, we would never have noticed a seam:

> $^{19(J)}$And Yahweh said to Moses in Midian, "Go, return to Egypt, for all the men seeking your *soul* have died."
>
> $^{18(E)}$So Moses went and returned to Jether his father-in-law and said to him, "I would go and return to my brothers who are in Egypt and see if they still live."
>
> And Jethro said to Moses, "Go in peace."

Perhaps Redactor^{JE} simply did not consider this solution, although it parallels Jacob's leave-taking in Gen 31:3–21 (JE). If, however, the editor consciously rejected this arrangement, it was perhaps because he conceived of Mount Horeb as lying beyond the borders of Midian. Moses had to return to Jethro before Yahweh could speak to him "in Midian."

Another oddity is that Redactor^{JE} appears to have transferred 4:27–28 (E), the call of Aaron, from its logical location between 4:17 and 18. This created the impression that Moses stops again at Horeb to meet Aaron on his way back to Egypt (see NOTE to 4:27). Presumably, in the original E text, Moses is still talking to Yahweh when Aaron arrives. *Then* Moses goes to Jethro and tells him he must visit his family in Egypt, implying that Aaron has summoned him back. Thus, as it stands, 4:24–28 (JE) treats in sequence the symbolic circumcision of Moses (J) and the call of Aaron (E). This in turn, in conjunction with 4:9 (Moses' "heavy" mouth), apparently inspired the Priestly Writer to imagine Aaron as appointed to remedy Moses' "uncircumcision" of lips (see NOTE to 6:12).

The combination of J and E changes the meaning of the text and invests certain episodes with new significance. Moses' hesitancy in E acquires poignancy when contrasted with his impetuosity in J (Exodus 2). As a young hothead, he was ready to take on the Egyptians one at a time. Now, faced with the serious prospect of liberating his people, he proves diffident (cf. Dillmann 1880: 29).

Redaction also lends the mystifying vignette 4:24–26 (J), the Bridegroom of Bloodiness, many new nuances and ambiguities. By stitching together vv 22–23 (E) and 24–26 (J), Redactor^{JE} made Pharaoh's firstborn implicitly parallel to Moses' (v 25 [J]). Thus the editor created ambiguity as to the victim of the attack (Kaplan 1981). In J, it was Moses, but from JE, we might understand that Yahweh acts out his threat upon Moses' *son*, as if the unleashed powers of destruction turn at once against the nearest object (cf. ibn Ezra; Blau 1956–57: 1–2; Kosmala 1962; Greenberg 1969: 113). This reinterpretation, in turn, makes 4:24–26 a foreshadowing of the paschal night, when the Israelites will be endangered along with the Egyptian firstborn (Fishbane 1979: 71; COMMENT below). One might even infer that in 4:24–26, Yahweh is enforcing his claim upon the firstborn, a custom associated with the *Pesaḥ* in 13:1–2, 11–16 (cf. Morgenstern 1963: 57). The appearance of *higgîaʿ* 'apply' in both 4:25 (J) (blood of circumcision) and 12:22 (E) (paschal blood) strengthens the analogy (see COMMENT, pp. 238–39).

But JE is not quite clear; Yahweh's victim might still be Moses, as in J. By this reading, since both Yahweh's (hostile) encounter with Moses (4:24) and Aaron's (friendly) encounter with Moses (4:27) are denoted by the root *pgš* 'meet' (Cassuto 1967: 59), 4:24–26 would be more closely bound to what follows than to what precedes. Compare Genesis 32–33, where Jacob wrestles with a "man"/"deity" before meeting his brother Esau (cf. Hendel 1987a: 158–62).

By any reading of JE, 4:24–26 continues the theme of tension between Yahweh and Moses, evident in the Elohistic sections of chap. 4. Even after Moses agrees to go, he still, like Balaam (Num 22:22–35), needs reminding that he is not a free agent (Talmon 1954a: 94). Yahweh has not yet forgiven Moses for his stubbornness at the Burning Bush.

Since 18:2 (E) alludes to a previous parting of Moses and his family, redaction also creates the impression that Moses leaves his family after 4:24–26 (J) (ibn Ezra on 18:2). Thus in JE, having saved Moses' life, Zipporah quietly exits—perhaps with new doubts about her husband (see COMMENT, pp. 233–38).

The most momentous change wrought by the combination of J and E involves the divine name. In E, the scene at Horeb is the climactic moment when God first reveals his proper name to Moses, Israel and the world. In JE, the meaning of the scene is entirely changed. Since the name "Yahweh" was already known to the Patriarchs (e.g., Gen 15:2 [J]), Moses' request for God's true name (3:13 [E]) implies either that Moses is testing the bush (cf. Deut 18:20–22; Judg 13:17) or that the name of the ancestral god had been forgotten by Israel, or at least never been taught to Moses. If Moses himself never learned the name, he is presumably preparing himself for interrogation by a skeptical people (Jacob 1992: 65–67; Schmidt 1988: 168; Blum 1990: 12; see COMMENT, pp. 223–24).

To conclude, we must observe several contributions of the final Redactor of the Torah. He is probably responsible for 4:21b, "But I, I will strengthen his heart, and he will not release the people." We have already been advised that Pharaoh will be uncooperative (3:19 [E]); now we are assured that this is God's plan. Had the Redactor inserted his comment between vv 23 and 24, he would have destroyed Redactor^{JE}'s association of Pharaoh's son with Moses' son. Instead, he set his interjection between references to the coming "wonders" (i.e., the Plagues) and the slaying of the firstborn. Exod 4:21b later becomes the refrain of the Plagues cycle (7:13, 22; 8:11, 15; 9:12, 35; 10:20, 27; 11:10–11); see further SOURCE ANALYSIS to 7:8–11:10.

The Redactor's work also created new implications and associations. "Aaron your brother [i.e., fellow] Levite" (4:14 [E]; see NOTE) becomes Moses' full brother (6:20 [R]). The valuables taken from the Egyptians (3:22; 11:2–3; 12:35–36 [J?]) are no longer mere booty. In the composite Torah, they are presumably used for building the Tabernacle (chaps. 25–31, 35–40 [P]).

NOTES

3:1. *Moses, meanwhile.* Calvin and Jacob (1992: 48) call attention to the disjunctive syntax: *ûmōše(h) hāyâ rōʿe(h)* (vs. *wayhî mōše[h] rōʿe[h]* or *wayyērᵃʿ mōše[h]*). One might also regard the disjunction as signaling the start of a new narrative unit: "Now, Moses was herding . . ." (Waltke and O'Connor 1990: 650–52 [§39.2.3]).

herding. One might well meet the unexpected while tending the flock or herd: Saul finds the kingship (1 Samuel 9), and Anah finds *yēmim* — whatever they may be (Gen 36:24) — both while herding donkeys (on the symbolism of the shepherd, see COMMENT, pp. 221–22). Buber (1946: 60) notes that Moses has reverted to the pastoral nomadism of the Patriarchs, whom Yahweh invokes in 3:6, 15; 4:5.

Jethro. This is E's name for Moses' father-in-law; J calls him Reuel (see NOTE to 2:18). *Yitrô* is a presumedly Midianite form of the common Israelite name *yeter*. *Yeter* in fact replaces *yitrô* in 4:18 (MT) and may have been read throughout by LXX, which consistently calls Jethro *Iothor* (cf. LXX *Bosor* = MT *beṣer*, *Bochor* = *beker*, *Mosok/Mosoch* = *mešek*, *Odom* = *ʿēden*, *Rhobok* = *rebaʿ*, *Rhokom* = *reqem*, *Soros* = *šereš*, *Chobol/r* = *ḥeber*). The suffix -ô is probably an optional, fossilized case ending (Cassuto 1967: 52), as in the name of the Arabian king Geshem/Gashmu (Neh 6:1–2, 6) (cf. ibn Ezra on 4:18). The root *wtr/ytr* 'to be excessive' is common in Semitic names, usually accompanied by a divine title (for parallels, see Loewenstamm 1965: 956–57); cf. David's son *yitrᵊʿam* 'The (divine) Kinsman is greatness' (2 Sam 3:5). Other biblical names formed on this stem are *yitrāʾ* and *yitrān*.

behind the wilderness. Does *ʾaḥar* mean "into" (Vg), "in the direction of " (LXX) or "west of, the west side of " (Plastaras 1966: 60; Hyatt 1971: 71)? Perhaps the sense is that Moses drives his flock through and beyond Jethro's desert, into another region, the "far side of the wilderness" (Bekhor Shor; cf. 18:5). Qimḥi and Cassuto, however, interpret *midbār* as "pasturage" (Aramaic *dabrāʾ*, Hebrew *dōber*), translating the phrase as "after [i.e., in search of] pasturage." *Tg. Ps.-Jonathan* and some MSS of *Tg. Onqelos* even combine these

two interpretations of *midbār*, paraphrasing: *l'tr/btr špr r'y' lmdbr'* 'to a place
of/after good pasturage, into the wilderness.' For the conjectural emendation
"he drove behind the flock into the wilderness," see TEXTUAL NOTE.

the Deity's mountain. Horeb is so called because of Yahweh's revelation there,
first to Moses and later to all Israel (cf. Rashi). It is unclear whether Horeb was
also considered the Deity's proper, immemorial and permanent home (Josephus *Ant.* 2.265); compare Elijah's journey thither to confront Yahweh (1 Kgs
19:8). On the disputed location of Horeb, see APPENDIX B, vol. II.

Horeb. This is the name of the mountain of revelation in E and D; J and P
call it Sinai.

3:2. *Yahweh's.* This is the first appearance of the Deity's personal name in Exodus. On its vocalization and meaning, see NOTE to 3:15 and APPENDIX C,
vol. II.

Messenger. The Greek term for messenger (Hebrew *mal'āk*) is *angelos*,
whence English "angel." The relation between Deity and angel is somewhat
ambiguous in 3:2–4. One might initially identify the angel with the flame that
burns in the bush. Having captured Moses' attention, Yahweh himself then
calls down from heaven. This is probably incorrect, however. God himself is
within the bush.

Admittedly, sometimes angels are independent divine beings and are even
called "gods" (Ps 82:1, 6; 95:3; 96:4) or "sons of gods/deity" (e.g., Gen 6:2;
32:29, 31; Deut 32:8 [see TEXTUAL NOTE to 1:5]; Ps 29:1; 89:7; Job 38:7).
Often, however, an angel is a visible manifestation of God (Gaster 1962a;
Licht 1962; Greenberg 1969: 70). This explains the striking confusion (to our
minds) of angel and the Deity in such passages as Gen 16:11, 13; 22:11–12;
48:15–16; Exodus 3–4; Num 22:35, 38; Judg 6:11–24. The quasi-identity between Yahweh and his emissaries also explains why, except in latest Old Testament literature (i.e., Daniel), angels are anonymous (cf. the angels' reluctance
to reveal their names in Gen 32:30; Judg 13:6, 17–18).

The angel's ambiguous status arises from at least three factors. First, "Yahweh's Messenger" may be an early example of Judaism's tendency to avoid
direct reference to God, especially to his physical manifestations. Second,
while many ancient Near Eastern gods employ minor deities as messengers,
in Israelite monotheism these necessarily are, to an extent, absorbed into the
unique Deity (see APPENDIX C, vol. II). In later Judaism, the angels will
emerge as full-fledged individuals whose names all terminate in *-'ēl* 'god' in
memory of their former quasi-identity with the Deity (Gabriel, Raphael, etc.).

The third factor is the most important. Since a messenger speaks for his dispatcher, there is an inevitable transfer of identity. Thus prophets, also "messengers" (Isa 42:19; 44:26; Hag 1:13; 2 Chr 36:15, 16), speak in the divine voice
and merge into the divine persona (cf. Exod 7:17; 11:8). They are human angels, garments of the divine spirit (Judg 6:34; 1 Chr 12:19; 2 Chr 24:20). The
paradoxical interpenetration of Yahweh and angel, or Yahweh and prophet,
also recalls the relationship between deity and idol in Egypt, Mesopotamia

and Canaan. The statue is not the god, but can become the god and be referred to by the god's name (Jacobsen 1987a). The Egyptian "Report of Wen-Amon" 2.55 (*ANET* 28) in fact calls a portable idol a "messenger." Idol, angel and prophet are essentially localizations of a divine presence, or theophanies. The Bible's emphasis on angelic revelation may be directly related to Israel's avoidance of (male) divine icons (see APPENDIX C, vol. II).

flame. MT *labbat* is apparently derived from a root **lbb*, rather than the expected *lhb* 'burn' (see TEXTUAL NOTE). We may compare Akkadian *labābu* 'to rage,' used once with *išātu* 'fire = fever' (*CAD*). On the other hand, perhaps the daghesh in the beth was inserted to compensate for a lost he', as *bāttîm* 'houses' may come from **bahtîm* (cf. Ugaritic *bhtm*).

the bush. I.e., a certain bush, known to the narrator but not necessarily to the reader (*pace* Buber 1946: 39; Richter 1970: 81; Pixley 1987: 16). The word *sane(h)* occurs only here and perhaps in Deut 33:16, *šōkanî sane(h)* 'sane(h)-dweller' (but see Cross and Freedman 1975: 116). We do not know if *sane(h)* is a generic term for a bush or denotes a particular species; on real and imagined botanical cognates, see Tournay (1957). The earliest parallel comes from the Aramaic "Tale of Aḥiqar" (fifth century B.C.E.), where *sny'* (later Aramaic *sanyā'*) denotes a spiny plant (ll. 65–66) (Cowley 1923: 218; trans. in *ANET* 429–30). Perhaps, too, a sharp rock called *sene(h)* is named for the thorns of this bush (1 Sam 14:4). Some even speculate that the *sane(h)* lent its name to the whole Wilderness of Sin (16:1; 17:1; Num 33:11, 12) and/or Mount Sinai (ibn Ezra). (If *sane(h)* does allude to Sinai [Gressmann 1913: 24; Fohrer 1964: 34], then "from within the bush" [3:4] must be attributed to R^JE, since E calls the mountain "Horeb.")

Growing from "holiness ground," the *sane(h)* may be comparable to the sacred trees characteristic of ancient and modern Palestinian holy places (see COMMENT to 13:17–15:21, pp. 569–71). Smith (1927: 193, 562–63 [note by S. A. Cook]) and Gressmann (1913: 26–28) cite various parallels, all postbiblical, to the motifs of the burning but unconsumed tree, and the spirit-possessed tree (for a humorous Arabian example, see Doughty 1936: 2.231). One might also identify the bush with Yahweh's tree-emblem, the Asherah — but this is most uncertain (see NOTE to 34:13). Others compare the flaming bush to the rami-form candelabrum of the Tabernacle (see the discussion of 25:31–40 in vol. II).

burning . . . consumed. Combustion (*b'r*) is generally accompanied by consumption (*'kl*) (Num 11:1; 2 Sam 22:9 = Ps 18:9; Isa 9:17; 10:17; Job 1:16; Lam 2:3). But here, surprisingly, the result is nonconsumption. The anomalous form *'ukkal* 'eaten, consumed' is a Qal passive participle, probably originally pronounced **'ukal* (see Barth 1894: 273 n. 1).

3:3. *I would turn.* Yahweh's mode of self-revelation requires that Moses exercise free will, if only out of curiosity. He must choose to turn aside and approach the bush, where another might have passed by. Yahweh does not call Moses by overpowering him, but entices him with an uncanny flame, a benevolent *ignis fatuus.*

vision. Moses intends *mar'e(h)* in the sense of "sight" or "phenomenon." But it also has the nuance of "divine manifestation, prophetic vision"—which, unbeknownst to him, is wholly appropriate.

not . . . burn. Moses' words seem illogical or, at best, ill chosen. He should say, "Why is the bush not *consumed* (**yə'u[k]kal*)?" (cf. LXX; Syr; *Tg. Onqelos*). Still, the context makes the sense clear.

There are also ways to "fix" the problem, though I think them unnecessary. Since the Qal of *bʿr* can mean "to be (partially) consumed" (Judg 15:14), while the Piʿel connotes total consumption (1 Kgs 14:10), we might revocalize *yəbāʿēr (vs. MT *yibʿar*). Another solution would be to regard *lō(')*, ordinarily meaning "not," as an emphatic asseverative paralleled in Ugaritic: "Why, indeed, does the bush burn?" (Freedman 1969). But this seems far-fetched; the wonder, after all, is not the combustion, but the nonconsumption, of the bush. And others, surely overreacting to a minor problem, resort to source analysis (see Schmidt 1988: 104).

3:4. *Moses, Moses.* We do not know the significance of the repetition; compare Gen 22:11 (E); 46:2 (E); 1 Sam 3:10.

See me. *Hinnēnî* is the proper response, equivalent to "at your service" (Speiser 1964: 162). LXX renders, as elsewhere, "what is it?"

3:5. *Pull your sandals from upon your feet.* In Josh 5:15, Joshua likewise encounters an angel and is told to remove his sandal(s) because the site is holy. McNeile (1908: 17) compares the Muslim and Samaritan practice of removing shoes in holy places. In fact, as Ramban and others observe, it is likely that the Tabernacle priests ministered barefoot; Exodus 28 prescribes no footgear (*Exod. Rab.* 2:6), while 30:18–21; 40:30–32 require priests to wash their feet (Jacob 1992: 53). According to *m. Ber.* 9:5, one might not wear shoes on the entire (Second) Temple Mount. For a Greek parallel, see Milgrom (1991: 654); for extensive analogies worldwide, see Gaster (1969: 231–32).

The simplest explanation for this restriction is that one should not track dirt into God's house (Bekhor Shor; Cassuto 1967: 33). Perhaps shoes were not in general worn indoors, both for reasons of cleanliness and, suggests Morgenstern (1966: 292), to avoid bringing in bad luck. Moreover, ancient Egyptians removed their shoes before social superiors (Erman 1969: 227), and there is evidence that bare feet symbolized humility and mortification in Israel (2 Sam 15:30; Isa 20:2; Ezek 24:17, 23). Thus it would be presumptuous to appear before Yahweh shod. Milgrom (1991: 654) further suggests that leather sandals, made from dead animals, bear minor ritual impurity and contaminate holy ground.

place . . . holiness. Both *māqôm* 'place' and *qōdeš* 'holiness' can independently connote a sanctuary. Even in the absence of a surrounding structure, the vicinity of the Burning Bush is like a temple; the very ground is sacred. According to Num 5:17, the dust of the Tabernacle's floor possesses magical properties.

Many believe that the basic meaning of *qdš* is "separate, set apart" (e.g., BDB; Mowinckel 1953: 32; Gruber 1986: 133; Cogan and Tadmor 1988: 56). This is questionable, however (Luzzatto [on 15:11]; Mettinger 1988: 154). More likely, *qdš* means "to be numinous, imbued with a divine quality."

3:6. *your father's.* The phrase "father's deity" is paralleled in Gen 26:24; 31:5; 43:23; 46:3; 50:17; Exod 15:2; 18:4. In general, "god of the father" was an ancient Near Eastern designation for a clan's divine patron (Alt 1968: 3–100; Cross 1973: 3–43). "Father" in 3:6 is conceivably collective, connoting all of Moses' ancestors (cf. NOTE to 15:2). Or it may refer to the clan father Levi (cf. David in Isa 38:5). Most likely, however, *'ābîkā* is Moses' long-estranged true father. Calvin imagines that invocation only of the ancient Patriarchs would have had less effect; Moses might think the promises to them had lapsed during the centuries. Therefore, Yahweh first avers he is the god of Moses' own father.

Abraham. Gen 17:5 relates the name *'abrāhām to 'abrām* 'The [divine] Father is exalted' (cf. also *'abîrām* 'My Father is exalted'). Most scholars infer that *rāhām* and *rām* are simply synonymous dialectal variants. This is not quite certain, however. While an interchange of the roots *rwm* and **rhm* would have many parallels (GKC §77*f*), **rhm* remains unattested for Hebrew and related languages.

Liverani (1979) takes an entirely different approach. Noting that the Beth Shean stele of Seti I, c. 1300, mentions an ethnic group *rhm* (*ANET* 254), he proposes that *'abrāhām* originally meant "Father of *rhm*" (But then the vocalization should be ** 'abīrāhām*).

Isaac. The name *yiṣḥāq* means "He laughs/is pleased," the presumed subject being God (but see Martin-Achard 1992: 463).

Jacob. The name *ya'ăqōb* means either "He follows [in support]" or "He protects," the subject again being God. For a discussion and parallels to the name from all periods, see Thompson (1974: 36–51).

hid his face. The Israelites believed that close contact with a deity was dangerous (see Gen 32:23–33; Exod 19:21–24; 20:19; 24:11; 33:20, etc.). Later in E, Moses will be granted a vision of God (24:9–11) and will even request another viewing, presumably more intimate (33:18–23; cf. Num 12:8). Thus it is ironic that Moses hides his face from his first theophany (cf. *b. Ber.* 7a; Ramban). He has not yet achieved his matchless familiarity with Yahweh. Moses' act will later be imitated by Elijah, who wraps his face in his cloak at Horeb (1 Kgs 19:13).

3:7. *from the face of.* Mippənê means both "in the presence of" and "because of."

indeed. The Versions render *kî* as "for," which is possible but unlikely in this context. Presumably, Yahweh does not perceive because he knows, but knows because he perceives. Saadiah takes *kî* as tantamount to "and." But it is more likely simply an emphatic particle (Muilenburg 1961).

3:8. *I will descend/have descended.* The tense of the verb is uncertain. To judge from *Samaritan Tg. w'y't* 'and I will descend,' Sam *w'rdh* is future/cohortative: "I *will* descend," i.e., from heaven/Horeb/the desert into Egypt (cf. Gen 46:4 [E]). On the other hand, MT, LXX and Syr all read "I *have* descended" (*wā'ērēd*), i.e., to earth (cf. Gen 11:5, 7; 18:21; 28:12;) Exod 19:11, 18, 20; 34:5, etc.). By either reading, there is a contrast with Yahweh's intent "to bring him up." But following Sam sharpens the comparison: Yahweh goes *down to* Egypt to take Israel *up from* Egypt (cf. Ehrlich 1908: 268). Ackerman (1974) finds death-and-resurrection symbolism in this descent-ascent imagery. But topography provides an adequate explanation: Egypt is a low country, while Canaan is hilly.

arm. *Yād* 'arm, hand' often connotes "power."

to a land. Canaan is described by its qualities, but not actually named.

milk and honey. This cliché refers to two of the three bases of the Israelite economy: herding and horticulture (Rashi on 13:5; Dillmann 1880: 29). (The third and most important is cultivation of grains.) *Dəbaš* here is probably not bees' honey, but a syrup made from grapes or dates, Arabic *dibs* (Caquot 1978). The sense of the metaphor is that Israel is so fertile, its springs exude, instead of water, nutritious fluids ready for consumption. The same image is found in the medieval legend of Cockaigne and the "Big Rock Candy Mountain" of American folk song, as well as in Ugaritic literature (*KTU* 1.6.iii.6–7, 12–13) and the Bible (Deut 32:13–14; Joel 4:18; Amos 9:13; Ps 36:9) (see COMMENT to 17:1–7; Propp 1987a: 26–28; Schmidt 1988: 164–65).

We need not take this hyperbole too seriously. Although the Egyptian "Tale of Sinuhe" (*ANET* 19) lauds Syria-Palestine's marvelous fertility, and although Canaan's natural wealth was an article of faith for biblical authors, in fact the abundance of Egypt dwarfed that of Canaan. In Num 16:13, the regretful Israelites more realistically call *Egypt* a "land flowing of milk and honey." Canaan is outstandingly fertile only in contrast to the desert. Indeed, the reason for the Hebrews' presence in Egypt is Canaan's vulnerability to famine (Calvin).

Canaanite . . . Jebusite. Simultaneously enticing and intimidating, Yahweh assures Moses that Canaan is broad and fertile, but not unoccupied. On the pre-Israelite inhabitants of Canaan, see APPENDIX B, vol. II.

3:9. *Egypt are oppressing.* "Egypt" (*miṣrayim*) is often collective. The verb *lḥṣ* 'oppress' is used similarly in 23:9: "And a sojourner do not oppress; for you, you have known the sojourner's *soul,* for sojourners you were in the land of Egypt" (cf. 22:20). In other words, the Egyptians have violated Israelite standards of conduct toward foreigners.

3:10. *go, for I send.* One might expect sending to precede dismissal, but biblical style often inverts the temporal order of actions (hysteron proteron). The identical phrase appears in Gen 37:13 (cf. also 1 Sam 16:1).

take . . . out. Ehrlich (1908: 268), Yaron (1959: 165 n. 15) and Wijngards (1965: 92–94) suggest that *hôṣîʾ* 'take out' bears the connotation "liberate," inasmuch as *yṣʾ* 'go out' can describe manumission (21:3, 7, 11) (cf. also Akkadian *šūṣû*). Still, the basic meaning is literal: Moses is to take Israel out of Egypt into the desert.

3:11. *Who am I.* The correct response to "Go, for I send" should be *hinnēnî* 'See me' (Gen 37:13). Instead, Moses asks, "Who am I?" This is not necessarily a *faux pas.* When David (1 Sam 18:18; 2 Sam 7:18) and Solomon (2 Chr 2:5) ask "Who am I?" in response to various opportunities and divine commissions, the words signify humble acquiescence (cf. also 2 Kgs 8:13). In Exodus, however, the ensuing discussion proves that Moses really is trying to evade his commission. (For a full study of the formula, see Coats 1970.)

that . . . that. Bekhor Shor perceives intensification *a fortiori:* if unfit to appear before Pharaoh, how much more unfit am I to liberate Israel!

3:12. *Because.* Or "this is because"; cf. Durham's (1987: 28) colloquial "the point is." *Kî* seems to have a dual function, continuing the divine speech from 3:10 and responding to Moses' interruption. Alternate renderings would be an emphatic "indeed" or nothing at all, since *kî* can introduce direct as well as indirect speech (see Muilenburg 1961). L. Garber (privately) observes that Yahweh may be playing upon Moses' repeated *kî . . . kî* 'that . . . that' (v 11).

I will be with you. Since God arguably calls himself in 3:15 *'ehye(h)* 'I-will-be,' one might translate *'ehye(h) 'immāk* as "I-will-be is with you." But I will argue below that 3:15 is sarcastic (see pp. 224–26). In any case, *'ehye(h) 'immāk* is a ubiquitous formula of divine reassurance (Gen 26:3; 28:15; 31:3, etc.; see Preuss 1968). Although it does chime with 3:14, the cliché need not be overinterpreted.

Moses has just asked, "Who am I (to do all this)?" (3:11). Yahweh does not answer directly but responds, as it were: "The question is not who *you* are, but who *I* am, and I will be with you" (cf. ibn Ezra; Calvin; Durham 1987: 33, 37). Moses, dissatisfied, next demands, "Then who are *you?*" (3:13), a question that the Deity initially rejects (3:14) but finally answers seriously (3:15) (see COMMENT).

this is the sign. What is the sign? Upon first reading, one thinks of Israel's safe arrival and worship at Horeb, fulfilled in 18:12; 24:4–5. Worship at the mountain would be evidence of Providence after the fact, proof that God, not chance, freed Israel. If such is Yahweh's intent, Moses' dismay is understandable (4:1). Prophetic signs are generally of more immediate, practical use (e.g., 4:8; 2 Kgs 20:8–11; Isa 38:7–8) (Scharbert 1989: 22). Even if Moses himself trusts, how will the people blindly follow? After further importunings, the Deity gives Moses two wonders on the spot and the promise of a third, as if implicitly accepting Moses' complaint (Fretheim 1991a: 68).

There are other plausible readings of 3:12, however. Rashi and Rashbam suggest that the sign is the Burning Bush, marking precisely where Israel is to worship. Thus the sign is for Moses alone; it will not help him to convince the people. (If, however, the bush is not proper to E, then the sign must originally have been something else.) Another possibility is that at this point, Moses receives the divine rod (see COMMENT, pp. 227–29).

Taking a more abstruse approach, Ehrlich (1969: 138) argues that the sign is "that I, I sent you" — but this would be a highly unusual use of *kî.* More plausibly, *Exod Rab.* 3:4 raises the possibility that the sign is Yahweh's presence with Moses, promised in the first part of the verse (also anonymous Gaon quoted by ibn Ezra; Coats 1988: 64). D. N. Freedman (privately) suggests that the very name "I-will-be" (*'ehye[h]*) is to be Moses' sign.

It is also possible that worship at the mountain is a sign of some *subsequent* event. Ibn Ezra compares Isa 37:30–32 = 2 Kgs 19:29–31, while Childs (1974: 57) adduces 1 Sam 2:34; 1 Kgs 13:3–5; Jer 44:27–30. Rashi, as an alternative to his above-cited interpretation, suggests that safe arrival at the mountain will certify the imminent giving of the Torah. Similarly, Kravitz (*apud* Greenberg 1969: 78) proposes that reaching Horeb will vouchsafe Israel's future arrival in the promised land of v 8 (which may, however, come from a different source). Finally, Noth (1962: 42) and Fohrer (1964: 39–40) brutally sever the Gordian knot: the original sign has fallen from the verse by scribal error.

that I, I sent you. We are unsure where the emphasis lies: "this is the sign that *I* (and none other) have sent you," or "this is the sign that I sent *you* (and none other)." The stress on the first person pronoun suggests the former, but, given the people's anticipated skepticism, both are probably meant. Thus v 12 serves as a transition from v 11, where Moses doubts his own worth, to vv 13–15, concerning Yahweh's identity.

serve. To "serve" (*ʿbd*) a deity is to worship.

3:13. *Your fathers' deity.* Who are the "fathers"? They may, of course, be the three Patriarchs (or the Matriarchs and Patriarchs). But they might also be the parents of each individual Israelite (cf. 3:6).

Nowhere in J, E or P does Moses call Yahweh "*our* fathers' deity" (but note Deut 26:7). (Some LXX MSS have "*our* fathers'" in 3:13, 15, 16, but this is a confusion of Greek *hymōn* 'your' and *hēmōn* 'our.') By his choice of words, Moses stands apart from his people. Arguably, this alienation is a side effect of Moses' assumption of Yahweh's persona. But Joseph similarly distances himself from his brothers, calling Jacob "my father" (Gen 45:13) or "your father" (Gen 45:18–19), never "our father."

What is his name. Does the ancestral deity have no name? On the contrary, he has many, especially in E: God the Eternal (*ʾēl ʿôlām*), God of Bethel/the god Bethel (*hāʾēl bêtʾēl*), Fear of Isaac (*paḥad yiṣḥāq*), etc. (see Cross 1973: 3–75). Even the name "Yahweh" appears in several forms: *yahwe(h)*, *yāh*, *yāhû*, *yəhô*, *yô*. Thus the gist of Moses' question may be "Which name will I give them?" (Greenberg 1969: 80).

In the original Elohistic document, God's answer is unexpected, since heretofore the name "Yahweh" has not been used (on Gen 22:14, 15, see Davila 1991). That is, 3:15 represents the first disclosure of the name to Israel and humanity (see INTRODUCTION). In the redacted Torah, however, both Moses' question and Yahweh's answer require reinterpretation, since the name "Yahweh" has been known since antediluvian times (Gen 4:26 [J]); see REDACTION ANALYSIS. On inquiring after a deity's name, see COMMENT, pp. 223–26.

3:14. *I will be who I will be . . . I-will-be.* The most familiar translation of *ʾehye(h) ʾăšer ʾehye(h)* is KJV "I am that I am," or, in modern English, "I am what I am." Other efforts include LXX *eimi ho ōn* 'I am the existing one,' Mettinger's (1988: 36) "[My name will be] *Ehyeh* [I AM], because I am" and Davies's (1967: 72) rapturous "I AM *who and what, and where and when, and how and even why you will discover* I AM" (capitalization and italics his); for further attempts, see Mettinger (pp. 33–36).

Hebrew expresses "I am X," however, with a nonverbal sentence (e.g., *ʾānōkî yahwe[h]* 'I am Yahweh'). The imperfect of *hyy* always refers to the future (Abba 1961: 324; de Vaux 1970: 66). If one could say "I am that I am" in Hebrew at all, it would probably be through some such barbarous circumlocution as **'ānōkî hû' 'ăšer 'ānōkî hû'*. Likewise, if the meaning were "I am *'ehye(h)*," as the second half of the verse might suggest, we would expect **'ānōkî (hû')* *'ehye(h)*. And if the intention were *"'ehye(h)* is who I am" (Andersen and Freedman 1980: 199), again assuming this could be conveyed in Hebrew at all, we should get something like **'ehye(h) 'ăšer 'ānōkî hû'*. We still have the option of rendering *'ehye(h) 'ăšer 'ehye(h)* as *"'ehye(h)* is who I will be," but this seems a strange way for the Deity to identify himself. I follow, therefore, the translation of Aquila and Theodotion: *esomai (hos) esomai* 'I will be who I will be' (see Field 1875: 1.85). Or, if the intent is evasion, an attractive alternative is "I may be who I may be" (see COMMENT).

3:15. *further said.* Notice how gradually Yahweh approaches the explicit pronouncement of his name: "I will be who I will be (*'ehye[h] 'ăšer 'ehye[h]*) . . . 'I-will-be' (*'ehye[h]*) has sent me to you . . . Yahweh . . . has sent me to you." Only the last truly answers Moses' question (see COMMENT).

Yahweh. Because uttering the Tetragrammaton became taboo among the Jews before the common era and its pronunciation was forgotten (Fitzmyer 1979: 115–42), our vocalization of the consonants *yhwh* is somewhat speculative. *Yahwe(h)* (originally **yahwi?*) is simply the most likely reconstruction. For further discussion of the name "Yahweh," its etymology and history, see APPENDIX C, vol. II.

Why does MT vocalize *yhwh* as *yəhōwāh* (Codex L *yəhwāh*)? Because in reading aloud, Jews replace the divine name with *'ădōnāy* 'my Lordship' (if, however, *yhwh* is preceded by *'ădōnāy*, one says *'ĕlōhîm* 'Deity,' to avoid **'ădōnāy 'ădōnāy*). To signal the substitution, the Massoretes inserted the vowels of *'ădōnāy* (or sometimes *'ĕlōhîm*) into the consonants *yhwh*, yielding the hybrids *yəhōwāh* and *yĕhōwih* (in *yəhōwāh*, the change *ă > ə* is necessitated by the replacement of *'* with *y*; for *yĕhōwih*, however, we would expect **yəhōwih*). English "Jehovah," current since the sixteenth century, is simply a misguided transliteration of *yəhōwāh* (*j* = *y*, *v* = *w*).

this is my name. Since Hebrew lacks quotation marks, these words might still be part of Moses' announcement to Israel. My punctuation, however, takes them as directed to Moses alone. Jacob (1992: 75) suggests that the Deity's full name is "Yahweh, your fathers' [or *'ăbōtênû* 'our fathers''] deity, Abraham's deity, Isaac's deity and Jacob's deity" (also Van Seters 1972: 457). If so, Yahweh has already disclosed half of his name in 3:6.

designation. Here, as often, *zēker* functions as a quasi-synonym for *šēm* 'name,' with additional connotations of speaking and remembering. Implausibly, Rashbam differentiates between God's *zēker* (Yahweh) and his *šēm* (I-will-be). If there is such a distinction, more likely his "name" is Yahweh, while his "designation" is "the deity of Abraham . . . Isaac . . . Jacob."

age (by) age. Literally, "to age-age" (*lədōr dōr*), with reduplication conveying "each and every." For *'ōlām* 'eternity' parallel to *dōr (wā)dōr* in Ugaritic and Hebrew, see *KTU* 1.2.iv.10; 19.iii.154, 161–62, 167–68; Deut 32:7; Isa 34:10, 17; 51:8; Ps 33:11; 61:7–8; 77:8–9; 85:6, etc.

Dōr derives from a Proto-Semitic root **dwr* referring to expanse of space and time, or to circularity of the same. The usual rendering, "generation," can be misleading; see NOTES to 6:20 and 12:40.

Fuss (1972: 46) observes that "this is my name to eternity,/and this is my designation age (by) age" exhibits quasi-poetic parallelism; compare Ps 102:13; 135:13. Thus in 3:15, Yahweh reveals himself in elevated style (Jacob 1992: 75).

3:16. *appeared.* In the composite text, this refers to the fiery Messenger of 3:2 (J). But in E, too, Yahweh appears visibly to Moses (3:6b; cf. Num 12:8).

the deity of Abraham, Isaac and Jacob. The author varies the formula in 3:6, 13, 15, 16 to avoid monotony.

acknowledge. Difficult to translate, *pqd* refers both to mental action or perception and to consequent physical action. Thus it can be rendered "perceive, reckon, remember, feel an obligation" as well as "visit, muster, entrust, appoint, be absent, punish, reward" (cf. Lübbe 1990). *Pāqōd pāqadtî* echoes Gen 50:24-25: "Joseph said to his brothers, 'I am dying, but Deity will acknowledge, acknowledge (*pāqōd yipqōd*) you and take you up (*wǝheʿĕlâ ʾetkem*, cf. Exod 3:17) from this land to the land which he swore to Abraham, to Isaac and to Jacob.' So Joseph adjured Israel's sons, saying, 'Deity will acknowledge, acknowledge you. . . .'"

3:17. *said.* As in 2:14, "say" means "intend, propose." But here the nuance may be "I said (long ago)," i.e., promised.

3:18. *they will heed your voice.* But not at once, apparently, since Moses must first perform the signs (4:30). Calvin connects these words with what follows: "after they shall have heeded your voice, you will come to Egypt's king. . . ."

come. Moses both "comes" (*bwʾ*) and "goes" (*hlk*) before Pharaoh. The former connotes entry into the palace, the latter describes outdoor encounters (J. C. Geoghegan, privately).

you and Israel's elders. As affairs turn out, Moses and the elders meet separately with Pharaoh; see COMMENT to 5:1-6:1.

Yahweh the Hebrews' deity. The term *ʿibrîm* 'Hebrews' often appears in conversation with foreigners, or in the mouths of foreigners; see NOTE to 1:15 and APPENDIX B, vol. II.

happened upon us. The verb *qry/qrʾ* connotes a theophany in 5:3; Num 23:3, 4, 15, 16. The elders, together with Moses, are to tell Pharaoh that they all have met Yahweh. Although for the elders the experience will have been indirect, theirs is the greater prestige and credibility (see COMMENT, pp. 232-33).

three days' way. "Three days" is a biblical cliché for a duration greater than a day and less than a week. In 3:18, it is slightly unclear whether "three days" limits the time of absence or the distance of the journey. The latter appears more likely, since that is the normal meaning of *derek* 'way' plus a measure of time (e.g., Num 10:33; 11:31) (Jacob 1992: 125). Thus Moses is requesting a furlough of a week or more (Bekhor Shor on 5:4). Supposed cultic obligations seem to have been favored as polite excuses in Israel, presumably because to challenge them was impious (cf. Rashbam); compare 1 Sam 16:2; 20:6; 2 Sam 15:7; Prov 7:14–20.

Whether or not the writer knew it, the Egyptians did give their laborers vacations of a week or two, sometimes explicitly for religious holidays (Kitchen 1966: 156–57). So Moses' request would be, by Egyptian standards, quite reasonable. Since Pharaoh will not dismiss the Hebrews for an ordinary excuse, it is clear he would never have freed them voluntarily (Abarbanel).

By any interpretation, "three days' way" is at best a half-truth. Moses never promises to return (ibn Ezra on 11:4; Jacob 1992: 125). The Egyptians begin to catch on in 10:10, and they discover only in 14:5 that the Hebrews are bent on escape—in fact, on the third day (Rashi).

Another reason for the tradition of Moses' and Yahweh's equivocation is the inherent appeal of Trickster tales (see Niditch 1987). At the expense of God's dignity—he, after all, does not need to fool Pharaoh—tradition has created an enjoyable story of the Hebrews and their god outwitting a tyrant (cf. 1:15–21). For the sake of drama, even Yahweh briefly becomes an underdog vis-à-vis Pharaoh.

the wilderness. Pharaoh would naturally understand this as the desert surrounding the Nile valley, whose outer limit was three days from Egypt proper (see NOTES to 13:20 and 14:5). He would never imagine a trek into the Sinai.

sacrifice. This desert pilgrimage festival (note 5:1 *wəyāḥōggû* 'celebrate') may foreshadow the paschal offering and Festival (*ḥag*) of Unleavened Bread, which will ever after commemorate the departure from Egypt (Haran 1978: 300–3). It could also allude to pilgrimages hypothetically made by later Israelites to Horeb (cf. Noth 1940; Meshel 1981; Cross 1988; Coote and Ord 1989: 224–25). By the plain sense, however, Yahweh is simply equivocating. Israel will indeed worship God in the wilderness—but at Sinai, three *months* out of Egypt (19:1).

3:19. *unless.* Following 4QExod[b] and LXX (see TEXTUAL NOTE) and Ska's (1994) detailed study, I take *wəlō(')* as equivalent to *'im-lō(')* or *kî 'im* (cf. 1 Sam 20:2; 2 Sam 13:26; 2 Kgs 5:17). See also Luzzatto and, for further bibliography, Schmidt (1988: 106).

strong arm. I.e., physical force, as in English "strong-arm." Although *yād* is usually rendered "hand," that really corresponds to *kap* (often mistranslated "palm"); note that the earliest form of the letter yodh (= *yād*) is a bent arm. Sometimes *yād* does refer to the hand (e.g., 4:2), but more often it is the arm, just as *regel* is usually the leg but sometimes the foot (properly, *kap regel*).

The owner of the arm in 3:19 is somewhat uncertain. If it is Yahweh (*Memar Marqah* 1:2 [MacDonald 1963: 1.9; 2.9]), we note that in the ancient Near East, a deity's "arm" connoted his power to cause wonders, often catastrophic (Roberts 1971; Görg 1986). In Num 20:20, however, *yād ḥăzāqâ* refers to *Israel's* military might; and 6:1 may mention the "strong arm" with which *Pharaoh* expels Israel (see NOTE). Thus the sense of 3:19 might be "Pharaoh will not just let (*ntn*) you go; he will expel you by force." Still, 3:19 is most naturally taken as referring to Yahweh's arm (cf. 3:20; 7:4–5, etc.).

3:21. *emptily.* I.e., empty-handed. *Rêqām* bears two associations here. On the one hand, Israelite *mores* prohibited releasing a servant "emptily." Rather, he was to be liberally endowed (Gen 31:42; Deut 15:13). On the other hand, Israelite men were forbidden to appear "emptily" before Yahweh at pilgrimage festivals (23:15; 34:20; Deut 16:16).

3:22. *a woman.* Why are women singled out? Are they considered more materialist than men, or more generous toward children? When this command is reiterated (11:2), it applies to both men and women; there is no mention of the young at all.

ask. Often *š'l* has the sense of "borrow," but here there is no thought of returning the goods. "Request," if not "demand," is rather the implication.

woman sojourner of her house. Daube (1963: 53–54) conjectures that these temporary, non-Israelite tenants are in fact slave-concubines, comparing the sequence "men sojourners of my house . . . maidservants . . . slaves" (Job 19:15–16). One thinks particularly of Hagar, the *Egyptian* maidservant-concubine of Abraham and Sarah (Gen 16:3).

you will place. The commands are ostensibly masculine plural, addressed to all Israel. In light of v 22a, however, they could apply to the woman alone; i.e., we may have gender incongruence.

your sons and . . . daughters. Ehrlich (1908: 271) and Greenberg (1969: 87) rescue the decorum of the passage (somewhat) by emphasizing that at least the despoiled property is bestowed upon others (see also following).

despoil Egypt. There is likely wordplay: *wəniṣṣaltem* can also mean "you will be rescued." That Israel would bear great wealth from Egypt was perhaps foreshadowed in Gen 12:10–20 (J) and explicitly predicted in Gen 15:14 (J).

The plundering of Egypt has occasioned much embarrassed eisegesis. Sforno argues that the riches were honestly borrowed, to be returned later (cf. NOTE to 14:2). Once the Egyptians pursued Israel in hopes of plunder (15:9), however, turnabout was fair play. Entering a more popular avenue of interpretation, Philo (*Moses* 1.141–42), Ezekiel the Tragedian 162–66 and Jub 48:18 claim that the "spoils" are really back payment for Israel's servitude (also *b. Sanh.* 91a). Daube (1963: 18, 57), too, notes that released slaves were entitled to gifts upon release (Deut 15:13; cf. Genesis 31) (see also Cassuto 1967: 44).

Others adopt an anthropological stance. Morgenstern (1966: 220, 297–98) discerns a general Semitic pattern of ritualized borrowing of clothing, originally meant to deceive evil spirits. And Segal (1963: 148–49, 260) raises the possibility that "despoiling the Egyptians" in fact began as a springtime children's game (NOTE to 12:36).

All these approaches have merit, but skip over the surface meaning. The author's *Schadenfreude* at the exploitation of Israel's imperialist neighbor is palpable. Childs (1974: 201) aptly compares the departing Hebrews, laden with the Egyptians' goods, to a triumphant army returning home (also Van Seters 1994: 98). The season of Israel's departure may also be relevant, for New Kingdom Pharaohs received tribute from their Canaanite vassals each spring (Liverani 1990a; on springtime taxation in general, see Segal 1963: 136–37).

4:1. *suppose.* *Hēn* could also be translated more emphatically: "*Look*—they will not believe me."

4:2. *What's this.* Yahweh's response seems at first a change of subject. He does not say, "Here is a sign," to warn Moses. Instead, he gives him a small scare, punishment for his stubbornness (cf. *Exod. Rab.* 3:12–13). Like a stage magician, the Deity first asks Moses to identify his own property, to ascertain that it is nothing out of the ordinary (Rashi; but see pp. 227–28 for the possibility that the rod has just materialized). Other prophets, too, are asked to identify objects (Jer 1:11–14; Amos 7:8; 8:2). But these function paronomastically as omens; they undergo no transformations.

MT writes the interrogative pronoun as prefixed *m-*, rather than the expected *mh* (Sam). Cassuto (1967: 46) suggests that *mzh* 'what's this' is a graphic pun with *mṭh* 'rod.'

A rod. The shepherd's staff supports his steps, guides his flock and smites his foes. It is a fitting symbol for God's presence (see further NOTE to 4:20).

4:4. *grasp its tail.* If the Elohist knew anything of snake-handling, he would surely have known that one grasps potentially poisonous snakes behind the head. For Cassuto (1967: 47) and Durham (1987: 45), God's command is a special test of Moses' faith and fortitude. I think it more likely the author had never handled a snake.

4:5. *So that.* This is the continuation of Yahweh's speech in v 3a (made explicit in some LXX witnesses). In its immediate context, however, *ləma'an* is elliptical: "*this is* so that." There is no need to see the verse as an addition (*pace* Richter 1970: 60).

4:6. *məṣōrāʿ.* Once again Yahweh neglects to warn Moses in order to give him a scare (cf. NOTE to 4:2). *Məṣōrāʿ* describes a person (or limb) afflicted with the skin disease *ṣāraʿat.* Such men and women were secluded from the community (Num 12:14 [E]), for skin disease, though nonfatal, was considered both contagious and ritually defiling (Leviticus 13–14). (To explain why, Jacob [1992: 86] hypothesizes that snow-white *ṣāraʿat* was associated with death's pallor.)

I have declined to translate *məṣōrāʿ* and *ṣāraʿat.* The usual renderings, "leprous" and "leprosy" (i.e., Hansen's disease), are inaccurate. Both Hebrew *ṣāraʿat* and Greek *lepra* originally denoted a variety of ephemeral, snowlike (i.e., white and/or flaky) skin ailments such as psoriasis and fungus, perhaps as well as the more severe Hansen's disease. Only in the Middle Ages was the term "leprosy" restricted to the last affliction (Mull and Mull 1992). According to Lev 13:33–53; 14:34–47, even garments and buildings could contract *ṣāraʿat*, which must be rot or mold. For further discussion, see Hulse (1975) and Avalos (1995: 311–16).

We may wonder why Moses is described as even a temporary *məṣōrāʿ.* The most reasonable answer is that Yahweh wishes to prove, on Moses' person, his ability to send disease and healing (see COMMENT to 15:22–27). Perhaps that the prior miracle involved a rod and a snake is no coincidence. Throughout the ancient Mediterranean world, the serpent on a pole symbolized healing (cf. the bronze serpent of Num 21:4–9; the rod of Aesculepius) (Astour

1967: 240–41). And, within the Elohistic source, ṣāra'at appears to be the specific penalty for doubting Moses' authority. In Numbers 12, Miriam is the skeptic, but in Exod 4:6–7, it is Moses himself.

4:7. *like his flesh*. This is generally taken to mean "like his previous, healthy flesh" (cf. 2 Kgs 5:14). But Saadiah's interpretation, "like the rest of his healthy flesh," is possible, too (also Ehrlich 1908: 272).

4:8. *voice*. I.e., import, meaning. We might also take *šāma' bəqōl* 'hear the voice' as a cliché meaning "pay attention." O'Connell (n.d.) notes how the signs' "voice" will validate Moses' own "voice" (4:1, 9). But Moses remains concerned about his ability to communicate, as the following verses show.

4:9. *will become . . . will become*. After the parenthesis "you take from the Nile," the main verb is repeated; Ramban compares Gen 46:2; Exod 1:15–16.

blood. This third sign, which Moses cannot test in the desert, adumbrates the first plague, when all the waters of Egypt, not just what Moses spills, turn to blood (7:14–24). See SOURCE ANALYSIS to 7:8–11:10.

4:10. *my Lordship*. Literally "my Lords," the plural connoting abstraction as well as power (GKC §124g–i).

words man. The Versions paraphrase in various ways, the most interesting being LXX^AB "competent" (perhaps taking *dəbārîm* as "affairs" [O'Connell n.d.]). But the plain sense is that Moses is a poor communicator. (Jacob [1992: 98] notes that, at the bush, Yahweh does almost all the talking.)

One wonders how the original audience took the demurral of Moses, renowned as lawgiver, orator and poet—is there a touch of irony? Moses certainly finds his tongue by Deuteronomy (Greenberg 1969: 95; cf. the midrash that his impediment was removed when he received the Torah [*Deut. Rab.* 1:1]).

Moses' objection evinces a misunderstanding of the nature of prophecy, as Yahweh hastens to point out. The prophet need not be a "words man" at all. His message comes from Yahweh (see further under COMMENT).

yesterday . . . the day before. I.e., in the past. *Təmôl šilšōm* is an old Canaanite expression; compare Amarna *tumāl šalšāmi* (EA 362.16).

nor since your speaking. Moses indirectly blames his condition on Yahweh, who has neglected to heal him (see further below).

but. Alternative renderings would be "as," "because" (*kî*).

heavy of mouth and heavy of tongue. The pairing of "mouth" and "tongue" is formulaic in Canaanite and Hebrew literature (*KTU* 1.93.2–3; Isa 57:4; Ps 10:7; 37:30; 66:17, etc.).

There is a tragic aspect to Moses' plaint. The man closest to God is the least able to communicate his experience. Hallo (1991: 48) compares Moses' "heavy" (*kābēd*) mouth and lips to Pharaoh's "heavy, firm" (*kābēd*) heart (7:14; 8:11; 28; 9:7, 34). Both conditions hinder the transmittal of Yahweh's word.

Commentators are divided among three basic approaches to "heavy of mouth and tongue," one literal and two metaphorical. It is certain that the phrase primarily connotes a speech impediment, for Hebrew and other ancient languages often call defective bodily organs "heavy" (Tigay 1978). Most traditional and contemporary interpreters think this is the sense here. LXX witnesses have "shrill-voiced/stammering and slow of tongue," while Syr paraphrases "stammering of speech and difficult of tongue."

A second approach sees "heavy of mouth and heavy of tongue" as a hyperbolic metaphor for ineloquence, described as a physical impediment. To explain the self-deprecation, Luzzatto cites Moses' innate modesty (cf. Num 12:3).

A third approach is inspired by Ezek 3:5–6, where "heavy of tongue" means "speaking a foreign language." Tigay observes that terms properly denoting speech impediments in many languages also connote the sounds made by foreigners. Many exegetes have inferred that Moses has forgotten Egyptian; after all, according to 6:12, 30 (P, R), his "uncircumcised" lips prevent communication with Pharaoh. For precritical scholars, this was a reasonable surmise. I would carefully distinguish, however, between E and P. In E, Moses' heavy mouth and tongue hinder him from talking with the *people*, not necessarily with Pharaoh (4:1, 29–31). Thus, if foreign languages are at issue, in P Moses cannot speak *Egyptian*, but in E he cannot speak *Hebrew*—either because of his long absence or because, as in J, he was raised apart from his people.

It seems to me most likely, however, that Moses really has a physical problem. First, Yahweh's claim to control human faculties would be irrelevant without an actual impediment (unless the Deity argues, *a fortiori*, that for Omnipotence it will be trivial to impart fluency). Note, too, that Moses' interpreter, Aaron, who assists in addressing the people, also accompanies Moses before Pharaoh in E (5:1, 4, 20; 8:4, 8, 21; 9:27; 10:3, 8, 16). A likely inference is that Moses' condition hinders his communication with both Pharaoh and Israel. This excludes the possibility that he has simply forgotten his Hebrew.

Moses' objection seems to be twofold: (a) he is ineloquent ("not a words man") *because* (*kî*) (b) he is "heavy of mouth . . . and tongue," i.e., speech-impaired. Yahweh's response in 4:12 is a mirror image (chiasm): he (b') will be with Moses' mouth and (a') will tell him what to say, i.e., give him words. Exod 4:11, in which Yahweh vaunts his mastery over human faculties, serves as the complement or introduction to elements (b) and (b'): the God who gives a mouth or makes dumb will be with Moses' mouth.

The precise nature of Moses' impairment could be almost anything, from a soft voice to severely slurred speech. At least it is clear that, while his kinsman Aaron understands him sufficiently, Moses is ineffective as a public speaker. Since the Elohist abandons this theme after Israel leaves Egypt and rarely mentions Aaron, Fretheim (1991a: 73) infers that Moses grows into his office. Yahweh's original plan of using him alone is eventually realized (cf. *Deut. Rab.* 1:1).

4:11. *made/makes.* The aspect/tense of *śām* is uncertain. It could be the perfect, describing the past (*Tg. Ps.-Jonathan*), or a participle, indicating habitual action (LXX; *Tg. Onqelos*). We might make a virtue out of this ambiguity: Yahweh created a mouth for the first man (*'ādām*) and ever after has been endowing each human (*'ādām*), including Moses, with speech. Yahweh's creation of the faculties is also celebrated in Ps 94:9; Prov 20:12.

Yahweh appears to accept Moses' oblique blame for his handicap (v 10).
Not only did God refrain from curing Moses during their conversation but he
admits that he created Moses impaired to begin with (cf. Bekhor Shor).

SPECULATION: Some believe, however, that Yahweh is offering to *cure*
Moses (cf. Luzzatto and other Jewish sources cited by Tigay [1978: 61–62]).
Otherwise, is he not simply bullying the handicapped? Moses himself has
raised the issue of healing in v 10. Thus Yahweh may be implying that,
should Moses accept his mission, the impediment will be removed. But
Moses declines to be healed, in hopes he will be excused from service.
Undeterred, Yahweh appoints a surrogate mouth: Aaron (4:16).

percipient. *Piqqēaḥ* most often connotes seeing, but sometimes hearing, e.g.,
Isa 42:20 (ibn Ezra; R. Isaac the Proselyte [*apud* Bekhor Shor]). Another example comes from Lachish Ostracon 3.4–5: *wʿt hpqh nʾ ʾt ʾzn ʿbdk* 'and now,
let be opened, pray, the ear of your servant' (*AHI* 1.003.4–5; Cross 1985). Further examples of *pqḥ* 'hear' are *m. Yebam.* 14:1, 3, 4; *Giṭ.* 2:6; *Bab. Qam.* 4:4;
see Speir (1960). Therefore, the common emendation *pissēaḥ 'lame' in 4:11
is unwarranted (*pace* McNeile 1908: 25; Lachs 1976: Valentin 1978: 52 n. 5).
On the contrary, *piqqēaḥ* makes excellent sense: as "mouth" and "dumb" are
opposite, so are "deaf" and "blind" each the opposite of the "percipient" that
separates them.

4:12. *your mouth*. Moses' demurral and Yahweh's response recall such passages as Deut 18:18, "I [Yahweh] will raise a prophet . . . and I will put my
words in his mouth," and Isa 51:16, "I will put my words in your mouth." The
image is made concrete in Ezek 3:1–3: in a vision, the prophet absorbs Yahweh's word by eating a scroll (cf. Jer 5:14; 15:16; 2 Esdr 14:38–41). Exod 4:12
particularly resembles the exchange in Jer 1:6–7: "I said, 'Ah, my Lordship
Yahweh, I do not know to speak, but rather I am a child.' But Yahweh said to
me, 'Do not say, "I am a child," but go wherever I send you and speak all I
command you.'" Here, too, a prophet vainly tries to excuse himself from service by claiming a physical limitation. Our scene also recalls the initiation of
Isaiah, terrified to behold Yahweh since he is unclean-lipped (Isa 6:1–8). Unlike Moses and Jeremiah, however, Isaiah volunteers for service (see further
COMMENT below; NOTE to 6:12).

4:13. *send through the hand you would send*. I.e., "send through the hand *of
him whom* you would send." *Tišlāḥ* 'you would send' functions as a one-word
relative clause.

To send through a person's "hand" is to entrust him or her with delivering a
thing (Gen 38:20; 1 Sam 16:20) or a message (1 Sam 11:7; Esth 8:10), or with
performing a task (1 Kgs 2:25). Thus Moses in effect says, "Send whatever
messenger you like." This seeming diffidence suits E's Moses, who is "very
humble, more than any human on the face of the earth" (Num 12:3).

Out of context we would take this response as polite acquiescence (cf. 1 Sam
14:36, 40). (On Moses' polite demurrals, see also NOTE to 3:11 "Who am I.")

But Moses begins with the particle *bî* 'please,' employed in petitions, complaints and excuses. And Yahweh certainly takes his words as another refusal (v 14). How do we resolve the contradiction between the particle of entreaty and Yahweh's anger, on the one hand, and Moses' humility, on the other? The solution does not lie in such remote paraphrases as "Send, I pray, some other person" (RSV).

In the Garden of Gethsemane, Jesus says, in reference to his imminent tribulation, "My Father, if it may be, let this cup pass from me; but not as I wish, but as you [wish]" (Matt 26:39; cf. Luke 22:42). In other words, Jesus accepts his fate, but unwillingly. In Moses' case, while *šəlaḥ-nā' bəyad-tišlāḥ* alone might express acquiescence, the initial *bî 'ădōnāy* 'please, my Lordship' adds a querulous tone, indicating that Moses, like Jesus, would not freely accept his fate. In the New Testament, God is not offended by Jesus' words. But in Exodus, Moses' faintheartedness arouses Yahweh's anger.

SPECULATION: Perhaps "send through the hand you would send," though acquiescent, is not humble at all, but hostile. Lundbom (1978) has shown that the *idem per idem* construction (defining a thing by itself) tends to sever discussion (see also below, pp. 224–26). If so, Moses' words may convey an effrontery inappropriate before God. Even his curt diction, *šəlaḥ-nā' bəyad-tišlāḥ* instead of **šəlaḥ-nā' bəyad-hā'îš 'ăšer tišləhennû* 'send through the hand of the man whom you would send,' arguably betrays sullenness.

4:14. *nose.* I.e., anger. The image is of flaring nostrils, or perhaps of a nose breathing fire (cf. Job 41:10–13) and/or smoke (cf. 2 Sam 22:9 = Ps 18:9; Job 41:12). For a general discussion of the metaphorical connotations of body parts, see Dhorme (1920–23).

grew angry. Although the lexica claim that *ḥry* means "to burn," it exclusively describes rage, never combustion (see Rabin 1961: 390–91). Since, however, anger is frequently likened to a fire (Isa 7:4; Ezek 21:36; Ps 89:47; Lam 2:4, etc.), *ḥry* may after all be a variant of *ḥrr* 'to be burnt' (see also NOTE to 15:7).

When Yahweh is *ḥry* at persons, the outcome is generally violent. The only exceptions are Job 42:7 and our passage. Thus, after the opening of 4:14, we might expect Moses finally to be blasted for his obstinacy. That he escapes unscathed shows the Deity's great forbearance. (Note, however, that in the composite text, Yahweh in fact attacks Moses in 4:24 [J]).

Still, the deputation of Aaron is in some sense a punishment, a diminution of Moses' dignity. In fact, all Israel will suffer, since Aaron will construct the Golden Calf (Exodus 32).

Aaron. The derivation of *'ahărōn* is unknown. The suffix *-ôn* looks Hebraic, but no root **'hr* is attested. It may be a variant of *'wr* 'shine' (cf. *nhr/nwr* 'shine'), in which case the name means "Brilliant." (D. N. Freedman [privately] compares the names of the first Patriarch, *'abrām* and *'abrāhām;* see NOTE to 3:6 "Abraham.")

your brother Levite. Another translation might be "is not Aaron your brother Levite?" In the composite Torah, Moses and Aaron are true siblings, but all the passages where this is explicit are Priestly or Redactorial (e.g., 6:20 [R]). E's language in 4:14 indicates, however, that Moses and Aaron are nothing more than *fellow* Levites (Ginsberg 1982: 85 n. 103; Friedman 1987: 190). Otherwise, why say "the Levite" at all? Compare the expressions "brother Hebrew" (Deut 15:12; Jer 34:14) and "brother priest/Levite" (Num 16:10; Deut 3:18; 18:7; Ezra 6:20; Neh 3:1; 5:8; 1 Chr 6:33; 2 Chr 35:15). In confirmation, we note that 15:20 (E) calls Miriam "Aaron's sister," implying that she is more closely related to Aaron than to Moses. Only in P are the three full siblings (Num 26:59).

Since the Levites would become a sacred tribe (32:26–29) entrusted with teaching (Lev 10:11; Deut 33:8–11), many perceive in 4:14 a foreshadowing of Aaron's priestly ordination and/or the Levites' pedagogic mission (Sforno; Luzzatto; Baentsch 1903: 31–32).

I know that he will speak. That Yahweh "knows" Aaron will speak suggests to Jacob (1992: 93) that at issue is not Aaron's ability to talk, which would have been common knowledge, but his willingness.

As the nature of Moses and Aaron's prior acquaintance in E cannot be determined, we cannot tell why Aaron is particularly able to understand Moses. In the composite Torah, the answer is simple: they are brothers, albeit raised apart.

moreover . . . him coming out. This itself is a miracle. Evidently, while talking to Moses, Yahweh is simultaneously calling Aaron—or, more likely, in his prescience he has already summoned him. Report of Aaron's call is deferred to 4:27, however, so as not to interrupt the conversation at the bush (cf. Thompson 1987: 137; see also REDACTION ANALYSIS).

Gen 32:4–7 offers an interesting parallel to Exod 4:14. Jacob sends messengers to Esau in Edom, who hasten back, reporting, "We came to your brother, to Esau, and moreover he is going to meet you." But, as time passes between Gen 32:6 and v 7, no chronological difficulty obtains.

4:15. *his mouth . . . his mouth.* For the first "his mouth," MT has *pîw*, and for the second, *pîhû* (Sam *pyw*). It appears that the archaic form *pîhû* is used for emphasis, heightening the parallel "your mouth" (*pîkā*).

you will do. "You" is plural, suggesting that both Moses and Aaron are involved not just in speaking but also in producing the signs (see NOTES to 4:13, 17, 30). Alternatively, the sense may be simply that Yahweh will tell them how to proceed.

4:16. *he will speak.* The verb may also be jussive: "let him speak" (Valentin 1978: 67 n. 4).

mouth. In Jer 15:19, "mouth" connotes a prophet; cf. Exod 7:1: "Aaron your brother will be your prophet." This is the seventh occurrence of the theme word *pe(h)* 'mouth' in this section. For the image of a surrogate organ, cf. Num 10:31, "Be as eyes for us."

Deity. Or "a deity."

4:17. *signs.* As Greenberg notes (1969: 90), the plural *'ōtōt* must refer to the Plagues, not just to the snake trick (cf. also Valentin 1978: 78–79). See also NOTE to 4:21.

4:18. *went and returned.* I.e., went back.

Jether. I.e., Jethro; see NOTE to 3:1.

brothers. Whoever these "brothers" may be, why should Moses doubt that they are alive? The implication is that many years have passed (cf. 4:19 [J]), as in the analogous case of Jacob and Joseph (Gen 43:7, 27, 28; 45:3, 26, 28; 46:30) (Jacob 1992: 101; Fox 1986: 31); cf. also 1 Kgs 20:32. "Seeing one's brothers" may simply be a cliché for a family reunion (1 Sam 20:29).

Moses' words bear multiple meanings. At one level, by citing a spurious pious duty he simply employs a polite equivocation (see NOTE to 3:18; cf. Thompson 1987: 137). At the same time, Moses is truly leaving to join his "brother" Aaron and later his "brother" Hebrews (cf. 2:11), whose survival is indeed tenuous.

How Jethro takes Moses' words is another matter. A natural inference is that Moses has never admitted the circumstances of his emigration. Why else would he conceal the encounter at the bush? (Calvin's commonsense suggestion: Moses fears Jethro's incredulity.) Jethro may assume that Moses' brothers are Egyptians, not Hebrews (cf. Exod 2:19 [J]).

Moses' mild deception of his father-in-law is also a fixture in the literary genre of the Sojourner's Tale (see COMMENT). Such stories often involve hostility and deception between sojourner and patron, as in the relationships between Jacob and Laban and between Israel and Pharaoh. But even when Abraham's servant departs amicably from Laban (Gen 24:54–56), or when the Levite leaves his father-in-law (Judg 19:4–10), or when Uriah returns to the front (2 Sam 11:11–12), or when Pharaoh dismisses Hadad of Edom (1 Kgs 11:21–22), there is a brief dispute. My inference: to discourage a guest's departure was polite, and leave-takings were consequently somewhat tense, entailing a sort of ritual combat of courtesy comparable to our "picking up the check." (In fact, Jewish legend envisions considerable hostility between Moses and his father-in-law, even recounting Jethro's imprisonment of Moses [Ginzberg 1928: 2.293–94].)

Exod 4:18 serves an important function in the pentateuchal narrative. By invoking his "brothers," Moses weakens his Midianite ties and reclaims the Hebrew identity he had shed in 2:22: "A sojourner *was* I in a foreign land"— but no longer. (In E, Moses in fact leaves his family behind with Jethro [18:2].)

4:19. *Go, return.* I.e., go back. Yahweh's command seems redundant with the preceding revelation at the bush, but the solution is not to render in the pluperfect ("but Yahweh *had* said" [Calvin]). Rather, we have a switch from E to J (see SOURCE ANALYSIS). The hendiadys *hlk . . . šwb* also appears in 4:18, 21, and in 1 Kgs 19:15, likewise situated in the vicinity of Midian and Mount Horeb.

men. I do not find a contradiction with 2:15, where Pharaoh alone tried to kill Moses (vs. Fohrer [1964: 25] and others). The reference is either to the slain Egyptian's kin or, more likely, to Pharaoh and his constabulary (cf. 2 Sam 4:11). Surely the sense of 2:15 is that Pharaoh *gave orders* to have Moses killed.

4:20. *his woman*. The Hebrew word for "wife" is "woman" (*'iššâ*). "Husband" is either "man" (*'îš*) or "owner" (*ba'al*).

his sons. So far in J, Moses has but one son; only in E does he have two (18:4). Therefore, we would expect the original J text to have read "his *son*" (Hyatt 1971: 86)—unless the Yahwist ascribed to Moses other, anonymous children. One possibility is that Redactor^JE harmonized his sources by pluralizing an original *bənô (Plastaras 1966: 102). Another possibility is innocent scribal confusion. In the Yahwist's day, "his son" would have been spelled *bnh*, "his sons" *bnw*. In later, standard biblical spelling, however, "his son" is *bnw* and "his sons" is *bnyw*. There must have been a transitional phase in which *bnw* could be read as either *bənô* 'his son' (new style) or *bānāw* 'his sons' (old style) (cf. Andersen and Forbes 1986: 62). Thus if the original were *bnh 'his son' (or 'her son'; cf. 4:25), a scribe might have modernized this as *bnw. Then another copyist might have mistaken *bnw for an archaic plural and modernized again as *bnyw* 'his sons.'

the ass. I.e., "a certain ass," or perhaps "his ass" (Ehrlich 1969: 44). LXX, however, takes *haḥămōr* as collective, paraphrasing "the beasts of burden."

Why mention the ass at all? First, it represents Moses' improved status. He arrived in Midian without property or family; now he has a wife, a child or children and an ass. Moreover, the animal may be a narrative convention; we also read of a family's journey from Egypt, an ass and a night-stop in Gen 42:27 (J) (cf. Fuss 1972: 90). Probably, too, the scene is meant to illustrate Moses' solicitude for his family (cf. Jacob 1992: 103). (In contrast, E's Moses seems apathetic to his domestic ties; see COMMENT to chap. 18.)

the Deity's rod. The expression *maṭṭē(h) hā'ĕlōhîm* occurs again in 17:9 (E). It can be taken in one of two ways. Ostensibly, it implies that the rod properly belongs to God. Occasionally, however, *'ĕlōhîm* functions as an abstract noun connoting the supernatural (e.g., Job 1:6; Ezek 1:1; 8:3; 40:2). Therefore, *maṭṭē(h) hā'ĕlōhîm* might mean that the rod gives its wielder miraculous powers; note *Tg. Onqelos*, "the rod with which miracles may be worked from before Yahweh." We shall consider at length the relationship between the rods of God and Moses under COMMENT.

4:21. *In your going to return*. I.e., "as you go back"; cf. 4:18, 19. The phrase is somewhat surprising. We expect Moses to "see" the wonders *after* he reaches Egypt, not on the way. One possibility is that the text is corrupt (see TEXTUAL NOTE). Another is that Moses is to rehearse his performance during the journey, or to contemplate its meaning.

see. In the context, *rā'â* must refer either to concerning oneself (cf. Gen 39:23) or to remembering.

wonders. Since the "strengthening" of Pharaoh's heart immediately follows, "wonders" probably includes not only the tricks of 4:1-9 but also the Plagues (see NOTE to 4:17). Since *'ōtōt* 'signs' and *môpətîm* 'wonders' constitute a common word pair (7:3; Deut 4:34; 6:22; 13:2; 26:8, etc.), the sequence "signs . . .

wonders" links 4:21 with 4:17 (Jacob 1992: 104). The verses are also connected by the repetition of "in your hand" and *'śy* 'perform, work.'

to Pharaoh's face. I.e., in Pharaoh's presence. This is a good example of biblical narrative imparting information piecemeal. Previously, Yahweh had commanded Moses to *speak* to the Israelite elders and to Pharaoh (3:16–18). After Moses requests proof of his commission for the *Israelites* (4:1), Yahweh gives him the three signs (4:2–9). The mission to Pharaoh is forgotten for the moment. Finally, in 4:21 we learn that the signs are for Pharaoh as well as the people (although we are only told of their performance before the people [4:30]); see COMMENT to 5:1–6:1.

strengthen. The traditional translation "harden" is misleading, since we use "hard-hearted" to connote cruelty. The Hebrew does not mean "I will make Pharaoh cruel," but rather "I will strengthen his resolve" or "make him stubborn" (cf. Deut 2:30; Josh 11:20; Ezek 2:4; 3:7). Zech 7:12 makes the image graphic: "They have made their heart *šāmîr* (a hard stone)" (cf. also Ezek 36:26).

4:22. *My son, my firstborn, is Israel.* This statement contains many implications. Most obviously, it expresses Yahweh's love for Israel (cf. Deut 1:31; Jer 3:19; 31:9, 20; Hos 11:1–4) and Israel's filial duty of love (1 Esdr 6:58) and obedience (Deut 8:5; 32:5, 19; Isa 1:2; 30:1, 9; 63:16; Mal 1:6). Given the connotation of "son" as "vassal" (2 Kgs 16:7), there may also be a hint of covenant relationship (Fensham 1971; contrast Liverani 1990b: 190–99). On another level, 4:22 suggests that Yahweh is bound by kinship duty to rescue or ransom his enslaved son (Gen 14:12–16; Lev 25:39–43; Neh 5:8; see NOTE to 15:16). (On redemption in the ancient Near East, see Yaron 1959.) On a third level, the verse implies that Pharaoh, by conscripting Israel, has violated the law that all firstborn are Yahweh's (13:2, 11–15, etc.; see COMMENT to 12:1–13:16, pp. 454–57) (Meyer 1906: 40; Fretheim 1991a: 77). And, although 4:22 is patently chauvinistic, Bekhor Shor proffers a universalistic reading: if Israel is Yahweh's *first*born, all creatures must be God's other children.

Exod 4:22 is crucial to the Elohist's understanding of the plague of the firstborn. Yahweh kills the Egyptian firstborn but redeems his own firstborn, the entire nation of Israel (see COMMENT to 12:1–13:16, pp. 454–57).

4:23. *serve.* The verb *'bd* 'work, serve' has connotations of both bondage and worship. Yahweh demands that Israel no longer *'bd* Egypt as slaves, but *'bd* him as worshipers.

Exod 4:22–23, like Mal 1:6, mixes two metaphors for the relationship between Israel and Yahweh: son and father, slave and master. One does not enslave one's own son, the literal import of 4:23. But in the language of covenant, the terms are synonymous. A vassal may be called the suzerain's "slave" and "son," even in the same breath (2 Kgs 16:7).

As Daube (1963) emphasizes, the Bible's governing conception of the Exodus is redemption (*g'l*), i.e., reversion of Israel's ownership from Pharaoh to Yahweh. Compare Lev 25:39–55 (P): "Should your brother with you decline and be sold to you, do not work him as slave labor . . . they may not be sold in the slave trade . . . for to me are Israel's sons slaves . . . whom I took from the land of Egypt." To enslave an Israelite is tantamount to thieving from Yahweh. Even if Israel were Yahweh's runaway slave, ancient Near Eastern (but not biblical) law would mandate returning him to his legal owner (Liverani 1990b: 106–12).

Yahweh does not politely suggest Israel's release, nor does he offer any compensation. He addresses Pharaoh as a great king commanding a lesser ruler (on asymmetrical extradition treaties, see, briefly, Liverani 1990b: 108). Yahweh's demand to Pharaoh, conveyed by his accredited ambassadors, particularly recalls the admonition of ancient Near Eastern kings to their vassals: "Do not detain (Akkadian *kalûm*) my messenger!" (*CAD* 8.97). The king's servants are rather to be "sent forth with dispatch" (*wuššurum*).

I am going to kill your son, your firstborn. Now the battle becomes personal, Yahweh against Pharaoh (Meyer 1983: 58). But what is the crime of Pharaoh's son? Harming a second party's child in revenge for a crime against one's own is more reminiscent of Mesopotamian than biblical law (cf. Hammurapi §209–10, 230 [*ANET* 175, 176]; Middle Assyrian Laws, tablet A §55 [*ANET* 185]). Exod 4:23 is one of the few biblical passages to take the principle of talion (symmetrical retribution) to the extreme (cf. Exod 21:23–25; Lev 24:19–20; Deut 19:21). One might object that the punishment (death) is in fact *more* severe than the crime (kidnap, enslavement). But the latter are capital offenses (21:16; Deut 24:7).

Although he repeatedly transmits the first part of the message ("Release my people"), Moses does not actually deliver God's threat until 11:4–6. Why the delay? Many commentators suggest that vv 22–23 are misplaced, since they would more logically be set just before the plague of the firstborn, in either 10:29 or 11:4 (e.g., Hyatt 1971: 85; cf. Sam [TEXTUAL NOTE to 11:4]). Rather than suppose violent editorial transposition, however, I would regard vv 22–23 as foreshadowing later events and creating a framework for the Plagues cycle. In its arrangement of references to both the despoiling of Egypt and the slaying of the firstborn, the text displays an interlocking structure: 4:22–23 is fulfilled in 11:4–8, 11:2–3 is fulfilled in 12:35–36. The separation of command and fulfillment both avoids monotony and creates coherence.

4:24. night-stop. Often translated "inn," a *mālôn* (< *lwn* 'spend the night') is not necessarily a permanent structure (note Josh 4:3, 8). The ready availability of a flint might suggest an outdoor setting (Luzzatto; Houtman 1983: 81–82). At any rate, the choice of word establishes both place and time.

SPECULATION: Gunkel (*apud* Gressmann 1913: 58 n. 4) conjectures that *mālôn* rather means "place of circumcision" (< *mwl* 'circumcise'); Morgenstern (1963: 68–69) similarly translates "circumcision." This approach is quite far-fetched (on the symbolism of the *nocturnal* attack, see COMMENT). Still, it at least raises the possibility of wordplay with *mwl*.

put him to death. Hămîtô (Hiph'il). Although the causative of *mwt* 'die' can be synonymous with *hrg* 'kill,' *hēmît* often has judicial connotations comparable to English "execute" (e.g., Num 35:19, 21). The subject of *hēmît* is frequently Yahweh, whose decrees are by definition justice; cf. 2 Kgs 5:7: "Am I Deity, to put to death (*ləhāmît*) or to let live?"

4:25. *flint.* On the use of this mineral for performing circumcisions, compare Josh 5:2. The usual inference is that the stone tool bespeaks the rite's primeval origin (e.g., Ehrlich 1969: 144). But, in fact, flints were still used in Iron Age Israel for a variety of purposes (Rosen 1996).

her son. In ancient spelling, "her son" and "his son" would both have been written *bnh.* The Massoretic vocalization *bənāh* 'her son' emphasizes the role of Zipporah.

applied to. A more literal translation of *wattaggaʿ* might be "she brought near" (so *Tg. Ps.-Jonathan* and a Palestinian Targumic Tosephta fragment [Klein 1986: 1.173]). In this context, however, *higgîaʿ* may specifically mean to dab or smear; cf. 12:22, "*wəhiggaʿtem* to the lintel and to the two doorposts from the blood that is in the bowl/threshold" (cf. Ben-Shabbat 1956–57).

There are other possible interpretations, although I think them less likely. First, since *higgîaʿ* ordinarily means "draw near," *Tg. Onqelos* renders, "she approached his feet." LXX, in a similar vein, translates, "she fell at his feet," while Syr paraphrases, "she seized his feet." Presumably, Zipporah is throwing herself upon Yahweh's mercy. On the other hand, Houtman (1983: 85) understands *higgîaʿ* as "to cast down," comparing Isa 25:12; 26:5; Ezek 13:14; Lam 2:2. By this reading, *raglayim* must be actual feet, although Houtman strangely retains the common interpretation "genitals" (see below).

his legs. What are these "legs," and whose? *Raglayim* may also denote feet or genitalia, and it is probably Moses' penis that is meant here (see COMMENT). Less likely, the "feet" are Yahweh's (LXX; *Tg. Onqelos*; Syr; Scharbert 1989: 28).

For. Kî may introduce direct quotation or simply add emphasis (Muilenburg 1961). Since Zipporah has just performed an unusual act and is about to comment upon it, an explanatory "for" seems the most suitable rendering (cf. the function of *ləmaʿan* 'so that' in 4:5).

bridegroom/son-in-law. Ḥātān etymologically means "male relative by marriage" (Mitchell 1969). Most often, however, it connotes a son-in-law or bridegroom. The translation "bridegroom" is usually preferred for our passage, since it appears that Zipporah is addressing Moses (see COMMENT). Even if this is correct, however, "bridegroom" is somewhat misleading. In English, a man is a "bridegroom" only on his wedding day. But *ḥātān* can denote, as here, a recently married husband, just as the counterpart *kallâ* 'daughter-in-law, bride' may be a young wife (Hos 4:13, 14; possibly 2 Sam 17:3 [OG]). (Oddly, it appears that *ḥātān* and *kallâ* describe a lifelong relationship with one's parents-in-law, but only a temporary relationship with one's spouse.)

bloodiness. I would translate the plural *dāmîm* as "bloodiness" or even "blood-guilt," to distinguish it from the singular *dām* 'blood' (cf. *Tg. Onqelos* "the bridegroom would *deserve killing*"). The abstract plural (GKC §124d–f) describes either the blood shed by a killer (Gen 4:10, 11; 1 Kgs 2:5; 2 Kgs 9:26, etc.) or the miasma of guilt clinging to perpetrators of heinous crimes and to their land (22:1-2; Lev 20:9, 11, 12, 13, 16, 27, etc.). Admittedly, for P and Ezekiel, *dāmîm* also connotes the defiling blood of menstruation (Lev 20:18) and of childbirth (Lev 12:4, 5, 7; Ezek 16:6, 9 [but cf. the singular in v 22]). Perhaps for J, too, the blood of male circumcision bears utmost impurity, or *dāmîm*. I will argue under COMMENT, however, that Zipporah's act actually *purifies* Moses.

4:26. *he slackened from him.* I.e., let him alone.

Then she said. Many take 4:24–26 as an etiology (see COMMENT). Some scholars, troubled by the redundancy of vv 25–26, even emend *'āz 'āmərâ* 'then she said' to **'āz 'āmərû* 'then [in those days] they said' (e.g., Ehrlich 1908: 277). Indeed, there is no need to emend. One might simply take *'āmərâ* either as an impersonal feminine singular ("one [f.] said") (Morgenstern 1963: 67–68; cf. 1 Kgs 1:6) or else as a uniquely archaic 3 f. pl. ("they [f.] said"). But in any case, by this approach we would expect the imperfect *tō(')mar/ tō(')marnâ* 'she/they would say' (Morgenstern 1963: 68).

The redundancy of vv 25–26 should not disturb us. De Groot (1943: 14) compares 1 Sam 4:21–22: "And she called the child Ichabod, saying, 'Glory has gone into exile from Israel' concerning the taking of the Deity's ark and concerning her father-in-law and husband. And she said, 'Glory has gone into exile, for the Deity's ark has been taken.'" So Exod 4:26 should probably be translated "then she said" or "that was when she said." The repetition in vv 25–26 may simply put an emphatic end to the narrative, like 1 Sam 4:22.

by circumcision. I tentatively regard *mûlōt* as another plural of abstraction: "the act of circumcision" (cf. *dāmîm* 'bloodiness'). The preposition *l-* might also be rendered "in reference to" (Childs 1974: 100), "by means of" or "because of."

4:27. *Yahweh said to Aaron.* Since Aaron is already on his way (4:14), *way-yō(')mer yahwe(h)* must be retrospective and concomitant with, or even prior to, Yahweh's conversation with Moses (see NOTE to 4:14). I have refrained, however, from translating in the pluperfect, which technically would correspond to **wəyahwe(h) 'āmar.* On the likelihood that 4:27–28 was moved by Redactor^JE from its original location after 4:17, see REDACTION ANALYSIS.

The manner of Yahweh's revelation to Aaron is of no interest to the author (although it exercised the Rabbis; see *Exod. Rab.* 5:9). Aaron should be no less surprised than Moses to hear a disembodied voice, and no less inclined to doubt. When Aaron again hears God's voice (Num 12:4 [E]), the writer inserts *pit'ōm* 'suddenly.'

at the Deity's mountain. In the present text, Moses must stop again at Horeb (see REDACTION ANALYSIS). Apparently, it is important that Aaron, too, be commissioned at God's mountain (on Horeb, the "Mountain of Meeting," see COMMENT to chap. 18). We are not told whether Aaron also sees the Burning Bush.

kissed him. Although Moses and Aaron will one day be antagonists on this very mountain (Exodus 32), the two begin as loving cousins. Their kiss more than fulfills God's prediction (4:14). Aaron does not only "rejoice in his heart," he demonstrates his affection. Also, assuming lip-to-lip contact, their mouths merge; Moses breathes the divine word into Aaron, his surrogate mouth.

4:30. *he did.* Who is "he"? The nearest person named is Moses, but the subject of the previous clause is Aaron. In E, it is Moses who works the signs (4:17), and so he is probably the subject. In 4:15, however, God speaks as if both Moses and Aaron will work wonders (see NOTE).

4:31. *trusted.* There may be a pun between the roots *'mn* 'trust' (said of Israel) and *m'n* 'refuse' (said of Pharaoh [4:22]). From the very fact that Moses is obliged to perform the signs, I would infer the Hebrews' initial *dis*belief (cf. 4:1, 8, 9) (Josephus *Ant.* 2.280; vs. *Exod. Rab.* 5:13; Noth 1962: 51). P, too, records Israel's first skeptical response (6:9). The Elohist, however, emphasizes their eventual conviction. He barely hints here at their lack of faith, to be described more fully in 5:20–21; 14:12, etc.

and they heard. Assuming the correctness of MT, this is hysteron proteron; belief should follow hearing, not vice versa (Van Seters [1994: 69] observes the same sequence in 4:1, 8, 9). Conceivably, this very "problem" generated the LXX variant "rejoiced" (see TEXTUAL NOTE).

knelt and bowed down. This is the first mention of worship in Exodus. Now that Yahweh has broken his long silence, the people acknowledge his divinity.

COMMENT

A SHEPHERD

At the end of Exodus 2, Moses' "identity crisis" seems to be resolved by marriage and fatherhood. He is finally at home in Midian. One would think his tale is finished.

Years pass. Moses, tending his father-in-law's flock in the wilderness, suddenly hears a voice from a Burning Bush: "I am your father's deity, Abraham's deity, Isaac's deity and Jacob's deity." By invoking the ancestors, the voice reminds Moses of his real identity. He may be Egyptian by adoption and Midianite by choice, but he is Hebrew by birth. Moses' initial efforts to succor his people had been ineffectual, leading to his separation from them. Now he must return to Egypt, bringing permanent salvation.

That Moses is called while tending the flock is most significant. Throughout the ancient Near East, the shepherd symbolized leadership (Greenberg 1969: 67–68; cf. Philo *Moses* 1.60–62; Clement of Alexandria *Strom.* 1.156). Conversely, the people are often compared to a flock or herd (Eilberg-Schwartz 1990: 120–21). The best biblical example is David, called from tending his father's sheep to become king over Israel (1 Sam 16:11–13; 17:34–37; 2 Sam 7:8; Ps 78:70–72). Compare also Saul, who finds kingship while seeking his father's stray asses (1 Samuel 9), and the prophet Elisha, chosen while plowing with oxen representing the twelve tribes (1 Kgs 19:19).

The image of the shepherd is polyvalent. Usually it conveys power, authority and concern, as when applied to Yahweh (e.g., Psalm 23). But sometimes it betokens humility and obedience. Often a shepherd does not own his flock, but works for another. By emphasizing that Moses' sheep are actually Jethro's, the text underscores the parallels between Moses' present and future occupations. As he brings Jethro's flock to Horeb, so will he one day bring Yahweh's "flock" to God's mountain.

A BUSH

Why should Yahweh's angel appear in a Burning Bush, rather than assume human form or speak from thin air? Mysterious, beneficial, dangerous, uncontainable, cleansing, radiant—fire is a popular symbol for the divine. Sometimes combustion is a side effect of Yahweh's presence (2 Sam 22 = Ps 18:9, 13; Isa 29:6, etc.) or the medium through which one travels to heaven (Judg 6:21; 13:20; 2 Kgs 2:11). Elsewhere fire is personified as God's servant (see Miller 1965; Hendel 1985). Within Exodus, the Burning Bush on the Deity's mountain seems to foreshadow the later pyrotechnics at Sinai/Horeb (on fire as a theme in Exodus, see INTRODUCTION, p. 36).

There are several possible interpretations of the theophany in the thornbush that burns but is not consumed. We have already considered a pun between sɔne(h) 'bush' and Sinai, and mentioned a possible relationship to sacred trees and the Tabernacle menorah (see NOTE to 3:2). For Philo (Moses 1.67–69), the bush represents Israel, unconsumed by the fire of Egyptian oppression (also Augustine Sermons 6, 7; Calvin; Johnstone 1990: 48); note the comparison of Egypt to an "iron furnace" (Deut 4:20; 1 Kgs 8:51; Jer 11:4). Rashi quotes Ps 91:15, "I am with him in trouble": as Israel is humbled in slavery, so Yahweh shares their humiliation by condescending to appear in the meager bush (cf. Jacob 1992: 50). We could also view the bush as representing Moses himself, by nature no more suited to receive Yahweh's spirit than a desert shrub. Rashi sees in the bush's nonconsumption a promise: Moses, like the dry wood, will not be harmed by God's spirit.

I believe the most important function of the Burning Bush is to signal a change in God's interaction with Creation. Since the Flood (Genesis 6–9), he has mostly left nature alone. The sole exception is when brimstone rains upon Sodom and Gomorrah (Genesis 19). But Moses and his contemporaries will see, among other prodigies, water turned to blood, light made darkness, a sea split, torrents from a rock and a mountain aflame. The humble thornbush that burns unconsumed, like the modest signs of 4:2–9 (see below), are, so to speak, warm-up exercises for both God and humanity. Moses, the conduit of divine power, must gradually be inured to wonders (cf. Greenberg 1969: 71). And Yahweh's first interventions in nature should be modest, in preparation for the greater wonders to follow, and in proportion to the size of his audience.

THE NAME OF GOD

After warning Moses of the site's sanctity, Yahweh opens his address proper with *'ānōkî* 'I (am)' (v 6). In an age when gods talked with men and women, it was important to know whose voice one was hearing (Mowinckel 1961: 123; for neo-Assyrian parallels, see Wilson 1980: 117). For example, in 1 Sam 3:4–8, the boy Samuel mistakes God's disembodied voice for his master Eli's.

But in Exod 3:6, Yahweh's words are cryptic. He does not name himself, but rather Moses' ancestors: "I am your father's deity, Abraham's . . . Isaac's . . . Jacob's." This is not the identification Moses might have expected, and so he presses the voice further: "Suppose I come to Israel's Sons . . . and they say to me, 'What is his name?'"

Moses' desire to learn the Deity's name seems to be born, not of idle curiosity, but of a persistent aspiration to know God. In 33:18, he will request an even more direct experience. Yet in Exodus 3, Moses inquires obliquely, citing, not his own wishes, but his audience's anticipated skepticism (cf. *Lev. Rab.* 11:5; Jacob 1992: 69, 73). Why should Israel ask for God's name?

The answer depends on whether we read the story in its current setting or in the reconstructed Elohistic source. In the composite Torah and in JE, the name "Yahweh" has been in use since Enosh's day (Gen 4:26). The point of Moses' request is thus somewhat obscure. Most likely, the divine name functions somehow as a password. If Moses already knows God's name, he may be testing the voice, to see if it really belongs to Yahweh. If, however, raised as an Egyptian, Moses is as ignorant as Pharaoh himself (5:2), he may anticipate that Israel will test both him *and* the voice (Calvin; Jacob 1992: 65–67; Schmidt 1988: 168; Blum 1990: 12). The trial is appropriate: the legitimate prophet is quintessentially one who speaks "in Yahweh's name" (Deut 18:19–22; Jer 11:21, etc.) (Burns 1983: 47).

For E, on the other hand, Exodus 3 describes Yahweh's first revelation of his name to humanity (see INTRODUCTION, pp. 50–51). Moses implies that Israel will expect him to bring a new name—i.e., a heightened knowledge of and closeness to the Deity. An ancient mystery will be cleared up, as, on the eve of liberation from slavery and reconstitution as nation, the Hebrews finally learn the name of their Patriarchs' god.

In a sense, the divine name functions as a shibboleth for the Elohistic source itself—not among the characters, but between text and reader. Just as a prophet speaking in the name of another god than Yahweh is to be killed and his oracles disregarded (Deut 18:20), so a text not speaking in Yahweh's name might be discarded and ignored. So far, the E source has left its Deity nameless (Gen 22:15–16 may be an exception, but see Davila 1991). At the bush, the reader is told explicitly that the god of E is none other than the national deity, Yahweh. This serves as E's *imprimatur*, lending credence to whatever historical or ideological claims the work may make.

To narrate Moses' call, the Elohist employs a type-scene with important parallels in Gen 32:23–33 and Judges 13. In the former passage, Jacob wrestles in the fords of the Jabbok with an astral deity, i.e., an angel (cf. Hos 12:5). Between early light and sunrise, his opponent begs to be released. Jacob agrees, on condition that he be blessed. The divinity then asks Jacob's name and complies. But when Jacob in return seeks the being's name, he is rebuffed: "Why is it you ask for my name?" (Gen 32:30).

Similarly in Judges 13, a being variously called "Yahweh's Messenger," "the Deity man," "the man" and "a deity" appears to Manoah and his wife. He will not reveal his name, even when asked point-blank, responding only, "Why is it you ask for my name, as it is wondrous (pl'y)?"—i.e., beyond human ken (Judg 13:6, 17–18). Manoah seems to take this evasion as an indirect answer and sacrifices to "Yahweh the Wonder Worker" (Judg 13:19, reading *yahwe(h) hammaplî' la'ăśôt; cf. LXX^A and the divine title [?] pele' in Isa 9:5).

According to Exod 33:12, 17, a uniquely intimate relationship exists between Moses and God, for Yahweh knows Moses "by name"—which probably really means that Moses knows Yahweh's name (see NOTES). Why such fascination with deities' names? The noun šēm can also mean "self" or "essence," and scholars often observe that to know an object's name is, in the world of magic, to possess power over it. This is the likely import of Adam naming woman and the beasts (Gen 2:19; 3:20) (Vawter 1977: 75), or of Yahweh renaming the Patriarchs (Gen 17:5, 15; 32:29; 35:10). But what about a deity's name? In ancient Egypt, knowing the gods' secret names gave humans a degree of mastery over them (Erman 1969: 354; Hornung 1982: 86–91). Similarly, in later magical folklore both Jewish and gentile, God possesses a secret name (not "Yahweh"), the knowledge of which confers some of his power upon humans; it was supposedly engraved, for example, on Moses' staff. Humans in the Bible, then, are understandably eager to learn the names of deities, and the latter are understandably chary of disclosing them. (For a study of the significance of names in the Bible and the ancient world, see Porter and Ricks 1990.)

Unlike Jacob and Manoah, Moses ultimately succeeds in wheedling the divine name out of Yahweh. Thereby he transmits to Israel and humanity a mighty trust, dangerous to misuse (cf. 20:7; Deut 5:11; Ps 24:4). The spreading knowledge of Yahweh's name is a major theme of Exodus, and of the Hebrew Bible as a whole (see INTRODUCTION, p. 36).

REVELATION OR OBFUSCATION?

To his simple question, "What is his name?" Moses receives a redundant and obscure answer: "I will be who I will be ('ehye[h] 'ăšer 'ehye[h]). . . . Thus you will say to Israel's Sons: '"I-will-be ('ehye[h])" has sent me to you.' . . . Thus you will say to Israel's Sons: 'Yahweh your fathers' deity, Abraham's deity, Isaac's deity and Jacob's deity—he has sent me to you'; this is my name to eternity, and this is my designation age (by) age." So what is his name: "I will be who I will be," "I-will-be" or "Yahweh?" Only the last is explicitly called "my name."

Much contemporary scholarship since Haupt (1909) has taken 'ehye(h) 'ăšer 'ehye(h) as a distortion of Yahweh's original name, 'ehye(h) alone being an abbreviated, transitional form. Followers of this approach resort to linguistic reconstruction and/or textual emendation to arrive at such readings as **'ahye(h) 'ăšer yihye(h)* 'I cause to be what comes into existence' (Haupt 1909; Albright 1924), **'ahye(h) 'ăšer 'ahye(h)* 'I create what I create' (Freedman 1960), **'ahwe(h) 'ăšer 'ahwe(h)* 'I create what I create' (from which the deity's original name is reconstituted as **yahwī ḏū yahwī* 'he creates what he creates' [Cross 1973: 68–69]). The obvious weakness of this approach is that it relies so heavily upon conjecture (see Brownlee 1977).

Alternatively, many take "I will be who I will be" and "I-will-be" as *interpretations* of the name "Yahweh." Scholars call sentences with two identical (or nearly identical) verbs, usually connected by the relative pronoun *'ăšer*, *idem per idem* formulae (Gen 43:14; Exod 3:14; 16:23; 33:19; 1 Sam 23:13; 2 Sam 15:20; 2 Kgs 8:1; Ezek 12:25; Esth 4:16; also, without *'ăšer*, Exod 4:13; Zech 10:8) (see Ogden 1992). The main function of this rhetorical device is to be vague, whether to convey infinite potentiality or to conceal information, by defining a thing as itself. In Driver's (1911: 363) words, *idem per idem* is employed "where the means or desire to be more explicit does not exist." One possible inference is that "I will be who I will be" means "I can be and can do anything," providing an interpretation of the name "Yahweh."

The stories of Jacob's and Manoah's encounters with secretive divinities suggest another interpretation, however. Lundbom (1978) has exposed the most important contextual function of *idem per idem*: to terminate discussion by eliminating the option of a response. This is highly suggestive in light of the evasions of Gen 32:23–33 and Judges 13. Perhaps by responding "I will be who I will be," Yahweh *diverts* Moses' inquiry. Some past commentators have read 3:14 in this manner (e.g., Philo *Moses* 1.75; Köhler 1957: 242 n. 38; for bibliography, see Schmidt 1988: 175). But they find profundity in the evasion itself: the mystery of the *deus absconditus*, the "hidden God." I think that Yahweh is simply being cagey.

But what about v 14b, "'Thus you will say to Israel's Sons: "I-will-be (*'ehye[h]*)" has sent me to you'"? Does this not prove that *'ehye(h)* is a divine name? Not necessarily. We have already seen that 3:14a cannot mean "I am *'ehye(h)*" (see NOTE). Perhaps, nonetheless, God is revealing two different names in 3:14–15: *'ehye(h)* and Yahweh. If so, the best analysis is Rashbam's: Yahweh calls himself *'ehye(h)* 'I-will-be,' while others refer to him in the third person as *yahwe(h)*, assumed to be a form of *yihye(h)* 'he will be.' But it is not clear that *'ehye(h)* is the first person of *yahwe(h)*, and nowhere else does God plainly refer to himself as *'ehye(h)* (Bekhor Shor). Admittedly, many compare *kî 'attem lō(')* *'ammî wə'ānōkî lō(')-'ehye(h) lākem* (Hos 1:9), rendering "for you are not my people, and I am not Ehyeh for you" (e.g., Andersen and Freedman 1980: 4). Delcor (1990: 87), moreover, points to a possible god **'hyw* featured in the common Nabatean name *'bd'hyw*. The Nabatean data, however, are post-Israelite and difficult to interpret. As for Hos 1:9, it is a negative form of a biblical cliché existing in several variants; compare *wihyîtem lî lə'am wə'ānōkî 'ehye(h) lākem lē(')lōhîm* 'you will be for me a people, and I will be for you a deity' (Jer 11:4;

30:22; cf. Lev 26:12; Ezek 11:20, etc.). Hos 1:9 thus should probably be translated, "You will not be my people, and I will not be for you [i.e., belong to you]," the verbless first clause deriving its tense from *'ehye(h)* in the second. So the evidence for a divine name *'ehye(h)* remains scant. Most likely, in Exod 3:14b, it is simply a verb, "I will be."

But if *'ehye(h)* is a verb, then is not 3:14b nonsense? Just so. I have argued that 3:14a, "I will be who I will be," is an evasion. It seems to me that Yahweh displays more anthropopathic petulance, continuing in this sarcastic vein: "Just tell them 'I-will-be' sent you." Still, v 14b is half-serious, for *'ehye(h)* approaches the Deity's true name.

Why would the Elohist have written such peculiar dialogue? It may be enlightening to compare other biblical stories of namings (cf. Vriezen 1950: 506–7). Such narratives often do not provide a linguistically correct derivation for a proper noun. Rather, they tell a story in which a character does or says something that *sounds like* the term to be explained (cf. Jacob 1992: 32; Garsiel 1992). Exod 3:14–15 may belong to this genre. Rather than being interpretations or archaic forms of the name "Yahweh," *'ehye(h) 'ăšer 'ehye(h)* and *'ehye(h)* may simply be puns, utterances that sound like the divine name but do not explain its meaning. If so, Yahweh discloses his name in his very effort to conceal it. Compare Judg 13:18–19, where the angel's demurral that his name is too "wondrous" for humankind reveals a new divine epithet, "Wonder Worker." Somewhat similar, too, is Judg 6:11–24: an angel appears to a frightened Gideon, whom God reassures, "Peace to you (*šālôm ləkā*)." Gideon proceeds to build an altar to *yahwe(h) šālôm*.

It remains odd that, having rejected Moses' question in 3:14, Yahweh should answer in 3:15, "Yahweh . . . is my name to eternity." Are we to imagine that God is tricked à la Rumpelstiltskin? Or does the odd rhythm of vv 14–15 — "Deity said . . . and he said . . . Deity further said" — depict the subsiding of Yahweh's anger as he shifts from irony to a serious demeanor? However that may be, in 3:14, the Elohist is winking at his audience (cf. McCarthy 1978: 316). We, after all, already know the answer to Moses' question and appreciate the puns in *'ehye(h) 'ăšer 'ehye(h)* and *'ehye(h)*. I am not certain we are actually supposed to find the scene humorous, but it is not inconceivable. There is a further hint of levity later on, when God without warning works frightening wonders upon Moses, and the poor shepherd appears quite the buffoon (4:1–7).

MOSES THE MAGICIAN

As Yahweh's ambassador, Moses needs diplomatic credentials whose "voice" can support his own (4:1, 8, 9). One of these, as we have seen, is the divine name. But Moses is not satisfied. To reinforce Moses' authority, then, Yahweh gives him three magic tricks. He can turn his rod into a snake and back again, he can make his hand diseased and whole again and he can turn water into blood. One could interpret the first two wonders also as tests of Moses' nerve.

Heroes of folktale are often proved before receiving magic weapons (Forsyth 1987: 447; see also INTRODUCTION, p. 33).

These tricks are not particularly impressive. They stand in relation to the Plagues of Egypt as the Burning Bush does to Mount Sinai aflame. That the first two miracles are reversible makes them slightly more showy (compare Gideon's fleece [Judg 6:36–40] or Marduk's test in *Enūma eliš* IV: 19–26 [Gressmann 1913: 45]; see also Bertman 1964). Even if, as Hamlin (1974) argues, the snake symbolizes Chaos, and skin disease and blood symbolize death—still, an animated rod, a scaly hand and some red fluid do not compare with the death of the Egyptian firstborn and the parting of the Sea.

Parallel wonders abound in extra-biblical literature. We possess both ancient (McNeile 1908: 42) and modern (Sarna 1986: 69, 229) reports of magicians who make snakes rigid as rods (Moses, however, does the opposite). As for the miracle's reversibility, Bertman (1964: 325–26) compares the Egyptian magician who animates and de-animates a wax crocodile (Erman 1927: 37–38). There are ample parallels, too, for the sanguification of water (see COMMENT to 7:8–11:10, pp. 348–49). And any mountebank claims to cause or cure disease. No wonder the Priestly Writer portrays Pharaoh's magicians as able to duplicate Moses' feats.

In short, Yahweh provides Moses with miracles that make him seem an ordinary conjuror and even smack of fakery. Understandably, he is disappointed (4:10–12). Like the Burning Bush, these minor prodigies may stimulate faith, but they will not compel it. Moses should know: a prophet's true power and authentication lie in speaking God's word. Deut 13:2–4 addresses just this issue: "Should a prophet or a dream dreamer arise among you and give you a sign or a wonder, and if the sign or wonder should come to pass in connection with which he spoke to you, saying, 'Let us go after other deities [or another deity],' whom you have not known or worshiped—do not heed the words of that prophet or that dream dreamer, for Yahweh your deity will have been testing you." Although the folktales about Elijah and Elisha stress thaumaturgy, the main tradition deemphasizes this aspect of prophecy (note, however, 2 Kgs 20:8–11; Isa 7:9–25).

ROD OF MOSES OR ROD OF GOD?

As we have seen, *maṭṭē(h) hā'ĕlōhîm* might be rendered either "the supernatural rod" or "the Deity's rod" (NOTE to 4:20). Elsewhere, E refers to Moses' rod (7:15, 17, 20; 9:23; 10:13; 17:5). Are these distinct objects? Does Moses even own a rod before meeting Yahweh? At what point might he receive *maṭṭē(h) hā'ĕlōhîm?* The word order in 4:17, *wa'et-hammaṭṭē(h) hazze(h) tiqqaḥ bayādekā* 'and *this rod* you will take in your hand,' suggests to some the introduction of a new staff (Ehrlich 1908: 274; cf. Fohrer 1964: 29; for bibliography, see Valentin 1978: 74 n. 3). Alternatively, one might infer from 4:2, where Yahweh asks "What is this in your hand?" and Moses answers "A rod," that a staff has magically appeared (*Memar Marqah* 1:2 [MacDonald 1963: 1.6–7, 9; 2.6–7, 10]). (See NOTE, however, for Rashi's more likely explanation.) The rod could even be the mysterious *'ôt* 'sign, standard' that Moses receives in 3:12 (see NOTE).

At any rate, taken at face value, 4:20 implies that Moses has somehow acquired Yahweh's own staff (*Exod. Rab.* 8:1; cf. Cassuto 1967: 51–52; Loewenstamm 1992a: 147–54). There is nothing inherently implausible in this. As Gressmann (1913: 48) observes, Gideon's angel carries a staff (Judg 6:21), and Loewenstamm (1962b: 827–28; 1992a: 149–50) notes references to Yahweh's rod, associated with divine wrath and the storm, in Isa 10:24–26 and 30:30–32. Similarly, Ezek 20:37 and Mic 7:14 describe God as a staff-wielding shepherd.

Moreover, ancient parallels abound. At Ugarit, the storm god Ba'lu-Haddu brandishes a "lightning tree (i.e., spear shaft)" (*'ṣ brq* [*KTU* 1.101.4]) or "cedar" (*'arz* [*KTU* 1.4.vii.41]) (see Weinfeld 1983: 139 n. 94). He also possesses two magic clubs with which he defeats the Sea (*KTU* 1.2.iv.11–25; see *ANET* 131). In Egypt, too, Canaanite Baal is renowned for his staff or spear (*ANET* 249; Helck 1971: 448–49). The chief Ugaritic deity "God" (i.e., *'Ilu*) also has a "rod," or possibly a spear or bowstaff (*ḥt, mṭ*), which occasions phallic jesting (*KTU* 1.23.37, 40).

Moreover, the storehouses of myth are well stocked with magical weapons properly belonging to supernaturals, but bestowed on worthy mortals. A Hittite seal of Tudḫaliyas IV depicts the storm god and a man together grasping a mace (Loewenstamm 1958: 138; 1992a: 149; *Ug* 3 figs. 24, 26 [pp. 19, 21]). A letter from Mari claims that the god Addu (= Haddu) of Aleppo gave King Zimri-Lim the weapon with which Addu had defeated the Sea (Charpin and Durand 1986: 174; Durand 1993: 45). Similarly, Assyrian monarchs claim to wield various gods' weapons, including their rods (e.g., *CAD* 6.153–55; 8.52, 54; 17.II.377; Luckenbill 1926–27: 1.85, 141, 212; 2.259). It was even possible in Old Babylonia to "rent" a god's weapon, which functioned as a portable symbol of legal sanction (Harris 1965). Perhaps, then, just as Zimri-Lim receives the weapon of Adad/Haddu, efficacious against the Sea, so does Moses receive Yahweh's own staff, powerful over waters (7:17; 14:16; 17:5). (Compare, too, Ezekiel's statement that Yahweh has given his sword to Nebuchadnezzar [Ezek 30:24–25].)

What, then, of Moses' own rod? It is a reasonable assumption that Moses, as a shepherd, enters the scene already bearing a staff. Does he carry away two rods at the story's end (cf. Jacob 1992: 94)? Probably not. If Moses leaves and enters with one staff, his own rod must be replaced by or transubstantiated into God's own. Henceforth, it is called both "the Deity's rod" and Moses' rod.

The ambiguity is not surprising. Moses, after all, is the Deity's vicar. Whereas the ordinary prophet only speaks for God, Moses also acts for God. Consider the confusion of persons in 7:17 (E): "Thus has Yahweh said: 'By this you may know that I am Yahweh. See: I am going to strike with the rod that is in my hand upon the waters that are in the Nile, and they will turn to blood.'" As Moses speaks in the divine persona, his rod becomes God's own (cf. Valentin 1978: 75).

Moses' rod in E, and Aaron's rod in P, are projections onto the terrestrial plane of Yahweh's incorporeal arm, i.e., his power (Gressmann 1913: 158; cf. Roberts 1971; Fishbane 1994). The association is natural, since the main function of a rod is to extend (*maṭṭe[h]*) one's reach, and "arm" and "rod" frequently interchange (SOURCE ANALYSIS to 7:8–11:10). Thus, when we read of God's *zərôaʿ nəṭûyâ*, the "extended arm" with which he rescues Israel, it is impossible not to think of Moses or Aaron with arms outstretched (*nṭy*) or holding a staff (*maṭṭe[h]*) as God sends calamities upon Egypt. Similarly, while the Song of the Sea describes Yahweh killing the Egyptians with his "right hand" (15:6, 12), the prose account has Moses extend his arm or rod (14:16, 26–27). Isa 30:30–32 appears to associate Yahweh's rod with his arm, and both with the storm. Consider, too, Isa 63:11–12: "Where is he that raised them from the Sea, with (?) the shepherd of his flock? Where is the one who put inside him [Israel? Moses?] the wind/spirit (*rûaḥ*) of his holiness, who made his glory's arm go at Moses' right hand/side (*lîmîn mōše[h]*), cleaving the waters from before them?" The text seems deliberately ambiguous, but a reasonable interpretation is that Yahweh and Moses together cleft the Sea with their right hand(s). (David's arm, too, is accorded the power of Yahweh's arm to rule the waters [Ps 89:22, 26].)

IS MOSES AMONG THE PROPHETS?

Moses ostensibly accepts Yahweh's right to command him. He humbly calls the Deity "my lord" and himself "your slave" (4:10). Yet throughout Exodus 3–4, Moses tries to evade his commission. Even after accepting, he will frequently complain to Yahweh, most often in E (5:22–23; 17:4; Num 11:12–15; also 6:12 [P], 30 [R]). When Moses imputes doubts to the people (3:13; 4:1), we might even infer that he is voicing his own. In comparable commissioning scenes, Yahweh gives his chosen ones signs to fortify their faith (Judg 6:36–40; 1 Sam 10:1–13; cf. Exod 3:12). Perhaps, then, the miracles in Exodus 4 are intended as much to encourage Moses as to convince Israel.

Given his bitter experience in 2:11–15a, no wonder Moses doubts the efficacy of his mission from the start. In this he is not alone. The prophet Jeremiah (Jer 1:6; cf. 20:7), the judge Gideon (Judg 6:15, 36–40) and the monarch Saul (1 Sam 10:21–22; cf. 15:17) are all described as having hesitated to accept Yahweh's call. Solomon, too, is somewhat diffident (1 Kgs 3:7). Similarly, Samuel (1 Sam 16:2), Elijah (1 Kgs 19:4, 10), Ezekiel (Ezek 4:14; 21:5), Jonah (Jonah 1:3; 4:1–3, 8–9) and especially Jeremiah (1:6; 15:10–11, 15–18; 17:14–18; 18:18–23; 20:7–18) periodically try to shirk their missions, or grumble bitterly about them. Their protests are almost always in vain, for "A lion roars; who cannot fear? My Lordship Yahweh speaks; who cannot prophesy?" (Amos 3:8) (for fuller treatment of the Call Narrative genre, see Habel 1965; Richter 1970; Schmidt 1988: 123–29).

Why this perennial reluctance to serve Yahweh? One obvious factor is the periodic doubt experienced by many persons of faith. And, as the biographies of Elijah, Jeremiah and Ezekiel attest, prophets' lives could be full of conflict, even danger. No wonder if at times they regretted their prophetic gift, an ambivalence shared by mantics of other cultures (Wilson 1980: 49). Yet a prophetic career held attractions. Inspired men and women attained influence and respect, and some were remunerated (1 Sam 9:7-8; 2 Kgs 5:15-27; Mic 3:11). Even a Jeremiah, who offended almost everyone, retained his prestige, his life and (most of the time) his liberty. In fact, there were hundreds of Israelite prophets (1 Kgs 18:4, 19; 22:6)—some sincere, some doubtless charlatans—competing for the people's ear. Not surprisingly, they were highly factionalized (Jer 5:13, 31; 14:13-16; 23:13-40; 27:9-18; 28:15-17; 29:8-9; Ezekiel 13; 22:25, 28; Hos 9:7-8; Mic 3:5-7, 11; Zech 13:2-5).

Given their great numbers, frequent disagreements, eccentric behavior, political entanglements and the fact that some were paid, it was perhaps inevitable that the Israelites would come to mistrust their prophets. Amid a torrent of conflicting oracles, all supposedly issuing from the same divine font, how was one to distinguish the true prophet from the false? Deut 18:21-22 and Jer 28:9 agree: the best test is whether the prophet's predictions are materialized. But years might pass before a seer's inspiration could be retroactively certified. No wonder the Elohist imagined Moses as fearing the people's rejection. Such incredulity must have often met prophets of the author's day.

This social background illuminates the pervasive theme of prophetic reluctance. One way to establish credentials as a true prophet, or any other kind of leader, is to avow indifference or inaptitude for one's calling. This is why, for example, Amos claims not to be what he palpably is: a prophet (Amos 7:14).

Though a historian, not a prophet, the Elohist, too, purported to speak for Yahweh. He recounted Yahweh's interventions in history and put words into the mouths of God and his servants. A writer's assertion that one of his characters was a true prophet would have required the same legitimation as the claims of a Jeremiah or an Ezekiel. Thus, just as Jeremiah's putative antipathy to prophecy legitimated his preaching, so did the story of Moses' reluctance legitimate the Elohist's implication that his text, as well as his protagonist, spoke with divine authority.

The same motives may also account for Moses' native inarticulateness, which he claims should disqualify him from service. By laying a humiliating disability upon his hero, the Elohist in fact exalts both Moses and his god. The important point about Demosthenes' stammer or the illiteracy of Akiva and Muḥammad—whether actual or legendary—is that these men overcame their handicaps. In the cases of Moses and Muḥammad, that God used such flawed vessels implicitly validates their messages.

Moses may be considered the archetypical Israelite prophet, transmitting God's word to kings and peoples and working miracles in an international arena (cf. Buber 1946: 62-64; Fohrer 1964: 58; Plastaras 1966: 113; Childs 1974: 144-49). Yet in the Torah, only Deuteronomy calls Moses a *nābî'* 'prophet' (Deut 18:15; 34:10; cf. Hos 12:14). The E source *compares* Moses to prophets, but puts him in a class apart. Moses alone directly experiences God (Num

12:6–8), possessing more than seventyfold prophetic powers (Numbers 11). Only Moses, God's most trusted courtier, is privileged to speak with him "mouth-to-mouth" as a virtual equal (Num 12:8). We might more accurately describe E's Moses as a superprophet, a once-in-history phenomenon (contrast Dtr's recurring "prophet like Moses" [Wilson 1980: 157–252]). And, like the later Samuel, Moses is no less judge and priest than prophet. To have given him any title at all would have been to circumscribe his unique authority.

AARON

Aaron is a cipher in the non-Priestly Torah. He emerges as a character only in rebellion (Exodus 32, Numbers 12 [E]). Why include him at all? To be sure, Moses' speech impediment necessitates an interpreter. But this does not fully account for Aaron's role.

I would cite two factors in particular. On the one hand, the dispatch of paired messengers conforms to Near Eastern social and literary convention. Multiple envoys were often used as insurance against mishap (see Meier 1988: 96–119); compare the two spies of Joshua 2 (called "messengers" in Josh 6:25). In particular, a god's dispatch of two messengers is a cliché of Ugaritic literature (Meier 1988: 119–28); a biblical parallel may be the two angels sent to Sodom (Genesis 19). Overall, our closest parallel to the Moses-Aaron tradition is the Ugaritic myth of the storm god and Prince Sea (see INTRODUCTION, p. 34). Sea sends two ambassadors to 'Ilu (God) demanding the delivery of Ba'lu into his service (ANET 129–35). Convert Sea into Yahweh, 'Ilu into Pharaoh, and the divine envoys into Moses and Aaron, and you have the Exodus tradition.

On the other hand, E's portrayal of Aaron constitutes a critique upon a prominent priestly family claiming Aaronic pedigree. One branch is assumed to have run the Jerusalem Temple; another may have officiated at Bethel (Cross 1973: 199; see COMMENT to Exodus 32). The tense relations among Moses, Aaron and the Levites in the pentateuchal sources probably reflect actual rivalries and alliances among the Israelite clergy (Cross 1973: 195–215). The Priestly Writer pushes Aaron to the fore and upholds the exclusive prerogative of his descendants, in opposition to the Elohistic and Deuteronomic assertion that all Levites are potential priests (see COMMENTS to 6:2–7:7 and 32).

E's Aaron is a complex yet shadowy figure. He is Moses' sidekick, not sibling as in P (NOTE to 4:14). He acts and speaks under Moses' supervision, standing in relation to Moses as Moses does to Yahweh. Essentially, he is Moses' "mouth" (4:16). He is never called priest, but is just a Levite (4:14). Numbers 12 implies that Aaron is also a prophet, but stresses his inferiority to Moses. Twice Aaron engages in activity hostile to Moses, in the affairs of the Golden Calf (Exodus 32) and Snow-White Miriam (Numbers 12). Both times, while his confederates suffer, Aaron himself escapes the consequences of his cowardice and spite. In short, while E's Aaron plays an important role, he is a subordinate and foil to Moses, altogether a different creature from P's uncanny superpriest. It appears that, although the Elohist honored the Aaronids' prerogatives as Levites, he rejected their more extreme claims. (Whether he had in mind a particular branch of the family or the whole clan remains moot; see COMMENT to Exodus 32). Given the relative dates of E and P, the Elohist cannot have been refuting the Priestly source per se. But he doubtless responded to the tradition from which P would emerge (see APPENDIX A, vol. II).

We must not let the occasional friction between Moses and Aaron overshadow their overall cooperation. In fact, neither can function without the other. Without Aaron, Moses cannot be understood. Without Moses, Aaron has nothing to say. Only united can they mediate between the people and the unapproachable divine.

SPECULATION: Although the text makes it clear that Moses' inarticulateness is innate and chronic, his use of an interpreter recalls the practice of many mantics worldwide. One individual, possessed by spirits and/or intoxicated by drugs, babbles inspiredly; another translates. Christian glossolalia (speaking in tongues) is merely the most familiar example (cf. Johnson 1992). While the author is not describing such a practice, conceivably it underlies the tradition that Aaron served as Moses' medium.

THE ELDERS

The Bible's zəqēnîm are "elders" in honor and wisdom, not necessarily in years. Israelite settlements were typically inhabited by a small number of extended families (Stager 1985), over whom the elders constituted a sort of local administration. Under foreign rule, elders might also represent their people before imperial authorities (e.g., Ezra 5:9; 6:7). (For general discussion, see Wolf 1947, McKenzie 1959, van der Ploeg 1961, Reviv 1989 and Willis 1990.)

Though the elders are often considered a quasi-democratic institution, in Exodus quite the opposite is true. In a democracy, authority ascends from the people to its delegated rulers. But E envisions theocratic political authority *descending* from Yahweh to Moses to Aaron to the elders to the clans. The common Israelite ordinarily hears no direct communication from Moses or Aaron, let alone from God.

When Moses enters the scene in Exodus 2, the elders are the standing authority in Israel. The wicked slave questions Moses' right to intervene among Hebrews, or between Hebrews and foreigners, on the grounds that Moses is not a "ruler and judge," i.e., not an elder (see NOTE to 2:14). Among other things, the exchange demonstrates that, to move the people and impress Pharaoh, Moses will have to court Israel's traditional leadership. Yahweh cannot work effectively through Moses and Aaron alone.

So Moses continually convokes the elders at crucial moments (3:16, 18; 4:29; 12:21; 17:5-6; 18:12; 19:7; 24:1, 9, 11). But they are no deliberative body. They represent the tribes — but only inasmuch as they report Moses' words and wonders to their people. Their office, in short, is to disseminate information (Calvin on 3:16). The elders' social status is clear in their physical position at

Mount Sinai (chaps. 24 and 32): Moses stands at the top; Joshua may be somewhat beneath him; lower still are Aaron and Hur. They oversee the elders, who control the people at the mountain's base.

In Exodus 18, however, the tribal leaders appear to regain independence, for some are appointed surrogate judges. And in Num 11:16–29, seventy of them share Moses' overabundant prophetic power. They also assist Moses in quashing the rebellion of Dathan and Abiram (Num 16:25).

Aaron is associated with the elders in 18:12; 24:1, 9, 14 and perhaps is among their number. After the seventy elders receive prophetic powers (Num 11:16–29), Aaron claims that he, too, is a prophet (Num 12:2). And, in the P source, Aaron is explicitly the head of the tribe of Levi (Num 17:18).

The complex relationship among Moses, Aaron and the elders, particularly within E, reflects competition and cooperation between the recognized authorities in ancient Israel: the village elders, the priests, the judges, the king. Although one might read into E an anti-elder polemic, I rather infer that the Elohist viewed Israel's foundational epoch as one in which norms were suspended, in which direct theocracy temporarily superseded traditional authority. (Admittedly, the question is quite complex and depends upon how much of the legal material in chaps. 20–23 is Elohistic.)

A BRIDEGROOM OF BLOODSHED

According to the Heroic Tale narrative archetype, the Hero may be "branded" before his final showdown with the Adversary with either an injury or a protective sign (see INTRODUCTION, p. 33). The sign may even be received from a friendly princess. Thus the traumatic experience of Moses' family at the night-stop (4:24–26) is not entirely unexpected.

But it remains terribly mysterious (for Rabbinic interpretations, see Greenberg 1969: 111–14; for modern opinions, see Houtman 1983). The difficulties of identifying the actors and explaining their actions lend the vignette a nightmarish surrealism. It sounds like a leaf from Freud's casebook: "I dreamed that God tried to kill my father; my mother cut off the end of my penis to save my father's life, saying to both me and my father, 'You are my bridegroom'" (see further Propp 1993: 496–98).

Our first question is who is "him" in "Yahweh met *him* and sought to put *him* to death": Moses or his son? In the context of J, it seems likely that Moses is the victim (Kutsch 1977: Propp 1993: 498–99). Were it Gershom, the text would read "(he) sought to put *Moses' son* to death." The reason it is Zipporah who acts, then, is that Moses is incapacitated (ibn Ezra). It also follows that "he slackened from him" refers to the cessation of Yahweh's aggression against Moses. (The identity of the victim in the composite text, however, is less clear; see REDACTION ANALYSIS.)

Next, why should Yahweh attack the man he has just commissioned to liberate Israel? Moses is not the only biblical hero to be unexpectedly opposed by the Deity or his angels. Talmon (1954a) compares Jacob's wrestling in the fords of the Jabbok (Gen 32:23–33) and Balaam's confrontation with an armed angel (Num 22:22–35). In general, the Bible reflects a conviction that encounters with divinities are fraught with peril. But if Yahweh is often portrayed as volatile, his actions are rarely if ever irrational. We still need a motive.

According to early Jewish interpreters, God is provoked by Moses' failure to circumcise his son on the eighth day, as per Genesis 17 (see Vermes 1957–58; Le Déaut 1963: 209–12; Shinan 1992: 128). Zipporah quickly remedies the situation, and God is appeased. But this explanation, while possible for the redacted Torah, is problematic for J. The strict command to circumcise boys on the eighth day is from P (Genesis 17). Even if the Yahwist, too, presupposed infant circumcision (see below), his document nowhere commands it. While the Bible is often elliptical, it seems unfair that readers be expected to infer both the requirement of circumcision and Moses' omission of the rite between the lines of 4:24–26. A more convincing interpretation would find a reason for Yahweh's attack in events prior to Moses' departure from Midian actually mentioned in the text.

Many modern commentators approach our story through its "moral," the repeated phrase ḥătan dāmîm. They focus primarily on the meaning of ḥātān (ordinarily, 'bridegroom' or 'son-in-law') and the identity of its referent (Moses? the boy? Yahweh?). Dāmîm 'blood' (pl.), on the other hand, has been largely neglected. Almost all assume that the reference to blood is fully explained by "she applied to his legs" (4:25). That is, with either the flint or the foreskin, Zipporah transfers Gershom's blood to Moses.

This is undeniably the simplest reading, but other possible nuances of dāmîm have not gone unexplored. Some, for instance, find an allusion to the blood of defloration, as the mention of a "bridegroom" might suggest (Meyer 1906: 59; Gressmann 1913: 57–61; Auerbach 1975: 48–50). This approach has not proved productive, however (see Junker 1950: 121; Propp 1993: 501). Schneemann (1980) more plausibly defines ḥătan dāmîm as "a bridegroom who has shed blood," noting that the plural dāmîm, as opposed to the singular dām, almost always connotes bloodguilt (see NOTE on 4:25). Unfortunately, Schneemann identifies the bridegroom as Yahweh (in turn to be identified with Christ the Bridegroom!). Schneemann cannot be correct in imputing bloodguilt to Yahweh, however. In the first place, Yahweh does not actually kill Moses. Secondly, only unjust homicide creates bloodguilt, whereas the Bible in general considers Yahweh to be just by definition. Unlike the Hindu gods, he is inherently immune to bloodguilt. Finally, in no sense is Yahweh Zipporah's bridegroom or son-in-law. But Schneemann's "a bridegroom who has shed blood" fits Moses perfectly. He is Zipporah's husband, and, as Yahweh reminds him (4:19), he has until recently been wanted in Egypt for murder (Middlekoop 1967).

Before proceeding, we must consider briefly Israelite concepts of murder, bloodguilt, asylum and atonement. According to Gen 4:10 (J), the blood of the (unjustly) slain cries out to Yahweh from the ground. The ordinary punishment is execution, preferably by the victim's kin (see de Vaux 1961: 10–12). Only this will lift the curse from the land (Num 35:33–34; Deut 19:10; 21:1–9;

cf. Gen 4:11). Monetary restitution, the usual redress for crime, is forbidden for intentional homicide (Num 35:31–32). And the victim's nationality is irrelevant. Whether for the Hittite (2 Samuel 12) or the Gibeonite (2 Samuel 21), Yahweh demands blood for blood.

It is crucial to note, however, that Israelite law distinguishes between premeditated and accidental homicide (manslaughter). Capital punishment applies only to first-degree murder. For cases of manslaughter, there is a special provision (21:12–14): "Whoever strikes a man and he dies must be put to death, death. But in the case that he did not lie in wait, and the Deity by happenstance brought it to his hand, then I will set for you a place that he may flee thither. But when a man presumes against his fellow to kill him by premeditation, from my altar you may take him to die." The altar might provide temporary asylum for the manslayer (cf. 1 Kgs 1:50–53; 2:28–34), but, for the longer duration, there were to be six cities of refuge (Num 35:9–34; Deut 4:41–43; Deut 19:1–13; Joshua 20).

Is Moses the manslayer entitled to asylum? Today he might get off with a conviction of second-degree murder, inasmuch as his violence was basically impromptu. Admittedly, the laws of refuge do not protect the second-degree murderer; and Moses did peer this way and that, implying brief premeditation. Nevertheless, he did not really "lie in wait" (21:13; Num 35:20). His was essentially a crime of passion. While an Israelite legist might not grant Moses asylum, an Israelite storyteller could perhaps be more lenient.

For the moment, let us assume that Moses would be classified as an accidental manslayer, and explore the consequences. By the law of asylum, the killer is safe from avengers only as long as he remains inside the city of refuge, in a sort of internal exile (Num 35:26–27). He may safely depart, however, upon the death of the incumbent high priest (Num 35:25, 28; Josh 20:6), which perhaps atones vicariously for unavenged murders (*b. Mak.* 11b; Greenberg 1959). I suggest that Moses' flight to Midian, in or near which is "holiness ground" (3:5 [J]), is essentially a quest for asylum. Moses eventually outlives his victim's avengers, be they kin or civil authorities (4:19). But, without atonement for homicide, he is not free to go home.

If so, it is Moses' attempt to return bearing unexpiated bloodguilt that elicits Yahweh's attack. Note that *hēmît* 'put to death' often connotes the execution of a criminal by God or man (see NOTE to 4:24). Moreover, the *Leitwort bqš* 'seek' ties together 4:24 (Yahweh *seeks* to put Moses to death), 4:19 (unspecified men have *sought* Moses' life) and 2:15 (Pharaoh *seeks* to kill Moses) (Blum 1990: 52). I infer that in all three verses the reason for "seeking" is the same: Moses killed an Egyptian. A popular midrash (cf. Jude 9) even describes the quarrel of Michael and Satan/Sammael over Moses' body, with Satan claiming Moses was an unabsolved murderer (Ginzberg 1928: 6.159–60).

By this analysis, the expression "bridegroom of bloodguilt" takes on new meaning. When Yahweh attacks Moses, Zipporah realizes that the violent stranger she married is a felon (Middlekoop 1967). Had she known, she might have hesitated to marry a man with both a price and a curse on his head.

But if by God's own laws, Moses may not return, why does God send Moses back? Yahweh's problem is that he has two irreconcilable plans for Moses: he wants to dispatch him to Egypt to liberate the people, and he wants to punish him for his old crime. How can he accomplish both? Should Moses return home bearing his guilt, he must be executed, lest he pollute the community on the eve of the Exodus (on ritual purity and the paschal rite, see COMMENT to 12:1–13:16). This impasse results in the Deity's bizarre behavior. (Compare the predicament of the Greek gods vis-à-vis Orestes: there is no way to absolve him of even justifiable matricide, save by negating the very concept of maternity [Aeschylus *Eumenides* 657–66].)

Zipporah evidently solves Yahweh's problem. Since the attack ceases after her action, I infer that by shedding Gershom's blood, Zipporah has performed a rite of expiation/purification. Moses is cleared and may return home. (Among the Arabs, whose rite of *'aqīqa* [first haircut] corresponds in many ways to Israelite circumcision, blood vengeance may be analogously exacted with a haircut [Morgenstern 1966: 84–86].)

This analysis also clarifies whom Zipporah touches in v 25. Since it is Moses' crime that is being atoned for, it must be to him that Zipporah applies the bloodied flint or foreskin. The expiatory virtue of nonlethal bloodshed is transferred from son to father; the child's blood substitutes for his father's, theoretically forfeit. This in turn raises two questions: why should the atoning blood come from the penis, and why should it come from the innocent son, not the guilty father?

There is some evidence that Israelites, Arabs and Phoenicians attributed to circumcision an expiatory or purificatory function. Leviticus 12 (P) implies that a boy's circumcision removes his mother's childbirth impurity (see, however, Milgrom 1991: 744). Also, the equivalence of purification and circumcision is implied by the phrase *'ārēl waṭāmē'* 'uncircumcised and impure' (Isa 52:1); note, too, the parallel expressions "uncircumcised of lips" (6:12, 30) and "impure of lips" (Isa 6:5) (see also NOTE to 6:12). Moreover, both circumcision and ritual purity are requirements for celebrating the *Pesaḥ* (see COMMENT to 12:1–13:16). For the Arabs, Wold (1978: 259) notes that *ṭhr* 'to be pure' connotes circumcision. Finally, in a Phoenician myth recorded by Philo of Byblos and transmitted by Eusebius (*Praep. evangelica* 1.10.33), "At the occurrence of a fatal plague, [the god] Kronos immolated his only son to his father Ouranos ['Heaven'], and circumcised himself, forcing the allies who were with him to do the same" (Attridge and Oden 1981: 57). Here, too, circumcision seems to be propitiatory.

But if Kronos corresponds to Moses, we would expect Moses, not his son, to be circumcised. Moses' penis is at least involved somehow, for *raglā(y)w* 'his legs' (4:25) probably connotes Moses' genitals (see NOTE). The natural inference is that, either by touching the bloodied flint to Moses' penis or by applying and removing Gershom's foreskin, Zipporah *symbolically* circumcises her husband (cf. Driver 1911: 33; de Groot 1943: 14–15; Houtman 1983: 98). (Compare the later Jewish rite of drawing the "Covenant Blood" from the penis of a previously circumcised proselyte [b. Šabb. 135a].) By this act, Zipporah transfers the purifying power of blood from son to father. (She may also simultaneously remove guilt or impurity the son has inherited from his tainted parent [F. I. Andersen, privately]; see below.)

Why not circumcise Moses directly? One possibility is that Moses is already circumcised; cf. Josh 5:5. But I think the true answer is bound up with the original meaning of ḥătan dāmîm, forgotten by the Yahwist's day. I have argued that in the context of 4:24–26, the phrase alludes to Moses' bloodguilt. But I also share the common opinion that 4:24–26 is an etiological narrative explaining an obscure expression (e.g., Childs 1962: 60–61; Schmid 1965; Kutsch 1977). As innumerable scholars since Wellhausen (1897: 175) have observed, it can be no coincidence that in Arabic, while ḥatana means "to become related by marriage," the base form ḥatana means "to circumcise." Current Muslim practice varies widely, but the ambivalence of ḥtn suggests that pre-Islamic Arabs circumcised adolescents soon before marriage (see Propp 1993: 507, 515–18).

There are three stories in the Bible featuring circumcision, marriage and the root ḥtn. The first is Gen 34:14–17 (Shechem must be circumcised to marry [ḥtn] Dinah), the second is our tale and the third, more subtle, is 1 Sam 18:25–27 (David pays a bride-price of foreskins to his prospective ḥōtēn Saul [Ehrlich 1969: 145 n.; Propp 1987b: 361; Hallo 1991: 49]). In light of these traditions, it seems likely that in Hebrew as in Arabic, ḥtn originally connoted both circumcision and marriage.

We know, however, that the age of Israelite circumcision had shifted from adolescence to early infancy by the time of P (Genesis 17) (Propp 1987b). Why this happened is unknown, but I suspect the process of detribalization charted by Halpern (1991) played a crucial role. Circumcision was no longer a rite of solidarity among the youths of a clan, but a solitary, domestic observance. At any rate, the result of this shift would have been lexical confusion: some uses of ḥtn adhered to the marriage rite and others to circumcision. Specifically, ḥātān might have meant both "relative by marriage" and "circumcised boy" (on passive qāṭāl, see Barth 1894: 433 n. 1). If we hypothesize that by the Yahwist's day, circumcision had already moved at least to childhood if not infancy, 4:24–26 makes sense as the author's attempt to explain a fossilized expression whereby a young boy is seemingly called "son-in-law/bridegroom."

A story depicting this semantic transition should in theory bring into contact a new husband and a circumcised child — precisely what we find in 4:24–26. If the author is trying to explain why son and father are both called ḥātān 'bridegroom/circumcised,' it makes sense that each should have a bloody penis. The father receives dāmîm 'blood' from his son and, as it were, bestows the title ḥātān in exchange. We know nothing about the Israelite circumcision ritual, but it is even possible that 4:24–26 mirrors actual practice, with the mother playing a crucial role (in many cultures, however, women are banned from circumcisions). Further: Eilberg-Schwartz (1990: 162–63) speaks of circumcision creating a "blood brotherhood" between fathers and sons, whose relatedness is of necessity presumptive, not provable. On one level, then, Zipporah is affirming that the child is Moses', as well as her own.

If a circumcised adolescent was originally called ḥătan dāmîm, what was the import of the second word? We have seen that the plural of dām 'blood' connotes the defilement of bloodshed, primarily from murder but also from menstruation and childbirth. Thus there are many possibilities. If a man's in-laws became his blood avengers at marriage or at the birth of his first child, then ḥătan dāmîm might mean "in-law protected by blood-vengeance" (cf. Akkadian ḥatānu 'defend'); Herodotus (Histories 3.8) reports that blood rituals conferred clan protection among the Arabs of his day. Alternatively, if only a circumcised man was fair game in a blood feud, as among the Bedouin (Murray 1935: 174), then ḥătan dāmîm may have meant "circumcised one capable of bearing bloodguilt." Another possibility is that, as in Leviticus 12, circumcision purified the mother of her dāmîm from childbirth. Or maybe dāmîm simply connoted the blood of circumcision, after all. Only with the development of the nuance "bloodguilt" did it become necessary to frame a story linking marriage, circumcision and murder.

SPECULATION: A final possibility is that, like later baptism, circumcision was believed to block the inheritance of guilt, specifically bloodguilt, from father to son. If so, the Rabbinic theory that Moses' crime was not circumcising Gershom is compatible with my approach.

However that may be, I think those who identify the ḥātān as Moses and those who identify the ḥātān as the son are equally right. Our story chronicles a shift in meaning: in 4:25 ḥātān 'bridegroom/circumcised' is addressed to the symbolically circumcised Moses, but in v 26 it applies to the actually circumcised child.

To summarize: Although Yahweh commands Moses to return to Egypt (4:19), he still holds him accountable for the death of the Egyptian. Zipporah sheds the blood of their son and dabs Moses' penis with it, thereby expiating her husband's sin. Contrary to the view of almost all exegetes, 4:24–26 is well integrated into the J narrative, as it presupposes 2:11–12. And, as we shall presently see, it also points forward to the mighty deeds of the Exodus.

PASCHAL SYMBOLISM

Because by my reckoning, the Yahwist is largely absent from Exodus 11–13, I am not sure that 4:24–26 (J) originally foreshadowed the paschal ritual and the Exodus—although I think it likely. At least in the composite text, the effect is unmistakable.

First, by inserting the episode after the threat to Pharaoh's firstborn (4:23 [E]), Redactor^JE created the impression that it was Moses' firstborn, Gershom, not Moses himself, whom Yahweh attacked. This in turn recalls the plague of the firstborn, from which Israel will be spared by virtue of the paschal rite (see REDACTION ANALYSIS). In other words, the blood of Gershom's circumcision is homologous with the blood of the paschal lamb. Indeed, the same verb, *higgîaʿ*, describes the application of both (4:25 [J]; 12:22 [E]) (cf. ibn Ezra; Smith 1906). One might even understand that Zipporah redeems her firstborn from Yahweh, just as God's firstborn, Israel, is redeemed during the paschal night (cf. 13:1–2, 11–16; 34:20; Num 18:15) (Fretheim 1991a: 80). Alternatively, one may still consider Moses the victim in JE. If so, one might say that Gershom's blood, which substitutes for Moses' own, parallels that of the paschal lamb, by whose death Israel lives (see COMMENT to 12:1–13:16).

The later addition of P strengthened the paschal connection. Exod 12:44, 48 enunciates a key requirement for the *Pesaḥ*: "Any man's slave, a purchase by silver, and you will circumcise him; then he may eat of it. . . . If a sojourner sojourns with you and would do a *Pesaḥ* for Yahweh, every male of him must be circumcised, and then he may approach to do it and be like the land's native. But any uncircumcised may not eat of it." Josh 5:2–11, too, associates circumcision and the paschal ceremony (see COMMENT to 12:1–13:16, pp. 452–54). The implication for 4:24–26 is that, were Moses and/or his son uncircumcised, they would be ineligible to participate in the paschal meal and the departure from Egypt (cf. Smith 1927: 609; de Groot 1943: 16). (The parallel between the blood of circumcision and the paschal blood was not lost on the Rabbis. The Midrash tells of the Hebrews marking their doorways with the mixed blood of circumcision and *Pesaḥ* [*Exod. Rab.* 19:5; *Tg. Ps.-Jonathan* Exod 12:13; *Tg. Neb.* Ezek 16:6].)

As I have noted, we cannot say how much of this paschal foreshadowing existed in J and how much was a consequence of later editing. But already in JE, and certainly in the final Torah, 4:24–26 plays an important structural role, being both prospective and retrospective. Through the transfer of blood from the son's penis to the father's, and the transfer of the epithet "bridegroom of bloodguilt" from father to son, 4:24–26 links Moses' limited, unauthorized act of violent protest, killing one Egyptian taskmaster, to Yahweh's grand act of violent protest, killing all the Egyptian firstborn. And as Moses' deed causes him to flee to God's mountain in the desert, so Yahweh's deeds will enable Israel to escape to Sinai.

INITIATION AND REBIRTH

We learn from Gen 17:10–14 (P) that circumcision was a sign of Israelite identity. Not that the lack of a foreskin was uniquely Israelite; many neighboring peoples were also circumcised (Propp 1987b). Rather, in earliest Israel, the operation acquired special significance as a rite of socioreligious initiation and a perpetual reminder of the Covenant. Performed upon adolescents, it betokened eligibility not only for marriage but for *all* rights and responsibilities of an Israelite man, including celebration of the *Pesaḥ* (see COMMENT to

12:1–13:16; for cross-cultural parallels, see van Gennep 1960: 70–73, 81, 85–86). Moses' symbolic circumcision on the way back to liberate Israel is his own personal rite of passage.

It is indeed striking in how many respects the tale of Moses' Midianite sojourn is comparable to rituals of male initiation in other cultures (cf. Hendel 1987a: 158–61). A young man, previously surrounded by women, goes alone into the desert, meets a dangerous spirit, learns its secret name and the history of his people, receives his life's mission and a symbolic wound, then returns to the men of his tribe—this is terrain familiar to ethnographers. If the story of Moses in Midian is not directly inspired by Israelite rites of initiation, it must draw upon the same wellsprings in the human psyche.

Initiation ceremonies frequently feature elements of danger, acted out or real, and a symbolic death and rebirth into adulthood (Turner 1967: 96). J has already featured two "births" of Moses—literally to his Hebrew mother and figuratively to Pharaoh's daughter, who draws him from the water and names him (see COMMENT to 1:22–2:10). In 4:24–26, Moses nearly dies and is rescued by a symbolic circumcision. His Midianite wife gives him an epithet properly applied to circumcised boys and daubs him with the blood of circumcision. Thus, Zipporah is a third mother figure for Moses.

SPECULATION: Perhaps Zipporah is not just a symbolic mother but is also usurping the role of father-in-law. For, if Moses is her ḥātān 'bridegroom/ son-in-law/circumcised,' she is conversely his ḥōtēn 'father-in-law/circumciser.' In the Bible, marriage is in many respects an economic exchange between two men: the bridegroom (or his father) and the woman's father (or other male guardian) (de Vaux 1961: 24–38). When Moses fathers a son, he is implicitly initiated as a Midianite and full member of Jethro's household, hence his words "I was a sojourner in a foreign land" (2:22).

Is it too much to imagine that Zipporah, in protest, initiates Moses as her own ḥātān, not her father's? Note her words: ḥătan . . . lî . . . lammûlōt 'a son-in-law . . . to me . . . by circumcision.' If so, she is unsuccessful. Moses' deepest personal relationship continues to be with Jethro, not with his own wife and children (see COMMENT to chap. 18).

IS YAHWEH AMONG THE DEMONS?

Yahweh's violence in 4:24–26 is often described as "demonic." In fact, Jub 40:2 attributes the attack to Mastemah, the archfiend, while *Fragmentary Targum* blames the Angel of Death. Some of the tale's nightmarish quality might reflect an author's (or storyteller's) memories of his own circumcision. But the text might also be making a point about the nature of God.

Explaining evil and chaos was as much a challenge to ancients as to us. There are two basic rationalizations for disorder and injustice: either one sees divinities (gods, spirits, demons, etc.) working at cross-purposes, or else one attributes psychological instability to individual gods. Judaism and Christianity, influenced by Persian dualism, opted for the first approach, creating a hierarchy of evil angels and purging the Godhead of malicious attributes. The Israelites, on the other hand, were forced to impute to Yahweh a degree of maleficence in order to explain reality: "Can there be harm in a city, and Yahweh has not done it?" (Amos 3:6); "I am Yahweh, and there is none other, who fashions light and creates dark, who makes well-being and creates harm; I, Yahweh, make all this" (Isa 45:6–7).

It is common human experience that "power tends to corrupt and absolute power corrupts absolutely." Lord Acton was speaking of humans, but it follows that an anthropopathic being of limitless power should possess an exaggerated dark side. Although the Bible generally depicts its deity as equitable, the Book of Job probes the seemingly irrational cruelty of the universe and its Master. Exod 4:24–26, too, depicts Yahweh's dread unpredictability, even for his closest intimate.

THE SOJOURNER'S TALE

The overall literary character of 2:11–4:31 deserves comment. Again our authors, or their sources, have employed stereotypical plot elements to structure and flesh out Moses' biography. We might call the ideal type the "Sojourner's Tale." It is most fully exemplified in the Bible by the stories of Jacob in Aram, Moses in Midian and Israel in Egypt. Hendel (1987a: 137–65) has already exposed the extraordinary similarities between the stories of Moses and Jacob, while Daube (1963: 63–72) has demonstrated equally deep analogies between Jacob and Israel (the nation). I will combine their observations, with slight modifications (see also King 1987).*

The plot of Jacob in Aram may be summarized as follows: Jacob commits a crime (Gen 27:1–30 [J]), flees abroad as a refugee (Gen 27:41–45 [J]; 27:46–28:5 [P]) and experiences Yahweh (Gen 28:10–22 [JE]). He proves his heroism at a well (Gen 29:10 [J]) and marries into a native family (Gen 29:15–30 [J]), acquiring a powerful patron whose service he enters as a shepherd (Gen 29:15–30 [J]). He becomes wealthy (Gen 30:31–43 [J]; 31:1–2, 4–16 [E]), though essentially a slave, and begets many children (Gen 29:31–30:24 [JE]). He asks permission of his tricky, fickle (Gen 30:23–27 [J]; 31:41 [E]) father-in-law/master to leave with wives and children (Gen 30:26 [J]) but is refused (Gen 30:27 [J]). Nonetheless, Yahweh commands him to return home (Gen 31:3 [J]; 31:13 [E]). Jacob neglects to inform his master but steals his family and the cattle he is owed both as a released servant (Daube 1963: 49–51) and as a relative by marriage (Gen 31:17–18a [J]); 31:16, 26–43 [E]). Jacob is pursued and overtaken

---

*The following synopses cross source boundaries frequently. I infer that both J and E hewed to the prototypical Sojourner's Tale even before combination into JE. The Priestly Writer naturally imitated what he found in JE. After editing, however, the full pattern is visible only in the composite.

(Gen 31:22–5 [E]), but, protected by Yahweh (Gen 31:24 [E]; 31:49–53 [JE]), he becomes dominant over his former master, whom Jacob's wife repulses with (purported) blood (Gen 31:35 [E]). Jacob crosses a river border (Gen 32:23 [J]) and has a hostile encounter with a deity at night in a quasi-rite of passage (Hendel 1987a: 63). He defeats the being at dawn but receives a symbolic wound (Gen 32:25–33 [E?]). He meets his brother, an old adversary (Gen 32:14–22 [J]; 32:4–13 [J?]; 33:1–17 [E]). Finally, fully mature, he arrives home in Canaan (Gen 32:22–32 [JE?]).

Here is the plot of Moses in Midian: Moses commits a crime (Exod 2:11–12 [J]), flees abroad (Exod 2:15 [J]; cf. Exod 18:4 [E]) and proves his heroism at a well (Exod 2:17 [J]). He marries into a native family (Exod 2:21 [J]), acquiring a powerful patron whose service he enters as a shepherd (Exod 3:1 [E]), and begets a child (Exod 2:22 [J]). He experiences Yahweh (Exod 3:2–4:17 [JE]), who commands him to leave his exile (Exod 3:10 [E?]; 4:19 [J]). He informs his father-in-law of his intention to depart but conceals the true reason (Exod 4:18 [E]). He then leaves with his family (Exod 4:20 [J]) and has a hostile encounter with Yahweh at night in a quasi-rite of passage (Exod 4:24); his wife repulses the attack with blood, and Moses is symbolically wounded (Exod 4:25–26). Moses meets his brother (Exod 4:27 [E]), a future adversary (Exodus 32, Numbers 12 [E]), then meets his brethren, the Hebrews (Exod 4:30 [E]), and a substitute adversary, the new Pharaoh (Exodus 5–11 [EP]). Fully mature, he has arrived home in Egypt (Exod 4:29).

Now for Israel in Egypt: Jacob's sons commit a crime (Gen 37:18–33 [JE]), whereby Joseph becomes a slave (Gen 37:36 [E]); 38 [J]). But Joseph acquires powerful patrons in Potiphar and Pharaoh (Gen 37:36; 41:37–44 [E]; 39 [J]) and marries into a native family (Gen 41:45 [E]). Jacob's sons, refugees from famine (Gen 42:1; 43:1 [J]), also gain Pharaonic patronage, entering royal service as shepherds (Gen 46:32–34 [J]) and perhaps marrying native women (Daube 1963: 53–54). They begat many children (Exod 1:7 [P]; 1:8 [J?]; 1:20 [E]) but become slaves to their patron, a new Pharaoh (Exod 1:11 [J?]; 1:13 [P]). Yahweh commands them to leave (Exod 3:8 [J?]; 3:10 [E]; 6:6 [P]), and they ask permission of their master to depart along with wives, children and cattle (Exod 10:9, 24–26 [E]), concealing the true reason (Exod 3:18; 5:1, 3, etc. [E]). They are rebuffed (Exod 10:10, 24 [E]) by their fickle oppressor (Exodus 7–14 *passim* [EPR]). They nonetheless take their families and their masters' property (Exod 11:2–3; 12:35–36 [J?]), while Yahweh attacks at night (Exod 11:4; 12:21, 29 [E]). Blood averts the attack from Israel, as their houses are symbolically wounded (Exod 12:23 [E]). Israel is pursued and overtaken, but, protected by Yahweh (Exodus 14 [JEP]), Israel becomes dominant over its former master. The Hebrews cross the sea/border while Yahweh attacks the Egyptians (Exod 14:15–15:21 [JEP]). Israel repeatedly encounters Yahweh, often hostilely, and is tested in the desert in a quasi-rite of passage (all sources; see INTRODUCTION). Finally, a mature Israel arrives home in Canaan (Joshua 1–4).

Another biblical tale that follows the pattern, albeit with greater deviation, is that of Joseph (King 1987). The young shepherd alienates his family and leaves them, symbolically wounded (the bloodstained garment). He gains a powerful patron abroad, has a (nonconsummated) liaison with a female in his patron's house, incurs his master's enmity, acquires an even greater patron, marries well, is reunited with his brothers and returns home, albeit as a corpse (cf. Levenson 1993b: 144).

And there are other stories from Antiquity that, space permitting, could be compared to our Sojourner's Tale: the *Odyssey*, the *Epic of Gilgamesh* (*ANET*[3] 72–99, 503–7; Dalley 1989: 39–153), the "Shipwrecked Sailor" (Lichtheim 1973: 211–15), the "Tale of Sinuhe" (*ANET* 18–22; Lichtheim 1973: 222–35), the "Report of Wen-Amon" (*ANET* 25–29; Lichtheim 1976: 224–30), the "Story of Idri-mi" (*ANET*[3] 557–58). I assume that in the ancient world, impoverished commoners, especially younger sons, would often indenture themselves to wealthy cattle owners, hoping for enrichment and restoration to their patrimony. The popularity of the Sojourner's Tale would lie in its romanticized dramatization of a common plight.

What sets the tale of Moses apart, however, is the lack of a happy ending. Moses returns to his home, but not to rest. The end of his Sojourner's Tale is the beginning of a new story: Israel's Exodus from Egypt (chaps. 5–15).

VIII. *A sword in their hand to kill us* (5:1–6:1)

5   [1(E)]And afterwards Moses and Aaron came and said to Pharaoh, "Thus has Yahweh Israel's deity said: 'Release my people, that they may celebrate to me in the wilderness.'"

[2]But Pharaoh said, "Who is Yahweh, that I should heed his voice by releasing Israel? I have not known Yahweh; moreover, Israel I will not release."

[3]Then they said, "The Hebrews' deity happened upon us. We would go a three days' way into the wilderness and sacrifice to Yahweh our deity, lest he strike us with the plague or with the sword."

[4]But Egypt's king said to them, "Why, Moses and Aaron, should you distract the people from his work? Go to your tasks." [5]And Pharaoh said, "See: the land's people are now many, and you will interrupt them from their tasks."

[6]So on that day Pharaoh commanded those overseeing the people and his officers, saying, [7]"Do not continue to give the people straw to brickmake the bricks as yesterday and the day before. They, they shall go and scrabble straw for themselves. [8]But the volume of the bricks they were producing yesterday and the day before you shall lay upon them; do not deduct from it. For they

are lax; therefore they cry, saying, 'We would go sacrifice to our deity.' [9]Let the work be hard upon the men; so let them do it, and not look to words of deceit."

[10]Then the people's overseers and his officers went out and said to the people, saying, "Thus has Pharaoh said: 'I am not going to give you straw. [11]You, you go get for yourselves straw from wherever you can find, for not a whit is deducted from your work.'"

[12]So the people scattered in all the land of Egypt to scrabble stubble for the straw, [13]and the overseers were urging, saying, "Finish your tasks, a day's matter in its day, just as when the straw was being given to you." [14]And the officers of Israel's Sons, whom Pharaoh's overseers had placed over them, were beaten, saying, "Why have you not completed your quota of brickmaking as yesterday and the day before, both yesterday and today?"

[15]And the officers of Israel's Sons came and cried to Pharaoh, saying, "Why do you do so to your slaves? [16]Straw is not being given to your slaves, yet 'Bricks,' they say to us, 'make!' Now, see: your slaves are being beaten, and your people is the fault."

[17]But he said, "Lax are you, lax; therefore you are saying, 'We would go sacrifice to Yahweh.' [18]And now, go work; and straw will not be given to you, but the full volume of bricks you must give."

[19]And the officers of Israel's Sons saw them in trouble, saying, "Do not deduct from your bricks, a day's matter in its day." [20]And they encountered Moses and Aaron stationed to meet them in their going out from with Pharaoh. [21]And they said to them, "May Yahweh look on you and judge, who have fouled our odor in Pharaoh's eyes and in his slaves' eyes, placing a sword in their hand to kill us."

[22]So Moses returned to Yahweh and said, "My Lordship, for what have you done badly to this people? For what is it you sent me? [23]For ever since I came to Pharaoh to speak in your name, it has gone badly for this people, and rescued, you have not rescued your people."

6 [1]And Yahweh said to Moses, "Now you will see what I will do to Pharaoh. For by a strong arm he will release them, and by a strong arm he will expel them from his land."

ANALYSIS

TEXTUAL NOTES

5:1. *came and said to Pharaoh.* LXX paraphrases: "came *to Pharaoh* and said *to him.*"

†5:2. *Who is Yahweh.* Most LXX MSS have *tis estin* 'who is he,' as if reading *hw'* for *yhwh* (other witnesses either have *theos* 'God' or have been corrected to match MT). It is hard to decide what is original. Either of the two, *my yhwh 'šr* (MT) or **my hw' 'šr* (LXX *Vorlage*), could have generated the other, and both make sense. As the LXX *Vorlage* remains hypothetical, I follow MT. (On

hû' 'he' as a substitute for "Yahweh" in the Bible and the Dead Sea Scrolls, see de Vaux 1978: 344–45.)

releasing Israel. Probably independently, LXX and Rossi 592 read "releasing Israel's *sons.*"

5:3. *they said.* LXX and Rossi 440 add "to him." This seems a simple expansion—or two independent expansions—but O'Connell (n.d.) raises the possibility that *'lyw* 'to him' fell out before *'lhy* 'the deity of' by homoioarkton; alternatively: *'lyw* could have dropped by homoioteleuton after *wy'mrw*.

The Hebrews' deity. Syr "*the Lord,* the Hebrews' deity" is a secondary expansion.

happened upon us. As in 3:18 (see TEXTUAL NOTE), several MT MSS read etymologically correct *nqrh* for standard MT-Sam *nqr'* (Kennicott 1776–80: 114) (see NOTE). LXX and Vg have "the Hebrews' god has *called* (Hebrew *qr'*) us," indirectly supporting standard MT.

†*into the wilderness.* Instead of MT *bammidbār*, Sam reads *hmdbrh* and places it after "we would go." Either could be original.

†*Yahweh.* The divine name is missing in many LXX witnesses and seems not to have appeared in the original LXX. Compare the variants of v 17, where LXX has "our deity," missing from MT.

with the plague or with the sword. These are reversed in Syr. Syr, LXX and Tgs. Onqelos and Ps.-Jonathan paraphrase *deber* 'plague' as "death," while LXX and the Tgs. interpret *ḥereb* 'sword' as "murder."

†5:4. *distract.* Perhaps correctly, 4QExod[b] and Sam read *tprydw* 'separate.' If MT *tpry'w* 'distract' is a corruption, it was probably influenced by the proximity of *pr'h* 'Pharaoh' and *gr'* 'deduct.'

his work. Tg. Onqelos and Syr have "*their* work," while LXX has "*the* works."

†5:5. *the land's people are now many.* Our three major textual witnesses are in dissent. MT has *rabbîm 'attâ 'am hā'āreṣ* 'the land's people are now many' (also 4QExod[b]); Sam reads *rbym 'th m'm h'rṣ* '(they are) now more numerous than the land's people'; LXX reflects **rbym 'th h'm* 'the people are now numerous' (LXX[A], however, agrees with MT). Which, if any, is correct?

In theory, each of these could be a corruption of **rbym 'th h'm m'm h'rṣ* 'the people are now more numerous than the land's people' (cf. 1:9). But this is somewhat clumsy and entirely conjectural. And one might ask: of what pertinence are the relative numbers of Israel and Egypt?

Of our three attested readings, Sam is the least attractive, since *rabbîm* lacks a clear antecedent within the sentence. And, again, why repeat that Israel outnumbers Egypt? We could elaborately derive Sam from MT as follows: *rbym 'th 'm h'rṣ > *rbym 'm h'rṣ* (homoioarkton) > **rbym m'm h'rṣ* (dittography) > *rbym 'th m'm h'rṣ* (partial correction to MT).

Most likely, then, either LXX or MT preserves the original reading. LXX is fairly attractive, for there is no obvious motivation for the omission of *h'rṣ* 'the land' in LXX, while one can imagine a proto-MT copyist expanding "the people" into "the land's people" (on the meaning, see NOTE). My translation nevertheless follows MT, since LXX is uncorroborated by Hebrew MSS.

you will interrupt. LXX reads "let *us* not interrupt them," either a paraphrase or reading *whšbtm* as **wəhišbattim* 'and shall *I* interrupt them?'

†5:6. *on that day.* The phrase is missing in LXX, whose shorter text might be original (Cross 1994: 95).

†5:7. *continue.* The form in the consonantal text (Kethibh), *t'spwn*, means "gather" and should be vocalized **te'espûn.* More likely to be original, however, is the received vocalization (Qere) **tōsîpûn* 'continue, add' (= Sam; Kenn 9, 17, 69, 80, 111, 132, 193; LXX; Tgs.). As for the extraneous 'aleph, either *'sp* is a genuine linguistic variant of *ysp* (cf. *'sp* = *ysp* in 1 Sam 18:29), or a scribe absentmindedly inserted 'aleph (subconsciously recalling that the Israelites had to *gather* [*'sp*] their straw?).

†*the bricks.* Sam has "bricks" (no article), perhaps correctly (contrast v 18).

day before. Some LXX witnesses add "and today," presumably borrowed from 5:14 (Wevers 1990: 62).

†*scrabble.* For MT *wqššw*, Sam has *wyqššw*, with the same meaning. Syr lacks the conjunction entirely, perhaps reading **yqššw*. Sequential waws and yodhs were as easily doubled as omitted by careless scribes, for in Herodian times, the letters were indistinguishable (Cross 1961a; Qimron 1972). That the previous word ends in waw makes the situation all the more precarious.

5:8. *yesterday and the day before.* For MT *təmôl šilšōm*, LXX has "each day." Either this is a paraphrase, or it reflects a variant Vorlage **dəbar-yôm bəyômô* 'a day's matter in its day' (= v 13). 4QExod^b supports MT, with the byform *'tmwl.*

†*lay . . . deduct.* These verbs are plural in MT, but singular in most LXX MSS, as if reading **tāśîm . . . tigra'.* Since the parallel v 19 uses the plural *tigrə'û,* and since in the prior verse *tō(')sîpûn* is plural in MT (but perhaps singular in LXX), the singular may be preferable in 5:8 as *lectio difficilior.*

do not deduct from it. LXX and 4QExod^b add "a whit" (*dābār*) (cf. v 11).

sacrifice. LXX and 4QGen-Exod^a have "*and* sacrifice," as do some witnesses to MT and the Tgs. (see Kennicott 1776–80: 114; de Rossi 1784–85: 50). Sam, Syr and most Tg. MSS agree with standard MT.

†5:9. *let them do it . . . deceit.* In MT (supported by Tg. Ps.-Jonathan; Vg), the verse contains distinct but punning verbs, *ya'ăśû* 'do' and *yiš'û* 'look' (Cassuto 1967: 68; Cross 1994: 95). If MT is original, the verbs have been leveled in the Versions. Sam, LXX and Syr read *yš'w* twice: "let them *look* to it [the work] and not look to words of deceit." Tgs. Onqelos and Neofiti I, on the other hand, probably read *y'św* twice: "let them *engage in* it and not engage in idle affairs." 4QExod^b, extant for only the first verb, supports Sam-LXX-Syr (*wyš'w*); 4QGen-Exod^a, extant for only the latter verb, supports MT (*y'św*). MT seems preferable on account of its variety, but Sam-LXX-Syr is possibly correct.

†5:10. *went out.* For MT *wyṣ'w* 'went out,' LXX has "harried them," as if reading **wy'ṣw.* Either could be original. On the one hand, *'wṣ* 'urge' (LXX) is a far less common root than *yṣ'* 'go out' (MT) (*lectio difficilior*). On the other hand, LXX may anticipate v 13, where we find *'wṣ* along with *nōgəśîm* 'overseers' and *'mr* 'say.'

The object "them" in LXX is probably an addition both for ease of translation and to match v 13. But the *Vorlage* may actually have read **wy'ṣwm* 'and
they urged them.' Since the next letter, nun, resembles mem in paleo-Hebrew
script, either haplography (*mn* > *m*) or dittography (*m* > *mn*) may have occurred.

†*said . . . saying*. Where MT is redundant (*wayyō['
]mərû . . . lē[']mōr*),
4QExod[b] and Sam read *wydbrw . . . l'm(w)r* 'they *spoke . . . saying*' (also Soncino Bible 1488). Either could be original.

†5:11. *go get*. By a likely reconstruction, 4QExod[b] reads *[lkw] wqḥw* '[go] *and
get*' (= Kenn 236). Haplography to generate MT (*ww* > *w*) and dittography to
generate 4QExod[b] (*w* > *ww*) are equally possible.

yourselves. Strangely, LXX has "*them*selves," presumably under the influence
of v 7.

straw. "Straw" is missing from Rossi 16, 592. Since it is unsupported in
other traditions, this short reading is probably the result of scribal error.

5:12. *scattered*. *Wayyāpeṣ* looks to be a Hiph'il, but the intransitive Hiph'il
of *pwṣ* is exampled only here, in 1 Sam 13:8 and perhaps in Job 38:24. Otherwise, *hēpîṣ* is transitive. (Ibn Ezra's solution, to make Pharaoh the subject [i.e.,
"he scattered Israel"] is unconvincing.) As all Versions render intransitively,
perhaps we should revocalize **wayyāpoṣ* (Qal) or **wayyippōṣ* (Niph'al).

land of. *'Ereṣ* is unrepresented in some LXX MSS.

†5:13. *urging*. LXX adds "them"; Sam adds *b'm* 'the people.' These are probably clarifying expansions, but O'Connell (n.d.) observes that LXX could conceivably represent **'ṣwm* (**'āṣûm*) 'they urged them' for MT *'ṣym* (waw-yodh
confusion). If so, Sam's meaningless *'ṣwym* conflates the two readings.

††*being given to you*. MT lacks the words *ntn lkm* (*nittān lākem*) 'being
given to you' that conclude the verse in Sam, LXX, Syr, Tg. Onqelos, Tg. Ps.-
Jonathan and, to judge from space requirements, 4QGen-Exod[a]. It is hard to
say whether this longer reading or MT's *lectio brevior et difficilior* is original.
"Being given to you" may be an explanatory plus derived from v 16. My translation, however, follows Sam etc., assuming that, because of the similarity of
n and *m* in paleo-Hebrew script, *ntn lkm* dropped from proto-MT by homoioteleuton after *htbn* 'the straw.'

5:14. *Israel's Sons*. LXX has "the people [*genos*] of Israel's Sons," i.e., **'am
bənê yiśrā'ēl*, as perhaps does 4QGen-Exod[a]. This longer reading presumably
derives from 1:9. Wevers (1990: 66), moreover, suggests that "people" was
inserted to stress the difference in ethnicity between the Egyptian overseers
(*nōgəśîm*) and the Israelite officers (*šōṭərîm*).

†*both yesterday*. These words are missing in LXX, present in other Versions.
This could be a classic haplography in either Greek (*kai . . . kai*) or Hebrew
(*gam . . . gam*). Or the words might have been purposely excised to relieve a
seeming contradiction: in MT, v 14 literally asserts that "yesterday" Israel's production was both adequate and inadequate. The difficulty is illusory, however,
as "yesterday and the day before" is a cliché for the past in general. Still, v 14
remains syntactically odd; see NOTE.

†5:15. *do so.* Syr translates, "Why is thus done," as if reading **tēʿāśe(h)* (vs. MT *taʿāśe[h]*). While this is possible, the masculine **yēʿāśe(h)* would be expected (GKC §144b).

††5:16. *your people is the fault.* Symmachus "you have fault" appears to read **wǝḥaṭṭā(ʾ)t ʿimmāk* 'fault is *with you*' for MT *wǝḥāṭā(ʾ)t ʿammekā* 'your people has sinned' (?) (see NOTE). I have vocalized the first word after Symmachus and the second after MT: **wǝḥaṭṭā(ʾ)t ʿammekā* 'the fault is your people (i.e., your people's; cf. GKC §141c, d).' Less attractive is LXX-Syr "you will wrong your people," presumably **wǝḥāṭā(ʾ)tā ʿammekā*. The object of *ḥṭ'* is always the sin committed, never the person wronged.

5:17. *said.* LXX adds "to them" to make explicit the change of speakers (Wevers 1990: 68). For the same reason, Syr has "*Pharaoh* said *to them*" (also some LXX MSS).

†*Lax . . . lax.* Though attested in all Versions, *nirpîm ʾattem nirpîm* may conflate two variants, *nirpîm ʾattem and **ʾattem nirpîm.

sacrifice. Kenn 1, 84, 129, 181, Rossi 11, 554, LXX^A and some Sam MSS have "*and* sacrifice."

Yahweh. LXX, Kenn 13, 181, Rossi 440, 503 and Tg. *Ps.-Jonathan* read instead "our deity"; Rossi 404 have "Yahweh our deity."

5:18. *go work.* Many Syr MSS have "go *and* work."

†*bricks.* It is tempting to follow Sam *hlbnym* 'the bricks,' which is what we would expect. But MT *lbnym* is *lectio difficilior* (contrast v 7).

give. While L reads the irregular *tittēnnû*, other MSS and editions have the expected *tittēnû*. One assumes that the punctator simply got carried away, since, apart from the nun, all the other letters contain points. (On extraneous daghesh, see also TEXTUAL NOTES to 2:3 and 15:17.)

†5:19. *saw them in trouble.* Because it is so awkward, I suspect the first half of v 19 is corrupt (see NOTE). A conjectural emendation might be **wayyir'û šōṭǝrê bǝnê-yiśrā'ēl bǝrā'ātām* 'And the officers of Israel's Sons saw their trouble'; cf. 2 Sam 16:8, *hinnǝkā bǝrā'āteka* 'see: you in your trouble.'

saying. To ease the difficulty (see NOTE), Syr paraphrases "and said *to them*."

†*deduct.* For MT *tigra'û*, Sam has *ygr'* (*yiggāra'*) 'let it not be deducted' (cf. *Samaritan Tgs.*), carrying over the passive construction from v 11 (*nigrā'*). Sam is supported by some LXX witnesses and Vg. Other LXX MSS, however, support MT, as do Syr and Tg. Onqelos. Either MT or Sam might be correct.

5:20. *stationed.* For MT *nṣbym* 'standing,' LXX has *erchomenois* 'coming,' apparently reflecting **yṣ'ym* 'going, going out,' a corruption born of graphic similarity to *nṣbym* and the presence of *bṣ'tm* 'in their going out' later in the verse.

†*Pharaoh.* Sam has *m't pny pr'h* 'from with Pharaoh's face [i.e., presence]' (cf. 10:11), probably an expansion. Not impossibly, however, MT *m't pr'h* is the product of haplography by homoioarkton (*pny pr'h* > *pr'h*).

5:21. *Yahweh.* LXX reflects **(h)'lhym* '(the) Deity.' This is probably an error caused by the presence of **'lhm* 'to them' previously in the verse.

†*look on*. MT *yēre'*. *Pace* Schmidt (1988: 244), Sam *yr'h* (= Kenn 9) is probably not a Niph'al, but a Qal imperfect (cf. *Samaritan Tg. yḥzy* 'he will see'). On the other hand, *Tg. Onqelos* "may the Lord reveal himself to you" does read a Niph'al *yērā'/yērā'e(h)* (cf. *Tg. Ps.-Jonathan*). This is a possible interpretation; see NOTE.

†*their hand*. Here we find great variety. MT has *yādām* 'their hand,' supported indirectly by Syr and *Tgs*. *Neofiti I* and *Onqelos* "their hands" (pluralized collective). Sam, however, reads *ydw* 'his hand' (cf. Vg "to him"). LXX "his hands" also reflects *ydw*, now interpreted as archaic *yādāw*. I would reject LXX, since in ancient depictions swords are gripped one-handed. But there is no basis for choosing between *ydm* 'their hand' (MT) and *ydw* 'his hand' (Sam).

5:22. *My Lordship*. LXX^B prefixes "please," as in 4:10, 13, etc., but other LXX MSS agree with MT. Many witnesses to MT replace *'ădōnāy* 'my Lordship' with *yahwe(h)* (Kennicott 1776–80: 115; de Rossi 1784–85: 50; cf. TEXTUAL NOTE to 15:17).

†*For what* (second time). Sam, LXX, Syr, *Tgs*. *Onqelos*, *Ps.-Jonathan* and *Neofiti I* and many exemplars of MT (Kennicott 1776–80: 115; de Rossi 1784–85: 50) read "*and* for what." Kenn 13, Rossi 174, 592 lack *zh* 'is it,' either lost by homoioteleuton after *lmh* or simply omitted as unnecessary.

6:1. *Now*. For MT, LXX and Syr *'attâ* 'now,' Sam reads *'attâ* 'you.' Confusion of *'aleph* and *'ayin* is common in the Qumran scrolls and in Northwest Semitic dialects generally about the turn of the era (Propp 1987c: 378 n. 12, 379 n. 18).

†*strong arm*. LXX and Syr, instead of the second "strong arm," read "outstretched limb" (**zərōa' nəṭûyâ*; cf. Deut 4:34; 5:15, etc.). This may well be the original text, but it remains unsubstantiated by any Hebrew MS.

SOURCE ANALYSIS

Many find in Exodus 5 two sources (e.g., McNeile 1908: 30–34; Gressmann 1913: 61–62; Fohrer 1964: 55–58; Thompson 1987: 139; for further bibliography, see Schmidt 1988: 237). The primary evidence is the redundancy of vv 4 and 5: "But Egypt's king said to them, 'Why, Moses and Aaron, should you distract the people from his work? Go to your tasks.' And Pharaoh said, 'See: the land's people are now many, and you will interrupt them from their tasks.'"

Moreover, one could argue that 5:1 and 3 are also doublets: "Thus has Yahweh Israel's deity said: 'Release my people, that they may celebrate to me in the wilderness.'. . . The Hebrews' deity happened upon us. We would go a three days' way into the wilderness and sacrifice to Yahweh our deity, lest he strike us with the plague or with the sword." Were these originally by the same author, we might expect Moses and Aaron to respond with "Yahweh is the Hebrews' god" to meet Pharaoh's objections. Instead, v 3 sounds like the opening of a new address.

When we attempt, however, to analyze the remainder of chap. 5, we soon realize that we cannot reconstruct two complete or nearly complete narratives.

Rather, 5:6–6:1 constitutes a seamless whole. Perhaps, then, we have been too quick to dissect vv 1–5.

In fact, vv 1, 3 are not true doublets. In v 1, Moses demands an unqualified release in Yahweh's name. In v 2, Pharaoh refuses, ostensibly since he does not recognize Yahweh. In v 3, Moses clarifies and mollifies his demands: Yahweh is the Hebrews' god, and the release sought is only a short jaunt from Egypt (cf. Greenberg 1969: 123). In fact, 5:1 and 3 together fulfill the commission to tell Pharaoh, "Yahweh the Hebrews' deity happened upon us; and now, we would go a three days' way into the wilderness and sacrifice to Yahweh our deity" (3:18). Similarly, Jacob (1992: 123) argues that vv 1 and 3 together anticipate 8:4: "I will release the people, that they may sacrifice to Yahweh."

Why, then, does v 3 sound so like the opening of an oration? Perhaps the intended effect is that Moses saves face with a fresh start, rather than answer Pharaoh directly. More important, this time Moses uses the very words Yahweh had given him (3:18), adding only the threat "lest he strike us with the plague or with the sword." However we understand the relation between 5:1 and 3, they are probably by one author.

We are left with vv 4 and 5, where the case for partition is strongest. Are these true doublets? Note, first, that the content is different; although the verses are interchangeable, they are not synonymous. In fact, were they reversed, we would not notice any redundancy at all. Pharaoh may simply be presenting his arguments out of logical order: he has many slaves (5:5a), whom Moses and Aaron are making idle (v 5b); therefore they should stop distracting the people (v 4a), and everyone should get to work (v 4b). At any rate, we find similar redundancy in Gen 15:2–3; 20:9–10; 37:21–22; 41:39–41; Exod 16:6–8. Considering each case in isolation, we might be tempted to regard the second clause as a doublet or scribal gloss. The ubiquity of the pattern requires a more general explanation, however (cf. Greenberg 1969: 123). Sometimes, it appears, a biblical writer, finding a phrase unsatisfactory, would supplement it with a second, clearer expression, rather than delete. By any analysis, the redundancy of vv 4, 5 is largely illusory and is not a valid source-critical criterion. The sequence "Egypt's king said . . . Pharaoh said" presents not the slightest problem. Examples of superfluous wayyō(')mer 'and he said' from Genesis alone are 1:29; 9:8, 12, 17; 17:9, 15; 18:20; 20:10; 21:7; 31:51; 35:11; 37:22; 41:41.

In short, all of Exodus 5 probably comes from one writer, most likely the Elohist. Pharaoh's ignorance of Yahweh comports with E's theory that God has so far concealed his name from all but Moses and Israel (cf. Dillmann 1880: 48). The presence of Aaron, too, is a sign of E (cf. 4:14–16, 27–31), and the šōṭərîm 'officers' reappear in Num 11:16 (E). Exod 6:1 is probably still Elohistic, since 11:1 (E) likewise refers to Israel's release (šlḥ) and expulsion (grš) from Egypt, while yād ḥăzāqâ 'strong arm' appears also in 3:19 (E). Moreover, in Num 11:23 (E), Yahweh again assuages Moses' doubts with 'attâ tir'e(h) 'now you will see.'

That chap. 5 is Yahwistic is not, however, impossible. In 3:19 (E by my analysis), Yahweh had already warned Moses that Pharaoh would not heed him.

Why should Moses be so upset in 5:22–23, unless chap. 5 is from another source, i.e., J? I do not find this argument compelling, however. Moses is displaying natural, spontaneous disappointment, whatever he knows intellectually of God's plan. Moreover, Yahweh had predicted only Pharaoh's intransigence. He had not mentioned an intensification of the oppression or the Hebrews' rejection of Moses.

A more substantive argument for the Yahwistic authorship of 5:1–6:1 is the resemblance between 5:5 ("See: the land's people are now many, and you will interrupt them from their tasks") and 1:9, 11 ("See: the people of Israel's Sons is greater and mightier than we. . . . So they set over him corvée masters in order to oppress him with their tasks"), which I have tentatively assigned to J. But E also records Israel's multiplication (1:20), and the similarity of 5:5 and 1:9, 11 is in any case slight.

One could also argue for Yahwistic authorship on the basis of vocabulary. The verb *lāban* 'brickmake,' with the cognate accusative *ləbēnîm* 'bricks' (5:7, 14), also appears in Gen 11:3 (J), and nowhere else in the entire Bible. For the Torah, *teben* 'straw' appears only in Exodus 5 and in Gen 24:25, 32 (J); *ś^ey* 'look (favorably)' only in Gen 4:4, 5 (J) and Exod 5:9; *'wṣ* 'urge' only in Exod 5:13 and Gen 19:15 (J). But these words are so rare in the Torah, and for the most part so common outside it, that I regard them as poor source indicators.

And one can also frame a lexical case for Elohistic authorship. The expression "yesterday and the day before" (5:7, 8, 14) appears in the Torah only in E (Gen 31:2, 5; Exod 4:10; 21:29, 36), although outside the Pentateuch it is common enough. More important, "the Hebrews' deity" (5:3) is paralleled in 3:18; 7:16; 9:1, 13; 10:3 — all Elohistic — and nowhere else in the Bible. I would also note the similarity of 5:23 to 4:10 (E), both featuring *mē'āz* 'ever since' followed by a complaint.

Finally: the theme of Israelites seeking liberty to worship Yahweh in a pilgrimage, only to be rebuffed by their sovereign, recalls somewhat the circumstances surrounding the secession of Northern Israel. In 1 Kings 12, the Northerners demand relief from their corvée duties, but King Rehoboam rejects their suit. The people withdraw and, at some later point, hold a pilgrim festival. Thus Exodus 5 suits well E's Northern patriotism (see Friedman 1987: 61–87; Coote 1991; COMMENT to chap. 32).

REDACTION ANALYSIS

The Elohist's story of Moses' childhood, if it ever existed, is lost. In J, however, Moses is raised as an Egyptian. For JE and JEP, then, Pharaoh's seeming unacquaintance with Moses is striking. If Moses was raised in the court of the preceding ruler, the king should regard him as a sort of foster nephew (O'Connell n.d.). Is Moses changed beyond recognition (cf. Gen 42:8)? In any case, Moses has fully shed his Egyptian persona. Now Pharaoh considers him just another presumptuous slave (5:4 [E] by one reading).

NOTES

5:1. *Moses and Aaron.* Where are the tribal elders who were supposed to come along (3:18)? According to *Exod. Rab.* 5:13, they indeed set out for the palace but fell back one by one on the way, so that Moses and Aaron arrived alone. For further discussion, see COMMENT.

Thus has Yahweh . . . said. Even if Pharaoh does not recognize it, this is the formulaic opening of a prophetic oracle. Moses apparently expects the divine name to impress Pharaoh, as it did the Hebrews (3:13–15) (Jacob 1992: 155–56).

Release my people. This command, along with the call for a wilderness celebration, will resound throughout the Plagues narrative—a total of seven times (5:1; 7:16, 26; 8:16; 9:1, 13; 10:3) (cf. Leibowitz 1976: 232).

According to 4:23, at this point, Moses is supposed to threaten Pharaoh's firstborn with death. But he does not do so until 11:4–6. The delay frames the entire Plagues cycle and allows Pharaoh to exhibit his cruelty, fully justifying Yahweh's vengeance. (On Moses' noncompliance with Yahweh's commands, see COMMENT.)

celebrate. Wəyāḥōggû might also be rendered "that they may make a pilgrimage." See NOTES on 3:18 "sacrifice," 12:14 "festival."

5:2. *Israel.* This is the last time Pharaoh will use the people's proper name until their release (12:31). Meanwhile, the king always calls them "the people" (5:4, 7; 8:4), "the men" (5:9) or "you" (8:24; 9:28; 10:10). This may be read as a refusal to recognize Israel's national legitimacy (cf. Jacob 1992: 121).

I have not known. Comparing Deut 11:28 ("other gods you have not known"), Luzzatto observes, "Even if he had in fact heard his name, he still said, 'I have not known him,' as if to say, 'I do not acknowledge his divinity.'" Exod 5:2 (E) somewhat recalls 1:8 (J?), where a previous Pharaoh did not "know" Joseph (Tanḥuma šəmôt 5; Ackerman 1974: 79). The cumulative import: the Egyptian monarchy is oblivious to Israelite history and religion.

In fact, the biblical author has probably cast Pharaoh in his own intolerant image. A true Egyptian (excepting Akhenaten and his circle) would not spurn foreign gods or their messengers. The Egyptians adopted many Asiatic deities (Helck 1971: 446–73), and the traveler Wen-Amon respected Asiatic prophets (*ANET* 26).

Apropos of Pharaoh's parallelistic "Who is Yahweh, that I should heed his voice by releasing Israel?/ I have not known Yahweh; moreover, Israel I will not release," D. N. Freedman (privately) suggests, "The upper classes in the Bible speak more elegantly, just as they do in Shakespeare; and since in the Bible they are often also the more wicked people, there may be a certain opprobrium attached to elegant speech" (see also NOTES to 1:10 and 5:18).

Pharaoh will come to rue his hauteur, whereby, as it were, he calls down the Plagues upon his own head. Knowledge of Yahweh becomes the *Leitmotif* of the Plagues narrative: God repeatedly afflicts Pharaoh and his people so that they may "know" Israel's god (7:5, 17; 8:6, 18; 9:14, 29; 10:2; 11:7; 14:4, 18)

(Fretheim 1991a: 86). Pharaoh will explicitly acknowledge Yahweh's power in 8:4, 24; 9:27–28; 10:17 (Blum 1990: 14).

moreover. In context, the particle *gam* may convey more than the usual "in addition." It might be an emphatic explicative "therefore, of course." Sforno paraphrases, "Even if I were convinced of Yahweh's existence, I still would not release Israel."

5:3. *The Hebrews' deity.* Moses and Aaron now amend their mistaken assumption that Pharaoh would recognize the names "Yahweh" and "Israel." Moses makes no universal or monotheistic claims for his god; Yahweh is merely "the Hebrews' deity." (The Midrash remedies this modesty; cf., e.g., *Exod. Rab.* 5:14.)

happened upon. The diction conveys the happenstance aspect of the encounter at the bush. The spelling is slightly unusual—*nqr'* for expected *nqrh* (cf. TEXTUAL NOTE to 3:18). On the one hand, III-' and III-*y* alloform roots are common in Hebrew, especially with this stem (see BDB 896–97); e.g., the preposition "toward" (< *qry*) is spelled *lqr't* throughout the Bible, but *lqrt* in the Siloam inscription (*AHI* 4.116.4). On the other hand, the orthography may also imply a pun. Since *nqr'* is properly the passive of *qr'* 'to call,' one might paraphrase: "(the name of) the Hebrews' deity *is called* upon us" (so *Tg. Ps.-Jonathan*; compare Num 6:27; Deut 28:10; 1 Kgs 8:43; Isa 43:7; 63:19; 65:1; Jer 7:10, 11, 14, 30; 14:9; 15:16; 25:29; 32:34; 34:15; Amos 9:12; Dan 9:18, 19) (cf. Rosenmüller *apud* Luzzatto on 3:18).

lest he strike us. We might have expected "lest he strike *you*," which is what actually happens (cf. Rashi). Instead, Moses and Aaron appeal to Pharaoh's interest as a slave owner (Bekhor Shor; Meyer 1983: 6). And they may be hinting that Yahweh is dangerously arbitrary. If Israel would suffer for failing to worship God, not by their own fault, how much more might Pharaoh suffer!

Greenberg (1969: 128 n. 1) detects the irony between 5:3 and vv 20–21. Moses threatens that Yahweh will *pg'* 'strike' Israel with the sword. Instead, Moses' own people *pg'* 'encounter/reproach' him with the metaphorical "sword" he has given the Egyptians.

the plague or . . . the sword. Which might threaten not just the Hebrews but the Egyptians themselves (Luzzatto). Notice the assonance of "plague" and "sword," whether in Massoretic pronunciation (*deber, ḥāreb*) or in reconstructed Israelite (**dabr, ḥarb*). In fact, *baddeber 'ô baḥāreb* sounds like a proverb or cliché.

5:4. *distract.* The tense is simultaneously present and future: "you are distracting and will continue to distract." Assuming MT is correct (see TEXTUAL NOTE), the root *pr'* puns with the king's own title *par'ō(h)* (Schmidt 1988: 243). O'Connell (n.d.) suggests that Pharaoh may paronomastically accuse Moses and Aaron of usurping his own authority.

the people. To the extent that Pharaoh accuses Moses and Aaron of distracting the people in the present (see previous NOTE), and assuming the elders are in attendance (see COMMENT), "the people" may be the tribal leaders, interrupted in their labors due to Moses' mission (cf. Luzzatto). But more likely, the reference is to all Israel.

tasks. Here and in the next verse, an alternative translation of *səbālōt* is "labor gangs"; see NOTE to 1:11.

5:5. *said.* While this is conceivably a silent comment, Syr adds "to them," as in the previous verse.

land's people. The sense of *ʿam hā'āreṣ* is unclear and depends upon which Version one follows. The phrase is entirely absent from LXX (see TEXTUAL NOTE).

In non-Israelite contexts, *ʿam hā'āreṣ* usually connotes natives, as one might expect (Schmidt 1988: 243). This is clearly the import of Sam: the "land's people," whom Israel outnumbers, must be Egyptians. What MT might mean by *ʿam hā'āreṣ* is less clear. If the "land's people" are Egyptians, then either (a) Pharaoh is calling the Hebrews Egyptians, so to speak, to assert his authority over them or (b) he is not referring to Israel at all, but rather to his own people, whose labors are also being impeded.

And there is another possibility. If the opinion of many scholars is correct, that "land's people" later connotes an aristocratic social stratum, then Pharaoh might be referring anachronistically to the Hebrews' elders as landed magnates (on *ʿam hā'āreṣ*, see Daiches 1921, 1929; de Vaux 1961: 70–74; Talmon 1986: 68–78). In that case, having commented upon Israel's great population (v 5), Pharaoh says to Moses and Aaron, "Their leaders alone constitute a large group, and, look, you have caused them to be idle. Go, you leaders, to your tasks!" (cf. Daiches 1921). But it is uncertain that the elders are present at all; see COMMENT.

you will interrupt. In the Yavneh Yam Ostracon (*AHI* 7.001.5), the root *šbt* may similarly connote cessation of forced labor, although the text is susceptible to other interpretations (Talmon 1986: 82). *Hišbattem* in any case evokes the day called *šabbāt* 'cessation, Sabbath' (Janzen 1989: 398). Moses and Yahweh will not only bring Israel's servitude to an end; they will cause Israel to rest once a week forever, in commemoration of their ancient liberation (Deut 5:15).

5:6. *on that day.* Unlike LXX (see TEXTUAL NOTE), MT emphasizes that Israel's increased affliction is due directly to Moses and Aaron's intervention (Cassuto 1967: 68).

overseeing. The *nōgəśîm* are Egyptians, as opposed to the Israelite *šōṭərîm* 'officers' (but see next NOTE).

his officers. While "his" probably refers to collective Israel, Jacob (1992: 132–35) argues that "his officers" in vv 6, 10 are *Pharaoh's* Egyptian henchmen. Only v 14 refers to Hebrew *šōṭərîm*.

Šōṭēr derives from *šṭr* 'write'; hence, both LXX and Syr call the *šōṭərîm* "scribes." But the officers' authority is broader than the etymology would suggest (Weinfeld 1977b). Van der Ploeg (1954: 196) distinguishes between *šōṭərîm* and mere *sōpərîm* 'scribes.' The officers reappear in Num 11:16 (E) as a subgroup of elders, while Deuteronomy and Joshua often link *šōṭərîm* with elders, heads, judges and rulers (Deut 1:15–16; 16:18; 29:9; 31:28; Josh 1:10; 3:2; 8:33; 23:2; 24:1) (cf. Weinfeld). In our passage, too, it seems that the officers are elders.

5:7. *straw . . . bricks*. For a detailed study of Egyptian brick architecture, see Spencer (1979); for New Kingdom representations of brickmaking, see *ANEP* 35 (no. 115); Ball (1899: 111–12). Particularly evocative of Exodus is a New Kingdom text complaining of a lack of sufficient personnel and straw for brick-making (Pap. Anastasi 4.12.5) (Redford 1992: 206). Nims (1950: 26–27) gives the following description of brickmaking in pre-industrial modern Egypt, which manifestly perpetuates ancient technology:

A patch of ground roughly three to four meters on a side is dug up to the depth of twenty five to thirty centimeters, the alluvium being broken up into small pieces. The proper amount of *tibn* ['straw'] is scattered on top and water let into the area from canals dug for the purpose. The alluvium, *tibn* and water are thoroughly mixed together and allowed to stand for two or three days, until the mass becomes easily workable. The mud is carried on a round woven mat made of strips of palm leaf, having handles on opposite sides, and is placed where it is convenient for the brick maker to reach it with the minimum of effort. There are usually two carriers and two brick makers working from one trough of mix, and the mud paste is piled in a long heap between the two makers in the amount they will use as they work down the brick yard.

The brick maker dips his hands in a jar of water, takes mud for a single brick, the amount of which he has learned by experience, dips one hand in the water again and wets the outside of the lump, and pushes it into the mold which is resting on the ground. The area has been dusted with fine dry mud and fine chaff to prevent sticking to the ground. When the bricks are to be used for vaulting, the top is scored with two or three fingers to give a good key. The ancient bricks in the vaults about the temple of Ramses II, which were larger than the modern ones, were scored with all the fingers of the hand.

One brick having been molded, the mold is removed, placed at its side, and another brick struck. Thus, as the workman progresses he covers the area with bricks, spaced the thickness of the mold apart. The brick maker is a skilled craftsman and receives a higher wage as such. The brick maker and his helper turn out two to three thousand brick [*sic*] in the usual seven to eight hour day.

The bricks are left in position for two or three days, then turned on side and end for three consecutive days to insure thorough drying. They are then loosely piled and cured for a minimum of ten to fifteen days, and usually for a month or more.

yesterday and the day before. The Canaanite cliché *təmôl šilšōm* (*tumāl šal-šāmi*) first appears in a cuneiform letter from fourteenth-century Byblos (EA 362.14; see Rainey 1978: 18).

scrabble. The verbal root *qšš* is derived from *qaš* 'stubble, straw' and properly denotes the gathering of straw.

5:8. *from it*. Although *matkōnet* 'volume' is feminine, *mimmennû* has a masculine suffix, doubtless because of the wide separation from its antecedent and the general predominance of the masculine in Hebrew (cf. Holzinger 1900: 18).

5:9. *deceit*. Šeqer connotes lying in general and false prophecy in particular (Isa 9:14; Jer 5:31; 14:14; 20:6; 23:25–26; 27:10, 14, 15, 16; 29:9, 21; Hab 2:18; Zech 10:2) (Fuss 1972: 110).

5:10. *Thus has Pharaoh said*. While *kō(h) 'āmar* is a ubiquitous message formula, in this context, it ironically echoes the prophetic cliché *kō(h) 'āmar yahwe(h)* 'thus has Yahweh . . . said' (5:1) (Fretheim 1991a: 86).

5:12. *scattered*. The verb *pwṣ* was perhaps chosen to chime with *qaš* 'straw, chaff'; cf. Jer 13:24, *'ăpîṣēm kəqaš* 'I will scatter them like chaff.'

stubble for the straw. Although *qaš* and *teben* may denote the same substance, the words bear different connotations. *Teben* is straw used for brickmaking or cattle fodder (Gen 24:25, 32; Judg 19:19; 1 Kgs 5:8; Isa 11:7; 65:25). When straw is described as particularly inflammable, however, it is called *qaš* (15:7; Isa 5:24; 33:11; 47:14; Joel 2:5; Obad 18; Nah 1:10; Mal 3:19). Like *mōṣ* 'chaff,' *qaš* is quintessentially lightweight, easily blown (Isa 40:24; 41:2; Jer 13:24; Ps 83:14; *teben*, too, is windblown in Job 21:18). In Exodus 5, the Israelites must forage like starving cattle, traversing all Egypt to amass enough *qaš* to use as *teben*.

5:13. *a day's matter in its day*. Both here and in v 19, *dəbar-yôm bəyômô* seems to connote a daily quota. Syr, however, renders "as ordinarily."

just as when. In MT, v 13 ends "just as when the straw was," probably the overseers' words or, less likely, the narrator's (Luzzatto). But for the variant adopted here, "just as when the straw *was being* given to you," the speakers must be the overseers. To Luzzatto's question—why should they flaunt their own cruelty?—sheer sadism seems a sufficient answer.

5:14. *saying*. Lē(')mōr refers to the Egyptian overseers, not the Israelite officers (Rashi). It is as if the sentence read, "Pharaoh's overseers beat the officers whom they had placed over them, saying. . . ."

both yesterday and today. As observed under TEXTUAL NOTES, LXX omits "both yesterday," probably by homoioarkton. But MT itself is slightly awkward by the usual interpretation. Conceivably, *gam . . . gam* 'both . . . and' expresses coordination. That is, *gam-təmôl gam-hayyôm* might be an elliptical command: "As (you did) yesterday, so (do) today!"

5:15. *your slaves*. There is a nice ambiguity in *'ăbāde(y)kā*. The Hebrews are true slaves. But all subjects are a king's slaves, especially his inner circle of nobles (e.g., 7:20, 29, etc.). Thus, to style oneself the king's slave, though in one sense abject, is also to claim a relation of intimacy and mutual dependence. Jacob (1992: 136) observes that Moses, in contrast to the Hebrew officers, never uses this humiliating form of address before Pharaoh. Moses is rather *God's slave* (4:10, etc.).

5:16. *your people is the fault*. Or "your personnel are the problem," taking *ḥāṭā(')t* as equivalent to the noun *ḥaṭṭā(')t*. Many, however, understand *ḥāṭā(')t* as a verb, "your people *have sinned*" (for bibliography, see Schmidt 1988: 244). The problem is that *ḥāṭā(ʾ)t* would be a feminine verb (see GKC §74g), while *ʿam* 'people' is almost always masculine (exceptions are Judg 18:7 and possibly Jer 8:5). Other vocalizations of *wḥṭʾt ʿmk* also yield acceptable interpretations (see TEXTUAL NOTE). By any analysis, the basic point appears to be "we officers are beaten as if guilty, whereas in fact others are to blame."

> SPECULATION: To judge from Gen 31:39 (*ʾăḥaṭṭennâ miyyādî*), the Piʿel of *ḥṭʾ/ḥṭy* might connote reparation, or bearing a financial loss. Perhaps the officers in 5:16 are saying, "the harm is your people's," or "your people is paying the cost."

5:18. *go work.* Greenberg (1969: 128) catches the irony: Pharaoh will eventually utter the same words *ləkû ʿibdû* in the sense "Go worship [Yahweh]" (10:8, 24; 12:31). The point of contention is whom Israel will *ʿbd* 'serve/worship': Yahweh or Pharaoh?

straw . . . give. Pharaoh's words are noteworthy for assonance, i.e., the repetition of *n* and *t* (and, to a lesser degree, bilabial *b/m*): *wəṭeben lō(ʾ) yinnātēn lākem wəṭōken ləbēnîm tittēn(n)û* (see TEXTUAL NOTE). It was presumably to heighten the effect that the Elohist used *tōken* 'volume,' rather than *matkōnet* 'volume' (v 8) or *ḥōq* 'quota' (v 14). On Pharaoh's elegant speech, see also NOTES to 1:10 and 5:2.

5:19. *saw them in trouble.* The text is difficult, perhaps corrupt (see TEXTUAL NOTE). LXX, ibn Ezra, Cassuto (1967: 72) and Waltke and O'Connor (1990: 305 [§16.4g]) take *ʾōtām* 'them' as "(the officers) themselves," a rare usage paralleled in Jer 7:19; Ezek 34:2, 8, 10. Rashi and Calvin, however, see "them" as all Israel. Either way, the syntax feels un-Hebraic; see TEXTUAL NOTE for a conjectural emendation.

Another approach would be to consider *rāʾâ bərāʿ* a unique idiom meaning "look with malevolence." This would suit the context excellently: the Israelite officers *glared* at the Egyptian overseers.

saying. If "them" refers to Pharaoh's henchmen, the sense is "since they said to them" (Schmidt 1988: 244); cf. v 14. But if the speakers are the officers or the Hebrews in general, "saying" might mean either "since they had to say" (Durham 1987: 67) or "since they were told" (Vg; O'Connell n.d.).

5:20. *encountered.* *Pgʿ* can also mean "rebuke" and even "strike, attack." On the reference to 5:3, see NOTE.

5:21. *May Yahweh look.* Evidently, the people's faith in Yahweh is not diminished, only their faith in Moses (cf. 14:10–12). Perhaps, as Blum (1990: 13) suggests, these words contain ironic skepticism, especially if we read after *Tg. Onqelos* (see TEXTUAL NOTE): "May Yahweh *really* appear to you who have illegitimately spoken in his name."

you . . . who. We could alternatively take *ʾăšer*, ordinarily the relative pronoun, as a conjunction: "*inasmuch as* you have fouled our odor . . ." (cf. Seidl 1991).

odor in Pharaoh's eyes. A mixed but expressive image.

sword. A metaphor for "pretext."

5:22. *returned.* This means that Moses literally went somewhere else (Rashbam). Greenberg (1969: 125) notes that Moses will commune with Yahweh outside the city during the subsequent negotiations with Pharaoh (9:29; cf. 8:8, 25–26). Jacob (1992: 138) even supposes that Moses goes all the way back to Horeb, but this seems extreme; Balaam withdraws only a short distance from Balak to meet Yahweh (Num 23:3–6, 15–17). However great or small the separation, the image is that of a messenger shuttling between negotiating sovereigns (cf. NOTE to 4:22). There may also be an implication that solitude is conducive to prophetic inspiration.

5:23. *in your name.* On one level, this means "as your representative." But it also recalls Moses' vain attempt to impress Pharaoh with the name "Yahweh" (5:1).

it has gone badly. Syr, *Tg. Ps.-Jonathan* and Childs (1974: 92) render *hēra*ʿ impersonally, as do I. In contrast, LXX, *Tg. Onqelos*, Rashi and most modern translators render, "*he* has done badly," to parallel "you have done badly" (v 21). Either is possible.

this people. Compare Jonah's complaint (Jonah 4). Like Jonah, Moses gripes that Yahweh has wasted his servant's time and effort. But his primary concern is not for himself, but for his people.

6:1. *Now.* In many languages, thanks to invincible procrastination, "now" acquires the secondary meaning "soon" (cf. English "presently," etc.).

For. Although this is the most likely translation of *kî,* "that" is also possible (Ehrlich 1969: 282).

strong arm. Whose is this mighty limb? If Yahweh's, then "by a strong arm" might mean "compelled by wonders" or "accompanied by wonders" (cf. Rashi). But this seems a little forced. Rashbam's reading is more plausible: *Pharaoh* will forcibly expel Israel; cf. 12:33, "So Egypt *grew strong* (*wattehĕzaq*) toward the people, hastening to release them from the land." (Exod 3:19, too, may refer to Pharaoh's "strong arm"; see NOTE.) If so, Israel's liberation is accomplished by the "strong arms" of both Pharaoh and Yahweh.

expel. Luzzatto paraphrases, "Through my strong arm he will release them, and through my strong arm he will not just release them, but expel them from his land." In light of Israel's later regrets and recriminations (14:11–12; 17:3, etc.), the implication may be that they will leave whether they wish to or not (Bekhor Shor).

COMMENT

MOSES' NEGLIGENCE

Exodus 4 ended with a situation rare in the Torah: Israel, Moses and Yahweh in harmony (cf. also 14:31). The narrative rests there but for a moment.

In Exodus 5, things immediately go wrong. Perhaps the cause is Moses' inattention to his instructions. He had been told to bring the elders before Pharaoh; to say, "Yahweh the Hebrews' deity happened upon us . . . we would go a three days' way into the wilderness and sacrifice to Yahweh our deity"; to work wonders before the king, and to threaten Pharaoh's firstborn. Yahweh also predicts the king's intransigence (3:18–19; 4:21–23).

Moses seems to forget all this. First, he probably does not lead the elders to the king (see below, however). Second, he initially demands more than Yahweh had commanded, without considering that Pharaoh may never have even heard of Yahweh. Third, he works no wonders, missing an opportunity to impress the king. Fourth, he does not deliver the threat against Pharaoh's firstborn. Indeed, Moses does not fully execute his office until 11:4–6, when, after working wondrous Plagues against Egypt, he finally transmits God's words from 4:22–23. Finally, although Moses' dejection at the end of the chapter is understandable, Yahweh had forewarned him (see SOURCE ANALYSIS).

When biblical narratives feature minor divergences between command and fulfillment, sometimes we must regard the versions as completing, not contradicting, one another. Thus it is not quite certain that the elders are absent; their presence might be implicit in the verb "(they) came" (5:1) (Jacob 1992: 112–13; Van Seters 1994: 74). Aaron, on the other hand, needs explicit mention, because he was appointed Moses' interpreter only to the people, not to the king (4:16; cf. Cassuto 1967: 65). By this reading, the idle "people" Pharaoh mentions may be the elders standing before him, not all Israel (see discussion in Leibowitz 1976: 85–86). The words "go to your tasks" would then be addressed to them, not to Moses and Aaron, who are not otherwise described as slaves (Luzzatto; Jacob 1992: 130; Blum 1990: 28 n. 95; cf. the tradition of *Exod. Rab.* 5:16 that the tribe of Levi was exempt from servitude). Nevertheless, I do not believe the elders to be present in 5:1. There are four clear cases of Moses forgetting his commands, so why not a fifth? By my reading, Exodus 5 continues the theme of Moses' lack of faith from chaps. 3–4.

SPECULATION: Fretheim agrees that the elders are absent, but he plausibly suggests that the cause is not Moses' absence of mind. Rather, "Aaron replaces the elders. . . . When Moses continues to object to the divine commission [4:10, 13], *God adjusts to new developments* and appoints Aaron to stand with him" (Fretheim 1991a: 66). If so, Yahweh's original plan has been thwarted by Moses' hesitancy. Although the elders were supposed to obey Moses, Yahweh's servant, and help Moses deliver Israel, instead they obey the overseers, Pharaoh's servants, and help the king oppress Israel.

Yahweh's words "you will come, you and Israel's elders, to Egypt's king" (3:18) are in a sense fulfilled. Moses and the elders do confront Pharaoh. But they do so separately (5:15), and to no good effect. (Noth's [1972: 156–88] claim that the elders were the original protagonists in the Exodus account, later displaced by Moses and Aaron, cannot be substantiated.)

DIVIDE AND CONQUER

Although Yahweh had meant them to work in concert, by the end of Exodus 5, the tribal leaders are estranged from Moses and Aaron. The elders berate the self-proclaimed liberators, "May Yahweh look on you and judge, who have fouled our odor in Pharaoh's eyes and in his slaves' eyes, placing a sword in their hand to kill us."

The division in the Hebrew ranks is the triumph of Pharaoh's policy. By making Israel's servitude even harsher, the king impugns Moses' claim to a divine charter, magic tricks notwithstanding. With consummate cunning, he appoints the Hebrews' own clan leaders to mediate Egyptian control, both strengthening and undermining their position. Although they wield authority over Israel and can intercede on the people's behalf (vv 15–16), the Hebrew officers are also collaborators, subservient to Pharaoh's overseers and subject themselves to corporal punishment. The officers also undercut Moses' efforts by seeking, not a liberation, but mere relief from the increased workload. As a result, the officers and the people resent one another, and all blame Moses and Aaron (cf. Pixley 1987: 32; Fretheim 1991a: 83–85). Moses in turn reproaches Yahweh (5:22–23). Thus, while Pharaoh will later appear stupid, he is initially portrayed as a ruthless and effective strike-buster.

Admittedly, one might think that Exodus 5 already depicts the king as a fool, hampering his own slaves' efficiency. But in real life, a self-interested employer might well temporarily oppress his laborers, to discredit agitators and intimidate the rest, planning eventually to relent and restore productivity. We are not told Pharaoh's long-range program, but what we see of his behavior cannot be called stupid. Rather, he is "a no-nonsense ruler, completely sure of himself, whose time is being wasted. . . . [Moses and Aaron] are outclassed and overwhelmed by this Pharaoh" (Durham 1987: 64). Even his language bespeaks his cultural superiority to Moses and Aaron (see NOTE to v 2).

The Torah is not an eyewitness account, nor even a chronicle based upon eyewitness accounts, but an imaginative reconstruction of the past (Halpern 1988; see APPENDIX B, vol. II). The verisimilitude of Exodus 5 may reflect less what really happened in Egypt, and more the Elohist's own experience (or that of his sources) with politics and labor-management relations. As a Northern patriot, he may have particularly recalled Solomon's and Rehoboam's onerous corvée, which led to Northern Israel's secession (1 Kings 12). Like Pharaoh, Rehoboam thought he could cow his workers. Like Pharaoh, he ultimately lost them (cf. Crüsemann 1978: 175–76, 180).

A TEMPORARY SETBACK

Whereas chap. 4 ended in hope, 5:1–6:1 concludes in debacle. Moses has lost his credibility and finds himself in his old plight: as a non-elder, he lacks legitimacy before Pharaoh and his own people. Moses must return to Yahweh in order to begin again, armed with fresh wonders.

Despite the recurrent setbacks of chaps. 5–14, we never doubt that Pharaoh's intransigence will eventually crumble. Yahweh will even repay the monarch in his own coin. As Pharaoh makes Israel suffer on account of Moses and Aaron, alienating the Hebrews from their leaders, so Yahweh will make all Egypt suffer for Pharaoh's stubbornness, dividing the king from his people (9:20; 10:7; 11:3, 8; 12:33).

IX. *I am Yahweh* (6:2–7:7)

6 [2(P)]And Deity spoke to Moses and said to him, "I am Yahweh. [3]Now, I appeared to Abraham, to Isaac and to Jacob in God Shadday, but I, my name Yahweh, was not known to them. [4]And I both made stand my covenant with them to give them the land of Canaan, the land of their sojournings in which they sojourned; [5]and I also have heard the groan of Israel's Sons, because the Egyptians are making them work, and I have remembered my covenant. [6]Therefore, say to Israel's Sons: 'I am Yahweh. And I will take you out from under Egypt's burdens. And I will rescue you from their work. And I will redeem you with an extended limb and with great judgments. [7]And I will take you to me as a people, and I will become to you as a deity. And you will know that I am Yahweh your deity, who takes you out from under Egypt's burdens. [8]And I will bring you to the land that I raised my arm to give it to Abraham, to Isaac and to Jacob, and I will give it to you as an inheritance. I am Yahweh.'" [9]And Moses spoke so to Israel's Sons. But they did not heed Moses, from shortness of spirit and from hard work [10]Then Yahweh spoke to Moses, saying, [11]"Come, speak to Pharaoh Egypt's king, so that he will release Israel's Sons from his land." [12]But Moses spoke before Yahweh, saying, "If Israel's Sons have not heeded me, then how will Pharaoh heed me, as I am uncircumcised of lips?" [13(R)]And Yahweh spoke to Moses and to Aaron and commanded them to Israel's Sons and to Pharaoh Egypt's king, to take Israel's Sons from the land of Egypt.

[14]These are the heads of their fathers' house. The sons of Reuben Israel's firstborn: Hanoch and Pallu, Hezron and Carmi; these are Reuben's families. [15]And Simeon's sons: Jemuel and Jamin and Ohad and Jachin and Zohar and Shaul the Canaanitess's son; these are Simeon's families. [16]And these are the names of Levi's sons in their generations: Gershon and Kohath and Merari; and the years of Levi's life: seven and thirty and one hundred year. [17]Gershon's sons: Libni and Shimei in their families. [18]And Kohath's sons: Amram and Yizhar and Hebron and Uzziel; and the years of Kohath's life: three and thirty and one hundred year. [19]And Merari's sons: Mahli and Mushi. These are the Levite's families in their generations. [20]And Amram took Jochebed his aunt as a *woman* for him, and she bore him

Aaron and Moses; and the years of Amram's life: six and thirty and one hundred year. [21]And Yizhar's sons: Korah and Nepheg and Zichri. [22]And Uzziel's sons: Mishael and Elizaphan and Sithri. [23]And Aaron took Elisheba Amminadab's daughter, Nahshon's sister, as a *woman* for him, and she bore him Nadab and Abihu, Eleazar and Ithamar. [24]And Korah's sons: Assir and Elkanah and Abiasaph. These are the Korahite's families. [25]And Eleazar Aaron's son took for himself (one) of Putiel's daughters as a *woman* for him, and she bore him Phinehas. These are the heads of the Levites' fathers in their families. [26]That is Aaron and Moses to whom Yahweh said, "Take Israel's Sons out from the land of Egypt by their brigades." [27]They are the speakers to Pharaoh Egypt's king to take Israel's Sons out from Egypt; that is Moses and Aaron.

[28]And it happened, on the day Yahweh spoke to Moses in the land of Egypt, [29]and Yahweh spoke to Moses, saying, "I am Yahweh. Speak to Pharaoh Egypt's king all that I speak to you."

[30]But Moses said before Yahweh, "As I am uncircumcised of lips, then how will Pharaoh heed me?"

7 [1(P)]And Yahweh said to Moses, "See, I have made you a deity to Pharaoh, and Aaron your brother will be your prophet. [2]You, you will speak all that I command you, and Aaron your brother will speak to Pharaoh, that he should release Israel's Sons from his land. [3]But I, I will harden Pharaoh's heart and multiply my signs and my wonders in the land of Egypt. [4]And Pharaoh will not listen to you, and I will lay my arm upon Egypt and take out my brigades, my people, Israel's Sons, from the land of Egypt with great judgments. [5]And Egypt will know that I am Yahweh, in my extending my arm over Egypt. And I will take out Israel's Sons from their midst."

[6]And Moses and Aaron did, as Yahweh commanded them, so they did. [7]And Moses was a *son of* eighty years, and Aaron was a *son of* three and eighty years, in their speaking to Pharaoh.

ANALYSIS

TEXTUAL NOTES

†6:2. *Deity.* So MT. Sam, Rossi 476, 592, Vg and *Tgs. Onqelos* and *Ps.-Jonathan* read "Yahweh." LXX supports MT, while Syr MSS are mixed (cf. Wevers 1990: 72). Rossi 262 even has both names. We expect P to use "Deity" here (see INTRODUCTION, p. 50), although, in light of Gen 17:1, "Yahweh" is not inconceivable.

†6:3. *to Isaac.* Sam, LXX and Syr read "*and* to Isaac."

I, my name Yahweh, was not known to them. The rendering of LXX, Syr and *Tg. Onqelos*, "I did not *make known* my name (Syr and *Fragmentary Targum*: 'the name of') Yahweh to them," either is a paraphrase or else reads *ḫôdaʿtî* for MT *nôda'tî*. (*Tg. Ps.-Jonathan*, though periphrastic, supports the Niph'al of MT.) MT is by far preferable as *lectio difficilior* (see NOTE).

6:5. *heard*. Some LXX MSS read "seen," as in 3:7, 9.

groan. For MT *n'qt*, Sam has *nq't*—a simple misspelling of a rare word.

my covenant. LXX paraphrases: "I have remembered *your* covenant."

6:6. *Therefore*. For MT *lākēn*, LXX *badize* 'go' seems to read a form of *hlk*: *lēk, *ləkâ or possibly **lēk-nā'* (but contrast LXX Gen 27:9; 37:14). The sequence *lākēn 'ĕmōr* 'therefore, say' is characteristic of P and Ezekiel and should be retained (cf. Num 25:12; Ezek 11:16, 17; 12:23, 28; 14:6; 20:30; 33:25; 36:22).

Sons. LXX adds "saying."

Yahweh. Syr MSS add "the/your Deity."

extended limb. Syr inserts "with a strong arm and."

judgments. Here and in 7:4, Sam reads *bmšptym* for the more unusual MT *bšptym* (also Rossi 296 [6:6]). In 12:12 and Num 33:4, in contrast, Sam supports MT *šptym*. In MT, *mišpātîm* denotes laws and *šəpātîm* acts of judgment, while Sam blurs the distinction. 4QpaleoExod^m supports MT in 7:4 but is not extant here. For a discussion of these variants, see Sanderson (1986: 59–60).

6:7. *from under Egypt's burdens*. Many LXX MSS insert "from the land of Egypt and."

6:8. *raised my arm*. 4QGen-Exod^a unexpectedly paraphrases: *nšb't[y]* 'I swore.'

to Isaac. LXX and Syr have "*and* to Isaac."

6:9. *hard work*. Sam has a harmonistic plus at the end of 6:9, brought forward from 14:12: "And they said to Moses, 'Let us alone that we may serve Egypt, for serving Egypt is better for us than our dying in the desert.'"

6:12. *then how*. Syr omits the conjunction, either for ease of translation or by haplography (waw-yodh confusion); cf. 6:30.

6:13. *to Israel's Sons and*. These words have fallen from LXX by haplography (*to* Israel . . . *to* Pharaoh). While in theory this could have happened during Greek transmission, more likely the phrase was already absent from the *Vorlage*, as its omission affected the interpretation of *ləhôṣî'* (see below).

Egypt's king. Missing in some Byzantine LXX MSS.

to take . . . from. Without "to Israel's Sons" (see above), the subject of *ləhôṣî'* would be Pharaoh, rather than Moses and Aaron. Accordingly, LXX translates *exaposteilai* 'to release.' For "Israel's Sons," some Byzantine LXX MSS abbreviate, reading simply "his people."

6:14. *These*. LXX, Sam and Syr read "*and* these"; cf. NOTE to 1:1.

Hezron. Syr has "*and* Hezron."

6:15. *Jemuel*. LXX^B reads *Iemiēl*, while LXX^A *Iemouēl* supports MT *yəmû'ēl*. The variation between *yəmû'ēl* and **yəmî'ēl* may reflect waw-yodh confusion (cf. Cross 1961a; Qimron 1973). Syr and Sam support MT and LXX^A; we also find Jemuel in Gen 46:10. In Num 26:12, the name appears as *nəmû'ēl* (also 1 Chr 4:24), likely a confusion with Nemuel the Reubenite (Num 26:9).

and Zohar. Instead of MT *waṣōḥar* (also *Tgs.* and Syr), Sam, Kenn 166, 260 and Soncino Bible (1488) have *wṣhr*, possibly under the influence of *yṣhr* in v 18. Waw and yodh are almost indistinguishable in Herodian-period script (Cross 1961a; Qimron 1972), while ḥeth and heʾ are similar in all periods.

Simeon's families. LXX and *Tg.* Neofiti I have "the families of Simeon's *sons*," probably an expansion based upon the beginning of the verse.

6:16. Gershon. Syr confuses Gershon with Gershom, Moses' son. LXX has *Gedsōn*, reflecting a confusion of resh and daleth in Hebrew script (LXXᴬ has *Gersōn* here, but *Gedsōn* in the next verse). For further mutations, see Wevers (1990: 82).

†*and Kohath.* Sam and Kenn 173 omit the conjunction, perhaps rightly.

year. For ease of translation, LXX drops entirely the second, superfluous occurrence of this word.

†*6:17. Gershon's sons.* Sam, Syr and several exemplars of MT (Kennicott 1776–80: 117) begin "and." LXX has a still longer plus: "*and these are* Ge[r]shon's sons," as in v 16. While we ordinarily prefer the shortest reading, here LXX is conceivably correct, *wʾlh having fallen out by homoioteleuton with the preceding *šnh*.

†*6:18. and Hebron.* Sam and LXX omit the conjunction, thereby dividing the sons into two groups, as in v 14. This might be correct.

three. *Šālōš* 'three' has fallen from the LXX *Vorlage*, a victim of haplography within the sequence *šālōš ûš(ə)lōšîm* 'three and thirty.'

6:20. Aaron and Moses. Kenn 686, LXX and Sam append "and Miriam their sister," as in Num 26:59. Syr, however, inserts "and Miriam" between the brothers. Both readings seem to be expansions of the shorter, original MT.

††*six.* Sam and LXXᴬ have "six" (*šš*) for MT-Syr-*Tgs.* "seven" (*šbʿ*) and LXXᴮ "two" (*štym) (note that "six," "seven" and "two" all begin with shin; for rarer variants "three" and "five," see Wevers 1990: 85). Of these readings, MT is the least likely to be original, since "seven and thirty" also occurs in v 16. I accordingly follow Sam-LXXᴬ.

6:22. Mishael. The name has dropped from LXX by haplography (homoioteleuton) with Uzziel.

††*Elizaphan.* MT has *ʾelṣāpān*, as in Lev 10:4. Sam, LXX, Vg and Syr, however, reflect an older pronunciation *ʾeliṣāpān* (cf. *ʾeliṣāpān* in MT Num 3:30). Compare the alternation *ʾabnēr/ʾăbînēr*, *ʾabšālôm/ʾăbîšālôm* in MT.

6:23. Elisheba. LXX *Elisabeth* seems to reflect a variant *ʾĕlîšabʿat; compare the alternation between *yəhôšebaʿ* (2 Kgs 11:2) and *yəhôšabʿat* (2 Chr 22:11) (Dillmann 1880: 59).

Eleazar. LXX, Syr, *Tg.* Neofiti I, Vg and various MT MSS (Kennicott 1776–80: 117) read "*and* Eleazar," thus eliminating the division between the wicked and righteous sons of Aaron.

6:24. Assir . . . Abiasaph. For *ʾassîr*, Sam has *ʾswr*, i.e., *ʾassûr*; instead of *ʾbyʾsp*, it reads *ʾbysp* (cf. 1 Chr 6:8, 22; 9:19).

6:25. Levites'. Sam has the singular "Levite's" as in 6:19.

6:26. *Yahweh.* LXX has "the God."

Take. While MT uses direct quotation of Yahweh, LXX has indirect speech: "*to take.*"

the land of Egypt. LXX[A] and Kenn 223 omit "land," as in v 27.

by their brigades. LXX reads "*together with* their [military] force," as if the army were an entity distinct from the people (cf. 7:4; 12:17, 41, 51). Syr "*all* their brigades," if not a paraphrase, reflects **kl ṣb'tm* (cf. 12:41), rather than MT *'l ṣb'tm*. So also 12:51.

6:27. *to take.* LXX, presumably paraphrasing, has "and they took."

out from Egypt. Sam, LXX[B], Tgs. and many MSS of Syr and of MT have an expanded reading, "out from *the land of* Egypt" (Kennicott 1776–80: 117; de Rossi 1784–85: 51; see TEXTUAL NOTE to 3:10). The standard MT, other LXX witnesses and 4QpaleoExod[m] have the shorter text.

Moses and Aaron. LXX reverses the order to match 26; other Versions support MT. One assumes that the ABBA structure of MT is original, with LXX imposing greater consistency.

†6:28. *spoke.* The consonants *dbr* are ambiguous. Ordinarily, we would read the infinitive construct *dabbēr, but MT has a perfect *dibber* (for the construction, compare Num 3:1; also Gen 1:1; Lev 7:35). There is no difference in translation.

6:29. *all.* Absent in LXX, most likely for ease of translation (Wevers 1990: 90).

6:30. *before.* Syr and Rossi 419, 754 have "to" (*'el*).

then how. Syr omits the conjunction (cf. 6:12).

heed me. For MT and 4QpaleoExod[m] *yišmaʿ 'ēlay*, Sam reads *yšmʿny*, as in v 12 (LXX *eisakousetai mou* and Syr *nšmʿny* could reflect either variant). The MT is likely original; see also NOTE.

7:2. *he should release.* Instead of MT *wšlḥ*, Kenn 158, 196, 223 and a Cairo Genizah fragment (*BHS*) have *wyšlḥ* with no difference in meaning. This is presumably a secondary reading influenced by 6:11.

†*from his land.* 4QpaleoExod[m] apparently lacks *mē'arṣô* 'from his land.' Sanderson (1986: 56) argues that this shorter reading is preferable to MT et al., since there is no obvious reason why a scribe's eye should have skipped, and *mē'arṣô* may well have been imported from the parallel in 6:11 (also 11:10). Nevertheless, my translation follows MT, since the 4QpaleoExod[m] reading is reconstructed (and unique).

7:4. *my brigades, my people.* Although *'et-ṣib'ōtay 'et-ʿammî* seems to be a clear case of apposition, LXX takes only the second *'et-* as the direct object marker. The first *'et-* is translated "with." Thus, LXX renders, "I will lead out my people, *together with* my force" (cf. the Greek translation of *ʿal-ṣib'ōtām* in 6:26; 12:17, 41, 51: "*together with* its force"). Syr, following a similar line of interpretation, inserts "and" between the troop and the people.

†*from the land of Egypt.* A Genizah fragment (*BHS*) and Kenn 9 read simply "from Egypt." On the one hand, this is *lectio brevior*; on the other hand, it echoes 6:27 and so is *lectio facilior*.

judgments. See TEXTUAL NOTE to 6:6.

7:5. *Egypt.* Here and in 14:4, 18, LXX and Sam have a variant *kol-miṣrayim* 'all Egypt' (see, however, TEXTUAL NOTE to 14:4). This is apparently an expansion based on 7:24; 10:6; 12:30.

Israel's Sons. Sam inserts *ʿmy* 'my people' before "Israel's Sons"; cf. 3:10; 7:4.

7:7. *Aaron.* Many LXX MSS expand: "his brother."

their speaking. Some LXX MSS have "*he* spoke," while others agree with MT. It is hard to know which was the original Greek. On the one hand, "he spoke" (*elalēsen*) could be an inner-Greek corruption of "*they* spoke" (*elalēsan). But the change could well have been in the reverse direction, with an original *elalēsan* influenced by *epoiēsan* 'they did' at the end of 7:6 (Wevers 1990: 95). As Wevers observes, the reading "*he* spoke" acknowledges that, technically, only Aaron addressed Pharaoh.

SOURCE ANALYSIS

Exod 6:2–7:7 is basically Priestly, with Redactorial supplementation. The passage originally continued from 2:25 and was P's alternative to JE's bush theophany (Exodus 3–4). Lexical evidence of Priestly or Redactorial authorship abounds (Holzinger 1900: 18; McNeile 1908: 35): *hēqîm bərît* 'made stand a covenant' (6:4); *ʾereṣ məgurîm* 'land of sojournings' (6:4); *lākēn ʾĕmōr* 'therefore, say' (6:6) (see Wimmer 1967: 409–10); *šəpāṭîm* 'judgments' (6:6; 7:4); *nāśāʾ(ʾ) yād* 'raise an arm' (6:8); *môrāšâ* 'inheritance' (6:8); *məʾat* (vs. *mēʾâ*) 'hundred' (6:16, 18, 20); *tôlədôt* 'generations' (6:16, 19); *ləmišpəḥôtām* 'in their families' (6:17, 25); *ʿal-/bəlləṣibʾôtām* 'by their brigades' (6:26; cf. 7:4). Also characteristic of P is the expression "Moses and Aaron did, as Yahweh had commanded them, so they did" (7:6). Finally, the divine name *(ʾēl) šadday* appears in the Torah primarily in P (Gen 17:1; 28:3; 35:11; 48:3); note, however, Gen 43:14 (JE) and Gen 49:25 (independent poem).

Moreover, we find specific lexical links between 6:2–7:7 and the foregoing Priestly matter. In both 2:24 and 6:5, God "hears" (*šmʿ*) Israel's "groan" (*naʾăqâ*); both 2:23 and 6:6 call Israel's labor *ʿăbōdâ*; 2:24 and 6:4–5 alike speak of God remembering his covenant (*zākar bərît*) (Scharbert 1989: 32). Finally, both 1:13 and 6:5 use the Hiphʿil of *ʿbd* 'enslave.'

We also find contacts with Priestly portions of Genesis, in which God Shadday promises the land of Canaan to the Patriarchs (Gen 17:1; 28:3; 35:11; 48:3). Notice in particular the parallelism with Gen 17:1, "Yahweh appeared . . . and said, 'I am God Shadday.'" Now we read "I am Yahweh . . . I appeared . . . in God Shadday" (6:2–3). On the striking parallels in vocabulary between Gen 17:7–8 and Exod 6:4, 7, 8, see further Wimmer (1967: 416).

As usual, there is some dissonant evidence: Greenberg (1969: 149) observes that *səbālôt* 'tasks/burdens' (6:6) otherwise appears only in JE (1:11; 2:11; 5:4, 5). Rather than see a non-Priestly hand in Exodus 6, however, it is simpler to suppose P has borrowed JE's term.

As well as the language, the contents of 6:2–7:7 bespeak Priestly and/or Redactorial authorship. We find genealogies, chronology and Aaronic partisanship (see COMMENT). Most important, we find P's introduction of the name "Yahweh" (see INTRODUCTION).

The only unevenness in 6:2–7:7 involves 6:13–30. Vv 29–30 repeat matter from 6:2, 11–12, albeit with abbreviation and modification; and 6:13 introduces Aaron, not commissioned until 7:1–2. I would assign 6:13–30 entirely to R. The redundancy of 6:12 and 6:30 is a parade example of *Wiederaufnahme*, or epanalepsis, a technique of concluding a digression by repeating the words preceding it to reacquaint the audience with the context (Kuhl 1952). *Wiederaufnahme* is often evidence of editorial interpolation, but not necessarily (Long 1987). As Rashi observes, we do it constantly in free conversation.

Four additional clues within 6:13–30 betray the Redactor's hand. First, the reference to Aaron (6:13), anticipating his appointment in 7:1–2 (P), assumes familiarity with 4:14–16 (E). Second, the phrase "in the land of Egypt" (6:28) is unnecessary for P, in which, as far as we know, Moses never leaves Egypt at all (cf. Ezek 20:5).

The third clue goes back to medieval exegesis. Ibn Ezra and Rashbam ask why the sons of Yizhar and Uzziel are named, but not those of Hebron. Their answer: a son of Yizhar (Korah) and two sons of Uzziel (Mishael and Elizaphan) appear later in the Torah. This is also why only one great-great-great-grandson of Levi is named: Phinehas plays a major role in Numbers. As for Korah's sons (6:24), they are at least mentioned (but not named) in Num 26:11. Since Num 26:9b–11 is Redactorial, reflecting the composite narrative of Numbers 16, it follows that Exod 6:24, too, is R.

The fourth clue is the verbal similarity of 6:26–27, "that is (*hû'*) Aaron and Moses . . . that is Moses and Aaron," to Num 26:9b (R), "that is (*hû'*) Dathan and Abiram" (cf. Ehrlich 1969: 147). See also 12:42 (R?), "It (*hû'*) is a night of observance for Yahweh . . . it (*hû'*), this night, is for Yahweh an observance for all Israel's Sons."

It is instructive to compare P and JE so far. Overall, they are quite similar: Yahweh reveals himself as the ancestral god to the purebred Levite Moses. Moses must inform Israel that Yahweh is cognizant of Israel's sufferings and has determined to restore his people to Canaan. Moses must then demand that Pharaoh release the Hebrews from servitude. But when Moses doubts his fitness, being naturally inarticulate, Yahweh elects his kinsman Aaron to be Moses' spokesman. Moses, in turn, will become a quasi-deity, speaking through a prophetic mouthpiece. Yahweh forewarns Moses that Pharaoh will be obdurate and that the king and his people will suffer wondrous chastisements, so that all may know Yahweh.

Yet the differences are also glaring, reflecting the biases of the documents' authors (see COMMENT). So far as it is preserved, in P, Moses has no personal history. He never kills anyone, never travels to Midian, never encounters Yahweh in a bush. God simply addresses him in Egypt (Gressmann 1913: 51; cf. Ezek 20:5). In P, Yahweh is not shy to reveal his name to Moses (see COMMENT to chaps. 3–4). P also recasts the wonders that Moses receives in Exodus 4. The snake trick is performed, not before Israel with *Moses'* rod (4:2–5

[E]), but before Pharaoh with *Aaron's* rod (7:8–12 [P]); the water-to-blood trick (4:9 [E]) becomes the first plague (7:19–20, 21b–22 [P]); the *ṣāraʿat* trick (4:6–8 [E]) becomes the plague of *šəḥîn*, a related skin disorder (9:8–11 [P]). P's Moses is not just "heavy of mouth and heavy of tongue" (4:10 [E]) but "uncircumcised of lips" (6:12 [P]; see NOTE). In JE, Aaron is commissioned because Moses anticipates failure, but in P, Moses has already failed. In JE, Aaron is to help Moses address Israel, although in fact he accompanies Moses before Pharaoh; in P, Aaron is appointed to speak before Pharaoh (see, however, NOTE to 12:1). P's Aaron is not just Moses' kinsman but his literal brother (see NOTE to 4:14 [E]). He serves as Moses' "prophet," not just as his "mouth" (4:15 [E]); Moses is a god, not to Aaron, but to Pharaoh. (E, too, implies that Aaron is a prophet, but in a story to Aaron's discredit [Numbers 12].) In P, the release that Moses and Aaron demand is unconditional—no ruse of a three-day journey (3:18; 5:3; 8:23 [E]). Neither is there any despoiling of Egypt (3:21–22; 11:2–3; 12:35–36 [J?]). In P, Moses, seems to have no wife or children (see COMMENT). Finally, only P refers to Yahweh fulfilling a "covenant" with the Patriarchs (Wimmer 1967: 416). Although JE, too, knows of the ancestral covenant (Genesis 15 [J]), Exodus 3–4 (JE) speaks merely of liberation.

REDACTION ANALYSIS

The early chapters of Exodus presented the Redactor with problems that he only partly overcame. Before him were two descriptions of Yahweh's first revelation to Moses, one of them (chaps. 3–4) itself composite (JE). In theory, the Redactor could have inserted 6:2–7:7 into chaps. 3–4. But this would have entailed drastic rearrangement of the Priestly matter, as well as changing the verb in 6:12 from *šmʿw* 'have (not) heeded' to **yšmʿw* 'will (not) heed.' Instead, by placing the P matter after Pharaoh's rebuff of Moses (JE), the Redactor converted P's call theophany into a scene of reassurance (Beegle 1972: 90). Now, after Pharaoh's "Who is Yahweh, that I should heed his voice by releasing Israel? I have not known Yahweh; moreover, Israel I will not release" (5:2), the Deity reconfirms his name and support. He promises that soon all Egypt will know Yahweh. In effect, he "strengthens" Moses' heart, as he will soon strengthen Pharaoh's (cf. Calvin on 7:14).

   The combination of P and JE, however, entirely negated the original sense of 6:2–3 (P), that God was revealing his true name for the first time in history (see INTRODUCTION). In the composite Torah, the Patriarchs indeed know the name "Yahweh" (Gen 15:2; 27:27; 28:13, etc. [JE]). The reader is forced either to ignore the contradiction or to develop a nonliteral interpretation, e.g., that the ancestors knew Yahweh's name, but not his essence or fidelity (Rashi; see NOTE to 6:3).

   Other changes wrought by the combination of JE with P are less significant. For example, the Hebrews' "shortness of spirit" (P) is due not only to enslavement but also to the stiffening of their oppression brought about by Moses' interference (chap. 5 [E]). And Moses' protests in 6:12, 30 (P, R) represent a *second* failure of nerve. First he feared his "heavy . . . mouth and . . . tongue" would impair communication with his people (4:10 [E]); now he argues *a fortiori* that his "uncircumcised . . . lips" will never convince Pharaoh. Redaction also entailed a double commissioning of Aaron, but the difficulty was minor. The first time, Aaron was to speak only to Israel (4:14–15 [E]); now he must address Pharaoh, too (7:1–2 [P]) (Cassuto 1967: 83). Redaction also altered somewhat the meaning of 6:17; 7:5 (P). In the original Priestly context, the mighty act by which Egypt would "know" Yahweh was the Sea crossing. In the composite Torah, however, the Plagues are also part of Pharaoh's lesson (see NOTE to 7:5).

As for the Redactor's own contribution, the genealogical digression (6:13–30) befits P's theme of the promise to the Patriarchs. Moreover, suggests Thompson (1987: 14), the genealogy in a sense answers Moses' "Who am I?" (3:11 [E]). The insertion of 6:13–30 also changes the meaning of other passages in the Torah by affecting the relationship of Moses and Aaron (see NOTE to 4:14). We must assume that Aaron is born, as it were, between 2:1 and 2:2 (J) and that the anonymous parents in 2:1 are Amram and Jochebed. Lastly, in 7:1 (P), Aaron is ordained only to be Moses' *prophet*, with no mention of his future priestly office. By tracing his line through the priest Phinehas, however, R foreshadows Aaron's consecration (see COMMENT).

We also find the Redactor wrestling with an intractable chronological dilemma. According to Gen 15:13, 16 (J), the Hebrews would be slaves and sojourners for four hundred years, returning to Canaan in the fourth generation. Four overlapping generations covering four centuries would require men to father their children beyond the age of one hundred, which does not fit with even biblical chronology. The Redactor's recourse was apparently to count the years of Levi, Kohath and Amram as if *sequential*, rather than overlapping (see NOTES to 6:20 and 12:41).

Of some relevance to the editing process is the partition of the text by chapter and verse, and much earlier by space and paragraph (on *pətûḥâ* and *sətûmâ*, see Perrot 1969; Oesch 1979). On the one hand, the thirteenth-century Christian cleric who divided the Bible into chapters joined 6:1 (E) to 6:2 (P), thus reinforcing the Redactor's transformation of P's call scene into a theophany of reassurance. On the other hand, the earlier Jewish scribe who inserted a space between 6:1 and 6:2 unconsciously responded to the change in tone between E and P.

In MT, there is also an unexpected paragraph break (*pətûḥâ*) between 6:28 and 29. It struck ibn Ezra as either mysterious or foolish, depending on whether one takes as humble or sarcastic his disclaimer, "Perhaps the divider of the portions had a reason why he did this, for his wisdom was greater than ours." The real cause is the *Wiederaufnahme* beginning in v 29. The Redactor tried to be subtle by supplying an introduction with v 28. But a later scribe chose to emphasize the resumption by inserting a break before v 29.

NOTES

6:2. *I am Yahweh.* The expression *'ănî/'ānōkî yahwe(h)* serves several purposes in discourse (cf. Greenberg 1969: 130–31; Zimmerli 1982: 1–28). Beginning a divine address, particularly God's first communication with a human, it bears its surface meaning, identifying the invisible speaker (Mowinckel 1961: 123–24). But throughout the Bible, especially in P, Ezekiel and Second Isaiah, the phrase often occurs in the midst of or concluding a divine speech, and so must have other functions. Beyond self-identification, "I am Yahweh" serves to confirm promises (or threats), commands and declarations that people "will know that I am Yahweh" as a result of God's miraculous deeds.

All these uses are exemplified in 6:2–7:5. In 6:2, "I am Yahweh" primarily identifies the speaker, but also affirms the ensuing promises. In 6:6, "I am Yahweh" both identifies the god speaking through Moses and confirms his promise of deliverance. In 6:7, "you will know that I am Yahweh your deity" means that Israel will behold and understand Yahweh's wondrous deliverance. In 6:8, the concluding "I am Yahweh" confirms Yahweh's promise to give Israel the land of Canaan. In 6:29, "I am Yahweh" serves three purposes: identifying the speaker, summarizing the discussion of vv 2–8 (see NOTE) and intensifying the following command to go to Pharaoh. Finally, in 7:5, Yahweh's speech ends where it had begun: the Egyptians will learn that "I am Yahweh," a rhetorical device summarizing and framing the preceding matter (inclusio) (Wimmer 1967: 413).

What connects these uses of *'ănî/'ānōkî yahwe(h)?* Greenberg (1969: 130–33) regards "I am Yahweh" as a statement of power, comparing Gen 41:44 ("I am Pharaoh; no other man than you will raise his arm . . .") and Jer 16:21 ("I will make them know my *arm* [i.e., power] and my might, that they may know that my name is Yahweh"). To be more specific, "I am so-and-so" often functions as an oath (Greenberg pp. 134–35). Compare Ezek 20:5: "On the day I chose Israel and raised my arm [i.e., swore] to the seed of Jacob's House and made myself known to them in the land of Egypt, I raised my arm to them, saying, 'I am Yahweh your deity.'" Rashbam paraphrases Exod 6:2, "I am Yahweh, and my name means that I can fulfill my promises."

We may compare another common formula of oath/asseveration: *ḥê* '(by) the life (of).' The idiom affirms either that something is true or that the speaker will do (or not do) something (for ancient Near Eastern parallels, see Lehmann 1969). Significantly, a human swears only by the life of his/her addressee ("[by] *your* life") or of God ("[by] *Yahweh's* life"). The only being that may swear "as *I* live" with absolute credibility is Yahweh, whose eternal existence is the truth by which other truths are measured (Num 14:21, 28; Deut 32:40; Isa 49:18; Jer 22:24; 46:18; Ezek 5:11, etc.). The exception that proves the rule is Gen 42:15, 16, where Joseph exclaims, "as Pharaoh lives." This is in fact how Egyptians swore, since their king was divine (Wilson 1948). It is no coincidence that the only human to use the "I am" formula is this same Pharaoh (Gen 41:44).

In sum, "I am Yahweh" and "as I [Yahweh] live" appear to have much the same force. Not that they are interchangeable—"I am Yahweh" has wider functions and exists in several permutations. Nevertheless, the near-synonymity of the two expressions is evident in their clustering in Ezek 5:11–17; 14:4–20; 17:16–24; 20:3–44; 33:27–29; 35:4–15.

Other ancient deities besides Yahweh and Joseph's Pharaoh use "I am." Greenberg (1969: 130–31) cites the following Egyptian examples: "See, look at me, my son Thutmose. I am thy father, Harmakhis-Khepri-Re-Atum. I shall give thee my kingdom upon earth"; "I am Khnum, your creator. My arms are round about you" (for comparable theophanic statements, see Morenz 1973: 32–33, 41). From Assyria, we read, "I am Ishtar of Arbela, O Esarhaddon. . . . In the cities of Ashur, Nineveh, Calah, protracted days . . . unto [you] shall I grant"; "I am the great divine lady, I am the goddess Ishtar of Arbela, who will destroy your enemies from before your feet. What are the words of mine, which I spoke to you, that you did not rely upon? I am Ishtar of Arbela. I shall lie in wait for your enemies" (for further parallels, see Ringgren 1978: 346–47).

6:3. *I appeared.* As Rashi and Sforno observe, the verb *nir'â* describes Yahweh's manifestations to Abraham (Gen 12:7; 17:1; 18:1), Isaac (Gen 26:2) and Jacob (Gen 35:1, 9; 48:3). *Wā'ērā(')* 'and I appeared' (< *r'y* 'see') seems to connote a less intimate experience than *nôda'tî* 'I was known' (< *yd'* 'know') (see below).

in. I have translated *bə-* as "in," not "as," to emphasize that Yahweh was not fully equivalent to God Shadday, Rather, God Shadday was a partial manifestation of Yahweh.

God Shadday. The interpretation of *'ēl šadday* is disputed. The greater problem is the meaning of *šadday*, which I consider unknowable. The most we can say is that the name may originally have connoted a Transjordanian god of storm and fertility (see APPENDIX C, vol. II).

The lesser problem is the grammatical relationship between the two elements. *'Ēl šadday* is comparable to several other epithets from Patriarchal times: *'ēl 'elyôn* (Gen 14:18–22), *'ēl 'ĕlōhê yiśrā'ēl* (Gen 33:20), *'ēl rŏ'î* (Gen 16:13), *'ēl 'ôlām* (Gen 21:33) and *'ēl bêt-'ēl* (Gen 35:7; cf. 31:13). Assuming one explanation covers all names, the two elements might be a noun and an adjective, two nouns in apposition or two nouns in a genitival relationship (Cross 1973: 46–60). Since *'elyôn, 'ôlām, bêt-'ēl* and *šadday* are attested as independent divinities inside and outside the Bible (see Cross), the appositional interpretation is the most likely: God Elyon, God Olam, God Bethel and God Shadday. Note that, if these titles truly originated in the Middle Bronze Age, then case endings, obsolete by the Israelite period, would have eliminated ambiguity.

I, my name Yahweh. This phrase has generated a large literature (see Garr 1992). My translation, borrowed from Garr, attempts to capture a syntactic peculiarity of the original. In Hebrew, a verb may agree with the pronominal suffix on a noun denoting an inalienable attribute (a body part, the soul, a name). As it were, 6:3b combines two ideas—"my name Yahweh was not known to them" and "by my name Yahweh I was not known to them"—or, rather, it does not distinguish between them. We will meet further examples of this syntax in 32:29 and probably 15:6; 17:12 (see NOTES). The closest analogue may be Ps 83:19, "They will know that you, your name, Yahweh, alone are highest over all the earth" (other renderings are possible, however). Akkadian, too, uses this syntax (e.g., *Atra-ḥasīs* I:109, "What do I, my eye, see?"; OB *Gilgamesh* X:5, 8 "Who is your name? . . . My name, Gilgamesh, am I").

The Bible, especially Deuteronomistic literature, lays great stress upon Yahweh's "name," almost but not quite identical to God himself (e.g., Deut 28:58; Isa 24:15; Jer 10:6; Ps 5:12; 9:3; 68:5; 69:37; 83:17; 92:2) (McBride 1969; Mettinger 1982: 38–79). A god's name is, so to speak, an acoustic icon. Like an idol, it represents a theophany, a projection of the divine onto the terrestrial plane; it is and is not the deity (cf. Mettinger 1988: 8–9). Thus, when Moses requests a vision of God's Glory or Face (33:18, 20, 23), he receives instead knowledge of God's name, implicitly equated with Yahweh's back (33:12, 17, 19; 34:5–7). Deuteronomy will speak of Yahweh's "name" living in the Temple's sanctum (Deut 12:11; 14:23; 16:2, 6, 11; 26:2)—again, like the polytheist's idol.

Was not known. Yd° 'know' has connotations beyond intellectual knowledge, describing the intimacy between marital or covenant partners (Huffmon 1966; Huffmon and Parker 1966). The Patriarchs did not "know" Yahweh, both because they were unacquainted with his proper name and because their experience of the Covenant was incomplete. They had only an unfulfilled promise. The following is Garr's (1992: 408) paraphrase of 6:3: "I appeared to Abraham, Isaac, and Jacob (in limited form) as El Shaddai (who makes covenantal promises). But I was not the object of (full) covenantal knowledge to them as conveyed by my name Yahweh (who keeps covenantal promises)."

6:4. *made stand my covenant.* The Qal verb *qām* 'stand,' in the context of obligations, bears two connotations. It can mean "to be binding or valid" (Num 30:5–12 [P]; cf. Isa 40:8) or "to be fulfilled, proven" (Deut 19:15; Isa 14:24; 46:10; Jer 44:29; 51:29; Prov 19:21; Job 22:28). The first sense is limited to P (Numbers 30) and perhaps Isa 40:8 (where, however, *qām* could also be interpreted as "persist"). And for the Hiph°il *hēqîm*, P and Ezekiel again employ distinctive terminology. In Gen 6:18; 9:9, 11, 17; 17:7, 19, 21; Exod 6:4 (P) and Ezek 16:60, 62, *hēqîm bərît* means "*establish* a covenant" (cf. Ps 78:5). In other sources, however, to *hēqîm* an obligation means to *fulfill* it. (In P, *hēqîm* means "fulfill" only in Lev 26:9.) These two usages are not as distant as may appear at first. The English word closest to *hēqîm* is "confirm," describing both the initial establishment of a pact and its ongoing or eventual fulfillment.

Unlike Ezekiel (Ezek 17:13; 34:25; 37:26), P never uses the ordinary Hebrew verb for making a covenant: *krt* 'cut.' P largely reserves the root, in the Niph°al and Hiph°il conjugations, for the penalty of *kārēt* (see NOTE to 12:15). Why P should shun the idiom *kārat bərît* is unclear. If one "cuts" a covenant because the ceremony involved dismembering symbolic animals (cf. Genesis 15; Jer 34:18–19)—which is not certain (Weinfeld 1977a: 253–55)—then the Priestly Writer may have rejected the implication that, should he violate his Covenant, God himself would be dismembered.

6:5. *because the Egyptians are making them work.* Or "(their cry) *that* the Egyptians are making them work" (cf. Rashi and NJV; on *'ăšer* as a conjunction, see GKC §157c and Seidl 1991). RSV "*whom* the Egyptians hold in bondage" is also possible, but feels unidiomatic to me.

6:6. *I am Yahweh.* Moses is to address the Hebrews in the divine persona, just as he is to be a "deity to Pharaoh" (7:1). On the interchange of Deity and prophet, see COMMENT to Exodus 3–4, p. 228; NOTES to 7:17 and 11:8.

redeem. Durham (1987: 72) emphasizes that *g'l* often connotes fulfillment of kinship duty (see Johnson 1953, but also Ringgren 1977). *G'l* has particular associations with repatriation and blood feud, both pertinent here (see also NOTES to 4:22–23). Surprisingly, the verb is rarely applied to the Exodus—explicitly only in 6:6; 15:13; Ps 106:10 and probably in Ps 74:2; 77:16; 78:35 (Hyatt 1971: 94).

extended limb. The arm is usually "extended (*nṭy*)" to wield a rod or weapon, or to strike a blow with the fist—in any case, to act aggressively; cf. Job 15:25: "He extended his arm toward God, and vaunted himself toward Shadday."

judgments. I.e., acts of judgment, punishments (LXX *krisei* 'judgment' [sing.] apparently takes *šəpāṭîm* as an abstract plural). The theme also appears in Gen 15:14 (J), albeit with different language: "And also the nation that they will serve I am going to judge (*dān*)."

6:7. *I will take you to me as a people, and I will become to you as a deity.* Variations upon this sentence, expressing the essence of Israel's Covenant with Yahweh, recur throughout the Bible, especially in Jeremiah and Ezekiel (e.g., Lev 26:12; Jer 7:23; 11:4; 24:7; 30:22; Ezek 11:20; 14:11; 36:28; 37:23, 27; Zech 8:8). It has already appeared, truncated, in Yahweh's promise to Abram, "I will become to them as a deity" (Gen 17:7, 8 [P]), here reiterated (Wimmer 1967: 414).

6:8. *raised my arm.* In swearing.

6:9. *shortness of spirit.* "Shortness of spirit/breath (*rûaḥ*)" connotes despair or impatience (see Childs 1974: 110), or perhaps simple fatigue (Rashi). The idiom is paralleled in Num 21:4; Judg 10:16; 16:16; Mic 2:7; Job 21:4 and, in Ugaritic, *KTU* 1.1.vi.34, 47; 21.i.8, 14, 23, 31 (Cassuto 1967: 82; Haak 1982).

6:12. *before.* Or "in the presence of"—literally, "to the face of" (*lipnê*).

uncircumcised of lips. This is P's equivalent for "not a man of words . . . heavy of mouth and heavy of tongue" (4:10 [E]). The expressions are not synonymous, however. "Heavy of mouth and . . . tongue" has many parallels in ancient medical literature (see Tigay 1978 for details). "Uncircumcised" organs, however, apart from the obvious, are uniquely biblical. Other body parts described as *'ārēl* are the ear (Jer 6:10) and the heart (Lev 26:41; Jer 9:25; Ezek 44:7, 9; cf. Deut 10:16; 30:6; Jer 4:4), both associated with communication and understanding. In these passages, at issue is neither deafness nor a cardiac condition, but *rl* moral imperviousness to the divine word. (The opposite of *'rl* is *mwl* 'circumcise,' and perhaps also *gly* 'uncover,' said of the eye [Num 24:4, 16] and ear [1 Sam 9:15; 20:2, 12, 13; 22:8, 17; 2 Sam 7:27; Job 33:16; 36:10, 15; Ruth 4:4; 1 Chr 17:25].)

It follows that P's metaphor, while possibly connoting impeded speech, primarily describes inherent unfitness to transmit Yahweh's word—unfitness which Moses has just demonstrated in failing to convince the Hebrews. His lips are "uncircumcised," i.e., they do not allow Yahweh's words to pass freely, whether by reason of ineloquence or physical impediment.

The Priestly Writer probably invented the image of an "uncircumcised," rather than a "heavy," mouth, in order to denigrate Moses (see further COMMENT). In Priestly circles, uncircumcision was a major transgression (cf. Genesis 17) and, for Ezekiel, a disqualification for Temple worship (cf. P's laws on handicapped priests [Lev 21:16–24]). Ezek 44:7, 9 links metaphorical uncircumcision (of the heart) with actual uncircumcision. Similarly, the expression ʿārēl waṭāmēʾ 'uncircumcised and impure' (Isa 52:1) equates uncircumcision with ritual defilement. This condition is an impediment to prophecy, for, according to Ps 12:4–7, Yahweh's words are too pure (ṭāhôr) for sinful lips. When Isaiah has a problem like Moses'—he is "impure (ṭāmēʾ) of lips"—a seraph cauterizes his mouth with a coal. Ezekiel, too, has a "stuck" tongue that Yahweh looses—but it is God who disabled it in the first place (Ezek 3:25–27; 24:27; 33:22).

The specific image of uncircumcision in P is probably inspired by 4:24–31 (JE), where Moses must be vicariously circumcised before meeting Aaron and carrying out his mission to Israel and Pharaoh. In JE, Moses undergoes at least symbolic circumcision. But in P, his uncircumcision is never remedied. Instead, Aaron, whose lips are more pure, is appointed as his spokesman (cf. Mal 2:6–7, "iniquity was not found on his lips . . . a priest's lips preserve knowledge").

The condition of Moses' mouth is critical. Like the polytheist's idol, a prophet's body temporarily houses the divine presence. Thus, just as Mesopotamians animated their icons with a ritual "opening of the mouth," so must an Israelite prophet possess a pure, unimpeded, "circumcised" mouth. (Throughout the Near East, cultic functionaries as well as laymen underwent periodic oral purification rites—admittedly, without necessarily becoming receptacles for the divine spirit [Hurowitz 1989].)

We have observed that P's Aaron is commissioned to speak for Moses *to Pharaoh*, while in E, Aaron is Moses' spokesman *to Israel*. It is unclear whether in P we are also to suppose that Aaron interprets Moses' words to the people. This may be implied by 16:9 (P), "Moses said to Aaron, 'Say to all the congregation of Israel's Sons.'" But there is no indication elsewhere in P that Moses needs an interpreter with Israel.

6:13. *Aaron.* His introduction is abrupt and premature, anticipating his appointment in 7:1–2 (cf. Greenberg 1969: 136). Yet 6:13 is not superfluous. Within 6:2–7:7, only here are we told that Yahweh commissioned Aaron directly, addressing him as well as Moses (cf. 4:27 [E]).

commanded them to Israel's Sons. The language is probably elliptical; i.e., God commanded Moses and Aaron *to command* Israel (and Pharaoh). Taking ʾel 'to' as equivalent to ʿal 'on, about,' however, one might alternatively understand that Yahweh instructed Moses and Aaron *concerning* Israel and Pharaoh.

6:14. *their fathers' house.* Like *mišpāḥâ* 'family' and *bayit* 'house,' *bêt-'āb* 'father's house' literally denotes a small family unit but can be metaphorically extended to connote much larger kinship groups (Dillmann 1880: 58). The plural of *bêt-'āb* is *bêt-'ābōt* 'fathers' house,' not the expected **bāttê-'āb* 'father's houses'; i.e., *bêt-'āb* is a compound (cf. GKC §124p–r).

Who is "their"? In the present context, it could be all Israel or Moses and Aaron alone (Greenberg 1969: 136). Another possibility is the entire tribe of Levi. But if, as many suspect, 6:14a once headed an independent genealogical document, then the original antecedent was probably Israel.

sons of Reuben. Why begin with Reuben and Simeon if the focus is on Levi? That the writer mechanically copied a preexisting genealogy is surely an incomplete explanation. Rather, the genealogist, wishing to show Levi's status vis-à-vis all Israel, conceded Levi's traditional subordination to Reuben and Simeon (cf. Cassuto 1967: 84). Since Reuben and Simeon had vanished as tribes by the Redactor's day, little prestige was at stake (see APPENDIX A, vol. II).

Hanoch. *Ḥănôk* (often Anglicized "Enoch") means "Trained," "Dedicated" or possibly "Dedication." Hanoch is also the name of a Kenite/Midianite clan (Gen 4:17; 25:4; 1 Chr 1:33). Conceivably, then, the Hanochites fissioned into Israelite and Midianite branches.

Pallu. "Wondrous"; the Reubenite Pelet (Num 16:1) may be a variant.

Hezron. The name probably derives from either *ḥāṣēr* 'village' or **ḥṣr* 'to be green.' Hezron is also the name of two Judahite cities (Josh 15:3, 25).

Carmi. "Of the vineyard," also a Judahite name (Josh 7:1, 18; 1 Chr 2:7; 4:1).

6:15. *Jemuel.* *'Ēl* means "god," but *yəmû/yəmî* is unexplained; *pace* Layton (1990: 65–66), the shewa makes derivation from either *yôm* 'day' or *yām* 'sea' unlikely. For other names of this pattern, see NOTE to 2:18.

Jamin. *Yāmîn* means "Right hand" or "South" (Israelites, like Europeans, "oriented" themselves to the sunrise).

Ohad. As this clan is not mentioned elsewhere, ibn Ezra infers it died off either in Egypt or during the desert wanderings. The root **'hd* may also be attested in the name *'ehûd*, unless that is a dialectal form of **'ê-hôd* 'Where is glory?' (cf. the synonymous *'î-kābôd*). Conceivably, Hebrew **'hd* = Arabic *'yd* 'to be strong.'

Jachin. "He established."

Zohar. "Tawniness" is also a clan name in Judah (1 Chr 4:7 [Qere]) and the father of Ephron the Hittite (Gen 23:8; 25:9).

Shaul. The same name is borne by Israel's first king, Saul, and by an Edomite ruler (Gen 36:37–38; 1 Chr 1:48–49). It is also a Levitic name (1 Chr 6:9). *Šā'ûl* means "Borrowed" or "Besought."

the Canaanitess's son. Presumably, the Shaulites were considered to be of partly foreign extraction; cf. the tradition of Judahite-Canaanite intermarriage in Gen 38:2; 1 Chr 2:3.

6:16. *Gershon.* The name may refer to exile (< *gērēš* 'expel') or conceivably fertility (cf. *gereš* 'yield'). For other possibilities, see Propp (1992a) and NOTE to 2:22.

Kohath. Qəhāt appears related to the noun *yiqqəhat* 'obedience (?)' (Gen 49:10; Prov 30:17 [but see Thomas 1941]) and the name of the Ugaritic hunter-hero *'Aqht*, whom Astour (1967: 163–68) ingeniously connects with Greek Actaeon. Also potentially related is the name of Huldah's father-in-law, *tiqwâ* in 2 Kgs 22:14 but *to(w)qhat* in 2 Chr 34:22.

Merari. In theory, *mərārî* might be a Hebrew name "Bitter" (or "Strong" or "Blessed"; on *mrr*, see Dietrich, Loretz and Sanmartín 1973; Pardee 1978; Ward 1980; Kutler 1984). More attractive, however, is association with the Egyptian name *mrry/mrrî*, from the root "to love" (Cody 1969: 40 n. 4).

seven and thirty and one hundred. Fox (1986: 41) observes that, at least in MT, all the ages in this passage consist of multiples of three, seven and ten, special numbers in the Bible. On the prodigious life spans, see NOTE to 6:20.

6:17. *Libni.* "The one from Libnah," a Levitical city in southwest Judah (Josh 21:13; 1 Chr 6:42).

Shimei. "Obedient," a common Israelite name; cf. Simeon.

6:18. *Amram.* "The (divine) Kinsman is lofty"; for parallels, see RSP 3.491–92. We are accustomed to thinking of Amram and Jochebed as *Moses'* parents, but, since only in P are Moses and Aaron brothers, and since Moses' parents are unnamed in JE, Amram and/or Jochebed may originally have been connected more closely to *Aaron* (see also NOTES to 4:14 and 6:20).

Yizhar. "Olive oil." With further discoveries, perhaps *yiṣhār* will prove to be a divine name, like *dāgān* 'grain' and *tîrōš* 'wine,' with which it is often associated (cf. Astour 1966: 284).

Hebron. As the root *ḥbr* means "to join" or "associate," *ḥebrôn* may mean "League." Hebron is the chief city of Judah, where the national ancestors were buried in the Cave of Machpelah (Genesis 23). The family of David's priest Zadok may have been from Hebron (Cross 1973: 207–15; see, however, Olyan 1982). Hebron's children are not listed, probably because they play no further role in the Torah (ibn Ezra; Rashbam; see SOURCE ANALYSIS and COMMENT).

Uzziel. "God is my strength."

6:19. *Mahli.* The derivation is uncertain; one possibility is "Of forgiveness" (< Rabbinic Hebrew *mḥl*). The female name *maḥlâ*, perhaps originally a Manassite town, may be related (Num 26:33, etc.).

Mushi. The root *mwš* means "depart." As this seems unlikely to generate a personal name, many derive Mushi from *mōše(h)* (e.g., Wellhausen 1885: 143; Cross 1973: 195–215). If so, Mushi originally meant "Descended from Moses." Why Mushi is conceived as Moses' *cousin* will be considered under COMMENT.

6:20. *Jochebed.* The most plausible interpretations are "Yo (= Yahweh) is Glory" or "Yo is glorified," like Akkadian names in which a god is *kabit* 'reverend, important' (Stamm 1939: 225). While the name presents no problem for R (6:20), which acknowledges pre-Mosaic Yahwism, it is most surprising for P (Num 26:59), in which God's name is unknown before Moses' day (6:3) (see INTRODUCTION). Since the Priestly Writer changed the pre-Mosaic Yahwistic name "Joshua" (*yəhô-šûaʿ*) into "Hoshea" (Num 13:8, 16), we might have expected similar treatment for "Jochebed." Many, admittedly, skirt the difficulty by parsing the name as a verbal form of *kbd*: **yukbad* or **yukabbid* 'He is glorified' or 'He glorifies.' But this otherwise attractive approach founders on the *plene* spelling *ywkbd* (not **ykbd*).

SPECULATION: A simple solution, probably too simple, would be to take 6:3 at face value. The name *Yahweh* is a new revelation. This does not necessarily preclude knowledge of its short forms *yô* or *yəhô*. While one might infer from his censorship of *yəhô-šûaʿ* that the Priestly Writer excluded the short names, too, he may have been more troubled by the element *šûaʿ* (see NOTE to 17:8).

aunt. Although elsewhere *dôdâ* can mean "kinswoman" (cf. 2:1), the Priestly Writer uses it only in the sense of "aunt" (Lev 18:14; 20:20). Num 26:59 (P) confirms that Jochebed is Amram's father's sister. Since such a union is forbidden by Lev 18:12; 20:19 (P), by Priestly canons Aaron, Miriam and Moses are of illegitimate birth! This must be why LXX, Syr, Vg and *Tg. Neofiti I* make Amram and Jochebed mere cousins in 6:20, even though they cannot avoid the plain sense in Num 26:59.

In fact, many pre-Mosaic marriages are technically incestuous. According to Gen 20:12, Abraham and Sarah are wedded half siblings, in violation of Lev 18:9, 11; 20:17; Deut 27:22; Ezek 22:11. Jacob's marriage to two sisters (Genesis 29) contravenes Lev 18:18, and the intercourse between Judah and his son's betrothed (Genesis 38) transgresses Lev 18:15; 20:12; Ezek 22:11. Note, too, the xenophobic satire of Lot's intercourse with his own daughters (Gen 19:30–38). The point of such stories, apart from the realization of illicit fantasies, is to establish that the stock in question—Israel, Judah, Moab, Ammon—is purebred. So, too, Moses and Aaron are pure Levites.

Still, all of the above traditions are from JE, while the genealogy of Aaron and Moses is from P itself (Num 26:59). Why would the Priestly Writer cast doubt on the legitimacy of Moses, Miriam and especially Aaron? The only possible answer is that Amram and Jochebed are conceived to be exempt from the yet ungiven Law. (When it comes to sacrifice, however, there is no dispensation; P does not admit that any offerings were made prior to the establishment of the Aaronic priesthood [Friedman 1987: 191].)

woman. *'Iššâ* is the normal Hebrew term for wife. The husband is called either "man" (*'îš*) or "lord, owner" (*baʿal*, *'ādôn*).

The inclusion of wives in a genealogy is somewhat unusual. Exod 6:20–25 names Aaron's mother, wife and daughter-in-law both to draw attention to the high priestly lineage and to establish the purity of Aaronic descent, since there were special restrictions on priestly marriage (Lev 21:7, 13–14; Ezek 44:22). Luzzatto compares the prominence of queen mothers in the Books of Kings.

Aaron and Moses. Given the role of women in this chapter, Miriam's absence is somewhat surprising (contrast Num 26:59). But our genealogy is concerned with females only as wives or mothers in the direct Aaronic line (see COMMENT).

years. The preternatural life spans of Levi, Kohath and Amram fit the Torah's overall scheme. The earliest humans live almost a millennium. Longevity then gradually decreases, reaching its contemporary measure after the conquest of Canaan (on ancient parallels, with much greater life spans, see Speiser 1964: 41–42; Fritz 1990). That the Hebrews of Egypt live beyond their "threescore and ten" implies that we are still in mythic, not historical, time. The Torah is inconsistent in this regard, however. If all those born in Egypt were as long-lived as Levi, Kohath and Amram, then forty years' wandering would not have sufficed to kill them off.

Since we are not told the ages of Levi, Kohath and Amram at fatherhood, it seems impossible from 6:16–20 alone to calculate the duration of the Egyptian residence (contrast T. Levi; Demetrius; see Kreuzer 1991: 256). According to Gen 15:13, 16 (J), the Israelites would spend 400 years in sojourn and servitude, with the fourth generation returning to Canaan. Exod 12:40 (P) allots 430 years for the sojourn. How does this fit with 6:16–20?

At first glance, not well. The life spans of Levi, Kohath and Amram are far too short to cover four centuries. Levi and Kohath spend their early years in Canaan, Amram presumably dies in the desert and the lives of all three must overlap considerably (Rashi on Gen 15:13; Exod 12:40). Many ancient interpreters "fix" the problem by making 430 years include the Patriarchal era. Thus, the Israelites spend only 215 years in Egypt (see TEXTUAL NOTE to 12:40). More plausible, however, is Luzzatto's inference that 6:16–20 assumes some missing generations. How else, he asks, can there already be 8,600 Kohathites in the desert (Num 3:28)?

In fact, the life spans of Levi, Kohath and Amram are all curiously close to 133⅓, i.e., one third of 400, the approximate duration of the sojourn (cf. Rashbam). Following Luzzatto, we might simply infer that, while there were intervening generations, Kohath was born the year Levi died, and Amram the year Kohath died. But the plain sense is that Levi, Kohath and Amram are grandfather, father and son (see further NOTE to 12:40).

6:21. *Korah.* "Baldness" (?). Korah is both a Levitic and an Edomite name (Gen 36:5, 14, 16, 18; 1 Chr 1:35); cf. Aramaic *qarḥā'* (Tallqvist 1966: 183). There is also a Judahite Korah associated with Hebron and Caleb (1 Chr 2:43). Caleb in turn is called a Kenizzite (Num 32:12; Josh 14:6, 14; cf. Josh 15:17; Judg 1:13; 3:9, 11; 1 Chr 4:13), i.e., an Edomite (Gen 36:11, 15, 42; 1 Chr 1:36, 53). Thus the southern Korahites were variously considered Levitic, Edomite or Judahite, and exemplify the complex ethnic composition of early Judah (see Axelsson 1987: 71–73, 79–81).

To "Korah's sons," presumably Levites, tradition attributes Psalms 42; 44–49; 84–85; 87–88. In Chronicles, they are Temple singers (2 Chr 20:19), gatekeepers (1 Chr 9:19; 26:1, 19) and bakers (1 Chr 9:31). 1 Chr 6:18–23 even seems to place Samuel among their number. Apparently, Korahite Levites were prominent among the postexilic minor clergy.

Before the exile, however, "Korah's sons" appear on an eighth-century os-tracon from the Arad shrine, which competed with Solomon's Temple (*AHI* 2.049.1; see Aharoni 1981: 180–82). We assume, then, that the Korahites were *personae non gratae* in preexilic Jerusalem. P's animus against the Korahites is evident in Numbers 16, which tells of Korah leading a Levite revolt against Aaron and Moses. Yahweh kills Korah and his followers for claiming the priest-hood—but a postexilic Redactorial insertion conciliatingly reports the survival of Korah's sons (Num 26:11).

Nepheg. The Arabic cognate refers to "leaping" or "rising." The Levitic tribe Nepheg appears only here, but a son of David bears the same name (2 Sam 5:15; 1 Chr 3:7; 14:6).

Zichri. "Masculine" or perhaps "Remembrance." Although Zichri is a com-mon name in the Bible, this Levitic clan appears only here.

6:22. *Mishael.* As it stands, *mîšā'ēl* could be interpreted as "Who is what God (is)?" (BDB), or, assuming Hebrew *ša* here functions like Akkadian *ša*, "Who is of God?" (cf. *mîkā'ēl* 'Who is like God?').

Elizaphan. On the vocalization, see TEXTUAL NOTE. *'Eliṣāpān* may mean "My god has hidden" or "My god has treasured" (cf. *ṣəpanyâ* [Zephaniah] 'Yahweh has treasured' and the common epigraphic name *ṣpn* [*AHI* p. 477]). Alternatively, assuming either (intentional?) misvocalization or an archaic or dialectal variant, *'eliṣāpān* might mean "(the divine mountain) Zaphan/Zaphon is my god" (D. N. Freedman *apud* Milgrom 1991: 605). As Rashbam notes, Mishael and Elizaphan play a minor part in Lev 10:4 (see SOURCE ANALYSIS).

Sithri. The name is attested only here; it means "Secret one." The semantic similarity to the previous name is striking but probably coincidental (*str* paral-lels *ṣpn* in Jer 16:17; Ps 10:8; 27:5; 31:21; Job 14:13).

6:23. *Elisheba.* *Ělîšebaʿ* seems to mean "My god is Seven" (cf. the names *batšebaʿ* 'Seven's daughter,' *yəhôšebaʿ/yəhôšabʿat* 'Yahweh is Seven,' *bə'ēr šebaʿ* 'Seven's well' and *šebaʿ* 'Seven'; compare also the Byblian king Sibitti-bēl 'Baal is Seven' mentioned in inscriptions of Tiglath Pileser III [*ANET* 282, 283]). Is *šebaʿ* an Israelite manifestation of the Mesopotamian god/gods/demons Sebettu 'the Seven,' on whom see Edzard (1965: 124–25)? For other etymologies, see Loewenstamm (1950).

Elisheba is identified by both father and brother because these were an un-married woman's primary guardians, and perhaps because, in cases of polygyny, naming a brother in effect identified a woman's mother. In light of the empha-sis on Moses' and Aaron's pure Levitic ancestry, it is surprising that Aaron should marry a Judahite (cf. Num 1:7, etc.). But Elisheba is the daughter and sister of David's ancestors Amminadab and Nahshon (Ruth 4:20–22; 1 Chr 2:10–15). The tradition may reflect the close ties between the royal house of David and the Jerusalem priesthood (Friedman 1987: 213).

Holzinger (1900: 20) observes that Aaron may be considerably older than his wife. He is of the fourth generation from Jacob, she of the sixth.

Amminadab. "My (divine) Kinsman is generous."

Nahshon. The meaning is uncertain. *Naḥšôn* might mean "Little snake" or "Luxuriant" (cf. Akkadian *nuḫšu* 'luxury'). A third possibility is a connection with the putative Qal of *niḥḥēš* 'to divine.'

Nadab. "Generous" or "Noble."

Abihu. "He is my Father." The pronoun probably refers to a deity; cf. *'ĕlîhû'* "He is my god." Nadab and Abihu die in Leviticus 10, after offering "strange fire before Yahweh." Presumably, they were the ancestors of Aaronic lines that either died out or were considered illegitimate by the Priestly Writer.

Eleazar. "God has helped." From Eleazar will descend the Aaronic high priests (Ezra 7:1–5; 1 Chr 5:30–41; 6:35–38). On the resemblance to Moses' son Eliezer, see COMMENT.

Ithamar. "He [i.e., God] has appeared," a Gt of the root *'mr* in its Ugaritic-Akkadian sense "to see." The house of Eli, which in premonarchic times served at Shiloh, may have been Ithamarite (so 1 Chr 24:3, 6; see Propp 1992b).

6:24. *Korah's sons.* On the omission of Moses' family, see COMMENT.

Assir and Elkanah and Abiasaph. Contrast 1 Chr 6:22, where Ebiasaph [*sic*] is Assir's *father.* Assir might be a form of *'āsîr* 'captive,' assuming the clan originated as prisoners of war. Considering the Egyptian derivation of other Levitic names, however—Moses, Merari, Hophni, Phinehas, Hanamel, Pashhur—a connection with Osiris cannot be ruled out (Kerber *apud* Holzinger 1900: 20). *'Elqānâ* means "God has engendered/acquired" (see NOTE to 15:16). The meaning of *'ăbî'āsāp* is "My (divine) Father has gathered," or, reading with Sam *'ăbiyāsāp,* "My Father has added (a child)."

6:25. *(one) of Putiel's daughters.* The Redactor evidently did not know the name of Phinehas's mother.

It is unclear whether Putiel is a person or a tribe. The second element is Hebrew/Canaanite for "God." The first element seems to derive from Egyptian *pȝ dy* 'the given,' paralleled in biblical *pôṭîpar/pôṭî pera'* (Potiphar/Poti phera) 'Given of Re'' and epigraphic *pṭ's* 'Given of Isis' (Zadok 1986: 363; Hestrin and Dayagi-Mendels 1979: 65). Thus the name probably arose in a Semitic-Egyptian milieu and means "Gift of God" (Noth 1928: 63). The hybrid name "Putiel" is paralleled exactly by epigraphic Hebrew *ptyhw* 'Given of Yahweh' from Ein-Gedi (*AHI* 20.001); cf. also *ḥnm'l* 'Khnum is God.' It is probably no coincidence that Putiel's grandson also bears an Egyptian name; see next NOTE (A. C. Feliu, privately).

Phinehas. The genealogy culminates in Phinehas, Aaron's grandson and supposed ancestor of the priestly house of Zadok. The name, which recurs in the genealogy of the house of Eli (1 Sam 1:3) and among the postexilic clergy (Ezra 8:33), derives from the common New Kingdom Egyptian name *pȝ-nḥsy* 'The Nubian' (Lauth 1871: 139–40; Cody 1969: 71). Like the Hebrew name *kûšî* 'The Nubian, Cushite,' *pînəḥās* presumably connotes either a person with unusually dark skin or a true African.

SPECULATION: Some Levites, to judge from their names (NOTE to 6:24), did actually come out of Egypt. Perhaps some were also of Nubian extraction.

Moses, for example, is said to have had a Cushite wife (Num 12:1). Admittedly, many equate this "Cush" with Cushan = Midian (Hab 3:7), identifying the wife with Zipporah (e.g., Albright 1944: 205; Cross 1973: 204). I doubt this is correct, however. Num 12:1 implies that the Cushite is a new wife, and Miriam's snow-white condition is a fitter punishment if the new wife is dark. Perhaps some of the multitude that left Egypt along with Israel (12:38; Num 11:4), or the women sojourning among the Hebrews (3:22), were Nubians. On later legends associating Moses with Nubia, see Redford (1992: 419).

heads of the Levites' fathers. This is ellipsis for "heads of the Levites' fathers' *house*" (cf. v 14) (Holzinger 1990: 19).

6:26. *Aaron and Moses.* Listed here in birth order (MT); contrast v 27.

brigades. To judge from Num 1:3, *ṣəbā'ōt* refers primarily to adult males, although the entire people is clearly intended by synecdoche. The Priestly Writer, followed by R, imagines Israel as an army divided into tribal brigades (cf. Numbers 1–3; 10:14–28; Josephus *Ant.* 2.312). P thus emphasizes the dignity and order with which Israel left Egypt—as an army marching out to battle, not as a fleeing mob (Ehrlich 1969: 147; see also NOTE to 12:17). According to Hecataeus of Abdera (*apud* Diodorus Siculus *Bibliotheca Historica* 40.3), Moses was the first to divide Israel into tribes for administrative purposes.

SPECULATION: P's identification of Israel as Yahweh's "brigades" (7:4) may respond to the non-Priestly divine epithet "Yahweh of Brigades" (*yahwe[h] ṣəbā'ôt*), where the *ṣəbā'ôt* are probably minor deities (Deut 4:19; 17:3; Josh 5:14–15; 1 Kgs 22:19; 2 Kgs 17:16; 21:3, 5; 23:4, 5; Jer 8:2; 19:13; Zeph 1:5; Ps 103:21; 148:2; Dan 8:10, 11; see also NOTES to 15:3, 11). For P, however, Yahweh's *ṣəbā'ôt* are either Israel or the depersonalized elements of Creation (Gen 2:1).

One might initially infer that the Priestly Writer was sensitive to the mythological overtones of *yahwe(h) ṣəbā'ôt*, comparing P's aversion to angels (cf. Friedman 1987: 192, 204). But Ezekiel, too, never uses "Yahweh of Brigades," even though he describes heavenly beings in detail. We require a fuller explanation.

If, as some believe, the title *yahwe(h) ṣəbā'ôt* originated in the cult of Shiloh, and especially if its full form was "Yahweh of brigades, enthroned upon the cherubim," then P and Ezekiel may shun the term for theopolitical reasons (cf. Seow 1989: 9–21). That is, the Zadokite tradition represented by Ezekiel and probably P rejected the legitimacy of the house of Shiloh. The Priestly Writer even tried to obscure the very notion that Yahweh sits upon cherubim; P's cherubim rather form a canopy (25:17–22; 37:6–9) (Mettinger 1982: 80–97). Ezekiel, less sensitive to the issue, still depicts God as seated, but on a mobile cherub throne-chariot (Ezek 1:26–28; cf. chap. 10).

6:28. *in the land of Egypt.* As we observed under SOURCE ANALYSIS, in P, Moses first receives God's word while dwelling among his people. Unlike the

Moses of JE, he is not, so far as we know, an adopted Egyptian prince, nor does he flee to Midian. He is just a Hebrew in Egypt. I would compare the differing locations of the sacred Tent in JE and P. In JE, it is outside the camp (33:7–11; Num 12:4 [E]), while P's Tabernacle stands in the center (Numbers 2). Although separating the sacred and the profane was vital for the Priestly Writer, it was equally essential that Yahweh's place of revelation be in the midst of his people.

6:29. *I am Yahweh.* Cassuto (1967: 88) takes "I am Yahweh" as summarizing the earlier speech that began and ended with these words (vv 2–8).

6:30. *heed me.* With *yišma' 'ēlay* (MT), the Redactor blends two phrases from 6:12 (P), *šāmə'û 'ēlay* and *yišmā'ēnî*, presumably for the sake of variety. Exod 6:12 and 30 chiastically frame the material between (see SOURCE ANALYSIS): "How will Pharaoh heed me, as I am uncircumcised of lips? . . . As I am uncircumcised of lips, then how will Pharaoh heed me?"

7:1. *deity.* Cassuto (1967: 89) detects irony: Moses is to be a god to the god-king of Egypt.

prophet. Exod 7:1 excellently illustrates P's ambivalence toward Moses and toward prophets in general (see COMMENT). On the one hand, Moses is Aaron's superior, a quasi-deity. Yet he is unfit to address Pharaoh. Aaron the priest-to-be must serve as prophetic intermediary, delivering Yahweh's oracle against a foreign nation to its hostile ruler and performing wonders with his staff. On the one hand, we might regard P as *polemicizing* against prophets, claiming that Aaronic priests are superior intermediaries (7:1 is P's sole mention of *nābî'* 'prophet'). If so, the prophets' antipathy toward the hereditary clergy was fully reciprocated. But one could also read 7:1 as *legitimating* prophets by including Aaron among their number. Ezekiel is the only other figure described as both Aaronic priest and prophet.

7:3. *harden.* *Hiqšâ* means "give courage," not "make cruel." Out of this idiom, Ezekiel creates the image of a "stone heart" (36:26; cf. also Zech 7:12). Elsewhere, P and R describe Pharaoh's heart as, not "hard" (*qšy*), but "strong" (*ḥzq*) (4:21; 7:13, 22; 8:15; 9:12, 35; 10:20, 27; 11:10; 14:4, 8, 17).

7:4. *arm.* Exod 7:4 is connected to 6:6 both by their common mention of "great judgments" and by the parallelism of *zərôa'* 'limb' and *yād* 'arm.' Both terms often connote "power," but in the context of the Exodus, they also bear their proper meanings. Moses and Aaron, Yahweh's representatives, repeatedly extend their arms and rods over Egypt to bring down calamity. See also NOTES to 3:19 and 7:5; COMMENT to 13:17–15:21.

upon. Or "against" (*'al*).

Egypt. *Miṣrayim* may mean "the Egyptians," as in the next verse; see NOTE.

judgments. See NOTE to 6:6.

7:5. *Egypt will know.* Egypt's (and Israel's) "knowledge" of Yahweh is tantamount to recognition of his sovereignty. In ancient Near Eastern treaties, vassals and suzerains are said to "know" one another (Huffmon 1966; Huffmon and Parker 1966).

in my extending my arm. In the context of P, this probably refers to the crossing of the Sea, where Egypt finally learns to "know" Yahweh (14:4, 18; Childs

1974: 140). In the composite text, however, 7:5 refers also to the Plagues, enacted with an outstretched arm or rod. All God's wonders teach both Egypt and Israel to "know" Yahweh (7:17; 8:6, 18; 9:14, 29; 10:2; 11:7 [E]).

over. Or "against."

Egypt. That *miṣrayim* refers to the people of Egypt, rather than the land, is indicated by the plural *wəyādə'û* '(they) will know.'

7:6. *Moses and Aaron did* . . . The syntax, awkward to us, emphasizes that the two did precisely according to Yahweh's word.

7:7. *son of.* This is how Hebrew expresses age. Cassuto (1967: 90–91) notes that we are often told a character's age after (s)he undergoes a significant experience (Gen 16:16; 17:24–25; 25:26; 41:46, etc.).

eighty. In Israel, full (male) adulthood began at twenty (e.g., 38:26). Forty years was considered sufficient time for a generation of adults to die off, assuming a life span of sixty years (Num 14:29, 33–34). Moses has already completed two forty-year cycles and will eventually complete two sixty-year cycles, dying at 120 (Deut 34:7 [J?; cf. Gen 6:3]). Thus Moses is two-thirds through his life when he begins his most important work.

COMMENT

I AM YAHWEH

In some biblical theophanies, God changes a human's name (e.g., Abraham, Sarah, Jacob). The new appellation betokens, among other things, deeper intimacy with the Deity. In 6:2–3, however, God himself assumes a new name — or, rather, reveals an old name.

This is the final stage in P's chronicle of divine evolution/revelation. As Deity (*'ĕlōhîm*), a title not unique to Israel, God created and ordered all the Cosmos. As God Shadday, he restricted his concern to a band of seminomads who, despite their portable wealth, owned as heritable real estate a single burial site. In this manifestation, God promised two things to the Hebrews: numerous progeny and the land of Canaan (Gen 17:1–8) (Wimmer 1967: 416–17). As God Shadday, he fulfilled the first promise (1:7). Now, fully manifest as Yahweh, he is ready to free Israel and wrest Canaan from its current occupants.

GENEALOGICAL FORM AND FUNCTION

As Yahweh is defined by his covenantal relationship with Abraham, Isaac and Jacob (6:3–4, 8), so Moses and Aaron are defined by their genetic relationship with the ancestors (6:14–27). Biblical genealogies are not necessarily accurate records of paternity and maternity. Their function is to assign status, to establish reciprocal responsibilities and privileges among social groups (Wilson 1977). Many "persons" in biblical genealogies are really clans or even cities. Exod 6:14–27 traces the Levite lineage that will produce the holy personnel of the

Tabernacle and Temple. It proceeds generation by generation, gradually adding information on life span and maternity to limit our focus onto one man. Although ostensibly the pedigree of Moses and Aaron, the true "hero" of 6:14–27 is Aaron's grandson Phinehas, ancestor of Israel's high priests.

Exod 6:14 begins with Israel (i.e., Jacob) and gives an overview of the families of Reuben and Simeon, accorded their traditional primacy. There are no ages or wives, nor are their lines traced beyond one generation (hence the absence of "in their generations"). Reuben and Simeon are included merely to introduce and locate the third son, Levi (Cassuto 1967: 84).

In contrast, the Levites are enumerated "in their generations"; the genealogy never does get to Israel's next son, Judah. With Levi, we first find a life span. Although the writer is mainly concerned with Levi's second son, Kohath, he must follow birth order, so he names Gershon and his sons, but without life spans. Only when we return to Kohath do we find a life span. After naming Kohath's sons, the genealogy proceeds to Levi's third son, Merari, and his two sons. As in the case of Gershon, no extra details are provided.

Then the genealogist backtracks to Kohath's son Amram. To further heighten our interest, he not only tells us Amram's age at death but also names his wife. Amram's younger brothers, Yizhar and Uzziel, are then listed, along with their sons, but without detail. Hebron's children are ignored, because they play no further role in the Torah (see SOURCE ANALYSIS).

In the next generation, only two figures interest the genealogist: Aaron and Korah. The sons of each are named, but only Aaron has a wife. (His life span is omitted, presumably because he is still alive.) Surprisingly, Moses' children are passed over (see below).

The genealogy ends with Aaron's grandson Phinehas, the only member of his generation included—even though he is not yet born (witness his survival of the forty years' wandering). Phinehas will be a major character later in the Torah, and most likely both the Priestly Writer and the Redactor claimed descent from Aaron through Phinehas (Friedman 1987: 214–25). Ithamar's sons go unnamed (contrast 1 Chr 24:3, 6; Ezra 8:2; 1 Esdr 8:29).

MOSES VS. AARON

It is generally recognized that biblical depictions of the interactions among the Levites, Moses and Aaron reflect a centuries-long battle over the right to the priesthood waged between the Levites and the house of Aaron (COMMENT to chap. 32; cf. Cross 1973: 195–215). In E (Exodus 32; Numbers 12) and D (Deut 9:20), Aaron comes in for criticism, while Moses and the Levites are heroes. In P, however, the Levites are consecrated as the priests' *servants* (Num 3:6–9; 8:19; 18:1–7) and are even punished for seeking higher office (Numbers 16). Moses, too, is somewhat discredited or diminished in P (Friedman 1987: 197). He is Aaron's *younger* brother (Num 26:59; contrast Exod 4:14 [E]), "uncircumcised of lips" (6:12; cf. 4:10 [E]), unable to convince Israel (6:9; cf. 4:31 [E]) and possibly disfigured (34:29–35; see Propp 1987d). His hot temper brings about both his own death and Aaron's (Num 20:2–13; cf. Exod 17:1–7 [E]). Moses, lastly, does not react to the sin of Baal Peor, deferring to Phinehas (Num 25:6–9; cf. vv 1–5 [E]). P's animosity toward Midianites is also, most likely, an implicit denigration of Moses; see COMMENTS to 2:15b–23a (p. 176) and chapter 18 (p. 635).

But there is also a tendency in P to *apotheosize* Moses and hence to dehumanize him. Moses is the Founder, Lawgiver and Aaron's superior throughout P. He is a quasi-deity, explicitly to Pharaoh and implicitly to Aaron, his prophet (7:1; cf. 4:16 [E]). By one reading of 34:29–35, Moses is transformed into a radiant demigod from whom Aaron and the tribal princes flee. Another important aspect of Moses' dehumanization is his apparent lack of family in P (Num 26:59–61), in contrast to JE (2:16–22; 4:20, 24–26; 18:2–6) and 1 Chr 23:15–18. True, Num 3:27 (P) alludes to Amramite Levites, i.e., Moses' descendants, but the reference is rather oblique. Even the Redactor, who knows of Moses' family from JE, lists no children in 6:14–27. In P, Moses' authority is passed on, not to his sons, but to Joshua, and in much diminished measure. Joshua does not answer only to God; he must consult and obey Aaron's son Eleazar (Num 27:21).

The diminution and the exaltation of Moses probably served the same purpose: to make Moses irrelevant to the reality of the Priestly Writer's day (cf. Gunneweg 1965: 140). Why? Cross (1973: 195–215) provides one plausible answer: the author was attacking a priestly family claiming Mosaic lineage. According to Judg 18:30, the priesthood of Dan in the North was descended from Moses (OG; MT "Me^{n}asseh" is bowdlerized), although there is also an unclear Judahite connection (Judg 17:7; see Cody 1969: 54–55 n. 54). Note, too, that Josh 21:23–24 places non-Aaronid Kohathites, perhaps descendants of Moses, near Dan. And even though the Torah never calls him *kōhēn* 'priest,' Moses exercises priestly functions in JE (24:5–8; 33:7–11) and even in P (Exodus 29; 40:20–33; Leviticus 8). In fact, Ps 99:6 identifies both Moses and Aaron as Yahweh's priests. Finally, 1 Chr 26:24–26, though suspect on account of its lateness, claims that descendants of Moses were part of David's cultic establishment, overseeing the sacred treasury.

In short, there is convincing evidence that an influential Levitic clan claimed Mosaic descent. But I do not agree with Cross that the anti-Aaron stance of E and D or the anti-Moses tendency in P necessarily reflects direct conflict between the houses of Moses and Aaron. The only characters in P that vie with Aaron for the priesthood are *Levites* (Numbers 16–18); Moses, in fact, sides with Aaron. In E and D, on the other hand, Moses claims no exclusive priestly rights. His sons are insignificant in E and entirely absent from D. The Moses of E and D functions rather as a *pan-Levitic hero*, not as the progenitor of a Mosaic priesthood.

P's Moses is more complicated, however. In some respects, he may be a pan-Levitic villain, the denigration of whom is part and parcel of P's hostility toward the Levites. But in other respects, Moses is Aaron's legitimating ally against the Levites. Overall, it seems that the Priestly Writer, though uncomfortable with it, could not deny the primacy tradition ascribed to Moses. At most, he could enlarge Aaron's role somewhat and diminish Moses', making Aaron morally perfect and Moses flawed.

What, then, about P's elevation of Moses almost beyond humankind? What about Moses' lack of progeny? Here, perhaps, we may detect P's particular animus against the Mosaic Levites. Cross, among others, plausibly identifies the Levitic house of Mushi (*mûšî*) as derived from *mōše(h)* 'Moses.' But in the standard Priestly genealogy (e.g., 6:19), Mushi is Moses' *cousin*. The natural inference is that the Priestly Writer is attempting to discredit Mushite claims to Mosaic paternity by fabricating "Mushi," the last and presumably least of Levi's grandsons. Moreover, it cannot be coincidence that the name of Moses' first son, Gershom (JE), resembles so closely Levi's eldest son, Gershon (P, R); witness their confusion in 1 Chronicles 6; 15:7. It is also hard to ascribe to chance the similarity between Moses' other son, Eliezer (JE), and Aaron's Eleazar (P, R) (see Gunneweg 1965: 164). In short, the Priestly Writer attempted to dismember the house of Moses by making Mushi, Gershom/n and Eliezer/Eleazar independent one of another and of Moses.

SPECULATION: It is also conceivable that the house of Eliezer/Eleazar was divided into a Mosaic and an Aaronic branch—although we would have expected Eliezer/Eleazar to be Moses and Aaron's *father*, not son. Did the Aaronids win over some of this clan? If so, by what process did Eliezer/Eleazar come to be the chief Aaronid family, displacing Nadab and Abihu? Our data fail just as conjecture grows most intriguing.

X. But Pharaoh's heart was strong; he did not release Israel's Sons (7:8–11:10)

7 [8(P)]And Yahweh said to Moses and to Aaron, saying, [9]"When Pharaoh speaks to you, saying, 'Give yourselves a wonder,' then say to Aaron, 'Take your rod and cast before Pharaoh. Let it become a serpent.'"

[10]And Moses and Aaron came to Pharaoh and did so, as Yahweh commanded. And Aaron cast his rod before Pharaoh and before his slaves, and it became a serpent. [11]But Pharaoh, too, called to the sages and to the wizards, and they, too, Egypt's *ḥarṭummîm*, did with their mysteries likewise. [12]And each threw down his rod and they became serpents. And Aaron's rod swallowed their rods. [13]But Pharaoh's heart was strong, and he did not heed them, as Yahweh had spoken.

[14(E)]And Yahweh said to Moses, "Pharaoh's heart is firm; he has refused to release the people. [15]Go to Pharaoh in the morning; see: (him) going out to the waters. And you will station yourself to meet him on the Nile's *lip*, and the rod that turned into a snake you will take in your hand. [16]And you will say to him,

'Yahweh the Hebrews' deity sent me to you, saying, "Release my people, that they may serve me in the wilderness"—but, see: you have not hearkened till now. [17]Thus has Yahweh said: "By this you may know that I am Yahweh. See: I am going to strike with the rod that is in my hand upon the waters that are in the Nile, and they will turn to blood. [18]And the fish that is in the Nile will die, and the Nile will reek, and Egypt will be unable to drink waters from the Nile."'"

[19(P)]And Yahweh said to Moses, "Say to Aaron, 'Take your rod and extend your arm over Egypt's waters—over their rivers, over their "niles" and over their marshes and over every reservoir of their waters, that they become blood.' And blood will be in all the land of Egypt, in the stocks and in the stones."

[20]And Moses and Aaron did so, as Yahweh commanded. [(E)]And he raised with the rod and struck the waters that were in the Nile to Pharaoh's eyes and to his slaves' eyes, and all the waters that were in the Nile were turned to blood. [21]And the fish that was in the Nile died, and the Nile reeked, and Egypt were not able to drink waters from the Nile, [(P)]and the blood was in all the land of Egypt. [22]But Egypt's ḥarṭummîm did likewise with their mysteries, and Pharaoh's heart was strong, and he did not heed them, as Yahweh had spoken. [23(E)]And Pharaoh turned and came into his house and did not set his heart to this either. [24]And all Egypt dug waters to drink from the Nile's surroundings, for they could not drink from the Nile's waters.

[25]And seven days were filled after Yahweh's smiting the Nile. [26]And Yahweh said to Moses, "Come to Pharaoh, and you will say to him, 'Thus has Yahweh said: "Release my people, that they may serve me. [27]For if you refuse to release, see: I am going to strike all your territory with the frogs. [28]And the Nile will breed frogs, and they will ascend and come into your house and into your bed room and onto your bed and into your slaves' house and among your people and into your ovens and into your dough pans. [29]And upon you and upon your slaves and upon your people the frogs will ascend."'"

8   [1(P)]And Yahweh said to Moses, "Say to Aaron, 'Extend your arm with your rod over the rivers, over the "niles" and over the marshes, and raise the frogs upon the land of Egypt.'"

[2]And Aaron extended his arm over Egypt's waters, and the frog ascended and covered the land of Egypt. [3]But the ḥarṭummîm did likewise with their mysteries, [(P/E)]and they raised up the frogs upon the land of Egypt. [4(E)]And Pharaoh called to Moses and to Aaron and said, "Pray to Yahweh, that he remove the frogs from me and from my people, and I will release the people, that they may sacrifice to Yahweh."

[5]And Moses said, "Assume honor over me as to for when I should pray for you and for your slaves and for your people, to cut off the frogs from you and from your houses; only in the Nile they will remain."

[6]And he said, "For tomorrow."

And he said, "According to your word, that you may know that none is like Yahweh our deity. [7]And the frogs will depart from you and from your houses and from your slaves and from your people; only in the Nile they will remain."

⁸And Moses and Aaron went out from with Pharaoh, and Moses cried to Yahweh on the matter of the frogs that he put upon Pharaoh. ⁹And Yahweh did according to Moses' word, and the frogs died from the houses, from the yards and from the fields. ¹⁰And they piled them as heaps, heaps, and the land reeked. ¹¹But Pharaoh saw that there was respite, and he made firm his heart, ⁽ᴾ⁾and he did not heed them, as Yahweh had spoken.

¹²And Yahweh said to Moses, "Say to Aaron, 'Extend your rod and strike the dirt of the land, that it become lice in all the land of Egypt.'"

¹³And they did so. And Aaron extended his arm with his rod and struck the dirt of the land, and the louse became on man and on animal; all the dirt of the land became lice in all the land of Egypt. ¹⁴And the ḥarṭummîm did likewise with their mysteries, to bring forth the lice, but they were not able. And the louse became on man and on animal. ¹⁵And the ḥarṭummîm said to Pharaoh, "It is a divine finger." But Pharaoh's heart was strong, and he did not heed them, as Yahweh had spoken.

¹⁶⁽ᴱ⁾And Yahweh said to Moses, "Rise early in the morning and station yourself before Pharaoh; see: (him) going out to the waters. And you will say to him, 'Thus has Yahweh said: "Release my people, that they may serve me. ¹⁷For if you do not release my people, see: I am going to send against you and against your slaves and against your people and into your houses the ʿārōb; and Egypt's houses will be full of the ʿārōb, as well as the land on which they are. ¹⁸But I will separate on that day the land of Goshen, on which my people stands, and there will be no ʿārōb there, that you may know that I am Yahweh in the land's midst. ¹⁹For I will put a redemption between my people and between your people; tomorrow this sign will occur."'"

²⁰And Yahweh did so, and heavy ʿārōb came to Pharaoh's house and his slaves' house. And in all the land of Egypt the land was being devastated from before the ʿārōb.

²¹And Pharaoh called to Moses and to Aaron and said, "Go, sacrifice to your deity in the land."

²²But Moses said, "It is not possible to do so, for Egypt's abomination we would sacrifice to Yahweh our deity. If we sacrifice Egypt's abomination to their eyes, will they not stone us? ²³A three days' way we would go into the wilderness and sacrifice to Yahweh our deity as he may say to us."

²⁴But Pharaoh said, "I, I will release you, that you may sacrifice to Yahweh your deity in the wilderness. Only far, do not go far. Pray for me."

²⁵And Moses said, "See: I am going out from with you, and I will pray to Yahweh, and the ʿārōb will leave from Pharaoh, from his slaves and from his people tomorrow. Only let not Pharaoh continue to toy by not releasing the people to sacrifice to Yahweh."

²⁶And Moses went out from with Pharaoh and prayed to Yahweh. ²⁷And Yahweh did according to Moses' word and removed the ʿārōb from Pharaoh, from his slaves and from his people; not one remained. ²⁸But Pharaoh made firm his heart this time, too, and did not release the people.

9 ¹And Yahweh said to Moses, "Come to Pharaoh, and you will speak to him: 'Thus has Yahweh the Hebrews' deity said: "Release my people, that they may serve me. ²For if you refuse to release, and you still hold them, ³see: Yahweh's arm is about to be upon your cattle that are in the field, upon the horses, upon the asses, upon the camels, upon the herd and upon the flock—a very heavy plague. ⁴But Yahweh will separate between Israel's cattle and between Egypt's cattle, and of all belonging to Israel's Sons no thing will die."'" ⁵And Yahweh set a time, saying, "Tomorrow Yahweh will do this thing in the land."

⁶And Yahweh did this thing on the next day. And all Egypt's cattle died, and of Israel's Sons' cattle not one died. ⁷And Pharaoh sent, and, see: so much as one of Israel's cattle had not died. But Pharaoh's heart was firm, and he did not release the people.

⁸(P)And Yahweh said to Moses and to Aaron, "Take for yourselves oven ash, the fullness of your fists, and let Moses cast it heavenward to Pharaoh's eyes. ⁹And it will become dust over all the land of Egypt, and it will become upon man and upon animal a *šəḥîn* blossoming with boils in all the land of Egypt."

¹⁰So they took the oven ash and stood before Pharaoh, and Moses threw it heavenward, and there was a *šəḥîn* of boils blossoming upon man and upon animal. ¹¹And the *ḥarṭummîm* could not stand before Moses because of the *šəḥîn*, for the *šəḥîn* was upon the *ḥarṭummîm* and upon all Egypt. ¹²But Yahweh strengthened Pharaoh's heart, and he did not heed them, as Yahweh had spoken to Moses.

¹³(E)And Yahweh said to Moses, "Rise early in the morning and station yourself before Pharaoh. And you will say to him, 'Thus has Yahweh the Hebrews' deity said: "Release my people, that they may serve me. ¹⁴For this time I am going to send all these my afflictions against you and against your slaves and against your people, in order that you may know that none is like me in all the world. ¹⁵For now, I could have sent forth my arm and smitten you and your people with the plague, so that you would have vanished from the land. ¹⁶However, for this I have let you stand: in order to show you my strength, and to tell my *name* in all the world. ¹⁷You still exalt yourself over my people without releasing them. ¹⁸See: I am going to rain at this time tomorrow very heavy hail, whose like never was in Egypt from the day, her founding, and until now. ¹⁹And now send, shelter your cattle and all in the field that is yours. Every man or animal that will be found in the field and will not have been gathered into the house—then the hail will descend upon them and they will die."'"

²⁰He who feared Yahweh's word from Pharaoh's slaves, he sheltered his slaves and his cattle in the houses. ²¹But he who did not put his heart to Yahweh's word, then he left his slaves and his cattle in the field.

²²And Yahweh said to Moses, "Extend your arm toward the heavens, and let there be hail in all the land of Egypt, upon man and upon animal and upon all the field's herbage in the land of Egypt."

²³So Moses extended his rod toward the heavens, and Yahweh, he gave *voices* and hail, and fire went groundward, and Yahweh rained hail on the land

of Egypt. ²⁴And there was hail, and fire caught up within the hail, very heavy, whose like was not in Egypt since she became a nation. ²⁵And the hail struck in the land of Egypt everything that was in the field, from man and to animal, and all the field's herbage the hail struck, and every tree of the field it smashed. ²⁶Only in the land of Goshen, where Israel's Sons were, there was no hail.

²⁷And Pharaoh sent and called to Moses and to Aaron and said to them, "I have been wrong this time. The justified one is Yahweh, and the guilty are I and my people. ²⁸Pray to Yahweh, that it will be enough of being divine *voices* and hail, and I will release you, and you will not continue to stand still."

²⁹And Moses said to him, "As my leaving the city, I will spread my hands to Yahweh. The *voices* will cease, and the hail will be no more, that you may know that the earth is Yahweh's. ³⁰But you and your slaves, I know that you do not yet fear before Yahweh Deity."

³¹Now, the flax and the barley were smitten, for the barley was young ears and the flax was buds. ³²But the wheat and the emmer were not smitten, for they were *dark*.

³³And Moses left the city from with Pharaoh and spread his hands to Yahweh, and the *voices* and the hail ceased, and rain was not shed groundward. ³⁴And Pharaoh saw that the rain and the hail and the *voices* had ceased, and he continued to do wrong, and he made firm his heart, he and his slaves. ^{35(R?)}**And Pharaoh's heart was strong, and he did not release Israel's Sons, as Yahweh had spoken through Moses' hand.**

10   ^{1(E)}And Yahweh said to Moses, "Come to Pharaoh, for I, I have made firm his heart and his slaves' heart, so that I might set these my signs in his core, ²and so that you may tell into your sons' ears and your son's son's how I lorded it in Egypt, and my signs that I set among them, that you may know that I am Yahweh."

³And Moses and Aaron came to Pharaoh and said to him, "Thus has Yahweh the Hebrews' deity said: 'Until when do you refuse to humble yourself before me? Release my people, that they may serve me. ⁴For if you refuse to release my people, see: I am going to bring tomorrow locust in your territory. ⁵And it will cover the land's *eye*, and one will not be able to see the earth, and it will eat the excess of the remnant remaining to you from the hail, and it will eat every tree that sprouts for you from the field. ⁶And they will fill your houses and your slaves' houses and all Egypt's houses—that which your fathers and your fathers' fathers never saw, from the day of their being upon the ground until this day.'" And he turned and went from with Pharaoh.

⁷And Pharaoh's slaves said to him, "Until when will this be a snare to us? Release the men, that they may serve Yahweh their deity. Don't you yet know that Egypt is dying?"

⁸So Moses and Aaron were brought back to Pharaoh, and he said to them, "Go, serve Yahweh your deity. *Who and who* are going?"

⁹And Moses said, "With our youths and with our elders we would go, with our sons and with our daughters, with our flocks and with our herds we would go, for it is Yahweh's festival for us."

¹⁰But he said to them, "May Yahweh be so with you, as I would release you and your dependents. See: for evil is before your face. ¹¹Not so. Go, you males, and serve Yahweh, for that is what you are seeking," and he expelled them from before Pharaoh.

¹²And Yahweh said to Moses, "Extend your arm over the land of Egypt with the locust, and let it ascend upon the land of Egypt and eat all the land's herbage, all that the hail left behind."

¹³So Moses extended his rod over the land of Egypt, and Yahweh, he drove a *forward* wind into the land, all that day and all the night. The morning happened, and the *forward* wind bore the locust, ¹⁴and the locust ascended over all the land of Egypt and alit in all the territory of Egypt, very heavy. Before it there was never such locust as it, and after it never will be such. ¹⁵And it covered all the land's *eye*, so that the land was dark, and it ate all the land's herbage and all the tree's fruit that the hail had left; not any greenery was left on the tree or on the field's herbage in all the land of Egypt.

¹⁶And Pharaoh hurried to call to Moses and to Aaron and said, "I have wronged Yahweh your deity and you. ¹⁷And now, *lift* my fault only this time, and pray to Yahweh your deity that he remove from upon me just this death."

¹⁸So he went out from with Pharaoh and prayed to Yahweh. ¹⁹And Yahweh turned back a very strong sea wind, and it bore the locust and blew it into the Suph Sea. Not one locust was left in all Egypt's territory. ^{20(R?)}**But Yahweh strengthened Pharaoh's heart, and he did not release Israel's Sons.**

^{21(E)}And Yahweh said to Moses, "Extend your arm into the heavens, and let there be darkness over the land of Egypt." ²²And Moses extended his arm into the heavens, and there was a darkness of gloom in all the land of Egypt three days. ²³Man could not see his *brother*, and no man stood up *from under himself* three days. But for all Israel's Sons there was light in their dwellings.

²⁴And Pharaoh called to Moses and said, "Go serve Yahweh. Only your flock and your herd will be detained. Your dependents, too, may go with you."

²⁵But Moses said, "Both will you, you put into our hand *slaughter sacrifices* and *ascending sacrifices* that we may make to Yahweh our deity, ²⁶and also our own cattle will go with us; not a hoof will remain. For from them we will take to serve Yahweh our deity, since we, we do not know with what we will serve Yahweh until our arrival there."

^{27(R?)}**But Yahweh strengthened Pharaoh's heart, and he did not release them.**

^{28(E)}Then Pharaoh said to them, "Go from before me. Watch yourself, see my face no more. For on the day of your seeing my face you will die."

²⁹And Moses said, "You spoke right. I will see your face no more."

11 ¹And Yahweh said to Moses, "Yet one more plague I will bring upon Pharaoh and upon Egypt. After this, he will release you from here; when he releases completely, he will expel, expel you. ^{2(J?)}Speak in the people's ears, that they should ask, man of his friend and woman of her friend, silver objects and gold objects. ³And Yahweh will put the people's favor in Egypt's eyes.

Also, the man Moses will be very great in the land of Egypt, in Pharaoh's slaves' eyes and in the people's eyes." [4(E)]And Moses said, "Thus has Yahweh said: 'At midnight I am going to set forth in Egypt's midst. [5]And every firstborn in the land of Egypt will die, from the firstborn of Pharaoh sitting on his throne to the firstborn of the maidservant that is behind the two millstones, and every animal firstborn. [6]And a great cry will be in Egypt, whose like never happened nor whose like will ever recur. [7]But for all Israel's Sons not a dog will *sharpen his tongue*, from man to animal, that you may know that Yahweh will separate between Egypt and between Israel.' [8]And all these your slaves will go down to me and bow to me, saying, 'Go out, you and all the people that are at your *feet*,' and then I will go out," and he went out from with Pharaoh with anger of *nose*.

[9(R?)]And Yahweh said to Moses, "Pharaoh will not heed you, that my wonders may be multiplied in the land of Egypt."

[10]And Moses and Aaron, they did all these wonders before Pharaoh. But Yahweh strengthened Pharaoh's heart, and he did not release Israel's Sons from his land.

ANALYSIS

TEXTUAL NOTES

7:8. *said.* Sam and Kenn 176 instead have "spoke" (*wydbr*).

saying. Absent in Syr and Vg.

7:9. *When.* LXX inserts "and."

Give yourselves. LXX "Give *us*" is probably an inner-Greek corruption: *hymin 'for you' > *hēmin* 'for us' (cf. Wevers 1990: 96). But conceivably, the LXX *Vorlage* read *lnw 'to us' (= Kenn 109), reduplicating the final letters of *tnw* 'give.' Syr "give *me*" is unlikely to reflect yet another Hebrew variant but is a commonsense emendation (see NOTE).

a wonder. In Sam, Kenn 109 and LXX, the verb has two objects: "*a sign or* a wonder" (*'ôt 'ô môpēt*). As the shorter reading, MT is preferable.

Aaron. LXX expands: "your brother."

cast. LXX adds "on the ground," borrowed from 4:3.

before Pharaoh. LXX adds "and before his servants," as in the next verse.

†*Let it become.* Sam, LXX and Syr read *wyhy* (*wîhî*) '*and* let it become,' vs. MT *yəhî.* On the one hand, *wyhy* is more idiomatic, and waw could easily have dropped from MT before the similar-appearing yodh (haplography). On the other hand, the following verse contains *wyhy* (*wayhî*), which may simply have slipped forward. MT is slightly preferable as the shorter and more difficult text.

7:10. *came.* The verb is singular in MT, plural in Syr. Syr also omits "and" at the beginning of the verse.

to Pharaoh. Against MT *'el-par'ō(h)*, 4QpaleoExod^m, 4QGen-Exod^a, Sam and LXX read *lipnê par'ō(h)* '*before* Pharaoh,' perhaps repeated from 7:9. LXX again adds "and his servants."

commanded. Syr adds "them."

7:11. *too.* *Gam* is not reflected in LXX or Syr and is absent in Kenn 185.

the sages. Some LXX MSS expand: "*Egypt's* sages."

7:12. *his rod.* Syr adds "before Pharaoh" as in 7:9, 10.

7:13. *heed them.* For MT *šāma'* '*ălēhem*, Syr has "*release* them," harmonizing with 8:28; 9:7, 35; 10:20, 27; 11:10.

7:14. *said.* Sam and 4QpaleoExod^m have instead "spoke" (*wydbr*).

he has refused. For the MT perfect *mē'ēn*, we could also read **mā'ēn* 'is refusing'; cf. 9:2; 10:4. LXX has *mē* 'so as not to,' which we would ordinarily regard as a loose translation of MT (Wevers 1990: 99). Since, however, LXX renders *mē'ēn* literally in 7:27; 9:2; 10:3, 4, I suspect that in fact LXX reads **mē'ēn* 'so as not to.'

7:15. *see: (him).* 4QpaleoExod^m and Kenn 84, 129, 186, 196 have "*and* see." "Him" (*hû'*) is explicit in Sam, 4QpaleoExod^m and perhaps the LXX *Vorlage*; cf. 8:16.

†*to the waters.* For MT *hammaymâ*, Sam reads *hmym* (cf. 8:16; 9:8, 10; 10:19; 15:27; 16:33). The meaning is unaffected.

7:18. *from the Nile.* Sam and 4QpaleoExod^m have a major plus derived from vv 16–18: "Moses and Aaron went to Pharaoh and said [sing. in 4QpaleoExod^m, pl. in Sam] to him, 'Yahweh the Hebrews' deity sent us to you saying, "Release my people, that they may serve me in the wilderness"—but, see: you have not hearkened till now. Thus has Yahweh said: "By this you may know that I am Yahweh. See: I am going to strike with the rod that is in my hand upon the waters that are in the Nile, and they will turn to blood. And the fish that is in [4QpaleoExod^m: the midst of] the Nile will die, and the Nile will reek, and Egypt will be unable to drink waters from the Nile."'" The intent is to make explicit that Moses did exactly as told, in contrast to the laconic MT. Sam and 4QpaleoExod^m will follow a similar procedure throughout the Plagues (see TEXTUAL NOTES to 7:29, 8:1, 19, 9:5, 19 and 10:2, 5).

7:19. *Aaron.* LXX adds "your brother."

†*over . . . over.* The Versions put conjunctions in various places throughout the verse (Kennicott 1776–80: 119; de Rossi 1784–85: 51). My translation reflects standard MT.

every reservoir. Syr, Kenn 109 and 166 omit "every."

†"*that they become blood.*" *And blood will be.* Tg. Ps.-Jonathan omits the second of these similar-looking clauses (*wyhyw dm, whyh dm*) by either haplography or deliberate compression. For MT *wəhāyâ dām*, Sam has a variant *wyhy hdm*, i.e., **wayhî haddām* 'and the blood was' (*pace* BHS; cf. *Samaritan Tg.* J, LXX, Theodotion). Thus, in this tradition, the end of v 19 narrates the fulfillment of Yahweh's command. There is little doubt that MT *whyh* is correct, however, for the reading of Sam et al. breaks the time flow. The corruption of *whyh dm* into *wyhy hdm* is easy to explain; waw and yodh are similar in Herodian script

(Cross 1961a; Qimron 1972), and there are many cases of letters overleaping word divisions (Tov 1981: 174–77). Most important, the reading of Sam and LXX exactly anticipates v 21: *wayhî haddām bəkol-'ereṣ miṣrāyim* 'and the blood was in all the land of Egypt.' Evidently, a scribe simply brought these words forward.

7:20. *commanded.* Syr adds "them."

he raised. LXX^A and Syr clarify: "*Aaron* raised."

†*with the rod.* For MT *bmṭh*, LXX, Sam and most Syr MSS have *bmṭhw* 'with his rod.' Since the next word begins with *w*, either reading might be original; that is, either haplography or dittography may have occurred.

7:21. *the blood was.* 4QExod^c omits "the."

7:22. *mysteries.* For MT *lāṭêhem*, Sam and Kenn 5, 69, 150, 155, 189, 226, 228 have *lhṭyhm*, as in 7:11 (see also TEXTUAL NOTES to 8:3, 14).

†7:25. *were filled.* Where MT has the singular *wayyimmālē'*, Sam has the plural *wyml'w*. Either is grammatically acceptable; the former, however, is *lectio difficilior.*

7:26. *and you will say.* Sam has instead "and you will *speak*" (*wdbrt*).

7:27. *to release.* Kenn 18, 109, 150, 170, 686 and Rossi 262 append "my people."

all your territory. Kenn 69, 103, 109, Rossi 754 and the Arabic Version of LXX omit "all."

7:28. *your house . . . your bed room . . . your bed and . . . house.* In the Versions, the nouns are quite diverse in respect of number. 4QExod^c, only partly preserved, has *w'l mṭwtk . . . wbbyt* 'on your beds . . . and in the house of.' Sam has "your house [v 29 'houses'] . . . the rooms of your beds . . . your beds . . . your slaves' houses." And LXX puts all the nouns in the plural. Assuming the MT singulars are original, the other Versions have extended the language to include all Egypt.

into your slaves' house and among your people. The LXX equivalent for MT *wbbyt 'bdyk wb'mk* is "in your slaves' houses and your people's," as if reading *wbbyt 'bdyk w'mk* (which is bad Hebrew; see GKC §128a).

ovens and . . . dough pans. Reversed in LXX.

††7:29. *upon your slaves and upon your people.* My translation follows LXX, reading *ûba'ăbāde(y)kā ûb(ə)'ammekā* (vs. MT *ûb[ə]'amməkā ûb[ə]kol-'ăbāde[y]kā* 'and upon your people and upon all your slaves'). LXX is superior on two counts: it is the shorter reading; and wherever else the text mentions Pharaoh, his servants and his people or land, they appear in that order (8:5, 7, 17, 25, 27; 9:14; 10:6; 12:30; cf. 8:4; 9:15, 30, 34; 11:1), generally without "all" (except MT 10:6 and standard MT 12:30 [see TEXTUAL NOTES]). While MT is admittedly *lectio difficilior*, it may be too difficult.

Syr has an even shorter text than LXX: "and upon all your people," as if reading *ûb(ə)kol-'ammekā*. Most likely, all these readings reflect free variation of a formulaic list. If, however, we require mechanical explanations, to produce MT we might posit an earlier, expanded text: *ûb(ə)kol-'ăbāde(y)kā ûb(ə)'ammekā* 'and upon all your slaves and upon your people.' The words *ûb(ə)kol-'ăbāde(y)kā* fell out by homoioarkton and were then reinserted in the wrong place. And Syr would be a corruption by homoioarkton of another unattested, expanded variant: *ûbaʿăbāde(y)kā ûb(ǝ)kol-ʿammekā 'and upon your slaves and upon all your people' > *ûb(ǝ)kol-ʿammekā 'and upon all your people.'

ascend. At the end of v 29, Sam and 4QpaleoExod^m narrate the fulfillment of Yahweh's command in words derived from 7:26–29: "And Moses and Aaron came to Pharaoh and spoke to him, 'Thus has Yahweh said: "Release my people, that they may serve me. For if you refuse to release, see: I am going to strike all your territory with the frogs. And the Nile will breed frogs, and they will ascend and come into your houses [*sic*] and into the rooms [*sic*] of your beds [*sic*] and onto your beds [*sic*] and into your slaves' houses [*sic*] and among your people and into your ovens and into your dough pans. And upon you and upon your slaves and upon your people the frogs will ascend."'"

8:1. *Aaron.* LXX, Kenn 109 and Syr add "your brother."

†*over the* "*niles.*" LXX, Sam, Syr, Vg and some MSS of MT and of the *Tgs.* (Kennicott 1776–80: 120; de Rossi 1784–85: 52) insert "and."

upon the land of Egypt. These words are missing in LXX, probably by homoioteleuton in the *Vorlage*, since "frogs" (*ṣprdʿym*) and "Egypt" (*mṣrym*) end in the same consonants.

At the end of the verse, Sam adds "and Moses said to Aaron, 'Extend your arm with your rod and raise the frog upon the land of Egypt.'" While it is conceivable that Sam is original and MT haplographic, far more likely Sam is filling out the text (cf. TEXTUAL NOTES to 7:18, 29, 8:19, 9:5, 19 and 10:2, 5).

8:2. *the frog ascended.* Before this phrase, LXX inserts "and he raised up the frogs," increasing the parallelism with God's command (v 1) and with the act of the *ḥarṭummîm* (v 3).

8:3. *ḥarṭummîm.* Sam and LXX add "of Egypt/the Egyptians."

mysteries. For MT *lāṭêhem*, Sam and Kenn 155 have *lhṭyhm*, as in 7:11 (cf. 7:22; 8:14).

†*they raised.* So MT (*wayyaʿălû ʾet-haṣpardǝʿîm*). Sam and Kenn 152, 389 A *wyʿlw hṣprdʿym* is ambiguous and could also be rendered "the frogs ascended."

the land of Egypt. Some LXX MSS insert "all."

8:4. *said.* Syr and some LXX witnesses add "to them."

Pray to Yahweh. LXX adds "for me," as in 8:24.

the people. LXX^B has a shorter reading: "them."

8:5. *from you.* LXX adds "and from your people," as earlier in the verse and as in v 7.

†*your houses.* Here and in v 7, Syr and Vg have "your house"; in v 17, however, some Syr MSS agree with MT "houses." Sam and Vg add "and from your slaves and from your people," to agree with v 7. While MT is the shorter and less regular text, it is entirely possible that the repetition of the 2 m.s. suffix -*yk* caused corruptions, and that originally both vv 5 and 7 read "from you and from your houses and from your slaves and from your people."

†*only in the Nile they will remain.* As the clause is missing in Syr, perhaps the other traditions borrowed it from v 7. But it would be unusual for Syr alone to preserve an authentic reading.

8:6. *he said.* Both times, Syr adds "to him."

†*According to your word.* For standard MT *kdbrk*, Sam and some MT witnesses have *kdbryk* 'according to your words' (Kenn 9 [first hand], 84, 132, 193, 248, 686; Rossi 592).

our deity. Missing in LXX, which, unlike MT, makes a vigorously monotheistic and universalistic claim: "There is none other than the Lord" (Wevers 1990: 110).

8:7. *from your houses.* So MT-Sam. Syr has "your (sing.) house." LXX puts "your" in the plural and adds "and from your (pl.) yards"; cf. v 9.

8:8. *that he put upon Pharaoh.* LXX *hōs etaxato Pharaō* is ambiguous (Wevers 1990: 112). It might mean either "as Pharaoh commanded" (**'ăšer-śām par'ō[h]*) or "as was commanded for Pharaoh" (**'ăšer-śîm/śûm/śām ləpar'ō[h]*). In the Hebrew, at least, it seems best to take Yahweh as the subject.

†8:9. *from the yards.* LXX, Sam, Tg. Ps.-*Jonathan*, Syr and many MT MSS (see Kennicott 1776–80: 121; de Rossi 1784–85: 52) insert "and."

8:11. *made firm.* MT has a Hiph'il infinitive absolute *wəhakbēd*; Sam and Kenn 3, however, read *wykbd*, apparently Hiph'il *wayyakbēd (cf. *Samaritan Tg.* A; Syr). LXX and Tg. *Onqelos* seem also to read *wykbd, but as a Qal *wayyikbad 'and (his heart) became heavy' (see TEXTUAL NOTE to 9:34; on *'ēt* with an intransitive verb, cf. 10:8). As the most difficult reading, MT is probably correct.

spoken. Syr adds "to Moses."

8:12. *your rod.* Kenn 18 and 160 have "your *hand*," while Sam and LXX read "your hand *with* your rod" (*yādəkā bəmaṭṭəkā*), as in 8:1 (cf. 8:13).

that it become. For MT *wəhāyâ*, Sam reads *wîhî*, with no difference in meaning.

†*lice.* Throughout vv 12–14, there is confusion over the spelling and vocalization of this word. 4QpaleoExod^m and Sam have *knym* throughout. Standard MT has *knm* in v 12, *knm* and *knym* in v 13, *knym* and *knm* in v 14. The MSS, however, present a gamut of alternatives (Kennicott 1776–80: 121). LXX uses the plural *skniphes* 'mosquitoes,' except in v 14a, where, however, the Hebrew has the plural.

For *knym*, the vocalization is necessarily *kinnîm*. H*knm* is always vocalized *hakkinnām* and appears only with "was on man and animal." The difficult case is *lknm* in v 12: should we read *ləkinnîm* (MT) (plural) or **ləkinnām/lakkinnām* (singular)?

LXX also features a plus derived from the next verse: "on man and on animal and" (cf. 8:13, 14; 9:9, 10).

8:13. *they did so.* These words are absent from LXX. Ordinarily, we prefer the shorter text, but here there is probably haplography by homoioarkton from *wy'św* 'and they did' to *wyṭ* 'and [he] extended.' Kenn 84, Rossi 766 and Syr resemble MT, but put the verb in the singular: *wayya'aś*.

all the dirt. Kenn 125, 155, 181 and some Syr MSS insert "and." 4QReworked Pentateuch^c, LXX and Rossi 233 read **ûb(ə)kol-'ăpar* 'and in all the dirt.' This might be a scribe's answer to the naive question "If *all* the dirt had turned to insects, on what did the sorcerers try their spells?" But more likely, the copyist was influenced by *bəkol-ʾereṣ* 'in all the land' in 8:12, 13. In any case, MT is preferable.

8:14. *with their mysteries.* For MT *bəlāṭêhem*, Sam and 4QReworked Pentateuch^c have *blhtyhm(h)*, as in 7:11 (see also 7:22; 8:3).

lice. LXX reads a singular **knm* (cf. Kenn 5, 18, 84, 109, 129, 168, 175, 260, 264), perhaps vocalized **kinnām*, as in the latter part of the verse (MT)— where, however, LXX has a plural (= Kenn 153, 253).

the louse became. 4QpaleoExod^m has a masculine verb *wyhy* for the MT feminine *wthy*. For the MT singular noun, Sam, 4QpaleoExod^m, Kenn 153, 253 and probably the LXX *Vorlage* have the plural *hknym*.

8:16. *Moses.* 4QpaleoExod^m adds "saying" (*lʾmwr*).

and station yourself. Instead of the MT imperative, 4QReworked Pentateuch^c has a converted perfect *whtyṣbth* 'and *you will* station yourself.'

see. Kenn 17 and 18 have *whnh* 'and see,' while LXX^B, Sam, 4QReworked Pentateuch^c and *Tg.* Neofiti I have *whnh hwʾ* 'and see: he'; cf. 7:15.

†*to the waters.* For MT *hammaymâ*, Sam reads *hmym*. The meaning is unaffected (cf. 7:15; 9:8, 10; 10:19; 15:27; 16:33).

serve me. LXX adds "in the wilderness"; cf. 5:1; 7:16; 8:24.

8:17. *For if.* 4QReworked Pentateuch^c and, most likely, the LXX *Vorlage* read *wʾ[m]* 'and if.'

going to send. Where MT has a rare Hiph^cil participle *mašlîaḥ*, 4QExod^c, Sam, Kenn 1, 84, 109 and 4QReworked Pentateuch^c have the more common Pi^cel *mšlḥ* 'release,' probably under the influence of *məšallēaḥ* earlier in the verse.

†*and against your slaves.* Absent in Syr and Kenn 69, either by free variation or by homoioteleuton (*wbʿbdyk wbʿmk*). Conceivably, this shorter reading is original; cf. TEXTUAL NOTES to 7:28–29.

your houses. While MT puts "your" in the singular (*bātte[y]kā*), LXX has "your" in the plural (*tous oikous hymōn*). LXX seems to be a correction *ad sensum*: Pharaoh lives in only one house, so "houses" must belong to all the Egyptians (Wevers 1990: 116). But in LXX 8:20, Pharaoh himself has "houses" (vs. MT "house"). 4QReworked Pentateuch^c, *Tg.* Ps.-*Jonathan* and some Syr MSS have "and in your (sing.) house" (*wbbytk[h]*).

8:18. *stands.* Vs. MT *ʿōmēd*, 4QReworked Pentateuch^c and Syr paraphrase: *ywšb* 'sits, resides.'

I am Yahweh in the land's midst. LXX and *Tgs.* paraphrase: "I, the Lord, am the lord of all the earth." The translators seem troubled by the spatial limitation implicit in the Hebrew; cf. *Tg. Onqelos* 9:14. See also NOTES to 8:17, 20.

8:19. *tomorrow.* At the end of the verse, LXX appends "upon the land," presumably inspired by 8:20. Sam and 4QpaleoExod^m lack this addition, but add instead: "And Moses and Aaron came to Pharaoh and said to him, 'Thus has Yahweh said: "Release my people, that they may serve me. For if you do not release my people, see: I am going to send against you and against your slaves and against your people and into your houses the *ʿārōb*; Egypt's houses will be full of the *'ārōb*, as well as the land on which they are. But I will separate on that day the land of Goshen, on which my people stands, and there will be no *'ārōb* there, that you may know that I am Yahweh in the land's midst. For I will put a redemption between my people and between your people; tomorrow this sign will occur"'" (cf. vv 16–19).

†8:20. *heavy.* Sam, 4QpaleoExod^m and Vg have "*very* heavy" (*kbd m'd*). We ordinarily prefer the shorter reading, but *kbd m'd* could have become *kbd* by haplography (homoioteleuton).

†*came.* Perhaps correctly, Syr and Tg. *Ps.-Jonathan* read **wayyābē'* 'and he brought,' vs. MT *wayyābō'*.

house. Both times, LXX has the plural, correctly taking *bêt(â)* as collective.

and his slaves' house. For standard MT *ûbêt*, Kenn 129, 181 and Rossi 549, 789 read *ûb(ə)bêt* 'and in (his slaves') house,' a variant also preserved in the marginal Massorah to the standard MT (Sebhirin).

†*And in all the land of Egypt the land was being devastated.* The initial "and" is absent in Sam. Moreover, by later reading *wattiššāḥēt* (vs. MT *tiššāḥēt*), Sam, LXX and Syr imply a different clause division: ". . . (and) in all the land of Egypt. The land was devastated. . . ." I.e., "all the land of Egypt" culminates the list of sufferers, instead of beginning a new clause (cf. 10:6; 11:1; also TEXTUAL NOTE to 7:29). But to me, at least, MT makes more sense, implying that Egypt proper, as opposed to Goshen, was ravaged. If so, the corruption of Sam, LXX and Syr may be due to unconscious influence from Gen 6:11, *wattiššāḥēt hā'āreṣ* 'the land was (morally) devastated.' See also NOTES to 8:17, 20.

8:21. *called to Moses and to Aaron.* Sam and many witnesses to MT read *ləmōše(h) ûl(ə)'ahărôn*, while other MT exemplars have a synonymous *'el-mōše(h) wə'el-'ahărôn* (see Kennicott 1776–80: 122; de Rossi 1784–85: 52). Standard MT has the most varied and hence most likely reading: *'el-mōše(h) ûl(ə)'ahărôn*.

said. Syr adds "to them."

your deity. LXX^A, Syr and Tg. *Neofiti I* insert "Yahweh." Wevers (1990: 119) rejects this variant as "dramatically wrong. . . . The real struggle between the Lord and Pharaoh is Pharaoh's constant refusal to recognize *hoti egō eimi kyrios* ['that I am the Lord']"—but see "Yahweh" in 8:4, 24, etc.

8:22. *abomination.* LXX *bdelygmata* 'abominations' may read a plural **tô'ăbōt* for the MT singular *tô'ăbat*, as in some MSS of Sam, *Samaritan Tg. A* and Syro-Hexaplaric Theodotion and Symmachus (in Syr only the second *tw'bt* is plural). Alternatively, LXX may understand *tô'ăbat* as a collective singular (Wevers 1990: 120).

will they not. LXX, Syr, Tg. *Ps.-Jonathan* and Vg omit the negative, translating: "we will be stoned" (LXX) or "they will stone us" (Syr, Vg, Tg. *Ps.-Jonathan*). This is probably not a variant, but an attempt to avoid a misreading, "they will *not* stone us."

8:23. *and sacrifice.* For MT *wəzābaḥnû*, Sam reads *wnzbḥ* with no difference in meaning.

Yahweh. Absent in LXX^B—or, rather, the divine name has migrated within the verse (see following).

as he may say. LXX has "as he (LXX^B 'Yahweh') *said,*" apparently reading *ʾmr for MT *yʾmr* 'he will say.' Syr MSS are divided between the two readings. MT better suits the context, as the Hebrews do not yet know what animals they will sacrifice (cf. 10:26).

8:24. *Yahweh.* Absent in LXX^B.

Pray. LXX adds "to Yahweh," as in 8:4, 25, 26; 9:28; 10:17, 18.

8:25. *Moses said.* Syr adds "to Pharaoh."

pray to Yahweh. Here and in the next verse, LXX reads "the Deity."

leave from Pharaoh. LXX paraphrases the entire sentence in the second person: "leave from *you* and from *your* slaves and *your* people . . . only *do not* continue, O Pharaoh. . . ." Apparently, the translator found Moses' addressing Pharaoh in the third person awkward (or overreverent).

†*from his slaves.* LXX, Sam, Vg, Syr and many witnesses to MT (see Kennicott 1776–80: 122; de Rossi 1784–85: 52) read "*and* from his slaves." (*Tg. Ps.-Jonathan* omits the slaves entirely through haplography [homoioarkton: *mᶜ* . . . *mᶜ*].)

8:26. *Yahweh.* LXX reads "the Deity," as in the previous verse.

†8:27. *from his slaves.* LXX, Sam, Syr, *Tg. Ps.-Jonathan* and many MSS of MT and of *Tg. Onqelos* (Kennicott 1776–80: 122; de Rossi 1784–85: 53) read "*and* from his slaves."

not one remained. LXX and Rossi 716 insert "and."

†9:1. *and you will speak.* Sam, LXX, Syr and Kenn 69, 129 and possibly 75 have *wəʾāmartā* 'and you will *say*,' as in MT 7:26—where, however, Sam reads *wdbrt* 'and you will *speak.*'

9:2. *release.* LXX adds "my people"; Syr adds "them."

9:3. *field.* Syr "desert" is an inner-Syriac corruption: *dbrʾ* > *mdbrʾ*.

upon . . . upon. LXX puts "and" between all the animals; Syr puts "and" before all except the horses. Sam has "and" in front of the donkeys and the camels as well as the flock. On variant MT MSS, see Kennicott (1776–80: 122); de Rossi (1784–85: 53).

†9:4. *Yahweh will separate.* LXX "I will work a miracle at that time ('at that time' missing in LXX^B)" reflects (a) the translator's ignorance of the rare *plyʾ* 'separate' (see NOTE to 8:19) and (b) a possible *Vorlage* **wəhipêtî bāʿēt hahîʾ*. Here LXX might be correct, for *bāʿēt hahîʾ* could have fallen out in MT by homoioarkton with the following *bên* 'between.'

Israel's cattle. No doubt independently, Rossi 296 and many LXX witnesses read "Israel's *Sons'* cattle." I follow the shorter MT. LXX reverses "Israel" and "Egypt" vis-à-vis MT.

of all belonging to Israel's Sons. Syr has "of all Israel's House's cattle." See TEXTUAL NOTE to 3:11.

9:5. *Yahweh set.* LXX: "the Deity set."

in the land. At the end of the verse, Sam and 4QpaleoExod^m add "And Moses and Aaron came to Pharaoh and said to him, 'Thus has Yahweh the Hebrews' deity said: "Release my people, that they may serve me. For if you refuse to release and you still hold them, see: Yahweh's arm is about to be upon your cattle that are in the field, upon the horses and upon the asses and upon the camels, upon the herd and upon the flock—a very heavy plague. But Yahweh will separate between Israel's cattle and between Egypt's cattle, and of all belonging to Israel's Sons no thing will die. Tomorrow Yahweh will do this thing in the land" '" (cf. 9:1–5).

9:6. *Israel's Sons'*. Syr has "Israel's House's." See TEXTUAL NOTE to 3:11.

9:7. *sent*. LXX seems to read "saw" (*wayyar[']*) for MT *wayyišlaḥ*. This might be a paraphrase, taking "sent" in the sense of "learned by report, perceived at second hand." But Syr reads "Pharaoh sent and saw," as if conflating MT and a variant LXX *Vorlage*. Still, it seems more likely that Syriac *ḥzā* 'he saw' paraphrases *hinnē(h)* 'see' and that the resemblance to LXX is coincidental.

of Israel's cattle. LXX has "of (LXX[B] inserts 'all') Israel's *Sons*' cattle," as if reading *mimmiqnē(h) bənê yiśrā'ēl*, supported by Sam, 4QpaleoExod[m], Syr, Tg. Ps.-Jonathan, many MSS of MT (Kennicottt 1776–80: 123; de Rossi 1784–85: 53) and the Soncino Bible (1488). Syr witnesses are divided between "Israel" (= MT) and "Israel's House." I have followed standard MT.

9:8. *Aaron*. LXX adds "saying," supported by 4QpaleoExod[m] (*l'mwr*).

†*heavenward*. Sam and 4QpaleoExod[m] have *hšmym*, vs. MT and 4QGen-Exod[a] *haššāmaymâ*. (cf. 7:15; 8:16; 9:10; 15:27; 16:33).

to Pharaoh's eyes. LXX adds "and before his slaves"; cf. 5:21; 7:20.

†9:9. *over all the land*. 4QpaleoExod[m] uniquely has "over the land." While attractively short, this variant may be haplographic: *'l kl* 'over all' > *'l* "over" (homoioteleuton).

†*šəḥîn blossoming with boils*. Here, MT has *šəḥîn pōrēaḥ 'ăba'bū'ōt* 'a *šəḥîn* blossoming with boils.' The following verse, however, has *šəḥîn 'ăba'bū'ōt pōrēaḥ* 'a *šəḥîn* of boils blossoming.' Is one of these a corruption of the other? LXX paraphrases both expressions with *phlyktides anazeousai* 'boiling blisters.' After "boiling blisters," LXX adds "upon man and animal and." This is presumably a secondary expansion based upon v 10, and increases the chances that in both verses the LXX *Vorlage* read *šəḥîn 'ăba'bū'ōt pōrēaḥ*. That is, a scribe's eye skipped between identical phrases in vv 9 and 10. (Admittedly, the error might have occurred later, during Greek transmission.) At any rate, I follow the diverse MT.

9:10. *they took*. LXX[B] has "he took." MT "they" is superior, for the mention of Moses in midverse indicates a change of subject from plural to singular.

†*and stood*. The verb is absent in LXX, which might be superior on account of its brevity.

†*heavenward*. Sam has *hšmym*, vs. MT *hšmymh* (cf. 7:15; 8:16; 9:8; 15:27; 16:33). Syr adds "to Pharaoh's eyes."

9:11. *because of the šəḥîn, for the šəḥîn*. Syr paraphrases (?): "because of the *šəḥîn* that was great."

and upon all Egypt. LXX, 4QReworked Pentateuch[c], Kenn 80 and Rossi 754 read "and in all the land of Egypt" (*wbkl 'rṣ mṣrym*), as in MT v 9.

9:12. *to Moses.* These words are missing from LXX[B], in which 9:12 matches 7:13, 22; 8:11, 15. In MT, however, there seems to be a progression from "as Yahweh had spoken" to "as Yahweh had spoken *to Moses*" (9:12) to "as Yahweh had spoken *through Moses' hand.*" This is presumably original.

††9:14. *all these my afflictions against you.* All Versions more or less support MT *kol-maggēpōtay 'el* (Sam *'al-libbəkā* 'all my afflictions *to your heart*' (Syr omits "all"). But I tentatively adopt Driver's (1911: 72) emendation **kol-maggēpōtay 'ēlle(h) bəkā,* which makes good sense and better parallels the following. Compare, too, 10:1: *'ōtōtay 'ēlle(h) bəqirbô* 'these my signs in his core.' The error is more likely aural (*'ēlle[h] bəkā > 'el-libbəkā*) than graphic (*'lh bk > 'l lbk*). I hesitate, however, because the emendation eliminates a fine nuance in MT: Pharaoh's heart, the very cause of his stubbornness, suffers directly in the Plagues. If MT is correct, it should be interpreted with LXX: "your heart and (that of) your slaves and your people."

9:16. *in order to show you my strength.* For the MT infinitive construct *har'ōtəkā,* 4QExod[c], Sam and Kenn 152 have *hr'tyk* 'I have shown you.' Presumably, this latter reading is influenced by the preceding perfect *h'mdtyk* 'I let you stand'; perhaps, too, an intermediate plene spelling **hr'wtk* suffered metathesis and waw-yodh confusion (cf. Cross 1961a; Qimron 1972). The reading of LXX (cited in Rom 9:17), "that I might show my strength *through* you," seems to be a theological reinterpretation, not a true variant.

9:18. *from the day, her founding.* On the Sam variant *lmywm hysdh,* see NOTE.

9:19. *or animal.* Kenn 95, 109 and perhaps 193 expand: "or *every* animal."

they will die. Sam and 4QpaleoExod[m] append "And Moses and Aaron came to Pharaoh and said to him, 'Thus has Yahweh the Hebrews' deity said: "Release my people, that they may serve me. For this time I am going to send all my afflictions against you and against your slaves and against your people, in order that you may know that none is like me in all the world. For now, I could have sent forth my arm and smitten you and your people with the plague, so that you would have vanished from the land. However, for this I have let you stand: in order to show you my strength, and to tell my *name* in all the world. You still exalt yourself over my people without releasing them. See: I am going to rain at this time tomorrow very heavy hail, whose like never was in Egypt from the day of [sic] her founding and [sic] until now. And now send, shelter your cattle and all in the field that is yours. Every man or animal that will be found in the field and will not have been gathered into the house—then the hail will descend upon them and they will die"'" (cf. 9:13–19).

†9:20. *his slaves and.* Missing in LXX, perhaps correctly.

houses. Syr has "house."

9:21. *to Yahweh's word.* Sam reads "upon (*'l*) Yahweh's word."

†*his slaves and.* Missing in LXX. As the shorter text, LXX might be superior in vv 20–21.

9:22. *In all the land of Egypt.* Kenn 94, 181, 189, 226 and Rossi 503, 554 have "*upon* (*'al*) the land of Egypt," apparently under the influence of "toward (*'al*) the sky" previously.

†*field's herbage.* LXX has "herbage that is *upon the earth,*" as if reading *ḥāʿēśeb ʾăšer ʿal-hāʾāreṣ* or *ʿēśeb hāʾāreṣ* (cf. 10:12, 15). Since "field's herbage" may have been brought forward from v 25 by MT, LXX is the shorter and more attractive reading. I do not adopt it only because it is uncorroborated by Hebrew evidence.

†*in the land of Egypt.* Kenn 5, (6), 80, 107, 150, 206 and 389 A have "in *all* the land of Egypt," as earlier in the verse. Perhaps correctly, LXX lacks "in (all) the land of Egypt" entirely.

9:23. *his rod.* LXX "his *arm*" agrees with Yahweh's command in v 22. MT is superior as the more varied text.

†9:24. *there was hail.* LXX and Sam read *hbrd* 'the hail,' i.e., "*the aforesaid* hail." This is presumably an assimilation to "the hail" later in the verse (cf. TEXTUAL NOTES to 9:26, 33). LXX paraphrases the entire awkward sentence: "There was the hail, and fire burned in the hail, and the hail was very, very great."

very. LXX has "very, very,"

††*in Egypt.* I adopt the *lectio brevior* of Kenn 107, Rossi 5, Sam and LXX. Rossi 16 and the Arabic Version have "in *the land of* Egypt," while standard MT, 4QExodᶜ and Syr read "in *all the land of* Egypt," presumably influenced by 9:25.

since she became a nation. LXX paraphrases: "since there was a people upon it [i.e., the land of Egypt]."

††9:25. *in the land of Egypt.* I have adopted the short text of Sam; other Versions have "in *all* the land of Egypt."

everything . . . in the field. LXX lacks these words, perhaps skipped because of the repeated sequence mem-ʾaleph: *(mṣry)m ʾt . . . mʾdm.*

†*from man and to animal.* Sam, Kenn 82 and apparently a fragmentary Palestinian Targumic Tosephta (Klein 1986: 1.183) omit "and."

9:26. *hail.* LXX has "*the* hail" (*hbrd*). Since the previous word ends in *h*, either haplography to produce MT (*hh > h*) or dittography to produce LXX (*h > hh*) is possible. Since LXX and Sam also read *hbrd* in 9:24 (vs. MT *brd*), where the previous letter is not *h*, and since in 9:26 *hbrd* is slightly more expected than *brd*, I have followed the shorter, more difficult MT (cf. TEXTUAL NOTES to 9:24, 33).

9:28. *Pray.* Here and in 8:4, LXXᴮ adds "for me"; cf. MT 8:24.

†*hail.* LXX (not LXXᴬ) and 2QExodᵃ add "and fire," i.e., *wʾš.* Because the next word, *wʾšlḥh* 'and I will release,' begins with *wʾš*, either haplography (producing MT) or dittography (producing the LXX *Vorlage* and Qumran) might have occurred. If the short MT is original, the apparent dittography in LXX was doubtless influenced by the sequence *brd wʾš* 'hail and fire' in 9:24.

9:29. *the city.* Rossi 825 has "*from (min)* the city."

to Yahweh. LXXᵃ modifies and expands: "to God *toward the sky.*"

†*The voices.* Sam and LXX have "*and* the voices," whereas 2QExodᵃ, 4QExodᶜ and MT lack the conjunction.

hail. LXX adds "and rain," as in v 33.

†9:30. *Yahweh Deity.* This may be a conflation in MT, as LXX MSS vary between "God" and "Yahweh." 4QExod^c and Sam have an attractively unusual *'dny yhwh* 'my Lord Yahweh'; *Tg.* Neofiti I has "the Lord, our deity."

9:31. *were smitten.* For the MT singular *nukkātâ*, Sam has the plural *nukkû*. Both are grammatically acceptable, but the former reading is the more difficult, as *nukkû* also appears in the next verse.

barley was young ears and the flax was buds. 4QExod^c reverses the crops, so that the verse treats "flax . . . barley . . . flax . . . barley." In all other Versions, we find a chiastic "flax . . . barley . . . barley . . . flax."

9:33. *to Yahweh.* Syr expands: "*heavenward* before the Lord"; cf. LXX^A 9:29.

rain. Sam, Kenn 136, 193 and LXX read *whmṭr* 'and *the* rain' (cf. TEXTUAL NOTES to 9:24, 26). Since the preceding terms have the definite article *ha-*, and since *hammāṭār* appears in the next verse, MT is preferable. *Tg.* Onqelos paraphrases: "Rain that had been falling did not reach the ground."

9:34. *the rain and the hail.* These are reversed in Sam, but almost all other MSS and Versions support MT (for further variants, see Sanderson 1994: 109).

†*he made firm his heart.* We might revocalize MT *wayyakbēd* as **wayyikbad* (so Syr; cf. 9:7) and translate: "his heart *became firm*, his and his servants'." The absence of the direct object marker *'et* before *libbô* 'his heart' supports this emendation (Kenn 18 and 244, however, have *'et*) (cf. TEXTUAL NOTE to 8:11).

he and his slaves. Syr clarifies: "both *Pharaoh* and his slaves."

9:35. *spoken.* Syr paraphrases: "sent."

10:1. *Moses.* LXX adds "saying."

heart (second time). Omitted by LXX, most likely for ease of translation and to increase the parallelism with the next verse.

so that I might set. LXX paraphrases: "one after another there will come (*epelthēi*)," diminishing Yahweh's explicit involvement in events.

these my signs. Syr omits "my."

in his core. LXX, Syr and *Tgs.* Onqelos and *Ps.-Jonathan* translate as if reading **bəqirbām* 'in *their* midst.' Either they take MT *bəqirbô* 'in *his* midst' as collective, or else they reflect a *Vorlage *bqrbm.* If the latter is so, this might be a superior reading, mem having become waw in MT-Sam by ink abrasion. But, in the absence of Hebrew attestation for the variant, we must follow MT-Sam.

10:2. *you may tell.* MT has a singular verb, while LXX is plural (see also next TEXTUAL NOTE). Apparently, the translator pluralized all second persons to agree with *wîda'tem* 'that you [pl.] may know.'

your son's . . . and your son's son's. LXX has "your sons' and your sons' sons'." A variant *Vorlage* is unlikely; rather, LXX pluralizes Hebrew collectives.

my signs. Syr and LXX omit "my."

Yahweh. Sam adds "your deity" and continues with a long plus shared by 4QpaleoExod^m: "And you will say to Pharaoh, 'Thus has Yahweh the Hebrews' deity said: "Until when do you refuse to humble yourself before me? Release my people, that they may serve me. For if you refuse to release my people, see:

I am going to bring tomorrow locust in your territory. And it will cover the land's *eye*, and one will not be able to see the earth, and it will eat the excess of the remnant remaining to you from the hail, and it will eat all the land's herbage [*sic*] and all the fruit of [*sic*] the tree that sprouts for you from the field. And they will fill your houses and your slaves' houses and all Egypt's houses—that which your fathers and your fathers' fathers never saw, from the day of their being upon the ground until this day"'" (cf. 10:3-6).

10:3. *came.* Tg. *Ps.-Jonathan* seems to read **wayyābē'* 'and he [Yahweh] brought Moses and Aaron,' unless Aramaic *wə'ā'ēl* is an error for *wə'al* 'and (he) entered.'

to Pharaoh. LXX has "*before* Pharaoh"; cf. 7:10.

10:4. *bring.* LXX adds "at this time" (**kā'ēt*), as in 9:18.

locust in your territory. LXX expands: "*many* locusts in *all* your territory," as if reading **'arbe(h) kābēd bəkol-gəbūlekā*. Syr, too, has "*all* your territory."

10:5. *one will not be able.* LXX and Tg. Neofiti I paraphrase: "*you* [sing.] will not be able."

excess of the remnant. LXX inserts "all."

†*every tree.* Sam and 4QpaleoExod^m read instead "all the land's herbage and all the tree's fruit" (cf. 10:15, etc.). Although conceivably Sam-4QpaleoExod^m is correct, I adopt the shorter text of MT-LXX. Compare Sam's supplementation of v 12.

††10:6. *your slaves'.* MT, Sam and 4QpaleoExod^m have *kol-'ăbāde(y)kā* 'all your slaves.' I follow LXX and Syr, however, since the parallels lack "all" and I in general prefer a shorter text (see TEXTUAL NOTES to 7:29 and 12:30). (One could argue, however, that MT is superior as the more difficult reading.)

all Egypt's houses. LXX doubly expands: "*all* the houses in *all the land of* (the) Egypt(ians)."

upon the ground. A Genizah MS expands: "upon the ground's *surface* (*pny*)" (BHS).

he turned and went. LXX^B reads "*Moses* turned," while Syr has "*they* turned, (some MSS add 'and') they went." In MT, doubtless original, the narrator forgets Aaron, who had accompanied Moses into Pharaoh's presence (10:3).

10:7. *Yahweh.* LXX^B lacks the divine name.

10:8. *Go, serve.* LXX^B inserts a conjunction: "go *and* serve."

Yahweh. Again, LXX^B omits Yahweh.

10:9. *Moses said.* Syr adds "to him."

with our flocks. LXX inserts "and."

Yahweh's . . . for us. LXX^A, probably transmitting the original Greek reading, has "the Lord our god." All witnesses to LXX omit "for us" (*lānû*). Seemingly, an original *lyhwh lnw* 'of Yahweh for us' (MT) was expanded into **lyhwh 'lhynw lnw* 'of Yahweh our deity for us' (unattested), from which the last word dropped by homoioteleuton to create the LXX *Vorlage*: **lyhwh 'lhynw* 'for Yahweh our deity.' The short reading of LXX^B, "the Lord" (= Kenn 169), though attractively brief, is probably secondary (Wevers 1990: 149).

10:10. *May . . . be.* For MT *yhy*, Sam reads *"will . . . be"* (*yhyh*), supported (coincidentally?) by LXX^C *estai.*

†10:11. *Not so. Go.* Instead of MT-4QpaleoExod^m *lō(')* *kēn ləkû-nā'*, Sam reads *lkn lkw n'* *'therefore go'* (cf. the Versions on Gen 4:15; 2 Sam 18:14). Whichever is original, the corruption is probably aural. In many traditional pronunciations of Hebrew (Ashkenazic, Yemenite, medieval Tiberian), *lō(')* *kēn* 'not so' and *lākēn* are pronounced similarly.

Yahweh. LXX^B: "the Deity."

he expelled them. LXX, Sam and Syr read *"they* [Pharaoh's slaves] expelled them,"* to match 12:39 in these Versions (see TEXTUAL NOTE).

†10:12. *Extend your arm . . . with the locust, and let it ascend.* Although MT is probably corrupt, I can proffer no convincing emendation (see NOTE). Did the author or a later scribe begin to write *bammaṭṭe(h)/bəmaṭṭəkā* 'with the/ your rod,' and in midword switch to locusts? Did an original **whb' 'rbh* 'and bring locust' or **wyb' 'rbh* 'and let locust come' collapse into *b'rbh* (cf. Holzinger 1900: 30)? In fact, *Tg. Onqelos* has "raise your arm over the land of Egypt and *let the locust come* and let it ascend upon the land of Egypt"—but it would be astonishing for a Targum to uniquely preserve an authentic reading. More likely, the translator followed our line of reasoning and paraphrased.

LXX has a much easier text: "Let the locust ascend," as if reading **wəya'al hā'arbe(h)* (cf. 10:14), vs. MT *bā'arbe(h) wəya'al* 'with the locust, and let it ascend.' This eliminates the problem nicely and parallels the phrasing of the other episodes. But it is also suspect as the easiest reading.

†*land of Egypt.* LXX, perhaps correctly, omits "of Egypt."

all the land's herbage . . . left behind. LXX and Sam have a longer reading: *'t kl 'śb h'rṣ w't kl pry h'ṣ 'šr hš'yr hbrd* 'all the land's herbage *and all tree's fruit* that the hail left behind,' based upon 10:15; cf. 10:5 (Sam). Syr, many MSS of MT and Soncino Bible (1488) have "all the land's herbage *and* all that the hail left behind" (de Rossi 1784–85: 55).

For standard MT "all that," some MT MSS (Kenn 150, 228; see also de Rossi p. 55) read simply "all." Presumably, *'šr* 'that' fell out due to its graphic similarity to the following *hš'yr* 'left behind.'

10:13. *his rod.* Sam and some LXX MSS have *ydw* 'his *arm*,' to match 10:12.

over the land of Egypt. LXX reads instead "heavenward," as in 9:22, 23; 10:21, 22.

†*bore.* For MT *nāśā(')* (masc.), Sam has the feminine *nś'h*. Either is grammatically acceptable, since *rûaḥ* 'wind' is of ambivalent gender.

10:14. *ascended over.* On the LXX interpretation, see NOTE.

†10:15. *all the land's.* Kenn 170, Rossi 16, 296 and LXX omit "all." This variant is attractively short but may be a harmonization with 10:5; Num 22:5, 11.

†*so that the land was dark.* Against MT *wattehšak hā'āreṣ*, 4QExod^c and LXX read *wattiśśāḥēt hā'āreṣ* 'so that the land was *devastated*,' as in 8:20 (*pace* Wevers 1990: 153; cf. LXX Gen 6:11). Most likely the error was aural. As for which is original, MT is preferable as the more diverse text. It is also the more graphic.

†*not any greenery was left.* This clause is preceded by the conjunction in MT but not in LXX (= Kenn 84, 110, 225). Syr omits *kol* 'any.'

on the . . . herbage. LXX repeats "on *all* the herbage," as previously in the verse (cf. 9:22, 25; 10:12).

10:16. *said.* Syr adds "to them."

†10:17. *lift.* 4QExod^c, LXX, Sam and most Syr MSS read the command in the plural (*śǝ'û*), addressed to Moses and Aaron (cf. the preceding *lākem* 'to you (pl.)' and the following plural imperative *ha'tîrû* 'pray'). MT *śā'*, however, is slightly preferable as *lectio difficilior.* Throughout the Torah, Aaron tends to pop in and out of narratives about Moses—an inconsistency the Versions often rectify.

and pray. Sam omits the conjunction.

just. Omitted in LXX, probably for ease of translation.

†10:18. *he went out.* Many witnesses to MT, some Targumic MSS (de Rossi 1784–85: 55), a Sam MS, LXX and Syr specify "*Moses* went out." While we ordinarily would regard this as an expansion, its presence even in the Massoretic tradition may indicate its authenticity, since Rabbinic scribes rarely expanded in this fashion. If original, *mōše(h)* 'Moses' fell out by homoioarkton with the following *mē'im.*

Yahweh. LXX^B: "the Deity."

†10:19. *very strong.* LXX simply has "strong," either a paraphrase or reflecting a shorter *Vorlage.*

†*into the . . . Sea.* Sam omits the locative suffix on "Sea," reading simply *ym* (vs. MT *yāmmâ*) (cf. 7:15; 8:16; 9:8, 10; 15:27; 16:33).

Not one. LXX, Syr, Kenn 18, 69, 181, 226 and Targumic MSS (de Rossi 1784–85: 55) insert "and."

Egypt's territory. LXX: "land of Egypt."

10:21. *said.* 4QpaleoExod^m and Kenn 129 instead have *wydbr* 'and (Yahweh) spoke.'

††*Egypt.* MT continues with the unintelligible *wǝyāmēš ḥōšek* (Sam *hḥšk*), with which the Versions and commentators grapple variously (see NOTE). The phrase is entirely lacking in 4QpaleoExod^m, however, and the text makes sense without it. Although I have no neat explanation for an interpolation, I would observe that *ḥōšek* 'darkness' appears twice in proximity and that *wymš* could be a corruption of *mšh* 'Moses.' Admittedly, 4QpaleoExod^m may well be haplographic, since the following word also begins *wy-* (homoioarkton). But, as I cannot translate MT in any case, I follow 4QpaleoExod^m.

SPECULATION: Perhaps the original was **ûmiṣrayim yǝmaš(ǝ)šû (ba)ḥōšek* 'and Egypt will grope in the dark' (see NOTE). We could easily account for the loss of "and Egypt" either through haplography with the preceding word (*mṣrym wmṣrym*) or by homoioarkton with the following word (*wmṣrym ymššw*) (*w* = *y* in Herodian script). But the corruption of **ymššw (b)ḥšk* into *wymš (h)ḥšk* remains difficult.

10:23. *Man.* LXX and Kenn 75 insert "and."

his brother. LXXᴮ adds "three days," probably borrowed from the preceding and following clauses.

in their dwellings. LXX "in *all* (places) in which they lived" may reflect a variant *Vorlage:* *bəkol-môšəbōtām (cf. 12:20; 35:3; Lev 3:17; 7:26; 23:3, 14, 21, 31; Num 35:29; Ezek 6:6, 14; 37:23). Syr and *Tg. Onqelos* translate, "in their *dwelling,*" perhaps reading *bəmôšabtām, although no singular *môšebet is attested.

10:24. *Moses.* So MT, 4QExodᶜ and Syr. LXX, 4QpaleoExodᵐ, Sam, Kenn 17, Rossi 661, *Tg. Neofiti I* and Vg add "and Aaron." This is not a capricious expansion. After redaction, *ʾălêkem* '(to) you (pl.)' in 11:9 (R) indeed implies Aaron's presence in 10:24 (E). But see NOTE to 11:9.

and said. Syr adds "to him."

Yahweh. Rossi 296, LXX and many witnesses to Syr add "your deity," as in vv 25, 26. Wevers (1990: 157) observes that LXX reflexively adds *theos* 'God' with *latreuein* 'worship.'

Your dependents, too. Syr and Kenn 155 (first hand), 198 insert "and."

10:25. *Moses said.* Syr MSS variously add "to him/Pharaoh."

†*our hand.* While L and other MT MSS have the singular *bydnw,* many others read "into our hands" (*bydynw*) (de Rossi 1784–85: 55), as does the Soncino Bible (1488). We cannot tell which is correct.

slaughter sacrifices and ascending sacrifices. LXX and Kenn 18 reverse the order.

†10:26. *Not a hoof will remain.* LXX reads "we will not leave a hoof" (Syr, too, begins with a conjunction). We would ordinarily take this as mere paraphrase, but 4QpaleoExodᵐ proves that *l' nš'r* (*naš'îr*) 'we will not leave' is a genuine variant. Either MT or LXX-4QpaleoExodᵐ might be original.

with what we will serve Yahweh. LXX adds "our deity," as previously.

10:28. *to him.* Absent in LXXᴮ. Syr has "to Moses."

†*Go.* Sam and Syr read *lēk ləkā* 'go you.' It is as likely that *lk lk* generated *lk* (haplography) as vice versa (dittography). In this context, however, probability favors MT, since Sam and Syr might also be influenced by the following command, *hiššāmer ləkā* 'watch yourself.'

††*no more.* Codex L reads *ʾel-tōsep rəʾôt* 'in respect of (?) your continuing to see,' possibly supported by LXX (see, however, Wevers 1990: 159). Most other MT MSS and editions, however, have the expected *ʾal-tōsep,* supported by *Tgs.,* Syr, Vg and the parallel *lō(ʾ)-ʾōsîp* in v 29. This latter reading is adopted here.

seeing my face. Both times in v 28, Syr paraphrases: "appear to me." The second time, so does LXX; see below.

10:29. *Moses said.* Syr adds "to him."

I will see your face no more. LXX paraphrases: "I will not again appear to you in the face." Syr, however, agrees with MT (contrast TEXTUAL NOTE to 10:28). Here and in v 28, LXX correctly perceives that the problem is not Moses seeing Pharaoh, but Pharaoh seeing Moses (Wevers 1990: 160).

†11:1. *After this.* Preceded by "and" in LXX, Sam, Syr, many MT MSS (Kennicott 1776–80: 128; de Rossi 1784–85: 56) and *Tg. Ps.-Jonathan;* cf. 3:20; 5:1; 11:8; 34:32.

he will release. Syr: "*I* will release."

when he releases completely. See NOTE for the interpretations of LXX and Syr and for the proposed emendation **kallâ* 'bride' instead of MT *kālâ* 'completely.'

†*†expel you.* I follow the shorter text of LXX. MT continues "from here," but the redundancy of MT *'etkem mizze(h)* . . . *'etkem mizze(h)* looks like an expansion. Syr paraphrases with a command: "You (pl.) get out."

11:2. *Speak.* MT *dabber* is singular, addressed to Moses alone. Sam, which includes Aaron in the scene (10:24), correspondingly puts the command in the plural: *dbrw.*

the people's ears. LXX adds an explanatory "secretly," unlikely to have a basis in the *Vorlage.*

that they should ask. Syr omits the conjunction.

gold objects. LXX reads simply "gold," probably for a smoother rendering (cf. 3:22; 12:35). LXX, Sam and Kenn 109 add "and robes," as in 3:22; 12:35.

†††11:3. *And Yahweh will put.* The consonants *wytn* may be vocalized either *wayyittēn* 'and (he) put' (MT) or, more likely, **wəyittēn* 'and (he) will put' (cf. Sam *wntty* 'and *I* will put'). See further NOTE.

Also. Sam, LXX, Syr, Kenn 355 (?) and Rossi 419 insert "and."

the people's. LXX has "*his* people's," while Kenn 129, 150, 173, 206, 293, Rossi 419 and Sam expand: "*this* people's" (*h'm hzh*).

†*in Egypt's eyes.* To match 12:36, LXX adds "and they lent to them," for which we would normally reconstruct a *Vorlage *wayyaš'ilûm* (converted imperfect). Sam, however, has *whš'lwm*, a converted *perfect*, i.e., a future (so *Samaritan Tg.*). This must also have stood in the LXX *Vorlage.* Apparently, LXX's interpretation of *wytn* as a converted imperfect (= MT) necessitated reading *whš'lwm* as a nonconverted perfect. By my interpretation, however, *wytn* is an ordinary imperfect, and *wəhiš'îlûm* is converted as expected.

Might LXX-Sam preserve the correct reading? The symmetry with 12:36 (see NOTE to 11:3) favors *whš'lwm* in 11:3. And given the similarity of *w* and *y* in Herodian script (Cross 1961a; Qimron 1972), *whš'lwm* could well have dropped by homoioteleuton with the preceding *mṣrym*. But we cannot exclude the possibility that the parallelism with 12:36 is the creation of a later scribe. My translation follows MT.

Sam also contains a long plus, definitely not original: "At midnight I am going to set forth in the midst of the land of [*sic*] Egypt. And every firstborn in the land of Egypt will die, from the firstborn of Pharaoh sitting on his throne and to the firstborn of the maidservant that is behind the two millstones, and every animal firstborn. And a great cry will be in Egypt, whose like never happened nor whose like will ever recur. But for all Israel's Sons not a dog will *sharpen his tongue*, from man to animal, that you may know that Yahweh will separate between Egypt and between Israel; and" (cf. 11:4–7). This is Sam's solution to the discrepancy between Yahweh's command to Moses and Moses' address to Pharaoh (see SOURCE ANALYSIS).

in the land of Egypt. Some MT MSS (Kennicott 1776–80: 128) and the LXX *Vorlage* read "in *Egypt's* eyes," presumably repeated from the first half of the verse. See also following.

†*in Pharaoh's slaves' eyes . . . people's eyes.* The LXX *Vorlage* appears to have read **bʿyny mṣrym wbʿyny prʿh wbʿyny kl ʿbdyw* 'in Egypt's eyes and in Pharaoh's eyes and in all his slaves' eyes,' vs. MT *bʾrṣ mṣrym bʿyny ʿbdy prʿh wbʿyny hʿm* 'in the land of Egypt, in Pharaoh's slaves' eyes and in the people's eyes.' Either might be correct. Throughout, we have encountered considerable mutability in the sequence "Pharaoh . . . slaves . . . people" (see TEXTUAL NOTES to 7:10, 28, 29, 8:5, 17, 9:20, 21 and 10:6).

Here Sam has another addition, a close paraphrase of 4:22–23: "And Moses said to Pharaoh, 'Thus has Yahweh said: "My son, my firstborn, is Israel. And I have said to you, release my son that he may serve me. And if you refuse to release him, see: Yahweh is going to kill your son, your firstborn."'"

11:4. *Moses said.* 2QExod[a] and *Tg. Ps.-Jonathan*, perhaps independently, add "to Pharaoh." This is probably an explanatory plus, although haplography by homoioteleuton (*mšh . . . prʿh*) is not inconceivable (D. N. Freedman, privately).

midnight. For MT *kaḥăṣōt hallaylâ*, Sam has *kḥṣyt hlylh* by waw-yodh confusion (cf. Cross 1961a; Qimron 1972), perhaps also inspired by the nouns *ḥăṣî* and *maḥăṣît* 'half.'

Egypt. Sam reads "*the land of* Egypt."

†11:5. *to the firstborn of the maidservant.* LXX[B], Sam and Syr insert "and."

and every animal firstborn. LXX and Sam have an unidiomatic *wʿd bkwr kl bhmh* 'and *to* the firstborn of every animal,' vs. MT *wəkōl bəkôr bəhēmâ*. Most likely, behind LXX-Sam lies **wʿd kl bkwr bhmh* 'and to every animal firstborn,' which was corrupted either in one stage by metathesis or in two stages by the omission (through homoioarkton) and erroneous reinsertion of *bkwr*.

††11:6. *in Egypt.* So Sam, Kenn 184, Rossi 2, 669. Syr reads "in *the land of* Egypt," while MT has "in *all* the land of Egypt."

11:7. *all Israel's Sons.* Syr has "all Israel's *House*"; see TEXTUAL NOTE to 3:11.

from man to animal. Missing in LXX[B], perhaps reflecting a Hebrew *Vorlage* that lost these words by homoioteleuton (*lmʾyš . . . lmʿn*).

†*you may know.* MT and 4QpaleoGen-Exod[l] have a plural *tēdəʿûn*, while Sam and LXX have the singular *tdʿ*. The latter is expected, since Moses is addressing Pharaoh (Wevers 1990: 165). But v 8 indicates that the court is also present. Either might be correct.

11:8. *and bow.* For MT *wəhištaḥăwû*, Sam, Kenn 110 (?) and Rossi 419 have *wyšthww*. The meaning is unaffected.

saying. Syr adds "to me."

all the people. LXX "all *your* people" is presumably a paraphrase. "All" is missing in some LXX witnesses.

he went out. LXX, Kenn 650 B and Syr specify "*Moses* went out."

11:9. *my wonders may be multiplied.* LXX[B] expands: "multiplying, I will multiply my signs and wonders," as if reading **harbâ 'arbe(h)* (cf. Gen 3:16; 16:10; 22:17) *'ōtōtay ûmôpətay* (cf. 7:3, etc.).

†11:10. *all these wonders before Pharaoh.* Syr omits "all," while LXX (not LXX[A]) expands: "all these *signs and* wonders *in the land of Egypt* before Pharaoh." *his land.* LXX specifies "the land *of Egypt.*"

SOURCE ANALYSIS

Most scholars detect three sources in 7:8–11:10 (e.g., Holzinger 1900: xvi–xvii; Driver 1911: 55–57; McNeile 1908: xv–xvii; Fohrer 1964: 60–72; Childs 1974: 130–42; for further bibliography, see Steingrimsson 1979: 9–23). I, however, find mainly two (cf. Rudolph 1938: 18–24; Mowinckel 1952; Noth 1962: 62–84; Greenberg 1969: 183–92; 1971). (Unitary authorship has few defenders among critical scholars, but see Cassuto 1967: 94–135.)

Evidence that the text is composite abounds. For example, *'ārōb* (an insect) and lice constitute a doublet and are paired in Ps 105:31. The plagues of blood and frogs each appear to contain two fused accounts. In some episodes, Moses' arm or rod produces the miracle; in others, it is Aaron's. Only scenes featuring Aaron's rod mention a contest with Pharaoh's *ḥarṭummîm*.

Moreover, the sections giving prominence to Aaron and the *ḥarṭummîm* use vocabulary not found in J or E, but characteristic of P and Ezekiel: *tannîn* 'serpent' (7:9, 10, 12; cf. Gen 1:21; Ezek 29:3; 32:2 [MT *tannîm*]); *yĕ'ōrîm* '"niles"' (7:19; 8:1; cf. Ezek 29:3, 4, 5, 10); *miqwē(h) mayim* 'reservoir of waters' (7:19; cf. Gen 1:10; Lev 11:36); *ḥopnayim* 'fists' (9:8; cf. Lev 16:12; Ezek 10:7), especially with *ml'* 'be full' (9:8; cf. Lev 16:12; Ezek 10:2); *pāraḥ* 'blossom' (9:9, 10; cf. Leviticus 13 *passim*; 14:43). In general, the stereotyped language is typically Priestly: e.g., the divine command followed by "and so they did" (7:10, 20; 8:13). Throughout the Torah, Aaron's rod is a sure sign of P (Num 17:16–26; 20:1–13; see Propp 1988; Blum 1990: 273–74), for one of P's main aims is elevating Aaron vis-à-vis Moses (see Friedman 1987; COMMENT to 6:2–7:7).

There is no explicit passage of time in the Priestly Plagues. They could even be the events of a single day (cf. Holzinger 1900: 32; Schmitt 1989: 203). Or, if my count of seven Plagues is correct (see below), we might think of a week, given P's penchant for seven-day spans (D. Kirsch, privately). In fact, these afflictions are never removed, so that Aaron and his Egyptian rivals appear to bring down cumulative misfortunes upon Egypt—possibly a humorous touch (Thompson 1987: 141; Fretheim 1991a: 113). This, too, may indicate that the Plagues are of brief duration. How long could Egypt survive without potable water? And we do not know what happens to the Hebrews. Do they suffer along with the Egyptians? Perhaps so, since they, too, doubt Moses' authority (6:9; see below). But more likely, the reader is to assume the tradition that the Hebrews were spared—a rare case of P presupposing, not superseding, JE (cf. Lohfink 1994: 136–72).

In P, Moses and Aaron never address Pharaoh, although they had been commanded to do so in 6:10–12; 7:1–7 (Greenberg 1969: 187). Taken alone, this might suggest that P is not an independent narrative source, but presupposes the intervening Elohistic material (Cross 1973: 293–325). Since, however, overall analysis of P suggests it *was* an independent source (Friedman 1987; Propp 1997), we more likely have narrational economy and deliberate variation between command and fulfillment. That is, from the repeated "and Pharaoh did not heed them" (7:13, 22; 8:11, 15; 9:12), we are to infer Moses' repeated demand to let Israel go (for a general study of this phenomenon, see Vater 1980).

His delightful Plagues narrative belies the Priestly Writer's reputation as a cult-obsessed pedant or abstracted theologian. The sublime Creator of Genesis 1 condescends to engage in a contest with Egyptian sorcerers, and at first it seems a fair fight. The style is both spare and repetitive; McEvenue's (1971) comparison of P to children's literature is nowhere more apt. Yet the episodes' very similarity directs our attention to differences among them. Most obviously, the *ḥarṭummîm* are progressively discomfited. We also observe the changing commands to Aaron — "take your rod and cast" (7:9), "take your rod and extend your arm" (7:19), "extend your arm with your rod" (8:1), "extend your rod and strike" (8:12). This is variety for variety's sake. Similarly, within each episode, P uses slightly different diction for injunction and execution. The command may be more elaborate than the fulfillment (blood, frogs, *šəḥîn*) or vice versa (serpents, lice).

The episode of *šəḥîn* (skin disease) features the greatest deviation from the pattern. Moses, not Aaron, works the miracle, and he employs no rod. The omission of the staff makes sense — his hands must be free to cast ashes — but Aaron's marginality is harder to understand (see NOTE to 9:8). The episode of *šəḥîn* also varies the concluding cliché: instead of Pharaoh's heart being strong (7:13, 22; 8:15), Yahweh strengthens Pharaoh's heart (9:12) (see COMMENT).

Exod 8:3 requires brief comment on two counts. First, we would expect at the end "and Pharaoh's heart was strong," as in all other Priestly episodes. The phrase was presumably removed by the Redactor to accommodate the non-Priestly statement that Pharaoh made his heart "firm." Also, I am not sure how to assign the second half of 8:3. Possibly both JE and P reported, "They raised up the frogs upon the land of Egypt."

As for the non-Priestly narrative, it is as verbose and variegated as P is terse and redundant. No two episodes are told in the same way, although each shares features with others. This is worth exposing in detail, as minor divergences are often wrongly touted as evidence of multiple authorship. Moses addresses Pharaoh in the morning as the latter goes to the Nile (7:15 [blood]; 8:16 [*'ārōb*]; probably 9:13 [hail]). He invokes "Yahweh the Hebrews' deity" (7:16 [blood]; 9:1 [murrain]; 9:13 [hail]; 10:3 [locusts]). He demands, "release my people, that they may serve me" (7:16 [blood]; 7:26 [frogs]; 8:16 [*'ārōb*]; 9:1 [murrain]; 9:13 [hail]; 10:3 [locusts]). Moses asks to leave Egypt (10:25 [darkness]), to go into the wilderness (7:16 [blood]; 8:23 [*'ārōb*]) to sacrifice (8:4 [frogs]; 8:21–25 [*'ārōb*]). But Pharaoh's heart is "firm" (7:14 [blood]; 8:11 [frogs]; 8:28 [*'ārōb*]; 9:7 [murrain]; 9:34 [hail]; 10:1 [locusts]). His refusal to release the people is characterized as *mē'ēn ləšallaḥ* (7:14 [blood]; 7:27 [frogs]; 9:2 [murrain]; 10:3–4 [locusts]) or *'ên mašallēaḥ* (8:17 [*'ārōb*]). Moses works a miracle with his arm and/or rod (7:15, 17 [blood]; 9:22–23 [hail]; 10:12–13 [locusts]; 10:21–22 [darkness]), or else Yahweh sends the plague directly (8:20 [*'ārōb*]; 9:6 [murrain]). The miracle begins at a set time (8:19 [*'ārōb*]; 9:18 [hail]; 10:4 [locusts]; 11:4 [firstborn]). The affliction "ascends" (*'ly*) upon Egypt (7:28–29 [frogs]; 10:12–14 [locusts]). It enters the Egyptians' very houses (7:28; 8:7 [frogs]; 8:17, 20 [*'ārōb*]; 10:6 [locusts]; 12:30 [firstborn]). The crops of Egypt are devastated (9:25, 31 [hail]; 10:5, 12, 15 [locusts]). The cattle, too, are killed (9:3, 6 [murrain]; 9:19–21, 25 [hail]; 11:5; 12:29 [firstborn]). The sky is darkened (10:5, 15 [locusts]; 10:21–23 [darkness]) or it is night (11:4; 12:29 [firstborn]). Yahweh ensures that the afflictions beset only Egyptians, not Israelites (8:19 [*'ārōb*]; 9:4, 6–7 [murrain]; 9:26 [hail]; 10:23 [dark]; 11:7; 12:23 [firstborn]). Yahweh teaches that he is God (7:17 [blood]; 8:6 [frogs]; 8:18 [*'ārōb*]; 9:14, 16, 29 [hail]; 10:2 [locusts]). Temporarily contrite, Pharaoh begs Moses and Aaron to entreat Yahweh to lift the plague (8:4 [frogs]; 8:24 [*'ārōb*]; 9:28 [hail]; 10:17 [locusts]). The plague is removed at a set time (8:5–6 [frogs]; 8:25 [*'ārōb*]).

The author thus avoids the monotony to which a repetitive narrative is liable. No two non-Priestly Plagues are the same, and yet none is unique. This characteristic of Hebrew prose storytelling stands in contrast to the *verbatim* repetitions of Mesopotamian and Ugaritic epic poetry (Alter 1981: 88–113; Sternberg 1985: 365–440). The parade example of deliberate variation is the fivefold assertion that such a calamity was unprecedented: "from the day, her founding, and until now" (9:18 [hail]), "since she became a nation" (9:24 [hail]), "from the day of their being upon the ground until this day" (10:6 [locusts]), "before it there was never such . . . and after it never will be such" (10:14 [locusts]), "whose like never happened nor whose like will ever recur" (11:6 [firstborn]). (For the trope, cf. 2 Kgs 18:5; 23:25; Joel 2:2.)

Each individual episode is also liable to monotony, as it theoretically contains both command and fulfillment. To achieve greater interest and brevity, the author omitted certain details. For all the Plagues except locusts, hail and darkness, Moses is given a message to deliver to Pharaoh, but we are left to assume that he does so. In the case of the locusts, Moses is not given a message in 10:1, but we learn in vv 3–6 that he received one. In the plague of darkness, there is neither message nor delivery—though there may be missing text (see REDACTION ANALYSIS). And in the slaying of the firstborn, we have a message to Moses (11:1–2/3) and Moses' completely unrelated words to Pharaoh (11:4–8). In this last case, however, we may in fact have a change of author (see below).

In particular, like P, the non-Priestly source varies Moses' use of the arm or rod. In the plague of blood, Moses announces he will strike with the rod in his hand, and he duly lifts the rod to strike. For the plagues of hail and locusts, he is told to extend his arm, but he extends his rod. For the plague of darkness, he is told to extend his arm, and he extends his arm. The episodes of frogs, *ʿārōb*, murrain and firstborn involve neither rod nor arm.

A complication is that four of the non-Priestly episodes contain P-like references to the "strengthening" (*ḥzq*) of Pharaoh's heart (9:35; 10:20, 27; 11:10–11). These are probably Redactorial sutures in the style of P (see REDACTION ANALYSIS). But we must note the expression's previous occurrence in a JE context (4:21b). If 4:21b is JE, then 9:35; 10:20, 27; 11:10–11 might be JE, too. Or, in a more complicated scenario, P may have drawn its theme of "strengthening" from 4:21b (JE), after which the Redactor inserted it into the non-Priestly Plagues. But the simplest solution is to identify 4:21b, too, as a Redactorial insertion (see SOURCE ANALYSIS to Exodus 3–4).

In addition to its greater variety vis-à-vis P, the non-Priestly narrative puts events into a time frame: "in the morning" (7:15; 8:16; 9:13; 10:13), "seven days" (7:25), "tomorrow" (8:6, 19, 25; 9:5, 18; 10:4), "three days" (10:23). We are even apprised of the progress of the harvest (9:31–32; 10:5). As these Plagues progress, we note a general trend toward greater length and complexity of description, portraying Pharaoh's gradual degradation (Greenberg 1969: 176). Moreover, some of the episodes are bound together not only by shared themes and chronology but by explicit cross-references: hail refers backward to murrain (9:15) and forward to locusts (9:32), while locusts alludes to hail (10:15). And pervading and unifying the entire narrative is the elevenfold use of the root *kbd* 'to be firm, heavy' (7:14 [blood]; 8:11 [frogs]; 8:20, 28 [*ʿārōb*]; 9:3, 7 [murrain]; 9:18, 24, 34 [hail]; 10:1, 14 [locusts]) (Fox 1986: 45). Another theme word is *ydʿ* 'to know,' appearing seven times in non-P (7:17; 8:6, 18; 9:14, 29; 10:2; 11:7); see also INTRODUCTION, p. 37.

As we shall directly see, the non-P matter contains some internal inconsistencies. But there is no pattern of *consistent* inconsistency to warrant isolating separate strands. For example, one might wonder why the Israelites are not explicitly exempted from the first two plagues and from the locusts (7:28; 10:6, however, may implicitly exempt Israel [ibn Ezra on 7:29]). Perhaps the author simply did not consider the problem until after writing the first two episodes, or he may have regarded blood and frogs as bearable for the Israelites. As for the locusts, they would not have directly affected the Hebrews, who were shepherds and builders, not farmers (Greenberg 1969: 174 n. 1).

Another oft-observed problem within the non-P matter is that the Egyptian cattle, supposedly killed *en masse* in 9:6, are resurrected to die again in the plague of hail (9:25) and to be offered to the Hebrews as sacrificial victims (10:25). Some perish once more in the plague of the firstborn (11:5; 12:29), and the horses also drown in the Sea (14:28; 15:1, 4, 19, 21). This inconsistency, however, is a by-product of the author's penchant for hyperbole (see NOTE to 9:6; COMMENT). Source criticism does not provide a solution.

The most glaring difficulties within the non-P matter pertain to Moses and Pharaoh's exchange of bluster in 10:28–29 (Otto 1976: 7–13). Pharaoh commands, "Go from before me. Watch yourself, see my face no more. For on the day of your seeing my face you will die." And Moses responds, "You spoke right. I will see your face no more." We should expect these to be the antagonists' parting shots, immediately followed by "and he went out from with Pharaoh with anger of *nose*" (11:8) (cf. Van Seters 1994: 108). Instead, we find intervening a message from Yahweh to Moses (11:1–2/3), a possible comment by the narrator (11:3; see NOTE) and Moses' words to Pharaoh (11:4–8a), quite different from Yahweh's command in vv 1–2.

There are several possible explanations for this disjointedness. I doubt that all of 11:1–8a is interpolated from another source, for then it should have followed 10:27, allowing 10:28 to flow directly into 11:8b. More important, this section displays links to other non-Priestly matter: e.g., the incomparability formula and the separation of Israel and Egypt. I would rather take the text at face value: Yahweh interrupts in v 1 to inform Moses of the coming plague (*Exod. Rab.* 18:1; Rashi). As for the lack of agreement between Yahweh's command and Moses' oracle, it may arise from the author's desire to avoid *verbatim* repetitions. Moses was already told in 4:23 that Yahweh would kill Pharaoh's firstborn, so there was no need to be explicit in 11:1 (on 4:23 and 11:4–5 as a frame, see NOTE to 4:23). In vv 2–3, however, which are quite difficult to interpret (see NOTES), I do suspect the incursion of another hand (see below).

A still greater difficulty in the non-Priestly corpus is the apparent inconsistency between 10:29 ("I will see your face no more") and Pharaoh's address to Moses and Aaron in 12:31–32, giving the lie to Moses' prediction. But, however we reconcile the contradiction, it cannot be explained by a change of source (see NOTE to 10:29).

If the non-Priestly matter is primarily of one source, is it J or E? The lexical and stylistic clues are ambivalent. Some evidence might suggest the Yahwist's hand. For example, *ṭap* 'dependent(s)' (10:10, 24) does not otherwise appear in E, while it is common in J (Gen 34:29; 43:8; 45:19; 46:5; 47:12, 24; 50:8, 21; Num 16:27). The syntax and content of 10:28 — "on the day of your . . . you will die" — recalls Gen 2:17 (J), "on the day of your eating from it you will die, die." Most strikingly, *tōʿăbat miṣrayim* 'Egypt's abomination' (8:22) is paralleled only in Gen 43:32; 46:34 (J?). But other data point rather to the Elohist. E refers to the "*forward* wind" (10:13) in Gen 41:6, 23, 27; J never does. Moreover, *ṣbr* 'pile up' (8:10) occurs in the Torah only in E (Gen 41:35, 49). And the fish of the Nile (7:18) reappear in Num 11:5 (E).

Since stylistic evidence is inconclusive, we must look to content for evidence of authorship. The non-Priestly Plagues cycle fits best with texts I have previously assigned to E. Aaron acts as Moses' assistant (cf. 4:14–16, 27–30); Moses performs wonders before Pharaoh (cf. 4:21) with his rod (cf. 4:17, 20; 17:1–7), and Yahweh demonstrates his power to reverse miracles (cf. 4:4, 7). Particularly characteristic of E is the theme of God-fearing (cf. 1:21; see Wolff 1975). In 11:1, Yahweh repeats his prediction that Pharaoh will detain Israel until Yahweh punishes him (3:19–20). And, above all, in 11:4–6, Moses finally delivers God's message from 4:22–23, whose language resounds throughout the entire non-Priestly Plagues narrative: "My son, my firstborn, is Israel. And

I have said to you, 'Release my son that he may serve me.' And if you refuse to release him, see: I am going to kill your son, your firstborn." (Friedman's [1998] theory of the Greater J source presents a problem, however: 1 Sam 6:6 appears to cite the non-Priestly Plagues material [note particularly Exod 10:2]. If 1 Sam 6:6 is Yahwistic, we may have to rethink our analysis of Exod 7:8–11:10 [see further APPENDIX A, vol. II].)

The one place I detect J is in 11:2–3, which, by any reading, sits awkwardly in its context. Of what relevance is the despoiling of Egypt, and why should the narrator intrude in v 3, if indeed he does (see NOTES)? True, the expressions "the man Moses" and "Moses the man" reappear in 32:1, 23; Num 12:3 (E). Still, the connection to Gen 15:14, predicting Israel's enrichment, inclines me somewhat toward J for 11:2–3 and the parallel passages 3:21–22 and 12:35–36 (see SOURCE ANALYSES to Exodus 3–4 and 12:1–13:16).

Whether we consider P, E or the composite text, the number of the Plagues is unclear (see also REDACTION ANALYSIS). In P, there initially appear to be six: serpents, blood, frogs, lice, *šəḥîn* and firstborn. One might object that the transformation of rods into reptiles is not a "plague," but the loss of their staffs is at least an inconvenience to the magicians and surely a blow to their prestige (cf. Jacob 1992: 215). And, in any case, *makkâ* 'blow, plague' is a postbiblical term. The Bible calls the Plagues *'ōtōt* 'signs' (4:17 [E]; 7:3 [P]; 8:19 [E]; 10:1–2 [E]) and/or *môpətîm* 'wonders' (4:21 [E]; 7:3, 9 [P]; 11:9–10 [R?]; also Ps 78:43; 105:27) (cf. Childs 1974: 138–39). The trial of the serpents is explicitly a "wonder" (7:9).

But can the total really be six? The Bible in general and P in particular evince a marked penchant for sevens (Pope 1962b) — suffice it to mention the seven days of Creation (Genesis 1) and the exponentially sevenfold plagues punishing Covenant violators (Lev 26:14–38). In fact, although their interpretation is disputed, both Psalms 78 and 105 record seven Plagues against Egypt (see APPENDIX D, vol. II). There *must* have been a seventh Priestly plague — but where?

Before answering, let us note another difficulty. In E, we appear to have eight Plagues (blood, frogs, *'ārōb*, murrain, hail, locusts, darkness, firstborn). Again, we might have expected seven. Moreover, the first six Elohistic episodes follow an alternating pattern: for blood (1), *'ārōb* (3) and hail (5), Moses is told to "take his stand" to meet Pharaoh "in the morning"; for frogs (2), murrain (4) and locusts (6), Yahweh simply commands, "come to Pharaoh" (Schmidt 1990: 1). But the pattern breaks down with darkness (7), which begins with the enactment of the plague. It is also the only episode from E's latter Plagues lacking the incomparability formula.

These anomalies impel Greenberg (1969: 184–87) toward an obvious solution. If we transfer darkness to P, each source has the expected tally of seven. In confirmation, Greenberg notes that, like the episodes universally assigned to P, the plague of darkness begins without a warning to Pharaoh.

This may convince those who attend more to structure than to content (e.g., Norin 1977: 18). But for me, the absence of Priestly traits (Aaron, the *ḥarṭummîm*, "and so they did") and the prominence of Elohistic themes (Moses as miracle-worker, the lapse of time, the distinction between Egypt and Israel, the haggling with Pharaoh, the sacrifice in the wilderness) make this solution unacceptable.

A more attractive analysis was foreshadowed in 1801 by Wessely (see Luzzatto; Jacob 1992: 191) and later propounded by Holzinger (1900: 32; cf. McCarthy 1966); it may already be implicit in Wis 19:1–22 (see Loewenstamm 1992a: 107): P's seventh plague is the drowning of Egypt in the Suph Sea. Note that 14:4, 17, 18 (P) feature two themes associated with P's Plagues cycle: Yahweh "strengthening" Pharaoh's heart and the Egyptians learning that "I am Yahweh" (cf. 7:5). To be sure, this seventh plague differs slightly in form from its predecessors—e.g., we might have expected *Aaron* to split the Sea—but so does the Sabbath from the six days of Creation (Gen 1:1–2:4a).

Reducing the Elohistic Plagues to seven is more difficult, and perhaps unnecessary. One arbitrary expedient would be to exclude the death of the firstborn as a separate incident. But there *is* something odd about the darkness episode, as Greenberg observes. First, the action begins *in medias res*, unlike the other E Plagues. Second, Ps 105:28, which otherwise follows the order of Exodus (minus murrain and *šəḥîn*), makes darkness the *first* plague. Third, Ps 78:44–51 basically parallels E, but lacks darkness entirely (see further APPENDIX D, vol. II). Perhaps, then, the darkness plague is a later addition in the style of E—or an insertion from J—and the Elohistic Plagues originally numbered seven.

But our attempt to reduce the Elohistic Plagues may be misguided from the start. While far less common than seven, the number eight is not unparalleled. Loewenstamm (1992a: 85 n. 31) cites the eight days of Aaron's investiture (Lev 8:33–9:1), Amos' eight oracles against the nations (Amos 1–2) and the parallelism of seven and eight in biblical (Mic 5:4; Eccl 11:2) and Ugaritic literature (*KTU* 1.3.v.11, 26; 4.vii.10–11; 5.v.8–9, 20–21; 12.ii.44–45, 48–49; 14.i.8–9; 15.iv.6–7; 19.i.42–43; 23.66–67; 45.2–3; 101.3–4). One should also mention circumcision on the eighth day (Gen 17:12), the eighth day of the Festival of Shelters (Lev 23:36), the eight-day consecration of the Temple (1 Kgs 8:66) and Jesse's eight sons (1 Sam 16:10). Indeed, Yahweh's words in 9:14–16 seem designed to demarcate two symmetrical sets of four Plagues, the second round more severe than the first. Under REDACTION ANALYSIS, I shall explain the deviation of the darkness episode as a consequence of final editing.

As elsewhere, in the Plagues cycle we find indications that the Priestly Writer based his work upon JE (see Friedman 1981). The similarities are obvious and need not be spelled out. But the differences are both interesting and significant. The most blatant is Aaron's prominence in P, as opposed to his shadowy presence in JE. As we have seen, this distinction reflects the competing theopolitical agendas of the Priestly Document and E (COMMENT to 6:2–7:7).

It is fascinating to observe P reworking traditions inherited from JE. The transformation of Aaron's rod into a serpent, P's first plague, imitates the analogous mutation of *Moses'* rod, intended as a sign, not to Pharaoh, but to Israel (4:2–4). The cannibalistic voracity of Aaron's rod may also be inspired by the dreams of Joseph's Pharaoh, in which cows eat one another and likewise ears of grain (Gen 41:4, 7). P derives its plagues of blood, frogs and lice from the corresponding Elohistic episodes, but P's plague of blood is more severe than E's, affecting not just the Nile but all the water in Egypt. For the insects, P simply replaces the term *ʿārōb* with *kinnîm*. Behind P's plague of *šəḥîn* stands Moses' skin disease *ṣāraʿat*, originally not a plague against Egypt but a sign for the Hebrews (4:6–7) (cf. Fretheim 1991a: 70, 123; NOTE to 9:9). And P's sixth and seventh plagues, the death of the firstborn and the drowning of Egypt, draw directly upon JE prototypes (see SOURCE ANALYSES to 12:1–13:16 and 13:17–15:21).

Moreover, unlike the Elohistic Plagues, P's are unreversed (except for the parting of the Sea). This enhances Pharaoh's apparent courage. Whereas in E his firmness of heart generally either follows the removal of an affliction (8:11, 28; 9:34) or precedes its imposition (7:14; 10:1), in P Pharaoh stands fast in the face of mounting disaster (7:13, 22; [8:3], 8:15; 9:12). But, as if to compensate, P's Plagues are initially less severe than E's. No one dies until the slaughter of the firstborn.

The reason for this last difference lies in the respective purposes of the Elohistic and Priestly Plagues. In E, the goal of each affliction, and of the whole series, is to inculcate "knowledge" of Yahweh (7:17; 8:6, 18; 9:14, 29). For P, in contrast, only the culmination at the Sea teaches Egypt "that I am Yahweh" (7:5; 14:4, 18) (Childs 1974: 140). It seems that the Priestly Plagues are intended to inure Pharaoh gradually to hardship, lest he relent before Yahweh can show his full power (7:3–4; cf. Childs 1974: 139). For E, however, each individual plague is to convince Pharaoh of Yahweh's supreme Godhood.

REDACTION ANALYSIS

Just as it is surprisingly difficult to enumerate the twelve tribes of Israel or to list the Ten Commandments, so it is unclear how to count the Plagues of Egypt—not only in E and P but in the composite Torah. The Redactor never gives us a tally; the number ten first appears in Jub 48:7.

As we have seen, JE apparently told of eight wonders (blood through firstborn), while P contained seven (serpents through drowning). The Redactor fused four of these—blood, frogs, firstborn, drowning—leaving it unclear where the series begins and ends. Tradition, partly confirmed by Psalm 105 (see APPENDIX D, vol. II), follows E in considering blood the first plague and the slaying of the firstborn the last. Thus, there are ten Plagues. But one could also follow P and count *twelve* wonders (*môpətîm*), from serpents through drowning; note the references to "wonder(s)" in 7:9; 11:10 (Wessely *apud* Luzzatto; see discussion of Jacob [1992: 191]). Nevertheless, even for the Redactor, the traditional count of ten is probably correct. Exod 11:1 (E) calls the death of the firstborn "yet one more plague"—i.e., the last. Accordingly, the Redactor probably conceived of P's first round, the trial of the rods (7:8–13), as prefatory to the Plagues proper. For a series of ten trials, we may compare the ten times Laban changed Jacob's wages (Gen 31:7, 41) or the ten times Israel tried Yahweh's patience (Num 14:22).

However we define its limits, we can easily reconstruct the Redactor's procedure in creating the Plagues narrative. He clustered the Priestly episodes toward the beginning, for several reasons. First, by letting the magicians fall by the wayside early, the Redactor made it clear that they were no match for Yahweh. Moreover, by putting P's shorter, milder episodes at the front, the Redactor created an impression of mounting severity throughout the cycle. We may assume that each P section originally ended, "Pharaoh's heart was strong, and he did not heed them, as Yahweh had spoken." (The formula is now partly missing from 8:11 and entirely absent from 8:3, while 9:12 features a variant: "Yahweh strengthened Pharaoh's heart.") To lend consistency to his composite text, the Redactor reused the Priestly cliché to conclude the Elohistic episodes of frogs, hail, locusts, darkness and firstborn as well (8:11b; 9:35; 10:20, 27; 11:9–10).

For the plagues of blood and frogs, the Redactor fused E with P. This was practicable for three reasons, aside from the obvious one of shared subject: (a) P's narrative was much briefer than E's and, in effect, could fit inside it; (b) each episode theoretically consisted of two parts, a commission and an execution, creating an expectation of redundancy and an opportunity for conflation; (c) E's commission scenes focus on words, P's on deeds.

In the plague of blood (7:14–24), the Redactor created a double commission scene, with remarkably little jarring. The phrase "Pharaoh's heart is firm" (7:14 [E]) refers, in its present context, not to the debacle of Exodus 5 (E), but to the king's intransigence in 7:13 (P). Yahweh commands Moses to announce the sanguification of the Nile, a wonder that, in the original E, was worked with Moses' rod. But then follows P's command: Moses is to have Aaron work the miracle with a rod. The awkwardness is minimal, as E had merely implied that Moses would enact the plague. Note that, in the composite text, the "rod that turned into a snake" (7:15 [E]), even though held by Moses, appears to be Aaron's (see NOTE).

Next the Redactor included P's laconic fulfillment formula, "Moses and Aaron did so, as Yahweh commanded," probably displacing an Elohistic comment, "Moses did so," originally standing between 7:18 and 20b. Through redaction, the subject of "he raised the rod" (7:20 [E]) became Aaron, whereas in E it had been Moses. As a consequence of this gesture, first the Nile alone is turned to blood (E), and then there is blood throughout Egypt (P). Thus, in the composite text, the pollution of all Egypt seems an afterthought, an intensification of God's initial plan. A careful reader might even infer that Yahweh has maliciously concealed his full intent from Pharaoh.

The redacted text next tells of the magicians' duplication of the feat (P), only returning to E to conclude the episode: the Egyptians must dig for water. This *seems to* contradict P, which implies the absence of any water—but perhaps not, since 7:19 does not specify that subterranean water was affected (cf. ibn

Ezra on 7:22). Finally, to enhance coherence, the Redactor probably inserted *gam* 'also' into 7:23: "Pharaoh . . . did not set his heart to this either (*gam-lazzō[']t*)," referring to P's trial of serpents. (Alternatively, *gam* may be an originally Elohistic allusion to Pharaoh's rejection of Moses and Aaron in chap. 5.)

The Redactor followed an analogous procedure for the next vignette (7:25–8:11). He first quoted E's commissioning, consisting mostly of a speech, and then cited P, which focused on an act. The Redactor was particularly clever in 8:3. He probably dropped E's "Moses (and Aaron) did so" before *wayya'ălû* 'and they raised.' This made the subjects of *wayya'ălû* the magicians, not Moses and Aaron (but see TEXTUAL NOTE on Sam). Since only the Elohist spoke of removing the frogs, the Redactor stayed with E, shifting P's final comment "he did not heed them, as Yahweh had spoken," to the end. But he probably excised the first half of P's cliché "Pharaoh's heart was strong," which would have been redundant with 8:11 (E), "he made firm his heart." (Admittedly, the editor let stand just such a redundancy in 9:34–35.)

Next the Redactor faced a choice. He might have combined lice (8:12–15) and *'ārōb* (8:16–28), since both are biting insects (they are equated in Ps 105:31). The result would have been this:

(E)And Yahweh said to Moses, "Rise early in the morning and station yourself before Pharaoh; see: (him) going out to the waters. And you will say to him, 'Thus has Yahweh said: "Release my people, that they may serve me. For if you do not release my people, see: I am going to send against you and against your slaves and against your people and into your houses the *'ārōb*; and Egypt's houses will be full of the *'ārōb*, as well as the land on which they are. But I will separate on that day the land of Goshen, on which my people stands, and there will be no *'ārōb* there, that you may know that I am Yahweh in the land's midst. For I will put a redemption between my people and between your people; tomorrow this sign will occur." ' "

(P)And Yahweh said to Moses, "Say to Aaron, 'Extend your rod and strike the dirt of the land, that it become lice in all the land of Egypt.' "

And they did so. And Aaron extended his arm with his rod and struck the dirt of the land, and the louse became on man and on animal; all the dirt of the land became lice in all the land of Egypt. (E)And heavy *'ārōb* came to Pharaoh's house and his slaves' house. And in all the land of Egypt the land was being devastated from before the *'ārōb*.

(P)And the *ḥarṭummîm* did likewise with their mysteries, to bring forth the lice, but they were not able. And the louse became on man and on animal. And the *ḥarṭummîm* said to Pharaoh, "It is a divine finger."

(E)And Pharaoh called to Moses and to Aaron and said, "Go, sacrifice to your deity in the land."

But Moses said, "It is not possible to do so, for Egypt's abomination we would sacrifice to Yahweh our deity. If we sacrifice Egypt's abomination to their eyes, will they not stone us? A three days' way we would go into the wilderness and sacrifice to Yahweh our deity as he may say to us."

But Pharaoh said, "I, I will release you, that you may sacrifice to Yahweh your deity in the wilderness. Only far, do not go far. Pray for me." And Moses said, "See: I am going out from with you, and I will pray to Yahweh, and the *'ārōb* will leave from Pharaoh, from his slaves and from his people tomorrow. Only let not Pharaoh continue to toy by not releasing the people to sacrifice to Yahweh." And Moses went out from with Pharaoh and prayed to Yahweh.

And Yahweh did according to Moses' word and removed the *'ārōb* from Pharaoh, from his slaves and from his people; not one remained. But Pharaoh made firm his heart this time, too, and did not release the people. **(P)And Pharaoh's heart was strong, and he did not heed them, as Yahweh had spoken.**

This incorporates all of E and P except "and Yahweh did so" (8:20 [E]), difficult to combine with "and they did so" (8:12 [P]).

Why did the Redactor decline this course? First, in order to achieve a round number of wonders, be it ten or twelve. As for why he put P's lice before E's *'ārōb*, it may simply have been to avoid anticlimax, given the greater detail of E. Another factor was perhaps reluctance to introduce the theme of the separation of Israel and Egypt too soon. If *'ārōb* (E) came first, the reader might wonder whether the Israelites, too, were bitten by the lice (P). And, as we shall see below, the triple triad structure of the first nine plagues also necessitated the present arrangement.

After *'ārōb*, another choice confronted the Redactor. Should he proceed to murrain (9:1-7 [E]) or to *šəḥîn* (9:8-12 [P])? He elected to put murrain first, most likely in order to have Yahweh afflict animals before humans, creating a sense of mounting severity. As for E's theme of the separation of Israel and Egypt, while it is absent from P's *šəḥîn* episode, the quarantine of the magicians might imply that only Egyptians were afflicted (Greenberg 1969: 174 n. 1). And again, the triple triadic structure of the first nine plagues was likely a consideration (see below).

The remainder of the Plagues narrative, through chap. 11, is Elohistic. To unify the cycle, the Redactor merely added to each episode a comment that Pharaoh's heart was strong (9:35) or was strengthened (10:20, 27; 11:9-10). (Exod 9:35 is slightly surprising, however: given P's comment in 9:12, we would expect R to continue with "Yahweh *strengthened* Pharaoh's heart," not "Pharaoh's heart *was strong*.")

Assuming that the Redactor counted ten Plagues beginning with blood, he shifted hail, E's fifth plague, to the seventh position. Consequently, God's pivotal warning of increased severity (9:14-16), which originally marked the midpoint of the Elohistic Plagues cycle, took on a new structural function, setting off the seventh plague (cf. Leibowitz 1976: 175; on the special qualities of seven, see Pope 1962b).

Finally, in 11:9-10, the Redactor summarized the proceedings. By repeating "Pharaoh will not heed you," he created a frame (cf. 7:4), detaching the paschal legislation and the death of the firstborn (chap. 12) from the prior plagues (cf. Bekhor Shor).

As for overall structure, several commentators since Rashbam have noted a pattern of three triads for the first nine plagues as traditionally enumerated: (I) blood-frogs-lice, (II) ʿarob-murrain-šəḥîn, (III) hail-locusts-darkness (e.g., Cassuto 1967: 92–93; Greenberg 1969: 171–72; Sarna 1986: 77). Within each triad, the first episode begins with God's command to "station yourself . . . in the morning" before Pharaoh (wəniṣṣabtā [7:15]; wəhityaṣṣēb [8:16; 9:13]); the second episode opens with "come to Pharaoh," and the third contains no warning at all.

What conclusions may we draw from this phenomenon? Cassuto (1967: 93) infers unitary authorship for the Plagues cycle, but I would instead attribute the pattern to the craftsmanship of the Redactor and to the traits of his sources (cf. Schildenberger 1961: 251–54; Greenberg 1969: 183–92). We have already observed that the first six Elohistic plagues feature alternating commands to "station yourself . . . in the morning" and to "come to Pharaoh" (SOURCE ANALYSIS). Because he rejects source analysis, Cassuto does not realize that, in each triad, the first two episodes begin with E matter. In contrast, the third episode of the first two triads, lice and šəḥîn, begin with P. Since P never contains any forewarnings for Pharaoh, the first two triads inevitably end with unheralded plagues.

Did the Redactor know what he was doing? I think so (vs. Childs 1974: 150; Durham 1987: 96). Notice that, considering only the authorship of opening verses, we find the following pattern in the first nine plagues: (I) EEP, (II) EEP, (III) EEE. The ninth, deviant episode is the plague of darkness, whose strangeness we have already noted (see p. 315). Unlike the other Elohistic episodes, darkness opens *in medias res* (10:21), as if the Redactor had lopped off the beginning. But why should he have done so? The triadic structure suggests an answer: to perpetuate the pattern established by the first two triads, whose third elements were Priestly. In other words, having exhausted P, the Redactor trimmed the Elohistic plague of darkness to resemble a Priestly plague. Drastic Redactorial intervention at this point might also explain why the episode of locusts does not end with E's expected obduracy formula, "Pharaoh's heart was firm," but rather with R's "Yahweh strengthened Pharaoh's heart" (10:20).

NOTES

7:8. *to Aaron.* The words that follow are addressed to Moses alone, but are really meant for Aaron. Jacob (1992: 252) compares Num 20:23–24; cf. also Exod 12:1; Lev 11:1–2; 15:1–2.

7:9. *When Pharaoh speaks.* Yahweh says "*when* (*kî*) Pharaoh speaks," not "*if* (*ʾim*) Pharaoh speaks," implying that God is in control throughout (*Exod. Rab.* 9:1). Admittedly, *kî* may also be translated "if," but it is less specifically conditional than *ʾim*.

Give yourselves a wonder. We might rather have expected "give *me* a wonder" (so Syr; cf. LXX). It is as if Pharaoh says, "I'm not interested in your tricks, but perform one if you must" (cf. Leibowitz 1976: 163). Fretheim (1991a: 113) catches the irony: Pharaoh, who first suggests a wonder, will get many more than he bargained for.

serpent. In 4:3 (E), Moses' rod became a mere *nāḥāš* 'snake.' Here in P, Aaron's rod becomes a veritable *tannîn* (on the "competition" between Moses and Aaron, see COMMENT to 6:2–7:7). Both *nāḥāš* and *tannîn* denote reptiles (Propp 1990: 195), but *tannîn* is grander, describing the great beings believed to inhabit the seas. *Tannîn* means "snake" only in the elevated diction of poetry (Deut 32:33; Ps 91:13). What does it connote here?

In light of the Egyptian setting, some suggest that the author had in mind the crocodile (Gressmann 1913: 88; Cassuto 1967: 94). Ezek 29:3–7; 32:2–10 liken Pharaoh to a *tannîn (MT *tannîm*) who sounds rather crocodilian (cf. Bekhor Shor). Egyptian literature, too, compares Pharaoh to a crocodile (on the symbolism, see, briefly, Eyre 1992: 281). Jacob (1992: 214), however, more plausibly associates the *tannîn* with the cobra, a ubiquitous symbol of the Egyptian monarchy. This better parallels 4:3 (Moses' rod) and evokes the implicit opposite of the biblical miracle: charming a snake into rigidity.

Aaron's rod will undergo a further transformation, becoming an almond branch deposited in the Tabernacle (Numbers 17 [P]); compare the deposition of sacred rods in Phoenician shrines (Sanchuniathon *apud* Eusebius *Praep. evangelica* 1.10.10 [Attridge and Oden 1981: 42–43]). Aaron's sacred rod/serpent/tree may in fact be P's counterpart to Moses' magical serpent ensign (Num 21:6–9 [J?]), later erected near the Temple (2 Kgs 18:4). It may also be related to the holy pole/tree called Asherah (Smith 1990: 81–85), especially if the theories that associate the cult symbol with the goddess Asherah, and associate the goddess with serpents, are both correct (Cross 1973: 32–33; Olyan 1989: 70–71).

7:11. *sages.* Egypt was renowned for its ancient wisdom (e.g., Isa 19:11–12; Acts 7:22). As in the Joseph story (Gen 41:8), Pharaoh's savants seem to exist for the sole purpose of being bested by Hebrew virtuosi—on their own turf. But here the focus is less on wisdom and more on sorcery. M. S. Smith (privately) compares the Egyptian literary tradition of competition between native and foreign magicians (e.g., "Setne II" [Lichtheim 1980: 138–51]). One thinks, too, of the rivalry between "true" and "false" prophets endemic in preexilic Israel and Judah.

ḥarṭummîm. The foreign term is glossed as "sages and wizards" (cf. Gen 41:8 [E]). Almost certainly, *ḥarṭōm* derives from Egyptian *ḥry-tp* 'he that is at the head, chief,' a title often borne by Egyptian priests (Redford 1970: 203–4; Quaegebeur 1985; *pace* Lambdin 1953: 150–51).

mysteries. Here and in 7:22; 8:3, 14, *lahaṭ/lāṭ* connotes magic spells. Theoretically, the root might be either *lhṭ* 'burn' or *lwṭ* 'be wrapped up, hidden.' From the former derives the noun *lahaṭ* 'flame,' but this does not fit the context. More likely, *lahaṭ/lāṭ* is an alloform of *lāṭ/lā(ʾ)ṭ* 'secrecy' (< *lwṭ*) (GKC

§77*f*). But, given the root meaning of *lwt*, it is not impossible that *lahat/lāt* denotes a magic scroll.

7:12. *And Aaron's rod swallowed.* Fox (1986: 45) observes that the behavior of Aaron's rod leaves "no doubt as to whether optical illusion or sleight of hand is involved." That one *tannîn* devours several others, presumably of its own size, demonstrates how easily Yahweh's power encompasses that of the *hartummîm*. The prodigious swallowing abilities of reptiles (Jer 51:34) is not necessarily at issue. After all, in Gen 41:4, cows swallow one another, and in Gen 41:7, so do ears of grain. The Freudian symbolism in Exodus is hard to miss: Aaron's alternatingly rigid and supple implement overpowers and ingests its rivals. Note, throughout the Exodus tradition, the ambivalence between "rod" and "arm" (*yād*) and the latter's additional connotations of "power" and "penis" (Isa 57:8; Cant 5:4; 1QS 7:13 [?]; cf. *KTU* 1.4.iv.38–39; 23.33–35, 37, 40) (on phallic euphemism, see Paul 1995: 593 n. 30).

We learn from the following episodes that the rod, having ingested the magicians' staffs, reverts to its original shape (Van Seters 1994: 54).

7:13. *strong.* A "strong" heart is courageous, of firm resolve. The common English rendering "hard" misleadingly suggests cruelty (e.g., RSV).

he did not heed. Wilson (1979: 31–32) notes the parallel to 6:9, "they [Israel] did not heed Moses," inferring that the story of Pharaoh's stubbornness contains a message for Israelite readers. They, like Pharaoh and his people, must learn "that I am Yahweh" (10:2; cf. 7:17; 8:6, 18; 9:14, 29; 11:7). Exod 15:26 makes the connection explicit: "If you listen, listen to Yahweh your deity's voice, and what is straight in his eyes you do, and give ear to his commands and observe all his rules, all the disease that I set in Egypt I will not set upon you" (see further under COMMENT).

7:14. *is firm.* On the one hand, *kbd* connotes weight and mass; a *kābēd* heart would be difficult to sway. On the other hand, defective bodily organs are often called *kābēd* (Tigay 1978). The text implies that Pharaoh's heart, the seat of his mental faculties, does not function properly, is "an organ of perception that is no longer receiving outside stimuli" (Wilson 1979: 22). In 4:10, Moses' "heavy" mouth and tongue hinder his speaking the divine word; in 7:14, Pharaoh's "heavy" heart prevents him from heeding it. (*Pace* Ben-Reuben 1984, I do not find a reference to the Egyptian belief in the postmortem weighing of the heart.)

7:15. *Go. hlk* implies an outdoor encounter (see NOTE to 3:18).

in the morning. Moses is again commanded to confront Pharaoh "in the morning" in 8:16; 9:13, and Samuel, too, confronts Saul "in the morning" (1 Sam 15:12). We should probably infer that Yahweh has spoken to his prophet in a night vision (Gressmann 1913: 68), notwithstanding E's denial that Moses hears God in dreams (Num 12:6–8). Yahweh frequently communicates with humans by night (e.g., Genesis 15; 20:6–7; 28:11–15; 31:24; 46:2–4; 1 Sam 3:2–18; 1 Kgs 3:5–14; Job 33:15–16).

going out to the waters. Several times JE depicts Egyptian royalty going to the Nile (Gen 41:17; Exod 2:5; 7:15; 8:16; presumably 9:13), apparently to wash

(2:5) and/or to cool off (Palestinian Targumic Tosephta fragment [Klein 1986: 1.179]). Herodotus, too, comments on the Egyptians' frequent baths (*Histories* 2.37), and Ezekiel envisions Pharaoh as a huge reptile wallowing in the river (Ezek 29:3–5; 32:2–6). In any event, the plot of Exodus requires the presence of the princess and the king by the water. On the trip to the river as a structural device in the Plagues, see REDACTION ANALYSIS.

to meet. So *Tg. Onqelos*, taking *liqra(')t* in its etymological sense (< *qry* 'meet'). But *liqra(')t* also bears a prepositional nuance: "toward."

lip. I.e., "bank."

snake. Now the term is *nāḥāš*, since in JE, the reference is to the Burning Bush (4:3). The composite Torah, however, implies that Moses has borrowed Aaron's rod, which had just become a serpent (*tannîn*) (7:9 [P]) (see REDACTION ANALYSIS; NOTE to 7:17).

7:16. *saying.* Or "to say."

7:17. *you may know that I am Yahweh.* Yahweh responds to Pharaoh's hauteur in 5:2: "Who is Yahweh? . . . I have not known Yahweh."

the rod that is in my hand. Since Aaron works the miracle, in the composite text, the first person must refer to God. In E, however, the rod and hand might belong to either Moses or Yahweh. Since a prophet often speaks in the Deity's persona, since Moses' rod is equally God's (4:20; 17:9) and since Moses is a "deity to Pharaoh" (7:1), no distinction is necessary (cf. Friedman 1995: 40–42). Thus, according to 7:25, *Yahweh* struck the Nile, while 17:5 credits *Moses* (Van Seters 1994: 110). Greenberg (1969: 152 n. 1) pertinently compares Jer 43:10: "I [Yahweh] will take Nebuchadrezzar king of Babylon, my slave, and I [Yahweh] will set his seat above these stones that I [Jeremiah] hid" (MT). See also NOTE to 11:8 below.

7:18. *Egypt.* Here, as often, *miṣrayim* is collective.

unable. So LXX, supported by v 21 (P), where *lō(')-yākəlû* 'were not able' in effect glosses the rare *nil'û*. The root *l'y* connotes debility (cf. Holzinger 1900: 22; Jacob 1992: 257), hence Vg "they became sick from drinking" (also Josephus *Ant.* 2.294).

7:19. *Take.* In the composite text, this is the necessary translation. In the original P, however, the implication may have been "pick up," assuming Aaron's rod was left on the ground in 7:12.

over Egypt's waters. Presumably, Aaron is to wave his staff in all directions (ibn Ezra).

rivers . . . "niles." Hebrew *yə'ōr*, like Egyptian *itrw* 'river' from which it derives (Lambdin 1953: 151), functions grammatically as a common noun (contrast *pərāt* 'Euphrates,' *ḥiddeqel* 'Tigris'). It refers primarily to the Nile River (*hay'ōr, yə'ōr miṣrayim*), but also to a river channel (e.g., Isa 33:21) or an underground shaft (Job 28:10). Dan 12:5–7 even calls the Tigris *hay'ōr* (cf. Dan 10:4). My neologism "niles" tries to capture this ambiguity. "Rivers . . . 'niles'" connotes either the major branches of the Nile delta, of which there were two in antiquity, or else irrigation canals (LXX).

stocks and . . . stones. ʿĒṣ and *'eben* are often parallel, whether as the building materials wood and stone or the landscape elements tree(s) and rock(s), as far back as Ugaritic (*KTU* 1.3.iii.23, iv.14–15; 82.43; see *RSP* 1.387). Here, although LXX, Vg and *Tg.* Onqelos interpret "in wood and in stone *vessels*," more likely we have synecdoche connoting wood and in stone *buildings* (cf. 35:33; Lev 14:45; 1 Kgs 5:32; 15:22; 2 Kgs 12:13; 22:6; Ezek 26:12; Hab 2:11; Zech 5:4; Eccl 10:9; 1 Chr 22:14–15; 2 Chr 2:13; 16:6; 34:11) (Houtman 1986).

7:20. *he raised.* In the redacted Torah, the subject is clearly Aaron (cf. v 19) (Greenberg 1969: 152). In E, however, it might be Moses or Yahweh (Durham 1987: 93–94); cf. NOTE to v 17.

with the rod. The language is elliptical: "he raised (his arm) with the rod."

7:21. *the blood was in all the land of Egypt.* This fulfills the prediction of 7:19 (see TEXTUAL NOTE to 7:19). "*The* blood" is tantamount to "*the aforesaid* blood."

For Israelite readers, the image of a land bleeding from its main artery would be particularly disturbing (Zevit 1975–76: 201 n. 31). Like frogs, murrain, šəḥîn and the death of the firstborn, the plague of blood ritually defiles Egypt.

7:22. *likewise.* Various commentators engage the question of how the magicians could duplicate Aaron's feat if there was no water. Jacob (1992: 208) observes that the magicians might work their wonder *before* Aaron works his, while Bekhor Shor and Dillmann (1880: 73) suppose that the waters return to their natural state immediately after the demonstration. Augustine suggests that, assuming the Hebrews' supply remains unaffected, the magicians might take from Israel's dwellings. In the redacted Torah, at least, the real answer appears in 7:24: the Egyptians can obtain water by digging. On hyperbole in the Plagues narrative, see COMMENT.

mysteries. *Lāṭ is also spelled lā(')ṭ and *lahaṭ; see NOTE to 7:11.

7:23. *set his heart.* I.e., took to heart, paid heed.

7:25. *seven days . . . Nile.* LXX and both Rabbinic and Samaritan scribal traditions place a break after 7:25. More likely, however, v 25 should be regarded as the preface to v 26. We could even translate, "*when* seven days had been filled . . ." (cf. NJV).

Why are we told that a week passes? One possibility is that conditions of serious defilement, such as blood contamination, last for seven days (or multiples thereof) (Leviticus 12; 15:19, 28; Num 19:11–19 [P]; Ezek 44:26). E, too, hints at seven-day defilement for social shame and for the skin disease ṣāraʿat (Num 12:14–15; cf. Lev 13:5–6; 14:9 [P]). Another possibility, assuming that the Nile is eventually healed, is that seven days pass after Yahweh *finishes* smiting the Nile (Jacob 1992: 259).

7:26. *Come.* Bw' implies that the meeting will be indoors (see NOTE to 3:18).

7:27. *if you refuse.* The form mā'ēn is slightly anomalous. Holzinger (1900: 23) suggests that wə'im-mā'ēn is a scribal corruption of *wə'im-məmā'ēn. This cannot be so, however, for we find precisely the same expression in 9:2; 10:4;

Jer 38:21. In fact, the expected Pi'el participle *məmā'ēn is unattested; perhaps it was reduced to mā'ēn in speech.

frogs. In this passage, *ṣəpardēa'* is both masculine (7:29; 8:9, 10) and feminine (8:2, 5, 7). A degree of randomness is expected in matters of gender (Levi 1987).

7:28. *breed.* The root *šrṣ* combines the notions of abundant breeding and creeping; a common rendering is "swarm" (RSV, NJV). In the composite text, there is a humorous association with the Hebrews' teeming, denoted by the same verb (1:7 [P]) (Fox 1986: 47). In fact, *'ālâ* 'ascend' is likewise used of both Israel (1:10) and the frogs (7:28, 29; 8:1, 2, 3). There may also be a paronomastic association between *šrṣ* and *šqṣ* 'unclean animal' (cf. Lev 11:20, 23), as this plague, like its predecessor, brings ritual defilement upon Egypt (see following).

ovens. The reference to ovens and dough pans is probably meant to disgust readers for whom frogs were unclean to eat (Leviticus 11: Deuteronomy 14). Certainly, piles of rotting frog carcasses (8:10) would be highly defiling (cf. Lev 11:29–38).

dough pans. Both here and in 12:34 (see NOTE), LXX renders *miš'ārōt* as *phyramata* "lumps of dough." But in light of the parallelism with *ṭene'* 'container, basket' in Deut 28:5, 17, the more likely translation is "dough pans." Probably, we should read **miś'eret* with a *śin* throughout MT; cf. *maśrēt* 'dough pan,' *śə'ōr* 'leaven' (KB). The pointing *miš'eret* with a *šin* may have arisen through an association with *š'r* 'to be left over' (cf. LXX Deut 28:5, 17, *enkataleimma* 'remnant'; Tg. Onqelos Exod 12:34 *mwtr 'ṣwthwn* 'the remainder of their dough [pans]'); see also TEXTUAL NOTE to 12:34.

7:29. *upon you.* That is, the frogs will climb onto humans and perhaps get stuck in their garments (Luzzatto).

ascend. Cassuto (1967: 101) translates more graphically as "climb." Elsewhere in this section, I have rendered the same root *'ly*, when used in the causative, as "raise."

8:2. *the frog ascended.* Hebrew often uses a collective when referring to animals; cf. "the louse," "the locust."

8:3. *they raised.* In the composite text, the subjects are the magicians, while in E, they are either Moses and Aaron or perhaps, if we read with Sam, the frogs; see TEXTUAL NOTE, SOURCE ANALYSIS and REDACTION ANALYSIS.

8:4. *Pray to Yahweh.* An alternative translation would be "appease Yahweh." This is the first time Pharaoh acknowledges the power and name of Israel's god. He is beginning to "know" Yahweh (contrast 5:2) (Calvin on 8:8).

remove. The ultimate display of power is the *reversal* of a miracle; cf. 4:2–7; Judg 6:36–40. For a general treatment with comparative material, see Bertman (1964).

I will release. That is, Pharaoh will grant a temporary leave. He does not say he will release the people *from Egypt* (cf. 8:21) (Jacob 1992: 22).

8:5. *Assume honor.* An alternative rendering would be "take control." With mock humility, Moses puts himself at Pharaoh's service. He allows the king to participate in the miracle, assuring him that God will do Pharaoh's bidding (cf. 8:27, where Yahweh does Moses' bidding). Compare also Isa 7:10–13, where Yahweh allows King Ahaz to request a sign.

for when. Rashi distinguishes between *ləmātay* and *mātay*. *Mātay 'a'tîr* would mean "When should I pray?" while *ləmātay 'a'tîr* means "For when should I pray?" The answer, then, is "for tomorrow." Moses is to pray at once that the frogs disappear the next day (see below).

your houses. The plural *bātte(y)kā* (MT) may imply that Pharaoh lives in more than one residence. On the other hand, in Ugaritic poetry, the plurals of architectural terms, particularly *bt* 'house,' may connote single, complex edifices (Gordon 1965: 54, §8:7).

remain. An alternative translation of *tiššā'arnâ* would be "survive."

8:6. *For tomorrow.* This means either that the frogs should be gone "by tomorrow" or that they should disappear all at once on the following day. In either case, why the delay? Gunn (1982: 91 n. 6) writes, "To have said 'today' would have been to ask the impossible; 'tomorrow' is both a concession . . . and a demand." In other words, Pharaoh's lack of faith unnecessarily prolongs his suffering. D. Kirsch (privately), however, more plausibly cites Pharaonic bravado: so as not to appear desperate, he casually answers, "Oh, tomorrow would be fine."

Both these interpretations, in any case, apply to the artificial world of the narrative. The "real" reason for the delay is the Elohist's consistent effort to impede the flow of time. Nothing is instantaneous (cf. 8:19, 25; 9:5, 18; 10:4; see SOURCE ANALYSIS).

8:8. *went out.* See NOTE to 5:22.

matter. So *Tg. Onqelos.* One could also translate *dābār* as "word," referring to Pharaoh's answer, "for tomorrow"; cf. LXX "limitation (*horismos*) [of the frogs]."

he put upon Pharaoh. It is unclear whether the antecedent of *'ăšer* is *dābār* 'matter' (Dillmann 1880: 77) or *haṣpardə'îm* 'the frogs.'

8:10. *reeked.* Bekhor Shor notes that, between this plague and the last (7:21), all Egypt, land and river, must have stunk.

8:12. *dirt.* Like stars and sand, dirt (*'āpār*) often serves in the Bible as a metaphor for the innumerable (Gen 13:16; 28:14; Num 23:10; Isa 40:12; Zeph 1:17; Zech 9:3; Ps 78:27; Job 27:16; 2 Chr 1:9) (Noth 1962: 77–78). Gressmann (1913: 91) detects sympathetic magic, since a swarm of tiny insects resembles a dust cloud.

lice. This is the rendering of *kinnîm* in Syr and Tgs. (*qalmā'* 'louse'); Leslau (1958: 26–27) proffers several Ethiopic cognates in support. Driver (1911: 65), however, suggests "mosquitoes," on the basis of LXX *sknips.* And Jacob (1992: 264) identifies *kinnîm* as sand fleas, noting that they come from the dirt (cf. Bekhor Shor). In any case, *kinnîm* are biting insects.

The word *knm* is anomalous in form. To judge from MT, the plural is *kinnîm*, while the singular is *kinnām*, rather than the expected **kēn* (*kēn* conceivably means "louse" in Isa 51:6). Since the nominal suffix *-ām* is unusual (see GKC §85t, 87h), Dillmann (1880: 77) supposes that *kinnām* is the creation of the Massoretes, who were misled by the singular *wattəhî* 'became' (vv. 13, 14).

But Rabbinic Hebrew *kənimmâ* 'moth/caterpillar,' too, may reflect a root *knm*, in which case *kinnîm* might derive (irregularly, to be sure) from **kinmîm* < **kinnəmîm*. (Moths and caterpillars are admittedly not lice, but species names tend to be fluid in ancient languages.)

8:14. *did likewise.* Not that they produced lice, which they could not, but that they tried, perhaps striking the ground with their rods (Ramban). Bekhor Shor, however, supposes the magicians tried to *eliminate* the insects (*ləhôṣî'* 'bring, send forth') (also Jacob 1992: 264–65). This interpretation enhances the connection with the final clause of v 14 and makes the magicians' behavior more rational. But it does not explain in what sense they "did likewise."

8:15. *divine finger.* I.e., a supernatural agency; on this use of *'ĕlōhîm*, cf. 9:28; Ezek 1:1; 8:3; 40:2; Job 1:16. Other possible renderings of *'eṣba' 'ĕlōhîm* are "a deity's finger" or "Deity's finger." The image is related to the ubiquitous hand/arm metaphor for supernatural calamity and disease (see Roberts 1971). In the composite text, there is also an allusion to Aaron's rod, equated in 7:4, 5, 17 with Yahweh's hand (Fretheim 1991a: 118).

8:17. *I am going to send.* Cassuto (1967: 107) observes that the rare form *mašlîaḥ* puns with *məšallēaḥ* 'release.'

'ārōb. This obscure term seemingly derives from *'rb* 'mix.' Already in *Exod. Rab.* 11:3, we find two competing interpretations: (a) assorted beasts of prey, an image paralleled in Lev 26:22 (with *hišlîaḥ* 'send') (also *Tg. Ps.-Jonathan*); (b) biting insects (LXX). (A third proposal, "crows" [Samariticon], inspired by *'ōrēb* 'raven,' does not suit the context.)

The Bible itself supports understanding (b). First, Ps 78:45 recalls: "he released against them *'ārōb*, and it ate them." Since there is no indication in Exodus that the *'ārōb* are deadly, it follows that they can devour without killing, i.e., are biting insects. Second, P replaces *'ārōb* with *kinnîm* 'lice,' apparently synonymous; cf. Ps 105:31, "*'ārōb* came, *kinnîm* in all their territory." Cassuto (1967: 107) further observes that entering houses is easy for insects, but not for beasts of prey (8:17, 20). As for etymology, Jacob (1992: 267) tentatively compares Talmudic Aramaic *'irbûbîtā'*, an affliction of the head, body or clothing caused by uncleanliness. This might refer to lice (although Jacob thinks not).

as well as the land. LXX paraphrases, "and in the land," i.e., in Egypt proper, as opposed to Goshen (Wevers 1990: 117). This interpretation is confirmed by the parallelism of vv 17 and 18; see also NOTE to 8:20.

8:18. *Goshen.* See APPENDIX B, vol. II.

stands. Syr renders, "dwell," but the nuance of *'ōmēd* is more "stand firm."

I am Yahweh. The phrase can also be translated, "I, Yahweh, am in the land's midst."

land. This probably refers not just to Goshen but to all Egypt.

8:19. *redemption.* Rashbam, like other Jewish commentators, understands *pədūt* as combining the notions of distinction and salvation (see Macintosh 1971: 549–50). The *Tgs.* try to convey this via paraphrase: "I will put a redemption for my people, but upon your people I will bring an affliction." I think this is basically correct: it is Yahweh's *redeeming* Israel from the affliction that *dis-*

tinguishes them from Egypt. We may compare the paschal blood, which both redeems and separates (see COMMENT to 12:1–13:16).

LXX, however, followed by Syr and Vg, renders, "division" (*diastolē*). Some infer that the translators were reading an otherwise unattested noun **pəlūt* (< *pl'/y* 'divide'), the confusion of **pəlūt* and *pədūt* presumably being aural (cf. Dillmann 1880: 80). It is highly unlikely, however, that LXX is reading any such word. The translator does not even know this meaning of *pl'/y*, but only the more common "to be miraculous, glorious" (cf. LXX 8:18; 9:4; 11:7; 33:16). The sole passages in the entire Greek Bible to betray an awareness of *pl'/y* 'separate' are (wrongly) Judg 13:19 (LXX[B]) and Isa 29:14; Jer 32:27 (OG 39:27). In Exod 8:19, then, LXX "division" is probably a guess to fit the context. If the translator had had **pəlût* before him, he would probably have translated it "miracle." Davies (1974), however, suggests that the original reading behind LXX is **pāredet* 'separation,' also otherwise unattested (by this theory, the similar-looking *r* and *d* coalesced in MT). And Macintosh (1971) approaches the problem via comparative philology: on the basis of Arabic *fdd* 'be separate' (which should, however, correspond to Hebrew *pzz*), he conjectures that MT *pdt* may indeed mean "separation." I find the Targumic interpretation far superior.

tomorrow. Asking why Yahweh announces he will wait a day before acting (cf. 8:6; 9:5), Rashbam plausibly explains, "Lest you say it is a coincidence." Part of a prophet's miraculous power is the ability not just to cause but accurately to predict supernatural events (Deut 13:1–12). On another level, the narrator lets time pass in order to generate suspense, as elsewhere in the Plagues cycle (see NOTE to 8:5; SOURCE ANALYSIS). D. Kirsch (privately) observes that the delay also affords Pharaoh an opportunity to relent.

8:20. *the land of Egypt the land.* The first *'ereṣ* connotes "land, country," while the second refers to the ground, tantamount to *'ădāmâ* in v 17.

8:21. *your deity.* Jacob (1992: 225) detects condescension in Pharaoh's choice of words, as if to say, "the minor deity of . . . poor slaves."

in the land. Abarbanel observes that Pharaoh may be quite clever here, exploiting Moses' statement "that you may know that I am Yahweh in the land's midst" (8:18). If Yahweh is in the land, why leave it? Whether or not this was the author's intent, it is notable that both Pharaoh and, implicitly, Moses agree that Yahweh may be worshiped anywhere. His presence is not confined to the wilderness.

8:22. *It is possible to do so.* Cassuto (1967: 109) detects punning irony in *lō(') nākôn la'ăśôt kēn.* Since *nākôn* 'possible' and *kēn* 'so' both derive from *kwn* 'stand firm, exist,' in effect Moses is saying "it is not *kwn* to do *kwn*."

abomination. As far as we know, nothing in Israelite sacrificial practice would have horrified a second-millennium Egyptian. Greenberg (1969: 203) emphasizes that the New Kingdom was most hospitable to Asiatic cults (see Helck 1971: 446–73). So how do we explain Moses' claim? On the one hand, the author could be projecting Israelite intolerance onto the Egyptians; Greenberg (p. 202) observes that stoning sounds more Israelite than Egyptian. Or Moses may simply be lying to Pharaoh; cf. the midwives' prevarication about the vitality of Hebrew women (1:19), or Moses' misleading request for a short furlough (3:18; 5:3; 8:23).

But Egyptian fastidiousness had probably increased by the first millennium, the time of the Elohist. In the fifth century, Herodotus (*Histories* 2.18, 41) reports that the Egyptians would not eat or sacrifice cows, and therefore shunned contact with Greeks and their cooking utensils (cf. Gen 43:32). Like the Greeks, the Israelites sometimes offered cows to Yahweh (Lev 3:1; 1 Sam 6:14; cf. Gen 15:9). Herodotus goes on to describe certain Egyptian cults that never sacrificed goats or sheep (2.42, 46), also staples of Israelite worship (cf., too, the Egyptians' supposed abhorrence of shepherds [Gen 46:34]). He also reports that only specially marked bulls might be offered (2.38, 45), a distinction presumably neglected by Israelites.

This phase of Egyptian culture was long-lasting. In the first century B.C.E., Diodorus Siculus (*Bibliotheca Historica* 1.83.6–9) notes that it was a capital offense to slaughter a sacred animal, and claims to have witnessed the lynching of a cat-killer. In the second century C.E., Plutarch records taboos like those known to Herodotus (*Isis and Osiris* 4–8); in the third century C.E., Porphyry adds that the Egyptians did not eat doves (*De abstinentia* 4.7), also sometimes sacrificed by Israelites (Lev 1:14; 5:7, 11, etc.).

Overall, Herodotus et al. describe the Egyptians as fanatical in matters of ritual and physical cleanliness—which may explain the frequent baths of royalty in Exodus. Even if, as many believe, Herodotus's knowledge of Egypt was secondhand and often wrong (Oertel 1970; Armayor 1978), it is still significant that Greeks and Israelites viewed Egypt similarly. As for the violent reaction Moses expects from the Egyptians, we should note that in the Persian period, Egyptian priests in fact destroyed a Jewish temple in Elephantine (*ANET* 492; Porten 1968: 284–89), although their provocation may only be guessed (see NOTE to 12:12).

The idea that Hebrew ritual was intrinsically abhorrent to Egyptians is taken up by later, anti-Jewish gentile writers. Tacitus (*Histories* 5.4–5) alleges that Moses ordained animal sacrifice purposely to scandalize the Egyptians. Earlier, Manetho indicts the Hebrews not just of sacrificing some sacred animals but of wantonly butchering all (Josephus *Ap.* 1.239, 249). (For archaeological evidence of Egyptian purity requirements in the Greco-Roman era, see Sauneron 1962: 340–50.)

will they not. This is probably the correct understanding, although Nötscher (1953: 375) suggests *l'* is an emphatic particle.

8:23. *he may say*. Moses explains in 10:26 that the Israelites will learn how to serve Yahweh only once they reach the wilderness. Thus 8:23 and 10:26 dimly foreshadow the Lawgiving at Sinai/Horeb.

8:24. *Only far, do not go far*. Is the intent "Go, but no more than a three days' way" or "Go, but not so far as a three days' way" (Gressmann 1913: 72)? Note the assonance: *raq harḥēq lō(')-tarḥîqû*.

8:25. *going out*. On Moses' comings and goings between Yahweh and Pharaoh, see NOTE to 5:22.

Only. Moses responds to Pharaoh's qualifying *raq* (v 24) with a condition of his own.

8:27. *removed. Wayyāsar* might be either Hiph'il or Qal. If Qal (as in 8:25), 8:27 would mean "the *ʿārōb* left Pharaoh. . . ." But all ancient translations parse the verb as a Hiph'il, hence my "removed."

9:3. *see . . . is about to be.* Ogden (1967) argues that the rare participle *hôyâ* has been, in effect, "manufactured" to match the participles in 7:17, 27; 9:14; 10:4 (cf. also 4:23). It ostensibly means "about to be." But we might alternatively interpret *hôyâ* on the basis of Arabic *hwy* 'fall' (cf. Hebrew *hawwâ, hōwâ* 'destruction') (Cassuto 1967: 111), perhaps emending **hōwâ* or **hōwiyyâ* (Knobel *apud* Dillmann 1880: 82). If so, 9:3 may mean "Yahweh's arm is about to fall" (cf., in a different sense, Ezek 8:1 [MT]). By any interpretation, there is assonance between *hwyh* and the divine name *yhwh* (Cassuto 1967: 111).

camels. This is an anachronistic projection of Asian custom upon Egypt. In Palestine and environs, domestic camels have been common since the Iron Age (Firmage 1992: 1139). But, despite possible earlier experiments (Ripinsky 1983), domesticated camels were scarce in Egypt before the Greek period (Driver 1911: 70; Hyatt 1971: 114; Midant-Reynes 1977). No Egyptian term for the beast is even known; it has no hieroglyph.

plague. The episode of murrain, like blood, frogs, *šəḥîn* and the death of the firstborn, brings ritual impurity upon Egypt—this time by the abundance of animal carcasses (cf. Lev 11:39–40, etc.).

9:4. *no thing.* A creature is not usually described as *dābār* 'thing, item'; we would rather expect *'eḥād* 'one' (cf. 8:27; 9:6; 10:19). Perhaps *dābār* in 9:4–5 was chosen to pun with *deber* 'plague' (Cassuto 1967: 111).

9:5. *Yahweh set.* God names a time to impress Pharaoh (Rashbam).

9:6. *all Egypt's cattle.* This seems a clear case of hyperbole, as the livestock reappear in 9:19; 10:25; 11:5; 12:12, 29; chap. 14 (horses) (see COMMENT). Ibn Ezra explains that "all" really means "most," observing that, according to 9:22, 25, "all the field's herbage" was smitten, whereas 9:31; 10:5 explain that some vegetation was left. Dillmann (1880: 83) proffers a further elucidation, much in the rabbinical spirit. It is not the case that all the cattle died; rather, we are to interpret v 6 by v 3, "your cattle *that are in the field.*" That is, sheltered cattle survived, as in the plague of hail (9:19–21).

9:8. *ash.* This is the second P plague to be caused by particles; recall that the lice came from dirt (8:12–13). Why ash? For one thing, it easily wafts through the air (an intimation of the germ theory?). Moreover, assuming the principle of sympathetic magic, the result should be a burning, flaking, gray-white condition—i.e., *šəḥîn* (but see NOTES to 9:9). A good parallel is Akkadian *saḥar-šubbû,* connoting both ash and psoriasis and related to the generic skin disease *epqu* (Adamson 1988: 169–70); compare, too, Greek *anthrax* 'coal, blister.'

let Moses. Both Moses and Aaron are told to collect the ash, but only Moses is to work the wonder. This violates P's pattern; we would expect Moses to command *Aaron* to cast the ashes (Durham 1987: 120; see SOURCE ANALYSIS). Perhaps the Priestly Writer found it unfitting that the priest-to-be Aaron should cause a defiling skin disease (cf. Leviticus 13–14; Num 12:12, 14–15; 2 Chr 26:20–21) which if contracted would indeed disqualify a priest from service (Lev 21:20–21). Again, when Aaron and Miriam later rebel against Moses, only Miriam is smitten with the skin disease ṣāraʿat (Numbers 12 [E]). (That priest and leper are polar opposites is suggested by the similarity between rituals for consecrating the former [Exodus 29; Leviticus 8] and cleansing the latter [Leviticus 14].) But if the author does not wish to associate Aaron with disease, why involve him at all? Presumably to obtain four fistfuls, which may represent the four compass points.

to Pharaoh's eyes. In Pharaoh's presence, but out of doors.

9:9. *Šəḥîn.* The root *šḥn* refers to heat in Rabbinic Hebrew, with cognates in Arabic, Aramaic, Ugaritic (*KTU* 1.12.ii.38) and Akkadian (Elman 1976; Milgrom 1991: 787). *Šəḥîn* is probably named for the sensation of burning itch, here appropriately caused by ashes. Bekhor Shor and Abarbanel even infer that the ashes are still hot—but then how can Moses and Aaron hold them? A related condition, *ṣārebet* (Lev 13:23), similarly derives from *ṣrb* 'scorch' (for further parallels, see Waldman 1974: 43–45).

The inexactitude of biblical medical terminology makes precise definition of *šəḥîn* difficult (cf. NOTE to 4:6). Lev 13:18–23 describes *šəḥîn* as a possible precursor to *ṣāraʿat.* Deut 28:27 refers to "Egypt's *šəḥîn*"—evidently the affliction was particularly associated with that country—in association with *ḥeres* 'itch,' *ʿŏpālîm* 'buboes, tumors (?)' and *gārāb* 'scab' (cf. Akkadian *garabu*, associated with *epqu* and *saḥaršubbû* [see NOTE to 9:8]). According to Deut 28:35; Job 2:7, *šəḥîn* affects the entire body, but especially the thighs and knees. The lower limbs may be a euphemism for genitalia (Jacob 1992: 217), but more likely *šəḥîn* is the ulceration of the lower body that the British in Egypt called "Nile sores" (Doughty 1936: 2.511; also Dillmann 1880: 84).

From the foregoing, one gets the impression that *šəḥîn* is a mere inconvenience. According to 2 Kgs 20:1–7; Isa 38:1–21, however, it is symptomatic of a fatal condition; Cassuto (1967: 113) identifies *šəḥîn* with smallpox. (Thucydides similarly describes a plague originating from Egypt characterized by feverish heat and external blistering, among other symptoms [*Peloponnesian War* 2.48]. And Pliny calls elephantiasis, a combination of skin eruptions and swelling of the lower parts, the particular disease of Egypt [*Natural History* 26.5].)

Whatever its precise nature, we may say that *šəḥîn*, as a skin disease, brings ritual defilement upon Egypt, no less than blood, frogs, murrain and the death of the firstborn (cf. Leviticus 13–14; Numbers 12; 2 Kgs 7:3–10; 2 Chr 26:20–21).

blossoming. "Blossoming" is a technical term for the spread of skin eruptions (Leviticus 13 *passim*; 14:43).

boils. "Boils" (*ʾăbaʿbūʿōt*) do not seem consistent with the scaly, ashlike skin of psoriasis (cf. above), which the OED describes as "characterized by the appearance of dry reddish patches covered with glistening imbricated scales." Perhaps these are *ʾăbaʿbūʿōt*. But *šəḥîn* may well be something more serious than psoriasis (see above), and "boils" remains the most likely interpretation of *ʾăbaʿbūʿōt*, since the root *bwʿ* connotes bulging and bubbling.

9:11. *the ḥarṭummîm.* The author neglects to say whether Pharaoh, too, is afflicted.

could not stand. As often, *ʿmd* bears the connotation "resist." Whether they are simply bedridden or quarantined as lepers, the *ḥarṭummîm* are eliminated from the contest (Zevit 1975–76: 207; cf. Num 12:10–15; 2 Kgs 7:3–10; 2 Chr 26:19–21).

9:13. *station yourself.* The implication is that Moses should stand outside the palace, where Pharaoh will encounter him. Presumably, the king will be on his way to the Nile, as in 7:5; 8:16.

9:14. *in all the world.* Throughout vv 14–16, *hāʾāreṣ* is ambiguous, perhaps deliberately. The meaning might be "in all the land [of Egypt]," or "in all the world" (cf. Cassuto 1967: 115). On Yahweh's incomparability and international reputation, see NOTES to 15:11, 14.

9:15. *For now . . . the plague.* "Had I wished, when my hand was against your cattle and I struck them with disease, I could have sent it forth and stricken you and your people, together with the cattle" (Rashi) (on the syntax, see GKC §106p; compare 1 Sam 13:13; 14:30). There is an alternative rendering, however. It is true that, for E, humans are not yet directly afflicted; the reference is solely to murrain. But in the composite Torah, one might interpret *deber* 'plague' as alluding to the preceding episode of *šǝḥîn* (P). If so, all of v 15 might be translated in the past tense: "For just now, I sent forth my arm and smote you and your people with the plague, so that you were vanishing from the land." But the first interpretation is the more likely.

from the land. Or "from the earth."

9:16. *to tell my name.* The idiom to "tell (Yahweh's) name" is paralleled in Ps 22:23; 102:22. *Šēm* 'name' often has the nuance of "fame" and here connotes both God's greatness and his mighty deeds (cf. 10:2), as well as the fact that, at least in P and perhaps in E, he has recently adopted a new name (see COMMENT to Exodus 3–4). The sense is probably not that Yahweh will proclaim his own name, but that it will be proclaimed by others (LXX, Syr, Tg. Onqelos).

world. Here *hāʾāreṣ* probably means the "world," rather than the "land [of Egypt]" (Saadiah). According to Josh 2:10, news of Yahweh's defeat of Egypt reaches as far as Canaan (see also NOTE to 15:14). *Hāʾāreṣ* in the sense of "land [of Egypt]" (Jacob 1992: 156), while possible, would be anticlimactic.

9:17. *exalt yourself.* Tg. Ps.-Jonathan correctly derives *mistôlēl* 'build yourself up, exalt yourself' from *sll* 'lift up.' LXX, Syr and Tg. Onqelos, however, have "detain," presumably a guess to fit the context and inspired by *sal* 'basket, container' and/or *sll* 'pile stones' (cf. "stonewall"). Rashi's translation "tread on" compounds the error by taking Tg. Onqelos *kǝbēšat* 'detain' as "trample," because of the association of *sll* with roads (cf. *Exod. Rab.* 12:1).

9:18. *from the day, her founding.* MT *lǝmin-hayyôm hiwwāsǝdâ* is grammatically difficult. Most likely, *hiwwāsǝdâ* is an inflected Niphʿal infinitive construct (*pace* Cassuto 1967: 117)—but then we must restore a *mappîq* to the suffixal he' (**hiwwāsǝdāh*). We must also explain the definite article in *hayyôm*, since, with sporadic exceptions (GKC §127f–g), Hebrew does not tolerate defined nouns in construct. Apparently, "the day" is in apposition to "her founding" (cf. GKC §127h), hence my translation (compare ibn Ezra on Gen 6:17). Alternatively, we may adopt Sam's *lectio facilior: lmywm hysdh* [*sic*] 'from the day *of* her founding.' A final, more drastic expedient would be to vocalize *hwsdh* as a Hoph'al perfect **hûsədâ* and translate the clause, "from the day she was founded."

Whatever the correct reading, Couroyer (1960) suggests that 9:18 preserves a borrowed Egyptian concept, since Egyptian texts also speak of Egypt's founding (*grg*).

9:19. *the field.* *Śāde(h)* connotes both a cultivated plot and the outdoors in general. Here, the latter is intended (Saadiah).

9:23. *rod.* In this episode, Moses' rod most closely resembles its mythic forebears, controlling meteorological phenomena (see COMMENT to Exodus 3–4, p. 228). Compare especially Ugaritic Ba'lu's *'ṣ brq* 'lightning tree/shaft' (*KTU* 1.101.4; for representations, see *ANEP* 168 no. 490, 170 no. 500).

Yahweh, he gave. Niccacci (1990: 63) directs due attention to the inverted word order: *wəyahwe(h) nātan* vs. **wayyittēn yahwe(h).* But his inference that the acts of Moses and Yahweh are simultaneous is incorrect. On the contrary: first Moses gestures, then God responds. More likely, the inversion emphasizes the Deity's agency.

voices. Or "sounds" (*qōlōt*). This is the idiom for "thunder" in Hebrew (see NOTE on 9:28) and Ugaritic (*KTU* 1.4.v.70, vii.29, 31).

went. *Tihălak* is a rare example of *hlk* conjugated in the imperfect as a strong verb (GKC §69x).

rained. To judge from 9:33–34, Yahweh sends down not just hail but also rain (see NOTE to 9:33).

9:24. *fire caught up.* *Mitlaqqaḥat* could be rendered either reflexively, "taking hold of itself," or passively, "caught up." Cassuto (1967: 119) sees a reference to lightning "taking hold of itself" by following a jagged trajectory. But the same expression occurs in Ezek 1:4: "a storm wind coming from the North, a great cloud, and fire *mitlaqqaḥat*, with radiance around it, and from its midst like the appearance of electrum from within the fire." Although we cannot be certain, this sounds more like a radiant cloud than a cumulonimbus shedding thunderbolts. In what sense, then, is "fire caught up within the hail"? Does each ball contain both fire and ice (ibn Ezra)? Or is the "hail" not frozen at all, but completely ablaze (cf. Gen 19:24; Ezek 38:22; Ps 11:6; 18:13–14; Job 18:15)? Is the image after all that of lightning falling through a hailstorm? We cannot tell, although to me the second interpretation appears the most probable (see COMMENT).

9:27. *this time.* Either Pharaoh is too proud to admit he has been wrong all along, or only now does he realize the truth (Luzzatto).

The justified . . . the guilty. The language (*ṣaddîq . . . rəšā'îm*) implies legal innocence and guilt.

I and my people. Perhaps Pharaoh is trying to spread the blame (Luzzatto).

9:28. *divine voices.* I.e., noises (*qōlōt*) of supernatural origin (cf. *'ĕlōhîm* in 8:15; Ezek 1:1; 8:3; 40:2; Job 1:16). The reference is to thunder, which the Bible, taking up an ancient trope, calls Yahweh's "voice" (2 Sam 22:14; Isa 30:30, 31; Jer 10:13; Joel 2:11; 4:16; Amos 1:2, etc.).

9:29. *As my leaving the city.* Cassuto (1967: 121) infers that Moses requires solitude for communion with God (see also NOTE to 5:22).

spread out my hands. A posture of prayer (1 Kgs 8:22; Isa 1:15; Ezra 9:5).

the earth is Yahweh's. Some interpret *hā'āreṣ* as "the land [of Egypt]" rather than "the earth" (e.g., Wevers 1990: 140). But I think that here, as in 9:14, Moses is claiming universal authority for Yahweh. Compare Ps 24:1: "'The earth (*hā'āreṣ*) is Yahweh's and its contents; the world and those that dwell in it."

9:30. *your slaves . . . do not yet fear.* A minor inconsistency. According to 9:20, some Egyptians have begun to fear Yahweh's word; see NOTE to 10:7.

9:31. *flax . . . barley.* Note the chiasm: "flax . . . barley . . . barley . . . flax" (but see TEXTUAL NOTE).

were smitten. As vocalized by MT, *nukkātâ* and *nukkû* (v 32) exemplify the rare Nuph'al conjugation, the internal passive of the Niph'al better attested in postbiblical Hebrew (Moreshet 1980; Qimron 1988). Most Nuph'als are of I-*n* roots. If the Nuph'al is anachronistic for the Bible, we have the option of re-vocalizing **nikkātâ* and **nikkû*, ordinary Niph'als.

barley was young ears and the flax was buds. The author explains why some vegetation survives and also establishes a chronological framework. But here there is a possibility of confusion. The Hebrews leave Egypt in the month of *'ābîb* 'young ear(s) of barley,' roughly March–April (13:4). Yet the plague of hail falls in the season of *'ābîb*—weeks, at least, before the Exodus.

The Elohist has not lost track of the calendar. He is thinking in terms of the Egyptian agricultural year, where crops ripen earlier than in Canaan. Egyptian flax blooms and barley is harvested in February or early March (McNeile 1908: 56), while Palestine begins to reap its barley in April, the month of *'ābîb* (Borowski 1987: 37). Similarly, the locusts destroy Egypt's wheat crop shortly before the harvest in March–April (10:5) (Greenberg 1969: 161), roughly the time of the Exodus and the season in which locusts are common (Borowski p. 154). Canaan's wheat is reaped in May (Borowski p. 37).

The Elohist's expertise in these affairs is less surprising than it might seem. One assumes that, from time immemorial, in lean years Asiatics purchased Egyptian grain (cf. Gen 12:10; 41–47). During the Late Bronze Age, Egypt supplied Canaan and Anatolia with food (Helck 1971: 371; Halpern 1983: 66 n. 5).

9:32. *emmer.* Kussemet is a species of wheat, often translated "spelt" but more likely to be emmer (Borowski 1987: 91). It frequently parallels *ḥittâ* 'wheat' (9:32; Isa 28:25; Ezek 4:9; KTU 1.16.iii.9–10; 4.269.30, 32; 345.4–5; 400.7, 9, 12, 13, 16, 17).

dark. LXX, Syr and Tg. Ps.-Jonathan paraphrase *'ăpîlōt* as "late," while ibn Ezra explains that "dark" means underground (*pace* Rashi). This sounds forced, but no one has discovered a better explanation.

9:33. *left the city.* This is one of only two instances of *yṣ* 'go out' plus direct object; ordinarily, one leaves "from (*min*)" a place. Curiously, both here and in Gen 44:4, the object is "the city." Because of the unusual usage, *Tg. Ps.-Jonathan* and *Exod. Rab.* 12:7 appear to read *'ēt* II 'with, nearby, at,' instead of the direct object marker *'ēt* I.

rain. Not, as Cassuto (1967: 122) observes, *hammāṭār 'the rain,' since it is here mentioned explicitly for the first time. But see TEXTUAL NOTE.

Upon first reading, one might think the "rain" is in fact hail, which Yahweh "rained" down (9:23). But v 34 proves that we have a mixture of water and ice (cf. Ezek 38:22).

9:34. *he made firm his heart.* If MT is correct (see TEXTUAL NOTE), it is critical to observe that Pharaoh's hardening of his heart (9:34) and Yahweh's making Pharaoh's heart hard (10:1) are the same process (see COMMENT).

9:35. *through Moses' hand.* Here *yād* 'hand' connotes agency. Perhaps the image was originally that of a messenger bearing written orders.

10:1. *his slaves'.* Here is a minor incongruency. From 9:20; 10:7, we infer that not all the servants' hearts have been "strengthened."

in his core. MT *bəqirbô* presumably refers to the location of Pharaoh's heart (cf Jer 31:33; Ps 39:4; 55:5; 109:22; Prov 14:33; Lam 1:20). Dillmann (1880: 90) and Driver (1911: 88), however, take *bəqirbô* as "in its [Egypt's] midst" (cf. LXX; Syr; *Tgs.*; see TEXTUAL NOTE).

10:2. *how.* Unusually, the reflexive Hithpaʿel conjugation takes a direct object (*'ăšer* 'that which'), indicating an "action . . . performed with regard to or for oneself" (GKC §54f).

I lorded it. The nuance of *hitʿallēl* is to act with capricious power; cf. Childs's (1974: 126) "I toyed."

that you may know. By abruptly switching to the second person plural, the Elohist implicitly addresses later readers.

10:3. *do you refuse.* We would expect the imperfect **təmā'ēn* 'will you refuse,' instead of the perfect *mē'antā*. The full implication may be "how long have you refused and will you continue to refuse?" (GKC §106h).

to humble yourself. MT points *lʿnt* as *lēʿānōt*, a Niphʿal infinitive construct with he' syncope. It is also possible to read a Qal *laʿănōt* with little change in meaning (GKC §51l).

10:5. *land's eye.* We find the identical expression in Num 22:5, 11. *Pace* the Targumim and Saadiah, this is probably not the sun; rather, *ʿayin* 'eye' connotes "surface, appearance" in Lev 13:5, 37, 55; Num 11:7; 1 Sam 16:7; Ezek 1:4–27; 8:2; Prov 23:31; Dan 10:6. The idiom seems to exchange the organ of perception for the thing perceived (but see Hurowitz 1990). (1 Sam 16:7, too, mingles the notions of "eyes" and "appearance": "Do not regard his appearance . . . for Man sees *lāʿênayim* 'with his eyes/ at appearances,' while Yahweh sees *lallēbāb* 'into the heart.'") The imagery in 10:5 seems playful: Yahweh covers Egypt's "eye" in a manner previously "unseen" (v 6), so that the land cannot be "seen" (v 5).

every tree that sprouts for you. A looser translation would be "all your trees that grow."

10:6. *fathers.* The Egyptians' "fathers and . . . fathers' fathers," sources of tradition from the past, balance the Hebrews' "son . . . and your son's son" (10:2), through whom tradition will be transmitted for posterity (Jacob 1992: 282).

10:7. *Until when.* The courtiers' complaint echoes Moses' words, "Until when? . . . Release my people, that they may serve me" (10:3).

this. The referent could be Moses (KJV) or Israel, but I find attractive the interpretation of LXX: "this matter," namely, Israel's detention.

snare. The *môqēš* is a hunter's trap. The term connotes an inextricable predicament.

Release the men. We might expect "release the *people*" (*šallaḥ 'et-hā'ām), to echo Moses' repeated demand. The word *'ănāšîm* means "persons, men," i.e., Israel as a collection of individuals. This apparently evokes Pharaoh's question in v 8, "Who are going?" and suggests to him releasing only the *gəbārîm* 'men, adult males' (10:11).

Yahweh. Assuming MT is correct (see TEXTUAL NOTE), by this point in the story, not only Pharaoh but his people know the name of Israel's god. For the composite Torah, 10:7 fulfills 7:5: "And Egypt will know that I am Yahweh, in my extending my arm over Egypt" (on the meaning of 7:5 within P, see NOTE to 7:5).

Don't you yet know. Hăṭerem tēda' may refer to 9:30: "you and your slaves . . . do not yet fear (ṭerem tîrə'ûn) before Yahweh Deity" (Cassuto 1967: 124). Now the slaves, at least, have learned to fear. With incredulous insolence, they upbraid their master's obtuseness, the effect of Yahweh's "strengthening" his heart (Van Seters 1994: 91).

is dying. 'Ābədâ could also be rendered "has perished."

10:8. *Who and who.* The idiom seems to convey "exactly who?" (GKC §137a). Previously, Pharaoh had lightly released and lightly recanted. Here, he finally begins to bargain in earnest—although, after so many miracles, to haggle now suggests detachment from reality (see Gunn 1982: 78). Moses' response in v 9 is to demand, as it were, too high a price—women, children and cattle—to which Pharaoh responds in v 11 with a ridiculously low price—men only. An ordinary negotiation would end in compromise, but Moses never budges. Indeed, he raises his demands in v 25.

10:9. *festival.* Often ḥag (cf. Arabic ḥajj) has the connotation "pilgrimage festival" (see NOTE to 12:14). Moses' demand will be met when he leads the people out of Egypt during the Festival of Unleavened Bread (12:17).

10:10. *May Yahweh be so with you.* The tone is sarcastic, tantamount to "God help you if I release all of you." But, since Pharaoh in fact releases Israel completely, his benison proves ironically valid: Israel is indeed blessed (Cassuto 1967: 125). Pharaoh's language in vv 10-11 is jerky, disjointed and difficult to translate. May we imagine the once cool monarch sputtering in frustration (cf. NOTES to 1:10 and 5:2, 18)?

dependents. As Cassuto (1967: 125) observes, *ṭap* can connote both women and children (and perhaps the elderly, too [R. Jonathan *apud Mek. pisḥā'* 14; Philo *Moses* 1.147; Josephus *Ant.* 2.317; Loewenstamm 1992a: 225]). In any case, Pharaoh demands Israel's most defenseless as hostages.

evil is before your face. Rashbam paraphrases, "you intend evil in your hearts," citing Isa 5:21, "Woe to the wise in their own eyes, that are clever before their own faces." Cassuto (1967: 126), however, interprets, "evil is in store for you" (also LXX, ibn Ezra, Ramban, Sforno, Luzzatto). Bekhor Shor seems to have the best approach: "the evil you plan is visible on your faces."

10:11. *Not so.* MT *lō(')* *kēn* probably revokes Pharaoh's sarcastic blessing in the previous verse, "May Yahweh be so (*yəhî kēn*) with you." The assonance in 10:11 is striking, whether we read *lō(')* *kēn* *ləkû-nā'* (MT) or *lākēn ləkû-nā'* (Sam) (see TEXTUAL NOTE).

males. Pharaoh maintains that Israelite pilgrimage and worship are incumbent only upon adult males (cf. 23:17; 34:23; Deut 16:16) (*Exod. Rab.* 13:5; Gressmann 1913: 73). Moses, however, claims that the festival requires the attendance of all (v 9), as per Deut 16:11, 14; 31:12; 1 Sam 1:3–19. The dispute between Pharaoh and Moses may reflect dissent within Israel as to women's religious obligations, comparable to later debates within Judaism, Christianity and Islam. In the narrative context, Pharaoh's real aim is to detain the women and children as hostages.

expelled them. Naturally, Pharaoh did not bodily expel Moses and Aaron, but had them expelled by others (cf. TEXTUAL NOTE); we could even translate, "*one* expelled them." Sforno (on 11:1) perceives an anticipation of the Exodus, when Pharaoh will expel all Israel (11:1; 12:39).

10:12. *Extend your arm . . . with the locust, and let it ascend.* MT may be corrupt, for in what sense can Moses extend his arm "with the locust" (see TEXTUAL NOTE)? Keeping to MT, perhaps *bā'arbe(h)* means "*for* the locust" or "*in such a manner as to bring on* locusts" (Knobel *apud* Dillmann 1880: 92). But this seems forced. Another solution would be to revocalize **bə'arbe(h)* 'with *a* locust.' Moses is to brandish a stray hopper as sympathetic magic (we must then also follow Sam-LXX in v 13: "Moses extended his *arm*").

10:13. *Yahweh, he drove.* Pace Niccacci (1990: 63), the inverted syntax highlights the divine causation of the wonder, not the simultaneity of Yahweh's and Moses' actions (see also NOTE to 9:23).

forward wind. Because the Israelites "oriented" themselves toward the sunrise, *qādîm* 'forward' is ordinarily east. But locusts actually enter Egypt from the southwest (Dillmann 1880: 92–93; Gressmann 1913: 74); indeed, LXX Exod 10:13 translates *rûaḥ qādîm* as "south wind" (see also NOTE to 14:21). If *qādîm* connotes the east in 10:13, the Elohist must have projected upon Egypt the conditions of Canaan, which locusts enter from the southeast (cf. NOTE to 10:19). The LXX reinterpretation would then reflect Alexandrian Jewry's greater familiarity with the Egyptian clime.

We may be misinterpreting the evidence, however. In Ps 78:26, *qādîm* parallels *têmān* 'south (wind),' supporting LXX Exod 10:13. Perhaps *rûaḥ qādîm* simply connotes a mighty wind from any direction (see NOTE to 14:21).

10:14. *ascended over.* *Wayya'al,* interpreted as Qal, might also be rendered "came upon, attacked, gained control over." Or the form might be Hiph'il, as in LXX and Kenn 125: "it [the wind] raised the locust."

10:15. *land's eye.* See NOTE to 10:5.

fruit. Do these miraculous locusts literally eat fruit? Perhaps. But the more likely interpretation is that, by devouring leaves and buds, they *prevent* the trees from bearing fruit.

10:17. *lift.* I.e., pardon.

only this time. I.e., jut this once. Childlike, Pharaoh forgets that he has already wronged God repeatedly and received pardon.

from upon me. Pharaoh speaks as if he alone were suffering, in contrast with his previous mention of himself and his people (8:4; 9:27) (Jacob 1992: 239). *L'état c'est moi.*

this death. Pharaoh's overstatement proves prophetic. He does not suspect the true death about to strike Egypt.

10:19. *sea wind.* Again, the terminology betrays a Palestinian context (cf. NOTE to 10:13). From Egypt's perspective, the "sea wind" is a north wind from the Mediterranean. For Canaan, however, *rûaḥ yām* connotes the *west* wind. Here a west wind blows the locusts into the Suph Sea.

blew. *Tq'* ordinarily means "thrust," which fits here perfectly. But since wind is at issue, and since *tq'* can also mean "sound a horn," I venture "blew."

Suph Sea. *Yam sûp* probably means "Reed Sea" or conceivably "Weed Sea" (cf. Jonah 2:6). The name was probably applied to a variety of bodies of water. Here, however, it is presumably the Gulf of Suez or the Red Sea, although reeds grow in neither (see further NOTE to 13:18; APPENDIX B, vol. II).

Fretheim (1991a: 128) views the plague of locusts as foreshadowing the Egyptians' fate at the Suph Sea. The similarities are the following: (a) both the advent of the locusts and the recession of the Sea are caused by a "*forward wind*" (10:13; 14:21); (b) Yahweh "drives, makes drive" (*nihag*) both the wind bearing the locusts and Pharaoh's cavalry (10:13; 14:25); (c) both the locusts and the Egyptian cavalry are drowned in the Suph Sea (10:19; 14:27–28; 15:1–10); (d) of both we are told "not one was left" (*lō[']* *niš'ar . . . 'eḥād*) (10:19; 14:28). These resemblances might seem accidental, but in fact armies are often compared to locusts and vice versa (Judg 6:5; Isa 33:4; Jer 46:23; 51:27; Joel 1; 2:25; Nah 3:15; *KTU* 1.14.iii.1, iv.29–30).

10:21. *darkness.* God's first act of Creation was to call light into being (Gen 1:3). Removing light symbolizes return to Chaos (Fretheim 1991a: 129; cf. Isa 45:19; Jer 4:23). On the one hand, darkness can imply God's absence, whether in the underworld (Ps 49:20; 88:11–13; Job 10:21–22; Eccl 6:4) or in captivity (Isa 42:7, 16; 49:9; Ps 107:10, 14). On the other hand, Yahweh's advent as storm god may be accompanied by darkness, representing his destructive power (Isa 13:10; Joel 2:2; Amos 5:18, 20; 8:9; Zeph 1:15; Zech 14:6). And Israelite knowledge of Egyptian religion may have been a factor, too. The Egyptians' extreme reverence for the sun was already well known in Late Bronze Age Canaan, where Pharaoh's vassals repeatedly call him "my Sun" (Moran 1992 *passim*).

Egypt. In MT, the verse ends *wayāmēš ḥōšek* (Sam *wymš ḥḥšk*). Under TEXTUAL NOTES, I opined that these words are a corruption. That may be too facile a dodge, however. We must at least try to make sense of the received text.

The three attested roots that might produce the verb *ymš* are *mšy* 'draw (from the water),' *mwš* 'depart' and *mšš* 'grope, feel.' The first is clearly irrelevant, but the latter two have been brought to bear. *Tg. Onqelos*, probably asking how one would recognize the plague's onset by night, translates: "and after the dark of night will *pass*," i.e., **wayāmūš ḥōšek* 'and dark will depart.' Sforno, however, paraphrases, "he will *remove* the natural dark of night," apparently reading a Hiphʿil *wayāmiš*.

Others, attributing the dark to airborne particles (see COMMENT), take the root as *mšš*, either in Qal **wayāmōš* ("and one will feel darkness" [Buber 1946: 65]) or Hophʿal **wayūmaš* ("and darkness will be felt"; cf. LXX "palpable darkness"). MT *wayāmēš*, however, is ostensibly a Hiphʿil, suggesting an interpretation "darkness will cause [the Egyptians] to grope" (Luzzatto; cf. *Fragmentary Targum* "they will grope about in the dark"). In fact, the Piʿel *miššēš* describes blind groping in Deut 28:29; Job 5:14; 12:25 (cf. also *giššēš* in Isa 59:10). But, were this the sense of 10:21, we might have expected **wayāmēš (ha)ḥōšek ʾet miṣrayim* '(the) darkness will make the Egyptians grope,' or, more idiomatic still, **ûmiṣrayim yəmaš(ə)šû (ba)ḥōšek* 'and the Egyptians, they will grope about in the dark' (see TEXTUAL NOTE).

And perhaps the root is neither *mwš* nor *mšš*. Rüger (1970) compares Arabic *massa* 'strike, meet, befall,' otherwise unknown in the Hebrew Bible (although Rüger spots it again in Sir 40:10). Alternatively, one might posit a root *nmš*, attested in the name "Nimshi" (epigraphic *nmš[y]* [AHI 39.001; 41.001; 100.622; 100.852]). Arabic *namasa* in fact means "hide"—but unfortunately in the sense of confide, rather than occlude.

Finally, Rashi views *wymš* as a defective spelling of **wyʾmš*, from a putative root **ʾmš* 'to be dark' (on the loss of ʾaleph, see GKC §68i). Although *ʾemeš* ordinarily means "yesterday, last night," it may connote darkness in Job 30:3 (Pope 1973: 220). We could even extend Rashi's theory and eliminate the syncopated ʾaleph by invoking Akkadian *mūšu* 'night,' Arabic *masāʾ* 'evening' and Ethiopic *mesēt* 'evening,' which might imply a root *mwš/mšy* 'to be dark.' Two pieces of evidence support this interpretation. The first is Ps 105:28, which says, apropos of the plague of darkness, "he sent darkness and it was dark (*wayyaḥšik*)," as if glossing 10:21. And Syr in fact renders *wayāmēš ḥōšek* as *wneʿmaṭ ḥeškāʾ* 'let the dark grow dark.' There is only one objection to this approach, but it is a strong one: I find in no Semitic language a *verbal* usage of the root *mwš/mšy*. It rather appears to be a primitive nominal root, and one not clearly attested in Hebrew.

10:22. *three days.* Why mention the duration at all? While a timely eclipse would have been impressive enough, the text implies that the plague of darkness was a phenomenon even more awesome.

10:23. *brother.* I.e., fellow.

from under himself. I.e., "from his place" (Syr, *Tg. Ps.-Jonathan*; cf. 16:29; Lev 13:23, 28; Judg 7:21). LXX "from his bed" is overprecise.

in their dwellings. This might indicate that lamps still functioned inside Israelite homes (cf. Philo *Moses* 1.124). More likely, however, "in their dwellings" means "*among* their dwellings," i.e., where they lived (LXX, Luzzatto; cf. Gen 10:30; 36:43; Num 35:29; Ezek 28:2; Ps 132:13).

10:24. *Only your flock . . . will be detained.* Were Moses bargaining in earnest, this would be the correct compromise between the extremes proposed in 10:9, 11. Josephus (*Ant.* 2.307) notes that the Egyptians truly need the Israelites' cattle, as theirs have been killed by plague and hail.

10:25. *slaughter sacrifices and ascending sacrifices.* Zəbāḥîm and ʿōlōt are partly and wholly burnt meat sacrifices, respectively (the narrator has forgotten that the Egyptians no longer possess any cattle!). The fulfillment of this prediction that Pharaoh would endow offerings is nowhere recorded (cf. Ramban). But it may be implicit in Pharaoh's plea for a blessing (12:32; see NOTE).

10:26. *we do not know.* Moses' (feigned?) ignorance reminds us of Abraham in Gen 22:7–8: when Isaac inquires as to the nature of the sacrifice on Moriah, Abraham evasively/presciently answers, "Deity will show [reading *yarʾe[h]*] the sheep/goat for the offering" (J. G. Propp, privately). In fact, the Israelites do not learn what sacrifices Yahweh desires until the Lawgiving at Sinai.

10:28. *seeing my face.* On this idiom, see NOTES to 10:29; 23:17; 34:23.

10:29. *I will see your face no more.* This is a problematic statement, since Moses and Pharaoh seem to meet again in 12:31–32. As diversity of authorship is unlikely (see SOURCE ANALYSIS), how do we account for the contradiction? There are several potential explanations.

First, we should note the possibility that Moses begins to function as a prophet only in 11:1, and that in 10:29 he is speaking for himself (cf. 1 Kgs 22:15–17). Elsewhere in the Pentateuch, Moses erupts in spontaneous anger without explicit divine sanction (2:12; 32:19; Num 20:10). Perhaps Moses is simply exceeding his authority, making an uninspired prediction. But this is counterintuitive, for the narrative is intended to exalt Moses over Pharaoh.

Another possibility is that Moses does speak with implicit divine sanction but that Pharaoh's (temporary) change of heart negates the prophecy. Jonah's threat, "forty days more, and Nineveh is destroyed" (Jonah 3:4), likewise is unfulfilled—not because it is uninspired, but because the Assyrians wholeheartedly repent (Jonah 3:5–10) (cf. also Jer 26:18–19). But this, too, is counterintuitive.

Possibly, then, we misunderstand Moses' words. At first they seem clearly to mean "I will not even once again see your face," an appropriate response to "on the day of your seeing my face you will die." But *hôsîp* 'continue,' with or without *ʿôd*, is ambiguous. It can be punctual, "to do something again," or durative, "to go on doing something." While the sense of Pharaoh's threat is clearly "do not see my face even once again," one might argue that Moses' answer means "I will not go on seeing your face," i.e., "soon I will have seen you for the last time." One might even regard 14:13 as disclosing the correct exegesis of the ambiguous 10:29: "you will see them no more (lō[ʾ] tōsîpû) to eternity." But this, too, is not the surface interpretation.

I find most attractive Abarbanel's approach. "Seeing the face" is a special idiom: "to wait upon, have an official audience" (cf. Gen 43:3, 5; 2 Sam 3:13; 14:24, 28, 32; 2 Kgs 25:19; Jer 52:25; compare Akkadian dāgil pāni 'servant, subject,' literally 'face-seer' [Cogan and Tadmor 1988: 320]). In 11:8, Moses predicts, "all these your slaves will go down to me and bow to me," and, according to 12:30–31, "Pharaoh arose by night, he and his slaves and all Egypt. . . . And he called to Moses and to Aaron." Since, however, Moses has forbidden any Israelite to go outside (12:22), he and Aaron presumably parley from their doorway (see NOTE to 12:22) (cf. Jacob 1992: 336). This would not constitute "seeing the face" of Pharaoh, i.e., attending an official audience. Rather, the Egyptians "see the face" of Moses.

11:1. *one more.* Emphasizing the urgency of the command to accept the Egyptians' valuables, for not much time remains. "One more" also implies that for E, and probably for the redacted Torah, the plague of the firstborn is to be the last (see REDACTION ANALYSIS).

plague. Fretheim (1991a: 130) correctly observes that negaʿ (< ngʿ 'touch, strike') ordinarily refers to disease, but can connote a wound or blow (see BDB). Both meanings operate here.

when he releases completely. The rare kālâ has the same meaning in Gen 18:21. LXX explicates, "when he sends you forth *with all*," i.e., not detaining the Hebrews' dependents or property (Wevers 1990: 162; so also Rashbam, Luzzatto; cf. Syr).

Several scholars, however, emend *kallâ 'bride' after Coppens (1947). Daube (1963: 58), for example, translates "as you would let go [i.e., divorce] a slave-wife." Indeed, both šillaḥ 'release' and gērēš 'expel' can connote divorce. By this interpretation, the Egyptians will treat the Hebrews as a despised concubine. Morgenstern (1949), however, does not see the relationship as so acrimonious. Excising the men from 3:22 and forgetting entirely about the children, he argues that the image behind the despoiling of the Egyptians is *showering a bride* as she is released into her husband's custody—here, presumably, Yahweh. But the plain sense of MT is satisfactory.

he will expel. The subject is not quite clear. It would appear to be Pharaoh, but, according to LXX, Sam and Syr (12:39), it is all Egypt (see TEXTUAL NOTE to 12:39).

11:2. *friend . . . friend.* A man asks from a male friend (rēʿēhû), a woman from a female friend (rəʿûtāh). While here rēaʿ must describe a foreigner, elsewhere it denotes a kinsman (e.g., 2:13). The unexpected diction has stimulated speculation that Israelites practiced a mock "despoiling of Egypt" among themselves as a springtime folk custom (Segal 1963: 148–49, 260; NOTE to 12:36). In the immediate context, however, the implication of rēaʿ must be "fellow human."

11:3. *Yahweh will put.* MT, LXX and Syr have wayyittēn yahwe(h) 'and Yahweh put' in the narrator's voice. I, however, read *wəyittēn yahwe(h) 'and Yahweh will put' in God's voice, comparing Sam wntty 'and I will put.' (Yahweh often speaks of himself in the third person, e.g., 9:5; 11:7.) If we read "and Yahweh put" (MT), the narrator's intrusion is awkward. Were the point that Yahweh had made or was then making Israel pleasing to Egypt, we would expect inverted syntax: *wəyahwe(h) nātan or *wəyahwe(h) yittēn.

The Sam plus *whš'lwm* 'and they will lend to them' also makes better sense if we interpret the initial verb as an unconverted imperfect (see TEXTUAL NOTE). In fact, reading *wəyittēn at the beginning and wəhiš'ilûm at the end would make 11:3 perfectly symmetrical with 12:36. *Wəyittēn 'and he will put' (11:3) mirrors nātan 'he put' (12:36); wəhiš'ilûm 'and they will lend to them' (11:3) mirrors wayyaš'ilûm 'and they lent to them' (12:36). Moreover, the third verb in 12:36, waynaṣṣəlû 'and they despoiled,' mirrors wəniṣṣaltem 'and you will despoil' in 3:22.

the man Moses will be very great. As a verbless clause, hā'îš mōše(h) gādôl mə'ōd derives its tense from context. In MT, we must translate, "the man Moses *was* very great." My reading *wəyittēn 'and he will put,' however, puts the second clause into the future and into God's voice (see previous NOTE).

SPECULATION: Alternatively, we might posit that part of 11:3 was originally situated within 12:36, where we indeed would expect it: "And Yahweh put (*wayyittēn* = MT) the people's favor in Egypt's eyes, and also the man Moses was very great in the land of Egypt, in Pharaoh's slaves' eyes and in the people's eyes. And they lent to them, and they despoiled Egypt." Before the combination of JE with P, 11:3 and 12:36 would have been sufficiently close that a scribe's eye might have skipped.

the people's. Hā'ām likely refers to the Egyptians. Less plausibly, Ramban thinks it is Israel.

11:4. *At midnight.* Literally, "at night's dividing" (kaḥăṣōt hallaylâ). For diurnal creatures such as humans, the night is a time of terror, when demons kill the weak, particularly the very young (Ziegler 1950; Fields 1992; see COMMENT to 12:1–13:16).

11:5. *firstborn.* Bəkôr must refer here to juveniles, or at least to those whose parents are living. After all, Pharaoh himself is probably a firstborn (Mek. pišā' 13). Given the specific reference to sons in 4:23; 13:12, most interpreters assume that only firstborn *males* are threatened. On all Israel as Yahweh's firstborn son, see COMMENT to 12:1–13:16, p. 457.

die. Moses finally discharges his commission, threatening Pharaoh's firstborn with death (4:23). Because the king has repeatedly demonstrated his cruelty, we now accept the fairness of the sentence. Like the plagues of blood, frogs, murrain and šəḥîn, the slaying of the firstborn brings defilement upon the houses of Egypt.

sitting on his throne. Since "firstborn" and "Pharaoh" are both grammatically masculine, it is unclear who sits (hayyōšēb) on the throne. Pharaoh naturally possesses a throne, but might not the crown prince also have a special seat? Tgs. Onqelos and Ps.-Jonathan compromise with paraphrase: "the firstborn of Pharaoh *destined to sit* upon the throne of his [Pharaoh's] kingship" (likewise in 12:29). But parallelism suggests it is Pharaoh who sits, just as it is the maidservant, not her son, who grinds (cf. NOTE to 12:29).

the maidservant that is behind the two millstones. Cassuto (1967: 133) observes that this is a common Egyptian expression found, for example, in the "Instructions of Ptah-ḥotep" (*ANET* 412). In Egypt, as in Israel and Greece (*Odyssey* 20:105–19), slave women often did the grinding (cf. Isa 47:2). This explains the parallelism with 12:29, "the firstborn of the captive that is in the pit house" (so Rashbam, who notes that Samson, too, "had to grind in the captives' house" [Judg 16:21]).

every animal firstborn. This allusion sets up the consecration of Israel's firstlings in 13:1–2, 11–16 (Van Seters 1994: 121; see COMMENT to 12:1–13:16, pp. 454–57).

11:6. *cry.* Ṣ'q was previously used of the Israelites (3:7, 9); now it is Egypt's turn to wail (Fretheim 1991a: 131). Indeed, if we take the incomparability formula literally, the Egyptians' cry surpasses Israel's.

whose like. "Cry" (ṣə'āqâ) is feminine, yet kāmōhû refers to a masculine noun (Sam, however, has feminine kmwh). Evidently, the usage is carried over from 9:18, 24; 10:14, where the antecedents are correctly masculine.

11:7. *not a dog will sharpen his tongue.* Jub 49:4 takes this as a promise of immunity to the Hebrews' domesticated dogs. But "man's best friend" has negative associations in the Bible (1 Sam 17:43; 24:15; 2 Sam 9:8; Ps 22:21; 59:7, 15; Prov 26:11; Eccl 9:4; Jdt 11:19, etc.) (Keel 1978: 87). Canines are not lovable pets, but noisy, scavenging street denizens.

To "sharpen the tongue" probably means to extend it in hostile utterance— here, to bark threateningly. The Bible elsewhere compares a malicious tongue to a weapon (Jer 18:18), a sharp sword (Ps 57:5; 64:4; Prov 12:18; Ben Sira 28:18) or a bow and arrows (Jer 9:2, 7). We also read of a lengthened (Isa 57:4) or sharpened tongue, as in Ps 140:2–4: "Keep me from the man [i.e., men] of violence, who have conceived evil things in the heart . . . they have sharpened their tongue like a snake." By a likely restoration, we also find the image in Ugaritic: ḥrb.lṭšt [lš]nhm 'their tongue a sharpened sword' (*KTU* 1.2.iii.32–33).

In Ugaritic myth, dogs' barking and the noisemaking of other animals presage ill (*KTU* 1.14.v.7–12). According to modern Middle Eastern folklore, dogs are able to scent Death's presence (Burton 1856: 193). The import of 11:7, then, is that all Goshen, man and beast, will be tranquil (Calvin). Not even the wild dogs will bark—in contrast to the cacophonous wailing of the Egyptians and their animals.

you may know. The verb is plural in MT (but see TEXTUAL NOTE). Moses is saying that Pharaoh, the Egyptians and perhaps the Hebrews and the reader, too (cf. 10:2), will all know that "Yahweh separates between Egypt and between Israel."

11:8. *these your slaves.* I.e., Pharaoh's court is in attendance.

will go down. I.e., from the palace (cf. 2 Sam 11:9, 10, 13). Holzinger (1900: 32) infers that the author projects onto Egypt's alluvial plain the topography of Canaan, where palaces are indeed elevated. There is an implication of condescension, too, if not degradation, in the court's "descent" to Goshen.

to me. Because Hebrew lacks quotation marks, we almost miss the change of speaker, from Yahweh to Moses (Friedman 1995: 42). Compare 7:17, where the personae of Deity and prophet merge. The prediction of 7:1, that Moses would become "as a deity to Pharaoh," thus is literally fulfilled.

people that are at your feet. I.e., "your followers" (cf. LXX; Syr; *Tgs. Onqelos* and *Ps.-Jonathan*). Exod 12:37 will describe the adult Hebrew males as *raglî* 'infantry'—literally, "the one of the foot"; see NOTE.

nose. I.e., "anger"; see NOTE to 4:14.

11:9. *you.* "You" (*'ălêkem*) is plural, referring to both Aaron and Moses, although there has been no indication of Aaron's presence (see, however, TEXTUAL NOTE to 10:24). Exod 11:9–10 (R) summarizes the entire Plagues narrative, in which Aaron has played a large role.

COMMENT

ANTI-CREATION?

In the beginning, God created light, restricted the waters, uncovered the dry land and fashioned heavenly bodies, plants, animals and humanity (Genesis 1 [P]). Now, to punish Egypt, Yahweh harms or removes each element constituting the natural order: water, animals, plants, sunlight and humans. Not surprisingly, the Plagues of Egypt have been characterized as a deliberate inversion of cosmogony: "It is a picture of creation gone berserk. The world is reverting to a state of chaos. It is a kind of flood story in one corner of the world" (Fretheim 1991a: 110; cf. Zevit 1975–76; Fretheim 1991b). We in fact find substantial lexical contact between the Priestly Plagues and Creation: *tannîn* 'serpent,' *miqwe(h)* 'collection of water,' *dāg* 'fish,' *'ereṣ* 'earth, land,' *šāraṣ* 'teem, swarm,' *mālē'* 'be full,' *'ădāmâ* 'earth, soil,' *'āpār* 'dirt, dust,' *hôṣî'* 'bring forth,' *'ādām* 'Man, humanity' and *bəhēmâ* 'animal.' One could even draw a parallel between the seven Priestly Plagues and the seven days of Creation.

Yet I am not quite convinced. Granted, biblical authors could and did write of Uncreation. P's Flood is one example: the primordial waters restricted in Gen 1:6–10 are let loose again (Gen 7:11). Similarly in Jer 4:23–26, the land reverts to darkness and "chaos-and-void" (*tōhû wābōhû*); it is uninhabited by man or fowl, an utter waste. And in Zeph 1:2–3, God removes from the earth man and beast, fish and fowl. In these passages, the theme of anti-Creation is blatant. Had Exodus described a series of divine acts whereby the humans, animals and plants of Egypt were killed, the land flooded (alternatively: desiccated) and light finally removed, the anti-Creation imagery would have been clear and presumably intentional. But the Plagues narrative is so complicated, so studded with features extraneous to anti-Creation, that the theme's very existence becomes conjectural. Is not any act of destruction in a sense "anti-Creation"?

Some plagues (blood, frogs, biting insects, šəḥîn) have no cosmogonic allusions whatever; indeed, frogs and insects really involve Creation, not Uncreation. As for the vocabulary common to the Priestly Creation and Plagues, most items are either so insignificant, occurring only once, or so common, attested throughout the Bible, that they are useless as literary allusions. I would cite stereotypical Priestly style rather than deliberate reference.

HUMANITY AND NATURE

The Plagues cycle, like the stories of the Flood (Genesis 6–9), Sodom and Gomorrah (Genesis 19) and Nineveh (Jonah), portrays God as Universal Judge (Gen 18:25), weighing crimes and assessing penalties. Yahweh punishes not only guilty humans but animals, crops and lands. It might seem strange or unfair that these, too, should suffer.

The Bible evinces a marked empathy for our fellow creatures. Animals and the very soil must enjoy rejuvenating Sabbaths (20:10; 23:10–11; Lev 25:1–7; 26:34–35; Deut 5:14). An animal must not be denied its gleanings (Deut 25:4) or be given a task beyond its strength (Deut 22:10). War must not be waged against trees (Deut 20:19–20). The mother bird may not witness her chicks' death (Deut 22:6–7). And the kid must not be boiled in its own mother's milk (Exod 23:19; 34:26; Deut 14:21).

This projection of human qualities upon all Creation complements another type of biblical anthropocentrism. As humanity was created to rule nature (Gen 1:26, 28; 9:2 [P]; cf. 2:19–20 [J]), so may humanity be punished through nature. In the plague of hail, the cattle (and slaves) of God-fearing Egyptians are spared, while those of impious Egyptians perish. Whether animals, plants and land are blessed or cursed depends directly upon the righteousness of their human stewards (see Frymer-Kensky 1992: 100–7). Leviticus 26 and Deuteronomy 28 most graphically describe the social and ecological disasters that will befall a sinful people and their land. Some even recall the Plagues of Egypt: "Cursed is your . . . dough pan. Cursed is your belly's fruit and your soil's fruit, your oxen's spawn and your flock's offspring (?). . . . Yahweh will make the plague (deber) cling to you . . . Yahweh will strike you with Egypt's šəḥîn . . . and with blindness . . . and you will grope at noon as the blind man gropes in the dark. . . . Yahweh will strike you with bad šəḥîn . . . you will gather in but little, for the locust will destroy it . . . the sojourner that is in your midst will ascend over you upward, upward; and you, you will descend downward, downward . . . and Yahweh will make distinct (hiplā[']) your plagues . . . and turn back against you all Egypt's illness" (Deut 28:17–43, 59–60 passim; cf. Exod 15:26; Deut 7:15).

Israelite belief modifies an immemorial Near Eastern ideology, whereby a ruler's piety determines his land's prosperity (Frankfort 1978: 307–12). Yahweh judges the Egyptians by their own principle: although the entire nation comes in for opprobrium (1:13; 3:9, etc.), it is clear that the cause of ruin is Pharaoh himself. The Torah will reject this ideology for Israel, however. Yahweh's blessing is contingent upon the fidelity of all society, not only of the king (Frankfort p. 343).

A TALL TALE

One of the outstanding features of the Exodus story, beginning already in chap. 5, is hyperbole (Plastaras 1966: 131–32). We find frequent assertions of totality: "not one remained," "not one was smitten," "not a hoof," "not a house," "man and animal." Fretheim (1991b: 386) counts over fifty appearances of *kōl* 'all.' These exaggerations both delight and offend our overfastidious sensibilities and are frequently noted by commentators. Do the Hebrews gather stubble "in *all* the land of Egypt," from border to border (5:12)? Does Aaron extend his rod "over *all* Egypt's waters," up and down the length of the Nile (7:19; 8:1)? If there is no water in *all* Egypt, what do the magicians convert to blood (7:22) (Gressmann 1913: 90)? If *all* the dirt turns to lice (8:13), on what do the magicians attempt to operate (8:14) (Gressmann p. 91)? Is the land really "devastated" by the swarms of tiny *ʿārōb* (8:20; cf. Ps 78:45) (Cassuto 1967: 107)? How can *all* the cattle die from murrain (9:6; but see NOTE) if some are later killed by hail (9:19–21), if Moses demands from Pharaoh sacrificial animals (10:25), if the firstborn cattle die during the paschal night (11:5; 12:12, 29) and if the horses drown in the Sea (chaps. 14–15)? Does Yahweh send *all* his afflictions against Egypt (9:14), or are some held in reserve (Jacob 1992: 230)? How can *every* servant of Pharaoh, throughout *all* Egypt, receive warning of the plague of hail in a single day (9:18–20) (Gressmann p. 74)? Can *every* household of Egypt contain a dead, firstborn male (12:30)?

Listing these is trivializing, but important given the history of biblical scholarship (see SOURCE ANALYSIS). Only a pedant would carp at such "contradictions," or, worse yet, use them in isolation as source-critical criteria. We must not hold the Bible to anachronistic standards of journalistic accuracy.

NOT NECESSARILY SO

The modern historian's method precludes acknowledgment of supernatural phenomena, onetime suspensions of physical law (see APPENDIX B, vol. II). When considering prodigies recorded in ancient texts—texts centuries younger than the events they purportedly chronicle—it is only prudent to credit human imagination with the majority of "miracles." In addition, a small proportion may be based on direct observation or secondhand knowledge of real events—misunderstood natural phenomena or ordinary occurrences of unusual magnitude or timeliness.

Any rigorous attempt to explain the whole Plagues narrative as a naive but basically accurate report of a chain of natural calamities is doomed from the start (e.g., Hort 1957–58). Rationalistic explanations for miracles, common in Hellenistic times (e.g., Artapanus) and revived to counter Enlightenment skepticism, are anachronistic today (Jacob 1992: 406). To believe that the Bible faithfully records a concatenation of improbable events, as interpreted by a prescientific society, demands a perverse fundamentalism that blindly accepts the antiquity and accuracy of biblical tradition while denying its theory of supernatural intervention. It is particularly unmethodical to discern causal links between events narrated in different documentary strata, all the more since Psalms 78 and 105 prove that the Plagues' number and sequence were fluid in Israelite tradition (Zevit 1975–76: 196). Exodus itself never refers to written sources about the Plagues, but rather implies a chain of oral tradition (10:2). Not surprisingly, many aspects of the biblical Plagues find parallels in world folklore (Dumermuth 1964).

I would single out, however, one natural event that lately has been associated with the Plagues of Egypt and/or the parting of the Suph Sea: the titanic explosion of the Aegean volcano Thera/Santorini (Wilson 1985: 115–27). Though skeptical of its pertinence (geologists now date the blast well before Israel's origins), I shall mention Thera where it may be relevant (on Thera, see Stiebing 1987; McCoy and Heiken 1990). I will also entertain the notion that some plague episodes are etiological, explaining the origins of certain well-known features of the Egyptian clime (Jacob 1992: 219). Compare Jer 32:20, "You set signs and wonders in . . . Egypt *until this day*" (MT).

Let us now consider the Plagues of Egypt in order, exploring the origins of each in oral/literary tradition, on the one hand, and in observable phenomena, on the other.

Serpents. In P's first plague (SOURCE ANALYSIS), the miraculous ability of Aaron's serpent to swallow others its own size evokes the awesome mandibular flexibility of snakes and crocodiles (see NOTE to 7:9). Scholars have also noted the circulation of similar motifs in ancient Near Eastern tradition. For example, an early Egyptian spell animates a knife, perhaps turning it into a serpent and causing it to swallow a threatening snake (*ANET* 326). The Middle Kingdom Westcar Papyrus similarly tells of a magician animating and enlarging a wax crocodile and having it seize a man; when the sorcerer grasps it, it reverts to wax (Erman 1927: 37–38). Furthermore, that Aaron's serpent swallows its competitors recalls the myths of sundry monsters or gods, often serpentine, that threaten to swallow the pantheon or Creation (Apophis in Egypt [*ANET* 6, 7, 11, 12, 366], Tiāmat in Babylon [*ANET*³ 60–72, 501–3], Death at Ugarit [*ANET* 138]).

But these connections are fairly remote. The immediate literary antecedent of P's episode of serpents is E's story of Moses' rod becoming a snake (4:2–4). And behind *that* story lies a real phenomenon, albeit quite the opposite of the biblical miracle: charming a serpent into rigidity (on ancient and modern Egyptian snake charming, see Dillmann 1880: 68–69; cf., too, Jer 8:17; Ps 58:5–6; Eccl 10:11).

Blood. Biblical tradition is probably inspired by memories or reports of a natural occurrence: the harmless reddening of the Nile each June, caused by sediment acquired upstream (Dillmann 1880: 72–73; Driver 1911: 62). Exod 7:14–25 may even be etiological, explaining the origin of this phenomenon. If so, the rubefaction has intersected with a universal literary motif: bloodied or bloodlike water as an omen or curse. Compare Isa 15:9, "the waters of Dimon will be filled with blood"; see also 2 Kgs 3:22–23; Rev 8:8; 11:6; 16:3–4. Akkadian texts, too, regard bloodlike water as portentous (*CAD* 3.79). And in the Egyptian "Admonitions of Ipu-wer," a bloodied Nile betokens hard times: "The River is blood. If one drinks of it, one rejects (it) as human and thirsts for waters" (*ANET³* 441; for a different rendering, see Lichtheim 1973: 151). The Roman-period Egyptian tale "Setne II" narrates a Nubian sorcerer's journey to Egypt. He tells his mother, "If it happens that I am defeated, then when you are drinking [and eating], the waters will take on the color of blood before you, the food before you the color of meat, and the sky will have the color of blood before you" (Lichtheim 1980: 148; Sarna 1986: 69). But the closest ancient parallels to the plague of blood, especially in its Priestly version, come from Sumer. A gardener has intercourse with the sleeping goddess Inanna. Upon awakening, she brings three plagues upon the land. In the third, all the water in the land turns to blood (Kramer 1981: 73). Another Sumerian text, the "Exaltation of Inanna," depicts in similar terms the suffering of a land that failed to revere the goddess: "Its rivers ran with blood because of you, its people had nothing to drink" (*ANET³* 580).

Perhaps the most telling description of a sanguified river comes from a second-century C.E. text dubiously attributed to Lucian of Samosata: "Each year the river [Adonis] becomes blood red and, having changed its color, flows into the sea and reddens a large part of it. . . . They tell the story that on these days Adonis is being wounded up on Mt. Lebanon and his blood . . . alters the river." The author goes on to cite, however, a variant explanation he has heard: "Mt. Lebanon has a quite ruddy soil. The strong winds come up on these days and deposit the earth . . . in the river, and the soil makes it blood red." The author's mediating judgment: even if the rationalistic explanation is correct, the timing of the event betokens its supernatural origin (Attridge and Oden 1976: 14–17).

The plague of blood arguably has mythic antecedents as well. The Israelite tradition of Yahweh drying or cleaving the Sea manifests deep roots in Canaanite myth, particularly the story of Baʿlu's victory over Prince Sea (COMMENT to 13:17–15:21). Since Prince Sea's other name is Judge River, perhaps the bleeding Nile, too, represents Yahweh's stricken, ancient adversary. (On "Sea" and "River" in Israelite-Canaanite mythopoeic thought, see Keel 1978: 21.)

Frogs. This episode is both the most original of the Plagues and the most humorous, more of a prank than an attack. As we have observed, the multiplication of frogs may be a whimsical reflection of Egyptian attitudes toward the burgeoning Israelites (note *šrṣ* 'swarm, breed' in 1:7; 7:28). In Egyptian literature, too, frogs symbolize spontaneous procreation. Heqet, the frog goddess of Antinoë, is associated with childbirth (Frankfort 1978: 45; Morenz 1973: 262, 264). And, according to the Hermopolitan Theogony, eight snakes and frogs emerge from the primordial slime to engender the sun (Frankfort p. 155).

While there are no known literary antecedents for the amphibious assault of Exodus, it is a fact that the Nile is well stocked with frogs, which "every year with the Nile's subsidence begin to invade the land to celebrate their wedding in the noisiest way possible, making [the] end of September–October into the month of frogs" (Hort 1957–58: 95). Curiously, Exodus does not mention potentially the most annoying aspect of a plague of frogs: their incessant peeping (cf. Origen *Homiliae in Exodum* 4.6; the midrash *Exod. Rab.* 10:6 even reads in Exod 8:8 **ʿal-dibbūr* [MT *dəbar*] *haṣpardəʿîm* 'concerning the frogs' *speech*'). At any rate, the biblical account may be implicitly etiological, explaining the profusion of Nile frogs in certain seasons.

Rationalist commentators often connect the plagues of blood and frogs causally (e.g., Hort 1957–58: 94–98). If the fish died (7:21), presumably the frogs came up on the land to escape the pollution. It is not impossible that the biblical authors, too, made some such connection, but the text is silent.

Lice and ʿārōb. The Priestly Plagues feature slightly more Egyptian "color" than the Elohistic episodes (Knobel *apud* Dillmann 1880: 66). Both sources, however, know a plague of biting insects, which are and were extremely common in Egypt (e.g., Herodotus *Histories* 2.95; Isa 7:18; 18:1 [Gressmann 1913: 71]). Thus these episodes, too, may be etiological (Jacob 1992: 219). And they surely are humorous. Calvin points to the ignominy of a nation conquered, not by a foreign army, but by minuscule vermin.

To be sure, one might find various mythological precedents for lice and ʿārōb: e.g., *Enūma eliš*, where Tiāmat's army includes a monstrous fly (I:142 etc. [ANET 62]), or the Ugaritic Baal Epic, in which ʿAnatu boasts of conquering *ʾil ḏbb* 'the divine Fly (?)' (*KTU* 1.3.iii.46; cf. *ANET* 137; Gibson 1978: 50 n. 11). 2 Kgs 1:2 calls the god of Ekron *baʿal zəbûb* 'Lord Fly' (probably a perversion, however, of **baʿal zəbûl* 'Exalted Lord' [cf. Matt 10:25; 12:24, 27; Mark 3:22; Luke 11:15, 18–19]). But none of these seems truly relevant.

Murrain. Deber can connote any epidemic, as in 9:15. In 9:1–7, however, it refers specifically to cattle plague. Egypt is not particularly unhealthful for cattle, and so the tradition is unlikely to be etiological. Rather, the antecedents are literary-mythic. *Deber* (among humans) is a Covenant curse in Lev 26:25; Deut 28:21 and also appears as a minor deity in Yahweh's retinue (Hab 3:5). Apropos of murrain, Origen proffers a most appealing eisegesis: cattle plague is the fit punishment for Egyptian animal worship (*Homiliae in Exodum* 4.6).

Šəḥîn. On the one hand, skin disease is a stereotypical Near Eastern covenant curse; cf. the treaty between Asshur-Nirari V of Assyria and Mati-ilu of Arpad (*ANET*³ 533), the succession treaty of Esarhaddon (*ANET*³ 538) and the treaty of Sin-shar-ishkun with his Babylonian allies (Parpola and Watanabe 1988: 72). On the other hand, the Israelites associated Egypt in particular with skin afflictions (Deut 28:27; for classical parallels, see Driver 1895: 309). Thus this plague, too, might be etiological (Jacob 1992: 219). The direct literary inspiration, however, is probably E's story of Moses' temporarily afflicted hand (4:6–7; see SOURCE ANALYSIS; NOTE to 9:9).

Ironically, Hellenistic Egyptian historians attributed the Israelites' expulsion from Egypt to the *Hebrews'* skin diseases (Josephus *Ap.* 1.229, 279, 304). Perhaps we have a case of neighboring nations blaming each other for a shared medical problem. Compare "Neapolitan disease," "Italian disease," "Haitian disease," "Christian disease" and "French pox" — all names for syphilis (Parron 1937: 36).

While the use of ashes to spread the disease is probably sympathetic magic (see NOTE to 9:8), conceivably the Israelites preserved a dim memory of the explosion of Thera (c. 1600), whose ash may have reached both Egypt and Canaan (Stiebing 1987; McCoy and Heiken 1990).

Hail. Hail is more typical of Canaan than of Egypt (Fohrer 1964: 78; Hyatt 1971: 119; but see Redford 1992: 420). It is among Yahweh's weapons when he is manifest as storm god (e.g., Josh 10:11; Isa 30:30; Ezek 13:11, 13; Ps 18:13–14). Hail is often associated with fire, whether in the form of lightning (Isa 30:30; Ps 148:8), burning sulfur (Ezek 38:22; cf. Gen 19:24; Job 18:15) or coals (Ps 18:13–14; cf. Ps 11:6). The motif of fiery precipitation also appears in the Sumerian "Exaltation of Inanna" II:13 (Hallo and van Dijk 1968: 16–17), the succession treaty of Esarhaddon (*ANET*³ 539) and an inscription of Asshurbanipal (Rassam Cylinder 9.81 [Mann 1977: 250]) (see further *CAD* 1.i.60; 11.i.26; 21.43). Given the popularity of the motif and the geology of the region, vulcanism is unlikely to be a factor. Rather, we have the association of opposites: fire and water or ice.

Locusts. This plague is obviously based upon a natural phenomenon. Throughout the Near East, locusts were and are a perennial menace (cf. Joel 1–2; Amos 7:12). Sarna (1986: 70) cites a modern (1889) infestation covering about two thousand square miles. According to Brodsky (1990: 35), a single swarm may contain over a billion grasshoppers. Locusts as a divine punishment are also a common literary theme, appearing in the succession treaty of Esarhaddon (*ANET*³ 538) and other Mesopotamian texts (see *CAD* 4.257), as well as the treaty text from Sefire (*KAI* 222.A.27). (A positive aspect of such plagues, however, generally goes unmentioned: the ready availability of edible insects [cf. Doughty 1936: 1.381].)

Darkness. Darkness, too, is a generic curse, inspired by periodic solar eclipses. The "Prophecies of Neferti" from Eighteenth Dynasty Egypt predict: "Re (the sun god) will withdraw from mankind: though he will rise at his hour, one will not know when noon has come; no one will discern his shadow, no face will be dazzled by seeing [him]" (Lichtheim 1973: 142–43). Closer to the Plagues of Exodus, "Setne II" tells of a contest between magicians during which the sky is darkened for three days (Lichtheim 1980: 144). Other Egyptian myths describe the gods' nightly battle with Apophis, an underworld serpent embodying the forces of dark and destruction (*ANET* 6, 7, 11, 12, 366). And, most suggestively, Egyptian sources recall a period of dark and storm about the time of the Hyksos' expulsion (Redford 1992: 420; see APPENDIX B, vol. II). Chronologically and geographically closer to Israel, the Jordanian Deir ʿAllā texts (eighth century) cite the following divine command: *šm. ḥšk. wʾl ngh ʿlm* 'make darkness and not light forever' (Combination I.6–7; cf. Hackett 1980: 25, 29, 43–44). The motif also appears in the Assyrian succession treaty of Esarhaddon

(*ANET*³ 538) and in the Mesopotamian Flood tradition; in fact, *Gilgamesh* XI:111 and *Atra-ḫasis* III:3.13 duplicate Exod 10:23 *verbatim:* "Man did not see his brother" (Lambert and Millard 1969: 94–95). There is also a Hittite myth about the sun god's disappearance (Hoffner 1990: 26–28), and parallels could be multiplied from around the world.

Here, too, we cannot exclude the memory of Thera, especially if 10:21 means that the darkness could be felt (see NOTE). According to Josephus (*Ant.* 2.308), the Egyptians could not even breathe, and Ezek 30:18; 32:7–8, probably alluding to the plague of darkness, mention thick clouds over Egypt (see APPENDIX D, vol. II), But I agree with Fohrer (1964: 78): true absence of light seems to be at issue in Exodus, rather than volcanic fallout or, as many suggest, sand or dust storms (e.g., Sarna 1986: 70). Since the Israelites "had light in their dwellings" (10:23), the most natural inference is that even the Egyptians' lamps do not shine (see, however, NOTE to 10:23).

Firstborn. The death of the Egyptian firstborn, man and beast, has no underlying natural cause. The tradition rather evolved out of themes connected with the paschal rite and Yahweh's claim upon the firstborn (see COMMENT to 12:1–13:16, pp. 454–58).

Drowning. As we have seen, the drowning of the Egyptian host probably constituted P's seventh plague (SOURCE ANALYSIS). Below, we shall discuss the background of the Sea event in ancient myths of cosmogony (COMMENT to 13:17–15:22). On relevant natural phenomena, see also APPENDIX B, vol. II).

Why, one might ask, does Yahweh send so many plagues against Egypt? Would not one great demonstration have sufficed? The Plagues cycle exemplifies an ancient literary motif of multiple disasters, of which examples may be found in the Mesopotamian *Epic of Atra-ḫasis*, in Egyptian "pessimistic literature" and, above all, in the manifold curses concluding ancient Near Eastern inscriptions, particularly treaties (Bickermann 1976: 1.1–32; Mendenhall 1954a; Baltzer 1971; Gevirtz 1961; Van Seters 1986). In Exodus itself, the immediate reason for the multiplication of the Plagues is to enhance the drama by giving Pharaoh repeated opportunities for repentance, and to demonstrate Yahweh's mastery over the land and climate of Egypt, "that you may know that none is like me in all the world" (9:14). Egyptians immediately learn to fear Yahweh (9:20; 10:7; 12:33), and distant nations, too, quake at his mighty deeds (9:16; 15:14–16). Yahweh's fame will resound through space (9:16) and time (10:2).

But, fundamentally, the reason Yahweh sends so many plagues against Egypt is that the author(s) wished him to. The Plagues narrative is surely the most entertaining portion of Exodus. We sense true *Erzählungsfreude* ("joy in narration"), not to mention *Schadenfreude*. Pharaoh is a pure villain whose desperate "Pray for me" (8:4, 24; 9:28; 10:17) evokes more contempt than pity. (On the contrast with the villain-victims of Greek literature, see Robertson 1977: 16–32.)

FAIRNESS AND JUSTICE

The lavish narration of Egypt's mortification is predicated on the recurrent "hardening," "strengthening" or "becoming firm" of Pharaoh's heart (cf. Wilson 1979: 25–26). The king may bend, at least in E, but he always springs back. Each episode ends where it began, with Pharaoh still defiant and Israel still enslaved. Each time there follows a new, escalated round of punishment. The cycle ends only when Israel has crossed the Sea and Egyptian corpses litter the shore.

The hardening of Pharaoh's heart is more than a device to prolong the narration, however. While all concede that "the passage is not intended as an essay on the theological and philosophical issue of human freedom and divine determinism" (Meyer 1983: 77), nonetheless, underlying the tale is a theory of the interplay between human and divine will that requires brief exposition. For centuries, the Plagues of Egypt have been the quintessential text on biblical theodicy (Beale 1984: 129; see already Origen *Peri archōn* 3.1; *Exod. Rab.* 13:3).

Most commentators distinguish between two idioms: either Pharaoh hardens his own heart, or Yahweh hardens it for him. Since the first is gradually replaced by the second, with an overlap in chap. 9, many infer that Pharaoh's intransigence is primarily self-generated. God intervenes only toward the end, to push him over the brink (e.g., *Exod. Rab.* 13:3; Rashi on 7:3; Sarna 1986: 63–65). But this analysis misses an important point. It assumes that, when the text says "Pharaoh's heart was firm/strong," Pharaoh, not Yahweh, has made it so. Since Yahweh predicted Pharaoh's stubbornness (3:19; 11:9) and even claimed he would make Pharaoh unyielding (4:21; 7:3), it is at least as likely that Yahweh is to blame from the start (Beale 1984). It would be more accurate, therefore, to distinguish among three descriptions of the hardening of Pharaoh's heart: (a) it becomes hard with no indication of agent (7:13, 14, 22; 8:15; 9:7, 35); (b) Pharaoh hardens his own heart (8:11, 28; 9:34 [Syr]); (c) Yahweh hardens Pharaoh's heart (4:21; 9:12, 34 [MT]; 10:1, 20, 27; 11:10; 14:4, 8, 17). The gradual shift from (a) to (b) to (c) reflects, not a change in the relationship between Yahweh and Pharaoh, but our own deepening understanding of why the king resists (10:7).

Taken as a whole, the Old Testament is unclear on whether sin is produced by human initiative (e.g., 2 Kgs 17:14; Jer 6:28; 9:13; 11:8; 13:10; 15:6; 16:12; 18:12; 2 Chr 36:13) or by divine intervention (e.g., Deut 2:30; Josh 11:20; Judg 9:23; 1 Sam 2:25; 1 Kgs 12:15; 18:37; 22:19–23; Isa 6:9–10; 29:10; 63:17; Ps 105:25; 2 Chr 25:16; cf. 2 Sam 15:31; 17:14). The implication of the composite Plagues cycle is that both factors can be at work (cf. 1 Sam 2:25). The situation really differs little from what we find in Homeric epic. The gods breathe cowardice or courage into mortals who are already brave or fearful; they punish humans for sins that ultimately should be blamed upon the gods themselves.

In sum, from the Plagues narrative and other biblical passages we may abstract the following understanding of sin: while people are often spontaneously evil, God may encourage or tempt them to err, until they become so wicked that his own attribute of justice compels him to destroy them. In other words, God ensures in advance that the wicked deserve their fated punishment. He may be just, but he is not necessarily fair.

In most of the Hebrew Bible, God plays the role later Judaism reserves for Satan (cf. Forsyth 1987: 121). *Haśśāṭān* 'the Adversary' first appears in early postexilic writings as an officer in Yahweh's angelic court entrusted with presenting human behavior in the worst light (Zech 3:1–2; Job 1–2). But when Judaism encountered Zoroastrianism, Persian dualism evidently attracted thinkers troubled by Yahweh's role in creating evil and misfortune. Beginning in the Persian period, various spirits—Belial, Mastemah, Asmodai, Sammael, the Evil Impulse, Satan—assumed the task of seducing humanity toward evil and launching attacks against individuals. For example, although it is Yahweh who tempts David into sinfully ordering a census (2 Sam 24:1), a later retelling (1 Chr 21:1) makes the instigator Satan (or perhaps an anonymous celestial adversary; see Day 1988: 127–45). Similarly, while it is Yahweh who attacks Moses in 4:24, in Jub 40:2, the adversary is Mastemah. Even the command that Abraham sacrifice his son (Gen 22:2) is, according to Jub 17:15–16, Mastemah's doing.

Although in Judaism, Satan et al. relieved Yahweh of some "demonic" aspects, diabolic influence was never consistently invoked to explain sin. St. Paul honestly confronts the plain sense of the hardening of Pharaoh's heart: God "has mercy on whomever he wishes, and he hardens the heart of whomever he wishes." But after raising the hypothetical question "Why does [God] still blame, for who can resist his desire?" Paul can only reject the question with a hauteur borrowed from Job's Deity: "Who are you, a man, to answer back to God?" (Rom 9:18–20).

Paul stands squarely in the Old Testament tradition: God himself may lead sinners to sin. But at least Paul acknowledges the attendant moral problem ignored by the Elohist and Priestly Writer. It is curious that no postbiblical tradition blames the hardening of Pharaoh's heart on Satan. This is presumably because Pharaoh is, after all, the villain. So far as we know, no one before Paul had thought to question the justice of his plight.

Although not a philosophical treatise, the Plagues narrative contains an implicit, practical warning. Just as medieval Europeans punctiliously feared the Devil, so readers are to guard against the impulses Yahweh instills in those he would destroy. Several commentators take Pharaoh's stubbornness and travails as paradigmatic: you, too, can be a Pharaoh (Wilson 1979; Durham 1987: 99–100, 109, 130). Even a Philistine might ask, "Why should you make firm your hearts as Egypt and Pharaoh made firm their heart?" (1 Sam 6:6).

PART II. LIBERATION FROM EGYPT (EXODUS 12:1–15:21)

XI. *And you will observe this day as an eternal rule* (12:1–13:16)

◆

12 ¹⁽ᴾ⁾And Yahweh said to Moses and to Aaron in the land of Egypt, saying, ²"This month is for you a *head* of months; it is the first for you of the year's months. ³Speak to all Israel's congregation, saying, 'On the tenth of this month, and they will take for themselves, (each) man a sheep/goat for a fathers'-house, a sheep/goat for the house. ⁴But if the house is insufficient for being for a sheep/goat, then he and his neighbor, the one nearest his house, will take; in proportion to the *souls*, (each) man according to what he eats, you will apportion the sheep/goat. ⁵A perfect male sheep/goat, *son of* a year, shall be for you; from the sheep or from the goats you will take. ⁶And it will be for you as a kept thing until the fourteenth day of this month. Then all the community of Israel's congregation will slaughter it *between the two evenings.* ⁷And they will take from the blood and put onto the two doorposts and onto the lintel, onto the houses in which they will eat it. ⁸And they will eat the meat in this night, fire-roasted; with unleavened bread and bitter lettuce they will eat it. ⁹Do not eat from it raw or cooked, boiled in water; but rather fire-roasted, its head with its shanks and with its innards. ¹⁰And leave none of it over until morning, but what remains of it until morning in fire you must burn. ¹¹And thus you will eat it: your loins girt, your sandals on your feet and your staff in your hand, and you will eat it frantically. It is *Pesaḥ* for Yahweh.

¹²'And I will pass through the land of Egypt in this night and strike every firstborn in the land of Egypt, from man and to animal, and upon all Egypt's gods I will execute judgments; I am Yahweh. ¹³And the blood will be for you as a sign on the houses where you are. And I will see the blood and protect over you, and harm from destruction will not be upon you in my striking the land of Egypt.

¹⁴⁽ᴿ/ᴾ⁾'And this day will be for you as a memorial, and you will celebrate it as a festival for Yahweh *to your ages*; as an eternal rule you will celebrate it.

^{15(P)}Seven days you will eat unleavened bread. Even on the first day you will eliminate leaven from your houses, for anyone eating what is leavened, then that *soul* will be cut off from Israel, from the first day until the seventh day. ¹⁶And on the first day a calling of holiness, and on the seventh day a calling of holiness will be for you. Any work may not be done on them; only what is eaten by any *soul*, it alone may be done for you. ¹⁷And you will observe the Unleavened Bread, for on the *bone* of this day I took your brigades out from the land of Egypt. ^(R)And you will observe this day *to your ages* as an eternal rule. ^{18(P)}In the first (month), on the fourteenth day of the month in the evening, you will eat unleavened bread, until the twenty-first day of the month in the evening. ¹⁹Seven days leaven will not be found in your houses. For anyone eating what is leavened, then that *soul* will be cut off from Israel's community, among the sojourner and among the land's native. ²⁰Anything leavened you will not eat. In all your dwellings, eat unleavened bread.' "

^{21(E)}Then Moses called to all Israel's elders and said to them, "Draw out, take for yourselves small cattle for your families and slaughter the *Pesaḥ*. ²²And you will take a marjoram bunch and dip in the sheep's/goat's blood and apply to the lintel and to the two doorposts from the blood that is in the bowl/threshold. But you, do not go out, (any) man from his house's doorway, until morning. ²³And Yahweh will pass to harm Egypt and will see the blood on the lintel and on the two doorposts, and Yahweh will protect over the doorway and will not allow the Destroyer to come into your houses for harm. ^{24(R)}And you will observe this matter as a rule for you and for your sons to eternity. ^{25(E/D-like)}And it will happen, when you come to the land that Yahweh will give to you as he has spoken, then you will observe this service. ²⁶And it will happen, when your sons say to you, 'What is this service to you?' ²⁷then you will say, 'It is the *Pesaḥ slaughter sacrifice* for Yahweh, who protected over Israel's Sons' houses in Egypt in his harming Egypt, but our houses he rescued.' "

And the people knelt and bowed. ^{28(P/R)}And Israel's Sons went and did; as Yahweh commanded Moses and Aaron, so they did.

^{29(E)}And it happened at half the night, and Yahweh, he struck every firstborn in the land of Egypt, from the firstborn of Pharaoh sitting on his throne to the firstborn of the captive that was in the *pit house*, and every animal firstborn. ³⁰And Pharaoh arose by night, he and his slaves and all Egypt, and there was a great cry in Egypt, for there was no house that there was not a dead one there. ³¹And he called to Moses and to Aaron by night and said, "Rise, go out from my people's midst, both you and Israel's Sons, and go serve Yahweh according to your speaking. ³²Both your flocks and your herds take, as you have spoken, and go. And bless me, too."

³³So Egypt *grew strong* concerning the people, hastening to release them from the land, for they said, "We all are dead." ³⁴And the people picked up its dough before it could rise, their dough pans wrapped in their robes upon their shoulder. ^{35(J?)}And Israel's Sons had done according to Moses' word and asked silver objects and gold objects and robes. ³⁶And Yahweh had put the people's favor in Egypt's eyes, and they lent to them, and they despoiled Egypt.

37(R)**And Israel's Sons set forth from Raamses to Succoth,** (E/R)about six hundred thousand *foot-men*—the males, besides the dependents. 38And also many foreigners went up with them, and flock and herd—very *heavy* cattle. 39(E)And they baked the dough which they took out from Egypt as cakes of unleavened bread, because it had not risen, because they had been expelled from Egypt and could not tarry, and also they had made no provisioning for themselves. 40(P)And the dwelling of Israel's Sons that they dwelt in Egypt: thirty year and four hundred year. 41And it happened at the end of thirty year and four hundred year, and it happened on the *bone* of this day, all Yahweh's brigades went out from the land of Egypt. 42(R?)It is a night of observance for Yahweh, as he takes them out from the land of Egypt; it, this night, is for Yahweh an observance for all Israel's Sons *to their ages.*

43(P)And Yahweh said to Moses and Aaron, "This is the *Pesaḥ* Rule: any foreigner's son may not eat of it. 44And any man's slave, a purchase by silver, and you will circumcise him; then he may eat of it. 45A resident or a hireling may not eat of it. 46In one house it must be eaten; do not take from the house from the meat to the outside, and a bone of it you must not break. 47All Israel's congregation must do it. 48And when a sojourner sojourns with you and would do a *Pesaḥ* for Yahweh, every male of him must be circumcised, and then he may approach to do it and be like the land's native. But any uncircumcised may not eat of it. 49One Direction will be for the native and for the sojourner residing in your midst."

50And all Israel's Sons did; as Yahweh commanded Moses and Aaron, so they did. 51And it happened on the *bone* of this day, Yahweh took Israel's Sons out from the land of Egypt in their brigades.

13   1(P?)And Yahweh spoke to Moses, saying: 2"Sanctify to me every firstborn, *loosening of* every womb among Israel's Sons, among man and among animal—he is for me."

3(E/D-like)And Moses said to the people, "Remember this day, when you went out from Egypt, from a slaves' house, for with arm strength Yahweh took you out from this; and anything leavened may not be eaten.

4"Today you are going out in the month of the New Grain. 5And it will happen, when Yahweh brings you to the land of the Canaanite and the Hittite and the Amorite and the Hivvite and the Jebusite, which he swore to your fathers to give to you, a land flowing of milk and honey, then you will serve this service in this month. 6Six days you will eat unleavened bread, and on the seventh day will be a festival for Yahweh. 7Unleavened bread you will eat for the seven days, and anything leavened may not be seen for you, and leaven may not be seen for you in all your territory. 8And you will tell to your son on that day, saying, 'For the sake of what Yahweh did for me in my going out from Egypt.' 9And it will be for you as a sign on your arm and as a memorial *between your eyes,* so that Yahweh's Direction will be in your mouth, for with a strong arm Yahweh took you out from Egypt.

10(R)"And you will observe this rule at its occasion, *from days to days.* 11(E/D-like)And it will happen, when Yahweh brings you to the Canaanite's land, as he swore to your fathers, and gives it to you, [12]then you will make each *loosening* of the womb pass over to Yahweh, and each *loosening*, animal spawn, that may be for you, the males, to Yahweh. [13]But each *loosening* of an ass you will redeem with a sheep/goat, or, if you do not redeem, then *neck* it; and each human firstborn among your sons you will redeem. [14]And it will happen, when your son asks you tomorrow, saying, 'What is this?' then you will say to him, 'With arm strength Yahweh took us out from Egypt, from a slaves' house. [15]And it happened, when Pharaoh was too hard to release us, then Yahweh killed each firstborn in the land of Egypt, from the human firstborn and to the animal firstborn. Therefore I sacrifice to Yahweh each *loosening* of the womb, the males, and each firstborn of my sons I redeem.' [16]And it will be as a sign on your arm and as a circlet *between your eyes*, for with arm strength Yahweh took us out from Egypt."

ANALYSIS

TEXTUAL NOTES

12:1. *and to Aaron.* LXX "and Aaron" might but need not represent a variant *wə'ahărôn, possibly the product of haplography (cf. TEXTUAL NOTES to 12:28, 43, 50).

12:2. *head of months.* Sam has "head of *the* months" (*hhdšym*).

the year's months. Syr paraphrases: "*all* the year's months."

12:3. *Speak.* Where MT has the plural imperative *dabbərû*, LXX and some Syr MSS put the command in the singular, as if reading *dabbēr, addressed to Moses alone. Whether this is a real variant or loose translation, the plural is preferable as the rarer, more difficult reading (only three parallels in the Massoretic Torah). Sam supports MT *dbrw* but adds the particle *n'*, also reflected in some LXX witnesses (Wevers 1990: 168) and paralleled in Gen 50:4; Judg 9:2 (MT). This perhaps lends the injunction a degree of formality.

Israel's congregation. 4QpaleoGen-Exod[l], LXX, Sam, Syr, *Tg. Neofiti I* and many MSS of MT and of *Tg. Onqelos* read *'ădat bənê yiśrā'ēl* 'the congregation of Israel's *Sons*' (see de Rossi 1784–85: 56), a more common expression. Since there is no reason why *bənê* should have dropped from the Hebrew, the shorter Massoretic reading is likely original; see also TEXTUAL NOTES to 12:6, 47.

†*a sheep/goat for a fathers'-house, a sheep/goat for the house.* Comparison of the Versions exposes two problems. The first is the absence or presence of "and" between the parallel phrases (lacking in standard MT, 4QpaleoGen-Exod[l] and LXX; present in some MT MSS [de Rossi 1784–85: 56] and Syr). The second, more significant variation is in the order of the phrases. 4QpaleoGen-Exod[l] has *[śh.l]byt.ś[h.l]byt.'[bwt]* '[a sheep/goat for] the house, a she[ep/goat for] a fa[thers']-house," supported by Syr "a sheep/goat for the house and [sic] a sheep/goat for his [sic] fathers'-house." Whichever is original, it is likely a scribe skipped from one *śh* 'sheep/goat' to the next, after which the omitted matter was

erroneously reinserted. Alternatively, all surviving traditions may conflate ancient, synonymous readings: "a sheep/goat for a fathers'-house" and "a sheep/goat for the house." My translation follows standard MT.

12:4. *in proportion to the souls*. Sam has "in proportions [*sic!*] to the *souls*" (*bmkswt npšwt*), vs. MT *bəmiksat nəpāšōt*. Apparently, the *-at* of the first word was attracted to and corrupted by the *-ōt* of the second.

†12:5. *from the sheep*. While MT has *mn hkbśym*, 4QpaleoGen-Exod¹, Sam and Kenn 1, 80, 99, 129 have *mn hkśbym*. Both *keśeb* and *kebeś* are well-attested terms for "sheep," the former arising from the latter by metathesis, presumably in Proto-Hebrew (**kibśu* [cf. Arabic *kabš*] > **kiśbu* > *keśeb*). Either could be original here, although *kśbym* is slightly preferable as the rarer word. Particularly close to 12:5 is Lev 1:10, where MT has *min-hakkəśābîm*.

12:6. *day*. Missing in LXX, probably for ease of translation.

†*the community of Israel's congregation*. So standard MT. Most other Versions (including Kenn 18, 80, 109), however, have "the community of the congregation of Israel's *Sons*," reflecting the common tendency to lengthen *yiśrā'ēl* into *bənê yiśrā'ēl* (see TEXTUAL NOTES to 12:3, 21, 47). Vg shares this expansionistic reading but has only one term, *multitudo*, for *qəhal 'ădat* 'community of . . . congregation.' Most likely, Jerome has paraphrased MT (cf. Vg Num 14:5), but conceivably his Hebrew *Vorlage* was shorter (Kenn 665 and a Genizah MS [*BHS*] also lack *'ădat*).

SPECULATION: Perhaps two variants once circulated: *qəhal yiśrā'ēl* 'Israel's community' (Vg?) and *'ădat bənê yiśrā'ēl* 'the congregation of Israel's Sons' (unattested). Their conflation would account for the preserved readings. As for which might be original, *qəhal yiśrā'ēl* would have the slightly better claim as *lectio difficilior et brevior*, since *'ădat (bənê?) yiśrā'ēl* appears in 12:3, 47 (see TEXTUAL NOTES).

slaughter it. While MT and LXX have the singular, 4QpaleoExodᵐ uniquely reads "slaughter *them* (*'wtm*)." In 12:7, 9, 21, however, LXX refers to the animals in the plural, while we find the singular in MT and 4Qpaleo-Exodᵐ (to the extent that the latter is preserved).

12:7. *onto the houses*. Syr, Syro-Hexaplaric Symmachus, Aquila and Theodotion and some MSS of MT and of the *Tgs*. (Kennicott 1776–80: 129; de Rossi 1784–85: 57) prepose "and."

in which. For MT *bāhem*, a Cairo Genizah MS (*BHS*) reads *šām* 'there, where,' as in 12:30 (MT; see TEXTUAL NOTE).

it. So MT (*'ōtô*). The majority LXX reading is *auta* 'them' (LXXᴬ, however, has *auto* 'it,' presumably revised to match either MT 12:7 or LXX 12:6). Similarly, in 12:21, some LXX witnesses render *ṣō(')n* 'small cattle' as a plural, while others treat it as a singular (see TEXTUAL NOTE). The plurals in the various MSS and traditions all arise from the same exegetical consideration: if there are many households, there must be many animals. Although certainty is impossible, the singulars of MT seem original.

††12:8. *with unleavened bread and bitter lettuce they will eat it.* My translation rests upon a semiconjectural emendation. All Versions read *ûmaṣṣôt ʿal-mərōrîm yō(ʾ)kəlûhû* 'and unleavened bread with bitter lettuce they will eat it,' which makes little sense. Num 9:11, however, has the expected *ʿal-maṣṣôt ûm(ə)rōrîm yō(ʾ)kəlûhû* 'with unleavened bread and bitter lettuce they will eat it.' I have adopted this reading for 12:8 as well (with Kenn 650 B, 651). It is easy to imagine a scribe's eye or memory converting **ʿal-maṣṣôt ûm(ə)rōrîm* into *ûmaṣṣôt ʿal-mərōrîm* as a spoonerism.

12:9. *from it.* LXX has *ap' autōn* 'from them,' referring to the paschal animals of all Israel (cf. TEXTUAL NOTES to 12:6, 7).

raw. 4QpaleoGen-Exod[l] uniquely reads *nw* for *nʾ*, under the influence of the preceding *mmnw*.

cooked. For MT *wbšl mbšl*, 4QpaleoGen-Exod[l] uniquely has *wbšl wmbšl*.

†12:10. *and leave none.* LXX and Kenn 4, 9, 129, 674 omit "and." Since the prior word ends in waw, dittography and haplography are equally likely, and either reading might be original.

morning (first time). LXX expands: "and a bone you must not break of it," apparently borrowing from 12:46.

12:11. *your sandals.* LXX, Kenn 84, 181 and Syr prefix "and."

†*your staff in your hand.* LXX, Sam and Tgs. Neofiti I and Ps.-Jonathan read "your staffs in your hands" (*mqlykm bydykm*), against MT *mqlkm bydkm* (Tg. Onqelos compromises: "your staffs in your hand"). MT is probably original, the other Versions reflecting attraction to the plural imperative verbs and, more specifically, to the "sandals" and "feet" mentioned previously. Each Israelite wears two sandals—on two feet—but holds one staff in one hand.

12:12. *and strike every firstborn.* Syr, perhaps to avoid anthropomorphism, reads "all firstborn will die." But in v 13, Syr is literal.

†*from man and to animal.* Sam, Kenn 81, 132, 200 and perhaps the LXX *Vorlage* lack the conjunction: *m'dm 'd bhmh.*

12:13. *the land of Egypt.* While standard MT has *b'rṣ mṣrym*, Rossi 262 (first hand) reads *'t mṣrym*, and Kenn 388 and Rossi 503 have *'t 'rṣ mṣrym.*

12:14. *to your ages.* Many LXX witnesses read "to *all* your ages," an idiom not attested anywhere in MT. It may be an inner-Greek expansion.

12:15. *for.* Here and in 12:19, LXX does not reflect *kî*. Either the translators took *kî* as a colorless particle not requiring rendering, or else it had dropped before *kol* by homoioarkton in one verse, after which the corruption spread to the other (D. N. Freedman, privately).

what is leavened. Syr adds "from your houses," duplicated from the first half of the verse. This is an inner-Syriac corruption. While Hebrew *śə'ōr* 'leaven' and *ḥāmēṣ* 'what is leavened' are quite distinct, their Syriac equivalents *ḥmîrā'* and *ḥmî'ā'* are all but identical. A scribe's eye simply skipped back.

until the seventh day. Sam, Kenn 69, 129, 199 and Syr insert a conjunction.

††12:16. *on the first day.* While standard MT begins v 16 with *w*, many MSS of Sam, Syr and MT lack the conjunction (de Rossi 1784–85: 57). The shorter reading is slightly superior, assuming waws are more often added than deleted.

We might also cite the similar-looking yodh ending the previous word, and the presence of *ûbayyôm* '*and* on the . . . day' later in the verse.

a calling of holiness (first time). LXX has "will be called holy," apparently reading *niqrā' *qōdeš/qādōš* for MT *miqrā*' *qōdeš* (*m* and *n* are similar in both sound and, in paleo-Hebrew script, appearance). Elsewhere, however, LXX properly renders *miqrā*' with a noun.

work. LXX has *ergon latreuton* 'work for hire,' its ordinary equivalent for *məle(*')*ket* '*ăbôdâ* 'work of labor.' Whether in the LXX or its *Vorlage*, this is an assimilation to the formulaic Sabbath law (cf. Lev 23:7, 8, 21, 25, 35, 36; Num 28:18, 25, 26; 29:1, 12, 35).

may . . . be done. Major LXX witnesses (A, B, M) render the second *yē'āśe(h)* literally in the third person passive but treat the first *yē'āśe(h)* as if second person active: "you (pl.) will do." Other Greek witnesses, however, have a third person passive like MT. The simplest explanation is inner-Greek confusion between *poiēsetai* 'will be done' and *poiēsete* 'you will do,' with the former the original LXX (Wevers 1990: 177; 1992: 230–31).

†*what is eaten*. Syr "what a person eats" may paraphrase *'*šr y*'*kl* (*yō[*']*kal*) *kl npš* 'what any soul eats,' vs. MT '*šr y*'*kl* (*yē'ākēl*) *lkl npš* 'what is eaten *by* any soul.' Since haplography and dittography are equally likely amid this profusion of kaphs and lamedhs, either reading might be correct. LXX–Tg. *Neofiti I* "whatever is *done*" seems to have repeated *yē'āśe(h)* from earlier in the verse (breaking, incidentally, the pattern of fourteen repetitions of '*kl* 'eat' in 12:1–20; see NOTES to 12:11, 20). Tg. *Ps.-Jonathan* appears to combine MT with LXX–Tg. *Neofiti I*, paraphrasing: "what is done for eating"—which is what MT really means (see NOTE).

†*12:17. the Unleavened Bread*. We must choose among four readings: (a) *hmṣwt* (*hammaṣṣôt*) 'the Unleavened Bread' (MT); (b) the same consonants vocalized *hammiṣwōt 'the commandments' (R. Josiah *apud Mek. pisḥa*' 9; NEB); (c) *hmṣwh* 'the commandment' (Sam); (d) *hmṣwh hz'*t* 'this commandment' (LXX, unless LXX *Vorlage* = Sam). The first, a classic *lectio difficilior*, is almost certainly correct. But since we expect a commandment as the object of *šmr* 'observe,' *hammaṣṣôt* must be the festival, not the comestible (see NOTE). The ambiguity of *hmṣwt* (*hammaṣṣôt/hammiṣwōt*) stems from Persian-period orthographic developments (see Cross and Freedman 1952). The original text probably had an unambiguous *hmṣt (*hammaṣṣōt*).

SPECULATION: Since in all periods, *h* and *ḥ* are similar in appearance, possibly an original **ḥg hmṣ(w)t* 'the *Festival of* Unleavened Bread' became *hmṣ(w)t* by haplography (*ḥ . . . h*). But the posited variant is unattested.

I took. LXX "I will take" adopts the perspective of Moses' generation, removing the seeming anachronism (see NOTE). It does not reflect a variant *Vorlage*.

your brigades. LXX renders as a collective "your force"; cf. 6:26; 7:4; 12:41, 51.

†*And you will observe*. LXX reads "and you will do," i.e., **w'śytm*, against MT *ûš(ə)martem*. Here LXX may preserve the superior reading, since MT's

double *ûš(ə)martem* is suspect. It would be unusual, admittedly, to "do" a "day"; one rather "does" festivals or rituals (e.g., 12:48; 31:16; Num 9:4, 6, 13; Deut 16:10, etc.). This argues both for and against LXX. "Do" is difficult, but perhaps too difficult.

Initially, Sam *wšmrtm w'śytm* 'and you will observe and do' seems a conflation of MT and LXX. But Sam might be original, with LXX and MT having suffered respective haplographies by homoioarkton (*w-* . . . *w-*) and homoioteleuton (*-tm* . . . *-tm*). Note, too, that "observe" and "do" are often coordinated (e.g., Lev 19:37; 20:8, 22; 22:31; Deut 4:6; 7:12; 29:8, etc.). Still, the chance of double error seems remote. It is better to follow LXX or MT.

12:18. *In the first (month), on the fourteenth day of the month.* LXX paraphrases "*beginning* on the fourteenth day of the first month," in effect doubly rendering *bāri(')šōn* 'in the first.'

twenty-first. Instead of *hā'eḥād*, Sam has *'ḥd.*

12:19. *For.* Again, LXX ignores *kî*; cf. 12:15.

12:20. *dwellings.* Here LXX translates collectively, "dwelling"; contrast 10:23 (see TEXTUAL NOTE).

†12:21. *Israel's elders.* So MT and Sam; Syr has "the elders of Israel's *Sons.*" LXX MSS are divided between the readings of MT and Syr; I presume the *Vorlage* agreed with Syr and that some MSS were corrected to MT.

Which, then, is original: *zqny yśr'l* (MT, Sam) or *zqny bny yśr'l* (LXX, Syr)? While we ordinarily prefer the shorter text, *zqny* 'elders of' and *bny* 'sons of' end in the same consonants, raising the possibility of haplography. Moreover, the longer text finds a parallel in MT 4:29. Nevertheless, MT and Sam are almost certainly correct. We find systematic expansion of the phrase "Israel's elders" throughout non-Massoretic tradition; compare TEXTUAL NOTES to 3:16, 18 and 17:6.

††*Draw out, take.* LXX paraphrases: "going out, take," while Syr has "immediately take." Both Versions are apparently confused by the obscure *miškû* (see NOTE). They also seem to share the asyndetic reading of Sam: *mškw qḥw* 'draw out, take' (vs. MT *mškw wqḥw* 'draw out *and* take'). It is hard to say whether the conjunction *w-* is original, as dittography (*w > ww*) and haplography (*ww > w*) are equally likely to have occurred. But, since asyndeton is unusual, I follow Sam.

small cattle. LXX witnesses are divided between *probata* (plural) and *probaton* (singular) (cf. TEXTUAL NOTES to 12:6, 7, 9). Since Hebrew *ṣō(')n* is a collective singular, *probata* is really the more accurate rendering (see NOTE).

12:22. *take.* A Genizah fragment adds *lkm* 'for yourselves' (*BHS*), derived from *qəḥû lākem* 'take for yourselves' in the preceding verse.

and dip in the . . . blood. LXX "dipping *from* the blood" (*bapsantes apo tou haimatos*) may anticipate "from the blood" later in the verse. The sense is probably partitive: "apply *some of* the blood" (contrast Wevers 1990: 180). There is, in any case, no reason to doubt the accuracy of MT.

††*the sheep's/goat's.* Reading **haśśe(h)* with Syr. All other Versions have instead *'ăšer-bassap* 'that is in the bowl/threshold,' which thus appears twice in

the verse. While it is hard to see how MT could have generated Syr, one can easily imagine a scribe skipping from the first *dm* 'blood' to the second and automatically duplicating *'šr bsp* to produce MT et al.

to. Both times, Sam has *'al* 'upon,' vs. MT *'el* 'to.' MT is probably correct, Sam having conformed 12:22 to 12:7, 23, "on the lintel and *on* the two doorposts."

12:25. *observe this service.* Sam continues *bḥdš hzh* 'in this month,' an expansion inspired by 13:5.

†12:26. *What is this service to you?* LXX, Kenn 111 and Syr omit "to you," a shorter reading that might be original.

†12:27. *say.* LXX and Syr have "to them," apparently expanding.

bowed. Syr adds "to the Lord."

†12:28. *and Aaron.* Sam (Baillet 1982: 28) and many MT MSS (Kennicott 1776–80: 131) put the direct object marker *'et-* before Aaron's name, thus matching 12:50. If original, it could have dropped from MT by homoioarkton (*'t 'hrwn*) or simply because it was superfluous (cf. TEXTUAL NOTES to 12:1, 43, 50).

"And Aaron" is entirely missing from LXX[AB]. This shorter text is conceivably original, with other Versions expanding 12:28 to match 12:50, "as Yahweh commanded Moses and Aaron" (cf. also 12:1). In the absence of Hebrew evidence corroborating LXX, however, I follow MT.

†12:29. *to the firstborn.* Many witnesses to LXX, Sam and Syr insert a conjunction. While this is a ubiquitous phenomenon, here a contributory factor might have been the waw ending the prior word.

†*in the pit house.* While MT features the unusual expression *bəbêt habbôr*, LXX simply has "in the pit," as if reading **babbôr* (contrast OG Jer 44:16 [MT 37:16] *oikian tou lakkou* 'the house of the pit'). One might even regard **babbôr* as the superior text, assuming that a scribe inserted "house" (MT) to clarify the reference to a prison, rather than a natural pit. But it is also possible that *bbyt hbwr* (MT) collapsed into *bbwr* (LXX) by quasi-homoioarkton; note, too, the visual similarity of *bbwr* and *bkwr* 'firstborn,' occurring four times in the verse. Since no extant Hebrew MS supports the putative LXX *Vorlage*, I retain MT.

12:30. *he.* LXX omits the pronoun, most likely for ease of translation. On the function of *hû'*, see NOTE.

†*his slaves.* Standard MT has "*all* his slaves," matching "all Egypt." I have followed the shorter reading of LXX[B], Kenn 69 and Rossi 174: *wa'ăbādā(y)w*. Note that the parallels in 8:5, 7, 17, 25, 27; 9:14 lack "all"; it appears only in MT 7:29; 10:6 (see TEXTUAL NOTES).

in Egypt. So MT-Sam. Kenn 181 and Syr have "in *the land of* Egypt," while LXX has "in *all the land of* Egypt" (cf. Kenn 136). I have followed the short, standard MT.

dead one there. LXX and Syr, if not paraphrasing, seem to reflect **bô* 'in it,' vs. MT *šam* 'there.' Some MSS of *Tg. Onqelos* support MT, while others try to have it both ways: *lyt byt' tmn dl' hwh byh myt'* 'there was no house *there* that there was not a dead one *in it*' (cf. *Tg. Neofiti I: l' hwh tmn byt dy l' hwh tmn mytyn*). Most likely, MT is correct, and the other Versions are harmonizing with 12:7 (compare TEXTUAL NOTE to 12:7).

12:31. *he called.* LXX, Kenn 193 and Syr expand: "*Pharaoh* called."

by night. Syr "that night" may be a contamination, either during Syriac transmission or in the *Vorlage,* from v 30 *blly' hw/*bəlaylâ hû'* (see NOTE to v 30).

and said. LXX and Syr add "to them."

Rise, go. LXX "rise *and* go" perhaps reflects a *Vorlage* *qwmw wṣ'w,* vs. MT *qwmw ṣ'w.*

and go serve. LXX and Kenn 152 lack the initial conjunction, while LXX^B inserts a conjunction between the imperatives.

Yahweh. LXX expands: "your god."

†*according to your speaking.* Instead of MT *kədabberkem,* Sam has *kdbrykm* 'according to your *words.*' Either might be correct.

†12:32. *as you have spoken.* Lacking these words, LXX is arguably superior; perhaps MT has expanded by duplicating the sentiment, though not the syntax, of 12:31. Wevers (1990: 185), however, suggests that LXX has purposely omitted the phrase as redundant, while D. N. Freedman (privately) conjectures that LXX is imitating Gen 12:19; 24:51; 42:33 "take and go."

12:34. *dough pans.* Tg. Onqelos renders *miš'ărōtām* as *mwtr 'ṣwthwn* 'the remainder of their dough (pans),' presumably drawing an etymological connection between *miš'eret* and *š'r* 'remain, be left over.' (On repointing *miš'ărōtām* with a śin, see NOTE to 7:28.) Tg. Ps.-Jonathan, pursuing this approach further, paraphrases: "what was left over for them from the unleavened bread and bitter lettuce." On the renderings of LXX and Syr, see NOTE.

†*their robes.* While both MT and Sam read *śmltm,* 4QExod^c has a synonymous *ślmtm* (see also TEXTUAL NOTE to 22:25). As *śalmâ* is rarer than *śimlâ,* this might be the superior reading (cf. Sanderson 1986: 60–61).

upon their shoulder. Syr, for ease of translation, paraphrases: "and put under their shoulders."

††12:35. *asked.* Reading with 4QExod^c (*lectio brevior*). All other Versions and MSS add "of Egypt."

and gold objects. LXX omits "objects," presumably for ease of translation; cf. 3:22; 11:2. Some LXX MSS transpose the metals.

12:36. *the people's.* LXX has "*his* people's."

†12:38. *many foreigners.* Most Versions support MT *'ēreb rab.* It is possible, however, that we should read a single word *'ărabrāb* with some Sam MSS, especially if the "foreigners" are the group Num 11:4 calls *'spsp* 'riffraff' (Kethibh), similarly reduplicated (Geiger *apud* Ehrlich 1908: 308; Cassuto 1967: 147–48; cf. GKC §84^b n). MSS of Tg. Onqelos Num 11:4 in fact translate *'spsp* as *'ērabrəbîn,* again suggesting a reading *'rbrb* for Exod 12:38.

In this case, however, I hesitate to emend MT. Aramaic *'ērabrəbîn* is probably a conflation of *rabrəbîn* 'great ones' and *'irbûbîn* 'mixtures,' both also attested for Tg. Onqelos Num 11:4 (note, too, *Fragmentary Targum* Exod 12:38 *'rbrwbyn*). And there is no certain example of *'ărabrāb* in Hebrew, while Jer 50:37; Neh 13:3 use *'ēreb* to describe gentiles (also perhaps 1 Kgs 10:15; Jer 25:24).

very heavy cattle. LXX, Kenn 69, 84, 129, 193, Rossi 592, 597, Syr and Tg. Ps.-Jonathan prefix "and."

†12:39. *they had been expelled from Egypt.* So MT (*gōrəšû mimmiṣrayim*). 2QExodᵃ, LXX, Sam and Syr reflect a different division and vocalization of *gršmmṣrym*: **gērəšûm miṣrayim* 'Egypt/the Egyptians had expelled them.' Either could be original, but MT is somewhat suspect, since *mimmiṣrayim* occurs twice in the verse.

†12:40. *Israel's Sons.* Sam and LXX add "and their fathers" (*w'btm*), referring to the Patriarchal era. See following TEXTUAL NOTE.

†*in Egypt.* 4QExodᵇ and some Syr MSS have "in *the land of* Egypt," while other Syr MSS support MT. This is a minor matter. More serious is the LXX variant "in the land of Egypt *and in the land of Canaan,*" paralleled by Sam's more logical "*in the land of Canaan and* in the land of Egypt" (cf. also Kenn 651, "in Egypt *and in the land of Canaan and in the land of Goshen*"); see also previous TEXTUAL NOTE. The tradition that 430 years is the duration from Abraham to Moses also appears in Jubilees; *Bib. Ant.* 9:3; Demetrius the Chronographer; the Qumran Testaments of Levi and Qohat; the Vision of Amram (Grelot 1975); Josephus *Ant.* 2.318 (contrast *Ap.* 1.299); Gal 3:17; *Tg. Ps.-Jonathan*; *Exod. Rab.* 18:11, and various early church historians (see Dillmann 1880: 120–21). The opinion of some commentators notwithstanding (e.g., Johnson 1969: 33–34), the shorter MT is preferable. One can easily envision the pristine text undergoing progressive expansion, while it is harder to account for the MT as abbreviated (Kreuzer 1991). See further under NOTE.

thirty . . . and four hundred. Here and in v 41, LXXᴮ has a variant "four hundred, thirty-*five,*" perhaps reflecting a particular scribe's or group's understanding of biblical chronology (see Kreuzer 1991: 258).

12:41. *thirty . . . and four hundred.* See previous TEXTUAL NOTE.

†*and it happened on the bone of this day.* The phrase is missing in LXX, perhaps rightly, assuming it was borrowed from 12:51 in MT et al. On the other hand, LXX may have suffered haplography by homoioteleuton (*šnh . . . hzh*).

†*from the land of Egypt.* Sam and LXX put *lylh* 'night' at the end of v 41, whereas in MT *lyl* 'night of' begins v 42. We are thus presented with variants "all Yahweh's brigades went out from the land of Egypt *by night.* It is an observance . . ." (Sam; LXX) and "all Yahweh's brigades went out from the land of Egypt. It is a *night of* observance . . ." (MT). Either is possible, although Sam and LXX may be harmonizing with Deut 16:1 (see below). (On the implications for the timing of the Hebrews' departure, see next TEXTUAL NOTE and REDACTION ANALYSIS.)

†12:42. *It is a night of observance.* So MT. Sam and LXX have "it is an observance," joining "night" to the preceding verse (see previous TEXTUAL NOTE). It is difficult to choose between these readings. (A third, remote possibility is that the original had a double **lylh lyl* and that all surviving versions are defective.) However we judge, we must take into account the parallel in Deut 16:1, "In the month of the New Grain, Yahweh your deity took you out from Egypt *at night* (*laylâ*)." Either Sam and LXX have harmonized 12:41–42 with Deut 16:1, or MT has modified 12:41–42 to fit E's implication that the Hebrews spent the night at home (12:22). See further under REDACTION ANALYSIS.

†12:43. *and Aaron*. Sam, Kenn 84, 111, 150, 206, 325, 674, Rossi 6, 10 (first hand), 16, 18 (first hand), 198, 407, 611, Syr and *Tgs*. *Onqelos* and *Ps.-Jonathan* read "and *to* Aaron" (*w'l 'hrn*), which, if original, might have become *w'hrn* (MT) either by parablepsis or in the interests of concision (cf. TEXTUAL NOTES to 12:1, 28, 50). LXX also adds "saying," possibly reflecting **l'mr*.

†12:44. *And any man's slave, a purchase by silver*. All textual witnesses except XQPhyl1, Kenn 89, Rossi 419 and some Sam MSS begin v 44 with the conjunction *w*. Since the previous verse ends in *w*, either dittography (*w* > *ww*) or haplography (*ww* > *w*) may have occurred. But given the unusualness of asyndeton, on the one hand, and the lack of conjunctions throughout vv 43–49, on the other, XQPhyl1 et al. may indeed preserve the original text (cf. TEXTUAL NOTE to 12:48).

LXX and XQPhyl1 read "any man's slave *and* a purchase by silver" (**w'bd 'yš wmqnt ksp*). The conjunction was probably added to break up a slightly awkward and ambiguous phrase (see NOTE).

Sam *kspw* 'his silver' (= 4QPhyl1 *kśpw*) also skirts the potential grammatical ambiguity of MT, and may betray the influence of Gen 17:23, *yəlîdê bêtô wə-* . . . *miqnat kaspô* 'the [slaves] born of his house and . . . the purchase by his silver.' *Kspw* could also be the result of simple dittography, since the next word begins in *w*. But we cannot eliminate the possibility that Sam is correct and MT etc. haplographic.

and you will circumcise him. These words are missing from 4QPhyl1, probably due to homoioteleuton between *kspw* 'his money' (see previous TEXTUAL NOTE) and *'tw* 'him.'

12:46. *do not*. Kenn 75, XQPhyl1, Syr and many LXX MSS prefix "and."

†*take*. LXX, Sam, XQPhyl1 and Syr have the plural imperative *tôṣî'û*, vs. MT *tôṣî'*. The discrepancy is due to a shift, not apparent in English translation, between commands in the singular (12:44) and the plural (12:46). Either version could be original, but MT is more likely; see TEXTUAL NOTE to 12:48.

from the house. XQPhyl1 has a nonsensical *mn hbyth* 'from to the house.' Doubtless, the scribe was influenced by the following *ḥwṣh* 'to the outside.'

†*to the outside*. For MT *ḥûṣâ*, Sam has a synonymous *hḥwṣh* and 4QDt¹ has *lḥwṣ* (Duncan 1992: 211). Many LXX witnesses continue, "and do not leave any of the flesh until the morning," borrowing from LXX Lev 22:30 (cf. Exod 12:10; Num 9:12).

12:47. *Israel's*. Various exemplars of MT and the Targumim (de Rossi 1784–85: 58), LXX and some Syr MSS read "Israel's Sons'"; cf. TEXTUAL NOTES to 12:3, 6.

12:48. *And if*. 4QPhyl1 omits the conjunction. Since v 47 ends in *w*, both haplography and dittography are theoretically possible—or the phylactery text may simply have been written from memory.

with you. "You" is singular in standard MT (*'ittəkā*), plural (*'tkm[h]*) in 4QExod^c, 4QDt¹, 4QPhyl1, XQPhyl1, Sam, LXX, Syr, *Tg. Neofiti I* and some MSS of MT and *Tg. Onqelos* (de Rossi 1784–85: 58). In fact, apart from "circumcise" (v 12:44), all the second person forms in these Versions are plural.

Since MT varies between singular and plural (*ûmaltā* . . . *tôṣî'* . . . *tišbərû* . . . *'ittəkā* . . . *bətôkəkem*), most likely the other witnesses have leveled an originally uneven text.

†*But.* Kenn 181, 674, XQPhyl1 and LXX lack the conjunction, perhaps rightly, paralleling the other commands in 12:45-47 (cf. NOTE to 12:44).

12:49. *will be.* The verb *yihye(h)* is masculine in form, although *tôrâ* is feminine; contrast 13:9. 4QPhylM in fact reads feminine *thyh* in 12:49, but is probably a secondary correction. On gender incongruence in Hebrew, see Levi (1987).

†12:50. *all.* So MT. *Kol* 'all' is absent from 4QPhylA, Kenn 18, 150, Rossi 10, 19, 340, 483, 503, 588, 643, 699, LXX and a Genizah fragment (*apud BHS*), thus matching v 28. This shorter reading is conceivably original (but see NOTE). Kenn 84, 129 and Rossi 404, 440, 609, however, replace *kol* with *kēn* 'thus,' creating a mirror effect with the end of the verse.

as. Rossi 198 reads *kl 'šr 'all that'* (vs. MT *ka'ăšer* 'as'); XQPhyl1 expands *kkl 'šr* 'as *all* that' (cf. Esth 3:12; 8:9), while Kenn 84 has a nonsensical conflation *kkl k'šr.*

and Aaron. A Genizah MS lacks *'et* (cf. TEXTUAL NOTES to vv 1, 28, 43). Most LXX witnesses add a clarifying "toward *(pros)* them [Israel]"—i.e., God's command was transmitted to Israel through Moses and Aaron.

12:51. *in their brigades.* Syr "*all* their brigades," if not a paraphrase, might reflect **kl ṣb'tm* (cf. 12:41), rather than MT *'l ṣb'tm.* So also 6:26.

13:2. *firstborn, loosening.* LXX[A] inserts a conjunction between the nouns.

every womb. Kenn 80, 111 and Rossi 699 omit "every."

†13:3. *Remember.* Where MT uses the infinitive absolute *zkwr*, Sam has the plural imperative *zkrw.* It is hard to say which is original. Infinitives absolute are generally rarer than imperatives, but for this verb the opposite is true.

when you went out. MT and 4QExod[c] have a slightly unusual *'ăšer yəṣā(')tem.* Sam, 4QPhyl[A],I,M, the LXX *Vorlage* and some MSS of Syr feature more typical syntax: *'ăšer yəṣā(')tem bô* 'that you went out *in it.*'

Egypt. Sam, 4QPhylA,M, 4QExod[c], 4QPhyl1 (sublinear correction) and some MSS of LXX and of Syr read "*the land of* Egypt."

†*from a slaves' house.* M*byt 'bdym* is missing from 4QExod[c]. While often we prefer the shorter text, in this case the phrase probably dropped by homoioteleuton after *mṣrym* 'Egypt' (in all periods, -*rym* and -*dym* would have been virtually indistinguishable; cf. the Versions on 1 Sam 2:27).

arm strength. LXX and Syr "strong hand" might reflect a variant **bəyād ḥăzāqâ* (cf. 3:19; 6:1; 13:9; 32:11, etc.) but is more likely periphrastic (also in 13:14, 16).

†13:4. *Today you.* With MT and LXX. By inserting "and" before "you" (*w'tm*), Sam joins "today" to 13:3: "anything leavened may not be eaten today."

13:5. *Yahweh.* LXX, 4QExod[c], 4QDt[j], 4QPhylM,R, Sam, Kenn 107, Rossi 405, 668 and some MSS of *Tg. Ps.-Jonathan* add "your deity," probably an expansion (see TEXTUAL NOTES to 12:31 and 13:8, 9, 11). Here, however, it is barely possible that *'ĕlōhe(y)kā* dropped by homoioarkton with *'el* 'to' (also in 13:11).

the land. 4QPhylC has an ungrammatical *h'rṣ,* which often follows *'el* but cannot do so here (cf. 6:8; 12:25, etc.).

You . . . your . . . you. Throughout 13:5–8, the second person pronouns are singular in MT-Sam-LXX, but plural in most Syr MSS. Syr presumably harmonizes with 13:3–4, where the second persons are plural. Syr finally changes to the singular in v 9.

†*Hittite . . . Jebusite.* As always, the list of pre-Israelite Canaanite nations exhibits various permutations in the Versions, in regard to order and number of peoples and the presence or absence of "and" (see, provisionally, O'Connell 1984). Kenn 18, 84, 152, 260, 264 and early printed Bibles (Ginsburg 1894: 122) basically support standard MT, but lack "and" before "the Hittite" (Kenn 18 also omits "and" before "the Amorite"). 4QPhylI,R, to the extent preserved, also resemble MT in sequence, but lack any conjunctions except before the final "Jebusite." Syr agrees with MT, but adds "and the Perizzite" at the end. Sam reads "the Canaanite, the Hittite and the Amorite and the Perizzite and the Girgashite and the Hivvite and the Jebusite." 4QExod^c and 4QPhylA omit all conjunctions; the former lacks "the Hivvite," and the latter includes "the Girgashite." 4QPhylA and 4QPhylM put the Perizzites after the Amorites, and the Girgashites after the Jebusites (cf. 4QDt^i). 4QPhylM has a conjunction only before the Hivvites. The fragmentary 4QPhylQ mentions the Perizzites, but the context is lost. LXX witnesses add the Girgashites and Perizzites in various places and otherwise differ from MT and Sam in the order of nations.

Ordinarily, I would adopt the shortest reading, in this case MT minus conjunctions. Since, however, opportunities for parablepsis abound, a longer form might be original. The quest for an *Ur*-text underlying all versions of the catalog is, in any case, futile. My translation follows standard MT.

which. Instead of MT-Sam *'ăšer,* Syr seems to reflect **ka'ăšer* 'as,' the reading of 4QExod^c, 4QDt^i, 4QPhylM and a Genizah fragment (*apud BHS*).

††13:6. *Six.* I read *šēšet* 'six' with 4QPhylE,I,M,Q,R, Sam and LXX. Other Versions, including MT, 4QpaleoExod^m and 8QPhyl, have *šib'at* 'seven.'

Many biblical passages command, "For six days do such-and-such, and on the seventh day do so-and-so" (16:26; 20:9–10; 23:12; 31:15; 34:21; 35:2; Lev 23:3; Deut 5:13–14; 16:8; Josh 6:3–4). Other texts narrate, "For six days such-and-such happened, and on the seventh day so-and-so happened" 20:11; 24:16; 31:17; Josh 6:14–15). Thus, on the one hand, MT "seven" may be correct, and Sam-LXX may have harmonized 13:6 with the more common idiom, and especially with Deut 16:8, "*Six* days you will eat unleavened bread, and on the seventh day will be a cessation (*'ăṣeret*) for Yahweh." But I think it more likely that MT replaced "six" and "seven" because of 13:7, "Unleavened bread you will eat for the *seven* days"; cf. also 12:15; 23:15; 34:18; Deut 16:3. That is, I assume that the original text prescribed eating unleavened bread for six days plus a day (13:6), for a total of seven (13:7), as in Deut 16:3, 8. (An analogous error occurred in Gen 2:2, with MT reading "seventh day" and LXX, Sam and Syr more plausibly reading "sixth day.")

you will eat. The verb is singular in MT, plural in LXX, 4QPhylM and Syr. In general, I consider singulars more original than plurals. The ancient translations tend to pluralize Hebrew collectives.

†† 13:7. *Unleavened bread you will eat.* MT *maṣṣôt yēʾākēl* 'unleavened bread will be eaten,' though paralleled in Ezek 45:21, is grammatically difficult: the subject is feminine plural and the verb masculine singular. LXX and Syr, however, have a plural, active command "you will eat," as if reading **tʾklw* (plural) or, more likely, **tʾkl* (collective singular). If so, a plene writing **mṣwt twʾkl* may have produced MT *mṣwt yʾkl* by haplography (*tt > t*) and waw-yodh confusion (cf. Cross 1961a; Qimron 1972). I reconstruct **maṣṣôt tō(ʾ)kal*, the basis for my translation.

†*and* (first time). Absent in Sam (Baillet 1982: 29), LXX, 4QPhylQ, Kenn 18, 69, 80, 150, 674, Rossi 262 and 669.

anything leavened may not be seen for you. Most Syr MSS replace "for you (singular)" with "among you (plural)," as if reading **bākem* for *lǝkā*. But this is probably paraphrase (cf. TEXTUAL NOTE to 13:5 "you . . . your . . . you").

†*leaven may not be seen for you.* MT "may not be seen . . . may not be seen" is suspiciously redundant. LXX has a superficially attractive variant, "there will be no leaven for you" (on Syr, see below). We might infer that the original had **yihye(h)* 'will (not) be,' with MT duplicating *yērāʾe(h)* 'may (not) be seen' from earlier in the verse. But the equivalent command in Deut 16:4 also features *yērāʾe(h)*, confirming MT Exod 13:7. Wevers's (1990: 197) judgment that LXX 13:7 is a deliberate alteration for variety's sake is sound.

SPECULATION: Still, MT remains peculiarly repetitive. I would surmise that it conflates two variants: (a) "anything leavened (*ḥāmēṣ*) may not be seen for you" and (b) "leaven (*śǝʾōr*) may not be seen for you." Which of these might be original, however, is hard to say. That Deut 16:4 refers only to "leaven" might support (b) as the older variant. But one could alternatively argue that the pristine text of 13:7 referred only to *ḥāmēṣ* and that the verse was later expanded to match Deut 16:4. The prime support for such an argument would be Syr, which lacks entirely the clause with *śǝʾōr*. But Syr has probably suffered parablepsis from *ḥmîrāʾ* 'leavened thing' to *ḥmîʿāʾ* 'leaven' (cf. TEXTUAL NOTE to 12:15).

your territory. "Your" is singular in MT and other Versions, plural in Syr; see TEXTUAL NOTE to 13:5.

13:8. *Yahweh did for me.* 4QPhylM modifies the word order: *ʿśh ly yhwh*, perhaps the result of writing from memory. LXX adds "Lord, *the* God"; cf. TEXTUAL NOTE to 13:5 "Yahweh."

Egypt. Some LXX witnesses read "*the land of* Egypt," presumably an expansion. In general, LXX is at pains to distinguish the land of Egypt from the Egyptians (D. N. Freedman, privately).

13:9. *And it will be.* Here and in 13:16, Sam has *whyw* 'and *they* will be.' The plural may refer to the wearing of phylacteries (see NOTE). Or it might simply be an assimilation to "sign . . . and . . . memorial."

your arm. Rossi 265, XQPhyll and 4QPhylB,C,E,I,M,R read "your arms" (*ydyk[h]*), as does Sam (*ydyk*) both here and in 13:16. This is probably an assimilation to '*ynyk* 'your eyes.' Cf. TEXTUAL NOTES to 12:11 and 13:16.

with a strong arm. 4QPhylC has "with arm strength" (*bḥwzq yd*), as in MT 13:14.

Yahweh (second time). Some LXX MSS expand: "the Lord the/your God"; see TEXTUAL NOTE to 13:5 "Yahweh."

13:10. *observe.* The command is singular in MT, plural in LXX. LXX, or its *Vorlage*, is probably influenced by the plural injunctions to "observe" in 12:17, 24, 25.

this rule. Syr adds "and this law," as if reading **wə'et-hattôrâ hazzō(')t.* This is presumably a secondary expansion, although haplography (*hazzō[']t . . . hazzō[']t*) in the other Versions remains a remote possibility.

at its occasion. LXX[B] omits this expression entirely, while other LXX witnesses paraphrase MT: *kata kairous hōrōn* 'according to the seasons' times.'

13:11. *Yahweh.* Sam, LXX and Kenn 388 add "your God." See TEXTUAL NOTE to 13:5.

as. For standard MT *ka'ăšer* 'as,' Kenn 75 and Rossi 18, 669 read *'ăšer* 'which.'

††*to your fathers.* So LXX; MT has *ləkā wəla'ăbōte(y)kā* 'to you *and* to your fathers.' Wevers (1990: 199) views LXX as a pedantic correction of the Hebrew, in consideration of the fact that the promises were made to the Patriarchs alone. But ordinarily we prefer the shorter text, in this case LXX. Moreover, all other references to God's oath to the fathers support LXX (13:5; Num 11:12; 14:23; Deut 1:8, etc.). These parallels may make MT attractively difficult, but to my mind they make it too difficult. I think MT inserted *ləkā wə-* 'to you and' both because *ləkā* appears later in the verse and because we have several cases of Yahweh "giving" (but not "promising") the land "to you and to your fathers" or "to us and to our fathers" (Num 20:15; Jer 7:14; 23:39; 24:10; 25:5; 35:15; 2 Chr 6:25).

and gives it. Some LXX MSS have "and *I* will give it," ending the sentence in 13:11. MT, in contrast, continues the utterance into 13:12.

13:12. *loosening of the womb.* Before this phrase, Syr inserts "firstborn," as if reading **bəkôr peṭer.* This is most likely an expansion based on 13:2 (see also TEXTUAL NOTE to 13:13). LXX, after "*loosening* of the womb," adds "the males," who are thus mentioned twice in the verse. This is probably a harmonization with 13:15.

†*and each loosening, animal spawn.* LXX has "each that opens *the womb, from the herds or among your cattle*" (see Wevers 1990: 200). The lack of an initial conjunction might be a superior short reading (= Kenn 84, 674). As for the rest of the phrase, LXX may expand a *Vorlage* reading *šgr bbhmh 'spawn among the animals' with 4QPhylC,G and 4QMezG (cf. MT 13:2).

8QPhyl has a much shorter reading than MT or LXX, probably haplographic: *wh'brt kl pṭr rḥm [bhmh/bbhmh] 'šr yhyh lk hzkrym lyhwh* 'then you will make each *loosening* of the womb [of/among the animals] that you may have, the males, pass over to Yahweh.' Assuming the restoration is correct, it is easy to imagine a scribe's eye skipping from *(b)bhmh* to *bhmh*, thereby omitting *wkl pṭr šgr*. (This argument is circular, however, since *(b)bhmh* has been reconstructed precisely to account for such an error.)

SPECULATION: MT is suspiciously redundant. I suspect that the second *peṭer* 'loosening' is a secondary gloss on *šeger* 'spawn,' and that the original text was *wǝhaʿăbartā kol-peṭer reḥem lǝyahwe(h) wǝkol-šeger bǝhēmâ . . .* 'You must make each *loosening* of the womb pass over to Yahweh, and each animal spawn . . .' (see NOTE). Since this is hypothetical, however, my translation follows MT.

that may be for you. The verb is singular in MT, plural in Sam (*yhyw*).

†*to Yahweh.* LXX supplements the last clause of 13:12 with a singular command to "sanctify" (*hagiazeis*), the direct object being "each that opens the womb . . . the males." Combined with the lack of an internal conjunction (see previous TEXTUAL NOTE), this divides v 12 into two independent clauses: "And make each that opens the womb pass over . . . to the Lord. Each that opens the womb . . . the males, you must consecrate to the Lord." *Tgs. Onqelos* and *Ps.-Jonathan* similarly have *taqdēš* 'you must sanctify' plus the object *dikrîn* 'males.' Most likely, LXX and *Tgs.* have expanded after 13:2; Num 3:13; 8:17; Deut 15:19, which mention sanctification (*qiddēš/hiqdîš*) of the firstborn. We might alternatively discern a double rendering of *wǝhaʿăbartā* as both "make pass" and "sanctify." In any case, MT is probably correct. But we should note a remote possibility: the original had a verb, *tzkr/hzkr* 'consecrate as male,' corrupted into *hzkrym* in MT (cf. TEXTUAL NOTE to 34:19). If so, LXX conflates the variants *tzkr/hzkr* and *hzkrym*.

†13:13. *But each loosening of an ass . . . redeem.* LXX and Kenn 129 lack the initial conjunction, perhaps rightly. LXX and *Tgs. Neofiti I* and *Ps.-Jonathan* read "*loosening* of an ass's *womb*"; cf. "*loosening* of the womb" in 13:2, 12, 15, etc. The short MT is likely to be original, with the other Versions paraphrasing (but see below).

Syr has an interesting variant, "but every firstborn male, *loosening* of the womb of cattle, you will redeem," the result of scribal error and conscious expansion. The Syr *Vorlage* must have been identical to MT, save that *ḥmr* 'ass' had been miswritten (or misread) as *rḥm* 'womb,' which follows *pṭr* 'loosening' in 13:2, 12, 15; 34:19; Num 18:15; Ezek 20:26. When the Hebrew was rendered into Syriac, the expressions *peṭer reḥem*, *peṭer šeger* and *peṭer ḥămōr* all came out as *ptḥ rḥm* 'opening the womb.' Then, since *rḥmʾ dbʿyrʾ* 'the womb of cattle' appeared in 13:12, a scribe inserted *dbʿyr* 'of cattle' into v 13 as well. The reference to the "male" is also inspired by 13:12, 15. This complex history in turn raises the possibility that "*loosening* of an ass's womb" (LXX, *Tgs. Neofiti I* and *Ps.-Jonathan*) is not free paraphrase but accurately renders a *Vorlage* *pṭr rḥm ḥmr*. (It is even possible that this is original and that *rḥm ḥmr* underwent haplography in both MT [dropping *rḥm*] and Syr [dropping *ḥmr*].)

or. 4QPhylC and Kenn 84 lack the conjunction *w-*.

if you do not redeem. Sam, 4QMezG and 4QPhylC supply the implicit object: *tpdnw* 'redeem *it*.'

neck. The LXX interpretation is unexpected: "exchange it (for money)." Wevers (1990: 201) discerns an attempt to minimize the destructiveness mandated in the Hebrew (see NOTE). Perhaps, however, the translator read, not *ʿrp*, but **ʿrb* 'pledge, exchange.' When the same command appears in 34:20, LXX translates "estimate," now apparently reading *ʿrk* (cf. Lev 27:27; Num 18:16) (in the square script, *p*, *k* and *b* all look quite similar). In Deut 21:4, 6, however, LXX translates *ʿrp* as *neurokopeō* 'hamstring,' which is somewhat closer to the correct meaning, "break the neck."

†*and.* The conjunction *w-* is absent in LXX and Kenn 196, perhaps rightly; cf. MT 34:20 (see TEXTUAL NOTE). Because the previous word ends in waw, dittography (*w > ww*) and haplography (*ww > w*) are both possible.

13:14. *And it will happen, when.* While standard MT has *wəhāyâ kî*, Syr (*wkad* 'and when') conceivably reflects **wəkî*, the reading of a Genizah fragment (*apud BHS*). But Syr also has *wkad* for *wəhāyâ kî* in 13:11, 15, where there is no evidence for a Hebrew variant.

tomorrow. LXX paraphrases: "after these things." This is unlikely to reflect a variant *Vorlage*, but rather emphasizes that "tomorrow" is used figuratively. (Perhaps, too, LXX is engaging in folk etymology, deriving *māḥār* 'tomorrow' from *ʾaḥar* 'after.') Elsewhere, the Greek translates *māḥār* literally, even when used metaphorically (Deut 6:20; Josh 4:6; 22:24, 27, 28).

saying. Syr adds "to you."

to him. 4QPhylC has a synonymous *lw* for MT *ʾlyw*.

With. 4QPhylC,[F],H insert *ky* 'for,' as in 13:16.

arm strength. LXX and Syr render, "strong hand"; see TEXTUAL NOTES to 13:3, 16.

Egypt. LXX has "*the land of* Egypt."

†13:15. *Yahweh killed.* LXX has a shorter, more difficult reading: "*he* killed." If LXX is original, then MT "Yahweh killed" is a clarifying expansion. In the absence of Hebrew evidence corroborating LXX, however, I have translated after MT.

†*and to.* "And" is absent in LXX, Sam, 4QPhylC, Kenn 9, 125, 200 and even Syr MS 5b1, despite its strong revision toward MT.

I sacrifice. All MT MSS read *ʾănî zōbēaḥ*, but 4QPhylH reverses the two words. 4QExod^d and 4QPhylB,C support the MT word order, but have a synonymous *ʾn(w)ky* for MT *ʾănî* 'I.'

each loosening of the womb. LXX^B inserts "every firstborn," presumably on the basis of 13:2 (cf. Syr in 13:12; see TEXTUAL NOTE). And 4QPhylB,C,H and some Sam MSS add a conjunction: *wkl pṭr rḥm* '*and* each loosening of the womb,' harmonizing the two *kl*s in v 15b.

each firstborn of my sons. Sam and 4QPhylB,C read *wkl bkwr 'dm bbny* 'and each *human* firstborn among my sons,' probably assimilating to 13:13.

†13:16. *And it will be.* Here, as in 13:9 (see TEXTUAL NOTE), Sam has "and *they* will be." Moreover, Sam, Kenn 193, 686, 4QPhylB,C,[H] and Syr add *lk(h)* 'for you.' While this could be a harmonization with 13:9, that the next word (*l'wt*) also begins with lamedh raises the possibility of haplography in MT. I follow MT, however.

your arm. Sam and 4QPhylB,C,H read *ydyk(h)* 'your arms' (cf. TEXTUAL NOTE to 13:9). But 8QPhyl *ydkh* 'your arm' supports MT *yādəkâ*.

††*circlet.* Reading **ṭôṭepet* (vs. MT *ṭôṭāpōt* 'circlets'); see Tigay (1982a: 893; 1982b). Although we find the plural *ṭṭpwt* in 4QExod^d, the word is consistently spelled *ṭwṭpt* in the Qumran phylacteries and mezuzoth, where we would expect the plural to be **ṭwṭpwt* (Milik 1977: 38). Note, too, that *b. Sanh.* 4b; *Menaḥ.* 34b take the consonants *ṭwṭpt* as singular in Exod 13:16; Deut 6:8 (also *Mek. pishā'* 17). The MT plural *ṭôṭāpōt* was probably created unconsciously in order to rhyme with the parallel *'ôt* 'sign.' (Since the verse is inscribed on phylacteries, which may be written by memory, corruptions of this sort are not surprising.)

arm strength. LXX and Syr paraphrase, "strong hand," this time supported by Kenn 181 *yad ḥăzāqâ* (vs. MT *ḥōzeq yād*) (cf. 13:3, 14).

†*took us out.* LXX, Sam and Syr have a significant variant, *hwṣy'k* 'took *you* out,' vs. MT *hôṣî'ānû* 'took *us* out.' Since both words are found earlier in the chapter—*hôṣî'ānû* in 13:14, *hôṣî'ăkā* in 13:9—either could be a harmonization. The real question is where the father's response to his son ends. If, as I assume, the quotation runs through 13:16, then it makes sense for the father to speak in the first person ("took *us* out"), as in 13:14–15. If, however, the father's answer ends in 13:15, and 13:16 is the legislator's recapitulation of 13:9, then *hôṣî'ăkā* 'took you out' is likely original. (It is also barely possible that the father's words continue in 13:16, and that LXX, Sam and Syr are nevertheless correct, assuming that the son is instructed to regard himself as having participated in the Exodus [cf. Deut 29:13–14 and the Passover Haggadah].)

SOURCE ANALYSIS

Exod 12:1–13:16 is primarily an amalgam of P and one other source, most likely E. The clearest evidence of multiple authorship is the redundancy of 12:1–13 and 21–27: each passage commands the Israelites to select a sheep or goat for the paschal meal and to dab protective blood on the door frame. Exod 12:15–19 and 13:3–9 manifest further redundancy, each ordaining the Festival of Unleavened Bread. The following discussion will deal first with the sections ascribed to P and the related R stratum; then we shall turn to JE. (For a very different microanalysis of this and other passages treating the *Pesaḥ*, see Laaf 1970; on Knohl's [1987, 1995] theory that 12:1–20, 43–49 derive from a "Holiness School," see APPENDIX A, vol. II).

Many expressions from 12:1–20, 40–51 appear in Driver's (1891: 133–34) catalog of Priestly language: *ʿēdâ* 'congregation' (vv 3, 6, 19, 47), *bêt-ʾābōt* 'fathers'-house' (v 3), *bên hāʿarbāyim* 'between the two evenings' (v 6), *wǝnikrǝtâ hannepeš hahî* 'that *soul* will be cut off' (vv 15, 19), *ṣǝbāʾōt* 'brigades' (vv 17, 41, 51), *ʿeṣem hayyôm hazze(h)* 'the *bone* of this day' (vv 17, 41, 51), *lǝdōrōt* 'to ages' (vv 17, 42), *bǝkol-môšābōt* 'in all dwellings' (v 20), *miqnâ* 'purchase' (v 44; compare esp. Gen 17:13 [Ehrlich 1908: 310]) and *tôšāb* 'resident' (v 45). Another Priestly cliché is *beʿāśōr laḥōdeš (hazze[h])* 'on the tenth of (this) month' (v 3). Also characteristic of P, Ezekiel and the postexilic prophets is referring to months by ordinal number alone ("in the first," v 18). *Ḥuqqat ʿōlām* 'eternal rule' (vv 14, 17), too, is Priestly, as are *miqrāʾ qōdeš* 'calling of holiness' (v 16), *ʾezrāḥ* 'native' (vv 19, 48) and "according to what he eats" (v 4). The ritual detail in vv 3–20, 43–49 is typically (but not exclusively) Priestly, as is the precise chronology of vv 2–3, 40–41. (The redundancy of vv 40–41 might suggest an internal source break, but compare Deut 9:9, 11; Judg 11:38–39; Isa 23:15; Ezek 29:12–13.)

We also find in 12:1–13:16 a few verses pertaining to the R stratum. First, 12:24 is somewhat redundant with v 25 (P) and employs language reminiscent of but not identical to P (cf. 29:28; 30:21; Lev 6:11, 15; 7:34; 10:13–15; 24:9; Num 18:8, 11, 19). Since it falls within a JE context, I would assign 12:24 to the Redactor (see further NOTE).

Exod 13:10 is similar to 12:24 in both diction (*šāmar* 'observe,' *ḥōq/ḥuqqâ* 'rule') and transitional function. I infer that it, too, is R. Exod 12:28 is also probably Redactorial, since it concludes an E section, yet is Priestly in style (cf. Gen 50:12; Exod 7:10, 20; 39:32; Num 1:54; 2:34; 5:4; Deut 34:9). (In fact, 12:28 may be both P and R—i.e., Priestly matter shifted during editing from its proper position after 12:17a or 12:20.) Exod 12:14 is another candidate for Redactorial authorship, but here I am less certain. The hortatory tone recalls 12:17b, 24; 13:10, suggesting R. But the parallelism with v 13, *wǝhāyâ haddām . . . wǝhāyâ hayyôm* 'and the blood will be . . . and this day will be,' might indicate that both verses are Priestly (cf. Jacob 1992: 313). Exod 12:18–20 may also be R, since it is somewhat redundant with 12:15 (P). But I rather take vv 18–20 as the Priestly Writer's own amplification of v 15 (see NOTES).

The syntax of 12:42 is peculiar, whether one reads with MT or with Sam-LXX (see TEXTUAL NOTE): "It is a (night of) observance for Yahweh, as he takes them out from the land of Egypt; it, this night, is for Yahweh an observance for all Israel's Sons *to their ages*." The awkward *hûʾ hallaylâ hazze(h)* 'it, this night' is reminiscent of other Redactorial texts: "That (*hûʾ*) is Aaron and Moses . . . they (*hēm*) are the speakers to Pharaoh, Egypt's king, to take Israel's Sons out from Egypt; that (*hûʾ*) is Moses and Aaron" (6:26–27); "That (*hûʾ*) is Dathan and Abiram" (Num 26:9b). Thus, even though the context is Priestly, it is likely that 12:42 is Redactorial. Like 12:14, 17b, 24; 13:10, Exod 12:42 enjoins observance of the festival upon future generations.

Exod 12:43–51 presents a special problem. The vocabulary is essentially Priestly (compare v 50 to 12:28 and v 51 to 7:4; 12:17, 41). But the terse style is not at all Priestly. The *Wiederaufnahme* (resumptive repetition) in v 51 (cf. 12:28, 41–42) strengthens our impression that the framed material, the *"Pesaḥ Rule,"* is an insertion (Beegle 1972: 136; Fox 1986: 71; on *Wiederaufnahme*, see Kuhl 1952). But by whom and from where? While it is possible that vv 43–51 were incorporated by the Redactor (Scharbert 1989: 54), the more likely culprit is the Priestly Writer himself, who explicitly quotes the "Rule" in Num 9:12–14. It may seem odd that the "Rule" should be separated from P's other paschal instructions, but, when we remove JE, 12:43 follows closely upon 12:20.

The *"Pesaḥ* Rule" is probably based upon an independent source older than P, containing seven apodictic (direct) commands expanded in casuistic ("if . . . then") style with a strong Priestly cast (cf. Cassuto 1967: 150). These additions may be the work of the Priestly Writer himself, or an older author in his tradition (for the phenomenon, compare Deuteronomic expansions of earlier laws studied by Haran [1978: 333–41]; see also SOURCE ANALYSIS to Exodus 19–24). The primal *"Pesaḥ* Rule" might be reconstructed as follows, with alternating negative and positive injunctions:

I. Any foreigner's son may not eat of it.
II. Any slave may eat of it.
III. A resident or a hireling may not eat of it.
IV. In one house it must be eaten.
V. A bone of it you must not break.
VI. All Israel's congregation must do it.
VII. Any uncircumcised may not eat of it.

We now turn to the Elohistic strand, probably represented in 12:29–34, which continues the narrative of 11:1–8 (E). Compare in particular 12:29 to 11:4–5: "At midnight I am going to set forth in Egypt's midst. And every firstborn in the land of Egypt will die, from the firstborn of Pharaoh sitting on his throne to the firstborn of the maidservant that is behind the two millstones, and every animal firstborn." Similarly, 12:30 describes the "great cry" predicted in 11:6 (E).

A shred from the largely absent J source may be 12:35–36, which abruptly returns to the despoiling of Egypt, predicted in 3:21–22; 11:2–3. These passages perhaps connect back to Gen 15:14 (J), where Yahweh had promised that Israel would leave servitude with "much property."

We have yet to attribute the two most difficult sections of Exodus 12: vv 21–27 and 37–39. The latter is the less problematic. Exod 12:37a is almost identical to Num 33:5, "and Israel's Sons set forth from Raamses and camped in Succoth," and belongs to the itinerary sequence running through Exodus and Numbers (see provisionally Cross 1973: 308–17; Friedman 1981: 98–119; 1987: 230–31; also APPENDIX A, vol. II). Most or all way station notices come from the Redactor's hand (see also SOURCE ANALYSES to 13:17–15:21 and 15:22–26).

Exod 12:39, on the other hand, is Elohistic, continuing v 34, which introduced the unrisen dough. The verb *grš* 'expel' described Egypt's release of Israel previously in E (6:1; 11:1).

Exod 12:37b–38 could plausibly be assigned to either E or R. On the one hand, the passage resembles Num 11:21 (E), which likewise mentions "six hundred thousand *foot-men.*" And the "many foreigners" (*'ēreb rab*) of 12:38 recalls the "riffraff" (*'spsp*) of Num 11:4 (E). Finally, the root *kbd* 'heavy' has occurred eleven times in the Elohistic Plagues narrative (7:14; 8:11, 20, 28; 9:3, 7, 18, 24, 34; 10:1, 14). As it reappears in 12:38, perhaps the Elohist used an even dozen purposely. But assigning 12:37b–38 to E also creates difficulties. First, why should 12:38 and Num 11:4 use different terms for the mixed multitude? Moreover, if 12:37b–38 is Elohistic and v 37a Redactorial, we must posit a lost Elohistic description of Israel's departure, displaced by the Redactor's comment in v 37a. Perhaps, then, all of vv 37–38 is R, partly inspired by Num 11:4, 21 (E).

Upon first inspection, 12:21–23, 25–27 appears to be entirely Elohistic, despite a possible contradiction between v 22 and 12:31 (E) (see NOTE to 10:29). Exod 12:21 begins with Moses addressing the elders, whom I provisionally consider characteristic of E (see INTRODUCTION, pp. 50–52). And 12:26, with its theme of instructing posterity, recalls 10:2, "so that you may tell into your son's ear and your son's son's" (E). Moreover, 12:27, "the people knelt and bowed," echoes 4:31 (E). Finally, in terms of content and context, vv 21–23, 25–27 fit well within E, linking 11:1–8 with 12:29–36. Without the passage, E would lack any reference to the paschal offering.

Some, admittedly, attribute all of 12:1–27 to P (May 1936: 70–72; Wambacq 1976: 316–19; Van Seters 1983: 173–75; 1994: 114–19; Levenson 1993b: 45). If so, 12:1–27 as a whole simply features varied command and fulfillment (on the phenomenon, see Alter 1981: 88–113; Sternberg 1985: 365–440). But, since in these situations P tends to repetition or abridgment, rather than paraphrase and elaboration (see SOURCE ANALYSIS to 7:8–11:10), I follow the majority and regard 12:1–20 and 21–27 as true doublets from P and JE, respectively.

In 12:21–23, 25–27, we encounter an important problem: language in Genesis–Numbers resembling that of Deuteronomy (D) and the associated editorial framework of Joshua–Kings and the prose narratives of Jeremiah (Dtr) (see Noth 1981). This D-like material might be attributed to the Elohist (Friedman 1987: 258), Redactor ᴶᴱ (Wellhausen 1899: 74, 86) or a later hand, perhaps the final Redactor (cf. Lohfink 1994: 51–63). A popular theory holds that a Deuteronomic/Deuteronomistic Redactor inserted D-like matter throughout the Torah (Noth 1962: 93, 97, 101; Fohrer 1964: 86–87; Perlitt 1969; Hyatt 1971: 141–44; Schmid 1976; Smend 1978: 65–66; Rendtorff 1990; Blum 1990: 167–69; Peckham 1993; Vervenne 1994). While this view has certain attractions, it does not explain well the following: (a) D-like interjections are usually next to or within E material (Wright 1953: 319–20); (b) lexically, they differ somewhat from true Deuteronom(ist)ic style (Lohfink 1963: 121–24; Caloz 1968); (c) sometimes they disagree with Deuteronomy in substance. For example, the concept of *Pesaḥ* in 12:21–23, 25–27 differs sharply from Deut 16:2–8 (see COMMENT, pp. 445–47). For an older survey of the Dtr debate, see Brekelmans (1966); I shall return to the matter in APPENDIX A, vol. II.

However we explain it, the phenomenon is undeniable. Wellhausen (1899: 74; cf. 86) already notes the Deuteronomic cast of 12:25–27a. The sequence wəhāyâ 'and it will happen,' followed by a "when" or "if" clause, followed in turn by a second or third person injunction, is ubiquitous in Deuteronomy (6:10; 7:12; 8:19; 11:13, 29; 15:16; 20:2; 21:14; 23:12; 24:1; 26:1; 27:2, 4; 28:1, 15; 30:1; 31:21). Again, the phrase hā'āreṣ 'ăšer yittēn yahwe(h) 'the land that Yahweh will give' (12:25) finds numerous parallels in D and Dtr (Deut 1:20, 25; 2:29; 3:20; 4:1, 21, 40; 5:16, 31; 11:17, 31; 12:9; 13:13; 15:4, 7; 16:5, 18, 20; 17:2, 14; 19:2, 10, 14; 20:16; 21:1, 23; 24:4; 25:15, 19; 26:2; 27:2, 3; 28:8; 32:49; Josh 1:2, 11, 15). Exod 12:25 particularly resembles Deut 6:10; 11:29; 26:1; similar, too, are Deut 17:14 and 18:9.

The theme of the son's question (12:26) is often considered Deuteronom(ist)ic. Compare Deut 6:20–21, "(Sam and LXX: And it will happen) when your son asks you tomorrow, saying, 'What are the laws . . . that Yahweh our deity commanded you?' then you will say. . . ." Joshua 4 contains two further parallels, of which the first, at least, belongs to the Deuteronomistic stratum of Deuteronomy–2 Kings (Noth 1981: 37): "When your sons ask tomorrow, saying, 'What are these stones to you?' then you will say . . ." (vv 6–7); "When your sons ask their fathers tomorrow, saying, 'What are these stones?' then you will inform your sons . . ." (vv 21–22). But equally pertinent is Josh 22:24–28, a passage often ascribed to P (e.g., by Weinfeld [1972: 181]). Thus, there is reasonable doubt as to whether the theme is uniquely Deuteronom(ist)ic (see further below).

Where does the D-like matter in Exodus 12 end? To judge from the parallels, it should extend through the first word of 12:27: wa'ămartem 'then you will say.' But the remainder of 12:27 seems to continue 12:23 (E): note psḥ 'protect,' ngp 'et-miṣrayim 'harm Egypt' and the sparing of Israel's houses. Thus the D-like matter cannot easily be extracted from its Elohistic context. This does not comport with the theory of a Deuteronom(ist)ic redaction, but rather suggests that all of 12:21–23, 25–27 is Elohistic, with the author quoting a D-like document or more likely using D-like language himself (on links between D and E, see Friedman 1987: 128, 258). We might impute the D-like diction to a literary topos rooted in didactic tradition (Soggin 1960: 341–47; Lohfink 1963: 121–24; Caloz 1968; cf. Van Seters 1983: 175–76). It need not be specific to a single source.

To be sure, one might attribute the D-like matter to the final Redactor, since the preceding verse (12:24) is R. Two considerations argue against this, however. First, as we have seen, the D-like material cannot easily be excised from E. Second, the case of 12:24 cannot be settled without examination of 13:10 (R), which is framed by D-like matter (see below) and thus is not an editorial splice between E and a D-like source or insertion. More likely, both 12:24 and 13:10 are Redactorial interjections into older material, presumably Elohistic.

In 13:3–16, we meet more D-like exhortation: the injunction that Israel "remember" (zkr) (13:3) is paralleled in Deut 5:15; 7:18; 9:7; 15:15; 16:3, 12; 24:9, 18, 22; 25:17. Exod 13:3, 14 refer to Yahweh's rescuing Israel from bêt 'ăbādîm 'a slaves' house,' a common expression in Deuteronomic and related literature (Deut 5:6; 6:12; 7:8; 8:14; 13:6, 11; Josh 24:17; Judg 6:8; Jer 34:13). In Exod 13:5, 11, we have two more occurrences of D-like "and it will happen, when Yahweh brings you" (see above on 12:25). Moreover, besides 13:5, 11, almost all references to Yahweh's oath to the Fathers come from D or Dtr (Deut 1:8; 6:10, 23; 7:8, 12, 13; 8:1, 18; 10:11; 11:9, 21; 13:18; 19:8; 26:3, 15; 29:12; 31:7, 20; Josh 1:6; 5:6; 21:43; Judg 2:1; Jer 11:5; 32:22). The full phrase "swore to your fathers to give to you" (13:5) is duplicated *verbatim* in Deut 7:13 and closely paralleled in Deut 1:8; 6:10; 10:11; 11:9, 21; 26:3; 31:7; Josh 1:6; 5:6; 21:43; Jer 11:5; 32:22. (For many scholars, calling Canaan "a land flowing of milk and honey" [13:5] and listing its inhabitants are Deuteronom[ist]ic traits [see Schmidt 1988: 137–42]; I, however, am unconvinced [note 3:8, 17; see APPENDIX A, vol. II].) Finally, the injunctions to teach one's children and to wear Yahweh's law as a "sign on your arm and a memorial/circlet *between your eyes*" (13:9, 16) are closely paralleled in Deut 6:6–9; 11:18–20. Exod 13:3–16 thus comes from the same D-like source as 12:25–26, to which it is linked by the unique phrase *hāʿăbōdâ hazzō(ʾ)t* 'this service' (12:25, 26; 13:5).

Within this section, I find unevenness at only two points. First, 13:4 opens abruptly, as if beginning a speech, and breaks the natural flow between vv 3 and 5. (This awkwardness may have generated variants in LXX and Sam; see TEXTUAL NOTES to 13:4.) My impression—and it is no more than that—is that we have ancient, variant versions of Moses' speech to the people: "Remember this day, when you went out from Egypt . . . anything leavened may not be eaten" (v 3) and "Today you are going out in the month of the New Grain" (v 4).

A second point of unevenness is 13:6–7, which twice commands a week's abstinence from leavened food. Here, too, we might discern a Deuteronom(ist)ic hand. Both vv 6 and 7 find parallels in Deuteronomy 16: compare Exod 13:6 to Deut 16:8, and Exod 13:7 to Deut 16:4. But conclusions are hard to form. On the one hand, D is apparently influenced by JE (see Driver 1891: 75–82). On the other hand, the theory of a Deuteronom(ist)ic redaction of the Torah posits influence flowing in the opposite direction, with JE being revised in the style of D. Thus 13:6 might be Elohistic, cited in Deut 16:8, while Exod 13:7 might be a Deuteronom(ist)ic expansion after Deut 16:4. Or the opposite might be true. (Johnstone [1992] concludes that all of 13:3–7 originally belonged to D[tr], but that a *Priestly* editor introduced some eight modifications! This is more than we could possibly know.)

Finally, we must consider 13:1–2, which might be Elohistic, Redactorial, Priestly or even Yahwistic. Given the redundancy with vv 12–13 (E), most argue that 13:1–2 is P. But one might with equal or greater plausibility regard 13:1–2 as the Redactor's heading to 13:3–16 (Van Seters 1994: 122–23). Still, Num 3:13 and 8:17 (P?) recall that "On the day of my striking every firstborn in the land of Egypt, I sanctified to me every firstborn in Israel, from man to animal they will be for me." Therefore, we might well posit something like 13:1–2 in the original P. Admittedly, the verses fit awkwardly with the Priestly material in chaps. 12–13, but something may be missing (see below). (Num

3:13; 8:17 may themselves be Redactorial, however, in which case Exod 13:1–2 might belong to any stratum.)

Let us now characterize E and P, our basic sources, and explore the relationship between them. The last event in the Elohistic strand was Moses' conversation with Pharaoh, during which Yahweh interrupted to tell Moses of the imminent death of the Egyptian firstborn, and that Israel should prepare for departure (10:24–11:8). Now Moses, presumably still speaking for God, informs the people how to escape Yahweh's Destroyer (*mašḥît*) by the *Pesaḥ* ritual. They must mark their houses with the blood of a sheep or goat. They are not at first told what to do with the rest of the animal (Hyatt 1971: 136), but 12:27 indicates that the *Pesaḥ* is a cooked sacrificial meal (*zebaḥ*). Among the procedures presupposed by 12:21–22 may even be burning part of the *Pesaḥ* upon a makeshift altar (Haran 1978: 344; cf. 1 Sam 14:32–34). When the Egyptians urge Israel to depart, so quickly do the Hebrews leave, their leavened dough has no time to rise (see NOTE to 12:34), and they have made no other provision—most likely because they never believed Moses to begin with (see NOTE to 12:39). Moses commands that, once Israel inhabits Canaan, they must forever commemorate the Exodus by avoiding leavened food and by eating *maṣṣôt* for seven days in the month of the New Grain. Moreover, Moses requires that Israelites dedicate each firstborn, animal and human, to Yahweh, in memory of the culminating plague against Egypt. The E narrative will continue in 13:17, explaining Israel's unexpected route out of Egypt.

P follows E's basic outline. The Hebrews are to apply the blood of a sheep or goat to their lintels and doorposts, averting "destruction" (*mašḥît*) from Yahweh. They must avoid leavened bread and eat *maṣṣôt* for seven days in the first month, although it is unlikely this law applies to the generation of Egypt (see REDACTION ANALYSIS; NOTE to 12:34; cf. Jacob 1992: 292). The P section probably ends abruptly with the Consecration of the Firstborn (13:1–2).

Overall, it appears that the Priestly instruction is a commentary, supplying details absent from the older Elohistic legislation: when to begin preparations (12:3), the date of the festival (12:1, 6, 18), provisions for the poor (12:4), which animals are suitable (12:5), when the *Pesaḥ* is killed (12:6), how it is cooked and eaten (12:8–9), what is done with leftovers (12:10), how to dress for the meal (12:11), the punishment for eating leavened food (12:15, 19), which days of the Festival of Unleavened Bread are most important (12:16), how those days should be distinguished (12:16), who is obliged to observe the leaven taboo (12:19), how long Israel had been in Egypt (12:40–41) and who may eat the paschal meal (12:43–49). To what extent the Elohist already had these particulars in mind is unknowable. It is possible, for example, that E's paschal victim is a mature animal, not a yearling as in P.

P also alters certain details. E's bare mention of the "month of the New Grain" (13:4) becomes the establishment of a new calendar (12:2; see NOTE). Though still called *mašḥît*, E's personal "Destroyer" becomes abstract "destruction" (see NOTE to 12:13). E's command not to leave (*tēṣəʾû*) the house (12:22) becomes in P a less stringent prohibition: not to remove (*tôṣîʾ*) the paschal animal from the house (12:46) (cf. Hyatt 1971: 136). Israel's haste, E's explanation for *maṣṣôt* (12:34, 39; cf. Deut 16:3), becomes the manner in which one eats the paschal meal (12:10–11). P's blood rite is to be performed only by the generation of the Exodus, while E leaves this unclear (see COMMENT, pp. 445–52).

Although, in some respects, P is an expansion of E, it also omits certain details. There are no elders. P never explains with what to apply the paschal blood (contrast 12:22) — either because the Priestly Writer reserved marjoram for priestly spargings (Lev 14:4, 6, 49, 51, 52; Num 19:6, 18) or, more likely, because the blood rite would never be repeated (see COMMENT). E's careful instruction of posterity (12:26–27; 13:8, 14–15) goes unmentioned, possibly because the Priestly Writer envisioned priests, not elders, as religious educators. Unlike E, P gives no reason for eating unleavened bread (12:15–17a). P also drastically curtails the firstborn law (13:1–2). Significantly, P never calls the paschal meal a sacrifice in Exodus 12, in contrast to 12:27 (E) (see COMMENT, pp. 448–51).

Most strikingly, P predicts but does not narrate the death of the firstborn (12:12). P's Moses does not see Pharaoh grovel (contrast 12:29–33 [E]); Israel simply leaves. One might infer that this omission is for the sake of economy; a mere prediction suffices. But in all the other plagues, P reports not only command but also fulfillment, however briefly. I suspect, therefore, that the Redactor replaced P's account of the death of the firstborn with E's, contrary to his usual practice. As we have observed, 13:1–2 lacks a clear context in P; perhaps it originally belonged to the lost Priestly narrative of the plague of the firstborn.

SPECULATION: Ezek 20:5–10, loosely based upon P (see TEXTUAL NOTE to 2:25; APPENDIX A, vol. II), recalls an episode of idolatry on the eve of the Exodus, as do Ezek 23:3, 19, 27 (Batto 1992: 163) and Josh 24:14 (Eichrodt 1970: 266). Admittedly, the incident is probably a figment of Ezekiel's petulance, an oblique attack on his backsliding contemporaries. But there could conceivably have been a basis in the original Priestly document, now censored.

REDACTION ANALYSIS

To produce 12:1–13:16, the editor had to combine two accounts of the departure from Egypt, as well as two bodies of legislation, each treating *Pesaḥ*, the Festival of Unleavened Bread and the Consecration of the Firstborn. Evidently, redundancy in law was tolerable. But it was hard to pile narrative atop narrative without obscuring the plot. To impose structure on this complex, the Redactor probably inserted five exhortations to "remember" and "observe" (12:14, 17b, 24, 42; 13:10).

Throughout 12:1–13:16, most of the Redactor's dispositions of text are logical, indeed inevitable. The P law in Yahweh's voice (12:1–17a) must precede the E law in Moses' voice (12:21–23, 25–27). By shifting P's conclusion to 12:28 — or by composing his own conclusion in Priestly style — the Redactor fashioned a continuous, composite narrative: the people obey (P/R) after hearing Moses' report (E) of Yahweh's command (P). True, in the composite, Moses' words differ from Yahweh's. But this is a minor problem, since E and P are similar to begin with and since biblical authors often present slightly varying accounts of command and fulfillment (Childs 1974: 199; Alter 1981: 88–113; Sternberg 1985: 365–440). Thus, if the Redactor stretched the forms of Hebrew narrative, he did not break them.

Jettisoning P, the Redactor then used E's narration of the death of the firstborn and the people's flight from Egypt (12:29–39), inserting new itinerary material (12:37) and replacing part or all of E's description of the departure (see SOURCE ANALYSIS). He then returned to P (12:40–41, 43–51), which precisely dates Israel's sojourn and enacts the "Pesaḥ Rule." Into this Priestly section, the Redactor probably inserted his own interpretation of Pesaḥ as "guarding" (12:42; see NOTES to 12:11, 42).

In chap. 13, the Redactor began with P's law of Firstborn Consecration, but continued with Elohistic legal and hortatory material (13:3–16). These now appear to be Moses' expansions of Yahweh's brief instructions in the prophet's own style, as best exemplified in Deuteronomy. Although 13:1–2 might have been more appropriately placed before 13:11, the Redactor presumably did not wish to break up continuous E matter.

Redaction of parallel strands necessarily led to the recurrence of certain words, which became thematic. For example, šmr appears in both P (12:6, 17a) and E (12:25); the Redactor himself added 12:17b, 24, 42 [2x]; 13:10, for a total of eight (on the significant number eight, see above, p. 316). The varied nuances of šmr are all pertinent to the context: ritual observance, vigilance, protection and possibly wakefulness (see NOTE to 12:42). The Redactor also (consciously?) created a pattern of seven occurrences of ʾkl 'eat' in the laws of Pesaḥ and of Unleavened Bread (see NOTES to 12:11, 20 and, on the importance of seven, Pope 1962b).

Redaction also created new meanings, resonances and internal allusions. The Priestly laws on the participation of foreigners (12:43–49) seem directed, in their present context, at the "foreigners" accompanying Israel from Egypt (12:38 [E]) (cf. Childs 1974: 202; Durham 1987: 172). Although mašḥît 'destruction, Destroyer' originally meant different things in 12:13 (P) and 23 (E), in the composite text one tends to equate them (although LXX and Syr do not; see NOTES). The reference to Egypt "growing strong (ḥzq) concerning the people," i.e., urging them to leave (12:33 [E]; see NOTE), becomes an ironic inversion of the Priestly/Redactorial refrain of 7:8–11:10: "Pharaoh's heart was strong/Yahweh strengthened (ḥzq) Pharaoh's heart, and he would not release them." From 13:11 (E), one might infer that the firstborn of the desert period were not consecrated at all (Resh Laqish, b. Bek. 4b–5a). But 13:1–2 (P?) precludes such an interpretation for the composite Torah (Ramban). Finally, E never tells us exactly where the unleavened bread is baked (12:39); in the received Torah, this occurs at Succoth (12:37; Dillmann 1880: 123).

These are all consequences of the redaction of JE with P. We can also observe some results of the earlier combination of the Yahwistic and Elohistic narratives, though neither source is fully preserved. Pharaoh's "Bless me" (12:32 [E]) may echo Gen 47:7, 10 (J), where Jacob had blessed a kindlier Pharaoh upon their first meeting (Cassuto 1967: 145–46). Other Yahwistic passages in Genesis foreshadow events probably once described in J, but now preserved only in E and P. For example, Yahweh's promise to Abram, "And also the nation whom they will serve I am going to judge" (Gen 15:14 [J]), anticipates the Plagues and Exodus. The story of Abram's and Sarai's sojourn in Egypt (Gen 12:10–20 [J]) also seems to foreshadow Israel's departure from Egypt: two Hebrews descend to Egypt because of a famine, they are taken into Pharaoh's house, Yahweh afflicts the Egyptians and their cattle, and the Hebrews leave with flocks and herds. Finally, the Bridegroom of Blood incident (4:24–26 [J]) adumbrates the events of the paschal night (E and P), with blood averting a nocturnal attack (see COMMENT to chaps. 3–4, pp. 238–39).

The text does not only gain by redaction; at times its coherence is impaired. For example, 12:34 (E) implies that the Israelites' dough had been leavened, in apparent defiance of 12:15–20 (P) (see Ehrlich 1969: 159; NOTE to 12:34). The jarring is only momentary, however, since 13:5 (E) makes it fairly clear that Unleavened Bread is to be observed in Canaan, not in Egypt (cf. ibn Ezra; Jacob 1992: 292).

There is also some chronological confusion. In E, the blowup between Moses and Pharaoh (10:24–11:8) is followed immediately by the command for the Pesaḥ (12:21–27). A superficial reading of the redacted text would give the same impression. But if we take the received Torah literally, then at least four days, and more likely two entire weeks, must pass to accommodate P's calendrical commands (Mek. pisḥā' 3). (Jacob [1992: 301] ingeniously solves the problem by dating the plague of darkness to the night of the tenth day of the first month. Then the three days of darkness pass between the tenth and the fourteenth [10:22], and Moses and Pharaoh spar on the eve of the Pesaḥ.)

It is moreover unclear just when Israel leaves Egypt. In E, since the Hebrews must spend the entire night at home (12:22), most likely they leave by day. According to D, however, "in the month of the New Grain, Yahweh your deity took you out from Egypt at night" (Deut 16:1; cf. Exod 13:4 [E]). R seems to contain both ideas: "on the morning/day after (mohŏrat) the Pesaḥ, Israel's Sons left" (Num 33:3); "it is a night of observance for Yahweh, as he takes them out from the land of Egypt; it, this night, is for Yahweh an observance for all Israel's Sons" (Exod 12:42). As for P, in Sam and LXX the Hebrews depart at night (12:41), while in MT we cannot tell when they leave (see TEXTUAL NOTES). My guess is that the varied tradition reflects dissent as to when the Israelite day began (see NOTE to 12:6).

NOTES

12:1. And Yahweh said. The following paschal legislation severely disrupts narrative chronology. Two weeks must pass within Exodus 12, from the first to the fifteenth, yet the logic of the Plagues narrative requires that Israel leave immediately after negotiations are broken off (chap. 11). Perhaps we are to assume that the laws of chap. 12 were issued during the Plagues, but that the report was deferred (cf. Jacob 1992: 301). Still, as the Rabbis say, "in the Torah there is no earlier and later."

Moses and . . . Aaron. Mek. *pišā'* 3 infers that Yahweh directly addresses only Moses, while his spokesman Aaron speaks to the people. This is a logical reading of the redacted text, in which Aaron is Moses' interpreter, not only to Pharaoh (6:29–7:2 [P]) but also to the people (4:16, 30 [E]). Moreover, on a symbolic level, Moses' "uncircumcised" lips (6:12, 30 [P, R]) hinder transmission of the laws of *Pesaḥ*, one of which is the requirement of circumcision.

in the land of Egypt. This explicitly distinguishes the paschal instruction from other Mosaic laws, promulgated at Sinai, in the Tabernacle or on the plains of Moab (Ramban, Rashbam).

12:2. *This month.* Hebrew possesses two nouns for "month": *yeraḥ* 'moon' and *ḥōdeš* 'newness, new moon.' Elsewhere, P uses *ḥōdeš* in the sense "month." But here the original meaning, "new moon," may also operate, since Yahweh is speaking some time before the tenth of the month, most likely on the first. The Book of Exodus ends exactly one year later, with the consecration of the Tabernacle on the first of the first month (40:17).

In a lunar calendar, a month (i.e., a lunation) lasts about 29.5 days, a twelve-month year about 354 days. Since, however, the Israelites linked their festivals to both the lunar and the agricultural cycles, it is a reasonable surmise that they somehow conformed their calendar to the sun, on which the crops depend (Sforno on 13:4). The Babylonians, pioneers in this field, reckoned lunar months of both 29 and 30 days, with an extra month intercalated every few years to restore approximate correspondence to the solar year (this lunisolar system survives as the "Jewish" calendar). But the Bible never explicitly mentions intercalation, fundamental to a lunisolar calendar and important, too, for a usable solar calendar.

The Israelite lunar month began approximately on the new moon, but we are not surely exactly when. Ps 81:4 refers to a festival on the full moon (*kēse[h]* = *kese'*; cf. Job 26:9?), while the holidays of Unleavened Bread (*Maṣṣôt*) and Shelters (*Sukkôt*) fall on the fifteenth of the month (see NOTE to 12:18). Day 15 on average coincides with the true full moon only if months are reckoned either from the first invisibility of the old moon (de Vaux 1961: 183; Goldstein and Cooper 1990: 22), as in Egypt (Parker 1950: 10), or from total conjunction determined by calculation (cf. Gandz 1970: 136 on 1 Samuel 20). Reckoning from the first new crescent, as in Babylon, puts the average full moon on day 13 (cf. McKay 1972). But it is quite possible that, like the Egyptians, the Israelites considered the fifteenth day the full moon, irrespective of astronomical reality (cf. Parker pp. 9, 12).

for you. Both times, "you" is masculine plural (*lākem*), ostensibly referring to Moses and Aaron. But the words are obviously meant for all Israelites, including later readers (Ehrlich 1908: 303).

head of months. I.e., "first month." Philo (*Quaest. in Exod.* 1.1) and Durham (1987: 153), however, also discern a qualitative distinction: the month containing *Pesaḥ* is the most important month. Just as our civil reckoning of years points continually to Christ, and just as the Jewish calendar recalls Creation, in the Priestly calendar all dates implicitly commemorate the Exodus (Ramban).

Sarna (1986: 85) observes that P's calendar is grounded neither in mythology nor in nature, but in history. It is striking that, although the Priestly Writer's interest in chronometry is apparent in Gen 1:14–18, no calendar is instituted there. God establishes the day, the week and the year—but not the month. Except for the Flood account, P ignores the measure of months until Exodus 12. The implication may be that the birth of the Israelite nation and the concomitant establishment of a calendar are themselves acts of cosmogony, completing the unfinished Creation.

Barring new epigraphic discoveries, we shall never fully understand the Israelite measure of time (see VanderKam 1992; Cohen 1993: 20). Although the Bible presupposes a calendar, maybe several calendars (see below), nowhere does it reveal their principles. This silence cannot be attributed to indifference. Either the biblical authors were not privy to the secrets of chronometry, or, more likely, they purposely declined to share the measure of time with the masses. (They may also have been offended by the association of astronomy and astrology; cf. Isa 47:13.)

Throughout history and in many societies, astronomical expertise has been jealously guarded and sometimes abused. In Rome, priests were accused of regulating the calendar to benefit special interests—e.g., to manipulate repayment dates—and similar abuses apparently existed in pre-Islamic Arabia (O'Neil 1975: 47). For Israel, setting the dates of festivals must have been crucial (Talmon 1958b; see 1 Kgs 12:32); in later Judaism, it was a matter of prestige, even of life and death. For example, the "Wicked Priest" of Dead Sea Scrolls infamy attacked the "Righteous Teacher" on a day that the latter, but not the former, considered Yom Kippur (1QpHab 11:4–8). And *m. Roš Haš.* 2:9 tells an equally dramatic, if less sanguinary, tale: Rabban Gamaliel II required Rabbi Joshua to profane a day that Joshua considered Yom Kippur, but Gamaliel did not. The Samaritan, Rabbanite, Boethusian and Qara'ite branches of Judaism followed and still follow different calendars (Talmon 1958a: 70, 74; 1958b: 196). The Church is in comparable disunity.

To return to Exodus: most likely, 12:2 proclaims a *new* first month (May [1936: 76] and most others), hence the solemnly parallelistic diction noted by Cassuto (1967: 140). Creation of a calendar is an exercise of sovereign power, an affirmation that Yahweh's reign over Israel has begun and Pharaoh's has ended (cf. *Exod. Rab.* 15:13). Since P's calendar is particularly associated with the festival cycle, there is also the implication that Yahweh has begun to teach his worship to Israel. (Admittedly, one might interpret 12:2 as "*whereas* this is the first month . . . ," in which case there is no innovation [Cassuto 1967: 137].)

By the usual interpretation, 12:2 may imply the prior existence of a different calendar, now abolished. But this is a vexed question (for further detail, see

Tadmor 1962; de Vaux 1961: 190–92; Thiele 1951: 14–41, and, for some healthy skepticism, Snaith 1947: 18–23, 28–38; the most recent treatment is Cohen 1993). There were in fact two competing first months in Israel, as throughout the ancient Near East. The "month of the New Grain (*'ābîb*)," corresponding more or less to Babylonian Nisan (March–April), followed the vernal equinox; this was the anniversary of the Exodus (13:4). The "month of the Perennial Streams (*hā'ētānîm*)," roughly Babylonian Tishri (September–October), followed the autumnal equinox. Each might be considered the first month.

The evidence is, admittedly, of varying quality. Many scholars have drawn unwarranted conclusions as to when the year began from such expressions as *təqûpat haššānâ* 'the year's revolution' for the autumn (34:22) (cf. 1 Sam 1:20; Isa 29:1; Ps 19:7; Job 1:5); *ṣē(')t haššānâ* 'the year's departure' also for the autumn (Exod 23:16); **bō' haššānâ* 'the year's coming' for the spring (?) (2 Kgs 13:20); *qēṣ yāmîm* 'days' [i.e., year's] end' for the spring (?) (Gen 4:3; 2 Sam 14:26; 1 Kgs 17:7; Neh 13:6; cf. 2 Chr 21:19), and *təšûbat haššānâ* the year's return' for the spring (2 Sam 11:1; 1 Kgs 20:22, 26; 1 Chr 20:1; 2 Chr 36:10) (see de Vaux 1961: 190–91; vs. Snaith 1947: 32–34). In fact, each of these terms might plausibly connote either the beginning or the midpoint of a year. They cannot tell us when the year began.

We first find unambiguous evidence for a spring-based year in the seventh century. (Auerbach [1959, 1960] boldly dates the institution of the vernal New Year exactly to 604 B.C.E.!) Jer 36:22 places the "ninth month" in winter, implying a spring reference point. And 2 Kgs 25:8 (= Jer 52:12) dates the Temple's destruction, which we know occurred in summer, to the fifth month, again indicating a spring New Year (de Vaux 1961: 191). If we correlate Babylonian records with Jer 25:1; 46:2, we similarly find a spring-based reckoning. Finally, the calendrical contents of Ezek 40:1 and perhaps 33:21 assume a spring New Year (see Zimmerli 1983: 2.192, 345–46 for arguments pro and con). From later literature, 1 Macc 10:21; 16:14 also imply a spring-based reckoning—but by now the system is Babylonian, not Israelite (Goldstein 1976: 541). Most important, all pentateuchal lists of festivals begin with Unleavened Bread in the spring (23:14–16; 34:18–22; Leviticus 23; Num 28:16–29:39; Deuteronomy 16; see also 4QMišmārôt [Talmon 1958b: 170–72]). And Exod 12:2 is explicit: the first month of the year is in the spring.

In contrast, Israel's autumn-based calendar is scantily documented, having been largely supplanted. It may be an heirloom from the Canaanites, assuming that their New Year was coincident with the annual resurrection of the storm god in the autumn (Morgenstern 1924; de Moor 1972). The "Gezer Calendar" (c. 1000) lists the tasks of the agricultural year, beginning in the autumn (*AHI* 10.001). We should also note the biblical cliché *yôre(h) ûmalqôš* 'autumn rain and spring rain,' always in that order (Deut 11:14; Jer 5:24; Joel 2:23) (Sarna 1986: 84). Again: since time passes between Josiah's Temple audit in his eighteenth year (2 Kgs 22:3) and the celebration of *Pesaḥ* that same year (2 Kgs 23:23), the year cannot have begun in spring (see, however, Tadmor 1962: 266). As late as the fifth century, Nehemiah strangely uses month names from the spring-based Babylonian calendar for an autumn-based system (Neh 1:1; 2:1) (de Vaux [1961: 192], however, argues that the text is corrupt). The autumn New Year will be decisively reinstated in the postbiblical Jewish festival of Rō(’)š haššānâ 'the Year's Head' — paradoxically, on the first day of the seventh (spring-based) month (cf. Lev 23:24–25; Num 29:1–6).

What is the relationship between the spring-based and fall-based calendars? Some infer that the older system was autumn-based and that the spring New Year was brought west in the eighth–sixth centuries by Mesopotamian conquerors. (Cohen [1993: 14–20], however, argues for the primacy of the spring New Year throughout the Near East.) Others posit that Judean kings reckoned from fall to fall, while Northern kings reckoned from spring to spring (Thiele 1951; Borowski 1987: 43). If either of these views is correct, then the Priestly Writer must be polemicizing in 12:2. While allowing that another first month may have existed, since Moses' day, he asserts, any competing system has been heterodox. (On the implications for the date and setting of P, see APPENDIX A, vol. II.)

The most plausible inference, however, is that the two New Years had different functions: the autumnal was for agricultural activity, the vernal for religious observances (Tadmor 1962: 264–65; Sarna 1986: 84). Which is the older system is moot and not pertinent to our discussion. I would further suggest that Israel's fall-based, agricultural calendar was closely bound to the sun, on which planting and harvesting depended, while the spring-based festival calendar bowed more to the moon (Ps 104:19; cf. Gen 1:14). This is not inherently implausible; for administrative purposes, Egypt followed a solar calendar, while certain festivals were lunar (Parker 1950). And why, after all, observe only one New Year? The important point is not when the year begins, but how long it lasts. We, too, superimpose a solar fiscal year on a solar civil year, while traditional Jews, Muslims, Buddhists, etc., additionally superimpose their respective religious calendars, more closely tied to the moon. Ancient Egyptians actually maintained three calendars simultaneously, variously calibrated to the sun and moon (Parker). And, according to m. Roš Haš. 1:1, the Rabbis reckoned with four New Years!

We know, moreover, that various Jewish communities of the Greco-Roman period, including the Dead Sea sect, used a schematic solar calendar of 364 (sic) days (see Talmon 1958b). This system may date back to ancient Israel (Morgenstern 1924, 1935; Jaubert 1953), although the evidence is flimsy (Hendel 1995a). I shall argue below that corresponding to the two types of year were two definitions of the day: sunrise-to-sunrise and sunset-to-sunset (see NOTES to 12:6, 18).

Although I have spoken of a "New Year," the reader should not infer the existence of an associated festival. While all new moons were minor holidays, neither the vernal nor the autumnal equinox was originally followed by a special New Year's Day. P places an anonymous festival on the first of the seventh month, in the fall, which would later become Jewish Rosh Hashanah, but for P, it is really Midyear's Day. In ancient Israel, the New Year, whether vernal or autumnal, was a theoretical reference point only.

This is because both lunisolar and solar calendars require periodic adjustment. Since the start of a new year was presumably determined, as in later Judaism, by both astronomical observation and calculation, an interval was required for proclaiming a new year *retroactively* (see also NOTE to 12:3; for further discussion of the calendar, see NOTES to 12:3, 6, 18 and 13:4).

SPECULATION: Perhaps we err to assume that a full year was the primary calendrical unit. Observing the frequency of parallel festivals in the spring and fall throughout the ancient Near East (see COMMENT), Cohen (1993: 6–7) argues that the "concept of a six-month equinox year appears to have been a major factor in the establishment of the cultic calendar throughout the Near East." Somewhat similarly, Ewald (1876: 337–39, 348) infers that the Bible's dual system reflects its obsession with the number seven (cf. Pope 1962b), Tishri being the seventh month from Nisan, and Nisan the seventh from Tishri (Ewald coins the term "Sabbath-month").

first . . . of the year's months. Exod 13:4 (E) dates *Pesaḥ* to *ḥōdeš hāʾābîb* 'the month/new moon of the New Grain' in early spring, when ears of barley are green and tender (see NOTE). Rabbinic Judaism, following the Babylonian calendar, celebrates Passover at the sunset beginning the fifteenth day of Nisan (Nisan 1 falls between March 25 and April 21 in the Gregorian calendar, within a month after the vernal equinox [see O'Neil 1975: 92–93]).

12:3. *On the tenth of this month.* In the punctuation of MT, with the pause under *hazze[h]*, "on the tenth of this month" is when Moses is to command the people. This cannot be right. Since *lē(ʾ)mōr* 'saying' almost always immediately introduces direct quotation, "on the tenth of this month" must be the opening of Moses' speech (Rashi, Luzzatto). That is, on the tenth of the month, the paschal animal is designated, as in modern Samaritan practice (Jeremias 1932: 76). Why select the victim on the tenth? Lest, says Philo, the sacrifice be casual or rushed, rather than the result of pious deliberation (*Quaest. in Exod.* 1.2). Philo also supposes that the Hebrews of the Exodus needed an interval to prepare themselves spiritually for liberation.

Philo asks a good question but does not provide the full answer. The tenth of the first and seventh months apparently held a special significance in Israel (see also COMMENT, p. 443–44). Segal (1982: 206) notes that the Israelites enter Canaan on the tenth of the first month (Josh 4:19), and they may also be circumcised on this day (Segal 1963: 3; Jacob 1992: 300–2), although this is not quite clear (Josh 5:2–9). Ezekiel receives a vision of the reconstructed Temple on the tenth of the first month (Ezek 40:1). As for the seventh month, its tenth is the Day of Expiation, *Yôm hakkippūrîm* (Leviticus 16; 23:26–32), also the beginning of the Jubilee year (Lev 25:9). (The tenth day of the first month of the Muslim calendar, *muḥarram*, is also a festival, perhaps inspired by Yom Kippur [Dalman 1928: 1.27].)

Segal (1963: 143–45) surveys various theories about the original significance of the tenth day. First: ten days is one-third of a lunation of c. 29.5 days (ibn

Ezra), and in fact the Egyptians reckoned a ten-day "decade" (O'Neil 1975: 45, 66)—but there is no further evidence of Israel marking such a unit. Segal (1957: 269), positing a lunisolar calendar for Israel, has a more attractive suggestion. Since the Babylonians generally intercalated before Nisan (month 1) or Tishri (month 7) (see Rochberg-Halton 1992), he hypothesizes that Israel, too, intercalated in spring or autumn (the later Jewish calendar intercalates only in the spring). If so, during the first ten days of the month, leaders would determine by observation whether intercalation was required (cf. *b. Sanh.* 10b–11a). Lastly, we should note Morgenstern's (1924: 73) theory: the first ten days of Nisan/Tishri correspond to the gap between the 364-day schematic solar calendar and the 354-day lunar year. That is, the interval between Nisan/ Tishri 1 of one lunar year and Nisan/Tishri 10 of the next approximated one solar year.

sheep/goat. Hebrew *śe(h)* is ambiguous, denoting both caprines and ovines (cf. v 5; Num 15:11; Deut 14:4). Unlike Exod 12:3, 21, Deut 16:2 allows a bovine victim as well (see COMMENT, pp. 446–47).

Since Late Antiquity, many have sought astrological significance in Passover's occurrence under the sign of Aries the Ram (e.g., Ramban on 12:3; Samaritan tradition *apud* Dalman 1928: 1.450; cf. Josephus *Ant.* 3.248). But we do not know if the Israelites made any such connection, or even saw the constellation as a ram. Note, too, that Passover and Aries coincided only from c. 1000 B.C.E. to 1000 C.E. (Bickermann 1968: 58). Still, some association remains possible (cf. Langdon's [1935] discussion of astronomy, astrology and mythology in Mesopotamia).

for. Here as in 21, the preposition *lə-* is ambiguous. The surface meaning is "one animal *per* household." But, since the animal's death is redemptive (see COMMENT, pp. 434–39, 452–58), an interpretation "one animal *substituting for* the household" is not excluded.

Fathers'-house . . . house. *Bêt-'ābōt* 'fathers'-house' usually connotes an extended family (Stager 1985). Here, however, "a sheep/goat for the house" limits "fathers'-house" to the inhabitants of a single domicile (on the possibility of scribal conflation, see TEXTUAL NOTE). Stager estimates that the average early Israelite house contained about four residents, while the family compound, the *bêt 'āb* 'father's house' proper, might contain a dozen or more, too many to eat a single lamb or kid (cf. *Mek. pisḥā'* 3).

12:4. *the house.* Bayit connotes both "house" and "household."

insufficient for being for a sheep/goat. Pace Ehrlich (1908: 304), this is probably not a textual corruption, just slightly unusual syntax. *Yim'aṭ . . . mihyôt miśśe(h)* combines, as it were, two simpler phrases: **yim'aṭ mihyôt śe(h)* 'insufficient for (there) being a sheep/goat' and *yim'aṭ miśśe(h)* 'insufficient for a sheep/goat.'

We do not know what the Priestly Writer considered "insufficient." According to Josephus (*War* 6.423), the minimum was ten persons, and there might be as many as twenty. The Rabbis, however, set no limits (*b. Pesaḥ.* 89ab, 99a), so long as each participant received a mouthful (*m. Pesaḥ.* 8:3). For P, the main issue is the family's ability to consume the animal completely, lest any be left over (12:10).

nearest his house. In an Israelite village, a neighbor would probably be either a relative (Stager 1985; cf. Segal 1963: 141 n. 3) or a *gēr* 'sojourner,' whose participation will be addressed in vv 43–49.

take. That is, take an animal.

souls. *Nepeš* 'soul, life force, self' also connotes "person, individual." It is unclear whether the phrase "in proportion to the *souls*" is connected with what precedes (Massoretic trope) or what follows (Childs 1974: 182). I prefer the latter interpretation, regarding the basic sentence as *bəmiksat nəpāšōt tākōssû ʿal-haśśe(h)* 'in proportion to the souls you will apportion the sheep/goat,' with *bəmiksat . . . tākōssû* a cognate genitive construction analogous to the cognate accusative (GKC §117*p–r*). The full, complex sentence then glosses the rare word **mikkəsâ* 'proportion' as *ʾîš ləpî ʾoklô* '(each) man according to what he eats.' Still, we cannot rule out the interpretation "let him and his neighbor, the one nearest his house, take in proportion to the souls" (MT).

(each) man according to what he eats. The nuance of *ʾîš* 'man, each man, each one' is not quite clear. It could imply "each man" or "each house." The common idiom *ləpî* 'according to'—literally "to the mouth of "—is admittedly a dead metaphor. But here and in 16:16, 18, 21, it particularly befits the act of eating.

you will apportion. In other words, one divides the cost of the meal in proportion to the relative sizes of the two households.

12:5. *perfect*. As we shall see, the *Pesaḥ* is a sacrifice (COMMENT, pp. 445–52). Naturally, one offers to Yahweh only healthy animals (29:1; Leviticus 1, etc.).

male. Sacrificial animals may be of either gender, depending upon the sanctity of the offering and the social status of the offerer. At least for P, males are required for the most holy holocaust (Lev 1:3, 10; contrast 1 Sam 6:14) and the special festival offerings (Numbers 28–29). To atone for unintentional violations, however, while a prince sacrifices a male animal, a commoner offers a female (Lev 4:23, 28, 32). The preference for the male may reflect general biblical esteem for masculinity (Segal 1963: 142). But we should not underestimate practical considerations: only a few males are necessary to maintain a herd (Firmage 1992: 1123).

son of a year. P in general prefers animals of this age for sacrifice (29:38; Lev 9:3; 12:6, etc.; cf. Ezek 46:13; Mic 6:6). Ugaritic gods, too, eat "calves of a year" (*ʿglm dt šnt* [*KTU* 1.1.iv.31, 4.vi.42, 22.ii.13]). Tenderness aside, young animals were probably preferred for sacrifice because they had not been profaned by work or breeding (cf. Num 19:2; Deut 21:3).

The precise significance of "son of a year" is disputed. Rashi reasonably supposes that the animal should be *at most* a year old (so also Haneman 1980), the lower limit being eight days (Lev 22:27; cf. Exod 22:29). By Samaritan interpretation, however, the animal must be born in the same calendrical year, i.e., since the previous Rosh Hashanah (Dalman 1928: 1.268–69). And Gray (1971: 348–51) argues that the sense is *at least* a year old. At any rate, since many sheep are born in spring, it would be possible to find paschal victims almost exactly one year old (Henninger 1975: 27–28 n. 13; Firmage 1992: 1127).

12:6. *kept thing. Mišmeret* is usually the functional equivalent of *ḥōq/mišpāṭ/ miṣwâ* 'commandment.' Here, however, there is probably an implication that the animal itself, as well as the command, must be "kept" (ibn Ezra; Ehrlich 1908: 305; Fox 1986: 62). Ehrlich (1969: 155) compares the reservation of Manna as a *mišmeret* (16:23). (*Mek. pišḥā* 5 and *b. Pesaḥ.* 96a further infer that the days between the tenth and the fourteenth should be spent examining [*šmr*] the animal for flaws.)

fourteenth. This is approximately the night of the full moon, which rises as the sun sets (see NOTE to 12:2). For Philo, the day is particularly sacred because the world is continuously lit (*De spec. leg.* 2.155).

this month. By a dispensation for the ritually impure and travelers, *Pesaḥ* may also be observed on the fourteenth of the following month (Num 9:6–13 [P]; cf. 2 Chr 30:2–3).

community of . . . congregation. There is no discernible difference between *qāhāl* 'community' and *ʿēdâ* 'congregation' (on the possibility of a conflate text, see TEXTUAL NOTE). The redundancy appears to stress the participation of all Israel. While ritual purity will later be requisite for celebrating *Pesaḥ* (see COMMENT), the urgency of the first *Pesaḥ* brooks no deferral.

between the two evenings. We are not sure what the Priestly Writer means by this curious phrase, paralleled in 16:12; 29:39, 41; 30:8; Lev 23:5; Num 9:3, 5, 11; 28:4, 8 (all P), as well as by Arabic *bayna (ʾ)l-ʿišāʾayni* 'between the two evenings' (GKC §88c). The standard Jewish view is that *bên hāʿarbayim* extends from late afternoon until sunset (Jub 49:1, 10, 12; 11QTemple 17:7; Josephus *War* 6.423; Philo *De spec. leg.* 2.145; *m. Pesaḥ.* 5:1; *b. Ber.* 26b). In biblical terms, this is the interval between *panôt ʿereb* 'evening's turning' (late afternoon) and *bō' haššemeš* 'the sun's entering' (sunset) (cf. Deut 23:12). Practical considerations may have affected Jewish interpretation, for, at least in the Second Temple, three afternoon shifts were required to accommodate the thousands of worshipers (*m. Pesaḥ.* 5:5–7). R. Ulla even defines the "two evenings" as the sunsets beginning and ending the entire day before *Pesaḥ* (*b. Zebaḥ.* 11b; cf. also Wevers 1990: 170). Samaritan tradition (Jeremias 1932: 80) and Segal (1963: 131), however, equate the "two evenings" with evening itself; the dual conveys that sunset is both the end of one day and the start of the next (cf. also Sternberg's observations in Gandz 1970: xx–xxv). P's dawn-to-dawn orientation, however, militates against these approaches (see below).

More attractive is the opinion of the Sadducees, Qaraʾites, Samaritans and ibn Ezra: *hāʿarbayim* is the "twi-light" between sunset and dark and synonymous with *ʿereb* 'evening' (see Segal 1963: 253; Jeremias 1932: 80). This appeals to common sense and fits all available evidence. While 12:6 puts *Pesaḥ* "between the two evenings," Deut 16:4, 6 requires that the paschal victim be slaughtered "at evening . . . at the sun's *entering* (setting)"; see also Josh 5:10. In Exod 16:12, Moses predicts that Israel will eat meat *bên hāʿarbayim*, and the quails duly arrive "at evening" (vv 6, 8, 13). Ibn Ezra further observes that, when Aaron lights the Tabernacle candelabrum *"between the two evenings"* (30:8), it is in fact evening (27:21). According to 12:18, the Festival of Unleavened Bread begins on the fourteenth "at evening," apparently concomitant with the *Pesaḥ* (see NOTE). And the "Passover Letter" from Elephantine, Egypt, inaugurates the holiday at *mʿrb šmš* 'the sun's setting' (Cowley 1923: 62–63; Porten and Yardeni 1986: 1.54).

SPECULATION: Perhaps we should not render *ʿarbayim* as "two evenings," but rather as "two *entrances*," the original meaning of *ʿereb*. Conceivably, Israelites imagined two portals to the underworld below the horizon. When the sun enters the vestibule, its light still tinges the sky. Then the sun enters the underworld proper, the gates shut and light disappears. Possibly reflecting an analogous concept, Ugaritic may call the beginning and end of the evening *ṣbu špš* 'the sun's settling down' and *ʿrb špš* 'the sun's entry' (Tarragon 1980: 18–19; Margalit 1982; contrast Levine 1981a: 248–50); *špšm* 'two suns(?)' is the division between one day and the next (*KTU* 1.14.iii.3, 14; iv.33, 46). Note, too, the odd Talmudic phrase "between the suns" (*bên haššəmāšôt/ šimšayyāʾ*) for the period between sunset and the appearance of three stars (Luzzatto).

Rather than connote twilight, however, *bên hāʿarbayim* might mean "exactly at sunset," as if *ʿarbayim* could be split down the middle (Holzinger 1900: 36). One wonders if there existed an equivalent expression **bên haṣṣohŏrayim* 'exactly at noon.' (In Jonah 4:10, *bin-laylâ . . . ûbin-laylâ* means "during the night," but it is not clear that *bin* is a form of *bên* 'between.')

Some would argue that *ʿarbayim* is not dual at all, comparing *ṣohŏrayim* 'noon' (*pace* Ramban). It is even possible that *bəqārîm* 'mornings' (Isa 33:2; Ps 73:14; 101:8) should be read as a singular **boqrayim*, since the plural makes little sense (cf. Gandz 1970: 238). Still, if *-ayim* is not the dual suffix, we do not know what it might be. The oft-made comparison with adverbial *-ām* is not apposite, since *ṣohŏrayim* means "noon," not "at noon" (contrast *yômām* 'by day'). At any rate, *bên* 'between' proves that P, at least, takes *ʿarbayim* as a dual.

To explain why *Pesaḥ* is performed in the evening, we must return to the Israelite calendar (see NOTES to 12:2, 3). It may be that, like the Egyptians, Israelites began their day at dawn. Only the latest biblical strata reckon from evening to evening in the Babylonian and later Jewish mode (Morgenstern 1935: 15–19; de Vaux 1961: 181–82; Talmon 1994). For example, in preexilic sources, a twenty-four-hour day is almost always called "day and night" (1 Sam 30:12; Isa 28:19; Jer 33:20, etc.), whereas late biblical and postbiblical texts often reverse the formula (Deut 28:66–67; Isa 34:10; Esth 4:16; Jdt 11:17). Gen 19:34; Judg 19:5–8; 1 Sam 28:8, 18–19 and perhaps 1 Sam 19:11 also presuppose a dawn-to-dawn day, with the nighttime belonging to "yesterday" and the morning to "tomorrow." The Priestly Writer, in particular, reckons from dawn to dawn. In Genesis 1, for example, the first day begins with light breaking forth; then there is evening and morning, and the day is done. On each day that follows, Yahweh does his work, then night falls, and the day finally ends in the morning. Dawn is the boundary between one day and the next. We can deduce the same from Lev 7:15, "the flesh . . . on the day of its sacrifice must be eaten; one must not leave any of it until morning"; Lev 22:30, "on that day it must be eaten; do not leave any of it until morning." Similarly, Lev 6:13 and Num 28:4 (P) mention the morning offering before the evening offering. In fact, were P following an evening-to-evening reckoning, Exod 12:6; Num 9:11–12 should command the slaughter of the Pesaḥ on the evening of the *fifteenth* day, not the fourteenth.

On the other hand, although the evidence is incomplete, it appears that all Israelite festivals begin at sunset (e.g., Unleavened Bread [12:8, 18; Deut 16:4] and the Day of Expiation [Lev 23:32]). Why should festivals begin at dusk if the day starts at dawn?

We have already noted the competition, so to speak, between the sun and moon over the measure of time. One reflection of this struggle may be the acknowledgment of two New Years: for the sun in the autumn and for the moon in the spring (NOTES to 12:2, 3). Analogous problems pertain to the definition of a day. I conjecture that the days of the Israelite fall-based agricultural calendar were "solar," i.e., dawn-to-dawn, as in Egypt. In the spring-based cultic calendar, however, days were "lunar," i.e., dusk-to-dusk, as in Mesopotamia. (Admittedly, in Egypt the day always began with sunrise, whether one was using the lunar or the solar calendar [Parker 1950: 10].)

Assuming that two definitions of a day coexisted in Israel, giving calendrical dates for festivals would inevitably have been cumbersome, witness Lev 23:27, 32: "On the tenth of this seventh month is the Day of Expiation . . . on the ninth of the month at evening, from evening to evening." This seems to be an effort to superimpose a lunar day upon a solar day, as the middle of the solar ninth is the start of the lunar tenth (cf. Olivarri 1971–72: 310–14; VanderKam 1992: 814). Similarly, in Exod 12:6, *"between the two evenings"* of the fourteenth solar day is the evening that begins the fifteenth lunar day. In fact, although the Bible always dates Pesaḥ to the fourteenth (12:6; Lev 23:5; Num 9:3, 5, 11; 28:16; Josh 5:10; Ezek 45:21; Ezra 6:19; 2 Chr 30:15), Rabbinic Judaism celebrates Passover on Nisan 15 (see NOTE to 12:18). (For a modern parallel, note that American Christians begin their calendrical day at midnight, yet certain holidays, such as Christmas and All Souls' Day, may be celebrated the night before.)

The Exodus narrative, of course, provides a different reason why the paschal lamb/kid should be slaughtered at sunset. Its protective blood must be in place by dark, because Yahweh will strike at night—in fact, precisely at midnight. Nocturnal danger is a common theme throughout the Bible; see studies by Ziegler (1950) and Fields (1992).

12:7. *doorposts.* Philo (*Quaest. in Exod.* 1.12) proffers an interesting if unconvincing explanation of why blood is applied specifically to the doorways. Moses previously claimed that Israelite animal sacrifices would horrify the Egyptians (8:22). Now, no longer afraid, the Hebrews flaunt their foreignness (cf. ibn

Ezra). Ibn Ezra rejects this understanding on two grounds: (a) he assumes the Hebrews' doorways are behind courtyards, beyond public view; (b) the blood would be invisible at night.

More important, the blood is a sign for Yahweh and his Destroyer, not for the Egyptians. The doorway in particular must be bloodied because it is a house's point of vulnerability, whereby misfortune can enter (see COMMENT, pp. 434–39). It is unclear, however, whether all four sides of the doorway are marked, or only three, the threshold being omitted (see NOTE to 12:22).

The houses in which they will eat it. If two households share the meal, the visitors need not bloody their own doorway, since they presumably spend the whole night with their neighbors.

12:8. *eat.* As Cassuto (1967: 140) observes, the root *'kl* 'eat' appears seven times in the laws of Pesaḥ (12:1–13) and seven times more in the laws of Unleavened Bread (12:14–20); see NOTE to 12:20. This may or may not be intentional. After all, one can count other repeated words (e.g., "seven," "sheep/goat")—and no doubt Cassuto did—without discovering any pattern. It is worth noting, nonetheless, that *'kl* occurs another seven times in 12:43–13:7, which further treats Pesaḥ and Unleavened Bread. The numbers seven, fourteen and twenty-one are, of course, prominent in the holiday legislation.

unleavened bread. This is presumably true unleavened bread, not the unrisen cakes Israel bears from Egypt (see NOTE to 12:34). Maṣṣôt accompany the paschal meal for two reasons. First, once Israel reaches Canaan, they will observe the Festival of Unleavened Bread concomitant with the Pesaḥ. Second, the Priestly Writer wished to make the paschal meal as much like a sacrifice as possible, and unleavened bread often accompanies offerings to Yahweh. These matters, as well as the multiform symbolism of leaven, will be explored at length under COMMENT.

Apart from the Festival of Unleavened Bread, *maṣṣôt* appear mainly in two contexts. They were (and are) ordinary Palestinian fare when the preparation is hurried (Gen 19:3; Judg 6:19; 1 Sam 28:24; cf. Gen 18:6) (Wellhausen 1885: 87; Licht 1968a: 226). And all baked goods presented to Yahweh are unleavened (23:18; 29:2; 34:25; Lev 2:5, 11; 6:9–10; 7:12; 10:12; Judg 6:19–21; 2 Kgs 23:9, etc.; cf. Amos 4:5 [MT; OG different]). Maṣṣôt were generally made from barley, but sometimes from wheat (Borowski 1987: 7).

The etymology of *maṣṣâ* is uncertain. Some posit a connection with Greek *maza* 'barley bread' (< Greek *massō* 'knead'), but the resemblance is probably coincidental. The Hebrew roots *mṣy* 'drain, press out' and *mṣṣ* 'sip, suck,' though occasionally cited, do not seem relevant. Recently, Goldstein and Cooper (1990: 21–22) have proposed that *maṣṣôt* is a plural of abstraction (cf. GKC §124g) meaning "strife" (< *nṣy*), connoting the contest between Yahweh and Death over the life of the firstborn, which must be redeemed from both (cf. *maṣṣâ* 'strife' in Isa 58:4; Prov 13:10; 17:19). Maṣṣôt, they claim, was originally the name of the festival, only secondarily applied to the bread. It is admittedly striking that the term *maṣṣâ* is unique to Hebrew, as if it bore a special religious significance. But the theory of Goldstein and Cooper generates more problems than it solves. Is it plausible that unleavened bread, eaten throughout the year in a variety of circumstances, should have been named after a particular festival? For the etymology, I would instead compare Arabic *naḍā* 'to be thin, poor,' quite appropriate to the flat "bread of humility" (Deut 16:3). The development **manḍatu > maṣṣâ* would be as expected.

bitter lettuce. Generally rendered "bitter herbs," *mərōrîm* (< *mrr* 'to be bitter') is probably a variety of lettuce (Licht 1968b; on the difficulties of biblical botany, see Jacob and Jacob 1992: 804). Vg translates *mərōrîm* as *lactucae agrestes* 'lettuce of the field,' and Samaritans still eat wild lettuce for *Pesaḥ* (Dalman 1928: 1.346–47). The linguistic cognates point in the same direction: Akkadian *murāru* 'bitter lettuce' and colloquial Arabic *murêr*, identified by Zohary (1982: 100) with dwarf chicory and/or reichardia (see also Dalman). The Mishnah allows a range of herbs as *mərōrîm*: *ḥāzeret* 'lettuce,' *ʿûlšîn* 'endive,' *tamkā'* 'chervil,' *ḥarḥăbînā'* (?) and *mārôr* itself (*Pesaḥ*. 2:6; cf. *b. Pesaḥ*. 39a).

Mərōrîm is not just the name of a plant but also an abstract plural, "bitterness." To eat *mərōrîm* is thus to suffer pain or humiliation (Lam 3:15). Later Jews inevitably saw the bitter herbs of *Pesaḥ* as recalling the Hebrews' travails in Egypt, citing 1:14: "They embittered (*waymārərû*) their lives" (*m. Pesaḥ*. 10:5; *y. Pesaḥ*. 16b; also Holzinger 1900: 37). This might be a very ancient tradition.

Some, however, assign a magical function to the *mərōrîm*. Beer (1911) lists classical texts attributing apotropaic virtue to certain herbs, to which we may add the plant Marduk bears to battle against Tiāmat in Mesopotamian mythology (*Enūma eliš* IV:62 [*ANET* 66]). Recently, van der Toorn (1988) has implausibly conjectured that the herbs were a mild toxin administered as an ordeal.

The paschal meal in fact features several characteristic and for Israelites slightly unusual flavors: roast meat, unleavened bread, bitter herbs. Perhaps, like the first two, the lettuce was considered a primitive, ascetic repast, consumed in mortification and penance (see COMMENT, pp. 433–34). But we may be thinking too hard about the matter. If the species in question sprouted in the springtime, it may simply have been part of the holiday's season symbolism (Dalman 1928: 1.347). Or lettuce may have been a pungent condiment that ultimately became canonical (anonymous Spanish rabbi *apud* ibn Ezra; Ehrlich 1969: 157; Zohary 1982: 95).

12:9. *raw.* The Massoretic cantillation puts a stop after *nā'* 'raw,' but I take "raw or cooked" as a single phrase. Since this would seem to exclude all meat, however, "cooked" is immediately limited by "boiled in water" (D. N. Freedman, privately). Although *nā'* occurs only here in Biblical Hebrew, its meaning is relatively assured; compare Arabic *na'* 'raw' (ibn Ezra).

Why is this proscription necessary? Raw meat is forbidden in all situations (cf. Lev 17:15), since it contains blood and fat (Gen 9:4; Lev 3:17; 7:23–26; 17:13–14; Deut 12:16, 23; cf. 1 Sam 14:32–34), which are Yahweh's food (Ezek 44:7). Perversely, many scholars have inferred from 12:9 that raw meat *was* sometimes eaten. The search for Near Eastern parallels has been disappointing, however. Segal (1963: 166) invokes a Sumerian description of Amorites eating uncooked meat (Chiera 1934: 58.4.26–27; Buccellati 1966: 331). But this source, like the "St. Nilus" account of the early Arabs' consumption of raw camel, is tainted with xenophobia (Henninger 1955). Segal also mentions the use of raw meat in a Hittite ritual (*ANET* 355–56), but this is extremely remote chronologically, geographically and culturally from Israel. Malamat (1956: 78) conjectures that the *pagra'i* meat offerings on the fourteenth of the month at Mari (ARM II: 90) were raw, but proffers no supporting evidence. Lastly, somewhat reminiscent of Exodus 12 is an Assyrian text forbidding to the king cooked meat and baked bread on the fourteenth of Nisan, when there is also a nocturnal offering (Langdon 1935: 77). Analogous taboos, however, without the nocturnal sacrifice, apply to the seventh and perhaps the twenty-first and twenty-eighth days of the month, so the parallel is less impressive than it at first appears (Langdon pp. 75, 81).

There is really no reason to think 12:9 alludes to a forbidden ritual. Most likely, the text simply emphasizes roasting by eliminating the theoretical alternatives: boiling the meat or not cooking it at all. Perhaps the point is also that the meat must be well cooked, not raw in any parts (Jacob 1992: 306). (Bekhor Shor sees 12:9 as limiting 12:11: eat the *Pesaḥ* in haste, but not so quickly as to eat it raw.)

cooked. Biblical *bšl* can mean specifically "boil," as in postbiblical Hebrew (cf. *m. Ned.* 6:1; *b. Ned.* 49a), but only when the context makes this clear. *Bšl* more properly refers to the transformation whereby things become edible (Loewenstamm 1965: 90 n. 33); cf. Akkadian *bašālu* 'boil, roast,' Ethiopic *basala* 'cook.' Thus it denotes the ripening of fruit as well as the cooking of meat. (*Bšl* apparently does not, however, include the baking of bread [16:23; Ezek 46:20; note, however, Num 11:8].) Sacrificial meat eaten by humans is routinely *bšl*-ed (e.g., Lev 6:21; Num 6:19; Deut 16:7; 1 Sam 2:13; Ezek 46:20–24; Zech 14:21; 2 Chr 35:13).

Thus the oft-cited contradiction between Exod 12:9 and Deut 16:7 may be illusory (so *Mek. pišḥā'* 6; Jacob 1992: 307; Segal 1963: 205–6; Loewenstamm 1992a: 209 n. 41). The injunction to "cook (*ûbiššaltā*) and eat" the paschal animal (Deut 16:7) need not exclude roasting and authorize boiling alone; cf. 2 Chr 35:13, *waybaššəlû happesaḥ bā'ēš* 'they *bšl*-ed the paschal animal with fire.' In any case, Deut 16:7 is more concerned with *where* the *Pesaḥ* is cooked than *how*. It is only in postbiblical Hebrew, where *bšl* connotes primarily boiling, that Deut 16:7 *necessarily* contradicts Exod 12:9. (Both LXX and *Tg. Ps.-Jonathan* "fix" this perceived difficulty: the former expands Deut 16:7, "boil *and roast* and eat," while the latter simply translates *bšl* as "roast" [*ṭwy*].) Nonetheless, since Deuteronomy presents *Pesaḥ* as an ordinary sacrifice, it is likely that boiling is envisioned. The common view that 2 Chr 35:13 harmonizes Exod 12:9 and Deut 16:7 may be correct, after all (cf. COMMENT, p. 447).

water. The text creates the fleeting impression that one may boil the animal in some other liquid, such as milk (cf. 23:19; 34:26; Deut 14:21). The next clause removes all ambiguity.

fire-roasted. P attempts to maximize the resemblance of the paschal meal to an offering, without using the sacrificial terms *ʿôlâ, zebaḥ* or *qorbān* (see following NOTES and COMMENT, pp. 448–51). Thoroughly roasting the animal minimizes the presence of two substances reserved for Yahweh: blood and fat (Dillmann 1880: 105; McNeile 1908: 70; Segal 1963: 167). We should note, however, that the Samaritans remove fat and blood *before* roasting (Jeremias 1932: 26; Gaster 1949: 81), and this might have been biblical practice, too. After all, some blood must be drained for application to the door frames.

The requirement to roast the victim may be related to various other commandments: to cook the animal whole, not to break the bones, and to eat it in haste (12:11). Boiling would require extensive butchering (Mic 3:3; Segal 1963: 166), and, in the modern Middle East, meat dishes are seethed for hours. Hence, boiling may have been a slower procedure than roasting (Philo *Quaest. in Exod.* 1.13; ibn Ezra; Bekhor Shor; vs. Jacob 1992: 309). But roasting, too, can be slow. Modern Samaritans spit the animals, then plant the poles, with the animals head-down, in a fire pit. They seal the pit and leave the meat to roast over the dying fire for about three hours (Jeremias 1932).

head . . . shanks . . . innards. On *kərāʿayim* as the lower legs, see Milgrom (1991: 159–60). The special treatment of head, legs and innards is not uniquely Israelite. According to Herodotus (*Histories* 2.39–40), the Egyptians removed these parts from their sacrificial victims.

It is not clear whether the text demands that head, shanks and innards be merely *roasted* (*b. Pesaḥ.* 74a), or also *eaten* (Vg; Smith 1927: 406). In the sacrificial cult, these parts are generally detached and burnt, reserved for Yahweh (29:17; Lev 1:8–9, 12–13; 4:11–12; 8:20–21; 9:13–14). Thus 12:9 may permit Israel, this once, to eat Yahweh's food. But the intent of 12:9 is more likely that the animal is to be roasted intact. This comports with the theme of unity pervading the paschal legislation: the animal must be eaten in one night (12:8, 10) and in one house; its bones may not be broken (12:46) (Niditch 1993: 55–56). And if the paschal sacrifice was originally vicarious, perhaps it was roasted whole in order to resemble a living human as closely as possible (see further NOTE to 12:46; COMMENT, pp. 434–39). The Samaritans, however, whose execution of the *Pesaḥ* is generally quite literalistic, eviscerate the victim before roasting its body whole (Jeremias 1932: 26).

12:10. *until morning.* In the immediate context, the point is that the Hebrews will have no time to eat the next morning (cf. 12:39). But a greater ritual principle is at issue. The Torah often commands that sacrificial meals be consumed within a *set* time. For priestly consecration offerings (29:34; Lev 8:32) and *šəlāmîm* sacrifices of gratitude (Lev 7:15; 22:30), it is within a day. According to *m. Zebaḥ.* 5:6 (but not Num 6:19), the Nazirite's ram, too, must be eaten within one day. For *šəlāmîm* in fulfillment of vows, however, worshipers have two days to consume the meat (Lev 7:16–18; cf. Lev 19:6–7). And 23:18 enunciates a related law: all fat of a festival offering (or is it just the *Pesaḥ?*) must be burnt before morning, presumably upon the altar (see NOTE). Hittite law, too, imposes a time limit (three days) for consumption of consecrated foods (Milgrom 1991: 323–24).

There is an implicit logic to these restrictions — quite apart from hygiene. An offering should be eaten not only at or near sacred space but during or near sacred time. Leftovers possess a sanctity that forbids extended contact with profane time; compare Manna's rapid decay during the week with its preservation during the holy Sabbath (16:19–24). Milgrom (p. 220) notes, moreover, that the *Pesaḥ*, the *šəlāmîm* of gratitude, the priestly consecration and the Nazirite's ram are all accompanied by unleavened bread. I would infer a requirement of maximal purity and avoidance of putrefaction, the latter represented by leavened bread and slightly spoiled meat (cf. Segal 1963: 207; COMMENT) (compare, too, the time limit on exposing a criminal's corpse, lest the land be defiled [Deut 21:23]).

In the non-Priestly legislation, since the *Pesaḥ* is a true sacrifice, the one-day limit is expected (34:25; Deut 16:4). Although P's *Pesaḥ* is not yet a sacrifice in Exodus 12, the same principles apply. Again we see P attempting to lend the first paschal meal the formalities of a burnt offering (see COMMENT, pp. 448–51).

SPECULATION: The Manna incident suggests another interpretation of 12:10. According to 16:19–24, any food the Israelites gather, except on the Sabbath eve, must be consumed that very day. The prohibition of hoarding is a test of Israel's faith in Providence. Perhaps for sacrifices, too, one must eat the meat one shares with Yahweh heartily, without concern for the morrow.

in fire you must burn. This redundant idiom is a cliché in the Bible (32:20; Lev 13:55, 57, etc.) and at Ugarit (*KTU* 1.6.ii.33, v.14).

12:11. *loins girt . . . staff in your hand.* The Samaritans still dress for *Pesaḥ* as prescribed in 12:11 (Jeremias 1932: 49, 98). What does this garb represent? The girdle is donned in preparation for a hasty departure; cf. 1 Kgs 18:46; 2 Kgs 9:1; Jer 1:17 and especially 2 Kgs 4:29, which also mentions a staff. Such belts were apparently worn on long journeys, perhaps with various items attached, freeing the hands and supporting the back (Seale 1974: 83; Edwards 1992: 233). Soldiers, especially, wear girdles (e.g., 1 Sam 2:4; Isa 8:9; Ezek 23:15; Ps 93:1; Job 38:3, 40:7; see also NOTE to 13:18 "resolute"). As for sandals, one assumes that they were normally shed indoors (cf. NOTE to 3:5). Wearing them would be exceptional, in anticipation of instant departure. The pair "girdle and sandals" may be formulaic; cf. 1 Kgs 2:5 (MT).

frantically. Ḥippāzôn connotes a combination of fear and haste. Jacob (1992: 310–11) cites Ezek 12:18–19, which refers to eating and drinking in *raʿaš* 'disturbance,' *rogzâ* 'tumult,' *daʾăgâ* 'disquiet' and *šimmāmôn* 'devastation.' But 12:11 may simply command one to eat quickly; the Samaritans still wolf down the paschal meal (Jeremias 1932: 98). The motif of frantic haste, but not the root ḥpz, also appears in E's etiology for unleavened bread (12:33–34, 39). Deut 16:3, however, explicitly associates unleavened bread with Israel's ḥippāzôn. (Should the South Semitic root ḥbz 'bake' ever turn up in Northwest Semitic, we might consider this a pun.)

We naturally assume that eating with ḥippāzôn is unusual, indeed, a violation of table manners. The busy, dangerous eve of the Exodus is not the time for a calm repast. Or perhaps the requirement is ritual: since roast food is generally God's, one eats it quickly, with guilty fear (see COMMENT, p. 439). But rapid eating need not be bad manners at all. The nineteenth-century Arabs with whom Doughty dined impressed him with the speed with which they ate, so that those of lesser rank need not wait long (Doughty 1936: 1.606, 2.378; also Burton 1856: 478).

By placing ḥippāzôn immediately before pesaḥ in 12:11, the Priestly Writer may be punning on the roots ḥpz and psḥ (Holzinger 1900: 37; Laaf 1970: 135); note that we find the same collocation in 2 Sam 4:4. George (apud Dillmann 1880: 107) even infers that ḥpz 'hurry' is P's etymology for the word pesaḥ.

Pesaḥ. The term is usually rendered "Passover," but, given its uncertain derivation, I have elected to transliterate. The original pronunciation was probably *pasḥ (less likely *pisḥ), whence English "paschal" (< Greek-Latin pascha < Aramaic pasḥā').

The term Pesaḥ connotes both the paschal rite and the animal killed; compare ḥag 'pilgrimage festival, sacrificial victim' (for the latter sense, see Mal 2:3; Ps 118:27; Rabbinic ḥăgîgâ). Pesaḥ is almost always qualified in some way: either pesaḥ ləyahwe(h) 'Pesaḥ for Yahweh' or happesaḥ 'the Pesaḥ' (Segal 1963: 134). The only exception is 2 Chr 35:18: "a Pesaḥ like it was not made. . . ."

Whether Pesaḥ connotes a true festival (ḥag) as in later Judaism is debated. The terms Pesaḥ and ḥag are very rarely associated; rather, the seasonal ḥag is Unleavened Bread. Nicolsky (1927: 172–74), in fact, denies that Pesaḥ was a ḥag before Jesus' day, but this is surely extreme. Ezek 45:21 appears to call Pesaḥ a ḥag, equivalent to Unleavened Bread. Haran (1978: 317–18 n. 2) also infers that Pesaḥ is a festival from the analogy between the expressions pesaḥ ləyahwe(h) 'Pesaḥ for Yahweh' (12:11, 27, 48; Lev 23:5, etc.) and ḥag ləyahwe(h) 'festival for Yahweh' (12:14; 13:6; 32:5, etc.). He argues, moreover, that in 23:18 ḥaggî refers to the paschal offering (pp. 327–41; see NOTE). Lastly, 34:25 explicitly calls Pesaḥ a ḥag—but here Haran admits that, since ḥag is the only word in 34:25b not echoed in Deut 16:4, it may be a later insertion (Haran's analysis is somewhat more complex, however; see NOTE). But, these arguments notwithstanding, I doubt that Pesaḥ originally connoted a festival day. Rather, the sacrificial ritual gradually lent its name to the following Maṣṣôt festival, completely supplanting it by the Rabbinic period.

We are uncertain of the original derivation and meaning of Pesaḥ. Exodus provides an explanation of sorts: the blood of Pesaḥ caused Yahweh to pāsaḥ over Israel's houses (12:13 [P]; 23, 27 [E]). This bears all the earmarks of folk etymology yet cannot be dismissed out of hand. But even accepting the Bible's explanation, we are not certain what the crucial verb means (see NOTE to

12:13). If *pāsaḥ* means "pass (over)," then "Passover" is an acceptable transla-tion for *Pesaḥ*. If, however, *pāsaḥ* refers specifically to hopping or skipping, matters are less clear. Some posit an archaic, limping dance connected with the holiday, comparing the dance of Baal's priests in 1 Kgs 18:26 (Engnell 1969: 190; on limping dances in general, see Cook in Smith 1927: 671–72). The ul-timate in conjecture is Keel (1972): the limping dance imitated the progress of the deformed demon of the East Wind, the "Destroyer." Others imagine a pas-chal ritual of skipping over a threshold (Zeph 1:8–9; cf. 1 Sam 4:5). But if *pāsaḥ* means "protect," then *Pesaḥ* simply means "protection" (see NOTE to 12:13).

Some moderns circumvent this ambiguity by dismissing the connection with Hebrew *pāsaḥ* and seeking instead ancient Near Eastern parallels. But all ef-forts in this direction have been quite speculative, since there is no ritual with a name resembling *Pesaḥ*. McNeile (1908: 65) and others (see Segal 1963: 96 n. 4) associate *Pesaḥ* with Akkadian *pašāḫu* 'to be appeased,' Mendenhall (1954b: 29) citing the adjective *pašḫu* 'appeased' (EA 74:37), which arguably corre-sponds to old Hebrew **pash*. Still, although "appeasement" or "appeased" would be an excellent name for an offering, we would expect **pešaḥ* or more likely **pāšēaḥ* to correspond to Amarna *pašḫu*. (Given, however, the confusing development of the sibilants in Hebrew [note Judg 12:6] and in Semitic in general [Rustum-Shehadeh 1969], we cannot rule out this approach entirely). Another potential Akkadian cognate, *pesû* 'rejoice,' would also suit, but is ex-tremely rare and not necessarily derived from **psh* (cf. Syr *pṣh* 'rejoice').

Others resort to Arabic. Ehrlich (1969: 157) proffers *fsh* 'to be wide, spacious, free' as befitting a celebration of freedom. Kopf (1976: 166–67) similarly sug-gests a semantic evolution "to make room" > "to protect," thus returning to a traditional etymology. Another Arabic root that could correspond to Hebrew *psh* and fits the holiday theme is *fsḫ/fṣḫ* 'dislocate, dismember, tear, abolish.' Wen-sinck (1925: 37), in fact, suggests that *Pesaḥ* was originally a festival, like the fourteenth of the Arab month *šab'ān*, during which God separated (*fsḫ*) the living from the dead by deciding destinies. Ultimately, all these Arabic con-nections are as questionable as they sound—although the last is suggestive, in light of the tenth plague.

Others have proposed even more dubious Egyptian derivations. The fact re-mains that no analogous Egyptian sacrifice has been discovered, and the best effort, that of Couroyer (1955), suffers from phonological difficulties as well. His Egyptian prototype *p3 sḫ* 'the blow' should have yielded Hebrew **pîsāḥ*, not **pash* (cf. *pînəḥās* < *p3 nḥsy*). This approach, though lately revived by Görg (1988), should be abandoned (de Vaux 1961: 488; Segal 1963: 100). My own opinion is that *Pesaḥ* is Hebrew for "Protection"; see NOTE to 12:13. For fur-ther bibliography on the etymology, consult Laaf (1970: 142–47).

for Yahweh. I.e., ordained by Yahweh and holy to him (Dillmann 1880: 107). Haran (1978: 317–18 n. 2) notes the analogy with *ḥag ləyahwe(h)* 'festival for Yahweh' (12:14; 13:6; 32:5, etc.).

12:12. *upon all Egypt's gods I will execute judgments.* "Judgments" (*šəpāṭîm*) here are penalties, presumably for enslaving and abusing the Hebrews (Daube

1963: 36–37). In 6:6, Yahweh promised to work "great judgments" without specifying against whom. Now we learn that the Egyptian pantheon will suffer along with their devotees (cf. Num 33:4; Isa 19:1; Jer 43:8–13; 46:25–26; Ezekiel 30). *Pace* Sarna (1986: 78–80), this cannot mean that Yahweh uses the Plagues to humiliate the natural elements Egyptians worshiped: snakes, the Nile, frogs, cattle and the sun. Nor can God be punishing the Egyptian gods by defeating the magicians (*pace* Holzinger 1900: 38; Elliger 1966: 193). In 12:12, Yahweh announces that he *will* punish all of Egypt's gods, not that he *has* punished some of them.

To what, then, does 12:12 refer? Perhaps to an interruption of the cult caused by the ensuing calamity. Or "gods" might here be idols, which Yahweh intends to smash (1QM 14:1; Jub 48:5; *Tg. Ps.-Jonathan; Mek. pisḥā'* 7). Ibn Ezra compares 1 Samuel 5, where Yahweh dismembers Dagon's image, and one thinks, too, of Jer 50:2, predicting the shattering of Babylon's idols (cf. Jer 43:8–13). Dillmann (1880: 107) further cites the late Egyptian tradition that King Amenophis, threatened by the Hebrews, hid the divine statuary and took the sacred animals in flight to Ethiopia (Josephus *Ap.* 1.244). And, in a similar vein, Jerome records a legend that all temples in Egypt were destroyed during the paschal night by storm and earthquake (*Epist. ad Fabiolem* [PL 22.701]). All this is midrash, however. The real meaning of 12:12 is more likely that Yahweh will humiliate the Egyptian gods by having his way with their land and people. (On the remote possibility that 12:12 refers to the discrediting of the Egyptian gods in the eyes of their *Israelite* worshipers, see SOURCE ANALYSIS.)

However that may be, not far beneath the surface of 12:12 lies the image of Yahweh presiding in a celestial court (1 Kgs 22:19–23; Isaiah 6; Zechariah 3; Ps 89:6–9; Job 1–2). God's judgment and punishment of gods and kings is the burden of Isa 24:21–23 (Ramban) and Psalm 82; cf. also Isa 14:12–23. The theme's Canaanite precedents are well known. At Ugarit, "God" (*'ilu*) is president and judge of the divine assembly (Cross 1973: 13–75, 186–90), with authority to deliver even Baʻlu into servitude and to appoint a new god-king in his stead (*ANET* 129–42).

As it happens, at least one of Egypt's gods would have his revenge. In 410 B.C.E., the priests of Khnum looted and destroyed the Jewish temple at Elephantine, Egypt (Porten 1968: 284–89). While we do not know their grievance, the Bible contains many passages that could have provoked pious and patriotic Egyptians. In particular, the paschal sacrifice would have horrified devotees of the ram god Khnum (see Porten pp. 280–82, 286 and NOTE to 8:22).

I am Yahweh. We might also render with LXX, "I, Yahweh."

12:13. *for you as a sign.* Within the narrative context, this must mean a sign to distinguish Hebrews from Egyptians. If, however, P intends the blood rite for reenactment by future generations, then the blood on the door has a further significance. All other "signs" in P are perennial reminders: the rainbow (Gen 9:12), circumcision (Gen 17:11), the Sabbath (Exod 31:13, 17), the tassel (Num 15:39 [reading *lə'ōt* with BHS]), Korah's censers (Num 17:3) and

Aaron's rod (Num 17:25). The same might be true of paschal blood. But in my opinion, P intends the blood rite solely for the generation of Egypt (see COMMENT, pp. 445–51).

I will see. Yahweh is presumably omnipercipient whenever he wishes to be; in the other plagues, he easily distinguished Israel from Egypt (Jacob 1992: 312). The blood, then, may be less for Yahweh's benefit than for Israel's, who are thereby entitled to participate actively in their own redemption (Kaufmann 1942–56: 2.430). The paschal command is, as it were, both a test of Israel's obedience and a demonstration of piety's rewards. It is thus a prologue to the legislation of Sinai (see also COMMENT to 15:22–26).

But this reading may be excessively homiletical. Elsewhere, the Bible restricts Yahweh's capabilities in order to enhance drama (e.g., Genesis 2–4). Here, one could argue that Yahweh's semi-autonomous baneful aspect, the Destroyer, is essentially demonic, blindly killing unless magically repelled (see COMMENT). That, at any rate, makes a better tale.

protect. There are two ancient renderings of *psḥ*, either of which might be correct (in fact, both are found in LXX; for a detailed study, see Brock 1982). One emphasizes the parallelism with *ʿbr* 'pass by,' the homonym *psḥ* 'limp' and the near-homonym *psʿ* 'step over' (Loewenstamm 1992a: 219–20). Yahweh "skips" or "passes over" Israel's houses (LXX 12:23; Aquila; Symmachus *apud* Theodoret [PG 80.252A]; Ezekiel the Tragedian 187; Jub 49:3; Josephus *Ant.* 2.313; R. Josiah *apud Mek. pishāʾ* 7). The best defense of this approach is Segal (1963: 186).

The other traditional interpretation, to which I and many moderns incline, takes *psḥ* to mean "protect" (LXX 12:13, 27; *Tgs.*; Symmachus *apud* Syro-Hexapla [Field 1875: 1.100]; Loewenstamm 1992a: 197–202, 219–21; Hyatt 1971: 134). This suits the context—Yahweh protects the Israelites' houses—and is supported by Isa 31:5, "as flying birds, so will Yahweh of Brigades defend over Jerusalem: defending (*gānôn*), and he will rescue; protecting (*pāsōaḥ*), and he will save." In Exod 12:42, we might even translate *šimmūrîm hûʾ ləyahwe(h)*, not as "it is an observance for Yahweh," but as "it is Yahweh's guarding" (cf. Rashi on 12:42; Hyatt 1971: 140; Fretheim 1991a: 145). If so, this might be R's gloss on *pesaḥ hûʾ ləyahwe(h)* (12:11, 27). Similarly, we might take *wəʾet-bāttēnû hiṣṣîl* 'but our houses he rescued' (12:27) as the Elohist's paraphrase of 12:23, *ûpāsaḥ yahwe(h) ʿal-happetaḥ* 'and Yahweh will protect (*ûpāsaḥ*) over the doorway.'

harm from destruction. The word *mašḥît* is ambiguous, both here and in 12:23 (see NOTE). Sometimes, especially in later texts, it connotes destruction in the abstract (e.g., Ezek 21:36; Prov 18:9). Elsewhere, however, it refers to a personal Destroyer, often supernatural (cf. *malʾāk mašḥît* 'destroying Messenger' in 2 Sam 24:16; 1 Chr 21:12, 15). My translation assumes that *mašḥît* is abstract destruction in 12:13, but a personal destructive force in 12:23 (with LXX, Syr, Holzinger [1900: 38] and others). Theoretically, one could render 12:13 as "no blow from the/a Destroyer will be against you" (cf. *Tg. Ps.-Jonathan*), and, conversely, 12:23 might mean "Yahweh will not allow destruction to come into your houses" (*Tg. Onqelos*). My interpretation, however, is based upon the considerations that (a) elsewhere *ləmašḥît* refers to destruction in the abstract (Ezek 5:16; 9:6; 25:15; Dan 10:8; 2 Chr 20:23; 22:4) and (b) P generally does not acknowledge Yahweh's supernatural servants (Friedman 1987: 191).

will not be upon. There is a remote possibility of translating "will not *fall* upon," since the root *hyy/hwy* may carry both meanings (cf. NOTES to 9:3; 15:3). "To be," however, is vastly the more common connotation.

in my striking the land of Egypt. Because of the ambiguity of the preposition *bə-*, we could also render "in my striking *in* the land of Egypt."

12:14. *this day.* It is difficult to tell whether "this day" is the *Pesaḥ* or the first day of Unleavened Bread. The answer is presumably both, since the paschal offering begins the weeklong Festival of Unleavened Bread, reckoned by lunar days from evening to evening (see NOTES to 12:6, 18; COMMENT, pp. 428–44). But *Pesaḥ* is almost never called a *ḥag* '(pilgrimage) festival,' while Unleavened Bread is a true *ḥag* (see NOTE to 12:11 "*Pesaḥ*"; COMMENT, pp. 428–34). On the structural function of 12:14, 17b, 24, 42; 13:10, see REDACTION ANALYSIS.

memorial. *Zikkārôn* can be translated either "commemoration" or "reminder" and can also connote a written memorandum. See Freund (1989) and NOTE to 13:9.

festival. A *ḥag* is generally understood to be a pilgrimage feast, cognate to Arabic *ḥajj*. Most believe the term originally referred to traveling or dancing in a circuit; Segal (1963: 128–29) argues, however, that a *ḥag* is properly a recurrent festival tied to the astronomical cycles, not necessarily a pilgrimage. But the theme of pilgrimage fits the narrative context well. The Hebrews now begin their trek to the Holy Mountain and ultimately the Holy Land, where all *ḥaggîm* can be properly observed.

to your ages. *Dōr* means "period" and "life span," as well as "generation" (cf. Latin *saeculum*). The older form of this idiom, found in 3:15 (MT) and in Ugaritic, is *dōr dōr* 'age (by) age, forever' (see NOTE to 3:15 [E]). *Lədōrōtêkem* 'to your ages' is unique to Hebrew, combining the ideas of "forever" and "for your posterity."

It seems that the Festival of Unleavened Bread is to be observed only by future generations. There is no impression that the Hebrews pause to observe a weeklong holiday, and in fact their bread already contains leaven (see REDACTION ANALYSIS; NOTE to 12:34). Moreover, according to Deut 29:5, the Hebrews did not eat bread at all for the entire wilderness period, again implying that the Festival of *Maṣṣôt* was reserved for the Holy Land.

12:15. *on the first day.* Due to the broad semantic range of the preposition *bə-*, the rendering of LXX and Syr is also possible: "(starting) *from* the first day."

eliminate. Here and in 5:5 (see NOTE), *hišbît* may resonate with *šabbāt* 'Sabbath,' ostensibly derived from the same root (see NOTE to 20:8). The first and last days of Unleavened Bread are days of rest (12:16).

leaven. *Śə'ōr* is old, fermented dough used as a starter (*m. Men.* 5:1–2). Here is Pliny the Elder's description of the production of leaven in first-century C.E. Rome, probably similar to Israelite practice:

Millet is specially used for making leaven; if dipped in unfermented wine and kneaded it will keep for a whole year. A similar leaven is obtained by kneading and drying in the sun the best fine bran of the wheat itself, after it has been steeped for three days in unfermented white wine. . . . Moreover though these kinds of leaven can only be made in the vintage season, it is possible at any time one chooses to make leaven from water and barley, making two-pound cakes and baking them in ashes and charcoal on a hot hearth or an earthenware dish till they turn brown, and afterwards keeping them shut up in vessels till they go sour; then soaked in water they produce leaven. But when barley bread used to be made, the actual barley was leavened with flour of bitter vetch or chickling; the proper amount was two pounds of leaven to every two and a half pecks of barley. At the present time leaven is made out of the flour itself, which is kneaded before salt is added to it and is then boiled down into a kind of porridge and left till it begins to go sour. Generally however they do not heat it up at all, but only use the dough kept over from the day before; manifestly it is natural for sourness to make the dough ferment, and likewise that people who live on fermented bread have weaker bodies, inasmuch as in old days outstanding wholesomeness was ascribed to wheat the heavier it was.
(*Natural History* 18.26; trans. H. Rackham [LCL])

cut off. Thirty-two times P and R describe a sinner's fate with a variant of the phrase *wənikrətâ hannepeš hahî(w)' miqqereb ʿamme(y)hā* 'that *soul* [individual] will be cut off from its kin' (for an exhaustive classification of the variations, with similar formulae from the Bible and the ancient Near East, see Wold 1978: 4–7, 17–34). Jewish tradition calls this penalty *kārēt* 'cutting off.' The derivation of the Rabbinic term is uncertain; some see an apocopated Niphʿal infinitive: *ləhikkārēt > likkārēt*, whence *kārēt* by "clipping." *Kārēt* may alternatively be a form particular to legal abstractions; cf. *gāzēl* 'theft' (Waldman 1989: 118).

Crimes evoking *kārēt* are neglect of circumcision (Gen 17:14), neglect of Unleavened Bread (Exod 12:15, 19), neglect of the *Pesaḥ* (Num 9:13), neglect of purification after contact with the dead (Num 19:13, 20), bootlegging holy oil or incense (Exod 30:33, 38), eating from sacrifices in a state of impurity (Lev 7:20, 21), eating sacrificial fat or blood (Lev 7:25, 27), slaughter or sacrifice outside the Tabernacle (Lev 17:4, 9), the approach of a defiled priest to the Tabernacle and its appurtenances (Lev 22:3), various sexual violations (Lev 18:29; 20:17, 18), necromancy (Lev 20:6), child sacrifice (Lev 20:2–5), Sabbath violation (Exod 31:14), neglect of the Day of Expiation (Lev 23:29, 30) and any intentional sin (Num 15:30–31). Quite possibly, *all* violations of Priestly law bring *kārēt* upon the malefactor, whether or not the text makes this explicit.

The Priestly Writer never explains what it means to be "cut off." Perhaps it is a vague aspersion devoid of concrete meaning: the sinner is not a "true" Israelite. But many have supposed *kārēt* to be physical banishment or excommunication, a cutting off from one's contemporaries by human agency (Morgenstern 1931–32: 47–48; von Rad 1962: 1.264 and n. 182). Others argue that *kārēt* betokens execution, whether by human or divine agency (e.g., *Sipre Numbers* 125 [on Num 19:13]). None of these explains all the evidence.

A consensus has now emerged that the *kārēt* penalty is a complex, entailing the premature death of the individual and the future eradication of his lineage and alienation from their land (Loewenstamm 1962a: 330; Brichto 1974: 25 n. 37; Wold 1978; cf. Milgrom 1991: 457–60). Thereby, the sinner's afterlife is also impaired (Propp 1987b). P's fullest elucidation of *kārēt* is Lev 20:10–24, which enumerates punishments for various sexual crimes: execution (vv 10–18), "cutting off" (vv 17–18), lack of descendants (vv 19–21) and exile (v 22; cf. Lev 18:28). In sum, *kārēt* betokens alienation from what Brichto (1974) calls the "kin-cult-land-afterlife complex." The notion is not unique to P. Compare Genesis 15 (J): the childless Abram fears for his future (v 2), but God promises him progeny (vv 4–5), future possession of the land (vv 7, 18–21) and a peaceful death (v 15) (Wold 1978: 40). And a most poignant example of a "cut off" ancestor is Rachel, weeping from the grave for her vanished children, the exiled houses of Joseph and Benjamin (Jer 31:15).

On the one hand, it is sometimes clear that Yahweh himself imposes *kārēt* (e.g., Lev 20:2–6). On the other hand, Exod 31:14 associates "cutting off" with judicial execution. (Ezra 7:26 also mentions a judicial penalty called *šərōšî* [Qere] 'uprooting,' probably the Aramaic equivalent of *kārēt*.) This is not necessarily a contradiction. If *kārēt* is the analogue on the divine plane to execution on the human plane, then the two can but need not coincide. In other words, all *kārēt* may involve execution, but not vice versa. Lev 20:17, "they shall be cut off before the eyes of their people's sons," may even imply a public cursing ceremony activating *kārēt*—but the point might also be that Israel will witness Yahweh's judgment.

12:16. *calling.* The precise significance of *miqrā'* is uncertain. It is probably derived from *qr'* I 'call' (cf. Isa 1:13, *qərō' miqrā'*), although *Tg. Onqelos* appears to associate it with *qr'* II = *qry* 'meet, happen.' Assuming derivation from *qr'* I, *miqrā'* might connote either an assembly of people called together (a "convocation") or the proclamation of a festival day (Milgrom 1991: 20–21). Since the domestic Sabbath is also a "calling of holiness" (Lev 23:3), the latter appears more likely. Jacob (1992: 322) observes that the phrase "calling of holiness" is always associated with the prohibition of work (Leviticus 23 *passim*; Num 28:18, 25, 26; 29:1, 7, 12).

done. The verb *yē'āśe(h)* is masculine, although its subject, *məlā(')kā* 'work,' is feminine. We would rather expect **tē'āśe(h)*, a reading found, presumably as a correction, in Kenn 80, 82, 84, Rossi 503. (On LXX^{ABM} "you [pl.] may do," see TEXTUAL NOTE.) Apparently, the verb has been attracted to the two following masculine Niph'als, especially *yē'āśe(h)* 'may be done.' But, in any case, gender "errors" are common in Biblical Hebrew (Levi 1987).

what is eaten. This elliptical expression must mean "work necessary to prepare what is eaten" (cf. *Tg. Ps.-Jonathan* [see TEXTUAL NOTE]).

soul. Here, in contrast to 12:15, 19, *nepeš* is tantamount to "living thing" (cf. Gen 1:20–30; 2:19; 9:10–16; Lev 11:10, 46; Ezek 47:9; Ps 104:29, 30; Job

12:10). This includes animals, who, like humans, require daily feeding (*Mek. pisḥā'* 9; Ehrlich 1908: 306; Jacob 1992: 322). The original meaning of *nepeš,* "throat," is also quite apposite, as is the extended connotation "life force."

12:17. *observe the Unleavened Bread.* This phrase has needlessly exercised many translators and commentators. The forced interpretation of *Mek. pisḥā'* 9—one must watch (*šmr*) the dough carefully lest it rise—and the confusion of the Versions (see TEXTUAL NOTE) arise from a misunderstanding of "Unleavened Bread." In this context, *hammaṣṣôt* must be not the food, but the holiday, elsewhere called *ḥag hammaṣṣôt* 'the Festival of Unleavened Bread' (Childs 1974: 179; Wambacq 1980: 47; Fox 1986: 64). Compare other injunctions to *šmr* 'observe' festivals (23:15; 31:13, 14, 16; 34:18, etc.), and note the parallelism within the verse: "observe the Unleavened Bread. . . . observe this day."

There is unmistakable assonance in the repetition of *ṣ* and *m* throughout the verse: *ûš(ə)martem . . . hammaṣṣôt . . . bə'eṣem hayyôm . . . hôṣē(')tî . . . ṣib'ôtêkem mē'ereṣ miṣrayim.*

the bone of this day. Hebrew uses *'eṣem* 'bone' to mean "body" and then, by extension, "self, selfsame." Modern Hebrew grammarians differentiate between the two definitions by gender ("bone" is feminine, "essence, self" is masculine), but there is no evidence for such a distinction in biblical times.

I took. Since the legislation also addresses future generations (cf. ibn Ezra), one should perhaps render, "I shall have taken."

your brigades. This refers to the tribes in battle array; cf. 6:26; 7:4; Numbers 1–3; 10:14–28; Josephus *Ant.* 2.312; see NOTE to 6:26. Noting the military terminology associated with the Exodus, Segal (1963: 136–38) observes that the spring, the anniversary of Israel's liberation, was also the season of ancient military campaigns and the census.

this day. I.e., the fifteenth of the month, the first day of the Festival of Unleavened Bread (see NOTE to 12:18); cf. "this day" in 12:14 (see NOTE).

12:18. *first.* I.e., the first month. P uses the same abbreviated style of dating in Gen 8:13; Num 9:5 (see also Ezek 1:1; 8:1; 20:1; 29:17; 45:18; 30:20; 31:1; 45:21, 25; Zech 7:5; Hag 1:15; 2:1, 10, 18).

fourteenth. This seems to contradict Lev 23:6 and Num 28:17, where Unleavened Bread begins on the fifteenth, like the parallel holiday of Shelters (*sukkôt*) in the autumn (Lev 23:34, 39; Num 29:12; Ezek 45:25; cf. 1 Kgs 12:32–33; see COMMENT, pp. 443–44). Our oldest extra-biblical witness, a fifth-century B.C.E. papyrus from Elephantine, Egypt, also begins the Festival of Unleavened Bread on the fifteenth of Nisan (Cowley 1923: 62–63; Porten and Yardeni 1986: 1.54). Why, then, does Exod 12:18 begin *maṣṣôt* on the fourteenth?

After long wrestling with this problem, I have come to a tentative conclusion that the contradiction is more apparent than real. By my theory of the dual calendar of Israel, bowing to both moon and sun (see NOTES to 12:2, 6), any dating would inevitably be ambiguous. The first lunar day of Unleavened Bread, from evening to evening, overlaps solar days fourteen and fifteen of the month, just as the Day of Expiation is dated to both the tenth (lunar) day

(Lev 16:29; 23:27) and the evening of the ninth (solar) day (Lev 23:32) of the seventh month (cf. VanderKam 1992: 814). Aramaic scribes in Egypt encountered comparable difficulties when dating documents by both the Egyptian solar and the Babylonian lunar calendars—particularly when they wrote at night (Porten 1990).

12:19. *will . . . be found.* There is likely wordplay between *maṣṣâ* 'unleavened cake' and *yimmāṣē'* 'may be found.'

what is leavened. In vv 19–20, the noun is not *ḥāmēṣ* but the unique *maḥmeṣet* (contrast 12:15; 13:3, 7, etc.). By context, *ḥāmēṣ* and *maḥmeṣet* should be synonyms, but *maḥmeṣet* is formally causative: "what causes to rise." Thus it may technically be the equivalent of *śə'ōr* 'leaven' (Rashi), rather than of *ḥāmēṣ* 'leavened, risen.' Still, *maḥmeṣet* must here connote leavened food, if only by synecdoche, since leaven itself is inedible (*Mek. pisḥā'* 10).

sojourner. A *gēr* is a person living off his ancestral territory, the opposite of an *'ezrāḥ* 'native' (see next NOTE). Generally, the *gēr* differs in nationality, ethnicity or clan affiliation from those among whom he resides (for a more refined treatment, see van Houten 1991). In 12:19, the "sojourner" is a non-Israelite (see NOTE to 12:48).

Although the positive requirement of the *Pesaḥ* is optional for the foreign *gēr* (12:48), the negative command to avoid leaven is incumbent on all foreigners, presumably lest they supply leaven or leavened bread to Israelites after the festival is over (see COMMENT, p. 434). It is unclear whether, in addition to abstaining from leavened food, the sojourner must consume unleavened bread (cf. Holzinger 1900: 38). I would imagine not.

native. An *'ezrāḥ*, the opposite of a "sojourner," is one living on his ancestral territory. The root *zrḥ* ordinarily means "shine" and perhaps "sprout" (*'ezrāḥ* is a tree in Ps 37:35 [MT]; cf. Greenfield 1959). We might infer that *'ezrāḥ* means "autochthonous, arising from the soil" (Dillmann 1880: 124). Smith (1927: 75), however, convincingly relates *'ezrāḥ* to Arabic *ṣariḥ* 'pure blooded (kinsman)' < *ṣrḥ* 'to be pure.' So the connection to *zrḥ* 'shine, sprout (?)' would be at most folk etymology.

12:20. *In all your dwellings.* Exod 12:15–17a, 18–20 expounds the laws of *Maṣṣôt* in a leisurely, redundant fashion, each iteration adding new detail. We are told first to eat unleavened bread for a week and to remove leaven from our houses (v 15a)—the basic requirements of the holiday. In v 15b, we learn that not only leaven itself but all food made with leaven is banned (cf. NOTE to 12:19). In v 15c, we learn the sanction for disobedience—*kārēt*—and how long it is in effect—a week. In v 16a, we find not only that the festival lasts a week but that it begins and ends with special days of rest. But, the reader might ask, how can one eat on those days? Cooking, then, is exempted (v 16b). In v 18, we learn on what days and at what times the festival begins and ends. Vv 19–20 recapitulate the essential requirements—to avoid leaven and leavened food and to eat *maṣṣôt*—along with the penalty for negligence. In addition, the text specifies that these laws are incumbent on both citizens and sojourners. Lastly, in v 20, the author explains the geographical extent of the statute: Israel's entire territory (cf. *môšāb* in Gen 10:30; 36:43; Exod 10:23; Num 35:29).

unleavened bread. Knohl (1987: 79 n. 35) observes a chiastic pattern in vv 18–20: *maṣṣōt . . . maḥmeṣet . . . maḥmeṣet . . . maṣṣôt* 'unleavened bread . . . leavened . . . leavened . . . unleavened bread.'

12:21. *elders*. If the clan elders preside over the rite, the Elohistic *Pesaḥ* may be performed by larger groups than the single households envisioned by P (12:3). But perhaps the elders are simply to transmit Moses' instructions to the heads of households (ibn Ezra).

Draw out. The precise sense is uncertain. Ramban supposes that the Israelites must literally "draw in" their scattered sheep. The verb *mšk* 'pull,' however, is sometimes used in hendiadys, modifying another verb in the manner of an adverb. Compare Judg 4:6, *lēk ûmāšaktā* 'go and you will draw out'; Judg 20:37, *wayyimšōk . . . wayyak* 'and he drew . . . and struck,' and perhaps Cant 1:4 *moškēnî . . . nārûṣâ* 'draw me . . . let us run.' BDB (p. 604) suggests that in Exod 12:21; Judg 4:6; 20:37, *mšk* means "proceed, march." Another possibility, raised by Cant 1:4, is that *mšk* connotes quick action (cf. Jacob 1992: 326). That, in fact, is Syr's rendering of 12:21: "quickly take" (*bᶜgl sbw*).

small cattle. Fox (1986: 66) renders *ṣō(')n* as "a sheep." But, while this suits the context, *ṣō(')n* is always collective. The proper term for a head of small cattle is *śe(h)* (12:3, 5; 13:13). Therefore, in 12:21, *ṣō(')n* must denote sheep and/or goats in the plural (RSV, NJV, etc.), just as the elders are addressed collectively, not individually (cf. Jacob 1992: 326).

Unlike P (12:5), the sources E and D (Deut 16:2) do not specify the age of the paschal victim. Perhaps a mature sheep or goat is envisioned.

for. Alternatively: "in exchange for"; see NOTE to 12:3.

12:22. *marjoram*. The LXX rendering, *hyssōpos* 'hyssop,' is based on the phonetic similarity to Hebrew *'ēzôb*, a common translation technique for LXX (Tov 1979). But even when Hebrew and Greek words are truly related via borrowing, their meanings may differ slightly. *'Ēzôb* is "Syrian hyssop" (*Origanum syriacum l.*) or marjoram, still used by Samaritans for *Pesaḥ* (Saadiah; Crowfoot and Baldensperger 1931). Greek *hyssōpos* is a different plant altogether (Zohary 1982: 96). A literalist might object that we should seek a native *Egyptian* plant, rather than a Palestinian, but no doubt later Israelite practice has been transplanted into an Egyptian setting.

The marjoram tuft, readily available (cf. 1 Kgs 5:13), is essentially a brush (Cassuto 1967: 143). Segal (1963: 159) and Jacob (1992: 328) plausibly infer that it insulates lay officiants from the dangers of the holy; true priests, in contrast, manipulate blood with their fingers. Marjoram is also used to apply blood in ritual purifications (Ps 51:9), particularly from skin disease (Leviticus 14 *passim*) and death (Num 19:18; cf. v 6) (on *Pesaḥ* and ritual purity, see COMMENT). According to Heb 9:19, it was also used for the Covenant ceremony of Exod 24:8.

apply. The usual verbs describing blood applications are *zāraq* 'cast,' *šāpak* 'pour,' *yāṣaq* 'pour,' *nātan* 'give, put,' *hizzâ* 'sprinkle' and *hēbî'* 'bring.' *Higgîaᶜ*

408   NOTES   12:1-13:16

in this sense is unique to 4:25; 12:22 (see COMMENT to Exodus 3–4, p. 239). Segal (1963: 159) also cites Isa 6:7, where purifying fire is applied (*higgîaʿ*) to Isaiah's mouth.

bowl/threshold. Unfortunately, *sap* can mean "bowl" or "threshold." Either would fit 12:22, and tradition is divided. "Bowl" is favored by R. Aqiba (*Mek. pishā'* 11), Saadiah, Rashi and Rashbam; "threshold" is the choice of LXX, Vg and R. Ishmael (*Mek. pishā'* 11). Plainly, some information is assumed, since E never says what is done with the animal just after it is killed. We are already supposed to know either that the blood is caught in a bowl (cf. 24:6; 1 Kgs 7:50; 2 Kgs 12:14; Jer 52:19) or that the animal is slaughtered in the doorway (Trumbull 1906: 206–9; Auerbach 1975: 54).

Given the biblical parallels, the former seems more likely. As Morgenstern (1966: 289) observes (against his own interpretation), the preposition *ba-* 'in,' rather than *ʿal* 'upon,' suggests a receptacle such as a pot. Still, the alternative is quite credible. Although the Bible does not explicitly describe threshold sacrifice, Trumbull (1906: 118–21) notes that the altars of both the Tabernacle (40:6, 29, etc.) and Temple (2 Kgs 12:10) were by the entrance. Moreover, we find many analogies among peoples akin to Israel (Morgenstern 1966: 168–69, 290–92). In particular, modern Middle Eastern bridal and seasonal rites often involve doorway sacrifices (Rihbany 1927: 98; Jaussen 1948: 54 n. 3; Canaan 1963: 20; Lane 1978: 537). If the paschal victim is slaughtered on the threshold, then the entire doorway is framed with blood. (For further ethnographic parallels, see Trumbull 1906; on the magical associations of doorways and thresholds, see COMMENT, pp. 440–41.)

do not go out . . . until morning. Jacob (1992: 329) compares Lev 8:33, 35 (P), forbidding Aaron and his sons to leave the Tent until the completion of their ordination. Similarly in Josh 2:18–19, Rahab's family is protected by the scarlet cord in their window as long as they stay indoors. The house in which the paschal sacrifice is eaten becomes a sacred asylum from the powers of destruction (COMMENT, p. 437). On night as a time of danger, see Ziegler (1950) and Fields (1992).

This command is slightly difficult within the context of E. Moses and Aaron seem to converse with Pharaoh in 12:31, but how can they do so without leaving home (cf. Meyer 1906: 34; Johnstone 1990: 41)? Most likely, Pharaoh sends messengers (Calvin) or goes himself to Moses and Aaron (Rashbam), who respond from their doorway (see NOTE to 10:29). Alternatively, Moses and Aaron may be exempt from the curfew.

12:23. *protect over the doorway.* This is probably a pun; Cassuto (1967: 143) catches the assonance in *pāsaḥ . . . ʿal-happetaḥ*. There is still greater assonance between *petaḥ* 'doorway' (properly pronounced *peṭaḥ*) and the noun *pesaḥ*. In ancient Israelite pronunciation, however, *petaḥ* was probably *pitḥ (or *piṭḥ), while *pesaḥ* was *pash (less likely *pish). We previously noted punning between *pesaḥ* and *ḥippāzôn* (NOTE to 12:11).

Destroyer. This is the rendering of LXX and Syr. A possible alternative is "destruction" (*Tg. Onqelos*; see NOTE to 12:13), but *ntn* 'permit' seems to imply a personal object (contrast Gen 20:6; 31:7; Exod 3:19, etc.). Most likely, in 12:23, the *mašḥît* is a personalized, quasi-independent aspect of Yahweh. According to 12:23, 29, Yahweh himself attacks the Egyptian firstborn, while the paschal blood averts the Destroyer from Israel. The difference of emphasis is significant: Yahweh assumes the glory of striking Egypt, while the "dirty job" of threatening Israel is delegated to his semi-autonomous dark side (cf. Loewenstamm 1992a: 208–16).

SPECULATION: We often read of destructive angels dispatched or restrained by God (Genesis 19; Num 22:22–35; 2 Sam 24:16; 2 Kgs 19:35; Ps 35:5–6; 1 Chr 21:15). Sometimes multiple entities act in concert (Ezekiel 9; Ps 78:49). Since in 1 Sam 13:17; 14:15, *mašḥît* means "(human) strike *force*," it is even possible in 12:23 that Yahweh's Destroyer is an angelic host, rather than a single being (Jub 49:2–3; *Tg. Ps.-Jonathan* 12:12–13; Brettler 1989: 10, 33 n. 50).

The image of a night spirit or spirits going from house to house for good or ill has many parallels in folklore. On the positive side, one thinks in Judaism of the prophet Elijah or Queen Sabbath, and in European Christianity of various Christmas sprites. And contagious diseases are often envisioned as house-calling demons (cf. Jer 9:20). On *Pesaḥ* as an apotropaic rite against such beings, see COMMENT.

12:24. *observe.* There is a grammatical problem not apparent in English. The injunction *ûš(ə)martem* 'and you will observe' is plural, while the "you" in "for you and for your sons" (*ləkā ûl[ə]bāne[y]kā*) is singular (Noth 1962: 97). Redactorial authorship of 12:24 provides an explanation of sorts: the plural *ûš(ə)martem* both refers back to v 17 (P) and anticipates v 25 (E). The phrase "for you (sing.) and for your sons," however, was adapted from other materials available to the Redactor, e.g., Lev 10:15; Num 18:8, 9, 11, 19; Deut 4:40; 12:25, 28; Josh 14:9.

12:25. *service.* Since *ʿăbōdâ* connotes both servitude and worship, Fox (1986: 67) perceives a transition in 12:25. The Israelites henceforth perform *ʿăbōdâ* for Yahweh, no longer for Pharaoh (cf. Durham 1987: 164).

12:26. *when your sons say. Bānîm* 'sons' may here include daughters, assuming they, too, were given at least rudimentary indoctrination (note that Proverbs esteems mothers and fathers alike as teachers [Prov 1:8; 6:20; 31:1]). We might have expected an injunction to instruct the young whether they ask for it or not (cf. 13:8). Rather, the text attributes the initiative to children intrigued by exotic rites and taboos (cf. 13:14; Deut 6:20–21; Josh 4:6–7, 21–23). These rituals are performed not only in the service of Yahweh but for the perpetuation of tradition.

12:27. *slaughter sacrifice. Zebaḥ* is a sacrificial meal shared by humans and Deity. The other common type of meat offering, *ʿōlâ*, is a holocaust consumed entirely by fire, i.e., by God. Although it is not mentioned, an altar may be involved in the Elohistic *Pesaḥ* (cf. Haran 1978: 344).

who protected. On the meaning of *pāsaḥ*, see NOTE to 12:11. While *'ăšer* is ordinarily a relative pronoun, it can sometimes be a conjunction (Seidl 1991). Thus an alternative rendering would be "*inasmuch as* he protected." (LXX MSS are in fact divided between *hōs* 'as' and *hos* 'who,' but the confusion is presumably inner-Greek.)

the people knelt and bowed. As the Elohist is a parsimonious narrator, we must infer that the elders have transmitted Moses' commands to the populace (Noth 1962: 96). Israel's genuflection expresses not only adoration but obedience (cf. 4:31).

What is the significance of prostration? Keel (1978: 310) proffers a striking interpretation: "Proskynesis is at base a fear-response. Faced with the overpowering experience of the holy, man escapes into death. Regarded thus, falling down is equivalent to the death-feigning reflex well-known to behavioral research. . . . No man can see God and live. . . . Should a man live nonetheless, it is only due to the grace of God . . . being lifted up is an integral part of what takes place." In other words, bowing down is a quasi-death and resurrection.

12:29. *Yahweh, he.* The emphasis is conveyed by inversion: *wǝyahwe(h) hikkâ* (vs. **wayyak yahwe[h]*).

sitting on his throne. On the inherent ambiguity of the Hebrew and the renderings of Tgs. Onqelos and Ps.-Jonathan, see NOTE to 11:5. In both 11:5 and 12:29, it is probably the king, not the son, who sits on the throne, just as in 11:5 it is the maidservant, not her son, who grinds, and just as here it is the prisoner who properly belongs in captivity.

captive. Hebrew *šǝbî* is formally masculine, but in fact neutral. LXX, however, has a feminine *aichmalōtis*, presumably to match the "maidservant" of 11:5 (see further NOTE to 11:5).

pit house. I.e., prison.

12:30. *by night, he.* This understanding is imposed by the accents of MT and perhaps also implied by LXX's nontranslation of *hû'* 'he' (see TEXTUAL NOTE). One may, however, alternatively read *laylâ hû'* 'that night' (cf. Gen 19:33; 30:16, etc.). The Syr consonantal text (*blly' hw wklhwn 'bdwhy*) is as ambiguous as the Hebrew, with vocalized MSS varying between *hū(w)* (pronoun) and *haw* (adjective). (In v 31, Syr has *blilyā' haw* 'on that night,' suggesting a similar reading in v 30.)

no house. On the hyperbole, see COMMENT to 7:8–11:10, p. 347.

12:31. *he called to Moses and Aaron.* This probably implies that Pharaoh and/or his servants leave the palace to confront Moses and Aaron at home, not that Pharaoh summons the pair to an official audience (see NOTE to 11:8).

by night. For Cassuto (1967: 145), the threefold repetition of *laylâ* in 12:29–31 evokes the inherent terror of the dark (cf. Ziegler 1950; Fields 1992). It may also highlight the strangeness of the situation. Throughout the Bible, including the Plagues cycle, business is ordinarily conducted "in the morning" or "on the next day." *Pesaḥ* is the only nocturnal sacrificial meal (Haran 1978: 320).

both ... and. The fourfold *gam ... gam ... gam ... gam* 'both ... and ... and ... and' in vv 31–32 may emphasize Pharaoh's complete acquiescence to Moses' demands (Fox 1986: 69). But see NOTE to 12:32 "too."

go serve Yahweh. These words might also be the author's exhortation to readers—ironically, in Pharaoh's mouth—with reference to the surrounding ritual legislation (Fretheim 1991a: 136).

according to your speaking. Even now, Pharaoh is evidently releasing the people for only a brief desert celebration. In 14:5, he seems surprised by Israel's flight (ibn Ezra; Holzinger 1900: 39). Greenberg (1969: 165), however, argues that the king knows exactly what is going on (note his suspicions already in 8:24; 10:5). He is simply too proud to admit capitulation.

12:32. *bless me.* Departures are in general the occasions for blessings (Gen 24:60; 47:10; 1 Kgs 8:66). Durham (1987: 167) suggests that "blessing" here is tantamount to lifting the curse that has befallen Egypt. And, assuming sacrifice is involved (cf. Balaam and Balak in Numbers 23–24), 12:32 might fulfill Moses' prediction that Pharaoh himself would donate sacrificial animals (10:25) (cf. ibn Ezra; Bekhor Shor; Luzzatto).

Most convincing, however, is Daube's (1963: 52–53) interpretation. Observing that a master who emancipates his slaves will be blessed (Deut 15:18; cf. Deut 24:13), he argues that "Pharaoh *malgré lui* releases the Israelites in the manner of a generous master." (And there is conceivably a hidden joke, for *bērak* can also euphemistically mean "curse" [1 Kgs 21:10, 13; Job 1:5, 11; 2:5, 9].)

too. The referent of *gam* is unclear. Rashbam relates it to the verb: "and *also* bless me" (in addition to taking the animals and leaving). But, since *gam* precedes *'ōtî* 'me,' one might understand "bless me, *too*" (in addition to being yourselves blessed). It is also uncertain whether this *gam* is somehow coordinate with the two *gams* of the prior clause: *gam-ṣō(')nəkem gam-bəqarkem qəḥû* 'both your flocks and your herds take.' Perhaps the intent is: as for your animals, take them; as for me, bless me.

12:33. *grew strong.* The verb *ḥzq* 'to be(come) strong' also has the nuance "urge" (cf. 2 Sam 24:4; 2 Kgs 4:8; perhaps Jer 20:7). Previously, *ḥzq* described the "strengthening" of Pharaoh's heart. Now, ironically, his people are "strong" to release Israel (Fox 1986: 69). Some Jewish sources claim that the Egyptians were more enthusiastic than the Hebrews themselves (Ginzberg 1928: 5.438 n. 239).

Surprisingly, the verb *wattehĕzaq* is feminine singular. Throughout the early chapters of Exodus, Egypt has been treated as a masculine plural, since the Egyptian *people* are generally under discussion (1:13; 3:9; 6:5; 7:5, 19, 24; 14:4, 9, 18, 23). The sole exception is 10:7, *'ābədâ miṣrāyim* 'Egypt is dying,' where the referent is the *land* of Egypt. Since in 12:33 the subject is again Egypt's *people*, we would expect the masculine plural **wayyehezqû*. Presumably, the mention of *hā'āreṣ* 'the land' later in the verse is a factor in the choice of the feminine. And there may even be an effort to portray, by hyperbole, the very land of Egypt as expelling the Hebrews (cf. Canaan "vomiting" out Israel in Lev 18:25, 28; 20:22).

dead. Mētîm might also be rendered "dying" (LXX; Tg. Onqelos; Bekhor Shor) or even "about to die." The latter may well be the intent; the Egyptians fear that further escalation will finish them off (Durham 1987: 167). In any case, they exaggerate their plight (D. N. Freedman, privately).

12:34. *picked up.* The Hebrews' dough does not rise, not because it is leaven-free, but because it has been jostled (ibn Ezra; Luzzatto; Ehrlich 1969: 159; Durham 1987: 167). Cf. Hos 7:4, "the baker refrains from stirring up the dough, till it rises." The Festival of Unleavened Bread is meant for observance, not in Egypt, but in Canaan (vs. Jub 49:22–23; see also REDACTION ANALYSIS; COMMENT, p. 445). There, as a memorial of an ancient bakers' mishap, one prepares true unleavened cakes each spring (13:3–9).

before it could rise. Although he goes too far in denying any connection between 12:34 and the Festival of Unleavened Bread, Jacob (1992: 348–49) acutely observes that the preparation or eating of food may describe the passage of a brief time (cf. Num 11:33; 1 Sam 2:15; Isa 7:15–18). Jacob paraphrases our verse as if it were proverbial: "the redemption took place between 'kneading and baking.'"

dough pans. LXX and Syr both render *miš'ārōt* as "pieces of dough," like LXX 7:28 (see NOTE). This is conceivably correct, although the parallelism with *ṭene'* 'receptacle' in Deut 28:5, 17 suggests rather a container. As observed in NOTE to 7:28, we should probably repunctuate **miš'ārōt*.

wrapped in their robes upon their shoulder. Dillmann (1880: 117) compares the modern Middle Eastern use of a burnoose as a sack. The text leaves it slightly unclear whether the dough pans borne in the robes contain the unrisen dough, or whether Israel "picked up its dough before it could rise" *because* their (empty) pans were already packed (Segal 1963: 47, 72). The former appeals more to common sense. Segal's reading generates an unnecessary contradiction with v 39: was the dough unrisen because the pans were packed or because time ran out?

robes. Since the Israelites are using garments to wrap the dough pans, the Egyptians' "borrowed" clothes may be of practical as well as monetary value.

12:35. *had done.* That vv 35 and 36 are pluperfective is indicated both by logic—the Israelites would hardly pause at this stage, and the Egyptians would hardly be friendly—and by grammar. Were the tense simple past, we would expect waw consecutive: **wayya'ăśû bənê yiśrā'ēl . . . wayyittēn yahwe(h)*. Rather, the narrator pauses to inform us that the Israelites had already fulfilled Yahweh's command (11:2–3) (Jacob 1992: 342; Weimar 1985: 14 n. 26).

12:36. *despoiled.* The spoliation of Egypt, foretold and commanded in 3:21–22; 11:2–3, is now executed. For various explanations, see NOTES to 3:21–22.

SPECULATION: The theme of despoiling Egypt may have arisen from a seasonal observance. Exodus envisions children asking, "Why do we slaughter a sheep/goat, eat unleavened bread and consecrate firstborn animals?" (12:26; 13:14; cf. 10:2; 13:8). Perhaps the plundering of Egypt, too, is etiological. Near the equinoxes, many cultures observe carnival holidays with special appeal for the young. Examples from Judaism would be Purim in the spring and *Śimḥat tôrâ* in the fall. In addition, among the folk customs of Passover is the children's "theft" of a piece of *maṣṣâ*, the Afikoman, for ransom. Possibly, the Israelite paschal ceremony already possessed a carnival aspect. Certainly, with its humor, broad characterization, exaggeration and redundancy, the Plagues narrative reads as a children's story. And the reference to mothers giving their children valuables demanded or borrowed from friends, neighbors and sojourners (3:22)—terms making little sense in the Egyptian context—might indicate a custom of gift giving or lending *among Israelites*, comparable to our Halloween "trick or treat" (see Segal 1963: 148–49, 260). Even if these conjectures are dismissed as fantastical, I would maintain that, with its good humor and thematic inversion of status, the Exodus story provides an emotional release comparable to that afforded by the carnival holidays of other cultures.

12:37. *Raamses . . . Succoth.* On the location and modern exploration of these sites, see APPENDIX B, vol. II.

SPECULATION: *Sukkōt* is probably the city Egyptians called *ṯkw.* The Israelites converted the foreign name into the ordinary Hebrew word for "shelters"; in fact, there was a prominent Transjordanian city of the same name.

But there was also an Israelite festival called *Sukkôt*, which involved living in temporary huts (Lev 23:42–43; Deut 16:13–17; 31:10, etc.). I believe that the Redactor sought to associate these *sukkôt* with the city of 12:37 (cf. *Mek. pisḥāʾ* 14). In his supplement to the laws of *Sukkôt* (Lev 23:39–43), the Redactor explains, "so that *your ages* will know that in *sukkôt* I caused Israel's Sons to dwell in my taking them out from the land of Egypt" (Lev 23:43; see Friedman 1987: 222–23). The problem is that the Torah nowhere describes the Israelites as living in "shelters" in the wilderness (*ʾōhālîm* 'tents,' however, are frequently mentioned). But Israel's first stop outside of Egypt is the *town* of Succoth (12:37; Num 33:5–6 [R]). In other words, Lev 23:43 may be explaining the holiday's name with a pun (cf. Gen 33:17 for wordplay on *sukkōt*). As for the true origin of the Festival of Shelters, the conventional explanation, that the Israelites lived in outdoor huts during this part of the harvest, seems adequate (e.g., Rylaarsdam 1962, but see Meshel 1971: 88–90 for possible nomadic antecedents). We should note, too, that pilgrimage festivals may have involved outdoor camping (Pedersen 1940: 2.388, 703 n. 1; Segal 1963: 210–11), although the references are again to "tents," not "shelters" (Hos 12:10; Josephus *Ant.* 17.217). The Samaritans still camp at Mount Gerizim for *Pesaḥ* (Jeremias 1932: 7).

about six hundred thousand. These "six hundred thousand *foot-men*" reappear in Num 11:21 (E). Segal (1963: 136–37, 258) infers from cross-cultural parallels that the spring festival of *Pesaḥ-Maṣṣôt* was the occasion of an annual census. Adapting an idea from Mendenhall (1958) and others, one might argue that here *'elep* means, not "thousand," but "clan" or even "squad" (cf. Num 31:4–6, etc.). Thus the number of Hebrew men leaving Egypt could have been much less than 600,000. On the other hand, in Num 11:21, six hundred *'ălāpîm* is imagined to be a huge number. And P records that exactly 625,550 adult men left Egypt (Exod 38:26; Num 3:39). It seems, therefore, that we must take 12:37; Num 11:21 literally (see Halpern 1983: 114–16; Loewenstamm 1992a: 227–28 n. 5).

As for the discrepancy between E's round 600,000 and P's 625,550, I assume *a priori* that the former number was original and schematic, while the latter was fabricated to lend verisimilitude (cf. NOTE to 12:40). Sixty myriads appears to be a stereotyped number, influenced by the Mesopotamian sexagesimal (60-based) system (Cassuto 1967: 147). It is probably an amplification of the common unit of six hundred warriors (14:7; Judg 3:31; 18:11, 17; 20:47, etc.), identified by Malamat (1954) with the *gədûd* 'cohort' (see also Loewenstamm 1992a: 226–27). This cohort may in turn be an amplification of a unit of sixty warriors (Cant 3:7) or noblemen (2 Kgs 25:19; cf. also the sixty queens in Cant 6:8). Doughty (1936: 2.456–57) observes a Bedouin tendency to hyperbolically magnify numbers by factors of ten.

foot-men. Raglî, literally, "he of the leg," is ordinarily a singular collective noun connoting infantry. Most likely E, like P, envisions the Hebrews as an army. But conceivably, *raglî* here simply means "men" (cf. Arabic *rajul* 'man' < *rijl* 'leg, foot').

dependents. See NOTE to 10:10.

12:38. *many foreigners.* Notice the assonance of MT *'ēreb rab* (in reconstructed Israelite pronunciation **'irb rabb*). The term *'ēreb* '(ethnic) mixture' is quite rare, paralleled only in Neh 13:3; Jer 50:37. Ps 106:35, too, uses the verb *hit'ārēb* to connote mixing with foreign nations (ibn Ezra). In 12:38, the *'ēreb* might be foreigners living among Israel as temporary or long-term sojourners (see NOTE to 12:43) or simply "fellow travelers" (cf. Philo *Moses* 1.147). That alien females lived among the Hebrews in Egypt is suggested by 3:22, "the woman sojourner of her house" (Meyer 1906: 35 n. 35). Indeed, if these women are concubines, perhaps they and their children are the *'ēreb* (Daube 1963: 53–54). Lev 24:10 in fact refers to a half-breed, but he is the son of a Hebrew mother and an Egyptian father. Num 11:4; Deut 29:10; Josh 8:35 also refer to non-Israelites traveling with Israel in the desert.

Exod 12:38 gives no indication of how numerous the *'ēreb* was conceived to be. According to *Mek. pishā'* 14, they vastly outnumbered the Hebrews themselves! Various Hellenistic Egyptian historians agree that many Egyptians joined the Israelite Exodus. For example, Manetho (*apud* Josephus *Ap.* 1.234) alleges that some 80,000 Egyptian lepers and other diseased persons gathered about Moses and allied themselves to Jews already settled in Jerusalem (*sic!*); Cheremon (*Ap.* 1.290) puts the number of diseased at 250,000. For further discussion of non-Israelite participation in the Exodus and of the accounts of gentile Hellenistic historians, see APPENDIX B, vol. II.

heavy. Here *kābēd* 'heavy' combines the nuances of "numerous" and "valuable." On the root *kbd* as thematic in Exodus 7-12, see SOURCE ANALYSIS above and INTRODUCTION, p. 36.

12:39. *they had been expelled from Egypt.* This verse fulfills the prediction of 11:1.

made no provisioning. Mek. pishā' 14 imputes Israel's improvidence to trust in God. But why, then, take any food at all? If an explanation is required, I would rather attribute Israel's unpreparedness to incredulity.

12:40. *thirty year and four hundred year.* P's figure is presumably derived from the 400 years of sojourn and servitude predicted in Gen 15:13 (J). Just as 600,000 adult men (E) become 625,550 (P) (NOTE to 12:37), so 400 years become 430 (12:40). Many find a contradiction between Gen 15:13; Exod 12:40, on the one hand, and Gen 15:16, "and a fourth generation will return hither," on the other. Can a generation last a century? Holzinger (1900: 40), Talmon (1990) and others observe that, at least in Abraham's case, a generation really is a century (Gen 21:5). But Abraham's age is from P, not J, so this is probably not the Yahwist's intent (although it is valid for the composite text).

SPECULATION: The confusion may arise from a misunderstanding of *dôr*, which, like Latin *saeculum*, can mean "life span" rather than "generation" (cf. Talmon 1990). The Yahwist gives us his idea of a maximum and presumably ideal life span in Gen 6:3: 120 years, the age attained by Moses (Deut 34:7 [J?]) (cf. Herodotus *Histories* 1.163, 3.23). If we define J's *dôr* thus, three maximum life spans total 360 years. When we add 40 years in the desert (Num 14:33, 34, etc.), we find that in the 400th year the fourth *dôr* returns to Canaan. To confirm that "generations" may be added, even where it seems illogical to us, note that the Redactor apparently summed the life spans of Levi, Kohath and Amram to cover approximately 400 years (see NOTE to 6:20 "years"). As for why the Yahwist (or his source) chose the number 400, it is most likely an amplification of the round number 40 (see Pope 1962a: 565). There may also be a connection with the 400th anniversary of the storm god Seth's rule at Tanis, celebrated in the reign of Ramesses II (*ANET* 253-54); see Halpern (1993: 92*) and APPENDIX B, vol. II.

Why exactly 430 years? It may represent a doubling of the 215-year Patriarchal age, from Abram's migration to Jacob's death (Gen 12:4; 21:5; 25:26; 47:9) (Dillmann 1880: 120). But this begs the question: why 215? If it is simply half of 430, we return to our starting point. Cassuto (1967:86) suggests that 430 is the sexagesimal round number 360 plus the equally round 70. A better hypothesis is that of Plastaras (1966: 34 n. 17): the basic number is 480, or 40 times 12 (cf. 1 Kgs 6:1), from which are deducted 40 years in the desert and 10 years for the conquest of Canaan. But the ten-year conquest, unfortunately, is conjectural.

In many traditions, the 430 years include the Patriarchal era (see TEX-TUAL NOTE). Thus the Israelites spend only 215 years in captivity (the number 210 in *Exodus Rab.* and *Tg. Ps.-Jonathan* appears to be a miscalculation). This is probably a secondary attempt to rationalize the life spans in 6:14–25 by readers who did not realize the figures were to be summed.

SPECULATION: The figure 430 may appear once again in the Bible, but by implication only (Dillmann 1880: 12). In Ezek 4:4–6, Yahweh commands the prophet to spend 390 days lying on his left side, bearing Israel's sins at a ratio of one day per year (OG has 190, however; see Zimmerli 1979: 165–68; Greenberg 1983a: 105–6). Then he must lie 40 days on his right for Judah's guilt. The total, for MT, would be 430 days = 430 years of sin. This, in turn, is quite close to the total of 433½ for all the kings of Judah from Solomon through Zedekiah, if we add their reigns and assume no coregencies (Zimmerli, p. 166). Since the Temple was built in Solomon's fourth year (1 Kgs 6:1) and stood 430 years, Zimmerli plausibly infers that this is the sin Ezekiel has in mind. Thus, if Exod 12:40 is of exilic or postexilic date, perhaps the author critically compares the Judean monarchy or the Temple establishment to Israel's Egyptian sojourn and servitude (see further under APPENDIX A, vol. II).

12:41. *bone . . . brigades.* See NOTE to 12:17.

12:42. *observance.* The significance of *šimmūrîm* is uncertain. On the possibility that it is to be translated "guarding," to gloss *Pesaḥ*, see NOTE to 12:11. Others find a reference to a vigil: Ehrlich (1908: 309), for example, understands that Yahweh was up all night killing Egyptians, while ibn Ezra infers a custom of wakefulness during the paschal night (cf. *t. Pesaḥ.* 10:11–12; Passover Haggadah). According to Segal (1963: 132), one originally stayed up on *Pesaḥ* to make astronomical observations—but all this is sheer speculation. There is really no evidence that *šmr* means "stay awake" in Hebrew (although the Arabic cognate does bear this connotation).

In any case, 12:42 features *double entente* between the better-established meanings of *šmr*: "guard" and "perform an obligation." As Yahweh *kept watch* over Israel during the first paschal night, so ever after must Israel *observe* the commemorative *Pesaḥ* ritual (Noth 1962: 100).

12:43. *Moses and Aaron.* See NOTE to 12:1.

Pesaḥ Rule. Ḥuqqat happāsaḥ may well be a document, also cited in Num 9:12 (P); see SOURCE ANALYSIS.

foreigner's son. This probably simply means "foreigner." It is conceivable, however, that *ben-nēkār* connotes the son of an Israelite woman and a foreign man, as in Lev 24:10. In any case, the *ben-nēkār* was distinct from the *gēr* 'sojourner' (12:48; Lev 22:18, 25; Deut 14:21) (see Weinfeld 1968; NOTE to 12:48). The *gēr* was a long-term, free resident, whereas the *nēkār* 'foreigner' was either a slave (Gen 17:12, 27) or what the Greeks called a *xenos*: an alien temporarily in the land for mercantile, military, diplomatic or administrative purposes (Deut 29:21; 2 Sam 15:19; 1 Kgs 8:41).

12:44. *any man's slave, a purchase by silver.* Another conceivable rendering is "any slave, a man purchased by silver." My translation follows the accentuation of MT as well as the slightly variant texts of LXX, Sam and the Qumran phylacteries (see TEXTUAL NOTE).

Why is it necessary to define a slave as a bought person? Not all slaves were purchased: some were bred (cf. Gen 17:12, 13, 27; Exod 21:4; Lev 22:11), received as gifts or bequests (Lev 25:46), seized in payment for debt (2 Kgs 4:1; Jer 34:14) or captured in war (Num 31:9–18; 31:35, 40; Deut 20:11–14). But 12:44 presumably applies to all these. Most likely, P adds "a purchase by silver" to heighten the distinction between the slave, on the one hand, and the semifree "resident" and "hireling," on the other (see next NOTE).

The slave is included in the family *Pesaḥ* as part of the freeman's household. Compare Lev 22:10–11: "No foreigner may eat *holiness* [sacrificial food]; the resident (*tôšab*) of a priest and a hireling (*śākîr*) may not eat *holiness*. But a priest who buys a *soul* [person], purchased by his money, he [the slave] may eat of it, and the one born of his house [i.e., as a slave], he may eat of his food." We may also compare Lev 25:6, which lists various dependents, apparently in order of descending intimacy: "your slave and your maidservant and your hireling and your resident that sojourn with you." Naturally, to include one's slaves befits the liberation theme of *Pesaḥ* (Luzzatto).

circumcise. According to P, all Israelite males must be circumcised on the eighth day. Moreover, all foreign slaves, whether bought or bred, must be circumcised, although no time limit is set (Gen 17:11–13). If the "*Pesaḥ* Rule" presupposes Genesis 17 or similar legislation, then 12:44 can refer only to the foreign slave whom, for whatever reason, one has neglected to circumcise. Since a "foreigner's son" can but need not be a slave, v 44 in effect restricts v 43: no foreigner may eat the *Pesaḥ*—*unless* he is a circumcised slave.

12:45. *resident . . . hireling.* These are probably distinct persons, although Houtman raises the possibility of hendiadys (*apud* Grünwaldt 1992: 99 n. 181). For recent discussions of the *gēr* 'sojourner,' *tôšab* 'resident' and *śākîr* 'hireling,' see Ahituv (1982), Reviv (1982) and van Houten (1991). The *tôšab* sometimes appears, as here, parallel to the *śākîr* (12:45; Lev 22:10; 25:6, 40). But he is more often associated with the *gēr* (Gen 23:4; Lev 25:23, 47; Num 35:15; Ps 39:13; 1 Chr 29:15), and in Lev 25:6, 40, the "resident" and "hireling" are both said to "sojourn (*gwr*) with you." My tentative opinion is that *tôšab* is a functional synonym for *gēr*. He is a freeman, generally of foreign extraction (see, however, Lev 25:35), living amidst Israelites (see NOTE to 12:19). He has not inherited the land on which he "sojourns" (*gwr*) or "resides" (*yšb*), nor can he bequeath it to his own heirs in perpetuity (Lev 25:8–34). Often the *gēr* and *tôšab* are described as impoverished (22:20–23; Deut 10:18–19; 14:29; 24:14–22; Jer 22:3; Zech 7:10; Mal 3:5; Ps 94:6; 146:9). But this need not be the case (Genesis 29–33; Lev 25:47). The *śākîr*, on the other hand, is a "sojourner" in the paid employ of an Israelite; he, too, is generally but not necessarily (Lev 25:40) a non-Israelite. The *śākîr* is definitely impoverished and has little recourse when oppressed (Lev 19:13; Mal 3:5). His "days" or "years" are proverbially difficult (Isa 16:14; 21:16; Job 7:1).

Just as P's *gēr* is almost always non-Israelite (see NOTES to 12:19, 48), so, too, are the "resident" and "hireling" foreign in 12:45 (with *Tg. Neofiti I*; *Fragmentary Targum*; *Tg. Ps.-Jonathan*; Grünwaldt 1992: 99). Since "all Israel's congregation must do it' (v 47), the excluded *tôšāb* and *śākîr* cannot be Israelites. (Were the point that any Israelite *except* the "resident" and "hireling" Israelite is eligible, v 45 should follow v 48.) See further under NOTE to v 48.

12:46. *one house*. That is, if two families share the repast (12:4), they must consume it together (12:10). Gaster (1949: 18) writes, "The original purpose of the paschal meal was to re-cement ties of kinship, infuse new life into the family, and renew the bonds of mutual protection at the beginning of each year" (cf. Nicolsky 1927: 179). But the family hardly needed reinforcing. On the contrary, if the *Pesaḥ* was ordinarily eaten by small households, the effect would have been to weaken broader clan ties (cf. Halpern's [1991] discussion of detribalization).

do not take from the house from the meat to the outside. I.e., do not take any of the meat outside. The Priestly stricture *lō(')-tôṣî'* corresponds to, and is presumably inspired by, E's "do not go out (*lō[']* *tēṣə'û*), (any) man from his house's doorway" (12:22); see SOURCE ANALYSIS. Compare also 12:8, 10, which prohibit consuming the meal outside of sacred time.

a bone . . . you must not break. Why break bones? Either in order to suck marrow (*Tg. Ps.-Jonathan*) or to facilitate boiling. Mic 3:3 describes the typical preparation as requiring flaying the carcass and breaking its bones, prior to boiling in a pot. The roasting of the paschal animal whole obviates this procedure (12:9).

Why not break bones? Ehrlich's (1969: 160) argument that sucking marrow is unworthy of freemen smacks of subjectivity. Rashbam and Bekhor Shor do somewhat better: if one must eat in panic (12:11), there is no time to suck bones (see also Jacob 1992: 356). It is also possible that the prohibition simply reinforces the command to roast the animal whole, rather than dismember it for boiling.

Most, however, interpret the proscription by the principle of "sympathetic magic." For Jub 49:13, keeping the paschal bones unbroken protects the Hebrews themselves (see Delcor 1990: 74–77). To this we may compare the Islamic *'aqîqa* sacrifice upon a child's first haircut: the victim's bones may not be broken, lest the child himself suffer harm (Curtiss 1903: 201; Morgenstern 1966: 12, 16, 38, 41, 43; Henninger 1975: 148–49). By a related approach, the paschal animal represents, not the individual Hebrew, but each family, whose unity ought to be unbroken (Beer 1939: 71; cf. 12:46 and COMMENT). Still others suggest that nonbreakage of the victim's bones would protect flocks and herds for the coming year (see Henninger 1956: 451 n. 3). These theories, though speculative, possess a commonsense appeal.

SPECULATION: Kohler (1910), Morgenstern (1916), Henninger (1956; 1975; 147–57) and Stendebach (1973) take a radically different approach. They note that similar taboos against bone-breaking prevail not only among Israelites and Arabs but worldwide. These are often associated with a belief that the animal must be reincarnated whole after death, whether in this world or the next. Inevitably, these scholars also compare Jesus, the resurrected Lamb whose bones were not broken (John 19:36). In fact, the Bible often associates death with crushing or scattering bones (Ps 31:11; 32:3; 34:21; 51:10; 53:6; Lam 3:4), and Ezekiel's vision of the Valley of Bones (37:1–14) describes the reverse process.

Initially, this seems quite implausible. Scripture nowhere mentions, in approbation or condemnation, belief in animal reincarnation (Segal 1963: 170–71), although Eccl 3:21 does attribute souls to beasts. Nor do I know any conclusive archaeological evidence (Freedman privately cites the mummified animals of Egypt and Ashkelon). Given our ignorance of Israelite popular religion, we should keep an open mind. As always, multiple interpretations probably coexisted.

12:47. *Israel's congregation.* I assume that this includes females, since males are not singled out (contrast Lev 6:11, 22). Whether it also includes children is less clear. Jub 49:17 and 11QTemple 17:8 set the age of obligation at twenty.

12:48. *sojourner.* Is this an Israelite or a foreign sojourner (see NOTE to 12:19)? If non-Israelite, he would already be excluded by 12:43. But if Israelite, how can he be uncircumcised (cf. Gen 17:12 [P])?

For P, a *gēr* is almost always a non-Israelite man living among Israelites and participating in their religion. Only Lev 25:35, 47 envisions an Israelite *gēr*. If the *"Pesaḥ* Rule" likewise uses *gēr* to denote an alien, we might view v 48 as restricting v 43 (the "foreigner's son" is excluded *unless* he is a circumcised sojourner). Since, however, the "resident" and "hireling" are types of sojourner (see NOTE to 12:45), we should probably take v 48 as restricting v 45 instead. That is, neither "resident" nor "hireling" may eat of the *Pesaḥ—unless* circumcised. (Although one might alternatively take v 45 to restrict v 48 [any circumcised sojourner may eat *unless* he is a "resident" or "hireling"], we expect a restriction to follow, not precede, its law.) Compare the import of 12:43–44: no "foreigner's son" may eat the *Pesaḥ unless* he is a circumcised slave (see NOTES to 12:43, 44).

These provisions for the sojourner and slave resonate with the narrative context. Elsewhere, Israel will be enjoined to treat these classes well, since they themselves had been sojourners and slaves in Egypt (23:9; Lev 19:34; 25:55; Deut 5:15; 10:19; 15:15; 16:12; 24:18–22). Also, after the mention of "foreigners" in 12:38, one naturally wonders about their participation in the *Pesaḥ.* Exod 12:43–49 provides an answer.

Thanks to the Israelites' sense of "corporate identity," it is possible to understand the terms *gēr, tôšāb* and *śākîr* in vv 45, 48 as connoting not just individuals but entire families (cf. Robinson 1967). Such an interpretation is suggested by the following reference to "every male" (see below).

would do a Pesah. I.e., intends to participate in the paschal rite.

every male . . . must be circumcised. A sojourner must have all males of his household circumcised, probably including his own slaves (cf. Gen 17:12), to be eligible for participation (Ehrlich 1908: 311). As observed above, the requirement to circumcise slaves before admitting them to the *Pesah* should rarely have been invoked, since slaves were supposed already to be circumcised (NOTE to 12:44). The same would be true for the "sojourner," as most of Israel's neighbors practiced circumcision (Propp 1987b). This clause of the *"Pesah* Rule" thus treats an exceptional case.

approach. The exact nuance of *yiqrab* is unclear. It might mean to join an Israelite family near which the *gēr* sojourns, or to enter a shrine as in Lev 22:3 (cf. Dillmann 1880: 124), or simply to be qualified (Milgrom 1991: 577). At any rate, the sojourner shares the meal. (Jacob [1992: 357] observes that "approach" in v 48 parallels "eat" in v 44, since both are preceded by *'āz* 'then.')

any uncircumcised may not eat of it. This is the essence of the *"Pesah* Rule": all men, whether free Israelite, slave or sojourner, must be circumcised to celebrate the *Pesah.* On the rite of circumcision and its relation to the *Pesah*, see COMMENT, pp. 452–54.

SPECULATION: Josh 5:2–9 reports that the Israelites left Egypt circumcised, but that the desert generation neglected the rite, presumably due to the journey's rigors. Joshua, therefore, circumcises the people "again . . . a second time" (MT; Greek different). Is the point that Joshua is reviving a lapsed custom, or was there a specific first time? One possibility is that somewhere in the missing P matter (see SOURCE and REDACTION ANALYSES), or perhaps in J (see pp. 238–39), was a record of a mass circumcision before the first paschal meal. If so, later Jewish legends to this effect (e.g., *Exod. Rab.* 17:3; 19:5) may preserve authentic Israelite tradition (Jacob 1992: 300–1). But, of course, the men could not have been circumcised immediately before the Exodus, since they would have been incapacitated (cf. Genesis 34).

It is surprising that the *"Pesah* Rule" does not mention ritual purity, elsewhere a requirement for participation (Num 9:6–13; Ezra 6:19–22; 2 Chronicles 29–30). Within the context of P, the reason must be that the first *Pesah* is not yet a sacrifice, but simply a meal; moreover, there is no time to wait for the impure. Only with the erection of the Tabernacle will the *Pesah* become a regular offering, with ritual purity mandatory (see COMMENT). Still, since the "Rule" is directed at future generations and may even have arisen independently of the Exodus account (see SOURCE ANALYSIS), its omission of purity is striking. Evidently, the "Rule" is concerned with permanent states such as circumcision and social status, not with transitory conditions such as purity and impurity.

12:49. *One Direction*. *Tôrâ* means "law," "teaching" and "way"; here the nuance of "law" predominates. In general, P insists that Israelites and sojourners are equal in both rights (Num 35:15) and responsibilities (Lev 16:29; 17:8–15; 18:26, etc.).

12:50. *all Israel's sons*. Assuming the word "all" is original (see TEXTUAL NOTE), there is a heightening vis-à-vis 12:28, which reported merely that "Israel's Sons went and did."

did. This refers, not to the "*Pesaḥ* Rule," aimed at future generations, but to all the contents of chap. 12.

12:51. *in their brigades*. I.e., organized by tribe and marching in file, not fleeing in a rout (Ehrlich 1908: 311) (see NOTE to 12:17).

13:2. *Sanctify*. If the firstborn is already inherently holy to Yahweh (Lev 27:26), how can a human "sanctify" him? Perhaps *qaddeš* connotes formal announcement of holiness (Luzzatto; on "delocutive" verbs, see Hillers 1967). Alternatively, one might say that 13:2 commands *imitatio Dei*, sanctifying what Yahweh has already made holy (cf. Levine 1989: 256). But the main intent is doubtless more practical: do not profane the animal through ordinary use.

firstborn. Usually, *bəkôr* connotes a man's eldest son, his principal heir (e.g., Deut 21:15). Here, however, the qualification "loosening the womb" makes it clear that the *bəkôr* is a woman's male firstborn. A son with an older sister does not count, since he did not "loosen" his mother's womb. Thus a man with several wives might have to redeem several sons (*m. Bek.* 8:4; *Mek. pishā'* 18); Levenson (1993b: 56) notes in this connection 13:15, "*each* firstborn of my sons."

loosening. *Peṭer* may mean "(the act of) loosening," and then, by extension, "that which loosens." Presumably, that which is loosened or released is the womb (cf. Gen 20:18; 29:31; 1 Sam 1:5, etc.). Tur-Sinai (*apud* Hartom 1954: 123), however, sees a nuance of redemption: the surrendered firstborn, by ensuring a woman's future fertility, redeems his potential siblings. On the special status of the *bəkôr*, see COMMENT, pp. 454–57.

13:3. *Remember*. The root *zkr* connotes not only mental preservation but also commemoration by positive act. Thus it overlaps semantically with *šmr* 'observe' (see NOTE to 20:8). But *zkr* may cover a broader semantic field, referring not only to observance but also to teaching (13:8); cf. Akkadian *zakāru* 'speak.'

slaves' house. *ʿĂbādîm* might rather be a plural of abstraction (GKC §124), hence: "house of *slavery*" (LXX; *Tg. Onqelos*); *Tg. Ps.-Jonathan* has it both ways: "house of slaves' bondage." The implication may be that in Pharaonic Egypt all men and women, natives and foreigners alike, are slaves (F. I. Andersen, privately).

from this. I.e., from here.

13:4. *month of the New Grain*. Unleavened Bread/Pesaḥ is dated to *ḥōdeš hā'ābîb* n 13:4; 23:15; 34:18; Deut 16:1. Often simply transliterated "Abib," *'ābîb* denotes the young ear with soft grains (Ginsberg 1982: 44). (Mahler's [1947: 58] theory that *'ābîb* derives rather from the Egyptian month Epiph [*ipip*] is implausible, since Epiph falls in autumn, not spring.) From the same root is *'ēb, referring to tender young reeds (Job 8:12) or fruit blossoms (Cant 6:11). Durham (1987: 178) comments that the very name "New Grain" contains a promise of residence in Canaan.

Ḥōdeš 'month' literally means "newness" and additionally connotes the new moon and the day of the new moon. There are consequently three reasonable interpretations of 13:4: (a) one may begin Unleavened Bread at any time during the month of New Grain, depending upon the harvest's progress (Noth 1962: 95) and to avoid overcrowding at the central shrine (Wambacq 1976: 396); (b) the festival begins precisely on the new moon (Hitzig apud Dillmann 1880: 127; Ehrlich 1908: 312–13; Morgenstern 1924: 59; 1966: 264 n. 268; May 1936: 74–75; Auerbach 1958: 1–10; Ginsberg 1982: 44; Goldstein and Cooper 1990: 21; cf. Luther in Meyer 1906: 170–73); (c) the festival falls on a specific day within the month which the text declines to specify, either because it was already known to the reader or because it was subject to annual proclamation. The first two explanations imply that P's dating the holiday to the fifteenth of the month is an innovation, while the last may be compatible with 12:6, 18.

It is difficult to choose among these possibilities. Against (a), it seems strange not to have a fixed date for a festival—but this is probably the case for Šābūʿōt 'Weeks'; See COMMENT, pp. 430–32. Against (b), we know of no ḥaggîm 'festivals' on the new moon, while there are many references to midmonth festivals (Lev 23:6, 34, 39; Num 28:17; 29:12; 1 Kgs 12:32–33; Ezek 45:25; Ps 81:4)—but the new moon itself is a minor holiday (Num 10:10; 28:11–15), as is the first of the seventh month (Lev 23:24–25; Num 29:1–6). As for explanation (c)—to which I incline—it rests upon unprovable assumptions but at least removes the contradiction with P.

Before the adoption of Babylonian month names in the Persian period, the Israelites followed a version of the Canaanite calendar. At most, the Bible preserves only four old month names: zîw 'Sprouting (?),' bûl 'Produce (?),' hā'ētānîm 'the Perennial Streams' and hā'ābîb 'the New Grain' (see Gordon and Tur-Sinai 1965: 38; on Ziw in Greek guise, see Brock 1973). 1 Kgs 6:1, 37–38; 8:2 helpfully correlate the Canaanite calendar with the more common ordinal system: Ziv is the second, Bul the eighth and Ethanim the seventh month. We may also infer from Exod 12:2; 13:4 that "New Grain" corresponds to the first month.

Admittedly, it is not quite certain that Abib was a Canaanite month. (Hā)'ētānîm, bûl and probably zîw are actually attested in Canaanite texts, but not (hā)'ābîb. Abib may not even be a name at all. Perhaps (hā)'ābîb is simply a description, just as the "Gezer Calendar" (AHI 10.001) refers to months, not by name or number, but by characteristic agricultural activity (cf. Segal 1963: 193, 207). If so, 13:4 simply means that Israelites should keep Pesaḥ-Maṣṣôt on the new moon after the grain begins to form ears.

13:5. service. The noun ʿăbōdâ has nuances of "practice" and "worship," as well as "labor." In 12:25, ʿăbōdâ referred to the paschal offering; here it connotes the Festival of Unleavened Bread (pace Rashi; Jacob 1992: 365).

in this month. Though somewhat awkward in flow (see SOURCE ANALYSIS), vv 3–5 are bound together by the progression *hayyôm hazze(h)* 'this day' . . . *hayyôm* 'today' . . . *bəḥōdeš* 'in the month' . . . *baḥōdeš hazze(h)* 'in this month' (Jacob 1992: 365).

13:6. *on the seventh day.* Unlike P (12:16), E accords explicit sanctity to the seventh day alone. Ginsberg (1982: 45) infers that E commands a pilgrimage (*ḥag*) *after* the week of Unleavened Bread. More likely, however, the pilgrimage lasts seven days, with the first and last days *ḥaggîm*, just as in P. E's non-mention of the first day, in other words, is an accident.

13:7. *for the seven days.* *'Ēt šibʿat hayyāmîm* exemplifies the rare accusative of duration of time (Joüon 1965 §126*i*; cf. Deut 9:25; Lev 25:22 and possibly Exod 14:20 [see NOTE]; for inscriptional parallels, see Elwoude 1994: 175).

In my reading, vv 6–7 are chiastic: "Six days you will eat unleavened bread . . . unleavened bread you will eat for the seven days" (see TEXTUAL NOTE to 13:7).

may not be seen for you. This is more graphic than "eliminate" (12:15) or "may not be found" (12:19). But it theoretically leaves open the possibility of merely hiding one's leaven — surely not the author's intent. Since *ləkā* 'for you' implies possession, an equally valid translation would be "none of your leaven may be seen."

13:8. *For the sake of what.* The father's words are elliptical: "(This I do) for the sake of what Yahweh did. . . ." LXX and *Tg. Onqelos* "because of *this*, Yahweh acted for me" cannot be correct. Did God take Israel from Egypt *because* they avoided leaven? *Ze(h)* is rather a relative pronoun equivalent to *'ăšer* and *zû* (Luzzatto; Holzinger 1900: 40; cf. Ramban). Admittedly, all other examples are poetic, but at least the context is liturgical-pedagogical, not narrational.

13:9. *sign on your arm . . . memorial between your eyes.* The idiom "*between the eyes*" connotes the head or forehead in Hebrew (Deut 14:1; Dan 8:5, 21), Syriac and Ugaritic (*KTU* 1.2.iv.21–25). But it is unclear whether the "sign" is worn or tattooed (cf. Isa 44:5; 49:16; Ezek 9:4); the former, as we shall see, is more likely. In this context, *yādəkā* might denote either the hand (cf. Prov 7:3) or the arm (cf. Hag 2:23; Cant 8:6). For the *zikkārôn* 'memorial (amulet)' upon the forehead, cf. Zech 6:14 (compare also Isa 57:8).

Commentators are divided on whether the "sign" of 13:9, 16 is worn literally or only metaphorically. Here parallels from Deuteronomy and Proverbs are instructive (Miller 1970c). In Deut 6:6, 8; 11:18, Israelites are enjoined to set Moses' words upon their hearts, and to "bind them as a sign on your arm, and they will be as a circlet *between your eyes.*" Similarly, Proverbs commands, "My son, observe your father's command, / And do not forsake your mother's direction. / Bind them on your heart perpetually, / Wear them on your throat" (Prov 6:20–21); "My son, observe my sayings; / Store up my commands by you. / Bind them on your fingers; / Write them on your heart's tablet" (Prov 7:1–3). For the signet on the hand or arm and the circlet about the brow, see also Isa 62:3; Prov 1:9; 4:9; for the pendant on the breast and the necklace, compare Prov 1:9; 3:3, 22; Cant 8:6. These passages imply that such accessories are particularly dear to the wearer, constitutive of his or her identity (cf. also Gen 38:18, 25; Jer 2:32). Tigay (1982a: 891; 1982b: 327) compares Ishtar's necklace in *Gilgamesh* XI:163–65, worn as an eternal reminder of the Flood (*ANET* 95).

It is fairly clear that all the nonpentateuchal parallels to 13:9, 16 speak metaphorically. It is unlikely, for example, that Proverbs advises a son literally to wear parchments bearing parental injunctions. Many also take Exodus and Deuteronomy in this manner (LXX; the Qara'ites; Menahem ben Saruq; Rashbam; Tigay 1982a: 890–91).

At least since Second Temple times, however, Jews have prayed and studied while wearing *təpillîn* 'phylacteries,' capsules containing scriptural verses bound to arm and forehead, in literal compliance with Exod 13:9, 16; Deut 6:8; 11:18. Similarly, the command to write Moses' words on doorposts and gates (Deut 6:9; 11:20) has led to the placing of a box of verses, the mezuzah, in the doorway of the Jewish home (see COMMENT, p. 441). (Tradition takes the injunction to wear Moses' words "upon the heart," however, as metaphor—although in modern times one sees mezuzoth as chest pendants.) The use of sacred text as charm has many parallels in the Near East and Mediterranean regions (verses from Akkadian epic, Homer, Plato, the Gospels, the Qur'ān [Tigay 1979: 51–52 n. 33; 1982a: 886]). And silver plaques bearing the Priestly Benediction (Num 6:24–26) have been unearthed in Israel (*AHI* 4.301–2; Yardeni 1991; Barkay 1992), apparently worn in literal fulfillment of Num 6:27, "and they shall put my name upon Israel's Sons, and I will bless them." Thus it is possible that 13:9, 16; Deut 6:8; 11:18 are meant literally (Speiser 1965; Weinfeld 1972: 301; Scharbert 1989: 56). Elsewhere in P, the expression *hāyâ lə'ôt* 'be as a sign' refers to visible objects: Gen 9:13 (rainbow); 17:11 (circumcised penis); Exod 12:13 (paschal blood); Num 17:3 (incense pans); 17:25 (rod); many also emend Num 15:39 (fringe) to fit the pattern (cf. Weinfeld 1972). We find much the same elsewhere in the Bible: Isa 19:20 (altar); 55:13 (trees); Ezek 14:8 (apostate); 20:12, 20 (Sabbath [cf. Exod 31:17]). So, too, Exod 13:9 may prescribe wearing a visible sign to remind the Israelite of his obligation to keep Unleavened Bread.

But what might the sign be? One is surely not commanded to wear unleavened bread itself, let alone enjoined to don animal limbs (vv 9, 16). One is led to Kaufmann's (1942–56: 2.430, 487) conjecture: the *blood* of the *Pesah* and of the firstling was smeared on worshipers' heads and arms, as in certain Arab practices (see COMMENT). To me, it seems more likely that our text speaks metaphorically—or perhaps it was always ambiguous.

Whether the language is literal or metaphorical, 13:9 stipulates that the law of Unleavened Bread should be a constant part of one's identity and consciousness, like a signet or a circlet. It is a Covenant sign for the individual and his children. And Deut 6:6–9 and 11:18–20 broaden the command: *all* Moses' words are to be kept in perpetual consciousness, not merely on head and hand, but in the heart and on the doorway (this last expansion is probably inspired by the proximity of the paschal legislation in Exodus 12–13).

Since biblical MSS use no punctuation marks, it is unclear where the father's words conclude and Moses' address resumes in 13:8–10, 15–16 (cf. Rashbam). My translation ends the subquotations with vv 8 and 15, but it is possible that the *father* enjoins his son to wear Yahweh's law and to regard himself as having participated in the Exodus (see TEXTUAL NOTE to 13:9). This interpretation would strengthen the analogy with Proverbs, which advises a son to "bind on" his *parents'* teaching. But the parallels from Deuteronomy suggest that the command to "wear" Moses' words is addressed to his immediate listeners by Moses himself, who thus becomes a father figure (cf. Deut 32:7).

Direction. In light of the parallels from Proverbs (see above), *tôrâ* may here connote "teaching" rather than a particular "law." *Tôrat yahwe(h)* could mean both "teaching *from*" and "teaching *about*" Yahweh (Ehrlich 1908: 314).

mouth. The reference is probably to speech, although Jer 15:16 and Ezek 3:1–3 describe prophets as *ingesting* God's words. Fox (1986: 73) observes that the arm, eyes and mouth are respectively organs of action, perception and speech.

took you out. Here and in 13:16, we could render, "will have taken you out."

13:10. *this rule.* Scribal tradition, by placing a break after v 10, understands "this rule" as the Festival of Unleavened Bread. The parallel with 12:24–27 suggests, however, that the reference is rather to Firstborn Consecration.

occasion. Mô'ēd is a technical term, often connoting a meeting. Here, however, it is the date of a festival.

from days to days. "Days" (*yāmîm*) often connotes a year in Biblical Hebrew (e.g., Lev 25:29; Num 9:22; Judg 17:10; 1 Sam 27:7; Job 1:5; 2 Chr 21:19), inscriptional Hebrew (*AHI* 7.001.5, 7, 9 [Yavneh Yam]) and Phoenician (Karatepe III.1. [*KAI* 26]; see Bron 1979: 99 and, for a different interpretation, Haran 1978: 313. *Miyyāmîm yāmîmâ* thus means "from year to year, annually" (cf. Judg 11:40; 21:19; 1 Sam 1:3; 2:19).

13:12. *make . . . pass.* The causative of '*br* 'pass' refers to transfer of ownership (Num 27:7, 8). When the recipient is a deity, *he'ĕbîr* means "dedicate, consecrate." Scholars debate whether this necessarily entails full sacrifice, particularly when the object is a human; see NOTE to 22:28.

spawn. The meaning of *šeger* (13:12; Deut 7:13; 28:4, 18, 51; Ben Sira 40:19) is disputed. Most compare Aramaic *šəgar* 'throw' (e.g., Rashi; Luzzatto; Dillmann 1880: 129), hence my rendering "spawn" (cf. also English "cast," German *werfen* and possibly *hošlak* in Ps 22:11). But Syr renders *šeger* as *raḥmā'* 'womb' (also Cassuto 1967: 153); note the parallelism between *peṭer reḥem* and *peṭer šeger* in 13:12. We are thus left uncertain whether *šeger* is that which casts (the womb) or that which is cast (the spawn).

SPECULATION: Further support for Syr may be available from Ugaritic, but the connection is extremely tenuous. In Deut 7:13; 28:4, 18, 51, Yahweh promises to bless "your cattle's *šeger* and your flock's *ʿaštārōt*." The last term is otherwise the name of the goddess Astarte. Ugaritic *rḥmy* is also a goddess, possibly the same as Astarte; her name might mean "She of the womb." Assuming, then, that Astarte is a womb goddess, perhaps both *ʿaštārōt* and *šeger* in Deuteronomy mean "womb(s)." (On the possibility that *šgr* is itself a deity, see Hoftijzer and van der Kooij 1976: 273–74; Levine 1981b; *RSP* 3.415–16.)

the males. It is necessary to specify the sex, since neither *peṭer* 'loosening' nor *šeger* 'spawn' is gender-specific.

13:13. *ass.* Under normal circumstances, Israelites ate and sacrificed, among domestic mammals, only sheep, goats and bovines. Horses, pigs, camels and especially asses were sacrificed elsewhere in the ancient world, but not in Israel (Leviticus 11: Deut 14:3–21) (on the ass, see Smith 1927: 486; Dossin 1938: 108–9; Firmage 1992: 1137). Asses were eaten only in desperation (2 Kgs 6:25). It is unclear whether 13:13; 34:20 mention the ass as a paradigm for *all* unclean domestic animals (Luzzatto), or whether the ass is singled out as the *only* unclean animal requiring special treatment (*Mek. pishaʾ* 18; *b. Bek.* 5b). According to Lev 27:27; Num 18:15 (P), the firstborn of *all* unclean animals are either redeemed, with one-fifth added to their value, or sold by the priests.

neck. The precise meaning of *ʿrp* is uncertain. It seems related to *ʿōrep* 'neck,' hence my neologism "neck" (cf. "hamstring," "kneecap," "gut"). Some understand *ʿrp* as "break the neck by twisting" (e.g., Baentsch 1903: 113), but Aquila has "cut the neck," and, according to *m. Soṭa* 9:4; *b. Bek.* 10b, *ʿrp* is performed with a hatchet. The verb can also describe the demolition of an altar (Hos 10:2).

Why this particular mode of slaughter? Baentsch argues that twisting the neck, rather than slitting the throat (*zbḥ*), minimizes bloodshed, making the killing a profane rather than a sacred act (cf. Deut 21:4–6; *b. Ḥul.* 23b–24a). We may similarly infer from the elliptical Isa 66:3 that *ʿrp* connotes the opposite of proper sacrifice: "He who slaughters (*šḥṭ*) bull(s) [is, as it were,] striking down a man; he who sacrifices (*zbḥ*) small cattle [is, as it were,] *necking* (*ʿrp*) a dog; he who offers up a grain offering [offers, as it were,] pig's blood; he who burns incense blesses [, as it were,] sin."

However wasteful 13:13 may seem, we may be sure it was almost never applied—which is probably why it follows, rather than precedes, the mandate of redemption (Jacob 1992: 372). As Dillmann (1880: 13) observes, an ass is worth far more than a sheep or goat—at Ugarit, roughly ten times (Heltzer 1978: 21–22). One would therefore always choose redemption over slaughter. Num 18:15 in fact commands redemption of unclean animals without mentioning the option of profane slaughter.

Human . . . you will redeem. It is not clear what the text has in mind by "redeem" (*pdy*). The natural inference, both from the preceding law of the ass and from the paschal rite, is that a sheep or goat is literally sacrificed instead of the child (see also 34:20). P will later propose, however, that the redemption is monetary, at a rate of five shekels per firstborn (Num 3:47–51; 18:16). This money is paid to the Tabernacle, whose personnel, the Levites, are "donated" to Yahweh in place of Israel's firstborn (Num 3:11–13, 40–51; 8:14–18). Even the Levites' cattle somehow replace Israel's firstborn cattle (Num 3:45)—exactly how is unclear. On the implicit connection between the redemption of first-born humans and child sacrifice, see COMMENT, pp. 454–57.

13:14. *your son asks.* Whenever one offers a firstling, one should seize the opportunity to commemorate the Exodus (Johnstone 1990: 46, 108).

13:15. *Pharaoh was too hard.* Perhaps we should translate *hiqšâ parʿō(h)* as "Pharaoh *hardened*," taking as the implied object either his heart (cf. 7:3) or, less likely, his neck (cf. 32:9; 33:5; 34:9, etc.) (Jacob 1992: 373). Either way, the point is that Pharaoh repeatedly reneged on his promise to release Israel (Luzzatto).

13:16. *circlet.* Tigay notes the frequency with which Egyptian and Assyrian art depicts Syro-Palestinians wearing headbands (*ANEP* figs. 2, 4, 7, 46, 47, 52, 53, 54). Biblical references include Prov 1:9; 4:9 and especially Exod 28:36–38, describing the golden head plaque worn by the chief priest (Luzzatto).

Ṭôṭepet (see TEXTUAL NOTE) derives from a root *ṭwp* 'surround' attested in Arabic, but not otherwise in Hebrew (Gesenius *apud* Dillmann 1880: 130; Luzzatto; Tigay 1982b). The development was *ṭapṭapt* > *ṭawṭapt* > *ṭôṭapt* > *ṭôṭepet* (cf. *kabkab* > *kawkab* > *kôkāb* 'star'; also Mishnaic *lablab* > *law-lab* > *lûlāb* 'twig, frond, Lulav').

COMMENT

THE FUNCTION OF RITUAL

The Exodus narrative is nearing a climax. Negotiations are severed, and Israel stands on the brink of liberation. To our surprise, the text pauses to describe in detail the paschal ritual, digressing further to ordain the Festival of Unleavened Bread and the Consecration of the Firstborn. Aside from their obvious didactic function, these technical and hortatory materials work a literary effect. The minute cultic description both creates suspense (Fretheim 1991a: 135) and pulls readers into the events. As centuries of bondage draw to an end, we huddle with the Hebrews behind their blood-spattered doorways, tasting the roast meat, unleavened bread and bitter herbs (cf. Durham 1987: 180). Outside, Yahweh's Destroyer stalks the firstborn. Isa 26:20–21 may evoke the terror of this first paschal night (Füglister 1963: 32–33):

Go, my people, come into your rooms
And shut your door(s) behind you;
Hide just a little while, till wrath shall pass.
For, see: Yahweh coming forth from his place
To avenge the sin of the land's inhabitant(s) against him.
And the land will reveal her bloodiness,
And no longer cover over her slain.

While many modern readers find ritual detail unengaging, Rashi (on Gen 1:1) wondered why God did not simply begin the Torah at Exod 12:2. Here at last one encounters useful instruction, not mere history!

Locating the first *Pesah* in Egypt makes each subsequent celebration not just a historical commemoration but an actual reenactment. The tastes, smells and practices project celebrants backward in time (cf. Mann 1996: 242). All merge into their common ancestors and thus into one another. Conversely, Egypt, the "slaves' house," is drawn forward, becoming a universal symbol for physical or emotional oppression. In every generation and in every year, Israelites must perform the drama and undergo a national catharsis (on myth, ritual and the transcendence of time, see Eliade 1954).

PESAH AND *MAṢṢÔT*—INDEPENDENT FESTIVALS?

The relationship between the paschal meal and the Festival of Unleavened Bread remains a vexed question. To most readers, the answer will seem obvious: *Pesah* is the observance introducing the week of *Maṣṣôt* (Ewald 1876: 353; Segal 1963: 175). Many commentators, however, posit independent origins for the two institutions: *Pesah* was a holiday of nomadic Hebrew shepherds; *Maṣṣôt* was celebrated by farmers, possibly Canaanite (Oesterley 1933; Morgenstern 1935: 43–44; Pedersen 1940: 2.400–1; Füglister 1963: 41; Hyatt 1971: 134, 145–46; Haag 1971: 43–57, 64–67). As these populations merged to create Israel, their springtime rituals also merged.

I find this hypothesis untenable, not to say untestable (for a critical survey, see Segal 1963: 78–113; for further bibliography, Henninger 1975: 53–56). While there may be some truth to the underlying reconstruction of Israelite origins, modern research has blurred the once-sharp distinction between peasant and pastoralist (Segal 1963: 93–95; Gottwald 1979; see APPENDIX B, vol. II). Unleavened Bread, moreover, is not really an agricultural festival (see below), and shepherds are not exclusively carnivorous, no more than farmers are vegetarian. Lastly, the Torah was written and compiled over a half-millennium after Israel's emergence (see APPENDIX A, vol. II). The supposition that social tensions of the Late Bronze and Early Iron Ages left their traces in inconsistencies within and among biblical texts sounds like wishful thinking.

Far from being a late development, the *Pesah-Maṣṣôt* complex makes most sense in early Israel. Prior to cultic centralization in Jerusalem, Israelites could keep the paschal night at home and visit the local shrine the next morning (23:15; 34:23; Deut 16:16). *Pesah* would have been a yearly, domestic sacrificial meal, perhaps the *zebah mišpāhâ* 'family slaughter-sacrifice' (1 Sam 20:6, 29; compare 1 Sam 1:3; Job 1:4–5) (cf. Haran 1978: 304–16). Late monarchic centralization of worship, however, would create a rupture between *Pesah* and *Maṣṣôt*, as well as an exchange of status. *Pesah* became a Temple sacrifice, *Maṣṣôt* a domestic observance.

GROUNDS FOR SKEPTICISM

The Bible presents an unambiguous history and interpretation of *Pesaḥ-Maṣṣôt:* the rites, ordained by Yahweh and Moses, commemorate and reenact Israel's liberation from Egypt. Historians reflexively mistrust such foundation legends. For the case at hand, positive evidence suggests that later practices and beliefs have been foisted upon Moses, either by the biblical authors or more likely by their received tradition.

First, the laws of Unleavened Bread sit awkwardly in their narrative context. It is unlikely that the seven-day festival could have been celebrated with Egypt in hot pursuit (Noth 1962: 97; Durham 1987: 159). And no "Just So Story" could be more contrived than E's account of the disturbed dough (12:34, 39). In some respects, the *Pesaḥ*, too, is hard to square with its narrative context: e.g., if housebound (12:22), how do Moses and Aaron communicate with Pharaoh (but see NOTES to 10:29 and 12:22)? Ethnographic evidence to be presented below also suggests that *Pesaḥ*'s origins belong to Semitic prehistory and long antedate the historical Moses.

In the following analysis, therefore, I assume that *Pesaḥ* and *Maṣṣôt* only gradually evolved into commemorations of the Exodus. I also entertain the possibility that more "primitive" interpretations of the rites survived alongside the "official" understanding of the biblical authors.

THE LEAVEN OF MALICE AND EVIL

Apart from Exodus 12–13, biblical sources consistently describe the Festival of Unleavened Bread as a pilgrimage festival, a *ḥag*. Unleavened Bread (*Maṣṣôt*), Weeks (*Šābūʿôt*) and Shelters (*Sukkôt*) are the three annual holidays upon which all males must present themselves before Yahweh at a sanctuary (23:14–17; 34:18–23; Deut 16:1–17). Most scholars assume that originally one could worship at any nearby "high place" (e.g., Segal 1963: 133). Because Weeks and Shelters are primarily harvest festivals, interpreters generally assign to *Maṣṣôt* an analogous agricultural aspect (e.g., Wellhausen 1885: 83–99). To be sure, Exodus 12 presents Unleavened Bread as a historical commemoration, not as a harvest or seasonal celebration. But one has only to consider Christmas, Easter, Thanksgiving and Passover to realize that these categories are not incompatible.

At first, the characterization of *Maṣṣôt* as an agricultural festival seems reasonable. The holiday approximately coincides with the beginning of the barley harvest in the "month of the New Grain." But objections have been raised, some more cogent than others (Segal 1963: 108–13; Olivarri 1971–72; Halbe 1975; Wambacq 1980; 1981). Wambacq (1981: 503–4), for example, argues that any holiday with a fixed date, especially in a lunisolar calendar, cannot be agricultural, as crop-ripening is unpredictable. Yet *Sukkôt*, clearly a harvest festival, falls on a fixed date. In fact, for ritual purposes, minor divergence between the festival calendar and agricultural reality may have been tolerable (see below, however).

The real problem lies in the grain from which *maṣṣôt* were baked. As the Festival of *Maṣṣôt* coincides with the new barley crop, one might expect this to be the source of the flour. But tender new grain cannot be ground; it must be eaten parched (Lev 23:14; Josh 5:11) (Segal 1963: 111; Ginsberg 1982: 44). *Maṣṣôt* were rather made from the *old* crop. Hence, they were independent of the agricultural cycle.

There is one ritual, however, that may lend the Festival of Unleavened Bread an agricultural aspect: the Presentation of the first *ʿōmer* of barley to Yahweh (*ʿōmer* means either "sheaf" or "measure"; see Licht 1971a). Consideration of the Presentation of the *ʿōmer* will entail a long digression, but there is no help for it. It is the sole credible prop for the agricultural interpretation of *Maṣṣôt*.

After prescribing offerings for *Pesaḥ* and Unleavened Bread in Lev 23:5–8, Yahweh commands (vv 10–16):

> When you come to the land . . . and harvest its harvest, then you will bring an *ʿōmer* of the first of your harvest to the priest. And he will elevate the *ʿōmer* before Yahweh to propitiate for you on the day after the Sabbath. . . . And bread and roasted grain and produce do not eat . . . until your bringing your deity's sacrifice. . . . Then count for yourselves, from the day after the Sabbath, from the day of your bringing the *ʿōmer* of elevation: seven complete Sabbaths there shall be. Until the day after the seventh Sabbath you will count fifty days. Then you will *bring* [i.e., sacrifice] a new offering to Yahweh.

"New offering" refers to the Festival of Weeks (*Šābūʿôt*), Christian Pentecost, celebrating the end of the grain harvest and the ingathering of firstfruits. (The antiquity of the *ʿōmer* ritual is difficult to gauge, but it may be alluded to in Deut 16:9; for a possible Ugaritic antecedent, see de Vaux 1937: 549–50; 1961: 491; Worden 1953; Gray 1965: 68–69.)

The crux lies in the command to present the *ʿōmer* on "the day after the Sabbath." Which Sabbath? Traditional and critical sources offer five different answers (see Snaith 1947: 124–28; Haran 1976; Fishbane 1985: 144–51): (a) the eve of the festival (Fishbane); (b) the first day of the festival (LXX; Rabbis; Josephus); (c) the seventh day of the festival (Boethusian Jews; Jub 15:1; 44:1–5; Syr; Ethiopian Jewry); (d) the Sabbath falling during the festival (Sadducees; Samaritans; Qaraʾites; Christians; Wellhausen 1885: 86); (e) the first Sabbath during the grain harvest (Meshwi of Baalbek; Licht 1971a; Olivarri 1971–72: 266). If any of the first four explanations is correct, then *Maṣṣôt* has an agricultural aspect—at least indirectly, at least for P. But if (e) is correct, then the Presentation of the *ʿōmer* is a completely independent rite. As so often, our ignorance of the Israelite calendar frustrates our efforts. We are uncertain, for example, whether we are dealing with a solar or lunisolar calendar (see NOTES to 12:2, 3, 6, 18), and we do not know how the days in the month were counted (see below).

Fishbane strongly defends theory (a): the *ʿōmer* is presented on the first day of Unleavened Bread, the fifteenth of the month. Granted, Lev 23:10–16 is strikingly reminiscent of Josh 5:10–12, where the Israelites, having crossed the Jordan, eat the *Pesaḥ* on the evening of the fourteenth day, and on the morrow eat "the land's produce, unleavened bread and roasted grain." Specific lexical contacts are *qālî/qālûy* 'parched grain' (Lev 23:14; Josh 5:11), *moḥŏrat* 'morrow' (Lev 23:11, 15; Josh 5:12) and *šbt* 'cease' (Lev 23:11, 15, 16; Josh 5:12). Several caveats are necessary, however. First, despite Fishbane's characterization of Josh 5:10–12 as a commentary on Lev 23:10–16, the order of composition is not clear (see APPENDIX A, vol. II). But the greater difficulty is the assumption that *šabbāt* in Lev 23:11, 15 denotes the day of the paschal offering, the fourteenth of the month. Fishbane invokes Akkadian *šab/pattu*, the fifteenth of the month (cf. Goldstein and Cooper 1990: 20–21; for further bibliography, see Andreasen 1972: 94–99). But why should *šabbāt*, a common Hebrew noun, bear its Mesopotamian significance only here? (Admittedly, some scholars find other traces of a midmonth Sabbath; see NOTE to 20:8.) And why should *šabbāt* denote the fourteenth, rather than the fifteenth as in Mesopotamia?

Even without the *šab/pattu* connection, Fishbane could be right under either of two assumptions. Either Leviticus 23 follows a 364-day solar calendar beginning the year on Sunday (see NOTE to 12:2), so that the eve of Unleavened Bread is always the Sabbath (the Jewish solar calendar, however, started the year on Wednesday [Jaubert 1953; Talmon 1958b; Fishbane 1985: 145–46]). Or else, like the Assyrians, perhaps the Israelites began their count of weekdays anew each month, with days 29 and 30 omitted from the reckoning (cf. Langdon 1935: 83–89). If so, the eve of *Maṣṣôt* again would always be the Sabbath. But a problem remains. If the day before the festival is always a Sabbath, so is the last day of the festival. How would the reader know which Sabbath is meant? We will encounter comparable objections to the next two approaches.

Explanation (b)—the "Sabbath" is the first day of *Maṣṣôt*—suffers from even greater difficulties, although it is the norm in Rabbinic Judaism. The Rabbis emphasize the fact that the first day of the festival is a Sabbath-like day of rest, a *šabbātôn*. But why the imprecision? Why not simply say "the first day of the festival"? Clarity is crucial, since the seventh day of Unleavened Bread is equally a rest day. Still, it is possible that the first day of Unleavened Bread always fell on the Sabbath, if we assume that Unleavened Bread began on the fourteenth of the month, rather than the fifteenth (see NOTE to 12:18), and that we have either a Sunday-based 364-day solar calendar, with the fourteenth always the Sabbath, or an Assyrian-style reckoning of weekdays (see above).

Explanation (c) may be subdivided into two approaches, one unlikely and the other plausible. Some maintain that the seventh day of Unleavened Bread is called a "Sabbath" because it is a day of rest. But this is not cogent, since the first day of *Maṣṣôt* is equally a "Sabbath." More relevant is the observation that, as in Rabbinic Hebrew, Biblical *šabbāt* can mean "week"; cf. Lev 23:15, "there shall be seven complete *Sabbaths*" (Segal 1963: 197). The "Sabbath" of *Maṣṣôt* would thus be its seventh day. To dispose of Josh 5:10–12, Segal (p. 4) argues that there, as in Rabbinic Hebrew, *Pesaḥ* connotes a *seven*-day festival, on the morrow of which the Israelites ate "the land's produce." I find this forced, although it may be supported by Ezek 45:21 (OG), *"Pesaḥ,* a feast of seven days." An important objection to Segal's theory, however, is the oddity of *šabbāt* bearing an unusual meaning in v 11 which is explained only in v 15. Moreover, Rabbinic *šabbāt* connotes a Sunday–Saturday week, not *any* seven-day period. Still, if *Maṣṣôt* began on the fifteenth (see NOTE to 12:18), and if the Israelites used either the solar calendar or the Assyrian system, it is possible that Unleavened Bread *always* began on Sunday and ended on Saturday (Haran 1976). But by this scenario the law would still be ambiguous: is the "Sabbath" the eve of the festival (approach [a]) or its seventh day?

All the foregoing interpretations assume a frustrated effort to be precise on the author's part. Elsewhere, however, the Priestly Writer shows himself quite capable of calendrical specificity. Is it not strange, then, that he declines to date clearly the *ʿōmer* ritual as well as the dependent Festival of Weeks?

The last two interpretations assume that the text is sufficiently clear: a Sabbath is simply a Sabbath. Theory (d), that the Sabbath in question falls during *Maṣṣôt,* posits continuity with the preceding *Pesaḥ*-Unleavened Bread legislation (Lev 23:5–8). It also presupposes either a lunisolar calendar or, conceivably, a 365-day solar calendar—in any case, a system in which the Sabbath falls on different dates each year. This seems, however, an extremely arbitrary way to determine the date of the major festival of *Šābūʿôt.* Moreover, in a lunisolar or even a solar calendar, setting exact dates for agricultural festivals would be problematic. What if, due to climatic variation, a crop were too early or late? In fact, Second Temple Jews sometimes had to import grain for the *ʿōmer* (*m. Menaḥ.* 10:2). This would have been a continual inconvenience for any of the aforesaid approaches.

Theory (e), in contrast, obviates this difficulty. The Sabbath of Lev 23:11, 15 is whatever Saturday follows the start of the grain harvest. Consequently, the festival of firstfruits, *Šābūʿôt,* is determined by the condition of each year's crop. Although Deuteronomy rarely refers to a calendar, Deut 16:9 also creates the impression that the reckoning of Weeks was agriculturally based: "Seven weeks you will count for yourself from the sickle's beginning/profaning (*hāḥēl*) the standing grain" (see also NOTE to 19:1). Unfortunately, solution (e) is not without its own complications. How was the date of the Presentation of the *ʿōmer* determined and publicized? Given that grain ripens at different times in different locales, were the Presentation and Weeks observed on different days throughout the nation? Or, if there was one fixed day, would that not override our principal objection to the other interpretations, that of practicality?

We have reached an impasse regarding the date of the *ʿōmer.* Consequently, we cannot definitively establish or reject the agricultural significance of the Festival of *Maṣṣôt.* By theories (a), (b), (c) or (d), Unleavened Bread has a clear if indirect agricultural component. But if we detach the Presentation from Unleavened Bread (theory [e]), no agricultural symbolism remains for *Maṣṣôt,* apart from the approximate coincidence with the beginning of the barley harvest.

If *Maṣṣôt* originated neither as a commemoration of the Exodus nor as a harvest festival, what was it? Both of these interpretations focus on the requirement to eat unleavened bread. But in fact the stipulations of *Maṣṣôt* are two: not just to eat unleavened bread but to remove all leaven. For, despite its name, it is not the eating of *maṣṣôt* per se that characterizes the Festival of Unleavened Bread. Unleavened cakes were baked the year round for various sacral and secular purposes (Sarna 1986: 86; see NOTE to 12:8). To judge from Exodus 12, neglecting to eat them during *Maṣṣôt* would be at most a peccadillo. Instead, the severest sanctions apply to the eating of leavened food (cf. Segal 1963: 178). Here may lie the holiday's original significance.

The process of fermentation must have seemed mysterious to the ancients. Fermentation of grain yields not only toothsome bread but also intoxicating spirits (on Israelite taboos associated with wine and fermented honey, see Lev 2:11; 10:9; Num 6:3; Judg 13:4; 14:8–10; 1 Sam 1:14; Jeremiah 35; also Segal's [1963: 167–68, 197, 202] thesis of a partial wine taboo during *Maṣṣôt*). Leaven in particular is fraught with poignant, multivalent symbolism. Leavening entails both putrefaction and growth, death and life; its pungent odor reaches every corner of the house. Leaven is incompatible with *qōdeš qŏdāšîm* 'ultimate holiness' (cf. NOTE to 12:10). Cereal offerings must be unleavened (23:18; Lev 2:11; 6:9–10; Judg 6:19–21; Amos 4:5), unless consumed by humans, not Yahweh (Lev 7:13; 23:17; see Sarna 1986: 90). During the week of Unleavened Bread, not just the home but the entire land of Israel becomes like a vast altar to Yahweh, leaven-free.

SPECULATION: While leaven and honey are never offered to Yahweh (Lev 2:11), salt accompanies every sacrifice (Lev 2:13). Eating one's overlord's salt has well-known covenantal overtones (Num 18:19; Ezra 4:14; 2 Chr 13:5). But salt may also be considered leaven's opposite. While one is the product and agent of decay and defilement, the other preserves. Salt, in the proper hands, can repel death itself (2 Kgs 2:20–21) and is compatible with God's absolute holiness.

In postbiblical Jewish literature, leaven symbolizes the power of evil and ritual impurity to eternally replicate themselves, tainting whatever they touch (Oesterley 1933: 113), hence Paul's warning against "the leaven of malice and evil" (1 Cor 5:6–8; cf. Matt 16:6–12; Mark 8:15; Luke 12:1; Gal 5:9; *b. Ber.* 17a; contrast Matt 13:33; Luke 13:20–21). (Leavened bread was also among the innumerable taboos of the Roman priest *flamen dialis* [Gellius *Attic Nights* 10.15.19].) I believe that ancient Israelites held comparable beliefs and that purging leaven symbolized moral and ritual purification and regeneration. Weeklong purification rites comparable to the Festival of *Maṣṣôt* are described in 29:35–37; Lev 8:33–35; 12:2; 14:8–9; 15:13, 19, 24; Num 6:9–10; 19:11–19; 31:19.

Apart from the association with purity, unleavened bread may have been considered more primitive, closer to the created order and hence more sacred than leavened (Philo *De spec. leg.* 2.160; Licht 1968a). Leaven and fermentation symbolized civilization. Deut 29:5 recalls Israel's desert wanderings as an austere time when "(leavened?) bread you did not eat, and wine or beer you did not drink." Josh 5:11–12 may imply a homology between *maṣṣôt* and Manna, the sacred "bread of heaven" that sustained Israel in the desert (Ps 78:24; 105:40); see COMMENT to 15:27–16:36. Note, too, that the primitivist Rechabites, though they presumably ate leavened bread, shunned wine (Jer 35:6), as did Nazirites (Num 6:3–4; Judg 13:4, 14; 1 Sam 1:11 [LXX]; cf. 1 Sam 1:14). By this approach, *Maṣṣôt* may be described as an ascetic holiday (Jacob 1992: 318–19). Just as one fasts on certain days or undertakes temporary vows of abstinence to show independence of food, so one periodically avoids leavened bread and eats the purer *maṣṣôt* to attain a higher spiritual-ritual state.

The disposal of leaven has still deeper significance. Yeast is in theory immortal. The Israelites' chronometric system, however, and their entire worldview presuppose that time is not a continuous stream. It is and must be periodically interrupted. Six workdays are punctuated by the Sabbath; six years of agricultural labor are punctuated by the Year of Release; forty-nine years of commerce are punctuated by the Jubilee; each life ends with a death. Israelite history itself is punctuated by periods of absence from Canaan. It may not be coincidence that the word used for the elimination of leaven, *hišbît* (12:15), evokes the Sabbath. The laws of Unleavened Bread ensure that the bread by which people live does not transcend time, at least within the Holy Land. Once a year, all yeast must be killed, with a week of separation before the souring of a new batch (see NOTE to 12:15). It is crucial that aliens within the land also comply, lest their old leaven be used after the holiday to circumvent the taboo.

In short, the Festival of Unleavened Bread is primarily a rite of riddance. Leaven symbolizes the undesirable: misfortune, evil intentions and especially ritual impurity. To purge it is to make a fresh start, to experience catharsis. This understanding fits well with the historical content of the holiday. In the month of the New Grain, the Hebrews cast off centuries of oppression and assumed a holier, more ascetic status for their desert wanderings and subsequent national life. It also fits the seasonal aspect, for, throughout the world, equinoxes are opportunities for fresh beginnings (see below).

One wonders whether the Festival of Unleavened Bread was believed, at the popular level or in an early period, to avert bad luck, personified as demonic. We know little about Israelite demonology. But it would not be surprising if some of the populace believed that demons were attracted to leaven, or to what leaven represented. I raise this possibility because, as we shall directly see, fear of demons has everything to do with the other major observance of the season: *Pesaḥ*.

DEMONS AND DOORPOSTS

Scholars have long noted the extraordinary similarity between *Pesaḥ* as described in Exodus 12 and a Muslim sacrifice called *fidya* 'redemption' (colloquially, *fedu*). *Fidya* is not uniquely Arab or Muslim. Analogous rites are performed by Jews and Christians throughout the Middle East, especially in the Holy Land. *Fidya* is essentially a sacrifice of atonement and purging (Arabic *kaffāra*; cf.

Hebrew *kippūr*). Along with the slaughter and consumption of the animal victim, there is often an additional procedure. Blood from the slain beast is applied to humans, animals, the ground, a pillar, a domicile—or a doorway.

Fidya is performed in times of danger. To judge from the name "redemption," it was originally a protecting rite of substitution. The animal was held to have died in place of a human. Here is a suggestive report from Transjordan: during a cholera epidemic, "each family chose for itself a victim for . . . sacrifice, immolated it, prepared it on the spot and distributed it to the poor, after having eaten of it themselves. Each family took some blood of the sacrifice in order to stain the front of its door with it" (Jaussen 1948: 362).

Plagues are times of obvious peril, but there are more routine openings for misfortune. According to folk beliefs common to Jews, Muslims and Christians, demons are attracted to and powerful against those undergoing major life transitions, e.g., marriage (Gen 38:7-11; Tobit; *b. Ber.* 54b; Morgenstern 1966: 115-16). *Fidya* is therefore typically associated with birth, first haircut, circumcision, marriage, travel and the inauguration of new projects. The following representative examples are drawn primarily from Morgenstern's (1966) anthology, but see also Ewald (1876: 353), Euting (1896: 1.62), Wellhausen (1897: 125-27), Curtiss (1903: 217-26), Smith (1927: 344-45 n. 3), Dalman (1928: 1.31-32, 141-42, 426, 430-31, 445-46, 579, 7.93-97), Doughty (1936: 1.177, 499, 547, 2.118), Jaussen (1948: 54 n. 3, 111, 316, 339-43, 354-55, 358, 361-63), Segal (1963: 163), Füglister (1963: 90 nn. 68-70), Gaster (1969: 153-55), Gray (1971: 359-63) and Henninger (1975: 133-34 n. 440). In some Arab communities, after a child is born, the doorway or the baby itself is anointed with blood. The doorway may also be bloodied when a boy is circumcised. A threshold sacrifice greets one returning from a long journey, and blood may be placed on the traveler's forehead. A new bride steps over a bloodied threshold, or through a bloodied doorway, into her new house, or newlyweds may be themselves anointed. Blood applications often accompany the dedication of a new house. For all these rites, red dye may replace actual blood (is it a coincidence that Hebrew *kōper* means both "ransom" and "henna"?). Death rites, however, do not feature *fidya* (Doughty 1936: 1.498)—it is too late for redemption—but Morgenstern (1966: 128, 135) cites blood applications around a house in which someone has died, presumably to avert ghosts.

In addition to *fidya* as a rite of social passage, blood applications are particularly common in the spring as a rite of seasonal passage (Dalman 1928: 1.32, 426). Rihbany (1927: 98) describes a Lebanese Christian custom of sprinkling sheep's blood on the threshold in the spring. Sometimes the blood rite is part of the memorial *ḍaḥiya* sacrifice, often performed in the spring and believed to atone for the sins of the dead or the living (in some locales, this memorial sacrifice is called *fidya*). Again, blood may be applied to doorposts and lintels or to animals and children. (On blood in Arab folkways, see Canaan 1963; for similar blood rites from around the globe, see Gomes 1911: 201; Trumbull 1906.)

How does blood repel demons? The name *fidya* 'redemption' implies that the animal's death is vicarious. Its blood deludes demons into thinking a human has already died (compare the Egyptian myth of Sekhmet mistaking beer for blood [ANET 11]). Rituals in which a slain animal substitutes for an endangered human are well attested worldwide, including Mesopotamia (Ebeling 1931) and the classical world (e.g., Pausanias 9.8.2; Porphyry De abstinentia 2.54, 56; for further references, see Frazer 1911: 166 n.1). A Punic stela from N'gaous (Algeria) explicitly states: "spirit for spirit, blood for blood, life for life . . . lamb as a substitute" (Alquier and Alquier 1931). That is, a lamb has replaced a child who, according to the Punic mode, might himself have been sacrificed (see below). In the Bible, we find comparable substitutionary sacrifices in the Binding of Isaac (Genesis 22) and the Redemption of the Firstborn (see below). The equations person = sheep and society = flock in fact pervade the Bible (see Füglister 1963: 53; Good 1983; Eilberg-Schwartz 1990: 115–40).

In a ritual of pure substitution, the immolated object should be wholly surrendered to the god(s), i.e., destroyed. But Muslim fidya, like Pesaḥ, is a sacrificial meal, not a holocaust. Arguably, sharing food creates fellowship both among celebrants and between celebrants and the demon or deity at whom the rite is directed. Ingesting the meat may also reinforce, or even actuate, the fictive equation of victim and sacrificer underlying vicarious sacrifice.

Pesaḥ is not the only biblical analogue to fidya, merely the most obvious. In Gen 37:31–33, a goat dies instead of Joseph, whose garment is deceivingly stained with animal blood (cf. Levenson 1993b: 149). We also have various Israelite rituals involving blood applications: the consecration of priests (Exod 29:12, 20–21), the cleansing of lepers (Leviticus 14), the entry into the Covenant (Exod 24:8) and the annual purification of the Tabernacle (Lev 16:14–19).

The usual and logical inference from the affinity of fidya and Pesaḥ is that the latter is of pre-Israelite origin. Indeed, the paschal blood rite seems out of character with biblical theology. Throughout Exodus 7–11, Yahweh easily distinguished between Hebrew and Egyptian households, without the help of blood. But now, even though the Destroyer is an aspect of God himself, Yahweh instructs Israel to treat it as an amoral being that slays blindly unless checked— i.e., a demon (see NOTES to 12:13, 23); compare Yahweh's quasi-demonic behavior in 4:24–26 (see COMMENT to chaps. 3–4). The very name Pesaḥ 'protection' suggests inherent apotropaic powers (see NOTE to 12:11). Not too far beneath the surface, then, we glimpse a primitive Israelite or pre-Israelite belief that, in some fashion, the paschal blood averts a supernatural threat (Morgenstern 1966: 176).

Many scholars believe that Pesaḥ was originally intended to ward off, not spirits in general, but a specific demon. Some identify him with the Destroyer of 12:23, who, by this theory, antedates Yahweh himself (Meyer 1906: 38; Rost 1943: 208–9; Laaf 1970: 154–55). For Keel (1972), however, the adversary is the personified East Wind. Since śāʿîr means both "goat" and "(prancing) demon" (Isa 13:21), one might even, in a quasi-totemistic fashion, posit that the paschal victim is the demon (on the "limping dance" theory of Pesaḥ, see NOTE to 12:11). Given the theme of the endangerment of children, however, stronger candidates, or rather analogies, would be various entities hostile to babies (Peckham 1987: 88–89): "Lamb-strangler" of Arslan Tash (see below); "Night Fear" (Ps 91:5; Cant 3:8; cf. Akkadian *muttalik mūši* 'night-stalker' [Gaster 1962b: 820]), and Lilith (Isa 34:14), a birdlike demoness of Mesopotamian origin (see Handy 1992; on avian demons in Arab folklore, see Morgenstern 1966: 18–21). (Note, however, that the demons of the ancient and modern Near East do not prey particularly on the firstborn. That theme, as we shall see, is rooted in Yahweh's special claim upon firstlings and firstfruits.)

None of this, of course, is the Bible's own interpretation of *Pesaḥ*. But the "demonic" *Pesaḥ* may have survived throughout Israelite history, though unacknowledged by the biblical authors. In striking contrast to ancient Near Eastern literature, on the one hand, and the later sacred texts of Judaism, Christianity and Islam, on the other, the Hebrew Bible is all but silent on the existence of malicious spirits (see Gaster 1962b; COMMENT to 15:22–27). Evidently, there was room in the biblical universe for but one supernatural Personality. Angels were depersonalized, and demons were banished. The recrudescence of angel- and demonology in postbiblical literature implies, however, a continuous popular tradition throughout the biblical period, all but unknown from the written record. In the second century B.C.E., Jub 49:15 can still articulate *Pesaḥ*'s primal significance: "the plague will not come to kill or to smite during that year when they have observed the Passover in its (appointed) time" (*OTP* 2.141).

If, then, demonism is excluded, how would the biblical authors have explained *Pesaḥ?* For the Torah, blood is no mere repellent. It is the current of life; its quasi-magnetic bipolarity both attracts and repels the divine, removing and causing impurity. Blood is dangerous in the wrong hands. Laymen must pour it out (Lev 17:13; Deut 12:16, 24; 15:23; cf. 1 Sam 14:32–34), while consecrated priests may sprinkle it on the altar (Exod 29:16, etc.). Under no circumstances may blood be eaten (Gen 9:4–6; Lev 17:10–14; 19:26). (For further discussion of blood in the Bible, see Füglister 1963: 77–105; 1977; McCarthy 1969; Milgrom 1976; Kedar-Kopfstein 1978; Eilberg-Schwartz 1990: 177–94; Sperling 1992; Vervenne 1993.)

The prominence of blood in rites of purification raises an intriguing possibility: *Pesaḥ purifies* the doorway. Note that Ezek 45:18–20, describing a blood rite similar to *Pesaḥ*, uses the verbs *ḥiṭṭēʾ* 'purify' and *kipper* 'purge.' The role of marjoram (12:22), too, recalls the use of that plant in ritual purifications (Leviticus 14; Num 19:18; cf. v 6). Moreover, the verb *higgíaʿ*, connoting the application of the paschal blood to the Hebrews' door frames and the blood of circumcision to Moses' penis (4:25), also describes the purification (*kipper*) of Isaiah's mouth by fire (Isa 6:7; Segal 1963: 159). In the Exodus account, then, the paschal blood may not avert the Destroyer by its own virtue. Rather, it may create a zone of ritual purity attractive to Yahweh's presence (on the function of purification rites, see Milgrom 1976). God then protects (*psḥ*) the household from his own demonic side (cf. Levine 1974: 74–75). Thus the doorway functions as an altar. It receives atoning blood, it demarcates a zone of purity and asylum and it bars leaven.

SPECULATION: The specific impurity purged by the paschal ritual might be guilt for slaughtering the victim itself. According to Lev 17:11, killing an animal for food creates defilement and the need for purgation (*kpr*) through applying its blood to the altar (cf. Brichto 1976: 28). And an alternative possibility is that the blood protects Israel not only from the Destroyer but from the death impurity he brings upon Egypt.

Significantly, the Bible never describes the paschal slaughter as vicarious. At most, such an interpretation is implicit in the association of the *Pesaḥ* with Firstling Consecration—particularly the substitution of a sheep or goat for a firstling ass (13:13). Nonetheless, the vicarious aspect virtually suggests itself: witness Christianity's application of paschal imagery to Jesus, God's firstborn slain on Passover to redeem humanity (John 19:36; 1 Cor 5:7; 1 Peter 1:18–19, etc.). One thinks, too, of the poem *ḥad gadyāʾ* 'One Kid' sung at the Passover Seder: the death of a kid leads to the death of Death himself. (There is comparable ambiguity in the function of the Yom Kippur "scapegoat," which, according to Leviticus 16, merely conveys impurity out of the community. Popular parlance, however, instinctively and plausibly recognizes the goat's death as vicarious [cf. Wright 1987: 15–74].)

SPECULATION: Fretheim (1991a: 149) raises the intriguing possibility that, even for the biblical authors, the Hebrews were saved by a vicarious death—but not the lamb's. From 13:15, "Yahweh killed each firstborn in the land of Egypt . . . therefore I sacrifice to Yahweh each *loosening* of the womb, the males, and each firstborn of my sons I redeem," Fretheim infers that the *Egyptians'* firstborn sons and animals, slain while the Hebrews consume the *Pesaḥ*, are the real substitutional victims (for foreign nations redeeming Israel, cf. Isa 43:3–4). If this is truly the Torah's interpretation, it is surely a rationalization of a popular belief in the redemptive virtue of the paschal sacrifice itself.

Why do E and P downplay the idea that the *Pesaḥ* is a substitutional sacrifice? Perhaps because it comes dangerously close to suggesting *human* sacrifice (Henninger 1975: 166–67; Delcor 1990: 90–104), witness Frazer's (1911: 174–79) wild speculations on the origins of *Pesaḥ* (see below). But more likely, E and P are simply combating the vulgar and original conception of *Pesaḥ* as a demon-repellent. Authorized explanations for overinquisitive children are even provided (12:26–27).

In short, the analogy of *fidya* 'redemption' suggests that the death of the paschal victim was originally or popularly conceived as substitutionary (Gressmann 1913: 104; Füglister 1963: 68–70). The blood on the doorway tricked the destructive spirit into passing on to the next domicile in search of a victim. This supposition may also explain the emphasis on the paschal victim's wholeness. As a stand-in for a healthy human, it must be flawless and whole, with no bones broken (12:5, 9, 46).

Though demons may be repelled or ignored, they are harder to kill. Our paschal demon survived, so to speak, by donning various disguises. Most obviously, he was absorbed into Yahweh's persona as the Destroyer. I also suspect that the characterization of the Pharaoh of the oppression as a would-be baby-killer (1:16, 22) owes an unconscious debt to the paschal demon. And the antique sprite is still with us, but defanged, as it were. He has become a kindly being, in fact a Jew.

The Hebrews of Egypt bloodied their door frames in order to shunt the Destroyer onto their enemies. Nowadays the traditional Passover Seder ends with the opening of a door and a call for the destruction of infidels (Ps 79:6–7; cf. Jer 10:25). But then a genial spirit is symbolically invited into each house to share the "blood of the grape": none other than the prophet Elijah, harbinger of the Messiah.

THE RAW, THE BOILED AND THE ROAST

Hendel (1989: 384–87) and Niditch (1993: 58–60) draw our attention to the unusual directions for cooking the paschal animal (12:9). An ordinary sacrificial meal is boiled in a pot (Lev 6:21; Num 6:19; 1 Sam 2:13–14; Ezek 46:20–24; Zech 14:21; 2 Chr 35:13). Beside the *Pesaḥ*, there are only two other biblical references to roast meat. In Isa 44:16, the idolmaker barbecues his dinner over his workshop scraps; in 1 Sam 2:13–16, while worshipers at Shiloh boil their sacrificial meat, the wicked priests demand raw flesh to roast for themselves. Hendel infers that, under normal circumstances, roasting is itself sinful. It is allowed for *Pesaḥ* because "the roasting of meat . . . contrasts with the boiling of meat . . . just as the foreign and abhorrent life of Egyptian captivity contrasts with the proper life of Israelite culture" (p. 386).

In many cultures, boiled and roasted meat are viewed as opposites, with one or the other preferred (Piganiol 1963). But it is not at all certain that roasting was actually forbidden in Israel. The Bible, after all, is not reticent in matters of dietary taboo, yet we find no such proscription. Roasting may simply not have been customary, or our data may be incomplete. As for Isa 44:16 and 1 Sam 2:13–16, the idolmaker and the priests are condemned on other grounds than eating improperly prepared meat. Their respective sins are idolatry and depriving both worshipers and Yahweh of their due (1 Sam 2:29).

Still, Hendel has rightly emphasized the unusualness of roast meat. He observes that the only "person" in the Bible who habitually consumes burnt food is God. Thus, one might say, in the *Pesaḥ* ritual Israelites eat food ordinarily reserved for Yahweh. I am uncertain how to interpret this fact, however. One possibility is that, for fortification, the Hebrews in Egypt are permitted God's food (Niditch 1993: 60); note that unleavened cakes are also divine fare (see NOTE to 12:8), while Manna is called "heaven's grain" (Ps 78:24; 105:40).

But another reading is suggested by Levi-Strauss's (1978: 478–95) demonstration that cooking is a highly symbolic act for many cultures. Finding an all-pervasive polarity between nature and culture, he posits a basic contrast between the raw and the cooked. And, within the category of cooked, he finds a comparable contrast between meat roasted over a fire (nature) and meat boiled in a vessel (culture). While his analysis may be overschematic, we may grant Levi-Strauss that roasting, presupposing only the discovery of fire, is a more primitive technique than boiling, which in the Near East requires pottery. Thus the requirement may be to eat the meat in a primitive manner, but not so primitive as to transgress the raw flesh taboo (see NOTE to 12:9, "raw").

Citing evidence from Europe and the Americas, Levi-Strauss (p. 482) further argues that boiling symbolizes not only culture but decay. We may add that cognates of Hebrew bšl 'cook, boil, ripen' also connote fermentation, i.e., being "overripe," in various Semitic languages (Arabic bsl, Galla bilčad; see Rabin 1977: 333). In fact, there is a notable symmetry between the two main dishes of the Pesaḥ-Maṣṣôt complex. Boiling and leavening both involve interpenetration of substances—broth and meat, yeast and dough—and both processes are associated with putrefaction. Note, for example, that Gideon is ordered to discard the broth he presents to the angel, leaving only meat and maṣṣôt (Judg 6:20). In Ezek 24:3–13, too, a pot of boiling meat symbolizes Jerusalem's impurities; afterward, the vessel must be cleansed by fire (likewise, in Rabbinic literature [e.g., m. Makš.], liquids are particularly liable to bear or cause impurity). Thus we can set up the following homologies: raw meat is the equivalent of raw grain; stewed meat is the equivalent of leavened bread; roast meat is the equivalent of unleavened bread. Unleavened cakes symbolize purity, and their analogue, roasted meat, is passed through fire, the ultimate purifier that sends sacrifices to heaven (cf., too, the association of unleavened bread and fire-roasted grain [Lev 23:14; Josh 5:11]).

THREE QUESTIONS

Many aspects of the Israelite Pesaḥ are explained by the assumptions that it is of common origin with Islamic fidya and was originally directed against a demon or demons. But Pesaḥ is, so to speak, a specialized form of fidya. Why is it limited to the evening, the doorway and the springtime?

Pesaḥ is performed just before nightfall, because night is when malefic influences are strongest. Fear of the dark is probably a human universal, exampled many times in the Bible (Ziegler 1950; Fields 1992). Morgenstern (1966: 58–59) cites a Jewish custom in some ways reminiscent of the Pesaḥ: during a boy's first eight days, before his circumcision, visitors are prohibited from entering the house after dark, presumably lest they attract demons (or be demons themselves). A comparable Albanian custom requires nighttime visitors to a newborn's home to vault a firebrand at the threshold; again, this probably filters out evil spirits (Morgenstern p. 13).

Why is the paschal blood applied to the doorposts, lintel and possibly the threshold (see NOTE to 12:22)? Doorways, especially thresholds, are places of danger and omen in worldwide folk belief (Trumbull 1906). The symbolism of the doorway lies in its being the boundary between internal and external, kin and stranger, familiar and foreign, safe and dangerous. It is a home's point of vulnerability (Milgrom 1976: 394–95). Crossing the threshold in either direction can be dangerous: one leaves the safety of home, or one risks importing the alien. According to Gen 4:7, "sin lies down [abides] at the doorway"—or, by another interpretation, "sin is a demon (rōbēṣ) at the doorway" (Speiser 1964: 32–33). The Bible attributes a custom of "skipping over the threshold" to both Philistines (1 Sam 5:5) and Israelites (Zeph 1:9), and even we do not allow a bride to cross her new threshold on foot, lest misfortune follow.

To keep evil outside, many peoples employ doorway charms. Colossal bull-men, genii of fortune, flank Assyrian palace entries. Archaeologists have discovered in Arslan Tash, Syria, two seventh-century amulets, most likely hung in a doorway (KAI 27; Cross and Saley 1970; Cross 1974: 486–90). They purportedly repel a she-demon, or perhaps several, named ḥnqt 'mr 'Lamb-strangler(s).' To judge from the plaque's illustration, the "lambs" in question are human babies (Keel 1978: 84, fig. 97a; ANEP fig. 662); Cross and Saley compare Ugaritic 'iltm ḥnqtm 'the two strangler goddesses' and Arabic ḥānūq 'al-ḥamal 'Lamb-strangler' (du Mesnil du Buisson 1939: 426). The plaque also mentions "Fliers" and "Night-demons," as well as a male demon, Sasam: "As for Sasam, let it not be opened to him, and let him not come down to (my) door posts. The sun rises, O Sasam: disappear, and fly away home" (Cross and Saley 1970: 47). These all must be close cousins of the original paschal demon.

Comparable customs and beliefs apparently existed in Israel, although they were controversial. Isa 57:8 appears to disparage doorway charms: "Behind the door and the doorpost you set your memorial (?)" (zikrōnēk; cf. zikkārôn as a head amulet in 13:9; Zech 6:14). And Jews, taking literally the exhortation to write Moses' commands "on your house's doorposts" (Deut 6:9; 11:20), still hang amulets containing scriptural verses beside their doors (see NOTE to 13:9).

Another way to fortify the entrance is to anoint it with blood or red dye, as in Pesaḥ or fidya. Layard (1849: 2.256) discovered dried black fluid, possibly blood, on the door frames of the oldest Assyrian palace at Nimrud. Trumbull (1906: 206) even finds paschal imagery in Rahab's scarlet cord—albeit suspended in a window, not a doorway—which protects her household from the Israelite conquerors (Josh 2:18). (On the apotropaic virtues of the color red, see Koenig 1985: 8–10.)

Lastly, what is the special relationship between Pesaḥ and the spring? Scholars committed to the nomadic derivation of Pesaḥ contend that the ritual originally protected the flock, since April marks the end of the lambing and inaugurates the migration to summer pasturage (Dalman 1928: 1.445; Brock-Utne 1934; Rost 1943; Loewenstamm 1992a: 196, 206; Laaf 1970: 154 n. 135). In particular, some compare Arab domestic sacrifices of sheep, often firstlings, in the month of Rajab, which fell in the spring in the pre-Islamic calendar (Wellhausen 1897: 98–101; Smith 1927: 227–28; Henninger 1975: 38–42 et passim). But this offering was not, so far as we know, accompanied by a blood ritual. And I have found no report of fidya performed in connection with the lambing or seasonal migration. The only datum supporting this theory is that, in the first *Pesaḥ*, the Hebrews are about to embark on a trek with their livestock in tow. But this more likely reflects historical reality than the historicization of seasonal transhumance (see APPENDIX B, vol. II).

In fact, we need not posit a nomadic basis for the *Pesaḥ* to explain its timing. The Arabs' sacrifices of Rajab fit a pattern of increased religious activity about both the vernal and the autumnal equinoxes throughout the Middle East: e.g., in Late Antique Hierapolis, Harran, Hawran, Palmyra and Bosra in Syria (pseudo-Lucian *De dea Syria* 49 [Attridge and Oden 1976: 53–54]; Smith 1927: 407 n. 1; Sourdel 1952: 109–11; Henninger 1975: 80; Chwolson 1965: 2.6–7, 23–25, 175–92). (Moreover, in Tyre, the resurrection of the god Melqart was celebrated in February–March [Lipiński 1969]—perhaps too early to be relevant—while in April, ancient Cypriotes made special sacrifices to Astarte of swine and sheep [Smith 1927: 290–91, 406, 470–79]—perhaps too distant to be relevant.) Palestinian peasants, both Christian and Muslim, still make offerings for the protection of the household in early spring (Henninger 1975: 32; for parallel customs worldwide, see Henninger pp. 103–28; Segal 1963: 118–21). The universality of springtime offerings may explain why the Bible's first sacrifices, those of Cain and Abel, are probably offered in the spring (*qēṣ yāmîm* 'end of *days*'; see NOTE to 12:2 "*head* of months").

Some springtime rites even include blood applications. There were evidently bloodsmearings in fourth-century C.E. Egypt associated with the vernal equinox (Epiphanius *Adv. haeres.* 18.3 [PG 41.260]). And we have already observed that the Muslim memorial sacrifice *cum* blood ritual *ḍaḥiyya* is often performed in the spring. Blood is also part of the most prominent ancient parallel to *Pesaḥ*, the Babylonian *Akitu* festival, celebrated during the first eleven days of Nisan. Most of our information comes from the first millennium B.C.E., but the festival has roots in the third millennium (for brief discussion and bibliography, see Klein 1992). During the *Akitu*, the creation myth *Enūma eliš* was recited and apparently acted out (*ANET*³ 60–72, 501–3; Dalley 1989: 233–74). Among many other activities not germane to our discussion, the temple was purified with sheep's blood in a rite called *kuppuru* (= Hebrew *kippūr*; see Wright 1987: 62–65, 291–98 and Ezek 45:18–20). In this season, the gods decreed fates for the coming year.

The parallels between the Babylonian *Akitu* and the Exodus tradition are acknowledged (Levenson 1988: 66–77 *et passim*). Both feature a celebration in early Nisan of a national storm god's triumph over his foes involving the splitting of a sea, the god's enthronement and the creation of a civilization. Indeed, both the Exodus tradition and *Enūma eliš* may be described as Creation Myths (see COMMENTS to 13:17–15:21 and 17:1–7). They were recounted in the spring, perhaps because that season recapitulates Creation (cf. Philo *De spec. leg.* 2.151–54). Note that two other biblical events with cosmogonic overtones are likewise dated to the spring: the reappearance of dry land after the Flood (Gen 8:13) and the erection of the Tabernacle (Exod 40:2, 17) (see Blenkinsopp 1976). Still, we must remember that the *Akitu* was celebrated at different times throughout Mesopotamia, often twice a year in a given city (Cohen 1993: 400–53). And, even in Babylon, *Enūma eliš* was recited again in the winter. Moreover, the paschal tradition, at least as embodied in Exodus, celebrates, not the crossing of the Sea and the foundation of the Israelite nation, but the protection of Israel from a plague and the departure from Egypt (*pace* Pedersen 1934; see Mowinckel 1952). So the parallels are imprecise.

Spring was the New Year for much of the Near East, although the autumn-based year is also well attested (see NOTE to 12:2). Segal (1963) characterizes the *Pesaḥ-Maṣṣôt* complex as a New Year's festival. Given the ambiguity as to when the year began, I would rather call *Pesaḥ-Maṣṣôt* an equinoctial festival dividing half-year from half-year (so already Philo *De spec. leg.* 2.151), leaving open the question of whether it celebrated the New Year as well (cf. Cohen 1993: 6–7).

In any case, *Pesaḥ-Maṣṣôt* is a rite of passage from season to season, perhaps from year to year. The weeklong celebration is what Turner calls a "liminal" period (1967: 93–111), a transitional interval set apart from quotidian activity. Throughout the Near East, both equinoxes were seasons of fate and danger, evoking special rites of purification and protection. In the lunisolar calendar, months were intercalated at the equinoxes—a procedure that strikes us as routine, but in antiquity was fraught with significance (see NOTE to 12:2).

We in fact find considerable symmetry between the biblical festivals associated with the equinoxes. The congruity of Unleavened Bread (*Maṣṣôt*) in the first month and Shelters (*Sukkôt*) in the seventh is blatant. Both begin on the fifteenth day, last for a week and are pilgrimage festivals. But the similarities are more extensive. Both *Maṣṣôt* and *Sukkôt* are liminal periods involving evacuation of the house. For the former, one removes all leaven; for the latter, one removes oneself, to live in a temporary shelter (Lev 23:42). Again, time must be punctuated: to live perpetually in a house or to keep yeast alive indefinitely would be unnatural. Both festivals, moreover, are characterized by quasi-ascetic or primitive practices: eating unleavened bread and living in rude shelters. Each festival is preceded by an unusual observance involving small cattle: *Pesaḥ* and *Yôm hakkippūrîm* (the Day of Expiation) (cf. Rost 1943: 212–16). These rituals, the only annual blood rites in the Bible, both begin in the evening (12:6; Deut 16:6; Lev 23:32) (Segal 1963: 162). Each in some manner placates a supernatural malefic agency: a demon or the Destroyer at *Pesaḥ*, the demon (or death god) Azazel on the Day of Expiation (see Tawil 1980; Wright 1987: 21–25). Both rituals have undertones of purification and vicarious offering played down by the biblical authors (cf. Johnstone 1990: 41–42). Since *Pesaḥ* is a domestic rite, while *Yôm hakkippūrîm* is a national rite, the two equinoctial observances annually cleanse the nation at the micro- and macro-levels. In fact, the verb *kipper* 'purge' is associated with *Pesaḥ* in Ezek 45:18–20, while its Akkadian and Arabic cognates are respectively associated with the *Akītu* festival and *fidya*, whose affinities with *Pesaḥ* we have explored (note, too, the apotropaic overtones of Hebrew *kipper* in Prov 16:14). We discover further homologies between *Yôm hakkippūrîm* and *Maṣṣôt*—both are rites of riddance—and between *Sukkôt* and *Pesaḥ*—both simulate nomadic lifestyle (i.e., dressing for the road and living in temporary shelters). The analogies are obviously inexact. For example, *Yôm hakkippūrîm* is observed on the tenth of the month, *Pesaḥ* on the fourteenth. But, even so, the paschal observance really begins on the tenth, with the victim's selection. (Goldstein and Cooper [1990] suggest that the *Pesaḥ* was originally eaten on the tenth, allowing a longer interval for the *Maṣṣôt* pilgrimage.) Another important difference between P's autumn and spring festival cycles is that the former includes a Day of Trumpeting on the first of the seventh month (Lev 23:24-25; Num 29:1-6), which would become the Jewish New Year, *Rō(')š haššānâ*. Why is there no comparable marking of the first day of the first month, the New Year proper? The best explanation is Segal's (1957: 269): intercalation was performed in the spring, and New Year's Day was proclaimed only retroactively (see NOTES to 12:2-3).

Some would object that *Pesaḥ* is generally considered the oldest of Israelite festivals, and the Day of Expiation among the youngest. But *Yôm hakkippūrîm* may be older than we realize. The notion that Israel developed feelings of guilt only after the Exile (a common caricature of Wellhausen's [1885: 110-12] more nuanced view) is *prima facie* absurd. And, if the Day of Expiation is after all late, it may have developed precisely to balance *Pesaḥ*. Compare the effort to maximize the symmetry of the equinoctial festivals in Ezek 45:18-20: the prophet envisions special rites of purification for the first days of the first and seventh months (reading v 20 with the Greek: "on the first day of the seventh month"); cf. also Jub 7:2-6; 11QTemple 14:9.

A FESTIVAL COMPLEX

Let us summarize the relationship between *Pesaḥ* and *Maṣṣôt*. Although many scholars distinguish sharply between the two, they form a coherent complex. It makes sense that Unleavened Bread should originally have been preceded by a blood rite, just as the weeklong purifications of the priest (Exodus 29; Leviticus 8) and the leper (Leviticus 14) are preceded by a blood rite. Both *Pesaḥ* and *Maṣṣôt* feature foods associated with a higher state of purity: roasted meat and unleavened bread. *Pesaḥ* was originally intended to appease or repel hostile powers, while *Maṣṣôt* removed accumulated impurity, liable to attract misfortune. The eve of *Maṣṣôt* was in effect the "dirtiest" day of the year, requiring the extraordinary paschal ritual for protection. Together, *Pesaḥ* and *Maṣṣôt* ensured domestic prosperity for the coming year or half-year, paralleling the *Yôm hakkippūrîm–Sukkôt* complex in the fall.

THE EXODUS CONNECTION

If the paschal blood rite dates back to hoary pan-Semitic antiquity, and if *Maṣṣôt* is originally an equinoctial observance, how did they come to be associated with the story of Israel's liberation?

One answer is that the historical Exodus may have occurred in the spring, as tradition maintains. But, even if so, this is an incomplete explanation, just as the date of the crucifixion does not fully account for the identification of Jesus and the paschal lamb (see below). And what if it is not true? What if the dating of the departure is after all based upon a prior association of the Exodus tradition with *Pesaḥ-Maṣṣôt?*

Let us briefly return to *fidya.* To judge from the name "redemption," it is primally a vicarious sacrifice: an animal dies so that a human may live. Like Arabic *fdy,* the Hebrew cognate *pdy* can describe redemption from Death (Hos 13:14; Ps 49:16). But more often it refers to liberation from servitude (Exod 21:8; Lev 19:20), particularly from the Egyptian bondage (Deut 7:8; 9:26; 13:6, etc.) (cf. Segal 1963: 164). Even though *pādâ* does not occur in Exodus 12, this seems an important point: redemption from death is homologous to redemption from slavery. The association of the Exodus tradition with the springtime paschal rite is perfectly natural.

THE *"PESAḤ* OF EGYPT" AND THE *"PESAḤ* OF GENERATIONS"

We may distinguish two ideal categories of biblical ritual: prescriptive ritual and historical ritual. Prescriptive ritual is to be performed in all generations; historical ritual is ritualized activity in the context of historical narrative (e.g., Abram's covenant with Yahweh in Genesis 15). Most pentateuchal legislation is prescriptive. If, however, a ritual makes sense in its narrative context, and if the text does not command its reenactment, we must consider whether it is historical ritual preserved out of antiquarian or other motives.

The laws of Unleavened Bread fall squarely into the category of prescriptive ritual. They make little sense in their narrative context, since the Hebrews cannot observe the festival in Egypt (see REDACTION ANALYSIS; NOTE to 12:34). And the commandment is explicitly *"to your ages;* as an eternal rule" (12:14), when "Yahweh brings you to the land" (13:5). For *Pesaḥ,* however, matters are less clear. First, we must distinguish between the sacrificial meal and its accompanying blood rite. Both E (12:25–27) and P (12:43–49) enjoin future generations to keep the *Pesaḥ,* but this might mean the meal alone. The blood rite may belong to the category of historical ritual. It makes good sense in its narrative context, protecting the Hebrews from a onetime endangerment. And there is no unambiguous command to perpetuate the custom.

Ancient authorities are divided on this question. The Samaritans maintained and still maintain that both the sacrifice and the blood rite are for all time (Jeremias 1932). On the other hand, according to Jub 49:19–21, the blood application was intended only for the liberated Hebrews, being replaced in the Temple cult by the priestly sprinkling of paschal blood upon the altar. The Mishnah, too, distinguishes the *"Pesaḥ* of Egypt" from the *"Pesaḥ* of [later] Generations," terminology I shall adopt (*m. Pesaḥ.* 9:5). Admittedly, much modern scholarship dismisses the Rabbinic distinction as a facile harmonization of contradictions both within Scripture and between Exodus 12 and later Jewish practice (e.g., May 1936: 73–74; Haran 1978: 317–18). But the distinction is in fact implicit in the Torah itself. The Book of Deuteronomy, widely considered a supplement to JE, describes the *Pesaḥ* of the future in terms quite unlike those of Exodus 12:

> Observe [or: watch for] the month of the New Grain, and you will make *Pesaḥ* for Yahweh your deity. For in the month of the New Grain Yahweh your deity took you out from Egypt at night. And you will sacrifice a *Pesaḥ* to Yahweh your deity, small cattle or large cattle, in the Place that Yahweh will choose to settle his Name there. Do not eat with it leavened food; seven days you will eat with it unleavened bread, bread of humility—for frantically you went out from the land of Egypt—so that you may remember the day of your going out from the land of Egypt all your life's days. And leaven may not be seen for you in all your territory seven days. And none of the meat that you offer in the evening on the first day may abide till the morning. You will not be able to sacrifice the *Pesaḥ* in any one of your *gates* [cities] that Yahweh your deity is going to give you. But at the Place that Yahweh your deity will choose to settle his name there—there you will sacrifice the *Pesaḥ* in the evening, at the sun's *entering* [setting], the date of your departure from Egypt. And you will cook and eat in the place that Yahweh your deity will choose; then you will turn in the morning and go to your tents [i.e., homeward, *pace* Segal 1963: 179, 210–12, 267; cf. 1 Kgs 8:66, etc.]. Six days you will eat unleavened bread, and on the seventh day a *cessation* [day of rest] for Yahweh your deity; do not do work. . . . Three times in the year all your males must see the face of Yahweh your deity in the place that he will choose: on the Festival of the Unleavened Bread and on the Festival of the Weeks and on the Festival of the Shelters. And Yahweh's face, he must not be seen [*sic* MT] emptily. For each man, his hand's gift should be in proportion to the blessing of Yahweh your deity that he will give you. (Deut 16:1–8, 16–17)

With a few modifications (see below), this is the *Pesaḥ* of later Israelite religion and Second Temple Judaism, as described in 2 Chronicles 30, 35; Ezra 6:19–22; the "Passover Papyrus" from Elephantine, Egypt (Cowley 1923: 62–63; Porten 1968: 122–33; Porten and Yardeni 1986: 1.54); 11QTemple 17:6–9; Josephus (*Ant.* 17.213–14; 20.106; *War* 2.280; 6.421–27); Philo (*De spec. leg.* 2.145–48); the New Testament (Matthew 26; Mark 14; Luke 2:41; 22; John 13; Acts 12:3–4), and the Mishnah (*Pesaḥ.*, esp. 5:5–7) (see Segal 1963: 225–69). These sources describe *Pesaḥ* as a massive pilgrimage to Jerusalem in a state of ritual purity. Each family's paschal lamb/kid is slaughtered and flayed in the Temple, beginning in the late afternoon. The priests throw blood on the foundation of the altar and burn the fat for God; then worshipers cook and eat the

Pesaḥ inside or near the Temple. The meat is not shared with the priests, who consume their own paschal meals. In addition to the roast lamb/kid, unleavened bread and bitter herbs stipulated by the Torah, drinking wine and singing hymns have become customary.

In short, the domestic ritual described in Exodus 12 has become little different from an ordinary sacrifice. This seems to be precisely the intent of Deuteronomy, which even allows bulls as well as sheep and goats (age unspecified) for the *Pesaḥ* (Deut 16:2; Ezekiel the Tragedian 177; on Ezek 45:18, see below). Moreover, Deut 16:7 seems to permit boiling the animal (see NOTE to 12:9 "cooked"). How the Deuteronomist and subsequently the Redactor rationalized these contradictions with Exodus 12 we can only guess. The simplest explanation is that of R. Moshe b. Amram the Persian (*apud* ibn Ezra): only the "*Pesaḥ* of Egypt" was restricted to small cattle. But this view did not become standard. Admittedly, 2 Chr 35:7–9, 12 mentions bulls—probably not for *Pesaḥ*, however, but rather for either *qŏdāšîm* (Segal 1963: 15) or, conceivably, *šəlāmîm* (ibn Ezra; cf. *Mek. pisḥā᾽* 4). (Even so, the mention of bulls is probably an attempt to harmonize Exodus 12 and Deuteronomy 16 [Ginsburg 1982: 58; Fishbane 1985: 136–37]; cf. NOTE to 12:9.)

Most interestingly, Deuteronomy mentions no paschal blood rite. Instead, *Moses' words* are to be set on doorposts at all times—whatever that might imply (Deut 6:9; 11:20; see NOTE to Exod 13:9). Neither does the bloodied doorway appear in any text apart from Exodus 12 (on Ezekiel 45, see below). And we know the blood application was not part of Second Temple practice. After all, with the *Pesaḥ* a pilgrimage festival, the celebrant was not even at home.

How and why did *Pesaḥ* come to be centralized? The process may have begun in the late premonarchic period, when Shiloh was an important pilgrimage center (Judg 21:19; 1 Sam 1:3). With Solomon's celebration of the major festivals in the new Temple (1 Kgs 9:25; 2 Chr 8:12–13), centralization would have received fresh impetus (cf. 1 Kgs 12:27). Cultic unification accelerated under Hezekiah (2 Chronicles 30) and reached its climax under Josiah (2 Kgs 23:21–23; 2 Chr 35:1–19), of whose reform Deuteronomy was probably the charter (Friedman 1987: 101–35). *Pesaḥ* became part of the royal cult.

The kings who sponsored *Pesaḥ* (note Ezek 45:22) presumably exploited its patriotic theme (Licht 1971b: 523). In particular, Josiah, who would fall in battle against Pharaoh (2 Kgs 23:29–30; 2 Chr 35:20–24), may have emphasized the anti-Egyptian message (Nicolsky 1927: 185–87). Meanwhile, the seasonal *Maṣṣôt* aspect was downplayed. Deut 16:1–8 makes Unleavened Bread subsidiary to *Pesaḥ*, not even using *maṣṣôt* as the name of a festival (contrast Deut 16:16, based upon Exod 23:14–15; 34:18). For Deut 16:7–8, the first day of *Maṣṣôt* is not a special observance, but a day of travel. Ironically, it seems that *Maṣṣôt* has become a domestic observance and *Pesaḥ* a national pilgrimage—a reversal of their original status. In time, the name *Pesaḥ* would entirely displace *Maṣṣôt* to denote the weeklong observance (see already Ezek 45:21).

THE PRIESTLY *PESAḤ*

Where does 12:1–20, 43–49 (P) fit into the evolution of *Pesaḥ* from domestic rite to national holiday? Like Deuteronomy, the Priestly source generally demands unification of worship (Friedman 1987: 171–72). Thus, while the centralized *Pesaḥ* of Deuteronomy 16 meets our expectations, P's domestic *Pesaḥ* is a surprise. In fact, many nineteenth- and a few twentieth-century critics have considered P the oldest pentateuchal source, based partly upon the archaic flavor of 12:1–13 (e.g., Kaufmann 1942–56: 1.122–23; on older scholarship, see Thompson 1970).

How can we explain the anomaly of P's domestic *Pesaḥ*? It is inadequate merely to observe that P preserves archaic law (Segal 1963: 70–77). Why? Why would the Priestly Writer turn a communal, centralized rite back into a domestic celebration, in contradiction to his overall ideology? Moreover, if redomesticating *Pesaḥ* was the Priestly Writer's goal, why did he fail? Why was the Second Temple *Pesaḥ* still a centralized ritual, as if P had never been written (Welch 1927: 26–27)?

Wambacq (1976: 323–26) and Van Seters (1983: 180–81) explore one possible answer, based upon their exilic dating of P (see APPENDIX A, vol. II). The Priestly *Pesaḥ* evolved in Babylon, where, in the temporary absence of a central shrine, the home became a temple. But, I would object, the rest of Priestly law presupposes a centralized cult, without accommodation for the Diaspora. Why was *Pesaḥ* alone adapted? Moreover, P will later require that the *Pesaḥ* be performed only in the land of Israel (Num 9:6–13), completely vitiating the argument of Wambacq and Van Seters—unless they consider Num 9:6–13 a snippet of pre- or postexilic law embedded within P. But the multiplication of literary strata should be a last resort.

Here is an alternative hypothesis: the Priestly Writer *reconstructed* the Mosaic *Pesaḥ* on the basis of the domestic *Pesaḥ*, a rite with which he was familiar but of which he did not approve (cf. Wellhausen 1885: 102–3; Friedman 1981: 95–96; Jacob 1992: 317). In other words, many aspects of 12:1–13 fall under the rubric of historical, not prescriptive, ritual.

The Priestly Writer was, admittedly, no disinterested antiquarian. He consistently advanced a partisan vision of Israelite religion and history (Friedman 1987: 188–206). Rather than always retrojecting his program into the past, however, he sometimes took a subtler approach. An informative parallel is P's history of the divine name. For the Priestly Writer as for all Israelites, God was Yahweh. But he knew that some called him *'ēl šadday* or *'ĕlōhîm* (see APPENDIX C, vol. II). Rather than dispute the authenticity of these appellations, P presents them as genuine, but as superseded by the Tetragrammaton (6:3). Likewise, most scholars believe that P does not really advocate Tabernacle worship, as one might initially think. Rather, the Priestly Writer uses the Tent as a prototype of the Temple (see APPENDIX A, vol. II).

I think the Priestly Writer pursued a comparable strategy in envisioning the first *Pesaḥ*. Tradition (as attested by E) recalled a domestic sacrifice plus a blood ritual, the latter an archaic practice tainted with demonism. However great the temptation, the Priestly Writer could not deny this tradition without impugning his own authority as historian. Instead, he presented an *evolution* of *Pesaḥ* from domestic ritual into centralized sacrifice. That P acknowledges both a "*Pesaḥ* of Egypt" and a "*Pesaḥ* of Generations" is clear from the "*Pesaḥ* Rule" (12:43–49). And P returns to the future observance of *Pesaḥ*-Unleavened Bread in Lev 23:5–8; Num 9:1–14; 28:16–25. Num 9:1–14 is particularly important, for it calls *Pesaḥ* a *qorbān* 'sacrifice' (vv 7, 13) and makes ritual purity and proximity to the shrine requirements for participation (cf. Josh 3:5; Ezra 6:15–22; 2 Chronicles 29–30; Elephantine; Josephus [see above, p. 446]; *m. Pesaḥ.* 6:6; 7:4, 6, 9; 8:5; 9:1, 4; also Safrai 1965: 135–41). This is quite different from Exodus 12 and much closer to Deuteronomy.

There is evidence that P's "*Pesaḥ* of Generations," like Deuteronomy's, excluded the blood application. Num 9:3 commands the Israelites at Sinai to celebrate *Pesaḥ* "according to all its rules and . . . statutes." This cannot refer to the entire ritual of Exod 12:1–13 for a simple reason: the blood rite presupposes residence in a *house*, whereas the Israelites are traveling in *tents* (e.g., Exod 16:16). Num 9:3 must refer to other rules—the meal, circumcision, ritual purity—but not the bloody doorway. One might counter that this is nit-picking: one could still smear a tent flap, as in the Samaritan *Pesaḥ* (Jeremias 1932: 89, 91). But another Priestly text, Lev 17:3–9, proves that, for future generations, the paschal rite of 12:1–13 would have been impossible, indeed heretical:

A man, (any) man from Israel's House who slaughters a bull or a sheep or a goat in the camp, or who slaughters outside the camp, and to the Meeting Tent's opening does not bring it to sacrifice a sacrifice (*qorbān*) to Yahweh before Yahweh's Tabernacle, blood will be reckoned to that man; he will have shed blood, and that man will be cut off from his people's midst. So that Israel's Sons will bring their slaughter-sacrifices (*zibḥêhem*) that they sacrifice/slaughter (*zōbəḥîm*) on the *face* of the field, and they will bring them to Yahweh, to the Meeting Tent's opening, to the priest, and they will sacrifice/slaughter (*wəzābəḥû*) them as *šəlāmîm* sacrifices. . . . And they will no longer sacrifice/slaughter their slaughter-sacrifices for the hairy/goat demons (*śəʿîrim*) after whom they whore. An eternal statute this will be for them. . . .

In the context of P, this legislation implicitly emends Exod 12:1–12. No longer may the family head slaughter a lamb/kid and apply its blood to his door, even for *Pesaḥ*. He must bring it, like any other meat meal, to the Tabernacle. There the priest will remove the fat and use the blood to cleanse the celebrant of bloodguilt for the animal's death (Lev 17:11; see Brichto 1976: 28). The archaic *Pesaḥ* has been silently abolished.

There are several potential objections to my interpretation. One might, for example, regard Leviticus 17 as articulating a general procedure from which Exodus 12 constitutes an annual exemption. Perhaps—but ordinarily we expect a law appearing later in the text to modify an earlier statute, not vice versa. One might also object that Leviticus 17 does not properly belong to P, but to the Holiness stratum (H). The question of H will be taken up in APPENDIX A (vol. II); I am currently unconvinced of its existence. Still, the case relies on more than Leviticus 17. P consistently requires centralization of worship and accordingly proscribes eating the *Pesaḥ* while away from the shrine or in a state of impurity (Num 9:1–14). Where would P expect the *Pesaḥ* to be slaughtered, if not at the altar? (For a contrary opinion, that P permits profane slaughter, see Milgrom 1991: 29.) Even 1 Sam 14:32–35, a source not interested in ritual, views neglect of altar slaughter as heinous, tantamount to eating blood. The requirement of ritual purity also presupposes the role of the Tabernacle in the "*Pesaḥ* of Generations" (cf. Lev 7:21; 22:3). In short, the form of *Pesaḥ* advocated by the Priestly Writer must have been centralized, not domestic.

We can understand the Priestly Writer's ambivalence. On the one hand, both tradition (i.e., JE) and common sense dictated setting the first *Pesaḥ* in Egypt. On the other hand, P consistently demands that all sacrifices be performed by an Aaronic priest in the Tabernacle. JE stories featuring lay sacrifice are either eliminated or bowdlerized in P (Friedman 1987: 191). The Priestly Writer cannot deny that humans, including the Israelites, were carnivorous before Sinai (Gen 9:2–6). But, prior to the enactment of Leviticus 17, all slaughter was perforce profane. Here was P's dilemma: to describe the "*Pesaḥ* of Egypt" as a sacral meal *sans* Tabernacle and priesthood.

The solution was to describe a ritual meal like and yet unlike a burnt offering (Holzinger 1900: 36; see NOTES to 12:5, 8, 9, 10). The victim is an unblemished male. Its head, legs and innards are burnt in fire. It is eaten with unleavened bread, finished within twelve hours. But there are no priests. Instead, presumably, each paterfamilias manipulates the blood. The paschal blood is not sprinkled on an altar, but smeared on the door frame, which, like an altar, affords sanctuary from death and bars leaven (see also NOTE to 12:22). The niceties of ritual purity are ignored: Yahweh has not yet settled among Israel, and in any case all Israel, the clean and unclean alike, require rescue. Indeed, the paschal blood may itself have purifying virtue (Levine 1974: 74–75). *Pesaḥ*'s quasi-sacrificial, quasi-profane aspect was evident to Philo of Alexandria, although he describes the "*Pesaḥ* of Generations," not the "*Pesaḥ* of Egypt": "In this festival many myriads of victims from noon till eventide are offered by the whole people . . . [who are] raised for that particular day to the dignity of the priesthood. . . . On this occasion the whole nation performs the sacred rites and acts as priest with pure hand and complete immunity." This unusual practice was instituted in memory of the Exodus, when, "in their vast enthusiasm and impatient eagerness, they naturally enough sacrificed without waiting for their priest. . . . On this day every dwelling-house is invested with the outward semblance and dignity of a temple. . . . The guests assembled for the banquet have been cleansed by purificatory lustrations" (*De spec. leg.* 2.145–48; trans. F. H. Colson [LCL]).

I have described P's *Pesaḥ* as the solution to a dilemma. That is surely inadequate. Viewed more positively, the Priestly *Pesaḥ* is a "type." Ever since Genesis 1, P has been foreshadowing the Tabernacle and its sacrificial ritual (cf. Blenkinsopp 1976). In Genesis 1, mankind, animals and plants are created, but humans are still vegetarian. In Gen 9:2–6, humanity is granted permission to take life in order to eat meat. Consuming blood, however, is strictly forbidden. In Exodus 12, Yahweh ordains a proto-sacrificial meat meal, including a blood rite. This is the penultimate prefiguration of the sacrificial cultus. Finally, at Sinai, Israel is instructed in the laws of slaughter and sacrifice, presided over by the priesthood (Leviticus 17). The domestic *Pesaḥ* is a dead institution.

While P does not envision any future performance of the blood rite, some injunctions from 12:1–13 may still be incumbent upon future generations. I assume that rules making the most sense for the Hebrews of the Exodus are historical ritual, while others may be prescriptive. Examples of the former category might be eating hastily and dressed for a journey; indeed, later Jewish law and custom commend consumption of the Passover in ritualized leisure (*m. Pesaḥ.* 10:1). In contrast, selecting a perfect, one-year-old animal on the tenth of the month and eating the meat roasted with bitter herbs and unleavened bread sound like prescriptive ritual, as Num 9:11 confirms. And in some cases, we cannot decide: e.g., finishing the animal by dawn makes sense in the narrative context, but is also a common ritual law (see NOTE to 12:10).

Ezekiel, in many ways the Priestly Writer's soulmate, faced the same difficulty. But he found a different way to adapt and neutralize the primitive *Pesaḥ:*

> In the first [month], on the first of the month, you will take a perfect bull, the son of the herd, and you will purify (*wəḥiṭṭē[ʾ]tā*) the Sanctum. And the priest will take from the blood of the purification offering (*ḥaṭṭā[ʾ]t*) and put [it] on the House's doorpost and on the four corners of the altar's *ʿăzārâ* (platform? barrier?) and on the doorpost of the inner court gate. And you will do likewise in the seventh [month], on the first of the month [so OG; MT different], against the unwitting man and the ignorant [sinner]. And you will purge (*wəkippartem*) the House. In the first [month], on the fourteenth day of the month, will be for you the *Pesaḥ*, a festival of seven [MT "weeks of"] days [when] unleavened cakes will be eaten. (Ezek 45:18–21)

Ezekiel is the first writer to call the weeklong observance *Pesaḥ*, rather than *Maṣṣôt*. But he denies any special character to the festival eve. The blood ritual is centralized, assimilated to the purification offering (*ḥaṭṭā[ʾ]t*) and transferred to the *first* of the first month, as well as the first of the seventh. One uses a bovine, not a sheep or goat (cf. Deut 16:2). The king is the protagonist, as in the national *Pesaḥ* of the historical books. The blood does not protect so much as purge. Little, in short, is left of the primitive *Pesaḥ*.

THE ELOHISTIC *PESAH*

If the Priestly Writer did not intend 12:1–13 wholly to apply to future generations, what about the Elohist (12:21–27)? E explicitly commands posterity to
perform the *Pesah* (vv 25–26)—but, again, is this the sacrifice alone, or sacrifice *cum* blood application? And, in either case, is the sacrifice performed
domestically or at a regional shrine?

Whatever its date and provenance (see APPENDIX A, vol. II), the Elohistic
source lies near the beginning of biblical literature, before radical cultic centralization. For the patriarchal period, E is interested in the regional shrines of
Shechem (Gen 33:18–20; 48:22) and Bethel (Genesis 28), but it never restricts
sacrifice to them or to any other site. E does assign the priesthood to the tribe
of Levi (Exod 32:29), but whether this entails proscription of lay sacrifice is
uncertain. Perhaps the Levite was simply the preferred priest (cf. Judg 17:7–
13). At any rate, the emphatic cultic centralization of P and D is absent. We do
not even know whether E's Meeting Tent possesses an altar (Exod 33:7–11;
Numbers 12; Deut 31:14–15). On the one hand, if E's readers already knew of
Pesah as a domestic sacrifice, nothing in 12:21–27 would contradict their expectations. But if, on the other hand, their *Pesah* was a sacrifice performed at
a regional shrine by Levitic clergy, readers would simply find in 12:21–27 the
historical ritual underlying their contemporary paschal sacrifice. It would not
be viewed as prescriptive (cf. Haran 1978: 344–48).

It is likewise unclear whether E's blood rite is historical or prescriptive.
While the child's question in 12:26 is often taken to address the unique blood
application rather than the sacrifice per se (cf. ibn Ezra), a similar question is
asked about routine firstling sacrifice (13:14). Moreover, the prescribed answer
refers to the paschal offering, not the blood. Probably all the child seeks is the
origin and etymology of the *Pesah* sacrifice.

ANY UNCIRCUMCISED MAY NOT EAT OF IT

There is a curious association between *Pesah* and circumcision. In Gen 17:12,
P requires that all males be circumcised on the eighth day. When P next
mentions circumcision (excluding Moses' "uncircumcised" lips [6:12, 30]), it
is as a precondition for participation in the *Pesah* (12:44, 48).

Josh 5:2–9 suggests quite a specific connection. Before celebrating the *Pesah*
at Gilgal, all Israelite men are circumcised at "the Foreskins Mountain." Even
the name "Gilgal" is associated with the rite of circumcision: Yahweh "rolled
back (*gll*) the Egyptians' contempt" (Josh 5:9; cf. Ps 119:22)—perhaps alluding to rolling back (*gll*) the foreskin to reveal (*gly*) the glans. It seems that
periodic mass circumcision of boys and men was part of the ongoing paschal
ceremony of Gilgal (Kraus 1951; Soggin 1966; Cross 1973: 103–5; Otto 1975),
just as Arab circumcision or baptism is often coincident with a major festival,
especially the first full moon of spring (Canaan 1926: 133–36, 142; Musil 1928:
244; Morgenstern 1966: 67, 72, 82–83). The entire festival complex was thus a

rite of passage for adolescent boys. (Only later would infant circumcision become the rule in Israel [Genesis 17]; see Propp 1987b; 1993 and COMMENT to chaps. 3–4, pp. 237–38).

At least in the cult of Gilgal, the national rite of passage out of Egypt into Canaan was powerfully combined with an individual's rite of passage out of juvenility into social maturity. According to the Midrash, prior to the first *Pesaḥ*, the Hebrews underwent a mass circumcision, mingling the paschal blood with human blood (*Exod. Rab.* 19:5; *Tg. Ps.-Jonathan* Exod 12:13; *Tg. Ps.-Jonathan* Ezek 16:6). This legend may be a reaction to the Greco-Roman world, where circumcision distinguished Jew from gentile as sharply as the paschal blood separated Israel from Egypt. But it also responds to an association implicit in the Bible itself (see NOTE to 12:48).

The connections between *Pesaḥ* and circumcision transcend the fact that each is a rite of passage. Above I analyzed *Maṣṣôt* as a festival of purification and *Pesaḥ* as an apotropaic ritual of redemption with possible purificatory aspects. There is evidence that circumcision, too, purifies. In fact, Arabic *ṭhr* connotes both purity and circumcision (see further Wold 1978: 257–61 for various African parallels). Above we intimated that circumcision purges Moses' bloodguilt in 4:24–26 (COMMENT to Exodus 3–4). And Isa 52:1 associates uncircumcision (*ʿrl*) with impurity (*ṭmʾ*); compare also the expressions "uncircumcised of lips" (Exod 6:12, 30) and "impure of lips" (Isa 6:5). Blood impurity (Num 9:6–14) and noncircumcision alike bar participation in the *Pesaḥ*. And the verb *higgîaʿ* describes the transfer of blood of circumcision (4:25), the application of paschal blood (12:22) and the purification of Isaiah's mouth by fire (Isa 6:6–7) (Segal 1963: 159).

Moreover, traces of a belief in the apotropaic virtues of circumcision survive in both the Bible (cf. Loewenstamm 1992a: 202–6) and early Judaism (Flusser and Safrai 1980). Most obviously, the blood of circumcision averts Yahweh's quasi-demonic attack in 4:25–26. From outside Israel, Philo of Byblos (*apud* Eusebius *Praep. evangelica* 1.10.33) preserves the following Phoenician myth: "At the occurrence of a fatal plague, [the god] Kronos immolated his only son to his father Ouranos, and circumcised himself, forcing the allies who were with him to do the same" (Attridge and Oden 1981: 57). This fragment suggestively combines themes from Exodus 12–13: a plague, the defense against which is circumcision and consecration (through sacrifice) of a firstborn son. (There is an even greater resemblance to the traditions surrounding Abraham, who nearly sacrificed his "only" son Isaac and circumcised himself and his household [Hall 1992: 1027]—but, we must remember, Genesis 22 is Elohistic and Genesis 17 Priestly.)

Regarded in isolation, Philo of Byblos provides strong support for scholars who believe that circumcision evolved out of human sacrifice as a sort of *pars pro toto* (Ghillany 1842: 592–603; Frazer 1911: 181; Smith 1906). This theory goes far beyond the evidence, however, since circumcision is a prehistoric rite practiced worldwide (Sasson 1966). Levenson's (1993b: 48–52) more nuanced treatment shows that circumcision came over time to be regarded as a ritual of substitution in Israel and Judaism. A parallel process may account for the Phoenician myth. That is, Phoenicians themselves may have believed that circumcision evolved from child sacrifice. But that does not make it true, or relevant for Israel.

SANCTIFY TO ME EVERY FIRSTBORN

Exod 13:2 enunciates a fundamental principle: the firstborn of man and beast are holy to Yahweh. To legitimate this claim, many passages invoke the Exodus tradition, at least implicitly (13:1–2, 11–16; 34:18–20; cf. Num 3:12–13; 8:5–9:14; Deut 15:19–23).

Some, most memorably Frazer (1911: 174–79), have posited that the paschal rite was primitively an infant sacrifice, with the bloodied doorway grisly proof of parental compliance. In a more civilized stage, supposedly, the child was replaced with the paschal lamb (cf. Hooke 1938: 49). One could even correlate the unique hour of the *Pesaḥ* with Punic nocturnal child sacrifice (see NOTE to 22:28). But Wellhausen (1885: 88) and almost every commentator since have rightly dismissed such conjectures. No human sacrifice, let alone a firstborn sacrifice, could have been performed annually by each family (cf. Loewenstamm 1992a: 196). The theory is nothing more (and nothing less) than modern midrash, highlighting an important association without plausibly explaining it. One suspects that Frazer, who found human sacrifice everywhere, owed a substantial if unconscious debt to Christianity's equation of God's slain Firstborn with the paschal sacrifice. Similarly, the medieval Christian slander that Jews' *maṣṣôt* were baked with children's blood (cf. already Josephus *Ap.* 2.89–102) makes an instinctual connection between homicide and the paschal lamb, the latter in turn associated with unleavened bread through Christianity's identification of both bread and lamb with Christ (see below).

Others have envisioned a more believable evolution: the paschal offering developed out of the sacrifice of firstling lambs and kids (Wellhausen 1885: 87–88; Guthe 1918; Pedersen 1940: 398–402; Füglister 1963: 69; for further bibliography, see Segal 1963: 104 n. 1; Schmidt 1983: 52). In the land of Israel, March–April marks the end of the lambing (Hirsch 1933: 26; Firmage 1992: 1127; see also Henninger 1975: 27–28 n. 13). Most goats, too, are born between December and April (Hirsch p. 58). As we have seen, many ancient and modern Near Eastern societies offer special sacrifices in this season. Pedersen (1934: 166) compares to *Pesaḥ* the Arabic *ʿatira* sacrifice of young animals born in the spring. The Bedouin, in particular, offer some (not all) firstlings of cattle, generally male, always perfect (see also Henninger 1975: 28–29, 39–42, 68 n. 139). (Frequently, however, the Arab springtime offering is not of meat, but of first dairy products.) By this theory, when the blood of firstlings was employed for *fidya*, a rite of desacralization assumed an apotropaic aspect and became *Pesaḥ*.

This theory is with good reason also rejected today (e.g., by Nicolsky 1927; Loewenstamm 1992a: 194–97; Laaf 1970: 122, 125, 148–49). At least in 12:1–

13:16, the paschal victim cannot be a firstling, because the Hebrew firstborn, man *and beast*, are still alive at the end of the night. More important, the law specifies only the species and age of the paschal offering, not its birth order. And if firstling sacrifice evolved into *Pesaḥ*, it is odd that the former survived as an independent practice (see below). The true connection between *Pesaḥ* and various Israelite beliefs and practices surrounding the firstborn is probably more complex.

It is a general principle that firstfruits and firstborn alike are sacred to Yahweh (Gen 4:4; Exod 13:2, 11–16; 22:28–29; 23:16, 19, etc.). Firstfruits are offered at the shrine (Deut 18:4), where, according to P and Ezekiel, they are consumed by the clergy (Num 18:12–13; Ezek 44:30). Male, firstling, clean animals are sacrificed by the priests (on unclean animals, see NOTE to 13:13). Part of the meat goes to God, but on the disposition of the rest there is disagreement. D permits owners to partake (Deut 12:6–7, 17–18; 14:23; 15:19–20), while P restricts the firstlings to the priests (Num 18:15–18; Josephus *Ant.* 4.70; see, however, Segal 1963: 181 for a different interpretation). This discrepancy is part of a larger difference between D and P. Whereas the Deuteronomist acknowledges profane slaughter (Deut 12:15–27), for the Priestly Writer, all slaughter is sacrificial (Lev 17:1–9). In D, because the firstling offering is particularly holy, the priests get *some* of it; in P, because the firstling offering is particularly holy, the priests get *all* of it.

The immolation of firstlings and firstfruits is common worldwide (Gaster 1962c: 149; Henninger 1968). Aristotle (*Nichomachean Ethics* 8.9.5) posits that humanity's first sacrifices were firstfruits, and the Yahwist may have held a comparable opinion vis-à-vis animal sacrifice (cf. Gen 4:4) (Henninger 1975: 179). In the custom of offering to God firstlings and firstfruits, we instinctively perceive an act of preemptive gratitude. One relinquishes property in hopes that more will accrue, giving one ever greater cause to be thankful. Sacrifice of firstfruits and firstlings may also be construed as redemptive, giving life to future crops and broods (Tur-Sinai *apud* Hartom 1954: 123). Curiously, however, the Bible largely ignores this commonsense interpretation of firstling/firstfruits sacrifice as an investment (note, however, 1 Sam 2:20–21). The text instead emphasizes that firstlings and firstfruits are *inherently* holy to Yahweh. They must be "desacralized" before humans may use the rest of the crop or flock (see Gaster 1962c: 149). Refusal would be embezzlement and a courting of catastrophe.

A special subcategory of sanctified firstling is the human male, firstborn to his mother (see NOTE to 13:2). In earliest times, human consecration may have been expressed through ordination to cultic office (cf. *m. Zebaḥ.* 14:4; *Tg. Onqelos* Exod 24:5; *t. Bek.* 4b; ibn Ezra [short commentary on 13:10]; Sforno; various moderns). While this stage is conjectural, the following cases are suggestive. The Patriarchs, firstborn sons to their mothers, commune directly with God, make sacrifice and erect sacred pillars. Manoah and his wife (Judges 13) and Elkanah and Hannah (1 Samuel 1–3) devote their firstborn sons, Samson and Samuel, as holy Nazirites (Judg 13:5; 1 Sam 1:11 [note Greek]). When

Micah (Judg 17:5), Abinadab (1 Sam 7:1) and David (2 Sam 8:18) establish shrines, they install their sons as priests—although we are not told their birth status.

This hypothetical phase of Israelite religion was temporary. While the Deuteronomist apparently rejected the entire notion of human Firstborn Consecration (Levenson 1993b: 44), in P, the Levites are ordained as minor clergy to substitute for Israel's firstborn (Num 3:12–13, 40–51; 8:16–18; compare Judg 17:10–13). There is a special ritual of redemption: either a sheep/goat is offered (13:13; 34:20), or five shekels are paid to the sacred treasury (Num 3:47; 18:16). (This is exactly how one redeems an unclean animal; cf. Segal 1963: 182–83; on humans as beasts, see Eccl 3:18–21.)

We have seen how easily the notion of redemption suggests a third manner whereby a child might be consecrated: through immolation. If a sheep or goat can substitute for a human, would not an actual child be more efficacious? The human offering would presumably be a holocaust (*ʿôlâ*), rather than a feast (*zebaḥ*) (note, however, Ezek 16:20; 23:37). Human sacrifice is not just a theoretical possibility. Several of the Canaanite peoples apparently practiced infant sacrifice, most notably the Phoenicians, along with their Punic colonists. This was an act of *imitatio Dei:* Death himself was probably imagined to be God's sacrificed firstborn (see NOTE to 22:28).

We must resist the temptation to posit a simple evolution from sacrifice to redemption, as do Ghillany (1842: 494–510) and Frazer (1911: 174–79). For nineteenth-century scholars, it was axiomatic that, the further one went back in time, the greater the divergence from contemporary mores. Many peoples in fact believe that animal sacrifice developed out of human sacrifice (for China and India, see Trumbull 1885: 150–59, 185–86; for Greece, see Theophrastus [*apud* Porphyry De abstinentia 2.27]; for classical writers on Egypt, see Trumbull p. 170). Henninger (1975: 168–69), however, shows that human sacrifice is more typical of "advanced," agriculturalist civilizations than of hunting or nomadic societies. And Carthaginian child sacrifice grew *more* popular over time, not less (Stager 1980). Wellhausen (1885: 89) and others have similarly argued that child sacrifice was a late development in Israel.

What was the purpose of dedicating children, particularly firstborn boys, to Yahweh, whether by ordination, redemption or sacrifice? Originally, we may assume, the rite was supposed to ensure fertility. Thus, in Gen 22:15–18, God promises Abraham numerous descendants in reward for his willingness to slaughter Isaac. In 1 Sam 2:20–21, Hannah is granted five more children after surrendering Samuel to Yahweh as a hierodule. Levenson (1993b), moreover, draws our attention to stories in which a beloved son is lost to a father, only to be replaced or restored (e.g., Abel, Isaac, Jacob, Joseph, Job's children, Jesus, etc.); these reflect the same ideology. But, overall, the Bible insists that the firstborn are *inherently* Yahweh's. There is no special reward for giving God what is God's, only punishment for withholding.

THE SON OF GOD

During the paschal night, Yahweh threatens both Israel and Egypt. Since he kills the Egyptian firstborn, symmetry requires that the imperiled Israelites, too, be the firstborn—a logic underlying Judaism's Fast of the Firstborn on the half-day before Passover (*Sop.* 21:3). The text reiterates, however, that *all* Israelite households are endangered, not only firstborn sons (12:13, 22, 23, 27) (Loewenstamm 1992a: 191). Where, then, lies the symmetry with the plague against Egypt?

Fretheim (1991a: 149) finds the key in 4:22–23 (E) (cf. Wis 18:5): "My son, my firstborn, is Israel. And I have said to you, 'Release my son that he may serve me.' And if you refuse to release him, see: I am going to kill your son, your firstborn." *All* Israel, man and woman, young and old, are Yahweh's collective firstborn son (cf. Reichert 1977: 346). Firstborn redemption thus becomes an act of *imitatio Dei*: because Yahweh redeemed his firstborn son, Israel, I redeem my own firstborn. (It is interesting to compare this with the Phoenician concept of child sacrifice as *imitatio Dei*; see Tertullian *Apology* 9.4 and Philo of Byblos, quoted above.) Deuteronomy's nonmention of Firstborn Redemption suggests, however, that the association with the Exodus tradition was not universally endorsed (Levenson 1993b: 44); see further below.

HYPOTHETICAL HISTORY OF TRADITION

To summarize the foregoing pages, I proffer, with due reservation, the following evolution of the tradition:

1. Originally, *Maṣṣôt* was a rite of annual purification; *Pesaḥ* was an associated redemptive sacrifice protecting either children or households from demonic attack. Neither had a strong connection with the Exodus tradition, and quite possibly they antedated Yahwism. But the irresistible tendency to root distinctive aspects of Israelite culture in the Mosaic period led to the reinterpretation of both rituals.

2. There arose the etiological legend of the first *Pesaḥ* of Egypt, when the rite redeemed Israel from two predicaments: a plague (*via* vicarious sacrifice) and servitude (cf. Loewenstamm 1992a: 207–18). The annual *Pesaḥ* became a commemorative reenactment. *Maṣṣôt* underwent a comparable reinterpretation, spawning the story of the Hebrews' unrisen dough.

3. The belief in God's special relationship with firstborn sons existed independent of the Exodus tradition and was probably also pre-Israelite. Again, there was an effort to attach the institution to Moses. The story arose that, on the paschal night, Yahweh killed Egypt's firstborn, while Israel, God's firstborn, was ransomed. A debt was created: henceforth, all firstborn sons must be offered to and redeemed from Yahweh.

4. While immemorial tradition acknowledged God's claim on firstborn animals as well as humans, there was originally no connection with the

paschal tradition. As Segal (1963: 183) observes, the mention of first-ling animals in 11:5; 12:29 seems an afterthought; technically, all the firstling cattle should already be dead, whether by murrain or hail (see NOTE to 9:6). Segal notices, moreover, that the consecration of first-ling animals is explicitly tied to the Exodus *only* when accompanied by reference to firstborn humans, suggesting that animal consecration is secondary (13:2, 11–16; 34:18–20; contrast Lev 27:26–27; Deut 12:6–7, 17; 14:23).

An exception that proves the rule is Deut 15:19–23. The mandate for firstling sacrifice is followed, as often, by paschal legislation (Deuteronomy 16), even if the text draws no explicit connection between the two. But Deut 15:19–23 is preceded by laws concerning, not the redemption of sons, but the manumis-sion of slaves and treatment of the oppressed. Implicit in this sequence is an analogy between firstborn redemption and the redemption of Israel from Egypt, even if D itself rejects the ritualized redemption of firstborn sons that consti-tutes the missing link.

PASCHAL FORESHADOWING

On rereading the preceding chapters of Genesis and Exodus, we find several possible adumbrations of the events of the paschal night and the departure from Egypt.

1. Inasmuch as they are setting out for Canaan at God's behest, the He-brews' departure from Egypt recalls Abram's departure from Haran (Gen 12:1–3). They have now reached a total of 600,000 adult men (Exod 12:37), fulfilling God's promise to Abram of many descendants (Gen 12:2; cf. Exod 1:7, 9).
2. Parallel to the Hebrews' Egyptian sojourn is Abram's sojourn at Pha-raoh's court, to which he, too, is driven by famine. Abram leaves after a plague, accompanied by slaves and livestock donated by the Egyptians (Gen 12:10–20).
3. Many themes connect the Binding of Isaac (Genesis 22) and the *Pesaḥ*-Exodus tradition: pilgrimage to a holy mountain, endangerment of a woman's firstborn son, the vicarious death of an ovine. These parallels led Jewish authors to associate *Pesaḥ* with the Akedah (e.g., *Mek. Pishaʾ* 7) and even to date the Binding to Passover (Jub 17:15–16; *Tg. Neofiti I* Exod 12:42; *Exod. Rab.* 15:11; see Le Déaut 1963: 131–208; Levenson 1993b: 176–83, 192–93).
4. Pharaoh's threat to the Hebrew boys (1:16, 22) is turned back upon Egypt, with the death of their own firstborn sons. The Egyptians will be fully repaid at the Suph Sea, when more Egyptian males will die by water, just as Pharaoh had tried to drown the Israelites' boys (see COM-MENT to 1:22–2:10).

5. Exod 4:22–23, foretelling the death of Pharaoh's firstborn, provides E's understanding of Firstborn Redemption and its relation to the *Pesaḥ*. Israel is Yahweh's firstborn, whom he will redeem from bondage.

6. The episode of the Bridegroom of Bloodiness (4:24–26), with its motifs of crossing the Egyptian border, Yahweh's nocturnal attack and the apotropaic power of blood of circumcision, implicitly presages the paschal night; see COMMENT to Exodus 3–4.

7. Moses' demand in 5:3, "We would . . . sacrifice to Yahweh our deity, lest he strike us with the plague or with the sword," is borne out in Exodus 12 (ibn Ezra)—but not as Pharaoh might have expected, with the Hebrews' death. Rather, by virtue of the paschal rite, Yahweh's wrath is shunted onto Egypt. The Hebrews' repeated request to sacrifice in the desert (3:18; 5:1, 3; 7:16; 8:23–24), though perhaps a ruse, seems, in light of Exodus 12, to allude to the pilgrim festival of Unleavened Bread (Haran 1978: 300–3).

The paschal theme also plays an important structural role in the rest of the Hebrew Bible. Licht (1971b: 519) observes that the *Pesaḥ*s of Moses and Joshua set off Israel's wilderness period, with water-crossings (the Suph Sea, the Jordan) constituting an interior frame. And we must not forget the central *Pesaḥ* at Mount Sinai (Num 9:1–5). The later *Pesaḥ*s under Solomon (1 Kgs 9:25; 2 Chr 8:12–13), Hezekiah (2 Chronicles 30), Josiah (2 Kgs 23:21–23; 2 Chr 35:1–19), Zerubbabel (Ezra 6:19–22) and perhaps Ezra (Ezra 8:31–35) also mark significant epochs in biblical history.

AGNUS DEI

In Christianity's twofold Scripture, Jesus' Passion culminates the paschal theme. Conversely, Exod 12:1–13:16 prefigures Christ's death. The various aspects of *Pesaḥ-Maṣṣôt*—substitutional sacrifice, the redeeming death of a firstborn male, the eating of unleavened bread and drinking of wine—all meet in Jesus. The timing of his historical trial and crucifixion, coincident with Passover, was one essential factor in this development. Another was the custom of combing Scripture for allegorical prophecies of the End, as in the Pesher literature of Qumran.

The result was a total reinterpretation of the Judean Messiah. No longer a conquering king in the style of David, the New Testament Christ is a paschal lamb (1 Cor 5:7) slaughtered with bones unbroken (John 19:36). His sacrifice redeems believers from death, not in this world but in the next (Rev 20:14), by atoning for transgression (Matt 20:28; Mark 10:45; John 1:29–36; Eph 1:7; 1 Tim 2:6; Titus 2:14; 1 Peter 1:18–19; Rev 5:6–14, etc.). Thus Jesus is also a sin offering, an association probably derived from early Jewish interpretations of Genesis 22 and Isaiah 53 (Vermes 1961: 193–227; Levenson 1993b: 173–219). After his death and resurrection, Jesus' essence enters into consecrated unleavened bread and wine, ingested by his followers in a periodic reenactment of the Last Supper (Luke 22:19; 1 Cor 11:23–26; see below). And, at the Eschaton, the Lamb's partisans will be distinguished by a protective mark reminiscent of the paschal blood (Revelation 7). In the second century C.E., the Aramaic equivalent of *Pesaḥ*, *Pasḥā'*, was even associated by felicitous pseudo-etymology with Greek *paschein* 'to suffer,' connoting the Passion (e.g., Melito of Sardis *Peri pascha* 46).

Jesus' Last Supper was no Passover Seder in the modern sense. The Haggadah did not achieve its traditional form until Judaism had assimilated the Temple's destruction. Moreover, it is uncertain that the meal took place on Passover at all (O'Toole 1992). On the one hand, the Synoptic Gospels make the Last Supper coincident with Passover eve (Mark 14:12–16; Luke 22:5), and their description of the proceedings is compatible with a paschal meal. The repast is nocturnal (Mark 14:17; cf. John 13:30; 1 Cor 11:23), the bread is preceded by an *hors d'oeuvres* (Matt 26:23; Mark 14:20; cf. John 13:26), wine is drunk (Matt 26:27–29; Mark 14:23–25; Luke 22:17, 20) and a hymn is sung (Matt 26:30; Mark 14:26). On the other hand, John 13:1–2 puts the Last Supper twenty-four hours *before* Passover (cf. 19:14, 31, 36). It is the crucifixion that coincides with the paschal sacrifice (19:14). John is the Gospel that most clearly attaches paschal significance to Jesus' death (see also 1 Cor 5:7), describing him as the expiatory "Lamb of God" (John 1:29, 36) whose bones were not broken (19:36) (see further Brown 1994: 1372).

Despite its obvious *Tendenz* in associating Jesus with the *Pesaḥ*, many scholars believe that in this matter John is historically accurate (e.g., Brown 1994: 1350–73). They point to a surprising omission in the Synoptic Last Supper. There is the wine and the unleavened bread, but where is the lamb for the offering? The Synoptic tradition took the liberty, supposedly, of adjusting the chronology of the Passion Week. But the Evangelists dared not add another dish to the Last Supper itself (cf. Segal 1963: 243–45).

I do not find this compelling. First, the Synoptics do make clear that the disciples are gathering to eat the paschal offering (Matt 26:17; Mark 14:12; Luke 22:8). As for why the lamb goes unmentioned in the descriptions of the meal itself, three answers are possible. First, Jesus may not have spoken memorably about the meat; i.e., he did not claim identity with the paschal lamb. It is only in light of John and 1 Cor 5:7 that we find this surprising. The second factor may be that, whether or not Jesus intended it (note Luke 22:19), the eating of the Eucharist early became traditional (1 Cor 11:23–26). How expensive and inconvenient would worship have been, had Jesus supposedly identified himself with the lamb instead of with the bread! Third and most likely, the presence of the main Passover dish may have been too obvious to require mention.

This is not to say that the Synoptic Gospels are necessarily more accurate than John. They, too, manifest a *Tendenz*, providing an etiology for a later ritual and implying that it replaces the Jewish Passover. In fact, it is hard to believe that the Romans would have performed executions in Jerusalem at any point during the Passover week. One might well conclude from the ambiguous data that Jesus was simply executed shortly before Passover (cf. Brown

1994: 1373). Early Christian tradition in various ways sought to make the most of the coincidence.

However that may be, we sense that formative Christianity faced a dilemma. To describe the Last Supper as a Passover—the Synoptic option—would have precluded identification of the still living Jesus with the paschal offering. Alternatively, Jesus slain might be equated with the paschal sacrifice—John's choice—but then the Last Supper precedes Passover and is not a prototype for the Eucharist.

This dilemma found its resolution in the compilation of the New Testament. With both versions standing side by side, we cannot read the Synoptics' Last Supper without finding in the nonmention of the sacrificial victim an implication that Jesus himself is the paschal offering. The magic words "this is my body" make the periodic consumption of the wafer equivalent to partaking of the paschal lamb (cf. the equation of Jesus and Manna, treated in COMMENT to 15:27–16:36).

XII. But Israel's Sons walked on the dry land in the Sea's midst (13:17–15:21)

13   [17(E)]And it happened, in Pharaoh's releasing the people, and Deity did not lead them the way of the land of Philistines, although it was near, but Deity said, "Lest the people repent in their seeing war and return to Egypt." [18]And Deity sent the people around the way of the wilderness of/toward the Suph Sea; and resolute went up Israel's Sons from Egypt. [19]And Moses took Joseph's bones with him, for he had adjured, adjured Israel's Sons, saying, "Deity will acknowledge, acknowledge you, and you will take up my bones from here with you."
[20(R)]**And they set forth from Succoth and camped at Etham, on the wilderness's edge.** [21(JE?)]And Yahweh was going before them by day in a cloud pillar to lead them the way, and by night in a fire pillar to illuminate for them, going by day and by night. [22]The cloud pillar would not depart by day, nor the fire pillar by night, before the people.

14   [1(P)]**And Yahweh spoke to Moses, saying,** [2]**"Speak to Israel's Sons, that they should** [(P?)]**turn back and** [(P)]**camp before Pi-hahiroth between Migdol and between the Sea before Baal-zephon; opposite it you will camp by the Sea.** [3]**And Pharaoh will say of Israel's Sons, 'They are confused in the land; the wilderness has closed against them.'** [4]**And I will strengthen Pharaoh's heart, and he will pursue after them. And I will glorify myself over Pharaoh and over all his force, and Egypt will know that I am Yahweh." And they did so.**
[5(E?)]And it was told to Egypt's king that the people had fled. And Pharaoh's and his slaves' heart was reversed concerning the people, and they said, "What is this we did, that we released Israel from our service?"

⁶⁽ᴱ⁾And he harnessed his chariotry and his people he took with him, ⁷⁽ᴶ/ᴾ⁾and he took six hundred choice chariotry and all Egypt's chariotry, and *thirds* over all of it. ⁸⁽ᴾ⁾And Yahweh strengthened the heart of Pharaoh, Egypt's king, and he pursued after Israel's Sons, ⁽ᴾ⁾and Israel's Sons were going out with raised arm. ⁹⁽ᴾ⁾And Egypt pursued after them and overtook them encamped by the Sea, all the horse of Pharaoh's chariotry and his horsemen and his force, at Pi-hahiroth before Baal-zephon.

¹⁰⁽ᴶᴱ⁾And Pharaoh, he led near. ⁽ᴶᴱ⁾And Israel's Sons raised their eyes and they saw, and, see: Egypt setting forth after them. And they feared greatly. And Israel's Sons cried to Yahweh. ¹¹And they said to Moses, "Is it from a lack of no graves in Egypt that you took us to die in the wilderness? What is this you did to us, by taking us out from Egypt? ¹²Is not this the word that we spoke to you in Egypt, saying, 'Let us alone that we may serve Egypt'? For serving Egypt is better for us than our dying in the wilderness."

¹³And Moses said to the people, "Do not fear. Station yourselves and see Yahweh's salvation that he will make for you today. For, as you have seen Egypt today, you will see them no more to eternity. ¹⁴Yahweh, he will fight for you; and you, you will be still."

¹⁵⁽ᴾ⁾And Yahweh said to Moses, "(For) what do you cry to me? ⁽ᴾ⁾Speak to Israel's Sons, that they should set forth. ¹⁶And you, ⁽ᴿ⁾raise your rod and ⁽ᴾ⁾extend your arm over the Sea and split it, and Israel's Sons will go in the Sea's midst on the dry land. ¹⁷And I, see, I am going to strengthen Egypt's heart, and they will come after them. And I will glorify myself over Pharaoh and over all his force, over his chariotry and over his horsemen, ¹⁸and Egypt will know that I am Yahweh, through my glorification over Pharaoh, over his chariotry and over his horsemen."

¹⁹⁽ᴱ⁾And the Deity's Messenger going before Israel's camp set forth and went behind them, ⁽?⁾and the cloud pillar set forth from before them and stood behind them. ²⁰And it came between Egypt's camp and between Israel's camp. And there was the cloud and the dark, and it illumined the night. And *this one* did not approach *this one* all the night.

²¹⁽ᴾ⁾And Moses extended his arm over the Sea, ⁽ᴶᴱ⁾and Yahweh conducted the Sea with a mighty *forward* wind all the night, and he made the Sea into the dry ground, ⁽ᴾ⁾and the waters were split. ²²And Israel's Sons entered in the Sea's midst on the dry land, and the waters for them a wall from their right and from their left. ²³And Egypt pursued and came after them, all Pharaoh's horse, his chariotry and his horsemen, into the Sea's midst.

²⁴⁽ᴶᴱ⁾And it happened during the morning watch, and Yahweh looked down toward Egypt's camp from inside a pillar of fire and cloud. And he panicked Egypt's camp, ²⁵and he diverted/bound/removed his chariot wheel and made him drive with heaviness. ⁽ᴱ⁾And Egypt said, "I must flee from Israel's *face*, for Yahweh is the fighter for them against Egypt."

²⁶⁽ᴾ⁾And Yahweh said to Moses, "Extend your arm over the Sea, and its waters will return upon Egypt, upon his chariotry and upon his horsemen."

²⁷**And Moses extended his arm over the Sea,** ⁽ᴶᴱ⁾and the Sea returned *at morning's turning* to its original course, and Egypt setting forth to meet it. And Yahweh tumbled Egypt in the Sea's midst. ²⁸⁽ᴾ⁾**And the waters returned and covered the chariotry and the horsemen of all Pharaoh's force coming after them into the Sea;** ⁽ᴱ⁾so much as one of them did not remain. ²⁹⁽ᴾ⁾**But Israel's Sons had walked on the dry land in the Sea's midst, and the waters for them a wall from their right and from their left.**

³⁰⁽ᴶ⁽?⁾⁾So Yahweh saved on that day Israel from Egypt's *arm*, and Israel saw Egypt dead at the Sea's *lip*. ³¹⁽ᴶᴱ⁾And Israel saw the great *arm* that Yahweh made in Egypt, ⁽ᴱ⁾and the people feared Yahweh and trusted in Yahweh and in Moses his slave.

15 ¹⁽?⁾Then sang Moses and Israel's Sons this song of Yahweh, and they said, saying:

I would sing of Yahweh, for he acted exaltedly, exaltedly!
Horse and his driver he hurled into the Sea.

²My strength and my power/music is Yah;
And he was for me as salvation.

This is my god, and I exalt him,
My father's deity, and I elevate him:
³Yahweh Man of War, Yahweh is his name.

⁴Pharaoh's chariots and his force he cast into the Sea.
And the choice of his *thirds* were sunk in the Suph Sea.

⁵Deeps, they cover them;
They went down in the depths like stone.

⁶Your right hand, Yahweh, strong in might,
Your right hand, Yahweh, you shatter enemy.

⁷And in your pride's greatness you break down your *uprisers*.
You release your anger; it consumes them as straw.

⁸And with your nostrils' breath waters were piled;
Streams stood like a heap.
Deeps congealed in Sea's heart.

⁹Enemy said,
"I'll pursue, overtake,
Apportion spoil.

My gullet will be full of them.
I'll *empty* my sword.
My hand will dispossess them."

¹⁰You blew with your breath; Sea covered them.
They sank like lead in strong waters.

[11]Who as you among gods, Yahweh,
Who as you is strong in holiness,
Dreadful of glory, worker of wonder?

[12]You extended your right arm;
Earth swallows them.

[13]You led by your grace the people which you redeemed;
You guided by your might to your holiness's pasture/camp/tent.

[14]Peoples heard. They shudder.
Convulsion seized Philistia's inhabitants.

[15]Then perturbed were Edom's princes.
Moab's *rams*, quaking seizes them.
Liquefied were all Canaan's inhabitants.

[16]Upon them fall fear and terror.
At your limb's greatness they are still as stone,

Till crosses your people, Yahweh,
Till crosses the people which you have gotten.

[17]May you bring them and plant them in your property mountain,
The firm seat for your sitting/throne/dwelling you devised, Yahweh,
The sanctum, my Lordship, your hands founded.

[18]Yahweh, he will reign, ever and eternity.

[19(R)]For Pharaoh's horse, with his chariotry and his horsemen, entered the Sea, and Yahweh brought back upon them the Sea's waters. But Israel's Sons walked on the dry land in the Sea's midst.
[20(E)]And Miriam the prophetess, Aaron's sister, took the drum in her hand, and all the women went forth behind her with drums and with dances. [21]And Miriam sang back to them:

"Sing of Yahweh, for he acted exaltedly, exaltedly!
Horse and his driver he hurled into the Sea."

ANALYSIS

TEXTUAL NOTES

13:17. *Deity.* Throughout vv 17–18, the *Tgs.* ostensibly reflect "Yahweh"—probably just loose translation.

††13:18. *from Egypt.* Following Kenn 18, 80, Rossi 2, 16, 296, 543, 766, supported by LXX[A] and the *n*-group of Greek MSS. Standard MT has "from *the land of* Egypt." LXX[B], before correction by a later hand, originally lacked any reference to Egypt at all, but this attractively short reading is unsubstantiated by any other Version.

13:19. *he.* Sam and many witnesses to LXX specify "Joseph," a gloss removing the fleeting misimpression that Moses had adjured Israel (Wevers 1990: 204). †*Deity.* LXX "Lord" might reflect a *Vorlage* *yhwh. The *Tgs.* also have "Yahweh," but here there is little likelihood of a variant *Vorlage*, since the *Tgs.* use "Yahweh" for "the Deity" throughout the passage. It is difficult to say which divine name is original. Gen 50:24, which 13:19 quotes, uses *'ĕlōhîm*. But that makes LXX attractively difficult.

13:20. *Etham.* Symmachus, Aquila and Theodotion read *'ētān*, a Hebrew word appearing in 14:27. MT *'ētām* is presumably original. After "Etham," Sam and most likely the *Vorlagen* of Syr and *Tgs.* add *'šr* 'which is.' I follow the shorter MT.

†13:21. *Yahweh.* Here LXX reflects "(the) Deity" (contrast 13:19). It is hard to say which is the superior reading. On the one hand, *'ĕlōhîm* is the less common divine name; on the other hand, it predominates in this passage. See also TEXTUAL NOTES to 14:13, 31; 15:1 and APPENDIX A, vol. II.

to lead them. Lanḥōtām is vocalized as a Hiph'il infinitive with he'-syncope (GKC §53*q*). We might be tempted to read *linḥōtām*, a Qal with the same meaning; compare 13:17 *nāḥām* 'led them.' But when our verse is quoted/paraphrased in Neh 9:19, we find the unambiguous Hiph'il *ləhanḥôtām*.

the way. The definite article is present in MT (*hadderek*), but absent from Sam (*drk*). MT is supported by Neh 9:19 *bəhadderek*.

to illuminate for them . . . night. These words are absent from LXX, presumably dropped by homoioarkton across vv 21–22 (*lh'yr . . . l'*) (Wevers 1990: 207).

†13:22. *The cloud pillar . . . the fire pillar.* While some Sam MSS support MT *'ammûd he'ānān . . . 'ammûd hā'ēš*, others read "*a . . . pillar*" both times, without the definite article (cf. Kenn 4, 111). This is probably secondary, borrowed from the previous verse. In 13:22, the definite article is tantamount to "the *aforesaid*" (GKC §126*d*) (on the absence of the article in 14:24, see SOURCE ANALYSIS).

would not depart. MT has *ymyš*, while Sam and Rossi 378 read *ymwš*. The latter variant is unambiguously intransitive ("it would not depart"), whereas the MT accommodates an alternate rendering: "he [Yahweh] would not remove" (Hiph'il) (see NOTE).

the people. LXX expands: "*all* the people."

14:1. *saying.* Syr paraphrases: "and he said to him."

†14:2. *before Pi-hahiroth.* Here and in 14:9, LXX has *apenanti tēs epauleōs* 'before the sheepfold,' vs. MT *lpny py hḥyrt*. When the same words reappear in Num 33:7, however, LXX has "the mouth of Eïrōth," now agreeing with MT but taking *pî* as the construct of *pe(h)* 'mouth' (cf. Syr Exod 14:2 *pwmh dḥryt'* 'the mouth of *ḥrîtā*,' which also apparently transposes yodh and resh).

LXX Exod 14:2 reflects two apparent differences from MT: (a) loss of *py* by haplography after *pny* in v 2 (and the spread of the error to v 9; cf. Num 33:8 in MT, LXX); (b) a likely reading of either *ḥṣr(t)* or *ḥwt* 'sheepfold' for MT *ḥyrt*. *Ḥṣr(t)* is closer to MT *ḥyrt* in appearance (on yodh-ṣadhe confusion in paleo-Hebrew, see Tov 1992: 245, 358) and is in fact a way station mentioned in Num 11:35; 33:17–18—but it is not in Egypt. *Ḥwt, on the other hand, recalls Egyptian ḥwt 'palace, temple,' a common element in place-names. It is also possible that the LXX Vorlage was after all identical to MT and that "sheepfold" was a translator's guess. Identifying the corresponding Egyptian toponym might settle the question, but this has proved difficult; see APPENDIX B, vol. II. (If MT py ḥḥyrt is not original, perhaps a copyist understood the name as postbiblical Hebrew *pî haḥērūt 'freedom's mouth' [cf. Rashi].)

†before Baal-zephon. LXX has "from before Baal-zephon," i.e., *millipnê for MT lipnê. Since the prior word ends in m, we might have either dittography (m > mm), producing the LXX Vorlage, or haplography (mm > m), producing MT. See also TEXTUAL NOTE to 14:9.

opposite it. LXX "opposite them" is probably periphrastic; see also NOTE.

†you will camp. The command is plural in MT (taḥănû), but singular in LXX, apparently addressed to Moses alone, or more likely to the people collectively (Wevers 1990: 208). Perhaps LXX is translating loosely. But if its Vorlage actually had a singular *tḥnh, this would be a superior reading; MT taḥănû would be an assimilation to yaḥănû earlier in the verse.

14:3. And Pharaoh will say. Syr has "and Pharaoh said" in the narrator's voice. See further below.

of Israel's Sons. To avoid potential misunderstanding (see NOTE), LXX^B has "Pharaoh will say, 'Israel's Sons. . . .'" Other LXX witnesses expand: "Pharaoh will say to his people: 'Israel's Sons. . . .'" LXX^AFM, however, correspond to MT.

14:4. And I will strengthen. Syr, which erroneously takes v 3 as the narrator's interjection, of necessity begins v 4 with "and the Lord said to Moses."

after them. Syr and some LXX read "after you."

Egypt. LXX and one Sam MS, presumably independently, expand: "all Egypt"; see TEXTUAL NOTES to 7:5 and 14:18.

14:5. Egypt's king. LXX^A instead reads "Pharaoh, saying."

heart. For MT ləbab, Sam has the synonymous and more common lēb.

†What is this. Rossi 16, Syr and Vg omit "is this."

Israel. Kenn 155, 384 and LXX read "Israel's Sons," presumably an expansion.

†14:6. he harnessed. LXX specifies "Pharaoh harnessed."

his people. LXX expands: "all his people."

14:8. Egypt's king. Many exemplars of LXX add "and his slaves," matching 14:5. While this is most likely an expansion, it is barely conceivable that MT lost *w'bdyw 'and his slaves' by homoioarkton with wyrdp 'and he pursued.'

†14:9. all the horse of Pharaoh's chariotry. The LXX Vorlage probably read *kol-sûs wərekeb par'ō(h) 'all Pharaoh's horse and chariotry,' less likely *kol-sûs par'ō(h) wərikbô 'all Pharaoh's horse and his chariotry' (so Syr; cf. MT 14:23). MT, in contrast, has the difficult kol-sûs rekeb par'ō(h) 'all the horse of Pharaoh's chariotry.' While sûs wərekeb 'horse and chariotry' (LXX) is a common phrase (Deut 20:1; Josh 11:4; 1 Kgs 20:1, etc.), sûs rekeb (MT) is unparalleled.

SPECULATION: Perhaps neither MT nor LXX is correct. Two ancient variants may underlie v 9: *kol-sûs par'ō(h) 'all Pharaoh's horse' and *kol rekeb *parʿō(h)* 'all Pharaoh's chariotry.' MT simply conflates the variants, while LXX smooths by inserting a conjunction. We expect such vicissitudes in the copying of a formulaic list.

at Pi-hahiroth. Syr inserts "encamped," presumably lest the reader forget the main verb after the parenthesis.

before. Again, LXX reads *"from before,"* i.e., **millipnê* (see TEXTUAL NOTE to 14:2). Here the previous word does not end in *m*, so the error should have originated in 14:2. But in both cases loose translation is an alternative and likely explanation.

14:10. *And Pharaoh, he led near.* Sam and Syr place a dramatic break (*pətûḥâ*) after these words, unlike MT. The inverted word order (*ûparʿō[h] hiqrîb*), however, suggests rather the beginning of a new section (Weimar 1985: 22), as does the frame created by 14:2, 9.

Israel's Sons. Syr paraphrases: "those of Israel's House." See TEXTUAL NOTE to 3:11.

††*and they saw, and, see.* So Sam and 4QReworked Pentateuchᶜ (*wyrʾw whnh*), supported by LXXᴬ. MT has simply *whnh* 'and, see,' presumably the product of haplography (*w . . . w*) (D. N. Freedman, privately). Most MSS of LXX and Syr have simply "and saw," perhaps a loose translation of **whnh* (= MT).

SPECULATION: LXX and Syr may preserve a third variant, however: **wyrʾw* 'and they saw,' conflated in Sam and 4QReworked Pentateuchᶜ with *whnh* (MT) (cf. *wayyar[ʾ] wəhinnē[h]* in MT 3:2). That would leave us with two older readings, *whnh* and **wyrʾw*. Of these, the former is more likely original. To create the latter, a scribe's eye could have skipped from ʿ*ynyhm* 'their eyes' to ʾ*ḥryhm* 'after them' (homoioteleuton). Then, since ʾ*ḥryhm* is followed by *wyrʾw* 'and (they) feared' (Kenn 13, 18, 69, 80, etc.), he brought the latter forward to follow ʿ*ynyhm*, where it would naturally be read *wayyirʾû* 'and (they) saw.' The scribe then resumed with *whnh*.

Egypt. LXX inserts "and" before "the Egyptians." This is either free translation or a dittography of the final waw of **wyrʾw* 'and they saw,' a possible reading in the LXX *Vorlage* (C.-P. M. Yu, privately; see above).

†*setting forth.* The participle is singular (*nsʿ*) in standard MT, but plural (*nsʿym*) in 4QExodᶜ, Sam, 4QReworked Pentateuchᶜ, Rossi 378 and the Vg *Vorlage*, which at some point lost **nsʿym* after *mṣrym* 'Egypt' by homoioteleuton. LXX, Tgs. and Syr may also have had the plural in their *Vorlagen*, but we cannot tell, as they regularly render "Egypt" with "the Egyptians." Since the prior verse treats *mṣrym* as a plural, the MT singular may be preferable as the more diverse, difficult reading. But the plural *nōsəʿîm* heightens the wordplay with 14:27, whether we read *nāsîm* 'fleeing' or *nōsəʿîm* 'setting forth' (see TEXTUAL NOTE).

14:11. *in Egypt.* LXX has "in *the land of* Egypt," presumably an expansion.

14:13. *Yahweh's salvation.* LXX has "salvation *from the God.*" Did the LXX *Vorlage* read **hāʾĕlōhîm* (cf. Kenn 186 *hʾlhym yhwh*), and, if so, might it be correct (cf. LXX 13:21; 15:1)? When 2 Chr 20:17 quotes Exod 14:13, both MT and the Greek read "*Yahweh's* salvation," confirming MT Exod 14:13. The change to "Deity" in LXX might reflect the influence of Isa 52:10 = Ps 98:3, "the earth's ends have seen our *deity's* salvation."

"God's/Yahweh's salvation" means, of course, Yahweh's saving Israel (cf. 15:2), not his being saved himself. It is presumably to bar blasphemous misinterpretation that LXX paraphrases: "salvation *from* the God."

for you. Most LXX MSS have "for *us*"—a confusion between Greek *hymin* and *hēmin* (cf. v 14).

For, as. Standard MT *kî ʾăšer*, though slightly awkward, is probably correct. 4QReworked Pentateuch^c, Sam, Kenn 69, 80, 101, 199, 674, Rossi 378, 730 and some Genizah MSS (*BHS*) read *kî kaʾăšer*, a longer, somewhat easier reading that may also underlie LXX, Syr and some exemplars of *Tg. Onqelos.*

no more to eternity. For MT *tōsîpû*, Sam and Kenn 9 have *twspwn*, probably inspired by *tḥryšwn* in the next verse. (We expect paragogic nun at the end of a clause, not in the middle.)

see them. 4QReworked Pentateuch^c has *[lrʾw]tw* 'see *him,*' i.e., Egypt.

14:14. *be still.* Syr adds at the end "and Moses prayed to the Lord," presumably to explain Yahweh's unexpected rebuke of Moses in v 15 (see SOURCE ANALYSIS; NOTE).

†14:17. *Egypt's heart.* Elsewhere, *Pharaoh's* heart is hardened (4:21; 9:12; 10:20, 27; 11:10; 14:4, 8). In fact, LXX reads "the heart of Pharaoh and all the Egyptians," while 4QReworked Pentateuch^c has "*Pharaoh's heart and* Egypt's heart." It is difficult to say which reading is the best. MT is shortest and most difficult, but could also be haplographic (**ʾt lb prʿh wʾt lb mṣrym > ʾt lb mṣrym*) (D. N. Freedman, privately).

over his chariotry. LXX, Syr and Vg (Clementine edition) prefix "and" (*w-*), absent in MT. Since the previous word ends in waw, either dittography (*w > ww*) or haplography (*ww > w*) might have occurred. More likely, however, these Versions are translating loosely, as in the next verse and in 14:23. In any case, the shorter, asyndetic MT is preferable.

14:18. *Egypt.* LXX and Sam expand: "*all* Egypt."

over Pharaoh. Sam and Syr add "and over all his force" (*wbkl ḥylw*), probably borrowed from 14:17. There is a slight chance, however, that the longer reading is original. In archaic spelling, **kl ḥylh* could have dropped by homoioteleuton after *prʿh* 'Pharaoh.'

over his chariotry. LXX, Syr and Vg (Clementine edition) prefix "and" (cf. TEXTUAL NOTES to 14:17, 23). Since here there is no chance of confusion from the previous word, we must suppose either that the translation is free (also possible in v 17) or that a corrupt reading migrated from v 17 to v 18. Exod 14:18 is entirely absent from 4QReworked Pentateuch^c, presumably because vv 17 and 18 both end in *brkbw wbpršyw* (homoioteleuton).

14:19. *Deity's Messenger.* Throughout this section, Syr and the *Tgs.* replace "the Deity" with "the Lord" (i.e., Yahweh).

Israel's. LXX has "Israel's Sons'," apparently an expansion.

14:20. *Egypt's camp.* LXX[B] reads simply "the Egyptians" (i.e., Egypt). This shorter text is the result of haplography by homoioarkton, probably in Hebrew (*mḥnh mṣrym*) but possibly in Greek (*tēs parembolēs tōn Aigyptiōn*).

Israel's camp. LXX[Bfz] add "and it stood still," as if reading **wayyaʿămōd.* This could be original, assuming *wyʿmd* fell out of MT etc. by homoioarkton with *wyhy* 'and it happened.' But more likely, LXX[Bfz] contain an inner-Greek exegetical expansion borrowed from v 19.

†*there was the cloud and the dark.* Where MT reads *wayhî heʿānān wahahōšek* 'and there was the cloud and the dark,' many Sam MSS read *wyhy hʿnn hḥšk*, which may be rendered as either "and there was the cloud, the dark" or perhaps "and there was the cloud; it became dark (**heḥĕšîk*)" (cf. Gressmann 1913: 109 n. 1). Other Sam MSS, however, support MT.

Both variants are quite awkward, and 4QReworked Pentateuch[c] is also odd, reading *wyh[y] hʿnn ḥwšk* 'and the cloud was darkness.' I suspect a transposition of some sort. Perhaps the original was **wayhî (ha)ḥōšek wayyāʾēr (heʿānān) ʾet-hallaylâ* 'and it was (the) dark, and it (the cloud) illumined the night,' with *heʿānān* probably a gloss that shifted position in MT (cf. Wellhausen 1899: 77). For further discussion of this difficult verse, see following, SOURCE ANALYSIS and NOTE.

it illumined the night. Some suspect that MT is corrupt (e.g., BHS). If so, what is the original? LXX *diēlthen hē nyx* 'the night came between' sounds like a guess to fit the context. Syr "there was the cloud and the dark all the night, and it shone all the night upon Israel's Sons" (similarly Tgs.) is probably a midrashic expansion inspired by the plague of darkness (10:21–23). I would keep to MT; its strangeness may be the result of redaction, not scribal error (see SOURCE ANALYSIS; cf. Fuss 1972: 314; Weimar 1985: 50 n. 71).

14:23. *his chariotry.* 4QpaleoGen-Exod[l], LXX, Kenn 69 and Syr prefix "and," in contrast to MT, Sam, Vg; see TEXTUAL NOTES to 14:17, 18.

†14:24. *looked down.* Syr reads Niphʿal **wayyiššāqēp* 'appeared,' vs. MT Hiphʿil *wayyašqēp* 'looked down.' Although the Niphʿal in this sense is first attested in Rabbinic Hebrew, we cannot entirely rule out Syr's interpretation, which fits the context quite well.

†*toward.* For MT and 4QpaleoGen-Exod[l] *ʾel*, Sam and Rossi 669 have the expected *ʿal*.

†14:25. *diverted/bound/removed.* See NOTE.

his . . . him. LXX, Tgs. and Syr refer to Egypt in the plural throughout v 25, while the Hebrew uses collective singulars. Sam supports MT, except in pluralizing the verb "said." The ancient translations tend in general to pluralize collectives, and may also attempt to bar a potential misunderstanding that the singulars refer to Pharaoh alone.

†*from Israel's face.* Kenn 18, 69, 129, 260, Rossi 378, 668. Soncino Bible (1488) and Syr read *mpny bny yśrʾl* 'from the *face* of Israel's *Sons*.' This is probably an expansion, although we cannot exclude the possibility that standard MT has suffered haplography (*mpny bny > mpny*).

††*Yahweh is the fighter.* Reading with Sam *yhwh hnlḥm,* vs. MT *yhwh nlḥm* 'Yahweh fights.' Sam's emphatic syntax is paralleled in 14:14 (see NOTE); Deut 1:30 and especially Deut 3:21: *yahwe(h)* . . . *hû' hannilḥām lākem* 'Yahweh . . . he is the fighter for you.' MT is probably haplographic (*h h > h*).

14:26. *return upon.* LXX "return *and cover*" is probably a translational-exegetical expansion based upon v 28. But even if its *Vorlage* had *"wǝyāšûbû hammayim wîkassû 'et-miṣrayim* (cf. v 28), MT is preferable as the shorter reading.

his . . . his. Syr and Tgs. continue in the plural: "their . . . their." LXX ignores the pronominal suffixes.

†14:27. *the Sea returned.* For MT *wayyāšob hayyām,* one might read *"wayyāšeb hayyām* 'and he [Moses] returned the Sea,' on the analogy of 14:19.

morning's. Sam has *hbqr* 'the morning's,' vs. MT-4QExod^g.

††*setting forth.* Reading *ns'ym* with Sam. MT *nsym* 'fleeing' probably arose due to the proximity of *'ānûsâ* 'I must flee' (14:25). Another factor may be the weakening of Hebrew laryngeals starting in the Greco-Roman period (D. N. Freedman, privately).

†*in the Sea's midst.* Sam reads *twk hym* 'the Sea's midst,' vs. MT *bǝtôk hayyām* 'in the Sea's midst' (cf. 14:16, 22, 27, 29; 15:19). If correct, this would be the sole case of *tôk* alone used prepositionally.

14:28. *of all Pharaoh's force.* LXX and Syr have "*and* all Pharaoh's force," perhaps a loose translation. But even if they reflect a variant *"wǝkol-ḥêl par'ō(h)* (vs. MT *lǝkol-ḥêl par'ō[h]*), MT is preferable as the more unusual reading, deviating from the "and . . . and . . . and" pattern (cf. 14:7, 9, 17, 18, 23, 26). See also NOTE.

so much as one of them. LXX^B, Kenn 69, 95, 251, 674, Rossi 198, 419 and Syr insert "and."

†14:31. *trusted in Yahweh.* LXX "trusted in *the God*" is attractively difficult, given the presence of "Yahweh" earlier in the verse. Cf. TEXTUAL NOTES to 13:21; 14:13; 15:1.

†15:1. *song of Yahweh.* LXX has "song to/of *the Deity*"; cf. TEXTUAL NOTES to 13:21; 14:13, 31.

I would sing. Where MT has the singular *'āšîrâ,* LXX, Vg, Tgs. and Syr have "*we* would sing," as if reading *"nāšîrâ.* Assuming the authenticity of MT, perhaps the alteration reflects adaptation of the text to liturgical use (cf. Wevers 1990: 227). Or the adaptation may rather be to the narrative context, in which the men sing together. This appears to be yet another case of the ancient translations pluralizing a Hebrew collective singular.

Sam agrees with neither MT nor LXX etc. It conflates an archaically spelled *"'šrh ('āšîrâ)* and *"šrw (šîrû)* to create the hybrid *'šrw,* apparently conceived as a causative imperative "make sing!" (Ben-Hayyim 1961: 37); cf. *Samaritan Tg.*

he acted exaltedly, exaltedly. At first glance, *g'h g'h* (15:1, 21) appears dittographic. But both words must be retained *metri causa.* The Sam variant *gwy g'h* 'a [gentile] nation was exalted' (cf. *Samaritan Tg.*^A) is probably midrashic (Ben-Hayyim 1961: 37).

†*Horse and his driver.* Although unexceptionable, this phrase is often emended. Haupt (1904: 158) reads **sûs wārekeb* 'horse and *chariotry*' (also Cross 1973: 127). Gressmann (1913: 351), somewhat more conservatively, reads **sûs wərikbô* 'horse and *his* [Pharaoh's? the horse's?] *chariotry*.' The Haupt-Gressmann approach has much to commend it, yet not enough to establish it. The narrative context, which shares much vocabulary with the Song of the Sea, repeatedly names Pharaoh's *rekeb* 'chariotry,' but never any *rōkēb* 'driver.' Outside the Song we find *sûs wərōkəbô* 'horse and his driver' (singular in Jer 51:21; Job 39:18; plural in Hag 2:22; cf. "horse driver[s]" in Ezek 23:6, 12, 23; 38:15; Amos 2:15; Zech 10:5; 12:4). But more often *sûs* parallels *rekeb* 'chariotry' (Deut 11:4; 20:1; Josh 11:4; 1 Kgs 20:1, 21, etc.). Another consideration in Haupt's favor is that Isa 43:16–17, which manifests verbal and thematic links with the Song ("mighty waters, sinking down, burning"), refers to *rekeb wāsûs* 'chariotry and horse.' Finally, LXX "horse and driver" may also support Haupt's consonantal reconstruction **sws wrkb*, if not his interpretation—but Hebrew pronominal suffixes are often unreflected in LXX. (Syr "horses and their horsemen" is not a true variant, but paraphrases MT.) See further under NOTE.

††15:2. *My strength . . . salvation.* This difficult line reappears in Isa 12:2; Ps 118:14. In all three passages, the Versions disagree within and among themselves:

1. MT Exod 15:2; Ps 118:14: *ʿzy wzmrt yh wyhy ly lyšwʿh*
2. Sam Exod 15:2: *ʿzy wzmrty wyhy ly lyšwʿh*
3. LXX, Kenn 573 Exod 15:2: *ʿz wzmrt (w)yhy ly lyšwʿh*
4. Syr Exod 15:2: **ʿz wzmrt yh yhwh wyhy ly lyšwʿh*. (Syr actually has *ln* 'for *us*,' a pluralized collective.)
5. MT Isa 12:2: *ʿzy wzmrt yh yhwh wyhy ly lyšwʿh*
6. 1QIsaᵃ 12:2: *ʿwzy wzmrtyʰ yhwh hyhʾ ly lyšwʿh*
7. OG, Syr Isa 12:2; Ps 118:14; Kenn 80, 488 Exod 15:2: *ʿzy wzmrty yh(wh) wyhy ly lyšwʿh*

Plainly, the clustering of waws and yodhs, virtually identical in Greco-Roman Hebrew script (Cross 1961a; Qimron 1972), interspersed with repeated he's, created fertile ground for textual corruption. Particularly unclear is whether there are two divine names (4, 5, 6 [corrected text]), one (1, 6 [original text], 7), or none at all (2, 3). I think that at least "Yah" must be original; it is a *Leitwort* in Ps 118:5, 17–19. Although the sequence *yh yhwh* (variants 4, 5) is suspect, it may be paralleled in Khirbet Beit Lei Burial Cave Inscription B (*AHI* 15.007). (One might consider *wyhy/hyh* in the second colon a miswriting of the divine name *yhwh*, comparing *yahwe[h] lî* in Isa 45:24 [?]; Ps 118:6, 7. But "to be as a salvation" is an idiom attested in 2 Sam 10:11; Ps 118:21 and all seven versions of our passage [cf. also Job 13:16].)

My translation adopts variant 7, which to me feels the most idiomatic (with Talmon 1954b). I take standard MT *zimrāt* to be the product of haplography (*yy* > *y*), though other explanations are possible: e.g., *zmrt* might be a hyper-archaic spelling of **zimrātī* (Cross and Freedman 1975: 55), or the suffix on

ʿozzî 'my strength' might govern zimrāt as well (cf. təhillāt/at 'glory' [Qere]
paralleling məśôśî 'my joy' in Jer 49:25).

†and I exalt . . . and I elevate. Both times, Syr lacks the conjunction w (also
Syr Ps 118:28). This contrasts with Syr's polysyndeton in vv 9, 10, 11, 12, 14 (but
cf. TEXTUAL NOTE to 15:7). Could Syr be correct here? Note that, for each
conjunction in 15:2, the previous word ends in y, similar to w in Herodian script.
Thus either dittography (y > yw) or haplography (yw > y) may have occurred.
Syr's shorter reading is more consistent with the asyndetic style of archa(ist)ic
poetry (see Cross and Freedman 1975: 126–27). And Ps 118:28, a virtual paraphrase of our verse, offers partial confirmation, using the conjunction only in
the first colon: ʾēlî ʾattâ wəʾôdekkā ʾĕlōhay ʾărôməmekkā 'you are my god, and
I praise you; my deity—I elevate you' (so MT; OG has two conjunctions).

†15:3. Man of War. For MT ʾîš milḥāmâ 'Man of War,' Sam reads gbwr
bmlḥmh 'Hero in War.' Syr g(n)br' wqrbtn' 'Hero and Warrior' presumably reflects a conflated *gibbôr wəʾîš milḥāmâ (but cf. Isa 3:2; Ezek 39:20 and similar
expressions in 1 Sam 16:18; 2 Kgs 24:16; Isa 42:13; 1 Chr 12:1; 2 Chr 13:3; 17:13).

LXX features the curious paraphrase "the Lord destroys (syntribōn) warfare"
(also Jdt 16:3). The closest biblical parallel is Ps 46:10, mašbît milḥāmôt 'making wars cease,' although here the Greek uses a different verb (antanairein).
Since syntribein most often corresponds to Hebrew šbr, conceivably an original *gbr mlḥm(w)t 'Hero of Wars' (cf. Ps 24:8 gbwr mlḥmh) was corrupted into
šbr mlḥm(w)t by ink abrasion (gimel resembles the middle of shin in paleo-
Hebrew; cf. Tov 1992: 92).

We are left to choose between MT and Sam. This is ultimately impossible
and perhaps unnecessary, assuming oral transmission (cf. Cross and Freedman 1975: 56).

†15:4. And the choice. The conjunction is absent in LXX, Kenn 69 and Vg.
Cross and Freedman (1975: 58) prefer this shorter reading.

his thirds. LXX appears to render šālîšā(y)w with two words, "riders, thirds,"
as if reading *pršyw šlšyw. More likely, however, the translators inserted "riders"
to clarify the nature of "thirds," on which see NOTE to 14:7.

†were sunk. Where MT and Tg. Onqelos have a passive Puʿal ṭubbəʿû (also
LXXᴮ, but see Wevers 1990: 228), the original LXX seems to have read an
active verb, presumably Piʿel *ṭibbaʿ 'he submerged' (also Syr, Fragmentary
Targum, Tgs. Ps.-Jonathan, Neofiti I). But LXX, Syr, etc., may be loosely translating to enlarge Yahweh's role. Even accepting the MT consonantal text,
there are other ways to parse ṭbʿw. Jacob (1992: 427) sees a Qal Passive rather
than a Puʿal, on the grounds that Biblical Hebrew lacks a corresponding Piʿel
ṭibbaʿ. Better still, we might read *ṭābəʿû as an ordinary Qal intransitive (Ehrlich 1908: 320).

†15:5. Deeps, they cover them. LXX "he covered them with the Sea" apparently reads *təhōmōt yəkassêmô/yəkassyēmô, vs. MT təhōmōt yəkasyūmû
(Dillmann 1880: 156). Again, LXX emphasizes God's active role (cf. previous
TEXTUAL NOTE). Sam yksmw could be interpreted as either *yəkassēmô
'he covers them' or *yəkassûmô 'they [the deeps] cover them' (Samaritan Tg.

supports the latter). (We find a similar ambiguity in MT Ps 140:10: Kethibh *ykswmw [yəkassûmû]* vs. Qere *yəkassêmô.*)

Which is correct here? One might argue against MT that it contains a gender error: *yəkasyūmû* is masculine, *təhōmōt* 'deeps' is feminine. But gender incongruence is ubiquitous in Hebrew and not, in general, grounds for emendation (Levi 1987). Perhaps LXX is trying to correct this "mistake."

went down. Syr has "went down *and sank*," an expansion apparently based upon v 16, where Syr renders *yiddəmû* as "sink," rather than "be still."

†*depths.* Although MT *məṣōlōt* and Sam *mṣlwt* are plural, LXX has a singular *bathos* 'the Deep.' Elsewhere OG translates *məṣû/ōlōt* with the plural *bathē* (Mic 7:19; Zech 10:11), while in OG Jonah 2:4, Greek *bathos* is the equivalent of the Hebrew singular *məṣûlâ.* Thus it is possible that LXX takes *mṣ(w)lt* in Exod 15:5 as a singular **məṣōlāt* (cf. *zimrāt* in v 2 [MT]; on such forms, see GKC §80g). If the singular is correct, then Sam and the Massoretic vocalization have matched *mṣ(w)lt* to the parallel *təhōmōt* 'Deeps' (cf. Jacob 1992: 429). See also TEXTUAL NOTE to 15:11 "glory."

15:6. *enemy.* LXX "enemies" and Syr "*your* enemies" are not true variants, but pluralizations of the collective singular.

†15:8. *And.* Cross and Freedman (1975: 59) follow Syr, which lacks a conjunction (cf. TEXTUAL NOTE to 15:2). If *w-* is indeed secondary, it was presumably borrowed from the following verse, which is syntactically parallel and begins with the same letters *wbr.* Adopting the Syr reading would help my argument that v 8 begins a new stanza (see NOTE), but Syr is not in general our best textual witness.

Piled. LXX "separated" is periphrastic, perhaps reflecting uncertainty as to the meaning of *ne'ermû.* The main intent, however, is to make the Song match the P account, in which the Sea is split (see also following).

stood . . . congealed. LXX translates both verbs with *epagō* 'congeal.' Wevers (1990: 230) suggests that the translator is trying to evoke two walls of water, as in the prose account (14:22, 29); see also previous TEXTUAL NOTE.

15:9. *of them . . . them.* LXX omits "them" because it is unnecessary in Greek. LXX also changes the person of the verb ("*I* will fill"), as if reading **'ămallē'/'emlā(')* to match the preceding and following verbs (note, too, that 'aleph and taw are somewhat similar in paleo-Hebrew [Tov 1992: 244–45]).

dispossess. LXX renders, "dominate," as if deriving a defective **trśmw* (MT *twrśmw*) from *rśy* 'have power' (*pace* Wevers 1990: 231; see Tournay 1958: 339).

15:10. *You blew.* For MT *nšpt,* a rare lexeme (15:10; Isa 40:24) with cognates in Akkadian, Arabic and Aramaic, Sam has the synonymous and more common *nšbt.* MT is preferable as the more difficult reading. Moreover, it makes a pun (see NOTE).

15:11. *among gods.* Absent in Syr, presumably by theological censorship.

in holiness. LXX "among the holy ones" is probably an interpretation of MT *bqdš,* not a literal rendering of a variant **bqdš(y)m* (*pace* Haupt 1904: 161; Cross and Freedman 1975: 61); see NOTE. Still, since the next word begins in *n*, similar to *m* in paleo-Hebrew script, haplography (*mn* > *n*) is not inconceivable.

dreadful. For MT *n'dr*, Sam has *n'dry*, as in v 6.

glory. MT has *təhillōt*, a plural of intensification or abstraction (GKC §124e, g). Conceivably, however, we should read an archaic singular *təhillāt (cf. *zimrāt* in MT 15:2), matching the singular *qōdeš* 'holiness' and *pele'* 'wonder.' See also TEXTUAL NOTE to 15:5.

wonder. For MT *pl'*, Sam has *pl'h*, probably to be read *pəli'ā* (cf. Ps 139:6 *pəli'ā* [Qere]).

15:12. *Earth*. Sam adds the definite article: "*the* earth."

15:13. *the people which*. Here and in 15:16, Syr and Tgs. render, "*this* people which," while LXX expands further: "*this your* people which" (cf. TEXTUAL NOTE to 15:16). "This . . . which" is a double rendering of MT *zū* (Sam *zh*), which can mean "this" or "which," but not both together (Wevers 1990: 232). See NOTE.

You guided. For MT *nhlt*, Sam MSS, Kenn 82 and *Tg. Ps.-Jonathan* read *nḥlt* 'you endowed.' There is little likelihood of this being original. It arises from the graphic and aural similarity of *h* and *ḥ* and the presence of *nḥyt* 'you led' at the beginning of the verse as well as the proximity of *nḥltk* 'your property' (15:17).

15:14. *They shudder*. 4QExod^c, LXX and Sam prefix "and" (*wə-*). The conjunction *w* may also be a dittography of the following *y*, similar to *w* in Herodian script (Cross 1961a; Qimron 1972). MT is presumably original, since asyndeton is archaic-poetic, polysyndeton prosaic (Cross and Freedman 1975 *passim*; Watson 1984: 37).

seized. Syr has "seized *them*," anticipating the next verse.

15:16. *fall*. For MT *tippōl* (Qal), one could in theory read *tappîl 'you cast' (Hiph'il) with *Fragmentary Targum, Tg. Neofiti 1* and Cross and Freedman (1975: 63 nn. 47–48). Supporting MT Exod 15:16, however, Josh 2:9 has *nāpəlā 'êmatkem 'ālênû* 'your fear has fallen upon us.'

fear. For the rare *'êmātā* (MT), 4QExod^c and Sam have simply *'ymh*.

greatness. Holzinger (1900: 49) and Cross and Freedman (1975: 63) read *bəgōdel (vs. MT *bigdōl*), but see NOTE.

†*are still*. On the vocalization of *ydmw*, see NOTE.

the people which. LXX "this, your people which" represents a double rendering of *zū* (see TEXTUAL NOTE to 15:13) as well as duplication of "your people" from the first colon. I prefer the shorter text of MT (with Freedman 1980: 197; vs. Cross and Freedman 1975: 63). MT feels more idiomatic and finds a parallel in Ps 78:54, *har-ze(h) qānətā yəmînô* 'the mountain which his right hand acquired' (not **hārô-ze[h]* 'his mountain which . . .').

†15:17. *bring them and plant them*. For both verbs, 4QExod^c has the ordinary, short suffix (*tby'm wtṭ'm*), vs. MT *tby'mw wtṭ'mw*.

Because the line is metrically overlong and features coordinate verbs in the same colon, Freedman (1980: 185, 214) reconstructs **təbî'ēmô ['el-gəbûl qodšekā] wətiṭṭā'ēmô bəhar nahălātekā* 'May you bring them [to your holiness's territory/mountain,] and may you plant them in your property mountain' (cf. Ps 78:54). I find this too radical (see NOTE).

†† *sanctum.* MT misplaces the daghesh, reading *miqqədāš* for *miqdāš. D. N. Freedman (privately) suggests that the punctator may have been thinking of the prefix *mi-* 'from,' which doubles the following consonant. For comparable forms, see TEXTUAL NOTES to 2:3; 5:18.

† *my Lordship.* 4QExod^c, Sam and many witnesses to MT, from both the Cairo Genizah (*BHS*) and elsewhere (Kennicott 1776–80: 138; de Rossi 1784–85: 60–61), as well as early printed Bibles (Ginsburg 1894: 127), read *yhwh* for (or in addition to) standard MT *'ădōnāy* 'my Lordship.' Whichever is original, the source of confusion is the Jews' replacement of the sacred name "Yahweh," in study and prayer, with *'ădōnāy* 'my Lordship' since at least the third century B.C.E. This practice has led to the occasional interchange of divine names (see Tov 1992: 214). I follow standard MT as the more difficult reading (vs. Haupt 1904: 163; Cross 1973: 131).

† 15:18. *Yahweh, he will reign.* LXX "the Lord is ruling" is a paraphrase conditioned on the presence of **w^cwd* 'and still' in the *Vorlage* (see following).

† † *ever and eternity.* While MT has *l^cwlm w^cd*, 4QExod^c, 4QReworked Pentateuch^c and Sam omit the preposition "to," reading *^cwlm w^cd*. This is the shorter and more unusual reading, and, as it finds a parallel in Ps 10:16 (*yhwh mlk ^cwlm w^cd*), I adopt it here.

Some Sam MSS read *^cwlm w^cwd* 'eternity and still' or 'ever and beyond.' While there is little chance that this is correct, the error is quite ancient. The LXX *Vorlage* appears to have read **^cwlm w^cd w^cwd* 'ever and eternity and still,' conflating MT and Sam.

15:19. *waters.* While 4QReworked Pentateuch^c has *mymy*, all other witnesses have *my.*

Sea's midst. 4QReworked Pentateuch^c contains a unique addition at the end of the verse: "with the waters for them a wall from their right and from their left" (partly reconstructed). It is barely possible that this is correct, having fallen out from the other witnesses by homoioteleuton (*hym . . . śm³lm*). But far more likely, we have a harmonizing borrowing from 14:22, 29. Sam and 4QpaleoExod^m feature comparable expansions throughout the Plagues pericope; see TEXTUAL NOTES to 7:8–11:10.

15:21. *to them.* "Them" is masculine in MT (*lhm*), but Syr and some witnesses to LXX have the feminine (*lhn). Given the similarity of *m* and *n* in sound and, in paleo-Hebrew script, shape, it is conceivable that an original *lhn mrym was corrupted into *lhm mrym*. But MT is probably correct (see NOTE). After "to them," LXX adds "saying."

Sing. While MT, Sam and *Tg. Onqelos* have an imperative *šyrw* 'sing!' LXX, Vg, *Fragmentary Targum* and *Tgs. Ps.-Jonathan* and *Neofiti I* have "we would sing" (see TEXTUAL NOTE to 15:1). Syr, curiously, has a feminine singular imperative *šbḥyn* 'praise!' as if reading *šyry (on waw-yodh confusion, see Cross 1961a; Qimron 1972). Thus, in Syr, Miriam exhorts the *women* to sing, addressing them in the collective singular.

he acted exaltedly, exaltedly. On Sam *gwy g'h,* see TEXTUAL NOTE to 15:1.
Horse and his driver. Syr pluralizes the collectives: "horses and *their*
horse*men*."
the Sea. Uniquely, 4QReworked Pentateuch^c contains a continuation of
Miriam's song. The text is incompletely preserved and almost certainly a secondary concoction (White 1992: 222).

SOURCE ANALYSIS

All critics regard 13:17–15:21 as composite (on past analyses, see Childs 1974:
219–20; Weimar 1985). Most likely, we have five sources or strata: J, E, P, R
and the Song of the Sea. Some, however, deny the presence of P (e.g., Fohrer
1964: 91, 98; for bibliography, see Weimar 1985: 2 n. 8). And others would
not consider 15:1b–18 an originally independent poem (see COMMENT,
p. 553, and APPENDIX A, vol. II).

Exod 13:17–19 is Elohistic, witness the divine name "Deity" (*'ĕlōhîm*) and
the quotation of Gen 50:24–25 (E): "and Joseph said to his brothers, 'I am dying,
but Deity will acknowledge, acknowledge (*pāqōd yipqōd*) you and take you up
(*wəhe'ĕlâ*) from this land to the land which he swore to Abraham, to Isaac and
to Jacob.' So Joseph adjured Israel's sons, saying, 'Deity (*'ĕlōhîm*) will acknowledge, acknowledge (*pāqōd yipqōd*) you; and you will take up (*wəha'ălitem*)
my bones from here'" (also cited in Exod 3:16; 4:31). Exod 13:20, on the other
hand, continues out of 12:37a (R) and is presumably the Redactor's contribution, excerpted from an itinerary document more fully preserved in Num
33:3–49 (Cross 1973: 293–325); cf. SOURCE ANALYSES to 12:1–13:16 and
15:22–26; APPENDIX A, vol. II.

Exod 13:21–22 is more difficult. Friedman (1987: 251) assigns the verses to
P, and Yahweh does appear in a cloud in 16:10 (P) (see NOTE). Nevertheless,
I prefer J or E, since the pillar of cloud by day and fire by night reappears in
Num 14:14 (J?) and Deut 1:33 (based on JE). The cloud pillar alone also appears in 33:9–10; Num 12:5; Deut 31:15 (all E). Note especially that Exod 33:11
(E), like 13:22, uses the phrase *lō(')* *yāmîš* 'would not depart'—albeit of Joshua,
not of the pillar (cf., too, Num 14:44 [J]). One might argue, too, that *lanḥōtām*
'to lead them' in v 21 is a lexical link with *nāḥām* 'led them' (v 17 [E]). To
complicate affairs maximally, one could attribute 13:21 to J and v 22 to E,
since they are somewhat redundant, and since 14:19–20, which again mentions the pillar, may itself be composite (see below). Because of these uncertainties, I simply assign 13:21–22 to JE with a question mark.

Exod 14:1–4 is either Priestly or Redactorial. The formula "Yahweh spoke
to Moses, saying, 'Speak to Israel's Sons . . .'" (vv 1–2) is typical of P. The
phrase "and X will know that I am Yahweh" (v 4c) is most closely paralleled in
the Torah in P (6:7; 7:5; 16:12; 29:46), although it also appears in E (7:17; cf.
5:2; 8:6, 18; 9:14, 29; 10:2; 18:11) and is a favorite theme of the prophets (e.g.,
1 Kgs 20:13, 28; Isa 60:16; Joel 4:17; Zech 4:9, etc.)—particularly Ezekiel,
whose style is so like P's (Ezek 6:7, 13; 7:4, 9; 11:10, 12; 12:20, etc.). Moreover,

the expression "and they did so" is frequently paralleled in Priestly sections of Exodus (7:10, 20, 22; 8:3, 14; cf. 6:9; 7:6, 11; 12:28, 50). The distinctive reference to "strengthening" Pharaoh's heart (v 4) is paralleled in both P (7:13, 22; 8:15) and R (4:21; 9:35; 10:20, 27; 11:10). That v 2 conveys geographical information initially suggests that it continues 13:20 (R) and belongs to the Redactorial way station sequence recapitulated in Num 33:1–49 (see Cross 1973: 309–17). Moreover, the command to "turn back" (v 2) is most easily related to 13:20: the Hebrews are to turn back from the desert. Nonetheless, 14:1–4 is more likely Priestly. All other Redactorial itinerary notices use the verb *nsʿ* 'set forth,' and none occurs within direct speech (see further APPENDIX A, vol. II).

SPECULATION: Although 14:3 fits its Priestly context well enough, I hesitate slightly as to authorship. "Pharaoh will say of Israel's sons, 'They are confused in the land; the wilderness has closed against them'" might be taken from JE, assuming the editor changed an original *wayyō(ʾ)mer parʿō(h)* 'and Pharaoh said' (= Syr) to *wəʾāmar parʿō(h)* 'and Pharaoh will say' (cf. Bacon *apud* Holzinger 1900: 43; Fuss 1972: 300). But since v 3 follows logically out of v 2 (see NOTE), it is better assigned to P.

Most consider 14:3 and 5 contradictory descriptions of Pharaoh's reaction to the Hebrews' departure. According to v 3, he will learn they are lost, and in v 5 he discovers they have fled. Taking the former as P, critics assign the latter to JE. But only v 5 is true narrative; v 3 is mere prediction. They can easily be read together: when Pharaoh learns Israel has fled, he repents their release (v 5), but rejoices that they are trapped (v 3). While this complexity is, I agree, probably a consequence of redaction, we must admit the possibility it was already present in P, which would then extend through 14:5.

But further evidence supports the attribution of 14:5 to JE, probably E. The Elohist frequently mentions Pharaoh's slaves (5:21; 7:20, 28, 29, etc.), although they are also known from P (7:10). Moreover, *šillaḥ* 'release' in the context of the Exodus is typical of E (3:20; 4:21, 23; 5:1, 2, etc.), although it occasionally appears in P (6:11; 7:2) and R (10:27; 11:10; 12:33). More important, *wayyuggad* 'and it was told' is never found in P, while it is attested in JE (Gen 22:20; 27:42; 38:13), even associated with *brḥ* 'flee' (Gen 31:22 [E]) (Fuss 1972: 301). To complicate matters further: although it is unnecessary (cf. Childs 1974: 220), one could theoretically divide 14:5 in two (Holzinger 1990: 43; Meyer 1906: 20; Noth 1962: 106). Such a partition might explain why no J Plagues account is extant: the people simply flee (14:5a) (cf. Noth 1962: 111–12; de Vaux 1978: 370–71).

We encounter comparable ambiguities in 14:6 and 7. Must these verses be of distinct authorship, merely because both describe the Egyptian muster (so Noth 1962: 106; cf. Weimar 1985: 34)? Not necessarily (Durham 1987: 191). But it is hard to resist the impression of separate hands, considering the other evidence of multiple authorship in the passage. If we take *wayyāsar* 'and he diverted/bound/removed' (14:25 [JE]) as a conscious pun with *wayyeʾsōr* 'and he harnessed' (14:6), then 14:6, at least, is JE. Perhaps it is E, for Fuss (1972: 302) notes the similarity to Gen 31:23 (E), "he took his brothers with him and pursued after him." That would leave v 7 for J or P. One could even divide vv 6 and 7 each in two, generating further permutations (cf. Holzinger 1900: 44).

Exod 14:8-9, with its itinerary and thematic "strengthening" of Pharaoh's heart, is basically Priestly, the continuation of vv 1-4. The only question pertains to the parenthesis concluding v 8, "and Israel's Sons were going out with raised arm," after which we are again told, unnecessarily, that Egypt is pursuing Israel. The sequence in 14:8-9 *wayyirdōp . . . wayyirdəpû* 'and he pursued . . . and [they] pursued' is an example of resumptive repetition framing a digression or interpolation (on *Wiederaufnahme*, see Kuhl 1952). It is possible that the description of the Hebrews' proud departure is from JE, with the *Wiederaufnahme* supplied by the Redactor in v 9. But a simpler analysis would attribute all of vv 8-9 to P, recognizing the Priestly Writer's attempt to replace the hasty flight of JE (12:34, 39; 14:5) with something more dignified.

By v 9, Israel has arrived at the seashore, at least in P. In contrast, 14:10, "see: Egypt setting forth after them," implies that the Hebrews are still moving *toward* the Sea. Their fear is dying "in the *wilderness*" (v 11), not in or by the Sea. And since Israel still appears to be traveling seaward in 14:15, 19, all these verses are probably JE. The expression "to raise the eyes" (14:10) is absent from P, though common in JE (Gen 13:14; 18:2; 22:4, 13, etc.). Similarly, "feared greatly" (14:10) is found in JE (Gen 20:8; 32:8), but never in P. People "cry out" (ṣʿq, 14:10, 15) throughout JE (Gen 4:10; 18:21; 19:13; 27:34; 41:55; Exod 3:7, 9; 5:8, 15; 8:8; 11:6; 12:30; 15:25; 17:4, etc.), but never in P, which deemphasizes prayer and stresses sacrifice (but see below for a likely exception).

There is little doubt that 14:11 is also JE. Exod 14:11b echoes ironically v 5 (E): the Egyptians say, "What is this *we* did?" and the Israelites say, "What is this *you* did?"

Exod 14:12-14 continues well enough out of the preceding and is likewise JE. To "station oneself" (*hityaṣṣēb*, v 13) is paralleled only in JE (2:4; 8:16; 9:13; 19:17; 34:5, etc.), never in P. Moreover, Moses' "do not fear" (v 13) responds to v 10 (JE), "they feared greatly," and *heḥĕrîš* 'be still' (v 14) contrasts with ṣʿq 'cry out' (v 10).

Still, 14:11-14 does not read quite smoothly, hence the widespread midrash that Moses responds to different parties among the Israelites (*Bib. Ant.* 10.3; *Memar Marqah* 4:8 [MacDonald 1963: 1.100-1, 2.167]; *Mek. bəšallaḥ* 3; see Olyan 1991). One suspects the presence in vv 11-14 of J and E intermingled, although it is difficult to decide what constitutes a source break. In the following hypothetical partition, the first version would be E and the second J:

A.   ¹¹ᵇ"What is this you did to us, by taking us out from Egypt? ¹²Is not this the word that we spoke to you in Egypt, saying, 'Let us alone that we may serve Egypt'? For serving Egypt is better for us than our dying in the wilderness." ¹³ᵃAnd Moses said to the people, ¹⁴"Yahweh, he will fight for you; and you, you will be still."

B.   ¹¹ᵃ"Is it from a lack of no graves in Egypt that you took us to die in the wilderness?" ¹³And Moses said to the people, "Do not fear. Station yourselves and see Yahweh's salvation that he will make for you today. For, as you have seen Egypt today, you will see them no more to eternity."

But other analyses are equally plausible (see, e.g., Noth 1962: 106; Weimar 1985: 52 n. 74). And we still have the option of assigning all of vv 11–14 to E, since the flow is adequate.

To 14:13, 31, Blum (1990: 31) compares 1 Sam 12:16–18: "Also now *station yourselves and see* this *great* thing that Yahweh is *going to make* before your eyes . . . and all the *people feared* greatly *Yahweh and Samuel*" (cf. also Josh 4:14, 24; 2 Chr 20:15, 17). The resemblance might be due to one text imitating the other, or to their common reliance upon the salvation oracle genre, or to common Yahwistic authorship (Friedman 1998), or to Deuteronomistic editing of both (Blum); compare, too, the similarity of Deut 1:29–30; 3:21–22 to Exod 14:13–14 (see APPENDIX A, vol. II).

Another example of potential unevenness, perceived by many, is the abruptness of 14:15a, "(For) what do you (sing.) cry to me?" As far as we know, Moses has not cried out at all. Rather, the *people* have panicked (14:10 [JE]), while Moses has attempted to pacify them (14:13–14 [JE]). Calvin suggests that v 15 is pluperfect, "But Yahweh *had* said to Moses," but the noninverted syntax indicates otherwise. One might rather infer that Moses' own cry to Yahweh, now missing, originally stood between 14:12 and 15 (*Bib. Ant.* 10:4, in fact, supplies Moses' prayer). But it is also conceivable that the author intended 15a merely to hint that, despite his bravado, Moses shared the people's doubts, or at any rate faithfully transmitted them to God. Or we could suppose that "you" is not Moses in particular, but each individual Hebrew, or Moses as their representative (ibn Ezra; Rabenau 1966: 14); compare 16:28–29, where Yahweh's words to Moses are clearly meant for all Israel. The temptation is great, nonetheless, to give v 15a to P, since it enhances the flow of P and disturbs the flow of JE (but this would be the sole case of *ṣʿq* 'cry out' in P).

The latter half of v 15 might be either JE or, more likely, P. The verb *nsʿ* 'set forth' often connotes breaking camp, and in P the Hebrews have been camping by the Sea (14:2, 9). Plastaras (1966: 171) also finds a contradiction with v 13 (J?): Moses had told the people to *stand still* and watch; now he tells them to move. But this is a misinterpretation of *hityaṣ(ṣə)bû* 'station yourselves' (see NOTE).

That 14:16–17 constitutes a single unit is evident in the emphatic antithesis: *'attâ . . . 'ănî* 'you . . . I.' Both verses are Priestly. Exod 14:17 continues the *Leitmotif* of "strengthening" Pharaoh's heart from 14:4, 8 (P). Moreover, the repetition of "I will glorify" links 14:17 with 18, and both with 14:4 (P). Sentence-initial *wa'ănî hin(ə)nî* is characteristic of P (Gen 6:17; 9:9; cf. Exod 31:6; Num 3:12; 18:6).

There is an important difficulty in considering v 16 entirely Priestly, however. *Moses'* rod is ordinarily a feature of E (4:2–4, 17, 20; 7:15, 17, 20; 9:23; 10:13; 17:5–6, 9); P instead celebrates *Aaron's* rod (7:9–12, 19; 8:1–2, 12–13). Even at Meribath-Kadesh (Num 20:2–13 [P]), the rod is probably Aaron's, not Moses' (*pace* MT; see Propp 1988; Blum 1990: 273–74). To judge from the Priestly Plagues narrative, then, we might expect Moses to command Aaron to split the Sea with Aaron's rod (Hyatt 1971: 153). We are faced with two possibilities: either in P Moses uses his rod just this once, for the culminating plague against Egypt; or else he uses his arm alone (cf. 14:21, 26, 27; *Exod. Rab.* 21:9), and the rod is R's insertion to create continuity with JE (Kohata 1986: 232–33). If the latter is correct, the command is probably the Redactor's own creation, not a snippet of JE (*pace* Dillmann 1880: 149; Holzinger 1900: 44; Gressmann 1913: 109 n. 1; Hyatt 1971: 148, 153). The reason is that 17:5 (E) refers to "your rod, with which you smote the *Nile*," passing over the wonder at the Sea. This would be inconceivable had E included the rod in its own Sea narrative.

Exod 14:19 contains two almost identical components, one featuring "the Deity's Messenger" (E) and the other "the cloud pillar." There are many possible explanations for the redundancy. We may have doublets, the first Elohistic and the latter Priestly or Yahwistic (Holzinger 1900: 44; Scharbert 1989: 60). We may have a single author explaining that the pillar is an angel. Or this could be an undatable conflation of variant readings unrelated to the redaction of J, E and P.

Exod 14:20 is difficult to interpret, textually suspect (see TEXTUAL NOTE) and conceivably composite. Josh 24:7, apparently based upon a version of Exod 14:20, does not refer to shining at all. And one could break 14:20 either after "Israel" or after "dark," to generate parallel passages. But any source-critical solution is so fraught with doubt, I would rather leave the verse unattributed.

Exod 14:21 reads smoothly, but is universally considered composite, given the evidence of multiple authorship elsewhere in the passage. In one strand, we read: "and Moses extended his arm over the Sea, and the waters were split." The other account differs significantly: "and Yahweh conducted the Sea with a mighty *forward* wind all the night, and he made the Sea into the dry ground (*ḥārābâ*)." The first follows out of v 16 (P), where Moses is commanded to split the Sea by raising his arm. The second version must be JE, perhaps E, since Yahweh uses the same wind in Gen 41:6, 23, 27; Exod 10:13 (E). *Ḥārābâ*, in any case, is a non-Priestly term for dry land; P prefers the synonym *yabbāšâ* (Gen 1:9–10; Exod 14:16, 22, 29). Note that in Josh 3:17, based upon JE, Israel crosses the Jordan on *ḥārābâ* (but contrast *yabbāšâ* in Josh 4:22).

Exod 14:22, with its looming walls of water, fits somewhat better P's notion of "splitting" the Sea than JE's "drying up." The Book of Joshua sheds more light, showing familiarity with JE and the Song of the Sea but not with P (except perhaps in Josh 4:22). When the Israelites cross the Jordan, its flow is stopped upstream and its waters mount "in one heap" (Josh 3:13, 16; cf. Exod 15:8); the people cross on dry land. This recapitulates the Suph Sea crossing, of which Josh 2:10 recalls, "Yahweh dried the waters of the Suph Sea from before you in your going out from Egypt." It seems that in JE, Yahweh drives back the water, piling it into *one* wall, as in the Song (15:8). The *two* walls of water in 14:22 should therefore be assigned to P. Exod 14:23 goes with v 22, and so is likewise Priestly. (For further discussion of the parting/drying of the waters and the Hebrews' and Egyptians' crossings, see COMMENT.)

An abrupt source break falls between 14:23 and 24. The reference in v 24 to Yahweh surveying the scene during the morning watch does not easily follow Egypt's seaward dash in v 22. The chronological notice instead links 14:24 with v 20b (JE) and with the JE section of v 21: "all the night . . . made the Sea into the dry ground . . . during the morning watch . . . panicked Egypt's camp." Exod 14:24, in turn, flows easily into 14:25b, describing Egypt's flight. Rabenau (1966: 12) observes that the formulaic sequence "panic . . . flee" connecting 14:24, 25b is paralleled in Judg 4:15. Moreover, 14:25b ("Yahweh is the fighter for them") alludes back to 14:14 (E): "Yahweh, he will fight for you." The intervening description of the Egyptians' malfunctioning chariotry (v 25a) might be J or E. It is in any case of the same hand as 14:6, to judge from the pun between *wy'sr* and *wy(')sr* (see TEXTUAL NOTE and NOTE). Because both vv 24 and 25 might but need not be partitioned between sources, I have labeled them JE (cf. Weimar 1985: 56 n. 89).

In 14:26, Moses is once again commanded to extend his arm, and we are back with P. Exod 14:27, like v 21, features P material surrounding JE, the latter characterized by precise chronology (*"at morning's turning"*) (cf. also 14:24). There is some tension within JE. According to v 25, the Egyptians are under attack and decide to flee from Israel; according to v 27, it seems they are traveling (or fleeing [MT]) toward Israel or the Sea (see TEXTUAL NOTE and NOTE).

Exod 14:28a is redundant after the end of v 27 ("And Yahweh tumbled Egypt in the Sea's midst. And the waters returned and covered . . . all Pharaoh's force"). This reflects a shift from JE back to P, at least for the first half of v 28. Note, too, the similarity in phrasing between v 26 (P) and v 28a. Exod 14:28b, however, is probably Elohistic. "So much as one of them did not remain" recalls hyperbolic statements in 8:27; 9:4, 6, 7; 10:26 (all E).

As for 14:29–31, v 29 repeats v 22 and is probably Priestly, although it might conceivably be a Redactorial summary connecting P with JE (Holzinger 1900: 44). Exod 14:30, however, I would attribute to JE, based on the similarity to v 13 ("today . . . that day" [Noth 1962: 106; cf. Cassuto 1967: 172]); there is also a *verbatim* parallel in 1 Sam 14:23. Exod 14:31b is likely Elohistic, since it resembles 4:31 (E), where Israel trusts in Moses and God. Moreover, the fear of Yahweh is a favorite theme of E (Wolff 1975). Exod 14:31a is either J or E, but probably not P, since it is paraphrased in Joshua 24 (v 7), which generally ignores Priestly tradition (but note Terah in Josh 24:2; cf. Gen 11:24–32 [P, R]).

We have yet to consider the authorship of the Song of the Sea (15:1b–18), the Song of Miriam (15:21b) and their narrative frame (15:1a, 19–21a). I am unpersuaded that 15:1b–18 itself is composite (vs. Schmidt 1931; Hyatt 1971: 163; Durham 1987: 202–10, et al.). Brenner (1991: 30–34) makes a convincing case for the Song's unity (also Tournay 1958: 337; Muilenburg 1966: 245);

see below, pp. 502–8. Most scholars consider the Song an older independent work incorporated by one of the pentateuchal authors or editors, rather than a fresh composition. The complex question of its original setting and date will come up in the NOTES and COMMENT, but full treatment must be reserved for APPENDIX A, vol. II.

Assuming the Song once circulated independently, we must ask when it was inserted into the prose account and by whom. Apparently, it already stood in JE. Deuteronomy 2–3, which knows JE, but not JEP (Driver 1891: 81–82), seems familiar with the Song: compare Deut 2:25 with Exod 15:14, and Deut 3:24 with Exod 15:11, 16 (Moran 1963: 340–42; cf. Foresti 1982). Similarly, Josh 2:9–10, 24 knows both the liquidation of the Canaanites and the drying of the Sea, themes from the Song and JE, respectively, but not P's split Sea. And Josh 3:13, 16 describe the Jordan's waters as standing in a *nēd* 'heap' (cf. Exod 15:8), while Josh 4:23–5:1 knows the drying of the Sea, Yahweh's arm, the liquidation of the Canaanites and their fear before Yahweh. All these data indicate that, by the time of Dtr's composition, JE contained the Song of the Sea. How did it get there?

Scharbert (1981: 404) suggests that the Song was incorporated by R^{JE}, while Foresti (1982: 67–69) invokes a Deuteronomistic editor. Most, however, assume that the Song formed an integral part of either J or E. Our principal clue is the reprise in 15:20–21, which may with relative assurance be assigned to the Elohist. Mention of prophecy is diagnostic for E (Jenks 1977), as is "Miriam . . . Aaron's sister" (see NOTE to 4:14; compare especially Num 12:1–15 [E]).

Most scholars conclude by elimination that 15:1b–18 is *not* from E, but from J (e.g., Kautzsch and Bacon *apud* Holzinger 1900: 45; Cross 1973: 123–24). Exod 15:1b–18 and 20–21 are thus taken as doublets, with vv 20–21 the continuation of 14:31. It is, arguably, hard to imagine E's tongue-tied Moses (4:10) bursting into song. We might even infer that in E, it is Miriam who sings, precisely because Moses is unable, just as her brother Aaron speaks for Moses (4:14–16).

It is at least as likely, however, that all of 15:1b–18, 20–21 is Elohistic. As we shall see, the brief songs of biblical women may be refrains to longer compositions. If so, Miriam's "song" is not redundant with the Song of the Sea, but complementary (see NOTE to 15:21). As for Moses' impediment, either the Elohist has dropped the theme—he often depicts Moses speaking without Aaron's help—or he believed, like the author of Wis 10:20–21, that at the Sea the mouths of the dumb and ineloquent gave forth inspired song (cf. Isa 35:6).

We have seen that both the Song of the Sea and the Song of Miriam belong to JE. On the basis of 15:19, however, one could make a case for the Redactor or Priestly Writer having incorporated 15:1b–18. Exod 15:19 forms a frame with 14:29 (P), both verses reporting in identical language that "Israel's Sons walked on the dry land in the Sea's midst." Ordinarily, one would attribute this repetition (*Wiederaufnahme*) to the hand that inserted the poem (Scharbert 1989: 66). Since he knows 14:29, the interpolator would be either the Priestly Writer himself or the Redactor (cf. Holzinger 1900: 45; Watts 1992: 59).

Yet we cannot deny the Song to JE. And if it existed already in JE, then it was not inserted by the Redactor. Conceivably, the Song stood in both JE and P, but P is not otherwise given to rhapsody. More likely, we are simply misunderstanding the epanalepsis in 15:19. The verse is Redactorial, but here *Wiederaufnahme* does not frame an interpolation. Rather, it summarizes the Song and supplies information only implicit in vv 1–18: that Israel crossed the Sea on dry land (cf. Dillmann 1880: 160). Exod 15:19 also returns the reader to the period of the Exodus, after the anticipated settlement at the holy mountain (v 17) (Watts 1992: 43–44; cf. Childs 1974: 248).

SPECULATION: A more complicated scenario is that all 15:1b–18 was originally JE's Song of *Miriam*, comparable to the Song of the prophetess Deborah (Judges 5). The Redactor shifted all but the opening lines to their present position, making his hero Moses the singer and relegating Miriam to the female chorus (see Van Dijk-Hemmes 1994).

Let us now compare the Song of the Sea, JE and P. As we noted in the Plagues cycle, JE marks the passage of time; P does not (see SOURCE ANALYSIS to 7:8–11:10). The Priestly material is characterized by redundancy in command/prediction and fulfillment (14:8–9 fulfills 14:2–4; 14:21–23 fulfills 14:15–16; 14:27–28 fulfills 14:26) (Burns 1983: 105). P's characters are more like automata than those of JE: Pharaoh is manipulated by Yahweh; Moses and Israel do as they are told; Israel marches out of Egypt in battle formation (cf. Hendel 1995b). JE, in contrast, describes the Egyptians' changes of attitude as spontaneous. The Israelites are timid, unfit to face border guards, quick to panic and to blame Moses. Only safely across the Sea do they believe. P's Deity is, in general, more remote than JE's and more in control.

While in both sources Israel has already left Egypt proper, P's Sea event points backward to the Plagues through the thematic "strengthening" of Pharaoh's heart (McCarthy 1966; see SOURCE ANALYSIS to 7:8–11:10). For JE, in contrast, Israel's "murmuring" (14:10–12) links the Sea event more closely with the following wilderness narratives (cf. Coats 1967; 1968: 133–37; Childs 1970; 1974: 222–23; Vervenne 1987). The Song, too, is prospective, culminating in the arrival at Yahweh's mountain (see NOTE to 15:17; COMMENT, pp. 562–68).

The most obvious difference among the Song, JE and P lies in the Sea's behavior. In P, it is split, while in JE and the Song, its waters are pushed back or dried up (see NOTE to 15:8 and COMMENT, pp. 550–54). In JE, the process takes all night, while in P, it is presumably instantaneous. Moses is uninvolved in the miracle in the Song and JE, while he is Yahweh's partner or proxy in P. Thus, in both JE and P, an assistant begins the attack on Egypt, while his superior takes over to drown the Egyptians. In JE, *Moses* works the Plagues, then *Yahweh* dries the Sea; in P, *Aaron* works the Plagues, then *Moses* splits the Sea.

For many exegetes, the most significant difference among the sources is that only P explicitly describes the Israelites crossing the Sea. But the Song (15:16) can easily be read in this way (Haupt 1904: 162; cf. Kloos 1986: 139; Halpern

1983: 39). And so can JE, since it after all includes the Song. This issue will be revisited under NOTE to 15:16 and COMMENT.

REDACTION ANALYSIS

Because it is so hard to distinguish J from E, I shall speak here only of JE, P and the Song of the Sea. Overall, the received text coheres well (see Auffret's [1983] structural analysis). Lacking outside evidence, we would never suspect an embedded, variant version in which the Sea is dried by Yahweh, not cleft by Moses' arm or rod. Only in spots is the flow lost (14:19–20, 24–25). Our confusion is greatest in 14:24–25. The implication of the composite account is that, after both the Hebrews and the Egyptians enter the Sea, Yahweh stampedes the Egyptian cavalry, simultaneously impeding their mobility. As the Egyptians attempt to reverse course, they meet the waters closing upon them like a zipper. Israel, meanwhile, completes its transit (see NOTES to 14:27, 29). Here JE and P each reads better than the composite.

In many respects, however, redaction has enriched the text, highlighting the tension between human free will, on the one hand, and divine precognition and omnipotence, on the other (see also COMMENT to 7:8–11:10, pp. 353–54; NOTE to 15:9). In 13:17 (JE), Yahweh fears that Israel will return to Egypt; in 14:4 (P), he promises to "strengthen" Pharaoh's heart; then in 14:5 (JE), Pharaoh decides on his own to pursue Israel—but, 14:8 (P) reminds us, this is all Yahweh's doing. The combination of Israel's hasty flight in JE with their triumphal march in P also creates psychological complexity (see, however, NOTE to 14:5). They leave confidently (14:8b [P?]), but their assurance crumbles under stress (14:10–13 [JE]), as Yahweh had foreseen (13:17 [E]). And yet God leads them back toward danger (14:2 [P])—even creates the danger by enticing the Egyptians (14:4, 8, 17 [P])—in order to fight on Israel's behalf (14:13–14, 30–31 [JE]) and strengthen their faith (14:31 [JE]). Throughout, the accumulation of Yahwistic, Elohistic and Priestly descriptions of Egypt's muster and pursuit screws the tension to an ever higher pitch: "(JE)And he harnessed his chariotry and his people he took with him, (?)and he took six hundred choice chariotry and all Egypt's chariotry, and *thirds* over all of it. . . . (P)and he pursued after Israel's Sons. . . . And Egypt pursued after them and overtook them encamped by the Sea, all the horse of Pharaoh's chariotry and his horsemen and his force, at Pi-hahiroth before Baal-zephon. (JE?)And Pharaoh, he led near. . . . (JE)see: Egypt setting forth after them."

Because the JE material is thematically bound with the wilderness accounts, and the P material with the Plagues cycle (see SOURCE ANALYSIS, p. 483), their combination smooths over the disjuncture between the two epochs. In other words, chaps. 14–15 in their present form are transitional (Vervenne 1987: 258 n. 3). The Hebrews at the Sea are neither in Egypt nor in the desert, neither enslaved nor free.

The Song of the Sea retards plot progress, but not so as to create suspense. We already know the outcome (14:30–31). Rather, 15:1b–18 sheds light on characters and events (Watts 1992: 34 *et passim*). The Song emphasizes Yahweh's role in defeating Pharaoh, diminishing that of Moses (Childs 1974: 249). It also enriches the psychological depiction of the Egyptians, who prove to be motivated by greed and bloodlust, not just the violation of their property rights. The Song also prophetically discloses the meaning and historical context of liberation. Salvation is incomplete with the defeat of Egypt. Israel must reach the holy mountain, where Yahweh will establish his eternal rule (see COMMENT).

Lastly, combining the various sources has changed the familial relationship among the human protagonists (cf. NOTES to 4:14; 6:20). Specifically, adding P to JE makes Miriam Moses' *sister*, not just his kinswoman (see NOTE to 15:20). This in turn creates a presumption that the anonymous sister-guardian of 2:1–10, too, was Miriam. Once, she protected the defenseless Moses until he was rescued from the river. Now she celebrates her brother's rescue of all Israel from the Sea. Her figure beside the waters frames the events of Exodus 2–15 (cf. Fox 1986: 86).

NOTES

13:17. *in Pharaoh's releasing the people.* We might have expected, "in *Deity's* taking the people out from Egypt," or "in *Israel's* going out from Egypt" (cf. Abarbanel). The emphasis on Pharaoh presumably contrasts his present acquiescence both with his previous intransigence and with his later reversion to hostility.

lead them. Cassuto (1967: 156) observes the wordplay between *nāḥām* 'led them' and *yinnāḥēm* 'repent' (cf. *Exod. Rab.* 20:11).

the way of the land of Philistines. Philistia is Egypt's gateway, from the opposite direction, in Gen 26:1–2 (J): "And Isaac went to Abimelech king of Philistines, to Gerar, and . . . Yahweh . . . said, 'Do not go down to Egypt'" (Rashbam; Bekhor Shor).

The phrase *derek 'ereṣ pəlištîm* is ambiguous. Since *derek* 'way' can also mean "through" (cf. Latin *via*), some translate "through the land of Philistines" (RSV; NJV). Thus the foes Israel might meet are Philistine (Noth 1962: 107; cf. Philo *Moses* 1.164). Others infer that the coastal route from Egypt was called the "Way of the Land of Philistines," although this appellation is otherwise unknown (so LXX; Vg; KJV). By this interpretation, the forces confronting Israel would likely be Egyptian border guards (Sforno; Sarna 1986: 105; Durham 1987: 185). (Bekhor Shor equivocates, imagining the Hebrews potentially caught between the hosts of Egypt and Philistia.)

In fact, Sforno, Sarna and Durham must be right: the "Way of the Land of Philistines" is a specific road. The immediate context explains, not why Israel did not go straight to Canaan, but why they left Egypt as they did, shunning the much-used and well-garrisoned northerly route the Egyptians called the "Ways of Horus" (see Oren 1987). Indeed, Yahweh never intended to take the people directly to Canaan, but planned a meeting at Horeb from the start (3:12; cf. Josephus *Ant.* 2.323). He may even have foreseen a lengthy desert sojourn

(Gen 15:16 [J]; see *Mek. bəšallaḥ* 1; Ginzberg 1928: 6.2 n. 8). And Philistia is scarcely closer to Egypt than is Canaan (a ten days' journey, according to the annals of Thutmosis III [see Katzenstein 1982]). Finally, if the text were explaining why Israel did not march directly to Canaan through Philistia, we would expect "although *it* was near" to be feminine (**kî qərôbâ hî[w]'*), since *'ereṣ* 'land' is feminine. On the geography of the Exodus and the probable anachronism in the reference to Philistia, see APPENDIX B, vol. II.

although. The concessive function of *kî* (ordinarily "for"), though doubted by Aejmelaeus (1986), is well documented (ibn Ezra; Joüon 1965: 525 §171*b*; Muilenburg 1961: 147 n. 37a). Still, with some reading between the lines, the usual meaning of *kî* is also possible: "Deity did not lead them the way of the land of Philistines—(which you might have expected) *because* it was near—for Deity said. . . ." Alternatively: Yahweh did not take the people directly to the "Way of the Land of Philistines" precisely *because* it was too near; i.e., they needed time to muster strength and courage (ibn Ezra).

it was near. "It" (*qārôb hû'*, masc.) is the "way" (*derek*, masc.), not the "land" (*'ereṣ*, fem.).

said. I.e., "said to himself, thought" (Niehoff 1992).

return to Egypt. "Egypt" is the Nile valley, not the territory of the modern state of Egypt, which is mainly desert. The Hebrews left Egypt proper after the paschal night. Still, they are not beyond Egypt's immediate sphere of influence.

Yahweh's fears that Israel might turn back to Egypt are not idle (Rashi; Rashbam). Already in 14:11–12, the people regret their departure. And in Num 14:3–4, perceiving their inferiority to the Canaanites, the Israelites complain, "Why is Yahweh bringing us to this land, to fall by the sword? Our wives and our dependents will become as spoil. Would not returning to Egypt be better for us? . . . Let us return to Egypt."

It is possible to take all of 13:17 as a series of subordinate clauses, the main verb coming in v 18 (Leibowitz 1976: 234–35): "When Pharaoh released the people, and Deity did not lead them the way of the land of Philistines, although it was near, for Deity had said, 'Lest the people repent in their seeing war and return to Egypt,' *then* Deity sent the people around. . . ." This is roughly the structure of Gen 1:1–3 and 2:4b–7.

13:18. *the way of the wilderness of/toward.* One could alternatively translate *derek midbar* as "*through* the wilderness," since it is uncertain a specific road is meant; see further under APPENDIX B, vol. II.

Equally ambiguous is the grammatical relationship between "wilderness" and "Suph Sea." Ibn Ezra and Coats (1967: 255) understand *derek hammidbār yam-sûp* as "by way of the wilderness *of the* Suph Sea." This analysis entails a minor anomaly, the definite article on a noun in construct, but this is permitted when the genitive is a geographical name (GKC §127*f*) But one might skirt the difficulty by understanding *yam-sûp* as "*toward* the Suph Sea" (cf. GKC §118*d*–*g*; Joüon 1965: 372 §125*n*).

Suph Sea. Since elsewhere *sûp* denotes reeds (2:3, 5; Isa 19:6) or seaweed (Jonah 2:6), most interpret *yam sûp* as "Reed Sea" (Rashi; ibn Ezra) or perhaps

"Weed Sea" (cf. Dillmann 1880: 136; *pace* Holzinger 1900: 45). *Sûp* is generally considered a loanword from Egyptian *ṯwf(y)* 'marsh plant, papyrus' (Lambdin 1953: 153), possibly via Phoenician (Ward 1974); some, however, see the borrowing in the reverse direction (references in Huddlestun 1992). Two other Hebrew terms for sedge, *gōme'* and *'āḥû*, are also of likely Egyptian origin. Presumably, the words were imported along with the papyrus on which Israelites wrote.

But what is the "Reed/Weed Sea"? One would expect a body of water characterized by lush vegetation, either along its shore or floating near the surface. The Red Sea, the traditional candidate (LXX; Vg), does not sustain coastal reeds. Many moderns, therefore, look to a papyrus marsh closer to Egypt proper (see further under APPENDIX B, vol. II). Others argue that the *sûp* in Suph Sea has nothing to do with plant life, but is a variant of *sôp* 'end.' Thus, *yam sûp* means "border, terminal sea" (Copisarow 1962) or "sea of extinction" (Batto 1983; Snaith 1965) — but see the convincing counterarguments of Kloos (1986: 153–57). Even if *sûp* originally bore another meaning, it is hard to believe the Israelites did not associate it with their own botanical term. I have simply transliterated "Suph" (with OG[B] Judg 11:16), both because we are unsure of the meaning and because *sûp* lacks the definite article expected on a common noun (ibn Ezra; but see Dillmann 1880: 137 for parallels). *Sûp* appears alone as a geographical name in Deut 1:1.

resolute. *Ḥămūšîm* is an old crux debated already in *Mek. bəšallaḥ* 1. The term is attested only here, Josh 1:14; 4:12; Judg 7:11 and Num 32:17 (LXX; MT *ḥūšîm*). At issue is whether there is a connection with *ḥāmēš* 'five.' LXX Exod 13:18 has "fifth generation," while *Tg. Ps.-Jonathan* Exod 13:18 renders "five families," and Theodotion has "on the fifth day." *Y. Šabb.* 6:4 infers that each soldier bore fifteen different weapons (*sic!*; but *Pesiqta de Rab Kahana* has "five"). An anonymous opinion in *Mek. bəšallaḥ* holds that only one Hebrew in five left, the rest presumably having died; i.e., *ḥămūšîm* is a fraction. None of these interpretations is plausible.

More worthy of consideration is OG Judg 7:11: "fifty." *Ḥmšym* could even be revocalized **ḥămiššîm* 'fifty,' the reading of many Sam MSS and Kenn 193. Perhaps the sense is "by units of fifty" (cf. 1 Sam 8:12; 2 Sam 15:1; 1 Kgs 1:5; 2 Kgs 1:9–14; 15:25) or "divided into fiftieths." (Compare Achilles' Myrmidons, divided into fifty groups of fifty, all led by five generals [*Iliad* 16:168–72].) Fifty units of 1,000 fighters (the *'elep*), multiplied by the twelve tribes, would equal 600,000 soldiers (12:37). Or we could derive *ḥămūšîm* directly from *ḥāmēš* 'five'; Calvin understands *ḥămūšîm* as "in ranks of five." Other Hebrew military terms with possible numerical etymologies are *šālîš* 'third' (see NOTE to 14:7) and *'elep* 'thousand' (NOTE to 12:37); compare, too, Arabic and Old South Arabic *ḥamīs* 'five-part army, troop' (BDB; Dillmann 1880: 137). But these interpretations do not optimally suit the contexts of 13:18; Num 32:17; Josh 1:14; 4:12; Judg 7:11.

The majority rendering, "well girt, armed, equipped" (Syr; *Samaritan Tg.* A; Vg; *Tgs. Onqelos* and *Neofiti I*; also OG Josh 1:14; 4:12), fits all attestations well enough and has been adopted into Modern Hebrew. Perhaps Judg 18:11 illuminates the meaning: six hundred Danite troops are described as "girt with weapons of war" (Loewenstamm 1992a: 226). But what might be the etymology? Ibn Janaḥ (*Book of Roots*), citing not the number five but the noun *ḥōmeš* 'belly,' explains that the soldiers' midriffs are girt; Qimḥi (*Book of Roots*) has a similar derivation, but understands *ḥōmeš* as the "fifth rib" (so KJV; but cf. Syriac *ḥumšā' '*abdomen'). Ibn Janaḥ also compares the relationship between *ḥălāṣayim* 'loins' and *ḥālûṣ* 'armed, equipped'; and ibn Ezra further observes that the soldiers of Reuben, Gad and Manasseh are called both *ḥămūšîm* (Josh 1:14) and *ḥălûṣîm* (Deut 3:18), suggesting that the terms are synonymous (note also Num 32:17 [LXX]; Josh 4:12-13). Thus 13:18 may illuminate 12:11: the *Pesaḥ* is eaten with girt loins in commemoration of the warlike garb of the Hebrews leaving Egypt.

If the meaning of *ḥămūšîm* is specifically "armed," then Sforno's observation is well taken: 13:17-18 informs us that, even though well equipped for battle, the Hebrews are psychologically unready (also Luzzatto). But, as Ehrlich (1969: 162) and Jacob (1992: 379) observe, this definition does not fit the other passages, for *all* Israel is presumably armed, not just certain squadrons. In fact, there is an ancient debate as to whether the Hebrews left Egypt under arms at all. Yea-sayers are Ezekiel the Tragedian (1.210), Philo (*Moses* 1.170, 172), Josephus (*Ant.* 3.18) and the Dura Europos artist (Goodenough 1964: pl. xiv); nay-sayers are *Bib. Ant.* 10:3 and other midrashim (see Loewenstamm 1992a: 226-32).

Last, there is the LXX Num 32:17 rendering of **ḥ[m]šym*: "vanguard." In Num 32:17; Josh 1:14; 4:12; Judg 7:11, the *ḥămūšîm* indeed go before the main army. Moreover, the apparently synonymous *ḥālûṣ* also connotes a vanguard (Josh 6:7, 9, 13). As for etymology, Arabic affords a suitable cognate in *ḥms* 'to be zealous, courageous' (Ehrlich 1969: 162). The difficulty is that "vanguard" will not work in Exod 13:18.

What is the solution? I believe that Hebrew possessed a productive verbal root *ḥmš* 'to be resolute,' generating **ḥāmūš* 'resolute,' *ḥōmeš* 'belly' and possibly *ḥallāmîš*, a hard stone (von Soden 1967: 297-300). In Num 32:17; Josh 1:14; 4:12, the adjective "resolute" describes a vanguard, and *ḥămūšîm* is even nominalized in Judg 7:11 to denote an elite force. But in Exod 13:18, *ḥămūšîm* is simply an adjective. The verse thus parallels 14:8, "Israel's Sons were going out with raised arm" (see NOTE). But I would not entirely rule out the ingenious explanation of ibn Janaḥ, Qimḥi and ibn Ezra.

13:19. *Moses took.* By Joseph's injunction (Gen 50:24-25), all Israel should have been responsible for Joseph's reinterment, not only Moses. Either Moses is singled out as particularly meritorious, or else he acts as the people's representative (Sforno). *Exod. Rab.* 20:19 observes that Moses is rewarded for this act of piety with burial at the hand of Yahweh himself (Deut 34:6). *Mek. bəšallaḥ* attractively develops this notion further:

Whom can we find greater than Joseph, who was buried by none other than Moses? Moses, than whom none was greater in Israel, accrued merit through

Joseph's bones. . . . Whom can we find greater than Moses, who was buried by none other than the Holy One, Blessed is He? . . . What is more, with [the deceased] Jacob, there went up [from Egypt] Pharaoh's servants and the elders of his house; but with [the deceased] Joseph, were the ark and the divine presence and the priests and the Levites and all Israel and the seven clouds of glory. And, what is more, Joseph's coffin traveled beside the Eternal's ark.

The passage goes on to imagine foreign nations inquiring about the contents of the two chests. They are told that the occupant of the one (Joseph) fulfilled the contents of the other (the Covenant).

Although Joseph's coffin goes unmentioned until Israel reaches Canaan (Josh 24:32), we must always bear in mind that the Israelites' wilderness trek is simultaneously Joseph's long-postponed funeral cortege. The piety of this act for Israelites cannot be overstated (see below and NOTE to 14:11 "to die in the wilderness"). It is an acknowledgment of duty toward the ancestors and an affirmation of Israel's continuing relationship with the "fathers' god" (3:6, 15 etc.).

bones. Pace ibn Ezra, ʿaṣmôt seems to connote the entire body by synecdoche (cf. Amos 6:10). Not only Joseph's bones but his very flesh were preserved by mummification (Gen 50:26) (Dillmann 1880: 137).

adjured. The oath is exacted in Gen 50:24–25 and fulfilled in Josh 24:32. Instead of arranging immediate burial in Canaan, as he had treated his father, Jacob (Gen 49:29–50:14), Joseph has his own remains preserved by the Hebrews as a token of faith in their repatriation. Since nonburial is the ultimate biblical curse, Joseph's act might be construed as one of extreme self-abnegation (cf. NOTE to 14:11). He postpones his own peaceful repose lest Israel come to settle permanently in Egypt (at Joseph's own behest!). (But if skeletal disarticulation was prerequisite to "joining one's fathers," perhaps mummification mitigated a deferred burial.)

13:20. *Succoth . . . Etham.* Rashi plausibly assumes that the Hebrews spend one night at each campsite, reaching the Sea on the third day; see NOTES to 14:2, 5. On the itinerary of the Exodus, see APPENDIX B, vol. II.

13:21. *cloud pillar . . . fire pillar.* Of how many pillars are we speaking: one pillar with two aspects, or two different pillars? Probably of one, since 14:20 may refer to the pillar turning from cloud to fire, while 14:24 likely describes the opposite transformation at dawn (see NOTES).

Exod 13:21 recalls a military practice attested from ancient Greece and modern Arabia, but not yet from the ancient Near East. Quintus Curtius (5.2.7) records that a beacon was borne atop a pole before Alexander's army, *ignis noctu fumus interdiu* 'fire by night, smoke by day' (Dillmann 1880: 137–38). Until recently, Arab caravans, including the *ḥajj*, were preceded by a signal brazier (Doughty 1936: 1.47). If ancient Israel knew such a custom, it might partly explain the symbol of the fiery-cloudy pillar. There may also be a Ugaritic parallel: the goddess ʾAṭiratu rides following her servant, who is *yʾuḥdm.šbʿr . . . kkbkb* 'caught on fire . . . like a star' (*KTU* 1.4.iv.16–17 [Mann 1977: 98]).

Wilson (1985) has revived an old suggestion: the biblical image of the cloud/ fire pillar originates in vulcanism (also Gressmann 1913: 112–13, 117–19). Indeed, he attempts to associate almost every supernatural event in the Book of Exodus with the explosion of Thera (see COMMENT to 7:8–11:10). Other difficulties aside, by current estimates, the blast occurred too early to be directly relevant to formative Israel; see Stiebing (1987); McCoy and Heiken (1990). For further discussion of the pillar, see NOTES to 14:19, 20, 24; COMMENT, pp. 549–50.

going (second time). My translation takes the pillar as the subject. One could also render *lāleket* as *"for* going," referring to the people's journey.

The parallelism in 13:21–22 is often noted; Mann (1977: 130–31) even sets the passage as verse (also Buber 1946: 76). But the Hebrew is too wordy for poetry. Rather, it is high-flying prose (cf. Kugel 1981).

13:22. *would not depart.* This applies to the whole desert period, not just the immediate crisis (*pace* Jacob 1992: 382); cf. 16:10; 40:34–38; Num 9:15– 23; 10:11–12; 14:14; Deut 1:33; Ps 78:14; Neh 9:12, 19 (cf. also the guiding angel in Exod 23:20, 23; 32:34; 33:2; Num 20:16; Judg 2:1–4).

My translation parses *yāmîš* as an intransitive Qal (with ibn Ezra). Rashi, however, sees a causative Hiphʿil, with Yahweh the implicit subject: "He did not *remove* the pillar. . . ." While this is morphologically unassailable, it is neither the plain sense nor the interpretation of any ancient Version. It is justly rejected by Luzzatto.

before. After the verb "depart," one might expect **millipnê 'from* before,' rather than *lipnê* 'before.' The diction thus implies a semantic carryover of *lāleket* 'going' from the previous verse. That is, v 22 combines two sentiments: "the cloud would not *depart from before* the people" and "the cloud would not depart, but rather *went before* the people."

14:2. *turn back.* I.e., change direction, most likely back to Egypt (*pace* Gressmann 1913: 110 n. 2). Jacob (1992: 384) understands *yāšūbû wəyaḥănû* as hendiadys, "let them camp again," presumably in addition to their previous camping at Etham (13:20). But, with so many references to camping, why should the idiom appear only here?

It may be Israel's about-face that suggests to Pharaoh the people are lost (Rashi). Bekhor Shor optimistically supposes that the Israelites are returning in order to restore the Egyptians' borrowed valuables (3:21–22; 11:2–3; 12:35– 36). But ibn Ezra's notion that Yahweh is feinting, enticing Egypt into pursuit, rings more true (also Durham 1987: 185, 187). Sforno compares Judg 4:7, "I [Yahweh] will draw Sisera toward you."

Pi-hahiroth . . . Migdol . . . Baal-zephon. Pi-hahiroth looks like a real Egyptian name; *pî* must be either Egyptian *pꜣ* 'the' or *pr* 'house.' But *haḥîrōt* remains mysterious (see TEXTUAL NOTE and APPENDIX B, vol. II). *Migdōl* is Hebrew/Canaanite for "fortress, tower," a common element in city names. There were in fact four Migdols on Egypt's eastern border (Redford 1987: 143, 154 n. 14). *Baʿal ṣapôn* is properly the name of a deity, "Lord of [Mount] Zaphon" in North Syria. At Ugarit, *bʿl ṣpn* is an epithet of the storm god Haddu;

he also appears in Esarhaddon's treaty with Tyre (IV.10) (*ANET*[3] 534; Parpola and Watanabe 1988: 27) and in a fifth-century Phoenician papyrus from Saqqarah, Egypt (*KAI* 50.3; Aimé-Giron 1941; Albright 1950b; Helck 1971: 447); see further under NOTE to 15:17; COMMENT; APPENDICES B and C. In Exodus, however, Baal-zephon is not a deity, but an Egyptian city also mentioned in classical sources (Eissfeldt 1932). Since *ṣpwn* is usually vocalized *ṣāpôn*, perhaps *ṣəpôn* reflects the later pronunciation of Aramaic-speaking Egypt (LXX, however, has *Sepphōn*, as if the local pronunciation were *ṣappōn*).

On the framing function of 14:2 and 9, see NOTE to 14:9. On the itinerary of the Exodus, and especially on the problem of Baal-zephon, see APPENDIX B, vol. II.

opposite it you will camp. The writer ends the sentence with assonance: *nikhô taḥănû*. I assume *nikhô* 'opposite it' means opposite Baal-zephon. Since this is redundant in context, however, we might alternatively understand "opposite him [Pharaoh]"; cf. LXX "opposite them [Egypt]."

For Israelites engaged in combating Baal worship, perhaps there was a spiteful emphasis on the locale. Yahweh works his greatest miracle opposite Baal's sacred city (Jacob 1992: 390), even appropriating Baal's prerogatives as master and conqueror of the Sea (see Eissfeldt 1932 and COMMENT).

14:3. *say of.* My translation follows Syr and Tg. Onqelos; *'āmar lə-* often means "say *regarding*" rather than "say *to*" (Gen 20:13; Deuteronomy 33 *passim*; Judg 9:54; Isa 41:7, etc.). Here "say" implies "say to oneself, think" (Niehoff 1992).

confused. The rare word *nəbūkîm* has occasioned some philological speculation. Norin (1977: 34), citing Arabic *nab(a)k* 'quicksand,' interprets *nəbūkîm* as "mired." But this fits the context poorly and is linguistically dubious (*nab[a]k* is probably related to Akkadian *nagbu*, Hebrew *nēbek* 'subterranean source'). Rabin (1961: 388), on the other hand, translates "distressed," invoking Arabic *bāka* 'press.' Actually, "hemmed in" would work even better, parallel to "the wilderness has closed against them." But in Joel 1:18; Esth 3:15, *nābôk* connotes mental perplexity, a meaning also paralleled in Arabic. "Confused" remains the most likely interpretation.

the land. What land? The quasi-poetic parallelism of 14:3 suggests that *hā'āreṣ* 'the land' is tantamount to *hammidbār* 'the wilderness.'

the wilderness has closed against them. There are two possible interpretations of *sāgar 'ălêhem*: "shut them *in*" and "shut them *out*." By the former understanding, the wilderness is compared to a prison (cf. Josephus *Ant.* 2.325; Rashi). Jacob (1992: 390), however, sees the wilderness as a barrier, not a cage. Jacob also takes Yahweh as the subject ("he [Yahweh] has shut the wilderness against them"), but a more plausible rendering would be "the wilderness has shut them out" (cf. Cassuto 1967: 160).

14:4. *I will strengthen.* Yahweh ensures that Israel will not return to Egypt (cf. 13:17) by fanning Egyptian hostility (see REDACTION ANALYSIS). On Yahweh's "strengthening" Pharaoh's heart, see COMMENT to 7:8–11:10, pp. 353–54.

they did so. I.e., they camped where Yahweh had told them (v 2).

14:5. *the people had fled.* For some, Pharaoh's sudden realization contradicts his previous release of the people (12:31–32) (e.g., Fohrer 1964: 99). But there is no indication that the king had meant to free Israel for good. He may still be expecting their return after a "three days' way into the wilderness" (see below).

heart was reversed. Like English "repent," *nehĕpak lēb* has connotations of both regret and vacillation (Bekhor Shor).

What is this we did . . . from our service. Rashi observes that the Israelites are now on their third day of travel (see NOTE to 13:20) and have reached the limit of a "three days' way" (3:18; 5:3; 8:23). For the first time, Pharaoh realizes that Moses' refrain, "release my people," does not mean "release them for a short religious festival," but "release them forever."

Israel. This is the Egyptians' first use of Israel's proper name (see also NOTE to 14:25) (Jacob 1992: 121, 393). Previously, they have been "the people" or "Hebrews," the latter apparently a term of derogation (see NOTE to 1:15).

14:6. *he harnessed his chariotry.* Pharaoh does not himself do the harnessing (ibn Ezra on Gen 46:29; *pace Mek. bašallaḥ* 2; Rashi; Durham 1987: 191), no more than Solomon builds his Temple (1 Kgs 6:14). The idiom *'āsar rekeb* also appears in Gen 46:29; 2 Kgs 9:21 and in an eighth-century plaque from Arslan Tash, Syria (l. 2; see Cross 1974: 486–90). The expression is elliptical; implicit is "to the horses" (cf. Jer 46:4).

his people. *'Am* 'people' often connotes "fighting force" (BDB 766), a collection of males representing the citizenry (Childs 1974: 218).

with him. Like 13:21–22, 14:6 features quasi-poetic diction, with a chiastic (ABB′A′) structure: "he harnessed his chariotry/his people he took." There is also paronomasia: *'ammô . . . 'immô* 'his people . . . with him' (Cassuto 1967: 162). These are features of elevated prose, not necessarily of poetry.

14:7. *six hundred.* Military forces of this size also appear in Judg 18:11; 1 Sam 13:15; 23:13; 2 Sam 15:18 (see Malamat 1954). One could also regard the number of Egyptian chariots as corresponding to 600,000 Israelite men (12:37), at a ratio of 1:1000 (compare Deut 32:30, "one will pursue a thousand").

choice chariotry. While this is the only occurrence of *rekeb baḥûr*, warriors are elsewhere called *'îš bāḥûr* 'chosen man' (Judg 20:15, 16, 34; 1 Sam 24:3; 2 Chr 13:3, 17) or simply *bāḥûr* 'chosen' (1 Sam 26:2; 2 Sam 10:9, etc.). This is the first of several instances of shared or similar vocabulary in the prose narrative and the Song of the Sea. Both 14:7 and 15:4 refer to Pharaoh's "chariots" (*rekeb, markɔbōt*) and his *šālišîm* 'thirds,' along with the root *bḥr* 'choose.'

thirds. *Šālîš* is ostensibly an ordinal number or fraction derived from *šālōš* 'three,' although this has been questioned (see below). A venerable tradition identifies the *šālîš* as the third man in the chariot, a shield-bearer or attendant (*Mek. bašallaḥ* 2; Origen *Homiliae in Exodum* 6.3; modern references in BDB). But Mastin (1979), the most comprehensive treatment to date, raises many objections: e.g., if the *šālišîm* are mere subalterns, why call them "choice" (15:4)? Why do they present a special threat (14:7)? One might also object that three-man chariot teams were more common in the first than in the second millennium — but the text could simply be anachronistic.

Biblical usage suggests, in any case, that a *šālîš* is a superior commander or hero (e.g., Ezek 23:15, 23), although the term may have undergone semantic development (Särko 1993). The theory that it derives from Hittite *sallis* 'great, powerful' is superficially attractive (Cowley 1920), but no Hittite officer is so designated (Rabin 1963: 133). Somewhat more plausible is Marzal's (1963) and Margalith's (1977–78) association with Ugaritic *ṯlṯ* 'bronze,' supposedly connoting a coat of mail and, by metonymy, an armored warrior.

It remains possible, too, that there is a connection with *šālōš* 'three.' We read of tripartite hosts in Judg 7:16; 9:43; 1 Sam 13:17; 2 Sam 18:2; 2 Kgs 11:5–7 (cf. Mendenhall 1958: 58). One might infer that in 14:7, Pharaoh leads three brigades of two hundred chariots, each under a general, the *šālîš*. David's military organization may also be based on three-ness—three paramount heroes among a group of thirty (2 Sam 23:8–23)—but the matter is quite problematic (see Na'aman 1988; Schley 1992). Alternatively, a "third" may be a commander of the third rank, beneath king and general (ibn Ezra; Mastin 1979; Na'aman 1988); compare Aramaic *taltā'* (Dan 5:16, 29) (cf. Cowley 1920: 327). Lastly, Schley (1990) has revived the notion of a three-man commando squad—but this is hard to reconcile with the language of 14:6–7.

Exod 14:7, like the previous verse, exhibits high rhetorical style. A thought is stated once, then expanded for emphasis and specificity with one or two parallel clauses. We are told: (a) Pharaoh gathered his select chariotry; (b) what is more, he took all the chariots of Egypt; (c) what is more, they were led by hero-commanders.

over all of it. This might mean that the *"thirds"* commanded "over all." But one could also interpret *'al-kullô* as "in addition to all [the chariotry]."

14:8. *raised arm.* The same expression is associated with the Exodus in Num 33:3. *Mek. bəšallaḥ* 1 imagines the Israelites raising their arms in prayer and praise. But in the Bible, to act with "raised arm" is generally to behave willfully (Gen 41:44; Num 15:30), to rebel or attack (1 Kgs 11:26–27) or to be powerful (Deut 32:27; Isa 26:11; Mic 5:8; Ps 89:14, 43; 118:16; Job 38:15). Exod 14:8 thus states that Israel left Egypt with powerful self-determination, not as skulking slaves (ibn Ezra; cf. Labuschagne 1982). (According to *Tgs. Onqelos* and *Neofiti I*, the Hebrews departed "bare-headed," i.e., disrespectfully [cf. the Jewish custom of covering the head in prayer].)

Israel's confidence is ill conceived and short-lived, based upon ignorance, not faith (Rashbam). The people seem unaware of Egypt's pursuit, as if Moses had not reported God's words from 14:3.

14:9. *pursued . . . overtook.* The sequence *rādap . . . hiśśîg* is formulaic (Gen 44:4; Exod 15:9; Deut 19:6; 28:45, etc.). "Egypt pursued" serves as a *Wiederaufnahme* or resumptive repetition with "he [Pharaoh] pursued after Israel's Sons" (v 8) (see Kuhl 1952). Together, the clauses frame the aside, "and Israel's Sons were going out with raised arm" (Cassuto 1967: 162).

all the horse of Pharaoh's chariotry and his horsemen and his force. Throughout 14:6–9, the accumulation of terms describing the Egyptian host emphasizes the inequality of the contest. "Horse" and "chariotry" are fairly clear. But scholars dispute whether *pārāšîm* 'horsemen' are charioteers, mounted scouts or true mounted fighters; in the Near East, soldiers fought from horseback beginning in the first millennium B.C.E. (Firmage 1992). As for *ḥayil* 'force,' we infer by elimination that it connotes infantry (Holzinger 1900: 47). Except for *pārāšā(y)w* 'his horsemen,' all these terms reappear in the Song (15:1, 4).

Pi-haḥiroth . . . Baal-zephon. The verbal parallels between 14:2 and 9 frame the action transpiring in Egypt. Exod 14:10 then opens a new episode taking place in the desert (see following).

14:10. *And Pharaoh, he led near.* *Ûparʿō(h) hiqrîb* is generally interpreted "and Pharaoh approached" (e.g., Luzzatto; also most ancient translations). But the Hiphʿil should be transitive, the implicit object being the Egyptian army (so ibn Ezra, but contrast his comment on Gen 12:11). (According to *Memar Marqah* 1:11, Pharaoh is not approaching, but *sacrificing* [*hiqrîb*] to the god Baal-zephon [MacDonald 1963: 1.27; 2.42]!)

The disjunctive reversal of verb and subject (*ûparʿô[h] hiqrîb*) may signify that these words open a new section, after the framed unit vv 1–9 (see previous NOTE and TEXTUAL NOTE). One could also regard the syntax as emphasizing the king's role or, conceivably, as putting the clause into the pluperfect ("now, Pharaoh *had* led near").

raised their eyes and they saw, and, see. In JE, the language conveys the Israelites' surprise (Childs 1974: 218). The effect is somewhat diminished in the composite text, since in 14:3–4 (P), Yahweh had foretold Pharaoh's pursuit. Did Moses keep this information to himself?

cried to Yahweh. "Cry [out]" need not signify panic; *ṣʿq* also connotes prayer (Coats 1988: 114). The Hebrews still believe in Yahweh; it is Moses they mistrust (Ramban; cf. 5:21). Ibn Ezra, observing that the Hebrews may outnumber their pursuers (12:37), imputes their timidity to their former servility, not their actual peril.

14:11. *Is it from a lack of no graves.* For the double negative, compare 2 Kgs 1:3, 6, 16. Cole (1973: 120) finds irony in questioning the existence of tombs in the Land of Pyramids. Compare the rhetorical queries "Is there no balm in Gilead?" (Jer 8:22) and "Is there no longer wisdom in Teman?" (Jer 49:7).

to die in the wilderness. The ancient ideal was to lie in one's ancestral tomb on one's hereditary land. The worst of fates was to lie unburied in no-man's-land, to "die in the wilderness" (Brichto 1974; see Deut 28:26; 2 Sam 21:1–14; 2 Kgs 9:10, 35–17; Isa 14:19–20; Jer 8:1–2; 14:16; 16:4–8; 22:18–19; 25:33; Ps 79:2–3).

What is this you did. The Israelites (rightly) take no responsibility for their own liberation. Nor do they blame Yahweh. It is all Moses' fault. With unconscious irony, the people echo the Egyptians' "What is this we did, that we released Israel from our service?" (14:5). All except Moses and Yahweh agree that Israel would be better off in bondage; the Hebrews are the Egyptians' equals for obtuseness (Cassuto 1967: 164; Childs 1974: 226). Daube (1963: 40) notes that the former slaves' ambivalence toward freedom mirrors an actual situation envisioned in the law codes: the slave who "loves" his master (21:5–6; Deut 15:16–17).

This incident inaugurates a series of "murmuring" episodes set in the wilderness. Whenever faced with a crisis, the people reject Moses' authority and/or wish they were back in Egypt. Yahweh always saves the day, sometimes punishing Israel as a lesson (14:10–14; 15:24–25; 16:2–3, 6–8; 17:1–7; Num 11:1–6; 14:2–4; 16:13–14; 20:2–13; 21:4–5; cf. Deut 1:26–28; Ezekiel 20; Ps 78:17–42; 95:7–9; 106; general studies are Coats 1968 and Buis 1978). Two prophetic texts, in contrast, appear to recall the wilderness period as a time of harmony (Jer 2:2; Hos 2:17). The effect of the "murmuring" stories is to make readers feel guilty for doubting religious authority and being ungrateful to God.

14:12. *the word that we spoke.* The people's statement could be taken in either of two ways, depending on whether we are meant to believe it. On the one hand, since the text registers no such complaint, they may be exercising creative hindsight. On the other hand, the non-Priestly authors are chary of unnecessary repetitions; we are expected to read into the silences. Here I think we are to believe that the people really did predict disaster (cf. Sam and SyrHex [TEXTUAL NOTE to 6:9]). They have been consistently skeptical, as Moses foresaw (3:13; 4:1–9). Even 4:31 may hint at Israel's initial disbelief (see NOTE), and in 5:21, they fear Pharaoh will kill them for troublemaking (cf. *Mek. bašallaḥ* 2). The author cites the people's words only in 14:12, once they have become pertinent (cf. Pixley 1987: 88–89).

For serving Egypt is better. It is hard to tell where the people's self-quotation ends. I tend to agree with Holzinger (1900: 47) and Ehrlich (1969: 164): "for serving Egypt . . ." is no longer self-quotation, but the people's current opinion. But the scribal tradition represented by Sam and SyrHex holds otherwise (see TEXTUAL NOTE to 6:9).

in the wilderness. The people's words "serving . . . in the wilderness" seem to parody Moses' repeated demand that Pharaoh release the people to serve Yahweh in the wilderness (3:18; 5:1, 3, etc.) (cf. Mann 1988: 92).

Egypt. "Egypt" occurs five times in vv 11–12; it is the Hebrews' favorite theme (Jacob 1992: 397). Weimar (1985: 53, 78) observes the chiasm: (A) ". . . to die in the wilderness"; (B) "What is this you did to us, taking us out from Egypt?"; (B′) "Let us alone that we may serve Egypt. For serving Egypt is better for us"; (A′) "than our dying in the wilderness." This entire sequence, moreover, is framed by symmetrical references to seeing and fearing (vv 10, 13) (Auffret 1983: 58).

14:13. *Do not fear.* Moses exercises the war leader's office of encouraging the people (cf. Deut 20:3; Josh 10:25; Judg 7:3; 1 Sam 23:17; 2 Sam 10:12; Isa 7:4) (Plastaras 1966: 175).

Station yourselves. I.e., hold firm and watch carefully (cf. Childs 1974: 226); compare Deut 7:24; 11:25; 2 Sam 21:5 and especially 1 Sam 12:16. The sense of *hityaṣ(ṣə)bû* is not "stand still"; that would be *ʿimdû*.

today. After decades of servitude and centuries of sojourning, and even after their departure from Egypt proper on the morrow of the *Pesaḥ*—this is the day on which Israel will become forever free.

as you have seen Egypt. "Egypt" is tantamount to "the Egyptians." Given the versatility of *ʾăšer*, we might paraphrase *ʾăšer rəʾîtem ʾet-miṣrayim* with "as for *the fact that* you have seen the Egyptians today" or "*in contrast to* your seeing the Egyptians today" (see also next NOTE).

see them no more. Is this a prediction or a command? And does it apply for all time, or only for Moses' contemporaries (cf. Deut 17:16; 28:68; *y. Suk.* 5:1)? In light of Israel's continued contact with their Egyptian neighbors, the sense might be "you will never again see Egypt as permanent residents" or "you will never see Egypt as slaves" (*Tg. Neofiti I*). For Dillmann (1880: 148) and Cassuto (1967: 164), however, the sense is rather that the Hebrews will never again see the Egyptians as an army. (In fact, Egyptian armies will continually march to and through the land of Israel until the Roman period.) In any case, Yahweh here ratifies Moses' retort to Pharaoh, "I will see your face no more" (10:29, but cf. NOTE).

Just as 14:2 and 9 frame the scene in Egypt, 14:13 and 14:30–31 frame the miracle at the Sea by virtue of shared vocabulary (Mann 1977: 134; Auffret 1983). Here are the two passages in translation, with common words italicized:

> *Do not fear.* Station yourselves and *see Yahweh's salvation* which he will *make* for you *today*. For, as you have *seen Egypt today*, you will *see* them no more to eternity. (14:13)

> So *Yahweh saved* on that *day* Israel from *Egypt's* arm, and Israel *saw Egypt* dead at the Sea's lip. And Israel *saw* the great arm that *Yahweh* had *made* in *Egypt*, and the people *feared Yahweh* and trusted in *Yahweh* and in Moses his slave. (14:30–31)

The parallel in 1 Sam 12:16–18, moreover, in effect runs together Exod 14:13, 30–31: "Now station yourselves and see this great thing that Yahweh is going to make before your eyes . . . and all the people feared greatly Yahweh and Samuel" (cf. Blum 1990: 31).

In both Exod 14:13, 30–31 and 1 Sam 12:16–18, we observe play between the roots *r'y* 'see' and *yr'* 'fear' (see also Exod 1:16–17; 1 Kgs 3:28). Note, too, the alliteration at the end of 14:13, *ʿôd ʿad-ʿôlām* (Cassuto 1967: 164; Childs 1974: 226).

14:14. *Yahweh, he will fight for you.* The inverted syntax (*yahwe[h] yillāḥēm lākem*, not **yillāḥēm lākem yahwe[h]*) emphasizes the contrast between "Yahweh" and *'attem* 'you' (cf. NOTE to 15:18). The word order also creates assonance; compare the alliteration in v 13 noted above. Cassuto (1967: 174) observes that *yahwe(h) yillāḥēm lākem* 'Yahweh, he will fight for you' anticipates 15:3, *yahwe(h) 'îš milḥāmâ* 'Yahweh Man of War.' It also foreshadows 14:25, *yahwe(h) hannilḥām lāhem* 'Yahweh is the fighter for them' (see TEXTUAL NOTE). On Yahweh as warrior, see Fredriksson (1945), Cross (1973: 91–111) and Miller (1973).

you, you will be still. It is unclear whether *'attem taḥărîšûn* means "you may stay calm," in contrast to "Yahweh, he will fight" (14:14) (Syr); or "you be quiet," in contrast to "Israel's sons cried" (14:10) (Bekhor Shor). R. Meir raises a third, less likely possibility: "Yahweh would fight for you *even if* you were still" (*Mek. bəšallaḥ* 3). In light of the emphasis placed upon "Yahweh," the first interpretation seems to me the best. However, the Israelites do cease complaining at this point, and will not break their silence until the Song of the Sea (cf. Halpern 1983: 43 n. 3). So perhaps Moses is simply saying, "Shut up!" (If so, it is striking that Yahweh forthwith tells *Moses* to be quiet.)

14:15. *(For) what do you cry.* God's words could imply that, despite his bravado, Moses shares his people's doubts, or at least has relayed them to Yahweh (Coats 1988: 114; SOURCE ANALYSIS). Lack of faith would be in character for Moses, particularly in E (cf. especially 5:22–23). Perhaps we are to understand that Moses has prayed between vv 14 and 15 (*Tg. Onqelos;* Syr), if only in his heart (Philo *Moses* 1.173; Origen *Homiliae in Exodum* 5.4). It may be better, however, to infer with ibn Ezra that Moses is addressed as the people's representative, even if he did not himself cry out (cf. 16:28–29; compare Moses suffering for the people's sin in Deut 1:37; 3:26; 4:21). But Sforno, citing parallel rebellion episodes, presents a credible alternative: Moses has indeed cried out—not about the danger, but about the challenge to his authority (cf. 17:4). If so, Yahweh simply tells him to act like a leader, with self-reliance. And a final possibility is that *tiṣʿaq* expresses potential, rather than actual fact: "Why *should* you cry to me?" At any rate, Yahweh's basic message to Moses is "Stop talking and get moving" (according to R. Eliezer [*Mek. bəšallaḥ* 4], it is Moses' long-windedness that irks Yahweh!). On the likelihood that 14:14 and 14:15 are of different authorship, see SOURCE ANALYSIS.

14:16. *you.* The emphatic *wəʾattâ* contrasts Moses both with Israel (v 16) (Ehrlich 1908: 318) and with the following *waʾănî* 'and I [Yahweh]' (v 17) (see NOTE).

extend your arm. Although it is Yahweh who works the miracle, 14:16, taken alone, suggests that Moses has the power to split the Sea. At least in choice of language, then, the author reserves the honor of rescuing Israel for Moses (Jacob 1992: 398–99).

According to the Song of the Sea, it is Yahweh who extends his arm at the Sea (15:12). The implication for 14:16 is that Moses' arm channels the power of, or even becomes, God's own arm; compare 7:17, where it is unclear whether the hand and rod are Yahweh's or Moses' (see NOTE). Isa 63:12 makes the connection explicit: "He makes his glory's arm go with Moses' right hand." And Ps 89:22, 26 similarly asserts of David, "My [Yahweh's] arm will be reliably with him. . . . I have put his arm upon the sea, and his right hand upon the rivers." David and Moses are each Yahweh's vicar, wielding godlike power over the waters (see also COMMENT to Exodus 3–4 and NOTE to 15:12).

split it. While in the Song and perhaps in JE, a wind retains the Sea, in P, the waters are literally split, a greater wonder (see also COMMENT). (Later legend fancies that, to facilitate the tribes' crossing, the Sea is parted in *twelve* places [e.g., *Tg. Ps.-Jonathan* Exod 14:21; Dura Europos frescoes]; see further Ginzberg 1928: 3.22).

14:17. *I, see, I.* "I" is emphatic (*waʾănî*) and coordinate with "you" (*wəʾattâ*) in v 16 (Cassuto 1967: 166). The implication is that Yahweh and Moses together will save Israel; cf. 14:31, "the people feared . . . and trusted in Yah-weh and in Moses."

strengthen. According to 14:4, only Pharaoh's heart would require fortifica-tion. But now Yahweh strengthens the resolve of all the Egyptians. We might infer that, while Pharaoh's courage was sufficient to initiate the pursuit, for all Egypt to enter between towering walls of water required an additional dose of "strengthening" (Jacob 1992: 399; Cassuto 1967: 165–66).

14:18. *my glorification over Pharaoh.* An equally valid rendering would be "my glorification *through* Pharaoh." The root *kbd* 'be heavy, numerous, glori-ous' is prominent throughout Exodus (see INTRODUCTION, p. 36).

14:19. *Messenger.* A *malʾāk* is most often a supernatural sending, i.e., an angel (see NOTE to 3:2). On the relationship between the Messenger and the pillar of cloud and fire, see SOURCE ANALYSIS and COMMENT.

stood behind. Compare Isa 52:12, prophesying a "second Exodus" from Babylon: "You will not go out frantically (*bəhippāzôn;* cf. 12:11; Deut 16:3) . . . for Yahweh goes before you, and your rearguard is Israel's deity." In Exod 14:19, the pillar standing between the two camps appears to hide the parting of the waters, giving Israel an interval in which to begin their passage (D. N. Freedman, privately). Rashi imagines the cloud also functioning as a force field, repelling Egyptian ballistics.

14:20. *It came.* Or "he [the Messenger] came."

cloud and the dark. We would expect cloudy darkness to be observable dur-ing the daytime, not at night (cf. 13:21–22). Philo (*Moses* 1.176), however, ac-cepts the plain sense of the received text: the cloud made for a particularly dark, starless night. See further below.

illumined the night. An alternative rendering might be "shone all the night"; for *ʾēt* indicating duration of time, see NOTE to 13:7.

The mention of cloud, dark, fire and night is somewhat confusing. Perhaps the cloud is radiant for Israel, dark for Egypt (Rashi; ibn Ezra; cf. NOTE to 14:24). Or perhaps the meaning is: by day the dark cloud separates the two camps (cf. Josh 24:7), and at night it begins to shine, still keeping them apart. Exod 14:20 might even describe nightfall, when the pillar is half cloud and half fire (cf. NOTE to 14:24); if so, one could loosely render, "(First) there was a cloud. (When it was) dark (reading *ḥōšek* or *heḥĕšîk*), it illumined the night" (see TEXTUAL NOTE). Finally, we should note the opinion of some medieval Jewish commentators that the root *ʾwr,* ordinarily "shine," can also mean "be dark" (ibn Janaḥ [*apud* ibn Ezra]; Bekhor Shor; Rashi on Ps 139:11). But the proof-texts, Ps 139:11 and Job 37:11, are susceptible to more plausible interpretations, and there is no corroboration from cognate languages. On the possibility that 14:20 is corrupt and/or composite, see TEXTUAL NOTES and SOURCE ANALYSIS.

this one . . . this one. I.e., "the one . . . the other."

14:21. *forward wind.* Rûaḥ qādîm is generally taken as the east wind, since the Israelites "oriented" themselves toward sunrise. LXX, however, has "south wind" (also 10:13; Ezek 27:26; 40:44; 42:10; Ps 78[OG 77]:26; Job 38:24; see NOTE to 10:13. Conceivably, the connotation of *qādîm* is simply "hot desert wind" (Syr) or "mighty wind," irrespective of compass direction (Clericus *apud* Dillmann 1880: 151; Cassuto 1967: 127). This *"forward* wind" is among Yahweh's favored weapons (Isa 27:8; Jer 18:17; Ps 48:8) (Loewenstamm 1992a: 265); Hos 13:15 calls it "Yahweh's wind." As a hot wind (Gen 41:6, 23), the *qādîm* is particularly suited to dry the Sea.

all the night. At least in the composite text, the wind blows all night to retain the waters while Israel crosses (ibn Ezra). The implication for vv 26–27 is that the *cessation* of the wind restores the waters (see NOTE). Thus Fretheim's (1991a: 159) inference that it takes all night simply to dry the Sea is probably wrong for JEP, although it might be correct for JE.

14:23. *Egypt pursued.* It may appear incredibly audacious of the Egyptians to rush between danger's jaws, without considering how and why the Sea has parted (cf. Josephus *Ant.* 2.342). Perhaps this is the result of Yahweh "strengthening" their hearts (14:17) (Jacob 1992: 399; Cassuto 1967: 165–66). Given, however, the cloud and the dark (v 20), the Egyptians may be partly blinded. Quite possibly, they do not perceive their peril until sunrise (Calvin).

14:24. *morning watch.* The biblical night was divided into three watches (Judg 7:19; 1 Sam 11:11; Lam 2:19). On morning as a time of salvation following nocturnal danger, see Ziegler (1950) and Fields (1992).

looked down. Yahweh does not just "see" (*rā'â*); he beholds from above (*hišqîp*). The diction conveys Yahweh's spatial and perhaps moral elevation over the Egyptians.

pillar of fire and cloud. We receive the distinct impression from 13:21 that the pillar is *either* cloud or fire, not *both.* But Rabbinic sources imagine the pillar as fire on the Israelite side and cloud on the Egyptian side (*Tgs.; Mek. bəšallaḥ* 5; also Wevers 1990: 222); see NOTE to 14:20. Cassuto (1967: 169) implausibly finds in 14:24 a new cloud, unrelated to that of 13:21–22. But I find Bekhor Shor's solution the most attractive: at dawn, the pillar is in transition between its two aspects. The same notion might clarify 14:20 (see NOTE).

panicked. The root *hwm* connotes divinely sent fear also in 23:37; Josh 10:10; Judg 4:15; 1 Sam 7:10; 2 Sam 22:15; Ps 144:6. We cannot tell how Yahweh frightens Egypt, however. Many suggest that he thunders (ibn Ezra; Rashbam; Luzzatto). And various midrashim imagine Yahweh hurling fire upon Egypt (see also Gressmann 1913: 177; NOTE to 15:7). In 2 Kgs 7:6, Yahweh simply causes the Arameans to hear the sound of an approaching host.

Where are the Egyptians when they panic? One might suppose that they have made it to the opposite shore; now they rush back into the Sea (Hyatt 1971: 155). (1 Sam 4:8 [MT] recalls that Yahweh smote Egypt *bammidbār* 'in the wilderness,' which might put the Egyptians on the shore in 14:24, at least for JE. But McCarter [1980: 104] reads **ûb[ə]mô dāber* 'and with plague,' finding an allusion rather to 7:8–11:10.) To me, it seems more likely they are still in transit.

Egypt's camp. Maḥăne(h) often connotes an army on the march, not necessarily at rest (cf. Gen 50:9; 2 Kgs 3:9, etc.). Thus there is no real contradiction between JE and P (vs. Halpern 1983: 43 n. 2; Soggin 1985: 382).

14:25. *diverted/bound/removed.* Just what happens to the Egyptians' chariot wheels is an old crux. In any case, Yahweh is probably the subject of the clause (but see Rashbam and Bekhor Shor). We possess two variants for the crucial verb: *wy'sr* (Sam) and *wysr* (MT). While the former can only mean "bound," the latter might mean "removed," "diverted" (< *swr*) or "bound" (< *'sr* with quiescent *'aleph* [GKC §23*f*; Yellin 1926]).

Perhaps Yahweh removes the chariot wheels. That is, he loosens the pins attaching the wheels to the axle (R. Nehemiah, *Mek. bəšallaḥ* 6; *Tgs.*). But would a wheelless chariot drive "with heaviness," or would it just grind to a halt (Dillmann 1880: 151)? If this is the correct interpretation, the diction is understated.

"Bound" (LXX; Sam; Syr) is also possible; NJV, supposing mechanical failure, renders "locked." Others, however, citing the equally difficult Judg 5:21, imagine mud clogging the wheels (e.g., Hay 1964; Wevers 1990: 222). Stek (1986) blames thick aquatic vegetation, presumably that which lent its name to the Suph Sea (see NOTE to 13:18). However that may be, although I know no Semitic parallel for this use of *'sr*, the posited semantic development "bind" > "lock" is quite plausible.

Another possible meaning of the Hiph'il of *swr* is "divert" (e.g., Deut 7:4; 2 Sam 6:10). Perhaps Yahweh causes the drivers to lose control of their chariots, so that they collide (cf. Rashbam *apud* Bekhor Shor). Several Jewish commentators imagine the Egyptians executing frantic U-turns in the narrow space between the walls of water.

By any interpretation, 14:25 ironically alludes to 14:6, where Pharaoh harnessed (*wayye'sōr*) his chariotry. Now Yahweh *y(')srs* the same vehicles. The pun underscores the delicious irony, that Egypt's superweapon proves their undoing (cf. Freedman 1980: 134). Many biblical passages evince mingled awe and contempt for chariots, intimidating but fairly useless in the Israelite highlands (Josh 11:4, 9; 17:18; Judg 1:19; 4:15; 5:21–22; 2 Kgs 19:23, etc.).

wheel. A collective reference to all Egypt's chariot wheels.

him. The referent is either Egypt or its collective "wheel."

heaviness. Yet another appearance of the theme root *kbd* (Fox 1986: 81); see INTRODUCTION, p. 36.

I must flee. In Judg 4:15, Yahweh similarly "panics" the Canaanite army, whereupon Sisera abandons his chariot and flees on foot. Perhaps something of the sort happens here.

from Israel's face. Less literal renderings might be "from Israel's presence," "from before Israel" or simply "from Israel."

Yahweh. In 14:25, the Egyptians use together two names that once seemed unfamiliar to Pharaoh (5:2): "Yahweh" and "Israel." Egypt has learned too late the lesson of the Plagues, that "I am Yahweh" (Cassuto 1967: 170).

the fighter for them. The Egyptians unwittingly testify to the fulfillment of Moses' promise, "Yahweh, he will fight for you" (14:14) (Jacob 1992: 404; Cassuto 1967: 170).

against Egypt. The phrasing is slightly odd; one might have expected "against me/us." Perhaps *bəmiṣrayim* was chosen for its ambiguity, as it can also be rendered "*in* Egypt." It may even evoke *bimṣārîm* 'in straits, distress' or *bəmēṣar yām* 'in Sea's strait.'

14:26. *its waters will return.* The next verse does not specify what brings the Sea back upon Egypt. Is it a cessation of the "*forward* wind" or a wind from the opposite direction? Exod 14:21 may suggest the former, but in the Song (15:10), a second wind restores the Sea, perhaps melting a wall of ice (cf. Philo *Moses* 1.179; ibn Ezra; NOTES to 15:7, 8, 10). Conceivably, the second wind is a storm, since Ps 77:17−19 and perhaps Ps 81:8 recall a thunder theophany at the Sea (also Josephus *Ant.* 2.343).

14:27. *at morning's turning.* When the sky begins to lighten. In Judg 19:26−27, *pənôt habbōqer* 'the morning's turning' precedes morning (*bōqer*) itself, just as "evening's turning" precedes sunset (Deut 23:12).

original course. Or "permanent, primordial course" (compare Ps 74:15). The diction heightens the sense of the miraculous, since, by definition, an *ʾêtān* stream never fails or deviates.

setting forth to meet it. The object of "meet" is probably the Sea, but possibly Israel. On the disagreement between MT and Sam, see TEXTUAL NOTE.

tumbled. I assume the reference is to Egypt's head-over-heels motion within the Sea (Dillmann 1880: 152). Alternatively, one could understand that the Egyptians are shaken off (*nᶜr*) like dust (cf. Isa 52:2) or insects (cf. Ps 109:23) from the shore *into* the Sea (cf. NOTES to 15:1, 4; Coats 1969: 13). Conceivably, too, the diction is influenced by *nᶜrmw* 'were piled' (15:8).

14:28. *of all Pharaoh's force.* The clause division is uncertain. My translation follows the MT cantillation, but one might alternatively punctuate: "And the waters returned and covered the chariotry and the horsemen; of all Pharaoh's force coming after them into the Sea, so much as one of them did not remain." And there is a third possibility. Luzzatto, comparing 27:3, 19, suggests that the preposition *lə-* is tantamount to "in short," summarizing a list. In that case, *ləkōl ḥêl parᶜō(h)* may be translated "*that is,* all Pharaoh's force."

coming after them. "Them" might be either the Hebrews or the Egyptian cavalry, which the infantry (*ḥayil*) follows. Since in 14:17, 23, Egypt "comes after" Israel, the former is more likely.

14:29. *had walked.* Given the inverted, disjunctive syntax, I would construe the clause as pluperfective. But one might alternatively perceive a contrast: *whereas* the Egyptians drowned, the Israelites walked on dry land. For this to work, however, we must assume that the Sea is closing like a zipper from the Egyptian side, so that the Hebrews complete their transit while Egypt founders (Sforno; De Mille 1956). Still, by this interpretation, we would expect the imperfect **yēləkû* 'were walking,' not *hāləkû* 'walked, had walked.'

on the dry land in the Sea's midst. The diction heightens the paradox: "dry land" and "Sea" are ordinarily opposites. Jacob (1992: 405) notes the chiasm in 14:22, 29 (also 15:19): "in the Sea's midst on the dry land . . . on the dry land in the Sea's midst."

14:30. *arm*. *Yād* 'arm, hand' connotes power—here, Egypt's worldly might, implicitly contrasted with the supernatural "hand" of God (14:31; 15:6, 12, 16, 17).

saw Egypt dead. As the night lifts (14:27), Israel witnesses Yahweh's promised rescue.

lip. I.e., "shore." *Śāpâ* connotes a rim bordering a moist cavity, be it a mouth, a vessel, a river or a sea. The only other shore mentioned in Exodus is the Nile's. Since Hebrew *yām* and *nāhār* are less distinct than English "sea" and "river" (Keel 1978: 21), 14:30 recalls a previous Pharaoh's plot to drown the Hebrew boys in the Nile (1:22–2:10). Now, in revenge, Yahweh has drowned the (male) soldiery of Egypt in the Sea (cf. *Exod. Rab.* 22:1; COMMENT to 1:22–2:10; REDACTION ANALYSIS to 13:17–15:21). Moses, once rescued from the river, saves Israel from the Sea, in accordance with his name's ostensible etymology: "He who rescues from water" (NOTE to 2:10).

It is unclear who is "at the Sea's *lip*"—Israel alone (ibn Ezra; Rashbam), the Egyptians' corpses or both? If the Egyptians' bodies have come aground, there may be a contradiction with the Song (see NOTE to 15:12).

14:31. *arm*. As in the previous verse, *yād* 'arm, hand,' connotes power—now, Yahweh's. On the theme of Yahweh's hand, see INTRODUCTION, p. 36; COMMENT to Exodus 3–4, p. 229; NOTE to 15:12.

made in. Or "worked against." The text refers primarily to the miracle at the Sea, worked *against* Egypt, but secondarily to the Plagues, worked *in* Egypt. On the framing function of 14:13 and 14:30–31, see NOTE to 14:13.

feared. The root *yr'* chimes with *r'y* 'see'; see NOTE to 14:13.

trusted. The same verb (*he'ĕmîn*) appeared in 4:31, where the people believed in Moses—but only briefly. Now it takes a divided Sea to restore their faith. The Hebrews were not saved from Egypt because they believed, but they believed because they were saved (Childs 1974: 238).

In Yahweh and . . . Moses. E puts God and Moses in apposition when treating either the people's faith (14:31) or lack of faith (17:2; Num 21:5). In contrast, on such occasions P pairs Moses with *Aaron* (16:2; Num 20:2). But the Elohist and Priestly Writer ultimately agree: obeying Yahweh's legitimate representative(s) is tantamount to obeying God himself.

EXCURSUS ON BIBLICAL POETRY AND THE SONG OF THE SEA (EXOD 15:1b–18, 21)

This is not the place to attempt a thorough characterization of Israelite poetry. Many good books on the subject appeared in the late 1970s and 1980s, by

Collins (1978), Freedman (1980, esp. pp. 23–50),[1] O'Connor (1980), Kugel (1981), Watson (1984), Alter (1985), Berlin (1985) and Alonso-Schökel (1988). On the debate over meter, see Cloete (1989) and, for further bibliography, Waldman (1989: 71–78). As for the Song of the Sea itself, the classic study is Cross and Freedman (1975: 45–65),[2] and a handy summary (in German) of more recent secondary literature is Zenger (1981: 452–60).

Hebrew verse consists of terse utterances (cola) generally grouped in pairs (bicola) or triplets (tricola). These in turn can form larger constellations: the strophe and the stanza (for the terminology, see Watson 1984). A colon may but need not contain an internal pause, the caesura. Factors determining the points of caesura and colon end are generally syntactical and somewhat subjective. If the caesura is sufficiently strong, we must consider whether a supposed colon is in fact a short bicolon. In the Song of the Sea, for example, it would be equally reasonable to analyze 15:6 as four short cola (*BHS*; Cross 1973: 127) or two long cola with strong internal caesurae (O'Connor 1980: 181). For this reason, scholars disagree over the number of cola in 15:1b–18 (see Zenger 1981: 454 n. 5). Jewish tradition, as enshrined in *Sop.* 12:11, distinguishes forty-two lines (see Kugel 1981: 119–27). O'Connor finds fifty-six, while Cross recognizes sixty-seven cola—even after excising 15:2a as an interpolation. For reasons to be explained below, I favor longer cola, of which I find forty-six (see NOTES to 15:4, 15).

Biblical poetry lacks metrical feet like those of English and classical verse. But there is usually a rough equality of length between cola in a bi- or tricolon, whether we count stresses, syllables or morae (hypothetical units of length). How the Israelites themselves measured length is unknown; sometimes one method works better than another. Israelite Hebrew was not pronounced like Modern Israeli Hebrew, nor even like the Hebrew of the medieval Massoretes. We can to a degree reconstruct or approximate ancient pronunciation, but this is naturally a speculative procedure.

An example of syllabic equality in Israelite Hebrew is the tricolon in v 8. In later Massoretic Hebrew, it runs as follows (approximate syllable counts are given within parentheses; the uncertainty factor is whether šewa' need be counted as a vowel in certain positions):

ûb(ə)rûaḥ 'appe(y)kā neʿermû mayim (11–12)
niṣṣəbû kəmô-nēd nōzəlîm (9)
qāpə'û təhōmōt bəleb-yām (9)

---

[1] This work is an anthology through which one can trace Freedman's evolving views. Citations of "Freedman (1980)" may therefore appear self-contradictory.

[2] *Ancient Yahwistic Poetry*, though published in 1975, was originally a 1950 Johns Hopkins University dissertation (the treatment of the Song of the Sea was also published separately as an article [Cross and Freedman 1955]). Thus, Cross (1973) was written more than two decades *after* Cross and Freedman (1975).

There is no real symmetry here. But in reconstructed Israelite pronunciation, we get something like the following:

*wabarūḥ 'appayk(a) na'ramū maym (9–10)
naṣṣabū kamō nid nōzilīm (9)
qapa'ū tihōmōt balibb yamm (9)

Now, counting syllables works quite well; our only uncertainty is whether the 2 m.s. suffix on the second word was pronounced -k (Kethibh) or -ka (Qere). Counting stresses in v 8 is more difficult, however: do we give kəmô-nēd/ *kamō nid 'like a heap' and bəleb-yām/*balibb yamm 'in Sea's heart' one accent each (MT) or two? If two, we have both syllabic (9 : 9 : 9) and accentual equality (4 : 4 : 4).

In v 17a–c, on the other hand, counting stresses yields greater symmetry than counting syllables. Reconstructed pronunciation would be something like this:

*tabī'imu wattaṭṭa'imu baharr naḥlatak(a) (14–15)
makōn lašibtak(a) pa'alt(a) yahwi (9–11)
miqdaš 'adōnay/yahwi kōninū yadayk(a) (9–11)

Stress analysis yields either 3 : 4 : 4 or 4 : 4 : 4, depending on whether bəhar nahălātəkā/*baharr naḥlatak(a) 'in your property mountain' is accorded one accent or two. Stress analysis also yields a better result in 15:2b (stresses 3 : 3; syllables 8 : 11).

What separated cola in acoustic reality is unknown. There could have been an actual pause, a change of intonation or merely a sense of grammatical closure. (I assume that performers breathed between, not within, bi- and tricola, since enjambment is very rare.) It appears that Israelite poetry was sung or chanted, not spoken, but the musical dimension is no longer accessible.

Beyond approximate equality of length, the device binding single cola into bi- and tricola is conventionally, but misleadingly, called "parallelism." Parallelism covers many analogies among lines of poetry: shared subject, similar grammatical structure, synonymous sentiment, opposite sentiment and so forth. Kugel (1981) and Alter (1985) argue that a second or third colon generally intensifies the meaning of the first; we shall note where this seems true for the Song of the Sea. Often there is more than one type of parallelism at work, and sometimes there appears to be none. Parallelism, moreover, is not an infallible guide to colonic division, since we must acknowledge "internal parallelism" within cola (Watson 1984).

Art lies in balancing the expected and the unexpected. Synonymous parallelism, verse after verse, would be trite; lack of parallelism for more than a few lines would no longer be poetic. In fact, prose is often parallelistic. Kugel persuasively argues that biblical language is a spectrum in whose middle we cannot tell elevated prose from poetry.

As scholars disagree on the delineation of cola within the Song of the Sea, so they differ on the larger units. Much study has been devoted to the structure of 15:1b–18, at the ascending levels of strophe and stanza. Since no such divisions are indicated in the text, these analyses are inevitably subjective (Coats 1969: 1–2), and in fact no two agree (see Zenger 1981: 455). All recognize, however, the important function of vv 6, 11, 16b (see below).

Some scholars put form first. I, however, analyze the Song initially on the basis of content, then seek formal devices that may be intentional division markers. For me, the poem falls into three stanzas of unequal length: vv 1b–7 (58 words), vv 8–12 (48 words) and vv 13–18 (62 words). The first stanza gives the *gist* of events the Song will celebrate: Yahweh cast the Egyptians into the Sea, where his anger consumed them. There is no clear substructure of strophae, although we find a cluster in vv 4–5, describing the drowning of Egypt.

The second stanza (vv 8–12) explains what happened in reality (Ramban): Yahweh did not literally hurl the enemy, but made a path in the Sea to entice them; then he brought the Sea back upon them so that they died. One might say that the first two stanzas of the Song are related in the manner of parallel cola within a bicolon: the first says in general what the second says in particular. In stanza II, the only apparent cluster of tricola (i.e., a strophe) is in v 9, revealing the enemy's thoughts.

This analysis yields a pattern of sorts for stanzas I and II. Each ends with a mineral comparison ("like stone" [v 5], "like lead" [v 10]), followed by a "staircase" bi/tricolon of praise (vv 6, 11; see NOTE to 15:6), followed by the enemy being metaphorically "eaten" (v 6 [consumed by anger], v 12 [swallowed by the underworld]). Both stanzas also climax in extolling the might of Yahweh and his right arm—but here the parallel is imprecise. In stanza I, Yahweh's right arm (*yāmîn*) appears in the "staircase" bicolon (v 6), while stanza II mentions his arm (*yād*) in the concluding bicolon (v 12).

The third stanza (vv 13–18) proceeds to new business: crossing the desert and reaching Yahweh's holy mountain. "Your holiness's pasture/camp/tent" and God's "sanctum" (vv 13, 17) constitute a frame more or less surrounding this section. A cluster of cola describes the fright of Israel's neighbors (vv 14–15), flanked by verses with ʿ*am zû* . . . -*tā* 'the people which you. . . .'

There is at least one structural/thematic link between stanza III and the previous stanzas. Once more, a mineral comparison (v 16 ["like stone"]) is followed by a "staircase" bicolon. But, in contrast to stanzas I and II, stanza III continues with several lines in which Yahweh does not *strike down* an enemy with his *right hand*, but *builds up* a shrine with *both hands*. Exod 15:17 thus creates a frame by antithesis with the beginning of the Song (15:1, 4), where Yahweh "casts down" the enemy—in terms that can also connote the laying of foundations (*rāmâ, yārâ*; see NOTES to 15:4, 5, 16)!

Although I partition 15:1b–18 into stanzas, I must acknowledge images and sound plays overlapping and blurring the divisions. These devices might be taken as evidence that my analysis is incorrect, or that there are really no stanzas at all. For example, I break between vv 7 and 8; yet each begins with *ûb(ə)r-*, and there is also syntactic parallelism ("in [bǝ-] your pride's greatness . . . with [bǝ-] your nostrils' breath"). Indeed, the fire imagery of v 7 ("consumes them as straw") makes more sense in connection with the windy blast of v 8 (stanza II) than with the arm of v 6 (stanza I); see NOTE to 15:7 "straw." For some, all this would forbid breaking between vv 7 and 8. Similarly, my other stanza break, between vv 12 and 13, is crossed by verbs of the pattern *n . . . tā* (15:10, 12–13). "You extended your right arm" (v 12), read in the light of the pastoral language in v 13, attractively suggests a shepherd's crook.

For me, however, the overriding consideration is that my partition makes temporal sense of the Song (see NOTES to 15:6, 7, 8, 12, 13). The images and devices crossing internal divisions do not necessarily disqualify the analysis. Rather, they unify the whole. Surely, the poet did not wish us to concentrate on dissecting his work. All elements are and should be mutually illuminating, as we shall repeatedly see in our interpretation below.

What other features characterize biblical poetry in general, and 15:1b–18 in particular? Hebrew poetry delights in assonance, i.e., the clustering of identical or similar sounds. Where relevant, I will transliterate the Hebrew, either in Massoretic or in reconstructed Israelite pronunciation, to enable non-Hebrew readers to enjoy the sound play.

I am among the scholars who devote great attention to polysemy, i.e., the many meanings associated with a set of sounds (see Herzberg 1979; Paul 1992a). I do not assume that all or even most instances of polysemy are intentional. But I believe that subliminal associations may influence a poet's diction. Making these explicit can enhance our appreciation, albeit crudely engaging the mind instead of the sensibility. The following NOTES will point out internal allusions and key words, as well as lexemes and concepts the Song does not mention explicitly but merely evokes, in order to reconstitute the web of unconscious and conscious associations shared by the poet and the original audience.

In addition to its characteristic structures, Hebrew poetry has its own peculiar grammar. Terseness, a hallmark of poetry in general, is achieved by under-use of "prose particles": the definite article *ha-*, the definite accusative preposition *'ēt* and the relative pronoun *'ăšer* (Andersen and Forbes 1983). (Sometimes, as we have seen under TEXTUAL NOTES, these are restored by later scribes, who in general tend to make biblical poetry more proselike.) A further peculiarity of the Song of the Sea is a paucity of adjectives, especially attributive adjectives (only *'addîrîm* in v 10) (Jacob 1992: 415). Relative to prose, we also find under-use of the conjunction *wǝ-* 'and.'

Biblical poetry also differs from prose in the use of verbs. Hebrew prose knows two tenses/aspects, conventionally (but misleadingly) called "perfect" (*kātab*) and "imperfect" (*yiktōb*). In prose, the former generally describes past action, the latter future or durative/habitual action. In Hebrew poetry, however, it often seems that tenses are used indiscriminately; it is upon the reader to supply the interpretation according to the context (cf. Niccacci 1990: 193–97). For prophetic poetry, the unfortunate result is that we sometimes cannot tell whether the writer is recalling the past, describing the present or predicting the future! For the Song of the Sea in particular, scholars are divided on whether v 17 originally described a future or a past event. Within the Book of Exodus, at least, only the former option exists (see NOTE). My recourse has been to render the Hebrew "perfect" with the English past tense, the "imperfect" with present, future or subjunctive verbs. The strange effect at least replicates the experience of reading the original from the perspective of Hebrew prose. I do not imagine it re-creates the experience of the ancient audience.

Until the 1930s, our understanding of Hebrew poetry was based mainly on the biblical corpus. We now know, however, that Israelite poetry shares techniques and even a few hundred verbal formulae with verse from Ugarit (see RSP). Our conclusion is that Israel inherited its poetic canons from Late Bronze Age Canaan. Such traditional clichés will be pointed out below.

The biblical and Ugaritic poetic corpora differ somewhat, to be sure. For example, we possess extensive narrative poems from Ugarit, but none from Israel. Many influential biblical scholars have suggested that epics like those of Ugarit underlay the pentateuchal prose sources (e.g., Cassuto, Noth, Albright, Cross). This is a plausible conjecture at best, however; the Bible always narrates in prose (see Talmon 1978c). Ugaritic-Hebrew poetry is in fact not well suited to narration, at least from our perspective. The laconic cola are rarely connected by the "thens," "therefores" and "meanwhiles" so helpful to storytelling (cf. Alter 1985: 39). Even taking into account our incomplete understanding of the language and the tablets' poor condition, the Ugaritic epics are extremely hard to follow.

An Israelite poetic form approaching narrative is the victory hymn, of which Exod 15:1b–18 and Judges 5 are our most extensive specimens. Still, the genre is lyric, not epic. It is impossible to extract from either work a clear or complete understanding of the events celebrated. Doings and happenings are alluded to, not recounted—as is appropriate, since the fictive, "implied" audience is supposed recently to have experienced them, while the poems expect of their "actual" audience (i.e., readers) prior familiarity with the tradition. Out of context, these hymns would be as enigmatic as paintings of forgotten historical incidents.

What makes reading the Song of the Sea so challenging is that, just as stanzas interpenetrate, so time blurs; events become metaphors for one another. In 15:16, what do the people cross: the Sea, the desert, a river, Canaan? All are possible, and all may be intended (see NOTE). And the goal of Israel's journey is equally unclear (see COMMENT). Throughout the Song, mixed metaphors and ambivalent language provoke multiple interpretations. In such a case, underreading may be more dangerous than overreading.

The date of the Song of the Sea is highly controversial. Modern estimates range from the thirteenth century (Albright 1968: 112)—in which case, the author is probably Moses himself—to the fifth century B.C.E. (Pfeiffer 1941: 281). Most American scholars consider the Song extremely early, i.e, premonarchic, while many Europeans date it to the late monarchic, exilic or even postexilic eras (for a summary, see Zenger 1981: 456–58). The most thorough linguistic study (Robertson 1972) upholds an early date (twelfth century), but we cannot rule out the possibility of competent forgery. The latest monograph sets the Song in the postexilic restoration, linguistic arguments notwithstanding (Brenner 1991). (For further discussion, see APPENDIX A, vol. II.)

A final methodological comment: based on particular theories about meter and parallelism, or yearnings for structural symmetry, or presuppositions about the development of Israelite thought, or a vision of What Really Happened, many commentators "fix" the text (e.g., Haupt 1904) or reconstruct its "original," shorter form (e.g., Norin 1977; Zenger 1981). I am skeptical of conjectural emendation where the Hebrew or some other Version makes adequate sense (see also Freedman 1980: 49–50, 187). And I consider efforts to recover a short, pristine Song utterly unconvincing. Exod 15:1b–18 makes excellent sense as a complete artwork, as we shall find throughout our discussion (see Tournay 1958: 337; Muilenburg 1966: 245; Durham 1987: 202–10; Brenner 1991: 30–34; Smith 1997: 205–26).

Notes (Resumed)

15:1. *Then sang.* Having silently beheld Egypt's overthrow (14:14), *then* (*'āz*) Israel bursts into song.

Moses. It is uncertain that Moses is considered the Song's author. All we are told is that, despite their former strained relations, people and leader are now literally in harmony. In any case, the association of the Song with Moses enhances the prestige of both the poem and Moses himself, who is remembered not only as a leader but as a singer/songwriter (on the contradiction with 4:10 [Moses' speech impediment], see SOURCE ANALYSIS).

Israel's Sons. Here *bǝnê yiśrā'ēl* are the men alone; the women respond with Miriam in 15:20 (contrast NOTE to 1:7). Arab and traditional Jewish celebrations still feature independent, simultaneous performance by the sexes. Since celebrating a male warrior's prowess is normally women's work, the act of singing a victory song arguably feminizes Moses and the men (Watts 1992: 52–53; see NOTE to 15:20). Male feminization is generally demeaning (e.g., 2 Sam 3:29), but here, since the hero is divine, it is appropriate for human males to subordinate themselves (cf. Judg 16:23–24; 2 Sam 6:14–22; for a different interpretation of feminization, see Eilberg-Schwartz 1994, esp. 137–62).

song. *Šîrâ* is distinguished in distribution but perhaps not meaning from the more common *šîr.* *Šîrâ* appears exclusively in prose comments introducing or framing poems (15:1; Num 21:17; Deut 31:19–22, 30; 32:44; 2 Sam 22:1; Isa 5:1; 23:15). It is uncertain whether *šîr/šîrâ* connotes primarily chant as opposed to speech, or poetry as opposed to prose—i.e., whether it is a performance style or a literary genre. Most likely it is both.

of Yahweh. Ləyahwe(h) is generally rendered "to Yahweh." This is quite possible, as the poem addresses God in vv 6ff. But since the main theme is Yahweh's mighty acts, "*of* Yahweh" is at least as appropriate, and perhaps both meanings are intended (see below). "Yahweh" is the Song's dominant word, appearing approximately ten times, especially toward the beginning (see Hauser 1987: 266–67; on *yāh* in v 2 and *'ădōnāy* in v 17, see TEXTUAL NOTES). Because of the prominence it accords the divine name, the Song of the Sea culminates the theme of the knowledge of Yahweh and his name pervading Exodus 3–15 (see INTRODUCTION, pp. 36–37).

I would sing. As in classical epic, the poet mentions himself in the opening lines (vv 1–2), then bows out (*Odyssey* 1:1; *Aeneid* 1:1; cf. *Iliad* 2:484–93). He may reappear in v 17, calling God "*my* Lordship"—but *'ădōnāy* is a common divine title; the singer does not mean that Yahweh is uniquely *his* master. Poetic self-address is common throughout the Bible (e.g., Deut 32:1–2; Judg 5:3; 1 Sam 2:1; 2 Sam 22:50; Isa 63:7), particularly in the Psalter (Ps 7:18; 9:2–3; 21:14, etc.). The Ugaritic myth of the wedding of the lunar god and goddess (*KTU* 1.24.1) likewise begins *'ašr* 'I would sing' (also ll. 38, [40]) (Cassuto 1967: 174). Akkadian hymns and epics, too, open with self-invocation (Wilcke 1977; Watts 1993).

In 15:1, "I" is not necessarily Moses. The singer might be each individual Israelite (cf. ibn Ezra). In fact, several Versions treat the verb as collective: "let *us* sing" (see TEXTUAL NOTE).

of Yahweh. The interpretation is Freedman's (1980: 199). All others render "*to* Yahweh," who is addressed in much of the poem below. But, because the Deity is described in the third person until 15:6, "*of* Yahweh" is more apposite to the immediate context; cf. Isa 5:1, *'āšîrâ nnā' lîdîdî* 'I would sing *of* my beloved,' and perhaps Judg 5:3, "Hear, O kings; lend ear, O leaders! I *of* Yahweh, I, I would sing (*'ānōkî ləyahwe[h] 'ānōkî 'āšîrâ*)." Isa 12:5 appears to paraphrase Exod 15:21 with *zammərû yahwe(h)* 'Sing [of] Yahweh.'

for. In the Bible, a call for hymnic praise is often followed by a *kî* clause explaining *why* God merits gratitude (e.g., Ps 13:6; 117:1–2; 148:5, 13). The most famous is *hôdû ləyahwe(h) kî ṭôb* 'praise Yahweh for he/it is good' (Ps 106:1; 107:1; 118:1, 29; 136). Kugel (1980) argues, however, that in such instances *kî ṭôb* may be adverbial, describing the manner of singing. Here, too, one could conceivably render *kî gā'ô(h) gā'â* as "Sing of Yahweh *in exaltation*." Also possible is "Sing of Yahweh, for *it* [singing] is exalted." Still, the traditional understanding remains the most likely (see following).

acted. The root *g'y* means either "to be exalted" or "to act exaltedly," with connotations of both elevation and pride. Here *gā'â* is more likely active ("he acted exaltedly") than stative ("he is exalted"). As Luzzatto observes, true stative verbs are not used with infinitives absolute (*mwt* might seem an exception, but the infinitive absolute *môt* is used only for the ingressive sense "to die," not the stative "to be dead"). Moreover, Isaiah 12, which evinces notable contacts with the Song of the Sea, in v 5a apparently paraphrases Exod 15:21

(cf. 15:1): *zammərû yahwe(h) kî gē'ût 'āśâ* 'Sing (of) Yahweh, for he *did* exaltation' (Jacob 1992: 425).

exaltedly, exaltedly. The infinitive absolute *gā'ô(h)* creates metrical balance between the cola, lends emphasis to the finite verb *gā'â* and enhances the alliterative pattern: *gā'ô(h) gā'â . . . rōkəbô rāmâ* 'acted exaltedly, exaltedly . . . his driver he hurled.'

Gā'â interacts semantically with two elements in the following colon. Since *g'y* often describes swelling waters (Ezek 47:5; Ps 46:4; 89:10; Job 38:11; cf. Isa 24:14), it chimes with *yām* 'sea' (cf. Alter 1985: 50). But *g'y* 'be exalted' also interacts antithetically with *rmy* 'hurl (down).' Yahweh brings low (*yrd, špl*) the haughty (*g'y*) in Isa 13:11; 14:11; 25:11; Ezek 30:6; Zech 10:11; Prov 29:23; Job 40:11–12. Moreover, synonymous to *g'y* is *rwm* 'to be high' (Isa 2:12; Jer 48:29), present in 15:2 (*'ărōməmenhû* 'I elevate him') and perhaps anticipated by *rāmâ* 'he hurled' (15:1).

Exod 15:1b–18 features many verbs connoting elevation and depression, rising and falling (L. Garber, privately). Egypt descends—literally from shore to Sea to underworld, metaphorically from glory to ignominy—while Israel ascends—from slavery, Egypt and the Sea to secure habitation on Yahweh's mountain. The more imaginative reader might feel the up and down of the Sea's waves (see also NOTES to 15:7 "uprisers," 15:8 "streams").

Horse and his driver. These are poetic collectives, or rather personifications (Luzzatto). The sense is "horses and *their* drivers" (Syr). (On the chariot as emblematic of Israel's enemies, see NOTE to 14:25.)

The traditional English rendering of *rōkəbô*, "his *rider*," is probably inaccurate. While the Egyptians occasionally used mounted horsemen as scouts as far back as the fifteenth century, the horse was used primarily for drawing chariotry until the ninth century (Schulman 1957), as in the prose accounts of Exodus. A *rōkēb* (literally, "one who mounts" [Moran 1962: 323–27]) must therefore be a "driver." The term may be elliptical; Kloos (1986: 128) observes that in Egyptian, too, to "mount a horse" can connote boarding a chariot.

To be sure, some date the Song after the ninth century and regard *rōkēb*, understood as "rider," as a naive anachronism. Brenner (1991: 82–84), for example, insists that *rōkēb* must be a rider, since the verse implies a one-to-one correspondence between horse and *rōkēb*, whereas a chariot is drawn by several horses. To this there are several possible responses. First, to stoop to Brenner's level of literalism and lower still: the text says "horse and his *rōkēb*," not "*rōkēb* and his horse"; i.e., each chariot-horse has only one driver, even if the opposite is not true. More important, the root *rkb* refers to mounting a chariot in Gen 41:43; 1 Kgs 18:45; 2 Kgs 9:16; 10:16; Hab 3:8; 2 Chr 35:24. Why, after all, would a chariot be called *rekeb/merkābâ*, if not because one *rkb*-ed in or onto it? In fact, *rōkēb* can denote a charioteer as well as a mounted rider (Jer 17:25 = 22:4; 51:21; Hag 2:22). (Brenner's interpretation can also be obviated by emending *rōkəbô* 'his rider/driver' to **rikbô/rekeb* '[his] chariotry' [see TEXTUAL NOTE].)

hurled. This must be meant figuratively. Yahweh did not bodily cast the Egyptians into the waters (*pace* Cross 1973: 132, who thinks the chariots fell from barges!). Rather, he fanned the Egyptians' native aggressivity, so that they entered the Sea and drowned. "Hurled" simply indicates that Yahweh was behind it all (cf. 14:17 [P]).

Although Hebrew *rmy* here must mean "throw," as in Arabic, Akkadian and Aramaic, otherwise it means "shoot" (Jer 4:29; Ps 78:9). Ibn Ezra therefore understands that Yahweh actually "shot" Egypt into the Sea. God is elsewhere described as an archer (Hab 3:9, 11; Zech 9:14; Ps 144:6) directing his missiles against the hostile Sea (2 Sam 22:15) (compare also *Enūma eliš* IV:101). In light of other similarities between 15:1b–18 and myths of divine combat, I would detect a variation upon a mythic motif: instead of subduing the Sea by shooting arrows into it, Yahweh subdues Egypt by shooting Egypt itself into the Sea (see NOTES to 15:4 "cast" and 15:7 "anger"; COMMENT, p. 560). We might also assimilate the Egyptians, not to arrows, but to slingstones, since they are compared to stones in vv 5, 16 (cf. Calvin; on [hail]stones as divine weapons, see 9:22–34; Josh 10:11; Ezek 38:22, etc.).

Rmy evokes still other images. The Akkadian cognate *ramû* can mean "lay a foundation," and, though still unattested for Hebrew, such a connotation would chime with nearby terms related to throwing and/or building (*rōmēm, yārâ, ṭābaʿ*) (see NOTES to 15:1, 2, 4). One could even perceive an allusion to *rimmâ* 'delude': "horse and his driver he *tricked* in(to) the Sea" (for the pun, cf. Hos 7:16; Ps 78:57; 120:3–4, *qešet rəmiyyâ* 'bow of deceit/shooting').

Above we noted the alliteration of *rōkəbô rāmâ* 'his driver he hurled,' echoing *gāʾô(h) gāʾâ* 'he acted exaltedly, exaltedly.' There is also a degree of vocalic assonance in *rāmâ bayyām* 'he hurled into the Sea' (cf. NOTE to 15:4 "cast"). At a greater remove, Watts (1992: 46) perceives play between *rāmâ bayyām* and *bəyād rāmâ* 'with raised arm' (14:8).

into the Sea. So familiar is the line, we scarce notice the paradox: *sailors* drown in the sea; *charioteers* should die on *land*. Moreover, one generally hurls a rider from his horse or chariot; one does not throw down horse and rider together (Rashi). The bizarreness underscores the wonder of Yahweh's salvation and raises the question answered by stanza II. What really happened?

15:2. *strength and . . . power/music.* This verse is extremely difficult and possibly corrupt (see TEXTUAL NOTE). It reappears almost *verbatim* in Isa 12:2 and Ps 118:14, both times in the context of praising Yahweh. Perhaps the line had an independent existence (cf. Cross 1973: 127 n. 49). But more likely, it is original to one of the works—probably Exod 15:1b–18—and the other two are quoting.

Here my concern is with the nouns *ʿōz* and *zimrâ*. Both are well attested; the former means "strength" and the latter "music," hence KJV "my strength and my song." That Yahweh should be one's "strength" is not surprising. But can he be "music" or a "song"? Perhaps the sense is "Yah is the *subject* of my song" (cf. Syr, "Yah is mighty and *praiseworthy*"). In fact, by a sort of metonymy, a song's subject can be the song itself. We often find God himself or his attributes as the direct objects of "sing" (Isa 12:5; Ps 21:14; 30:13; 47:7; 57:10; 59:17; 89:2; 108:4; 138:1; 147:1; the classical parallel is Virgil's *arma virumque cano* 'I sing weapons and the man'). Compare, too, "I have become their song (*nəgînātām*)" (Job 30:9; Lam 3:14; cf. Lam 3:63).

But, if so, how does "my song" comport with *ʿuzzî* 'my strength'? Is the point that "Yah is the source of my strength; therefore I sing of him"? Or is it that "Yah's strength is the subject of my song" (Good 1970; cf. Kloos 1986: 32–36 on Ps 29:1)? Or does the singer attribute both his martial and his artistic prowess to God? Perhaps he exclaims that Yahweh possesses a strength, like poetry, to cheer and transport the soul. Most intriguing is a special connotation of *ʿōz* 'strength' as a form of praise possibly sung or danced (2 Sam 6:14; Ps 29:1; 68:33, 35; 1 Chr 13:8; 2 Chr 30:21). Psalms 29; 68:33–36 imply that, when worshipers give Yahweh the *ʿōz* he inherently possesses, he returns *ʿōz* to them. But how might a word properly referring to strength come to describe music? One immediately thinks of *loud* music, but Biblical Hebrew does not otherwise use the root *ʿzz* in this manner. Perhaps *ʿōz* means "that which strengthens or rouses," a typical function of music. Or *ʿōz* might connote a hymn *about strength* (cf. Good 1970; Kloos 1986: 32–36). Seale (1974: 175, 201), however, suggests a nuance of "honor, glory, pride," comparing the extended meanings of Arabic *ʿizz* 'strength.'

On the other hand, Loewenstamm (1969a) argues that *zimrâ*, too, connotes "glory." Luxury trade items, he notes, are called a land's *zimrâ* (Gen 43:11)—not its "song," but its "glory" or "fame." He compares *təhillâ*, which can be a hymn of praise, Yahweh's glory or the glory Yahweh gives his adorants. A still better analogy would be *kābôd*, connoting glory, natural splendor, luxury exports and wealth, especially in late Biblical Hebrew (Isa 66:12; Eccl 6:2; Esth 5:11; 1 Chr 29:12, 28; 2 Chr 1:11, 12; 17:5; 18:1; 32:27). *Kābôd* is also associated with *šyr*/*zmr* 'sing' (Ps 30:13; 57:8–9; 66:2) and like *ʾōz* is rendered in tribute to Yahweh (Josh 7:19; Jer 13:16; Mal 2:2; Ps 29:1–2; Ps 63:3; 66:2; 96:7–8; 115:1; 145:11; 149:5). Comparable to Exod 15:2, Ps 62:8 calls Yahweh "my salvation and my *kābôd*, the rock of my strength." In short, "strength" and "song" are not as semantically distant as it might seem.

Nevertheless, most scholars now associate *zimrâ* in 15:2, not with song, but with a Semitic root *ḏmr* 'to be strong' (e.g., KB; Gaster 1936–37; Parker 1971; Barré 1992). We find probable derivatives in Arabic *ḏimr* 'courageous, capable man'; Ugaritic *ḏmr* 'strength, warrior' and Baal's epithet *ḏmrn*; note, too, the epigraphic Hebrew names *bʿlzmr* (AHI 3.012.2–3 [Samaria]) and *zmryhw* (AHI 100.054.2–3 [Egypt]) (Barré 1992: 626). The last is semantically identical to 15:2, "My . . . *zimrâ* is Yah." Other relevant names are Hebrew Zimri, Ugaritic *ḏmrbʿl* and *ḏmr(h)d* (RSP 3.499–500) and such Amorite names as Zimri-Lim 'My *zimru* is [the god] Lim.' Old South Arabic parallels have also been proposed, and, while some are dubious (Loewenstamm 1969a; Blau 1977: 82–83 n. 54), the evidence from personal names remains pertinent (Barré 1992: 626). And *zimrâ* may describe Yahweh again in 2 Sam 23:1; while the conventional interpretation of *nəʿîm zəmîrôt yiśrāʾēl* as "Israel's sweet singer" is not impossible, and while others translate "singer (cf. Arabic *nǧm*) of Israel's songs," Barré (1992: 627–28) is the latest to emend *zmrwt* to **zmrt* and interpret, "the Favorite of Israel's Strength/Strong One."

'Ōz and *zimrâ* together appear to constitute an Old Canaanite cliché. We find them again in *KTU* 1.108.21–22, 24, first in parallel and then in sequence (Loewenstamm 1969a). To Exod 15:2, compare in particular *KTU* 1.108.24: *'zk.dmrk* 'your *'z*, your *dmr*.' The singer seems to be praying that a god's attributes of *'z* and *dmr*, both probably connoting strength, will abide forever in Ugarit. (In l. 3 of the same tablet, however, *dmr* refers to musical performance.)

Accordingly, we should probably render *zimrāt(î)* in Exod 15:2 as "my power" or "my protection" (cf. LXX *skepastēs* 'refuge'); for other passages acclaiming Yahweh as "my strength, shield, aid," etc., see Muilenburg (1966: 240). Some, however, think that *zimrâ* has a more specific connotation of "stronghold" and take *'ōz wazimrâ* as hendiadys (e.g., Watson 1984: 325), hence Freedman's (1980: 195) "mighty fortress." Still, the considerable merits of this new interpretation notwithstanding, we should not be deaf to the pun with *zmr* 'sing' (cf. Herzberg 1979: 31–37). By the fullest interpretation, Yahweh is *both* the poet's defense and the subject of his song. In fact, God's name is the dominant theme of 15:1b–18.

Exod 15:2 is notable for sound play. First, we hear minor assonance in the repetition of zayin: *'ozzî wazimrāt(î)*. In this context, moreover, *'zz* 'be strong' evokes *'wz* 'shelter,' with which it is often confused. And the roots *'zz* and *zmr* together suggest a third term, equally apposite: *'zr* 'help, be powerful' (cf. *Mek. šîratā'* 3); compare Ps 118:13b–14: *wayahwe(h) 'azārānî 'ozzî wazimrāt* 'And Yahweh helped me; my strength and power/music. . . .'"

is. Or "was" or "will be," depending on how one takes the following *wyhy* (see below).

Yah. Yāh is evidently a short form of *yahwe(h)* (see APPENDIX C, vol. II).

was for me as salvation. In the narrative context, one most naturally renders *wyhy* as "and he became." But, given the fluid tenses and moods of poetry, we cannot exclude "he will become," "he [always] becomes" or "may he [ever] become" (cf. Syr Isa 12:2). To "become as a salvation" means to succor (Kloos 1986: 127); apart from Isa 12:2; Ps 118:14, the expression is paralleled in 2 Sam 10:11; Ps 118:21; cf. Job 13:16.

Arguably, this colon intensifies its predecessor. Not only is Yahweh a reliable source of power, but he grants victories.

This. As the sound *z* is relatively uncommon elsewhere in the poem, there is a phonetic connection with 15:2a: *'ozzî wazimrāt(î) . . . ze(h)*.

my god. The assertion "this is my god" raises several questions (see Eissfeldt 1945–48). First, to whom does "my" refer? Moses is one possibility. But I think rather of each individual Israelite (Eissfeldt pp. 7–8) or of Israel as a personified collective. Second, is Yahweh exclusively "*my* god" and no one else's? If we understand the singer to be all Israel, there is no problem; Yahweh is Israel's particular deity. The phrase "my god" has connotations of intimacy and protection (Vorländer 1975). Although Yahweh is the mightiest god (15:11), each

Israelite, and Israel *en masse*, are under his constant care. And, as Israel belongs to Yahweh, so Yahweh belongs to Israel.

What is the logical connection of "this is my god" to what precedes and follows? Presumably, the train of thought in v 2 is something like this: inasmuch as Yahweh has saved me, he has proved himself my personal god, worthy of my praise, just as he earned my ancestors' adoration (cf. Bekhor Shor).

exalt. '*Anwēhû* is a crux. Some compare Hebrew *n*'*y/nwy* 'to be beautiful' (Rashi; Rashbam; Foresti 1982: 43) and Ugaritic *šnwy* 'adorn' (Dahood 1978). Others invoke Arabic *nwy* 'intend' (Cross and Freedman 1975: 56) or Hebrew *nāwe(h)* 'pasture/camp/tent' (*Tg. Onqelos*). I, however, follow LXX, Syr and Vg, taking '*anwēhû* to connote praise. Compare Ps 118:28: '*ēlî* '*attâ* wə'*ôdekkā* / '*ĕlōhay* '*ărômamekkā* 'You are my god, and I praise you; my deity—I elevate you' (Brenner 1991: 68).

The verb '*anwēhû* is probably derived, not from *nwy*, but from *nwh* 'to be high' (admittedly, we would expect **'nwhhw*, not '*nwhw*). *Nwh* is attested in Arabic (Cassuto 1967: 174) and perhaps Hebrew *nōah* 'eminence' (Ezek 7:11 [MT]; but see Greenberg 1983a: 149). Arabic *nawwaha* means "to raise, elevate, acclaim, mention," all well suited to our context. By this analysis, '*nwhw* is an exact synonym for '*ărômamenhû* 'I elevate him' (< *rwm* 'be high'). It might be either Hiph'il or Pi'el.

There still remains an association by paronomasia, if not etymology, with *nāwe(h)* 'pasture/camp/tent' (v 13) (Cassuto 1967: 176). The fullest interpretation is that one exalts (*nwh*) Yahweh by building, beautifying and frequenting his *nāwe(h)* (note, too, that the parallel *rōmēm* 'elevate' also means "build" [Avishur 1981; see below]).

Exod 15:2b features repetition of the sequence *w*' beginning the last word of each colon (Brenner 1991: 28): *zh* '*ly* w'*nwhw* / '*lhy* '*by* w'*rmmnhw* (but see TEXTUAL NOTE). Also, as throughout the poem, the clustering of pronominal suffixes in 15:2b creates "poor" rhyme: '*anwēhû* . . . '*ărômamenhû* (see Alonso-Schökel 1988: 23–24).

My father's deity. Note the intensification within the bicolon: not only is Yahweh "my god," he was also "my father's deity." On '*ĕlōhê* '*ābî*, a pregnant expression in a patriarchal-tribal society, see Alt (1968: 3–100) and Cross (1973: 3–12). The "I" implicit in "my father" is probably not Moses (*pace* Dillmann 1880: 155; Jacob 1992: 427), but each individual Israelite or collective Israel (cf. Sforno). "Father" is in any case collective, referring to ancestors in general (Luzzatto)—including, for later readers, all the generations between the Exodus and themselves. The prose narratives also emphasize the identity of the god of the Exodus and the ancestral deity (2:24; 3:6, 15, 16; 4:5; 6:3).

I elevate. Like '*nwhw* 'I exalt,' '*ărômamenhû* refers primarily to elevation but has connotations of building in both Hebrew (Ezra 9:9) and Ugaritic (*KTU* [1.1.iii.27]; 2.iii.7, 9, 10 [?]; 4.v.52, 54, vi.17) (Avishur 1981). Yahweh has acted exaltedly for Israel (*g*'*y*, 15:1), and the poet reciprocally exalts him, both by singing and, implicitly, by building him a house (v 17). The root *rwm* 'be high' resonates in sound and sense with its quasi-opposite *rmy* 'hurl (down)' (15:1); see NOTE.

15:3. *Yahweh Man of War . . . name.* The image of Deity as a warrior defeating vast armies is common in biblical and ancient Near Eastern literature. Most evocative of 15:3 is Isa 42:13, comparing Yahweh to *'îš milḥāmôt* 'a man of wars.' One of God's most common epithets is *yahwe(h) ṣəbā'ōt*, probably meaning "Yahweh of Brigades." Sometimes God is said to battle alongside Israel (Deut 20:1–4; Josh 10:8–11; 23:9, 14; Judg 4:14 [cf. 5:20]; 2 Sam 5:24). But at the Sea he fights alone; the Hebrews need only stand and watch (14:14 [cf. also Josh 24:12]). Plastaras (1966: 191) calls this "the purest ideal of the holy war." In naming him "Yahweh Man of War" (15:3), the Song suggests that at the Sea Yahweh was fully manifest in his bellicose aspect. For further discussion of Yahweh as fighter, see Fredriksson (1945), Cross (1973: 91–111), Miller (1973), Weinfeld (1983), Kang (1989) and COMMENT.

Exod 15:3 is somewhat enigmatic in grammar and relation to context. It is generally translated, "Yahweh *is* a man of war; Yahweh *is* his name." But "Yahweh is his name" is flat and meaningless, unless the preceding colon tells us something *about* Yahweh's name. Compare: "as his name, so is he; Nabal is his name, and vice (*nəbālâ*) is with him" (1 Sam 25:25); "Yahweh the Zealous is his name; he is a zealous god" (Exod 34:14).

Hos 12:6 paraphrases or parallels Exod 15:3 particularly closely: *wəyahwe(h) 'ĕlōhê haṣṣəbā'ôt yahwe(h) zikrô* 'Yahweh the Deity of the Brigades, Yahweh is his name' (cf. Brenner 1991: 78). This in turn recalls the prophetic refrain *yahwe(h) ṣəbā'ôt šmô* 'Yahweh of Brigades is his name' (Isa 48:2; Jer 10:16; Amos 4:13, etc.). If "Yahweh the Deity of the Brigades, Yahweh is his name" is the equivalent of "Yahweh of Brigades is his name," then "Yahweh Man of War, Yahweh is his name" might simply mean "Yahweh Man of War is his name" (cf. Ehrlich 1908: 319–20). For the title, compare Ps 24:8, 10: "Yahweh the Mighty, the Hero [i.e., the Mighty Hero]; Yahweh the Hero of War . . . Yahweh of Brigades."

If the sense of 15:3 is "Yahweh Man of War is his name," what is the function in the larger context? Freedman (1980: 195) proffers "Yahweh—that man of war / Whose name is Yahweh / Pharaoh's chariot army / He cast into the Sea." I, however, would rather link v 3 with v 2. While often simply affirming a theological statement, the formula "Yahweh of Brigades is his name" sometimes seems tantamount to "none other than Yahweh," qualifying a *preceding* statement (Isa 47:4; 51:15; 54:5; Jer 31:35; 50:34; 51:19; Amos 4:13). Similarly, we could paraphrase Exod 15:2–4: "This is my god, whom I exalt . . . *none other than* Yahweh Man of War, who cast Pharaoh's chariots and his force into the Sea." (Alternatively: the proclamation of God's name (v 3) might be a subquotation, the praise mentioned in v 2 ["exalt . . . elevate"].)

Exod 15:3 does not merely reveal another title of God. *Šēm* 'name' also has the nuance of "fame" (cf. Gen 11:4; 12:2; 2 Sam 7:9, etc.). Yahweh's epithets are the means by which his reputation is spread and his nature expressed. Compare Isa 42:8: "I am Yahweh, that is my name; I will give my honor to none other, nor my glory to idols." Thus a condensation of 15:2–4 might be "I praise Yahweh, famous as the sole warrior who defeated Egypt."

For Israelites, Yahweh's "name" is more than the sound "Yah-weh" or the grapheme *yhwh*. It has special powers and is a quasi-independent entity. The Book of Deuteronomy and related works emphasize that Yahweh's "name," not Yahweh himself, resides in the Temple (McBride 1969; Weinfeld 1972: 193–98). Yahweh's "name" can also function as a talismanic weapon wielded by humans or God (1 Sam 17:45; Hos 1:7; Ps 20:8; cf. *Mek. šîrātā'* 4). The Covenant Ark, associated with the title "Yahweh of Brigades, Enthroned upon the Cherubim," may also have been called God's "name" (2 Sam 6:2; 2 Chr 13:6).

As for stichometry, although 15:3 seems at first a monocolon, my translation treats it as the conclusion of a tricolon (vv 2b–3). Taken alone, 15:3 somewhat resembles the three "staircase" bi-/tricola later in the poem (15:6, 11, 16). Like them, it begins each half-utterance with the same word and completes the thought only in the second part (see NOTE to 15:6). And all four examples feature prominently the name "Yahweh," otherwise absent in vv 3–16. But v 3 is much shorter than the others and does not employ the vocative (cf. Freedman 1980: 189). It seems too brief to stand alone.

Lastly, we should note sound play in v 3: the repeated cluster *šm* after the divine name. In reconstructed Israelite pronunciation, v 3 would sound like **yahwi 'iš malḥama yahwi šmuh* (running together *yahwi 'iš* as *yahwiš* heightens the effect).

15:4. *Pharaoh's chariots and his force.* Cross and Freedman (1975: 56) convey Albright's suggestion that this unwieldy phrase conflates variants "Pharaoh's chariots" and "Pharaoh and his force" (also Cross 1973: 127 n. 54). Freedman (1980: 203), however, now upholds MT. At issue is whether the phrase has too many syllables and hence disturbs metrical symmetry. But this is a problem only if we insist upon short cola:

Pharaoh's chariots and his force (8 syllables; 5 stresses)
He cast in the Sea. (4 syllables; 2 stresses)
And the choice of his *thirds* (6 syllables; 2 stresses)
Were sunk in the Suph Sea. (5–6 syllables [see TEXTUAL NOTE];
      2–3 stresses)

I, however, simply analyze v 4 as two long cola of 12 syllables each (or 12 : 11); see also NOTE to 15:15.

cast. The Egyptians are probably not literally thrown from the surface into the depths (*pace* Cross 1973: 132). Rather, they move from the seashore into the Sea or perhaps the seabed. It is not even certain that the primary meaning of *yārâ* here is "cast." As with *rāmâ* in v 1, ibn Ezra proffers a translation "shot" (see NOTES to vv 1 "hurled" and 7 "consumes"). And *yārâ* can also refer to laying a foundation, i.e., sinking something into the ground (see also NOTES to 15:1, 4). Arguably, then, v 4 anticipates both v 12, where the earth (i.e., the ocean floor) swallows Egypt (Jacob 1992: 427–28), and v 17, where Yahweh founds his habitation.

As we observed for the synonymous *rāmâ bayyām* (v 1), there is vocalic assonance in *yārâ bayyām* 'he cast into the Sea.'

thirds. On *šālīš* as a type of warrior, see NOTE to 14:7.

sunk. We are uncertain whether the correct reading is "were sunk" or "he sank" (see TEXTUAL NOTE). Moreover, it is not quite clear that the root *ṭbʿ* refers to sinking in water. In Biblical Hebrew, *ṭbʿ* otherwise connotes descending into the ground (Luzzatto; Jacob 1992: 427–28), while the Arabic cognate refers to imprinting. One might therefore infer that the Egyptians are *mired* in the Suph Sea bed (so Jacob; Luzzatto's reading is somewhat different); cf. Ps 69:3, 15–16. As we have observed, one could assign a similar meaning to *rāmâ* and *yārâ* in vv 1, 4 (see NOTES); in fact, *yry* parallels *ṭbʿ* in Job 38:6. Still, the context clearly favors the traditional understanding. *Ṭbʿ(w)* 'were sunk/he sank' may simply be an archaism, for the basic meaning of Semitic **ṭbʿ* does appear to be "to sink (in liquid)." Both Akkadian *ṭebû* and Ethiopic *ṭmʿ* refer to immersion, while Aramaic *ṭbʿ* means "sink (in water)" as well as "imprint." (Arabic presumably borrowed the connotation "imprint" from Aramaic, along with Persian-period coinage.)

Exod 15:4b lends specificity and emphasis to v 4a: "Pharaoh's chariots and his force" become the elite "choice of his *thirds*." The relatively vague *yry* 'cast' becomes the more precise *ṭbʿ* 'sink.'

15:5. *Deeps . . . depths*. The synonymous and rhyming nouns *təhōmōt . . . məṣôlōt* 'deeps . . . depths' frame the alliterative and rhyming verbs *yəkasyūmû yārədû* 'cover them; they went down.' The overall effect is chiastic: "(A) Deeps, (B) they cover them; (B′) they went down (A′) in the depths." The plural number in *təhōmōt, məṣôlōt* 'deeps, depths' conveys grandeur and complexity; compare the cliché *mayim rabbîm* 'many waters.'

cover. The third masculine plural suffix *-mû* in *yəkasyūmû* 'cover them' is unparalleled. Elsewhere we find *-m* or, occasionally, *-mô*. To explain the anomaly, Ewald (*apud* Dillmann 1880: 156) plausibly cites assimilation to the preceding *ū* vowel: *-ūmō* > *-ūmū*. Since the standard Biblical Hebrew form would be *yəkassûm*, *yəkasyūmû* is triply archaic/archaistic: the *-mû* suffix, the preservation of the third radical *y* and the defective spelling of *ū*. Note that, while the subject "deeps" is feminine, the verb is masculine—a typical case of incongruence (Levi 1987).

stone. On the possibility that the Egyptians are likened to slingstones or foundation stones, see NOTES to 15:1 "hurled," 15:4 "cast," "sunk" and 15:6 "crosses."

15:6. *Yahweh*. "Staircase" parallelism (also called "climactic" parallelism) is found occasionally in Hebrew poetry, more often in Ugaritic poetry (Watson 1984: 150–56). Such bi- or tricola typically begin a sentence, interject a vocative and then restart, completing the utterance in the parallel colon or cola (see further below).

strong in might. Cross and Freedman (1975: 59) translate *ne'dārî* as "fearsome," comparing Akkadian *adāru* 'to fear.' I rather regard *ne'dārî* as referring to strength, as elsewhere in Hebrew and Ugaritic. Note, too, the paraphrase in Isa 43:16; Neh 9:11: *mayim 'azzîm* 'strong waters.'

Luzzatto raises a third possibility, remote but deserving mention. He takes *'dr* as a variant of *'zr* 'gird' (cf. *ndr/nzr* 'vow'), comparing the garment called *'adderet* 'mantle.' He accordingly translates *ne'dārî bakkōah* as "girt with might," synonymous to *ne'zār bigbûrâ* (Ps 65:7; cf. also Isa 51:9; Ps 18:33, 40; 93:1). Luzzatto's theory works for 15:11, too (see NOTE). (In 15:10, however, he affirms the traditional understanding of *mayim 'addîrîm* as "strong waters," rather than "enveloping waters" or the like.)

The syntactic structure of v 6 is subject to debate. Most take *ne'dārî* 'strong' as predicative, seeing in v 6 two complete sentences: "Your right hand . . . is strong. Your right hand . . . shatters" (e.g., KJV; Jacob 1992: 428–29). Various objections have been raised, however. First, *ne'dārî* appears to be a masculine participle, whereas Yahweh's right hand is grammatically feminine (ibn Ezra [tentatively]; Rashbam; Driver 1911: 134; Cross and Freedman 1975: 59). But gender incongruence is common in Hebrew (Levi 1987), and, although *ne'dārî* is traditionally classified as a Niph'al participle plus *hireq compaginis* (a fossilized case ending), Moran (1961: 60) suggests that many such forms are in fact infinitives absolute. These may replace finite verbs, imperatives and, rarely, participles (Waltke and O'Connor 1990: 597, §35.5.3). If so, *n'dry* is probably to be vocalized *ne'dōrî* and would be genderless.

A more important objection is that, in comparable "staircase" structures, the entire bi- or tricolon forms a single, interrupted sentence (e.g., Ps 92:10; 93:3; 94:3; Prov 31:4; Cant 4:8) (Rashbam; see also Loewenstamm 1969b). Although in some examples, such as Exod 15:6, 11, 16b; Isa 26:15, the first colon bears construal as an independent clause upon first hearing, the thought is still incomplete until the following colon ends (Greenstein 1974). In 15:6, thus, we should take "strong" as an attributive adjective modifying either "Yahweh" or "your right hand," leaving the sentence incomplete until the next colon. In fact, Robertson (1969) has shown that, in twenty-nine of thirty-three cases, *hireq compaginis* is affixed to a noun or adjective in apposition, not in a predicate. The implication, again, is that 15:6 forms a single sentence (so RSV, NJV). See also next NOTE.

Your right hand . . . you shatter. Because the verb *tir'as* (< *r's* 'shatter') might be either second person masculine singular or third feminine singular, we are uncertain whether its subject is Yahweh (m.) or his hand (f.)—a fine point, admittedly. If the corresponding element in the previous colon, *ne'dārî*, refers to Yahweh, we should probably take the verb in v 6b as likewise addressed to Yahweh (Dahood 1972: 394–95; Freedman 1980: 188). This would also enhance the grammatical parallelism with vv 7–8, where the verbs are unambiguously 2 m.s. But we really need not choose. "Your right hand . . . you shatter/it shatters" is a construction analogous to "My name Yahweh I/it was not known to them" (6:3). That is, a verb may agree with the pronominal suffix on an inalienable attribute such as a body part; see NOTES to 6:3 and 32:29.

Grammar aside, there is some question as to the image evoked by 15:6. While one might think of Yahweh *pummeling* the enemy, Lohfink (1968: 76) argues, on the basis of ancient Near Eastern iconography, that Yahweh's hand implicitly holds a *weapon*. God is a soldier, not a brawler.

In 15:6–8, nouns with the 2 m.s. suffix -*kā* cluster, creating a rhyming pattern across the (likely) stanza break: *yəmînəkā* . . . *yəmînəkā* . . . *gə'ônəkā* . . . *qāme(y)kā* . . . *ḥărōnəkā* . . . *'appe(y)kā*. We should also observe the alliteration of the repeated *yəmînəkā yahwe(h)* 'Your right hand, Yahweh.'

enemy. "Enemy" is most likely Egypt (note the parallelism with the plural "uprisers," i.e., foes). But we cannot exclude the possibility that the referent is Pharaoh.

15:7. *in.* My translation assumes that the preposition *bə-* expresses manner. We could also take the beth as instrumental: "*through* your pride's greatness."

pride's. Gə'ônəkā echoes *gā'ô(h) gā'â* 'he acted exaltedly, exaltedly' (Cassuto 1967: 175). *Pace* Luzzatto, *gā'ôn* is unlikely to connote "irresistible might." Rather, it is the absolute self-esteem appropriate to a god. In a human, *gā'ôn* is essentially *hybris*, in both Hebrew (Isa 16:6 = Jer 48:29; Ezek 7:20; 16:49; Zeph 2:10; Ps 59:13; Prov 8:13; 16:18; Job 35:12) and Ugaritic, where it parallels *pš'* 'sin' (*KTU* 1.17.vi.44).

uprisers. Qāmîm, literally "those who stand up," are enemies. This relatively rare term contributes to the "up-down" theme of the poem: those who rise up are thrown down (see also NOTES to 15:1 "exaltedly, exaltedly," 15:8 "streams" and 15:17 "your property mountain"). Although the immediate referents are Egyptian soldiers, Lichtenstein (1984: 110) finds an allusion to Yahweh's foes in general (see below).

release. The verb *šillaḥ* generally connotes letting go that which is pent up. Here it implies the mounting pressure of Yahweh's wrath.

anger. Freedman (1980: 204) notes the use of rhyme: Yahweh's two attributes are *gə'ônəkā* 'your pride' and *ḥărônəkā* 'your anger,' together connoting high dudgeon.

While the verb *ḥry* 'be angry' describes either human or divine wrath, the derived noun *ḥārôn* is reserved for Yahweh's anger. The original meaning of *ḥry* is perhaps "to burn," assuming it is a variant of *ḥrr* 'to be burnt' (Luzzatto; for semantic parallels, see Waldman 1975: 45). But *ḥry* may simply mean "to rage" (see NOTE to 4:14).

consumes. The comparison of Yahweh's fury to a conflagration may be the source of a later, multiform tradition that the Egyptians encountered divine fire in the Sea (Wis 19:20; Artapanus *apud* Eusebius *Praep. evangelica* 9.27.37; *Memar Marqah* 2:3, 8, etc. [MacDonald 1963: 1.32, 41; 2.49, 64]). *Tg.* Neofiti I, taking *yārâ* in 15:4 as "shot," has angels shooting fiery arrows at Egypt (cf. 2 Sam 22:14–16; 77:18–19; see NOTES to 15:1 "hurled" and 15:4 "cast"). Similarly, according to Ezekiel the Tragedian 234, at the Sea fiery radiance descended from heaven. *Memar Marqah* 2:5 (MacDonald 1.36; 2.55), associating 15:7

and 8, supposes that, in addition to wind, fire dried the Sea (cf. Amos 7:4 and *Iliad* 21:333–82). And Rev 15:2 describes the chanting of the "song of Moses, God's servant" by a sea of mingled glass and fire (see Loewenstamm 1992a: 273–76). These are all survivals of an ancient, mythic motif of divine fire at the Suph Sea (see COMMENT).

The image of the *drowning* Egyptians also metaphorically *burning* may seem somewhat incongruous. In Isa 43:17, possibly based upon the Song (cf. Exod 15:1, 4), enemies "smolder, go out like a flax [wick]" in the Sea—but here, burning is life, extinguishing is death. For Lichtenstein (1984: 110), the incongruity of burning in the Sea proves that the objects of Yahweh's ire are *all* his potential enemies, not just the Egyptians. This is an overinterpretation. Fire and water together constitute a cliché for destruction, danger and testing (e.g., Isa 43:2). Fire and water also appear as purifying agents (Num 31:23; Ps 66:12) (see COMMENT; Norin 1977: 124–25), and God's super-hot flames can overcome water (1 Kgs 18:38). In any case, since in 15:7 the fire is only symbolic, at worst we have a mildly mixed metaphor.

SPECULATION: Below, I shall suggest that Yahweh *freezes* the Sea (NOTE to v 8 "congealed"). If so, the reference to Yahweh's *burning* anger in v 7 becomes more appropriate. Yahweh's first blast turns the Deeps to ice. His second (v 10) melts the gelid waters.

straw. Straw serves two functions in biblical imagery. It is either windblown (Isa 17:13; 40:24; Jer 13:24, etc.) or ignited (Isa 1:31; 5:24; 33:11, etc.). The later sense is primary in v 7: Yahweh's anger burns up the enemy like straw. But the very mention of straw evokes the wind (*rûaḥ*), which in the next verse inflates the Sea and in v 10 kills the Egyptians. Compare Isa 17:13, which associates the recession of the Sea with windblown chaff and the defeat of enemies. Exod 15:7 and 10 are also connected by thematic antithesis: straw and lead are the respective quintessences of lightness and heaviness (see NOTE to 15:10). In addition, we might detect a contrast between the straw of v 7 and the vegetation of v 17: the Egyptians are mere chaff, whereas Israel will be securely planted (cf. Ps 1:3–4).

15:8. *with your nostrils' breath.* 'Appayim 'nostrils, face' is the dual of 'ap 'nose.' Since 'ap has the further connotation of "anger" (snorting, flaring nostrils), 'appayim resonates with ḥārôn 'anger' (15:7); indeed, ḥārôn and 'ap are often conjoined as ḥārôn 'ap. The "breath" (*rûaḥ*) of Yahweh's nostrils, in mundane terms a mighty wind, is generally a destructive force (2 Sam 22:16; Job 4:9).

With Smend (1912: 143), I discern a stanza break before v 8—despite the fact that the line begins with a conjunction (but see TEXTUAL NOTE), despite the sound play and parallelism linking vv 7 and 8 (*ûb[ə]rōb . . . ûb[ə]rûaḥ*), despite the fact that the image of fire (v 7) goes well with the blast of Yahweh's nose (v 8). For me, the overriding consideration is that the enemies' furious pursuit (v 9) makes no sense unless it occurs *before* Yahweh smashes and kills them (vv 6–7) (this is why *Tg. Onqelos* translates v 9 in the pluperfect). There must be a temporal break before either v 9 or v 8.

My stichometry is guided by the prose account(s): the Egyptians pursue *after* Yahweh dries the waters. It follows that v 8 jumps backward in time and must be connected to v 9 (Rashbam; Ramban; Loewenstamm 1992a: 267; Childs 1970: 411). The unmistakable devices linking vv 7 and 8, therefore, must have been deployed precisely to blur the boundaries between stanzas and temporal settings. Similar phenomena obscure the stanza break between vv 12 and 13 (see NOTES).

SPECULATION: Alternatively, the break may fall in the middle of v 7. If so, v 7a goes with v 6 to form a "staircase" tricolon: "Your right hand, Yahweh, strong in might, / Your right hand, Yahweh, you shatter enemy. / And in your pride's greatness you break down your *uprisers*" (Watson 1984: 151 n. 106). If so, v 7b might describe the consumption not of the enemy, but of the waters (v 8). Or one could argue that v 7b is intentionally ambivalent, in accordance with the Song's overall tendency to equate Egypt and the Sea (see COMMENT).

piled. So LXX, Syr and modern translations. Although a verbal root ʿrm is otherwise unknown in Hebrew, the meaning is clear from the derived noun *ʿărēmâ* '(grain) pile,' from various Semitic cognates (see KB) and from the parallel with "stood like a heap." Perhaps, however, "piled" is not sufficiently specific. We might rather render "dammed," since ʿrm is used of damming in Syriac, Arabic and Sabaean; cf. also Akkadian *arammu* 'wharf, ramp, siege dike' (< *arāmu/erēmu* 'cover') (Hauser 1987: 283 n. 21). If so, Jacob's (1992: 429) observation is well taken: "We now have a surprising paradox, a dam of water rather than one which restrains water!"

There are other possible puns or associations. Since a homophonous root ʿrm means "to be or act craftily," *Tg. Onqelos* renders "the waters became cunning," i.e., they lured the Egyptians. This is rather far-fetched, but allusion to another root, ʿrm/ʿry 'to be naked,' is more believable: the sea bottom was *stripped* of its water (cf. 2 Sam 22:16, "The Sea's channels appear, / The earth's foundations are revealed, / At Yahweh's roar, / From the breath of his nose's wind"). Neʿermû also evokes nʿr 'shake, tumble' in 14:27.

Streams. Like all the Song's terms for water, except *yām* 'sea' itself, *nōzəlîm* is plural, expressing complexity and immeasurability. Compare the formulaic *mayim rabbîm* 'many waters.'

Properly, the root *nzl* means "flow *down*" (cf. Arabic *nazala* 'descend,' Syriac *nazzēl* 'hang down'). Calling sea water *nōzəlîm* is somewhat unexpected, since, unlike rain and river water, sea water cannot be said to descend, unless as wave crests. Presumably, the poet was aiming for alliteration with *niṣṣəbû . . . nēd* 'stood . . . heap' (see below). And we have more paradoxical "up-down" imagery (cf. NOTES to 15:1 "exaltedly, exaltedly," 15:7 "uprisers" and 15:17 "your property mountain"). At Yahweh's blast, *descending* waters (*nōzəlîm*) stand *up (niṣṣəbû)* (*Memar Marqah* 2:3 [MacDonald 1963: 1.34; 2.51]; ibn Ezra). Moreover, just as *nᶜrmw* conjures *nᶜr* 'shake,' *nōzəlîm* evokes *nəzallîm 'shaken' (Judg 5:5 [OG]; Isa 63:19; 64:2 [MT]). One imagines a wind-lashed, quivering wall of water.

stood. The literal meaning of *nṣbw* is confirmed by the paraphrase in Josh 3:13, 16, "the Jordan's waters were cut off . . . and stood (in) one heap (*wayyaᶜamdû nēd ʾeḥād*). . . . The waters descending from above stood (in) one heap (*qāmû nēd ʾeḥād*)." As for why Exod 15:8 uses *niṣṣāb* 'stand, be stationed,' rather than *ᶜmd* or *qwm*, the most obvious answer is for alliteration: *niṣṣəbû kəmô nēd nōzəlîm* 'streams stood like a heap.' The diction may also personify the waters, which stand at attention, awaiting Yahweh's command. (Watts [1992: 46] perceives play with *hityaṣ(ṣə)bû* 'station yourselves' [14:13], but for me this is too remote.) There is also a possible pun with *niṣbû 'were swollen,' although the form is attested only in Rabbinic Hebrew (*y. Soṭa* 20a; cf. Wolters 1990: 228). See also next NOTE.

heap. *Nēd* describes the stationary waters of both the Suph Sea (15:8; Ps 78:13) and the Jordan River (Josh 3:13, 16). In Ps 33:7 (MT), *nēd* seems also to describe the heavenly waters, but here we should probably read *nōd 'waterskin' (OG; cf. Job 38:37). Otherwise, *nēd* appears only in Isa 17:11, where, if the text is not corrupt, it connotes a pile of harvested produce (cf. NOTE to "piled" above). *Nēd* is probably related to *nō(ʾ)d* 'waterskin,' Arabic *nadd* 'hill' and *nhd* 'swell' (Dillmann 1880: 156) and perhaps Akkadian-Ethiopic *nʾd* 'praise' (Albright 1927: 180). For the comparison between a heap and the Sea, cf. *gal* 'mound, wave.'

Like *neᶜermû* and *nōzəlîm*, *nēd* has punning associations with shaking (*nwd/ ndd*). It also, as we have seen, evokes *nō(ʾ)d* 'waterskin,' which various Aramaic and Rabbinic sources read here (Syr; *Tgs. Ps.-Jonathan* and *Neofiti I; Mek. šîrətāʾ* 6; Aramaic paraphrase from the Cairo Genizah [Klein 1986: 245]). While *niṣbû kəmô nōd 'swelled up like a waterskin' is not the original sense (*pace* Wolters 1990: 229–35), there might well be paronomasia or allusion.

congealed. Despite critiques by Albright (1968: 45), Cross and Freedman (1975: 51, 60), Cross (1973: 128–29 n. 59) and Wolters (1990: 237–40), this traditional interpretation of *qāpəʾû* is probably correct (see Kloos 1986: 136–37); after all, it is presupposed by 14:22, 29. Part of the problem is the rarity of *qpʾ*, found in Biblical Hebrew only in 15:8; Zeph 1:12; Zech 14:6; Job 10:10 (also Sir 43:20). But *qpʾ* is more common in Rabbinic Hebrew and Aramaic, where it denotes the formation of solids in liquids (see Cross 1973: 128–29 n. 59). The liquid may predominate—as when solids rise to the surface as scum or ice—hence the extended connotations "float, rise" (cf. Sir 43:20). Alternatively, the solids may predominate, as in the curdling of cheese (Job 10:10). The common denominator is coagulation.

Returning to the biblical attestations, we find that, despite some ambiguities, the translation "congeal, solidify" fits all occurrences. Zeph 1:12 describes complacent drunkards as *qōpəʾîm ᶜal-šimrêhem* 'coagulated together with their lees,' i.e., as thick and slow as goblet sludge. As for Zech 14:6, while the context is obscure, we may read with the Greek *wəqārût wəqippā'ôn* 'and frigidity and rigidity' (cf. MT Qere and Kethibh; for the association of *qp'* with cold, see Sir 43:20 and Modern Hebrew *qp'* 'freeze'). Closest to Rabbinic usage is Job 10:9–11: ". . . You worked me like clay, / And you will return me to dirt; / Do you not pour me like milk, / *Qp'* me like cheese? / You clothe me in skin and flesh; / Cover me with bones and sinews." The image appears to be cheese setting.

In Exod 15:8, too, "congeal" fits well. The poet has been developing a progressively paradoxical and miraculous image: the waters are first piled up (*ne'ermû*), not unusual in a storm, but then they actually stand upright (*niṣṣəbû*)! How? Because some of the waters, the "Deeps," have congealed, presumably into ice (cf. Philo's *krystallōthentos* 'crystallized/frozen' [*Moses* 2.253]). To heighten the miracle, the ice does not float to the surface (cf. Sir 43:20), but remains vertical "in Sea's heart" until melted by Yahweh's second blast (v 10, cf. v 7). Later in the Song, the enemy's petrifaction will parallel the congealing of the waters (see NOTE to 15:16).

SPECULATION: Under COMMENT, we shall see that the Sea event symbolically recapitulates Creation. The congealing of the deep may be an overlooked part of that picture. After all, Zech 14:6, though scarcely intelligible, uses *qp'* in the context of cosmogony.

Congealing might be pertinent to Creation in one of two ways. According to Gen 1:9, the primordial waters simply withdrew to reveal the dry ground. But where did the land come from? Perhaps another version described the solidification of some of the Sea, just as, in the Babylonian *Enūma eliš*, Tiāmat's (Hebrew *təhôm* 'Deep') lower half becomes the solid earth (IV.137–V.62 [ANET³ 67, 501–2; Dalley 1989: 255–57]; see also Berossus *apud* Heidel 1951: 77) (cf. Stern 1989: 418). In some Egyptian cosmogonies, the primeval ocean coagulates to form the first hillock (Assmann 1995: 160 n. 20). And a similar concept existed in India: foam above the primordial waters congealed to form the dry land (Brihadaranyaka Upanishad 1.2.2), a process one text compares to the curdling of cheese (cf. Job 10:9–11) (Thompson 1955: motif A826).

When we think of congealed water, however, we ordinarily envision ice or possibly glass. Perhaps the translucent firmament, the barrier supporting the waters above, was believed to be frozen or crystalline, the product of a primordial "congealing in the Sea's heart" (cf. Exod 24:10; Ezek 1:22; Rev 15:3).

Sea's heart. Sometimes the location of the "Sea's heart" is submarine (Jonah 2:4; Ezek 27:27; 28:8; Ps 46:3). But it can also be at the surface, the location of an island (Ezek 27:4, 25; 28:2) or a ship (Prov 23:34 [?]; 30:19; also EA 114.19; 288.33 [Kloos 1986: 129]). In 15:8, both nuances apply. The frozen water is, miraculously, vertical.

15:9. *Enemy.* This might be Pharaoh (ibn Ezra) or, more likely, Egypt personified (note the plurals in vv 7, 10).

said. V 9 must be a flashback relative to vv 1–7, hence *Tg. Onqelos* "the enemy *had* said." As often, "said" is tantamount to "thought, intended" (Niehoff 1992).

pursue, overtake, Apportion spoil. Since Judg 5:30 also depicts an enemy's premature gloating, Hauser (1987: 276–77) draws the logical if speculative inference that this was a standard feature of victory hymns.

The staccato, alliterative *'erdōp 'aśśîg 'ăḥallēq* 'I'll pursue, overtake, apportion' (following *'āmar 'ōyēb* 'Enemy said') conveys haste, as well as confidence that conquest will be easy (see also NOTE to 2:16). Perhaps the effect is that of panting (cf. Trible's [1984: 40] comments on 2 Sam 13:4). In 15:15, however, *'*aleph alliteration conveys terror.

The first two acts, pursuit (*'erdōp*) and overtaking (*'aśśîg*), are expressed with one word each; the third, plundering, is described with two (*'ăḥallēq šālāl* 'apportion spoil'). From ancient parallels, we might have expected a three-word boast such as **'erdōp 'aśśîg 'āšōl* 'I'll pursue, overtake, despoil'; cf. Akkadian *akšud appul aqqur* 'I conquered, tore down, demolished' (*CAD* 11.i.273), *ašrup appul aqqur* 'I burned, tore down, demolished,' *(arkīšunu) ardud aḥmuṭ urriḥ* 'I pursued, harried, hastened (after them)' (*CAD* 1.ii.222), etc. (There is considerable variety in the formulation, and sometimes there are more than three verbs; see *CAD*.) Note also Ugaritic *ḥšk.ʿṣk.ʿbṣk* 'hurry yourself, press on, make haste' (*KTU* 1.3.iii.18; see Watson 1977: 274). And Luzzatto is one of many to invoke Caesar's *veni vidi vici* 'I came, saw, conquered' (Suetonius 1.37).

Why, then, does the third element in 15:9 contain two words (*'ăḥallēq šālāl*)? Presumably for variety's sake, like the Akkadian variant *appul aqqur ina išāti ašrup* 'I tore down, demolished, burned with fire.' Moreover, the poet needed two words to balance metrically *'erdōp 'aśśîg* 'I'll pursue, overtake.' Lastly, *ḥillēq šālāl* 'divide spoil' is an independent cliché (Gen 49:27; Judg 5:30; Isa 9:2; 53:12; Ps 68:13; Prov 16:19).

My stichometry rejects the traditional versification of Torah scrolls (see Kugel 1981: 119–27), followed by Cross and Freedman (1975: 51) and others, which puts a space after "overtake" and links "I'll apportion spoil" with "my gullet will be full of them." In contrast, the MT cantillation sets the break after "apportion spoil." To me, it makes more sense to analyze v 9 as two tricola, rather than three bicola.

gullet. Hebrew *nepeš,* originally denoting the neck or throat, usually means "soul, person, appetite, self." Luzzatto, Dillmann (1880: 157), Cassuto (1967: 175), Cross and Freedman (1975: 51) and others accordingly interpret: "my *greed* will be sated." O'Connor (1980: 182), however, shows that the reference is to eating, here and in Jer 31:25; Ps 107:9; Prov 6:30; Eccl 6:7. (Bender [1903: 27] also compares Ps 35:25; 41:3.)

Exod 15:9 likens pursuit and plunder to a predator's gorging on a carcass (Calvin). Compare Gen 49:27, "Benjamin, a wolf, ravens; in the morning he *eats plunder,* and by evening he *divides spoil,*" and Prov 1:12–13, "We will, like Sheol, *swallow* them alive. . . . We will fill our houses with *spoil.*" The enemy's intention to devour Israel proves ironic, however. He himself will be eaten, both by Yahweh's wrath (v 7) and by the underworld (v 12) (see also next NOTE). The comparison of the despoiler to a predator also evokes a familiar similitude: Israel is Yahweh's protected flock (see NOTES to 15:13).

will be full of them. Timlā'ēmô is a near-homophone with *tiblā'ēmô* 'swallows them' (15:12), enhancing the above-noted irony of the eater eaten. *Timlā'ēmô* initiates a chain of rhyming verbs running through vv 9–10, 12: *timlā'ēmô . . . tôrîšēmô . . . kissāmô . . . tiblā'ēmô*, all with the archaic/poetic third person masculine plural suffix *-mô* (not the enclitic mem, *pace* Cross and Freedman 1975: 60; contrast Freedman 1980: 207; on enclitic mem, see Hummel 1957).

empty. Exod 15:9 features semantic play between "empty" and "fill" (Ehrlich 1908: 320; Jacob 1992: 430). The idiom *"empty the sword"* is paralleled in Lev 26:33; Ezek 5:2, 12; 12:14; 28:7; 30:11; Hab 1:17 (1QPHab 6:8); cf. also Ps 35:3. The meaning is disputed. For LXX, to *"empty* the sword" is to kill (i.e., to empty the body of life *with* the sword; cf. Durham 1987: 201). Bekhor Shor, however, interprets *hērîq hereb* as "to arm oneself," comparing Gen 14:14, *wayyāreq 'et-hănîkā(y)w* 'and he armed (?) his troops' (so MT; LXX and Sam different). But it is far more likely that the sense is to empty the *scabbard* by extracting the sword (Tgs.); compare the synonymous idiom *pātaḥ ḥereb* 'open the sword' (Ezek 21:33; Ps 37:14). The fluidity of the concepts "blade" and "scabbard" is also evident in the word *ta'ar,* meaning both "knife" and "sheath." Moreover, if *ta'ar* derives from '*ry* 'pour out, empty, make bare,' the usage parallels *hērîq* 'empty' in 15:9.

sword. The enemy metaphorically attacks Israel both with jaws, like an animal, and with sword, like a soldier. The transition scarcely jars; after all, a sword is often said to "eat" its victims (Deut 32:42; 2 Sam 2:26; 11:25, etc.) with its *(pî)piyyôt* 'mouths,' i.e., edges (Judg 3:16; Ps 149:6; Prov 5:4; cf. Isa 41:15).

My hand. This is ultimate *hybris.* The might of *Yahweh's* hand is the theme of the Song and all of Exodus 3–15 (see INTRODUCTION, p. 36; NOTES to 14:30, 31 and 15:12). For *yād* 'hand' as a poetic complement to *ḥereb* 'sword,' cf. Deut 32:41; Isa 49:2; Ezek 39:23; Ps 22:21; 144:10–11; 149:6; Job 5:15; also *KTU* 1.15.iv.24–25; v.7–[8].

dispossess. Tôrîšēmô is polyvalent. Since *yrš* also means "acquire," Cassuto (1967: 175) understands that the Egyptians wish to retake their wayward slaves. But *yrš* is never otherwise used so. Assuming an original spelling **tršmw* (LXX *Vorlage;* see TEXTUAL NOTE), there may, however, be a graphic pun with the roots *ršš* 'beat down' and *ršy* 'master.'

Still, neither of these is the surface meaning. The basic sense of *hôrîš* is "cause to inherit" or "divert an inheritance," hence "dispossess," paralleling "divide spoil." *Hôrîš* specifically connotes dispossession from land (Num 33:53; Josh 13:13, etc.) and/or destruction of posterity (Num 14:12). In the context of the Song, the enemy aims not only to rob Israel of their portable possessions but also to destroy their hope of acquiring and settling Yahweh's *nahălâ* 'property, inheritance,' the holy mountain (v 17).

We have observed alliteration and rhyme throughout vv 9–10, 12. At the end of the foe's speech, we encounter rhyme again in the repeated first person suffix *-î*, perhaps indicative of arrogance: *napšî . . . harbî . . . yādî* 'my gullet . . . my sword . . . my hand.'

15:10. *blew.* I find *two* winds in vv 8 and 10 (*pace* Cross 1973: 131). Having heaped, retained and perhaps frozen the waters with his first breath (v 8), Yahweh brings them back with his second. The prose account, in contrast, does not specify what restores the Sea (see NOTES to 14:21, 26), perhaps because it presupposes the Song.

Nāšaptā 'you blew' puns with *napšî* 'my gullet' (Tournay 1958: 347). The enemy expected to fill his *throat*, but Yahweh instead *blows* him to death.

sank. The verb *ṣll* 'sink' occurs only here in Biblical Hebrew. If Isa 43:16–17 paraphrases the Song, then *ṣll* may be equivalent to *škb* 'lie down.' Akkadian *ṣalālu* in fact means "lie down, sleep," while the Ethiopic cognate means "swim" or "float" (Cross and Freedman 1975: 61). Given the context and the cognates, there is no doubt that some sort of descent is intended, possibly with overtones of dying or drowning. Also evoked, via paronomasia, is the homophonous root *ṣll* referring to darkness and covering.

Why use this unusual verb? Perhaps to chime with *maṣôlōt* 'Deeps' in 15:5, also part of a mineralogical simile ("went down in the depths like stone"). *Maṣôlōt* and *ṣll* are probably but not certainly related (cf. ibn Ezra; Dillmann 1880: 157).

lead. In 15:5, 16, Israel's enemies are likened to "stone," which would work here, too. Why bring in lead? The superficial motive is variety—or, rather, intensification. Since the category "stone" includes lead (Zech 5:8), v 10 makes the simile of v 5 more emphatic: "they sank like stone, nay, like lead," the proverbially heavy mineral (Tournay 1958: 348)—cf. Iris "plummeting" to Thetis in the sea (*Iliad* 24:80). As observed above, there is an implicit contrast with the quintessentially light "straw" of v 7 (see NOTE). And another factor may be wordplay: *ʿôperet* 'lead' (originally pronounced **ʿōpart/ʿōpirt*) chimes with both *parʿōh* 'Pharaoh' (originally **parʿō/pirʿō*) and *ʿāpār* 'dirt,' which often connotes the underworld (Isa 26:19; Ps 22:16, 30; 30:10, etc.).

strong waters. Isa 43:16 and especially Neh 9:11 appear to paraphrase the Song, replacing *mayim ʾaddîrîm* with *mayim ʿazzîm*. This confirms the interpretation of *ʾaddîr* as "mighty," not "dreadful" (see NOTE to 15:6).

15:11. *Who as you.* The customary translation is "Who *is like* you among gods, Yahweh? Who *is like* you . . . ?" But comparable examples of "staircase" parallelism are best taken as single, long utterances (Luzzatto; Rozelaar 1952: 225; see NOTE to 15:6). The sound of "who as you" is noteworthy, particularly if one runs together the words *mî-kāmōkā*.

gods. How is this statement compatible with Israelite monotheism? The sense might be "so-called gods," the traditional interpretation. But there is ample evidence that some biblical authors acknowledged the existence of divinities beside Yahweh (see TEXTUAL NOTE to 1:5; NOTE to 7:4; APPENDIX C, vol. II). Other biblical passages, however, deride foreign gods as mere statues, i.e., nonentities (e.g., Isa 42:17; 44:6–20; 46:1–2, etc.).

To what gods is Yahweh incomparably superior: the angels of his court or the gods of other nations? The answer is probably both (Bender 1903: 29). It appears that foreign gods were sporadically identified with Yahweh's retinue (see TEXTUAL NOTE to 1:5). In a xenophobic culture that would eventually outlaw the veneration of Yahweh's celestial servants, even while admitting their existence, statements of Yahweh's uniqueness would have patriotic overtones (cf. Halpern 1992b). In fact, Deut 4:7–8, 32–35; 33:29 and 2 Sam 7:23 explicitly associate Yahweh's incomparability with Israel's (Labuschagne 1966: 149–53).

strong. Ne'dār comes from the root *'dr*, already applied to water (v 10) and to Yahweh or his right arm (v 6). On Luzzatto's interpretation *"girt* in holiness," see NOTE to 15:6.

in holiness. The language is quintessentially polyvalent. One initially understands *baqqōdeš* as "in respect of holiness," comparable to "dreadful of glory . . . worker of wonder" (v 11) and parallel to "strong in might" (v 6). But *qōdeš* can connote any holy thing, place or being, and so other readings are possible. We could, for example, interpret "in the temple," foreshadowing *nawē(h) qodšekā* 'your holiness's pasture/camp/tent' (15:13) and *miqdāš* 'sanctum' (v 17). Or we could identify "holiness" with Yahweh's mountain (v 17), just as Ugaritic myth calls Ba'lu's mountain "holiness" (NOTE to 15:17). And "holiness" can also be heaven itself, sometimes called the "height of holiness" (Isa 63:15; Ps 102:20), "residence of holiness" (Deut 26:15; Jer 25:30; Zech 2:17; Ps 68:6; 2 Chr 30:27), "heavens of holiness" (Ps 20:7) or simply "holiness" (Ps 150:1).

Last and most important, "holiness" can connote the minor gods or *qədôšîm* 'holy ones' (so LXX Exod 15:11), whether celestial (Hos 12:1; Zech 14:5; Job 5:1; 15:15, etc.) or chthonian (Ps 16:3). Divine *qdšm* also appear in an amulet from Arslan Tash, Syria (*KAI* 27.12). By this reading, *baqqōdeš* parallels *bā'ēlim* 'among gods.' Citing the Phoenician cliché *'lm qdšm* 'holy gods' (*KAI* 4.5, 7; 14.9, 22). Freedman (1980: 208) finds in "gods . . . holiness" (15:11) the "breakup" of a formula, i.e., the distribution of a compound expression between parallel cola (see Melamed 1961). In Ugaritic myth, too, "gods" parallel "holiness"—in a sense. The Ugaritic pantheon is known by two ambivalent titles; *bn.'ilm* and *bn.qdš*. The former can be interpreted as either "sons of gods" (i.e., members of the category "god") or "sons of God (*'ilu*)" with enclitic mem (cf. Ps 29:1; 89:7). Similarly, *bn.qdš* might mean either "sons of holiness" (i.e., "holy ones") or "sons of [the goddess] Holiness (*qudšu*)," better known as *'Ilatu* 'Goddess' and *'Aṭiratu*/Asherah (see Maier 1986: 42–44, 81–96). In a way, it makes no difference: *'Ilu* and Qudšu-'Ilatu-'Aṭiratu respectively embody the divinity and holiness of the entire pantheon (cf. my comments on Hebrew *'ĕlōhîm* 'divinity, God' [NOTE to 1:17]; see also APPENDIX C, vol. II).

We find two illuminating parallels to 15:11 in the Psalter: "Deity, your might (derek) is in the qōdeš. Who is a great god like Deity? You are the god, worker of wonder" (Ps 77:14–15). Even closer is Ps 89:6–8a:

The heavens praise your wonder (pele'), Yahweh;
Your grace among the assembly of qədōšîm.
Who in the sky is equivalent to Yahweh,
Similar to Yahweh among God's sons [i.e., the gods],
A god reverenced in the privy council of qədōšîm
Great and revered above all around him?

Here qōdeš and qədōšîm connote the pantheon, heaven or, most likely, both. In Exod 15:11, too, we may take qōdeš as a collective reference to the gods, as well as a possible allusion to their heavenly abode.

In short: "holiness" in 15:11 equally parallels "glory . . . wonder," on the one hand, and "gods," on the other. Presumably, the poet wished to evoke all possible nuances. We are invited to equate holy temple, holy mountain, holy heaven, the gods and the abstract concept of holiness.

glory. The root hll can mean either "shine" or "sing, praise." The derived noun təhillâ connotes primarily fame, accomplishments or singing, but sometimes also radiance (Hab 3:3). What is the meaning here? "Terrible of songs" is one possibility, since victory hymns inspire dread of Yahweh (Ps 106:12 in fact calls the Song of the Sea təhillâ). But "terrible of fame" and "terrible of radiance" work equally well, if not better; to the latter, compare nôrā' hôd 'terrible of radiance' (Job 37:22). Another possible rendering would be "dreadful in praiseworthy accomplishments," to which Dillmann (1880: 157) compares Ps 9:15; 78:4; 79:13; Isa 42:12; 60:6; 63:7. (On the possibility that thlt is to be read as a singular *təhillāt, see TEXTUAL NOTE.)

worker of wonder. This is the essence of Yahweh's incomparability (cf. Deut 4:34–35): he alone performs miracles (Isa 25:1; Ps 72:18; 77:15; 78:12; 86:10; 88:11; 106:21–22; 136:4; Job 5:9; 9:10). The singular pele' 'wonder' is another example of our poet's penchant for collectives. The immediate referent is the Sea event (cf. Ps 77:12, 15; 78:12), but one also thinks of the Plagues. We may alternatively take pele' adverbially: "working wondrously."

Exod 15:11 is difficult to relate to its context. It seems an ecstatic interjection into the historical résumé of vv 10 and 12. But v 11 is important for the Song's overall structure: like 15:6, it praises Yahweh in "staircase" form (see NOTES to 15:3, 6).

15:12. You extended. Exod 15:12 is Janus-faced, linked with both the preceding and the following verses. In terms of content, it culminates the foregoing description of the drowning of Egypt; I accordingly assign it to stanza II. But v 12 also begins a sequence of main verbs beginning in n and ending in -tā: nāṭîtā . . . nāḥîtā . . . nēhaltā (Freedman 1980: 209). To those who elevate form over content, this indicates that the break lies before v 12 (see table in Zenger 1981: 455). I, however, would rather see sound play crossing a stanza break (Brenner 1991: 31); cf. next NOTE and NOTE to 15:8. In fact, the sequence of *n . . . tā* verbs already began with *nāšaptā* 'you blew' in v 10, clearly part of stanza II. Thus one might argue that vv 10 and 12 *nāšaptā . . . nāṭîtā* frame v 11, with v 13 beginning a new section.

That Yahweh extended his arm is nowhere stated in the prose accounts. But we have previously observed a quasi-identification of deity and prophet (4:16; 7:1, 17; 11:8). The moment in the prose narrative corresponding to 15:12 is 14:26 (P), where Moses extends his arm to bring the Sea back upon Egypt (Rashbam). The Song thus clarifies the symbolic nature of Moses' gesture: God is the real miracle-worker. Isa 23:11, perhaps influenced by the Song (or vice versa), also refers to Yahweh extending his arm over the Sea and frightening (*rgz*) the nations, including Canaan (cf. Exod 15:14–16). The Sea event is, *par excellence*, Yahweh's salvation "by a strong arm and by an outstretched limb" (Deut 4:34; 5:15; 26:8, etc.; cf. 3:19; 6:1, 6; 13:9; 32:11).

your right arm. Freedman (1980: 209) observes a series of rhyming nouns ending in the second masculine singular *-kā* (*yəmînəkā . . . ḥasdəkā . . . ʿozzəkā . . . qodšekā*), overlapping with the repetition of verbs ending in 2 m.s. *-tā.* Both devices cross the probable stanza break between vv 12 and 13 (Brenner 1991: 31). Jacob (1992: 416–17) and Goldin (1971: 39) find in this concentration of divine second persons a response to the enemy's arrogant first persons (v 9).

That Yahweh manipulates the waters with both his "right arm" (v 12) and his "nostrils' wind" (v 8) is less incongruous than at first appears. Yahweh's arm (*yād*) can be associated with his wind/spirit (*rûaḥ*) (Isa 11:15; 63:11), which in turn emanates from his nose (*ʾap*). Moreover, since "nose" (*ʾap*) often connotes anger, while "arm" (*yād*) connotes power, the cumulative point is that Yahweh acts in mighty wrath. We find the same association in Wis 11:17–21 and in the Isaianic refrain "His *nose* [anger] has not returned, and his *arm* is still extended" (Isa 5:25; 9:11, 16, 20; 10:4).

In addition to the divine name, the Song's major theme is Yahweh's "hand, arm," mentioned five times with varying terms (*yād, zərôaʿ, yāmîn*). This limb destroys (vv 6, 12), intimidates (v 16) and builds (v 17). Throughout the Bible, "arm" often appears in proximity to *yšʿ* 'save' (14:30–31; Judg 6:37; 7:2; 2 Kgs 14:27, etc.), suggesting that *yād* itself bears the connotation "salvation," as in 14:30–31: "So Yahweh *saved* Israel . . . and Israel saw the great *yād* that Yahweh had made in Egypt." Thus, by extolling Yahweh's "arm," the Song of the Sea praises Yahweh as Israel's savior, as is made explicit in v 2 (see NOTE to 14:16). For further discussion of Yahweh's hand, see Fredriksson (1945: 101–5), Roberts (1971), Ackroyd (1986: 419–26) and COMMENT below.

Earth swallows. In my analysis, stanzas I and II both end with the Egyptians being eaten. In v 7, they are metaphorically consumed by fire (see NOTE); in v 12, the earth swallows them. Both images may at first seem inappropriate to drowning in the Sea. According to *Memar Marqah* 2:8 (MacDonald 1963: 1.41; 2.64), Yahweh uses all-four elements to destroy Egypt: water (vv 1, 4, 5, 10), fire (v 7), air (vv 8, 10) and earth (v 12). Even if the four-element theory is fifth-century Greek B.C.E. (Empedocles), not ancient Israelite, we can still recognize in the mixed metaphors the poet's desire to have all nature participate in Egypt's demise.

Still, 15:12 is somewhat surprising. One might rather have expected "the *Deep* swallowed them" (Ps 69:16; 124:3-5). In what sense does the earth swallow Egypt? Like Ugaritic *'arṣ* and Akkadian *erṣetu*, Hebrew *'ereṣ* denotes not only the earth but also the subterranean underworld (1 Sam 28:13; Isa 29:4; Ezek 26:20, etc.) (Gunkel 1895: 18 n. 1). To enter the earth is thus to die (Ps 55:16; 63:10).

The image of Death eating or swallowing the living is common. "We will, like Sheol, swallow them alive" (Prov 1:12); "He widens his gullet like Sheol; and he, like Death, cannot be satisfied" (Hab 2:5); "Sheol widens her gullet, opens her mouth immeasurably" (Isa 5:14); "Firstborn Death will eat his limbs" (Job 18:13). The voracious Big Fish of Jonah 2:1, too, probably represents death (note Jonah 2:3). And Isa 25:8 ironically reverses the image: Yahweh will one day "swallow Death forever." We can trace this trope back to the mythology of the Canaanite death god, who devours with "a lip to earth and a lip to heaven" (*KTU* 1.5.ii.2-3; cf. Ps 73:9).

But there is also a specific connection between the Sea and the underworld, although its nature is difficult to grasp. Perhaps the ocean and Sheol are simply equivalent (cf. Reymond 1958: 212-14); note "death's breakers" (2 Sam 22:5; cf. Ps 18:5) and "the nethermost pit, darkness like the Deep" (Ps 88:7). Also potentially relevant is Ps 71:20, assuming *təhōmôt hā'āreṣ* means "the underworld's Deeps." At Ugarit, Death's realm is called *hmry, mk* and *ḫḫ*, perhaps meaning "ooze, decay, slime," evocative of the marine floor (*KTU* 1.4.viii.12-13; 5.ii.15-16); see Clifford (1972: 81 n. 55). Moreover, some texts associate entry into the underworld with drowning. "When I bring upon you the Deep, and the many waters cover you, I will bring you down with those who descend into the pit, to the folk of eternity, and make you dwell in the nethermost land" (Ezek 26:19-20; cf. 31:15). Note also Jonah 2:3, 6-7: "From Sheol's belly I prayed / . . . Waters engulfed me up to the neck; / Deep surrounded me; / Weeds are wrapped round my head. / To mountains' extremities I descended to the *earth*; / Its bolts over me forever." One might infer that drowning is simply tantamount to entering Sheol and vice versa.

SPECULATION: Although the Bible is inconsistent (Reymond 1958: 213), some passages locate the underworld directly beneath the sea bottom, e.g., Job 38:16-17, "Have you come to the Sea's sources, walked the Deep's recesses; have Death's gates been revealed to you?" and particularly Job 26:5-6, "The shades writhe under the waters and their denizens; Sheol is bare before him, there is no covering for Abaddon [Perdition]." The ocean is thus Hell's roof, just as the dry land ceils the Deep (Ps 136:6) and the firmament ceils the habitable hemisphere called "heaven and earth" (Gen 1:6-7). If the Song of the Sea shares this concept, then the Hebrews and Egyptians standing on the ocean bed are perilously close to the underworld. The Egyptians may simply sink down (cf. Luzzatto), or else the underworld gapes for Egypt, as for Dathan and Abiram (Num 16:30, 32, 34; Deut 11:6; Ps 106:17). Curiously, Mek. *bašallaḥ* 1 considers such quasi-inhumation a *reward* for Pharaoh's transitory piety in confessing Yahweh's justice (9:27)!

The prose account ostensibly reports that the Egyptians' corpses came aground (14:30 [J?]). Were they not swallowed by the underworld (15:12)? Some Jewish sources infer that the Song refers to burial *after* the Egyptians were washed up (e.g., Ramban; see Ginzberg 1928: 6.11 n. 56; cf. *Memar Marqah* 2:9 [MacDonald 1963: 1.44; 2.70]). But this is not the plain sense. We might solve the problem by interpreting 14:30 in light of 15:12: since the Egyptians are already swallowed up (15:12), "at the Sea's *lip*" (14:30) must be where the *Hebrews* stand, not where Egypt lies (ibn Ezra; Rashbam; see NOTE to 14:30). But, at least for the composite Torah, we do better to take "earth swallows them" figuratively. The Egyptians' souls, not necessarily their bodies, enter the underworld.

However we resolve this issue, or whether we choose to leave it unresolved, we should note the irony in v 12, heightened by paronomasia. The Egyptians, who planned to fill their throats (*timlā'ēmô*) with Israel (v 9), are instead swallowed (*tiblā'ēmô*) by the underworld.

SPECULATION: So far, I have been assuming with all commentators that the Egyptians are the object of the verb "swallow." But the interjection in v 11 evokes by allusion an alternate interpretation: the gods, incomparably inferior to Yahweh, are swallowed by the "earth." The minor gods are explicitly condemned to death in Ps 82:7, and one of their number, Helel, is hurled into the *'ereṣ* 'underworld' in Isa 14:15 (cf. vv 9–11). Similarly, in Ugaritic myth, two sons of 'Aṯiratu attempt to replace the storm god Ba'lu; neither is up to the job, and one of them, 'Aṯtaru the Morning Star, descends to the *'arṣ* 'underworld.' In the same myth, Ba'lu himself is swallowed by Death (*KAI* 1.5; *ANET* 140).

Even if fanciful, such a reading of 15:12 may underlie the midrash of God drowning Egypt's angelic patron in the Sea (*Exod. Rab.* 21:5; 22:2; 23:15). By this interpretation, 15:12 evokes 12:12, "Upon all Egypt's gods I will execute judgments."

15:13. *led.* As well as guidance in general, *nḥy* connotes specifically herding (Dillmann 1880: 158). In 15:13, the pastoral reference is clear from the goal of the journey: Yahweh's *nāwe(h)* 'pasture' (see below). This nuance also resonates across the stanza break with the gesture of v 12: Yahweh extends his hand not only to destroy enemies but also to guide his flock. Compare Ps 78:52–53, "He made his people journey like a flock and drove them like a flock in the wilderness, and he led them (*wayyanḥēm*) in security, and they did not fear," and Ps 77:21, "You led (*nāḥîtā*) your people like a flock through the hand of Moses and Aaron" (cf. also Ps 23:3). On Israel as God's flock or herd, see Eilberg-Schwartz (1990: 120–21).

In Hebrew poetry, we must determine verbal tense and aspect according to context. In their current literary setting, the perfect verbs in vv 13–15 must be taken as "prophetic perfects," i.e., the equivalent of future verbs (ibn Ezra). Israel has barely begun its journey. If, however, the Song arose independently as a commemoration of historical events, then these verbs might have been actual past tenses (Cross 1973: 125, 130 n. 67).

grace. Ḥesed usually implies the fulfillment of a moral obligation; its connotations include "kindness," "condescension," "reliability," "love," "pity," "piety" and, most prominently, "fidelity" (Glueck 1967; Sakenfeld 1978; Romerowski 1990; Clark 1993). Yahweh's obligation presumably arises from his relationship with Israel's ancestor(s) (15:2). Since *ḥesed* is an emotional state motivating action, the parallelism with *ʿōz* 'might' conveys Yahweh's power to effect his faithful benevolence.

people which you redeemed. The collocation of *gʾl* 'redeem' and *ʿam* 'people, kinsman' is significant, since *gʾl* often connotes performance of kinship duty (cf. NOTE to 4:22).

guided. Like the parallel verb *nḥy*, *nhl* has associations with herding (Isa 40:11; 49:10; Ps 23:2). *Nhl* might also be rendered "sustain" (Gen 47:17); BDB has "guide to a water-place," comparing Arabic *nahala* 'take a drink,' *manhal* 'watering place' (also Gaster 1936–37). If so, v 13 might allude to any of several accounts of Water in the Wilderness (15:22–26, 15:27; 17:1–7; Num 20:2–13; 21:16–18). But this is probably overspecific.

your holiness's pasture/camp/tent. Nāwe(h) means primarily "shepherds' abode, pasture" (on the Mari Akkadian cognate *nawûm*, see Edzard 1959 and Malamat 1988: 168–72). A *nāwe(h)* is generally the goal of a journey or a place of rest (Isa 32:18; 33:20; 65:10; Jer 23:3; 31:23; 33:12; 50:19; Ezek 34:14) (Brenner 1991: 13), and bears the additional connotations of "camp" (Isa 32:18) and "tent" (Isa 33:20; Job 5:24; 18:15). Albright (1968: 27 n. 63) translates *nāwe(h)* as "encampment" (also Cross and Freedman 1975: 52), while Cross (1973: 125) finds a reference to a specific tent shrine. The matter should be left open (see COMMENT). (On the relationship between *nāwe[h]* and *ʾanwēhû* 'I exalt him,' see NOTE to 15:2.)

Where is the *nāwe(h)* of 15:13? If it is a temporary abode, the obvious referent is Sinai/Horeb and its environs (ibn Ezra; Jacob 1992: 421; Cassuto 1967: 176; Freedman 1980: 136–40; 1981). There Moses pastures Jethro's flock (3:1); there he stands upon "ground of holiness" (3:5; cf. *qodšekā* in 15:13); there Israel camps (19:2) and tends its cattle (19:13; 34:3); there a spring is created to water humans and beasts (17:6); there Israel builds Yahweh's holy Tent (chaps. 25–31, 35–40). Other candidates are the oasis Kadesh (cf. *qodšakā* 'your holiness') or Shittim, the Hebrews' last station before crossing into Canaan (cf. v 16, "crosses") (Num 25:1; Josh 2:1; 3:1; Mic 6:5) (Cross 1973: 141). But a permanent habitation such as Jerusalem can also be a metaphorical *nāwe(h)*, and Yahweh's holy *nāwe(h)* may even be the entire land of

Canaan (Rashbam; Bekhor Shor; Lagrange 1899: 538; Freedman 1980: 214). Similar ambiguity obtains in v 17, and, to make matters worse, vv 13 and 17 may or may not refer to the same place (see COMMENT, pp. 568–69).

15:14. *peoples heard.* The Bible several times portrays Israel's neighbors as having heard of the Exodus from afar (Exod 18:1 [Midianites]; Numbers 22–24 [Moabites]; Josh 2:10; 5:1 [Canaanites]; 9:9 [Gibeonites]; 1 Sam 4:8 [Philistines]). Deut 2:25, seemingly a paraphrase of Exod 15:14, makes the rumor universal: "This day I will begin to set your fear and your dread upon the face of the peoples (*'ammîm*) under . . . the heavens who will hear (*šm'*) your report and shudder (*rgz*) and convulse (*hyl*)" (other biblical parallels include Josh 6:27; 9:1, 3, 9, 24; 10:1; Jer 33:9). The dismayed enemy hearing from afar is also a common motif in Assyrian royal annals, particularly those of Sargon II and his successors (e.g., Luckenbill 1926–27: 1.77; 2.17, 22, 28, 30, 31–32, 34, 36, 124, etc.).

In a sense, 15:14 is self-referential. The nations will hear of Yahweh's victory through paeans such as the Song itself (cf. Fretheim 1991a: 164–65). According to v 11, Yahweh is "dreadful of *təhillâ* 'glory, radiance, fame, song.'" In other words, songs of his exploits inspire terror (on the Song of the Sea as *təhillâ*, see Ps 106:12).

Exod 15:14 is notable for assonance of *m* and *'* in the first colon and *ḥ* in the second: *šámə'û 'ammîm . . . ḥîl 'āḥaz* 'peoples heard . . . convulsion seized.'

shudder. Like many Semitic stems beginning with **rg-*, *rgz* connotes perturbation. Compare Hebrew *rgm* 'stone,' *rgn* 'slander,' *rg'* 'disturb,' *rgš* 'be in a tumult'; Arabic *rjj* 'shake,' *rjb* 'fear,' *rjz* 'shake,' *rjf* 'shake', *rjm* 'stone, hit, banish'; Akkadian *rgm* 'make noise'; Ethiopic *rgm* 'stone, curse,' *rgṭ* 'move the feet' and perhaps *rgb* 'pigeon.' It is uncertain, however, whether *rgz* in Exodus describes primarily a behavior (trembling) or an attitude (agitation).

Rāgaz begins a series of seven verbs or expressions conveying terror, climaxing in petrifaction: "shudder . . . convulsion seized . . . perturbed were . . . quaking seizes . . . liquidated were . . . upon them fall . . . they are still." The nations are alternatingly subject and object of these verbs.

The sequence "hear . . . shudder" in response to military tidings may be a cliché; compare Hab 3:16 (also in the context of Yahweh's battle at the Sea): "I heard and my stomach shuddered." (On the physical manifestation of fear in the Bible, see Waldman 1976.)

Convulsion seized. Various maladies such as "sorrow," "fear" and "pain" are described as "seizing" the sufferer (15:15; 2 Sam 1:9; Isa 21:3, etc.). Gaster (1962b: 818) finds the idiom's origin in spirit possession. On the assonance within v 14, see NOTE to "peoples heard" above.

Philistia's. This is a notorious anachronism. By conventional chronology, the Philistines were not yet in Canaan when the Hebrews left Egypt (see Albright 1968: 46–47; Cross 1973: 124–25; Freedman 1980: 142). On the mention and nonmention of nations as evidence for the dates of the Song and of the historical Exodus, see APPENDICES A and B.

15:15. *Then*. The particle *'āz*, though unessential to the meaning, provides a stressed syllable to balance the following cola, whether we count stresses (4 : 4 : 4) or syllables (9 : 9 : 9). It also creates 'aleph alliteration within its own colon (see below) and with the beginning of the next colon (*'êlê*). In v 9, 'aleph alliteration described a hasty pursuit (see NOTE); here it evokes terror. We should also notice the resonance of *'āz* with *'āḥaz* 'seized' in the preceding and succeeding cola.

perturbed. LXX "hurried" is based upon the meaning of *bhl* in late Biblical Hebrew (e.g., Eccl 5:1; Esth 2:9; 2 Chr 35:21 [Wevers 1990: 233]). Here the verb describes an emotional state, not a rate of motion.

The sequence *'āz nibhălû 'allûpê 'ĕdôm* 'then perturbed were Edom's princes' is noteworthy for repetition of identical or similar sounds: 'aleph/he', lamedh, beth/pe'/mem and zayin/daleth.

princes. My rendering follows LXX, with minor reservations. In Zech 12:5, 6, *'allûp* indeed means "leader," like Ugaritic *'ulp*. But in Genesis 36; Zech 9:7; 1 Chr 1:51-54, *'allûp* appears to signify a "clan" (although "founding father" is also possible); Luzzatto compares *'elep* 'family' (Judg 6:15; 1 Sam 10:19; 1 Sam 23:23), apparently derived from *'elep* 'thousand' as a military unit (Num 10:36; 31:5; Josh 22:14; see Mendenhall 1958). Perhaps, then, a leader was called *'allûp* because he represented his clan and led its *'elep* into battle (BDB compares "chiliarch"). But it is equally possible that *'allûp* derives from *'elep* 'bull' (cf. Ps 144:14), since animal names often served as military honorifics (Miller 1970b; see next NOTE). There is also a verbal root *'lp* 'train,' relevant to both leadership and animal husbandry. (Most likely, these etymological streams meet in Proto-Semitic **'lp*, perhaps meaning "to be acquainted, associated" [Arabic *'lf*].) In sum: the rough parallelism of *'allûpê* with "peoples . . . inhabitants" (15:14-15) favors the translation "clans." But the closer parallelism with "rams" (see below) imposes the interpretation "princes," also evoking "bulls" (Cross and Freedman 1975: 62).

rams. *'Ayil* often connotes a leader; on animal names as military titles, see Miller (1970b). Perhaps the Moabite connection is more than fortuitous; Dillmann (1880: 158) cites Moab's rich flocks and herds (cf. 2 Kgs 3:4).

The mention of *'allûpê* 'princes, bulls (?)' and *'êlê* 'rams' continues the pastoral imagery of v 13. Lohfink (1968: 79) writes, "The other flocks are struck still when the great and good shepherd passes by with his flocks. They stand alongside the processional route like stone sphinxes."

seizes. The first two clauses of v 15 are a classic example of chiasm "(A) Perturbed were (B) Edom's princes; (B') Moab's *rams*, (A') quaking seizes them." There is slight assonance in *mô'āb yō(')ḥāzēmô* 'Moab . . . seizes,' matching the stronger assonance of the parallel *nibhălû 'allûpê* 'perturbed were . . . princes.'

Liquefied. *Mwg* can describe literal moistening, but more often it connotes loss of moral firmness, particularly of courage. In 15:15, the primary nuance is "lost their nerve," but allusion to liquidity is also apposite in several respects.

First: the nations' progressive discomfiture (vv 14–16) parallels the Sea's behavior (v 8). They are perturbed, they quiver, they run like water, they are petrified (see further below).

Second: throughout, the Song contrasts liquid and solid, water and mineral, Sea and mountain. "Liquefied" contrasts with "still as stone" in the next verse.

Third: to be "liquefied" can mean to run with water, rather than to become aqueous. The nations may be conceived as sweating, weeping or urinating in fear (cf. Ezek 7:17; 21:12).

Fourth: the reference to liquefaction at Yahweh's arrival recalls texts in which mountains "melt" before God. That is, they metaphorically lose their courage and literally run with fertilizing water (Judg 5:5; Isa 34:3; Mic 1:4; Nah 1:5; Ps 97:5; cf. Joel 4:18; Amos 9:13; also Kuntillet ʿAjrud *ymsn hrm* 'mountains melt' [Weinfeld 1978–79; *AHI* 8.023]). Thus v 15 may ironically allude to Canaan's fertility.

all. If we prefer short to long cola, we have a metrical difficulty here. *Nāmōgû / kōl yōšəbê kanaʿan* 'Liquefied were / All Canaan's inhabitants' is metrically unbalanced (1 : 3 in stresses; 3 : 6 in syllables). To solve the problem, Cross and Freedman (1975: 63) tentatively take *kōl* as an adverb, "wholly," so that one may read *nāmōgû kōl / yōšəbê kanaʿan* 'Liquefied totally / Are Canaan's inhabitants' (also Freedman 1980: 191). This restores metrical symmetry (2 : 2 in stresses; 4 : 5 in syllables). Cross and Freedman, however, cite no other examples of adverbial *kōl*. And the Bible itself affords evidence against their view. Josh 2:9, 24 paraphrases Exod 15:15 with *nāmōgû kol-yōšəbê hāʾāreṣ*, which, being prose, could only be rendered, "all the land's inhabitants were liquefied."

This has implications for the stichometry of 15:1b–18 as a whole. If *kōl* bears its normal meaning, "all," in v 15, then v 15c must be analyzed as one long colon, with either no caesura or a weak one after *nāmōgû*. All of v 15 must consequently be a tricolon. This is my basis for preferring long cola over short throughout the Song (see also NOTE to 15:4).

inhabitants. Cross (1973: 130 n. 65) argues that the parallelism within v 15 requires that *yōšəbê* be rendered "enthroned ones" (also Stuart 1976: 91; Freedman 1980: 185, 196). Admittedly, *yšb* often refers to enthronement (e.g., 15:17), and *yōšēb* may connote a ruler in Isa 10:13; Amos 1:5, 8. Moreover, throughout the Bible, *yšb* is associated with *mlk* 'rule' (15:17; 2 Sam 19:9; 1 Kgs 16:11, etc.); we find much the same at Ugarit (*KTU* 1.16.vi.37–38, 52–53). I doubt, however, that *yōšəbê* is used differently in vv 14 and 15 (*pace* Cross). Freedman (1980: 142–43) more consistently translates *yōšəbê* as "enthroned ones" in both verses. In support of this approach, we may cite Josh 5:1, "When all the Amorite's *kings* . . . and the Canaanite's *kings* . . . heard that Yahweh had dried the Jordan's waters from before Israel's Sons till their [Qere] crossing, then their heart melted."

But the matter is not so simple. After *kōl* 'all' one might expect a broad category such as "inhabitants," not just the ruling elite. And, as we have seen, Josh 2:9, 24 appear to paraphrase Exod 15:15 with "all the *yōšəbê* of the land were liquefied." Here, since *yōšəbê* parallels "us" (v 9) and "the land" (v 24), it is best rendered "inhabitants." In sum, it appears that Josh 2:9, 24 interprets Exod 15:15c in one way, and Josh 5:1 interprets it in another. Perhaps the phrase was always ambiguous (a similar uncertainty obtains for *yōšēb* in Isa 10:12; Amos 1:5, 8).

15:16. *Upon them.* Ibn Ezra identifies "them" as the Philistines, Edomites and Moabites, near whose territory Israel passes. He excludes the Canaanites, whose land Israel actually takes. This, I think, is overreading.

fear. The ordinary word for "fear" is *'êmâ.* *'Êmātâ* probably features a double feminine suffix (*pace* GKC §90g). The reduplicated suffix is regular in the 3 f.s. of the perfect III-*y* verb (e.g., *bānətâ* < **banatat*) and is occasionally found on nouns in poetry (*'ezrātâ* [Ps 44:27; 63:8; 94:17]; *yəšû'ātâ* [Jonah 2:10; Ps 3:3; 80:3]; *'awlātâ/'ōlātâ* [Ezek 28:15; Hos 10:13; Ps 92:16; 125:3; Job 5:6]; *ṣārātâ* [Ps 120:1]; *'êpātâ* [Job 10:22]). (I assume that such forms were originally accented on the ultima; the penultimate accent in MT may be an assimilation to the locative/directive suffix -*â* [cf. GKC].)

terror. As often in Hebrew poetry, synonymous terms fall, not in parallel cola, but within the same colon connected by "and" (see Watson's [1984: 158] discussion of "vertical" parallelism). Compare "strength and power/music" (v 2), "Pharaoh's chariots and his force" (v 4); also NOTE to 15:17.

As observed above, the description of the nations' terror is a literary *topos* with a clear propagandistic function. Egyptian and Mesopotamian texts often describe the dread that seizes foreign enemies at the advent of the king and his supporting gods (Freedman 1980: 135; Mann 1977: 128–29). Similarly, at the climax of the Ugaritic myth of Ba'lu and the Sea, the storm god thunders forth from his holy mountain and terrifies his foes (see COMMENT).

At your limb's greatness. *Gədōl* is a rare construct of *gōdel* 'greatness'; cf. *gəbōah* in 1 Sam 16:7, *qədōš* in Ps 46:5; 65:5 (see GKC §93h, and compare also the infinitive construct *qəṭōl* < **quṭl*). In Ps 79:11, however, we find the expected *kəgōdel zərô'ăkā* 'according to your limb's greatness.' Also related to 15:16 is Deut 11:2: *godlô . . . yādô haḥăzāqâ ûz(ə)rō'ô hannəṭûyâ* 'his greatness . . . his strong arm and his extended limb,' preceding an account of the Exodus (Tournay 1958: 353). Within the Song, the phrase recalls the semantically analogous *bərōb gə'ônəkā* 'in your pride's greatness' (v 7).

still. The verb *ydmw* (MT *yiddəmû*) is quintessentially ambiguous, due to an ancient mixing of the roots *dmm* 'be still' and *dmy* II 'cease' (GKC §77e). But of the many interpretations proposed, some are more likely than others. Quite implausible is the revocalization **yidmû* 'they resemble,' suggested by Alter (1985: 51) and probably underlying LXX (Cross and Freedman 1975: 63; *pace* Wevers 1990: 234). As Cross and Freedman note, *dmy* I 'resemble' is never otherwise used with *kə-* 'like.' And Dahood's (1962) analysis of *ydmw* as a Qal Passive or Hophal of *ndy* 'hurl' plus enclitic mem is far too speculative. But *ydmw* might well come from *dmm* 'be still, silent,' whether in Qal (*yiddəmû* [MT]) or Niph'al (**yiddammû*). It could also derive from *dmy* II 'cease, be destroyed,' again either in the Qal (**yidmû*) or Niph'al (**yiddāmû*). Overall,

MT *yiddəmû* appears to be the best reading, connoting cessation of both motion and sound, but primarily the former (cf. Symmachus "are unmoving," vs. Aquila "are silent" [Field 1875: 1.108]). See also following.

stone. The key to the verb *ydmw* is the simile *kā'āben* 'like stone': the nations are "petrified" (cf. 1 Sam 25:37). And the evocation of *dmy* II, connoting death and destruction, is equally apposite (see previous NOTE). The potentially hostile nations are not just still but "stone dead"; cf. Ps 31:18, *yiddəmû liš'ôl* 'they perish into Sheol' (also Lam 2:10?).

As in vv 7 and 12, the poet uses imagery that initially seems incongruous. The mineral metaphor (15:16) follows oddly on the comparison to water (v 15). But the effect is deliberate. First, that both the Egyptians (15:5) and the Syro-Palestinians (v 16) are likened to stone creates an equivalence between them, an implication that Yahweh subdues *all* of Israel's potential enemies (see COMMENT). Further: the peoples of vv 14–16 reenact the Sea's role (v 8): at first tumultuous and liquid, they stand petrified while Israel crosses (Lohfink 1968: 83; Loewenstamm 1992a: 259). The Bible often assimilates Israel's enemies to water or the Sea (e.g., 2 Sam 22:5–18; Isa 2:2 = Mic 4:1; Isa 17:12–14; Habakkuk 3; Ps 124:4–5; 144:5–7; Lam 3:52–54). And to confirm our interpretation, Ps 77:17, related to Exod 15:1b–18, transfers the nations' "shuddering" and "convulsion" to the waters themselves.

Till. '*Ad* might also be rendered "while," as in Syriac and sometimes in Hebrew. It begins an alliterative sequence: *'ad-ya'ăbōr 'amməkā*.

crosses. Like so many references in vv 13–18, *ya'ăbōr* seems intentionally polyvalent. What does the people cross? Even in biblical times, 15:16 was probably accorded multiple readings. First, in light of the prose context, one cannot but think of crossing the Sea (Haupt 1904: 162; cf. Kloos 1986: 139; Halpern 1983: 39). If so, mention of Israel's passage, notably missing from 15:1b–12, is simply deferred to v 16; i.e., we have another leap backward in time (cf. v 8). Josh 4:23, in fact, uses the phrase *'ad-'obrəkem* 'till your crossing' of Israel's passage through the Suph Sea. Similarly, Josh 2:9–11 cites Exod 15:15–16 ("fear fell on us . . . all the land's inhabitants were liquefied") apropos of the drying of the Suph Sea before Israel. Moreover, Ps 77:14–21, whose contacts with the Song are unmistakable, climaxes in a description of Israel's crossing: "Your way was in the Sea, / And your path in many waters, / Though your footsteps were unknown [unperceived?]. / You led your people like a flock, / Through the hand of Moses and Aaron" (vv 20–21). Isa 11:15, too, recalls that Israel crossed the dried seabed, before apparently quoting the Song (Isa 12:2, 5).

If this interpretation is correct, however, one might ask why the Song is so oblique. Why does it not simply mention Israel's transit at the beginning? Perhaps because, as we shall see under COMMENT, the Song plays upon a Canaanite mythic prototype: a storm god defeats the Sea and crosses to his mountain, there to build his habitation. There is no room for anyone, Israel or Egypt, to cross the Sea in vv 4–11 without disrupting this pattern. Mention of Israel's passage must be postponed to the point at which, in the mythic template, the victorious Deity crosses from the Sea to his mountain.

Israel "crosses" things other than the Sea, however. One might take 15:16 to foretell Israel's traversing the desert, whether to Sinai/Horeb or to Canaan (see COMMENT, pp. 562–69). But, curiously, the verb *'br* almost never describes the wilderness trek. The only possible example I have found is 17:5 (see NOTE).

If Israel does not "cross" through the wilderness per se, Deut 29:15 and Josh 24:17 refer to "crossing" among foreign nations in general, while Deuteronomy 2 lists places through which Israel "crosses": Edom, the desert of Moab, the Wadi Zered, Moab. And when Israel crosses the River Arnon (Deut 2:25), Yahweh says, in language evocative of Exod 15:14, 16, "I will begin to set your fear and your dread upon the faces of the peoples under all the heavens, who will hear your report and shudder and convulse before you." Yahweh then intimidates Sihon king of Heshbon, through whose domain Israel "crosses" in triumph. This might indicate that Deuteronomy takes Exod 15:16 to predict crossing the Arnon, or crossing through the Amorite territories of Transjordan.

And one can frame an equally cogent argument that 15:16 refers to crossing the Jordan, the boundary of Canaan proper. Compare Josh 5:1, "When all the Amorite's kings . . . and the Canaanite's kings . . . heard that Yahweh had dried the Jordan's waters from before Israel's Sons *till their crossing* (*'ad-'obrām* [Qere]), then their heart melted." The sequence *'d 'br* 'till cross' also describes the Jordan crossing in Deut 2:29; Josh 4:23; 5:1 (Josh 4:23, as we have seen, uses *'d 'br* of the Suph Sea). (Thus, Targumic tradition, in which the first "crosses" in Exod 15:16 refers to the River Arnon, the second to the River Jordan, is less fanciful than it at first appears.)

Israel's "crossings" continue in the land of Canaan. They *'br* before Jericho (Josh 6:7, 8) and throughout the territory of Judah (Josh 10:29, 31, 34). Conceivably, Exod 15:16 predicts that the peoples of Canaan will be still, as Israel passes in their midst (Loewenstamm 1992a: 259).

Lastly, the verb *'br* 'cross' can describe a change of status as well as location. According to Deut 29:11, Israel "crosses" into Covenant with Yahweh (cf. Ezek 20:37). In general, the causative Hiph'il *he'ĕbîr* connotes transfer of ownership (see NOTE to 22:28), and, although the intransitive *'ābar* is not ordinarily used in this sense, the reference to Yahweh's "getting" Israel (v 16) could imply that Israel "crosses" from Pharaoh's possession into Yahweh's.

In sum: Israel's progress is conceived as a *series* of "crossings"; hence, 15:16 is deliberately polyvalent. Since the Suph Sea, the Jordan River and Israel's enemies are equated or associated in the Song and other biblical texts, all interpretations of 15:16 may be equally valid. The ambiguity as to what Israel crosses mirrors ambiguity as to the journey's goal (see COMMENT).

SPECULATION: Cross (1973: 141) finds a plausible explanation for the polyvalence of v 16 in the cult of Gilgal, which supposedly featured a ritual crossing of the dammed Jordan representing the passage through the Suph Sea (see also Kraus 1951; Soggin 1966). If so, crossing the Sea and crossing the Jordan are symbolically identical acts (see also Batto 1992: 109, 136–44).

Compare the equation of the Jordan and the Sea in Ps 66:6; 114:3, 5, and note that the phrase *'d 'br* 'till crosses' describes passage through both the Jordan (Deut 2:29; Josh 4:23; 5:1) and the Suph Sea (Josh 4:23). Batto (pp. 141–42) observes, moreover, that Elijah and Elisha, who in other respects reenact Moses' career, cross the Jordan dry-shod (on Elijah, see Fohrer 1957: 55–58; Carroll 1969: 408–14; Carlson 1969: 431–39; Propp 1987a: 71–72 n. 11). And if the Gilgal rite included a triumphal march around the ruins of Jericho (C. L. Seow, privately), then there was also a symbolic occupation of the land, a "crossing" among the nations.

Cross's hypothesis may even explain the prevalence of mineral imagery in the Song. If the Jordan was actually dammed, then these stones would be, on the one hand, the physical realization of the piled waters (Exod 15:8). On the other hand, they would also correspond to the enemies who, petrified, permit Israel's passage (15:16). One might even speculate that ritualized dam building, entailing the sinking of many stones, symbolized Yahweh's hurling/implanting the Egyptians into the Sea (see NOTES to Exod 15:1, 4, 5).

But the disposition of the stones of Gilgal is not quite clear (Josh 4:5–9, 20–24). Given the difficulty of damming a river annually, not to mention the absence of material or textual evidence for such a practice, a more realistic scenario suggests itself. Perhaps the Gilgal rite involved passing by or between stones taken from the riverbed, relocated on the shore. These could have symbolized (a) the piled waters of the Suph Sea and Jordan, (b) Israel's Syro-Palestinian enemies and, possibly, (c) the Egyptians themselves (unless the drowned enemy is symbolized by yet other stones within the river [Josh 4:9]). Admittedly, Josh 4:5, 8 associates the twelve stones of Gilgal, not with Israel's enemies, but with Israel itself. Does their erection rather correspond, then, to the "planting" of Israel (Exod 15:17)? Whatever the details, the prominence of stones in both Exod 15:1b–18 and Joshua 4 may be more than coincidence, and strengthens Cross's case for the Song's origin. Even the name *gilgāl* (ancient **galgal*) may be related to *gal* 'heap, wave.'

people which you have gotten. English "get" barely captures the connotations of Hebrew *qny* 'acquire, purchase, engender.' On the one hand, an economic understanding of Israel's redemption underlies the Exodus tradition (Daube 1963): Pharaoh has misappropriated Yahweh's slaves, whom God will reclaim by whatever means necessary (see NOTE to 4:23). Thus, although *qny* usually means "buy," here the sense is more "repossess."

On the other hand, Cross and Freedman (1975: 64) translate: "people . . . whom thou hast created" (previously, Köhler 1934 et al.). Yahweh is elsewhere said to have created (*'śy, br', yṣr*) Israel (e.g., Isa 43:1, 7); note especially the evocation of Exod 15:16 in Isa 43:21: *'am zû yāṣartî lî* 'the people which I have fashioned for myself' (Mettinger 1982: 76). But *qny* does not mean precisely "create." Rather, it means "procreate, engender," in both Hebrew (Gen 4:1; Deut 32:6; Ps 139:13; Prov 8:22) (Irwin 1961) and Ugaritic, which calls the mother goddess ʾAṯiratu "the gods' *qnyt*" (*KTU* 1.4.i.22, etc.);

similarly, King Kirta hopes to *qny* sons (*KTU* 1.14.ii.4). Even in the title *'ēl* *'elyôn qōnē(h) šāmayim wā'āreṣ* 'God, Highest, *qōne(h)* of Heaven and Earth' (Gen 14:19, 22), *qōne(h)* originally meant "progenitor," for the Canaanite god *'Elyōn* is literally Father of Heaven and Earth (Philo of Byblos *apud* Eusebius *Praep. evangelica* 1.10.15; Attridge and Oden 1981: 46–47) (for parallels to this divine title, see Della Vida 1944; Avigad 1972: 195–96; 1983: 41; Cross 1973: 51 n. 25; *KAI* 26.A.III.18; 129.1; *ANET³* 519). Consequently, although "the people which you *created*" is imprecise, a rendering "the people which you *begot*" would be defensible. Yahweh does not merely repossess Israel as stolen chattel; he ransoms (*g'l*) Israel as a captive kinsman, indeed a firstborn son (NOTES to 4:22–23; 15:13). The parallelism of 15:13 and 16, *'am-zû gā'āltā . . . 'am-zû qānîtā* 'people which you redeemed . . . people which you have gotten,' suggests an equivalence or association between *qny* and *g'l*. Compare also Ps 74:2, "Remember your community which you got (*qānîtā*) of old, you redeemed (*gā'altā*) your property tribe," and Ruth 4:4, apropos of kinship duty, "Acquire (*qanē[h]*)! . . . if you would redeem, redeem (*gə'āl*)!" (Campbell 1975: 159).

SPECULATION: One way to synthesize the two connotations of *qny*, "acquire" and "beget," is to see a reference to adoptive sonship. Compare Deut 32:6–15, seemingly depicting an adoption gone awry: Yahweh *qny*-ed Israel, made and established him, found him, embraced him, taught and loved him, treated him as a bird treats its young, led him and suckled him, till Israel grew fat and became a rebellious child. Vv 18–20 then make explicit the parent-child relationship between Yahweh and Israel (for further reflections on Israel's adoption and adoption in general, see COMMENT to 1:22–2:10).

In Exod 15:16, however, the nuance "acquire" dominates over "procreate." Decisive is Ps 78:54, which appears to incorporate elements from Exod 15:16–17 (see also NOTE to 15:17; COMMENT, pp. 565–66; APPENDIX A, vol. II): "He brought them to his holiness's territory/mountain (*gəbûl* = Arabic *jabal?*), the mountain which his right hand got (*har-ze[h] qānətâ yəmînô*)." It is unlikely that Yahweh's right hand *engendered* this territory/mountain; rather, Yahweh *captured* it. Consider, too, Isa 11:11, "And it will happen on that day, and my Lordship will once again [use?] his hand (*yādô*) to acquire (*liqnôt*) his people's remnant that remains from Assyria and Egypt." The association of "hand" with *qny* again suggests acquisition, not procreation (cf. Humbert 1958: 166–74).

15:17. *plant them.* The complementary verbs *təbi'ēmô wətiṭṭā'ēmô* 'may you bring them and plant them' fall, not in parallel cola, but, somewhat surprisingly, in the same colon (cf. Watson 1984: 158). Luzzatto proffers an over-ingenious explanation: "bring them" goes with "(to) the firm seat for your sitting/throne/dwelling," interrupted by "plant them in your property mountain." To my ear, however, the coordinated verbs simply create a sense of fresh start through surprise. Previously, we met equivalent *nouns* within the same colon, but not verbs ("strength and power/music" [v 2], "Pharaoh's chariots and his force" [v 4], "fear and terror" [v 16]).

The translation *"may* you bring them and plant them" assumes that *təbiʾēmô wətiṭṭāʿēmô* expresses the singer's desire. One could also read a prediction, "you *will* bring and . . . plant," or simply a command, "bring and . . . plant." Cross (1973: 125), however, positing an original cultic function for the Song, regards the verbs as preterite: "You brought them and planted them." This may be possible if we read the Song in isolation. It is impossible in the current literary context.

SPECULATION: Although *nṭʿ* 'plant' refers primarily to the transplanting of Israel as a garden or grove onto Yahweh's holy mountain (see COMMENT, pp. 569–71), there may also be an implication that Israel will *camp* at God's mountain. The act of driving a tent peg naturally brings to mind planting and vice versa (cf. *nṭʿ* 'to drive a nail' [Eccl 12:11]). In fact, in later strata of Biblical Hebrew, *nṭʿ* acquires the secondary meaning "pitch a tent" (explicitly in Dan 11:45; implicitly in Isa 51:16 [cf. Ps 104:2]; compare Sabaean *nṭʿ[t]* 'tent [?]' [Biella 1982: 302]). Conversely, to break up a tent is to "uproot" (*sērēs*) its owner (Ps 52:7). Aside from the physical analogy between planting and implanting, an important factor is the homophony of *nāṭaʿ* 'plant' and *nāṭâ* 'extend, pitch a tent' (compare the merger of *zrʿ* 'sow' and *zry* 'scatter, winnow' in Hebrew [Zech 10:9] and Ugaritic [see Loewenstamm 1975: 339–40]). (Ps 94:9 also puns between *nṭʿ* and *nty*: *hannōṭēaʿ ʾōzen* 'he who planted the ear,' though incongruous, chimes with *hiṭṭâ ʾōzen* 'incline the ear.')

In Exod 15:17, there is little chance that *tiṭṭāʿēmô* literally means "make them pitch tents." But we should not rule out metaphorical *allusion* to camping, since that is Israel's current mode of habitation. We find biblical poets of all periods gracefully slipping from arboreal to tabernacular imagery: "The tent of the righteous will blossom" (Prov 14:11); "He is plucked up from the tent of his trust. . . . Sulfur is shed upon his pasture. From beneath his roots dry up, from above his bough withers" (Job 18:14–16). Sir 14:24–27 describes the wise man as one who "camps about her [Wisdom's] house . . . pitches his tent by her side . . . and makes his nest in her boughs and lives in her branches and takes shelter from the cold in her shade. . . ." Num 24:5–7 (MT) plays extravagantly upon the images of tent and tree, punning not only between *nṭʿ* 'plant' and *nty* 'spread' but also among *ʾŏhālîm* 'tents,' *ʾăhālîm* 'aloes' and *ʾărāzîm* 'cedars.'

Are there any positive indications that Exod 15:17 alludes to camping? First, Israel's initial goal is a *nāwe(h)* 'pasture, encampment' (see NOTE to 15:13). More important, Ps 78:54–55, which resembles Exod 15:16–17, refers to tenting explicitly:

And he brought them to his holiness's territory/ mountain,
The mountain which his right arm got.

And he expelled nations from before him
And allotted for them a property region
And settled Israel's tribes *in their tents.*

your property mountain. I.e., "your mountain that is your property" (cf. GKC §128*k–m*). "Property" (*naḥălâ*) refers to an eternal, inalienable possession.

Exodus 15:17 culminates two themes running throughout the Song of the Sea: the contrast between liquid and solid, and the contrast between down and up (see NOTES to 15:1 "exaltedly, exaltedly," 15:7 "uprisers" and 15:8 "streams"). The overall movement has been from the unruly Deeps to the stable mountain. On the disputed identity of the latter, see COMMENT.

firm seat for your sitting/throne/dwelling. Most English translations render *mākôn ləšibtəkā* as "a place for your residence" or the like (KJV; RSV; NJV). This is accurate but inadequate. *Mākôn* and *šebet* are both polyvalent: the former connotes a place of permanence and stability, a "station," "seat," "locus" or "foundation"; *šebet* is probably an infinitive construct meaning either "dwelling" or "sitting," often with a connotation of "enthronement" (see below).

Mākôn ləšibtəkā evokes the expression *məkôn kissē'* 'a throne's *mākôn*' (Ps 89:15; 97:2). What is the physical relationship between *kissē'* and *mākôn?* Some think of throne and dais (Syr Exod 15:17; Cross and Freedman 1975: 52; Cross 1973: 161). But *məkôn kissē'* is better understood as hendiadys, tantamount to "firmly and permanently supported throne" (cf. GKC §128*k–m*). The root *kwn* often describes the eternity of a throne, whether Yahweh's (Ps 9:8; 93:2) or David's (2 Sam 7:13, 16; Prov 29:14, etc.); *kwn* is also associated with *malkût/mamlākâ* 'reign' (e.g., 1 Sam 20:31; 1 Kgs 2:12, 45). The opposite of a *kwn* throne is one overturned or cast down (Hag 2:22; Ps 89:45; also *KTU* 1.2.iii.18, 6.vi.27–28). Isa 18:4 uses *mākôn* alone to connote a throne, as if the term described a throne's inalienable attribute—its stability, not merely its fundament. (Also of some relevance is the Ugaritic couplet *grdš.mknt* . . . *grdš.ṯbt* [*KTU* 1.14.i.11, 23], where *mknt*, cognate to Hebrew *mākôn*, parallels *ṯbt*, corresponding to *šebet* [*RSP* 3.104]. The parallelism suggests that the terms are synonymous, or nearly so. The context does not refer to enthronement, however, but rather to family or perhaps abode.)

Ugaritic provides further evidence, albeit indirect, that *mākôn* is the functional equivalent of *kissē'* 'throne.' Quite similar in meaning to *mākôn ləšibtəkā* is Ugaritic *ks'u.ṯbth* 'his throne/enthronement seat' (*KTU* [1.1.iii.1]; 3.vi.15–16; 4.viii.13–14; 5.ii.15–16). Arguably, Hebrew *mākôn* is tantamount to Ugaritic *ks'u*, in turn cognate to Hebrew *kissē'* 'throne.' As it were, *mākôn ləšibtəkā* in 15:17 combines Hebrew *məkôn kissē'* and Ugaritic *ks'u.ṯbt*, dropping the common denominator *kissē'/ks'u.* (One might object that, on the analogy of Ugaritic *ks'u.ṯbt* and Hebrew *məkôn kissē'*, we should have in 15:17 *məkôn šibtəkā, not *mākôn ləšibtəkā*. But, to judge from 1 Kgs 8:13, 39, 43, there is no difference in meaning; compare also *məkôn šibtô* [Ps 33:14].)

Šebet in the sense of "place of sitting, throne" is attested at most once in Hebrew (1 Kgs 10:19 = 2 Chr 9:18). Elsewhere it is simply the infinitive "to sit, sitting." It is the Ugaritic cognate *ṯbt* that means "throne" or "power" (Seow 1989: 125). Is it conceivable, then, that 15:17 uses *šebet* in a manner more characteristic of Ugaritic than of Hebrew? Certainly, for the Song's grammar and diction are in general archaic or archaistic, closer to Ugaritic than is standard Hebrew (Cross and Freedman 1975; Robertson 1972). And yet I cannot help feeling that *šebet* in 15:17 is after all an infinitive, which one would never have doubted before Ugaritic (Ugaritic *ṯbt*, too, may be a vestigial infinitive [*pace* Seow]; cf. *ṣ'at* [*KTU* 1.3.ii.8; 16.i.35]).

In short, *mākôn ləšibtəkā* connotes eternal enthronement, anticipating v 18, "Yahweh will *reign* ever and eternity." Yahweh's enthronement is associated with his kingship also in Ps 29:10; 47:9; 93:1–2; 97:1–2; 99:1, 5; for a study, see Mettinger (1982: 19–37).

So far we have given the motif of enthronement its due and more. We cannot ignore the tradition, as old as LXX, that 15:17 uses *šebet* in the sense of "residence"; compare the surrounding references to *miqdāš* 'sanctum, temple' and *naḥălâ* 'property' (cf. Judg 18:1; also *KTU* [1.1.iii.1]; 3.vi.15–16; 4.viii.13–14; 5.ii.15–16). Accommodating the notions of "sitting" and "dwelling" is not really a problem. If Yahweh lives on his mountain, there he must be enthroned. And where would he be enthroned, if not in his dwelling? Still, in a given context one connotation of *yšb* usually predominates. In 15:17, the immediate environment suggests primarily enthronement. Contrast Ps 68:17, "the mountain that Deity appropriated for his *šebet*; yes, Yahweh will dwell (*škn*) forever," where the preferred translation is "residence," and likewise 1 Kgs 8:13, "Yahweh *said* [intended] to dwell (*škn*) in cloud, but I have built a lofty house for you, a *mākôn ləšibtəkā* forever."

What is the relation between Yahweh's mountain and Yahweh's throne? In Ps 99:5, 9, Yahweh's footstool seems equivalent to his holy mountain, and a footstool is part of a throne (Metzger 1970: 153 n. 41); there are many Mesopotamian illustrations of gods using mountains as seats or footstools (Metzger; also Keel 1978: 330 fig. 441). The difficult Ugaritic verse *KTU* 1.101.1 may similarly equate Ba'lu's throne with Mount Zaphon (cf. Cross 1973: 147–48), but this is disputed (e.g., by Kloos 1986: 48). A later tradition evocative of 15:17 describes Yahweh's throne as consisting of seven mountains surrounded by trees (1 Enoch 24). To be sure, most texts locate Yahweh's throne in the sky (1 Kgs 8:27–49; Isa 40:22; 57:15; 66:1; Ps 2:4; 33:13–14; 93:2–4; 103:19; 123:1). But this is not a real contradiction, given the physical and conceptual interpenetration of "mountain" and "heaven" (see COMMENT, pp. 563–64, 568).

devised. The primary meaning of *p'l* is "make, do." Luzzatto, however, calls attention to another nuance: "plan, intend" (Mic 2:1; possibly Isa 41:4; Ps 58:3); compare *yāṣar* 'fabricate, intend.'

The sanctum. Or "*your* sanctum," assuming that the second person suffixes of *naḥălātəkā* 'your property' and *šibtəkā* 'your sitting/enthronement/dwelling' carry over to *miqdāš*.

A *miqdāš* is any holy place. The word generally denotes permanent temples, whether Israelite or foreign, but even the portable Tabernacle is called a *miqdāš* (Lev 16:33; 21:23, etc.). As we have already observed, much of the vocabulary in 15:17 is traditional Canaanite, also describing Ba'lu's palace in Ugaritic myth: *btk.ǵry.'il.ṣpn bqdš.bǵr nḥlty* 'in the midst of my mountain, divine Zaphon, in the sanctum, my property mountain' (*KTU* 1.3.iii.30, [iv.20]); see above and COMMENT.

Is the "sanctum" of 15:17 a palace or a tent? At Ugarit and Babylon, at least, the erection of a solid palace betokened the storm god's elevation to kingship. And throughout the Near East, monumental construction was the quintessential royal occupation (Hurowitz 1992). One might therefore conclude that v 17 refers to a true palace, be it celestial or mundane (see COMMENT). Still, the Ugaritic high god 'Ilu reigns from a tent, and by one interpretation, 15:13 refers to Yahweh's Tabernacle (see NOTE). The matter remains moot.

my Lordship. On *'ădōnāy* as an abstract plural, see GKC §124i and NOTE to 1:17. On the variant "Yahweh," see TEXTUAL NOTE.

your hands. For most exegetes, the reference to the sanctum built by Yahweh himself proves that there must be a physical temple on the mountain. For others, it proves the opposite: the sanctum must be as incorporeal as the hands that built it, like the abode of the Greek gods on Olympus (Freedman 1981). The distinction may be too sharply drawn, however. Ba'lu's palace on Mount Zaphon is presumably metaphysical, yet there was apparently once a structure at the summit (Schaeffer 1938: 325).

Whatever house Yahweh is said to have built, we must take seriously the poem's claim that he did it without intermediary. Ps 78:69 and 147:2 similarly credit Yahweh with building the Temple and Jerusalem, respectively. This is a familiar mythic theme: according to the Egyptian "Memphite Theology," the god Ptaḥ himself created Egypt's cities, nomes and idols (*ANET* 5). *Enūma eliš* similarly credits the gods with constructing the temples of Babylon (for other Sumero-Akkadian examples, see Hurowitz 1992: 333–34). We even have rituals from Mesopotamia (Jacobsen 1987a) and Hatti (*ANET* 356) whereby craftsmen disclaim any role in the fabrication of sacred images or buildings. Finally, like and yet unlike Exod 15:17 is the Ugaritic myth in which Ba'lu commissions the divine craftsman Kôṯaru to build him a house. Even though the storm god exults, "My mansion have I built of silver, my palace of gold," it is quite clear who did the work (*KTU* 1.4.vi.36–38, viii.35–37; cf. v.10–11). For further discussion, see COMMENT.

founded. Kônǝnû comes from the same root as *mākôn* 'seat, fixed place' (see above, pp. 542–43). In addition to connoting enthronement, the root *kwn* can appear in cosmogonic contexts (Isa 45:18; Ps 8:4; 24:2; 119:90; Prov 3:19). This might suggest that the founding of the sanctum is of comparable importance with Creation, and even coeval with it (cf. *Enūma eliš*).

SPECULATION: The difficult verse Ps 68:10 also associates *kōnēn* with Yahweh's *naḥălā*. I propose we read **naḥălātǝkā wǝtil'â* (MT: *wǝnil'â*) *'attâ kônantâ* (MT: *kônantāh*) 'your property and your power you founded,' on the analogy of Ugaritic *ǵr.nḫlty . . . gbʿ.tlʾyt* 'my property mountain . . . mountain of my power' (*KTU* 1.3.iii.30–31).

Each line of 15:17b–c contains three semantic units; the parallelism may be represented schematically as ABC : A'C'B'. Element A, a two-word phrase (*mākôn ləšibtəkā*) parallels the one-word A' (*miqdāš*). Conversely, the one-word B (*pāʿaltā*) corresponds to B' (*kônənû yāde[y]kā*). Element C (*yahwe[h]*) becomes C' (*ʾādōnāy*). The cola balance with four words and four stresses each.

15:18. *Yahweh, he will reign.* Yahweh has proved himself unique (v 11) as shepherd (v 13), farmer and builder (v 17) and most of all as warrior (vv 1–12)— all common metaphors for ancient Near Eastern kingship, which encompassed the sciences necessary for controlling the natural and political worlds (Masetti-Rouault n.d.). Now he is explicitly acclaimed king.

Exod 15:18 features emphatic inversion. Normal word order would be, not *yahwe(h) yimlōk*, but **yimlōk yahwe(h)*, as in Ps 146:10 (Goldin 1971: 47). Such inverted syntax typifies proclamations of kingship. The implication is that all rivals—and, for that matter, the previous king—have been eliminated from contention (e.g., 1 Sam 12:12; 1 Kgs 1:13, 17, 18, 24, 30; 2 Chr 23:3; for further discussion and bibliography, see Lipiński 1965: 336–461). Many commentators compare the Ugaritic passage in which, having defeated the Sea, Baʿlu is emphatically acclaimed king with inverted syntax and the enclitic: *bʿlm.yml[k]*): 'Baʿlu [and no one else] shall reign' (*KTU* 1.2.iv.32) (e.g., Norin 1977: 97). Similarly, we read in *Enūma eliš* IV:28, *Marduk-ma šarru* 'It is Marduk who is king' (for further Akkadian parallels, see Lipiński p. 368). In contrast, when ʿAttaru is merely nominated king, the word order is normal: *ymlk.ʿttr* 'Let ʿAttaru rule' (*KTU* 1.6.i.55). Exod 15:18 thus proclaims that Yahweh—not the gods, not Pharaoh, not the nations—will rule over Israel. (I do not find convincing Goldin's [1971: 48–57] *tour de force* argument that the intended contrast is between Yahweh and David.)

In 15:18, not only is the syntax inverted but the verb is in the "imperfect" form *yimlōk*. It cannot be jussive (*pace* Cross 1973: 131), since a jussive precedes its subject, while *yimlōk* follows (contrast Ps 146:16). Nor is it likely to describe an existing state: "Yahweh rules." The ordinary way to proclaim that someone has become king or reigns is with the perfect *mālak* (2 Sam 15:10; 1 Kgs 1:11, 13; Isa 24:23; Mic 4:7; Ps 47:9; 93:1; 96:10; 97:1; 99:1; possibly also Ps 10:16). At least in prose, the imperfect *yimlōk* refers only to the future. The man in question is not yet king, but will become king (1 Sam 12:12; 1 Kgs 1:13, 17, 24, 30; 2 Chr 23:3). Most likely, then, the verbs in vv 17–18 are true futures. Yahweh and Israel are not yet at the holy mountain. Once they arrive, and once Yahweh founds his throne, he will begin his eternal reign.

Over what should Yahweh rule? Over Israel, at least. In the Ugaritic parallel, however, Baʿlu is proclaimed king of the universe (*KTU* 1.4.vii.49–52). In the Song of the Sea, too, Yahweh's incomparability (15:11) implies world dominion. While Mic 4:7 (cf. v 5) and probably Ps 146:10 assert God's kingship over Israel in particular, most biblical parallels make it clear that his reign is universal (Ps 47:9; 93:1; 96:10; 97:1; 99:1). I assume the same for the Song of the Sea. (For further discussion of Yahweh's kingship, see Lipiński 1963, 1965 and Brettler 1989.)

ever and eternity. The root *mlk* 'reign' is often associated with expressions of perpetuity, whether the ruler is divine or human (see *RSP* 1.266).

15:19. *For Pharaoh's horse . . . Sea.* Presumably bothered by the superfluity of this verse, Rashi proffers, "When (*kî*) Pharaoh's horse . . . entered the Sea, *then* Yahweh brought back upon them the Sea's waters" (alternatively: *"when* Pharaoh's horse . . . entered the Sea, and *when* Yahweh brought back upon them the Sea's waters, *then* Miriam . . . took the drum" [Rashbam; Bekhor Shor]). Less plausible is Ramban's reading, connecting *"when* Pharaoh's horse . . . entered the Sea" (15:19) back to "then sang Moses" (15:1). We do best, however, to translate *kî* according to its usual meaning, "for," making 15:19 a prose summary of the preceding poem.

Jewish scribal tradition, defended by ibn Ezra, treats 15:19 as the Song's conclusion, versifying as follows:

> For Pharaoh's horse, with his chariotry and his horsemen, entered the Sea,
> And Yahweh brought back upon them the Sea's waters,
> But Israel's Sons walked on the dry land in the Sea's midst.

This counterintuitive treatment of v 19 as poetry (cf. also Judg 5:31) may stem from a desire to eliminate redundancy from the prose narrative, or to remedy the Song's perceived silence concerning Israel's passage (Lohfink 1968: 83; cf. NOTE to 15:16). The antiquity of the tradition is attested by 4QReworked Pentateuch[c], where, however, the versification is somewhat different.

15:20. *Miriam.* The only other person with this name in the Old Testament is a man, the son of an Egyptian princess (1 Chr 4:17). Since both Miriams have Egyptian connections, most scholars derive *miryām* from Egyptian *mrỉ* 'to love'—but without explaining the terminal *-ām*. Von Soden (1970), however, posits an old Canaanite root **rym* 'give' behind the Amorite names "Yarim-Lim" and "Yarim-Adad" and possibly Hebrew *tərûmâ* 'offering.' He accordingly interprets *miryām* as "Gift." There is also a Ugaritic noun *mrym* 'height, peak' (< *rwm* 'be high'); thus, *miryām* might mean "Eminence."

the prophetess. A prophet (*nābî'*) or prophetess (*nəbî'â*) transmits divine messages to humans. Only four other biblical women are so described: Deborah (Judg 4:4), Huldah (2 Kgs 22:14), Noadiah (Neh 6:14) and Isaiah's anonymous wife (Isa 8:3) (many suspect, however, that here "prophetess" means "Mrs. Prophet"). In addition, Ezek 13:17 and Joel 3:1 refer to prophetesses in general. Various female ecstatics are known from Mari and Mesopotamia: the *šā'iltu, maḫḫūtu* and *āpiltu.*

In Numbers 12, Miriam will claim prophetic powers like those of Aaron and Moses himself. Why is her vocation mentioned already in 15:20? Perhaps her prophetic office is directly related to her musical performance. Deborah, too, is singer and prophetess; Luzzatto argues that all praise singers are prophets, noting that 1 Chr 25:1–3 imputes prophetic powers to the choristers Asaph, Heman and Jeduthun. Conversely, prophets sometimes use musical accompaniment (1 Sam 10:5; 2 Kgs 3:15) (Zimmerli 1977: 202). Perhaps certain singers were considered inspired, like the Greek bards (*Odyssey* 22:349). But most likely, "Miriam the prophetess, Aaron's sister" is simply Miriam's full title, used here upon her first appearance.

Aaron's sister. Miriam is not called *Moses'* sister, because in E she is only his kinswoman (see NOTE to 4:14). For the redacted Torah, however, Aaron, Moses and Miriam are full siblings (Num 26:59 [P])—so the question remains: what is the implication of "Aaron's sister"? A woman is often identified by her relationship to a male guardian, be it husband, father or brother (cf. Gen 4:22; 25:20; 28:9; 36:3, 22; Exod 6:23; 2 Kgs 11:2; 1 Chr 4:19) (Bekhor Shor; Jacob 1992: 433). We must suppose that Miriam is associated particularly with Aaron because he is her *senior* brother (Ramban).

drum. *Tōp* is a Mediterranean word, attested not only in Hebrew, Phoenician and other Semitic languages (see Meyers 1994: 220), but also in Greek (*typtō* 'beat,' *tympanon* 'drum'). Evidently, musical instruments and terminology crossed the sea—unless we have independent lexicalizations of the sound *tap-tap-tap.* For depictions of women holding discoid objects, probably drums, see Keel (1978: 337–39, figs. 450–51, 453–54), Meyers (1987, 1991, 1994) and Beck (1990).

all the women. Songs, especially victory songs, were a special female province (Judges 5; 11:34; 18:6; 21:12; 29:5; 2 Sam 1:20; Jer 31:4; Ps 68:26; Cant 7:1; Jdt 15:12–13; cf. 1 Sam 2:1–10 [Watts 1992: 29–31]) (Bird 1987: 418–19; Meyers 1987, 1991, 1994; Poethig 1985). For a comparable Arab victory celebration, see Doughty (1936: 1.499).

Generally, when celebrating women greet male victors, there are erotic overtones. For instance, David the conqueror displaces Saul as the women's darling (1 Sam 18:7; 21:12), even acquiring Saul's own daughters (1 Sam 18:17–29) and wives (2 Sam 12:8). In Exodus 15, however, this aspect is muted, if present at all (see NOTES to 15:1 and 32:6, 18).

went forth. This is a cliché in female celebrations; cf. Judg 11:34; 21:21; 1 Sam 18:6; Jer 31:4. Since it seems that respectable women ordinarily remained indoors, "went forth" may originally have been meant literally. In 15:20, however, the phrase is *pro forma*, since the women are already outside. The sense rather is something like "stepped forward." I assume the women's performance is simultaneous with the men's (see below). Janzen's (1992) reading of 15:19–20 as temporally *preceding* vv 1–18 is unnatural.

and . . . dances. *Māḥōl* is particularly associated with women (Judg 11:34; Jer 31:4). It generally connotes a frolicking dance (Judg 21:21; 1 Sam 21:12; 29:5) or joy itself (Ps 30:12; Lam 5:15). The apparent root is *ḥwl* 'whirl, writhe' (for other possibilities, however, see Poethig 1985: 52–66). Elsewhere, *māḥôl* appears in lists of musical instruments (Ps 149:3; 150:3–5; perhaps also Ps 53:1; 88:1 [*BHS*]) (Luzzatto: Cassuto 1967: 182). One possibility is that the *māḥôl*-dance was accompanied by an instrument of the same name, whether whirled (*ḥwl*) or hollow (*ḥll*) (Qimḥi [*Book of Roots*] and Luzzatto compare *ḥālîl*, a woodwind). But more likely we have zeugma: the women step forth (beating) drums and (dancing) dances.

15:21. *sang back.* Proto-Semitic **ʿny* 'answer' and **ġny* 'sing' (cf. Arabic *ġny*, Syriac *ʿny*) merge into Hebrew *ʿny*, which usually means "answer" but often refers to music (15:21; 32:18 [?]; Num 21:17; 1 Sam 18:7; 21:12; 29:5; Isa 13:22; 27:2; Jer 25:30; 51:14; Ps 88:1; 119:172; 147:7; Ezra 3:11). In fact, LXX Exod 15:21 renders *wattaʿan* as "led them in song," perhaps parsing the verb as Hiphʿil (cf. Silbermann and Rosenbaum 1934: 2.242–43 n. 5). Hos 2:17, "she shall *ʿny* there . . . as [on] the day of her ascent from the land of Egypt," may also use *ʿny* with reference to Miriam's Song or the entire Song of the Sea.

It is striking how often *ʿny*-songs are only a line or two (15:21; Num 21:17; 1 Sam 18:7; 21:12; 29:5; Isa 27:2; Ezra 3:11) (Ehrlich 1908: 323). Perhaps the words were repeated *ad infinitum* (Burns 1987: 14–15), or maybe they were the intermittent chorus of a longer song, the "response" (*Memar Marqah* 2:7 [MacDonald 1963: 1.37–38; 2.57]; Scharbert 1989: 63, and many others); compare "for his loyal benevolence is forever" (Psalm 136), or "how heroes fell!" (2 Sam 1:19–27) (Calvin; Freedman 1980: 79). Many invoke Arabic or Bedouin parallels for songs improvised by a leader with a following chorus, whether of women or men (e.g., Smith 1912: 54). Doughty (1936: 1.384, 385, 412, 607) reports never having heard Arabian women sing more than a single stave. (See also Kugel 1981: 116–19 on Jewish antiphonal singing.) At any rate, the association of *ʿny* with short refrains vitiates the common thesis that 15:21 is only the *incipit* (opening line) of a longer poem (Bekhor Shor; Loewenstamm 1992a: 256–57; Cross 1973: 123–24).

to them. To whom Miriam sings is a little unclear. Reading in English, one at first thinks of the women. But both *lāhem* 'to them' and the imperative *šîrû* 'sing' are masculine. To be sure, gender incongruence is common in Hebrew (Levi 1987). Nevertheless, Miriam probably leads the women in singing back to Moses and the men. (Philo imagines the sweet harmony of treble and bass [*Moses* 1.180; 2.256]!) Compare the duet of Deborah and Barak in Judges 5.

Sing. Unlike 15:1, we now have the imperative *šîrû*, not the cohortative *ʾāšîrâ* 'I would sing,' because the Song is not really Miriam's (Luzzatto). Rather, she "sings back" to Moses and the men, encouraging them to praise Yahweh.

Noth (1962: 121–22) is among the majority who consider 15:21 the original poem, from which 15:1b–18 somehow grew (also Hyatt 1971: 169; Lauha 1963: 33; Coats 1988: 114; Fretheim 1991a: 161). But how could anyone claim to know this? As we have seen, 15:21 is more likely the refrain to 15:1b–18. The dogma "short is old and old is short" survives as a relic of nineteenth-century evolutionistic thought, despite perennial criticism (e.g., from Garofalo 1937: 6; Loewenstamm 1992a: 257; Cross 1973: 124).

COMMENT

A PILLAR OF CLOUD AND FIRE

Apparently, Yahweh has not told Israel the way to Canaan. He instead sends the pillar. Moses has already been to Horeb and could probably lead the way himself. But the miraculous apparition simultaneously legitimates his authority (cf. Gressmann 1913: 113) and tests Israel's faith. They do not know their path even a day in advance.

Cloud and fire are in a sense opposites, corresponding to the primal antithesis of dark and light (Gen 1:2–3). Cloud becomes visible by negating the daylight, and fire dispels the night. Yet, in another sense, cloud and fire are complementary: *'ānān* connotes smoke as well as cloud (Lev 16:13; Ezek 8:11), and the Israelites considered lightning a form of combustion (NOTE to 9:24). Thus the pillar simultaneously evokes images quite distinct for us: a storm cloud and a smoking fire.

Fire and cloud/smoke betoken the divine presence (e.g., Gen 15:17; Exod 19:18; 20:18; 24:16–18; Ps 97:2–4). Yahweh lives or travels in a cloud, from which he speaks to mortals (e.g., 24:16, 18; 33:7–11; 34:5; 40:34–35; Num 11:25; 12:5; 14:14; Deut 1:33; 5:22[19]; 1 Kgs 8:10–12; Isa 6:4; 19:1; Ps 99:7). Other passages liken Yahweh to fire or describe his manifestation in fire (e.g., Exod 3:2, 19–20; Deut 4:24; 9:3; see Miller 1965; Meyers 1976: 144–46; Weinfeld 1983: 138–40). As a vestige of Canaanite polytheism, Yahweh's fire may even be an independent being (Gen 3:24; Ps 104:4; see Hendel 1985). Throughout P in particular, light and cloud together constitute Yahweh's "Glory," his earthly manifestation (cf. Weinfeld 1983: 132–34). Beyerlin (1965: 134, 156–57) finds the physical reality behind this imagery in the clouds of incense believed to house and conceal the divine presence in the Tabernacle and Temple (Lev 16:2, 13) (also Plastaras 1966: 186; Sarna 1986: 112–13).

In Exodus 13–14, the precise relationship between Deity and pillar is not clear. Yahweh seems to be within or atop the pillar (14:24), apparently his vehicle (Jacob 1992: 383), somewhat like the fiery chariots of 2 Kgs 2:11; 6:17. Holzinger (1900: 46), however, renders *bə'ammûd* (13:21) as "*in the form of* a pillar"—i.e., the pillar *is* God or his angelic manifestation. Exod 14:19 in fact explicitly associates the pillar with God's *mal'āk* 'messenger, angel.' We may compare Ugaritic *'nn*, connoting a divine servant (*KTU* 1.1.iii.[17]; 2.i.[18], 35; 3.iv.76, etc.; see Mann 1971: 19–24) and apparently cognate to Hebrew *'ānān* 'cloud' (but cf. Cross 1973: 165–66 n. 86). Mann infers that the *'nn* is simply a personified cloud. For Mendenhall (1973: 54–56, 59), however, a god's *'nn* is the nimbus representing his or her presence. Thus it is a manifestation equivalent to an angel, precisely as in 14:19 (see also NOTE to 3:2).

Among an angel's important functions is to guide the wayfarer. In Gen 24:7, Abraham promises his servant, "Yahweh . . . will send his Messenger before you" (Mann 1977: 112; cf. Rendtorff 1990: 98). We frequently read of the *mal'āk* leading Israel out from Egypt and through the wilderness (13:21; 23:20, 23; 32:34; 33:2; Num 20:16), even through Canaan (Judg 2:1–4). (On the ancient Near Eastern motif of divine military guidance, see Lipiński 1965: 407–10 and Mann 1971.)

But the pillar of Exodus 13–14 does more than guide. It separates the Hebrews from the Egyptians (14:20) and apparently hides the drying of the Sea (cf. Josh 24:7; Ps 105:39; for ancient parallels, see Weinfeld 1983: 144–45). The pillar also has an offensive capacity: from it, Yahweh "panics" Egypt (NOTE to 14:24). Mendenhall (1973: 32–68) compares Akkadian *melammu*, the dread radiance of gods and kings (see Oppenheim 1943; Cassin 1968; on the motif of the refulgent warrior, see Thompson 1955: motif F969.3.2). In its bellicose aspect, God's fiery, cloudy conveyance also recalls stereotypic depictions of the Canaanite storm god, among whose epithets at Ugarit is *rkb.ʿrpt* 'cloud-rider' (on divine sky-riders, see Weinfeld 1973: 421–25; on Yahweh and Baal, see Cross 1973: 147–94). The pillar theme may even dimly reflect a tradition that Yahweh fully manifested himself at the Sea (compare Ps 77:12–21 and postbiblical references to Egypt being burnt in the Sea [NOTE to 15:7]). The pentateuchal narrative, however, reserves Yahweh's stormy appearance for Sinai (chap. 19).

We might also consider Yahweh's vehicle of fire and cloud the literary analogue to the Covenant Ark, equally symbolic of the divine presence (cf. Mann 1971; Van Seters 1994: 340–41). Like the cloud pillar, the ark travels before the people "to scout out for them rest" and guide them (Num 10:33–36; Josh 3:3–4). It also focuses Yahweh's protection over Israel (Num 14:44–45; Joshua 3–4; 6; 1 Samuel 4–6; 2 Sam 11:11; 15:24–29). Further: as the cloud is associated with the Suph Sea crossing, so is the ark associated with the Jordan crossing (Joshua 3–4). And the ark, too, appears to represent the storm, through its association with cherubim (25:19–20; cf. 1 Kgs 6:23–28)—not cupids, but winged monsters on which Yahweh sits enthroned and rides to battle (2 Sam 22:11; cf. Ps 104:3 [Mettinger 1978: 34–35; Greenberg 1983b]). The cherubim represent, among other things, the power and mobility of the storm (e.g., 2 Sam 22:8–16; Ezekiel 1; 10).

THE SEA EVENT ACCORDING TO THE SOURCES

In the composite text, it is clear what happens at the Sea. Yahweh parts the waters, and the Hebrews enter onto the seabed with Egypt close behind. Once Israel is safely across, or nearly so, Yahweh releases the waters, submerging Pharaoh's host (compare Ps 78:13–14, 53; 106:9–11; 136:13–15; Neh 9:9, 11).

Just as Exodus as a whole conforms to universal storytelling conventions (see INTRODUCTION, pp. 32–34), the miracle at the Sea exemplifies well-known narrational motifs. In many tales of magic, wet becomes dry or dry becomes wet (e.g., 17:1–7 and parallels). It is, moreover, a folkloric cliché that obstructing waters magically part or recede before a hero (Thompson 1955: motif D1551; see also Gaster 1949: 42–43). For example, in an oft-cited if rather homely parallel to Exodus, an Egyptian wizard parts a lake to retrieve a lost ring (Lichtheim 1973: 217). The biblical miracle is doubly wondrous, however, because reversible: wet becomes dry becomes wet again (on such miracles, see Bertman 1964).

That a story type is classified and cataloged does not imply that every case is wholly fictitious. For example, various classical writers record the recession of the Pamphylian Sea before Alexander (e.g., Josephus *Ant.* 2.348), and many critical scholars are willing to accept that the Macedonian exploited a natural phenomenon. Similarly, Scipio Africanus the Elder in the Second Punic War supposedly took advantage of the timely subsidence of a marsh (Livy, *History of Rome* 26.45). Interestingly, if Livy may be believed, Scipio was far from oblivious to his feat's mythic overtones: "What he had ascertained by painstaking and calculation, Scipio represented as a miracle and an act of the gods, who for the passage of the Romans were diverting the sea . . . opening up ways never before trodden by man's foot" (trans. F. G. Moore, LCL). Haupt (1904: 149) briefly recounts several similar, well-documented occurrences from modern times.

Much like Livy deflating Scipio, Hellenized Egyptian historians claimed that there was nothing miraculous in the Jews' escape from Egypt. Granting the basic historicity of the Torah, they inferred that Moses simply exploited his superior knowledge of the tides (Artapanus *apud* Eusebius *Praep. evangelica* 9.27.35). And many since have sought natural explanations for the prodigies of Exodus 14–15: tide, earthquake and tsunami (e.g., Haupt 1904: 149–50; Dayan 1977; Goedicke *apud* Shanks 1981; Wilson 1985: 128–41). While reserving further consideration of What Really Happened for APPENDIX B (vol. II), I would make a preliminary observation. The hydrologists, geologists, meteorologists and biblical scholars, amateur and professional, who reconstruct the actual Sea event rarely take into account the fruits of source criticism. The familiar picture of a dry path between looming walls of water comes from the latest source, P. As we shall see, what happened according to the older documents, JE and the Song, is less clear.

According to JE, "Yahweh conducted the Sea with a mighty *forward* wind all the night and made the Sea into the dry ground" (14:21). Although this somewhat resembles the younger Priestly account, it sounds more as if the wind simply deflects the water. Then the Egyptians drown in the returning waters while attempting to pass over the seabed (v 27). *But we are never told of the Hebrews' transit in JE.* This omission might be explained in one of four ways:

1. The tradition of Israel's crossing was so well known it did not need spelling out. This is almost but not quite impossible. On the one hand, many passages describe the Sea event only partially or piecemeal (e.g., Isa 43:16–17; 51:9–11; 63:12–14; Ps 66:6; 77:17–21; 78:13, 53; 114:3, 5). Even Psalms

universally regarded as based upon the composite Torah omit crucial episodes: 106 and 136 lack the Covenant at Horeb-Sinai, while 105 and 135 skip both the Sea and Sinai. Nevertheless, all these passages are lyric poetry, in which the writer assumes his audience's familiarity with primary tradition. We expect from historiographical narrative greater completeness.

2. The Hebrews in fact do not cross the Sea in JE. Rather, they stand near the shore, perhaps having circumvented an inlet. Then Yahweh makes the Sea recede, and the Egyptians unwittingly enter onto the seabed (confused by the cloud and fire? seeking a shortcut?). When Yahweh releases the waters, Egypt drowns, and Israel goes its way. This is unquestionably the most interesting of the four theories, and is the view of many influential commentators (e.g., Meyer 1906: 22; Noth 1962: 118; Scharbert 1981; Schmidt 1983: 63; Kohata 1986: 280–89). Some even take the command *hityaṣ(ṣə)bû* 'station yourselves' (14:13) as an order *not* to cross the Sea (e.g., Plastaras 1966: 171; see also Blum 1990: 257 n. 96). But this is a misinterpretation. The intent is rather "stand and watch" (see NOTE).

In fact, two texts apparently based upon JE, or sharing a common tradition, also omit the Sea crossing. Josh 24:6–7 recalls, "You came to the Sea, and Egypt pursued after your fathers with chariotry and with horsemen to the Suph Sea. And they cried out to Yahweh, and he put darkness between you and between the Egyptians, and he brought upon him [Egypt] the Sea, and it covered him." Deut 11:4 similarly reports, "He made the Suph Sea's waters overflow over *their faces* when they pursued after them." Still, these passages do not prove that JE lacked a crossing. Like the Psalms cited above, they allude to known events, without the necessity of a full recounting.

3. Israel's crossing *is* mentioned in JE. As I have argued under SOURCE ANALYSIS, JE contained the Song of the Sea, which at least hints at Israel's passage in 15:16 (see NOTE). By this theory, JE does not narrate the transit in the interests of economy (cf. SOURCE ANALYSIS to 7:8–11:10). I have trouble convincing myself, however, that this is the case.

4. The JE account of the Hebrews' crossing has been excised by the Redactor to accommodate P (14:22–23). Given the Redactor's overall affinity for P, this is plausible (although, with his evident tolerance for redundancy, he might have easily produced a passable composite).

We can, in fact, quote Joshua again to prove that JE *did* tell of Israel's passage. According to Josh 2:10; 4:23, "Yahweh dried the Suph Sea's waters from before you in your going out from Egypt . . . Yahweh . . . dried the Jordan's waters from before you . . . as Yahweh . . . did to the Suph Sea, which he dried from before us until our crossing." Since these sections of Joshua seem generally unrelated to P (note, however, the P-word *yabbāšâ* in Josh 4:22), we might infer that the author knew a form of JE, or some other pre-Priestly tradition, describing an Israelite crossing (Gressmann 1913: 116; for others, see Kohata 1986: 281 n. 20).

Furthermore: whence did the Priestly Writer receive the tradition that Israel crossed the Sea, if not from JE? A common answer is: from the Jordan crossing under Joshua (Scharbert 1981). But against this we may lodge several objections: (a) Josh 4:22–23, which models the Jordan crossing on the Sea crossing, would have to be reckoned a late addition; (b) the many parallels between Joshua and Moses make it reasonable that each would lead his people across a sea/river; (c) both Elijah and Elisha, whose careers also parallel Moses', cross the divided Jordan on *ḥārābâ* 'dry ground' (2 Kgs 2:8, 14) (see Fohrer 1957: 55–58; Carroll 1969: 408–14; Carlson 1969: 431–39; Propp 1987a: 71–72 n. 11); (d) P's picture of twin walls of water is rather different from the single "heap" in Josh 3:13, 16; (e) Ps 66:6 and 114:3, 5 poetically equate the Sea and Jordan events, as if the waters of both were not simply dried but also crossed; (f) no poetic text speaks only of Egypt's destruction, while many describe Israel's crossing. None of these arguments is decisive, but they cumulatively favor the proposition that JE did tell of the Israelites' passage, either in 15:16 or in another text now lost.

How does the Song of the Sea (15:1b–18) envision the episode at the Suph Sea? Can it be understood apart from JE and P? Cross and Freedman (1975), like most others, consider the Song to be originally independent of its narrative context, and far older in grammar and style (see APPENDIX A, vol. II). A minority, however, argue that the Song presupposes or is based upon its current narrative context (Bender 1903: 47; Herrmann 1973: 57; Thompson and Irvin 1977: 165–66; Alter 1985: 52; Brenner 1991: 51). I take something of a middle ground. I believe that the Song is originally independent (see APPENDIX A, vol. II). But I deny that it can be interpreted by internal criteria alone. Exod 15:1b–18 is not narrative poetry; indeed, none such exists in all the Bible. Rather, it is lyric poetry. Events are presented out of order, time is telescoped, crucial events are alluded to rather than narrated. For example, we are not told whom the Egyptians are pursuing or why, save that they hope for spoils. In other words, the Song of the Sea, like the Song of Deborah (Judges 5), presumes of its audience familiarity with the subject, whether from direct participation (the "implied audience") or from knowledge of tradition (the "actual audience," i.e., readers).

When we come to interpret the Song, then, we must look to the prose sources. While we cannot blindly trust their versions, we must respect their proximity to the Song in date and cultural context. We incur greater risks reading the Song in isolation than in intelligent consultation of JE and P, as well as extra-pentateuchal materials. This procedure might be disparaged as harmonistic, but it is mere prudence. At worst, we shall have correctly interpreted the Song in its current literary context, as the editor(s) intended. At best, we shall have understood the poem as did its ancient audience and author.

I find nothing in the Song contradictory to JE, and little different from P (*pace* Cross 1973: 132 n. 7). Yahweh drives back the Sea (cf. 15:8), leads Israel across (cf. 15:16), lures Egypt after them (cf. 15:9) and releases the waters (cf. 15:10). True, events are presented out of order, but that is a characteristic of the hymnic genre. I thus reject the claim that the Song describes a naval mishap (Cross and Freedman 1975: 47; Cross 1973: 112–44; Krahmalkov 1981;

Scharbert 1989: 64). In fact, Cross's overall thesis, that the Song originated and/or was transmitted in the context of a ritualized Jordan crossing at Gilgal, comports better with the traditional reading (see NOTE to 15:16 "crosses"). Moreover Cross explains the mythic resonances of the Exodus tradition by positing an actual event whose mythological overtones struck the Israelites (see below). A fortuitous shipwreck would not fit the bill at all (for other arguments against the chariots-on-barges hypothesis, see NOTES to 15:1 "hurled," 15:4 "cast," 15:8 "congealed" and 16:10 "blew").

THE STORM GOD AND THE SEA
IN THE ANCIENT NEAR EAST

Ancient Near Easterners found their world unsettling. On the one hand, the "Fertile Crescent" was bounded by encroaching deserts, ever-present reminders of the consequences of drought. On the other hand, the Sea ceaselessly nibbled the edge of the habitable earth. And overhead hung a fathomless mass of water, the sky—suspended, apparently, by nothing and always threatening to crash down in a new Flood.

In all ancient Near Eastern mythology, what created *Lebensraum* for terrestrial creatures was displacement of water: vertically to accommodate the atmosphere, and horizontally to unveil the dry land. Scrolls and tablets from Egypt, Syria-Palestine and Mesopotamia tell of titanic struggles by which various storm deities quelled and repelled the inimical, primordial waters, often pictured as serpentine. This is the so-called Combat Myth (important studies are Gunkel 1895; Fontenrose 1959; Wakeman 1973; Cassuto 1975: 2.80–99; Rummel 1981: 233–84; Day 1985; Kloos 1986; Forsyth 1987 and Batto 1992).

The association of seas and serpents may be explained in several ways. We might think of the ocean's glittering undulation and insatiable appetite. The circum-terrestrial sea may well have been conceived as a snake biting its own tail (for Egyptian depictions, see Keel 1978: 42, 44, 45, figs. 38–40; for a Phoenician parallel, see West 1971: pl. IIb). Or is the inspiration rather a river's twisting course (cf. the English "Serpentine" and American "Snake" Rivers)? Are waves caused by a giant tail lashing (cf. perhaps KTU 1.83.6–7)? All these images may be relevant—along with occasional encounters with eels and crocodiles.

The Egyptians believed that various gods each night warded off a subterranean sea monster threatening the sun (te Velde 1967: 99–108). This combat was also part of Creation. According to a late-second-millennium text, when the sun god "made heaven and earth . . . he repelled the water-monster" ("Instruction for King Merikare," ANET 417). In New Kingdom Egypt, when Canaanite cultural influence was strong and the god Seth was equated with Asiatic Baal (see below), Seth became the principal conqueror of the serpent Apophis (te Velde p. 123).

In late-third-millennium Mari, Syria, a seal may depict a god spearing a stream (see Vanel 1965: 73–74, 177 [fig. 30]; Keel 1978: 47–49). Also from Mari,

c. 1800, comes our oldest unambiguous evidence of the Northwest Semitic Combat Myth. A letter to King Zimri-Lim makes tantalizingly brief reference to the weapon with which the storm god Adad (= Ugaritic Haddu) battled the Sea (Charpin and Durand 1986: 174; Durand 1993; see also COMMENT to Exodus 3–4, p. 228).

Tablets from Ugarit, Syria, dating to c. 1300, recount the struggle of Baʿlu ("Lord," biblical Baal), also called Haddu ("Thunder"?), against Yammu the Sea (*KTU* 1.1–4; *ANET* 129–35). Because Ugaritic is not well understood and the tablets are damaged, we are unsure just how the story begins. When affairs become clear, Baʿlu is depressed by his lack of a permanent abode. To compound his problems, Prince Sea, also called Judge River, has sent messengers to the divine assembly demanding the gods' fealty and the delivery of Baʿlu as hostage. All the gods are cowed, except for Baʿlu himself. With two clubs provided by the divine craftsman Kôṯaru, he crushes Sea and—though this is disputed—probably dries him up (on *nšt*, see Montgomery 1935: 273; for other interpretations, see van Zijl 1972: 41–42). Then he is acclaimed king: *tqḥ.mlk.ʿlmk.drkt.dt.drdrk . . . ym.lmt.bʿlm yml[k]* 'Assume your eternal kingship, your everlasting power . . . Sea is dead! Baʿlu shall reign!' (*KTU* 1.2.iv.10, 32). Baʿlu celebrates by commissioning from Kôṯaru a dwelling atop Mount Zaphon (modern Jabal ʾal-ʾAqraʿ, north of Ugarit). Kôṯaru builds a vast edifice (*KTU* 1.4.v.56–57), featuring a window in the clouds from which Baʿlu thunders (*KTU* 1.4.vii.18–29, 25–30; cf. v.8) and presumably sheds precipitation (*KTU* 1.4.v.6–9; cf. Gen 7:11; 8:2; 2 Kgs 7:2; Isa 24:18; Mal 3:10). Kôṯaru also incorporates blue stone, perhaps as flooring (*KTU* 1.4.v.19, 34–35; cf. v.11 and Exod 24:10). Though the point is debated, I believe that Baʿlu's palace is equivalent to the sky itself (Propp 1987a: 1, 7 n. 5; cf. de Moor 1971: 162 n. 1). In this new dwelling, he hosts a banquet for the gods, thunders forth and routs his enemies.

Whether this is a true Creation account is a matter of definitions (see Fisher 1965; Mettinger 1982 n. 22). I myself would classify it as such. That it accounts for the theopolitical hierarchy in which Baʿlu rules the universe might alone suffice for a classification as "cosmogony" (< Greek *kosmos* 'order'). Moreover, we must remember that the text is poorly preserved and inadequately understood. If, as I believe, it describes the construction of the firmament, the cosmogonic character is explicit.

Less clearly cosmogonic, however, are passages in Ugaritic myth speaking of Baʿlu or his ally, the goddess ʿAnatu, conquering serpentine sea monsters: *tunnānu* 'Serpent' (*KTU* 1.3.iii.40; 6.vi.51; 83.8) and *lîtānu* 'Twister' (*KTU* 1.5.i.1–3, [28]; on the vocalization, see Emerton 1982). The first name appears in Hebrew as *tannîn* '[sea] serpent,' while the latter is Leviathan (*liwyā-tān*). While these snippets of Canaanite mythology do not mention Creation explicitly, their biblical analogues do (COMMENT to 17:1–7).

Ugarit is our richest mine of Northwest Semitic mythology, but it does not stand alone. A fragmentary mid-second-millennium Canaanite myth discovered in Egypt describes the Sea demanding tribute from the gods. Baal's combat with the Sea was also known in Hellenistic Phoenicia. Philo of Byblos recounts the tale briefly: "Then Ouranos [Heaven] again went to battle, against Pontos [Sea]. Demarous [Baal, cf. his Ugaritic epithet *dmrn*] revolted and allied himself with ⟨him⟩, and Demarous advanced against Pontos, but Pontos routed him" (Eusebius *Praep. evangelica* 1.10.28; translation by Attridge and Oden [1981: 53]). The outcome differs, however, from what we find at Ugarit (unless the Phoenician myth has a lost sequel).

The Northwest Semitic Combat Myth even found its way into Greece, borne by either the Phoenicians or the Anatolian Hurro-Hittites. The native storm god Zeus assumed or already possessed Baal's attributes of supremacy over seas and rivers (e.g., *Iliad* 21:184–99). In particular, he is said to have battled a serpentine-anthropoid giant named Typhon, whom Homer and Hesiod associate with the land of the Arimoi, presumably biblical Aram (Syria) (*Iliad* 2:782–83; Hesiod *Theogony* 304, 820–68). Reflecting the transfer of Canaanite culture from Syria-Palestine into Egypt, Apollodorus locates the combat with Typhon near Mount Casius in Egypt, i.e., the Baal-zephon of Exod 14:2 (*Library* 1.6; cf. Herodotus *Histories* 3.5) (see NOTE to 14:2; APPENDIX B, vol. II). Strabo, however, properly sets the combat in Syria, equating Typhon with the River Orontes (16.2.7) (cf. Ugaritic "Judge River").

Babylon's Creation Myth, *Enūma eliš*, is of disputed antiquity and antecedents (*ANET*³ 60–72, 501–3; Dalley 1989: 233–74; Lambert 1992). But it is well preserved and well understood. In the beginning, there exist only Tiāmat (Mother Ocean) and her husband Apsu (Abyss), conjugally mingled. Successive generations of children are born to mate with one another. When these young gods disturb their elders, Apsu loses patience and plots to destroy his progeny, despite Tiāmat's appeals for compassion. But the youngest god, crafty Ea, defeats Apsu by magic and builds his dwelling upon his ancestor's corpse. In the recesses of this shrine Ea and his wife engender Marduk, god of Babylon and master of the storm.

The story then repeats itself. Young Marduk's winds irritate Tiāmat herself, who spawns a race of monsters and, worse yet, elevates one Qingu as figurehead war leader, consort and king—the original wicked stepfather. Marduk strikes a bargain with the pantheon: if he defeats Tiāmat and Qingu, he shall reign. The gods give him a weapon to kill Tiāmat, and Marduk makes his own preparations, including bow and arrow, lightning, a mace, a net, the winds, an herbal antidote, radiant armor and four venomous chariot horses. Marduk then leads the gods against Tiāmat's cohorts and, ignoring Qingu, challenges her to single combat. Marduk confines Tiāmat in his net, inflates her when her mouth gapes and kills her with an arrow down the gullet. Marduk then proceeds to rout Tiāmat's army.

Next, Marduk splits Tiāmat's corpse "like a fish." Half, laid over the watery abyss—i.e., her slain husband Apsu—becomes the dry land; half becomes the aquamarine sky. Marduk makes Tiāmat's spittle into clouds, her eyes into the headwaters of the Tigris and Euphrates, her breasts into the sources of highland streams. He also builds sacred temples. When the gods ask what they might do in return, Marduk announces his intention to found a habitation for himself and the whole pantheon: the holy city of Babylon. Humanity is created at this point to relieve the gods of their labors. But before they rest forever, the deities perform one last task: they build Babylon and her temples. The gods also set Marduk's bow in the sky as a memorial constellation. The epic ends with a divine banquet and the ritual praise of Marduk.

The similarities between the Mesopotamian and Ugaritic myths are unmistakable. In both, a storm god defeats the Sea, is proclaimed king of gods and men and builds a new palace. Moreover, by my interpretation, both Marduk and Baʿlu-Haddu create the heavens. To explain the similarity, some argue that Enūma eliš derives from West Semitic prototypes (Jacobsen 1968; Durand 1993). Others, however, are dubious (Lambert 1992). It is best to keep an open mind, given the ubiquity of myths of theomachy.

Why should the universe be born from conflict? Freud would cite the immemorial struggle between parent and child. And these myths are also political propaganda, implying that, as the gods defeated Chaos, so will the king crush any who threaten his rule and disturb cosmic stability. Lastly, we should not overlook the obvious need to tell a good story. "The adversary . . . answers a basic human need—to cope with anxiety by telling ourselves stories in which the . . . origin of the anxiety may be located and defined and so controlled" (Forsyth 1987: 12).

The Combat Myth is not necessarily tied to cosmogony, even if the two genres continually overlap. We possess many Mesopotamian myths of battles among gods and monsters. Not all the enemies are marine, nor is the outcome inevitably Creation (cf. Kloos 1986: 70–86). Also in the Hittite myth of the gods' battle with Illuyankas (ANET 125–26; Hoffner 1990: 10–14), the connection with cosmogony is unclear. Still, at least in the Northwest Semitic realm, the gods' opponents tend to have marine associations, and the Combat Myth is usually cosmogonic (cf. Durand 1993: 56–57).

YAHWEH AND THE SEA

Unlike the Phoenicians and Greeks, the Israelites were not mariners (1 Kgs 9:26–28). Pervading biblical literature is terror of the sea and seafaring (e.g., Jonah; Ps 48:6–7; 107:23–29; Sir 43:24–25), mingled with some marvel (Ps 8:9; 104:25–26). Drowning was considered a particularly horrific death, and it symbolized general desperation—doubtless, a universal metaphor (2 Sam 22:17; Ps 42:8; 69:2–3, 15–16; 71:20; 88:7; 124:4–5; 130:1; 144:7; Lam 3:54). Some passages even assimilate the ocean to the realm of the dead, Sheol (see NOTE to 15:12). Israelites viewed sea travel much as we do space travel. The ocean was a remnant of the uncreated universe, a disquieting reminder of Chaos threatening the habitable realm.

The "Israelite Cosmos" should not and cannot be diagrammed in detail (Keel 1978: 56; Oden 1992). Nevertheless, we may venture a few generalizations. According to Genesis 1, all was originally formless water. God created a hemispherical air pocket, defined below by the earth and above by the firmament (see also Ps 24:2; 104:3–9; 136:6). The origin of the earth itself, however, is unclear (see NOTE to 15:8 "congealed"). Some texts view it as supported on pillars or foundations (1 Sam 2:8; Ps 18:8; 75:4; 82:5; 104:5; Job 9:6; 38:4–6), perhaps resting in the underworld beneath the waters (see NOTE to 15:12). At any rate, our world is bounded on all sides by water: in the heavens, underground and at the edges of the discoid earth. Some moisture, carefully regulated, trickles in as rain and groundwater (cf. Gen 8:2; Mal 3:10; Job 38:8, 10). An uncontrolled flow, however, would wreak havoc (Genesis 6–9). Israelites, like other peoples, marveled at the power that erected and sustains this seemingly fragile structure.

As Israel's image of the Cosmos was essentially identical to its neighbors', so its myths of Creation were similar. True, Genesis 1 (P) portrays a majestically peaceful process quite unlike the Combat Myth. Other biblical texts, however, envision a primordial battle between opposed forces of Order and Chaos. As we would expect, each version of the myth is different. But since Gunkel's (1895) pioneering work, all have acknowledged the mythic background of biblical allusions to hostility between Yahweh and the Sea or a sea monster named Rahab, Leviathan or the Serpent (a maximalist catalog of passages would include 2 Sam 22:5–18; Isa 11:15; 17:12–14; 27:1; 30:7; 37:25–26; 44:27; 50:2; 51:9–11, 15; Jer 5:22; 31:35; 46:7–8; Ezek 29:3–5; 32:2–10; Amos 7:4; 9:3; Nah 1:3–4; Hab 3:3–15; Zech 10:11; Ps 29:10; 44:20; 46:3–4; 65:7–8; 69:15–16; 74:12–15; 77:17–20; 87:4; 89:10–11; 93:1–3; 104:5–9; 114:3, 5; 124:4–5; 144:5–7; Prov 8:24–29; Job 7:12; 9:8, 13; 26:10, 13; 38:4–11; 40:25–41:26).

These mythic references are virtually restricted to biblical poetry, which, unlike the historiographic tradition, displays clear Canaanite roots (cf. Talmon 1978c). Thus the Combat Myth is absent from the prosaic Genesis 1. P's Deep (təhōm) is depersonalized. The wind is Yahweh's breath, about to speak the first, creative word (cf. John 1:1–2). Sea monsters do exist for P (Gen 1:21), but as mere marine fauna, not as Yahweh's adversaries (Cassuto 1975: 2.101). And J (Gen 2:4b–3:24) is even more antimythological, eliminating any account of the disposition of the waters and shrinking the ancient Serpent into a Garden pest (contrast Childs 1962: 46–48). Only by a later identification with Satan will the snake regain his original stature as Cosmic Adversary (see Forsyth 1987).

I agree with the many scholars who argue that the Exodus tradition evokes or builds upon the ancient Near Eastern Combat Myth (most recently, Batto 1992: 102–52). At a tolerable level of abstraction, the plot of Exodus as a whole, and of the Song of the Sea in particular, resembles Enūma eliš and the Baal epic. A battle is fought at the Sea, whose waters are pushed back or dried by God's wind (Exodus 14–15; cf. Ska 1981: 528–30). Yahweh is thereby proved greatest among gods (15:11). He marches in triumph to his holy mountain (15:17; chaps. 16–17). He releases waters, demonstrating his fructifying power (17:1–7; see Propp 1987a and COMMENT to 17:1–7). He also terrifies his enemies (15:14–16; 17:8–16) and thunders forth (19:16, 19;

20:18). There are several banquets (18:12; 24:5, 9–11). The Tabernacle is constructed (15:17; 25–31; 35–40), and a theopolitical structure is established: the Covenant between King Yahweh and Vassal Israel.

In particular, the motif of splitting (*bqᶜ*) the Sea, mentioned in P and Ps 78:13, is often claimed to have mythic antecedents (e.g., Cross 1973: 135; Eakin 1967). But here a qualification is necessary: in no biblical text does Yahweh "split" a sea serpent or the primordial Sea (Kloos 1986: 148, *pace* Childs 1970: 413). Two possible exceptions are Prov 3:20 and Ps 74:15, but in the first the Deeps are apparently celestial, while in the second the *land* is cleft for the sake of drainage (Emerton 1966). Nor does Baᶜlu cleave Sea in Ugaritic myth; rather, ᶜ*Anatu* cleaves *Death* (*KTU* 1.6.ii.32). The motif of the split Sea is actually paralleled only in Enūma eliš (*ANET* 67; cf. Scharbert 1981; Batto 1992: 110).

Biblical references to the Suph Sea event generally emphasize its paradigmatic aspect, speaking simply of "*the* Sea" without geographical specificity. The implication is that, when Israel left Egypt, Yahweh did more than modify the local topography. By drying or parting the Sea, he recapitulated his primordial deed, temporarily making more dry land (Ska 1981; Fretheim 1991a: 159; cf. *Exod. Rab.* 21:6, 8). (One could also describe the Sea event as an anti-Flood, in which wet becomes dry becomes wet again.)

Moreover, some passages evoke the Combat Myth explicitly by personifying the Suph Sea, e.g., Ps 106:9, "He shouted at the Suph Sea and it dried up." A still clearer case is Ps 114:1–3, "In Israel's going out from Egypt . . . the Sea saw and fled" (cf. Ps 104:6–9). And Ps 77:17–21 clearly articulates the mythic interpretation of the Exodus: "The waters saw you . . . they convulse; also, the Deeps shudder. . . . Your way was in the Sea. . . . You led like a flock your people, through the hand of Moses and Aaron." Second Isaiah, too, links the Combat Myth with the Sea event, and both with the anticipated rescue from Babylon (Isa 44:27; 50:2; 51:9–11).

In fact, the mythic pattern proves amazingly durable, growing stronger in post–Old Testament literature (Gunkel 1895). The text most closely resembling the myth of Baal and the Sea is 2 Esdras 13 (first century C.E.): a manlike figure rises out of the sea, breathes out fire and proceeds to a mountain, from which he chases his enemies. He is finally revealed as the Messiah. In the New Testament, the ancient Serpent Satan, imprisoned by God, proves to be an avatar of Sea/River/Serpent/Leviathan/Rahab (Revelation 12; 20:1–3): he spews forth rivers to overwhelm his victims, but the gaping earth swallows the effluent (Rev 12:15–16; cf. Ps 74:15 and Emerton 1966). Jesus' calming the sea (Matt 8:23–27; Mark 4:25–41; Luke 8:22–25) or treading upon it (Matt 14:22–33; Mark 6:45–52; John 6:16–21) may also dimly echo the Combat Myth (Forsyth 1987: 286; Batto 1992: 179–83). And the Rabbis tell of God killing Rahab, the Sea angel, when he presumed to argue Egypt's cause (see Ginzberg 1928: 6.8 n. 42 for references and a discussion of variants).

THE EXODUS AS MYTH AND HISTORY

To all appearances, consciously or unconsciously, Israel recycled an old mythological plotline as historiography (see INTRODUCTION, pp. 32–35). As the Combat Myth became the Exodus tradition, many modifications were introduced. First, the narrative medium was no longer poetry, but prose. The battle was set, not in primordial, mythic time, but in historic, human time. Not a world, but a single people was saved and made God's kingdom. The Sea was no longer the cosmic ocean, but a specific body of water. It became Yahweh's tool, not a personalized adversary. The role of antagonist was instead transferred to Pharaoh and his host, attacked by Yahweh's wind and metaphorical fire (see NOTE to 15:7) (for the transference, compare Habakkuk 3). Quelled at last by Yahweh, they sink to and perhaps through the sea bottom (NOTE to 15:12). Upon their demise is Yahweh's sovereignty predicated.

The assimilation of the primordial Adversary and Egypt was almost inevitable. Egypt is essentially defined by the River Nile, and, like Canaanites, Israelites did not sharply distinguish between sea and river (Keel 1978: 21). Ezekiel simply calls Pharaoh "the Serpent," simultaneously evoking the Combat Myth and the crocodiles that infest the Nile (Ezek 29:3–5; 32:2–10). Isa 11:15 speaks of Yahweh attacking "Egypt's Sea," presumably the Nile. Isa 37:25–26 and Zech 10:11 allude to the drying of the Nile, recalling both Creation and the Sea event, as well as the river's natural subsidence. Jer 46:7–8 associates the Nile's inundation with Sea/River's attempt to rule the world. And Isa 30:7; Ps 87:4 explicitly call Egypt "Rahab," the ancient sea monster.

The Song of the Sea, in particular, features several mythic vestiges, curiously recast. The verbs $rāmâ$ (15:1, 21) and $yārâ$ (15:4) describe Yahweh's action against Egypt. Although both must mean "hurl," in Hebrew they ordinarily refer to archery (see NOTES). In a sense, the Egyptian chariotry play the role of Yahweh's arrows, shot into the Sea's heart (cf. 2 Sam 22:15; Hab 3:9, 11; Zech 9:14; Ps 144:6). Further demythologizing is apparent in the prominence of chariotry. While in some versions of the Combat Myth, the storm god rides a chariot against or over the Sea, in Exodus the seabed is trampled by Pharaoh's cavalry (cf. Cassuto 1975: 2.100). A final mythic allusion may be the liquidation of Israel's petrified neighbors and enemies (15:15); this could correspond to the irrigation of the earth after the Divine Warrior's triumph (see NOTE to 15:15 and COMMENT to 17:1–7).

A consequence of this demythologization is the splitting, so to speak, of Canaanite Prince Sea/Judge River. In the Bible, Sea and River are each dried and crossed. But they are no longer the same. Sea is the Suph Sea, while River is the Jordan. They still appear coupled in poetry (Ps 66:6; 114:3, 5; see NOTE to 15:16), but the crossings remain distinct historical events.

These observations may answer the frequently asked question: where is the Combat Myth in the Torah? Not in Genesis 1–3, the Creation story proper. Rather, it has been displaced to Exodus 14–15, thrust forward from mythic time into (supposedly) historical time. The implication: Creation is complete only when God's reign on earth commences at Sinai. In effect, Exodus 14–15 and the entire Torah are a Creation Myth.

Does this mean there are no real events behind the Exodus tradition, that it is "myth" in the sense of tall tale? Some indeed consider the Exodus account myth-begotten pseudo-history (e.g., Kloos 1986: 158–212). Others posit actual events whose resemblance to cosmogonic myth impressed the Israelites gradually, but deeply (e.g., Cross 1973: 79–90). Given the paucity of evidence, either view might be correct (see the nuanced and open-minded synthesis of Loewenstamm [1992a: 233–92] and further under APPENDIX B, vol. II).

MORE MARINE METAPHORS

In addition to Creation imagery, we must explore other symbolic interpretations of the Sea crossing. The Samaritan *Memar Marqah* 2:3, 4 regards the Suph Sea as a judge separating the righteous from the wicked (MacDonald 1963: 1.34, 35; 2.51, 53). This curiously anticipates McCarter's (1973) thesis, that the language of drowning in the Psalter and Jonah 2 reflects a judicial ordeal.

In Mesopotamia and Mari, defendants in difficult legal cases might be thrown into a river (Frymer-Kensky 1977a; Bottéro 1981). Survivors were acquitted and the drowned posthumously convicted. In the Northwest Semitic region proper, evidence for the waters' judicial role might be found in the Ugaritic deity "Judge River" (*ṭpṭ.nhr*). Combining *Marqah* and McCarter, one could then argue that the Suph Sea crossing was a symbolic ordeal, which Israel passed and Egypt failed.

I would have reservations about such an approach, however. McCarter considers it immaterial whether the river ordeal was a living Israelite institution (p. 412). But even if the image is a literary fossil, we must posit a Northwest Semitic river ordeal in some period, and, for the moment, we lack any relevant evidence beyond the divine title "Judge River," which could also be interpreted "Chieftain River." Some of McCarter's biblical examples use legal terminology in a highly suggestive manner. But until we find evidence of the ordeal from Israel or Canaan, the hypothesis remains speculative. (Should future discoveries corroborate McCarter's argument, we should be alert to puns between *šṭp* 'overflow' and *špṭ* 'judge.')

A somewhat related approach views the passage through the Sea, not as an ordeal, but as a cleansing (Ska 1981: 525–28). This is more believable. Throughout the Bible, water purifies physically and spiritually (e.g., Gen 6:11–12; Exod 29:4; 2 Kings 5; Mic 7:19; Ps 26:6, etc.) (Reymond 1958: 197). Towers (1959) compares the Egyptian concept of the soul's postmortem purification in *š i3rw* 'the Pool/Sea/Lake of Reeds' (see also Wifall 1980) (*pace* Towers, however, this parallel is two millennia too old to be relevant to the "Reed Sea" problem [see NOTE to 13:18; APPENDIX B, vol. II]). The symbolism is so obvious it is easily overlooked: in Exodus 14–15, the Hebrews rinse off their slavery. Left floating in the bathwater are their erstwhile oppressors.

In addition to its associations with judgment and cleansing, water can symbolize both death (see NOTE to 15:12) and birth (see COMMENT to 2:1–10). Israel's emergence from the Sea might be regarded as a rebirth or resurrection (compare Jonah 2). 1 Cor 10:1–2 aptly analogizes the Sea crossing with Christian baptism, itself symbolic of birth (see further Daniélou 1960: 175–201). And some Christian writers regard the Sea event and baptism as symbolizing both death and resurrection (e.g., Origen *Homiliae in Exodum* 5.1; cf. Rom 6:3–4 and Daniélou pp. 184–90)—even though in Exodus the Egyptians alone do the dying, and the Hebrews alone are "reborn."

A modern, anthropologically informed critic could combine all these interpretations—ordeal, purification, death, rebirth—by invoking the "rite of passage" initiatory complex analyzed by van Gennep (1960), Turner (1967) and others (cf. Lohfink 1968: 85). In Exodus 14–15, as in the Jabbok incident (Gen 32:23–32), the initiate crosses a body of water tangibly separating the old life from the new (Segal [1963: 188 n. 1] also compares Isa 47:2). (For further discussion of the "rite of passage" apropos of the Exodus and wandering traditions, see INTRODUCTION, pp. 35–36.)

THE SONG OF THE MOUNTAIN

Exod 15:1b–18 in effect epitomizes the Book of Exodus. It begins with Pharaoh's forces sinking in the Sea and climaxes with Israel's arrival at Yahweh's holy mountain, where God's new abode is constructed and his kingship commences. Although it is traditionally known as the "Song of the Sea," since that is where it was first sung, 15:1b–18 could with equal justice be called the "Song of the Mountain."

The Song's original date and purpose are disputed (see APPENDIX A, vol. II). For those who put it late, i.e., after the Exile, the Song can have had no other function than that it now serves: interpreting and relieving the narrative flow of the Exodus account (Bender 1903: 47; Herrmann 1973: 57; Thompson and Irvin 1977: 165–66; Alter 1985: 52; Brenner 1991: 51). At the other extreme are those who regard the Song as an eyewitness response to historical events (Judeo-Christian tradition; cf. Albright 1968: 11–13, 45–47).

Most critics, however, posit an original setting in the Israelite cult, which periodically commemorated the departure from Egypt. By this theory, the Song was only secondarily inserted into its present context by one of the pentateuchal authors/editors (see SOURCE ANALYSIS). As for the original ritual setting, some associate 15:1b–18 specifically with the Pesaḥ (e.g., Pedersen 1934; Cross 1973: 112–44). Cross, who proffers the most detailed reconstruction, believes the Song of the Sea was sung at Gilgal in the context of a ritual reenactment of the Sea crossing (see NOTE to 15:16). Admittedly, we do not find explicit evidence of singing at Pesaḥ until after the Exile (2 Chr 30:21;

Jub 49:6; Wis 18:9; Philo *De spec. leg.* 2.148; Matt 26:30; Mark 14:26; *m. Pesaḥ.* 9:3; 10:2, 7). But the custom may be far older. Amos 5:23 already mentions festival singing, and some of the Psalms may have been composed for holidays (e.g., Psalm 81). In fact, Isa 30:29, possibly referring to *Pesaḥ* (note 31:5), mentions rejoicing, singing and flute playing "as on the night of sanctification for a pilgrim festival" (*lēl hitqaddeš-ḥāg*) (Rashi; Qimḥi; Ziegler 1950: 287; Füglister 1963: 31–32; Wambacq 1981: 514). Given its contents, the Song of the Sea is easily construed as the liturgy of a cultic procession to Yahweh's "property mountain, the firm seat . . . the sanctum." But what and where is this mountain shrine?

Ugaritic analogies are helpful but not decisive. In language anticipating 15:17, the storm god Ba'lu calls Mount Zaphon *qdš . . . ġr.nḥlty* 'the holiness, my property mountain' (*KTU* 1.3.iii.30, [iv.20]). Mount Zaphon was accorded divine status at Ugarit (Pope 1966: 461–62) and was apparently once the site of a temple (Schaeffer 1938). But it was also the location or foundation of Ba'lu's metaphysical, celestial abode, built for him by the craftsman god Kôṭaru. Moreover, it was the archetype for earthly temples devoted to Baal. Cities housing Baal shrines, however far from northern Syria, might be named after Zaphon or its god. The deity Baal of Zaphon was worshiped, for example, in Punic Marseilles (*KAI* 69.1), and we have read in 14:2 of the Egypto-Phoenician city Baal-zephon (see APPENDIX B, vol. II). In his classical guise of Zeus Kasios, Baal of Zaphon was also revered in Greece (Eissfeldt 1932). And Clifford (1972: 136) plausibly identifies Zaphon in the territory of Gad as yet another avatar (Josh 13:27). Lastly, because Yahweh inherits Baal's traits, Mount Zion itself may be called "Zaphon" (Ps 48:3; cf. Isa 14:13).

I have argued that Baal's palace atop Mount Zaphon, the prototype for all terrestrial Baal shrines, is also nothing other than the sky (p. 555). This ambivalence between temple, heaven and mountain is amply paralleled in ancient literature and art, including the Bible. Hebrew *qōdeš/miqdāš* 'sanctum' can refer to an earthly or celestial divine dwelling (see NOTE to 15:17), while *hêkāl* 'palace, temple' connotes heaven itself (2 Sam 22:7; Ps 11:4). Conversely, a Phoenician temple at Sidon was called *šmm rmm* 'high heavens' (*KAI* 15) or *šmm 'drm* 'mighty heavens' (*KAI* 14.16). And an Israelite sacred city was named "House of God" (Bethel), whence a ramp ascended to heaven (Gen 28:12). Some passages rationalize the connection between celestial abode and temple, claiming that lowly Mount Zion reaches into heaven (Jer 17:12; Ezek 40:2; Ps 78:69). Thus Yahweh is simultaneously enthroned in heaven and in the Jerusalem Temple (1 Kgs 6:23–28; 8:13; Jer 17:12; Ezek 43:7). Of course, a material temple is not literally heaven. It is heaven's image, a projection onto the terrestrial plane, a nexus for human and divine communication. The Deuteronomist clarifies the distinction by placing in the Temple, not Yahweh, but his "name," i.e., the concept of his Godhood (Deut 12:5, 11, 21, etc.; cf. Ps 74:2, 7 and NOTE to 15:3). Yahweh remains inviolate in heaven (1 Kgs 8:27–49). In Exod 15:17, the mountain might be Yahweh's proper abode, upon which he reigns in an invisible, heavenly sanctuary (cf. Freedman 1981). But the reference may simultaneously be to a terrestrial holy place patterned after this incorporeal sanctum.

Compounding our difficulty is the ambiguity of the terms *har* 'mountain' and *naḥălâ* 'ownership, property, inheritance.' Although *har* means primarily "mountain," it can also connote a mountainous region (e.g., Num 13:17, 29; Deut 1:7, etc.). And, while Yahweh's *naḥălâ* is generally either the land of Canaan or the people of Israel, occasionally the term connotes the Temple or Jerusalem (e.g., Jer 12:7; Ps 79:1; cf. Isa 57:13) (see von Rad 1965: 79–93; Malamat 1988: 172–76). We find much the same for Ugaritic *nḥlt*: Ba῾lu's *nḥlt* is a mountain, Zaphon, while Kôṯaru's *nḥlt* is a region, *kptr.ks᾽u.ṯbth.ḥkpt.᾽arṣ.nḥlt* 'kptr [Crete or Cyprus?] his enthronement seat, ḥkpt [Memphis] his property land' (cf. *KTU* 1.3.vi.15–16). The cliché *ks᾽u.ṯbth . . . ᾽arṣ.nḥlth* also describes Death's realm (*KTU* 1.4.viii.13–14; 5.ii.15–16).

The inherent impossibility of identifying the holy mountain of 15:17 has not deterred scholars from advancing candidates. The major contenders are Sinai (Tournay 1958: 355–56; Freedman 1980: 136–40; 1981), Zion (Mettinger 1982: 27; Scharbert 1989: 65–66), Gilgal (Cross 1973: 142), Shiloh (BDB 874 [under *miqdāš*]; Clifford 1981: 135–37), the land of Canaan (McNeile 1908: 92; Noth 1962; 125–26; Cassuto 1967: 177; Watts 1957: 377) and Israel's northern highlands (see Halpern 1983: 35). The most we can do is explore the manifold possibilities, acknowledging that several or all may be simultaneously correct.

1. *Sinai.* The parallel with Ugaritic Mount Zaphon suggests that 15:17 refers to a specific peak uniquely associated with Yahweh. The most obvious candidate is the mountain called "Sinai" in J and P, "Horeb" in E and D (Freedman 1980: 136–41; 1981). The name "Sinai" appears in other poetry dated early by Cross and Freedman (1975): Deut 33:2; Judg 5:5; Ps 68:9 (see, however, Robertson's [1972] strictures). In particular, Judg 5:5 and Ps 68:9 call God *ze(h) Sînay* 'Lord of Sinai' (Moran 1961: 61).

If we identify the mountain with Sinai, then the "sanctum" built by Yahweh's own hands might be one of several things. It could be the sapphire-paved celestial abode glimpsed by the Israelite elders (24:10) or the Tabernacle prototype shown to Moses (25:9, 40). But it might also be a physical shrine, whether the Tabernacle (called a "sanctum" in 25:8–9 [P]) or the altar-and-pillar installation of 24:4.

If there was an actual Exodus, if the participants went to Sinai to worship, if they did not know their ultimate destination and if the Song dates from this period, then Sinai is the only choice for 15:17. But, because each of these is at most a possibility, we cannot endorse this view to the exclusion of others. One might argue that 15:17 refers to a later Israelite cult center *symbolizing* Mount Sinai, like the various Canaanite temples called "Zaphon." There is in fact some evidence that Sinai/Horeb was associated with major Israelite shrines, including Gilgal (Cross 1973: 104), Shechem (Beyerlin 1965) and Zion (note Isa 2:3 = Mic 4:2; see also Clifford 1972: 154–55 on Ps 50:2).

2. *Zion*. To many, it is self-evident that 15:17 refers to Mount Zion. After all, Jerusalem housed Israel's most magnificent sanctuary, Solomon's Temple, which that king calls, in language reminiscent of Exod 15:17–18, *mākôn ləšibtəkā 'ôlāmîm* 'the firm seat for your eternal sitting/throne/dwelling' (1 Kgs 8:13). Similarly, the expression *har qōdeš* 'mountain of holiness' frequently connotes Zion (Isa 11:9; 27:13; 56:7, etc.). And Ps 74:2 describes Zion in vocabulary particularly recalling Exod 15:13, 16–17: "Remember your community which you got (*qānîtā*) of old, you redeemed (*gāʾaltā*) your property (*naḥălāte̊kā*) tribe, Mount Zion on which you resided." Likewise, Psalm 78, which exhibits many contacts with Exod 15:1b–18 (see below), includes a claim that Yahweh himself built Solomon's Temple (v 69; compare Exod 15:17). The image of Yahweh planting the people on his mountain, moreover, finds its closest parallel in Ezek 17:22–23, where the ostensible referent is again Zion (cf. Ezek 20:40). Lastly, given the parallels between the mountain of 15:17 and Mount Zaphon, it is significant that Ps 48:3 calls Mount Zion "Zaphon."

The nonmention of Zion in 15:1b–18 is no obstacle to this theory. Were the Song performed in Solomon's Temple, there could have been no doubt of the location of Yahweh's chosen abode. The chief difficulty is rather that modern linguistic studies consistently date the Song of the Sea to the premonarchic period (Cross and Freedman 1975; Robertson 1977; see APPENDIX A, vol. II). Unless the Song is a skillful forgery, Zion and its Temple cannot be the original referents. The application of certain themes from the Song to Jerusalem may simply reflect adaptation to a secondary context. Indeed, since almost all the terms used of God's "sanctum" have Canaanite prototypes, we must posit *some* intermediary between Ugarit in the fourteenth century and Jerusalem in the tenth. That is, there must have been a pre-Solomonic temple or temples, whether Canaanite or Israelite, preserving the ideology of Zaphon.

3. *Shiloh*. The Bible records that, before the institution of the monarchy, Israel's religious center was at Shiloh (Joshua 18; 1 Samuel 1). If the Song of the Sea is premonarchic, as the linguistic evidence suggests, one must ask whether it belonged to the Shilonite liturgy. The main data supporting this hypothesis come from Psalm 78, which shares both vocabulary and themes with Exod 15:1b–18. Since by linguistic criteria, the Song of the Sea is the older text (Robertson 1972), Psalm 78 probably depends on 15:1b–18, although a more complicated relationship is not impossible (see APPENDIX A, vol. II). We should at any rate seriously consider the possibility that Psalm 78 constitutes our earliest commentary on the Song. Note the following similarities:

Psalm 78	Exod 15:1b–18
təhillôt (v 4)	*təhillôt* (v 11)
nipləʾôtā(y)w . . . *ʿāśâ* (v 4)	*ʿōśē(h) peleʾ* (v 11)
ʿāśâ peleʾ (v 12)	
wayyaṣṣeb . . . *kəmô-nēd* (v 13)	*niṣṣəbû kəmô-nēd* (v 8)
təhōmôt (v 15)	*təhōmōt* (vv 5, 8)

yəšallaḥ bām ḥărôn 'appô (v 49)	təšallaḥ ḥărōnəkā . . . 'appe(y)kā (vv 7–8)
nōzəlîm (vv 16, 44)	nōzəlîm (v 8)
wayyanḥēm (v 53)	nāḥîtā (v 13)
kissâ hayyām (v 53)	bayyām . . . yəkasyūmû (vv 4–5)
	kissāmô yām (v 10)
pastoral imagery (v 52)	pastoral imagery (v 13)
ʿammô (v 52)	ʿam, ʿamməkā (vv 13, 16)
waybî'ēm (v 54)	təbi'ēmô (v 17)
gəbûl qodšô (v 54)	nəwē(h) qodšekā (v 13)
har (v 54)	har (v 17)
ze(h) qānətâ (v 54)	zû qānîtā (v 16)
yəmînô (v 54)	yəmînəkā (vv 6, 12)
	yāde(y)kā (v 17)
nahălâ (v 55)	nahălātəkā (v 17)
miqdāšô (v 69)	miqdāš (v 17)

Note, too, the Psalmist's appeal to tradition (vv 2–4). It would appear that the Song of the Sea is chief among the "riddles from the past, which we have heard, and we know them, and our fathers told us."

Clifford (1981: 135) argues strongly that the Israelites' first goal in Ps 78:54 is Shiloh, or perhaps the surrounding highlands—at any rate, the region that Yahweh would reject in favor of Judah and Jerusalem (Ps 78:59–72) (see also Halpern 1983: 35). Thus Psalm 78 may be not just a commentary but a corrective to Exod 15:1b–18, an accommodation to Davidic ideology. While applying the image of Yahweh building his own temple (Exod 15:17) to Zion (Ps 78:69), all other "quotations" from the Song refer to the abandoned region of Shiloh. It is as though the predictions of Exod 15:17–18 were realized in two stages: the initial, abortive choice of Shiloh and the second, permanent election of Jerusalem.

If the Psalmist was a proponent of the Jerusalem Temple, why did he not apply the language of Exod 15:13, 16–17 primarily to Zion? There must have been a tradition that the mountain of 15:17 was not Zion, a tradition too vital for the poet to deny (Halpern 1983: 35). And making Psalm 78 the source of Exod 15:1b–18, rather than vice versa, leads to the same conclusion: the author of the Song borrowed language from Psalm 78 that described Shiloh, not Zion (excepting v 69). As Halpern (p. 36) comments, "Exodus 15 composed in the light of a prior Psalm 78 reads like a legitimation of a demolished sanctuary (Shiloh)." We may not infer on the basis of Psalm 78 alone that the original referent of Exod 15:17 was Shiloh—only that the author and intended audience of the Psalm thought so. Still, we must respect the antiquity of this testimony.

4. *Gilgal.* Cross (1973: 143) plausibly situates Exod 15:1b–18 in the cult of Gilgal (see NOTE to v 16). Cross's theory is attractive, among other reasons, because it accommodates so many interpretations of 15:16–17. Gilgal was the

gateway to Canaan, the land of Yahweh's *naḥălâ* 'property' where Israel was "planted" (see following). One could also regard the temple of Gilgal as assimilated to Sinai (compare the pillars in Exod 24:4 and Josh 4:4–9, 20–24), just as the nearby Jordan is assimilated to the Suph Sea. True, Gilgal is not in the highlands; but Cross shows that any shrine, however lowly, may become God's "mountain."

5. *Canaan.* Many scholars equate Yahweh's "property mountain" with Canaan, often called Yahweh's *naḥălâ.* The terror of the neighboring peoples would be understandable, whether Israel passes through for violent conquest or for peaceful settlement (*pace* Freedman 1981: 23); see NOTE to 15:16. Moreover, the reference to "planting" sounds like long-term settlement (cf. Jer 24:6; 32:41; 42:10; Amos 9:15; Ps 44:3; 80:9). (See, however, NOTE to 15:7 for a contrary argument.)

The Song of the Sea is noteworthy for combining pastoral (v 13) and horticultural (v 17) imagery, quite appropriate for the "land flowing of [goats'] milk and [date] honey" (compare the imagery of Psalm 80). Just as the pastoral metaphor in v 13 functions on two levels—Israel is Yahweh's flock, possessing its own sheep—so might v 17 convey not only that Israel is Yahweh's plantation but that the Israelites themselves cultivate the hillsides of Canaan (see below). And the most important parallel to 15:16–17 is again Ps 78:54, "He brought them to his holiness's territory/mountain (*gəbûl* = Arabic *jabal* [Talmon 1978a: 431]?), the mountain that his right hand acquired" (Halpern 1983: 35). The reference to acquisition by the right hand suggests the conquest of Canaan or part thereof.

Yet the parallels for Canaan as Yahweh's mountain are few and ambiguous (e.g., Deut 3:25; Isa 11:9; 57:13). Were the referent Canaan, we might expect instead **'ereṣ naḥălātəkā* 'your property *land*' in 15:17 (cf. Josh 22:19; Ugaritic *'arṣ.nḥlth* [*KTU* 1.3.vi.16; 4.viii.14; 5.ii.16]). (We will below interpret Mount Horeb as symbolizing both the land of Canaan and, indeed, the whole earth [COMMENT to 17:1–7]. If so, the mountain in 15:17 may be simultaneously Sinai/Horeb *and* all Canaan.)

6. *Northern Israel.* Here again, Psalm 78 provides the mainstay of the argument. By the Psalm's internal logic, v 54 cannot describe all of Canaan, but only the part that Yahweh would reject: either the cult center of Shiloh or the whole Northern Kingdom (Clifford 1981: 135–37; Halpern 1983: 35). Can the entire North be Yahweh's mountain and throne? Note that Jeroboam I installs two calves at the opposite ends of Northern Israel (1 Kgs 12:26–30), arguably constituting a giant throne (cf. Halpern 1991: 68–69; see COMMENT to chap. 32). (If so, like the Song of Deborah, the Song of the Sea does not include Judah in Israel proper.)

What may we conclude for Exod 15:17? Rather than choose among the foregoing options, I would rather believe that the poet did not intend to limit his words to a single application. Unquestionably, its ambiguity has enabled the Song's survival. Wherever it is sung, there is Yahweh's mountain. And it remains, after all, but a plausible theory that the Song originated in communal worship. Today it exists only within a literary context—or rather within concentric literary contexts. Each of these, too, suggests its own referent for 15:17.

Within the Book of Exodus, Yahweh's mountain is most likely Mount Sinai, though Canaan is remotely possible (Smith 1996: 45). Within the Hexateuch (Genesis–Joshua), while Sinai remains possible, the balance tips toward Canaan. In the context of the entire Hebrew Bible, however, one might think of Sinai, Canaan or Zion. And, in the context of early Jewish literature, or in the context of the Christian Bible, one may identify Yahweh's mountain with the Kingdom of Heaven; on the notion of a celestial equivalent to Jerusalem and/or the Temple, see Gal 4:24–26; Heb 12:22–24; Revelation passim; Tob 13:9–18; 2 Bar. 4:1–7; 32:2–4; Test. Dan 5:12; 4 Ezra 7:26; 8:52; 10:25–54; 13:36; 4 Bar. 5:35 and, for Rabbinic parallels, Aptowitzer (1930–31).

We should experience this ambiguity as a virtue, not as a source of frustration. With its nonspecific language, the Song may teach the oneness of all historical experience (cf. Lohfink 1968: 83–86): Yahweh protected the Israelites from neighboring peoples, just as he saved them from Pharaoh and the Sea. Nations and the elements are equally in his power. Divine succor is ever available to Israel in distress; they can always win through to God's mountain. Indeed, later historical salvations, most notably the return from Babylon, are conceived as recapitulations of the Exodus (see APPENDIX D, vol. II). Some, ill-advisedly stretching the meaning of commonly used terms, even call 15:1b–18 "eschatological" or "proto-apocalyptical" (Bender 1903; Weimar 1985: 254–57; Brenner 1991: 39–40; for a true eschatological reading, see 11QTemple 29:7–10 [Yadin 1983: 1.185]).

YAHWEH'S PASTURE

To further complicate matters, we must now consider the relationship between the mountain shrine of v 17 and the holy nāwe(h) 'pasture/camp/tent' of v 13 (see NOTE). Are they one and the same? Or is the "camp" a temporary abode, preparatory to permanent settlement on the mountain? The similarity of ʿam-zû gāʾāltā 'people which you redeemed' (v 13) and ʿam-zû qānîtā 'people which you have gotten' (v 16) suggests some sort of congruity (see NOTE to 15:16). But congruity need not entail identity.

One may mount a fairly strong case for distinguishing the settlements of vv 13 and 17 (Cassuto 1967: 176–77; Cross 1973: 141). First, Israel's national history reckons with a nomadic period prior to settlement. Second, Yahweh's own biography involves a transition from tent shrine to permanent temple (e.g., 2 Sam 7:6–7). By this reading, the "crossing" in v 16 may be Israel's passage, not through the Sea, but from the temporary nāwe(h) to the permanent mountain (see, however, NOTE to 15:16). If we distinguish between Yahweh's "encampment" and Yahweh's "mountain," the identity of the first depends on the identity of the second. For example, if the mountain is Jerusalem or the Temple (see above), then the encampment might be Sinai, Kadesh, Shiloh (cf. Ps 78:54, 60) or David's sacred tent (2 Sam 6:17; note nāwe[h] in 2 Sam 15:25).

There are reasons, however, to think the "encampment" is the same as the "mountain." First: if 15:17 refers to Sinai, then the encampment (v 13) must also be Sinai (cf. my discussion of tent imagery, pp. 541–42). Moreover, Ps 74:2 ostensibly combines terms from Exod 15:13, 16–17, apropos of Zion: "Remember your community which you got (*qānîtā*) of old, you redeemed (*gā'altā*) your property (*naḥălātekā*) tribe, Mount Zion on which you resided." Freedman (1981: 24) also cites the collocation of terms from 15:13, 17 in Jer 31:23: *nawē(h) ṣedeq har haqqōdeš* 'pasture of righteousness, the mountain of holiness.' Similarly, Ps 93:5 calls an eternal, divine dwelling **nawē(h) qōdeš* 'encampment of holiness' (so 4QPs^b; MT different). And Mount Zion is Yahweh's *nāwē(h)* in 2 Sam 15:25; Isa 33:20, possibly also in Jer 10:25 (= Ps 79:7); 25:30. While one could argue that these passages are synthesizing language proper to distinct cult sites, the surface interpretation is that Exod 15:13, 17 were always taken to describe a single place.

In short, the relationship between Exod 15:13 and 17 is moot. Perhaps, again, the poet wished it so.

YAHWEH'S PLANTATION

According to 15:17, Israel is "planted" near or upon Yahweh's eternal sanctum. Smith (1927: 413) observes the frequency of tree imagery describing an extended family vertically, from ancestors through posterity—root (*šōreš*), stem (*gezaʿ*), branch (*ḥōṭer, maṭṭe[h]* [?]), fruit (*pərî*), seed (*zeraʿ*) (see esp. Isa 40:24). The cliché "root below . . . fruit above" is shared by Israel (Isa 37:31; Amos 2:9) and Phoenicia (*KAI* 14.11–12).

When Yahweh "plants" individuals, he rewards them with fertility and security (Jer 17:8; Amos 9:13–15; Ps 1:3; 92:13–15; cf. 52:10). The image of Israel transplanted fits especially well the identification of Yahweh's mountain with Canaan or the northern highlands. "You, your hand, dispossessed nations and planted them" (Ps 44:3); "A vine from Egypt you removed; you expelled nations and planted it" (Ps 80:9). We might even regard the "planted" people as replacing trees cleared for settlement (cf. Josh 17:14–18; Finkelstein 1988: 200). According to Isa 61:3 (cf. 60:21), Israel restored will be as "terebinths of vindication, Yahweh's plantation," while Isa 58:11 and Jer 31:12 also envision postexilic Judah as a lush garden. (For further discussion of vegetable metaphors for Israel and its kinship system, see Eilberg-Schwartz 1990: 115–76.)

But the image of a plantation would also fit Mount Zion. Compare 2 Sam 7:10, "And I will set a place for my people, for Israel, and I will plant him, and he will dwell *under himself* [i.e., in his own place] and not shudder any more." The reference is probably not to peaceful residence in Canaan, but to building the Jerusalem Temple, as the following verses make explicit (McCarter 1984: 202–4). A clearer parallel, proffered by ibn Ezra, is Ezek 17:22–23, "I will myself take from the top of the tall cedar . . . and I will myself transplant [it] on a tall, high mountain. On the mountain of Israel's height I will transplant it, and it will raise branch and make fruit and become a mighty cedar." This is a vision of the house of David restored to sovereignty either in Judah (cf. Ezek 34:14) or, more likely, in Zion (cf. Ezek 20:40). What if the mountain of Exod 15:17 is Sinai? Then the image of planting becomes problematic. I explore one solution under NOTE to 15:17: "plant" refers metaphorically to tent-dwelling. But this feels forced.

Whatever the geographical referent, the image of Israel planted on God's holy mountain possesses sacral overtones (cf. Metzger 1983, 1992; Stager n.d.). An integral part of ancient Near Eastern monumental architecture was the garden (Andrae 1947/52; Oppenheim 1965; Gallery 1978; Wiseman 1983). In Egypt, the Heliopolitan sun temple was landscaped (Schott 1950: 48–49), while Thutmosis III made a large botanical park at Karnak, also depicted on the temple walls (see Lalouette 1986: 363; Newby 1980: 83). Sumerian temples, too, featured gardens (Falkenstein and von Soden 1953: 131, 135), as did Asshur's festival house and, perhaps, Babylon's Ninmaḫ temple (Andrae 1947/52). Similarly, Asshurbanipal's palace reliefs portray a hilltop shrine surrounded by brooks and trees (Keel 1978: 150, fig. 202). Evidently, the Elamite temple of Susa pillaged by Asshurbanipal also featured secret groves (Luckenbill 1926–27: 310). The motif turns up in mythology, too: in the Gilgamesh tradition, the cedar forest of Lebanon is a divine abode, the gods' plantation (Stolz 1972: 149–53).

Why this recurrent theme? Gardens represent the ideal harmony of nature and culture. The Bible tells of Yahweh's garden (Gen 13:10; Isa 51:3) located on a holy mountain in Lebanon (Ezek 28:13; 31:8–9) or northeast of Mesopotamia (Gen 2:10–14). There humanity once resided in bliss (Genesis 2–3) (see Stolz 1972). In Isa 11:1–10, a passage replete with Edenic imagery, the house of David is likened to a tree on Yahweh's "holy mountain," now presumably Jerusalem (cf. Childs 1962: 65–69). Under the ideal Davidide, Edenic conditions will return to Zion: Israel will be granted longevity and harmony with the wild beasts (Isa 65:17–25). Prophets envision Mount Zion as the source of fertilizing waters, an image rooted in Genesis 2–3 and ultimately in Canaanite myth (see Propp 1987a; COMMENT to 17:1–7). Not surprisingly, trees and other plants constitute an important part of the Temple's ornamentation (1 Kgs 6:18, 29, 32; see Barker 1991: 57–103).

Whether the Temple compound itself was landscaped, however, is somewhat unclear. The bākā'-trees of Jerusalem (Ps 84:7) are associated with nesting birds, springs of water, pools and the Temple, while Isa 10:33–34 implicitly likens Jerusalem to the forest of Lebanon (Stolz 1972: 146). We also find horticultural imagery associated with the Temple in Ps 52:10, "And I, like a verdant olive tree in Deity's house . . . ," and in Ps 92:13–15, "The righteous man like the palm will blossom, like a cedar in the Lebanon rise high; transplanted in Yahweh's house, in the courts of our deity they will blossom; they will still yield in old age, sappy and verdant" (cf., too, the vision of the olive trees and the candelabrum in Zech 4:3). Admittedly, 1 Kings 6–7 is strangely silent on the landscaping of both Temple and palace. But we know that the palace featured a symbolic forest (1 Kgs 7:2) and, at least in later times, a real garden (1 Kgs 21:1–2; 2 Kgs 9:27; 21:18, 26; 25:4; Jer 39:4; 52:7; Eccl 2:4–6; Neh 3:15; cf. 2 Kgs 9:27). Still, we cannot be certain that the First Temple had a garden. The Second Temple did not, at least in the fourth century B.C.E. (Hecataeus *apud* Josephus *Ap.* 1.199).

As for Israelite temples outside of Jerusalem, we read of illicit worship in gardens (Isa 1:29; 65:3; 66:17; cf. Matt 26:36). In fact, the stereotypical "high place" was situated "on a high hill, under a verdant tree" (Deut 12:2; 1 Kgs 14:23, etc.). Various holy trees appear throughout the Bible (Gen 12:6; 13:18; 35:4, 8; Josh 24:26; Judg 4:5; 6:11, 19; 9:6, 37). And we should note that the cultic fixture called Asherah, until recently considered a sacred grove, was more likely a symbolic or actual tree (Deut 16:21) (see NOTE to 34:13).

In postbiblical Judaism, the image of the temple garden was translated to heaven. According to 1 Enoch 24–32, Yahweh's mountain-throne is surrounded by trees. Qumran fragment 4Q500 may also describe the gardens of Paradise (Baumgarten 1989). (Our very word "paradise" comes from Greek *paradeisos* and Hebrew *pardēs* 'garden,' both ultimately derived from Persian *pairidaēza* 'enclosure.') Traditional Jewish sources call heaven, or the afterlife, the "Garden of Eden."

THE ARCHITECTURE OF THE SONG

As we have repeatedly seen, the Song of the Sea counterpoises solid and liquid, up and down, life and death (NOTES to 15:1 "exaltedly, exaltedly," 15:7 "uprisers," 15:8 "streams" and 15:17 "your property mountain"). In overall structure, 15:1b–18 mirrors cosmic architecture. The Song begins in the Sea's depths (vv 1–10), where Yahweh's drowned enemies lie in the underworld (v 12). It ends on a mountaintop sanctum, from which Yahweh reigns forever.

We find a comparable progression in Jonah 2:3–10; Psalm 93 (Levenson 1993a: 140–41) and exemplars of the ancient Near Eastern Combat Myth considered above. Ancient art, too, depicts the gods as enthroned upon waters (Metzger 1970). Temples are said to reach from the underworld or the watery abyss into the very heavens (Hurowitz 1992: 335–37). According to Ps 29:10, "Yahweh is enthroned upon the Flood" — but here it is disputed whether *mabbûl* connotes abysmal or celestial waters (Kloos 1986: 62–66). Ps 24:1–3 states more clearly that both Yahweh's holy mountain and the whole earth are rooted in the Deep:

> Yahweh's is the earth and what fills it . . .
> For he, upon seas he founded it
> And upon rivers he established it.
> Who shall ascend in Yahweh's mountain,
> And who shall stand in his holiness's place?

The burden of Exod 15:1b–18, then, is that Yahweh's kingdom of Israel, founded in the Sea, stands unshakable like the eternal earth and like God's own throne.

LOOKING FORWARD

The Book of Exodus reaches a temporary climax in 15:21, with Israel exulting on the shore. But, the Song of the Sea reminds us, the desert is not Israel's goal. Liberation is but license without submission to Israel's proper Master at his mountain (cf. Fretheim 1991a: 20, 30; Levenson 1993a: 143–53). While the Sea crossing terminates Israel's physical bondage, it simultaneously inaugurates a period of rigorous testing that reaches an initial culmination at Sinai, where the people are socially and politically reconstituted as a mighty nation, the collective Vassal of King Yahweh. Israel's final reward comes under Joshua, when, as a disciplined host, they cross the Jordan to assume their inheritance (cf. *Exod. Rab.* 20:15; *Mek. bəšallaḥ* 1; Philo *Moses* 1.164).

PART III. SOJOURN IN THE WILDERNESS (EXODUS 15:22–18:27)
XIII. *I, Yahweh, am your healer* (15:22–26)

◆

15 ^{22(R?)}And Moses made Israel set forth from the Suph Sea, and they went out into the Shur Wilderness ^(?)and went three days into the wilderness, but did not find waters. ²³And they arrived at Marah (Bitter), but could not drink waters from Marah because they were bitter; therefore one called its name Marah. ²⁴And the people complained against Moses, saying, "What will we drink?"

²⁵So he cried to Yahweh, and Yahweh taught him a tree, and he threw into the waters, and the waters were sweetened.

There he set for him rule and law, and there he tested him. ²⁶And he said, "If you listen, listen to Yahweh your deity's voice, and what is straight in his eyes you do, and give ear to his commands and observe all his rules, all the disease that I set in Egypt I will not set upon you. Rather, I, Yahweh, am your healer."

ANALYSIS

TEXTUAL NOTES

15:22. *Israel.* LXX reads "Israel's Sons," while Syr has "those of Israel's House" (see TEXTUAL NOTE to 3:11).

†*and they went out.* So MT (*wayyēṣə'û*). Sam and LXX read *wywṣ(y)'hw* 'and he [Moses] *took* him [Israel] out.'

three days. Kenn 176, Syr and *Tg. Neofiti I* have "a three days' *way*," as in 3:18; 5:3, etc. And Num 33:8 (MT), paralleling our verse, also reads *derek šəlōšet yāmîm.* Nonetheless, in the absence of an easy mechanical explanation for the loss of *drk,* I follow the standard MT.

waters. LXX adds an explanatory "to drink."

†15:23. *Marah.* On the vocalization, see NOTE.

waters. The word is absent from some LXX MSS, including LXX[B]. Wevers (1990: 238; 1992: 255) cites assimilation to v 22, where "drink" is preceded, not followed, by "water" in the Greek. Equally possible, however, is that some LXX MSS render a defective Hebrew MS from which *mayim* had dropped by homoioarkton with *mimmārâ*.

†*its name.* I would ordinarily dismiss LXX-Syr "*that place's* name" as an expansion. But MT may be haplographic (*hm . . . hm*), assuming little or no space between words (*šmhmqwmhzhmrh* > *šmhmrh* > *šmh mrh*) (Lohfink 1994: 39 n. 8).

†15:24. *complained.* The verb is plural in MT, singular in 4QReworked Pentateuch[c], Sam and LXX (but see Wevers 1990: 238). It is hard to tell which is original. The Syr tradition in fact preserves both alternatives.

saying. Syr adds "to him."

15:25. *he cried.* 4QReworked Pentateuch[c], Sam, LXX, Kenn 69, Syr and *Fragmentary Targum* expand: "*Moses* cried."

†*taught him.* For MT *wayyôrēhû*, Sam has *wyr'hw* 'made him *see*,' a *lectio facilior* to be discussed further under NOTE. LXX *edeixen* and Syr *ḥawwî* appear to support Sam (cf. *Tg. Ps.-Jonathan*), although *deiknymi* can render *hôrâ* 'guide, teach, show' as well as *her'â* 'make see' (1 Sam 12:23; Mic 4:2; Job 34:32). *Tg. Onqelos 'alləpêh* 'taught him' supports MT. And the midrashic *Tg. Neofiti I* has it both ways: "The Lord *showed* him a tree, and he took from it *the word of the Lord, a word of the Law*"—i.e., God both made Moses see and instructed him. See NOTE.

rule and law. LXX, Syr and *Tg. Neofiti I* pluralize, treating *ḥōq ûmišpāṭ* as collective (Wevers 1990: 240) and/or harmonizing with the cliché *ḥuqqîm ûmišpāṭîm* 'rules and laws.'

15:26. *said.* Syr specifies "to him."

voice. For MT-Sam *lqwl*, several MT MSS (Kennicott 1776–80: 139) and a Cairo Genizah MS (*BHS*) have the synonymous *bqwl.*

SOURCE ANALYSIS

Exod 15:22a seems associated with the Redactorial sequence of itinerary notices in Exodus and Numbers, of which Num 33:1–49 presents a fuller enumeration (see provisionally Cross 1973: 308–17; Friedman 1981: 98–119; 1987: 230–31). But there is room for doubt. First, 15:22a does not follow the pattern "and they set forth (*nsᶜ*) from X and arrived/camped (*bw'/ḥny*) at Y." Second, the verse lacks a parallel in Num 33:1–49 (see also SOURCE ANALYSIS to 13:17–15:21 apropos of 14:1–4).

In contrast, the first words of v 23, "and they came to Marah," more closely resemble the itinerary genre. In fact, 15:22a and 23a, stitched together, would constitute a stereotypical interjection: "Moses made Israel set forth from the Suph Sea, and they arrived at Marah." But these clauses cannot be excised without leaving a gap; hence, it is uncertain they are secondary.

The Marah story proper is told in 15:22b-25a. In the absence of Priestly traits, one is initially inclined to attribute these verses to J or E (cf. Holzinger 1900: 53). After 15:25a, however, both tone and subject seem to change. What has drinkable water to do with testing, legislation and healing? Friedman (1987: 251) gives vv 22b-25a to J and 25b-26 to E, but, in the opinion of many, vv 25b-26 evince affinities rather with Deuteronomy and related literature (Holzinger 1900: 53; Noth 1962: 127, 129; Hyatt 1971: 171; Childs 1974: 266-67 [with reservations]; Johnstone 1990: 82; on "D-like" language in Exodus, see SOURCE ANALYSIS to 12:1-13:16 and APPENDIX A, vol. II). But how closely does 15:25b-26 resemble Deuteronomy? *Ḥōq ûmišpāṭ* 'rule and law' (15:25b) at first sounds Deuteronomic, but D in fact uses the plural *ḥuqqîm ûmišpāṭîm* (Lohfink 1994: 43 n. 22). Another motif recalling D is Yahweh "testing" (*nsy*) Israel. But in D/Dtr, Yahweh tests mortals by *travails* or *temptations* (Deut 8:16; 13:4; Judg 2:22; 3:1, 4); in E, he tests by *command* (Gen 22:1; Exod 16:4; 20:20). Weinfeld's (1972) Deuteronomic glossary does not even include *nsy*.

In 15:26, the resemblance to D is greater but still inconsistent. The phrase "if you listen, listen to Yahweh's voice" is common in D/Dtr (Bright 1951: 35; Weinfeld 1972: 337). And Deuteronomy frequently enjoins one to *šmr* 'observe' God's *miṣwôt* 'commands' and *ḥuqqîm/ḥuqqōt* 'rules,' as do other sources (Weinfeld p. 336). "Doing" (*ʿśy*) what is "straight in Yahweh's eyes" (*hayyāšār bəʿênê yahwe[h]*) is typical of Deuteronom(ist)ic literature (Deut 6:18; 12:25; 13:19; 21:9; 1 Kgs 11:33, 38, etc.). And "the disease that I set in Egypt" somewhat recalls Deut 7:15; 28:27, 60. On the other hand, the concluding "I (am) Yahweh" is typical of P and Ezekiel, not D (Lohfink p. 56; see Zimmerli 1982: 1-28).

Because it combines D-like and P-like language and may refer to the plague of *šəḥîn* (see NOTE to 15:26), Lohfink (pp. 35-95) regards 15:25b-26 as a Redactorial expansion. This is logical enough, although I am skeptical of the Deuteronomic stratigraphy underpinning his thesis. But, rather than dissect it, we might do better to give all of 15:22-26 to R, whose hand we detected in v 22a and possibly in v 23. Not that the Redactor necessarily worked from whole cloth; he may well have revised an older story, probably Elohistic. Such a scenario would explain why the R-like matter in vv 22-23 cannot be excised cleanly (on the unity of 15:22-26, see further under COMMENT).

Why the Redactor might have included this episode, I am not willing to say. It is easy to generate untestable conjectures: e.g., Babylonian Jewry required assurance of Yahweh's protection and the eternity of the Covenant before embarking on the trek back to Judah. For a speculative but heroic effort to ground the Marah incident in postexilic theology, see Lohfink (1994).

REDACTION ANALYSIS

Given the uncertainty of our source analysis, we can say little about the editing of 15:22-26. In APPENDIX B (vol. II), I shall explore the possibility that,

prior to redaction, both Exod 15:22-26 and Num 33:6-10 placed Elim and
Marah on the *Egyptian* side of the Sea.

NOTES

15:22. *Shur*. This desert, whose name might be Canaanite or Hebrew for "wall,"
separated Egyptian territory from the land of nomads (Gen 25:18; 1 Sam 15:7;
27:8); see further under APPENDIX B, vol. II.

three days. A biblical and ancient Near Eastern cliché for a stretch of time
more than a day and less than a week (Cassuto 1967: 183).

15:23. *Marah*. The resh of *mārâ* (< *mrr* 'to be bitter') was originally gemi-
nated: **marra* (cf. LXX *Merra*). At first, *mārâ* seems to be a feminine adjective
"bitter" (McNeile 1908: 94). LXX, however, more plausibly reads an abstract
Pikria 'Bitterness' (see GKC §122q). To judge from MT, LXX and Josephus
(*Ant*. 3.1.3), the original stem vowel was *a*. But the Syriac tradition has *ū/ō*,
perhaps reflecting a vocalization **mōrâ*, the usual Hebrew term for "bitterness"
(cf. Syr, Syro-Hexaplaric Symmachus and Theodotion of 15:23). On Marah's
location, see APPENDIX B, vol. II.

from Marah. There is *double entente*; one could also translate *mimmārâ*
as "*on account of* bitterness." The fourfold repetition of *mār(â)* 'bitter(ness)'
underscores the severity of Israel's plight (Jacob 1992: 435).

therefore. Some comparable stories of complaint and succor *conclude* with
an etiology introduced by *wayyiqrā(')* 'and he/one called' (e.g., 17:7; Num
11:3, 34). But Marah is explained in the middle, with *ʿal-kēn qārā(')* 'therefore one called' (cf. Gen 19:22; 21:31; 25:30, etc.). What does the distinction
signify?

In many etiologies, the featured name is an innovation, a reaction to a
novel circumstance. At Marah, however, the waters have always been bitter;
the change is their freshening. "Therefore one called its name Marah" is an
aside, explaining, not a new name, but an old. (On biblical etiologies, see
Long 1968.)

It is unclear whether the waters of Marah retain their sweetness after Israel's departure. Lohfink's (1994: 41) commonsense conjecture is that the
story explains why a spring called "Bitter" in fact yields sweet water. In the
parallel 2 Kgs 2:22, Elisha's spring is permanently "healed" (see COMMENT).

15:24. *complained*. The Marah incident is characteristic of Israel's wilderness period, featuring discontent with Moses' leadership and disobedience to
Yahweh (16; 17:1-7; 32; Num 11:1-14; 16; 20:2-13; 21:4-9, etc.; see already
Exod 5:20-21; 14:11-12). At Marah, the people's complaint is against Moses
alone. But the story ends with an ominous warning not to doubt Yahweh. The
very name *mārâ* evokes contention, chiming with *mry* 'rebel.'

15:25. *taught him*. Our witnesses are in dissent for this crucial verb. Because *wywrhw* (MT) and *wyr'hw* (Sam) look and sound alike, corruption in
either direction is imaginable (see TEXTUAL NOTE). Fortunately, there is

little difference in meaning. *Her'â* (< *r'y* 'see') (Sam) unambiguously means "caused to see." But *hôrâ* (< *yry* 'direct') (MT), too, can be associated with vision (e.g., Job 34:32). Their interchangeability is exemplified in the synonymous expressions *her'â derek* 'show the way' (Deut 1:33; Ps 50:23) and *hôrâ derek* 'teach the way' (1 Kgs 8:36; Isa 2:3, etc.). *Hôrâ*, however, covers a broader semantic field, also meaning "throw, shoot, rain, teach, direct."

If MT is correct, the implication may be that God shows or leads Moses to the tree and also instructs him in its use (cf. Ramban; Gressmann 1913: 122; Ehrlich 1908: 323; Childs 1974: 269). Less likely, Yahweh bodily hurls (*yry*) the tree/wood down from heaven (if so, note the resonance with *wayyašlēk* 'and he threw'). *Hôrâ* also forcefully suggests the derivative *tôrâ* 'Direction, Law,' absent in the passage but evoked by its synonyms *ḥōq*, *mišpāṭ* and *miṣwâ* (cf. Gressman 1913: 123); see *Tg. Neofiti I* and COMMENT. There is also some similarity to the toponym Marah itself.

tree. *'Ēṣ* can mean either "piece/object of wood" (LXX; Syr) or "tree" (*Tg. Neofiti I*); the parallel in Ezek 47:1–12 supports the latter interpretation (see COMMENT). *Tg. Ps.-Jonathan* even identifies the species: bitter oleander, to which Palestinian tradition accords the power of sweetening brackish water (Löw 1967: 1.211) (for healing bitterness by bitterness, cf. 2 Kgs 2:19–22). *'Ēṣ* perhaps puns with *'ēṣâ* 'counsel, wisdom,' an appropriate object for *hôrâ* 'teach' (*'ēṣâ* parallels *tôrâ* in Jer 18:18; Ezek 7:26; *hôrâ* parallels *yā'aṣ* 'advise' in Ps 32:8).

he threw. The subject is probably Moses, or perhaps God himself (cf. Gressmann 1913: 122). The object seems to be the tree or its wood, unless we are to think of pulverized leaves scattered into the spring.

he set. Who is the subject of the verbs "set" and "tested"? Most assume it is God, but Ramban, Dillmann (1880: 163) and Jacob (1992: 437) make a good case for Moses. In our closest parallels, the subject is a human (Gen 47:26; Josh 24:25; 1 Sam 30:25). But God, too, may "set a rule" (Jer 33:25; Prov 8:29). In a sense, it does not matter, given the frequent confusion between the personae of prophet and Deity (see NOTES to 7:17 and 11:3, 8).

for him. "Him" must be Israel, regarded collectively.

rule and law. Jewish tradition holds that several basic norms were enacted or reiterated at Marah: the Sabbath, filial piety, etc. (*Tg. Ps.-Jonathan*; *Mek. wayyassa'* 1; *b. Šabb.* 87b; *b. Sanh.* 56b). More likely, however, the "rule," "law" and "test" are simply the comprehensive commandment of obedience (Luzzatto). The closest parallel would be Josh 24:25, where "rule and law" refer to general exhortation. (In Gen 47:26 and 1 Sam 30:25, however, the "rule and law" are specific practices enacted by Joseph and David.)

he tested. The subject again might be either Moses or Yahweh (see NOTE to "he set" above). But what precisely is the test? Rashbam and Cassuto (1967: 184) think of the experience of thirst (cf. Deut 8:15–16; Judg 2:22; 3:1, 4). More likely, however, the commandment of total obedience constitutes the test (cf. Gen 22:1; Exod 16:4; 20:20). Thus, even before Sinai, Israel's faith is tempered by the discipline of Covenant duty.

The root *nsy* 'test' recalls the springs of Massah, where Israel will test Yahweh (17:2, 7). Modern scholars have devised vague yet complicated theories of mutual influence among the Water in the Wilderness traditions, generally positing a common historical origin at Kadesh (e.g., Wellhausen 1885: 342–44; Gressmann 1913: 419–48 *et passim*; most recently Blenkinsopp 1992: 137–38; for a critique, see Axelsson 1987: 113–18). I would rather consider the resonance between 15:25 and 17:2, 7 accidental—or, at most, literary foreshadowing (cf. Childs 1974: 268).

15:26. *listen . . . do.* The first part of Yahweh's speech is chiastic: "(A) If you listen, listen to (B) Yahweh your deity's voice, and (B′) what is straight in his eyes (A′) you do."

straight. Although often rendered "upright," *yāšār* probably connotes keeping "straight" to the path, as opposed to deviating (*swr*).

all . . . all. The repetition of *kōl* 'all' in vv 25–26 and the sequence *šām šām . . . wǝšām . . . śamtî . . . 'āśîm* 'there he set . . . and there . . . I set . . . I will (not) set' together suggest proportionality. The greater one's obedience, the stronger one's immunity to disease (Lohfink 1994: 46–47).

the disease that I set in Egypt. Or "upon Egypt." Though positive in tone, 15:26 bears an implicit threat (Durham 1987: 213–14; Fretheim 1991a: 179; Van Seters 1994: 179; cf. *Tg. Ps.-Jonathan*; ibn Ezra). Deut 7:15, too, promises immunity as the reward for fealty. But, conversely, the penalty for disobedience is the disease of Egypt (Deut 28:27, 60; cf. Lev 26:25; Amos 4:10). The Plagues are thus an object lesson for Israel.

Universally, patron saints, gods and spirits of healing also send disease (Eshmun, Apollo, St. Roc, etc.). Yahweh, too, is often extolled as a healer, yet illness is among his weapons. The moral of 15:26 is that Yahweh *controls* disease, dispensing blessing or harm according to his justice (cf. Isa 45:7).

"Disease" (*maḥălâ*) could refer to the Plagues or to Egypt's inherent unhealthfulness—or both, taking the Plagues tradition as etiological (see COMMENT to 7:8–11:10, pp. 348–52). Exod 15:26 particularly recalls the plague of the skin disease *šǝḥîn* (see Deut 28:27 and NOTE to 9:9). Israelite and late Egyptian tradition alike associate Israel's departure/expulsion from Egypt with epidemic "leprosy" (Josephus *Ap.* 1.227–320). And skin disease remained a source of concern in Israel (Leviticus 13–14; Numbers 12, etc.).

Rather. After a negative statement, this is the normal meaning of *kî* (usually "for") (Luzzatto).

I, Yahweh, am your healer. Equally accurate would be "I am Yahweh, your healer." The statement thus expands the emphatic "I am Yahweh" formula (see NOTE to 6:2). It also implies that no one else is Israel's healer (see COMMENT).

Like so much of his persona, Yahweh's title of Physician (*rōpē'*) may be an heirloom from Canaanite myth (see APPENDIX C, vol. II). Ugaritic religion knows a god *rp'u*, meaning either "Healer" or less likely "Dead One" (*KTU* 1.108.1, 19–21). Whether *rp'u* is a proper name or the epithet of a better-known deity remains moot, however (see Parker 1972).

COMMENT

TESTING IN THE WILDERNESS

The sojourn at Marah inaugurates a new epoch for God and Israel. Yahweh, the saving Warrior of the Suph Sea (15:3), must now sustain Israel in a parched land (for parallels from ancient military annals, see Luckenbill 1926–27: 2.60–62, 74–75, 122–23, 220; Kitchen 1982: 31–36, 49–50). To start with, at Marah, God merely desalinizes brackish water. With Manna (chap. 16) and Water from the Rock (17:1–7), he will actually produce food and drink from thin air and thick stone.

The episodes of Marah, Manna and Massah-Meribah (15:22–17:7) are connected by the theme of testing (*nsy*). At Marah, Yahweh tests Israel by insisting on total obedience. In 16:4, he ordains a specific command/test, on the nature of which see NOTE. At Massah-Meribah, Israel tests Yahweh by asking for water (17:1–7). The Amalek incident, too, may allude to testing (see NOTE to 17:15). And the theme continues in 20:20, where Moses offers a disquietingly paradoxical reassurance: "Fear not. Because for the sake of testing you has the Deity come, and . . . his fear will be *upon your face*." The rest of the Bible frequently associates the verb *nsy* with Israel's desert experience: Yahweh tested Israel through suffering (Deut 8:2, 16; 13:4) and with commandments (Exod 15:25; 16:4; 20:20; Deut 33:8), while Israel tested God's power and patience (17:2, 7; Num 14:22; Deut 6:16; Ps 78:18, 41, 56; 95:9; 106:14). Like prospective business or marital partners, Yahweh and Israel probe one another before entering into a permanent legal relationship (cf. INTRODUCTION, p. 34; for a general study of testing, see Licht 1973). Some also believe that *nsy* connotes tempering through discipline; cf. Eissfeldt (1955).

Israel's wilderness experience is both ordeal and rite of passage (see INTRODUCTION, pp. 35–36). Yahweh proves and purges Israel, and he establishes the norms of its civilization. The entire desert, not just Sinai, is really the site of lawgiving. The episode of Marah, where Yahweh miraculously sustained Israel and "set rule and law for him, and . . . tested him," both inaugurates and epitomizes the wilderness epoch.

MAGIC, MEDICINE, MONOTHEISM

Exod 15:22–26 acclaims God as Israel's healer (*rōpēʾ*). No one else, human or divine, may practice medicine unless as Yahweh's representative (ibn Ezra; Hempel 1957: 824). This is a common biblical attitude: Elijah condemns Ahaziah for seeking healing from an alien god (2 Kgs 1:2–4); 2 Chr 16:12 censures King Asa for consulting *rōpaʾîm* 'healers,' presumably mortal (some, however, read *rapaʾîm* 'the Shades'); Jeremiah repeatedly mocks medicine (8:22; 17:5, 14; 46:11; 51:8–9). And the Bible's most celebrated invalid never seeks professional help at all (see esp. Job 13:4). All approbatory references to healing involve either God himself or his priests and prophets (Gen 20:7, 17;

Exod 23:25–26; Num 12:13; 1 Kgs 13:6; 14; 17:17–24; 2 Kgs 4:8–41; 5; 8:7–15; 13:21; 20:1–7). Although Exod 21:19 appears to presume and sanction paid healing (see NOTE), the earliest explicit endorsement of lay, professional physicians—still as God's servants—is Sir 38:1–15 (second century B.C.E.).

Medical practice was doubly suspect. First, it infringed on Yahweh's sovereignty over life and death. Second, throughout the ancient world, medicine was indistinguishable from magic. Healing was affected by bizarre recipes, formulaic chants and obscure acts. But Num 23:23 boasts, "there is no divination in Jacob, and no sorcery in Israel." The Bible contains relatively few examples of what is generally considered magic.

Similarly, the Bible is all but silent on the existence of demons, the malevolent spirits upon which most premodern cultures blame disease and misfortune (Hempel 1957; see also COMMENTS to 3–4 and 12:1–13:16). Demons probably played a greater role in popular religion than our texts indicate, and magic and demonology would flourish in the post–Old Testament period. But, for the biblical authors at least, the concentration of all supernatural essence into Yahweh and the concomitant demotion of the pantheon into anonymous "angels" also entailed the demythologizing of illness and accident (see APPENDIX C, vol. II). Conversely, the postbiblical rise of magic, medicine and demonology coincided with the burgeoning of angelology and the remythologizing of Jewish literature, in which evil angels like Sammael are largely indistinguishable from demons. In this period, Exod 15:26 itself was employed as a medical incantation (m. Sanh. 10:1). (For further discussion of magic and the Covenant, see INTRODUCTION to vol. II.)

WATER AND HEALING

Water is inherently associated with healing throughout the ancient world. Medicinal springs might be either drunk from or bathed in (cf. 2 Kings 5; on sacred and medicinal springs in the Near East, see Smith 1927: 166–84; on Greece and Mesopotamia, see Avalos 1995: 48–50, 60, 63, 76–77, 182–84). If, as Meyer (1906: 102) suggests, later Israelites imputed medicinal powers to the waters of Marah, the transition from desalination to healing would be quite natural.

Water itself can be described as healthy or diseased. Fresh, flowing water is called "alive" (ḥayyîm). And, conversely, a bitter spring might symbolize disease; e.g., the root mrr 'to be bitter' is associated with death in 1 Sam 15:32; Eccl 7:26. (Note, too, that at Ugarit, Death's trappings include ṯkl w'ulmn 'bereavement and widowhood' [KTU 1.23.9; cf. Isa 47:8, 9], and that the biblical embodiment of both these misfortunes, Naomi, assumes the pseudonym mārā 'Bitter' [Ruth 1:20].) In Num 5:19, 24, 27, the ordeal of "bitter, cursing waters" has the power to sicken the adulteress.

A most illuminating parallel to 15:22–26 is 2 Kgs 2:19–22. Elisha "heals" (rpʾ/rpy) a spring causing sterility and death (škl, mwt) by casting in salt (thus, "like repels like" [Mek. wayyassaʿ 1]; on salt, see COMMENT to 12:1–13:16,

p. 433). Significantly, the incident occurs just after Elisha has crossed the parted Jordan, just as Marah is set after Israel's passage through the Sea.

Ezek 47:1–12 also illustrates the association between water and healing. The prophet envisions a river flowing eastward from beneath the Temple threshold into the brackish Dead Sea. The irresistible vitality of Yahweh's stream "heals" (*rp'*), i.e., desalinizes, the waters (v 8) and cures any diseased creature touching the river (v 9). Even the riverside trees take on medicinal virtues (v 12) (see following).

TREES AND HEALING

What is the tree whose secret Yahweh imparts to Moses? Is this a onetime prodigy, or can future generations still work the trick? In general, the wonders of Exod 15:22–17:16 are quite mundane, rooted in observable natural phenomena. That is, Manna and quails occur naturally in the Sinai (see COMMENT to chap. 16); experienced Bedouin can locate water behind a rock face (see COMMENT to 17:1–7); a military standard can direct an army (NOTE to 17:15). Similarly, 15:22–26 probably describes a tree whose wood or leaves were believed to desalinize (Philo *Moses* 1.185; *Mek. wayyassa'* 1). Many peoples use vegetable matter to make brackish water potable (Gaster 1969: 242).

The story's conclusion may imply that the tree in question is also medicinal. *Tg. Ps.-Jonathan* identifies the species as oleander, to which herb lore accords both healing and toxic powers as well as the ability to make water potable (Löw 1967: 1.206–12). The trees of Ezek 47:12 may also be oleanders, since they are medicinal and grow by water. According to *Bib. Ant.* 11:15 and *Fragmentary Targum*, however, the tree of Marah is none other than the quintessential medicinal herb, the Life Tree (Gen 2:9; 3:22).

COVENANT AND HEALING

Critics who partition 15:22b–26 among sources often ask: what has legislation to do with the sweetening of water and the banishing of disease? The simple answer is that, like the liberation from Egypt, Yahweh's gifts of drinking water and health are preconditions for the Covenant. That is, they put Israel in Yahweh's debt and oblige them to enter his servitude. Marah thus foreshadows Sinai (cf. Fretheim 1991a: 178–79). It is a covenant in miniature, with one benefit (water), one stipulation (obedience), one implicit curse (disease) and one explicit blessing (health) (on the covenant form, see Mendenhall 1954a; Baltzer 1971; INTRODUCTION to vol. II); compare 23:20–26.

Further evidence of the unity of 15:22b–26 is the convergence of similar themes in Ezekiel 34. Because Israel's leaders are faithless shepherds, Yahweh will himself tend his flock, gathering the strays, healing the sick and pasturing them by water sources, so that they may survive in the *midbār* 'wilderness/ pasturage,' here symbolizing Canaan. Yahweh will also test his flock, separating the good sheep from the bad. In Ezekiel, however, the climax is the appointment of a faithful shepherd of David's house—a theme absent from Exodus.

WISDOM AND HEALING

At Marah, God literally "instructs" (hôrâ) the magic tree to Moses (MT; see NOTE and TEXTUAL NOTE to 15:25). The odd diction appears to anticipate the legal terms ḥōq, mišpāṭ and miṣwâ (vv 25–26), also evoking tôrâ, beside which these nouns often appear (e.g., Gen 26:5; Exod 16:28; 18:16, 20, etc.). Tôrâ itself can be the object of hôrâ (Deut 17:11; cf. Exod 24:12) and is associated with testing (nsy) (16:4). Arguably, then, the healing tree of Marah symbolizes Torah. Note that Proverbs equates learning (i.e., Torah) with medicine (Prov 3:8; 4:22), while Prov 3:18 even identifies Wisdom with the Life Tree (cf. Prov 13:12; 15:4). Thus, if Eden's moral is that humanity has irrevocably chosen between Life and Knowledge, Proverbs teaches that one gains both through Torah. And water, too, has similar associations in Wisdom literature. Prov 13:14 elliptically calls the sage's Torah məqôr ḥayyîm 'font of life/living [waters]' (cf. Prov 10:11; 14:27; 16:22; 18:4). And Ps 1:2–3 compares the Torah student to an ever-verdant tree, nourished by waters (for postbiblical parallels [e.g., CD 3:16; 6:3–10], see Fishbane 1992).

SPECULATION: The Wisdom overtones of the Marah incident may also explain the quasi-Deuteronomic diction of vv 25a–26 (see SOURCE ANALYSIS). Much of what we consider Deuteronomic style may simply be sapiential exhortation, best represented in Deuteronomy but amply paralleled elsewhere (Soggin 1960: 341–47; Lohfink 1963: 121–24; Caloz 1968; see also Weinfeld 1972: 244–319). Wisdom's interest in medicine may well indicate that teaching and healing were practiced by the same social group, just as English "doctor" properly means "teacher" (see Prov 4:22; 6:15; 12:18; 13:17; 14:30; 15:4; 16:24; 29:1; Eccl 10:4; Sir 38:1–15).

In the New Testament, the incarnation of God's Word, i.e., his Wisdom (logos) and the fulfillment of his Law, is Jesus the Messiah. The inconspicuous Marah incident is therefore pivotal for the Christian Bible (Lohfink 1994: 35–95). It creates a symbolic context for Jesus' message and mission, realized primarily in curing the sick.

XIV. Bread from the heavens (15:27–16:36)

15   27(R)And they came to Elim, and there were twelve eye-springs of water there and seventy date palms. And they camped there by the water.

16 ¹And they set forth from Elim, and all the congregation of Israel's Sons came to the Sin Wilderness that is between Elim and between Sinai on the fifteenth day of the second month of their going out from the land of Egypt. ²⁽ᴾ⁾Then all the congregation of Israel's Sons complained against Moses and against Aaron in the wilderness, ³and Israel's Sons said to them, "Who *would give* our dying by Yahweh's hand in the land of Egypt, in our sitting by the meat pot, in our eating bread to satiety! Instead, you have taken us out into this wilderness to let all this community die of hunger."

⁴⁽ᴶ/ᴱ⁾Then Yahweh said to Moses, "See: I am going to rain down for you bread from the heavens; and the people may go out and collect a day's matter in its day, so that I may test him: will he walk by my Direction or not? ⁵⁽⁽ᐧ⁾⁾And it will happen on the sixth day, and they will prepare what they take in, and there will be a second amount, in addition to what they collect day (by) day."

⁶⁽ᴾ⁾Then Moses and Aaron said to all of Israel's Sons, "Evening: and you will know that Yahweh, he has taken you out from the land of Egypt; ⁷and morning: and you will see Yahweh's Glory, in his hearing your complaints against Yahweh—for what are we, that you complain against us?" ⁸And Moses said, "In Yahweh's giving you in the evening meat to eat, and bread in the morning to satiety, in Yahweh's hearing your complaints that you complain against him—and what are we? Not against us are your complaints, but against Yahweh."

⁹Then Moses said to Aaron, "Say to all the congregation of Israel's Sons, 'Approach before Yahweh, for he has heard your complaints.'"

¹⁰And it happened, with Aaron's speaking to all the congregation of Israel's Sons, and they faced toward the wilderness, and, see: Yahweh's Glory appeared in the cloud. ¹¹And Yahweh spoke to Moses, saying, ¹²"I have heard the complaints of Israel's Sons. Speak to them, saying, '*Between the two evenings* you will eat meat, and in the morning you will be sated with bread, that you may know that I am Yahweh your deity.'"

¹³And it happened in the evening, and the quail ascended and covered the camp, and in the morning the dew layer was about the camp. ¹⁴⁽ᴶ/ᴱ⁾And the dew layer ascended, and, see: on the wilderness's surface, fine as rime, fine as frost on the earth. ¹⁵And Israel's sons saw and said, (each) man to his *brother*, "That is What (*mān*)?" for they did not know what that was. ⁽ᴾ?⁾And Moses said to them, "That is the bread that Yahweh has given you for food. ¹⁶⁽ᴾ⁾This is the word that Yahweh commanded: 'Gather of it (each) man according to his consumption, an ʿōmer *per skull*; the number of your *souls*, (each) man for those in his tent, you may take.'"

¹⁷And Israel's Sons did so. And they gathered, he who did much and he who did little. ¹⁸And they measured it in the ʿōmer, and he who did much had no surplus, and he who did little had no deficit. (Each) man according to his consumption they gathered.

¹⁹And Moses said to them, "Let (each) man not leave any of it until morning." ²⁰But they did not heed Moses, and men left (some) of it until morning, and it bred worms and stank. And Moses was furious at them.

²¹And they collected it by morning by morning, (each) man according to his consumption, ⁽ᴶᴱ⁹⁾but the sun grew hot, and it melted. ²²⁽ᴾ⁾And it happened on the sixth day, they collected a second amount of bread, the two ʿōmer for the one, and all the congregation's leaders came and told to Moses. ²³And he said to them, "That is what Yahweh spoke. Tomorrow is a Sabbatical, a Sabbath of holiness for Yahweh. Whatever you would bake, bake; and whatever you would cook, cook; and all the remainder set by you as a kept thing until the morning."

²⁴So they set it by until the morning, as Moses commanded, and it did not stink, and a worm was not in it. ²⁵And Moses said, "Eat it today, for today is a Sabbath for Yahweh. Today you will not find it in the field. ²⁶Six days you may collect it; but on the seventh day, Sabbath, it will not be in it."

²⁷⁽⁹⁾And it happened on the seventh day, (some) of the people went out to collect but did not find. ²⁸⁽ᴶᴱ⁹⁾And Yahweh said to Moses, "Until when do you refuse to observe my commandments and my directions? ²⁹See that Yahweh, he has given you the Sabbath; therefore he gives you on the sixth day two days' bread. Sit, (each) man *under himself*; let (each) man not go out from his place on the seventh day." ³⁰So the people stopped on the seventh day.

³¹⁽ᴾ⁹⁾And Israel's House called its name *mān* ("What?"). And it was like white coriander seed, and its taste like a wafer in honey. ³²⁽ᴾ⁾And Moses said, "This is the word that Yahweh commanded: 'An ʿōmer-ful of it as a kept thing for your ages, so that they may see the bread that I fed you in the wilderness in my taking you out from the land of Egypt.'"

³³And Moses said to Aaron, "Take one container and put there the ʿōmer-ful of *mān* and set it before Yahweh as a kept thing for your ages," ³⁴as Yahweh commanded to Moses. And Aaron set it before the Covenant as a kept thing.

³⁵⁽⁹⁾So Israel's Sons ate the *mān* forty years, until their coming to a habitable land; the *mān* they ate, until their coming to the land of Canaan's edge.

³⁶⁽ᴾ/ᴿ⁾And the ʿōmer: it is the tenth of the *'ēpâ*.

ANALYSIS

TEXTUAL NOTES

†15:27. *And they came.* Conceivably, 15:27 once began "and they set forth from Marah" (cf. Num 33:9). If so, *wysʿw mmrh* dropped by homoioarkton before *wyb'w*.

to Elim. Sam lacks the locative suffix (cf. 7:15; 8:16; 9:8, 10; 10:19; 16:33).

were there. Sam, Tg. *Neofiti I* and a few witnesses to LXX explicate: "were *in* Elim."

16:1. *their going out.* Syr expands: "the going out *of Israel's Sons.*"

the land of Egypt. Syr and Kenn 199 have simply "Egypt."

† 16:2. *in the wilderness.* LXX lacks these words, perhaps correctly. But I hesitate to adopt LXX without corroboratory Hebrew manuscript evidence.

16:3. *pot.* Since the term is collective, LXX and *Tgs. Onqelos* and *Ps.-Jonathan* pluralize: "pots."

† *this wilderness.* *Tg. Onqelos* has "*the* wilderness," perhaps rightly assuming *hazze(h)* 'this' migrated forward within the verse. But a *Tg.* is unlikely to uniquely preserve an authentic reading. I follow MT et al.

16:4. *go out.* The verb is plural in Syr and *Tgs.*, since *'am* 'people' can take singular or plural modifiers (see also following TEXTUAL NOTES).

test him. LXX, Syr and *Tgs.* make the collective object explicitly plural: "test *them.*"

he walk. Sam, Syr and *Tgs.* again pluralize: "*they* walk."

16:5. *day (by) day.* Sam has "day *and* (by) day" (*ywm wywm*). Compare the evolution of Canaanite *dār-dār* 'age (by) age' into Hebrew *dôr wādôr* 'age *and* (by) age' (NOTE to 3:15).

16:6. *all of Israel's Sons.* LXX and Kenn 196, probably independently, have "all *the congregation* of Israel's Sons," as in vv 1, 2, 9, 10. The more varied MT-Sam is preferable.

the land of. Absent in Syr and Kenn 1.

16:7. *Yahweh's.* LXX^A has "the God's."

his hearing your complaints. To avoid anthropomorphism, Syr and *Tgs.* use the passive: "your complaints *are heard.*" Cf. vv 8, 9, 12.

against Yahweh. Here and in v 8, LXX reads "against *the God*" (see Wevers 1990: 246). Syr and *Tgs. Neofiti I* and *Ps-Jonathan* have "*before* the Lord," apparently to mitigate the shock of a grudge borne directly against the Deity (see previous TEXTUAL NOTE).

16:8. *said.* Syr explicates: "to them."

† *to satiety.* Here one might question the MT vocalization. The infinitive *liśbōaʿ* matches *leʾĕkōl* 'to eat,' but one could also read *lāśōbaʿ*, as in 16:3.

in Yahweh's hearing your complaints. Again, *Tgs.* avoid anthropomorphism: "when your complaints *are heard before the Lord*" (cf. vv 7, 9, 12).

against him. LXX reads "against *us*," apparently influenced by "against us" in vv 7, 8.

against Yahweh. LXX has "against *the God,*" as in v 7.

16:9. *Yahweh.* LXX has "the God."

he has heard your complaints. Some Syr MSS specify "*Yahweh* has heard." The *Tgs.* again paraphrase: "your complaints *are heard before him*" (cf. vv 7, 8, 12).

16:10. *and, see.* *Wǝhinnē(h)* is not reflected in LXX, but there is no need to posit a variant *Vorlage.*

† *appeared.* So MT (*nirʾâ*), but perhaps we should read the participle *nirʾe(h)* 'appearing.'

in the cloud. The consonants *bʿnn* are ambiguous. MT features the definite article (*beʿānān* 'in the [aforesaid] cloud'); LXX, however, renders: "in *a* cloud" (i.e., *baʿānān*). The difference is not trivial, since it is unclear whether this is the same as the theophanic cloud of 13:21–22, etc. (cf. Wevers 1990: 248; also NOTE).

16:12. *I have heard the complaints of Israel's Sons.* The Tgs. paraphrase: "the complaints of Israel's Sons *are heard before me*"; cf. vv 7, 8, 9.

†16:13. *the quail.* For MT *haśśəlāw*, Sam has *hślwy.* Cognates support Sam (Arabic *salwa[y]*, Syriac *salway*), but possibly have influenced its reading (see also BHS notes to Num 11:31; Ps 105:40). Most LXX MSS pluralize the collective and omit the article: "quails" (cf. Wevers 1990: 249).

dew layer was about the camp. In vv 13–14, LXX is shorter than MT. Most likely, the translator periphrastically combined the end of v 13 with the beginning of v 14, producing "when the dew about the camp was gone" (Wevers 1990: 249). But, given the repetition of *škbt hṭl* 'the dew layer,' one can also imagine a slightly unusual case of parablepsis (cf. Kenn 69): *wbbqr hyth škbt hṭl sbyb lmhnh wt'l škbt hṭl > *wbbqr wt'l škbt hṭl sbyb lmhnh.*

††16:14. *fine as rime.* Instead of MT *dq mhsps* 'fine, flaky,' I follow the unique reading of 1QExod, which creates better parallelism with the following "fine as frost": *dq khsps* 'fine *as* rime' (admittedly, this may be considered *lectio facilior*). LXX "fine like white coriander, white as frost" is a paraphrase based on v 31 and Num 11:7 (Wevers 1990: 250). Syr "fine and flaky and encrusted like frost" presumably reflects MT.

16:15. *saw.* Some LXX MSS add an explanatory "it."

16:16. *his consumption.* Here and in v 18, LXX has "each for the appropriate ones," i.e., his family (see also TEXTUAL NOTE to 16:21). Why LXX paraphrases is uncertain; it renders the same phrase literally in 12:4 (Wevers 1990: 251). Presumably, the translator thought it insufficiently clear that each family head had to gather for his dependents—even though the text is quite explicit. Is LXX also influenced by the similarity of *'oklô* 'his consumption' and the following *'ohŏlô* 'his tent'?

those in his tent. LXX smooths over the changes of person and number: "your (pl.) tentmates."

16:18. *his consumption.* On LXX, see TEXTUAL NOTES to 16:16, 21.

16:19. *morning.* Here and in v 20, LXX has "*the* morning," as in vv 23, 24.

16:20. *morning.* See above.

16:21. *according to.* Sam, MT MSS (Kennicott 1776–80: 141) and a Genizah text (*BHS*) read *lpy* 'according to' (vs. MT *kpy*), as in 12:4; 16:16, 18.

his consumption. Here LXX paraphrases: "according to his *custom*"; contrast vv 16, 18. Most likely filling out an awkward text *ad sensum* (see NOTE), Tg. *Onqelos* continues, "and whatever of it was left upon the field's surface. . . ."

†*grew hot.* Sam makes the verb feminine: *whmh*, vs. MT *whm* (masculine). Since *šemeš* 'sun' may be of either gender and since the next word begins with he', MT might be haplographic or Sam dittographic. (A complicating factor, at the subconscious level, could be that *hammâ* is also a noun meaning "sun.")

16:22. *bread.* LXX paraphrases: *deon* 'ration, portion.'

16:23. *he said.* LXX, Kenn 111, 190, Rossi 10, Syr and *Tgs. Ps.-Jonathan* and *Neofiti I* specify: "*Moses* said" (LXX^B "*Yahweh* said" is a senseless variant within the Greek tradition.) The short MT-Sam is presumably correct.

what. LXX, Kenn 110, Rossi 448 and *Tg. Neofiti I* expand slightly, "*the word* that" (cf. v 32).

by you. LXX does not render *lākem.*

16:24. *set it by.* LXX and Syr have "set *some of it* by," under the influence of vv 19, 20.

commanded. LXX and Syr add "them."

16:25. *said.* Syr adds "to them."

†*Eat it.* If LXX is not periphrastic, its *Vorlage* may have read **'klw* 'eat' (vs. MT *'klhw* 'eat it'). Since *w* and *y* look alike in Greco-Roman Hebrew script and since the next word begins *hyw-*, there is ample opportunity for metathesis and dittography (**'klwhywm* > *'klhwhywm*) or haplography (*'klhwhywm* > **'klwhywm*), especially assuming continuous writing. Alternatively: given the weakening of laryngeals in the Greco-Roman period (Propp 1987d: 378 n. 12), the confusion between *'iklūhû* and *'iklû* might be aural. See also TEXTUAL NOTES to "you will not find it" and "collect it" below.

†*Today* (third time). Absent in LXX. Wevers (1990: 256) favors MT, but I suspect that MT conflates ancient variants, each equivalent to LXX: **kî-šabbāt hayyôm ləyahwe(h) lō(') timṣā'ū(hû) baśśāde(h)* and **kî-šabbāt ləyahwe(h) hayyôm lō(') timṣā'ū(hû) baśśāde(h).* My translation, however, follows MT.

†*you will not find it.* Sam and some LXX MSS, including LXX^A, read *tmṣ'w* 'you will not find' without the accusative pronominal suffix (vs. MT *timṣā'ūhû*). Other LXX MSS, however, paraphrase: "it will not be found." It is therefore unclear whether the original LXX *Vorlage* supported Sam or MT. A somewhat comparable situation obtains for *'iklū(hû)* 'eat (it)' and *tilqəṭūhû* 'collect it'; see TEXTUAL NOTES to vv 25 (above), 26, 34.

†16:26. *collect it.* The pronoun is absent from LXX, which possibly had a variant *Vorlage;* cf. TEXTUAL NOTES to vv 25, 34.

Sabbath. Rossi 10 and Vg have "Sabbath *for Yahweh*," most likely an expansion (cf. 16:25; 21:10) but conceivably the result of haplography (*l . . . l*) (D. N. Freedman, privately).

†*in it.* In MT, *bô* 'in it (masc.)' refers to the field (*śāde[h]*, masc.). But in LXX, "it" is feminine, referring to the Sabbath (*šabbāt*, fem.). Is this simply careless translation? We must remember that in older orthography *bô* (masc.) and *bāh* (fem.) were both spelled *bh*; i.e., the autograph was ambiguous. It is therefore possible that the LXX *Vorlage* really was *bh* (*bāh*). If so, it is also possible that this was the original reading.

16:29. *the Sabbath.* LXX expands: "*this day,* the Sabbath."

he gives. LXX and Syr translate "he *gave*," as if reading **nātan*, as in the first clause (vs. MT *nōtēn*).

the seventh. Sam, LXX^F and the Ethiopic read "the Sabbath," presumably in anticipation of the following *wayyišbət(û)* 'stopped' (see next TEXTUAL NOTE).

†16:30. *the people stopped*. The verb is plural in MT, but singular in Sam and perhaps the LXX *Vorlage*. Either could be original.

†16:31. *Israel's House*. LXX, *Tg*. Neofiti I and other Targumic MSS, Syr and several MT MSS (de Rossi 1784–85: 61) read "Israel's Sons," as elsewhere in the passage. The principle of *lectio difficilior* favors MT, but we cannot be certain.

†16:32. *'ōmer-ful*. Sam and LXX have a plural imperative *ml'w* 'fill,' probably Pi'el. MT *malō'* is more difficult yet not impossible, and hence preferable (Holzinger 1900: 58). (Whichever is original, there may well have been an intermediate plene form **mlw'*.)

of it. LXX specifies "of Manna." This could be simple paraphrase, but I would rather cite interference from v 33 as well as the visual similarity of *mmnw* 'of it' and *(m)mn* '(of) Manna' (cf. BHS).

I fed you. LXX has "you yourselves ate." In LXX, Moses is not directly quoting God; see also next TEXTUAL NOTE.

in my taking you out. LXX has "when the Lord took you out," as if MT *bhwṣy'y* were understood as an abbreviation of *bhwṣy' yhwh* (cf. Talmon 1954a, 1954b). For LXX, Moses is the speaker, not God.

the land of. Absent in Syr.

16:33. *container*. While *Tg*. Ps.-*Jonathan* claims only a "*clay* container," LXX has a "*golden* jar" (also Heb 9:4).

†*there*. For MT *šmh*, Sam has *šm* without the locative suffix (cf. 7:15; 8:16; 9:8, 10; 10:19; 15:27).

Yahweh. LXX has "the God."

†16:34. *to Moses*. For standard MT *'el* 'to,' 4QpaleoExod^m, Sam, many MT MSS (Kennicott 1776–80: 142), a Genizah MS (BHS) and *Tgs*. Ps.-*Jonathan* and *Neofiti I* have the direct object marker *'et*. The sense is unaffected.

Troubled by Moses' self-reference in the third person, Syr paraphrases: "as the Lord commanded *me*." But the problem may also be solved by giving the words to the narrator (see NOTE).

†*set it*. The object pronoun is not reflected in LXX; cf. TEXTUAL NOTES to vv 25, 26.

SPECULATION: The beginning of v 34 is very awkward. I strongly suspect an ancient corruption of an original **wayya'aś 'ahărôn* (or *wə'ahărôn 'āśâ*) *ka'ăšer ṣiwwâ yahwe(h) 'el-mōše(h)* 'and Aaron did as Yahweh commanded to Moses' (cf. BHS). But no trace of such a reading survives.

SOURCE ANALYSIS

The basic source in the Manna episode is P (on various other analyses, see Maiberger 1983: 33–86, 809–16). Priestly terminology includes *'ēdâ* 'congregation' (vv 2, 9, 22), *qāhāl* 'community' (3), *'ereb . . . bōqer* 'evening . . . morning' (6–8, 12, 13), *kəbôd yahwe(h)* 'Yahweh's Glory' (7, 10), *lipnê yahwe(h)* 'before Yahweh' (9, 33), *bên hā'arbayim* 'between the two evenings' (12), *wîda'tem kî 'ănî yahwe(h)* 'that you may know that I am Yahweh' (12, cf. 6), *ze(h) haddābār* 'this is the word' (16), *('îš) lǝpî 'oklô* '([each] man) according to his consumption' (16, 18, cf. 21), *laggulgōlet* 'per *skull*' (16), *napšōtêkem* 'your *souls*' (16), *wayya'ăśû-ken* 'and they did so' (17), *'dp* 'be extra' (18, 23), *'ad (hab)bōqer* 'until (the) morning' (19, 20, 23, 24), *nāśî*' 'leader' (22), *šab-bātôn* 'Sabbatical' (23), *qōdeš lǝyahwe(h)* 'holiness for Yahweh' (23), *mišmeret* 'kept thing' (23, 32, 33, 34), *(ka)'ăšer ṣiwwâ* 'as (he) commanded' (24, 32, 34), *šēšet yāmîm . . . ûbayyôm haššǝbî'î* 'six days . . . and on the seventh day' (26) and *'ēdût* 'Covenant' (34). We also find P's characteristic redundancy, including the report of both command/prediction and fulfillment.

Not all of 15:27-16:36 is Priestly, however. First, the introduction (15:27-16:1) is Redactorial, part of the itinerary sequence more fully preserved in Num 33:1-49 (Cross 1973: 308-17; Friedman 1981: 98-119).

In 16:4-5, 14-15, 21b, 27-31, 35, we encounter the greatest redundancy and disorganization—though no more than we might expect for P. Still, it is somewhat odd that Yahweh should respond twice to Israel's complaints (vv 4, 11-12) and that Israel's leaders should appear surprised by the double portion on the sixth day (v 22) (Noth 1962: 132; see NOTES to 16:5, 23). Most likely, the Redactor has interpolated bits of JE into P. In vv 4-5, for instance, the theme of testing (*nissâ*) through commandment seems Elohistic (Gen 22:1; Exod 15:25; 20:20). And the phrase "a day's matter in its day," though found in other sources, last occurred in 5:13 (E). *Himṭîr* 'rain' appears in J (Gen 2:5; 7:4; 19:24) and E (Exod 9:18, 23), but not in P. (One might argue, too, that Num 11:4-9 [E] refers back to Exod 16:4—but this is not clear; Num 11:4-9 might be E's first mention of Manna.)

Exod 16:14-15a seems to be the continuation and fulfillment of v 4, hence also JE (cf. McNeile 1908: XXI-XXII). Moreover, 16:15a and 31 could be taken as doublets from JE and P, respectively, explaining the name *mān* (alternatively, we could assign one to J and the other to E). Exod 16:15b goes well with JE or P, but perhaps better with the latter.

Exod 16:21b is also JE. The reference to melting seems disjointed and digressive in its context, but suits the comparison to frost in v 14 (JE). In P, Manna does not melt, but rots (v 20) (Gressmann 1913: 124-25 n. 2).

Exod 16:27 cannot be easily separated from either JE or P. On the one hand, it closely parallels vv 20, 25 (P), yet it constitutes the necessary prelude to v 28 (JE). Apparently, then, both sources told of a Sabbath infraction, but the Redactor retained only P's account. Conversely, he preserved the JE version of Moses' chastening Israel (v 28) in preference to what must once have stood in P (cf. v 20).

Exod 16:28 resumes the theme of obedience from v 4 (JE); the verb *m'n* 'refuse' appears in JE, but never in P (Gen 39:8; 48:19; Exod 4:23; 7:14; 10:3; 22:16; Num 20:21; 22:13, 14). And 16:29 echoes v 5 (compare, too, 10:23 [E]). Although v 30 could go with either source, most likely it originally followed out of v 29 and is also JE. (Lohfink [1994: 89-90], however, gives 16:4b, 28 as well as 15:25b to R.)

Because of its redundancy with 16:35a, v 35b is often attributed to JE (e.g., Friedman 1987: 251). I do not find this compelling. First, we expect some redundancy in P. Second, the verb in 16:35b lacks a subject, which must be supplied from v 35a. Third, the inverted syntax of v 35b is inexplicable, unless there is a conscious effort to balance v 35a chiastically. Thus, all of v 35 is probably from one hand, whether the Priestly Writer's, the Elohist's or the Yahwist's. Lastly, 16:36 is a comment on the Priestly stratum. It might be P's own postscript or a later gloss on an obscure term.

The Priestly account features several well-known anachronisms. "Before Yahweh" (vv 9, 33) ordinarily refers to the Tabernacle, and v 34 refers explicitly to the "(ark of) the Covenant"—but neither has yet been constructed. The Sabbath is ordained in a rather offhand manner, as if already known (16:23-30). And meat eating (16:8-13) is problematic without the sacrificial cult (see COMMENT to 12:1-13:16, pp. 449-51). Many infer that, prior to redaction, P's Manna story *followed* Sinai (Dillmann 1880: 184-85, 192; Holzinger 1900: 54; Hyatt 1971: 174; cf. Cassuto 1967: 188). But then we must ask: what did Israel eat in the meantime? More likely, Exodus 16 simply *foreshadows* later institutions (Blenkinsopp 1976: 281). "Before Yahweh" (v 9) may well refer, not to the Tabernacle, but to the theophanic cloud, which later inhabits the Tent (Cassuto 1967: 193-94). And vv 33-34 must simply be taken as prospective. That is, v 34 jumps forward eleven months, assuring us that, once the Tabernacle was erected, Aaron fulfilled Moses' command of v 33, depositing the Manna beside the ark (Rashi).

P combines two distinct, yet related episodes from JE (Gressmann 1913: 125; Noth 1962: 131). In Num 11:4-15, 31-34 (E), the people's boredom with Manna leads them to crave meat, whereupon God sends quails (cf. Ps 78:18-31; 105:40). P, on the other hand, incorporates the quails into its own version of Manna, however briefly (conceivably, the Redactor truncated P after v 13 to minimize redundancy with Numbers 11). In fact, if the people's wish to have died "by the meat pot" (16:3) refers to death by overeating, then P's inspiration may have been Num 11:31-34, the "Graves of Appetite."

REDACTION ANALYSIS

Unaware of the Documentary Hypothesis, we would probably not suspect multiple hands in chap. 16. To achieve such coherence, the Redactor had to cut some material. For instance, v 4 (JE) may presuppose the people's complaint, now found only in P (v 3) (Noth 1962: 133). Again, the editor truncated JE after v 5; JE must once have contained a Sabbath command and a report of its violation, evoking Yahweh's outburst in v 28.

Some redundancies and contradictions, however, were inoffensive and so let stand. For example, the composite text states three times that Yahweh would provide bread. But in vv 4 (JE) and 12 (P), *God* speaks, while in v 8 (P), *Moses* speaks. Moreover, in the composite account, Moses already has a clear message from God (v 4 [JE]), which he seems inexplicably to mystify (vv 6-8

[P]). His nonmention of Friday's double portion (v 5 [JE]) evidently occasions the leaders' surprise (v 22 [P]) (Rashi; see NOTES to 16:5, 23).

Since Bekhor Shor, scholars have remarked that in vv 6–9, Moses appears already to know what Yahweh will tell him in vv 11–12. A radical solution would be to imagine that vv 6–8 originally *followed* vv 11–12, but that the Redactor rearranged the text to make vv 6–8 Moses' paraphrase of Yahweh's words in vv 4–5 (McNeile 1908: XXI–XXII; Hyatt 1971: 175). If so, P originally ran as follows:

> ²Then all the congregation of Israel's Sons complained against Moses and against Aaron in the wilderness, ³and Israel's Sons said to them, "*Who would give* our dying by Yahweh's hand in the land of Egypt, in our sitting by the meat pot, in our eating bread to satiety! Instead, you have taken us out into this wilderness to let all this community die of hunger."
> ¹¹And Yahweh spoke to Moses, saying, ¹²"I have heard the complaints of Israel's Sons. Speak to them, saying, '*Between the two evenings* you will eat meat, and in the morning you will be sated with bread, that you may know that I am Yahweh your deity.'"
> ⁶Then Moses and Aaron said to all of Israel's Sons, "Evening: and you will know that Yahweh, he has taken you out from the land of Egypt; ⁷and morning: and you will see Yahweh's Glory, in his hearing your complaints against Yahweh—for what are we, that you complain against us?"
> ⁸And Moses said, "In Yahweh's giving you in the evening meat to eat, and bread in the morning to satiety, in Yahweh's hearing your complaints that you complain against him—and what are we? Not against us are your complaints, but against Yahweh."
> ⁹Then Moses said to Aaron, "Say to all the congregation of Israel's Sons, 'Approach before Yahweh, for he has heard your complaints.'"
> ¹⁰And it happened, with Aaron's speaking to all the congregation of Israel's Sons, and they faced toward the wilderness, and, see: Yahweh's Glory appeared in the cloud. ¹³And it happened in the evening, and the quail ascended and covered the camp, and in the morning the dew layer was about the camp.

This is superficially quite plausible, and unquestionably ingenious. Still, one might quibble that, were he inclined to be so invasive, the Redactor would have done better to put v 12 within v 4, as follows:

> ⁴⁽ᴶ/ᴱ⁾Then Yahweh said to Moses, ¹²⁽ᴾ⁾"I have heard the complaints of Israel's Sons. Speak to them, saying, '*Between the two evenings* you will eat meat, and in the morning you will be sated with bread, that you may know that I am Yahweh your deity.' ⁴⁽ᴶ/ᴱ⁾See: I am going to rain down for you bread from the heavens; and the people may go out and collect a day's matter in its day, so that I may test him: will he walk by my Direction or not? ⁵And it will happen on the sixth day, and they will prepare what they

take in, and there will be a second amount, in addition to what they collect day (by) day."

I do not think, however, that P has been rearranged. Moses' self-abnegation "What are we?" (vv 7–8) should precede, not follow, God's appearance. And in comparable Priestly episodes, Yahweh's Glory appears with a solution only after the people rebel and Moses becomes frustrated (Num 14:10; 16:19; 17:7; 20:6); see also NOTE to 16:7. More likely, we have in vv 6–9 a case of prescience or of faith vindicated.

NOTES

15:27. *twelve . . . seventy.* These stereotypical numbers may parallel Israel's twelve tribes and seventy clans (Philo *Moses* 1.189; *Tgs. Neofiti I* and *Ps.-Jonathan*; *Mek. wayyassa'* 2). That is, each tribe has its own spring, and each clan its own tree. The image of twelve springs at Elim doubtless engendered the midrash that each tribe drank from its own stream at Massah-Meribah (Dura Europos Synagogue; Qur'ān 7:160; cf. *t. Suk.* 3:11).

eye-springs. Hebrew *'ayin* connotes primarily the ocular organ, but secondarily a fountain.

date palms. Dates are not only sweet but highly nutritious, a staple of the Near Eastern diet. Exod 15:27 curiously encapsulates the main themes of 15:22–17:7: the provision of honey-sweet food and drink. The sweet dates also contrast with the bitter waters at Israel's previous camp, Marah (ibn Ezra).

16:1. *Sin Wilderness. Sîn* is generally considered a short form of Sinai (e.g., Noth 1972: 133); compare the optional *-y* suffix on Ugaritic place-names (Richardson 1978: 304–12). Ahuviah (1991: 227 n. 1) further observes that, like Sinai, Sin is a place of lawgiving, since the Sabbath command is at least foreshadowed there.

fifteenth day . . . second month. One month has passed since Israel's departure from Egypt (12:17–18). Many commentators suggest that the unleavened bread the Hebrews bore from Egypt is now exhausted (*Mek. wayyassa'* 2).

It is a fine point whether the fifteenth marks Israel's arrival in the Sin Wilderness or the inception of their complaining. The versification of MT implies the former, but LXX infers the latter (Wevers 1990: 242–43). *Tg. Ps.-Jonathan* eliminates the problem: the people begin to gripe the moment they enter the desert.

16:3. *Who would give our dying.* The idiom means "would that we had died!"

by Yahweh's hand. Why mention Yahweh? Should not the people say, "Would that we had died . . . *in peace?*" Although the Israelites explicitly blame Moses and Aaron, they obliquely condemn God himself, as if to say, "Why did not Yahweh kill us then, rather than now? We might at least have received proper burial" (cf. 14:12).

meat . . . bread. Presumably, this refers to the Hebrews' dependence on Egyptian rations (Daube 1963: 24). In the desert, slavery's benefits—assured food, drink and lodging—appear to outweigh its disadvantages. While émigrés often yearn for the food of their native land (e.g., Num 11:5), this is extreme (Cassuto 1967: 189)! The people's mention of meat and bread elicits God's respective gifts of quails and Manna.

Instead. *Kî* could also be translated "for" or "in fact."

hunger. The worst form of death, according to Lam 4:9, is starvation (*Mek. wayyassaʿ* 2). One might think that Israel has exhausted its grain and lost all its cattle, too. But the livestock still live (e.g., 17:3; 19:13; 34:3) and will survive the forty years' wandering (Num 20:4; 32:1, etc.). Moreover, the cult will require regular grain and meat offerings. Dillmann (1880: 175) infers that Manna, while Israel's staple, is not their entire diet. In fact, since the characters, not the narrator, state that Israel is endangered, we are entitled to doubt their claim (Childs 1974: 284); contrast 15:22; 17:1. Perhaps, despite their ample provisions, they simply gaze into the wilderness and panic.

16:4. *bread.* For ibn Ezra and Ramban, this includes the quails. It is true that *leḥem* occasionally connotes meat, like Arabic *laḥm* (Cassuto 1967: 193), and that in Ps 78:24, 27 God "rains" down both Manna and quails. Still, it is hard to accept this as the plain sense.

from the heavens. This is a paradox: bread ordinarily comes from the earth, the sky's opposite (Ps 104:14; Job 28:5). The point is that, while grains are normally watered by the heaven's rain, Yahweh bypasses farming, directly raining down "bread" ready to cook (cf. *Mek. wayyassaʿ* 3).

in its day. Each day one may collect no more than a day's supply.

test. From v 4 alone, the test seems to be trusting Yahweh's providence instead of gathering extra Manna. What follows, however, suggests that the test is Sabbath observance. According to Deut 8:16, the diet of Manna itself is a test (cf. Num 11:6; 21:5 [?]) (Ramban).

Direction. *Tôrâ,* often tantamount to "teaching," "law," "way" or "wisdom," here refers either to the Sabbath ordinance or to all the commandments of Sinai. Deut 8:3 symbolically equates Torah with Manna: "He afflicted you and made you hungry, and fed you the *mān* . . . so that he might make you know that not by bread alone Man lives, but by all that comes from Yahweh's mouth [i.e., Torah] Man lives" (see COMMENT).

16:5. *prepare.* The sense of *hēkîn* is not "cook," but "set up, assemble" (cf. Josh 1:11; Ps 78:20; Prov 6:8; 30:25). To judge from the people's evident surprise in v 22, Moses does not immediately relay the contents of v 5 (see NOTE to 16:23).

second amount. Analogously, Lev 25:20–22 promises a double harvest in the sixth year of the agricultural cycle, since farming is forbidden in the seventh and there is no yield until the ninth.

16:6. *Moses and Aaron.* Moses presumably speaks to Aaron, who in turn addresses the people (v 9) (see NOTES to 4:10 and 6:12). Moses announces that Yahweh will respond miraculously and indeed sets a timetable—even while distancing himself and Aaron from the Deity.

you will know. What will Israel know? That God, not Moses and Aaron (v 3), has led Israel from Egypt and cares for them still (ibn Ezra; Ramban; Rashbam), and also that they can no longer loll by the fleshpots (Ehrlich 1969: 166).

16:7. *see.* R'y 'see' coordinate with *ydᶜ* 'know' (v 6) is a cliché for perception (Gen 18:21; Exod 2:25; 3:7; Lev 5:1, etc.).

Glory. We find the same sequence—murmuring, leaders' response, appearance of the Glory, an oracle—in the Priestly sections of Numbers 14 and 20 (Childs 1974: 279). But in Exodus 16, there is a chronological difficulty. V 7 is fulfilled in v 10, when Israel sees Yahweh's Glory in the cloud. It follows that v 10 is set in the morning. Then Yahweh proposes to begin to help Israel the *following* evening and morning (v 12). In other words, the relief Moses promises in the evening (vv 6, 8) actually arrives, not within the day, but after a day and a half—hardly the impression we get from his words.

There is no evading the problem. The suggestion of many since Rashi, that *kābôd* means different things in vv 7 and 10, is inherently implausible and does not solve the difficulty: v 12 indicates that God has not yet sent quails or Manna. And ibn Ezra's attempt to detach *bōqer* 'morning' from the rest of v 7 is even less convincing. The textual rearrangement suggested under REDACTION ANALYSIS does not remove the contradiction, either. The best approach may be to imagine that God's words in vv 11–12 do not emanate from the cloud of v 10, but had been said to Moses upon the people's complaint. The speech is simply reported out of sequence, as if to say, "Now, Yahweh *had* said" (v 11) (cf. Bekhor Shor; Calvin; Jacob 1992: 442). But this solution, too, is not without difficulties. First, for the pluperfect we expect inverted syntax: **wəyahwe(h) 'āmar.* More awkward still, we must unnaturally translate *bəšomᶜô . . . bišmōaᶜ yahwe(h)* as "inasmuch as he/Yahweh *has* heard" (LXX), rather than "in Yahweh's hearing," i.e., "when Yahweh hears." We would rather have expected **kî šāmaᶜ* 'for [Yahweh] has heard' (cf. v 9). Instead of forcing events into logical order, I would conclude that the Priestly Writer was simply confused.

in his hearing. This must mean "as soon as he shall have heard," since audition logically precedes revelation and response.

what are we. The implication is simultaneously "It is not our fault" and "We cannot help you."

16:8. *In Yahweh's giving.* V 8 resumes the discourse of v 7, interrupted by Moses' "What are we?" *Bətēt* 'in [Yahweh's] giving' (v 8) is coordinate with *bəšomᶜô* 'in his hearing' (v 7). But v 8 itself is an incomplete thought, as Moses again expostulates, "What are we?" Since 16:8 is so awkward, Vg makes the entire verse a prediction (Wevers 1990: 246), while *Tg. Ps.-Jonathan* inserts "Thus you shall know." The disjointedness is indeed so great that one suspects an ancient, irremediable textual corruption. Alternatively, we might have an effort to capture agitated speech (Jacob [1992: 447] blames Moses' native ineloquence [4:10; 6:12, 30]!).

There is nonetheless a logic of sorts. I would paraphrase as follows: "When God sends miraculous food, then it will become clear that Moses and Aaron, in contrast, are but flesh and blood" (cf. Wevers 1990: 246–47). We can even read vv 6–8 as one jumbled but continuous thought: "At evening, when Yahweh gives you meat to eat, you will know that Yahweh, not we, has taken you out from the land of Egypt; and in the morning, when Yahweh gives you bread to satiety, you will see Yahweh's Glory—for Yahweh will have heard your complaints" (Dillmann 1880: 168; Ehrlich 1969: 166).

16:9. *before Yahweh.* In this context, *lipnê yahwe(h),* which elsewhere refers to the Tabernacle, must mean in front of the cloud of v 10 (Cassuto 1967: 193–94).

16:10. *Glory.* *Kābôd* is tantamount to "weight," "honor," "splendor," "wealth" and "self." Yahweh's "Glory" is the portion of his essence visible on the terrestrial plane. In P, it appears as a fire (24:17), most often shrouded in cloud. Ezekiel, however, perceives the "Glory's . . . image" as a shining, fiery man (Ezek 1:27–28).

Fire represents Yahweh's danger, purity and intangibility, as well as his brightness. As first creation, light is of all things closest to God. The image of God as fire wrapped in cloud evokes both a thunderhead and true combustion—especially the sacred fire in whose smoke sacrifices ascend to heaven. Gideon's angel, a manifestation of Yahweh, actually merges with sacrificial flames (Judg 6:21).

the cloud. If the MT vocalization is correct, the meaning may be "the *aforesaid* cloud" (see TEXTUAL NOTE). But, by my analysis, this is the cloud's first mention in P. Either "before Yahweh" (v 9) already implied the cloud's presence, or else 13:21–22, describing the cloud pillar, belongs to P after all, not JE (see SOURCE ANALYSIS to 13:17–15:21). We can eliminate the problem, however, by reading *bə'ānān* 'in *a* cloud' (LXX) or by attaching less meaning to the definite article.

16:12. *Between the two evenings.* I.e., at evening (cf. vv 6, 8; on the idiom, see NOTE to 12:6). Although 16:12 features quasi-poetic parallelism, I would not call it poetry (vs. Kselman 1978: 169–70). Rather, it is high-flown prose (cf. Kugel 1981); we find much the same in v 8. Parallelism is fairly inescapable when evening and morning are contrasted.

16:13. *the quail.* As often with animal names, Hebrew uses the singular collective preceded by the definite article.

dew. Dew (*ṭal*) symbolizes divine favor (e.g., Gen 27:28, 39; Deut 33:13 [MT]; Hos 14:6) (Jacob 1992: 471); at Ugarit, it was venerated as the goddess Ṭallayu. Falling from the sky—or so Israelites imagined (cf. Num 11:9; Deut 33:28; Hag 1:10; Zech 8:12)—dew readily conveys dissolved Manna from heaven to earth. Manna is a gentle wonder, furtive as the dew (cf. 2 Sam 17:12).

16:14. *ascended.* Discharging its sugary burden, the dew evaporates and returns skyward.

rime. The meaning, etymology and reading of *ḥsps* are all uncertain (see TEXTUAL NOTE). Saadiah and Qimḥi find a reference to Manna's granularity (cf. Vg "as if crushed with a pestle"), but this is hard to sustain linguistically. Symmachus and Cassuto (1967: 195) relate *ḥsps* to *ḥśp* 'strip bare, reveal' (Ugaritic *ḥsp*), which might be relevant in one of two ways. Either Manna resembles peelings, or it "reveals itself" when the dew evaporates (*[m]ḥsps* might thus be a technical term for crystallization). But it is hard to resist correlation with Ethiopic *ḥśp* and Arabic *ḥśf*, referring to scaliness as well as snowiness. Most today follow the interpretation of the *Tgs.*, Aquila and Theodotion: "flaky." Even though Arabic-Ethiopic *ś* does not match Hebrew samekh, and even though the metathetic reduplication of a middle radical is anomalous (ibn Ezra)—a difficulty for any analysis—the gloss "fine as frost" appears to clinch the matter.

SPECULATION: The pairing of *dqq* and *ḥsp* may be paralleled in an Aramaic inscription from Elephantine, Egypt, where salt is called *dqq wḥsp* (Dupont-Sommer 1948: 109–16). While Dupont-Sommer takes the terms as antonyms, they might rather be synonyms meaning "fine." As for the problem of the sibilant (ṣadhe vs. samekh), we find the same ambivalence in Semitic terms for pottery: compare Biblical Aramaic *ḥăsap* and Syriac *ḥeṣpā'*.

16:15. *brother.* I.e., "fellow."
What. Deut 8:3, 16 also mention Israel's prior ignorance of Manna. To judge from the following gloss "what that was," *mān* is a primitive form of the Hebrew interrogative pronoun *ma(h)*; cf. Amarna *manna* 'what?' [EA 286:5], Ugaritic *mn* 'who, what?' and Syriac *mān* 'who, what?' Using a pronoun as a proper noun is a perennial joke; famous examples are Odysseus' *Outis* 'No-one' (*Odyssey* 9:408) and Abbott and Costello's "Who's on first."
The homophony with "what?" is fortuitous, however. *Mān* probably derives from a root **mwn* 'provide, feed,' attested in Arabic (Ellenbogen 1977: 93–94; for other views, see Maiberger 1983: 280–308). English gets "Manna" from LXX Num 11:6, 9; Deut 8:3, 16: *manna*. This, in turn, probably comes from the Aramaic emphatic form *mannā'*, with the encouragement of another pun: *manna* is Greek for "granules."
16:16. *according to.* *Ləpî* literally means "to the mouth of," befitting the act of eating (also 12:4; 16:17, 21).
'ōmer. The term properly denotes a sheaf and, by extension, an equivalent measure of grain, roughly one to two liters (Powell 1992: 903–4).
per skull. As we say, "per capita" (cf. also "poll tax," "head count," etc.).
16:18. *much . . . little.* That is, the Manna collectors only estimated their ration. Some took too much and others too little, but Yahweh miraculously ensured equity (Rashi, vs. ibn Ezra). Others, however, imagine a nonmiraculous redistribution while the Manna was being measured (cf. Bekhor Shor; Calvin).
16:19. *leave any of it.* At least in the early modern Middle East, one's "daily bread" was eaten on the day it was baked (Dillmann 1880: 173). Thus, the two-day freshness of Friday's portion is anomalous. On Manna's unusual fragility during the week and unusual durability on the Sabbath, see COMMENT.
16:21. *melted.* Like the frost Manna resembles (v 14).

16:22. *the one.* I take "one" as referring to each previous day's gleanings. *Tgs. Ps.-Jonathan* and *Neofiti I*, however, understand *lā'ehād* as "for each individual."

told to Moses. The leaders presumably speak in surprise and also some consternation. They must assume that half the yield will rot (Durham 1987: 225).

16:23. *That is what Yahweh spoke.* At first glance, *hû'* 'it, that' seemingly refers to the following Sabbath command. But, if so, we might rather have expected *ze(h)* 'this' (cf. v 32). Alternatively, Moses may be recalling an earlier command about the Sabbath—except that, so far as we know, none has been given. And if one was given, Moses should be furious that it has been ignored (cf. vv 20, 28).

How, then, may we make sense of 16:23? We previously found a *prediction* of a double portion on Friday (v 5)—a prediction apparently not relayed to the people. At least in the received text, the import of v 23 may be "Oh, that's what Yahweh meant; we are to keep the Sabbath!" In other words, Moses kept the matter of vv 4–5 to himself both because he did not fully understand it and because compliance did not require special action (Ahuviah 1991: 229).

Sabbatical. Šabbātôn refers to a day of rest, whether a festival or the Sabbath itself.

bake . . . cook. The people are to do all their Sabbath cooking a day in advance (Rashi, *pace* ibn Ezra). Cooking is apparently forbidden because it involves kindling fire (cf. 35:3). Sabbath thus differs from the first day of a festival, when a special dispensation permits food preparation (12:16; cf. Maimonides, *Mishneh Torah, hilkôt yôm ṭôb* 1:1).

Since *bšl* 'cook' ordinarily connotes boiling meat (but cf. NOTE to 12:9), one at first assumes that it here refers to the quails, not the Manna. But Moses' instructions probably apply to the entire wilderness period, during which Manna was eaten daily, whereas the quails were a short-term gift. More likely, then, both verbs refer to Manna, which, according to Num 11:8, might be baked or "cooked" (*Mek. wayyassaʿ* 5).

remainder. I.e., what is not consumed on the sixth day.

16:25. *Sabbath.* Jacob (1992: 374) notes that, for the wilderness generation, Sabbath observance was not optional or arbitrary. The seventh day differed intrinsically from the other six, since no Manna fell.

for Yahweh. God anciently desisted from Creation on the Sabbath (Gen 2:2–3) and accordingly will not create any Manna on his day off (Ahuviah 1991: 229). He instead produces a double share on Friday, rather like his double creation of man and beasts on the first Friday (Gen 1:24–31). The Manna cycle reestablishes the seven-day week, built into Creation but never before enjoined upon humanity.

16:26. *Six . . . seventh.* The wording recalls the Sabbath legislation (31:15; Lev 23:3), most famously the Decalogue: "Six days work . . . but the seventh day is Sabbath for Yahweh your deity" (20:8; Deut 5:13–14).

Sabbath. Or "a cessation."

16:28. *to Moses.* Moses is implicitly required to relay these words to the people (Luzzatto).

Until when. Or "how long?"

you refuse. The verb is plural, addressed to Israel, not Moses.

LXX uses the present tense for the Hebrew perfect, while *Tgs.* and Syr have a tenseless participle. As in 10:3 (see NOTE), the implication of *mē'antem* may be "how long have you refused and will you continue to refuse?" (GKC §106*h*).

16:29. *that.* *Kî* may also be translated "for" or "indeed."

Sit. Or "stay" (*šəbû*).

under himself. I.e., "in his place" (cf. 10:23). The Sabbath is to be spent at home (*m. 'Erubin*).

16:30. *the people stopped.* This is a conscious echo of Gen 2:2, "And he [Deity] stopped on the seventh day" (*imitatio Dei*).

16:31. *white coriander seed.* Coriander is not white—but, if it were, it would look like Manna (*b. Yoma* 75a; Rashbam; Bekhor Shor).

wafer. The meaning of *ṣappîḥit* is uncertain. Since the root *ṣpḥ* refers to flatness or making a thin layer, "wafer" or "flat cake" (*Tg. Ps.-Jonathan*) is most likely. But we cannot rule out "paste" (*Tg. Onqelos*).

honey. Ordinarily, *dəbaš* is molasses of grape or date, not bee honey (Caquot 1978). Manna's honey-sweetness betokens its heavenly origin, but also its fragility in this world, since honey was considered liable to fermentation and hence unacceptable upon the altar (Lev 2:11; cf. COMMENT to 12:1–13:16, p. 433).

According to Num 11:8, Manna resembles not only honey but also grain and oil (see Rashbam). A Canaanite mythic antecedent may be Baal's resurrection, whereupon "the heavens rained oil, the ravines ran with honey" (*KTU* 1.6.iii.6–7, 12–13). *Exod. Rab.* 25:3 ingeniously finds a reference to Manna in Ezek 16:19: "My bread that I gave you, fine meal and oil and honey I fed you."

16:33. *container.* The unique word *ṣinṣenet* must be related to Arabic *ṣwn* 'save, store, keep,' but Israelites may also have made a connection with *ṣnn* 'be cool' (*Mek. wayyassa'* 6). At any rate, the deposited Manna does not melt or decay (Noth 1962: 136–37). The Tabernacle's sanctity is like heaven's itself, whence Manna originates.

before Yahweh. I.e., in the yet-unbuilt Tabernacle.

16:34. *as Yahweh commanded to Moses.* I have given these words to the narrator, but they might well be the conclusion of Moses' speech, the third person reference to Moses notwithstanding. On the likelihood of textual corruption, see TEXTUAL NOTE.

Covenant. *'Ēdût* is traditionally translated "testimony" on the basis of Hebrew *'ēd* 'witness.' Most scholars today, however, equate *'ēdût* with Aramaic *'adê* 'covenant.' BDB and KB derive *'ēd*, *'ēdût* and *'ēdōt/'ēdwōt* 'laws' from **'wd* 'to repeat, endure, be customary.' But a more likely origin, at least for *'ēdût*, is **'hd*, which in Arabic means "entrust, promise, contract."

'*Ēdût* is often, as here, an elliptical or metonymic reference to *'ărôn hā'ēdût* 'the Covenant Ark.' The Manna pot is stored in the Tabernacle's inner chamber, along with Aaron's budding rod (Num 17:25). Like Water from the Rock, Manna offers a sweet foretaste of the blessings Yahweh will shower upon Israel in Canaan (von Rad 1965: 90; Jacob 1992: 474–75; COMMENT to 17:1–7; cf. Josh 5:11–12). But the preservation of a pot beside the Covenant is also a warning: Yahweh's promise to sustain Israel is conditional.

16:35. *forty years.* More precisely, forty years minus one month, since Israel will reach Canaan in the first month (Josh 5:10) (*b. Qidd.* 38a; Bekhor Shor). In the rest of the Torah, whenever the people rebel against Moses and God, we must imagine them rising in the morning, collecting their daily Manna and—incredibly!—complaining. Their wonder and gratitude grow dull by familiarity (cf. Num 11:6; 21:5 [?]).

16:36. *'êpâ.* This measure is apparently borrowed from Egyptian *ipt* (Lambdin 1953: 147). Its probable capacity was between ten and twenty liters (Powell 1992: 903–4); ten make one *hōmer* (Ezek 45:11).

COMMENT

MURMURING

The Israelites are inveterate doubters and whiners (3:13; 4:1, 8–9; 5:21; 6:9; 14:11–12; 15:24, etc.). While the Bible often speaks of Yahweh testing Israel in the desert, Yahweh is tested, too (17:2, 7; Num 14:22; Deut 6:16; Ps 78:18, 41, 56; 95:9; 106:14). Having proved his ability to make water drinkable, his next challenge is to "give bread . . . prepare flesh for his people" (Ps 78:20). (Water, bread and meat constitute, to the Israelite mind, a full diet; cf. 1 Sam 25:11; 1 Kgs 17:6.)

It may seem implausible, and it surely is, that a generation having witnessed the Plagues of Egypt and the parting of the Sea should lack faith. But the "murmuring" tradition, like the hardening of Pharaoh's heart, is essentially a parable aimed at readers: if Pharaoh and the liberated Hebrews would not believe in Yahweh, how much harder for us (cf. 1 Cor 10:6; Heb 3:7–4:13)! Although prior to the Covenant Yahweh graciously accedes to the people's demands (14:15; 15:25; 17:5), he later grows testy, slaying thousands for impiety (Exodus 32; Numbers 11; 16–17; 21:4–9) and dooming the remainder to expire in the wilderness (Numbers 13–14; 20:1–13) (Jacob 1992: 516). For further discussion of the "murmuring" theme, see Coats (1968), de Vries (1968), Fritz (1970) and Schart (1990).

NATURAL CAUSES

Like the Torah's other tales of desert sustenance, the legends of quails and Manna arise from natural phenomena. In the spring, quails migrating over the Sinai fall exhausted to the ground, becoming easy prey (Dillmann 1880: 170–71; McNeile 1908: 97). The miraculous in 16:15 thus lies, not in the phe-nomenon itself, but in its timeliness and magnitude. Similarly, despite some glaring differences (see ibn Ezra, Calvin, Luzzatto), there can be no doubt that Manna is a mythologization of "honey-dew," the sweet pellets (not neces-sarily white) secreted by plant lice (Bodenheimer 1947; 1957: 105–9).

In the Sinai, small quantities of honey-dew are found particularly in the summer and particularly in tamarisk trees; the Arabs call it *mann* (Maiberger 1983: 325–409). It does not rot or melt in the morning; rather, insects cart it off (Bodenheimer 1947: 5–6). *Mann* is not flaky, nor can it be made directly into cakes. But, gathered in sufficient quantities, it can be distilled into a flavoring syrup for confections. There is undeniable appeal to the image of Israel eating candy every day of its forty-year infancy!

But if Manna was a well-known substance, how did biblical tradition come to regard it as supernatural? Perhaps, for literate, urban Israelites, the desert and its peculiar features were as fabulously distant as Cathay. Or, more plausibly, the Manna of Exodus was regarded as the amplification or origin of a familiar phe-nomenon. Admittedly, the statement that Manna ceased when Israel entered Canaan, taken literally, would preclude identification with ordinary honey-dew (Josh 5:11–12). But the real point is that Israel in Canaan no longer needed Manna. Perhaps some was understood to dribble continually from heaven onto desert shrubbery as a memorial of an ancient miracle (cf. Josephus *Ant.* 1.33).

Unlike nonnutritious honey-dew, biblical Manna, or "heaven's bread" (Ps 105:20; cf. Ps 78:24; Wis 16:20; *b.* Yoma 75b), is supernaturally sustaining. It is a common folk motif that the gods' food lends mortals godlike vitality (Jacob 1992: 444); cf. Gen 3:22. Yet celestial Manna is also notably fragile in our cor-rupt sphere. Like sacrificial meat, it is inedible after a day (cf. NOTE to 12:10). Only in the sacred space of the Tabernacle or during the sacred time of the Sabbath can it endure.

MY FLESH IS FOOD

There may be an implicit homology between Manna and *maṣṣôt*, both ultra-pure forms of bread (Jacob 1992: 471; see COMMENT to 12:1–13:16, pp. 429–34). Conceivably, Manna was created specifically to replace the Israelites' exhausted unleavened bread (12:34, 39) (*Mek. wayyassaʿ* 2; Rashi). Note, too, that the day after the Manna ceases, Israel celebrates the Festival of Unleav-ened Bread under Joshua (Josh 5:11–12). Like the *Pesaḥ-Maṣṣôt* complex, Exodus 16 involves a meat meal eaten "*between the two evenings*," with the consumption of sacred "bread" on the morrow.

Maṣṣôt, Manna and meat converge in the New Testament's interpretation of Jesus. According to the Synoptic Gospels, Jesus identifies his body with *un-leavened bread* to be ritually consumed (Matt 26:26; Mark 14:22; Luke 22:19; see COMMENT to 12:1–13:16, pp. 459–61). In John 6:31–58, however, Jesus likens himself to *Manna* (cf. 1 Cor 10:3), again commanding that his flesh be eaten (note also that, for John, Jesus is God's Word [1:14], which Deut 8:3 identifies with Manna). The stories of Jesus feeding multitudes in the desert (Mark 6; Matthew 14; Luke 9; John 6) may also be refractions of the Old Testament Manna tradition. (For further discussion of Manna in Jewish and Christian literature, see Dumoulin 1994.)

XV. Is there Yahweh in our midst or not? (17:1–7)

17   ¹⁽ᴿ⁾And all the congregation of Israel's Sons set forth from the Sin Wilderness on their settings forth at Yahweh's *mouth*, and they camped in Rephidim. ⁽ᴶᴱ⁾And there was no water for the people's drinking, ²so the people quarreled with Moses and they said, "Give us water that we may drink."

But Moses said to them, "(For) what would you quarrel with me? (For) what would you test Yahweh?"

³But the people thirsted there for water, and the people complained against Moses and said, "For what is it you brought us up from Egypt, to let me and my children and my cattle die of thirst?"

⁴So Moses cried to Yahweh, saying, "What can I do for this people? Yet a little more and they will stone me!"

⁵And Yahweh said to Moses, "Cross before the people and take with you (some) of Israel's elders; and your rod, with which you struck the Nile, you shall take in your hand and go. ⁶⁽ᴱ⁾See: I will be standing before you there, upon the mountain, in Horeb. And you will strike the mountain, and waters will go out from it, and the people will drink."

And Moses did so, to the eyes of Israel's Sons' elders. ⁷⁽ᴶᴱ⁾And he called the place-name Massah (Testing) and Meribah (Quarrel), on account of Israel's Son's quarrel and on account of their testing Yahweh, saying, "Is there Yahweh in our midst or not?"

ANALYSIS

TEXTUAL NOTES

†17:1. *from the Sin Wilderness.* Vis-à-vis MT-Sam-LXX, 4QpaleoGen-Exod¹ and 4QExodᶜ reverse "on their settings forth" and "from the Sin Wilderness." Either order might be original.

17:2. *with Moses.* In place of MT-Sam ʿim-mōše(h), a Genizah MS (*apud* BHS) and perhaps the LXX *Vorlage* read ʿal-mōše(h) ʿagainst/before Moses.'

††*Give.* Reading tənâ, addressed to Moses alone (4QpaleoExodᵐ, Sam, LXX, Syr, *Tgs. Ps.-Jonathan* and *Neofiti I*, Vg, many MSS of *Tg. Onqelos* and

of MT [Kennicott 1776–80: 142; de Rossi 1784–85: 61]). In standard MT, the command is plural (*tənû*), probably addressed to Moses and Yahweh. Graphically, it is easier to imagine *tnh-lnw* becoming *tnw-lnw* than vice versa. Cf. TEXTUAL NOTE to 17:3 "brought us up."

†*(For) what* (second time). 4QpaleoExod^m, 4QExod^c, Sam, LXX, Syr, *Tg. Ps.-Jonathan* and many MSS of both *Tg. Onqelos* and MT (Kennicott 1776–80: 142; de Rossi 1784–85: 61) include a conjunction: *wmh* '*and* (for) what.' Whichever is correct, the resemblance (in Herodian script) of waw and the preceding yodh may be a factor (Cross 1961a; Qimron 1972). But the more important consideration is scribes' overall tendency to insert additional conjunctions. The principle of the shorter reading favors standard MT *mh*.

†17:3. *and said.* The verb is singular in MT, plural in many Sam MSS. Either might be right, since *'am* 'people' can be singular or plural. After "he said," Syr and *Tg. Neofiti I* expand: "to him."

†*is it.* Sam, Kenn 129, 177 and Rossi 419 lack *ze(h)*, as perhaps do the *Vorlagen* of Syr and Vg. This shorter text might be correct, but is more likely the result of haplography by homoioteleuton (*h* . . . *h*): *lmh zh* > *lmh*.

brought us up. The verb is singular in MT (*he'ĕlîtānû*) and other witnesses, but plural (**he'ĕlîtūnû*) in the majority reading of *Tg. Onqelos,* in which the people blame both Moses and Yahweh for their liberation (cf. TEXTUAL NOTE to 17:2 "give"). There is little likelihood that this is correct.

me . . . my . . . my. The collectives are pluralized in 4QReworked Pentateuch^c, LXX, *Tgs. Ps.-Jonathan* and *Neofiti I,* Vg and Syr: "us . . . our . . . our." This is simple paraphrase.

17:4. *stone me.* An eastern Massoretic variant has a Qere *yisqəlûnî* 'they will stone me' (no conjunction), replacing the converted perfect *ûs(ə)qālûnî* with the simple imperfect (Ginsburg 1894: 130).

17:5. *to Moses.* 4QExod^c uniquely lacks *'l mšh*, probably omitted by haplography (*h* . . . *h*): *yhwh 'l mšh* > *yhwh.*

the people. LXX "*this* people" imitates the prior verse.

†*Israel's elders.* LXX has "*the people's* elders" (**ziqnê hā'ām*), perhaps correctly (cf. 19:7; Num 11:16, 24; 1 Sam 15:30; Jer 19:1; Ruth 4:4). 4QReworked Pentateuch^c, however, has *zqny h'dh* 'the congregation's elders'; cf. Lev 4:15; Judg 21:16. This is unlikely to be original, since *'ēdâ* is a P word, and since 4QReworked Pentateuch^c is often periphrastic.

††*you shall take.* Where standard MT has the imperative *qaḥ* 'take,' Sam, Kenn 69, 80 and probably *Tg. Neofiti I* read the imperfect *tiqqaḥ* 'you shall take.' Either might be correct, but the principle of greater variety favors Sam, since *qaḥ* occurs earlier in the verse.

17:6. *I will be standing . . . there.* Disconcerted by the image of Yahweh standing before Moses, as if Moses were the superior, *Tg. Neofiti I* deletes "before you." For similar reasons, LXX changes the tense and paraphrases, "Here I *stand* before your *coming* there," implausibly taking "before you" in a temporal rather than a spatial sense (Wevers 1990: 266). (According to Rabbinic tradition, Gen 18:22 suffered a comparable emendation in MT; see McCarthy 1981: 70–76.)

the people. Some LXX MSS paraphrase: *"my* people."

††*Israel's Sons' elders.* My translation follows the presumed Syr *Vorlage:* **l'yny zqny bny yśr'l.* LXX presupposes **l'yny bny yśr'l* 'to the eyes of Israel's Sons,' while MT reads *l'yny zqny yśr'l* 'to the eyes of Israel's elders.' Admittedly, in parallel cases I have favored the shorter text (see TEXTUAL NOTES to 3:16, 18; 4:29; 12:21). But here we may best account for MT and LXX by assuming the originality of Syr. The source of corruption is homoioteleuton: *-ny . . . -ny . . . -ny.*

17:7. *the place-name.* LXX, Kenn 69, 150, 155 and Syr have *"that* place-name," as in Gen 21:31; 28:11; Num 13:24, etc.

or not. 4QExod^c has *"and* or not" (*w'm 'yn*).

SOURCE ANALYSIS

Exod 17:1a (through "Rephidim") belongs to the Redactorial way station sequence preserved more fully in Num 33:1–49 (Cross 1973: 308–17; Friedman 1981: 98–119). The notice presumably replaces an original geographical and/or temporal setting for the episode.

The ensuing story, vv 1b–7, is a doublet of Num 20:2–13, where Moses strikes a rock with Aaron's rod to produce the spring of Meribah/Meribath-Kadesh (see Propp 1988; Blum 1990: 273–74). Since Num 10:2–13 is Priestly, Exod 17:1b–7 is presumably JE. But is it J, E, or both?

For reasons strong though not compelling, many find two sources in vv 1b–7 (e.g., Holzinger 1990: 55; Noth 1962: 138–39; Hyatt 1971: 179–80). First and most obvious is the double toponym. Only 17:2–7; Deut 33:8 and Ps 95:8 mention Massah and Meribah together; other passages name either Massah (Deut 6:16; 9:22) *or* Meribah (Num 20:13; 27:14; Deut 32:51; Ezek 47:19; 48:28; Ps 81:8; 106:32; some [but not I] also read **mimməribat qādēš* in Deut 33:2). The names are not necessarily contradictory, however. We could infer that Massah and Meribah originally constituted a synonymous poetic pair, as in Deut 33:8; Ps 95:8.

Then there is the redundancy of the people's complaint in vv 2–3. One might argue that their anxiety first arises from the anticipation of thirst (v 2), then from thirst itself (v 3) (see NOTES). But it is theoretically possible to divide vv 1b–3 into parallel accounts, supplying only an extra "and Moses said":

⁽ᴶ⁾And there was no water for the people's drinking, so the people quarreled with Moses and they said, "Give us water that we may drink."
But Moses said to them, "(For) what would you quarrel with me?"

⁽ᴱ⁾But the people thirsted there for water, and the people complained against Moses and said, "For what is it you brought us up from Egypt, to let me and my children and my cattle die of thirst?"
[And Moses said,] "(For) what would you test Yahweh?"

This partition requires that v 7 also be a pastiche of E and J, explaining respectively the names Massah and Meribah (cf. ibn Ezra's theory that the Israelites were divided into two camps, one *striving* with Moses [Meribah], the other *testing* God [Massah]). On the other hand, we have only one version of Moses' prayer and Yahweh's response (vv 4–6). Given the mention of the rod, elders and Horeb, we may assign at least vv 4–6 to E (see INTRODUCTION, pp. 50–52). As for the rest, I am undecided whether the Massah-Meribah episode as a whole is better attributed to E, or regarded as a hash of J and E. We certainly cannot reconstitute two complete accounts out of 17:1b–7.

REDACTION ANALYSIS

Most issues pertaining to redaction have been treated under SOURCE ANALYSIS. The reference to Horeb (v 6) strikes some as anachronistic and is often deleted as a late gloss, perhaps Redactorial (see NOTE). But for many reasons it must be correct—not the least because glosses should solve problems, not create them.

I would rather take Exodus 17–19 at face value. Moses and the elders reach Horeb-Sinai in 17:7; Israel is attacked while awaiting Moses (17:8–16), then all Israel camps by the mountain and encounters Jethro (chap. 18). Thereafter, Moses and Yahweh finally begin the Covenant proceedings (chap. 19). The only puzzle is the Redactor's noting Israel's arrival at Sinai in 19:2, rather than in 18:1 (see REDACTION ANALYSIS to chaps. 19–24. (On the theory that the events of chaps. 16–18 are misplaced, see pp. 620–21, 628.)

NOTES

17:1. *Sin Wilderness.* See NOTE to 16:1.

their settings forth. Ləmasʿêhem probably refers to the two way stations between Sin and Rephidim: Dophkah and Alush (Num 33:12–14) (ibn Ezra).

Rephidim. The name presumably derives from *rpd* 'support, help, carry,' appropriate to the incident of Massah-Meribah and even more to the ensuing battle with Amalek (NOTE to 17:8). A town *bthrpd* 'House of the *Rpd*' appears in a Lachish ostracon (*AHI* 1.004.5) but is otherwise unknown. On the location of Rephidim, see APPENDIX B, vol. II.

17:2. *Give.* The people are not yet thirsty (cf. v 3); they merely anticipate thirst. In MT, the people demand water (*tənû*) from Moses and someone else, either Yahweh (cf. Num 21:5–7) or, less likely, Aaron (ibn Ezra; Cassuto 1967: 201; Jacob 1992: 476). In my preferred reading *tənâ*, however, the people address only Moses (see TEXTUAL NOTE).

me . . . Yahweh. Moses objects that to harass him is tantamount to testing God; cf. 16:7, 8 (P), "Not against us are your complaints, but against Yahweh." To test God is, of course, a great sin (cf. Isa 7:12). So Moses is really telling the people to shut up. He does not deign to address their concern until his own safety is threatened (cf. Fretheim 1991a: 188).

17:3. *thirsted*. The people's renewed complaint now arises from actual discomfort (*Mek. wayyassaʿ* 7). Their bitterness commensurately increases—would that they had never left Egypt at all! But God rescues them in their true need.

For what. The people mimic Moses' double "(for) what" in the prior verse.

you brought us up. "You" is singular, referring to Moses alone, as if to deny Yahweh's role and expose Moses as a charlatan (McBride 1990: 233); cf. Num 16:13. When Yahweh is annoyed, he himself will credit Moses with taking Israel from Egypt (32:7). The question of whether Moses acts with divine authority returns in v 7, "Is there Yahweh in our midst or not?"

me . . . my . . . my. The collective language may imply both that the people speaks with one voice and also that each man considers only his own family's welfare.

to let . . . die of thirst. The language parallels 16:3, only now the problem is lack of drink, not food.

17:4. *stone*. Acting as a mob (cf. Num 14:10; 1 Sam 30:6; 1 Kgs 12:18), not as a court of law (Exod 21:28–32; Lev 20:2; 24:15–16, etc.).

17:5. *Cross before*. Moses must first brave the people (Calvin), before leading a procession of elders to Horeb (Ramban). The masses, meanwhile, straggle behind (cf. Deut 25:17; Carmichael 1974: 244–45). For parallels to "cross before," see Mann (1977: 255); Jacob (1992: 477).

your rod. The implement that rendered the Nile undrinkable (7:15–18) now produces water (Wis 11:4–7; *Exod. Rab.* 26:2). The nonmention of the Sea event in 17:5 is important evidence that Moses' rod is a Redactorial insertion in 14:16 (see SOURCE ANALYSIS to 13:17–15:21, p. 480).

17:6. *I will be standing*. Yahweh's theophany shows Moses where to strike, and also reminds him (and readers) Who really works miracles (Fretheim 1991a: 190).

mountain. "Rock," the usual translation of *ṣûr*, is inadequate. A *ṣûr* is a large geological formation, not just a boulder (Propp 1987a: 21–22). The "*ṣûr* in Horeb" upon which Yahweh stands can be none other than Mount Horeb (or a part thereof); see following.

in Horeb. Gressmann (1913: 146 n.) calls *bǝḥōrēb* a "senseless gloss, inserted by a scribe who could only imagine Yahweh appearing at Horeb" (also Noth 1962: 140; Hyatt 1971: 181). Blum (1990: 55–56) agrees that "in Horeb" is secondary, but he associates it with a legalistic redactional stratum running throughout chaps. 15–18. I would rather take the text at face value: the springs of Massah and Meribah are really located at the Mountain of Lawgiving itself. They in fact reappear in 32:20, when Moses dissolves the Golden Calf in waters flowing from Horeb (cf. Deut 9:21). Moses also sanctifies the Levites by the waters of Massah-Meribah (32:26–29; Deut 33:8–11; see Propp 1987a: 61–63; COMMENT to 32). On the location of Horeb, see APPENDIX B, vol. II.

Moses did so. The language is prospective; i.e., once Moses arrived at Horeb, he performed Yahweh's command. Whether this was before or after the battle with Amalek is moot. The people, at least, probably drink after the battle, since they are en route to Horeb when attacked (see COMMENT to 17:8–16). Less likely, the waters run all the way from Horeb to Rephidim (Ramban).

eyes of . . . elders. When the people arrive, the water is already flowing; they see nothing more unusual than an oasis. But the elders can certify the spring's miraculous origin (*Mek. wayassa'* 7; *Exod. Rab.* 26:2).

17:7. *he called.* Alternatively: "one called."

Massah . . . Meribah. Water is and was the object of fierce contention in the rain-starved Middle East (cf. Exod 2:17; Judg 7:24); many springs bear names connoting strife (Gen 14:7; 26:18–23). A geographical name, *mrbh*, appears in the Sefire Inscription but is unrelated to the Meribahs of Exodus and Numbers (*KAI* 222.A.34, B.12).

Israel's Sons' quarrel. From v 7 alone, one might think that Israel quarreled with Yahweh, not with Moses. *Tg. Ps.-Jonathan* accordingly adds "with Moses," as was doubtless the author's intent. (v 2).

quarrel . . . testing. Ibn Ezra notes the chiasm: *massâ . . . mərîbâ . . . rîb . . . nassōtām* 'Massah (Testing) . . . Meribah (Quarrel) . . . quarrel . . . their testing.'

Is there Yahweh in our midst. The people voice a perennial religious doubt. Yahweh is clearly with them, however, for their salvation betokens his presence. It is sinful to ask for food or drink when Yahweh is "in your midst" (cf. Num 11:20), for the nation with which Yahweh travels will be perfectly secure (Num 14:14; Deut 7:21; Josh 3:10), providing it is righteous (Deut 6:15). Conversely, the nation without Yahweh is doomed to fail (Num 14:42; Deut 1:42; 31:17). After the Golden Calf (chap. 32), Yahweh resolves to abandon Israel, but then reluctantly agrees to remain in their midst (33:3, 5), now surrounded by the protective apparatus and ritual of the Tabernacle. Later on, Yahweh's residence in Zion's Temple will ensure, in the eyes of many, Jerusalem's invulnerability (e.g., Psalms 46, 48). (For an attempt to relate 17:7 to the exilic and postexilic crises of faith, see Herrmann 1992.)

Exod 17:7 articulates a major theme of the Book of Exodus and the entire Bible. How can God and Man coexist? The Torah's ethical and ritual law creates the condition for maximal closeness between Deity and humanity, with consequent blessing (and risk) for the latter. And, in the context of the Christian Bible, the question posed in 17:7 is answered by the Incarnation: Jesus is Emmanuel, "God-is-with-us" (Matt 2:23).

COMMENT
FOOD AND DRINK

In the desert, the need for drink is continual. The Torah features five spring narratives (15:22–26; 15:27; 17:1–7; Num 20:2–13; 21:16–18) which together spawned the legend of "Miriam's Well" following Israel through the desert (*Bib. Ant.* 10:7; 11:15; 1 Cor 10:4; *Num. Rab.* 19:25; Ginzberg 1928: 3.50–54). Generally, Yahweh leads Israel from oasis to oasis like a competent shepherd. But in water's absence he must improvise.

MIRACLE SPRINGS

Waters dramatically gushing forth to relieve thirst is a universal theme. As it happens, desert dwellers are adept at detecting subterranean waters, whether by scrutinizing soil and vegetation or by purported occult powers. Thus these stories have a basis in fact, however they may be elaborated (cf. Philo *Moses* 211).

Num 21:16–18 (the spring at Beer) is one biblical example of inspired dowsing. Yahweh, promising to provide water, tells Moses to assemble the people. The text then quotes an enigmatic song about "princes . . . the people's nobles" digging a well "with their staff and scepter." Although the poem's original context is forever lost, it seems the supernatural is restricted to Yahweh telling the princes where to dig. The same is true in Gen 21:19, where God simply reveals a spring to Hagar.

From these stories, it is a small step to the spring not discovered or excavated, but struck from the ground. This is both an observed practice of Bedouin (Koenig 1963; Cassuto 1967: 203) and a common folkloric motif (Thompson 1955: D1549.5; Gaster 1969: 233–34; for an Arab version, see Doughty 1936: 1.182). The implement varies; for instance, in *Mahabharata* 6.116, it is an arrow. In the Bible, the tool is a rod, be it Moses' or Aaron's (see Propp 1988; Blum 1990: 273–74). The wonder-staff that becomes a snake—or, in the case of Aaron's, a budding branch—seems to be a phallic symbol. A long, stiff weapon pierces the earth to produce a stream and, ultimately, life.

More impressive still is creation of a well, not by the sorcerer's wand, but by his word. According to flatterers of Ramesses II, "If you say to the water, 'Come from the mountain!,' then the waterflood shall come forth promptly after your word. . . . If you were to say to your father the Nile . . . 'Let water flow from the mountain!,' then he would do it in accord with all that you asked" (Kitchen 1982: 49–50). Similarly, at Meribath-Kadesh, Moses is commanded simply to *address* a crag to produce water (Num 20:2–13 [P]); compare Egyptian and Priestly doctrines of Creation by divine fiat.

Sometimes there is no human participation in the miracle at all. When the armies of Israel, Judah and Edom are stranded in the desert, Yahweh simply fills a ravine with drinking water (2 Kgs 3:9–22). Elisha is on hand to prophesy, but he does not activate the miracle by word or deed.

A most instructive parallel is Judg 15:18–19, virtually the prototype or ideal form of Exod 17:1b–7. After defeating the Philistines at Lehi, Samson "thirsted greatly and called out to Yahweh and said, 'You, you gave into your slave's hand this great victory. But now I will die of thirst and fall into the uncircumcised's hand.' So Deity cleft the *maktēš* [a geological formation] that is in Lehi, and waters went forth from it, and he drank, and his spirit returned, and he was revived. Therefore he called its name 'the Caller's *eye-spring*,' which is in Lehi until this day."

CREATION AND IRRIGATION

Ancient Near Eastern myths of cosmogony envision a two-stage Creation. First, the Creator establishes the basic physical and hierarchical distinctions in the Cosmos, separating heaven from earth and becoming king of the gods. These are onetime events. In the second stage, the Creator produces the conditions for life, and life itself, by irrigating the soil and engendering plants, animals and humanity. This second stage of Creation is never complete, but must be renewed daily.

For example, in the Babylonian Creation epic *Enūma eliš*, Marduk fashions the earth and heavens from the cloven corpse of Tiāmat (Ocean) (IV.137–40); the waters below already exist as the body of her slain husband Apsu (Abyss). Then Marduk creates clouds, rivers and springs from various parts of Tiāmat's body, to continually water the earth (V.47–58).

At Ugarit, the pattern is less clear, but still discernible (see Propp 1987a: 1). Ba῾lu subdues the Sea and builds his abode atop Mount Zaphon in the heavens, whence he eternally reigns and rains, providing groundwaters as well. In another myth, apparently a sequel, Ba῾lu battles Death himself, but this time the conclusion is ambiguous. The storm god is Death's equal, not his superior; each deity is killed and resurrected in turn. In Ba῾lu's absence, there is "no dew, no shower, no upwelling (?) of the two deeps, no sweetness of Ba῾lu's voice [i.e., thunder]" (*KTU* 1.19.i.44–46). When he revives, "the heavens rain oil, the wadis run with honey" (*KTU* 1.6.iii.6–7, 12–13). By my interpretation, the storm god represents the principles of life and, no less important, moderation. The teeming Sea is vitality uncontrolled. As its flood would make the earth uninhabitable, Ba῾lu must restrict Sea to its proper sphere. Instead, the storm god will provide moderate amounts of water through springs and precipitation (see Propp 1987a: 11); moreover, the now docile Sea will be traversible by sailors, thanks to Ba῾lu's winds (compare the treaty between Assyria and Tyre [*ANET*[3] 534; Parpola and Watanabe 1988: 27]). Ba῾lu's second adversary, Death, represents absence of life. The standoff between Ba῾lu and Death symbolizes the continual competition of Life and Death over time (rainy season and dry season) and space (the desert and the sown). (The image of the balanced powers of Storm, Sea and Death jointly administering the Cosmos, with Storm *primus inter pares*, is also known from Greece, where the brothers Zeus, Poseidon and Hades rule, respectively, the sky, sea and underworld [e.g., *Iliad* 15:185–92].)

Genesis 1–2 contains two Creation accounts. In P (Gen 1:1–2:3), God establishes the world's physical parameters and forms all its creatures. There is no particular emphasis on irrigation. The J source (Gen 2:4b–24), however, skips cosmogony proper, beginning on a vast, irrigated mud flat, from whose clay Yahweh molds humans and animals and in whose soil he plants vegetation. Read continuously, Genesis 1–2 describes a god first organizing the Cosmos, then providing the conditions necessary for life (cf. Casalis 1976).

Psalm 104 also features a bipartite cosmogony. Primordially, the Deep covered the earth (v 6). But Yahweh chased the waters uphill into the sky and downhill into the ground (vv 7–8), so that they could no longer dominate the land (v 9). Then Yahweh "set springs in the valleys, meandering amid the mountains; they water every beast of the field. . . . He waters the mountains from his upper chambers . . . the earth is satiated" (vv 10–13). Thus Yahweh created and continually re-creates the conditions for life by irrigating the dry land. (Isa 22:11 and 37:25–26 also refer briefly to Yahweh's creation of ancient springs.)

There was a Canaanite-Israelite myth dealing specifically with primordial irrigation. Although our best-attested Ugaritic cosmogony speaks of defeating the Sea, a variant tells of the serpent *ltn*, biblical Leviathan (*KTU* 1.5.i.1–3, [28]). Much is admittedly unclear, but the extant shreds of the Leviathan myth indicate, I submit, that his corpse, like Tiāmat's, irrigated the soil. First: according to a Canaanite myth in Greek guise, the dragon Typhon was struck by lightning; cleaving the earth to flee underground, he became the source of the River Orontes (Strabo 16:2.7). This particularly parallels Ps 74:13–15:

> You, you smashed Sea in your might.
> You broke the Serpents' heads upon the water.
> You, you shattered Leviathan's heads.
> You made him food for the desert (?) people.
> You, you cleft spring and ravine.
> You, you dried up perennial Rivers.

Although the cleaving of springs refers to drainage (Emerton 1966), by implication the process may be reversed, as in the Typhon myth: Leviathan can flow back to the surface, slaking humanity's thirst and feeding the multitudes.

Most other biblical references to Leviathan as irrigator are not proper cosmogonies, but evocations of Creation. In Isa 11:15–12:3, Yahweh promises to "sever the tongue of Egypt's Sea and lift his arm against the River with . . . (?) his wind, and smite it into seven ravines/brooks, and cause it to be trampled with sandals. . . . Then you will draw water in joy from victory's springs." While much is unclear, it again seems that the seven-headed Serpent is associated with irrigation. Ezekiel twice likens Pharaoh to the arrogant Serpent, i.e., a great crocodile, whom God will extract from the Nile and cast upon the desert. There birds and animals will feed upon him; his flesh will be upon the mountains (as rain), and his blood will fill valleys and watercourses, watering the entire earth (Ezek 29:3–5; 32:2–6).

These motifs evolve further in apocalyptic literature. The best-known example is Rev 12:15–16: the Dragon Satan spews water to threaten the Messiah, but the earth opens its mouth to swallow the flood. Moreover, Leviathan becomes the main dish at an eschatological banquet, along with the land monster Behemoth (1 Enoch 60:24; 2 Bar. 29:4; 4 Ezra 6:52; *b. B. Bat.* 74b–75a;

cf. Hab 3:14; on Behemoth's hypothetical Canaanite roots, see Wakeman 1973: 71–72 n. 2, 108–17; Pope 1973: 320–29; Batto 1992: 47). In short, we find a consistent association of the primordial Serpent with sustenance. It is not surprising, then, that in both E (4:2–4; 17:1–7) and P (7:9–12; Num 20:2–13), the staff that becomes a snake also produces water.

THE WET AND THE DRY

The Bible often compares the Exodus, Israel's national creation, to Creation proper. We have already rehearsed the cosmogonic symbolism in the drying/parting of the Sea (COMMENT to 13:17–15:21). But this corresponds only to the first stage of cosmogony. Creation is incomplete until Yahweh shows his power not only to make the wet dry but to make the dry wet, i.e., to sustain life: "He makes rivers into desert, water sources into thirsty land . . . he makes the desert a water swamp, the parched land water sources" (Ps 107:33–35). The antithetical parallelism between the Sea event and Massah-Meribah is implicit in Ps 78:13–16: "He cleft Sea . . . and stood up waters like a heap . . . he cleft mountain(s) in the wilderness, and watered like/with [see *BHS*] the great Deep(s); he brought forth streams from a crag, and brought down water like river(s)." The repetition of *bq^c* 'cleave' and the sequence *wayyaṣṣeb* 'stood up' . . . *wayyôred* 'brought down' indicate the symmetry of these acts.

We should also bring Manna into this picture. The Canaanite storm god irrigates the world with both springs and showers, likened respectively to honey and oil (see COMMENT to 15:27–16:36). Similarly, Yahweh sustains Israel in the desert with both Water from the Rock and Manna, the oily-sweet bread that "rains" from the sky (16:4). (Below we shall find water itself described as oil, wine, milk, fruit-honey, fat, wheat, etc.)

THE FLOWERING DESERT

We have come far from Exod 17:1–7. Is not Massah-Meribah after all a simple tale of thirst assuaged, like Samson's well (Judg 15:18–19)? Are we entitled to seek cosmic symbolism in the creation of a drinking fountain?

I think so. First, to support three million humans and their cattle, the waters of Massah-Meribah must be a mighty flow, not a mere trickle (the Midrash imagines twelve separate streams [see NOTE to 15:27]). Poetic allusions to the incident corroborate this impression. We read, for example, in Ps 114:8 that Yahweh "turned the mountain into a water swamp, hard stone into a water spring." Similarly, Ps 78:15–20 refers to "great Deep(s)," "streams," "rivers" and "flooding" emanating from the desert mountain. And Ps 105:41 recalls that Yahweh "opened a mountain, and waters flowed; they went in the wastes (as) a river." Thus, in the poetic tradition, God's gift of Water in the Wilderness is seen as transforming the desert clime, not just providing drink (see further below).

The irrigation of the desert is more than a renewal of Creation. It is equally a sign and promise of sustenance in the land of Canaan, the goal of Israel's journey. Psalm 81, after recalling Meribah (v 8), expostulates: "Widen your mouth that I [God] may fill it. . . . If only my people would listen to me . . . he [God] would feed him from wheat fat [i.e., finest wheat], and from a mountain I would sate you with fruit-honey" (vv 11, 14–17). The waters of Meribah are likened to grain and sweet syrup, the fruits of agriculture in Canaan.

Second Isaiah (chaps. 34–35, 40–66) interprets Massah-Meribah in a similar fashion. Israel undertakes a new Exodus from Babylon, but now there is no Sea to cross dryshod. The prophet emphasizes instead Water in the Wilderness:

Let desert and waste exult;
Let wilderness rejoice and blossom,
Like the flower let it blossom. . . .
The Lebanon's glory shall be given it,
The Carmel's splendor and the Sharon's . . .
For waters will be cleft open in the desert,
And brooks in the wilderness.
And the parched will become a swamp,
And the sere (will become) water fountains,
In jackal's abode a bog,
Grass (will become) reed and rush. (Isa 35:1–7)

Compare also Isa 41:18–20; 43:20, and especially 48:21: "And they will not thirst in the wastes (where) he leads them; / Water from a mountain he will make run for them, / And he will cleave a mountain, and waters will flow." Second Isaiah is not predicting the literal blooming of the desert. Rather, he speaks symbolically of the renewed cultivation of devastated Judah: "For Yahweh will comfort Zion . . . and make her desert like Eden, and her wasteland like Yahweh's garden" (Isa 51:3; cf. also Ps 107:35–38).

Deut 32:13–14 unfolds the meaning of Water from the Rock by elaborating on the cliché "land flowing of [or: secreting] milk and honey" (note Deut 31:20):

He made him mount on the land's *back/chest* [heights],
And fed him [see LXX, Sam] the field's produce.
And he suckled him (with) honey from a crag
And oil from a mountain's hard stone,
Cattle's curds and sheep's milk,
With fat of rams and of mountain goats
Sons of Bashan, and of billy goats,
With the fat of wheat *kidneys* [i.e., plump ears],
And grapes' blood you drank (as) wine.

While ostensibly describing Water from the Rock, the poem assimilates the flowing crag to Canaan, a Big Rock Candy Mountain oozing the fruits of agriculture and pastoralism (for the imagery, cf. Joel 4:18; Amos 9:13; Ps 36:9; 81:17; Job 20:17; 29:6). With the verbs "suckled" and "drank" and the reference to the land's *bāmōt* 'chest/back,' Deut 32:13–14 describes the mountain in the wilderness and simultaneously the highlands of Canaan as a mother's breast affording Child Israel complete nourishment (cf. Isa 66:7–14). There is even a pun between *śāday* 'field, highland' and *šād* 'breast' (Propp 1987c).

Isa 58:11, 14 appears to paraphrase Deuteronomy 32: "And Yahweh will lead you always, and sate your throat in the dry places . . . / And you will be like a moist garden, and like a water font whose waters never fail. . . . / Then you will luxuriate in reliance on Yahweh, and I will make you mount upon the land's *back/chest* / And feed you from Jacob your father's patrimony." Water from the Rock both recapitulates Creation and prefigures Settlement.

FOUNTAIN AND MOUNTAIN

In the texts surveyed above, Water in the Wilderness issues from a mountain, generally called *ṣûr*, *selaʿ* or *ḥallāmîš*. Exod 17:6 locates the springs of Massah-Meribah at the *ṣûr* of Horeb, the Mountain of Theophany and Lawgiving, and Yahweh's abode (see NOTE).

Israelite conceptions of Yahweh's residence display clear and well-known Canaanite roots (Clifford 1972). Ugaritic Baʿlu-Haddu 'Lord Thunder' and 'Ilu 'God' both live on mountains associated with water—Baʿlu upon Mount Zaphon and 'Ilu probably on Mount Amanus (Cross 1973: 26–28). 'Ilu is said to lodge "at the source of the two rivers, in the midst of the channels of the two deeps" (*KTU* 1.2.iii.4; 3.v.6–7; 4.iv.21–22; [5.vi.2]; 6.i.33–34; 17.vi.47–48; 100.3), or, in a Canaanite-Hittite myth, at the Euphrates' sources (*ANET*[3] 519; for pictorial parallels, see Keel 1978: 118, 140, 143, 207). Similarly, Baʿlu's enthronement on Zaphon is compared to both a mountain (*ǵr*) and a flood (*mdb*) (*KTU* 1.101.1–2; note the association of the Hebrew cognates *ṣûr* and *zwb* apropos of Water in the Wilderness [Isa 48:21; Ps 78:20; 105:41]). Baʿlu is the source of "the Deep's upwelling(?)" (*KTU* 1.19.i.44–46), the cosmic "canal inspector . . . giving pasturage and watering . . . fertilizing (*mʿdn*) all lands" (Tell Fekheryeh ll. 2–4 [Abou-Assaf, Bordreuil and Millard 1982: 23; see further Propp 1987a: 17 nn. 18, 19]).

In the Bible, when Yahweh appears as storm god, the mountains run with water (e.g., Judg 5:5; Isa 30:25; Mic 1:4; Hab 3:9–10; Ps 97:5). We would therefore expect his own mountain abode to be well watered. In fact, God's garden (Gen 13:10; Isa 51:3; Ezek 31:8–9) is both irrigated and located on a mountain or high ground—explicitly in Ezek 28:14, 16; 31:3, 15, 16, implicitly in Gen 2:10–14 (Gunkel 1910: 36; Cassuto 1961: 76–77). Its very name, "Eden" (*ʿēden*), means "Fertility."

The image of water emanating from God's mountain is particularly associated with Mount Zion, which Ps 48:3 simply calls "Zaphon." Prophetic oracles and psalms envision the Temple emitting a fructifying, healing stream (Ezek 47:1-12; Joel 4:18; Zech 13:1; 14:8; Ps 46:5; 65:10; 84:7 [?]; Rev 22:1-21; 1 Enoch 26). Ps 36:7-10 describes Zion in quasi-Canaanite terms: "Your righteousness is like God's (*'ēl*) mountain(s), your law is the great Deep (*təhôm*) . . . Gods and Man's sons . . . are fatted with your house's juice; the brook of your fertility (*'ădāne[y]kā*) you make them drink, for with you is the life/ flowing source (*məqôr ḥayyîm*)." And Isa 2:2-3 (= Mic 4:1-2) and Jer 31:11 play with the ancient image by reversing the current: one day the nations will "stream" *toward* Zion, whence Torah will emanate in return. True, Zion's spring of Gihon hardly resembles a cosmic ocean or mighty river. But it may have been considered part of a larger body, perhaps the Nile or Red Sea (Gen 2:13; on the underground linkage of rivers, see Pliny *Natural History* 6.128; Burton 1856: 226 n.; Pope 1955: 77-80). Isa 33:21 identifies the river of Zion as Yahweh himself (on water symbolizing God or his spirit, cf. Isa 44:1-4; 55:10-13; Jer 2:13; 17:13; Ps 42:2; John 4; 7:37-38; 1 Cor 10:3-4).

In short, the location of the springs of Massah-Meribah at Horeb, where Yahweh stands, is no "senseless gloss" (NOTE to 17:6). Rather, it is a key component in the imagery of the Mountain of Theophany. In later Jewish literature, water will represent the Sinaitic Covenant (Bienamé 1984; Fishbane 1992), and the notion that Torah is like sustaining water (cf. Ps 36:7-10) is implicit in Exodus, too: both water and Law flow from Horeb (Zenger 1982: 74; see also COMMENT to 15:22-26).

XVI. I will eradicate, eradicate the name Amalek from under the heavens (17:8-16)

17 [8(E)]And Amalek came and fought with Israel at Rephidim. [9]And Moses said to Joshua, "Choose for us men, and go forth, fight against Amalek tomorrow. I will be standing on the mountain's *head*, and the Deity's rod in my hand."

[10]So Joshua did as Moses said to him, to fight against Amalek. And Moses, Aaron and Hur, they ascended the mountain's *head*. [11]And it would happen, whenever Moses lifted his arms, then Israel would prevail. But whenever he rested his arms, then Amalek would prevail. [12]And Moses' arms grew heavy, so they took a stone and put under him, and he sat on it. And Aaron and Hur supported his arms, on this side one and on this side one, and his arms were steadiness until the sun's *entry*. [13]And Joshua cut down Amalek and his people by the sword's *mouth*.

¹⁴And Yahweh said to Moses, "Write this (as) a memorandum in the document and put into Joshua's ears, that I will eradicate, eradicate the name Amalek from under the heavens." ¹⁵And Moses built an altar and called its name, "Yahweh Is My Flag(pole)," ¹⁶and he said, "For an arm (is?) on Yah's kēs." Yahweh has had a war with Amalek *since age (by) age*.

ANALYSIS

TEXTUAL NOTES

17:9. *for us.* LXX, Syr and one *Tg. Onqelos* MS have "for *you*," an easier reading that is probably secondary (cf. Josh 24:15; 2 Sam 24:12; 1 Kgs 18:25; 1 Chr 21:10).

    men. Some LXX MSS have "men *of might*" (but LXXᴬ = MT); cf. 18:21, 25.

    I. While Syr reads "*and I*" (*wə'ānōkî), LXX and *Tg. Neofiti I* have "*and see, I,*" as if reading *wəhinnē(h) 'ānōkî. The more disjointed MT ('ānōkî) is probably original.

    17:10. *to fight.* LXXᴮ and Syr expand, "*and he went forth* to fight," on the analogy of v 9.

    Aaron. Sam, LXX, Syr, *Tgs. Ps.-Jonathan* and *Neofiti I*, Vg and many MT MSS (Kennicott 1776–80: 143; de Rossi 1784–85: 62) prefix the conjunction: "*and* Aaron."

    ascended. Sam, Kenn 4, 69 and 178 variously expand: "ascended *to* ('el, ʿal, lə-)."

    ††17:11. *his arms.* While MT and 4QExodᶜ have a singular *yādô*, I follow Sam, LXX, Syr, *Tgs.* and Kenn 107, reading the plural *yādā(y)w* (also Schmitt 1990: 337). All such forms are inherently ambiguous: *ydw* might be the archaic plural *yādāw* or the updated singular *yādô* (Andersen and Forbes 1986: 62; cf. TEXTUAL NOTE to 3:7). That the following letter is waw, similar to yodh in Greco-Roman-period script (Cross 1961a; Qimron 1972), only increases the opportunity for confusion.

    †17:12. *were.* For MT *wyhy* (masc. sing.), we find *wyhyw* (masc. pl.) in 4QExodᶜ, 4QpaleoExodᵐ, Sam, Kenn 4, LXX, Syr and *Tgs.* Whichever is correct—technically, neither matches the antecedent *yədê* (fem. pl.)—the source of error is waw-yodh confusion, compounded by the following yodh. See also NOTE.

    †17:13. *and his people.* So MT. LXX has a plus, "Amalek and *all* his people." 4QpaleoExodᵐ originally lacked *w't ʿmw* 'and his people' entirely; it was later inserted by a second hand.

    the sword's mouth. 4QpaleoExodᵐ and Sam feature a plus vis-à-vis MT-LXX: *wykm lpy ḥrb* 'and he smote them by the sword's mouth.' This is conceivably correct, although there is no obvious cause for parablepsis. But "and he smote them" may well be a gloss on the rare *wayyaḥălōš* 'and (he) cut down.'

†17:14. *in the document.* For MT *bassēper*, LXX may read *bəsēper 'in a document.' See NOTE.

Joshua's. Syr adds "Nun's son."

17:15. *altar.* Some LXX MSS add "to Yahweh."

My Flag(pole). LXX has "my refuge," as if reading **n(w)sy* (vs. MT *nissî*).

17:16. *and he said.* Not in LXX.

†*an arm (is?) on Yah's kēs.* The readings here are quite varied. For standard MT *yd ʿl ks yh*, Sam and Syr have *yd ʿl ks*' 'an arm (is?) upon a seat,' while *Tgs.* and Vg appear to read *yd ʿl ks' *yh* 'an arm (is?) upon Yah's seat.' Many MT MSS write *ksyh* as a single word (Kennicott 1776–80: 143), and LXX appears to read *ʿl yd ksyh 'by a hidden/covered hand' (for a more detailed discussion, see Houtman 1989: 111–14). On the frequent emendation *nēs yāh 'Yah's flag(pole)," see NOTE.

since age (by) age. 4QpaleoExod^m and most Sam MSS have "since age *and* (by) age" (*mdr wdr*), the younger form of the expression *middōr dōr* (see NOTE to 3:15). On the *lectio facilior* ʿ*d dr wdr* 'until age and age' (4QpaleoExod^m), see NOTE.

SOURCE ANALYSIS

Exod 17:8–16 is Elohistic (with Driver 1891: 30; Holzinger 1900: 55; Hyatt 1971: 182–83; vs. Noth 1962: 141; Grønbaek 1964; Eissfeldt 1961). The Amalek incident features Aaron, Joshua and the Deity's rod, elsewhere signs of E (see INTRODUCTION, pp. 50–52). Note, too, the association of *gbr* and *ḥlš* in both 17:11, 13 and 32:18 (E) (cf. Ramban on 32:18; Eissfeldt p. 139).

We must note an inconsistency, however. By the most likely interpretation of 3:13–15, the name "Yahweh" was not known in Joshua's generation. Yet the first element of Joshua's name, *yəhô-šūaʿ*, is a contraction of *yahwe(h)* (see NOTE to 17:9). Evidently, the problem did not trouble the Elohist, even if the Priestly Writer felt obliged to fix it, making Joshua's original name "Hoshea" (Num 13:8, 16; also Deut 32:44 [MT]). An analogous difficulty obtains for Moses' mother, Jochebed; see NOTE to 6:20.

REDACTION ANALYSIS

Exod 17:8–16 belongs to the continuous account of Israel's experiences in the vicinity of Mount Horeb prior to the Covenant (chaps. 17–19). Water comes from the rock, a battle is fought, the judiciary is established.

Many commentators believe that the material in Exodus 16–18 has been transferred from its original location *after* the Covenant. They note that chap. 16 presupposes the Sabbath and Tabernacle, that 17:1b–7 resembles P's Meribath-Kadesh account (Num 20:2–13) and that, according to Deut 1:9–18, Moses appointed judges just before Israel *left* Horeb. Some further argue that since Joshua is fully grown, not the "youth" of 24:13; 33:11, and since Moses is feeble, 17:8–16 must belong near the end of Israel's wanderings (McNeile 1908: 102). As for why an editor might have rearranged the text—perhaps it was to enhance symmetry by framing the Covenant with two Manna and quails accounts (Exodus 16; Num 11:4–34); two Meribah stories (Exod 17:1b–7; Num 20:2–13), each followed by holy war (Exod 17:8–16; Num 21:1–3); two less impressive water miracles (Exod 15:22–25; Num 21:16–18); two stories of Moses' delegation of authority (Exod 18:13–27; Num 11:10–17, 24–30) and two Midianite encounters (Exodus 18; Num 10:29–32) (cf. the varying analyses of Schart [1990: 52]; Blenkinsopp [1992: 163]; Levine [1993: 484]; Smith [1996: 32–33]).

These arguments are not convincing, however, neither individually nor *en masse*. References to the Sabbath and Tabernacle are not necessarily anachronistic, merely anticipatory (see SOURCE ANALYSIS to 15:27–16:36). As for Meribath-Kadesh, I would not accord greater antiquity to P than to JE (P may in fact associate Meribah with Kadesh in order to reconcile JE with Psalm 95 [Propp 1988]). As for Deut 1:9–18, the narrative differs in several respects from Exodus 18 (see REDACTION ANALYSIS). Lastly, in 24:13; 33:11, Joshua is not really a youth, but already a leader. And a man of any age might have trouble elevating his arms for twelve hours.

The events of chaps. 17–18 make most sense *before* the Covenant at Horeb, where they now stand. They are part of Israel's testing and tempering (see INTRODUCTION, pp. 34–36).

NOTES

17:8. *Amalek.* Early Israel's inveterate enemies were camel nomads (Judg 6:5; 7:12; 1 Sam 27:9) who ranged through the deserts south of Canaan (Gen 14:7; Num 13:29; 1 Sam 15:7; 27:8; 30:11–20; 1 Chr 4:43), launching occasional raids into the Israelite heartland (Judg 6:3–5, 33; 12:15; 1 Sam 30:1–2) and perhaps leaving behind small settlements (Judg 12:15). Amalekites would sometimes serve as mercenaries (Judg 3:13). Although Sarna (1986: 124) questions the tradition's antiquity, biblical genealogies link the Amalekites to the Edomites, descendants of Esau, brother of Jacob (Gen 36:12, 16; 1 Chr 1:36). That Amalek is implicitly Israel's "brother" makes their aggression the more heinous (Ehrlich 1969: 167). Num 14:45, perhaps a doublet of Exod 17:8–16, records yet another attack by Amalek upon Israel.

There appears to have been particular enmity between the Saulides and the Amalekites. Saul virtually exterminates Amalek (1 Samuel 15), while an Amalekite claims to have slain Saul (2 Sam 1:1–10; cf. 1 Sam 31:1–6; 2 Sam 4:9–10). In the Book of Esther, Mordecai of the house of Saul (Esth 2:5) outwits Haman, heir to Amalek (Esth 3:1), getting in the final blow.

Rephidim. Where Israel began to thirst (17:1). The root *rpd* means 'support,' quite apropos for the story of Amalek, in which Moses' supported arms help Yahweh support Israel (Eerdmans 1910: 3.55). On the location of Rephidim, see APPENDIX B, vol. II.

17:9. *Moses said.* Unlike the previous wilderness episodes, Moses responds to the crisis without seeking divine instructions, at least so far as we are told. But he gives God proper credit in the end (NOTE to v 15).

Joshua. The etymology of *yəhôšūaʿ* is uncertain. Although Joshua is called Hoshea in Num 13:8, 16 (P); Deut 32:44 (MT), the names are in fact unrelated. *Hôšēaʿ* is a verbal name derived from *yšʿ* 'save'; it may mean "Salvation," "Save!" or, conceivably, "He [God] saved."

In *yəhôšūaʿ*, however, *yəhô-* is the divine name, a contraction of *yahwe(h)* (see APPENDIX C, vol. II). And the stem of *šūaʿ* must be *šwʿ*, not *yšʿ*. *Šūaʿ* also appears in the names *ʾĕlîšûaʿ* 'My god is *šûaʿ*,' *ʾăbîšûaʿ* 'My father is *šûaʿ*' and *batšûaʿ* 'Daughter of *šûaʿ*'; also related may be biblical *ʾĕlîšāʿ* 'My god is *šāʿ*,' Canaanite/Phoenician/Israelite *ʾdnšʿ* 'My lord is *šʿ*' and Phoenician *šʿblˁ* 'Šʿ is Baal' or 'Baal is *Šʿ*' (Benz 1972: 423; Tarragon 1991; for further references, see Becking 1994: 113–14 nn. 3–4). Most likely, *šūaʿ* is equivalent to Hebrew *šôaʿ*, Ugaritic *tʿ* and Akkadian *šuwāʾu*, all meaning "ruler" (Greenfield 1969: 60–61). Despite some phonological problems, there may also be a connection with the pre-Islamic Arabian deity *Suwāʿ*, on whom see Wellhausen (1897: 18–19). (If so, P's censorship of *yəhôšūaʿ* may reflect discomfort not only with the first element but with the second; see NOTE to 6:20.)

Choose. The division of command between Moses and Joshua is quite natural (cf. Gressmann 1913: 155–56 n. 5). Joshua is considerably younger than Moses. And in antiquity, generals (e.g., Joshua) conducted battles, while diviners and priests (e.g., Moses, Aaron and Hur) examined the omens and besought the gods.

fight. At the Suph Sea, Yahweh fought alone for Israel. Now, against a lesser enemy, it is Israel's turn to fight, albeit still with supernatural assistance (Fretheim 1991a: 192). On the question of whether the Israelites bore weapons out of Egypt, see NOTE to 13:18. Apparently, they are armed now.

tomorrow. As observed already in *Mek.* *ʿămālēq* 1, *māḥār* could go with what follows (MT cantillation, Vg) or what precedes (LXX, Tg. *Neofiti* I, Syr). That is, "tomorrow" might be when Moses will stand on the mountain, or when Joshua is to fight Amalek. I prefer the latter approach. Otherwise, the meaning might be "go begin the battle (at once); tomorrow I will go up the mountain," which hardly makes sense.

mountain. The term is not *har* or *ṣûr*, but *gibʿâ*, often misleadingly rendered "hill." *Gibʿâ* is the poetic complement for *har* (e.g., Deut 33:15; Isa 2:2, 14; 10:32, etc.); there is no evidence that it is of lesser stature. In context, it would seem that the mountain is none other than Horeb (ibn Ezra; Houtman 1989: 118)—admittedly, nowhere else called a *gibʿâ*. In any case, to work his magic, Moses must be able to survey the scene from above, much as Balaam must overlook Israel in order to curse or bless (Numbers 22–24) (Gressmann 1913: 158).

17:10. *Hur.* The name probably derives from Egyptian *ḥr* 'Horus,' the falcon-headed god symbolizing Pharaonic divinity. As with Moses, Aaron and Joshua, E declines to specify Hur's paternity. Since he is Moses' and Aaron's associate (see also 24:14) and bears an Egyptian name, Hur may be a Levite (see APPENDIX B, vol. II). In P, however, Hur is a Judahite prince (31:2; cf. 1 Chr 2:19–20, etc.). For the composite text, at least, one naturally equates the two Hurs, and 17:12 thereby takes on political significance. Moses channels divine power, supported by Aaron (the priesthood) and Hur (the Davidic monarchy, or the nation of Judah).

17:11. *his arms*. That our textual witnesses vary between "his arm" and "his arms" reflects the ambiguity of Moses' gesture (see TEXTUAL NOTE). Is he raising one arm to smite symbolically with the rod, or two arms to pray? The first interpretation follows out of v 9, the second out of v 12.

My solution is simplistic. Since two arms include one arm, while the contrary is not true, I follow the majority and read the plural. That is, Moses raises two arms, one of which holds the rod. (I find appealing neither the view that Moses switches the rod from arm to arm [Pardo *apud* Luzzatto; Ehrlich 1908: 329; Jacob 1992: 482] nor the theory that Moses holds the rod first with one hand, then, as he grows tired, with two [Luzzatto].) See further under COMMENT below.

prevail. The image, but not the language, recalls Josh 8:18, 26: when Joshua points his spear at Ai, Israel prevails. On Joshua reenacting scenes from Moses' life, see also NOTE to 3:5.

17:12. *heavy*. *Kəbēdîm* is masculine, although *yədê* 'arms' is feminine. This is likely a simple case of gender incongruity (Levi 1987, but cf. Cassuto 1967: 205).

a stone. With Moses seated, Aaron and Hur can more comfortably support his arms without growing tired themselves (Luzzatto). One wonders whether the tradition is also etiological: i.e., was there a stone at Horeb bearing Moses' imprint, still displayed in the author's day? V 16 may also refer to this seat, but the text is very difficult (see TEXTUAL NOTE and NOTE).

were. Since "arms" are feminine, we would expect a feminine plural verb (**wattihye[y]nâ*), not the masculine singular *wayhî*. This could be simple lack of concord—many sentences, after all, begin *wayhî* 'and it was/happened'—but Rashi has an interesting idea: the subject is not Moses' arms, but Moses himself. The statement then is tantamount to "Moses was steadiness in respect to his arms" (on the construction, see NOTES to 6:2; 15:6; 32:29). Also possible is Ehrlich's (1908: 330) interpretation: "and it happened, (that) his arms. . . ."

steadiness. We might have expected an adjective here, but the language is metaphorical. Moses' arms were "steadiness itself" (Durham 1987: 236).

entry. In the Israelites' flat-earth cosmology, when the sun set it "entered" the netherworld.

17:13. *cut down*. Although in later Hebrew *ḥlš* generally connotes weakness, Bronznick (1977) argues that the primary meaning is "to cut," in particular to decapitate (vs. von Soden 1967: 296–97); on the parallel in 32:18, see NOTE. Jacob (1992: 483) and Cassuto (1967: 206) detect a possible pun in Deut 25:18, which describes the stragglers attacked by Amalek as *neḥĕšālîm*.

mouth. Hebrew describes a sword blade as a "mouth" devouring its victims; see also NOTES to 11:7 and to 15:9 "sword."

17:14. *the document.* The MT vocalization *bassēper* raises the question "What document?" We should not lay too much weight on the definite article, however, as this is the standard biblical idiom for writing (Dillmann 1880: 183).

Is the "document" a new scroll, or are we to imagine Moses as having recorded his experiences all along? Ibn Ezra, Spinoza (*Tract. theolog.-pol.* 8) and Garofalo (1937: 16) cite the mysterious "Document of Yahweh's Wars" (Num 21:14), but Luzzatto thinks God simply commands Moses to grab a handy writing surface. Perhaps the very stone on which Moses sits becomes a victory stele (cf. Cassuto 1967: 206).

Exod 17:14 is the Bible's first reference to literacy, oddly absent from the cultural achievements of Genesis 2–11. In the first century B.C.E., Eupolemus credits Moses with creating the alphabet! But this is probably not the Torah's intent.

ears. Like Moses' exhortations in Deuteronomy 31–32, the tradition about Amalek is to be handed down in both written and oral form. That which is written is permanent in a sense; but, precisely because it is set down, it may easily be forgotten. In contrast, that which is taught orally, "put into the ears," remains in the forefront of consciousness (Calvin). Our passage thus adumbrates the Jewish tradition of Oral Torah (*m. ʾAbot* 1:1).

name. *Zēker* is generally interpreted as "memory" < *zkr* 'remember' (e.g., LXX); thus, it chimes with *zikkārôn* 'memorandum.' By this translation, however, 17:14 is paradoxical: how can one remember to forget (Fretheim 1991a: 194)? Compare also Deut 25:17–19: "Remember what Amalek did to you . . . you must eradicate Amalek's *zēker*. . . . Do not forget!" In fact, *zēker* often means, not "memory," but "name" (cf. Akkadian *zakāru* 'speak'), and it additionally connotes posterity; compare *šēm* 'name, fame, posterity.' The point, therefore, is that Amalek will never be forgotten, but will survive *only* as a memory, not as a people. In other words, Amalek will suffer *kārēt* (see NOTE to 12:15).

17:15. *altar.* Presumably on which to render thanks for the victory (Josephus *Ant.* 3.59; Philo *Moses* 1.219). This might be the very altar Jethro will use in 18:12, although Houtman (1989: 110–11) thinks rather of a symbolic memorial altar (cf. Josh 22:26–29). At any rate, the name etiology implies an object visible in later times (Gressmann 1913: 157), perhaps Moses' stone seat. (For altars erected on special occasions, see also Gen 12:7; 13:18; 26:25; 33:20; 35:7.)

My Flag(pole). A *nēs* 'banner, pole' is generally a military standard (but note Num 21:8–9), often situated on a mountain (Isa 13:2; 18:3; 30:17; Jer 4:6). In Exodus, the divine rod functions as a kind of banner, rallying the people (cf. Rashbam, Bekhor Shor). But the words "Yahweh is my Flag(pole)" affirm that God himself, not the magic rod, bestows victory (Jacob 1992: 484). The banner-staff represents Yahweh's arm, i.e., his power to wreak harm (Fretheim 1991a: 194–95; see COMMENT to chaps. 3–4, pp. 227–29). Through wordplay, there may also be allusion to God testing (*nsy*) Israel (cf. 15:25; 16:4; 17:2, 7; 20:20).

Gressmann (1913: 157) conjectures that Moses' rod was permanently implanted by the altar. This may sound farfetched, but in fact JE never again mentions Moses' rod, while Deut 16:21 cites a custom of (im)planting an Asherah, i.e., a sacred tree or pole, beside Yahweh's altar (see NOTE to 34:13).

17:16. *arm*. Here *yād* probably means "arm, hand," although Cassuto (1967: 207) suggests "memorial pillar" (also Houtman 1989; see below). This key word occurs seven times in the vignette.

Yah's. Yah is a short form of Yahweh. On God's names, see APPENDIX C, vol. II.

Kēs. This term is otherwise unknown. LXX makes a connection with *ksy* 'cover,' while Cassuto (1967: 207) thinks of *kss* 'count.' More plausibly, Sam, Syr and Vg find a reference to a chair (*kissē'*), presumably Moses' seat (v 12) or perhaps all Mount Horeb (cf. 15:17). But nowhere else is a chair called *kēs*. And what would "an arm (is?) on Yah's seat" mean? A good effort in this line comes from Houtman (1989: 118): the altar is a "memorial (*yād*) on Yah's throne," i.e., the mountain. But even better is Rashbam's explanation: Yahweh's throne is heaven itself, by which God swears vengeance with elevated arm (cf. Deut 32:40).

But we are not certain *kēs* is the correct reading. Given the similarity of kaph and nun in the square script, many read **nēs yāh* 'Yah's flag(pole)' (see Dillmann 1880: 184; the best defense is Childs 1974: 312). "A hand (is?) upon Yah's flag(pole)"—i.e., the divine rod—makes adequate sense in explaining the name "Yahweh is my Flag(pole)." One could moreover, read the obscure Ps 60:6–7 as equating Yahweh's mighty arm with a banner: "You set for those who fear you a flag(pole) (*nēs*) to wave before the bow [i.e., against the enemy?] . . . so that your beloved may be saved. Rescue, O your right arm, and give us victory." Even more suggestive is Isa 49:22: "I raise my arm toward nations, and toward peoples I lift my flag(pole) (*nissî*)." Thus, Moses or Yahweh may be swearing vengeance by God's staff. Still, no MS or Version reads "flag(pole)" here. The emendation is conjectural.

since age (by) age. I.e., from ancient times. If attributed to Moses, the words are anachronistic (Ehrlich 1908: 330). From Moses' viewpoint, we would expect "*until* eternity," the reading of 4QpaleoExod^m (*'d dwr wdw[r]*). From the author's/narrator's viewpoint, however, Yahweh has been at war with Amalek "*since* eternity." The comment is therefore better given to the narrator than to Moses.

COMMENT

THE SEQUENCE OF EVENTS

Redaction (i.e., 19:1–2 [P, R]) has confused the fairly clear sequence of events within E. At Rephidim, the people demand water, and Moses and the elders go on to Horeb to produce the springs of Massah-Meribah. As the Israelites bring up the rear, they are attacked by Amalek between Rephidim and Horeb.

Moses sends back Joshua to muster the first army of the once timorous people (cf. 13:17; 14:10–13); he himself stands on Horeb (NOTE to 17:9), channeling divine power through the rod. After routing Amalek, Israel camps at the mountain and presumably drinks. Then Jethro arrives and helps Moses establish the first judiciary, prior to the Covenant itself. At Horeb, Israel acquires the trappings of nationhood: an army, a bureaucracy, a law code and a Sovereign.

MOSES' GESTURE

Atop the mountain, Moses raises two arms, one holding a rod (see NOTE to 17:11). The context suggests several interpretations for this gesture. First, the rod is a military standard from which Israel takes direction and encouragement (Bekhor Shor; Rashbam). Moreover, the rod is the conduit for Yahweh's power. Moses, as it were, impersonates God, with an arm upraised to strike the foe (cf. 7:17). But lifting *two* arms is an attitude of supplication, consonant with Moses' seeking divine protection (*Tgs.*; Keel 1974: 103–7; Zenger 1982: 100–7; Schmitt 1990: 341)—albeit the verb *rwm* is not ordinarily used in this connection (Sarna 1986: 122). Finally, in v 16, Yahweh (or Moses) appears to swear an oath, for which one arm is typically raised (cf. *Tg. Onqelos*). Thus readers must continually reinterpret Moses' gesture—as belligerent act, as prayer, as oath. (Inevitably, early Christians also discerned the Sign of the Cross [Letter of Barnabas; see Daniélou 1960: 168–69].)

HOLY WAR

The battle with Amalek may be regarded as Israel's prototypical "Holy War" (cf. Deut 25:17–19; 1 Samuel 15)—that is, a military action sanctioned by Yahweh, prosecuted in a state of ritual purity, involving total extermination of the foe and dedication of their property to God, whether by destruction or by donation to the Temple (Deuteronomy 20; 23:10–15) (see von Rad 1951; Grønbaek 1964: 43–44). Joshua's first victory over Amalek foreshadows his eventual conquest of Canaan, as well as Israel's repulsion of potential future invaders. Among the story's morals may be that successful Holy War requires both sensible military strategy and divine favor (cf. Joshua 8).

MYTHIC RESONANCE

The image of Moses lifting the divine rod atop Mount Horeb is probably mythological in origin. According to *KTU* 1.4.vii.41, after building his palace on Mount Zaphon, the storm god Baʿlu-Haddu brandishes a cedar to rout his enemies. This tree probably represents ramiform lightning; cf. the ʿṣ.brq 'lightning tree/shaft' Baʿlu wields (*KTU* 1.101.4; for a picture of him holding both club and tree, see *Ug* 2, pl. xxiii). Iconographically, Moses stands in for the old Canaanite storm deity.

Some maintain that the expulsion of Ba'lu's enemies from Mount Zaphon also underlies the biblical motif of *Völkerkampf* 'battle of nations,' i.e., the defeat of foreign armies massed against Mount Zion (Isa 17:12–14; 31:1–9; Ezekiel 38–39; Psalms 2; 48; 76; 83) (Clifford 1972: 142–60; see Stolz 1970: 72–101 for a general discussion of *Völkerkampf*). Moreover, like Exodus 17 taken as a whole, several passages associate the *Völkerkampf* with flowing waters (Joel 4; Zechariah 12–14; Psalm 46; cf. Psalm 110). In a variation, Isa 2:2–3 = Mic 4:1–2; Jer 31:12 even imagine the nations peaceably "streaming" *toward* Zion (see above p. 613). A postbiblical parallel is 2 Esdr 13:1–13, which, though a millennium and a half younger, reproduces the Ugaritic archetype almost exactly (see p. 559).

FROM EGYPT TO SINAI

The incidents of Marah, Manna, Massah-Meribah and Amalek are linked by more than *m*-alliteration. The key to their interpretation may be 23:20–26, which combines themes from 15:22–17:16:

> See: I am sending a Messenger before you to guard you on the way and to bring you to the place that I have prepared. Guard yourself from his *face* and heed his voice; do not rebel against him, for he will not *lift* [absolve] your sin, for my Name is within him. But if you heed, heed his voice and do all that I speak, then I will oppose your opponents and attack your attackers. . . . And you shall serve Yahweh your deity, and he will bless your bread and your water, and I will remove illness from your midst. There will not be a bereft or barren (woman) in your land; your days' number I will make full.

The text ostensibly describes Israel's trek from Sinai/Horeb to Canaan, led by an angel. But the language equally befits the journey from the Sea to Sinai (cf. Rashbam on 15:26). God's "Messenger" reminds us of Moses, against whom Israel should not rebel (cf. 15:24; 16:2–3; 17:2–4). If Israel is totally obedient (cf. 15:26), Yahweh will fight their battles (cf. 17:8–16) and provide bread (chap. 16), water (cf. 17:1–7) and health (cf. 15:22–26). Exod 23:20–26 implies, moreover, that these benefits are but a foretaste of what Israel may expect in Canaan.

XVII. Men of competence, fearing Deity, men of reliability, hating gain (18)

18 $^{I(E)}$And Jethro, Midian's priest, Moses' father-in-law, heard all that Deity did for Moses and for Israel his people, that Yahweh had taken Israel out from

Egypt. ²And Jethro, Moses' father-in-law, took Zipporah, Moses' *woman* since her marriage-gift, ³and her two sons, of whom the name of the one was Gershom—for he said, "A sojourner was I in a foreign land"—⁴and the name of the one was Eliezer—for, "My father's deity was as my help and rescued me from Pharaoh's sword." ⁵And Jethro, Moses' father-in-law, and his sons and his *woman* came to Moses, to the wilderness where he was camping, to the Deity's mountain. ⁶And he said to Moses, "I, your father-in-law Jethro, am coming to you, and your *woman* and her two sons with her."

⁷And Moses went out to meet his father-in-law, and he bowed and kissed him. And they inquired, (each) man of his fellow, about well-being, and they entered into the tent. ⁸And Moses told his father-in-law all that Yahweh did to Pharaoh and to Egypt on Israel's behalf; all the hardship that befell them on the way, and Yahweh rescued them. ⁹And Jethro rejoiced over all the good that Yahweh did for Israel, that he rescued him from Egypt's hand. ¹⁰And Jethro said, "Blessed is Yahweh who rescued his people from Egypt's hand and from Pharaoh's hand. ¹¹Now I know that Yahweh is greater than all the gods, for in the affair when they dealt wickedly with them—"

¹²And Jethro, Moses' father-in-law, took *ascending offering* and *slaughter sacrifices* for Deity, and Aaron and (some) of Israel's elders came to eat food with Moses' father-in-law before the Deity.

¹³And it happened on the next day, and Moses sat to judge the people, and the people stood about Moses from the morning till the evening. ¹⁴And Jethro, Moses' father-in-law, saw all that he was doing for the people, and he said, "What is this thing that you are doing for the people? Why are you sitting by yourself, and all the people standing about you, from morning till evening?"

¹⁵And Moses said to his father-in-law, "Because the people come to me to consult Deity. ¹⁶Whenever they have a matter coming to me, then I judge between a man and between his fellow, and I make known the Deity's rules and his directions."

¹⁷But Moses' father-in-law said to him, "The thing that you are doing is not good. ¹⁸You will wither, wither, both you and this people that is with you, for the thing is too heavy for you; you cannot do it by yourself. ¹⁹Now, listen to my voice—I will advise you—and may Deity be with you. You, be for the people *opposite* the Deity, and you, you will bring the matters to the Deity, ²⁰and you will clarify for them the rules and the directions, and make known to them the way they must walk in, and the deed that they must do. ²¹And you, you must see from all the people men of competence, fearing Deity, men of reliability, hating gain, and you will place over them rulers of thousands, rulers of hundreds, rulers of fifties and rulers of tens, ²²and they may judge the people at any time. And it will happen, all the big matters they will bring to you, and all the small matters they will judge themselves. And it will lighten from upon you, and they will bear with you. ²³If this thing you do, and Deity commands you, then you will be able to stand, and also all this people upon its place will come in well-being."

[24]And Moses listened to his father-in-law's voice and did all that he said. [25]And Moses selected men of competence from all Israel and set them heads over the people—rulers of thousands, rulers of hundreds, rulers of fifties and rulers of tens. [26]And they would judge the people at any time; the difficult matters they would bring to Moses, and all the small matters they would judge themselves. [27]Then Moses released his father-in-law, and he went him away to his land.

ANALYSIS

TEXTUAL NOTES

18:1. *Deity.* A Genizah MS (*BHS*), LXX and *Tgs.* read "Yahweh," while Kenn 356 has *yahwe(h)* '*ĕlōhîm.*

†*for Moses.* The phrase is absent from LXX. I ordinarily prefer the shorter reading, but the very unexpectedness of "for Moses" could be a sign of originality (*lectio difficilior*). It probably fell from LXX either by haplography (*l . . . l*) or by deliberate excision.

Israel (second time). Syr expands: "Israel's *Sons.*"

18:2. *Zipporah.* Syr and Kenn 109 add "his daughter."

18:3. *her.* Some LXX MSS read "his" as in v 5 (also Kenn 129; *Tg. Neofiti* I); other LXX witnesses have "her" (= MT).

†18:4. *one.* LXX-Syr "other" is probably free translation, less likely a confusion of '*ḥd* 'one' with '*ḥr* 'other' (daleth and resh are very similar in shape).

My father's deity. Syr takes this as collective: "my fathers' deity."

Some LXX MSS and *Tg. Ps.-Jonathan* appear to insert **kî 'āmar* 'for he said,' as in v 3. On the one hand, this could easily be a periphrastic expansion. On the other hand, MT could well have suffered haplography (*ky ' . . . ky '*). It is hard to say which is original.

sword. LXX has instead "hand," as in vv 9, 10.

18:5. *Deity's mountain.* To solve an exegetical problem (see NOTE), *Tg. Neofiti* I replaces this phrase with "where the Glory of the Lord's Presence camped."

†18:6. *And he said.* Since for LXX and Syr, Jethro is not the speaker, these Versions necessarily take *wayyō(')mer* impersonally: "one said, it was said" (see following).

†*I.* LXX, Sam, Syr and 4QpaleoExod[m] read *hinnē(h)* 'see,' vs. MT, 4QExod[c], *Tgs.* and Vg '*ănî* 'I.' The latter is adopted here as the more difficult reading (some might say, too difficult). "See" is what we would expect, and might be inspired specifically by Gen 48:2, "see (*hinnē[h]*): your son Joseph coming to you." And the acoustic similarity of '*ănî* and *hinnē(h)*, especially among Jews with weak gutturals (Propp 1987d: 378 n. 12), probably contributed to the corruption. But it remains quite possible that MT is wrong.

her two sons. LXX, Syr and Vg have "*your* two sons," apparently assimilating to "your wife."

with her. LXX, Syr and Tg. *Neofiti I* have "with *him.*" This is impossible for MT, however, since Jethro, not the narrator, is speaking (Tg. *Neofiti I,* which matches MT in other respects, is thus nonsensical). Note that in early Hebrew spelling, "with him" and "with her" were both written *ʿmh*; hence, the autograph was ambiguous.

18:7. *he bowed.* LXX and Syr add "to him [Jethro]"; Sam, however, adds "to Moses," no doubt because a scribe considered Moses' obeisance to a foreign priest inappropriate. For the same reason, Tg. *Neofiti I* replaces the reference to bowing with a less servile "he inquired after his welfare."

†*they entered.* For MT *wybʾw,* 4QExod^c, Sam and most LXX MSS have "he brought him [into]," i.e., *wyb(y)ʾhw* (LXX^AF have "brought *them,*" thereby including Moses' family). MT is probably original, the variant being the result of dittography, metathesis and misdivision (*wybʾwhʾhlh* > *wybʾhwhʾhlh*). The errant scribe may also have had in mind Gen 24:67, *waybiʾehā . . . hāʾōhĕlâ* 'and he brought her . . . into the tent.'

18:8. *Israel's.* Syr expands: "Israel's *Sons'.*"

all the hardship. LXX, Syr, Vg (Clementine edition), Kenn 4, 69, 129, 153 and a Genizah text (*BHS*) read "*and* all the hardship."

rescued them. LXX expands: "from Pharaoh's hand and from the Egyptians' hand."

†18:9. *for Israel.* The LXX *lectio brevior* "for *them*" might be correct, "Israel" in the other Versions being explicative. But in the absence of Hebrew evidence for the variant, I follow MT.

Egypt's hand. LXX and Syr add "and from Pharaoh's hand," as in v 10.

††18:10. *his people.* So LXX and Syr, vs. MT-Sam "*the* people." I translate v 10 as a whole after LXX^AFM (LXX^B = MT). In MT, Jethro says with triple redundancy, "Blessed is Yahweh who rescued you from Egypt's hand and from Pharaoh's hand, who rescued the people from under Egypt's hand" (the referent of *ʾetkem* 'you' [pl.] in v 10 [MT] is uncertain: is it all Israel, Moses and Israel [cf. 18:1] or Moses and Aaron [Rashbam]?).

Two scenarios, perhaps equally plausible, might account for the discrepancy between MT and LXX. Taking LXX as original, I consider MT as conflating synonymous variants in v 10 (Ehrlich 1908: 331). It is alternatively possible, however, that LXX has compressed MT (Wevers 1990: 279). But, if so, I doubt this was conscious, given LXX's overall fidelity in Exodus. Rather, I imagine the translator's (or later copyist's) eye skipping from one "rescued" to the next, yielding "blessed is Yahweh who rescued you from under Egypt's hand." Then the scribe, noting Pharaoh's omission, simply added him at the end.

18:12. *ascending offering.* LXX, Syr and Tgs. pluralize, either taking *ʿōlâ* as collective (Wevers 1990: 281) or actually reading **ʿōlōt.* In either event, MT is probably correct.

Deity. Syr: "the Lord."

††*and (some) of Israel's elders.* I follow Sam's *lectio difficilior: wmzqny yśrʾl* (vs. MT *wəkol-ziqnê yiśrāʾēl* 'and *all* of Israel's elders'). Syr expands further:

"and *all* of the elders of Israel's *Sons*"; cf. TEXTUAL NOTES to 3:16, 18; 4:29; 12:21; 17:6.

18:13. *the people stood.* LXX inserts "all."

†*the morning.* The fragmentary 4QpaleoExod[m] lacks definite articles on "morning" and, presumably, "evening."

†*till.* Sam, Syr, many MT MSS (Kennicott 1776–80: 144) and the Soncino Bible (1488) add a conjunction: "*and* till."

18:14. *Moses' father-in-law.* LXX has instead "Jethro," while the periphrastic 4QReworked Pentateuch[c] combines both variants: "Jether [*sic*] Moses' father-in-law."

said. Syr expands: "to him."

standing. For MT *niṣṣāb*, 4QReworked Pentateuch[c] and Tgs. have the plural *nṣbym.* *ʿAm* 'people' can be singular or plural, admittedly, but here I would follow MT, since 4QReworked Pentateuch[c] and Tgs. are given to paraphrase.

†*till.* Many MT MSS (Kennicott 1776–80: 144), Sam, 4QReworked Pentateuch[c] and Syr insert a conjunction: "*and* till."

†18:16. *coming.* Here the Versions display considerable variety. LXX, Syr and Tgs. have "(and) they come," as if translating *ûbā'û/bā'û, the latter being the majority Sam reading. 4QpaleoExod[m], however, has *w[b]'* 'and it comes.' I find MT *bā(')* 'coming' the most difficult, hence most attractive reading.

†*make known.* Sam has "I make *him* know" (*whwdʿtyw*), vs. MT *whwdʿty.* Since waw and yodh were once very similar (Cross 1961a; Qimron 1972), one might consider MT haplographic or Sam dittographic. Sam is the more difficult reading (who is "he"?), but perhaps too difficult to be correct.

his directions. For the MT plural *tōrōtā(y)w*, LXX has a singular, no doubt thinking of the Torah as a whole (see also TEXTUAL NOTE to v 20).

18:18. *this people.* LXX and Syr expand: "*all* this (LXX[A]: 'your') people."

the thing. LXX expands: "*this* thing."

do it. For the rare MT *ʿăśōhû* (see GKC §75n), Sam has the expected *ʿśwtw.*

18:19. *the matters.* LXX, Syr and Tg. Ps.-Jonathan expand: "*their* matters."

18:20. *the rules and the directions.* LXX ("the God's rules and his Law") and Sam ("the rules and the Direction") again find a reference to the entire Torah (cf. TEXTUAL NOTE to v 16 "his directions").

way . . . deed. LXX pluralizes, presumably taking the language as collective.

they must walk in. Sam, 4QpaleoGen-Exod[l], 4QpaleoExod[m] and many MT MSS (Kennicott 1776–80: 144) add the relative pronoun *'šr*: "*which* they must walk in."

18:21. *see.* Sam and the LXX *Vorlage* read *tḥzh lk* 'see *for yourself.*' On principle, I follow the shorter MT.

you will place over them. LXX (not LXX[B]) has "you will place *them* over them," partly harmonizing to v 25. This expansion also relieves an ambiguity in the original (see NOTE).

†*rulers . . . tens.* 4QpaleoExod[m], LXX, Syr, Vg, Tg. Neofiti I, Sam and MT MSS insert conjunctions in various places (Kennicott 1776–80: 145; de Rossi 1784–85: 62). My translation follows L.

18:23. *and Deity commands you.* LXX paraphrases "the God will *strengthen* you," apparently to suit the context (Wevers 1990: 289). *Tgs.* support MT, except that they ostensibly read "Yahweh"—but this is probably just loose translation.

†*upon.* For MT and 4QpaleoGen-Exod[l] *ʕl* 'upon,' 4QpaleoExod[m] and Sam read *ʾl* 'to.' The meaning is virtually unaffected (cf. 34:12; Num 11:12, etc.). Syr appears to reflect *ʾîš ʾel-məqômô "(each) man to his place," but is probably simply paraphrasing.

18:24. *he said.* Syr appends "to him."

18:25. *And Moses selected.* In Deut 1:9–18, Moses will remind Israel of his appointment of judges, and of what he said at that time. In accordance with their tendency to harmonize, 4QpaleoExod[m] and Sam simply replace Exod 18:25 with Deut 1:9–18, making the necessary adjustments in person and tense (cf. TEXTUAL NOTES to 7:8–11:10 *passim*).

set them. As in v 21, LXX adds "over them," and the Versions and MSS disagree over the placement of conjunctions (see TEXTUAL NOTE to 18:21).

††18:26. *they would judge.* I read with Sam *wyšpṭw* (*wəyišpəṭû*). MT *wəšāpəṭû*, which would ordinarily be rendered "and they *will* judge," is probably borrowed from v 22.

the difficult matters. Most LXX MSS (not LXX[A]) and Kenn 181 have "*all* the difficult matters," as in v 22 and subsequently in v 26.

†*all the small matters.* Kenn 109, Syr and *Tg. Neofiti I* lack "all," an attractively short reading uncorroborated by more authoritative witnesses.

††*they would judge.* Standard MT has the late spelling *yšpwṭw* (*yišpûṭû*; cf. *taʕăbûrî* in Ruth 2:8; *tišmûrēm* in Prov 14:3). Sam and many MT MSS (Kennicott 1776–80: 145), however, preserve the original *yšpṭw.*

†18:27. *went him away.* 4QpaleoExod[m] and Kenn 69 lack *lô* 'him,' perhaps rightly.

SOURCE ANALYSIS

Exodus 18 bears all the earmarks of E: Jethro, Horeb, *ʾĕlōhîm*, Aaron and the elders, and the motif of God-fearing (see INTRODUCTION, pp. 50–52). The naming of Gershom (v 3) is apparently a doublet of 2:22 (J). The entire episode may also be a doublet of Num 10:29–32 (J), where "Hobab the son of Reuel the Midianite, Moses' father-in-law," resists Moses' request that he accompany the people (cf. Van Seters 1994: 208–9). Within E, Moses and Jethro's affectionate meeting at "the Deity's mountain" recalls the previous reunion of Moses and Aaron on the same spot (4:27). And Moses' delegation of authority anticipates the sharing of his prophetic gift with the elders (Numbers 11).

REDACTION ANALYSIS

There are two opinions on the original placement of the Jethro encounter. One, which I uphold, accepts Exodus 18 in its current location. The other maintains that the events of chap. 18 really transpire immediately before Israel's *departure* from Sinai-Horeb. This latter view is first voiced by R. Eleazar of Modiim (*Mek. ʿǎmalēq* 3; *b. Zebaḥ* 116a) and is followed by Rashi, ibn Ezra and Rashbam. Similarly, many modern critics argue that an editor literally transferred the story from Numbers to Exodus (e.g., McNeile 1908: XXIV, 106–7; Glatt 1993: 152–57; Van Seters 1994: 208–9).

The evidence that Exodus 18 is out of place is superficially very strong. Israel's presence at "the Deity's mountain" (v 5), the references to Yahweh's laws (vv 16, 20) and a sacrifice without altar-building (v 12) cumulatively suggest the prior establishment of cult and Covenant. And, more important, in Deut 1:9–18 Moses appoints judges just before Israel leaves Horeb.

Naturally, this begs the question: why was the story moved? Many suggest that the author wished to balance the hostile Amalekites (17:8–16) against the friendly Midianite/Kenite Jethro (ibn Ezra; Cassuto 1967: 212; Sarna 1986: 128–29; see also COMMENT; on the relationship between Amalekites and Kenites, see Num 24:20–21; Judg 7:12; 1 Sam 15:6). And a more urgent motive might have been to minimize the scandal of Jethro sacrificing in front of Aaron by placing the episode before Aaron's consecration. Still, if the final Redactor shifted chap. 18 to its current location, one wonders why he purposely created confusion as to when Israel reaches Yahweh's mountain. R's itinerary insertion in 19:2, "and they set forth from Rephidim and arrived at the Sinai Wilderness," is hard enough to explain (see REDACTION ANALYSIS to chap. 19). Why would the Redactor have doubled the confusion by shifting chap. 18?

Internal evidence also tells against the theory. Why do vv 1, 8–10 refer to the liberation from Egypt and journey through the desert, but not the Covenant (Ramban)? Would not Jethro fetch Moses' family as soon as possible, rather than await Israel's departure (Jacob 1992: 494)? In fact, our story appears *not* to presuppose the Covenant stipulations, but rather describes the development of case law *ad hoc* (Luzzatto), highlighting the *need* for a law code (see COMMENT). As for the contradiction with Deuteronomy, Jacob (p. 502) observes that Deuteronomy often presents events out of order (e.g., 5:22b [cf. 9:9–10]; 9:22; 10:6–7), and, overall, the sequence of wilderness episodes seems to be fluid in biblical tradition (note Ps 78:14–31; Neh 9:12–15). Moreover, Deuteronomy does not mention Jethro's visit at all, but only the establishment of the judiciary; it may have quite a different conception of what went on. (To harmonize the two versions, Jacob infers that Exod 18:24–27 is prospective. That is, the implementation of Jethro's plan required considerable time, and was completed shortly before Israel left Horeb.)

NOTES

18:1. *for Moses.* This unexpected comment may hint at Jethro's pride in his son-in-law's accomplishments. Or the reference may be specifically to a missing Elohistic episode in which Yahweh rescued Moses in particular (cf. v 4; also 2:1–10; 4:19 [J]).

that Yahweh. One could render with LXX *"for (kî)* Yahweh. . . ." But the reader hardly needs a reminder of the Exodus.

18:2. *And Jethro . . . took.* The tense is somewhat uncertain. Were v 2 explaining how Jethro happened to be in company with Moses' family, we might have expected **wəyitrô lāqaḥ* 'now, Jethro had taken,' not *wayyiqqaḥ yitrô.* More likely, the point is not that Jethro *once* took Zipporah *in,* but that he *now* takes her *out.* Final assessment, however, depends on our understanding of *šillûḥe(y)hā* (next NOTE).

marriage-gift. Šillûḥe(y)hā is usually understood as Zipporah's "dismissal" (< *šillaḥ* 'release'), Moses having left her behind in the safety of Midian. (In the composite Torah, one can well imagine Zipporah's own second thoughts after the Bloody Bridegroom incident [4:24–26 (J)]!) Since *šillaḥ* can connote divorce (Deut 22:19, 29, etc.), some Rabbis even infer that Moses had dissolved his marriage after fulfilling the commandment to procreate (R. Joshua in *Mek. ʿămālēq* 3); he in fact takes another wife in Num 12:1. By either of the foregoing interpretations, however, we would expect inverted syntax signaling the pluperfect (previous NOTE).

There is probably no etymological relationship between *šillûḥe(y)hā* and *šlḥ* 'send, dismiss.' Rather, *šillûḥîm* denotes a wedding gift, as seen already by ibn Ezra, Bekhor Shor and Rashbam (cf. 1 Kgs 9:16 and Ugaritic *ṯlḥ* [KTU 1.24.47]). Thus, *'aḥar šillûḥe(y)hā* probably describes, not when Jethro took Zipporah in, but when she became Moses' wife: after the transfer of *šillûḥîm.*

18:3. *Gershom.* On the name, see NOTE to 2:22; on the similarity to Gershon son of Levi, see COMMENT to 6:2–7:7, p. 286.

18:4. *Eliezer.* The name means "My god is help," "My god is the Hero" or perhaps "'Ezer is my god." Unlike Gershom, Eliezer does not appear in 2:22 (J). On the similarity to Aaron's son Eleazar, see COMMENT to 6:2–7:7, p. 286.

for. MT is elliptical; we must understand "for (he said)" (ibn Ezra) (see, however, TEXTUAL NOTE).

as my help. Similar expressions are found in Ps 35:2; 146:5; compare also Ps 118:7 (MT *bəʿōzərāy* 'among my helpers'). In E as in J, Moses' flight to Midian was apparently precipitated by fear of Pharaoh. But the details are unknown.

18:5. *to the wilderness.* Since Jethro knows where to go, Jacob (1992: 495) infers that Moses had told him about the Burning Bush, after all (contrast 4:18).

the Deity's mountain. I.e., Sinai/Horeb. The reference is surprising in light of the Redactor's statement that Israel reached Sinai *after* the meeting with Jethro (19:2). But, within E, the Massah-Meribah incident has already brought the leaders to Horeb (17:6) (see REDACTION ANALYSIS).

18:6. *he said.* Either by letter (cf. 2 Chr 2:10) or by messenger (cf. 2 Sam 10:5) (*Mek. ʿămālēq* 3; Ramban; Jacob 1992: 486). (Were Jethro simply shouting, we would expect *wayyiqrā[']* 'and he called.')

I. Assuming MT is correct—which is uncertain (see TEXTUAL NOTE)—Jethro employs the formal diction of a royal inscription, beginning with the first person.

18:7. *to meet*. *Liqra(')t*, often translated "towards," here bears its etymological meaning (< *qry* 'meet'). Out of respect, Moses does not await Jethro's arrival, but goes out to escort him into camp.

he bowed. The subject is Moses, reverencing his father-in-law (*Mek. 'ămālēq* 3) (cf. TEXTUAL NOTE).

inquired . . . well-being. I.e., each asked about the other's welfare (*šālôm*).

tent. This is presumably Moses' home; he reciprocates the hospitality Jethro had once extended to him (2:21). On Zipporah's nonmention, see COMMENT.

18:8. *told*. For the first time ever, Moses fulfills the commandment to recount the Exodus story (9:16; 10:2) (Fretheim 1991a: 197).

hardship. I.e., thirst, hunger and battle.

befell. Two Semitic roots appear to have merged into Hebrew *mṣ'*: **mẓ'* 'find' and *mḏy 'arrive'; here the latter sense predominates. The idiom *tǝlā'â māṣǝ'â* 'hardship befell' reappears in Num 20:14, probably also from E.

18:9. *rejoiced*. The MT pointing combines alternative pronunciations *wayyiḥad* and *wayyiḥd* (cf. the III-guttural 2 f.s. perfect *šāma'at/šāma't*, etc.).

good. The ancient translations correctly treat *haṭṭôbâ* as a collective: good deeds.

that. I have taken *'ăšer* as a conjunction (see Seidl 1991), but it could also be the relative pronoun: "Yahweh . . . *who* rescued him."

18:10. *hand*. I.e., "power, authority" (*Tg. Onqelos*).

18:11. *Now I know*. Jethro's confession carries forward the main theme of Exodus (Fretheim 1991a: 196). Israel, Egypt and now Jethro must know Yahweh's might, not just intellectually but experientially (*yd'*) (see INTRODUCTION, p. 37).

all the gods. It is unclear whether the author conceives Jethro to be a monotheist, or a polytheist who confesses Yahweh's unique greatness (cf. 12:12; 15:11; compare Rahab in Josh 2:9–11 and Naaman in 2 Kgs 5:15). On Yahweh's incomparability, see Labuschagne (1966).

Some scholars take Jethro's words as preliminary to the establishment of a covenant with Israel, of which v 12 describes the ratification ceremony (cf. Gen 21:22–32; 26:28–31; Josh 9:6–15) (Brekelmans 1954; Fensham 1964; Cody 1968; Hyatt 1971: 189). Judg 4:17–22; 5:6, 24–27; 1 Sam 15:6 are indeed suggestive of such a relationship, but Exodus 18 barely hints at it.

the affair. The verse is odd, probably mutilated through ancient scribal error (Noth 1962: 149). Jethro's point seems to be that the Egyptians were requited for their wickedness, drowning in the Sea as they had conspired to kill the Hebrews' children (*Tgs. Ps.-Jonathan, Neofiti I*).

dealt wickedly. A better translation of *zādû* might be "plotted (to kill)" (cf. 21:14). Ehrlich (1969: 168) suggests that the subject is not the Egyptians, but their gods (cf. 12:12); the parallel in Neh 9:10, however, indicates otherwise.

18:12. *Jethro . . . took.* Polytheist or not (see NOTE to v 11), in the absence of another priest Jethro undertakes to lead Israel in sacrifice. But upon what stone? It might be the altar "Yahweh is my Flag(pole)" (17:15) or perhaps an improvised installation. At any rate, Jethro's act is the partial fulfillment of 3:12, the command/prediction of Israel's worship at the mountain (see also 24:4–5).

ascending offering . . . slaughter sacrifices. An *ʿōlâ* 'that which ascends' is a completely burnt offering; the *zebaḥ* 'slaughter' is shared by God and worshipers. Jethro necessarily makes many slaughter sacrifices to feed the elders. But it is unclear whether *ʿōlâ* is collective (cf. 2 Chr 7:1; also LXX, Syr and Tgs.) or a single holocaust to Yahweh (Jacob 1992: 498).

Aaron . . . elders. That is, Jethro celebrates with the people's representatives. One assumes that Moses, too, is present—unless he is too busy judging the people (Jacob 1992: 498). Rashbam supposes the sacrifice is eaten in Moses' own tent.

food. Here *leḥem* probably does not bear its particular meaning "bread," but rather its general meaning "food," including meat (cf. Arabic *laḥm* 'meat').

18:13. *the next day.* Moses may have taken off the previous day to honor his guest (Ehrlich 1969: 168). But the gratuitous marking of time's passage ("the next day," "on the third day," etc.) is in any case a convention of Hebrew narrative.

sat . . . stood. In the respective postures of judge and plaintiff (cf. 1 Kgs 3:16; Mal 3:3; Ps 9:8; Prov 20:8). *Mek. ʿămālēq* 4, however, finds in Moses' sitting presumptuous arrogation of a *royal* prerogative—surely not the author's intent.

18:14. *all that he was doing.* The echo of vv 1, 8, 9 may compare Yahweh's salvation of Israel to Moses' judging of Israel (Cassuto 1967: 218).

thing. *Dābār,* literally "word," is the theme of vv 13–27, appearing ten times; I have variously rendered it as "thing" or "matter." Arguably, this is a foreshadowing of God's words (*dəbārîm*) at Horeb/Sinai, in particular the "Ten Words" (*ʿăśeret haddəbārîm*).

18:15. *Because.* Moses misses the emphasis in Jethro's question. The priest asks, not why the people come to Moses, but why Moses has no assistance.

consult Deity. That is, every case, large or small, is judged by Moses acting both *in loco Dei* and, if necessary, in consultation with God. This is a waste of Moses' time and, implicitly, of Yahweh's time. On God as ultimate judge of legal cases, see 22:8.

18:16. *coming.* Rashi thinks the subject is the appellant: "one comes." But more likely it is the "matter" that comes; cf. 22:8; Isa 1:23 (Luzzatto; Ehrlich 1969: 168; Wevers 1990: 284).

18:18. *wither.* *Nbl* denotes not only vegetable decay and desiccation but also folly, irreligiosity, perversion—the characteristics least desirable in a judge. Bekhor Shor, moreover, finds a pun with the Niphʿal of *bll* 'to be perplexed' (cf. Rashbam).

this people. The Israelites, at least those in court, will be exhausted awaiting Moses' judgments. *Tg. Ps.-Jonathan*, however, implausibly takes "this people" as referring to Aaron and the elders alone.

18:19. *I will advise you.* Ignoring the MT cantillation, one could link *'î'āṣəkā* to what follows (Holzinger 1900: 62). Following the syntactic division implied by the MT trope, however, we would translate, "Listen to me, my voice, that advises you" (on the construction, see NOTES to 6:3, 15:6 and 32:29).

may Deity be with you. Jethro's intent is unclear. Is he blessing Moses (Luzzatto)? Is he predicting, "Pursue my plan and Yahweh will be with you" (ibn Ezra; Rashbam)? Or does he caution, "Pursue my plan only if Yahweh permits" (*Exod. Rab.* 27:6; *Mek. 'ămālēq* 4; cf. v 23)? By any interpretation, his interjection would be germane. When Moses judges, he especially requires divine assistance (cf. 1 Kgs 3:9). And Yahweh presumably must approve Moses' delegation of authority and inspire the lesser judges with wisdom.

opposite the Deity. That is, Moses alone will continue as Israel's intermediary before Yahweh. Ramban takes the text literally: once the Tabernacle is erected, Moses is to remain inside, perpetually in Yahweh's presence (contrast 33:7–11).

matters. Presumably, the *difficult* matters (ibn Ezra); cf. vv 22, 26.

18:20. *and you will clarify.* Wəhizhartâ, from the root *zhr* 'shine.' Moses is to explicate Yahweh's laws—an intimation of the Rabbinic theory of Oral Torah (cf. NOTE to 17:14).

18:21. *see.* The verb *ḥzy* may connote supernatural vision, requisite for choosing the best judges (Rashi); contrast *r'y* 'see' in Gen 41:33. Jacob (1992: 507) observes how much of Jethro's vocabulary is recherché: *zādû, nābōl tibbōl, 'ăśōhû, mûl, wəhizhartâ, 'ethem, teḥĕze(h)* and, in the narrator's voice, *wayyiḥad.* The effect, he suggests, may be ceremonious or dialectal (see also NOTE to 18:6).

men of competence. My translation is inspired by Ramban. *'Îš ḥayil* can connote a warrior, a rich man or a citizen of deserved respect and social influence. While the last dominates here, the judges also require physical stamina and material prosperity (cf. ibn Ezra; next NOTE).

hating gain. That is, immune to bribery because of their wealth. Perhaps Jethro is also recommending the appointment of men with the leisure to be full-time magistrates (*Mek. 'ămālēq* 4).

place over them. Although the language is somewhat ambiguous, the sense must be "over the Israelites," not "over the judges" (cf. LXX).

rulers. The term *śar* takes us back to 2:14 (J): "Who set you [Moses] as a man, ruler (*śar*) and judge (*šōpēṭ*) over us?" Moses himself is now the one who appoints rulers and judges.

thousands . . . tens. Ten people, even ten nuclear families, would not need their own judge. And if each high judge governed a thousand men, there would be six hundred supreme justices and a total of 78,600 magistrates, assuming an adult male population of 600,000 (*b. Sanh.* 18a) (cf. Abarbanel;

Luzzatto; Dillmann 1880: 188). This makes no sense. Either a quasi-military chain of command has been imposed upon the judicial system (Hyatt 1971: 194), or the numbers refer, not to men, but to clans.

18:22. *big.* Here *gādōl* must mean difficult, not necessarily important (cf. v 26).

matters. In vv 22, 26, *haddābār* is probably collective, hence my plural translation.

you. Presumably, Moses brings only the most difficult cases to Yahweh (cf. vv 15, 19; Num 27:5) (ibn Ezra, Bekhor Shor).

it will lighten. I take *hāqēl* impersonally (with Rashi). A valid alternative would be "*they* will lighten" (LXX, *Tgs. Onqelos* and *Ps.-Jonathan*). "Lighten" (*qll*) contrasts with "heavy" (*kbd*) in v 18 (Jacob 1992: 501).

18:23. *Deity commands.* Jethro seemingly returns to his proviso of v 19: the system will function only if God approves. Or the sense might be: God will guide Moses' judgment (Rashbam).

able to stand. The basic meaning is "survive," but there is also an implicit contrast to Moses' *sitting* (v 13). That is, Moses will finally be able to leave his judgment seat (Jacob 1992: 501).

this people. I assume the reference is to Israel reaching Canaan (Ehrlich 1899: 169). For ibn Ezra, however, the point is that those standing in Moses' court ("this people") may finally go home (also Rashbam; Luzzatto). See following.

come in well-being. A fair, efficient judiciary is the guarantor of social harmony (cf. Ehrlich 1899: 169). Jethro is either saying that Israel will reach Canaan in social tranquillity, or that, at day's end, each Israelite will go home satisfied that justice has been speedily rendered (Ehrlich 1908: 335) (see previous NOTE). Jacob (1992: 507) notes that *bašālôm* is Jethro's parting word, as if to say, "Go in peace" (cf. 4:18).

18:24. *listened.* Moses' obedience to Jethro implies divine confirmation of the plan (cf. vv 19, 23).

18:25. *heads.* Leaders.

18:27. *released.* I.e., said farewell. Perhaps Moses also escorted Jethro; cf. Gen 18:16, "and Abraham walked with them to release them" (ibn Ezra).

went him . . . to his land. Rather than join Israel, Jethro returns to minister among his own people—to what god(s) is unclear. Conceivably, he will be a missionary for Yahweh.

COMMENT

THE MOUNTAIN OF MEETING

Exodus 18 consists of two narratives (vv 1–12, 13–17), each set on its own day (Jacob 1992: 498). Between them falls a turning point in Israel's history. Exod 18:12 (also 24:4–5) fulfills the command/promise that Israel would worship

Yahweh at Horeb (3:12). But this itself was to be a sign that God would take Israel to Canaan (NOTE to 3:12). Thus Exodus 18 is a narrational pivot, looking both backward and forward.

The themes of meeting and dining at God's mountain (18:12) are rooted in Canaanite myth. The Ugaritic gods' *mpḫr m'd* 'assembly meeting' convenes on a mountain, apparently in ʾIlu's tent (*KTU* 1.2.i.14, 15, 17, 20, 31) (Clifford 1972: 35–57). The gods also banquet in Baʿlu's palace on Mount Zaphon (*KTU* 1.4.vi.40–59). Merging the images, Isa 14:13 calls Mount Zaphon *har-mô'ēd* 'mountain of meeting.'

We could also call Horeb a "mountain of meeting." There Moses encounters Yahweh, Aaron and Jethro; Israel meets God, and, centuries later, Elijah hears the small, still voice (1 Kgs 19:8–18). Exod 18:12; 24:5, 9–11, moreover, describe banquets on Horeb. And from Horeb, Israel bears the *'ōhel mô'ēd* 'Meeting Tent,' where humans can commune with the divine. For further discussion of Mount Sinai/Horeb and Canaanite myth, see NOTES to 15:17 and COMMENTS to 13:17–15:21, 17:1–7 and 17:8–16.

AMALEK AND MIDIAN, WAR AND JUSTICE

Cassuto (1967: 212), attempting to explain the slightly anomalous location of the Jethro encounter, perceives an intentional antithesis between the wicked foreigner Amalek and the righteous foreigner Jethro (see REDACTION ANALYSIS). Amalek "comes" to "fight" (17:8); Jethro "comes" to ask about "peace" (18:5, 7). Joshua "chooses" soldiers (17:9); Moses "chooses" judges (18:25). Moses "sits" to obtain victory (17:12); he also "sits" in judgment (18:13). The battle lasts till sunset (17:12); Moses judges till evening (18:13, 14). Moses' arms are "heavy" (17:12); his judicial duties, too, are "heavy" (18:18). Other lexical contacts are *nṣb* 'stand' (17:9; 18:14) and *māḥār/moḥŏrāt* 'the next day' (17:9; 18:13). Finally, the Amalek incident ends in a declaration of war (17:16), whereas Jethro's last words are "in peace" (18:23).

While acknowledging the force and insight of these observations, I do not think the intent is simply to contrast good and bad gentiles. Rather, the Elohist correlates military (17:8–16) and civil (chap. 18) administration, equally requisite to national security (*šālôm*) in the fullest sense: peace at home and abroad. For, although they have displayed military prowess (17:8–16), Israel is not yet prepared for nationhood under Moses' leadership. The difficulty was pointed out long ago by an anonymous compatriot: Moses is by nature no "ruler and judge" (2:14). Now his autocratic-theocratic regime harms both himself and his people.

As Jethro observes, Moses and Yahweh are dispensing judgment piecemeal, and Torah is *ad hoc*. A just and efficient administration requires a legitimate judiciary and a comprehensive law code. The former is established in Exodus 18; the code will occupy most of the remainder of the Pentateuch. With laws and magistrates, Israel will be ready to conquer Canaan and begin the next stage of its national history, ruled by regional judges. The system of local justice will survive into the age of kings (1 Kgs 21:8–14).

A FAMILY MAN?

Though narrating matters of utmost gravity, Exodus 18 also shows a lighter side to Moses. The Man of Power, who parted the Sea and produced Water from the Rock, is affectionately patronized by his father-in-law. It is a common literary theme, and perhaps the truth, that those best able to govern society are the worst stewards of their own affairs. And it is equally a truism that one's in-laws are liable to point this out.

When Jethro arrives, Moses greets him warmly and invites him into his tent. What about Zipporah and the boys? Is Moses glad to see them? Are they left outside? Is Zipporah immediately set to cooking, while the clergy talk shop? We cannot simply attribute this silence to ancient patriarchal mores. The women of Genesis are vivid characters, by and large cherished by their husbands; family life is richly depicted. The Elohist, then, probably had a particular reason to ignore Zipporah.

By depicting Moses as superior to sentiment and domesticity, perhaps the author meant to elevate him. The Patriarchs and Matriarchs of Genesis are important principally as ancestors; their private lives are of great consequence. In contrast, although some Levites claimed Mosaic descent (see COMMENT to 6:2–7:7, p. 285), the Torah is almost entirely indifferent to Moses' role as procreator. He is a unique leader: part prophet, part priest, part king, even part god. His office isolates him not only from his people but even from his own family (see also COMMENT to 2:15b–23a).

JETHRO

It is astonishing that, at God's very mountain, the priest of a nation later hostile to Israel (COMMENT to 2:15b–23a) should invent Israel's legal apparatus and lead the people in worship. The "Midianite Hypothesis" imputes to Jethro and his people a crucial influence upon formative Israel (see, briefly, Mettinger 1988: 24–28). How else could tradition have ascribed so great a role to Jethro, were it not historical fact? The force of this argument cannot be gainsaid, but neither can the dearth of evidence (for further discussion, see APPENDICES B and C).

INDEX OF AUTHORS

◆

INDEX OF SUBJECTS

◆

Festival of Unleavened Bread (*Maṣṣôt*) 337, 373, 379–83, 385, 391–93, 398, 402–3, 405–6, 412, 421–22, 424–25, 427–30, 432–34, 446, 600; as distinct from Festival of *Pesaḥ* 428; as domestic observance 428, 447–48; and equinox 443–44; as holiday of (Canaanite?) farmers 428; as liberation 444; and *Pesaḥ* 451; as pilgrimage festival 429; a prescriptive ritual 445; as protection ritual 444; as purification rite 444, 453, 457; as rite of riddance 434, 443; and roasted meat 444; and Sabbath 431–32; and unleavened bread 444

Festival of Weeks (*Šābūʿôt*) 422, 429–30, 446; as festival of firstfruits 432; Pentecost (Christian Festival of Weeks) 430

fidya or *fedu* ('redemption'), Muslim sacrifice of 434–36, 438, 441; and apotropaism 454; and demons 440; and marriage 435; and *Pesaḥ* 440, 443; as a vicarious sacrifice 445

Final Redactor (R; *see also* Redactor; Source criticism) 49, 50n.55, 53

Fire 36, 199, 489, 524, 529, 559; as motif 351; on night of the Exodus 498; as purification rite 437; as purifier 408, 440, 453, 520; Yahweh's 37, 180, 183, 194, 222, 499, 506, 519–20, 549, 560, 595

Fire pillar 489–90, 498–99, 549–50, 552

Firstborn 217–18, 239, 259, 308–9, 312–15, 317, 343–44, 347, 378–81, 393, 409, 413, 421, 427, 438; consecration of 379–81, 425, 427, 438, 453, 456; and demons 437; at *Pesaḥ* 426–27; plague of the death of 142, 154, 191, 196–97, 218, 227, 238–39, 252, 259, 308–9, 312–18, 321, 325, 331–32, 342–43, 347, 352, 455–58; redemption of 426; sacred to Yahweh 455–57; sanctification of 421, 454–55

Firstfruits; consecration of 438; and Aristotle 455; sacred to Yahweh 455

First haircut; and *fidya* 435

First haircut sacrifice, Islamic (*ʿaqiqa*) 418

Floating Foundling 150, 152, 155–56, 158

Flood 134–35, 146–47, 155, 159–60, 222, 345–46, 384, 424, 442; Mesopotamian Flood tradition 352

Foreshadow 458, 578, 581, 592, 621, 631

Forty 278, 283, 341, 415, 593, 599

Four hundred years 135–36, 269, 278, 365, 415

Fragmentary Targum 44, 46n.47, 581

Frogs; plague of 311–13, 315, 317–19, 321, 325–27, 331–32, 343, 346, 349–50; as Egyptian objects of worship 400

Garden of Eden 558, 570–71

Genealogy 135, 283–84

Generations 125, 415

Genubath 159

Gershom 170, 172, 174, 196, 216, 233–34, 236, 238–39, 264, 286, 627, 629

Gershon (son of Levi) 170, 174, 264, 275, 284, 286, 629

Gezer Calendar 385, 422

Gideon 121, 226–29, 440, 595

Gilgal 452–53, 538–39, 554, 562, 564, 566–67

Gilgamesh 159, 166, 272, 570

Glory, Yahweh's 36–37, 272, 512, 528, 533, 588, 592, 594–95

God (*see also* Yahweh); as an archer 511; Bethel 271; Elohim 448; El Shadday 271, 283, 448; Elyon 271; Olam 271; as shepherd 228–29

"God of the father" 201

Golden Calf 213, 231, 605–6

Goshen 124, 298, 328, 344–45, 365

H (*see* Holiness stratum)

Hadad/Haddu/Addu 228, 490, 555

Haddu (Ugaritic storm god; *see* Hadad/Haddu/Addu)

Haggadah, Passover 373, 416, 460

Hail, plague of 311–13, 315, 318, 320–21, 331, 334, 336, 346–47, 351, 458

Hand/arm (*see also* Right hand/arm) 36, 173, 193–94, 202, 207, 229, 249–50, 258, 263, 266, 270, 273, 282–83, 323, 328, 620; Aaron's 311, 325, 537, 559; Egypt's 496, 502; Moses' 310, 312–13, 336, 338, 480–81, 497, 529, 537, 559, 616, 618, 621, 634; raised 493, 511, 529, 609, 616, 618, 620–21; as symbol of power/strength 36, 536, 619; Yahweh's 328, 331, 333, 337, 496–97, 502, 525, 529, 531, 544, 592, 609, 619–20

Harden/hard-hearted (*see also* Pharaoh, strong heart) 217, 282, 336, 353–54

Harvest 432

Healing 575, 578–82, 613

Heart, hard or firm or heavy (*see also* Pharaoh, strong heart); Egyptians' 498–99

Hebrews; etymology of word 139; as a term for Israelites 206, 492

Helel 531

Helper (*see* Proppian character type)

Hero (*see* Proppian character type)

Herodotus 133, 149, 150, 154, 172, 238, 324, 330, 350, 396, 415, 556

Hesiod 556

Hezekiah 133, 447, 459

Hireling 417–19

Hittite 156, 186, 235, 275, 352, 368, 396, 493; eating of raw meat 395

Hobab (*see also* Jethro/Reuel) 172–73, 191, 627

INDEX OF SCRIPTURAL AND ANCIENT SOURCES

◆

Scripture is indexed according to Hebrew chapter and verse divisions. For all details on manuscripts and variants discussed, see the scripture reference in question.

17:1–7 175, 285, 495,
  558, 576, 579, 601,
  603, 606, 615–16
17:2 578, 599, 601, 604
17:2–7 51
17:3 605
17:4 605
17:5 51, 324, 579, 602,
  605
17:5–6 191
17:6 605, 612, 629
17:7 578, 599, 606
17:8 616, 634
17:8–16 52, 604, 613,
  615–16, 628, 634
17:8–18:27 34
17:9 216, 324, 617, 634
17:10 617
17:11 614, 618
17:12 36, 618, 634
17:13 618
17:14 619
17:14–18 229
17:15 579, 619
17:16 634
18 622
18:1 628
18:2 629
18:3 627, 629
18:4 162, 216, 629
18:5 629, 634
18:6 624, 629
18:7 630, 634
18:8 630
18:9 630
18:9–12 176
18:10 625, 630
18:10–11 171
18:11 37, 630
18:12 171, 173, 176,
  203, 559, 631,
  633–34
18:13 631, 634
18:13–26 168, 176
18:13–27 616
18:14 631, 634
18:15 631
18:16 631
18:18 631, 634
18:18–23 229
18:19 632
18:20 632
18:21 138, 632
18:21–26 163
18:22 633
18:23 633–34
18:24 633

18:24–27 628
18:25 633–34
18:27 633
19 604
19–20 52
19–21 52
19:1–2 37
19:2 628
19:3 52
19:6 34
19:7 52
19:16 36, 558
19:17 52
19:18 36
19:19 52, 558
20:1 52
20:2 37
20:7 36
20:7–18 229
20:8 597
20:10 346
20:18 138, 559
20:20 138, 579
20:24 36
21:2 139
21:5–6 494
21:13 235
21:16 218
21:19 580
21:20–21 167
21:23–25 218
23:9 202
23:10–11 346
23:14–17 429
23:15 208, 368, 421, 428
23:16 385
23:18 396, 398
23:19 346
23:20–26 622
24:4–5 203
24:5 559
24:5–8 285
24:9–11 201
24:10 523
24:13 52
24:13–14 52
24:16–17 36
24:17 36
25–31 559
25:17–22 281
27:19 37
28 200
29 332
29:39 390
29:41 390
29:43 36
29:46 37

30:8 390
30:16 37
30:18–21 200
31:13 37
31:15 597
32 49, 52, 213, 231,
  284
32:1 618
32:10 142
32:13 37
32:20 605
32:22 37
32:26–29 167, 214, 605
32:29 148
33:6 52
33:7–11 52, 282, 285
33:12 36–37, 224, 272
33:13 37
33:16 37
33:17 36–37, 224, 272
33:18 36, 223, 272
33:18–23 201
33:19 36, 272
33:20 272
33:22 36
33:23 272
34:5 36
34:5–7 36, 272
34:6–7 50
34:14 36
34:14–15 34n.10
34:18 368, 421
34:18–23 429
34:20 208, 239
34:22 385
34:23 428
34:25 397–98
34:26 346
34:29–35 284–85
35–40 559
35:21 37
35:24 37
36:1 37
36:3 37
36:5 37
37:6–9 281
38:21 37
38:26 122, 414
39:32 37
39:40 37
39:42 37
40:2 37, 442
40:17 37, 442
40:30–32 200
40:34–38 36
40:38 36

12:5 150
12:16 141
14:9 157
14:21 179
15:16 212
15:19 214
16:21 270
17:5 579
17:14 579
18:18 344
20–25 34n.10
20:7 229
22:15 150
28:9 230
31:9 157, 217
31:11 613
31:12 622
31:15 404
31:20 157, 217
31:23 569
31:35 558
32:20 348
34:9 139
34:13 378
34:14 139
38:7 164
43:10 324
44:27–30 203
46:7–8 558, 560
46:11 579
51:8–9 579
52:25 342

Ezekiel

1:1 328, 335
1:4 334
1:22 523
1:26 180
1:26–28 281
2:4 217
3:1–3 212
3:5–6 211
3:7 217
4:4–6 416
4:14 229
8:3 328, 335
10 281
13:11 351
13:13 351
16 34n.10
16:4–14 157
16:19 598
17:22–23 565
20 495
20:5 178, 267, 270
20:5–10 380

21:5 229
22:11 277
24:3–13 440
28:14 612
28:16 612
29:3–5 324, 558, 560, 609
29:3–7 322
30:18 352
31:3 612
31:8–9 612
31:15 612
31:16 612
32:2–6 324, 609
32:2–10 322, 558, 560
32:7–8 352
34 581
34:4 134
38–39 622
38:22 334, 351
40:1 387
40:2 328, 335
44:7 273–74
44:9 273–74
44:22 277
45:18–20 442–44
45:18–21 451
45:21 369, 398, 447
47:1–12 577, 581, 613
47:12 581

Hosea

1–3 34n.10
1:9 225–26
2:17 495
7:4 412
11:1 157
11:1–4 217
12:4–5 158
12:5 224
12:6 515
12:14 230

Joel

1–2 351
4 622
4:18 202, 535, 612–13

Amos

1–2 316
5:23 563
7:4 558
7:8 209
7:12 351
8:2 209

9:3 558
9:13 202, 535, 612

Jonah

1:3 229
2:3–10 571
2:6 339
4 258
4:1–3 229
4:8–9 229

Micah

1:4 535
3:3 396, 418
4:1–2 613, 622
5.4 316

Nahum

1:3–4 558
1:5 535

Habakkuk

3:3–15 558
3:5 350
3:7 281
3:14 610

Zephaniah

1:2–3 345
1:8–9 399
1:9 441
1:12 522

Zechariah

3:1–2 354
4:3 570
7:12 217
10:11 558, 560
12–14 622
13:1 613
14:6 522–23
14:8 613

Malachi

1:6 217
2:6–7 274
3:10 558

DEUTEROCANON-ICAL BOOKS

Baruch

4:6 189

INDEX OF HEBREW AND
ANCIENT LANGUAGES

◆